Diagnostic Manual – Intellectual Disability:

A Textbook of Diagnosis of Mental Disorders in Persons with Intellectual Disability

Second Edition

DM-ID-2

Edited by

Robert J. Fletcher, DSW, ACSW, NADD-CC, Chief Editor
Jarrett Barnhill, MD, DLFAPA, FAACAP
Sally-Ann Cooper, MD, FRCPsych

NATIONAL ASSOCIATION FOR THE DUALLY DIAGNOSED

132 Fair Street
Kingston, New York 12401
www.thenadd.org

LCCN: 2016917726

ISBN: 978-1-57256-134-2

Printed in the United States of America

Table of Contents

Editors

Robert J. Fletcher, DSW, ACSW, NADD-CC, Chief Editor
Founder and Chief Executive Officer
National Association for the Dually Diagnosed
Kingston, NY

Jarrett Barnhill, MD, DLFAPA, FAACAP
Clinical Professor, Department of Psychiatry
Clinical Professor, Department of Neurology
University of North Carolina School of Medicine
Chapel Hill NC

Sally-Ann Cooper, MD, FRCPsych
Professor of Learning Disabilities & Deputy Director - Institute of Health and Wellbeing
Institute of Health and Wellbeing
University of Glasgow
Mental Health and Wellbeing Research Group,
Gartnavel Royal Hospital
Glasgow, Scotland

DM-ID Work Groups

Anxiety Disorders

Sherva Elizabeth Cooray FRCPsych, DPM, MBBS, Chair
Chair, Working Group Faculty of Psychiatry of Intellectual Disability
Royal College of Psychiatrists UK
London, UK

Tim Andrews, MD, MB, ChB
Consultant Psychiatrist
Southern Health NHS Trust
Oxford, UK

Nicola M. Bailey MBBS, DM, MRCPsych
Consultant in the Psychiatry of Learning Disabilities
Dorset Healthcare University Foundation NHS Trust
Forston Clinic
Dorset, UK

John Devapriam MBBS, LLM, FRCPsych
Leicestershire Partnership NHS Trust
Agnes Unit
Leicester

Sujeet S. Jaydeokar MBBS, MD, MA, FRCPsych
Cheshire and Wirral Partnership NHS Foundation Trust
East Cheshire Community Learning Disability Team
HE, United Kingdom

Jennifer L. McLaren M.D.
Assistant Professor of Psychiatry
Geisel School of Medicine at Dartmouth
Department of Psychiatry
Lebanon, New Hampshire

Kiran N Purandare MBBS, MD, MRCPsych
Consultant Psychiatrist
Hon Clinical Senior Lecturer
Imperial College London
Faculty of Medicine
London, UK

Marc J. Tassé, PhD.
Director and Professor of Psychology and Psychiatry
The Ohio State University Nisonger Center
Columbus, Ohio

Anusha Wijerante MBBS, MRCPsych
Consultant Psychiatrist
Central and North West London NHS Foundation Trust
The Kingswood Centre
London, United Kingdom

Assessment and Diagnostic Procedure

Anne Desnoyers Hurley Ph.D., Chair
Associate Clinical Professor of Psychiatry
Tufts University School of Medicine, Boston Massachusetts
Northampton, Massachusetts

Elspeth A. Bradley Ph.D., MB, BS, FRCPC, FRCPsych
Associate Professor
University of Toronto
Department of Psychiatry
Toronto, Ontario, Canada

Nicola M. Bailey MBBS, DM, MRCPsych
Consultant in the Psychiatry of Learning Disabilities
Dorset Healthcare University Foundation NHS Trust
Forston Clinic
Dorset, UK

Andrew Levitas M.D.
Professor of Psychiatry
Rowan University School of Osteopathic Medicine
Department of Psychiatry
Center of Excellence for the Mental Health Treatment of Persons with Intellectual Disabilities
Stratford, NJ

James K. Luiselli Ed.D., ABPP, BCBA-D
Chief Clinical Officer
Clinical Solutions, Inc., and North East Educational and Developmental Support Center
Tewksbury, MA

Steve Moss, PhD
Estia Centre for Mental Health and Learning Disability
Health Service and Population Research Department
Institute of Psychiatry
King's College London
London, UK

Attention Deficit/Hyperactivity Disorder

Jessica A. Hellings, MB.Bch, M.Med. Psych. (S.A.), Chair
Professor of Psychiatry
University of Missouri-Kansas City School of Medicine
Kansas City, Missouri

Michael G. Aman Ph.D.
Professor Emeritus of Psychology
Ohio State University
The Nisonger Center UCEDD
Columbus, Ohio

L. Eugene Arnold
Professor Emeritus
Ohio State University Department of Psychiatry
Nisonger Center UCEDD
Columbus, Ohio

Benjamin L. Handen, PhD
Professor of Psychiatry and Pediatrics
University of Pittsburgh School of Medicine
Pittsburgh, Pennsylvania

Jennifer L. McLaren M.D.
Assistant Professor of Psychiatry
Geisel School of Medicine at Dartmouth
Department of Psychiatry
Lebanon, New Hampshire

Deborah A. Pearson Ph.D.
Professor
McGovern Medical School
The University of Texas Health Science Center at Houston (UTHealth)
Department of Psychiatry and Behavioral Sciences
Houston, Texas

Angela M. Reiersen, MD
Assistant Professor, Psychiatry
Washington University School of Medicine
Saint Louis, Missouri

Autism Spectrum Disorder

Terrence C. Bethea MD, Chair
Medical Director
The Hughes Center
Danville, Virginia

Marco O. Bertelli MD, Psychiatrist and Psychotherapist
MD, Scientific Director
CREA (Research and Clinical Centre)
San Sebastiano Foundation
Via Del Sansovino
Firenze, Italy

E. Richard Blumberg Ph.D.
Behavioral Psychologist/ Autism Clinical Specialist
Redwood Coast Regional Center
Ukiah, California

Lauren R. Charlot Ph.D.
Assistant Professor, Department of Psychiatry, UMass Medical School
Adjunct Professor, Brody School of Medicine, Eastern Carolina University
NC START East
New Bern, North Carolina

Jean A. Frazier, MD
Professor of Psychiatry and Pediatrics
UMASS Medical School/ University of Massachusetts Memorial Health Care
Department of Psychiatry
Worcester, Massachusetts

Andrew C Stanfield MB, ChB, Ph.D., MRCPsych
Senior Clinical Research Fellow
University of Edinburgh
Division of Psychiatry
Edinburgh, UK

Behavioral Phenotypes

Andrew Levitas M.D., Chair
Professor of Psychiatry
Rowan University School of Osteopathic Medicine
Department of Psychiatry
Center of Excellence for the Mental Health Treatment of Persons with Intellectual Disabilities
Stratford, NJ

Nathan Danker, MA
Doctoral candidate in Clinical Psychology
Vanderbilt University
Nashville, Tennessee

Elisabeth Dykens Ph.D.
Professor
Vanderbilt University
Departments of Psychology and Human Development, Pediatrics and Psychiatry
Vanderbilt Kennedy Center
Nashville, TN

Brenda Finucane MS. LGC
Professor
Autism & Developmental Medicine Institute, Geisinger Health System
Lewisburg, PA

Wendy R. Kates Ph.D.
Professor
State University of New York at Upstate Medical University
Department of Psychiatry and Behavioral Sciences
Syracuse, New York

Amy K. Olszewski, PhD
SUNY Upstate Medical University
Department of Psychiatry and and Behavioral Sciences
Syracuse, New York

Marcy Schuster, PsyD
Clinical Coordinator
Elwyn
Elwyn, Pennsylvania

Elliot W. Simon Ph.D.
Executive Director
Elwyn
Research and Quality Improvement
Elwyn, Pennsylvania

Bipolar and Related Disorders

Robert J. Pary MD, Chair
Professor Emeritus
Southern Illinois University School of Medicine
Springfield Illinois

Lauren R. Charlot Ph.D.
Assistant Professor, Department of Psychiatry, UMass Medical School
Adjunct Professor, Brody School of Medicine, Eastern Carolina University
NC START East
New Bern, North Carolina

Sherm Fox MD
Lecturer in Psychiatry
Geisel School of Medicine at Dartmouth
Sovner Center/ Bridgewell
Danvers, Massachusetts

Jessica A. Hellings, MB.Bch, M.Med. Psych. (S.A.), Chair
Director, Neurodevelopmental Psychiatry Study Program
The Ohio State University Nisonger Center
Columbus, Ohio

Anne Desnoyers Hurley Ph.D.
Associate Clinical Professor of Psychiatry
Tufts University School of Medicine, Boston Massachusetts
Northampton, Massachusetts

Communication Disorders

Jarrett Barnhill, MD, DLFAPA, FAACAP, Chair
Clinical Professor
Departments of Psychiatry and Neurology
University of North Carolina School of Medicine
Chapel Hill, North Carolina

Lee K. McLean, PhD, FASLHA, FAASAHP
Professor Emeritus
University of North Carolina
School of Medicine, Department of Allied Health Sciences
Chapel Hill, North Carolina

Billy T. Ogletree, PhD., CCC-SLP
Professor and Head
Department of Communication Sciences and Disorders
Western Carolina University
Cullowhee, North Carolina

Johanna R. Price Ph.D., CCC-SLP
Assistant Professor
Western Carolina University
Department of Communication Sciences and Disorders
Cullowhee, North Carolina

Linda R. Watson, EdD, CCC-SLP
Professor
University of North Carolina at Chapel Hill School of Medicine
Division of Speech & Hearing Sciences
Chapel Hill, North Carolina

Depressive Disorders

Lauren R. Charlot Ph.D., Chair
Assistant Professor, Department of Psychiatry, UMass Medical School
Adjunct Professor, Brody School of Medicine, Eastern Carolina University
NC START East
New Bern, North Carolina

Betsey A. Benson Ph.D.
Associate Professor
Ohio State University
Nisonger Center UCEDD
Columbus, Ohio

Sherm Fox MD
Lecturer in Psychiatry
Geisel School of Medicine at Dartmouth
Sovner Center/ Bridgewell
Danvers, Massachusetts

Angela Hassiotis MA, Ph.D., FRCPsych,
Professor
UCL Division of Psychiatry
University College London
London, UK

Robert J. Pary MD
Professor Emeritus
Southern Illinois University School of Medicine
Springfield Illinois

Marc J. Tassé, PhD.
Director and Professor of Psychology and Psychiatry
The Ohio State University Nisonger Center
Columbus, Ohio

Disruptive, Impulsive Control, and Conduct Disorders

Shoumitro (Shoumi) Deb MBBS, FRCPsych, MD, Chair
Professor
Imperial College London UK, Department of Medicine, Division of Brain Sciences
Centre for Mental Health, Imperial College Hammersmith Hospital Campus
London, UK

Terrence C. Bethea MD
Medical Director
The Hughes Center
Danville, Virginia

Susan M. Havercamp Ph.D., NADD-CC, FAAIDD
Associate Professor
The Ohio State University Nisonger Center
Columbus, Ohio

Arthur Rifkin MD
Clinical Professor of Psychiatry
Hofstra Northwell School of Medicine at Hofstra University
Hempstead, NY

Lisa Underwood BSc, Ph.D
Research Fellow
The University of Auckland
Faculty of Medical and Health Sciences
Auckland, New Zealand

Dissociative Disorder

Alya Reeve MD, MPH, FANPA, FAAIDD, Chair
Professor Emeritus
Department of Psychiatry, University of New Mexico
Continuum of Care
Albuquerque, New Mexico

Tim Andrews, MD, MB, ChB
Consultant Psychiatrist
Southern Health NHS Trust
Oxford, UK

Dora Calott Wang ,MD, MA
Historian and Associate Professor
University of New Mexico School of Medicine
Albuquerque, New Mexico

Eve Loren Wedeen, MA, ATR-BC, LPAT, LPCC
Art Therapist, Clinical Counselor
Eve Loren Wedeen and Associates
Los Ranchos, New Mexico

Elimination Disorders

Stephen L. Ruedrich MD, Chair
Professor of Psychiatry
Case Western Reserve University School of Medicine
Department of Psychiatry
Cleveland, Ohio

Kristen L. Kaelber MD, Ph.D., FAAP, FACP
Assistant Professor
Case Western Reserve University
The Metrohealth System
Cleveland, Ohio

Sarah M. Lytle MD
Senior Instructor
University Hospitals Case Medical Center
Division of Child and Adolescent Psychiatry
Cleveland, Ohio

Edwin J. Mikkelsen MD
Associate Professor
Department of Psychiatry
Harvard Medical School
Wellesley, Massachusetts

Feeding and Eating Disorders

Nellieke de Koning MBA-H, Chair
Director/ Child Psychiatrist
De Bascule
Duivendrecht, the Netherlands

Julie P.Gentile MD, Chair
Professor
Wright State University School of Medicine
WSU Department of Psychiatry
Dayton, Ohio

Frank Moreland MA
Finger Lakes Developmental Disability Service Organization (DDSO)
Rochester, New York

Pieter Troost MD, Ph.D.
Head of Psychiatric Training
De Bascule Academic Center for Child and Adolescent Psychiatry Amsterdam
De Bascule
Duivendrecht, the Netherlands

Gender Dysphoria

Georgina Parkes, MBBS, MRCPscyh, Chair
Hertfordshire Partnership University Foundation Trust
Specialist Learnng Disability Services
Watford, United Kingdom

James Barrett MB, BS BSc MSc FRCPsych
Consultant
Charing Cross National Gender Identity Clinic
London, UK

Nigel Beail Ph.D., FBPsS
Professor
South West Workshire Partnership NHS
Foundation Trust and University of Sheffield
Adult Specialist Learning Disabilities Health Service
Barnsley, UK

Sonika Bhasin M.B.B.S, MRCPsych, PGCert. Leadership academy
Consultant Psychiatrist in Learning Disabilities
Hertfordshire Partnership University Foundation NHS Trust
West Community Assessment Treatment Services
Hemel Hempstead, Hertfiordshire

Walter Pierre Bouman MD, MA, MSc, FRCPsych
Nottingham National Centre for Gender Dysphoria
Nottingham, United Kingdom

Annelou L.C. de Vires MD, Ph.D.
Child and Adolescent Psychiatrist
VU University Medical Center
Amsterdam

Daniel Wilson, RGN, RNLD, PG, dip Psychosexual therapy, Cert: Couple counselor, PG dip Practice education.
Psychosexual therapist/ Couples counselor
Relate
Essex, U.K.

Intellectual Development Disorders

Marc J. Tassé, PhD., Chair
Director and Professor of Psychology and Psychiatry
The Ohio State University Nisonger Center
Columbus, Ohio

Marco O. Bertelli MD, Psychiatrist and Psychotherapist
MD, Scientific Director
CREA (Research and Clinical Centre)
San Sebastiano Foundation
Via Del Sansovino
Firenze, Italy

Wendy R. Kates Ph.D.
Professor
State University of New York at Upstate Medical University
Department of Psychiatry and Behavioral Sciences
Syracuse, New York

Patricia Navas, Ph.D.
Assistant Professor
University of Salamanca-INICO
Salamanca, Spain

Elliot W. Simon Ph.D.
Executive Director
Elwyn
Research and Quality Improvement
Elwyn, Pennsylvania

Motor Disorders

Jarrett Barnhill, MD, DLFAPA, FAACAP, Chair
Clinical Professor
Departments of Psychiatry and Neurology
University of North Carolina School of Medicine
Chapel Hill, North Carolina

Elspeth A. Bradley Ph.D., MB, BS, FRCPC, FRCPsych
Associate Professor
University of Toronto
Department of Psychiatry
Toronto, Ontario, Canada

Brianna E.M. Cheyne, B.A.
St. Francis Xavier University
Antigonish, Nova Scotia, Canada

Heidi Diepstra Ph.D.
Surrey Place Centre
Toronto, Ontario, Canada

Neurocognitive Disorders

André Strydom MVChB, MRCPsych, MSc, Ph.D., Chair
Reader in Intellectual Disabilities
UCL Division of Psychiatry
London, United Kingdom

Shoumitro (Shoumi) Deb MBBS, FRCPsych, MD
Professor
Imperial College London UK, Department of Medicine, Division of Brain Sciences
Centre for Mental Health, Imperial College Hammersmith Hospital Campus
London, UK

Karen Dodd BSc, MSc, Ph.D., AfBPS
Surrey and Borders Partnership NHS Foundation Trust
Ramsay House
Surrey, UK

Lucille Esralew Ph.D.
Clinical Administrator
Trinitas Regional Medical Center
Department of Behavioral Health and Psychiatry
Elizabeth, NJ

Mark H. Fleisher MD, NADD-CC
Professor
University of Nebraska College of Medicine
Department of Psychiatry
Omaha, Nebraska

Tamara al Janabi Ph.D.
Research Project Manager
UCL Division of Psychiatry
London, United Kingdom

Howard Ring MD, FRCPsych
University Lecturer
University of Cambridge
Department of Psychiatry
Cambridge, UK

Julian Trollor MB BS, FRANZCP, MD
Professor
School of Psychiatry
Department of Developmental Disability Neuropsychiatry
UNSW, Australia

Sarah L. Whitwham, D Clin Psy C Psychol. PgDip AFBPsS
Consultant Clinical Psychologist
Cornwall Partnership Foundation Trust
Bodmin, UK

Obsessive-Compulsive and Related Disorders

Julie P.Gentile MD, Chair
Professor
Wright State University School of Medicine
WSU Department of Psychiatry
Dayton, Ohio

Betsey A. Benson Ph.D.
Associate Professor
Ohio State University
Nisonger Center UCEDD
Columbus, Ohio

Allison E. Cowan, MD
Assistant Professor
Wright State University
Dayton, Ohio

Mark H. Fleisher MD, NADD-CC
Professor
University of Nebraska College of Medicine
Department of Psychiatry
Omaha, Nebraska

Paulette Marie Gillig MD, Ph.D.
Professor
Wright State University Boonshoft School of Medicine
Department of Psychiatry
Dayton, Ohio

Paraphilic Disorders

Dorothy M. Griffiths C.M. O.Ont, Ph.D., Chair
Professor
Brock University
Department of Child and Youth Studies
Ontario, Canada

J. Paul Fedoroff MD
Professor of Psychiatry
University of Ottawa
Division of forensic Psychiatry
Ottawa, Canada

William R. Lindsay Ph.D., FBPS, FAcSS, FIASSIDD
Professor
Danshell Healthcare
Monroe House
Scotland, UK

Deborah A. Richards
M.A., PR
Consultant
Pelham Psychotherapy Practice
Fonthill, ON

Personality Disorders

William R. Lindsay Ph.D., FBPS, FAcSS, FIASSIDD, Chair
Professor
Danshell Healthcare
Monroe House
Scotland, UK

Regi T. Alexander MBBS, FRCPsych D
Professor
Partnerships in care LD Services
Department of Psychiatry
Norfolk, UK

Lawrence A. Dana Ph.D. ABPP
Regional Director
CHE Senior Psychological Services
Brooklyn, NY

Dorothy M. Griffiths C.M. O.Ont, Ph.D.
Professor
Brock University
Department of Child and Youth Studies
Ontario, Canada

Steve Wilkinson MBBS MRCPsych
Cumbria Partnership NHS Foundation trust
The Carlton Clinic
Carlisle

Schizophrenia Spectrum and Other Psychotic Disoders

Angela Hassiotis MA, Ph.D., FRCPsych, Chair
Professor
UCL Division of Psychiatry
University College London
London, UK

Anne Desnoyers Hurley Ph.D.
Associate Clinical Professor of Psychiatry
Tufts University School of Medicine, Boston Massachusetts
Northampton, Massachusetts

Mark H. Fleisher MD, NADD-CC
Professor
University of Nebraska College of Medicine
Department of Psychiatry
Omaha, Nebraska

Lucy Fodor-Wynne BSc
University College London
Division of Psychiatry
London, UK

Sexual Dysfunctions

Georgina Parkes, Chair
Hertfordshire Partnership University Foundation Trust
Specialist Learnng Disability Services
Watford, United Kingdom

Claire Reynolds, BSc, MBBS, MRCPsych
Higher Trainee on East of England Higher Training
Programme in Psychiatry of Learning Disability
United Kingdom

Peter E. Langdon
DClinPsy, Ph.D., AFBPsS, CPsychol
Senior Lecturer in Clinical Psychology and Disability
Tizard Centre
University of Kent
Canterbury, UK

Daniel Wilson, RGN, RNLD, PG, dip Psychosexual therapy, Cert: Couple counselor, PG dip Practice education.
Psychosexual therapist/ Couples counselor
Relate
Essex, UK

Sleep-Wake Disorders

Jarrett Barnhill, MD, DLFAPA, FAACAP, Chair
Clinical Professor
Departments of Psychiatry and Neurology
University of North Carolina School of Medicine
Chapel Hill, North Carolina

Jill A. Hollway Ph.D. MA
Research Scientist
Ohio State University
The Nisonger Center UCEDD

Ann Poindexter, MD
Consultant
Conway, Arkansas

Takahiro Soda MD, Ph.D.
Resident Physician
UNC Hospitals Department of Psychiatry
North Carolina Neurosciences Hospital
Chapel Hill, North Carolina

Somatic Symptom Disorders

Marco O. Bertelli MD, Psychiatrist and Psychotherapist, Chair
MD, Scientific Director
CREA (Research and Clinical Centre)
San Sebastiano Foundation
Via Del Sansovino
Firenze, Italy

Avril V. Brereton, PhD
Senior Research Fellow
Monash University
Center for Developmental Psychiatry
Clayton, Victoria, Australia

Bruce J. Tonge, MD, FRANZCP
Emeritus Professor
Monash University
Centre for Developmental Psychiatry and Psychology
Clayton, Victoria, Australia

Specific Learning Disorder

Susan M. Havercamp Ph.D., NADD-CC, FAAIDD, Chair
Associate Professor
The Ohio State University Nisonger Center
Columbus, Ohio

Sujeet S. Jaydeokar MBBS, MD, MA, FRCPsych
Cheshire and Wirral Partnership NHS Foundation Trust
East Cheshire Community Learning Disability Team
HE, United Kingdom

Jane McCarthy MD, MRCGP, FRCPsych
Visiting Senior Lecturer
King's College London
Institute of Psychiatry, Psychology & Neuroscience
London, UK

Andrea N. Witwer Ph.D.
Assistant Professor
Ohio State University Nisonger Center
Columbus, Ohio

Substance Use and Addictive Disorders

Edwin J. Mikkelsen MD, Chair
Associate Professor
Department of Psychiatry
Harvard Medical School
Wellesley, Massachusetts

William R. Lindsay Ph.D., FBPS, FAcSS, FIASSIDD
Professor
Danshell Healthcare
Monroe House
Scotland, UK

Joanne E.L. VanDerNagel MD
Tactus Addiction Medicine
Raiffeisentraat
The Netherlands

Trauma- and Stressor- Related Disorders

Jane McCarthy MD, MRCGP, FRCPsych, Chair
Visiting Senior Lecturer
King's College London
Institute of Psychiatry, Psychology & Neuroscience
London, UK

Valerie L. Gaus Ph.D.
Licensed Psychologist
Private Practice
Huntington, New York

Roberto A. Blanco MD
Assistant Professor
University of North Carolina School of Medicine
Department of Psychiatry
Chapel Hill, North Carolina

Daniel J. Tomasulo Ph.D., MFA, MAPP, TEP, NADD-CC
Adjunct Faculty - Columbia University, Teachers College, Department of Counseling and Clinical Psychology/ Positive Psychology
Adjunct Faculty – Master of Applied Positive Psychology Program University of Pennsylvania
Associate Professor of Psychology, New Jersey City University
Department of Psychology
Jersey City, New Jersey

Nancy J. Razza Ph.D.
Adjunct Assistant Professor of Pediatrics
The Boggs Center of Developmental Disabilities
Rutgers/Robert Wood Johnson Medical School
New Brunswick, New Jersey

Cautionary Statement

The *DM-ID-2* provides directions for applying the diagnostic criteria contained in the *DSM-5* for individuals with intellectual/developmental disability. The *DSM-5* classification system provides guidelines for making diagnoses of people with various mental disorders and is intended for use by qualified professionals. The directions for applying criteria contained in the *DM-ID-2* likewise is intended for use by qualified professionals and reflects the current best clinical practice arrived at by an expert consensus approach of clinicians who specialize in diagnosing mental disorders in persons with intellectual/developmental disability. The diagnostic categories listed in the *DM-ID-2* do not include all conditions for which people with intellectual/developmental disability may be treated. Future research may well change some of the expert opinions represented in this book.

The diagnostic criteria contained here are provided to improve treatment through accurate diagnosis and to support further research. These criteria may not be relevant to legal issues such as individual responsibility, competency, disability determination, or fitness to stand trial, nor does the inclusion of a diagnostic category within the *DM-ID-2* imply that the condition meets the legal or other non-medical criteria for a mental disease, impairment, disability, or mental disorder.

CHAPTER 1

An Introduction to the DM-ID-2

Robert J. Fletcher
Jarrett Barnhill
Sally-Ann Cooper

The Problem

Although psychiatric disorders in persons with intellectual/developmental disability (IDD) are common, they are often not appropriately identified (Reiss, 1994). The provision of adequate mental health treatment for people with ID continues to be lacking, in part, because reliable psychiatric diagnosis remains a clinical challenge. Determining an accurate psychiatric diagnosis becomes especially difficult at lower levels of intellectual functioning (Rush & Frances, 2000).

DM-ID-2 has been produced to help address this problem. in addition to adapting the *DSM-5* diagnostic criteria where appropriate, the *DM-ID-2* provides a wealth of information about and considerations for assessing and diagnosing individuals with ID and coexisting mental health needs. In some cases, it is not so much that the criteria need to be adapted as that a different method of eliciting the necessary information must be used. Information is provided in recognizing common behaviors of individuals with intellectual disabilities and in how to differentiate these behaviors from psychiatric disorders.

Review of Prevalence of Mental Illness in IDD

Individuals with IDD can experience the same mental disorders as the general population, as well as some disorders that are uncommon in the general population such as pica. Studies have indicated that psychiatric disorders in people with IDD are at a higher rate than in the neurotypical population. Studies on prevalence rates of psychiatric disorders have varied widely.

The variance of the data reflects a number of variables including: (1) the nature of the study sample, (2) the nature of the definition/classification system(s) used to identify psychiatric disorders and ID, (3) the particular tools used for assessment of potential psychiatric disorders, (4) the inclusion or exclusion of 'challenging behavior,' (5) the inclusion or exclusion of autism spectrum disorders under the general mantle of psychiatric disorders, (6) the inclusion or exclusion of biomedical conditions as a potential contributing/etiological factor in the presentation of behavioral or affective symptoms, and (7) the training and experience of the individual(s) applying assessment tools (Buckles, 2016), and the methodological quality of the study.

There have been a few studies that have employed rigorous methodological protocols. One such study conducted by Cooper, Smiley, Morrison, Williamson, and Allan (2007) used multiple measures. The method used a population-based adult sample (N=1023) with a comprehensive individualized assessment model. The data indicated a point prevalence of mental illness at 40.9% (clinical diagnosis); 35.2% (DC-LD); 16.6% (ICD-10); and 15.7% (DSM-IV-

TR). Similarly, high prevalence rates have also been reported for children and young people with intellectual/developmental disabilities, in whom mental health problems are about four times more common than in the general population (Einfeld, Ellis, & Emerson, 2011; Emerson and Hatton, 2007).

Although much of the prevalence data comes from Europe, and particularly the UK, the National Core Indicators from the USA has identified that a rate of 55% of people with IDD have a co-occurring psychiatric disorder (National Core Indicators, 2016). This study is based on patient charts from 30 states in the USA (N=13,466).

Another study that used a random sample (N=240) reported on different prevalence rates depending on the diagnostic classification system (Bailey, 2007). The data indicated that when using the DC-LD the rate was 57.0%; the ICD-10 reflected a rate of 24.8%; and 13.2% when using the DSM-IV.

These studies, as well as others, demonstrate that there is a higher prevalence rate when using diagnostic systems that are designed to assess mental disorders in people with IDD. Moreover, these studies indicate that the use of the DSM system reflects much lower rates than when using other diagnostic systems, even when compared to other nosology systems that are also not designed for assessing mental disorders in people with IDD (e.g. ICD-10). Hence the need for DM-ID-2, to consider and interpret how to use DSM-5 specifically from the perspective of people with intellectual disabilities.

Classification and Diagnosis of Mental Illness: Historical Perspective

The clinician is faced with certain challenges when an individual with ID presents with disturbed or disturbing behavior. Since at least as long ago as early Greek civilization, it has been acknowledged that not all abnormal behavior arises from a single, unitary cause. People might behave similarly or differently for a number of reasons, and knowing the specific reasons can be helpful not only in explaining the disturbing behavior but also in constructing an intervention that might alleviate the behavior. This is the reason that we attempt to classify behavior into discrete groupings, including syndromes.

Since the time of early Greeks, then, there have been a multitude of systems of nomenclature for mental disorders, each based upon underlying concepts of causation. Each of these systems was limited by the underlying theoretical and philosophical framework used to construct the system. It became increasingly difficult to clearly describe behaviors in terms that had some sort of common acceptance.

At the beginning of the twentieth century, Emil Kraepelin, a German psychiatrist, developed a systematic classification based upon manifest, observable behavior (Alexander & Selesnick, 1966). This classification system enabled psychiatrists from many different places to describe psychiatric disorders in a manner that could be duplicated elsewhere. Because the system was based on observable behavior, the theoretical approach of the psychiatrist would not determine the way he or she characterized the particular psychiatric disorder.

In the mid-twentieth century, the American Psychiatric Association (APA) published the *Diagnostic and Statistical Manual of Mental Disorders (DSM)* (American Psychiatric Association, 1952) as a systematic document containing descriptions of each of the disorders contained within this classification system. Although this system used the terminology of "reactions" and "syndromes," there was a clear effort to describe various disorders in behavioral and observable terms. In 1968, the *DSM-II* (American Psychiatric Association, 1968) eliminated the terminology of "reactions" in favor of such terms as Anxiety, Neurosis, and Schizophrenia, but in general there were few changes in the overall structure. Starting with the *DSM-III* in 1980 (American Psychiatric Association, 1980), diagnostic criteria sets were developed for each disorder, based whenever possible on observable phenomena. The *DSM-III-R* (American Psychiatric Association, 1987) and the *DSM-IV* (American Psychiatric Association, 1994) introduced some changes in individual categories, but in general the basic framework remained relatively unchanged.

The *DSM* diagnostic criteria are constructed to be "generic"; that is, they should ideally be applicable to all patient populations, independent of the patient's age, ethnicity, culture, gender, or the presence of comorbid medical or mental conditions. There have been many critiques of the *DSM*, however, arguing that developmental issues, cultural context, and other factors can affect the symptomatic expression of disorders.

Additionally, there has been controversy found in the literature concerning the issue of reliability in making specific *DSM* diagnosis in persons with ID, especially those with more severe impairment and intellectual function (Einfeld & Aman, 1995). Mickkelsen and McKenna (1999) assert that as intelligence decreases the validity of psychiatric diagnosis for individuals with ID tends to decrease. They explain this as the result of both an increase in nonspecific organic factors and the relative inaccessibility of the individual's inner life as productive speech decreases with the increased severity of impairment. Noting a general consensus that mental disorders can be diagnosed using standard diagnostic criteria for people with mild IDD and reasonably good communicative skills, Szymanski et al. (1998) acknowledge the increased difficulty for individuals with more severe IDD and poor verbal skills.

The *DM-ID* is not the first attempt to improve the diagnosis of mental disorders in individuals with ID. The Royal College of Psychiatrists in 2001 published a guide entitled *DC-LD [Diagnostic Criteria for Psychiatric Disorders for Use with Adults with Learning Disabilities/ Mental Retardation]* (Royal College of Psychiatrists, 2001). The *DC-LD* is a classification system that has been developed in recognition of limitations of the *ICD-10* Manual published by the World Health Organization (1992) and in its place the *DC-LD* reflects a consensus of current practice and opinion among psychiatrists from the United Kingdom and Ireland who specialize in ID (referred to there as *learning disabilities*). The *DC-LD* provides operationalized diagnostic criteria for psychiatric disorders and is intended primarily for use with adults with moderate to profound ID.

Recognizing the diagnostic challenges that clinicians face when attempting to arrive at an accurate psychiatric diagnosis for individuals with IDD co-occurring with mental illness, in 2007 the National Association for the Dually Diagnosed (NADD), in association with the American Psychiatric Association (APA), published *00*(Fletcher, Loschen, Stavrakaki, & First, 2007). The *DM-ID* was designed as a companion to the *DSM-IV-TR* and aimed to assist clinicians to arrive at a more accurate *DSM-IV-TR* diagnosis for individuals with IDD. In 2013, the American Psychiatric Association published the *DSM-5*, thus necessitating revision of the *DM-ID* to incorporate the changes from the *DSM-IV-TR* to the *DSM-5*.

Diagnostic Challenges

During the past few decades, there have been important developments in the field of mental health care for people with IDD. The National Association for the Dually Diagnosed has been instrumental in marshaling national and international attention, providing education and training, and disseminating relevant clinical and research policy issues. In spite of these encouraging developments, however, there remain significant obstacles hindering appropriate care and treatment for this underserved population. One key problem has been the lack of a diagnostic system appropriate for clinical use with the diverse population of people with IDD (Sturmey, 1999). As a result, individuals may receive no psychiatric diagnosis even when a mental disorder exists, or they may receive an inaccurate or inappropriate diagnosis. Because treatments, services, and supports are tied directly to the accurate evaluation and diagnosis of people who have IDD coexistent with mental disorders, the absence of psychiatric diagnoses is a central issue.

Clinicians need a system whereby they can recognize the presence of *DSM-5*-documented mental disorders in persons who have limited expressive and receptive language skills. The DSM system relies primarily on self-report.

Individuals report to the clinician their signs, symptoms, feelings, and experiences. A major advantage of the *DM-ID-2* is that it enhances the reliability of psychiatric diagnoses in persons with IDD which could ultimately improve treatment outcomes.

There are a number of factors associated with the difficulty of making an accurate diagnosis in people with IDD. The applicability of existing standardized classification systems (such as the DSM-5) for persons with IDD has been critically debated in professional literature (Sturmey, 1999). To determine whether a person within the general population has been experiencing psychiatric symptoms, a clinician typically relies on the person's description of his or her experiences and feelings. Individuals with cognitive impairments experience difficulties in receptive and expressive language to varying degrees. Mild limitations in cognitive and verbal skills make it difficult, and severe limitations may make it impossible, for people with IDD to articulate such abstract or global concepts as depressed mood or to communicate subtle differences among emotional or motivational states.

Other factors that increase the difficulty in making psychiatric diagnoses include the tendency for some people with IDD to attempt to hide their disabilities (to adopt a "cloak of competence"; Edgerton, 1967), the tendency not to be forthcoming with respect to self-descriptions, and the tendency for some to try to please the evaluator by answering falsely or in a manner that is inaccurate ("acquiescence bias"). Additionally, the symptoms of diverse psychiatric disorders are often expressed differently in people with IDD. Sovner (1986) has identified four processes that are common in persons with IDD that can influence the diagnostic decision-making process: (1) baseline exaggeration, (2) intellectual distortion, (3) psychosocial masking, and (4) cognitive disintegration.

Another diagnostic challenge is diagnostic overshadowing (Reiss, Levitan, & Szyszko, 1982). Having a diagnosis of IDD can overshadow coexisting mental disorders and may predispose practitioners to overlook the presence of psychopathology because unusual or anomalous behavior is attributed by the clinician to being artifacts of developmental or social delay. For example, a person with profound IDD who is very withdrawn and asocial might be less likely to be labeled as depressed than would a person with average intelligence (Sturmey, 1999). Adding further to this risk of diagnostic overshadowing is the considerable amount of physical disorders, impairments, and multimorbidity that people with intellectual disabilities experience (Cooper et al, 2015).

Accurate diagnosis is important because it provides a sound basis for effective treatment. Positive treatment outcome is based on an accurate diagnosis. Just as this is true concerning physical health, it is equally true in psychiatric health.

Severe behavioral disturbance in the form of verbal or physical aggression toward others, self-injury (aggression toward self), and property destruction frequently motivates referrals for diagnosis and treatment prescription. Such severe disturbance occurs at a clinically significant rate among people with ID, often threatens the stability of family living or the continuation of community living in a relatively nonrestrictive setting, and can precipitate admission to a public mental health or ID facility. Severe behavioral disturbance of various types occurs among people with mild to profound ID. However, it is important to understand that severe behavioral disturbances are not part and parcel of a diagnosis of ID. The presence of clinically significant behavioral disturbances mandates a thorough clinical diagnostic evaluation to determine the presence of comorbid mental and physical disorders that may be responsible for the behavioral disturbance. The extent to which behavioral disturbances represent symptom equivalents for symptoms such as depression and anxiety, especially in individuals with severe and profound ID, has been the subject of considerable debate, which remains to be elucidated by further research.

Diagnosis for an individual within the population without IDD generally relies upon the person's description of his or her experiences and feelings. Individuals with IDD have limited receptive and expressive language, thus limiting their ability to describe their symptoms. They may also lack the self-reflection to describe internal states. Furthermore, individuals with IDD who are experiencing mental illness may present in very different ways than their peers without IDD. The DM-ID-2 provides guidance for assessing and diagnosing specific disorders in individuals with IDD and provides information on recognizing challenging behaviors of individuals with IDD and how to differentiate between behavioral problems and psychiatric disorders. The DM-ID-2 is designed as a companion to the DSM-5 and aimed to assist clinicians to arrive at a more accurate diagnosis for individuals with IDD.

The DM-ID-2

The publication of the *DSM-5* (American Psychiatric Association, 2013) necessitated that the *DM-ID* be updated. NADD began putting together work groups to revise the *DM-ID* during the summer of 2012. One hundred and four experts from around the world were recruited to work in 26 work groups. A chairperson was identified for each work group.

Changes from *DSM-IV* to *DSM-5* reflect developments in genetic research and neuroimaging as well as efforts to promote ease of use. The disorders included in *DSM-5* have been reordered into a revised organizational structure, reflecting the fact that mental disorders do not always fit completely within the boundaries of a single disorder and that some symptom domains involve multiple diagnostic categories. DSM-5 recognizes developmental issues utilizing a lifespan approach and including descriptions of how the disorder presentation changes across the lifespan. The multi-axial approach has been dropped. A number of disorders that had been distinct in *DSM-IV*, such as autistic disorder, Asperger's disorder, and pervasive developmental disorder, have been consolidated in *DSM-5* and the *DM-ID-2* into autism spectrum disorder (ASD). Trauma- and stressor-related disorders in the *DSM-5* and *DM-ID-2* is an umbrella diagnostic area that now includes reactive attachment disorder, disinhibited social engagement disorder, posttraumatic stress disorder (PTSD), acute stress disorder, and adjustment disorder. The classification for bipolar and depressive disorders has been streamlined. Disorders previously referred to as "dementias" are now designated as major or mild neurocognitive disorders and have enhanced specificity.

Expert Consensus Model

Whilst there have been recent exploratory and confirmatory factor analyses that have delineated major grouping of psychopathology (depression, anxiety, psychosis, organic, emotional dysregulation/problem behaviours) in adults with intellectual disabilities (Melville, McConnochie, et al., 2016; Melville, Smiley, et al., 2016), there is a general dearth of research in the specific diagnostic categories of co-occurring IDD and mental illness. "Because many pertinent questions encountered in everyday practice are not well answered by the available research, expert consensus is a valuable bridge between clinical research and clinical practice" (Frances, Kahn, Carpenter, Frances & Docherty, 1988). In the absence of research, the collective opinion of experts is considered a useful and appropriate guide. For this reason, the authors of the DM-ID-2 relied upon an expert consensus model in much of their work. Grounded in the expert consensus model, each chapter grew out of a critical review of the available literature.

In the development of diagnostic systems and practice guidelines, consensus committees, consisting of experts, researchers, and practitioners, have been formed for various topics in medicine and behavioral healthcare. Consensus methods were an important aspect of the development of all editions of the DSM, and these methods have been applied within the field of developmental disabilities with respect to practice issues centering around the use of psychotropic medications (Reiss & Aman, 1998), integration of psychotropic medication and other treatments (Reiss & Aman, 1998), diagnosis and intervention for autism spectrum disorders (New York Department of Health [NY-

DOH], 1999a, 1999b, 1999c), and diagnosis and treatment of mental health problems in people with intellectual disabilities (National Institute for Health and Care Excellence, 2016).

Chapter Structure for DM-ID-2

A guideline was developed to structure the diagnostic chapters, allowing for clarity and uniformity. The diagnostic chapters in the DM-ID-2 generally follow this guideline. The primary elements of the guideline are listed below.

- Chapter summary
- Review of diagnostic criteria
  - General description of the disorder
  - Summary of DSM-5 criteria
  - Issues related to diagnosis in persons with ID
  - Development and course
  - Prevalence
  - Differential diagnosis
  - Functional consequences [if relevant]
  - Comorbidity
- Application of diagnostic criteria to people with ID
  - General considerations
  - Methodology
  - Review research applying to people with ID
  - Adults with mild to moderate intellectual disability
  - Adults with severe or profound intellectual disability
  - Children and adolescents with intellectual disability
  - Limitations in applying DSM-5 criteria to people with ID
- Etiology and Pathogenesis
  - Biological Factors
  - Psychosocial Factors
  - Developmental Factors
- Application of criteria
  - Table of Applied Criteria
  - References

The *DM-ID-2* encompasses seven types of applications of the *DSM-5* criteria. Unlike the *DSM* system, the *DM-ID* system does not rely on self-report. The *DM-ID* criteria subsets are principally concerned with observation of behaviors.

Table of Applied Criteria		
***DSM-5* Criteria**	Appling Criteria for Mild and Moderate ID	Applying Criteria for Severe and Profound ID

The seven applied criteria are:

1. Addition of symptom equivalents
   - Observed reports that are equivalent to self-reports as identified in the DSM system
2. Omission of symptoms
   - Symptoms that do not exist or cannot be identified in persons with IDD
3. Changes in symptom count
   - Indicated the frequency of a symptom that is required to meet the diagnostic criteria
4. Modification of symptom duration
   - The length of time a symptom has to be present in order to meet the diagnostic criteria
5. Modification of age requirements
   - Indicates change in age to take into consideration the developmental perspective of the individual with IDD
6. Addition of explanatory notes
   - Intended to communicate a criterion without an official modification of the criteria subset
7. Criteria sets that do not apply
   - Criteria sets that do not apply to persons with IDD

Some of the diagnostic chapters consolidated applied criteria ranging from mild-profound. As such, there will be two columns; one column lists the DSM-5 criteria, with another column listing applied criteria for mild-profound IDD, where applicable. Other diagnostic chapters have three columns; the left-hand column lists the DSM-5 criteria, the middle column lists applied criteria for mild-moderate IDD, and the right-hand column lists applied criteria for severe-profound IDD. It is important to note that there is not always a change from the DSM-5 criteria, and in these situations the applied criteria section will indicate that there is no change.

Limitations and Cross-Referencing

The American Psychiatric Association, publisher of the DSM-5, only allows for the reproduction of approximately 50% of criteria subsets. Therefore, the DM-ID-2 was restricted with regards to the number and extent of DSM-5 articulated diagnostic subsets. Thus we had to be selective with which criteria we chose to include in the DM-ID-2. We chose to exclude some criteria on the basis of their extreme similarity with another criteria set; in this case we comment at the bottom of the tables to this effect. Other criteria sets were omitted on the basis of rarity. Throughout several of the DSM-5 chapters, criteria are repeated for the specific mental disorders in question being due to another medical condition, and also for the specific mental disorder in question being induced by a substance/medication. Hence, rather than repeating the full criteria sets in several chapters, we provide them here, and cross-refer the specific chapter to these two tables where they apply.

DSM-5 Criteria for mental disorder due to another medical condition

DSM-5 Criteria for Mental Disorder Due to Another Medical Condition	Applying Criteria for Mild and Moderate ID	Applying Criteria for Severe and Profound ID
A. Symptoms/signs as reported in the relevant chapter.	A. Adaptations as reported in the relevant chapter.	A. Adaptations as reported in the relevant chapter.
B. There is evidence from the history, physical examination, or laboratory findings that the disturbance is the direct physiological consequence of a general medical condition.	B. No adaptation.	B. No adaptation.
C. The disturbance is not better explained by another mental disorder.	C. No adaptation.	C. No adaptation.
D. The disturbance does not occur exclusively during the course of a delirium.	D. No adaptation.	D. No adaptation.
E. The disturbance causes clinically significant distress or impairment in social, occupational, or other important areas of functioning.		

DSM-5 Criteria for substance/medication-induced mental disorder

DSM-5 Criteria for Substance/Medication-Induced Mental Disorder	Applying Criteria for Mild and Moderate ID	Applying Criteria for Severe and Profound ID
A. Symptoms/signs as reported in the relevant chapter.	A. Adaptations as reported in the relevant chapter.	A. Adaptations as reported in the relevant chapter.
B. There is evidence from the history, physical examination, or laboratory findings of: 1. the symptoms in Criterion A developed during, or soon after substance intoxication or withdrawal or after exposure to a medication. 2. The involved substance/medication is capable of producing the symptoms in Criterion A.	B. No adaptation.	B. No adaptation.
C. The disturbance is not better explained by a mental disorder that is not substance/medication induced. Such evidence of an independent mental disorder could include the following: The symptoms preceded the onset of the substance/medication use; the symptoms persist for a substantial amount of time (e.g., about 1 month) after the cessation of acute withdrawal or severe intoxication; or there is other evidence of an independent non-substance/medication-induced mental disorder (e.g. history of recurrent non-substance/medication-related episodes).	C. No adaptation.	C. No adaptation.
D. The disturbance does not occur exclusively during the course of a delirium.	D. No adaptation.	D. No adaptation.
E. The disturbance causes clinically significant distress or impairment in social, occupational, or other important areas of functioning.		

Added Value Chapters

In addition to all the major diagnoses that are found in the *DSM-5*, the *DM-ID-2* includes two additional chapters. Following this chapter, there is a chapter on assessment and diagnostic procedures. This chapter is important as it assists the reader in understanding the biopsychosocial developmental approach to conducting a psychiatric assessment with individuals who have an intellectual disability. Another added value chapter informs the reader about behavioral phenotypes that are associated with genetic disorders, which is intended to aid in the understanding of how a disorder's genotype affects its behavioral phenotype.

Neurodevelopmental Disorders

The *DSM-5* changes the "Disorders with Onset during Childhood and Adolescence" (*DSM-IV-TR* and *DM-ID*) to a new category "Neurodevelopmental Disorders." The reorganization adds stereotypic movement disorders and tic disorders to the neurodevelopmental disorders. There are major components of neurodevelopmental disorders: age of onset during the developmental period; diagnosis based on assessment based on a deviation from expected lines of development and differentiation from other medical or neurodegenerative disorders. Even when these basic criteria are met, there is still a high rate of overlap between them. This pattern of high rates of comorbidity also applies to other psychiatric disorders (American Psychiatric Association, 2013; Fletcher et al., 2007).

Because of these boundary issues, many affected children may have multiple developmental diagnoses. For example, child can have autism spectrum disorder, severe intellectual disability; attention deficit hyperactivity disorder and a tic disorder. The relationship between these neurodevelopmental disorders, challenging behaviors, and primary psychiatric disorders can also complex (American Psychiatric Association, 2013). In the *DM-ID-2*, intellectual disability is already established and serves as a starting point in the diagnosis. As a result, the diagnostician must consider how the severity of IDD limits our ability to clearly recognize many neurodevelopmental disorders (e.g. specific learning and communication disorders in nonverbal individuals). The presence of severe IDD can also affect the developmental trajectory of emerging motor co-ordination, communication, and specific learning disorders as well as the validity of many diagnostic instruments crucial to defining these disorders (Barnhill, 2014).

In recent years, it is becoming increasingly obvious that many primary psychiatric disorders are also neurodevelopmental in nature. The risk for early onset psychiatric disorders is related to gene-environmental interactions, the timing of early developmental stressors (e.g. trauma), and history of learning experiences and in some cases, the presence of a specific behavioral phenotype. In addition, the presence of IDD or autism spectrum disorder also alter the development, assessment, and treatment of schizophrenia, bipolar, depressive, anxiety and obsessive-compulsive/related disorders. Lastly, severity of IDD and autism spectrum disorder plays a critical role in the development of challenging behaviors (aggression, self-injury, anddisruptive and destructive behaviors) that frequently accompany primary psychiatric disorders (Barnhill, 2014). In order to negotiate these issues, the diagnostician needs a good working knowledge of diagnostic overshadowing, baseline exaggeration, and vulnerability to cognitive, emotional, and behavioral disorganization and cognitive distortions (Barnhill, 2014; Fletcher et al., 2007; Gardner, Griffiths, & Hamlin, 2012).

Other Disorders

Whislt neurodevelopmental disorders emerge in childhood and persist into adulthood, a large number of other types of disorders more typically have onset in youth, adulthood, or at older age. Chapters on these are presented in the DSM-5 after the neurodevelopment disorder chapter. Key changes include the streamlining of bipolar disorders and depressive disorders, the elimination of substance abuse and substance dependence which are replaced with a new overarching category of substance use disorders, and the enhanced specificity for major and mild neurocognitive disorders (formerly known as the dementias) to reflect scientific advances in this area. The categorization of personality disorders remains similar to that in DSM-IV, but section III of DSM-5 presents an alternative hybrid model of impairments in personality functioning and pathological personality traits.

Problem behaviors commonly present in children and adults with intellectual disabilities. *DSM-5* does not consider these as disorders, and hence it is essential to consider the underlying causes of the problem behavior and code accordingly. *DM-ID-2*, therefore, also follows this approach.

Summary

The *Diagnostic Manual – Intellectual Disability 2 (DM-ID-2): A Textbook of Diagnosis of Mental Disorders in Persons with Intellectual Disability* is designed to provide state-of-the-art knowledge of mental disorders and IDD. It provides a series of chapters that corresponds closely to the DSM-5 classification system, with specific directions for applying the existing criteria to make them apply to persons with dual diagnosis. The authors of the chapters were selected largely from among professionals who had made international contributions to the field of dual diagnosis. The DM-ID-2, therefore, represents a multicentered, multicultural, and multifaceted collaborative effort of many experts, an effort aimed at an improved understanding of mental disorders and their unique expressions in persons with IDD.

References

Alexander, F. G., & Selesnick, S. T. (1966). *The history of psychiatry: An evaluation of psychiatric thought and practice from prehistoric times to the present.* New York: Harper and Row.

American Psychiatric Association. (1952). *Diagnostic and statistical manual of mental disorders (DSM).* Washington, DC: Author.

American Psychiatric Association. (1968). *Diagnostic and statistical manual of mental disorders (DSM-II)* (2nd ed.). Washington, DC: Author.

American Psychiatric Association. (1980). *Diagnostic and statistical manual of mental disorders (DSM-III)* (3rd ed.). Washington, DC: Author.

American Psychiatric Association. (1987). *Diagnostic and statistical manual of mental disorders (DSM-III-TR)* (3rd ed., revised) Washington, DC: Author.

American Psychiatric Association. (1994). *Diagnostic and statistical manual of mental disorders (DSM-IV)* (4th ed.) Washington, DC: Author.

American Psychiatric Association. (2013). *Diagnostic and statistical manual of mental disorders (DSM-5)* (5th ed.). Washington, DC: American Psychiatric Publishing.

Bailey, N.M., 2007. Prevalence of psychiatric disorders in adults with moderate to profound learning disabilities. *Advances in Mental Health and Learning Disabilities,* 1, 36-44.

Barnhill J. (2014), Child development and intellectual disabilities: The challenge of hitting a moving target. In D. Baker & E. Blumberg (Eds.), *Mental health and wellness supports for youth with IDD* (pp. 223-237). Kingston, NY: NADD Press.

Buckles, J. (2016). The epidemiology of psychiatric disorders in adults with intellectual disabilities. In C. Hemmings & N. Bouras (Eds.), *Psychiatric and behavioral disorders in intellectual and developmental disabilities.* Cambridge, UK: Cambridge University Press.

Cooper, S.A., Smiley, E., Morrison, J., Williamson, A., Allan, L. (2007). Mental ill-health in adults with intellectual disabilities: prevalence and associated factors. Mental health services for adults with learning disabilities. *British Journal of Psychiatry, 190,* 27-35.

Cooper, S-A., McLean, G., Guthrie, B., McConnachie, A., Mercer, S., Sullivan, F. & Morrison, J. (2015). Multiple physical and mental health comorbidity in adults with intellectual disabilities: population-based cross-sectional analysis. *BMC Family Practice,* DOI: 10.1186/s12875-015-0329-3.

Edgerton, R. B. (1967). *The cloak of competence: Stigma in the lives of the mentally retarded.* Berkeley, CA: University of California Press.

Einfeld, S.L. & Aman, M.G. (1995). Issue in the taxonomy of psychopathology in children and adolescents with mental retardation. *Journal of Autism and Developmental Disorders. 25,* 143-167.

Einfeld, S. Ellis, L. & Emerson, E. (2011). Comorbidity of intellectual disability and mental disorder in children and adolescents: A systematic review. *Journal of Intellectual and Developmental Disability, 36,* 137-43.

Emerson E, & Hatton C. (2007). Mental health of children and adolescents with intellectual disabilities in Britain. *British Journal of Psychiatry, 191,* 493-99.

Fletcher, L., Loschen, E., Stavrakaki, C., & First, M. (Eds.). (2007). *Diagnostic manual–intellectual disability: A textbook of diagnosis of mental disorders in persons with intellectual disability.* Kingston, NY: NADD Press.

France, A., Kahn, D., Carpenter, D., Frances, C., & Docherty, J. (1998, July) A new method of developing expert consensus practice guidelines. *American Journal of Managed Care. 4 (7)*: 1023-9.

Gardner, W. I., Griffiths, D. M., & Hamlin, J. (2012). Biopsychosocial features influencing aggression: A multimodal assessment and therapy approach. In J. K. Luiselli (Ed.), *The handbook of high-risk challenging behaviors: Assessment and intervention* (pp. 83–102). Towson, MD: Brookes.

Melville, C., McConnachie, A., Johnson, P., Purves, D., Smiley, E. Simpson, N., & Cooper, S-A. (2016). Problem behaviours and symptom dimensions of psychiatric disorders in adults with intellectual disabilities: an exploratory and confirmatory factor analysis. *Research in Developmental Disabilities, 55*, 1-13.

Melville, C.A., Smiley, E., Simpson, N., Johnson, P., McConnachie, A., Purves, D., & Cooper, S-A. (2016). Statistical modelling studies examining the dimensional structure of psychopathology experienced by adults with intellectual disabilities. Systematic review. *Research in Developmental Disabilities, 53-54*, 1-10. doi.org/10.1016/j.ridd.2016.01.018

Mikkelsen, E. J. & McKenna, L. (1999). Psychopharmacologic algorithms for adults with developmental disabilities and difficult-to-diagnose behavioral disorders. *Psychiatric Annals. 29* (5), 302-314.

National Core Indicators. (2016). Mental illness or psychiatric diagnosis. Retrieved from www.nationalcoreindicators.org/charts/.

National Institute for Health and Care Excellence (2016) Mental health problems in people with learning disabilities. Prevention, assessment and management, https://www.nice.org.uk/guidance/indevelopment/gid-cgwave0684

New York Department of Health. (1999a). *Clinical practice guidelines: Report of the recommendations. Autism / pervasive developmental disorders, assessment and intervention for young children (age 0-3 years).* Publication No. 4215. Albany, NY: New York Department of Health (NYDOH).

New York Department of Health. (1999b). *Clinical practice guidelines: Quick reference guide. Autism/pervasive developmental disorders, assessment and intervention for young children (age 0-3 years).* Publication No. 4216. Albany, NY: New York Department of Health (NYDOH).

New York Department of Health. (1999c). *Clinical practice guidelines: The technical report. Autism / pervasive developmental disorders, assessment and intervention for young children (age 0-3 years).* Publication No. 4217. Albany, NY: New York Department of Health (NYDOH).

Reiss, S. (1994). *Handbook of challenging behavior: Mental health aspects of mental retardation.* Worthington, OH: IDS Publishing Corporation.

Reiss, S., & Aman, M.G. (Eds.). (1988). The international concsensus handbook: Psychotropic medications and developmental disabilities. Columbus, Ohio: Ohio State University –Nsonger Center.

Reiss, S., Levitan, G. W., & Szyszko, J. (1982). Emotional disturbance in mental retardation: Diagnostic overshadowing. *American Journal of Mental Deficiency. 86*, 567-571.

Royal College of Psychiatrists. (2001). *Diagnostic criteria for psychiatric disorders for use with adults with learning/mental retardation (DC-LD).* Occasional paper OP 48. London: Gaskell.

Rush, A. J., & Frances, A. (Eds.). (2000). Treatment of psychiatric and behavioral problems in mental retardation (Special issue). *American Journal on Mental Retardation, 105(3).*

Sovner, R. (1986). Limiting factors in using DSM-III criteria with mentally ill/mentally retarded persons. *Psychopharmacology Bulletin, 22*, 1055-1059.

Sturmey, P. (1999). Classification: Concept, progress and future. In N. Bouras (Ed.), *Psychiatric and behavioural disorders in developmental disabilities and mental retardation* (pp. 3-17). New York: Cambridge University Press.

Szymanski, L. S., King, B., Goldberg, B., Reid, A. H., Tonge, B. J. & Cain, N. (1998). Diagnosis of mental disorders in people with mental retardation. In S. Reiss & M. G. Aman (Eds). *Psychotropic and developmental disabilities: The international consensus handbook* (pp. 3-17). Columbus: Ohio State University, Nisonger Center.

World Health Organization (1992) ICD-10 International classification Diagnostic. 10th edition (ICD-10).

CHAPTER 2

Assessment and Diagnostic Procedures

Anne Desnoyers Hurley
Andrew Levitas
James K. Luiselli
Steve Moss
Elspeth A. Bradley
Nicola M. Bailey

The assessment of psychiatric disorder and challenging behavior problems in people with intellectual disability is clearly a vast topic. This chapter clearly cannot cover all the issues and challenges that arise. Rather, it focuses primarily on the application of DSM-5 in this population. As such, we will be concerning ourselves primarily with a psychiatric approach. Within this perspective, diagnosis is the paramount aim, collecting the necessary information to determine which diagnostic criteria the person meets.

While making these determinations reliably and validly for people with intellectual disability is the focus of this chapter, it is important to bear in mind that assessment often has aims beyond the production of a diagnosis. In most cases, the ultimate aim of assessment is hopefully to help the person. In this respect, diagnosis may often be a step towards a comprehensive formulation, rather than an end in itself.

Psychiatric diagnosis and treatment is always challenging due to the complexity of human nature, cultural differences, male-female differences, personality, and neuropsychological abilities as well as other ecological, social, and historical factors. There are no "lab" tests to help us diagnose a patient. When the patient is a person with a specific neurodevelopmental disorder such as intellectual disability, the process of diagnosis and treatment is that much more complicated. The aim of this chapter is to highlight specific differences and vulnerabilities unique to people with intellectual disability who are seeking psychiatric care, differences and vulnerabilities that can affect diagnosis and treatment.

The main format of psychiatric diagnosis is the *psychiatric diagnostic interview.* This is, ideally, an interview with the patient that is comfortable, builds a relationship, and offers critical information upon which to begin treatment. For those with intellectual disability, in most cases, this format is not ideal. Like young children or elderly people with severe dementia, most people with intellectual disability cannot fully participate in the question-answer framework of the interview. The practitioner cannot accept the discourse as reliable and, therefore, must use multiple sources of information to assist in the evaluation process. Reliance on third-party information is always given through the eyes of that person, not the patient. Even under the best of circumstances, the diagnosis can be quite provisional and might remain so throughout the course of treatment. The aim of any clinician who cares for persons with intellectual disability must be to try to see the world through their eyes; understand the difficulties imposed by developmental delay; be sympathetic to their difficulties navigating modern life; and understand their relationships and supports. Unlike a neurotypical person, those with intellectual disability are at great disadvantage in speaking for themselves in all areas of life, and none so obvious as the psychiatric diagnostic interview.

The aim of this chapter is to highlight the complexity of diagnosis for people with intellectual disability and offer suggestions to enhance diagnosis and treatment. Multiple perspectives are very important when using third-party information. Ideally, the person will be able to give some information, but all caregivers and support professionals will have their information as well, spanning different settings. We also advocate for the use of published rating scales and a constant documentation of symptom decrease or increase. In addition, special attention to psychosocial stressors and medical conditions must be emphasized for each person. Lastly, constant skepticism and "clinical uncertainty" must be accepted as "state of the art" when treating people with intellectual disability.

Psychiatric Diagnostic Interview

Special Considerations for Persons with ID

The first and obvious consideration is that many people with intellectual disability simply cannot undertake a clinical interview. Patel, Goldberg, and Moss (1993), using the PAS-ADD interview with older people with ID, found that 49% of subjects could complete the whole interview, with a further 13% being able to answer selected core items from the interview. Interestingly, this study found that the relationship between developmental level and ability to complete the interview was not as strong as might have been predicted. Some people with a low measured IQ were surprisingly good at being able to talk about symptoms, while some people with IQs over 60 found it very difficult. When the study was originally conceived, it was thought that some symptoms might be easier to discuss than others, so a subset of "core" items was identified. The idea was that the clinician would focus on these items in the case of poor linguistic ability; it was found that predictions about the ease or difficulty of specific symptoms were not borne out. Again, some people found some symptoms easier to discuss, while other symptoms were easier for other people.

Broadly speaking, it is of course easier to interview people with a higher developmental level. Paradoxically, however, the problems of interviewing may actually be more difficult to identify. For people with more severe intellectual disability, the communication issues are absolutely clear. For a person in the mild or borderline region, on the other hand, the language may appear to be perfect yet mask major problems in dealing with abstract concepts that the general population handles effortlessly. For instance, ask a member of the general population if he/she gets anxious and he/she will know all the various manifestations that this will include. The field trials of the PAS-ADD clinical interview found cases where high-functioning persons responded "no" in response to a question "Do you get anxious?" but subsequently reported anxiety symptoms. In one of these cases, the person went on to describe a panic attack on a bus that very week and reported actually listening every day to tapes for relaxation.

The mental health clinician must therefore exercise special care in several areas when interacting with an individual who has intellectual disability. First, the clinician must use language that is understandable to the individual and needs to verify the individual's comprehension. Because clinicians customarily talk rapidly, and use complex language in long sentences, individuals with intellectual disability can be at a disadvantage during the interview. The clinician should make the following adjustments: (a) Use very simple vocabulary words; (b) create short sentences; (c) ask one simple question at a time; (d) wait for the answer before proceeding; (e) check back with the individual for confirmation that he or she has correctly understood the question; and (f) use visuals to assist understanding and engagement, e.g., *Books Beyond Words* (Bradley & Hollins, 2013). For individuals with little or no language, using nonverbal strategies or body language will facilitate the therapeutic engagement and enrich the psychiatric evaluation (Boardman, Bernal, & Hollins, 2014). These adaptations obviously necessitate extra time, which may present serious problems in the healthcare settings where organizational factors may strictly limit the time available for screening or examination.

Intellectual disability limits the understanding of contextual implications. For example, when asked if he or she ever hears voices speaking inside his or her head, an individual with intellectual disability might answer affirmatively, referring to the self-talk we all have. The mental health clinician will, therefore, need to clarify explicitly — for example, by explaining that he or she is inquiring about when the individual is alone and not talking to himself or herself, even silently. To obtain the most reliable information, one sh [illegible] such a [illegible]

A m [illegible] of the i [illegible] agree to [illegible] of "yessi [illegible] vidual be [illegible] ever the a [illegible] of complia [illegible] la, 1997). [illegible] not frame [illegible] because this [illegible] understandi [illegible] ses. When yes-or-no qu [illegible] are necessary, the clinician should augment the individual'sresponses through more pointed requests for descriptions.

Sovner (1986) outlined four main difficulties in assessing a person with intellectual disability that are related to developmental delay and/or cognitive limitations (see Table 1 below).

Table 1.
Four Difficulties in Assessing Persons with Intellectual Disability

Presentation	Explanation
Baseline Exaggeration	Increase in challenging behavior frequency and/or intensity during the course of a mental illness. The most frequent situation that occasions the mental health evaluation appointment. For example, an individual may have a low rate of mild self-injurious behavior (SIB), but during a time of stress the frequency and intensity of this behavior escalates to a dangerous level, prompting a mental health appointment.
Intellectual Distortion	The individual cannot accurately understand the questions posed by the evaluator, nor assemble the correct information to respond. For example, when asked if he or she "hears voices," the individual might respond affirmatively without fully comprehending the implication in the question: The clinician meant abnormal phantom voices, whereas the individual was thinking of ordinary voices, including the clinician's, that he or she was able to hear. This example may seem understandable, but many responses are clearly inadequate or incorrect. Much like interviewing children, no answer can be taken at face value.
Psychosocial Masking	Due to developmental delay, the individual might present significant symptomatology that occurs within a developmental framework and would be common in, for example, a young child. For example, a manic individual with moderate intellectual disability might believe that he or she can drive a car, a skill well beyond such an individual's capability, and this is a manifestation of grandiosity.
Cognitive Disintegration	The individual may become grossly disorganized and psychotic due to the lack of "cognitive reserve" available to cope with the illness. For example, in a major depressive episode, the individual with intellectual disability is more likely than neurotypical individuals to be severely affected and suffer mood-congruent hallucinations and delusions. Thus, the clinician can be left with an inadequate amount of individual-generated information with which to conduct an assessment. Further, additional behavioral repertoires or thought patterns might be due to, or consistent with, other aspects of developmental delay. That is, they would be considered typical in a young child but would appear bizarre and abnormal in an adult.

...mplaint and ...mplaint

...blem, or chief complaint, is ...ultation or initial mental health ...n the outset, the mental health cli- ...d consider the presenting problem as ... constellation of changes in the individu- ...unctioning. The clinician should ask family ...nd direct support professionals about the onset and chronology of changes in any or all of the following: School, day services, residential services, and family life. This information, acquired not only from the individual but — more importantly — from all other possible sources, will comprise the history of present illness. It is important to not only elicit the presenting problem but also determine who has defined the problem, how long it has been observed, in what environments it is observed, and — if long-standing in nature — why evaluation is being sought at this time. It is crucial that the person or persons making the referral for evaluation are present to explain their concerns (Levitas, Hurley, & Pary, 2001). It is equally crucial to have available sources from which, or by which, the individual's premorbid functioning can be described.

Because individuals with intellectual disability cannot generally articulate their personal losses and feelings in detail or in specific terms, mental health clinicians must be alert to the presence of psychosocial stressors that occurred prior to the onset of the chief complaint. For example, the loss of a parent or a longtime friend might precipitate an episode of depressive disorder, which may manifest either as crying and sadness or with aggression and disruptive, challenging behavior. In addition, many medical conditions, including but not limited to genetic disorders, constipation, seizure disorders, drug interactions, and pneumonia, might cause symptoms suggestive of mental illness. Dental health, which is not fully covered by health insurance for most individuals with intellectual disability, can be an insidious cause of pain, discomfort, and feeling unwell; caregivers are often unaware of any dental issues.

Most importantly, psychosocial stressors experienced by persons with intellectual disability might be causing challenging behavior or emotional reactions that are mistaken for more serious mental disorders. It is essential that family and direct support professionals be knowledgeable about potential stressors, which can include: Placement in an inclusion classroom; transitioning from the educational system to a residential or vocational system; changes in routine at work; disruptions at home; staff turnover at home or at work; new personal relationships; moving to a new residence; changes in the frequency of family visits or in the quality of family interactions; the loss or death of friends, family, or direct support professionals; anniversary dates of losses; and medical conditions causing disability and/or pain (Levitas & Gilson, 2001). It is well known that changes in family care settings in childhood often result in a lifelong complex trauma (van der Kolk, 2005), and many people with intellectual disability experienced changes in family or "placements" during their developmental years. As adults, more changes exacerbate their stress and symptoms.

Challenging Behaviors

These are the most frequent cause for a mental health appointment. Challenging behavior is "culturally abnormal behavior of such intensity, frequency, or duration that the physical safety of the person or others is placed in serious jeopardy, or behavior which is likely to seriously limit or deny access to the use of ordinary community facilities" (Emerson & Einfeld, 2011). These behaviors that challenge services and service providers refer to a broad class of behaviors including aggression to self (e.g., self-injury), to others (e.g., hitting, biting), and to the environment (e.g., destructiveness); stereotyped mannerisms and a range of other behaviors that may be either harmful to the individual (e.g., eating inedible substances), challenging for care providers (e.g., persistent screaming, disturbed sleep patterns, overactivity, non-compliance), and/or objectionable to members of the public (e.g., smearing of feces or saliva on self and others, regurgitation of food) (Emerson & Enfield, 2011). Estimates of problem behavior range widely from "best estimate" of 15%-17.5% in general populations of people with intellectual disability (Koritsas & Iacono, 2012) to estimates of 42%-82% in those with profound intellectual disability and multiple disabilities (Poppes, van der Putten, & Vlaskamp, 2010). Problem behaviors may occur at any age, but those starting in childhood may persist into adult life and in adults may show a relapsing and remitting course such as aggression and SIB (Cooper et al., 2009a, 2009b).

A major problem in interpreting challenging and problem behavior by people with intellectual disability is the nature of their developmental delay. All people with intellectual disability are delayed, yet the field of psychiatry has done little to study or integrate how this affects people with intellectual disability and how this can change the presentation of symptoms at the psychiatric appointment. Dosen (2005a, 2005b) has carefully explained the integration of the developmental perspective to psychiatric diagnosis. Clinicians must conceptualize the patient's presenting problem through developmental lenses. For example, tantrums when frustrated are normal in a 3-year-old but seem quite dramatic and unacceptable in a grown man with severe intellectual disability.

When the presenting problem is challenging behavior, usually aggression, self-injury, property destruction, or inordinate recalcitrance (often termed as "noncompliance"), it is important to note all of the above, the antecedents of the behavior, the environmental responses to the behavior, and the individual's responses to any interventions already attempted. Symptoms of mental disorder can wax and wane in intensity or vary with the level of stress, but they will typically be observed throughout the day and in all environments. A behavior or symptom that occurs only at home, only at school or work, only on one shift, or only with specific caregivers is more likely to either be a systems problem or be complicated by a systems problem (Levitas & Gilson, 2001). As stated previously, these behaviors are not specific to a particular diagnosis, and they might only signal a problem for the person that is interpersonal, physical, or environmental — not necessarily a mental disorder.

The problem of aggression and self-injury is the most frequent cause for a mental health appointment (Charlot, Doucette, & Mezzacappa, 1993; Hurley, Folstein, & Lam, 2003; Hurley, 2008; King, DeAntoni, McCracken, Forness, & Ackerland, 1994). Indeed, aggression or self-injury is rarely the cause for a mental health appointment for intellectually normal adults, but it is a frequent cause for such an appointment for intellectually typical children (Tardiff & Koenigsberg, 1985). As with neurotypical children, the presentation of externalizing behavioral symptoms in individuals with intellectual disability is often not helpful in achieving a diagnosis. Aggression can result from multiple factors: Dissatisfaction with environmental circumstances, poor impulse control, physical illness or discomfort, interpersonal problems, and mental disorders.

Because challenging behavior is so often the central cause initiating a mental health appointment, the need for a thorough behavioral assessment may be essential. For example, a professional trained in applied behavior analysis (ABA) might be engaged to work with the individual (The details of an ABA assessment are covered later in this chapter). A behavioral evaluation might result in a recommendation for environmental changes, for positive behavioral support plans, or for both. In many cases, changing the precipitating stresses, or setting events, in the environment can prevent a recurrence of the behavior (Luiselli, 2006). The person's family, direct support professionals, and support network must work as a collaborative team to enact any plans for change productively. When this is done, the need for mental health intervention is often eliminated (Bradley & Caldwell, 2013; Gardner, 2007).

In considering these problem behaviors, the Royal College of Psychiatrists (2012) recommends a framework of "enabling environments," shifting the concept of problem behavior from an attribution of the individual to a circumstance that is co-constructed between an individual with unique needs and his/her environment of supports. From this perspective, assessment of problem behavior would also include assessment of the environment and supports available, while treatment would include making necessary accommodations. One might also subdivide behaviors into two categories, those that signal "distress" and those that pose social difficulties for others (Bradley & Korossy, 2015).

A. Distress problem behaviors are underpinned by pain or discomfort (e.g., gastroesophageal reflux disorder, emotional loss, or psychiatric disorder). Distress problem behaviors can include aggression to self, others and property, tantrums, pica, head-banging, wrist-biting, hair-tearing, and running away. Distress behaviors are often unique to the individual, and their characteristics may or may not give clues to the location of the body discomfort (e.g., constipation may cause increase in general aggression directed towards others rather than behaviors more obviously associated with the bowel). Likewise, the same problem behavior may be a final common pathway consequent to physical or emotional distress experienced in different parts of the body.

B. Social problem behaviors are a problem for care providers but may not be distressing to the individual. They include inappropriate touching, sniffing, tasting, repetitive behaviors, stereotypies, spitting, and smearing (Sullivan, et al., 2011).

Sometimes there is overlap between these two categories. Repetitive behaviors annoying to care providers can be pleasurable to the individual; on the other hand, repetitive behaviors giving rise to self-injury may be underpinned by a medical condition or may be a way to self-soothe in an environment that is too stressful. Distinguishing between (A) and (B) is crucial to formulating effective and ethical interventions.

Anxiety Symptoms

Anxiety symptoms might go unnoticed by family and direct support professionals, and individuals with intellectual disability might not even report them. Unless these symptoms can be specifically elicited during the interview, they will be overlooked. Obsessions, compulsions, and the signs of autonomic arousal indicative of panic disorder are all observable by family and direct support professionals, and they might be accessible to individual verification. Further, anxiety symptoms may be more of an internal experience, and without the ability to speak up to others, outward manifestations may be ignored. The anxious person may withdraw, stay away from others, rarely speak, rarely make eye contact, not indicate preferences, and not indicate discomfort when it is quite intense.

Obsessive-compulsive behavior, easily diagnosed in the typical population, is often overlooked although it is frequently observed in people with autism spectrum disorder. The difficulty is that people with autism spectrum disorder rarely meet the verbalization criteria. Leyfer et al. proposed using the term obsessive compulsive behavior (OCB), finding high rates of this condition in their child and adolescent study of autism spectrum disorder (Leyfer et al., 2006). Further, anxiety may be a prime cause of challenging and problem behavior.

Vegetative Symptoms

The assessment of sleep and appetite and the perception of internal energy are essential in the mental health interview. Family and direct support professionals can be an excellent source of information if they are willing to provide that assessment. The mental health clinician can use available sleep charts, mood charts, activity information from work or school, and dietary logs to identify onset or changes. The psychiatric clinician must remember how important sleep, appetite, and energy are to daily living. It should be obvious that poor sleep over time can lead to major difficulties functioning, and/or challenging and problem behavior as a symptom for people with intellectual disability. Thus, careful questioning of the person and any caregivers is essential in the psychiatric diagnostic interview.

Mood Symptoms

Individuals with intellectual disability might express depressed mood either typically or as changes in interpersonal relations that are implausible or clearly delusional (for example, a belief that important persons no longer care about oneself or are dead). Both mania and depression can present as irritability, sometimes with explosive anger. Abnormal ebullience and elation might be misconstrued as desirable and valued mood states by family and direct support professionals until either is replaced by irritability and unwanted behaviors.

Most psychiatric clinicians would agree that the diagnosis of depression or bipolar disorder is fairly straightforward in neurotypical patients. However, it was not that long ago when psychiatrists considered that people with intellectual disability could not experience, for example, depression. This was addressed by a classic paper, "Do the mentally retarded suffer from affective illness?" (Sovner & Hurley, 1983). In a literature review, they found cases meeting *DSM-III* criteria for all affective disorders at all levels of intellectual disability. They stressed that for patients with severe and profound intellectual disability, behavioral changes and vegetative symptoms were primary signals of affective disorders. Higher-functioning patients with depression rarely verbally complained of being depressed. Rather, they might appear sullen or apathetic, or had delusions of guilt or persecution. Patients with elated mood rarely had classic grandiosity but might present with aggression. Thus, analysis of history, many questions regarding mood, and careful examination of all vegetative symptoms are necessary for any patient with intellectual disability.

Hallucinations and Delusions

Reports of family and direct support professionals, as well as the individual's self-report, of hallucinations and delusions present very significant problems for the mental health interview. For those individuals who can communicate adequately and verbally, the clinician must first evaluate these self-reports within a developmental framework. Despite mild to borderline level of intellectual disability, these individuals might still retain some prominent features of early development throughout their adult lives. The clinician must, therefore, be certain that reports of self-talk out loud or monologue, fantasy play, and imaginary friends are not within normal limits and are not merely the baseline behavior for that person (Hurley, 1996).

Individuals might have hallucinations and delusions yet have difficulty articulating them. The clinician needs to spend time trying carefully to elicit reports of thoughts and perceptions, especially those that may be visual, somatic, or proprioceptive and related to seizure or neurological conditions. Delusional belief systems must be treated as such, even though they might be simplistic or have elements of a childlike view. For example, Hurley and Moore (1999) reported erotomania in a man with mild intellectual disability, and the object of his delusion was a fictional cartoon character. Plausible-sounding delusions must be distinguished from idiosyncratically reported reality, often by checking the report against history or caregiver observation. For example, a peer may indeed be "talking about" the patient; only caregivers might be able to report that the peer left the patient's life years ago.

A difficulty with hallucinations and delusions is that although they are psychotic symptoms, they may not indicate a psychotic disorder. Children under stress will have hallucinations or delusions. Flashbacks and illusions associated with posttraumatic stress disorder in a person with intellectual disability may result in a diagnosis of schizophrenia. We must also remember that some hallucinations and delusions are "normal," e.g., ones of a deceased loved one or visual hallucinations upon awakening. A recent study of the general population found that psychotic symptoms were more comment than thought (Ian, Jenner, & Cannon, 2010). Whereas a psychotic symptom not associated with a psychiatric disorder may not worry family or friends, when it occurs in a person with intellectual disability, it may result in a psychiatric appointment. Again, constant scepticism must be the rule when exploring symptoms in patients with intellectual disability.

Suicidal or Homicidal Ideation

Persons with intellectual disability are perfectly capable of forming ideas for, or even plans for, killing oneself or others. Threats might be either functional (designed to change the response of others, sometimes for needed attention, or associated with personality disorders) or genuine (associated with a psychotic illness, severe depression or grief, for example), and harm can come from either type of threat if ignored. The clinician needs to question the events surrounding any such threats or acts and explore them with family, direct support professionals, and the individual. Any credible plan must be investigated for its feasibility. The feasibility of a threat to shoot or overdose oneself depends upon whether an individual has access to a gun or drugs. Sometimes an individual engaging in apparently nonspecific aggression or self-injury can actually be expressing suicidality or homicidality (Hurley, 1998, 2002, 2003). Finally, any self-destructive behaviors must be understood in the context of a comprehensive evaluation of the individual and his/her support environment.

Medical History

During the psychiatric diagnostic interview, the patient is expected to detail physical problems and treatments, and communication with the primary care physician is expected. For those with intellectual disability, this information is unlikely to be relayed accurately. Moreover, family or direct support professionals might also be unable to give accurate reports, especially if the self-report of the person is necessary. It is obviously of critical importance to know the individual's current medications, their doses, and, where relevant, current serum levels. This list should include all medications prescribed, not just those prescribed for psychiatric treatment.

Medical problems are often the source of the chief complaint for the psychiatric diagnostic interview for an individual with intellectual disability, yet there may be little understanding of this relationship. Intellectually typical people understand that they have a medical condition that could be associated with a mental disorder, such as chronic pain leading to depression. For the person with intellectual disability, the association of medical condition with psychiatric disorder is not generally understood — not by family, not by direct support professionals, and not by clinicians. Furthermore, the symptoms, as explained in the foregoing paragraphs, might be nonspecific, such as "aggression." When a person with intellectual disability exhibits an increase in aggression, there is nearly always an underlying assumption that the increase has a psychiatric cause; the possibility of a medical or physical cause is not entertained. It is therefore extremely important that the clinician consider medical or physical causes, make every effort to get complete information, and conduct a baseline medical assessment (Abend & Silka, 1999; Silka & Hurley, 2003). At a minimum, full blood count, urea and electrolytes, liver function tests, and thyroid function tests are recommended.

Many genetic disorders and syndromes have known medical conditions associated with them that can provide valuable clues to what might be the problem. For example, Down syndrome is frequently associated with hypothyroidism, which can lead to depressive symptoms (Chase, Osinowo, & Pary, 2002); hypothyroidism can look like depressive disorder, and hyperthyroidism can look like a manic episode. Also, there is an emerging understanding of the mental disorders that are associated with syndromes, such as Down syndrome and dementia of the Alzheimer's type (see Chapter 3). Diabetes has well known behavioral and mental effects. Abnormalities in blood chemistry, such as unhealthy sodium and blood sugar levels, can also affect mood and cause confusion; this is more common in disorders such as Prader-Willi syndrome. Sleep apnea is a common problem, especially in Down syndrome and in any individuals who are obese.

There are also commonly observed medical problems that are often not considered by family or direct support professionals (Abend & Silka, 1999; Silka & Hurley, 2003). Constipation, whether chronic or severe, can cause extreme distress and in severe cases can cause an impaction that is potentially life-threatening. This condition can lead to agitation that is misinterpreted as a mental disorder, which would seem to justify the prescribing of inappropriate medications that actually might have the side effect of worsening the constipation. Other gastrointestinal problems such as ulcer disease or gastroesophageal reflux ("heartburn") can also cause significant distress. Infections can occur and cause either increased agitation or alterations in mental status such as confusion and lethargy; common examples include urinary tract infections, respiratory infections (bronchitis, pneumonia), ear infections, and skin infections.

Seizure disorders are frequently seen in this population, and they too can cause mental health symptoms (Barnhill, 2004; Benjamin, 2000). Involuntary movement disorders can sometimes be perceived as either volitional or symptoms of a mental decompensation. For example, akathisia is a movement disorder that causes severe motor restlessness, which can look like the increased motor activity seen in a manic episode or in attention-deficit/hyperactivity disorder (ADHD). Many of these conditions are in fact caused by psychotropic medications, most frequently antipsychotics, and the treatment is to taper the medications or to treat the side effects.

Another common complaint is physical pain, which can occur for a wide variety of reasons, from minor injuries, such as a muscle sprain or tendonitis, to more severe cases, such as unrecognized fractures or severe dental disease. A person of typical intelligence can usually identify these symptoms fairly well and will then initiate contact with a physician for help. However, people with even mild levels of intellectual disability are often unable to cognitively formulate their pain; they cannot identify the source of pain adequately. Their frustration often leads to increased agitation and aggression or self-injury.

The impact of vision and hearing abnormalities is often not considered, but they can cause problems that are misinterpreted as a mental disorder, especially when adequate supports are not in place. People whose sensory inputs are limited in this way can often become anxious or frustrated by not knowing what is going on around them and by misinterpreting their environment.

Substance abuse is often overlooked as a cause of abnormalities in mood or behavior for people with intellectual disability. Many of the higher-functioning individuals in the community who live more independently have access to alcohol and other drugs that can cause mental disorder symptoms. In addition, nicotine and caffeine effects can sometimes be a significant factor.

Another cause that is frequently overlooked is medication side effects and drug toxicities. Many medications can cause symptoms that are thought to be due to a mental disorder, a misdiagnosis that sometimes leads to the prescribing of more medications. Many medications also cause or worsen constipation, thyroid status, or metabolic abnormalities, and they might lower the seizure threshold. There might be important side effects and drug interactions for medications, or interactions with agents prescribed for general medical conditions, that can cause mental disorder symptoms. Recent medication changes might be crucial, especially if they have occurred rapidly; many medications can precipitate toxic or withdrawal symptoms if increased or tapered too rapidly. Intoxicants can interact with many drugs to produce symptoms suggestive of psychiatric disorder.

Lastly, advances in understanding genetics and behavioral phenotypes has shed light on many specific genetic conditions associated with psychiatric disorders (Chapter 3 on behavioral phenotypes will address this in detail). All clinicians should be aware of the possibility of a genetic disorder and refer the patient to clinical genetics if any dysmorphic features or unusual behavioral repertoires and/or family history are present.

Life History (Life Story)

The clinician's goal in understanding the individual's history is to construct as complete a picture as possible of how the individual became the person he or she is at the time of the evaluation. Parents are the ideal historians; see the following Checklist of Historical Information Needed for Effective Mental Health Evaluation (Table 2):

Table 2.
Checklist of Historical Information Needed for Effective Mental Health Evaluation

Adapted in part from Levitas & Silka, 2001
Pregnancy, birth
Early development
Behavioral adjustment in early school years
Educational interventions throughout childhood
Early family relationships, family members
Behavioral adjustment in adolescence
Level of educational interventions in high school years
Most recent Individual Educational Plan and full assessments
Friends and community contacts in adolescence-adulthood
Living situations in adulthood
Occupational history
Substance abuse history
Current social connections
Social history, hobbies, community activities
History of partners, marriage, or children
Psychological evaluations
Intelligence testing (IQ)
Adaptive behavior testing
Medical history (including current and past medications)
Illnesses in childhood
Disabilities, visual, hearing, physical
Seizure disorder (and associated medications)
Surgical procedures
Current conditions (including current and past medications)
Accidents, especially head trauma

Direct support professionals who have known the individual for significant time periods, siblings, and teachers can all be valuable sources of history. Relationships crucial to the individual's treatment can be forged in the shared task of gathering history. Often a single family member or direct support professional is the most important person in the individual's life, and it is that individual who is most likely to have the most accurate information and be the most crucial ally in treatment. It is important to educate people about what information is important to discuss and what records are important to bring to an appointment.

It is also important to take into account during the assessment the situation of the parents or support professionals. Many times, they are under a great deal of stress, dealing with very difficult situations, and they might be fearful that clinicians will judge them negatively and therefore be reluctant to speak freely. There can be underlying feelings of anger or guilt. There may also be preconceived notions about the causes of symptoms that color their presentation of information. It is helpful to try to make the parent, family member, or direct support professional feel comfortable and to encourage as objective a description of the situation as possible (Levitas & Silka, 2001).

Individual Educational Plans (IEPs) and Individual Service Plans (ISPs) seldom provide information that is useful for the mental health history. Most such plans are mechanically created to fit with the deemed educational or habilitative goals and objectives, and they do not provide information that is accurate and relevant for mental health purposes. The exception occurs where the IEP includes professional evaluations. The clinician should attempt to obtain the following past documentation: Developmental history, cognitive and communication evaluations, academic testing, mental health and psychological diagnostic reports, medical history, discharge summaries for any hospitalizations, and first and last IEPs for the school years if the individual is an adult. The Checklist of Historical Information Needed for Effective Mental Health Evaluation, provided above, is useful for obtaining this documentation.

Additional Evaluations Recommended

Because of the complexity of diagnosing a psychiatric condition for a person with intellectual disability, the addition of specific extra assessments is recommended for most situations. These may take extra time, and/or involve working carefully with the person evaluating the individual. It is important to have the assessor understand the importance of his/her work, how valuable it will be for the proper diagnosis of the individual, and to provide any encouragement if necessary (Moss & Hurley, 2013).

Applied Behavior Analysis (ABA) Assessment for Challenging and Problem Behavior

Applied Behavior Analysis (ABA) addresses several primary domains. First and foremost, there should be assessment of an individual's presenting problems through *direct observation and measurement*. For example, in the case of a man with intellectual disability who is diagnosed with a specific phobia, assessment might focus on the distance from which he approaches or the duration of time he comfortably tolerates close proximity to the phobic stimulus (Ricciardi, Luiselli, & Cammare, 2006). The man could also be asked to rate his level of anxiety, possibly combined with basic physiological monitoring of stress indicators. This tripartite model of assessment is intended to empirically document clinical measures that would be expected to change with therapeutic intervention.

Ideally, behavioral assessment should be initiated during a baseline phase that measures a person's pre-intervention level of impairment and to answer the question: What would happen if his/her problem were not treated? It is customary for behavioral assessment to continue throughout intervention in order to evaluate the impact of treatment and to adjust procedures according to clinical responsiveness. Behavior analysts make determinations about treatment effectiveness through visual inspection of assessment data trends and magnitude relative to baseline and intervention phases. Finally, the conducting of a post-intervention behavioral assessment is recommended to ascertain a long-term therapeutic outcome.

Functional behavioral assessment (FBA) is critical for informing treatment choices and matching intervention to the environmental "causes" of challenging behavior (Cipani & Shock, 2011). To illustrate, some individuals with intellectual disability display problems such as aggression and self-injury because these behaviors produce pleasurable tangible and social consequences (positive reinforcement). Other behavior-contingent consequences are pleasurable because they allow an individual to avoid or escape non-preferred situations (negative reinforcement). Non-social influences also affect challenging behavior, as depicted by a woman who engages in unusual stereotypic movements to produce pleasing sensory stimulation (automatic reinforcement). The purpose of FBA is to isolate and confirm these controlling contingencies as well as to pinpoint antecedent conditions that may provoke or set the occasion for the challenging behavior (Luiselli, 2006, 2008).

There are two FBA methodologies. *Indirect methods* include questionnaires that ask informants to identify conditions and interactions that are commonly present when a person displays challenging behavior. As well, informants are queried about situations in which challenging behavior never or rarely occurs. *The Motivation Assessment Scale* (*MAS*: Durand, 1986; Durand & Crimmins, 1988) and the *Questions About Behavior Function* (*QABF*: Paclawski, Matson, Rush, Smalls, & Vollmer, 2000) are two popular FBA instruments. Another indirect method is the *Functional Analysis Interview* (*FAI*: O'Neill et al., 1997), a semi-structured protocol that gathers information from face-to-face discussion with significant others. Indirect methods require that informants have spent reasonable time with an individual to be able to render opinions about challenging behavior, associated conditions, and possible behavior-function. Note too that indirect methods do not entail direct observation and they are frequently unreliable when comparing the information provided by two or more informants.

A second type of FBA uses *descriptive methods*. The basis for this approach is acquiring behavior data while observing an individual in relevant settings. The observer records challenging behavior and the antecedent and consequence conditions that preceded and followed the behavior respectively (e.g., A-B-C recording: Bijou, Peterson, & Ault, 1968). By linking behavior to consistent antecedents and consequences it is possible to derive correlational hypotheses about function.

Compared to FBA, a *functional analysis* involves "the direct observation of problem behavior while some event suspected of being related to problem behavior is manipulated" (Hanley, 2012, p. 57). The assessment objective is to document that an individual regularly performs challenging behavior when distinct antecedent and consequence conditions are present. When successful, a functional analysis yields the most confirmatory evidence of behavior-function. Though it is a more experimental approach than FBA, in practice functional analysis can be adapted efficiently and safely within a clinical context.

As indicated previously, the results of FBA and functional analysis inform treatment decisions. Typically, intervention for challenging behavior that is attention maintained will include rearranging reinforcing consequences to follow an individual's desirable responses, teaching new skills, and improving communication ability. Avoidance and escape motivated challenging behavior suggests intervention procedures that reduce and eliminate the aversive characteristics of non-preferred situations, particularly by training individuals to communicate their needs and desires more effectively and teaching them more adaptable behavior options. In cases of challenging behavior that is automatically reinforced through contingent sensory events, intervention usually provides an individual with equally pleasurable stimulation and response alternatives.

Another ABA assessment priority is knowing the personal preferences of the people receiving treatment. Through *preference assessment*, clinicians are able to select positively reinforcing objects and activities for intervention implementation. Observing and documenting what an individual does during free-time is one way to assess preferences. When warranted, a person could also fill out a preference rating scale. A more objective approach to preference assessment is presenting an individual with objects and activities, allowing her/him to pick from the available choices, granting access to what is chosen, and recording responding along the continuum of highest-ranked to lowest-ranked preference selections (Tiger & Kliebert, 2011). High-rank preferences presumably will be positively reinforcing when tested with the individual during treatment.

Lastly, ABA assessment is directed at the *social validity* of intervention procedures and outcomes (Wolf, 1978). On one hand, clinicians should be interested about whether the objectives of treatment are commensurate with behavior within the normative population. Individuals receiving and those administering treatment should participate in social validity assessment in order to measure their satisfaction with and acceptability of the behavior-change procedures they experienced. One additional assessment target is verifying whether intervention effects improve an individual's quality of life and are socially valued by the community at large. Thus, social validity assessment considers perceived appropriateness, efficacy, and effectiveness when evaluating treatment outcomes with individuals who have ID.

Cognitive & Neuropsychological Assessment

If the individual has not had a cognitive assessment within a reasonable number of years, a new assessment will be helpful to the diagnostic formulation. For example, in geriatric psychiatry, when an individual presents for the first time with a possible dementia, it is considered routine to refer that individual for a neuropsychological evaluation. This specialized assessment will provide detailed exploration of all cognitive abilities including memory, enabling a better diagnosis and possible treatment/support plan for the patient. If a person with intellectual disability is referred for a psychiatric evaluation, we might consider similarly that it will be important to understand that person's cognitive abilities in a deep and complex way. For example, people with Down syndrome may have a recorded IQ from childhood that is quite low, yet they as a group function at a much higher level than their predicted IQ. Similarly, a person with a nonverbal learning disability will be judged to be quite low functioning because we tend to judge others by their verbal acumen. Neuropsychological evaluations cover all aspects of cognition and memory, include a thorough history, and will evaluate social-pragmatic language as well as visual-spatial abilities and daily adaptive functioning. Thus, a neuropsychological evaluation will clarify ability levels, compare it to past records, and enlighten diagnosis as well as provide guidelines for treatment planning.

Projective Testing

The need to access the internal mental life of an individual during the diagnostic process is essential, and this is ordinarily accomplished through self-report data during the mental health diagnostic interview. It is assumed that the individual understands the purpose of the appointment, will comprehend the nature of the questions asked, and will be able to give reasonable answers to the best of his or her ability. It is expected that the experienced clinician will be able to discern psychopathology and parcel out the influences of education, culture, and socioeconomic class.

Formal projective tests can be helpful when the diagnosis is uncertain because the individual does not answer questions but instead responds to a stimulus that allows him or her to expound on his or her thoughts or to "project" feelings and view of the world. The ambiguous nature of projective tests is their main value, "pulling" from the unconscious and revealing defenses and adaptive mechanisms. Unfortunately, individuals with intellectual disability are rarely referred for projective testing. Most psychologists erroneously assume that individuals with intellectual disability cannot take such tests because of their significantly impaired intellectual and verbal abilities. Yet these tests, for individuals with borderline or mild intellectual disability, can often yield useful results either by ruling out a psychotic disorder or by identifying specific psychopathology and psychological issues for the individual.

The Rorschach (1981) is particularly useful for the identification of psychotic thought and understanding how cognitive distortion in reality testing alters the individual's perception of the world. Most importantly, it is nearly impossible to "fake" a psychotic response making the test very valuable. Researchers have found that Rorschach cognitive indicators correlated significantly with IQ—that is, in number of responses, pure form responses, human movement responses, animal movement responses, whole responses, number of popular responses, number of content categories, and number of color responses (Hurley, O'Brien, Chadwick, & Svenson, 1996). A variety of story-telling methods are widely used for diagnostic purposes as well as to establish themes to begin psychotherapy. The Thematic Apperception Test (TAT) is also among the most used of psychological test instruments (Murray, 1943). The underlying assumptions of the TAT are that the main character represents the individual and that the characteristics of the main character's environment also resemble those of the individual. It has a long history in use for individuals with mild to borderline intellectual disability (Hurley, et al., 1996).

Instrumentation

Instrumentation refers to the use of rating scales that either are administered to a third party or are encompassed in a self-report instrument administered to the individual. The rating scale can serve two purposes: it assists the clinician in quantifying observable symptoms and signs by assigning a number, and it may interface with procedural algorithms used in the *DSM* and ICD systems by including items that are related to diagnosis. Rating scales typically assign numbers to the gathered clinical data and sample one or more domains of behavior.

Most rating scales used for people with intellectual disability are informant rating scales; that is, a parent, teacher, or direct support professional typically completes the scales. Self-report instruments are mostly used with individuals with mild or borderline intellectual disability. Typically, a professional trained in the instrument interviews the person.

There are broad spectrum as well as individual area targeted instruments available. Scales vary in the content of items with regard to specificity or behavioral description of the item. Self-report scales can additionally refer to subjective internal states, whereas informant-based scales must refer to objective behavioral observations of the third party or to inferences that are closely linked to such observations. Multiple informants do not necessarily produce more accurate information. For example, research on parents and teacher reports found that self-report of feelings and sleep patterns did not agree well with the child's actual internal state and self-report. Thus, although informant-based information is valuable, it must be evaluated within the context of its inherent limitations.

Instrumentation should also ideally be designed to be accurate across settings—for example, from work, school, and home settings. Ideal informants are, therefore, people who have observed the individual in many different settings and who are familiar with persons with intellectual disability, have known the individual for a significant time, and can supply information that the clinician must have to consider a mental health diagnosis and to judge the effectiveness of pharmacotherapy. Rating scales also differ in the qualifications of the informant, and this must be taken into account when integrating the information for the diagnostic formulation.

We recommend published rating scales that have established psychometric data showing that they are reliable and valid. Briefly, reliability refers to the consistency of ratings (within the measures, across raters, and across time). The reliability of rating scales can decrease because of errors related to the rater and to the instrument. Factors related to the rater include different levels of training, experience, knowledge, and motivation to complete the scale. At the very least, choose motivated raters who are knowledgeable about the individual being rated. *Validity* refers to the extent to which the instrument measures what it claims to measure. There are three general types of validity: *content validity*, *criterion validity*, and *construct validity* . Briefly, measures of validity refer to the evidence that the instrument is measuring what it claims to measure. For example, a measure of aggression should measure aggression and not other behaviors.

Broad Spectrum Instruments. These instruments were designed to measure broad categories of mental health conditions, for example, often related to DSM categories such as major depressive episode. Instruments for children often measure categories related to school and development.

For example, the *Diagnostic Assessment for the Severely Handicapped–II* (DASH-II) (Matson, Gardner, Coe, & Sovner, 1991) is based on *DSM-IV-TR* taxonomy. The DASH-II is a widely used instrument intended for adults with severe or profound intellectual disability and consists of 84 items distributed on 13 subscales. The *Reiss Screen for Maladaptive Behavior (RSMB)* (Reiss, 1988) also is a broad spectrum scale that has good psychometric properties, and it can be administered for individuals of all level of ID (Aman, Tassé, Rojahn, & Hammer, 1996; Paclawskyj, Matson, Bamburg, & Baglio, 1997; Walsh & Shenouda, 1999).

The *Developmental Behaviour Checklist* (DBC) (Einfeld & Tonge, 1995) and the *Nisonger Child Behavior Rating Form* (NCBRF) (Aman et al., 1996; Tassé, Aman, Hammer, & Rojahn, 1996) are well-regarded instruments for children. Both the DBC and NCBRF are broadband empirically driven instruments with parent and teacher versions. The DBC contains 96 items distributed on five subscales. It has good psychometric properties and has been used in an increasing number of studies (Einfeld & Tonge, 2002). The NCBRF has 10 social competence items distributed on two subscales and 66 problem behavior items distributed on six subscales (Aman et al., 1996; Lecavalier, Aman, Hammer, Stoica, & Matthews, 2004).

The *PAS-ADD Assessments*

The *Psychiatric Assessment Schedules for Adults with Developmental Disabilities (PAS-ADD)* have been in continuous development since the late 1980s. The system has been designed to link knowledge and expertise between families, clinicians, and wide range of health, education, and social service personnel who may be involved in the care of the individual. The current hard-copy version of the PAS-ADD clinical interview produces full criterion by criterion diagnoses under ICD 10 and DSM IV. The new computer version, created and soon to be available, produces scores on ICD 10 and DSM . The system includes the follow instruments:

The *PAS-ADD Clinical Interview* (Moss & Friedlander, 2011). This is the top level assessment in this series, designed to maximize the ability of the person with intellectual disability to undertake a clinical interview. The validity of PASADD in relation to the clinical opinion of referring psychiatrists was reported by Moss, Prosser & Goldberg,(1996) and Moss et al,(1997). Interrater reliability of the lCD-10 version gave a mean Kappa of 0.65 for individual item codes of, and Kappa 0.7 for agreement on index of definition (clinical significance of the symptoms) (Costello, Moss, Prosser, & Hatton, 1997). The relationships between respondent (patient) and informant reports of symptoms, and the implications of deriving diagnoses solely from informant interviews, are discussed in Moss, Prosser, lbbotson & Goldberg (1996). The issues of using care staff as informants were discussed in Moss & Patel (1993).

The *Mini PAS-ADD* (Moss, 2002), designed for informant interviewing in relation to adults with intellectual disability. For the Mini PAS-ADD and the ChA-PAS, the primary aim is symptom identification and severity estimation. The scores to have thresholds giving a best-estimate diagnostic indication based on ICD 10 and DSM IV.

The Child and Adolescent Psychiatric Assessment Schedule (ChA-PAS) (Moss, Friedlander, & Lee, 2007) has is a similar format to the *Mini PAS-ADD*, but is extended to include ADHD and Conduct Disorder. Like the Mini PAS-ADD, the ChA-PAS uses a scoring system that provides a single score for each of the diagnostic constellations, each of the constellations having a corresponding threshold. However, a strong emphasis is placed on the importance of expert clinical judgement when interpreting the scores in relation to other pieces of information, e.g. history, environment, and family factors etc. The *PAS-ADD Checklist* (Moss, 2002), designed for non-trained users to enable them to make more informed judgements about the presence of a possible mental disorder requiring further assessment.

The *PAS-ADD Checklist* is a 25 item questionnaire, couched in everyday language, designed for use primarily by care staff and families—the people who have the most immediate perception of changes in the behavior of the people for whom they care. The *Checklist* aims to help staff and carers decide whether further assessment of an individual's mental health may be helpful. Thus, it was judged that the success of the *PAS-ADD Checklist* in detecting cases would be measured by the extent to which it identifies those individuals whom *expert clinicians* agree are the ones who should have been identified in relation to either the ICD or DSM diagnostic systems. Factor analysis of the *Checklist* completed on a community sample of 201 individuals yielded eight factors, of which seven were readily interpretable in diagnostic terms. Internal consistency of the scales was generally acceptable. Inter-rater reliability in terms of case identification, the main purpose of the *Checklist*, was quite good, 83% of the decision being in agreement. Validity in relation to clinical opinion was also satisfactory, case detection rising appropriately with the clinically judged severity of the disorder (Moss et al, 1998). Subsequent independent studies have further investigated the *Checklist*'s psychometric properties (Sturmey, Newton, Cowley, Bouras, & Holt, 2005) and established norms for an adult sample (Taylor, Hatton, Dixon, & Douglas, 2004)

Problem Area Specific Instruments

The most used instrument to measure challenging behavior is the *Aberrant Behavior Checklist (ABC)* (Aman, Singh, Stewart, & Field, 1985a, 1985b) and at last count was used in over 250 studies. Its robust psychometric properties are a main reason for its success and use. The ABC was originally developed to measure drug treatment effects in adults. It contains 58 items distributed on five subscales. Yet, the subscales have different numbers of items ranging from 4 to 16, and the subscales considered the most useful are Irritability, Lethargy, and Hyperactivity-Noncompliance.

A number of self-report instruments targeting specific mental health aspects have also been used in published studies, most of which have focused on mood disorders and anxiety disorders. For instance, Reynolds and Baker (1988) developed the *Self-Report Depression Questionnaire (SRDQ)*, a 32-item instrument designed specifically for adolescents and adults with mild to severe intellectual disability. The SRDQ was based on *DSM-III-R* symptoms of major depressive disorder, and its authors reported good psychometric properties. Two other instruments address depression and anxiety: The *Glasgow Depression Scale for People with a Learning Disability* (Cuthil, Espie, & Cooper, 2003) and the *Glasgow Anxiety Scale for People with Intellectual Disability (GAS-ID)* (Mindham & Espie, 2003). Both Glasgow Scales are useful for screening and monitoring treatment response.

The *Fear Survey for Children With and Without Mental Retardation* (FSCMR) (Ramirez & Kratochwill, 1990) is an adaptation of the FFSC-R for use by children with and without ID between the ages of 6 and 13. This measure contains 60 items assessing specific fear stimuli and intensity. The authors reported good psychometric characteristics in a sample of 271 children with and without intellectual disability.

Self-report measures should also be evaluated in terms of their reliability and their validity. One particular threat to reliability pertains to question content. Questions with abstract, socially reflexive, or unfamiliar content, as well as those requiring comparisons or quantitative judgments, can prove difficult for some individuals with intellectual disability (Finlay & Lyons, 2001). Attempts to overcome these threats to reliability include various strategies, such as reading the questions, simplifying the content of questions and rating scales, or using visual aids to facilitate judgments. These strategies could prove fruitful, but their efficacy has yet to be established (Finlay & Lyons, 2001). For instance, reading the questions in a face-to-face interview can lead to better comprehension, but it can also lead to the underreporting of certain behaviors. Adding visual aids to anchor points of rating scales could help people remember available options without increasing the reliability of their judgments. Modifications of item phrasing and administration procedures, however, might impact the reliability of the instrument as well as our ability to generalize findings between or among individuals.

Assessment of Psychosocial Stressors

This is an extremely important area, and in previous editions of the DSM, Axis IV was highlighted to evaluate stresses that may relate to the diagnosis and treatment plan for any patient. *DSM-5* has eliminated the axis system and stresses are listed using F codes. There are two instruments to assess stresses specifically for people with intellectual disability. We recommend that these instruments be considered as understanding current stressors may be an essential piece of information when trying to interpret psychiatric symptoms or challenging behavior.

Bramston and Fogarty developed the *Lifestress Inventory for Adults with Intellectual Disability* (Bramstson & Bostock, 1994; Bramston & Fogarty, 1995; Bramston, Fogaraty & Cummins, 1999). This is an interview scale for a person with intellectual disability who can respond to the questions and there are 30 items. The person identifies the areas of stress and the impact on his or her life on a 3-point scale. The inventory has adequate 2-week test-retest reliability, internal consistency, and validity (Bramston & Bo stock, 1994; Bramston & Fogarty 1995, Fogarty, Bramston, & Cummons, 1997). Subsequent studies showed a correlation with depression (Esbenson & Benson, 2006; Hartley & MacLean, 2005) An informant version of the Lifestress Inventory was developed and tested (Lunsky and Bramston, 2006) finding modest agreement between informants and self-report of individuals; families agreed more with the individual than professional carers. Self-report was concluded to be the most important source of information if possible.

Groden developed the *Stress Survey Schedule for Individuals with Autism and Other Pervasive Developmental Disabilities* (Groden et al., 2001). A carer is interviewee and items are those commonly experienced as stressful by persons with autism spectrum disorders, e.g. "receiving hugs and affection" or "waiting in line." These are rated on a 5-point scale. The items then score to important grouping for planning purposes: changes, anticipation, and unpleasant, positive, sensory-personal, food-related, social-environmental, rituals. A study of informants and self-report of persons showed modest agreement, and it is recommended that self-report is always an important factor. (Goodwin, Groden, Velicer, & Diller, 2007).

Summary

The assessment of an individual with intellectual disability requires that the clinician maintain a constant skepticism and continually reassess the diagnostic formulation. The individual with intellectual disability, compared with other individuals, will not have comparable verbal and intellectual ability with which to communicate the chief complaint, internal feelings states, and symptoms requiring details and accurate history. One must, therefore, rely heavily on third-party reports of observable behavior. As a result, the clinician should make every effort to obtain written historical information, medical information, utilizing information from formal psychological assessments, as well as using instrumentation to assess the individual.

References

Abend, S. L., & Silka, V. R. (1999). Medical care of patients with developmental disabilities. *Mental Health Aspects of Developmental Disabilities, 2* (2), 68–70.

Aman, M. G., Singh, N. N., Stewart, A. W., & Field, C. J. (1985a). The Aberrant Behavior Checklist: A behavior rating scale for the assessment of treatment effects. *American Journal on Mental Deficiency, 89*, 485–491.

Aman, M. G., Singh, N. N., Stewart, A. W., & Field, C. J. (1985b). Psychometric characteristics of the Aberrant Behavior Checklist. *American Journal on Mental Deficiency, 89*, 492–502.

Aman, M. G., Tassé, M. J., Rojahn, J., & Hammer, D. (1996). The Nisonger CBRF: A child behavior rating form for children with developmental disabilities. *Research in Developmental Disabilities, 17*, 41–57.

Barnhill, J. (2004). The differential diagnosis of anxiety in Individuals with Epilepsy and Intellectual Disability. Mental Health Aspects of Developmental Disabilities, 4, 123-131.

Benjamin, S. (2000). A neuropsychiatric approach to behavioral issues in epilepsy. *Clinical Nursing Practice in Epilepsy, 1*, 7–12.

Bijou, S. W., Peterson, R. F., & Ault, M. H. (1968). A method to integrate descriptive and experimental field studies at the level of data and empirical concepts. *Journal of Applied Behavior Analysis, 1*, 175-191.

Boardman, L., Bernal, J., & Hollins, S. (2014). Communicating with people with intellectual disabilities: A guide for general psychiatrists. *Advances in Psychiatric Treatment, 20*, 27-36.

Bradley, E., & Caldwell, P. (2013). Mental health and autism: Promoting autism favorable environments (PAVE). *Journal on Developmental Disabilities, 19(1)*, 8-23.

Bradley, E. & Hollins, S. (2013). Books Beyond words: Using pictures to communicate. *Journal on Developmental Disabilities, 19*, 24-32.

Bradley, E. & Korossy, M. (2015). Behaviour problems. In M. Woodbury-Smith (Ed.), *Clinical topics in the psychiatry of intellectual developmental disorders* (pp. 72-112). Royal College of Psychiatrists, Gaskell Press UK.

Bramston, P., & Bostock, J. (1994). Measuring perceived stress in people with intellectual disabilities: The development of a new scale. *Australia and New Zealand Journal of Developmental Disabilities, 19*, 149-157

Bramston, P. & Fogarty, G. (1995). Measuring stress in the mildly intellectually handicapped: The factorial structure of the Subjective Stress Scale. *Research in Developmental Disabilities, 16*, 117-131.

Bramston, P., Fogarty, G., & Cummins, R. A. (1999). The nature of stressors reported by people with an intellectual disability. *Journal of Applied Research in Intellectual Disabilities, 12*, 1-10

Cipani, E., & Schock, K. M. (2011). *Functional behavioral assessment, diagnosis, and treatment: A complete system for education and mental health settings.* New York: Oxford University Press.

Charlot, L. R., Doucette, A. C., & Mezzacappa, E. (1993). Affective symptoms of institutionalized adults with mental retardation. *American Journal on Mental Retardation, 98*, 408–416.

Chase, C. D., Osinowo, T., & Pary, R. (2002). Medical issues in patients with Down Syndrome. *Mental Health Aspects of Developmental Disabilities, 5*, 34–45.

Cooper, S.A., Smiley, E., Allan, L. M., Jackson, A., Finlayson, J., Mantry, D., & Morrison, J. (2009a) Adults with intellectual disabilities: Prevalence, incidence and remission of self-injurious behaviour, and related factors. *Journal of Intellectual Disability Research*, 53, 200-216.

Cooper, S.A., Smiley, E., Jackson, A., Allan, L., Mantry, D., & Morrison, J. (2009b) Adults with intellectual disabilities: Prevalence, incidence and remission of aggressive behaviour and related factors. *Journal of Intellectual Disability Research*, 53, 217-232.

Costello, H., Moss, S., Prosser, H., & Hatton, C. (1997). Reliability of the ICD 10 version of the Psychiatric Assessment Schedule for Adults with Developmental Disability (PAS-ADD). *Social Psychiatry and Psychiatric Epidemiology, 32*, 339–343.

Cuthill, F.M., Espie, C.A., & Cooper S.-A.. (2003) Development and psychometric properties of the Glasgow Depression Scale for people with a learning disability. Individual and carer supplement versions. *British Journal of Psychiatry*, 182, 347-353.

Dosen, A. (2005a). Applying the developmental perspective in the psychiatric assessment and diagnosis of persons with intellectual disability: Part 1 – assessment. *Journal of Intellectual Disability Research, 49*, 1-8.

Dosen, A. (2005b). Applying the developmental perspective in the psychiatric assessment and diagnosis of persons with intellectual disability: Part 2 – diagnosis. *Journal of Intellectual Disability Research, 49*, 9-15.

Durand, M.V. (1986). *Motivation assessment scale.* Topeka, KS: Monaco & Associates.

Durand, M.V., & Crimmins, D.B. (1988). Identifying the variables maintaining self-injurious behaviour. *Journal of Autism and Developmental Disorders, 18*, 99-117.

Einfeld, S. L., & Tonge, B. J. (1995). *The Developmental Behavior Checklist*: The development and validation of an assessment of behavioral and emotional disturbance in children and adolescents with mental retardation. *Journal of Autism and Developmental Disorders, 25*, 81–104.

Einfeld, S. L., & Tonge, B. J. (2002). *Manual for the Developmental Behaviour Checklist* (2nd ed.). Clayton, Melbourne, and Sydney, Australia: Monash University Center for Developmental Psychiatry and School of Psychiatry, University of New South Wales.

Emerson, E., & Einfeld, S. L. (2011) *Challenging Behaviour*, (3rd ed.), Cambridge, UK: Cambridge University Press.

Esbensen, A.J., & Benson, B.A. (2006). A prospective analysis of life events, problem behaviours and depression in adults with intellectual disability. *Journal Intellectual Disability Research, 50*, 248-58.

Finlay, W. M. L., & Lyons, E. (2001). Methodological issues in interviewing and using self-report questionnaires with people with mental retardation. *Psychological Assessment, 13*, 319–335.

Fogarty, G.J., Bramston, P.A., Cummins, R.A. (1997). Validation of the Lifestress Inventory for people with a mild intellectual disability. *Research in Developmental Disabilities, 18*, 435-456.

Gardner, W.I. (2007). Aggression in persons with intellectual disability and mental disorders. In J.J. Jacobson, J. Mullick, & J. Johahn (Eds.), *Handbook of intellectual and developmental disabilities*. Kingston, NY: NADD Press.

Goodwin, M.S., Groden, J., Velicer, W.F., & Diller, A. (2007) Validating the Stress Survey Schedule for Persons With Autism and Other Developmental Disabilities. *Focus on Autism and Other Developmental Disabilities*, 22, 183–189.

Groden, J., Diller, A., Bausman, M., Velicer, W., Norman, G., & Cautela, J. (2001). The development of a stress survey schedule for persons with autism and other developmental disabilities. *Journal of Autism and Developmental Disorders, 31*, 207–217.

Hanley, G.A. (2012). Functional assessment of problem behaviour: Dispelling myths, overcoming implementation obstacles, and developing new lore. *Behavioral Analysis Practitioner, 1*, 54-72.

Hartley, S.L. & MacLean, W.E. (2005). Perceptions of stress and coping strategies among adults with mild mental retardation: Insight into psychological distress. *American Journal on Mental Retardation, 110*, 285-290

Hurley, A. D. (1996). The misdiagnosis of hallucinations and delusions in persons with mental retardation: A neurodevelopmental perspective. *Seminars in Clinical Neuropsychiatry, 1*, 122–133.

Hurley, A. D. (1998). Two cases of suicide attempt by patients with Down's syndrome. *Psychiatric Services, 49*, 1618–1619.

Hurley, A. D. (2002). Potentially lethal suicide attempts in persons with developmental disabilities: Review and three new case reports. *Mental Health Aspects of Developmental Disabilities, 5*, 90–95.

Hurley, A. D. (2003). Delusions and hallucinations in Down syndrome: Literature review and comparison with non-Down syndrome patients. *Mental Health Aspects of Developmental Disabilities, 6*, 125–129.

Hurley, A.D. (2008). Depression in adults with intellectual disability: symptoms and challenging behaviour. *Journal of Intellectual Disability Research, 52*, 905-916.

Hurley, A. D., Folstein, M. F., & Lam, N. (2003). Patients with and without intellectual disability seeking outpatient psychiatric services: Diagnoses and prescribing pattern. *Journal of Intellectual Disability Research, 47*, 39–50.

Hurley, A. D., & Moore, D. (1999). A review of erotomania in developmental disabilities and new case report. *Mental Health Aspects of Developmental Disabilities, 2*, 12–22.

Hurley, A. D., O'Brien, M., Chadwick, K., & Svenson, S. (1996). The use of the Rorschach and Thematic Apperception Test in persons with mental retardation. *Seminars in Clinical Neuropsychiatry, 1*, 94–104.

Ian K., Jenner, J.A., & Cannon, M. (2010). Psychotic symptoms in the general population – An evolutionary perspective. *British Journal of Psychiatry, 197*, 167-169.

King, B.H., DeAntoni, C., McCracken, J.T., Forness, S.R., & Ackerland, V. (1994). Psychiatric consultation in severe and profound mental retardation. *American Journal of Psychiatry, 12*, 1802-1808.

Koritsas, S., Iacono, T. (2012a) Challenging behaviour and associated risk factors: An overview (part I). *Advances in Mental Health and Intellectual Disabilities, 6*, 199-214.

Lecavalier, L., Aman, M.G., Hammer, D., Stoica, W., & Matthews, G. (2004). Factor analysis of the Nisonger Child Behavior Rating Form in children with autism spectrum disorders. *Journal of Autism and Developmental Disorders, 34*, 709-721.

Levitas, A. S., & Gilson, S. F. (2001). Predictable crises in the lives of persons with mental retardation. *Mental Health Aspects of Developmental Disabilities, 4,* 89–100.

Levitas, A. S., Hurley, A, D., & Pary, R. (2001). The mental status examination in patients with mental retardation and developmental disabilities. *Mental Health Aspects Developmental Disabilities, 41,* 1–30.

Levitas, A. S., & Silka, V. R. (2001). Mental health clinical assessment of persons with mental retardation and developmental disabilities. *Mental Health Aspects of Developmental Disabilities, 41,* 31–42.

Leyfer, O.T., Folstein, S.E. Bacalman, S., Davis, N.O., Dinh, E., Morgan, J., ... Lainharat, J.E. (2006). Comorbid psychiatric disorders in children with autism: Interview development and rates of disorders. *Journal of Autism and Developmental Disorders, 26,* 849-961.

Luiselli, J. K. (Ed.). (2006). *Antecedent Assessment and Intervention: Supporting Children and Adults with Developmental Disabilities in Community Settings* .Baltimore, MD: Brookes Publishing.

Luiselli, J. K. (2008). Antecedent (preventive) intervention. In J. K. Luiselli, S. Wilczynski, D. C. Russo, & W. P. Christian. *Effective practices for children with autism: Educational and behavior support interventions that work* (pp. 393-412). New York, NY: Oxford University Press.

Lunsky, Y. and Bramston, P. (2006) A preliminary study of perceived stress in adults with intellectual disabilities according to self-report and informant ratings. *Journal of Intellectual and Developmental Disability, 31,* 20-27.

Matikka, L. M., & Vesala, H. T. (1997). Acquiescence in quality-of-life interviews with adults who have mental retardation. *Mental Retardation, 35,* 75–82.

Matson, J. L., Gardner, W. I., Coe, D. A., & Sovner, R. (1991). A scale for evaluating emotional disorders in severely and profoundly mentally retarded persons. *British Journal of Psychiatry, 159,* 404–409.

Mindhan, J. & Espie, C.A. (2003). Glasgow Anxiety Scale for people with an Intellectual Disability (GAS-ID): Development and psychometric properties of a new measure for use with people with mild intellectual disability. *Journal of Intellectual Disability Research, 47,* 22-30.

Moss, S. C. (2002). *The Mini PASS-ADD Interview Pack.* Brighton, UK: Pavilion Publishing.

Moss, S.C., & Friedlander, R. (2011). *The PAS-ADD clinical interview.* Brighton, UK: Pavilion Press.

Moss, S., Friedlander, R., & Lee, P. (2007). The ChA-PAS interview. *Handbook and clinical interview: For the assessment of mental health problems in children and adolescents: the Child and Adolescent Psychiatric assessment Schedule (ChA-PAS).* Brighton, UK: Pavillion Publishing.

Moss, S., & Hurley, A.D. (2014). Integrating assessment instruments within the diagnostic process. In E. Tsakanikos, & J. McCarthy. (Eds), *Handbook of psychopathology in intellectual disability, research, practice and policy.* New York: Springer.

Moss, S. C., Ibbotson, B., Prosser, H., Goldberg, D. P., Patel, P., & Simpson, N. (1997). Validity of the PAS-ADD for detecting psychiatric symptoms in adults with learning disability (mental retardation). *Social Psychiatry & Psychiatric Epidemiology, 32,* 344–354.

Moss, S. C., Patel, P., Prosser, H., Goldberg, D. P., Simpson, N., Rowe, S., & Lucchino, R. (1993). Psychiatric morbidity in older people with moderate and severe learning disability (mental retardation). Part I: Developmental and reliability of the patient interview (PAS-ADD). *British Journal of Psychiatry, 163,* 471–480.

Moss, S. C., Prosser, H., Costello, H., Simpson, N., Patel, P., Rowe, S., ... Hatton, C. (1998). Reliability and validity of the PAS-ADD Checklist for detecting psychiatric disorders in adults with intellectual disability. *Journal of Intellectual Disability Research, 42,* 173–183.

Moss, S. C., Prosser, H., & Goldberg, D. P. (1996). Respondent and informant accounts of psychiatric symptoms in a sample of patients with learning disability. *Journal of Intellectual Disability Research, 40*, 457–465.

Moss, S.C., Prosser, H., Ibbotson, B., & Goldberg, D.P. (1996).

Murray, H. A. (1943). *Manual for the Thematic Apperception Test.* Cambridge, MA: Harvard University Press.

O'Neill, R. E., Horner, R. H., Albin, R. W., Sprague, J. R., Storey, K., & Newton, J. S. (1997). *Functional assessment and program development for problem behavior: A practical handbook.* Pacific Grove, CA: Brookes/Cole.

Paclawskyj, T. R., Matson, J. L., Bamburg, J. W., & Baglio, C. (1997). A comparison of the Diagnostic Assessment for the Severely Handicapped – II (DASH-II) and the Aberrant Behavior Checklist (ABC). *Research in Developmental Disabilities, 18*, 189–298.

Pacpawskyj, T. R., Matson, J. L., Rush, K. S., Smalls, Y., & Vollmer, T. R. (2000). Questions About Behavior Function (QABF): A behavioral checklist for functional assessment of aberrant behavior. *Research in Developmental Disabilities, 21*, 223-229.

Patel, P., Goldberg, D.P., & Moss, S.C. (1993). Psychiatric morbidity in older people with moderate and severe learning disability (mental retardation). Part II: The prevalence study. *British Journal of Psychiatry, 163*, 481-491.

Poppes, P., van der Putten, A. J., Vlaskamp, C. (2010) Frequency and severity of challenging behaviour in people with profound intellectual and multiple disabilities. *Research in Developmental Disabilities, 31*, 1269-1275.

Ramirez, S. Z., & Kratochwill, T. R. (1990). Development of the Fear Survey for Children With and Without Mental Retardation. *Behavioral Assessment, 12*, 457–470.

Reiss, S. (1988). *The Reiss Screen for Maladaptive Behavior Test Manual.* Worthington, OH: International Diagnostic Systems Publishing Corporation.

Reynolds, W. M., & Baker, J. A. (1988). Assessment of depression in persons with mental retardation. *American Journal on Mental Retardation, 93*, 93–103.

Ricciardi, J. N., Luiselli, J. K., & Cammare, M. (2006). Shaping approach responses as intervention for specific phobia in a child with autism. *Journal of Applied Behavior Analysis, 39*, 445-448.

Rorschach, H. (1981). *Psychodiagnostics.* (P. Lemkau & B. Kronenberg, Trans.). New York: Grune & Stratton. (Original work published 1921).

Royal College of Psychiatrists, British Psychological Society & Royal College of Speech and Language Therapists (2012). *Challenging behaviour: A unified approach* (Publication # *CR 144*). London, UK. Banks, R., Bush, A., Baker, P., Bradshaw, J., Carpenter, P., Deb, S., ….Xeniditis, K. Available from: http://www.rcpsych.ac.uk/files/pdfversion/cr144.pdf

Silka, V.R., & Hurley, A.D. (2003). Differentiating psychiatric and medical problems in patients with developmental disabilities. *Mental Health Aspects of Developmental Disabilities*, 120-124.

Sovner, R. (1986). Limiting factors in the use of DSM-III criteria with mentally ill/ mentally retarded persons. *Psychopharmacology Bulletin, 22*, 1055–1059.

Sovner, R., & Hurley, A.D. (1983). Do the mentally retarded suffer from affective Illness? *Archives of General Psychiatry, 40*, 61-67.

Sturmey, P., Newton, J.T., Cowley, A., Bouras, N., & Holt, G. (2005). The PAS-ADD checklist: Intependent replicationof its psychometric properties in a community sample. *British Journal of Psychiatry, 186*, 319-323.

Sullivan, W., Berg, J., Bradley, E., Cheetham, T., Denton, R., Heng, J., … McMillan, S. (2011). Primary care of adults with developmental disabilities: Canadian consensus guidelines. *Canadian Family Physician, 57*, 541-53. http://www.cfp.ca/content/57/5/541.full

Tardiff, K., & Koenigsberg, H. W. (1985). Assaultive behavior among psychiatric outpatients. *American Journal of Psychiatry, 142*, 960–963.

Tassé, M. J., Aman, M. G., Hammer, D., & Rojahn, J. (1996). The Nisonger Child Behavior Rating Form: Age and gender effects and norms. *Research in Developmental Disabilities, 17,* 59–75.

Taylor, J., Hatton, C., Dixon, L., & Douglas, C. (2004). Screening for psychiatric symptoms: PAS-ADD Checklist norms for adults with intellectual disabilities. *Journal fo Intellectual Disability Research, 48,* 37-41.

Tiger, J. H., & Kliebert, M. L. (2011). Stimulus preference assessment. In J. K. Luiselli (Ed.), *Teaching and behavior support for children and adults with autism spectrum disorder: A practitioner's guide* (pp. 30-37). Baltimore, MD: Oxford University Press.

van der Kolk, B., (2005), Developmental trauma disorder: Towards a rational diagnosis for chronically traumatized children. *Psychiatric Annals, 35,* 401–408

Walsh, K. K., & Shenouda, N. (1999). Correlations among the Reiss Screen, the Adaptive Behavior Scale Part II, and the Aberrant Behavior Checklist. *American Journal on Mental Retardation, 104,* 236–248.

Wolf, M. M. (1978). Social validity: The case for subjective measurement or how behavior analysis is finding its heart. *Journal of Applied Behavior Analysis, 11,* 203-214.

CHAPTER 3

Behavioral Phenotypes of Neurodevelopmental Disorders

Andrew Levitas
Brenda Finucane
Elliott W. Simon
Marcy Schuster
Wendy R. Kates
Amy K. Olszewski
Elisabeth Dykens
Nathan Danker

Why Do We Need the Term Behavioral Phenotype?

The physical *phenotype* of a genetic syndrome is the set of biological characteristics produced by a genetic abnormality, or *genotype*. The most widely known example is the easily recognized face of a person with Down syndrome. Smith's "Recognizable Patterns of Human Malformation, 7th Edition" (Jones, Jones, & Casanelles, 2013), the standard text in the field, contains photographs of many currently known syndromes, with descriptions of other aspects of their respective phenotypes, including laboratory and X-ray findings.

Many syndrome diagnoses formerly dependent upon physical findings are now confirmed by laboratory evaluation. Unusual movements and behaviors—such as the distinct gait associated with Angelman syndrome, the active gaze avoidance apparent in people with fragile X syndrome, and self-mutilation patterns seen in Lesch-Nyhan and Smith-Magenis syndromes—have also been observed. In this context, it is appropriate to speak of these disorder-specific behavioral characteristics as a 'behavioral phenotype.'

In addition to maladaptive behavior, this term includes other aspects of biopsychosocial functioning—for example, learning style. Males with fragile X syndrome show an age-related decrease in measured IQ and a particular pattern of learning style development shows a gap between simultaneous and sequential processing abilities. Sequential processing abilities enable learning to occur in a stepwise sequential manner while simultaneous processing abilities enable holistic learning such as modeling. The former were found to develop less slowly than the latter in males with fragile X syndrome (Hodapp, Dykens, Ort, Zelinsky, & Leckman, 1991). This type of syndromic characterization differs from traditional IQ characterization of intellectual disability into levels of severity.

Specificity of Behavioral Phenotypes

IQ is a global, nonspecific measure of intellectual abilities and deficits: Two individuals with developmental disabilities due to different causes might have the same IQ yet have completely different patterns of abilities and deficits on the specific IQ test's subscales and still different patterns of abilities and deficits as revealed in detailed neuropsychological testing. The same is true of tests of adaptive functioning, in that two individuals scoring equivalently on global measures of adaptive functioning could have very different performance profiles in subdomains such as social functioning, communication, and daily living skills. DSM-5 recognizes as other specified neurodevelopmental disorder "presentations in which symptoms characteristic of a neurodevelopmental disorder that cause impairment in social, occupational, or other important areas of functioning predominate but do not meet the full criteria for any of the disorders in the neurodevelopmental disorders diagnostic class" (e.g. autism spectrum disorder), and gives as an example neurodevelopmental disorder associated with prenatal alcohol abuse. It also recognizes unspecified neurodevelopmental disorder for situations in which a specific biological association for such symptoms cannot be fully identified.

When one or more mental disorders (i.e., patterns of behavioral signs and symptoms that meet DSM-5 or ICD 10 diagnostic criteria) commonly occur in association with a genetic disorder, this occurrence, too, is part of the behavioral phenotype and can be called the mental health phenotype. The mental health phenotype is really, then, a subset of the behavioral phenotype, but the popularity of the term *behavioral phenotype* perhaps outweighs such exactitude, and leaves room for redefinitions as more is learned about the links between behaviors and mental disorders.

Mental health professionals working with individuals who have intellectual and developmental disabilities need to be aware of the contribution of behavioral phenotypes to diagnosis and treatment. To offer just two examples, they should be aware that a person with Down syndrome who is hallucinating is far more likely to have major depressive disorder with psychotic features, than to have schizophrenia or dementia of the Alzheimer's type, and that a cause might be hypothyroidism. Similarly, mental health professionals should be able to recognize Rubinstein-Taybi syndrome and avoid the use of older antipsychotic medications because of the high frequency of neuroleptic malignant syndrome in people with this genetic disorder (Levitas & Reid, 1998).

What Fits the Criteria of Behavioral Phenotype?

The phrase *behavioral phenotype* was coined by Nyhan (1972) to denote a behavior or a set of behaviors that was genetically determined, in the same way that the physical features of the phenotype were determined—a determination that made his paper the origin of what might be called the "research approach" to behavioral phenotype. A contrasting, more clinical, approach was embodied in Friedman (1969), describing what we would now call autism spectrum disorder in persons with phenylketonuria (PKU). Whereas Nyhan began with a specific pattern of self-mutilation unique to Lesch-Nyhan syndrome, Friedman was well aware, even in 1969, that autism spectrum disorder was not unique to PKU; by 1983, several syndromes, including congenital rubella syndrome and fragile X syndrome, had been shown to be associated with autism spectrum disorder. Flint and Yule (1994) defined behavioral phenotype as:

> the specific and characteristic behavioral repertoire exhibited by patients with a genetic or chromosomal disorder.

This was the beginning of the era of the search for genes associated with many specific human behaviors. To find genes for a behavior, that behavior had to be measurable and precisely defined. The Society for the Study of Behavioural Phenotype (SSBP), http://www.ssbp.co.uk, has proposed its own consensus definition:

> A characteristic pattern of motor, cognitive, linguistic and/or social abnormalities which is consistently associated with a biological disorder.

However, several studies have shown that people with an intellectual/developmental disability, irrespective of etiology, have executive function deficits. When individuals with known genetic syndromes are compared through neuropsychological testing with individuals without developmental disability, these same deficits are observed. These differences vanish, however, when their results are compared with executive function deficits of individuals with intellectual/developmental disabilities of unknown cause. In other words, there is likely a core set of deficits in neuropsychological functioning that is shared by all people with intellectual disability irrespective of associated genetic syndrome and more specific patterns of abilities and deficits associated with known genetic syndromes (Garner, Callias, & Turk, 1999).

Knight et al. (1999) suggested that "unknown cause" might actually be a matter of how closely one looks for causes; when more detailed DNA analysis was done on individuals with intellectual/developmental disabilities of unknown cause, including even those who had previous genetic evaluation, about 30% proved to have diagnosable genetic abnormalities, each of which might be associated with its own behavioral phenotype. This is particularly true today as Whole Exome Scanning (WES) is finding its way into clinical practice. Recent estimates of the "diagnostic yield" of WES approach 25% (Yang et al., 2014). In combination with chromosomal microarray and fragile X DNA analysis, current clinically available genetic tests reveal an underlying cause in up to 40% of people with neurodevelopmental disorders. Finding control groups for studies of behavioral phenotype is therefore a complex and controversial undertaking.

It is also possible that what look like differences in functioning could be due to differences in the ability to demonstrate a function depending on overall level of ability. Thus, to be considered a likely part of a behavioral phenotype, a characteristic should be present over the full range of ability seen in the syndrome, as Streissguth (1997) was able to demonstrate in adolescents with fetal alcohol syndrome. This suggested that the SSBP definition should be modified to read:

> A characteristic pattern of motor, cognitive, linguistic and/or social abnormalities which is consistently associated with a biological disorder *regardless of level of ability.*

Advances in the assessment of emotional states of children (Siegel & Smith, 2010), and of persons with severe and profound intellectual developmental disorder (intellectual disability) (reviewed in: Adams & Oliver, 2011) have begun to make this distinction realistic.

The path defined by Flint and Yule is the more rigorous and therefore the most useful to the researcher; the path implied by Friedman's work is of more immediate use to the clinician, the person with the syndrome, and that person's family. Dykens (1995) proposed a clinical definition of behavioral phenotype:

> . . . a heightened probability that people with a given syndrome will exhibit behavioral or developmental sequelae relative to others without the syndrome.

Theoretically, if there were no connection between genetic syndromes and mental disorders, any mental disorder should occur in individuals with any genetic syndrome, in the same frequency from one syndrome to another and in the same frequency as in the general population. Dykens's definition implies that, with respect to genetic syndromes, behavioral and personality traits, neuropsychiatric abilities and deficits, and mental disorders are distributed nonrandomly.

Is There a Link Between Genotype and Behavioral Phenotype?

The connection between genotype and behavior or mental disorder might be direct or indirect. There could be a direct molecular connection involved in the almost-unique self-mutilation pattern seen in Lesch-Nyhan syndrome. On the other hand, head banging is seen in some persons with Down syndrome because of pain from chronic sinusitis and otitis. Sinusitis and otitis have a higher probability of occurring in people with Down syndrome due to the flattening of the facial anatomy associated with the genetic abnormality; the behavior is a secondary result. Observing the presence of the behavior is immediately useful clinically; it is a signal to the clinician to look for sinusitis or otitis when a person with Down syndrome begins head banging, but it could never be said that Down syndrome *causes* head banging in the same sense that it causes short stature and decreased intellectual ability. The line of causation is indirect. In some other situations, such as the purported musical ability of many persons with Williams syndrome, the relationship is either complex or unknown.

Dykens and Hodapp (2010) note that phenotypes evolve over time, and may do so as a result of the interaction of genotypically determined neuropsychological traits with age, gender, and "a host of other subject and environmental variables" (Genetic X Environment interaction), for example "poor strategic thinking [i.e., poor means-ends thinking] and strengths in social relatedness are hypothesized to lead to less persistent and overly social personality-motivational orientation in this population" (Fidler et al 2006, quoted in Dykens and Hodapp, 2010). Similarly, psychiatric disorders associated with a neurodevelopmental syndrome may evolve over time, such as anxiety and specific phobias in adults with Williams syndrome not observed in children with the syndrome (Dykens, 2003).

Converging lines of evidence have overwhelmingly refuted the hope that a behavioral phenotype implies the existence of a unitary "behavioral genotype." Even when the concept of behavioral phenotype was proposed it was known that, as with other phenotypic characteristics, *phenocopies*—behavioral phenotypes that look very similar but are not identical might not be genotypically identical. Imagine an entity called "Darkness syndrome." The classic presentation would be that when one entered a dark room and turned on the wall switch, there would be no light. In classic Darkness syndrome, the cause would be a burned-out bulb, the replacement of which would cure the syndrome. In rare cases, however, the problem would be with the switch or with the fixture. Even more rarely, the problem would be in the wiring between the switch and the fixture, or between the switch and the fusebox, or in the fuse. Each of these causes of Darkness syndrome would produce the identical phenotype; together they would be a group of phenocopies.

This phenomenon occurs in well-known genetic disorders. For example, there are three different molecular mechanisms that produce Prader-Willi syndrome, and there are slight differences in phenotype depending upon the mechanism. A second example is that there are two different metabolic disorders—one disorder, the most common, depends upon a single gene, and the other disorder, one of the rarer versions, depends on one of seven different genes—that produce the identical phenotype of phenylketonuria (PKU) by interfering with the same chemical reaction; yet the standard diet is effective only with the common version (Levitas, 1998a, 1998b, 1999). Also, genes work in chains, controlling each other's expression in almost the same way as in the fuse–wire–switch–fixture–bulb chain in our hypothetical "Darkness syndrome." Waardenburg syndrome, for example, can be caused by the failure of any one of three genes; the first normally regulates the second, and the second regulates the third: Three different genotypes produce the same identical phenotype.

Phenotypes of all kinds—behavioral phenotypes, perhaps especially—can, then, be the final common pathway of multiple causes, just as with "Darkness syndrome." The broader the phenotype, the more likely it will be that there are multiple causes. This is the phenomenon of *Genetic Pleiotropy*, and its applicability to clinical understanding of neurodevelopmental syndromes is summed up by Skuse's Principles (Skuse, 2000):

1. The behavioral descriptions, like physical features of neurodevelopmental disorders, have increased probability of occurring and do not occur in all cases; they may not be fully expressed in all affected individuals.
2. The genetic background of any individual may affect the phenotypic expression.
3. Environmental factors may modify expression.
4. The behavioral presentation may be modified by the extent of intellectual disability associated with the disorder.

The beginning of an explanation for Genetic Pleiotropy lies in the advances in the understanding of the links between genes, neuropsychological traits, and psychiatric disorders being uncovered by genetic tests such as microarray analysis and WES. Copy Number Variations (CNVs) are changes in the number of copies of regions of DNA nucleotide bases, either deletions or duplications, which may extend over numerous genes. Single Nucleotide Variations (SNVs) are changes in single nucleotides in the DNA code. CNVs and SNVs can be pathogenic (e.g., disease-causing), benign, or of uncertain significance. Even when they are known to be pathogenic, however, there is no one-to-one correspondence between CNV or SNV and a particular psychiatric disorder. Rather, the same CNV or SNV may be identified in people with, for example, bipolar disorder, but also in those with schizophrenia and anxiety disorders (and persons with neither or no clinical psychiatric disorder). And, starting from a given CNV or SNV, persons with a variety of DSM-defined disorders may be found carrying the same mutation. In fact, numerous studies have associated these mutations with neuropsychological variables, not DSM-defined disorders (Moreno-Deluca et al., 2013), giving rise to the current understanding that these DNA mutations are more closely associated with *endophenotypes* (i.e., quantifiable, state-independent traits that are genetically correlated with disease liability and can be expressed in unaffected family members) than with a DSM-defined disorder per se. Moreover, neuropsychological traits that are risk factors for DSM-defined psychiatric disorders, and the exact nature of whose expression in any individual, will depend upon not only other genes but also *epigenetic factors*, such as developmental factors (e.g. toxic exposures, peri- and postnatal trauma) and Genetic X Environment interactions.

Several neurodevelopmental syndromes described in this chapter are in fact CNVs (one could consider Down syndrome a huge CNV: there is duplication of an entire chromosome). Moreover, some smaller CNVs associated with neurodevelopmental disorders (e.g., 22q11.2 deletion) may contain genes that, if disrupted, could by themselves result in a range of psychiatric symptoms associated with the neurodevelopmental syndrome.

Another way of putting this is that some CNVs are shared by intellectual disability, Autism Spectrum Disorder, psychoses and epilepsy (Pescosolido, Gamiscz, Nafgpal, & Morrow, 2013). Moreno-De-Luca et al (2013) propose a way to understand this overlap of neuropsychiatric Symptomatology: Variable Expressivity, or, more recently, *Genetic Multiformity.* They propose that neuropsychiatric traits are continuous variables, like IQ, rather than discrete, present/absent qualities, e.g. “sociability”, or “anxiety-proneness.” When these traits are quantified their measure produces the same sort of continuous distribution as IQ. Mutations like CNVs and SNVs, some alone, some in combination, some in combination with epigenetic factors, “shift the curves” toward pathology. Enough of them in the right combinations produce the familiar cognitive and psychiatric disorders of the DSM or ICD classification system. Such continuously-distributed variable traits have been found in persons with bipolar disorder and schizophrenia and to a less severe degree in unaffected family members (Hill et al., 2013).

This is very important to clinicians, because at present we do not have medication or behavioral interventions keyed to particular CNVs or SNVs, only to particular behaviors and disorders that may be the result of a chain of causation beginning with a mutation but running a developmental gauntlet of epigenetic modifications.

Patterns of mental disorders, then—for example, the peculiar grouping of mental disorders seen in Rubinstein-Taybi syndrome (Levitas & Reid, 1998)—might be directly or indirectly linked to a gene or mutation. Such a linkage does not imply that the behavior or disorder would be unmodifiable. There is no reason at all for such a conclusion, even if there is a direct link from a gene or CNV to a behavior; numerous studies support the modifiability of putatively phenotypic behaviors (reviewed in Tunnicliffe & Oliver, 2011), and psychiatric disorders respond, if perhaps with nontypical dose-response or side effect profiles, to medication specific to psychiatric diagnosis.

Conclusion

The term *behavioral phenotype* may not bring us closer to the genetic underpinnings of the behavioral features of disorders, but may be useful nonetheless in making a clinical diagnosis in patients with identified genetic and congenital syndromes. Behavioral phenotypes also provide a conceptual framework for the study and treatment of specific genetic disorders each of which is associated with a distinguishing, specific set of features.

The remainder of this chapter is devoted to capsule descriptions of the behavioral phenotypes of 12 ID syndromes. Wherever they exist, Internet resources are included. The following are four important general resources for the clinician:

- Jones,K.L., Jones, M.C., and Casanelles, M. deC. (Eds.). **Smith's Recognizable Patterns of Human Malformation**. This is the standard medical text in the field, an atlas of dysmorphology syndromes. It offers the diagnostic criteria for each syndrome, (analogous to the *DSM-5*) and, most valuable, photographs of individuals with each syndrome. It also contains an index of symptoms (for example, "Syndactyly") with lists of syndromes in which the symptom or dysmorphism occurs. (As in mental disorders, a symptom or dysmorphism can occur in many different and unrelated syndromes; a single symptom does not make a diagnosis. A review of relevant entries in this text is *not* a substitute for a clinical genetics evaluation.) Medical and sometimes behavioral consequences and comorbidities of syndromes are given.

  The book is an indispensable source of information and further references for physicians and other clinicians. This is a comprehensive source for pictures, rather than word descriptions, of these syndromes. Often a photograph clearly resembling the affected individual, accompanying other material, is the single most convincing factor in persuading families, primary care clinicians, and others to pursue a clinical genetics evaluation or to follow the recommendations after a diagnosis is made. A copy of the photograph and relevant pages in a person's chart or record will remain persuasive long after current caregivers are no longer involved.

- ***OMIM*** (sometimes simply said as a word, "*Omim*") is the acronym for the online version of McKusick's comprehensive text *Mendelian Inheritance in Man*, maintained by the National Center for Biotechnology Information at the National Library of Medicine. Constantly updated as new information becomes available, the database is searchable by name of syndrome or by location of chromosome abnormality. Within each entry the information available varies from the clinically relevant and immediately useful to the highly technical (useful only to specialists and research geneticists), with the useful clinical information at the head of each entry. Each entry offers links to the various levels of information. Pages are printable and can be added to charts. References can be followed, often to other online sources. Photographs and other images can be linked in some entries. Entries might contain links to relevant family and support groups and other relevant Web sites. Other sites and references often refer to a syndrome's "OMIM number."

  The URL (Internet address) is: https://www.ncb.nlm.nih.gov/omim. **Note:** The site cannot be accessed from some networks. When this is the case, a link to an alternate or mirror site is offered.

  Under the "Browsing OMIM" links, the first is: Search the OMIM Database. Clicking this option yields the search field. Simply enter the name of the syndrome you are looking up, or the chromosome location (for example, 17p), and click search or press Enter. Further down the home page are links to NCBI Medline, a searchable medical database, and to the next resource, the Alliance of Genetic Support Groups.

- GeneReviews (http://www.ncbi.nlm.nih.gov/books/NBK1116/) contains reviews of more than 650 conditions and the appropriate laboratory testing. This is a resource of choice among geneticists and genetic counselors, more so than OMIM.

- The ***Alliance of Genetic Support Groups*** is an organization made up of groups devoted to each particular syndrome. You can reach it at 202-966-5557, by E-mail at or at its Web page at http://www.geneticalliance.org/. There is a searchable database of support groups and informational newsletters, valuable in locating groups involved with especially rare syndromes. It is worth remembering in this connection that a person with ID/DD can have a genetic syndrome unconnected with the ID/DD, just as he or she can have any other disorder.

References

Adams, D., & Oliver, C. (2011). The expression and assessment of emotions and internal states in individuals with severe or profound intellectual disabilities. *Clinical Psychology Review* 31, 293–306

Dykens, E. M. (1995). Measuring behavioral phenotypes: Provocations from the "new genetics." *American Journal on Mental Retardation, 99*, 522–532.

Dykens E.M. (2003). Anxiety, fears, and phobias in persons with Williams syndrome. *Developmental Neuropsychol*ogy, 23,:291–316.

Dykens, E.M. & Hodapp, R.M. (2007). Three steps toward improving the measurement of behavior in behavioral phenotype. *Reseaerch Child and Adolescent Psychiatric Clinics of North America, 16*(3), 617-630.

Fidler, D.J. (2006). The emergence of a syndrome-specific personality profile in young children with Down syndrome. In: J.A. Rondal & J. Perera (Eds.), *Down syndrome: Neurobehavioural specificity* (pp. 139-152). London: John Wiley & Sons.

Flint, J., & Yule, W. (1994). Behavioural phenotypes. In M. R. Rutter, E. Taylor, & L. Hersov (Eds.), *Child and adolescent psychiatry* (pp. 666–687). Oxford, UK: Blackwell Scientific.

Friedman, E. (1969). The "autistic syndrome" and phenylketonuria. *Schizophrenia, 1(4)*, 249–261.

Garner, C., Callias, M., & Turk, J. (1999). Executive function and theory of mind performance of boys with fragile-X syndrome. *Journal of Intellectual Disabilities Research, 43(6)*, 466–474.

Hill, S.K., Reilly, J.L., Keefe, R.S.E., Gold, J.M., Bishop, J.R., Gershon, E.S., … Sweeney, J.A. (2013). Neuropsychological impairments in schizophrenia and psychotic bipolar disorder: Findings from the Bipolar-Schizophrenia Network on Intermediate Phenotypes (B-SNIP) study. *American Journal of Psychiatry, 170*, 1275-1284.

Hodapp, R. M., Dykens, E.M., Ort, S. I., Zelinsky, D. G., & Leckman, J. F. (1991). Changing patterns of intellectual strengths and weaknesses in males with fragile X syndrome. *Journal of Autism and Developmental Disorders, 21*(4), 503-516.

Jones, K.L., Jones, M.C., & Casanelles, M.deC. (Eds.). (2013). *Smith's recognizable patterns of human malformation* (7th ed.). Philadelphia: W. B. Saunders.

Knight, S. J. L., Regan, R., Nicod, A., Horsley, S. W., Kearney, L., Homfray, T., … Flint, J. (1999). Subtle chromosome rearrangements in children with unexplained mental retardation. *Lancet 354*, 1676–1681.

Kristian Hill, S.K., Reilly, J.L., Keefe, R.S.E., Gold, J.M., Bishop, J.R., Gershon, E. S., … Sweeney, J.A. (2013). Neuropsychological impairments in schizophrenia and psychotic bipolar disorder: Findings from the bipolar-schizophrenian on intermediate phenotypes (B-SNIP) study. *American Journal of Psychiatry, 170*, 1275–1284.

Levitas, A. (1998a). Phenylketonuria (PKU) and the hyperphenylalaninemias: I. *Mental Health Aspects of Developmental Disabilities, 1(2)*, 44–48.

Levitas, A. (1998b). Phenylketonuria (PKU) and the hyperphenylalaninemias: II. *Mental Health Aspects of Developmental Disabilities, 1(4)*, 113–118.

Levitas, A. (1999). Phenylketonuria (PKU) and the hyperphenylalaninemias: III: Psychiatric and behavioral aspects. *Mental Health Aspects of Developmental Disabilities, 2(4)*, 133–140.

Levitas, A., & Reid, C. S. (1998). Rubinstein-Taybi syndrome and psychiatric disorders. *Journal of Intellectual Disabilities Research, 42(4)*, 284–292.

Moreno-De-Luca, A., Myers, S.M., Challman S.D., Moreno-De-Luca, D., Evans, D. W., Ledbetter, H. (2013). Developmental brain dysfunction: revival and expansion of old concepts based on new genetic evidence. *Lancet Neurology*, 12: 406–14.

Nyhan, W. L. (1972). Behavioral phenotypes in organic genetic disease. *Pediatric Research, 6*, 1–9.

Pescosolido, M.F., Gamiscz, E.D., Nafgpal, S., & Morrow, E.M. (2013). Distribution of disease-associated copy number variants across distinct disorders of cognitive development. *Journal of the American Academy of Child and Adolescent Psychaitry, 52*(4), 414-430.

Siegel, M.S., Smith, W. E. (2010). Psychiatric features in children with genetic syndromes: Toward functional phenotypes. *Child and Adolescent Psychiatric Clinics of North America, 19*, 229–261

Skuse, D. H. (2000). Behavioural phenotypes: What do they teach us? *Archives of Diseases of Childhood*, 82, 222-225.

Society for the Study of Behavioural Phenotypes: http://www.ssbp.co.uk (accessed 18 January 2005), SSBP Office, Douglas House, 18b Trumpington Road, Cambridge CB2 2AH, UK.

Streissguth, A. (1997). *Fetal alcohol syndrome: A guide for families and communities.* Baltimore: P.H. Brookes.

Tunnicliffe, P, & Oliver, C. (2011). Phenotype–environment interactions in genetic syndromes associated with severe or profound intellectual disability. *Research in Developmental Disabilities, 32*, 404–418.

Yang, Y., Muzny, D.M., Xia, F., Niu, Z., Person, R., Ding, Y, … Eng, C.M. (2014). Molecular findings among patients referred for clinical whole-exome sequencing. *Journal of the American Medical Association.* doi:10.1001/jama.2014.14601. Published online October 18, 2014.

Behavioral Phenotypes of 12 ID Syndromes

This section describes behavioral phenotypes for the following 12 ID syndromes:

- ❑ Angelman syndrome
- ❑ Chromosome 15q11.2-13.1 duplication syndrome
- ❑ Down syndrome
- ❑ Fetal alcohol syndrome
- ❑ Fragile-X syndrome
- ❑ Phenylketonuria and other hyperphenylalaninemias
- ❑ Prader-Willi syndrome
- ❑ Rubenstein-Taybi syndrome
- ❑ Smith-Magenis syndrome
- ❑ Tuberous sclerosis complex
- ❑ 22q11.2 deletion syndrome
- ❑ Williams syndrome

Each of the subsections on these syndromes includes information on physical findings, diagnosis, cognition, behavioral and associated mental health disorders, and a table comparing the physical and laboratory phenotype features with childhood and adulthood manifestations.

Angelman Syndrome (OMIM # 105830)

Physical Findings

Angelman syndrome (AS) is associated with a lack of maternally derived information on the q11 - q13 region of chromosome 15. The prevalence of AS ranges between 1/15,000 - 1/20,000 live births and is known to occur by way of four different molecular etiologies. Approximately 75% of Angelman syndrome cases are the result of a deletion on the critical region of maternal chromosome 15q11-q13. Another 10-15% of cases result from a mutation in the maternally inherited ubiquitin-protein ligase E3A (*UBE3A*) gene. The remaining cases are due to either an imprinting defect, which causes a lack of expression of the maternal copy of *UBE3A*, or paternal uniparental disomy (pUPD) for chromosome 15, in which two copies of chromosome 15 are inherited from only the father, instead of one copy inherited from each parent.

Individuals with Angelman syndrome have microcephaly, an ataxic gait, dysmorphic facial features, seizures, a happy disposition which includes bouts of frequent laughter, severe developmental delays including motor and language impairments, as well as moderate to severe intellectual disability. Seizures typically begin in early childhood and then decrease in frequency throughout adolescence and adulthood. Some individuals with AS also experience gastrointestinal problems, including feeding disorders in infancy, gastroesophageal reflux disease (GERD), and constipation.

Diagnosis

DNA methylation analysis is the first step in confirming a clinically-suspected diagnosis of Angelman syndrome. A negative methylation result rules out Angelman syndrome. If positive, follow-up fluorescence *in situ* hybridization (FISH) can identify 15q11.2-13 deletions. For results that are methylation positive but FISH negative, targeted sequencing is indicated to look for *UBE3A* mutations.

Cognition

AS is associated with severe to profound intellectual disability, with most individuals reaching a plateau between 24-30 months. Adaptive behavior is variable among individuals with AS; however, many individuals show stronger receptive language skills than expressive language skills. Research indicates that the severity of ID varies with respect to the molecular etiology. For example, a recent study showed that the *UBE3A* mutation was associated with less cognitive and gross and fine motor impairment than the deletion. In addition, the study reported that cognitive skills in children with deletions do not appear to develop beyond 13 months of age, whereas children with other molecular etiologies continued to develop over time. As a result, the authors hypothesized that *UBE3A* may be integral in the development of expressive language skills.

Behavioral and Associated Mental Health Disorders

Individuals with Angelman syndrome typically show speech delay or minimal speech; a happy demeanor with frequent smiling and laughter unrelated to context; seizures; relatively strong socialization skills; relatively weak motor skills; a brief attention span and hyperactivity; excessive chewing/mouthing; stereotypies, such as hand flapping; and sleep disturbance, most often a reduced need for sleep. Irritability, including aggressive behavior, tantrums, and noncompliant behavior can also occur, secondary to the typically happy disposition. Research demonstrates that between 50-80% of individuals with Angelman syndrome show symptoms of autism spectrum disorder (ASD). Recent studies indicated that although a majority of individuals with Angelman syndrome met diagnostic criteria for autism spectrum disorder, their profile of social behavior was significantly different from autism spectrum disorder, as well as individuals with other genetic syndromes. Individuals with Angelman syndrome showed a higher level of social enjoyment and stronger motivation to seek adult contact and found adult eye contact to be particularly reinforcing. Although some studies have shown an association between Angelman syndrome due to deletion and more features of autism spectrum disorder, not all of them have used standardized instruments for diagnosing autism spectrum disorder, and longitudinal studies remain scarce.

In clinical settings, the combination of elated mood, overactivity, and sleep irregularity are difficult to distinguish from mania; when there appear to be cycles or waxing/waning of the behaviors bipolar disorder may be diagnosed (with unknown accuracy), and the most severe mood instability may (or may not) respond to mood stabilizing medication.

Phenotype and Behavioral Phenotype for Angelman Syndrome

Phenotype	Behavioral Phenotype: Childhood	Behavioral Phenotype: Adulthood
Ataxic gait	Attention Deficit/Hyperactivity Disorder (ADHD)	ADHD
Speech impairment	Seizure disorder	Less motor activity
Easily excited, happy disposition		Seizure disorder
Microcephaly		Bipolar Disorder?
Seizures		
Sleep disturbance		
Motor hyperactivity		
Stereotypies		
Gastrointestinal problems (feeding disorders in infancy, GERD, constipation)		

Sources

Bird, L. M. (2014). Angelman syndrome: Review of clinical and molecular aspects. *The Application of Clinical Genetics, 7*, 93-104.

Duca, D. G., Craiu, D., Boer, M., Chirieac, S. M., Arghir, A., Tutulan-Cunita, A.,...Budisteanu, M., (2013). Diagnostic approach of Angelman syndrome. *Maedica, 8*, 321-327.

Gentile, J. K., Tan, W.-H., Horowitz, L. T., Bacino, C. A., Skinner, S. A., Barbieri-Welge, R., ... Peters, S.U. (2010). A neurodevelopmental survey of Angelman syndrome with genotype-phenotype correlations. *Journal of Developmental and Behavioral Pediatrics, 31*, 592-601.

Mertz, L. G. B., Thaulov, P., Trillingsgaard, A., Christensen, R., Vogel, I., Hertz, J. M., & Ostergaard, J. R. (2014). Neurodevelopmental outcome in Angelman syndrome: Genotype-phenotype correlations. *Research in Developmental Disabilities, 35*, 1742-1747.

Moss, J., Howlin, P., Hastings, R. P., Beaumont, S., Griffith, G. M., Petty, J., ... Oliver, C. (2013). Social behavior and characteristics of autism spectrum disorder in Angelman, Cornelia de Lange, and Cri du Chat syndromes. *American Journal on Intellectual and Developmental Disabilities, 118*, 262-283.

Mount, R., Oliver, C., Berg, K., & Horsler, K. (2011). Effects of adult familiarity on social behaviours in Angelman syndrome. *Journal of Intellectual Disability Research, 55*, 339-350.

Rangasamy, S., D'Mello, S. R., & Narayanan, V. (2013). Epigenetics, autism spectrum, and neurodevelopmental disorders. *Neurotherapeutics, 10*, 742-756.

Chromosome 15q11.2-13.1 Duplication Syndrome
(OMIM #608636)

Physical Findings

The incidence of chromosome 15q11.2-13.1 duplication syndrome (dup15q) is believed to be approximately 1 out of every 15,000 births. The syndrome results from a duplication of the q11.2-q13.1 region of chromosome 15. When information from this same critical chromosomal region is deleted the result is either Prader-Willi syndrome or Angelman syndrome.

Dup15q occurs in one of two ways: a separate additional isodicentric 15 chromosome may be present, (idic(15)), or the duplicated information may be interstitial to an existing chromosome 15, (int(15)). People with idic(15) have 47 chromosomes instead of 46 but in some cases may have 48 or 49 chromosomes as 2 or even 3 idic 15 "extra" isodicentric chromosomes can occur. Some individuals with idic (15) are mosaic, as the extra chromosomal material is only present in certain cells. It appears that all idic(15) chromosomes are *de novo* and of maternal origin, while int(15) can be maternally or paternally inherited. The dup15q syndrome is specific only to maternally-derived duplications.

People with int(15) have the extra chromosomal material in one of their 2 copies of chromosome 15. If the duplicated material is from paternal chromosome 15, an individual may not have any developmental issues but if it is from maternal chromosome 15, developmental problems have a very high probability of occurring. Some individuals have an interstitial triplication of chromosome 15 as two extra copies of this region are present in a single chromosome 15.

Genes *UBE3A* and *ATP10A* are two maternally expressed genes that are in this region. They are being studied to determine their role in the development of the dup15q phenotype. The former is involved in the production of the ubiquitin protein ligase E3A enzyme that selects proteins for degradation to support cell function. The function of *ATP10A* is unknown but it is believed that it may be involved in between-cell calcium transmission.

Dup15q has its own specific physical phenotype that includes infant hypotonia that typically decreases with age, ataxia, scoliosis, and increased probability of a seizure disorder or EEG abnormalities. Survey data has shown that a seizure disorder is more common in people with idic(15) than in those with int(15). Physical growth is diminished in 20 to 30% of people with dup15q and fine and gross motor difficulties are often present.

There is a subtle but specific facial phenotype associated with dup15q that consists of a flat nasal bridge, a high palate, epicanthi at the inner corners of the eyes, and ears that are low set with unfolding at the edges.

A physician advisory has been issued for dup15q as children with the syndrome have died suddenly in their sleep. At this time the cause of death is unclear.

Diagnosis

While microarray testing will show duplicated material and precise CNV, it may not pick up the difference between idic(15) and int(15) so FISH is necessary to distinguish between idic(15) and int(15) .

Cognition

Decreased intellectual functioning and delayed language development are common and most children with dup15q have cognitive delay or will meet the full criteria for intellectual disability (intellectual developmental disorder). Language delay is often present and language may never fully develop although individuals with dup15q have been reported with minimal language delay. Echolalia is common.

Behavioral and Associated Mental Health Disorders

A strong association has been noted between dup15q and autism spectrum disorder. The incidence of dup15q has been found to be approximately 3-5% in cohorts of individuals with autism spectrum disorder. Many children with dup15q meet some of the criteria for autism spectrum disorder and were previously diagnosed with Pervasive Developmental Disorder NOS. An increased incidence of anxiety as well as attention deficit disorders has also been reported. These deficits often result in behavioral challenges such as self-injurious behavior and aggression.

Phenotype and Behavioral Phenotype for Dup15q Syndrome.

Phenotype	Behavioral Phenotype: Childhood	Behavioral Phenotype: Adulthood
Infant Hypotonia	Autism Spectrum Disorder	Autism Spectrum Disorder
Scoliosis	Seizure Disorder	Seizure Disorder
Ataxia	ADHD	ADHD
Decreased physical growth	Behavioral Challenges	Behavioral Challenges
	Language delay	Language delay
	Social Communication Deficits	Social Communication Deficits

Sources:

Baron, C. A., Tepper, C. G., Liu, S. Y., Davis, R. R., Wang, N. J., Schanen, N. C., Gregg, J. P. (2006). Genomic and functional profiling of duplicated chromosome 15 cell lines reveal regulatory alterations in UBE3A-associated ubiquitin-proteasome pathway processes. *Human Molecular Genetics, 15*, 853-69.

Battaglia, A. (2005). The inv dup(15) or idic(15) syndrome: A clinically recognizable neurogenetic disorder. *Brain and Development, 27*, 365-369.

Battaglia, A., Parrini, B., & Tancredi, R. (2010). The behavioral phenotype of the idic(15) syndrome. *American Journal of Medical Genetics Part C Seminars in Medical Genetics, 154C*, 448-55.

Bolton, P. F., Marijcke, W. M., Veltman, M. W., Weisblatt, E., Holmes, J. R., Thomas, N. S., … Brown, J. (2004). Chromosome 15q11-13 abnormalities and other medical conditions in individuals with autism spectrum disorders. *Psychiatric Genetics, 14*, 131-137.

Conant K. D., Finucane, B., Cleary, N., Martin, A., Muss, C., Delany, M., … Thibert, R. L. (2014). A survey of seizures and current treatments in 15q duplication syndrome. *Epilepsia*, *55*, 396-402.

Hogart, A., Wu, D., LaSalle, J. M., & Schanen, N. C. (2010). The comorbidity of autism with the genomic disorders of chromosome 15q11.2-q13. *Neurobiology of Disease, 38*, 181-91.

Miller, D. T., Shen, Y., Weiss, L. A., Korn, J., Anselm, I., Bridgemohan, C., … Wu, B. L. (2009). Microdeletion/duplication at 15q13.2q13.3 among individuals with features of autism and other neuropsychiatric disorders. *Journal of Medical Genetics, 46*, 242-248.

Mitchell, M. M., Woods, R., Chi, L. H., Schmidt, R. J., Pessah, I. N., Kostyniak, P. J., & LaSalle, J. M. (2012). Levels of select PCB and PBDE congeners in human postmortem brain reveal possible environmental involvement in 15q11-q13 duplication autism spectrum disorder. *Environmental and Molecular Mutagenesis, 53*, 589-98.

Piard, J., Philippe, C., Marvier, M., Beneteau, C., Roth, V., Valduga, M., … Leheup, B. (2010). Clinical and molecular characterization of a large family with an interstitial 15q11q13 duplication. *American Journal of Medical Genetics, 152A*, 1933-1941.

Rineer, S., Finucane, B. & Simon, E. W. (1998). Autistic symptoms among children and young adults with isodicentric chromosome 15. *American Journal of Medical Genetics, 81*, 428-33.

Schroer, R. J., Phelan, M. C., Michaelis, R. C., Crawford, E. C., Skinner, S. A., Cuccaro, M., … Stevenson, R. E. (1998). Autism and maternally derived aberrations of chromosome 15q. *American Journal of Medical Genetics, 76*, 327-336.

Simon, E. W., Haas-Givler, B., & Finucane , B. (2010). A longitudinal follow-up study of autistic symptoms in children and adults with duplications of 15q11-13. *American Journal of Medical Genetics Part B: Neuropsychiatric Genetics, 153B*, 463-7.

Thomas, J. A., Johnson, J., Peterson Kraai, T. L., Wilson, R., Tartaglia, N., LeRoux, J., … Hagerman, R. J. (2003). Genetic and clinical characterization of patients with an interstitial duplication 15q11-q13, emphasizing behavioral phenotype and response to treatment. *American Journal of Medical Genetics, 119A*, 111-120.

Thomas, N. S., Roberts, S. E., & Browne, C. E. (2003). Estimate of the prevalence of chromosome 15q11-q13 duplications. *American Journal of Medical* Genetics, *120*, 596-598.

Urraca, N., Cleary, J., Brewer, V., Pivnick, E. K., McVicar, K., Thibert, R. L., ... Reiter, L. T. (2013). The interstitial duplication 15q11.2-q13 syndrome includes autism, mild facial anomalies and a characteristic EEG signature. *Autism Research, 6*, 268-79.

Wegiel, J., Schanen, N. C., Cook, E. H., Sigman, M., Brown, W. T., Kucha, I., ... Wisniewski, T. (2012). Differences between the pattern of developmental abnormalities in autism associated with duplications 15q11.2-q13 and idiopathic autism. *Journal of Neuropathology & Experimental Neurology, 71*, 382-97.

Wolpert, C. M., Menold, M. M., Bass, M. P., Qumsiyeh, M. B., Donnelly, S. L., Ravan, S. A., ... Pericak-Vance, M. A. (2000). Three probands with autistic disorder and isodicentric chromosome 15. *American Journal of Medical Genetics Part B: Neuropsychiatric Genetics, 96B*, 365-372.

Additional Resource:

Dup15q Alliance 2014. P.O. Box 674, Fayetteville, NY 13066; phone: 855-dup-15qa; Web site: http://www.dup15q.org/

Down Syndrome (OMIM # 190685)

Physical Findings

Down syndrome is the most common congenital disorder associated with ID, occurring in about 1 in 700 to 1,000 births. People with Down syndrome have characteristic facial features, including: a small head with a flat-looking face, small ears and mouth, a protruding tongue, a broad neck, and an upward slant to the eyes, with epicanthal folds at the inner corners. Unlike most other syndromes, Down syndrome has wide public recognition. Neurological features of Down syndrome include reduced brain weight and volume in the frontal and temporal lobes. The decrease in brain size emerges in 4-5 month fetuses and continues during the last three months of development.

Individuals with Down syndrome are at increased risks for cardiac problems due to cardiac cushion defects and other congenital malformations, hearing loss, visual impairments such as strabismus, gastrointestinal problems, thyroid problems (most commonly hypothyroidism), dental problems, orthopedic concerns, and skin concerns. Many individuals with Down syndrome are also prone to being overweight, especially in adolescence and adulthood; even without obesity sleep apnea is frequent. Persons with Down syndrome may also develop seizures. It is estimated that 5-13% of children with Down syndrome have seizures. Seizures typically develop either before age one or after age thirty.

Down syndrome is caused in most cases (95%) by an extra chromosome 21 in all body cells. About 3% of individuals with Down syndrome have a mosaic form of the syndrome, in which some but not all of their cells have the trisomy 21 pattern. Still others (3% to 5%) have unbalanced translocations that involve chromosome 21. The remainder show unusual chromosomal arrangements. A child with Down syndrome can be born to a mother of any age; however, the chance of this occurring increases as a woman gets older.

Diagnosis

Definitive prenatal diagnosis of Down syndrome is available by amniocentesis and chorionic villus sampling. Non-invasive prenatal testing (NIPT) that analyzes fetal DNA extracted from maternal blood during pregnancy has largely replaced invasive prenatal testing as a reliable screening test for Down syndrome. Down syndrome is often identified at birth, or shortly thereafter, based on the characteristic physical features including hypotonia, a single crease across the palm of the hand, an upward slant to the eyes, and slightly flattened facial features. Follow-up laboratory analysis is needed to confirm the diagnosis and distinguish rare inherited forms of Down syndrome from the typical sporadic type.

Cognition

Individuals with Down syndrome have, on average, mild to moderate ID, with some individuals functioning in the range of borderline intelligence to low average cognitive ability, and others with severe or profound ID. Many individuals have a cognitive profile involving relative weaknesses in grammar and working memory. Individuals with Down syndrome are also prone to have deficits in articulation and intelligibility in terms of their expressive language abilities. Individuals with Down syndrome tend to exhibit impaired attention and impaired executive functioning. Areas of relative strength include visual-spatial tasks (motor, spatial, and visual memory). Use of gestures and signing, and new programs aimed at increasing the reading skills of those with Down syndrome, are thought to build on these strengths.

Behavioral and Associated Mental Health Disorders

Ever since Langdon Down described the syndrome named for him in 1866, people with DS have been cast as having a friendly, engaging nature. This personality stereotype is often called into question, yet parents and others continue to use such labels as "affable," "sociable," and "charming" to describe their children with Down syndrome. Compared with other children with ID, children with DS are less apt to show significant behavioral or emotional problems. Even so, they have more difficulties than do their siblings; common problems include inattention, noncompliance, impulsivity, social withdrawal, and high rates of self-talk. Some children with Down syndrome meet diagnostic criteria for autism spectrum disorders; the exact prevalence is unknown.

Such internalizing problems as withdrawal and decreasing animation or pleasure might increase in adolescence and young adulthood; such shifts may be subtle. Obsessional slowness in completing tasks has also been observed. Some young adults with Down syndrome appear at risk for significant psychopathology, including atypical psychotic disorders. Adults are at increased risk for depressive disorders, obsessive-compulsive disorder (which may present as obsessional slowness), and anxiety disorders, all of which may co-occur with hypothyroidism, and later for dementia of the Alzheimer's type. The depressive disorder is apt to be characterized by passivity, withdrawal, and mutism. Mania is rare. Although characteristic plaques and tangles are seen in most adults with Down syndrome, far fewer actually exhibit the clinical signs and symptoms of dementia of the Alzheimer's type.

Phenotype and Behavioral Phenotype for Down Syndrome.

Phenotype	Behavioral Phenotype: Childhood	Behavioral Phenotype: Adulthood
Small head, mouth	Oppositional and defiant	Depressive Disorders
Upward slant to eyes	Attention-Deficit/Hyperactivity Disorder (ADHD)	Obsessive-Compulsive Disorder
Epicanthal folds	Social, charming personality "stereotype"	Other Anxiety Disorders
Broad neck	Self-talk	Dementia of the Alzheimer's Type
Hypothyroidism		Mental disorders associated with hypothyroidism
Hearing loss, visual impairments		Atypical psychoses
Cardiac problems		Self-talk
Gastrointestinal, orthopedic, and skin disorders		
Obesity		

Sources

Capone, G. T. (2001). Down syndrome: Advances in molecular biology and the neurosciences. *Developmental and Behavioral Pediatrics*, *22*, 40–59.

Charlot, L., Fox, S., & Friedlander, R. (2002). Obsessional slowness in Down's syndrome. *Journal of Intellectual Disability Research*, *46*, 517–524.

Dykens, E. M., Shah, B., Sagun, J., Befck, T., & King, B. H. (2002). Maladaptive behavior in children and adolescents with Down syndrome. *Journal of Intellectual Disability Research, 46*, 484–492.

Fidler, D. J., Hepburn, S., & Rogers, S. (2006). Early learning and adaptive behavior in todders with Down syndrome: Evidence for an emerging behavioural phenotype. *Down Syndrome Research and Practice, 9*(3), 37.44.

Guihard-Costa, A. M., Khung, S., Delbecque, K., Menez, F., & Delezoide, A. L. (2006). Biometry of face and brain in fetuses with trisomy 21. *Pediatric Research, 59*, 33-38.

Hodapp, R. M., Evans, D. W., & Gray, F. L. (1999). Intellectual development in children with Down syndrome. In J. A. Rondal, J. Perera, & L. Nadel (Eds.). *Down syndrome: A review of current knowledge* (pp. 124–132). London: Whurr Publishers.

Holland, A. J., Hon, J., Huppert, A., & Stevens, F. (2000). Incidence and course of dementia in people with Down syndrome: Findings from a population-based study. *Journal of Intellectual Disability Research, 44*, 138–146.

Lott, I. T. (2012). Neurological phenotypes for Down syndrome across the life span. *Progress in Brain Research, 197*, 101-121.

Lott, I. T., & Head, E. (2001). Down syndrome and Alzheimer's disease: A link between development and aging. *Mental Retardation and Developmental Disabilities Research Reviews, 7*, 172–178.

Myers, B. A., & Pueschel, S. M. (1995). Major depression in a small group of adults with Down syndrome. *Research in Developmental Disabilities, 16*, 285–299.

Prasher, V. P., & Day, S. (1995). Brief report: Obsessive-compulsive disorder in adults with Down's syndrome. *Journal of Autism and Developmental Disorders, 25*, 453–458.

Rozien, N. J. (1995). Down syndrome and associated medical disorders. *Mental Retardation and Developmental Disabilities Research Reviews, 2*, 85–89.

Additional Resource

National Association for Down Syndrome, National Down Syndrome Society, 1666 Broadway, 8th Floor, New York, NY 10012; phone: 800-221-4602; Web site: http://www.ndss.org

Fetal Alcohol Syndrome and the Fetal Alcohol Spectrum Disorders

Physical Findings

Fetal alcohol syndrome (FAS) is not a genetic syndrome but rather a neuro-developmental disorder, first described by Jones, Smith, Ulleland, and Steissguth in 1973. It is caused by intrauterine exposure to alcohol (which is one of numerous known teratogens). The physical findings in the full, classic syndrome include: *prenatal and postnatal growth deficiency; short palpebral fissures; a smooth philtrum* (the space between the upper lip and the nasal root); *a thin, smooth upper-lip, maxillary hypoplasia*; and a short nose. (The features highlighted in italics are considered crucial to diagnosis, according to U.S. and Canadian national guidelines; all can be viewed in Jones [1997]). Microcephaly as well as digital, cardiac, and skeletal abnormalities might also be seen.

Varying amounts of alcohol, timing of exposure, and perhaps a varying sensitivity to the effects of alcohol are all thought to be factors in producing the spectrum of outcomes on brain and neurobehavioral development. Other factors that impact the severity of deficits include genetic background and nutritional status. Individuals can present with ranges of neurodevelopmental delay, now termed *Alcohol-related neurodevelopmental disorder (ARND)* or solely physical involvement, now termed *Alcohol-related birth defects (ARBD)*. These two new terms replace the earlier, *fetal alcohol effect (FAE)*. Growth deficits and facial and other physical anomalies are described, as well as individuals with symptoms that are mixtures of both neurodevelopmental and physical involvement. These complex possibilities have led to the increasing acceptance of the term *fetal alcohol spectrum disorders (FASD)*. Fetal alcohol spectrum disorders includes the full spectrum of outcomes observed among individuals with prenatal alcohol exposure (fetal alcohol syndrome, alcohol-related neurodevelopmental disorder, alcohol-related birth defects, and so forth). This is significant because many individuals who have been exposed prenatally to alcohol may demonstrate alcohol-related behavioral and brain dysfunctions but lack the facial features needed for a diagnosis of full fetal alcohol syndrome. Incidence and prevalence data for fetal alcohol syndrome fluctuate widely among nations and subcultures, in part because of diagnostic uncertainty, in part because of variations in alcohol intake and sensitivity, and in part because of variations in the cultural acceptability of revealing this information. Estimates vary from 1 in 300 live births to 1 in 3000 live births; the consensus suggests an incidence of at least 1 in 1000 live births in Europe and North America, with an estimated prevalence of alcohol-related neurodevelopmental disorder 5 to 10 times greater. The deficits associated with fetal alcohol spectrum disorder can be chronic and impact not only the affected individual but also his or her family and society at large.

Diagnosis

Fetal alcohol syndrome is currently the only diagnosis that is widely accepted as a result of prenatal alcohol exposure. The diagnosis of fetal alcohol syndrome includes the following three crucial features:

1) facial abnormalities of smooth philtrum, thin vermillion border, and short palpebral fissures,

2) prenatal and postnatal deficits in growth, and

3) abnormalities within the central nervous system.

Documentation of maternal alcohol use is also important for diagnosis; however, this criterion cannot always be met because an accurate history might be unavailable. The University of Washington's FAS Diagnostic and Prevention Network has proposed a multiaxial system, with rigorous criteria for growth, dysmorphism, and neurodevelopmental abnormalities, as well as a scale of alcohol exposure ranging from "No Risk" to "High Risk." This approach yields a range of diagnoses along the spectrum of fetal alcohol spectrum disorder. Currently this and similar systems are under consideration for consensus-based diagnostic guidelines to be issued by the Centers for Disease Control; it is likely that future diagnostic protocols for fetal alcohol spectrum disorder will incorporate this or a similar system.

Cognition

Deficits in intellectual functioning are common in individuals exposed to prenatal alcohol. Streissguth, Barr, Kogan, & Bookstein (1996) surveying 473 individuals with fetal alcohol spectrum disorder (ages 3 to 51), reported a range of Wechsler IQs from 29 to 120 (mean of 79; 29% with an IQ less than 70) in individuals with full fetal alcohol syndrome, and a range of 42 to 142 (mean of 90, 9% with an IQ less than 70) in individuals with other diagnoses along the fetal alcohol spectrum disorder spectrum. Neuropsychological testing (reviewed in Kodituwakku, Kalberg, & May, 2001; Mattson, Schoenfeld, & Riley, 2001) demonstrates executive function, learning, and memory deficits. These deficits contribute to the gaps between IQ and academic and adaptive functioning seen across the fetal alcohol spectrum disorder spectrum. Deficits in social skills are also often seen in individuals with FASD. A study conducted by Mattson and Riley (2000) utilized the Child Behavior Checklist (CBCL) to compare individuals with heavy prenatal alcohol exposure to individuals who had no prenatal alcohol exposure. Results demonstrated that children with fetal alcohol syndrome had significant impairments in social competence with social problems when compared to the control group.

Behavioral and Associated Mental Health Disorders

The challenges inherent in defining a behavioral phenotype in any syndrome are magnified in fetal alcohol spectrum disorder by variability in the following:

- The dosage as well as the timing of, and the sensitivity to, intrauterine alcohol exposure.

- Any exposure to other substances in utero.
- The comorbidity of alcohol abuse. The mother might have been using alcohol to "self-medicate" any of a range of mental disorders (for example, anxiety disorders, schizophrenia, or mood disorders), or she might in fact have been a member of a family with a Depressive Disorder; any of these possibilities could pose unknown heritability factors.
- The mother might have been using other drugs.
- Any exposure to abuse, neglect, or other family psychopathology, and the range of effects of the foster care and the adoption systems.
- Prenatal nutrition.
- Genetic background.

Therefore, a clear correlation of behavioral and mental health effects of intrauterine alcohol exposure is difficult to establish. However, a range of clinical conditions associated with FASD can still be described, irrespective of etiology.

Attentional problems, including short attention span, motor overactivity, impulsivity, and a peculiar deficit in comprehension of cause-and-effect relationships, are extremely common. Social skills and social behavior deficits exceed what can be accounted for solely on the basis of cognitive function (Thomas, Kelly, Mattson, & Riley, 1998), with an apparent plateau of social functioning at about the 4-to-6-year old level. Deficits in academic functioning are also apparent in individuals with FASD. Research suggests that individuals with FASD have specific impairments in numerical processing.

Formal study of psychopathology in adolescents and adults with FASD is limited to small studies. Famy, Streissguth, and Unis (1998) surveyed 25 individuals with FAS and other diagnoses on the fetal alcohol spectrum disorder spectrum (IQ>70) in a behavioral clinic population that showed high frequencies (>40%) of alcohol and other substance abuse, Mood Disorders (unipolar and bipolar depression), Psychotic disorders (including brief psychotic episodes), and lower but substantial (10–30%) rates of anxiety disorders, eating disorders, and dysthymic disorder (4%). Avoidant, antisocial and dependent personality disorders occurred at frequencies of 28%, 19%, and 14%, respectively. Clinical experience suggests mood and psychotic disorders to be the more common diagnoses in individuals with fetal alcohol spectrum disorder and an IQ < 70. An increase in negative life experiences for adults with prenatal alcohol exposure may be associated with deficits in adaptive functioning mainly in the areas of communication, daily living skills and socialization. Socialization deficits in children with fetal alcohol spectrum disorder do not appear to improve with age suggesting arrested as opposed to delayed development.

Phenotype and Behavioral Phenotype for Fetal Alcohol Spectrum Disorder

Phenotype	Behavioral Phenotype: Childhood	Behavioral Phenotype: Adolescence and Adulthood
Prenatal and postnatal growth deficiency*	Attention-deficit/hyperactivity disorder (ADHD)	Alcohol and other substance abuse
Short palpebral fissures*	Social skills deficits	Major depressive disorder
Smooth philtrum*		Bipolar disorder
Thin, smooth upper lip*		Other psychotic disorders
Microcephaly**		Anxiety disorders
Maxillary hypoplasia**		Eating disorders

Short nose**		Dysthymic disorder
Digital, cardiac, and skeletal abnormalities**		Personality disorders

*Crucial to diagnosis, according to U.S. and Canadian guidelines.

**Occasional findings.

Sources

Famy, C., Streissguth, A. M., & Unis, A. S. (1998). Mental illness in adults with fetal alcohol syndrome or fetal alcohol effects. *American Journal of Psychiatry, 155(4)*, 552–554.

Guerri, C., Bazinet, A., & Riley, E.P. (2009). Foetal alcohol spectrum disorders and alterations in brain and behavior. *Alcohol and Alcoholism, 44(2)*, 108-114.

Jacobson, J. L., Dodge, N. C., Burden, M.J., Klorman, R., & Jacobson, S. W. (2011). Number processing in adolescents with prenatal alcohol exposure and ADHD: Differences in the neurobehavioral phenotype. *Alcoholism: Clinical and Experimental Research,35(3)*, 431-442.

Jones, K. L. (Ed.). (1997). *Smith's recognizable patterns of human malformation* (5th ed.) (pp. 555–558). Philadelphia: W. B. Saunders.

Kodituwakku, W. P., Kalberg, W., & May, P. A. (2001). The effects of prenatal alcohol on executive functioning. *Alcohol Research and Health, 25(3)*, 192–198.

Mattson, S.N., Crocker, N., & Nguyen, T.T. (2011). Fetal alcohol spectrum disorders: Neuropsychological and behavioral features. *Neuropsychological Review, 21*, 81-101.

Mattson, S.N., & Riley, E.P. (2000). Parent ratings of behavior in children with heavy prenatal alcohol exposure and IQ matched controls. *Alcoholism: Clinical and Experimental Research, 36(4)*, 568-576.

Mattson, S. N., Schoenfeld, A. M., & Riley, E. P. (2001). Teratogenic effects of alcohol on brain and behavior. *Alcohol Research and Health, 25(3)*, 185–191.

Olson, H. C., Morse, B. A., & Huffine, C. (1998). Development and psychopathology: Fetal alcohol syndrome and related conditions. *Seminars in Clinical Neuropsychiatry, 3(4)*, 262–284.

Streissguth, A. P., Barr, H. M., Kogan, J., & Bookstein, F. L. (1996). *Understanding the occurrence of secondary disabilities in clients with fetal alcohol syndrome (FAS) and fetal alcohol effects (FAE)*. Final Report to the Centers for Disease Control and Prevention on Grant No. RO4/CCR008515 (Tech. Report No. 96-06). Seattle: University of Washington Fetal Alcohol and Drug Unit.

Thomas, S. E., Kelly, S. J., Mattson, S. N., & Riley, E. P. (1998). Comparison of social abilities of children with fetal alcohol syndrome to those of children with similar IQ scores and normal controls. *Alcohol Clinical and Experimental Research, 22(3)*, 528–533.

Warren, K.R., Hewitt, B. G., & Thomas, J.D. (2011). Fetal alcohol spectrum disorders: Research challenges and opportunities. *Alcohol Research and Health, 34(1)*, 4-14.

Additional Resources

National Organization on Fetal Alcohol Syndrome, 216 G St. NE, Washington, DC 20002; phone: 202-785-4585, tollfree: 800-666-6327, fax: 202-466-6456; Web site: http://www.nofas.org; E-mail: information@nofas.org

University of Washington Fetal Alcohol Syndrome Diagnostic and Prevention Network, Center on Human Development and Disability, PO Box 357920, Seattle, WA 98195; Web site: http://depts.washington.edu/fasdpn

Fragile X Syndrome (OMIM # 309550)

Physical Findings

Fragile X syndrome (FXS) is the designation for a broad spectrum of effects of a full mutation in the *FMR1* gene, located at Xq27.3. A sequence of the DNA bases Cytosine-Guanine-Guanine (CGG) normally repeats from 6 to 54 times in the gene's promoter region; expansion of this region to from 55 to <200 repeats ("premutation") causes increased messenger RNA (mRNA) production which can result in fragile X-associated tremor ataxia syndrome (FXTAS) and fragile X-associated primary ovarian insufficiency (FXPOI) in carriers. When the CGG number exceeds 200 repeats ("full mutation"), methylation of the promoter region typically occurs, preventing the gene from producing its protein product (FMRP). FMRP plays a role in synaptogenesis, especially in the cerebral cortex, cerebellum, and hippocampus and in modifying synaptic structure (Weiler & Greenough, 1999). The exact effect in any individual depends upon the amount of FMRP, in turn dependent upon mutation size (CGG repeat number), sex (affected females have one normal X and one fragile X chromosome), activation rate in females (% of active normal X chromosome vs. fragile X chromosome), mosaicism and methylation.

FMRP has been identified as a member of a family of post-transcription regulator proteins, the gene targets of which are at this point mostly unknown. It is speculated that differences in the regulated genes or perhaps in the other post-transcriptional regulators are additional factors in the variability of the syndrome. One aspect of neuroplasticity known to be regulated by FMRP is long-term potentiation vs. destruction of glutamate receptors (mGluR), affecting memory and executive functions.

Physical features in FXS males with full mutations (CGG>200) typically include prominent ears, long face, hyperextensible joints, flat feet, soft skin, and high arched palate and other connective tissue anomalies; affected individuals may not appear dysmorphic.

Fragile X syndrome (FXS) is the most common known cause of inherited intellectual impairment, with an estimated prevalence of 1/4000 males and 1/6000 females. Fragile X premutations occur in about 1 in 151 females and 1 in 468 males

Diagnosis

Fragile X syndrome is diagnosed using highly accurate DNA testing of the *FMR1* gene. Based on the wide spectrum of presentation of the syndrome plus the frequent lack of dysmorphism, testing for fragile X syndrome is recommended for any individual, male or female, with developmental delay, intellectual disability, or autism spectrum disorder of unknown etiology..

Cognition

From 50 to 70% of females with full mutations show cognitive deficits in the borderline to mild range of intellectual functioning; males are typically more severely affected. Individuals with fragile X premutations, defined as CGG repeat sizes of >54 and <200, do not have intellectual deficits but may show deficits in executive function as well as psychiatric symptoms, a progressive neurological disorder, fragile X-associated tremor ataxia syndrome (FXTAS), characterized by cerebellar ataxia and intention tremor, short-term memory loss, executive function deficits, cognitive decline and parkinsonism, and peripheral nervous system dysfunction, has been described in both males and females >50 years of age (Jacquemot et. al., 2003). As with FXS, males are more commonly affected by fragile X-associated ataxia syndrome due to the X-linked nature of the condition.

Behavioral/Psychiatric

Short attention span, impulsivity, and hyperactivity are extremely common.

Environmental sensitivities, active gaze avoidance, perseverative communication, echolalia, self-talking, cluttering, repetitive activity, motor stereotypy, gaze-avoidance, social anxiety (but not pervasive lack of interest in social contact) are all common and are estimated to rise to the level of clinical significance, with a diagnosis of an autism spectrum disorder, in 15% or more of males with fragile X syndrome. Autism spectrum disorder without cognitive or language impairment (DSM-IV Asperger's disorder) has also been described. The full range of comorbidity of the autism spectrum disorders (mood disorders panic disorder, other anxiety disorders) is seen in clinical populations. More recent work has raised the question of whether persons with fragile X syndrome and autism spectrum disorder differ from those with idiopathic autism spectrum disorder, and further, whether those who have fragile

X syndrome and meet diagnostic criteria for autism spectrum disorder represent the more severe end of the continuum of symptoms and deficits typical of all individuals with fragile X syndrome.

Full mutation females have been demonstrated to have increased rates of major depressive disorder, stereotypic movement disorder, avoidant disorder, and schizotypal personality disorder.

Phenotype and Psychiatric Phenotype for Fragile X Syndrome

PHENOTYPE	FULL MUTATION	PREMUTATION
long face	Attention Deficit / Hyperactivity Disorder	Attention deficit / hyperactivity disorder
prominent ears	Autism Spectrum Disorder	Avoidant Disorder
high arched palate	Generalized Anxiety Disorder	Schizotypal personality disorder
hyperextensible joints	Panic Disorder	Major depressive disorder
flat feet	Mood Disorders	Stereotypic movement disorder
soft skin and other connective tissue anomalies		(Autism spectrum disorders)
Post-adolescent full-mutation males: macroorchidism		Tremor/ataxia syndrome (FXTAS)

Sources

Berry-Kravis, E. (2014). Mechanism-based treatments in neurodevelopmental disorders: Fragile X syndrome. *Pediatric Neurology, 50*, 297-302.

Hagerman, R.J. & Cronister, A.C. (Eds). (1996). *Fragile X syndrome: Diagnosis, treatment, and research* (2nd ed., pp.3-87). Baltimore: Johns Hopkins University Press.

Hagerman, R.J. & Lampe, M.E. (1999). Fragile X syndrome. In: Goldstein, S. & Reynolds, C.R., (Eds). *Handbook of neurodevelopmental and genetic disorders in children* (pp. 298--316). New York: Guilford Press,.

Jacquemot, S., Hagerman, R.J., Leehey, M., Grigsby, J., Zhang, L., Brunberg, J.A., … Hagerman, P. (2003). Fragile X premutation tremor/ataxia syndrome: Molecular, clinical, and neuroimaging correlates. *American Journal of Human Genetics, 72*, 869-878.

Rogers, S.J.,Wehner, E.A., & Hagerman, R.(2001) The behavioral phenotype in fragile X:Symptoms of autism in very young children with fragile X syndrome, idiopathic autism, and other developmental disorders. *Developmental and Behavioral Pediatrics, 22*, 6: 409-417.

Smith, L.E., Barker, E.T. Seltzer, M.M., Abbeduto, L., & Greenberg, J.S. (2012) Behavioral phenotype of fragile X syndrome in adolescence and adulthood. *American Journal of Intellectual and Developmental Disabilities, 117*(1): 1–17.

Weiler, I.J. & Greenough, W.T. (1999). Synaptic synthesis of the Fragile X protein: Possible involvement in synapse maturation and elimination. *American Journal of Medical Genetics, 83*: 248522.

Wolff, J.J, Bodfish, J.W., Hazlett, H.C., Lightbody, A.A., Reiss, A.L., and Piven, J. (2012). Evidence of a distinct behavioral phenotype in young boys with fragile X syndrome and autism. *Journal of the American Academy of Child and Adolescent Psychiatry, 51*(12), 1324–1332.

Additional Resource

National Fragile X Foundation: www.nfxf.org/

Phenylketonuria (PKU) and the Hyperphenylalaninemias (HA) (OMIM #s 261600, 261630, 264070)

Physical Findings

Phenylketonuria and the other hyperphenylalaninemias are metabolic disorders caused by mutations in either the gene for the enzyme phenylalanine hydroxylase (PAH) or one of several genes involved in the formation of its coenzyme tetrahydrobiopterin (BH4). The PAH gene has been localized to Chromosome 12 (region 12q22-24.1) (Scriver, Kaufman, Eisensmith, Savio, & Woo, 1995)

Fölling (1934) linked the syndrome of mental retardation, hypopigmentation (paleness) of skin, eyes and hair, eczema, and odoriferous urine due to high levels of the amino acid phenylalanine in the blood (hyperphenylalaninemia) and excretion of its metabolite phenylketone in the urine. The latter symptom gave rise to the syndrome's common name, phenylketonuria (PKU). Deposition of phenylacetate crystals in skin and mucous membranes causes a pruritic eczema. By 1951 a dietary treatment was proposed and implemented. By 1969 most North American and Western European countries were screening newborns for hyperphenylalaninemia and dietary treatment through age 7 (now referred to as "early-treated PKU") was routinely instituted, resulting in a dramatic drop in institutional placement of persons with PKU. Discovery that behavioral, neurological, and fetal exposure problems resulted from discontinuation of the diet led by 1993 to firm governmental recommendations for earlier, stricter, and lifelong treatment (Medical Research Council 1993, Levitas, 1998a, 1998b) and became a firm NIH guideline in 2000. Proposed guidelines emerging from a NIH consensus document (Camp et. al., 2014) include recommendations for use of sapropretin (synthetic BH4) and large neutral amino acids (LNAA) to supplement and in some cases partially substitute for diet. The HA population thus consists of fully treated, partially treated ("early treated"), and untreated individuals.

Diagnosis

Hyperphenylalaninemia (HA) is defined as any elevation in plasma phenylalanine level. The overall incidence is about 1 in 10,000 live births (Scriver et al., 1995), of whom only a fraction have actual phenylketonuria, defined as plasma phenylalanine of over 1000 micromoles (16.5 mg.) per decaliter (dL.)) (Scriver et al., 1995).

Cognition

Average IQ's for strictly-treated children lag slightly behind averages for the population as a whole (Medical Resarch Council, 1993). While it is clear that the phenyl-free diet does not completely eliminate effects on IQ, since phenylalanine exposure begins in utero, IQ data for treated vs. untreated children show unequivocal gains for treated children and a decrement in IQ with cessation or poor compliance with diet (Smith, Beasley, & Ades, 1991). Neuropsychological testing has been shown to be a more sensitive indicator than global intellectual testing of effects of phenylalanine level on performance. It is possible to separate pretreatment effects from those due to concurrent phenylalanine levels, demonstrating the need for ongoing dietary treatment, and to correlate these results with known effects of high plasma phenylalanine levels on suppression of neurotransmitter synthesis (Krause et al, 1985; Waisbren, Schnell & Levy, 1980).

Behavioral and Psychiatric

Correlation of autistic disorder with PKU was one of the earliest instances of the phenomenon of behavioral phenotype. Severe mood dysregulation and aggression, stereotypy, hyperactivity, and "unresponsiveness" are seen in persons with untreated PKU. "Overt fidgetiness, behavior changes and psychotic illness" are described in children with early-treated PKU with high serum phenylalanine levels (reviewed in Levitas, 1999).

Woolf (1980) coined the term "Late Onset Phenylalanine Intoxication" for what was later called "early-treated PKU." He noted that the consequence of variable discontinuation of phenyl-free diet was an iatrogenic condition, heretofore unknown in nature, the hallmark of which is hyperphenylalaninemia beginning in late childhood, with consequences analogous to several neurodegenerative and metabolic disorders (e.g. Wilson's disease, neurosyphilis, the adrenoleukodystrophies) with onset in this age group. Typically, in these conditions there is dementia and IQ loss only late in their courses; early features were, rather, neuropsychological abnormalities, withdrawal, social inappropriateness, mood dysregulation, and, later, paranoid ideation and delusions. In fact, early-treated PKU has been associated with emergent stereotypy, behaviors associated with ADHD, anxiety, decreased responsiveness and communication, and social isolation, depressed mood, phobias including agoraphobia, and encopresis. Studies in adults have demonstrated significant rates of anxiety disorders (generalized anxiety disorder and agoraphobia), Dysthymic disorder and other depressive disorders (reviewed in Levitas, 1999).

Untreated children and adults showed decreased anxiety, hyperactivity and irritability, decreased stereotypy, spasticity, decreased eczema and marked developmental gains when started on the therapeutic diet. Successful institution of the diet was correlated with gradual (one patient at a time), flexible, carefully-supervised start-up. It was noted that more significant change in functioning was seen at home visits than in the institution (Bruhl, Arneson & Bruhl 1965), perhaps because of richer environment and opportunity for behavioral variety.

A hypothesis that the variety and severity of neuropsychiatric effects of untreated PKU is due to prolonged deficiency of DA, NE and 5HT activity, and resulting up-regulation of the corresponding receptors, proposed by Waisbren & Levy. (1991; Brumm, Bilder, & Waisbren, 2010), is consistent with the clinical data presented above. It is also consistent with the observation of Schuett, Brown, & Michals (1985) of a correlation between the benefit of resumption of the phenyl-free diet with return of serum phenylalanine to nearer-normal levels and time on the resumed diet. This would presumably be due to return of neurotransmitter synthesis to near-normal levels in the short term and the down-regulation of hypersensitive receptor systems in the long term (not unlike the time frame for benefits of neuroleptic withdrawal). Studies have demonstrated correlation of severity of psychiatric symptomatology with elevated serum phenylalanine levels, and that symptomatic individuals can benefit at any age from reduction of serum phenylalanine levels; low self-esteem and the stress of chronic disease and strict diet may also play a role (Brumm et al., 2010).

Phenotype and Behavioral Phenotype for Untreated PKU

Phenotype	Behavioral Phenotype: Childhood	Behavioral Phenotype: Adulthood
High levels of the amino acid phenylalanine in the blood (hyperphenylalaninemia) and excretion of its metabolite phenylketone in the urine	ADHD	ADHD
Odoriferous urine	Anxiety disorders	Autism spectrum disorders
Hypopigmentation (paleness) of skin, eyes and hair	Autism spectrum disorders	Stereotypic movement disorder
Eczema	Stereotypic movement disorder	Depression, bipolar disorder
	Unspecified schizophrenia spectrum disorder	Anxiety Disorders
	Unspecified bipolar disorder	
	Skin picking due to eczema	Skin picking due to eczema

Behavioral Phenotype for "Early-treated" and Treated PKU

Phenotype	Behavioral Phenotype: Childhood	Behavioral Phenotype: Adulthood
High levels of the amino acid phenylalanine in the blood (hyperphenylalaninemia) and excretion of its metabolite phenylketone in the urine	ADHD	Generalized anxiety disorder
Odoriferous urine	Generalized anxiety disorder	Panic disorder, agoraphobia; other phobias, other anxiety disorders
Possible hypopigmentation (paleness) of skin, eyes and hair	Phobic disorder	Dysthymic Disorder
Possible eczema	Obsessive-compulsive disorder	Major depressive disorder
	Autism spectrum disorders	Autism spectrum disorders
	Unspecified schizophrenia spectrum disorder*	
	Unspecified bipolar disorder*	

*Associated with poor dietary control, elevated plasma phenylalanine levels

Sources

Bruhl, H.B., Arneson, J.F. & Bruhl, M.G. (1965). Effect of a low-phenylalanine diet on older phenylketonuria patients (long range controlled study). *American Journal on Mental Deficiency* 69: 225-235.

Brumm, V.L., Bilder, D., Waisbren, S.E. (2010). Psychiatric symptoms and disorders in phenylketonuria. *Molecular Genetics and Metabolism, 99,* S59–S63

Camp, K.M., Parisi, M.A., Acosta, P.B., Berry, G.T., Bilder, D.A., Blaud, N., ... Young, J.M. (2014) Phenylketonuria scientific review conference: State of the science and future research needs. *Molecular Genetics and Metabolism.*

Fölling, I.A. (1934). Über ausscheidung von pheynylbrenztraubensäure in den harn als stoffwechselanomalie in verbindung mit imbezillität. (Urinary excetion of phenylpyruvic acid as a metabolic anomaly related to mental retardation.) *Hoppe Sylers Z. Physiol. Chem. 227,* 169-176.

Krause, W., Halminski, M., McDonald, L., Dembure, P., Salvo, R., Freids, D & Elsas, L. (1985). Biochemical and neuropsychological effects of elevated plasma phenylalanine in patients with treated phenylketonuria. *Journal of Clinical Investigation*: *75*, 40-48.

Levitas, A. (1998a). Phenylketonuria (PKU) and the hyperphenylalaninemias: I. *Mental Health Aspects of Developmental Disabilities*; *1*(2): 44-48.

Levitas, A. (1998b). Phenylketonuria (PKU) and the hyperphenylalaninemias: II. *Mental Health Aspects of Developmental Disabilities 1*(4): 113-118.

Levitas, A. (1999). Phenylketonuria (PKU) and the hyperphenylalaninemias: III: Psychiatric and behavioral aspects. *Mental Health Aspects of Developmental Disabilities 2*(4), 133-140.

Medical Research Council Working Party on Phenylketonuria (1993) Phenylketonuria due to phenylalanine hydroxylase deficiency: an unfolding story. *British Medical Journal*, 306:115-119.

Schuett, V.E., Brown, E.S. & Michals, K.(1985). Reinstitution of diet therapy in PKU patients from twenty-two US clinics. *American Journal of Public Health*; *75*(1), 39-42.

Scriver, C.R., Kaufman, S., Eisensmith, R.C., Savio, L & Woo, C. (1995). The hyperphenylalaninemias. In: C.R. Scriver, A.L., Beaudet, W.S. Sly. & D. Valle D (Eds.), *The metabolic bases of inherited disease, I* (pp. 1015-1075) New York: McGraw-Hill. 1015-1075.

Smith, I., Beasley, M.G. & Ades, A.E. (1991). Effect on intelligence of relaxing the low phenylalanine diet in phenylketonuria. *Archives of Diseases of Childhood, 66*, 311-316.

Waisbren, S.E. & Levy, H.L.(1991) Agoraphobia in phenylketonuria. *Journal of Inherited and Metabolic Diseases, 14*, 755-764.

Waisbren, S.E., Schnell, R.R. & Levy, H.L. (1980). Diet termination in children with phenylketonuria: a review of psychological assessments used to determine outcome. *Journal of Inherited and Metabolic Diseases*, 3, 49-153

Woolf, L.I. (1980) Late onset phenylalanine intoxication. *Journal of Inherited and Metabolic Diseases, 2*, 19-20.

Additional Resources

National PKU News
Virginia Schuett, Editor
6869 Woodlawn Avenue
Seattle, WA 98115-5469
Phone: 206-525-8140
e-mail: schuett@pkunews.org

Childrens' PKU Network
1520 State Street, Suite 111
San Diego, CA 92101-2930
e-mail: pkunetwork @aol.com

Association for Neuro-metabolic Disorders
P.O. Box 0202/L3220 Women's
1500 Medical Center Drive
Ann Arbor, MI 48109-0202
Phone: 313-763-4697

Prader-Willi Syndrome (OMIM # 176270)

Physical Findings

Prader-Willi syndrome (PWS), which is genetically related to Angelman syndrome (AS), is associated with a lack of paternally derived information on the q11-q13 region of chromosome 15. The prevalence of Prader-Willi syndrome ranges from 1/10,000 to 1/30,000, with several molecular etiologies. The most common etiology of Prader-Willi syndrome, accounting for approximately 70% of cases, is a deletion in the q11-q13 region of the paternally contributed chromosome 15. The deletions can be further subdivided into Type I deletions, which involve larger deletions between breakpoints BP3 and BP1, and Type II deletions, which involve smaller deletions between breakpoints BP3 and BP2. Another 25% of individuals with PWS have maternal uniparental disomy (mUPD), in which both copies of chromosome 15 come from the mother. The remaining 5% of individuals develop PWS as the result of an imprinting defect, which causes a lack of expression of the paternal copy of ubiquitin-protein ligase E3A (*UBE3A*), or via a mutation in the paternally inherited *UBE3A* gene.

Clinical features of Prader-Willi syndrome include: mild to moderate hypotonia starting in the neonatal period and lasting throughout life; decreased movement and lethargy in infancy; feeding difficulties, which often lead to failure to thrive; childhood onset hyperphagia; obesity; ritualistic behaviors; skin picking; small hands and feet; short stature; hypogonadism; delays in gross motor and language milestones, typically occurring at twice the normal age; and poor articulation. Hypothalamic disturbances have been implicated in many of these features, and disruptions in various neuroanatomical and neurotransmitter systems may help explain excessive appetite. Growth hormone therapy is often used to treat short stature and hypotonia, whereas behavioral interventions are indicated for the management of hyperphagia and obesity, the leading cause of morbidity and mortality among individuals with Prader-Willi syndrome. Obesity is associated with several health problems, including sleep disordered breathing, diabetes mellitus, and respiratory problems. A majority of individuals with PWS (between 75-85%) also engage in skin picking, which can lead to infections and other medical complications. Although research has shown that behavioral and pharmacological treatments can help improve skin-picking behavior in individuals with PWS, neither has been consistently or completely effective. The ritualistic behaviors seen in individuals with PWS have led many researchers to examine the presence of obsessive-compulsive disorder (OCD). These behaviors often include hoarding, ordering/arranging objects, and insistence on routines. However, some researchers believe the behaviors seen in Prader-Willi syndrome are more consistent with behavioral characteristics associated with Autism Spectrum Disorder, as compared to the more common checking, cleaning, or religious/sexual preoccupations seen in obsessive-compulsive disorder. In addition, research has shown that individuals with PWS do not appear to engage in ritualistic behaviors in order to reduce anxiety; rather, they appear to do so for the purpose of enjoyment.

A recent study showed possible neuroanatomical differences based on the molecular etiology of PWS, in that global volumes of gray matter, white matter, and total intracranial volume were significantly smaller in a deletion group than control group. In addition, individuals with PWS due to maternal UPD had significantly less white matter volume than healthy weight controls. The deletion subtype was also associated with more severe behavior problems than the UPD subtype. Another study examined the tryptophan hydroxylase 2 (*TPH2*) polymorphism, which is associated with serotonin biosynthesis. In PWS, individuals with a hemizygous genotype (G/T) had significantly higher ratings on hyperphagic behavior, drive, and severity scores. The T allele was also associated with higher IQ, and females with the T allele showed more internalizing symptoms.

Diagnosis

DNA methylation analysis is the first step in confirming a clinically-suspected diagnosis of Prader-Willi syndrome. A negative methylation result rules out PWS. If positive, follow-up fluorescence *in situ* hybridization (FISH) can identify 15q11.2-13 deletions. For results that are methylation positive but FISH negative, UPD is assumed and can be confirmed by targeted genomic sequencing.

Cognition

Mild ID and severe learning disabilities are common among children with PWS, with average IQs in the mid-60s to 70s. IQ remains relatively stable over time, with mild to moderate ID common in adulthood. Adults with PWS also demonstrate executive functioning difficulties, particularly with respect to planning/organization and set shifting. Some studies have suggested a relative strength in visuospatial ability among individuals with PWS due to their ability to complete jigsaw puzzles. However, a recent study indicated that individuals with PWS performed worse than typically developing controls on tasks involving the components of visuospatial ability (e.g., spatial perception, mental rotation, spatial visualization), and therefore concluded that these visuospatial abilities were not responsible for jigsaw puzzle solving skills in individuals with Prader-Willi syndrome. Other studies have determined that individuals with Prader-Willi syndrome show relative weaknesses in short term memory, processing speed, and/or social cognition.

Recent research has examined relationships between molecular etiologies and cognition, showing associations between Prader-Willi syndrome due to maternal UPD and higher verbal IQ/academic performance, as well as an association between maternal UPD and higher expressive as opposed to receptive language abilities. In addition, research has demonstrated an association between the *TPH2* G703-T polymorphism and higher IQ.

Behavioral and Associated Mental Health Disorders

Individuals with Prader-Willi syndrome often have a behavioral profile characterized by irritability, including temper tantrums, stubbornness, and difficulty with transitions; skin picking; and ritualistic behaviors, which may be, but are not necessarily related to, food hoarding and security. This profile begins in early childhood in approximately 80% of individuals with PWS. In addition, these behaviors may be associated with autism spectrum disorder in approximately 25% of individuals with PWS, which in turn is associated with the UPD genetic subtype. Individuals with the deletion subtype show higher rates of skin picking, nail biting, hoarding, and overeating. Some children and adults with Prader-Willi syndrome also display symptoms of attention deficit/hyperactivity disorder (ADHD), which can be exacerbated by sleep apnea associated with obesity. In addition, between 10-20% of adults with Prader-Willi syndrome develop psychotic disorders, which has also been associated with the UPD genetic subtype.

Phenotype and Behavioral Phenotype for Prader-Willi Syndrome

Phenotype	Behavioral Phenotype: Childhood	Behavioral Phenotype: Adulthood
Short stature	Autism spectrum disorder (ASD)	ADHD
Hypogonadism	Attention deficit/hyperactivity disorder (ADHD)	Psychotic disorders
Ritualistic behaviors		Mood disorders
Sleep disordered breathing		
Hyperphagia		
Temper tantrums		
Seizures		
Skin picking		
Dysmorphic facial features: narrow bifrontal diameter, narrow nasal bridge, almond-shaped palpebral fissures.		

Sources

Cassidy, S. B. & Driscoll, D. J. (2009). Prader-Willi syndrome. *European Journal of Human Genetics*, *17*, 3-13.

Cassidy, S. B., Schwartz, S., Miller, J. L., & Driscoll, D. J. (2012). Prader-Willi syndrome. *Genetics in Medicine*, *14*, 10-26.

Chevalere, J., Postal, V., Jauregui, J., Copet, P., Laurier, V., & Thuilleaux, D. (2013). Assessment of executive functions in Prader-Willi syndrome and relationship with intellectual level. *Journal of Applied Research in Intellectual Disabilities*, *26*, 309-318.

Dimitropoulos, A., Ferranti, A., & Lemler, M. (2013). Expressive and receptive language in Prader-Willi syndrome: Report on genetic subtype differences. *Journal of Communication Disorders*, *46*, 193-201.

Dykens, E. M., Lee, E., & Roof, E. (2011). Prader-Willi syndrome and autism spectrum disorders: An evolving story. *Journal of Neurodevelopmental Disorders*, *3*, 225-237.

Dykens, E. M., & Roof, E. (2008). Behavior in Prader-Willi syndrome: Relationship to genetic subtypes and age. *Journal of Child Psychology and Psychiatry*, *49*, 1001-1008.

Dykens, E. M., Roof, E., Bittel, D., & Butler, M. G. (2011). TPH2 G/T polymorphism is associated with hyperphagia, IQ, and internalizing problems in Prader-Willi syndrome. *Journal of Child Psychology and Psychiatry*, *52*, 580-587.

Ho, A. Y. & Dimitropoulos, A. (2010). Clinical management of behavioral characteristics of Prader-Willi syndrome. *Neuropsychiatric Disease and Treatment*, *6*, 107-118.

Honea, R. A., Holsen, L. M., Lepping, R. J., Perea, R., Butler, M. G., Brooks, W. M., & Savage, C.R. (2012). The neuroanatomy of genetic subtype differences in Prader-Willi syndrome. *American Journal of Medical Genetics B: Neuropsychiatric Genetics*, *159B*, 243-253.

Miller, J. L., & Angulo, M. (2014). An open-label pilot study of N-acetylcysteine for skin-picking in Prader-Willi syndrome. *American Journal of Medical Genetics Part A*, *164A*, 421-424.

Sinnema, M., Einfeld, S. L., Schrander-Stumpel, C. T. R. M., Maaskant, M. A., Boer, H., & Curfs, L. M. G. (2011). Behavioral phenotype in adults with Prader-Willi syndrome.

Research in Developmental Disabilities, 32, 604-612.

Spendelow, J. S. (2011). Assessment of behavioral and psychiatric problems in people with Prader-Willi syndrome: A review of the literature. *Journal of Policy and Practice in Intellectual Disabilities, 8*, 104-112.

Tunnicliffe, P., Woodcock, K., Bull, L., Oliver, C., & Penhallow, J. (2014). Temper outbursts in Prader-Willi syndrome: Causes, behavioural and emotional sequence and responses by carers. *Journal of Intellectual Disability Research, 58*, 134-150.

Rubinstein Taybi Syndrome (OMIM # 180849)

Physical Findings

Rubinstein Taybi syndrome (RTS) is a multiple congenital anomaly syndrome first recognized in 1963, characterized by intellectual disability, short stature, microcephaly (small head circumference), broad thumbs, broad great toes, and specific dysmorphic facial features including hypertelorism (widely-spaced eyes), beaked nose with tip overhanging the upper lip, and sometimes small jaw. Ophthalmologic and renal abnormalities are common; occasionally polydactyly is seen. Photographs of these features are available in (Jones, Jones, & Casnelles, 2013). Birth prevalence has been estimated at 1/125,000; frequency in ID clinic populations has been estimated to be about 1/600.

Diagnosis

The diagnosis of Rubinstein Taybi syndrome is usually made clinically based on the characteristic dysmorphisms. The syndrome has been mapped in some cases to a gene, CBP (formerly termed CREBBP, cyclic-AMP Protein Binding Protein), located within the chromosomal region 16p13.3. A specific abnormality of CREBBP can be detected in fewer than half of cases. With the increasing clinical availability of whole exome sequencing and targeted gene panels, laboratory confirmation of Rubinstein Taybi syndrome, as well as discovery of new causative genetic loci, are likely to become more common.

Cognition

Measured IQs range from 30 to 79 with an average of 51; 52% have IQ below 50.

Behavioral/Psychiatric

Short attention span, impulsivity, clinically non-significant stereotypy, withdrawal, and nonspecific "maladaptive behaviors" have all been identified in children with Rubinstein Taybi syndrome. Clinical experience and case reports suggest the possibility of a significant frequency of autism spectrum disorders., and stereotypy is reported in formal studies.

Prevalence of psychiatric disorders in Rubinstein Taybi syndrome is unknown and disputed. They may be relatively rare in non-referred populations and more common in adults than in children with Rubinstein Taybi syndrome. What appears significant is the clustering of diagnoses, into mood disorders, most strikingly bipolar disorder, and tic/obsessive-compulsive spectrum disorders. Autism spectrum disorder is also seen. Psychotic features were a striking component in all patients with mood disorders. With a single exception, reported patients with mood disorders did not have tic/OCD spectrum disorder; one patient with mood disorder had OCD symptoms insufficient to meet DSM-III-R criteria. Schizophrenia, panic disorder, generalized anxiety disorder and other acute psychiatric disorders were not observed.

A significant frequency of neuroleptic malignant syndrome is also reported, perhaps related to hypohydrosis reported in 38% of adults with RTS.

Psychiatric Phenotype for Rubinstein-Taybi Syndrome

Phenotype	Behavioral Phenotype: Childhood	Behavioral Phenotype: Adulthood
short stature	ADHD (attention deficit-hyperactivity disorder)	Tic Disorders
microcephaly	Tic disorders	Obsessive compulsive disorder
broad thumbs, broad great toes, occasional polydactyly	Obsessive compulsive disorder	Major depressive disorder
hypertelorism	Possible autism spectrum disorders	Bipolar disorder with psychosis
beaked nose with tip overhanging the upper lip	? Risk of neuroleptic malignant syndrome	Risk of neuroleptic malignant syndrome
Occasional maxillary hypoplasia (small jaw)	Stereotypy	
Ophthalmologic and renal abnormalities common	Motor control deficits	

Sources

Cantani, A., & Gagliesi, D. (1998) Rubinstein-Taybi syndrome. Review of 732 cases and analysis of the typical traits. *European Review for Medical & Pharmacological Sciences 2*(2), 8187.

Gale´ra, C., Taupiac, E., Fraisse, S., Naudion, S. Toussaint, E., Rooryck-Thambo, C., … Bouvard, M-P. (2009). Socio-behavioral characteristics of children with Rubinstein-Taybi syndrome. *Journal of Autism and Developmental Disorders, 39*, 1252–1260

Hennekam, R.C.M., Baselier, A.C.A.., Beyaert, E., Bos, A., Block, J. B., Jansma, H. B. M., Thorbecke-Nilsen, V.V. & Veerman, H. (1992) Psychological and speech studies in Rubinstein-Taybi syndrome. *American Journal on Mental Retardation, 96*(6), 645-660.

Hennekam, R.C.M., Van Den Boogaard, M.J., & Van Doorne, J.M. (1991) A cephalometric study in Rubinstein-Taybi syndrome. *Journal of Craniofacial Genetics and Developmental Biology, 20*, 33-40.

Jones, K.L., Jones, M.C., & Casanelles, M.deC. (Eds.). (2013). *Smith's recognizable patterns of human malformation* (7th ed.). Philadelphia: W. B. Saunders.

Levitas, A., & Reid, C.S. (1998) Rubinstein-Taybi syndrome and psychiatric disorders. *Journal of Intellectual Disabilities Research, 42*(4), 284-292.

Levitas, A., & Reid, C.S. (2003). Rubinstein-Taybi syndrome. *Mental Health Aspects of Developmental Disorders, 6*(4), 130-134.

Rubinstein J.H. (1990) Broad thumb-hallux (Rubinstein-Taybi) syndrome 1957-1988. *American Journal of Medical Genetics Supplement 6*, 3-16.

Stevens, C.A., Pouncey, J., & Knowles, D. (2011). Adults with Rubinstein–Taybi syndrome. *American Journal of Medical Genetics*, 155(Part A), 1680–1684.

Verhoeven, W.M.A., Tuinier, S., Kuijpers, H.J.H., Egger, J.I.M., Brunner H.G., (2010) Psychiatric profile in Rubinstein-Taybi Syndrome: A review and case report. *Psychopathology* : *43*,63–68.

Yagihashi, T., Kosaki K., Okamoto, N., Mizuno, S., Kurosawa,K., Takahashi, T., …,Kosaki, R. (2012). Age-dependent change in behavioral features in Rubinstein-Taybi syndrome. *Congenital Anomalies*, 52, 82–86.

Additional Resource

Rubinstein-Taybi Foundation: htttp://Tucson.com/rts/

Smith-Magenis Syndrome (OMIM # 309550)

Physical Findings

Smith-Magenis syndrome (SMS) was first described in 1986 as a contiguous gene deletion disorder involving chromosomal region 17p11.2. Males and females are affected equally. Individuals with SMS almost always have a cytogenetically visible deletion of chromosomal band 17p11.2. The finding of RAI1 gene mutations in 10% of nondeleted individuals with Smith-Magenis syndrome suggests that most of the major phenotypic features of this disorder, including its characteristic behavioral manifestations, are related to abnormalities affecting RAI1 gene function (Slager, Newton, Vlangos, Finucane, & Elsea, 2003).

Physical findings of Smith-Magenis syndrome include a characteristic facial appearance with underdeveloped cheekbones and a prominent jaw. Although recognizable to clinicians familiar with the disorder, the characteristic facial appearance in Smith-Magenis syndrome is often subtle, particularly in infants and young children. Mild postnatal growth retardation is usual, as is brachycephaly (a shortened skull shape). The fingers and toes are usually short (brachydactyly), and the skin on the hands and feet tends to be dry and leathery. There is significant clinical overlap with trisomy 21, especially in the newborn period, and many infants with SMS are initially thought to have Down syndrome. Congenital heart defects, urogenital anomalies, palatal clefts, and other structural abnormalities occur commonly but are rarely life threatening. Peripheral neuropathy results in an abnormal gait and is a likely underlying contributor to the self-mutilation of fingernails and toenails, which is characteristic of this disorder.

Diagnosis

The diagnosis of Smith-Magenis syndrome is confirmed by the detection of a deletion of the 17p11.2 critical region using FISH analysis when SMS is clinically suspected. More commonly, the diagnosis is revealed by chromosomal microarray analysis done as part of the etiological evaluation of developmental delay, ID, and/or behavioral disturbance. In cases where the diagnosis of Smith-Magenis syndrome is strongly suspected but FISH and microarray are negative, single gene mutation testing should be considered to check for mutations in RAI1 which are thought to account for ~10% of cases.

Cognition

As with many genetic syndromes, individuals with Smith-Magenis syndrome vary widely in cognitive and adaptive functioning, with the majority of those affected functioning in the Mild to Moderate range of ID. The cognitive profile of people with Smith-Magenis syndrome includes relative strengths in long-term memory and perceptual closure, with relative weaknesses in sequential processing and short-term memory.

Behavioral and Associated Mental Health Disorders

Infants with Smith-Magenis syndrome rarely cry and are often placid and lethargic, symptoms that are likely related to hypotonia and excessive sleepiness. Hypersomnolence and lethargy give way by age 4 to highly disturbed sleep patterns, which include difficulties falling asleep, frequent nighttime awakenings, waking up early, and excessive daytime sleepiness. Severely abnormal sleep patterns present a lifelong challenge for the majority of people with Smith-Magenis syndrome and are thought to be related to abnormalities in endogenous melatonin metabolism.

Maladaptive behaviors in Smith-Magenis syndrome begin to escalate by early childhood and most often include: a desire for constant attention from adults, prolonged outbursts and temper tantrums (often when attention is withdrawn), impulsivity, distractibility, adherence to routine, aggression, and self-injury. Maladaptive behaviors and sleep disturbance cause significant family stress and represent the major management problem for caretakers. The vast majority of children and adults with Smith-Magenis syndrome engage in some form of self-injurious behavior (SIB), most commonly head banging, face slapping, self-biting, and skin picking. The overall prevalence of SIB increases with age, as does the repertoire of different types of self-injurious behavior exhibited.

Two unusual forms of SIB distinguish SMS from other genetic syndromes: onychotillomania (pulling out fingernails and toenails) and polyembolokoilamania (inserting foreign objects into body orifices). These two behaviors, along with the "self-hugging" stereotypy that most people with SMS show when they are excited, represent key elements of the behavioral phenotype. Although the majority of people with SMS exhibit one or more of these three key symptoms at some point during their lives, these behaviors only rarely occur among people without Smith-Magenis syndrome.

Behavioral Phenotype for Smith-Magenis Syndrome

Phenotype	Behavioral Phenotype: Childhood	Behavioral Phenotype: Adolescence and Adulthood
Brachycephaly, underdeveloped cheekbones, prominent jaw	Attention-deficit/hyperactivity disorder (ADHD)	ADHD
Congenital heart defects	Tic disorders	Obsessive-compulsive disorder
Urogenital anomalies	Obsessive-compulsive disorder	Bipolar disorder with psychotic features
Palatal abnormalities	Possible autistic disorder	Anxiety disorder
Short fingers; dry, leathery skin on hands and feet	Oppositional defiant disorder	ID, usually mild to moderate
Peripheral neuropathy	Bipolar disorder with psychotic features	
Mildly short stature	Anxiety disorder	
	ID, usually mild to moderate	

Sources

Allanson, J. E., Greenberg, F., & Smith, A. C. (1999). The face of Smith-Magenis syndrome: A subjective and objective study. *Journal of Medical Genetics, 36*, 394–397.

Dykens, E. M., & Smith, A. C. (1998). Distinctiveness and correlates of maladaptive behaviour in children and adolescents with Smith-Magenis syndrome. *Journal of Intellectual Disability Research, 42*, 481.

Finucane, B., Dirrigl, K. H., & Simon, E. W. (2001). Characterization of self-injurious behaviors in children and adults with Smith-Magenis syndrome. *American Journal on Mental Retardation, 106*, 52–58.

Potocki, L., Glaze, D., Tan, D. X., Park, S. S., Kashork, C. D., Shaffer, L. G., … Lupski, J.R. (2000). Circadian rhythm abnormalities of melatonin in Smith-Magenis syndrome. *Journal of Medical Genetics, 37*, 428–433.

Slager, R. E., Newton, T. L., Vlangos, C. N, Finucane, B., & Elsea, S. H. (2003). Mutations in RAI1 associated with Smith-Magenis syndrome. *Nature Genetics, 33*, 466–468.

Smith, A. C., Dykens, E., & Greenberg, F. (1998). Sleep disturbance in Smith-Magenis syndrome (del 17 p11.2). *American Journal of Medical Genetics, 81*, 186–191.

Smith, A. C., McGavran, L., Robinson, J., Waldstein, G., Macfarlane, J., Zonona. J., … Magenis, E. (1986). Interstitial deletion of (17) (p11.2p11.2) in nine patients. *American Journal of Medical Genetics, 24*, 393–414.

Additional Resource

Parents and Researchers Interested in Smith-Magenis Syndrome (PRISMS); Web site: http://www.prisms.org

Tuberous Sclerosis Complex (OMIM # 191100)

Physical Findings

Tuberous sclerosis complex (TSC) is caused by a mutation in either the hamartin tumor suppressor gene *TSC1*, located at chromosome 9q34, or the tuberin tumor suppressor gene *TSC2*, located at chromosome 16p13.3. The protein products of *TSC1* and *TSC2* form a complex that modifies the mammalian target of rapamycin (mTOR) pathway, which helps regulate protein translation and cell growth. Individuals with tuberous sclerosis complex therefore experience a disruption in the mTOR pathway and develop multiple benign tumors on nearly all organs; however, lesions are most commonly found in skin, central nervous system (CNS), kidneys, heart, lungs, and eyes. The *TSC2* mutation is more common and has more severe effects than *TSC1*. The estimated prevalence of tuberous sclerosis complex is between 1/6,000 - 1/10,000 live births, and occurs by a spontaneous mutation in about 70% of affected individuals. Phenotypic expression of tuberous sclerosis complex is extremely variable, even among family members who carry the same mutation.

Skin findings are extremely common in tuberous sclerosis complex, with hypomelanotic macules (patches of lighter-colored skin) present in 90-98% of individuals with tuberous sclerosis complex. In addition, bilateral facial angiofibromas, often identified by a butterfly pattern across the nose and cheeks, occur in about 80% of children with tuberous sclerosis complex over 5 years old. Less common dermatological findings include shagreen patches on the back, trunk, and/or thighs; cephalic fibrous plaques; and ungual fibromas on toes and fingers.

Central nervous system findings in tuberous sclerosis complex include cortical tubers, subependymal nodules, fine-grained cerebral white and gray matter abnormalities, and subependymal giant cell astrocytomas. Cortical tubers occur in up to 95% of individuals with TSC and are best evaluated with magnetic resonance imaging (MRI). Subependymal nodules (SEN) also occur in the majority (between 85-95%) of individuals with tuberous sclerosis complex. They are often identified in early infancy and are most commonly found near the foramen of Monro. Fine-grained gray and white matter abnormalities (cerebral white matter radial migration lines) are less common, occurring in 20-30% of individuals with tuberous sclerosis complex. Subependymal giant cell astrocytomas (SEGA) are benign tumors that occur in about 10-20% of individuals with tuberous sclerosis complex. They are believed to originate from subependymal nodules near the foramen of Monro and may enlarge to the point of obstructing the flow of cerebrospinal fluid, resulting in obstructive hydrocephalus. The central nervous system findings are often associated with seizures, which occur in about 90% of individuals with tuberous sclerosis complex. Typical seizure onset occurs during infancy (infantile spasms) or early childhood.

Cardiac rhabdomyomas, relatively benign tumors that appear on the heart muscle, are common in the developing fetus and newborn with tuberous sclerosis complex. The tumors tend to recede over time, and most become undetectable during childhood. Approximately 80% of children with TSC develop renal complications such as angiomyolipomas, renal cystic disease, and polycystic kidney disease (PKD), which is associated with the *TSC2* deletion. Lymphangioleiomyomatosis, a cystic lung disease, typically occurs in mid-adulthood and is associated with mutations of the *TSC2* gene. Finally, retinal hamartomas occur in nearly 50% of children with TSC; however, they are typically asymptomatic and do not increase in size or number. The presence of other nonspecific findings, such as dental pits, gingival fibromas, and soft fibromas, are also minor criteria of tuberous sclerosis complex.

Recent research has led to FDA approval of everolimus, an orally-administered rapamycin derivative that acts as an mTOR inhibitor, for the treatment of SEGAs and renal angiomyolipomas. Everolimus has been shown to stop the growth of and decrease the volume of angiomyolipomas and SEGAs, with the most significant results occurring within the first year of treatment. Studies examining the use of topical sirolimus, a rapamycin preparation, have shown improvement in facial angiofibromas in the majority of treated individuals. Similar dermatological improvements were noted among individuals treated with everolimus for angiomyolipoma or SEGA. In addition, both sirolimus and everolimus have been shown to reduce seizure activity in individuals with tuberous sclerosis complex. Ongoing research continues to examine the long-term effects of everolimus and sirolimus, including the possibility that both may help prevent seizures and even ID, especially among very young individuals with tuberous sclerosis complex.

Diagnosis

Diagnosis of TSC is based on the presence of major features (e.g., facial angiofibromas, hypomelanotic macules, shagreen patch, cortical tubers, subependymal nodule, subependymal giant cell astrocytoma, cardiac rhabdomyoma) and/or minor features (e.g., pits in dental enamel, bone cysts, gingival fibromas, multiple renal cysts). A definite clinical diagnosis is made when either: (a) two major features or (b) one major and two minor features are present. Although the presence of major and/or minor features is enough to diagnose TSC, many studies stress the importance of an EEG in order to screen for seizures, in addition to regular MRI of the brain to confirm brain lesions. Targeted genetic testing of the TSC 1 and 2 genes responsible for TSC can be used to confirm diagnosis and guide genetic counseling; however, mutations are not detected in approximately 10-15% of individuals with tuberous sclerosis complex.

Cognition

Several studies have demonstrated the cognitive abilities of individuals with tuberous sclerosis complex follow a bimodal distribution. Approximately 30% of individuals with tuberous sclerosis complex are severely impaired, with a mean IQ ranging from 30-40, and more than 50% have average intelligence, with a mean IQ of about 93. The severity of ID has been associated with the number of brain lesions (particularly cortical tubers) present in individuals with tuberous sclerosis complex. In addition, earlier seizure onset is associated with poorer intellectual outcomes. Other studies have indicated memory and executive functioning difficulties among adults with tuberous sclerosis complex.

Behavioral and Associated Mental Health Disorders

Common behavioral problems associated with tuberous sclerosis complex include sleep disturbance, aggressive behavior, temper tantrums, and depressed mood. Approximately 40-50% of individuals with tuberous sclerosis complex meet criteria for autism spectrum disorder (ASD). Although the genotype-phenotype association remains largely unknown, research shows that autism spectrum disorder is more common in individuals with tuberous sclerosis complex and intellectual disability and is closely associated with epilepsy. A recent study found early developmental delays in infants with tuberous sclerosis complex, specifically in the visual domain, in addition to atypical social communication function at age 6 months. Attention deficit/hyperactivity disorder (ADHD) is also diagnosed in about 50% of individuals with tuberous sclerosis complex. Mood and anxiety disorders become more prevalent in adulthood; between 50-60% of adults with tuberous sclerosis complex meet criteria for these disorders.

Phenotype of Tuberous Sclerosis

Phenotype	Behavioral Phenotype: Childhood	Behavioral Phenotype: Adulthood
Skin lesions: facial angiofibromas, hypomelanotic macules, shagreen patch, cephalic fibrous plaques, ungual fibromas.	Autism spectrum disorder (ASD)	Mood disorders, anxiety disorders
Brain lesions: cortical tubers, subependymal nodules, giant cell astrocytomas, fine-grained white and gray matter abnormalities.	Attention deficit/hyperactivity disorder (ADHD)	Autism spectrum disorder
Other organ systems: cardiac rhabdomyomas, renal angiomyolipomas, renal cysts, lymphangioleiomyomatosis of lung, retinal hamartomas.	Seizure disorders	Attention deficit/hyperactivity disorder

Sources

Balestri, R., Neri, I., Patrizi, A., Angileri, L., Ricci, L., & Magano, M. (2015). Analysis of current data on the use of topical rapamycin in the treatment of facial angiofibromas in tuberous sclerosis complex. *Journal of the European Academy of Dermatology and Venereology, 29*, 14-20.

Cabrera-López, C., Martí, T., Catalá, V., Torres, F., Mateau, S., Ballarí, J., & Torra, R. (2012). Assessing the effectiveness of rapamycin on angiomyolipoma in tuberous sclerosis: A two years trial. *Orphanet Journal of Rare Diseases, 7*(87). doi:10.1186/1750-1172-7-87

Cardamone, M., Flanagan, D., Mowat, D., Kennedy, S. E., Chopra, M., & Lawson, J. A. (2014). Mammalian target of rapamycin inhibitors for intractable epilepsy and subependymal giant cell astrocytomas in tuberous sclerosis complex. *The Journal of Pediatrics, 164*, 1195-1200.

Curatolo, P., Bombardieri, R., & Jozwiak, S. (2008). Tuberous sclerosis. *Lancet, 372*, 657-668.

deVries, P.J. (2012). Targeted treatments for cognitive and neurodevelopmental disorders in tuberous sclerosis complex. *Neurotherapeutics: The Journal of the American Society for Experimental NeuroTherapeutics, 7*, 275-282.

Franz, D. N. (2013). Everolimus in the treatment of subependymal giant cell astrocytomas, angiomyolipomas, and pulmonary and skin lesions associated with tuberous sclerosis complex. *Biologics: Targets and therapy, 7*, 211-221.

Jansen, F. E., Braams, O., Vincken, K.L., Algra, A., Anbeek, P., Jennekens-Schinkel, A, … Nellist, M. (2008). Overlapping neurologic and cognitive phenotypes in patients with TSC1 or TSC2 mutations. *Neurology, 70*, 908-915.

Spurling Jeste, S. S., Wu, J. Y., Senturk, D., Varcin, K., Ko, J., McCarthy, B., … Nelson, C.A. (2014). Early developmental trajectories associated with ASD in infants with tuberous sclerosis complex. *Neurology, 83*, 160-168.

Kohrman, M. H. (2012). Emerging treatments in the management of tuberous sclerosis complex. *Pediatric Neurology, 46*, 267-275.

Krueger, D. A., Wilfong, A. A., Holland-Bouley, K., Anderson, A. E., Agricola, K., Tudor, C., … Franz, D.N. (2013). Everolimus treatment of refractory epilepsy in tuberous sclerosis complex. *Annals of Neurology, 74*, 679-687.

Mettin, R.R., Merkenschlager, A., Bernhard, M.K., Elix, H., Hirsch, W., Kiess, W, & Syrbe, S. (2014). Wide spectrum of clinical manifestations in children with tuberous sclerosis complex- Follow-up of 20 children. *Brain & Development, 36*, 306-314.

Moavero, R., Coniglio, A., Garaci, F., & Curatolo, P. (2013). Is mTOR inhibition a systemic treatment for tuberous sclerosis? *Italian Journal of Pediatrics, 39*:57. doi:10.1186/1824-7288-39-57

Ng, K.H., Ng, S.M., & Parker, A. (2014). Annual review of children with tuberous sclerosis. *Archives of Disease in Childhood, Education and Practice Edition, 0*, 1-8. doi: 10.1136/archdischild-2013-304948.

Pulsifer, M.B., Winterkorn, E.B., & Thiele, E.A. (2007). Psychological profile of adults with tuberous sclerosis complex. *Epilepsy & Behavior, 10*, 402-406.

Rosser, T., Panigrahy, A., & McClintock, W. (2006). The diverse clinical manifestations of tuberous sclerosis complex: A review. *Seminars in Pediatric Neurology, 13*, 27-36.

Yamada, H., Akiyoshi, K., & Izumi, T. (2014). The ominous sequence in patients with tuberous sclerosis complex. *Brain & Development, 36*, 254-258.

Additional Resources

http://www.tsalliance.org

22q11.2 Deletion Syndome (formerly known as Velocardiofacial Syndrome (OMIM # 192430 and DiGeorge syndrome)

Physical Findings

22q11.2 deletion syndrome (22qDS) is a relatively common genetic disorder that affects between one in 2500 and one in 4000 live births. It is characterized by a wide phenotypic spectrum that can include: characteristic facial features, cardiac defects, palatal anomalies, immune deficiency, cognitive deficits, and mental disorder. Although individuals with 22qDS do not have dysmorphic features per se, distinctive facial features can include: vertical lengthening of the face, a long pear-shaped nose, eyes that seem vertically narrow, small ears with overfolded helices and attached lobules (often protuberant), and reduced facial animation.

Approximately 75% of individuals with 22qDS exhibit conotruncal heart malformations, including: tetrology of Fallot, interrupted aortic arch, and ventricular septal defect. Palatal anomalies occur in about 70% of individuals with 22qDS, including: velopharyngeal incompetence (VPI), submucosal cleft palate, and cleft palate. Additional physical findings include: vascular anomalies, immune deficiency, hypocalcemia, feeding difficulties (secondary to pharyngeal hypotonia), hearing loss, renal anomalies, hernias, and skeletal abnormalities. Although the physical phenotype of individuals with 22qDS can vary significantly in the number of organs or systems that are affected, no anomaly occurs with 100% frequency.

Diagnosis

As its name implies, 22qDS is the result of a hemizygous microdeletion of approximately 40 genes at the q11.2 locus of chromosome 22. The diagnosis is confirmed using FISH analysis when 22qDS is clinically suspected, often based on the presence of congenital cardiac defects or other relevant physical findings. Although the clinical features of 22qDS were described as early as 1978, the mechanism for a genetic diagnosis did not become available until 1993. Historically, the diagnosis of VCFS had been made on the basis of fluorescent in-situ hybridization (FISH), a blood test that uses DNA probes to identify the microscopic deletion on chromosome 22. Referral for FISH was usually made on the basis of the presence of cardiac defects, palatal anomalies, hypocalcemia, immune deficiencies, or learning difficulties. With the widespread use of chromosomal microarray analysis for the etiological evaluation of developmental delay, ID, and/or behavioral disturbance, 22qDS is increasingly being identified in individuals without major structural defects.

Cognition

Although the mean IQ of individuals with 22qDS is in the borderline range, intellectual function can extend from average to moderate ID. Approximately 50% of individuals have IQ scores below 70. Verbal IQ scores are often (but not always) slightly higher than performance IQ scores, most likely due to difficulties in abstract reasoning and visual-spatial abilities. Individuals with IQ scores in the borderline to average range exhibit a wide variety of academic and neuropsychological deficits, primarily in the areas of language comprehension, mathematics, visual perceptual integration, working memory, and executive function.

Behavioral and Associated Mental Health Disorders

Children with 22qDS characteristically display inattention, impulsivity, temper outbursts, emotional lability, perseveration, and social withdrawal. More than two thirds of children with this syndrome are diagnosed with at least one mental disorder sometime during childhood. Most commonly, children present with attention-deficit/hyperactivity disorder, an anxiety disorder, simple phobias, or obsessive-compulsive disorder. Recent evidence suggests, however, that the frequency of occurrence of these disorders in children with 22qDS does not exceed that of children with nonsyndromic ID.

Depressive disorders tend to increase during late adolescence and adulthood. Moreover, up to 40% of individuals with 22qDS display symptoms of a severe mental disorder (i.e., psychosis) in adulthood. Most exhibit signs of thought disorder associated with schizophrenia or schizoaffective disorder, although a subset display the severe mood swings and affective lability that are associated with bipolar disorder. Research studies continue to investigate the natural history of severe mental disorder and psychotic disorder in individuals with 22qDS, in order to distinguish the behavioral phenotype in this disorder from schizophrenia and bipolar disorder in the general population. Current research, however, suggests few differences between 22qDS-associated and idiopathic Schizophrenia. In addition, several longitudinal studies have identified behavioral risk factors for psychosis in 22qDS, including the presence of an anxiety disorder at baseline, a lower full-scale IQ at baseline, and a decrease in verbal IQ scores over time.

An association has been postulated between the role of the COMT gene, which is located within the 22q11.2 region, and neuropsychiatric manifestations of 22qDS. Functional polymorphisms of the COMT gene, which codes for an enzyme involved in the breakdown of catecholamine neurotransmitters (dopamine, epinephrine, and norepinephrine), have been linked to neuropsychiatric disorders in the general population. It has been hypothesized that in patients with 22qDS, deletion of the COMT gene from one chromosome 22, combined with the low-activity COMT allele (COMT 108-met) on the nondeleted chromosome, results in an increase in catecholamine neurotransmission and consequent neuropsychiatric features in this disorder. This association has not yet been established empirically, however.

Behavioral Phenotype for 22q Deletion Syndrome.

Phenotype	Behavioral Phenotype: Childhood	Behavioral Phenotype: Adolescence	Behavioral Phenotype: Adulthood
Distinctive facial features (long face, a long pear-shaped nose, vertically narrow eyes, small ears with overfolded helices, reduced facial animation)	Attention-deficit/hyperactivity disorder (ADHD) (more prevalent in males)	Decrease in incidence of ADHD, but attention problems can persist	
	Social withdrawal	Increased incidence of positive and negative prodromal symptoms of psychosis	Schizophrenia or psychotic disorder
Velopharygeal insufficiency	Mood lability Temper outbursts	Mood lability Temper outbursts	Bipolar disorder, characterized by severe mood lability and temper outbursts
Conotruncal heart defects	Anxiety Disorders (also manifested by perseveration during childhood)	Anxiety disorders	Anxiety disorders (more prevalent in females) often comorbid with psychotic disorder or mood disorder
Hypocalcemia	Obsessive-Compulsive Disorder	Obsessive-compulsive disorder	Obsessive-compulsive disorder
Immune deficiency	Specific phobias (dark, thunderstorms) and Social phobias	Incidence of phobias decrease relative to childhood but still present	
Vascular abnormalities		Depressive disorder	Depressive disorder (more prevalent in females), often comorbid with psychotic disorder or anxiety disorder
Feeding difficulties (in infancy)	Autism Spectrum Disorder (no gender differences)	Autism spectrum disorder	Autism spectrum disorder

Sources

Antshel,, K.M., Shprintzen, R.J., Fremont, W., Higgins, A.M., & Faraone, S.V (2010). Cognitive and psychiatric predictors to psychosis in velocardiofacial syndrome: A 3-year follow-up study. *Journal of the American Academy of Child and Adolescent Psychitary, 49*, 333-343.

Bassett, A. W., & Chow, E. (1999). 22q11 deletion syndrome: A genetic subtype of schizophrenia. *Biological Psychiatry, 46*, 882–891.

Feinstein, C., Eliez, S., Blasey, C., & Reiss, A. L. (2002). Psychiatric disorders and behavioral problems in children with velocardiofacial syndrome: Usefulness as phenotypic indicators of schizophrenia risk. *Biological Psychiatry, 15*, 312–318.

Gothelf, D., Schneider, M., Green, T., Debbane, M., Frisch, A., Glaser, B., … Eliez, S. (2013). Risk factors and the evolution of psychosis in 22q11.2 deletion syndrome: A longitudinal 2-site study. *Journal of the American Academy of Child and Adolescent Psychiatry, 52*, 1192-1203.

Green, T., Gothelf, D., Glaser, B, Debbane, M., Frisch, A., Kottler, M., … Eliez, S. (2009) Psychiatric disorders and intellectual functioning throughout development in velocardiofacial (22q11.2 deletion) syndrome. *Journal of the American Academy of Child and Adolescent* Psychiatry, *48*, 1060-1068.

Lachman, H. M., Morrow, B., Shprintzen, R. J., Veit, S., Parsia, S. S., Faedda, G., … Papolos, D.F. (1996). Association of codon 108/158 catechol-O-methyltransferase gene polymorphism with the psychiatric manifestations of velo-cardio-facial syndrome. *American Journal of Medical Genetics, 67*, 468–472.

Murphy, K. C., Jones, L. A., & Owen, M. J. (1999). High rates of schizophrenia in adults with velo-cardio-facial syndrome. *Archives of General Psychiatry, 56*, 940–945.

Ryan, A. K., Goodship, J. A., Wilson, D. I., Philip, N., Levy, A., Seidel, H., … Scambler, P.J. (1997). Spectrum of clinical features associated with interstitial chromosome 22q11 deletions: A European collaborative study. *Journal of Medical Genetics, 34*, 798–804.

Schneider, M., Debbane, M., Bassett, A.S., Chow, E.W.C., Fung, W.L.A., ven den Bree, M.B.M., … Eliez, S. (2014) Psychiatric Disorders from Childhood to Adulthood in 22q11.2 Deletion Syndrome: Results from the International Consortium on Brain and Behavior in 22q11.2 Deletion Syndrome. *American Journal of Psychiatry, 171*, 627-639.

Shprintzen, R. J. (2000). Velocardiofacial syndrome: A distinctive behavioral phenotype. *Mental Retardation and Developmental Disabilities Research Reviews, 6*, 142–147.

Swillen, A., Devriendt, K., Legius, E., Prinzie, P., Vogels, A., Ghesquiere, P., & Fryns, J.P. (1999). The behavioural phenotype in velo-cardio-facial syndrome (VCFS): From infancy to adolescence. *Genetic Counseling, 10*, 79–88.

Additional Resource:

Velocardiofacial Syndrome Educational Foundation; Web site: http://www.vcfsef.org

Williams Syndrome

(OMIM # 194050)

Physical Findings

Williams syndrome (WS), first described by cardiologists as a clinical entity in 1961, is a relatively well-researched genetic cause of intellectual disability, primarily due to its unusual cognitive-behavioral phenotype. The condition is also associated with highly recognizable physical features and a range of medical concerns.

The distinctive facial appearance in Williams syndrome is easily recognized by clinicians familiar with the disorder and characterized by full lips, puffy cheeks, a long philtrum, small, upturned nose, and a small jaw. The eyes often show a starburst (stellate) iris pattern that is particularly noticeable in light-colored eyes. Youth and adults often have premature graying of hair and coarsening of skin.

WS is associated with several known medical

complications that can affect health and quality of life throughout the lifespan. Congenital cardiovascular anomalies, particularly supravalvular aortic stenosis, are found in 80% of those affected, and youth and adults are prone to hypertension. Approximately 15% of infants with Williams syndrome have transient hypercalcemia, a finding that sometimes results in early suspicion of Williams syndrome but is rarely of clinical significance. Gastrointestinal problems are common, including chronic constipation, stomach pain, and rectal prolapse. Many older children and adults with Williams syndrome experience incontinence and urinary tract infections, sometimes related to structural bladder changes such as diverticula. Subclinical low thyroid and glucose intolerance are also found. Short stature is typical, as is joint laxity and joint contractures that generally worsen with age. Although most of these associated medical issues can be successfully managed, early identification and monitoring is key for ensuring optimum health.

People with Williams syndrome have distinctive auditory features characterized by hyperacusis, or lowered hearing threshold, odynacusis, or pain in response to sounds, as well as auditory fascinations and aversions. Such auditory sensitivities may be associated with some of the fears and phobias seen in Williams syndrome, but do not fully explain them. Sensorineural hearing loss is common, and becomes more apparent with advancing age.

Diagnosis

Until 1993, when the underlying genetic basis for Williams syndrome was discovered, geneticists made the diagnosis based on known clinical criteria. The diagnosis of WS can now be confirmed by detection of a microdeletion (consisting of 26-28 genes) within the 7q11.23 chromosomal region using a molecular FISH probe. Laboratory testing is recommended for all children and adults meeting clinical criteria for Williams syndrome, particularly those with characteristic cardiovascular findings. Beyond the classic microdeletion found in the majority of WS cases, some individuals show duplications of the Williams syndrome critical region; these cases have extreme speech/language delay and features of autism spectrum disorder. As in other genetic disorders, individuals with atypical deletions in the Williams syndrome critical region have been reported. Although few in number, these atypical cases are instrumental in linking specific genes to key aspects of the Williams syndrome phenotype. With the widespread use of chromosomal microarray analysis for the etiological evaluation of developmental delay, ID, and/or behavioral disturbance, Williams syndrome is increasingly being identified in young children and those with subtle features in whom the diagnosis is not clinically suspected.

Cognition

Most children and adults with Williams syndrome have a distinctive cognitive profile that is masked by the average or overall IQ score. Individuals with Williams syndrome show mild to moderate levels of intellectual disability (IQs 50-60), and a minority has average IQs or more severe impairments. Importantly, Williams syndrome is characterized by relative strengths in expressive and receptive language abilities, facial recognition, and short-term auditory memory. In contrast, most people with Williams syndrome have significant, marked deficits in visuospatial construction, perceptual planning, eye-hand coordination and fine motor control. Impairments in these areas may explain their difficulty with relatively simple tasks, such as orienting blocks to match a model, or in everyday life skills (e.g., finding their way to the restroom, going up or down stairs, writing). Educational and vocational interventions for individuals with Williams syndrome are often complicated by their uneven cognitive profile. Relatively advanced language abilities may mask cognitive impairments and give the impression of higher overall functioning.

Despite early delays in language acquisition, most people with Williams syndrome eventually develop advanced verbal skills that are often higher than their overall level of functioning. Conflicting studies have yet to solidly define a profile of linguistic abilities, and there remains disagreement about the extent of deficits in semantics, syntax, and vocabulary in people with Williams syndrome. Most researchers agree that while linguistic abilities may not be completely spared, language represents an area of relative strength in people with Williams syndrome as compared to those with similar levels of cognitive impairment. In addition, exaggerated linguistic affect, such as the use of exclamations and dramatic inflection may add to the impression of highly developed language abilities.

Reflecting advances in the music cognition field, musicality in Williams syndrome has garnered increased research attention. The auditory sensitivities and very strong emotional responsiveness to music in those with WS has contributed to the belief that music perception and production are similarly enhanced in most with this syndrome. However, music perception and production skills in singing or playing an instrument actually vary widely in WS. In a large study of fundamental pitch processing, performance skills, and music perception, 74% scored above average (and similar to the general population) on music perception tests, and 11% met criteria for amusia, or "tone deafness." Rates of amusia are higher in Williams syndrome than in the general population (4%). Quality of music production (singing) varied widely and was better among those with formal music instruction. Thus, a more nuanced picture of musicality in Williams syndrome is emerging of strong emotional connections to music and variable performance skills that improve with instruction and practice.

Behavioral/Psychiatric

The friendly, outgoing demeanor of people with Williams syndrome has long been considered a behavioral hallmark of the disorder. Their happy, interested appearance can be partly explained by the syndrome's characteristic facial findings that include a wide mouth, upturned nose, and a stellate iris pattern resulting in "sparkly," animated eyes. People with Williams syndrome tend to have an unusual interest in faces from an early age, as well as a relative strength in their ability to recognize and remember faces. This interest, combined with heightened linguistic affect, gives the impression of an attentive, charming, and enthusiastic listener. Their friendly appearance may also engender positive reactions from those who interact with them, further reinforcing outgoing, gregarious behavior from an early age.

People with Williams syndrome perform better than mental age-matched controls, and in some cases as well as typical peers, on various tasks designed to assess theory of mind and empathy with others. Such findings, combined with the social orientation in Williams syndrome, creates an overall picture of a sensitive, caring personality in Williams syndrome. At times, however, this gregarious and caring approach remains relatively superficial, lacking the reciprocal give and take of deeper interactions or friendships.

Despite charming and friendly personalities, many people with Williams syndrome have difficulty with social interaction. They are overly friendly, even with strangers, to the point of being intrusive. They frequently have difficulty sustaining friendships and are often socially uninhibited, leading to indiscriminate and inappropriate interactions with others. Their desire for "friends" above all else lead to increased risks for sexual, interpersonal, or financial exploitation and abuse. In contrast to early assumptions, adults with Williams syndrome can learn appropriate ways to approach and interact with strangers, yet may need in-vivo "booster" trainings to reinforce these skills.

Reports of co-morbid psychiatric symptoms are remarkably consistent across children and adults with Williams syndrome. Approximately 65% of children and youth meet criteria for attention deficit hyperactivity disorder, and distractibility and attention difficulties persist over time. Studies have identified general problems with disengaging attention as opposed to inappropriate or deficient allocation of attention. Compared to others with intellectual disabilities, people with Williams syndrome show high rates of anxiety disorders, especially specific phobias (from 35-54%), and to a lesser extent, generalized anxiety disorder (12-16%). Worries about future events, loved ones, loss, uncertainty, noises, and scary things or situations are highly prevalent even among those who do not reach a diagnostic threshold for formal anxiety disorders. Somatic complaints are also exaggerated and may not necessarily be related to previous or current medical conditions that co-occur in Williams syndrome. Depression is less commonly encountered, and may be triggered by a loss or other major life event. Although not necessarily elevated compared to others with intellectual disabilities, adults with Williams syndrome may experience psychotic episodes and/or unusual preoccupations that impede adaptive functioning.

Phenotypic Features of Williams Syndrome

Physical/Medical Phenotype	Behavioral Phenoptype Childhood	Behavioral Phenotype Adolescence/ Adulthood
Full lips, puffy cheeks, long philtrum, small, upturned nose, small jaw, coarsening of facial features with age,	ADHD (attention deficit-hyperactivity disorder)	Attention deficits persist but with less hyperactivity; difficulties switching attention
Stellate iris, strabismus, altered depth perception,	Anxiety disorders: generalized anxiety disorder, specific phobias	Anxiety disorders persist and may worsen with age, new phobias may emerge; some depression
Cardiac abnormalities, supravalvular aortic stenosis, hypertension	Socially uninhibited, friendly outgoing personality, risks of inappropriate interactions	Social disinhibition persists, high risks for exploitation, abuse and social isolation
Musculoskeletal: Short stature, joint contractures that may worsen with age, sloping shoulders, lordosis, scoliosis, slumped posture	Auditory sensitivities: Hyperacusis, odynacusis, auditory aversions and fascinations, attraction to music	Progressive sensorineural hearing loss, auditory sensitivities and attraction to music persist
Endocrine: Glucose intolerance, hypothyroidism (subclinical), transient hypercalcemia,	Relative strengths in many aspects of language, auditory working memory, facial recognition	Cognitive profile appears stable over time
Renal: structural abnormalities, frequent voiding, enuresis, bladder diverticula, recurrent urinary track infections	Relative weaknesses and pronounced deficits in visual-spatial functions, motor planning and execution	Impaired visual-spatial skills may be complicated by joint contractures in adults and contribute to difficulties with some daily living skills

Sources

Bellugi, U., Wang, P., and Jernigan, T.L. (1994). Williams syndrome: An unusual neuropsychological profile. In S.H. Browman and J. Grafram (Eds.), *Atypical cognitive deficits in developmental disorders* (pp. 23-56). Mahwah, N.J.: Lawrence Erlbaum Associates.

Committee on Genetics, American Academy of Pediatrics. (2005). Health care supervision for children with Williams syndrome. *Pediatrics 107,* 1192-1204.

Dankner, N., & Dykens, E.M. (2012). Anxiety in Intellectual Disabilities: Challenges and next steps. *International Review of Research in Developmental Disabilities, 42,* 57-83.

Dykens, E.M. (2003). Anxiety, fears, and phobias in persons with Williams syndrome. *Developmental Neuropsychology 23,* 291-316.

Ewart, A.K., Morris, C.A., Atkinson, D., Jin, W., Sternes, K., Spallone, P., ... Keating, M.T. (1993). Hemizygosity at the elastin locus in a developmental disorder, Williams syndrome. *Nature Genetics,* 5, 11-16.

Fisher, M.H., Moskowitz, A.L., & Hodapp, R.M. (2013). Differences in social vulnerability among individuals with autism spectrum disorder, Williams syndrome and Down syndrome. *Research in Autism Spectrum Disorders, 7,* 931-937.

Fisher, M.H. (2014). Evaluation of a stranger safety training for young adults with Williams syndrome. *Journal of Intellectual Disability Research,* 58, 903-914. DOI:10.1111/jir.12108

Lense, M.D., Key, A.P, & Dykens E.M (2011). Attentional disengagement in adults with Williams syndrome. *Brain and Cognition, 77,* 201–207

Lense, M.D., Shivers, C.M., & Dykens, E.M. (2013). (A)musicality in Williams syndrome: Examining relationships among auditory perception, musical skill, and emotional responsiveness to music. *Frontiers of Psychology, 4*, 525;

Levitin, D.J., Menon, V., Schmitt, J.E., Eliez, S., White, C.D., Glover, G.H., ... Reiss, A.L. (2003). Neural correlates of auditory perception in Williams syndrome: An fMRI study. *Neuroimage* 18, 74-82.

Leyfer, O.T., Klein-Tasman, B.P., Fricke, J.S., & Mervis, C.B. (2006). Prevalence of psychiatric disorders in 4-16 year olds with Williams syndrome. *American Journal of Medical Genetics B Neuropsychiatric Genetics, 141B*: 615-622.

Martens, M.A., Wilson, S.J., & Reutens, D.C. (2008). Research review: Williams syndrome: A critical review of the cognitive, behavioral, and neuroanatomical phenotype. *Journal of Child Psychology and Psychiatry, 49*, 576–608.

Pober, BR. (2010). Williams-Beuren syndrome. *The New England Journal of Medicine 362*(3), 239-252.

Stinton, C., Elison, S., Howlin, P. (2010). Mental health problems in adults with Williams syndrome. *American Journal on Intellectual and Developmental Disabilities, 115*, 3–18.|

Additional Resources

Williams Syndrome Association: www.williams-syndrome.org

Gene Reviews: http://www.ncbi.nlm.nih.gov/books/NBK1249/

Vanderbilt Kennedy Center: Electronic Health Toolkit for Adults with intellectual Disabilities-Williams syndrome Watch Tables http://vkc.mc.vanderbilt.edu/etoolkit/

CHAPTER 4

Intellectual Disability (Intellectual Developmental Disorder)

Marc J. Tassé
Marco O. Bertelli
Elliott W. Simon
Wendy R. Kates
Patricia Navas

This chapter presents the *DSM-5* diagnostic criteria for intellectual disability (intellectual developmental disorder). This condition was previously known in the *DSM-IV-TR* as mental retardation. The diagnostic criteria are reviewed and discussed along with the etiology, course, specifiers, and issues related to making a differential diagnosis. We conclude with no proposed modifications to the *DSM-5* criteria for intellectual disability.

Intellectual Disability (Intellectual Developmental Disorder)

Review of Diagnostic Criteria

Intellectual disability (intellectual developmental disorder) occurs during the developmental period and is characterized by significant subaverage intellectual functioning and deficits in one or more of the following adaptive behaviors: Conceptual, social, and practice skills.

Intellectual disability (intellectual developmental disorder) is a complex developmental condition that is associated with significant impairment in intellectual functioning and adaptive behavior. The condition has its origin either prior to birth or during the developmental period. The etiology and course can be varied and is generally a lifelong condition.

Summary of DSM-5 *Criteria*

In the *Fifth Edition of the Diagnostic and Statistical Manual of Mental Disorders* (*DSM-5*), the definition of the condition formerly known as "mental retardation" contains several major changes. The chosen terminology is now Intellectual Disability (Intellectual Developmental Disorder). The use of "intellectual disability" brings the *DSM-5* in alignment with other diagnostic definitions (AAIDD; Schalock et al., 2010), other American professional and disability groups (American Psychological Association's Division 33, Arc of US) and the US Federal Government (President's Committee for Persons with Intellectual Disabilities, Rose's Law PL 111-256). The parenthesis containing "intellectual developmental disorder" is included in the *DSM-5* terminology in an effort to align the *DSM-5* with the draft version of the 11th edition of the International Classification of Diseases (ICD-11). However, it appears likely that the World Health Organization will be dropping the use of "intellectual developmental disorders" in favor of "disorders of intellectual development."

Intellectual disability (intellectual developmental disorder) is defined by the *DSM-5* as a neurodevelopmental disorder "with onset during the developmental period that includes both intellectual and adaptive functioning deficits in conceptual, social and practical domains" (American Psychiatric Association, 2013, p. 33). The following three criteria must be met (American Psychiatric Association, 2013, p.33):

A. Deficits in intellectual functions, such as reasoning, problem solving, planning, abstract thinking, judgment, academic learning, and learning from experience, confirmed by both clinical assessment and individualized, standardized intelligence testing.

B. Deficits in adaptive functioning that result in failure to meet developmental and sociocultural standards for personal independence and social responsibility. Without ongoing support, the adaptive deficits limit functioning in one or more activities of daily life, such as communication, social participation, and independent living, across multiple environments, such as home, school, work, and community.

C. Onset of intellectual and adaptive deficits during the developmental period.

"Intellectual functioning" is defined as cognitive processes that include reasoning, problem solving, abstract thinking, judgment, learning from instruction, learning from experience, and practical understanding. "Subaverage intellectual functioning" (Criterion A) is defined as an IQ score that is *approximately* two standard deviations or more below the population mean (i.e., a standard IQ score of 70 on a test with a mean = 100 and standard deviation = 15).

The term *approximately* is used purposefully in the *DSM-5* to highlight the need to take into consideration, when using one's clinical judgment in interpreting test scores, that all standardized tests of intelligence have some measurement error around the obtained scores. This test error around an obtained score includes the standard error of measurement. The often used rule of thumb representing a 95% confidence interval around any obtained IQ score has been plus or minus five points. Thus, a person can obtain an IQ score from 70 to 75 and still meet criteria for significant subaverage intellectual functioning (American Psychiatric Association, 2013). This is consistent with the AAIDD diagnostic system (Schalock et al., 2010) and a 2014 U.S. Supreme Court decision in Hall v. Florida.

Another source of measurement error cited in the *DSM-5* as a potential contributor to artificially inflating the estimate of an individual's true level of intellectual functioning is the obsolescence of the test's normative data, or the "Flynn effect."

It should be noted that there appears to be an effort on the part of the *DSM-5* to shift some of the overreliance on the individual's intellectual functioning in favor of the individual's adaptive behavior. The *DSM-5* has abandoned the determination of the levels of severity of intellectual functioning that was previously based on the person's IQ score, in favor of a severity system that is predicated on the person's level of adaptive functioning across social, conceptual, and practical adaptive skills.

Adaptive functioning is conceptualized as "how well a person meets community standards of personal independence and responsibility, in comparison to others of similar age and social background" (American Psychiatric Association, 2013; p.37). The *DSM-5* embraces the tripartite conceptualization of adaptive behavior proposed by AAIDD, which defines "adaptive behavior" as "the collection of conceptual, social and practical skills that have been learned and are performed by people in their everyday lives" (Schalock et al., 2010, p.15).

The *DSM-5* also acknowledges all the factors that could influence adaptive behavior (e.g., cultural experience, motivation, among others) and highlights the fact that deficits in adaptive deficits should occur across multiple environments, which has important implications for the assessment of adaptive behavior in controlled settings such as prisons or detention centers.

The *DSM-5* does not operationalize its definition of deficits in adaptive functioning (Criterion B) using a statistical criterion (e.g., two standard deviations below the mean), as it does for the intellectual functioning criterion. It does, however, recommend the use of psychometrically sound measures of adaptive functioning along with the use of clinical judgment. Criterion B is considered met when at least one domain of adaptive functioning (conceptual, social, or practical) is "sufficiently impaired that ongoing support is needed" (American Psychiatric Association, 2013, p. 38). Hence, deficits in one or more of conceptual, social, or practical adaptive skills is sufficient to meet the second criterion for a diagnosis of intellectual functioning.

These impairments are defined as mild, moderate, severe, and profound, and replace IQ-based levels of severity, arguing that adaptive functioning is a better predictor of an individual's support needs. Severity levels for intellectual disability based on adaptive functioning are shown in Table 1.

Table 1. Specifier: Severity of Intellectual Disability

	Conceptual Adaptive Behavior	Social Adaptive Behavior	Practical Adaptive Behavior
MILD ID	standardized scales, collateral case information, and clinical judgment.	standardized scales, collateral case information, and clinical judgment.	standardized scales, collateral case information, and clinical judgment.
Moderate ID	standardized scales, collateral case information, and clinical judgment.	standardized scales, collateral case information, and clinical judgment.	standardized scales, collateral case information, and clinical judgment.
Severe ID	standardized scales, collateral case information, and clinical judgment.	standardized scales, collateral case information, and clinical judgment.	standardized scales, collateral case information, and clinical judgment.
Profound ID	standardized scales, collateral case information, and clinical judgment.	standardized scales, collateral case information, and clinical judgment.	standardized scales, collateral case information, and clinical judgment.

Adopting deficits in adaptive functioning as severity specifiers has important implications. For many years, psychologists have persisted in relying solely on the results from standardized intelligence tests to make a diagnosis of ID or determine someone's eligibility for ID services (Greenspan, 2012; Lecavalier, Tassé, & Lévesque, 2002; Smith, 2005). As Haydt, Greenspan, and Agharkar (2014) point out, this new focus defines ID much more broadly than IQ scores and emphasizes what many researchers have reminded us for many years: That it is the deficits in adaptive behavior that constitute the major impediment to successful inclusion of individuals with ID (Greenspan, 2006, 2009, 2012; Harrison & Boney, 2002).

Standardized and psychometrically sound measures should be used for both the assessment of intellectual functioning and adaptive behavior, and should be administered along with clinical assessment or clinical judgment. Schalock and Luckasson (2013) defined it as "a special type of judgment rooted in a high level of clinical expertise and experience; it emerges directly from extensive data. Clinical judgment is based on the clinician's explicit training, direct experience with those with whom the clinician is working, and specific knowledge of the person and the person's environment" (pp. 5-6).

Clinical judgment is especially important in those situations in which no standardized measures are available and there are no other ways to analyze adaptive behavior or intellectual functioning but direct observation, review of academic reports and psychological assessments, or interviews with those people who know the person very well (Schalock et al., 2010).

The increased role of clinical judgment and adaptive behavior in the new definition of the *DSM-5* has been interpreted by some authors as an effort to make for greater flexibility, with less emphasis on IQ scores and IQ ceilings (see, for example, Haydt, Greenspan, & Agharkar, 2014).

Finally, one of the most notable changes compared to DSM manuals and the AAIDD diagnostic and classification system is the broadened age-of-onset criteria (Criterion C). Whereas in its revised fourth edition the *DSM* defined intellectual disability (formerly known as mental retardation) as a disorder that occurs before age 18 years, the current edition does not establish a cut-off age and defines ID as occurring *during the developmental period* (American Psychiatric Association, 2013, p. 33).

Specifier

When making a diagnosis of intellectual disability, the clinician should specify the current severity of the intellectual disability. Other specifiers are used to enrich the clinical description of the condition diagnosed. For example, along with a diagnosis of intellectual disability, the clinician should include the following specifiers: Age of onset, known etiology, associated genetic condition, the presence of chronic health problems, and psychiatric disorders.

A major paradigm shift occurred in this revision of the *DSM* with the dropping of level of intellectual functioning or IQ scores as the determinant for the severity levels of intellectual disability. The *DSM-5* retained the historical conceptualization of four levels of severity of intellectual disability: Mild, moderate, severe, and profound. However, the *DSM-5* proposed that the individual's level of adaptive functioning be the basis on which to determine the level of severity of ID (see Table 1). It argued that adaptive functioning is a more representative construct upon which to establish the severity level because it correlates more strongly with the determination of intensity of supports needed (American Psychiatric Association, 2013).

Adaptive functioning is discussed later in this chapter.

Issues Related to Diagnosis in Persons with ID

Development and Course

Intellectual disability originates during the developmental period and can be caused by prenatal, perinatal, or postnatal risk factors (Schalock et al., 2010), which result in life-long limitations in intellectual and adaptive functioning. Signs of cognitive impairment can be recognized as early as 2 years of age (American Psychiatric Association, 2013, p. 38) and are manifested by difficulties in reaching development milestones (e.g., language, fine and gross motor skills, and social milestones). In up to 60% of cases the etiological factors in ID are unknown (Rauch et al., 2006), and 80-90% of the population with ID has mild deficits (Schalock et al., 2010), which could explain why many individuals with ID are not identified until they reach school age and start having difficulties acquiring and learning new academic skills.

The development and course of this condition may vary depending on different etiological factors. Specific genetic conditions such as Down syndrome or Williams syndrome are associated with different health conditions that have a higher probability of appearing during the life of these persons (e.g., thyroid disorders, cardiovascular disease) than in people with ID without these syndromes. Other syndromes with known etiology such as Rett syndrome present progressive trajectories with periods of worsening (American Psychiatric Association, 2013). Early intervention can contribute to promoting the development of children with intellectual disability (Guralnick, 2005; Ramey & Ramey 1998), and, with appropriate supports across their lifespan and over a sustained period, the life functioning of individuals with ID generally will improve (Luckasson et al., 2002; Schalock et al., 2010). Deficits in intellectual functioning tend to remain stable (American Psychiatric Association, 2000), but improvements in adaptive behavior are more likely to occur, in which cases the diagnoses of intellectual disabilities may no longer be appropriate (American Psychiatric Association, 2013).

Prevalence

Although there have been some changes in terminology, intellectual disability (intellectual developmental disorder) covers the same population of individuals who were diagnosed previously with mental retardation (Schalock et al., 2010; Schalock, Luckasson, & Shogren, 2007).

Prevalence of ID has been reported to be around 1% of the general population (American Psychiatric Association, 2013; Fujiura, 2003; Harris, 2006; Larson et al., 2001; Maulik, Mascarenhas, Mathers, Dua, & Saxena, 2011). There are different factors that can affect the estimates of intellectual disability. Intellectual disability has been found to be higher in males than in females (average male-to-female ratio varies from 1.6:1 for mild intellectual disability to 1.2:1 for severe ID [American Psychiatric Association, 2013]), partly due to X-linked forms of intellectual disability (Harris, 2006, p. 85). Although Down syndrome is the most common genetic disorder associated with ID, fragile X syndrome is the most commonly inherited condition associated with ID (CDC, 2013). Some studies have also reported higher rates of Down syndrome in males (Esbensen, Seltzer, & Krauss, 2008; Shin et al., 2009).

Higher rates of intellectual disability have also been reported in lower income countries (Maulik et al., 2011) and in families with incomes below the US federal poverty level (Boyle et al., 2011; Emerson, 2012; Fujiura & Yamaki, 1997).

Prevalence may also vary depending on the diagnostic criteria used and IQ scores cut-off. Studies relying only on IQ scores or academic milestones may report higher prevalence (King, Hodapp, & Dykens, 2005; King, Toth, Hodapp, & Dykens, 2009).

Differential Diagnosis

■ *Autism Spectrum Disorder*

Approximately 30% to 40% of persons with ID have some autistic traits (Cooper, Smiley, Morrison, Williamson, & Allan, 2007; Morgan et al. 2002). The prevalence of ASD increased 269% between 1996 and 2010 (Van Naarden Braun et al., 2015). It has been reported that during this same period, the increase in prevalence of ASD without co-occurring ID was greater than the increase in prevalence of ASD with co-occurring ID (Van Naarden Braun et al., 2015). Although rates have fluctuated over the years, it has been recently estimated that approximately 38-41% of individuals with ASD have co-occurring intellectual disability (Centers for Disease Control and Prevention, 2009, 2012).

Although persons with ID and ASD share many common features, such as deficits of adaptive behavior and a high comorbidity of psychiatric disorders or challenging behaviors, ID and ASD have distinctive and specific core symptoms. ID is also defined by impairments in intellectual functioning, while ASD is characterized by qualitative deficits in socio-communicative skills and the presence of restricted and repetitive behaviors. Both have an onset during the developmental period. The *DSM-5* also notes that although the symptoms of ASD must be present in early childhood, they may not become fully manifest until the social demands exceed the individual's limited capacities. Anatomical anomalies of the central nervous system have been reported to be significantly different in ID and ASD, the former being variable from case to case, whereas the presence of diffused gray matter (Hazlett et al., 2011) and anomalies in the neuroanatomical networks (Lewis et al., 2014) are common in brains of individuals with ASD.

There is an increased risk of comorbidity of psychiatric disorders and ID. It has been estimated that as many as 40% of individuals with ID also present with a diagnosable psychiatric disorder (Cooper et al, 2007; Emerson, 2003; Reiss, 1994). When ID and ASD are present, the complexity of making a diagnosis of comorbid psychiatric disorders is increased. Approximately 40% of the items included in diagnostic tools used to screen for psychosis in persons with ID are more likely to be positively endorsed when ASD is present (Helverschou, Bakken, & Martensen, 2008).

More severe deficits in IQ were related to higher rates of challenging behaviors (Murphy, Healy, & Leader, 2009). High rates of stereotypies tend to be related to severity of autism (Goldmon et al., 2009) but not to severity of ID (Matson & Kozlowski, 2011). For severe and profound ID, the identification of autistic features or symptoms is particularly difficult, and the clinician should rely upon in-depth and longitudinal observations.

■ *Cerebral Palsy*

Cerebral palsy is distinguished from ID by the presence of abnormal neurological signs and motor delay disproportionate to cognitive functioning. Cerebral palsy is not always present with ID. However, when cerebral palsy is associated with significant limitations in both intellectual functioning and adaptive behavior, a diagnosis of cerebral palsy and ID is made.

■ *Sensory Impairment*

The presence of any impairment in development and skill acquisition is primarily attributable to the underlying sensory impairment (e.g., visual or auditory).

■ *Dementia*

There is a progressive loss of acquired cognitive abilities and skills that occurs with aging. Adults with ID are at greater risk of developing dementia in old age (Strydom, Hassiotis, King, & Livingston, 2009). Research has documented an increased vulnerability to developing dementia of Alzheimer type in persons with ID of Down syndrome etiology. This increased risk seems to be both in terms of increased comorbidity (50% over the age of 50 and 90% over the age of 70) and earlier average age of onset (40 years old versus 70 years old).

■ *Severe Psychosocial Deprivation*

Severe psychosocial deprivation is a risk factor for ID. Severe psychosocial deprivation can also mimic ID characteristics due to selective but severe impairments in personal functioning, including language, social interaction, and emotional expression.

■ *Severe and Persistent Psychiatric Disorders*

Severe and persistent psychiatric disorders may also interfere with an individual's intellectual functioning and adaptive behavior. For example, severe and disorganized schizophrenia can lead to cognitive deficits and significant limitations in adaptive functioning similar to ID.

■ *Global Developmental Delay*

Global developmental delay and ID are related but not synonymous diagnoses. If a diagnosis of ID cannot be reliably made in a very young child (i.e., before the age of 5 years), a diagnosis of global developmental delay may be more appropriate. This *DSM-5* category is an age-specific diagnosis. As the child grows older, a more definitive diagnosis should be made (Shevell, 2008).

■ *Neurodegenerative Disorders*

Neurodegenerative disorders such as Rett syndrome may cause ID, but they are usually progressive as opposed to other etiologies often associated with ID, where the individual's functioning typically remains static or may even improve over time with appropriate interventions and supports (Schalock et al., 2010). Other neurodegenerative disorders such as mucolipidosis I or Gaucher's disease type III can be distinguished from ID due to their late onset during the developmental period.

■ *Epilepsy/Epileptic Encephalopathy*

A complex relationship exists between ID and epilepsy. Intractable epilepsy such as Rasmussen's encephalitis, Sturge-Weber and Lennox-Gastaut syndromes are often associated with ID. On the other hand, absence seizures may hamper a developing child's learning ability and lead to reduced intellectual functioning, but appropriate and intensive early intervention should prevent significant subaverage intellectual functioning. Problem behaviors and other health conditions in persons with ID may at times be misdiagnosed as epilepsy.

■ *Adverse Side Effects of Medications*

The side effects of long-term use of some pharmacological agents may resemble the cognitive limitations seen in ID and should be carefully assessed. Certain medications, including antiepileptic drugs such as sodium valproate, may hamper learning in the developing child.

■ *Extensive Brain Damage*

Extensive brain damage caused by prematurity, multi-infarct, aneurysm, traumatic brain injury or acquired brain injury, cranial radiotherapy, or brain surgery (e.g., hemispherectomy) show a complex relationship with ID that requires careful clinical assessment and extended follow-up. Prematurity and cranial radiotherapy may be associated with mild intellectual impairments or cognitive delays but rarely reach the severity level to meet the diagnostic criteria for ID. Cranial hemispherectomy in children with intractable epilepsy has high individual variability, ranging from persistent ID to mild developmental delay with complete recovery of cognitive functioning in adulthood. The severity and location of bihemispheric damage and the developmental phase at which brain damage occurs play a critical role in prognosis and recovery.

Application of Diagnostic Criteria to People with ID

Significant Deficits in Intellectual Functioning

In all existing diagnostic systems, including the *DSM-5*, subaverage intellectual functioning has been operationally defined using full-scale IQ score obtained from the administration of an individually administered, comprehensive, reliable and valid test of intelligence. This criterion illustrates the primacy of existing mono-component ("g" = "general intelligence" factor) conceptualization of human intelligence within the international scientific community. Nonetheless, there is a growing body of literature questioning whether intelligence is best represented by a unified construct score or whether intelligence derives from overlapping component processes. In the last 20 years, there has been an increasing number of neuropsychological findings to support models of intelligence that consist of distinct but related processes. Cattell-Horn-Carroll, Das-Naglieri's PASS, and Gardner and Goleman models are some of the better known multidimensional models of intelligence.

The Cattell-Horn-Carroll model (McGrew, 2005) combines Cattell and Horn's concept of fluid and crystallized intelligence with Carroll's theory of triple stratification (Carroll, 1993), and postulates the existence of nine skills at a general level and over 70 skills at specific levels. The last enhancements of the Planning, Attention, Simultaneous, and Successive (PASS) processing model of intelligence (Naglieri & Das, 2002) also describe the existence of interdependent but separate functional systems, and would support clinical and experimental activity precisely in the field of ID and other neurodevelopmental disorders (Naglieri & Das, 1997). Also, Howard Gardner questioned the validity of full-scale IQ scores and traditional IQ tests as comprehensive indicators of intellectual functioning. According to his theory, IQ and related tools would assess only linguistic and logical-mathematical skills, while the characterization of individual human intelligence would require a specific combination of multiple "talents" (Gardner, 1993). Daniel Goleman's theory of emotional intelligence (1996) highlighted that people with a subaverage IQ score can equally achieve relevant levels of adjustment and satisfaction in life through a harmonious management of their relationship between themselves and others.

A recent literature review indicates that in people with ID, the same full-scale IQ score may be associated with very different profiles of cognitive indices, also based on the factors involved in etio-pathogenesis (Bertelli et al., 2014). As an example, persons with Down syndrome usually manifest impairments in specific areas of language, long-term memory, and motor performance while showing relative strengths in visuo-spatial construction (Edgin, Pennington, & Mervis, 2010). In contrast, persons with Williams syndrome show deficits in attention, visuo-spatial construction, short-term memory, and planning (Tiekstra, Hessels & Minnaert, 2009), while showing a distinctive pattern of auditory processing and relative strengths in music and concrete language (Thornton-Wells et al., 2010).

A deficit of a single cognitive function may have a neuropsychological overshadowing effect and determine low global performance scores. Similarly, erroneous conclusions may be drawn that any anomaly of neuropsychological functioning is explained by a lower than average IQ. In fact, the traditional standardized tests of intelligence were not originally developed for the evaluation of significantly below average performance and are not able to account for the complexity of cognitive and behavioral profiles of persons with ID, especially among those with severe/profound deficits, or in the presence of neuropsychiatric comorbidity. Furthermore, IQ scores may vary as a result of the specific test being used, the testing conditions, health and mental health status of the person being tested, the individual's life course, and even the age of the test norms. For example, the "Flynn effect" describes a substantial increase in average full-scale IQ scores on intelligence tests that may be about 3.0 IQ points per decade (Colom, Lluis-Font, & Andrés-Pueyo, 2005). Although the Flynn effect reportedly slowed in some Scandinavian countries after the 1990s, no such evidence seems to be available to support the same conclusion in the US population (Flynn, 2009). These variations are especially relevant for the diagnosis of ID and highlight the need for frequent renorming of IQ tests.

Other evidence suggests that limitations of functioning, behavior problems, and various neuro-bio-psychological factors that are associated with ID are more highly correlated with impairments of specific cognitive functions than with a reduction in overall IQ (Friedman et al., 2006; Johnson, Jung, Colom, & Haier, 2008). The functions most frequently studied were associative and working memory, orientation response, and attention to the task.

There is still no conceptual map or hierarchy of the cognitive functions and domains important in ID (Bilder et al., 2009). Different terms are often used for the same functions. However, a series of cognitive domains are significantly impaired in persons with ID; the most frequently reported in the literature are perceptual reasoning, verbal comprehension, working memory, and processing speed (Deary, 2001; Holdnack, Zhou, Larrabee, Mills, & Salthouse, 2011).

The current model of intelligence, based on an overall IQ score (or "g," for "general intelligence," factor), seems to be of limited utility with respect to the newly envisioned definitions of ID in the *DSM-5* and in the first products of the working group for ICD-11 (Salvador-Carulla et al., 2011) – especially given the wide range and variability of cognitive functions in ID related to neuro-bio-psychological factors and the wide range of adaptive functioning (Bertelli et al., 2014).

The International Classification of Functioning (World Health Organization, 2001) already considers intelligence an umbrella term that includes cognitive functioning, adaptive behavior, and learning, is age-appropriate, and meets the standards of culture-appropriate demands of daily life. The *DSM-5* proposes to assess intelligence across three domains (conceptual, social, and practical) and encourages clinicians to base their diagnosis on the impact of the deficits in general mental abilities on functioning needed for everyday life.

The impairment of intelligence should be evaluated in the most comprehensive way possible, and the tools to investigate specific intellectual functions should increasingly become part of standardized assessments for persons with ID (Bertelli et al., 2014). The assessment of intellectual functioning should be aimed at identifying those dysfunctions that have the highest impact on individual behavior, skills, adaptation, autonomy, and quality of life across the lifespan, highlighting personal cognitive strengths and weaknesses that can be useful to understand personal functioning and organize intervention. Indications regarding if, what, and why some functions should be further investigated can be determined by using neuropsychological screenings.

Significant Deficits in Adaptive Functioning

Adaptive behavior refers to the individual's *typical* ability to cope with and meet environmental demands for personal independence and responsibility (American Psychiatric Association, 2013), according to the expectations of his or her chronological age and cultural group (Schalock et al., 2010). Thus, adaptive behavior should be assessed in reference to the community settings that are typical for the individual's same-age peer group, as well as taking into account factors such as expectations within their cultural group.

Adaptive behavior consists of conceptual, social, and practical skills. Measurable indicators of each of these include the following:

Conceptual skills: Language; reading and writing; money use; understanding and using concepts such as time, numbers or measures; and problem solving.

Social skills: Creating and maintaining mutually satisfying social relationships; interactions with others; social engagement and participation; emotional competence; social problem solving; self-direction; responsibility, gullibility and naïveté; and self-esteem.

Practical skills: Instrumental and basic activities of daily living; work/vocational skills; domestic skills; and personal hygiene.

The *DSM-5* has maintained the four levels of severity of intellectual disability (mild, moderate, severe; and profound); however, these severity levels are no longer indexed on the individual's level of intellectual deficits; rather, the severity specifiers are determined based upon the individual's adaptive functioning (see Table 1).

Previous scientific studies have tried to delineate the adaptive behavior profile of those with mild, moderate, severe, and profound intellectual disability when severity levels were based on IQ scores. Most of the studies have focused on individuals with mild deficits due to their difficulties to get the services they need. Their support needs may be masked by the fact that these individuals are much more alike than different from the general population. Thus, they may present few difficulties in community use – e.g., communicating with persons outside of the family, instrumental activities of daily living such as shopping or getting around by themselves (Fujiura, 2003) – and many of them will be able to live independently, get a job, and build their own family (Schalock et al., 2010).

Some researchers also highlight that what differentiates individuals with mild deficits from the general population is that they may be especially vulnerable to risks such as social manipulation and maltreatment due to difficulties in social judgment or social competence (Greenspan, 2006). Other studies propose the existence of different subtypes of mild intellectual disability on the basis of intellectual, adaptive functioning, and behavior problems (Soenen, Van Berckelaer-Onnes, & Scholte, 2009).

Several research studies have described adaptive behavior profiles of individuals with different known etiologies. Knowing adaptive strengths and weaknesses yields important information for diagnostic purposes and may be important with regard to school-based interventions (Reilly, 2012). Down syndrome (Chapman & Hesketh, 2000; Dykens, Hodapp, & Evans, 2006; Fidler, Hepburn, & Rogers, 2006), Angelman syndrome (Brun et al., 2010; Peters et al., 2004), and Williams syndrome (Greer, Brown, Pai, Choudry, & Klein, 1997; Jones et al., 2000; Mervis, Klein-Tasman, & Mastin, 2001) are some of the conditions more commonly studied.

Age of Onset

The previously used age of onset of 18 years was considered arbitrary and was hence abandoned. It was agreed that a developmental perspective would be employed to distinguish ID as a persistent process that has an impact during early development (and hence dynamically influences further development), as opposed to onset during adult life.

Although ID is usually a stable and lifelong condition, there can be significant variability in intellectual and adaptive functioning across different clinical severity levels throughout the lifecycle. Therefore, ID is considered a dynamic health condition and, as such, should be reassessed at key developmental phases, life transitions (e.g., at school-entry age, puberty, early and later adulthood), other life events, and traumatic events. No specific temporal qualifier is necessary for the diagnosis.

Etiology and Pathogenesis

Biological Factors

While an ID diagnosis is made independent of etiology, biological factors clearly play a role in many individuals who meet the ID criteria. The *DSM-5* does not allow for a "due to" modifier in the case of ID (as it does in autism spectrum disorder, for example), so biological factors such as Down syndrome or other genetic disorders that impact intellectual functioning should be listed in the same manner as other "medical conditions." This difference in diagnostic protocol between ID and other neurodevelopmental disorders is in line with the view that the diagnosis of ID, as differentiated from impaired intellectual functioning, is "caused" by an interaction of the person and his/her environment.

Therefore ID as a diagnostic category is not due to an inherent biological "defect."

However, the AAIDD manual (Schalock et al., 2010) views an etiological understanding as an important part of understanding those variables that impact people with ID, and it should be part of the development of any person-centered support plan. Ten reasons are offered for the inclusion of etiology in a diagnostic workup, as follows:

1. Etiology may be associated with health-related problems that impact physical or psychological functioning;
2. Etiology may be treatable, increasing the value of interventions to minimize or prevent ID;
3. Etiology may provide information for programs to prevent specific etiologies;
4. Etiology may provide homogeneous groups for research, clinical, or administrative purposes;
5. Etiology may be associated with a specific behavioral phenotype, which would allow for anticipation of support needs;
6. Etiology may provide information that facilitates genetic counseling;
7. Etiology may be used to refer people with like etiologies to facilitate information acquisition and support;
8. Etiology may facilitate self-knowledge and life planning;
9. Etiology may clarify clinical issues for an individual in crisis; and
10. Etiology may clarify social, behavioral, and educational risks and offer an opportunity to prevent disability.

Biomedical factors are one of four interactional etiology types as proposed by Schalock et al. (2010). The four factors are biomedical, social, behavioral, and educational. Biomedical ID factors include genetic syndromes, prematurity, birth injury, malnutrition, and other situations that affect biology. It is further proposed that these four factors work together to result in an individual who through interaction with his/her environment meets the diagnostic criteria for ID. For example, a person born with trisomy 21 (Down syndrome) who does not receive early intervention services would be viewed as having both an educational and biomedical etiology to his/her ID.

Genetic Factors

Given AAIDD's (Schalock et al., 2010) conceptualization of etiology, genetic syndromes are a biomedical etiology factor and, as such, a recommendation for a referral to genetics professionals should be a part of any diagnostic workup for individuals with ID, at any severity level, for whom a genetic evaluation has not already occurred. This is especially crucial as increasing numbers of genetic syndromes are being linked to reduced levels of intellectual functioning.

Zigler and his colleagues (1967, 1969, 1984) postulated a two-group approach to ID etiology. "Cultural-familial" ID is viewed as due to deprived environments and other environmental factors or to polygenic inheritance (i.e., ID that "naturally" falls two or more standard deviations below the mean of the IQ bell curve). "Organic" ID includes people with genetic syndromes and other physical factors such as prenatal or birth injury. The "organic" grouping has traditionally been viewed as the smaller of the two groups.

Advances in genetic syndrome delineation, however, are now raising questions about the two-group approach. There are an increasing number of individuals who would previously have been determined to have "cultural-familial" ID who, given advances in genetic testing, would now be classified as having "organic ID." People with "cultural-familial" ID were also thought to have IQs greater than 50 and to make up the vast majority of the population of people with ID. However, we are now aware that certain genetic syndromes include a significant number of individuals with IQs well above 50 such as females with fragile X syndrome (Dykens, Hodapp, & Finucane, 2000; Behavioral Phenotype chapter, this volume). The belief that genetically determined syndromes account for a small percentage of people with ID has been shown to not be the case. This argues for a genetic evaluation for all people for whom the etiology of their ID is unknown.

Psychosocial Factors

Although, as noted above, genetic factors have been identified in cases that were otherwise thought to be "cultural/familial," it is well accepted that psychosocial and developmental factors can increase risk for intellectual disability, independent of genetic etiology. A multi-factorial approach to understanding etiology of ID is recommended, and therefore, etiological assessments should be broad-based and multi-disciplinary and include assessments of biomedical, genetic, psychosocial, and developmental risk factors.

The AAIDD manual (Schalock et al., 2010) includes several psychosocial factors in the etiologies of ID. During the prenatal period, these include maternal malnutrition, maternal substance abuse, and lack of access to prenatal care. In many cases, multiple psychosocial risk factors may contribute to the outcome. During the post-natal period, psychosocial risk factors can include child abandonment, abuse or neglect, domestic violence, and lack of availability of social services.

Developmental Factors

Developmental factors that could contribute to the etiology of ID include prenatal drug or alcohol exposure, post-natal exposure to lead and other environmental toxins, impaired parent-child interaction, difficult child behaviors, intellectual or social deprivation, and reduced access to early intervention or special educational services.

It should be noted that although poverty is often cited as a risk factor for ID, it may be more instructive to conceptualize it as a mediating factor in biomedical, psychosocial, and developmental risk factors (Emerson, 2007). For example, poverty is associated with biomedical risk factors of preterm birth and low birth weight (Leonard & Wen, 2002); psychosocial risk factors (Brooks-Gunn & Duncan, 1997) of maternal malnutrition and lack of access to prenatal care; and developmental risk factors of poor nutrition, exposure to environmental toxins, and reduced access to early intervention services and environmental supports. Poverty can also mediate the natural history of intellectual disability in that lower socio-economic status can result in reduced resources to cope with adverse environmental or biomedical events that contribute to ID.

Adaptation of Diagnostic Criteria

The parentheses used in the *DSM-5* containing the term "intellectual developmental disorder" was used to link the terminology of intellectual disability used by the *DSM-5* as a replacement for the former term "mental retardation" to the term used in the earlier drafts of the 11th edition of the International Classification of Diseases (American Psychiatric Association, 2013). It would appear that since then, the World Health Organization has dropped "intellectual developmental disorders" in favor of "disorders of intellectual development," or disorders of ID. Hence, we propose dropping the parentheses in the *DSM-5* and simply using "intellectual disability."

Intellectual Disability

DSM-5 Diagnostic Criteria	Applying Criteria for Mild-Profound ID
A. Deficits in intellectual functions, such as reasoning, problem solving, planning, abstract thinking, judgment, academic learning, and learning from experience, confirmed by both clinical assessment and individualized, standardized intelligence testing.	A. No modifications.
B. Deficits in adaptive functioning that result in failure to meet developmental and sociocultural standards for personal independence and social responsibility. Without ongoing support, the adaptive deficits limit functioning in one or more activities of daily life, such as communication, social participation, and independent living, across multiple environments, such as home, school, work, and community.	B. No modifications.
C. Onset of intellectual and adaptive deficits during the developmental period.	C. No modifications.

References

American Psychiatric Association. (2013). *Diagnostic and statistical manual of mental disorders (5th Ed.)*. Arlington, VA: American Psychiatric Publishing.

Bertelli, M. O., Salvador-Carulla, L., Scuticchio, D., Varrucciu, N., Martinez-Leal, R., Cooper, S. A., … Walsh, C. (2014). Moving beyond intelligence in the revision of ICD-10: Specific cognitive functions in intellectual developmental disorders. *World Psychiatry, 13*(1), 93-94.

Bilder, R. M., Sabb, F. W., Parker, D. S., Kalar, D., Chu, W. W., Fox. J., … Poldrack, R. A. (2009). Cognitive ontologies for neuropsychiatric phenomics research. *Cognitive Neuropsychiatry, 14*(4/5), 419-450.

Boyle, C. A., Boulet, S., Schieve, L. A., Cohen, R. A., Blumberg, S. J., Yeargin-Allsopp, M., ... Kogan, M. D. (2011). Trends in the prevalence of developmental disabilities in US children, 1997–2008. *Pediatrics*, peds-2010.

Brooks-Gunn, J., & Duncan, G. (1997). The effects of poverty on children and youth. *Future Child 7*, 55–71.

Brun Gasca, C., Obiols, J. E., Bonillo, A., Artigas, J., Lorente, I., Gabau, E., ... Turk, J. (2010). Adaptive behaviour in Angelman syndrome: Its profile and relationship to age. *Journal of Intellectual Disability Research, 54*, 1024-1029.

Carroll, J. B. (1993). *Human cognitive abilities: A survey of Factor-Analytic Studies.* Cambridge: Cambridge University Press.

Centers for Disease Control and Prevention (2009). Prevalence of autism spectrum disorders — Autism and developmental disabilities monitoring network, United States, 2006. *MMWR Surveillance Summaries, 58 (No. SS-10)*, 1–24.

Centers for Disease Control and Prevention (2012). Prevalence of autism spectrum disorders — Autism and Developmental Disabilities Monitoring Network, 14 sites, United States, 2008. *MMWR Surveillance Summaries, 61(3)*, 1–19.

Centers for Disease Control and Prevention (2013). Fragile X syndrome. Retrieved from http://www.cdc.gov/ncbddd/fxs/data.html

Chapman, R. S., & Hesketh, L. J. (2000). Behavioral phenotype of individuals with Down syndrome. *Mental Retardation and Developmental Disabilities Research Reviews, 6*, 84-95.

Colom, R., Lluis-Font, J. M., & Andrés-Pueyo, A. (2005). The generational intelligence gains are caused by decreasing variance in the lower half of the distribution: Supporting evidence for the nutrition hypothesis. *Intelligence, 33*, 83–91.

Cooper, S. A., Smiley, E., Morrison, J., Williamson, A., & Allan, L. (2007). Mental ill-health in adults with intellectual disabilities: Prevalence and associated factors. *British Journal of Psychiatry, 190*, 27-35.

Deary, I. J. (2001). *Intelligence: A very short introduction.* Oxford Paperbacks.

Dykens, E. M., Hodapp, R. M., Evans, D. W. (2006). Profiles and development of adaptive behavior in children with Down syndrome. *Down Syndrome Research and Practice, 9*, 45–50.

Dykens, E. M., Hodapp, R. M., & Finucane, B. M. (2000). *Genetics and mental retardation syndromes: A new look at behavior and interventions.* Towson, MD: Paul H. Brookes Publishing.

Edgin, J. O., Pennington, B. F., & Mervis, C. B. (2010). Neuropsychological components of intellectual disability: The contributions of immediate, working, and associative memory. *Journal of Intellectual Disability Research, 54*, 406-417.

Emerson, E. (2003). Prevalence of psychiatric disorders in children and adolescents with and without intellectual disability. *Journal of Intellectual Disability Research, 47*, 51-58.

Emerson, E. (2007). Poverty and people with intellectual disabilities. *Mental Retardation and Developmental Disabilities Research Review, 13*, 107–113.

Emerson, E. (2012). Deprivation, ethnicity and the prevalence of intellectual and developmental disabilities. *Journal of Epidemiology and Community Health, 66*, 218-224.

Esbensen, A. J., Seltzer, M. M., & Krauss, M. W. (2008). Stability and change in health, functional abilities, and behavior problems among adults with and without Down syndrome. *American Journal on Mental Retardation, 113*, 263-277.

Fidler, D., Hepburn, S., & Rogers, S. (2006). Early learning and adaptive behaviour in toddlers with Down syndrome: Evidence for an emerging behavioural phenotype? *Down Syndrome Research and Practice, 9*, 37-44.

Flynn, J. R. (2009). *What is intelligence? Beyond the Flynn effect.* Cambridge, UK: Cambridge University Press.

Friedman, N. P., Miyake, A., Corley, R. P., Young, S. E., DeFries, J. C., & Hewitt, J. K. (2006). Not all executive functions are related to intelligence. *Psychological Science, 17*(2), 172-179.

Fujiura, G. T. (2003). Continuum of intellectual disability: Demographic evidence for the "forgotten generation." *Mental Retardation, 41*, 420-429.

Fujiura, G. T., & Yamaki, K. (1997). Analysis of ethnic variations in developmental disability prevalence and household economic status. *Mental Retardation, 35*, 286-294.

Gardner, H. (1993). *Multiple intelligences: The theory in practice.* New York: Basic Books.

Goldmon, S., Wang, C., Salgado, M. W., Greene, P. E., Kim, M., & Rapin, I. (2009). Motor stereotypies in children with autism and other developmental disorders. *Developmental Medicine and Child Neurology, 51*, 30–38.

Goleman, D. (1996) *Emotional intelligence: Why it can matter more than IQ.* New York: Bantam Books.

Greenspan, S. (2006) Functional concepts in mental retardation: Finding the natural essence of an artificial category. *Exceptionality, 14*, 205-224.

Greenspan, S. (2009). Assessment and diagnosis of mental retardation in death penalty cases: Introduction and overview of the special "Atkins" issue. *Applied Neuropsychology, 16*, 89-90.

Greenspan, S. (2012). How do we know when it's raining out? Why existing conceptions of intellectual disability are all (or mostly) wet. *Psychology in Intellectual and Developmental Disabilities 37*(2), 4-8.

Greer, M. K., Brown, F. R., Pai, G. S., Choudry, S. H., & Klein, A. J. (1997). Cognitive, adaptive, and behavioral characteristics of Williams syndrome. *American Journal of Medical Genetics, 74*, 521-525.

Guralnick, M. J. (2005). Early intervention for children with intellectual disabilities: Current knowledge and future prospects. *Journal of Applied Research in Intellectual Disabilities, 18*, 313-324.

Hall v. Florida 134 S. Ct. 1986 (2014).

Harris, J. C. (2006). *Intellectual disability: Understanding its development, causes, classification, evaluation, and treatment.* New York: Oxford University Press.

Harrison, P. L. & Boney, T. L. (2002). Best practices in the assessment of adaptive behavior. In A. T. J. Grimes (Ed.), *Best practices in school psychology IV* (pp. 1167-1179). Bethesda, MD: National Association of School Psychologists.

Haydt, N., Greenspan, S., & Agharkar, B. S. (2014). Advantages of DSM-5 in the diagnosis of intellectual disability: Reduced reliance on IQ ceilings in Atkins (death penalty) cases. *University of Missouri-Kansas City Law Review, 82*(2), 359-387.

Hazlett, H. C., Poe, M. D., Gerig, G., Styner, M., Chappell, C., Smith, R. G., … Pivens, J. (2011). Early brain overgrowth in autism associated with an increase in cortical surface area before age 2 years. *Archives of General Psychiatry, 68*, 467–476.

Helverschou, S. B., Bakken, T. L., & Martinsen, H. (2008). Identifying symptoms of psychiatric disorders in people with autism and intellectual disability: An empirical conceptual analysis. *Mental Health Aspects of Developmental Disabilities, 11*, 105-115.

Holdnack, J. A., Zhou, X., Larrabee, G. J., Millis, S. R., & Salthouse, T. A. (2011). Confirmatory factor analysis of the WAIS-IV/WMS-IV. *Assessment, 18*(2), 178-191.

Johnson, W., Jung, R. E., Colom, R., & Haier, R. J. (2008). Cognitive abilities independent of IQ correlate with regional brain structure. *Intelligence, 36*(1), 18-28.

Jones, W., Bellugi, U., Lai, Z., Chiles, M., Reilly, J., Lincoln, A., & Adolphs, R. (2000). II. Hypersociability in Williams syndrome. *Journal of Cognitive Neuroscience, 12*, 30–46.

King, B. H., Hodapp, R. M., & Dykens, E. M. (2005). Mental retardation. In H. I. Kaplan & B. J. Sadock (Eds.), *Comprehensive Textbook of Psychiatry* (8th edition, vol. 2; pp. 3076-3106). Baltimore: Williams & Wilkins.

King, B. H., Toth, K. E., Hodapp, R. M., & Dykens, E. M. (2009). Intellectual disability. In H. I. Kaplan & B. J. Sadock (Eds.), *Comprehensive Textbook of Psychiatry* (9th edition; pp. 3444-3474). Baltimore: Williams & Wilkins.

Larson, S. A., Lakin, K. C., Anderson, L., Lee, N. K., Lee, J. H., & Anderson, D. (2001). Prevalence of mental retardation and developmental disabilities: Estimates from the 1994/1995 National Health Interview Survey Disability Supplements. *American Journal on Mental Retardation, 106*, 231-252.

Lecavalier, L., Tassé, M. J., & Levesque, S. (2002). Assessment of mental retardation by school psychologists. *Canadian Journal of School Psychology, 17*(1), 97-107.

Leonard, H., & Wen, X. (2002). The epidemiology of mental retardation: Challenges and opportunities in the new millennium. *Mental Retardation and Developmental Disabilities Research Review, 8*, 117–134.

Lewis, J. D., Evans, A. C., Pruett, J. R., Botteron, K., Zwaigenbaum, L., Estes, A., … Piven, J. (2014). Network inefficiencies in autism spectrum disorder at 24 months. *Translational Psychiatry, 6*, 4:e388.

Luckasson, R., Borthwick-Duffy, S., Buntinx, W. H., Coulter, D. L., Craig, E. M. P., Reeve, A., ...Tassé, M. J. (2002). *Mental retardation: Definition, classification, and systems of supports (10th ed.)*. Washington, DC: American Association on Mental Retardation.

Matson, J. L. & Kozlowski, A. M. (2011). The increasing prevalence of autism spectrum disorders. *Research in Autism Spectrum Disorders, 5*, 418–425.

Maulik, P. K., Mascarenhas, M. N., Mathers, C. D., Dua, T., & Saxena, S. (2011). Prevalence of intellectual disability: A meta-analysis of population-based studies. *Research in Developmental Disabilities, 32*, 419-436.

McGrew, K. S. (2005) The Cattell-Horn-Carroll theory of cognitive abilities: Past, present, and future. In D. P. Flanagan, J. L. Genshaft, & P. L. Harrison (Eds.), *Contemporary intellectual assessment: Theories, tests, and issues* (pp. 136-182). New York: Guilford.

Mervis, C. B., Klein-Tasman, B. P., & Mastin, M. E. (2001). Adaptive behavior of 4-through 8-year-old children with Williams syndrome. *American Journal on Mental Retardation, 106*(1), 82-93.

Morgan, C. N., Roy, M., Nasr, A., Chance, P., Hand, M., Mlele, T., & Roy, A. (2002). A community study establishing the prevalence rate of autistic disorder in adults with learning disability. *Psychiatric Bulletin, 26*, 127-129.

Murphy, O., Healy, O., & Leader, G. (2009). Risk factors for challenging behaviors among 157 children with autism spectrum disorders in Ireland. *Research in Autism Spectrum Disorders, 3*, 474–482.

Naglieri, J. A., & Das, J. P. (1997). *Das-Naglieri cognitive assessment system.* Itasca, IL: Riverside Publishing Co.

Naglieri, J. A., & Das, J. P. (2002). Practical implications of general intelligence and PASS cognitive processes. In R. Sternberg & E. Grigorenko (Eds.), *The general factor of intelligence. How general is it*? (pp. 55-84) New Jersey: Lawrence Erlbaum Associates.

Peters, S. U., Goddard-Finegold, J., Beaudet, A. L., Madduri, N., Turcich, M., & Bacino, C. A. (2004). Cognitive and adaptive behavior profiles of children with Angelman syndrome. *American Journal of Medical Genetics, 128*(2), 110-113.

Ramey, C. T., & Ramey, S. L. (1998). Early intervention and early experience. *American Psychologist, 53*, 109-120.

Rauch, A., Hoyer, J., Guth, S., Zweier, C., Kraus, C., Becker, C., ... Trautmann, U. (2006). Diagnostic yield of various genetic approaches in patients with unexplained developmental delay or mental retardation. *American Journal of Medical Genetics, 140*(19), 2063-2074.

Reilly, C. (2012). Behavioural phenotypes and special educational needs: Is etiology important in the classroom? *Journal of Intellectual Disability Research, 56*, 929-946.

Reiss, S. (1994). *Handbook of Challenging Behavior: Mental Health Aspects of Mental Retardation.* Worthington, OH: IDS Publications.

Salvador-Carulla, L., Reed, G. M., Vaez-Azizi, L. M., Cooper, S. A., Martinez-Leal, R., Bertelli, M., … Saxena, S. (2011). Intellectual developmental disorders: Towards a new name, definition and framework for "mental retardation/intellectual disability" in ICD-11. *World Psychiatry, 10(3)*, 175-180.

Schalock, R. L., Borthwick-Duffy, S. A., Bradley, V. J., Buntinx, W. H., Coulter, D. L., Craig, E.M., ... Yeager, M. H. (2010). *Intellectual disability: Definition, classification, and systems of supports (11th ed.).* Washington, DC: American Association on Intellectual and Developmental Disabilities.

Schalock, R. L. & Luckasson, R. (2013). *Clinical judgment (2nd ed.).* Washington, DC: American Association on Intellectual and Developmental Disabilities.

Schalock, R. L., Luckasson, R. A., & Shogren, K. A. (2007). The renaming of mental retardation: Understanding the change to the term intellectual disability. *Intellectual and Developmental Disabilities, 45*, 116-124.

Shevell, M. (2008). Global developmental delay and mental retardation or intellectual disability: Conceptualization, evaluation, and etiology. *Pediatric Clinics of North America., 55*, 1071-1984.

Shin, M., Besser, L. M., Kucik, J. E., Lu, C., Siffel, C., & Correa, A. (2009). Prevalence of Down syndrome among children and adolescents in 10 regions of the United States. *Pediatrics, 124*, 1565-1571.

Smith, T. (2005). Assessment of individuals with mental retardation: Introduction to special issue. *Assessment for Effective Intervention, 30*(1), 1-4.

Soenen, S., Van Berckelaer-Onnes, I., & Scholte, E. (2009). Patterns of intellectual, adaptive and behavioral functioning in individuals with mild mental retardation. *Research in Developmental Disabilities, 30*, 433-444.

Strydom, A., Hassiotis, A., King, M., & Livingston, G. (2009). The relationship of dementia prevalence in older adults with intellectual disability (ID) to age and severity of ID. *Psychological Medicine, 39(1)*, 13-21.

Tiekstra, M., Hessels, M. G., & Minnaert, A. E. (2009). Learning capacity in adolescents with mild intellectual disabilities. *Psychological Reports, 105*, 804-814.

Thornton-Wells, T. A., Cannistraci, C. J., Anderson, A. W., Kim, C. Y., Eapen, M., Gore, J. C., … Dykens, E. M. (2010). Auditory attraction: Activation of visual cortex by music and sound in Williams syndrome. *Ameri-*

can Journal on Intellectual and Developmental Disabilities, 115, 172-189.

Van Naarden Braun, K., Christensen, D., Doernberg, N., Schieve, L., Rice, C., Wiggins, L., ... Yeargin-Allsopp, M. (2015). Trends in the prevalence of autism spectrum disorder, cerebral palsy, hearing loss, intellectual disability, and vision impairment, Metropolitan Atlanta, 1991–2010. *PLoS ONE 10(4)*. e0124120.

World Health Organization (2001). *International classification of functioning, disability and health*. Geneva: World Health Organization Press.

Zigler, E. (1967). Familial mental retardation: A continuing dilemma. *Science, 155*(3760), 292-298.

Zigler, E., Balla, D., & Hodapp, R. (1984). On the definition and classification of mental retardation. *American Journal of Mental Deficiency*.

Zigler, E., & Harter, S. (1969). The socialization of the mentally retarded. *Handbook of socialization theory and research* (pp. 1065-1102).

CHAPTER 5

Communication Disorders

Jarrett Barnhill
Lee K.McLean
Billy T. Ogletree
Johanna R. Price
Linda Watson

The *Diagnostic and Statistical Manual-5 (DSM-5)* section on communication disorders includes speech sound (phonological), childhood-onset dysfluency (stuttering), language (expressive and mixed), and social communication (pragmatic) disorders. Understanding a communication disorder as a neurodevelopmental disorder necessitates an awareness of the developmental trajectory of motor control of speech (and fluency), the maturation of receptive and expressive aspects of language, and the expansion of social communication from dyadic to cultural contexts. This developmental path eventually results in a communication system that can generate a nearly endless supply of complex syntactical and semantic variations from relatively few phonemes.

A major challenge to the authors of this section is formulating an explanation of how the biopsychosociology of intellectual and developmental disabilities (IDD) and other neurodevelopmental disorders affect emerging communication skills (Barnhill & McNelis, 2012). To fully accomplish this requires a deconstruction of communication into its many constituent neurological systems; tracing the development of each component; reconstructing them into a coherent, functional neuro-linguistic system that accounts for the hierarchical organization of many interfacing subsystems, and then rerun the entire program to account for the many heterogeneous conditions associated with IDD (Domelloff et al., 2013; Van Battenburg et al., 2013). Unfortunately, developing such a grand unified theory of communication is beyond our reach. Instead, we contrive our diagnostic nomenclatures as a means of reducing these complex phenomena to functioning clinical disorders. As the reader shall see, the *DSM-5* is limited by an overly generalized criteria set that is designed for clinicians but falls short for the needs of those who are in research, or speech-language specialists. The authors provide a comprehensive update of available literature for persons with IDD.

Speech Sound Disorder

Review of Diagnostic Criteria

Most individuals with IDD communicate, with varying degrees of effectiveness, through *spoken* language. This is true even for those individuals diagnosed with severe IDD, many of whom are reported to use speech as a primary mode of communication (McLean, Brady, & McLean, 1996). However, the effectiveness and social acceptability of this speech can be seriously impacted by all the types of communication disorder that affect typically developing individuals. Among these is a disorder in the production of specific speech sounds. Even among typically developing children, diagnostic criteria for a speech sound disorder clearly exclude speech production errors that can be attributed to normal variation in speech sound development – which may continue until middle school age for the most complex sounds. For individuals with diagnosed intellectual disability, the identification of a true speech sound disorder becomes even more complex, in light of conflicting data on whether their spoken language reflects a delayed but typical course of speech and language development or actually deviates from typical development in terms of types of errors occurring at different development stages, including possible syndrome-specific error patterns (Berry-Kravis et al., 2013; Kent & Vorperian, 2013; (Van Borsel, 1996).

To further complicate the diagnosis of speech sound disorders in this population, the *DSM-5* criteria for this disorder exclude sound errors attributable to conditions that are commonly associated with IDD and that may share the same underlying genotype and phenotype. As noted previously, the relationship between these identifiable communication disorders and the neurological or genetic etiology of a co-occurring intellectual disability is complex and still poorly understood. Thus, the clinician will need to rely on clinical judgment, as well as input from appropriate specialists (e.g., speech-language pathologists) in determining whether an apparent speech sound problem is a true speech sound disorder.

General Description of the Disorder

Formerly known as phonological disorder, a speech sound disorder is a failure to use developmentally expected and culturally and dialectically appropriate speech sounds and to string those sounds together in meaningful ways to produce words and phrases. The actual production of speech sounds requires coordination of the speaker's respiratory system, tongue placement, and lip/mouth configuration. Specifically, every individual speech sound is produced with a unique combination of three elements: a) voice – voiced or voiceless sounds (e.g., /b/ vs. /p/); b) tongue placement – front, middle, or back (e.g., /t/, /d/, /k/); and c) overall manner of production – whether the speaker's breath is stopped or continued (/k/ vs. /h/) and whether air is released suddenly or with friction caused by narrowing of the air passage (e.g., /p/ vs. /f/). Production of vowel sounds further requires correct tongue placement relative to both the high-low and front-back dimensions of the oral cavity.

Typically developing children follow a rather predictable developmental sequence in their mastery of the speech sounds of their own language, and there are widely accepted norms for the correct production of specific sounds from early infancy through late childhood. There are also predictable and typical patterns of early errors in sound production, referred to as phonological processes. For example, "fronting" involves the substitution of sounds like /t/ for /k/ and is typically outgrown by about 3 years; and "weak syllable deletion" (e.g., the child says *nana* for *banana)* is usually outgrown by about 4 years.

In diagnosing a speech sound disorder in persons with IDD, the speech language pathologist (SLP) will thus need to consider that individual's specific sound errors in relation to his/her overall language and cognitive developmental status. However, as readers of this volume are all too aware, there are serious questions regarding the validity of "developmental age" or "language age" scores when these are assigned to children or adults beyond the chronological age range on which those age norms were developed. Thus, the clinician will also want to consider the degree to which a client's speech sound production ability is inadequate to communicate his or her linguistic messages so that they are intelligible and socially/developmentally appropriate (i.e., an adolescent who is stigmatized by toddler-like speech patterns).

Summary of DSM-5 *Criteria*

The new *DSM-5* criteria for a speech sound disorder differ from the previous *DSM-IV* criteria by placing greater emphasis on speech sound errors that have persisted over time and, critically, that interfere with effective communication and social participation. Like the previous criteria, the *DSM-5* stipulates that the speech sound difficulty must have emerged during the developmental period and that it not be directly attributable to the types of neurological and/or congenital conditions that are common among individuals with IDD. As noted above, this exclusion complicates the clinician's task in applying this diagnosis to clients with IDD.

Specifically, the new *DSM-5* criteria are:

A. Persistent difficulty with speech sound production that interferes with speech intelligibility or prevents verbal communication of messages.

B. The disturbance causes limitations in effective communication that interfere with social participation, academic achievement, or occupational performance, individually or in any combination.

C. Onset of symptoms is in the early developmental period.

D. The difficulties are not attributable to congenital or acquired conditions, such as cerebral palsy, cleft palate, deafness or hearing loss, traumatic brain injury, or other medical or neurological conditions.

Issues Related to Diagnosis in Persons with ID

Most studies of speech sound development and disorders among individuals with IDD focus on sub-populations identified by etiology. Historically, a majority of these studies have focused on individuals with Down syndrome, which is characterized by problems in speech production and intelligibility. A recent comprehensive review of this research (Kent & Vorperian, 2013) found that speech sound errors begin to be evident in this population by about 3 years of age, although there is some evidence that differences in speech development may be evident as early as infancy, in distinct patterns of infant vocalizations and babbling (Berry-Kravis et al., 2013; Kent & Vorperian, 2013).

There is substantial agreement, and evidence, that the speech sound errors produced by individuals with Down syndrome can be due to both developmentally delayed speech and language development and more specifically disordered patterns of speech sound production that are common among speakers with Down syndrome. These include errors in articulation and nasality, which seem attributable to phenotypic anatomical and physiological features characteristic of Down syndrome, including anomalies of the vocal folds, oral vault cavity and tongue size, and oro-buccal hypotonicity (Bunton & Leddy, 2011; Dodd & Thompson, 2001; Mahler & Jones, 2012). Further, many individuals with Down syndrome suffer chronic otitis media, which can result in hearing loss and subsequent phonological problems reflected in speech sound errors that are inconsistent in spontaneous speech, even though those sounds can be produced correctly in imitative speech (Dodd & Thompson, 2001).

Recently, a large number of studies have appeared that focus on speech sound development associated with the most common inherited form of ID: Fragile X syndrome (Bailey, Raspa, Holiday, Bishop, & Olmsted, 2009; Barnes, Roberts, Mirrett, Sideris, & Misenheimer, 2006; Berry-Kravis et al., 2013; Roberts et al., 2005). In this population, the emerging data suggest that there is a delay in speech sound development, commensurate with overall developmental delay. But there are also unique qualities of the connected speech produced by individuals with fragile X syndrome that negatively impact the perceived clarity of their speech and their overall intelligibility. Specifically, the speech of individuals with fragile X syndrome is often perceived as having a faster rate (measured in syllables spoken per second) and/or fluctuating rate of speech than that of typically developing children and children with Down syndrome. These atypical speech patterns are most common for individuals with a co-occurring autism spectrum disorder (Zajac, Harris, Roberts, & Martin, 2009). Such disorders of speech rate and prosody can definitely limit the effectiveness of an individual's communicative speech and so also constitute speech sound disorders. In their survey study of 981 parents of individuals with fragile X syndrome (ranging from infants to young adults), Bailey and colleagues (2009) found that 45% of adults with fragile X syndrome were described as not speaking clearly, and 25% were described as not producing words clearly.

While most available research on speech disorders in persons with IDD has focused on the

Down syndrome and fragile X syndrome populations, there have been a few studies looking at the speech production of individuals with IDD associated with low-incidence etiologies and syndromes. A review of research on speech and language development in people with cri du chat syndrome concludes that these individuals have problems with both consonant and vowel sound production, and their speech is characterized by frequent substitutions, omissions, and distortions of these sounds (Kristoffersen, 2008).

Prader-Willi is another low-incidence syndrome that has been the focus of some speech research. An early observational study by Kleppe and colleagues (Kleppe, Katayama, Shipley, & Foushee, 1990) provided detailed analyses of the speech and language characteristics of 18 children, ages 8-17, with Prader-Willi syndrome. All of these participants demonstrated mild to moderate developmental and language delays. The authors provide a detailed analysis of the specific types of articulation error found in each child's speech, as well as measures of overall intelligibility, which ranged from 68% to 93% of utterances. Oral examination revealed that many of these children exhibited higher than normal vaulted palatal contours and weakness of the oral musculature. More recently, in a study of 13 children and adults with Prader-Willi syndrome, Defloor and colleagues found high rates of articulation errors and that these rates were generally related to both IQ and chronological age (Defloor, Van Borsel, & Curfs, 2002). Clearly, these are preliminary findings and call for further research on the nature and, critically, the responsiveness to treatment of all of these syndromes. The growth of national and international registries of individuals with specific syndromes or disorders should increase the likelihood of more research on these low-incidence diagnoses.

Of course, there are still many more individuals with IDD for whom no genetic etiology or distinct syndrome has been identified. Further, we know that many children and adults with IDD will present with co-occurring sensory or neurological disorders that can further impact their speech sound development. In deciding about a diagnosis of speech sound disorder secondary to IDD, the clinician may ultimately find it most helpful to focus on the first two criteria for this diagnosis, which require consideration of how and whether the client's speech sound problems interfere with effective participation in social, educational, and other environments.

Application of Diagnostic Criteria to People with ID

General Considerations

The diagnosis of a specific speech sound disorder in an individual with IDD requires that his or her speech be evaluated by a team member with expertise related to typical and atypical speech sound development, as well as intellectual disability and associated syndromes. This will require an assessment by the team's speech-language pathologist, who will evaluate the client's speech sound production in various linguistic contexts, including different single words, imitated sentences, and spontaneous speech produced in an interactive language sampling session. Another important consideration in a speech evaluation, especially for an older client, will be determination of how intelligible and functional his or her speech is perceived to be across daily interactions at home, school, workplace, etc. This information may be gathered by any member of the team and should include input from parents and/or other communication partners.

These assessment data will allow the speech-language pathologist to determine whether an individual's speech sound errors reflect one or more phonological processes (e.g., fronting) that are common in typically developing children at the individual's approximate level of language development. Typically developing children outgrow these processes as they mature in both chronological age and language age, so they are not considered to have speech disorders. In the case of an older child or adult with ID, such delayed or immature speech and language may be identified as an area for intervention. However, using the *DSM-5* criteria, the clinician would not assign a differential diagnosis of a speech sound disorder because the speech sound errors are commensurate with the client's overall level of language development and, thus, attributable to his or her intellectual disability

Methodology

To identify recent research relevant to this diagnosis, the author used several online search systems: PubMed/MEDLINE, PsychINFO, ERIC, and PsycARTICLES. Key search terms were: intellectual disability OR mental retardation AND speech disorder OR articulation disorder. These searches were limited to articles published in peer-reviewed journals with publication dates between 2000 and 2014. This literature search produced a small number of articles reporting on some aspect of speech sound disorder in individuals with an intellectual disability, and these are cited above. However, none of these specifically reported use of the new *DSM-5* diagnostic criteria, or the previous *DSM-IV.*

Evaluating the Level of Evidence

Because the focus of this chapter is on diagnosis and not treatment, none of the articles cited meet the Cochrane criteria for Level I, Level II or Level III evidence. Most were "well designed observational studies" (Cochrane Level IV) and a few were "expert opinion, influential reports and studies" (Level V).

Adults with Mild to Moderate ID

Although adults with mild to moderate ID did participate in several of the studies cited here, they were selected based on confirmed diagnosis of a specific genetic syndrome (e.g., fragile X syndrome or Down syndrome) and not a formal ID diagnosis. As a result, no studies were found that specifically attempted to apply the *DSM-5* (or *DSM-IV*) criteria to adults with mild to moderate ID.

Adults with Severe or Profound ID

Many of the adult participants in the studies reviewed here seemed to be functioning at the severe or even profound level of ID, based upon information provided by the study authors. However, again, because the research focus was on describing speech sound disorders, none of these studies reported applying DSM criteria.

Children and Adolescents with ID

Again, studies involving children and adolescents with ID did not report, and apparently did not apply, the DSM (IV or 5) criteria to their young participants.

Etiology and Pathogenesis

While there are many known genetic and/or physiologic conditions that are associated with ID, the research related to speech sound disorders in this population is predominantly limited to the most common syndromes associated with ID: Down syndrome and fragile X syndrome. Many/most individuals with Down syndrome, and many with fragile X syndrome, do develop functional spoken language, and it is not surprising that research has focused on their speech development and disorders.

Speech Sound Disorder

DSM-5 Diagnostic Criteria	Applying Criteria for Mild-Moderate ID	Applying Criteria for Severe/Profound ID
A. Persistent difficulty with speech sound production that interferes with speech intelligibility or prevents verbal communication of messages.	No adaptation needed	No adaptation needed if client has functional speech. In cases in which the disorder has prevented development of any functional spoken communication, the clinician should determine if client uses or needs an alternative/ augmentative mode
B. The disturbance causes limitations in effective communication that interfere with social participation, academic achievement, or occupational performance, individually or in any combination.	No adaptation needed	
C. Onset of symptoms is in the early developmental period.	No adaptation needed	
D. The difficulties are not attributable to congenital or acquired conditions, such as cerebral palsy, cleft palate, deafness or hearing loss, traumatic brain injury, or other medical or neurological conditions.	For individuals with ID, a speech sound disorder may be attributable to the same underlying neurological and/or genetic condition[s] considered the cause of that individual's intellectual disability. If criteria A, B, and C are met, a diagnosis of speech sound disorder is still appropriate.	

Childhood-Onset Fluency Disorder (Stuttering)

Review of Diagnostic Criteria

Childhood-onset fluency disorder (stuttering) is a disturbance in the normal fluency and time patterning of speech, inappropriate for the individual's age, that is characterized by one (or more) of the following: a) sound and syllable repetition or prolongation; b) broken words (pauses within words); c) audible or silent blocking (i.e., filled or unfilled pauses in speech); d) circumlocutions (i.e., word substitutions to avoid problematic words); e) words produced with excess physical tension; and f) monosyllabic whole-word repetitions (e.g., "I-I-I-I see him"). Additionally, the dysfluency is of such severity as to interfere with the individual's participation and success in social, academic, and/or occupational contexts. It is estimated that stuttering affects about 1% of the general population (Yairi, 2005). By definition, this disorder manifests during childhood, usually by the age of 7. With increasing age and awareness of their stuttering, many children develop secondary or accessory behaviors (e.g., eye blinks or grimaces) and avoidance strategies (e.g., not speaking in a group conversation or class). It is common for stuttering to disappear when the individual is speaking pre-composed linguistic content (e.g., reading text aloud, reciting a memorized passage, or singing a familiar song).

Stuttering, although the most familiar, is not the only type of disfluency[1]. For purposes of this chapter, we will just briefly discuss two others: Normal disfluency and cluttering. Normal disfluency is so common in both child and adult speech that we typically don't even notice it. Any recording of adults (and older children/youths) in casual conversation will capture some normal disfluencies, as speakers reformulate a phrase to better capture the meaning (e.g., "Then *I . . . we* decided to buy the new sofa") or pause, often inserting fillers while deciding how to best express their meaning (e.g., "I thought that painting was ... *well, uh*, interesting"), or even interrupt their own utterance to interject another comment or question (e.g., "I'm going to visit my friend – *I think you met him when he was here last year* – while I'm in Paris"). And, we know that about half of all typically developing children will go through a period of "developmental disfluency" when their speech is characterized by a higher than normal rate of disfluencies (American Speech-Language-Hearing Association, 1999). This generally occurs during the preschool years and coincides with the period of very rapid lexical, morphemic, and syntactic language development.

Another type of dysfluency is cluttering, defined by the American Speech-Language-Hearing Association as a "fluency disorder characterized by a rapid and/or irregular speech rate, excessive dysfluencies, and often other symptoms such as language or phonological errors and attention deficits" (American Speech-Language-Hearing Association, 1999). More specifically, classic cluttering is characterized by excessive rates of normal disfluency, produced at a rapid and often variable mean articulatory rate (MAR), measured as the number of syllables produced per second. Cluttered speech is typically perceived as difficult to understand and yields a high percentage of utterances scored as unintelligible when recorded and scored by normal speakers. Clinical reports and research articles focused on cluttering have been in the speech pathology literature since the 1950s. However, over the past decade a growing body of research has appeared, suggesting the need for more accurate differential diagnosis and specifically addressing the issue of stuttering vs. cluttering in people with ID.

Summary of DSM-5 Criteria

The new DSM criteria for a diagnosis of fluency disorder are not much changed from the previous *DSM-IV* criteria and are very consistent with the definition and criteria used by speech-language pathologists for diagnosing stuttering. In addition to the specific types of speech disruptions and repetitions unique to stuttering (see summary in table below), true stuttering must be

[1]The spelling *disfluency* is generally used to refer to normal breaks in the continuity of spoken language, whereas *dysfluency* refers to stuttering or other patterns of broken or collapsed speech segments (e.g., cluttering) that disrupt effective communication.

of such severity and persistence as to cause the speaker distress and interfere with communication across multiple environments. And, while the stuttering may coincide with other developmental disorders, it must not be specifically attributable to any of those disorders.

The table below summarizes these new *DSM-5* criteria for childhood-onset fluency disorder (stuttering):

A. Disturbances in the normal fluency and time patterning of speech that are inappropriate for the individual's age and language skills, persist over time, and are characterized by frequent and marked occurrences of one (or more) of the following:
   1. Sound and syllable repetitions.
   2. Sound prolongations of consonants as well as vowels.
   3. Broken words (e.g., pauses within a word).
   4. Audible or silent blocking (filled or unfilled pauses in speech).
   5. Circumlocutions (word substitutions to avoid problematic words).
   6. Words produced with an excess of physical tension.
   7. Monosyllabic whole-word repetitions (e.g., "I-I-I-I see him").

B. The disturbance causes anxiety about speaking or limitations in effective communication, social participation, or academic or occupational performance, individually or in any combination.

C. The onset of symptoms is in the early developmental period. (Note: Later-onset cases are diagnosed as 307.0 [F98.5] adult-onset fluency disorder.)

D. The disturbance is not attributable to a speech-motor or sensory deficit, dysfluency associated with neurological insult (e.g., stroke, tumor or trauma) or another medical condition, and is not better explained by another mental disorder.

Issues Related to Diagnosis in Persons with ID

Perhaps the greatest issue facing the clinician evaluating a client with ID is recognizing and distinguishing a fluency disorder from other aspects of the client's general cognitive and linguistic development. Close attending and transcription of a client's responses are needed to determine if he or she is displaying normal developmental disfluency relative to overall level of language development, or is exhibiting true stuttering or cluttering that interferes with the client's participation in social interactions.

While limited, there is some evidence that children with Down syndrome, at least, do receive and benefit from speech therapy for their fluency disorders (Bray, 2003; Harasym & Langevin, 2012). Thus, it is important for the clinician diagnosing verbal individuals with ID to make note of any apparent fluency disorder and to seek assistance in diagnosis as needed. As discussed below, recent research on fluency disorders in persons with ID has suggested some unique patterns of dysfluent speech not found in clients who do not have ID (e.g., true stuttering without self-awareness or anxiety; greater incidence of cluttering). Again, it is recommended that the clinician involve a speech-language pathologist in the diagnosis if a fluency disorder is suspected.

Application of Diagnostic Criteria to People with ID

Methodology

To identify recent research relevant to this diagnosis, the author used several online search systems: PubMed/MEDLINE, PsychINFO, ERIC, and PsycARTICLES. Key search terms were: intellectual disability OR mental retardation AND fluency disorder OR stuttering. These searches were limited to English-language articles published in peer-reviewed journals with publication dates between 2000 and 2014. This literature search produced a number of articles reporting on some aspect of fluency disorder in individuals with an intellectual disability. None of these reported use of DSM diagnostic criteria for stuttering, although one (Coppens-Hofman et al., 2013) specifically mentioned the use of *DSM-IV* criteria for classifying research participants as having mild or moderate ID.

Review of Research Applying to People with ID

One clear finding is that fluency disorders are an issue for many speakers with intellectual disability, with varying prevalence rates reported by different investigators. In his classic study of 793 adults with ID, Stansfield (1990) reported that 6.3% of these participants had some type of fluency disorder. In a more recent study reported by Coppens-Hofman and colleagues (Coppens-Hofman et al., 2013) examining dysfluencies in the speech of 28 adults with mild to moderate ID (including 11 with Down syndrome), all of these individuals were referred for the study by caregivers because of concerns that poor intelligibility of these adults' speech was interfering with their daily interactions. The investigators collected speech samples and analyzed these for evidence of different types of dysfluency, using definitions based on percentages of normal and stuttered dysfluencies, mean articulatory rate, and rate variability. From this sample, they identified 7 individuals with no fluency disorder; 8 with cluttering-stuttering; 6 with classic cluttering; and another 7 who demonstrated a unique pattern of cluttering with normal articulatory rate. A multivariate ANOVA revealed no significant effect of ID level (mild vs. moderate), age, gender or syndrome/etiology on these results. If replicated, this study suggests that cluttering may be the most common type of fluency disorder in individuals with ID (Coppens-Hofman et al., 2013).

Several recent articles have focused on clinical dysfluency in children and adults with Down syndrome (Bray, 2003; Kent & Vorperian, 2013; Van Borsel & Vandermeulen, 2008). In their recent, systematic review of 17 studies published between 1955 and 2010, Kent and Vorperian found prevalence estimates ranging from 10% to 45%, with a mean of 31% of individuals with Down syndrome demonstrating some type and severity of clinical dysfluency. However, they note that there is inconsistency in the literature regarding how and if any distinction is made between stuttering and cluttering, and consideration of related features of dysfluent speech (e.g., rate variability, telescoping, and prosody disorder). They conclude that there is a need for more and better research into the nature of the fluency disorders that affect so many individuals with Down syndrome, beginning with professional consensus on definitions and criteria for these terms. Despite these concerns, they conclude that there is sufficient evidence now to suggest that cluttering may be more common than stuttering among speakers with Down syndrome.

Van Borsel and colleagues have written extensively about fluency disorders in Down syndrome (Van Borsel & Vandermeulen, 2008) and more generally in individuals with ID attributable to several genetic syndromes (Van Borsel & Tetnowski, 2007). The 2008 article reports results from a study in which 26 speech-language pathologists were provided with a cluttering screening instrument and asked to complete it for their clients with Down syndrome. Inventories were completed for 76 individuals with Down syndrome, ranging in age from 3.8 to 57.3 years. Analysis of these data indicated that, for these clients with Down syndrome, 79% would be diagnosed as clutterers and 17% as clutterer-stutterers. Based on their review of the inventory results, the authors conclude that there may be patterns of dysfluency that are unique to specific clinical sub-groups, including individuals with Down syndrome. More critically, they emphasize the need for professional consensus on the definition and criteria for the subtypes of fluency disorder, including cluttering.

Van Borsel and Tetnowski (2007) examined available data on dysfluencies in a number of clinical syndromes for which stuttering is considered a characteristic of that syndrome. Among the syndromes examined were Down, fragile X, and Prader-Willi. Once again, a major conclusion of this review is that there is a lack of clarity and consistency in the way fluency data are collected, analyzed, and matched up with different diagnoses based on often vague criteria. They do conclude that clinical dysfluency (stuttering, cluttering, and/or some unique pattern of both) is more prevalent in Down syndrome than other syndromes associated with ID, occurring in about one of every three children and adults with Down syndrome. Dysfluencies, including stuttering, are also common in fragile X syndrome and Prader-Willi syndrome and are more prevalent than in non-syndrome-specific ID, but are not as common as in Down syndrome.

Regarding Prader-Willi syndrome, a study published in 1990 by Kleppe and colleagues provided a comprehensive description of the speech and language characteristics of 18 children with Prader-Willi syndrome, ranging in age from 8.8 to 17.1. They collected and analyzed a 200-utterance language sample, as well as results from an extensive test battery administered to each child. Their analysis of speech fluency in each child's language sample revealed multiple types of normal and developmental disfluency (e.g., interjections, revisions, word repetitions), but only one child who presented with the types of dysfluency classified as true stuttering (Kleppe, Katayama, Shipley, & Foushee, 1990).

Evaluating the Level of Evidence

Because the focus of this chapter is on diagnosis and not treatment, none of the articles cited meet the Cochrane criteria for Level I, II or III evidence. Most were "well designed observational studies" (Cochrane Level IV) and a few were "expert opinion, influential reports and studies" (Level V). Additionally, all were published in refereed, archival journals in the fields of fluency disorders and more general speech and language disorders.

Summary of Limitations in Applying* DSM-5 *Criteria to People with ID

This review did not identify any studies that had applied DSM diagnostic criteria for fluency disorder. Rather, authors of these studies clearly described the behaviors and quantitative criteria (e.g., frequency/percent of stuttered utterances in a speech sample) used in their own research. In fact, there is general agreement among investigators in this field on the need for consensus on a standard set of criteria for diagnosis, and differential diagnosis, of different fluency disorders, including stuttering (Coppens-Hofman et al., 2013). While the literature reviewed here did document relatively high rates of fluency disorder among persons with ID, it also indicated that much of the dysfluency reported in persons with ID does not meet criteria for stuttering and is instead diagnosed as cluttering. Since the DSM criteria for childhood-onset fluency disorder is specific to stuttering, the diagnosing clinician can only be aware of this distinction and perhaps reflect it in clinical notes.

Etiology and Pathogenesis

While there are many known genetic and/or physiologic conditions that are associated with ID, the research related to fluency disorders in this population is predominantly limited to the most common genetic syndromes associated with ID: Down, fragile X, and Prader-Willi syndromes. As discussed above, there is some indication that fluency disorders are more prevalent in people with these syndromes than those with idiopathic ID, and differ in some aspects from the typical patterns of dysfluency reported in the normal literature.

Childhood-Onset Fluency Disorder (Stuttering)

DSM-5 Diagnostic Criteria	Applying Criteria for Mild to Profound ID
A. Disturbance in the normal fluency and time patterning of speech that are inappropriate for the individual's age and language skills, persist over time, and are characterized by frequent and marked occurrences of one (or more) of the following: sound and syllable repetitions, sound prolongations of consonants as well as vowels broken words (e.g., pauses within a word), audible or silent blocking (filled or unfilled pauses in speech), circumlocutions (word substitutions to avoid problematic words), words produced with an excess of physical tension monosyllabic whole-word repetitions (e.g., "I-I-I-I see him")	A. **Note:** Pay special attention to the specific aspects of speech sounds that are affected in the client's connected speech. We know that some persons with ID can present patterns of speech involving high rates of normal disfluency and unusual intonation patterns that can create the impression of stuttering but in fact represent a different type of fluency disorder.
B. The disturbance causes anxiety about speaking or limitations in effective communication, social participation, or academic or occupational performance, individually or in any combination	B. **Note:** Some persons with ID may have speech marked by high rates of true stuttering, which interferes with their intelligibility and, thus, social participation; however, they show no self-awareness or anxiety about their stuttering.
C. The onset of symptoms is in the early developmental period. (**Note:** Later-onset cases are diagnosed as 307.0 [F98.5] adult-onset fluency disorder.)	C. No adaptation.
D. The disturbance is not *attributable* to a speech-motor or sensory deficit, dysfluency associated with neurological insult (e.g., stroke, tumor, trauma), or another medical condition and is not better explained by another mental disorder.	D. Note that fluency disorders may co-occur with intellectual disability, but not be directly *attributable* to that disorder, or its underlying genetic syndrome.

Language Disorder

Changes in Classification

The *DSM-IV* distinguished two types of language disorders – expressive language disorder and mixed receptive-expressive language disorder. The *DSM-5* eliminated this distinction and settled on a single diagnostic category of language disorder. Individuals with language disorder demonstrate difficulties with comprehending and/or producing language across modalities. Language disorder interferes with academic and/or occupational achievement and often affects social participation.

Review of Diagnostic Criteria

General Description of the Disorder

The typical profile for expressive (output) deficits includes limited speech characterized by reduced vocabulary diversity, difficulty acquiring new words, word-finding or vocabulary errors, shortened sentences, simplified or limited grammatical structures, limited sentence variety, sentence part omission, unusual word order, difficulty with oral narratives or explaining complex topics, and slowed language development (Bortolini, Caselli, Deevy, & Leonard, 2002; Leonard, 1998). Input deficits involving receptive language affect perception or understanding of language. Receptive deficits are frequently underestimated and include difficulty with the understanding of words, sentences or word types (Hill, Hogben, & Bishop, 2005; McArthur & Bishop, 2004; Norbury & Bishop, 2002; Tallal, 2000).

Language disorder is diagnosed with the assistance of historical and observational data interpreted alongside scores on a battery of standardized individually administered measures of language. Language testing profiles for language disorder typically reflect scores substantially below those demonstrated in nonverbal intellectual testing.

Language disorder is typically categorized into acquired and developmental subtypes. The "acquired" specifier is used if the disorder follows a period of typical language development and can be attributed to a known neurological or other general medical condition. If no causal etiology is identified, the disorder is assumed to be "developmental" and is so indicated. Most recently, Paul and Norbury (2012) identified three distinct groups of children with developmental language disorders. These include children with: a) primary developmental language disorder, for whom no other diagnostic label is appropriate; b) secondary developmental language disorders, where language impairment is secondary to other developmental disorders; and c) developmental language disorders specific to language-learning problems associated with academic performance. Individuals with ID who have language disorders present secondary developmental language disorders.

Summary of DSM-5 *Criteria*

Using *DSM-5* criteria, language disorder is diagnosed when individuals present with persistent difficulties in the production and/or comprehension of language. Characteristics include reduced vocabulary, limited sentence structure, and impairments in discourse. Language abilities are substantially below age-expectation, which results in academic, social, and/or occupational limitations. Accurate diagnosis of language disorder occurs early in the developmental period and requires the diagnostic exclusion of sensory, motor, or other medical/neurological disorders as primary sources of the features mentioned above. These features must also not be best explained by intellectual disability or global delay.

Issues Related to Diagnosis in Persons with ID

If ID is present, a diagnosis of language disorder requires that the language difficulties be in excess of that which is expected with these problems. A valid diagnosis of developmental language disorder relies heavily on completion of standardized language and intellectual testing. This presents a significant barrier to diagnosis in individuals with ID. In ID populations, norms for language testing are limited, and the validity of intellectual testing can be suspect. Additionally, given the many etiologies of ID, known and unknown, with their own sets of individual dysfunctions, a complicated and confusing diagnostic picture often emerges. Until specific etiologies and characterizations of ID are understood (Abbeduto, Evans, & Dolan, 2001) and, subsequently, standardized norms for language testing are developed, it will remain difficult to diagnose these and other communication disorders in many individuals with ID using *DSM-5* criteria.

Application of Diagnostic Criteria to People with ID

General Considerations

DSM-5 diagnostic criteria specify that primary developmental language disorder should not best be explained by ID or global developmental delay. This is also the case for the International and Statistical Classification of Diseases and Related Health Problems 10th Revision (ICD 10, 2011). Accordingly, developmental language disorders in persons with ID must represent a secondary condition. Given that many of the receptive and expressive features of developmental language disorders are also core features of delayed language associated with ID, the co-existence of developmental language disorders and ID would necessitate unusual discrepancies between intellectual ability and actual language usage or understanding. Identifying these discrepancies relies on both valid observations and reliable and valid standardized testing. Unfortunately, reliance on standardized testing can produce suspect results.

Methodology

Searches were conducted in health, social science, and general science-focused information resources including M*EDLINE*, *Cumulative Index to Nursing and Allied Health Literature* (CINAHL), the *Cochrane Database of Systematic Reviews*, *SocINDEX*, *PsycINFO*, and *Science Citation Index*, as well as multidisciplinary resources such as *Academic Search Complete*. Resources were searched using terms related to ID and developmental language disorder. Resource-specific subject headings were mined for additional applicable terms. Although no findings surfaced specific to developmental language disorders and generalized ID, studies addressing language differences in genetic syndromes were identified. Findings are reviewed briefly in a section to follow (see genetic syndromes).

Review of Research Applying to People with ID

There are no empirical studies available in which *DSM-5* or other well-characterized diagnostic criteria for developmental language disorders were systematically applied to groups of individuals who have ID.

Evaluating the Level of Evidence

The strength of evidence of most available studies of developmental language disorders is Cochrane Type V.

Adults with Mild to Moderate ID

The impact of persistent acquired or developmental language disorders for individuals with mild to moderate ID has not been well studied. The form and course of the language disorder is impacted by the etiologic heterogeneity of ID, the developmental course associated with identified causes of ID, or both. For example, although the receptive and expressive difficulties associated with fragile X syndrome tend to be evident and persistent from childhood through adulthood (Abbeduto & Hagerman, 1997; Lewis et al., 2006), the verbal fluency associated with Williams syndrome (Lenhoff, Wang, Greenberg, & Bellugi, 1997; Mervis & Vellerman, 2011) can mask the extent of language disability until greater demands for abstract thought and comprehension, which the language of adulthood requires, expose the disparity between semantic and pragmatic communication.

Additionally, the acquisition and use of compensatory strategies as a means of developing pragmatic communication in the context of language disability can be expected to be limited in those with mild to moderate ID. The resultant frustration associated with communication difficulties can contribute to the development of disruptive behaviors or aggression. An appreciation of the lifelong developmental courses associated with these language impairments is essential in ruling out acute medical conditions, acquired aphasia, dementia, or degenerative disorders.

Adults with Severe or Profound ID

There is no body of literature that examines the relationship of *DSM-5* characterized communication disorders, including language disorder, with severe to profound ID. This is due to the paucity of speech and general language complexity typically observed from this population, as well as the limited appropriateness/reliability of standardized testing instruments. Communication-based assessment with this population typically utilizes naturalistic observations and criterion-referenced measures precluding the determination of significant discrepancies between cognitive functioning and language performance. Such discrepancies, if they exist, are likely less impactful given the overall reduced complexity of language in persons with severe or profound ID.

Children and Adolescents with ID

The issues described above specific to functioning and language disorder are relevant for both children and adults with ID. Obviously, the diagnosis of language disorder will likely occur later than with children who are typically developing, as the emergence of language itself may be somewhat protracted if not significantly delayed.

Summary of Limitations in Applying **DSM-5** *Criteria to People with ID*

The lack of assessment tools standardized for people with ID, as well as the etiologic heterogeneity and the limited data addressing the acquisition and use of language in individuals with ID, limit the use of *DSM-5* criteria for language disorder in people with ID.

Etiology and Pathogenesis

The cause of language disorders in ID is assumed to be multi-factored and will likely have roots in both the intellectual impairment itself and the social isolation frequently associated with ID (i.e., limited communication opportunities).

Biological Factors

Communication difficulties can be expected in individuals with ID and often are the initial indications of atypical development. There is evidence to support familial patterns of inheritance in the developmental subtype of language disorders (Kang & Drayna, 2011). These diagnoses have increased incidence in individuals who have a family history of communication disorders or learning disorders.

Genetic Factors

Certain well-characterized individual syndromes produce predictable communication deficits. For individuals for whom these syndromes are identified, a diagnosis of secondary developmental language disorders is appropriate if the language disability is beyond that which is expected for the degree of cognitive impairment. Language expectations associated with three common and fairly well studied syndromes are briefly discussed below.

Characteristic communication patterns for individuals with Down syndrome include relative strengths in word learning and social communication in the presence of disproportionately low morphological and grammatical skills (Abbeduto et al., 2003; Chapman, 1997; Estigarribia, Martin, & Roberts, 2012; Naess, Halaas Lyster, Hulme, & Melby-Lervag, 2011; Polisenska & Kapalkova, 2014; Stoel-Gammon, 2001). Generally, expressive language deficits are greater than receptive language deficits (Laws & Bishop, 2004; Roberts, Price, & Malkin, 2007).

Gender differences are expected in fragile X syndrome, with males displaying more severe impairments (Hagerman, 2002; Loesch et al., 2002, Reiss & Dant, 2003). Males with fragile X have deficits using and understanding grammar beyond those expected for their developmental levels, though these deficits generally are not as severe as those in individuals with Down syndrome (Kover & Abbeduto, 2010; Martin, Losh, Estigarribia, Sideris, & Roberts, 2013; Oakes, Kover, & Abbeduto, 2013; Price et al., 2008; Price, Roberts, Vandergrift, & Martin, 2007). Males also demonstrate expressive and receptive vocabulary skills either on par with or below developmental expectations (Roberts, Hennon et al., 2007; Roberts, Price, Barnes et al., 2007; Sudhalter, Scarborough, & Cohen, 1991). Pragmatic difficulties in both conversation and narration are well beyond those expected for developmental level (Estigarribia et al., 2011; Klusek, Martin, & Losh, 2014; Martin et al., 2013; Roberts, Martin, et al., 2007). Additionally, autism spectrum disorder is a common comorbid condition (Clifford et al., 2007; Hall, Lightbody, Hirt, Rezvani, & Reiss, 2010) and can negatively affect language performance (Estigarribia et al., 2011; Klusek, Martin & Losh, 2014; Martin et al., 2013; Roberts, Martin, et al., 2007).

Individuals with Williams syndrome are noted to present relative strengths with concrete vocabulary (understanding and use) and phonological processing with deficits in verbal short-term memory, relational/conceptual language, and pragmatics (Lenhoff et al., 1997; Majerus, Poncelet, Audrey, Zesiger, et al., 2010; Mervis & Velleman, 2011). Grammatical skills tend to be commensurate with developmental expectations (Mervis & Becerra, 2007).

Individuals with these and other syndromes can be expected to be different from one another, as well as from typically developing individuals, despite potentially similar results on basic cognitive testing.

Psychosocial Factors

A careful assessment of the individual's environment is at least as important in understanding communication in individuals with ID as it is in the general population. In fact, a tri-focus orientation to assessment is recommended including inquiry specific to the individual with ID, his/her partners, and his/her communicative environments (Siegel-Causey & Bashinski, 1997; Siegel & Cress, 2002). Expressive language is also predicated on internal motivation as well as adequate means for communication.

Developmental Factors

Protracted intellectual development can be a clear contributor to language disorders in persons with ID. This is especially true when confounding psychosocial variables specific to partners and environments are at play.

Application of Diagnostic Criteria

Below is a table specifying proposed modified criteria for language disorder for both mild to moderate and severe to profound ID.

Language Disorder

DSM-5 Diagnostic Criteria	Appliying Criteria for Mild to Moderate ID	Applying Criteria for Severe to Profound ID
A. Persistent difficulties in the acquisition and use of language across modalities (i.e., spoken, written, sign language, or other) due to deficits in comprehension or production that include the following: 1. Reduced vocabulary (word knowledge and use); 2. Limited sentence structure (ability to put words and word endings together to form sentences based on the rules of grammar and morphology); and 3. Impairments in discourse (ability to use vocabulary and connect sentences to explain or describe a topic or series of events or have a conversation).	A. Difficulties must manifest themselves in a manner that exceeds that expected of ID alone.	A. Difficulties must manifest themselves in a manner that exceeds that expected of ID alone. Given the lack of standardized testing norms for individuals with ID, estimation of intellect should incorporate clinically derived information such as compliance with simple directions or multi-step commands, understanding of abstract concepts, etc.
B. Language abilities are substantially and quantifiably below those expected for age, resulting in functional limitations in effective communication, social participation, academic achievement, or occupational performance, individually or in any combination.	B. Difficulties with language result in functional limitations in excess of those expected given an individual's ID and previous experience.	
C. Onset of symptoms is in the early developmental period.	C. Symptoms will appear later given that language emergence will be delayed. No general adaptation.	
D. The difficulties are not attributable to hearing or other sensory impairment, motor dysfunction, or another medical or neurological condition and are not better explained by intellectual disability (intellectual developmental disorder) or global developmental delay	D. No adaptation.	

Social (Pragmatic) Communication Disorder

Review of Diagnostic Criteria

Social (pragmatic) communication disorder (SCD) is characterized by difficulties in using both verbal and nonverbal communication for social purposes, such that an individual is impaired in the ability to maintain effective interpersonal interactions in social, academic, and/or occupational contexts. Symptoms include problems in following the rules for conversation and storytelling as well as difficulty in using nonverbal signals to regulate interaction (reciprocity), matching communication to the context and needs of a listener, and problems in making inferences and understanding nonliteral language.

Symptoms must first appear in early childhood, even if their impact on effective communication is not recognized until later. Also, the symptoms cannot be explained by structural language problems or by intellectual deficits; thus, if structural language or intellectual deficits are present, the social communication difficulties are in excess of what would be expected in light of these problems. A diagnosis of social communication disorder is given only after autism spectrum disorder has been ruled out, as individuals with social communication disorder do not show the patterns of restrictive and repetitive behaviors, interests, and activities that co-occur with symptoms of social communication impairment in autism spectrum disorder.

The addition of social communication disorder to *DSM-5* was based in part on prior research on individuals with similar symptoms, collectively labeled as reflecting "semantic-pragmatic disorder" (Rapin, 1996) or "pragmatic language impairment" (Bishop & Norbury, 2002).

Issues Related to Diagnosis in Persons with ID

The *DSM-5* is the first edition of the DSM in which diagnostic criteria for social communication disorder have been included. Social communication symptoms associated with social communication disorder also occur in autism spectrum disorder; in fact, under *DSM-IV-TR*, individuals meeting the current *DSM-5* criteria for social communication disorder were sometimes diagnosed with a pervasive developmental disorder (Greaves-Lord et al., 2013; Kim et al., 2014; Wilson et al., 2013). Given that ASD is diagnosed in individuals across a broad range of intellectual functioning, it seems likely that some persons with ID will display symptoms of social communication disorder. On the other hand, the criteria for diagnosing social communication disorder are not identical to the criteria for social communication symptoms used to diagnose autism spectrum disorder, and these differences have implications for the diagnosis of social communication disorder in persons with ID.

The primary issue in making a diagnosis of social communication disorder in persons with ID is determining whether the social communication difficulties exceed what would be expected based on the level of cognitive functioning. A second issue is that the criteria for diagnosing social communication disorder require that four types of symptoms be present, and some of these symptoms require verbal language to be present at a level allowing an individual to engage in conversations and narratives. Thus, whereas it may be clear that a given individual with severe to profound ID has difficulty in using communication for social purposes (e.g., the person may use gestures or words to make requests or protest, but not to initiate social interactions with others or to share information), such an individual may not have sufficient structural language skills to permit an evaluation of his or her knowledge of the rules for storytelling or conversation.

Application of Diagnostic Criteria to People with ID

There is a lack of data on the validity of applying the *DSM-5* diagnostic criteria for social communication disorder to people with ID. This lag in research studies is unsurprising, given that social communication disorder was recently disentangled from autism spectrum disorders and is first assigned syndrome status in this edition of the DSM. Many of the existing studies focused on individuals with pervasive developmental disorders, NOS. About 50% of these individuals are now rediagnosed with social communication disorder and most likely borderline to mild ID. In the only identified study providing evidence, two of 17 persons who met criteria for social communication disorder also had ID. The remainder of studies devoted to pragmatic language impairment excludes individuals with ID.

Methodology

PubMed and *PsycINFO* searches were conducted in an attempt to identify published work with data regarding the co-occurrence of ID and *DSM-5* social communication disorder. Secondary searches were conducted to identify work on the co-occurrence of ID and "pragmatics" or "social communication."

Review of Research Applying to People with ID

No empirical studies were found in which *DSM-5* or other diagnostic criteria for social communication disorder were systematically applied to individuals with ID. One identified study reported that two individuals with ID were diagnosed with social communication disorder in their sample, but the aims of the study did not include a systematic examination of the applicability of social communication disorder diagnostic criteria to persons with ID. There is a body of literature describing characteristics of social communication and pragmatic aspects of language use among people with ID.

Evaluating the Level of Evidence

There is insufficient evidence to evaluate its overall level.

Adults with ID

One study examined adult outcomes for a small sample of persons identified with pragmatic language impairment, specific language impairment, autism spectrum disorder or typical development as children, and found that social communication impairments associated with both pragmatic language impairment and autism spectrum disorder continued to be apparent in adulthood (Whitehouse, Watt, Line, & Bishop, 2009). Further, the social communication impairments in both disorders were associated with a lower quality of friendships and less independence in adulthood than individuals with a history of typical development (Whitehouse et al., 2009). All the individuals in that sample had nonverbal IQs within normal limits as children, however, and no direct assessment of their intellectual functioning as adults was completed. The indirect evidence suggests that, as a group, persons demonstrating pragmatic language impairment as children will experience some impairments in adaptive skills as adults.

Because symptoms of pragmatic language impairment persist into adulthood and are associated with adaptive functioning, the diagnosis of social communication disorder should be considered in evaluating adults with ID. Logically, a history of both ID and social/pragmatic communication impairments would have more impact on adult outcomes than either impairment alone, but no direct evidence was found to support or refute this assumption.

Children and Adolescents with ID

Criteria for the diagnosis of social communication disorder require symptom onset to be during the early developmental period. As a result, the assessment for social communication disorder should be considered in the evaluation of all children and adolescents with ID.

The diagnosis of social communication disorder is based on a discrepancy between the actual level of cognitive and language functioning and that expected based on age-stratified performance measures. The validity of the discrepancy scores is frequently suspect. For example, individuals with structural language abilities lower than what would be achieved in a typically developing child by the age of 3 to 4 years can invalidate the diagnosis of social communication disorder. Nevertheless, comparing functional impairments in the use of communication for social purposes (social interaction, sharing information and interests) with those serving instrumental purposes (requesting an object or actions, protesting, directing the behaviors of others) may sidestep the problems with *DSM-5* discrepancy criteria. This functional approach may be more useful for evaluating individuals with lower levels of functioning and generating habilitative programming.

Summary of Limitations in Applying DSM-5 Criteria to People with ID

The validity, reliability, and utility of *DSM-5* criteria for social communication disorder in individuals with ID are undetermined at this time.

Etiology and Pathogenesis

Risk Factors and Biological Factors

Studies of pragmatic language impairment consistently include more males than females (ratios ranging from 2:1 to 8:1), but no rigorous epidemiological studies have been published.

Psychosocial Factors

No evidence was identified related to psychosocial factors for individuals with ID who have social communication/pragmatic language impairments.

Genetic Syndromes

Among syndromes accompanied by ID, social communication and pragmatic skills in individuals with Williams syndrome, fragile X syndrome, and Down syndrome have been examined most.

Early descriptions of persons with Williams syndrome suggested that they might have language and social communication skills beyond what would be expected based on their cognitive functioning, but recent studies have presented convincing counter-evidence. Young children with Williams syndrome show difficulties with the use of communicative gestures, appropriate use of eye contact, and using communication to share interests – difficulties that are similar to those associated with autism spectrum disorder – and school-age children with Williams syndrome show varied impairments in pragmatic language, with a high proportion showing enough problems to be diagnosed with pragmatic language impairment (Laws & Bishop, 2004; Mervis & Becerra, 2007).

Persons with fragile X syndrome often meet criteria for a diagnosis of autism spectrum disorder, but even those who do not often exhibit weaknesses across a range of pragmatic language skills after accounting for structural language and cognitive abilities (Finestack, Richmond, & Abbeduto, 2009; Klusek et al., 2014; Martin et al. 2013).

Children with Down syndrome also show weaknesses in aspects of pragmatic language compared to typically developing children with similar language levels (Klusek et al., 2014; Martin et al., 2013). One study reported that 50% of a small sample of children with Down syndrome exhibited pragmatic language problems severe enough to be suggestive of pragmatic language impairment (Laws & Bishop, 2004). Another study found that preschoolers with Down syndrome more accurately comprehended the communicative intent expressed by others' pointing gestures and eye gaze than did preschoolers with Williams syndrome (John & Mervis, 2010), suggesting some relative social communication strengths in children with Down syndrome.

Social (Pragmatic) Communication Disorder

DSM-5 Diagnostic Criteria	Applying Criteria for Mild to Profound ID
A. Persistent difficulties in the social use of verbal and nonverbal communication as manifested by all of the following: 1. Deficits in using communication for social purposes, such as greeting and sharing information, in a manner that is appropriate for the social context. 2. Impairment of the ability to change communication to match context or the needs of the listener, such as speaking differently in a classroom than on a playground, talking differently to a child than to an adult, and avoiding use of overly formal language. 3. Difficulties following rules for conversation and storytelling, such as taking turns in conversation, rephrasing when misunderstood, and knowing how to use verbal and nonverbal signals to regulate interaction. 4. Difficulties understanding what is not explicitly stated (e.g., making inferences) and nonliteral or ambiguous meanings of language (e.g., idioms, humor, metaphors, multiple meanings that depend on the context for interpretation).	A. No adaptation. For individuals with insufficient structural language skills to support conversations or storytelling, note social communication deficits descriptively.
B. The deficits result in functional limitations in effective communication, social participation, social relationships, academic achievement, or occupational performance, individually or in combination (e.g., results in decreased independence or compromised safety beyond that expected given an individual's ID and previous experience)..	B. No adaptation
C. The onset of the symptoms is in the early developmental period (but deficits may not become fully manifest until social communication demands exceed limited capacities).	C. No adaptation.
D. The symptoms are not attributable to another medical or neurological condition or to low abilities in the domains of word structure and grammar, and are not better explained by autism spectrum disorder, intellectual disability (intellectual developmental disorder), global developmental delay, or another mental disorder.	D. No adaptation.

Unspecified Communication Disorder

DSM-5 also provides a category for unspecified communication disorder.

Summary and Conclusions

The evolution and development of communication represent a move from more generic modes of affective or nonverbal communication to increasingly specific and information-rich modes of information sharing. Communication disorders are the result of disturbances in brain development that undermine these developmental trends. This chapter focuses on specific issues related to communication in individuals with IDD. The impact of IDD on the processes associated with communication disorders may appear early during the developmental period but have ramifications across the life cycle.

Speech production and fluency, language, and social (pragmatic) communication are not static processes. They follow developmental courses that follow a sequence of progressive refinements, neurological specialization, and integration. Both typical and atypical patterns of perception, processing, planning, and expression are embedded in social interactions and, in general, serve social purposes.

The *DSM-5* does not expand upon these developmental aspects of human communication systems. Nor does it focus on their progressive and hierarchical organization and the extensive neuronal intercommunication (coherence) essential to linguistic and social pragmatic skills. Diagnostic criteria sets like the *DSM-5* or the *DM-ID-2* are not configured to capture the extensive developmental interrelationships between overlapping brain circuits devoted to multiple cognitive, attentional, executive, and social communication skills. Our understanding of these is incomplete, and we need to continue to seek a more comprehensive understanding of the relationships among ID, communication disorders, and behavioral and mental health disorders.

References

Abbeduto, L., Evans, J., & Dolan, T. (2001). Progress in understanding language and communication problems in mental retardation and developmental disabilities. *Mental Retardation and Developmental Disabilities Research Reviews, 1,* 45-55.

Abbeduto, L., & Haggerman, R. (1997). Language and communication in fragile X syndrome. *Mental Retardation and Developmental Disabilities Research Reviews, 3,* 313-322.

Abbeduto, L., Murphy, M. M., Cawthon, S. W., Richmond, E. K., Weissman, M. D., Karadottir, S., & O'Brien, A. (2003). Receptive language skills of adolescents and young adults with Down syndrome or fragile X syndrome. *American Journal on Mental Retardation, 108,* 149–160.

American Speech-Language-Hearing Association (1999). Terminology pertaining to fluency and fluency disorders: Guidelines. Retrieved from http://www.asha.org/policy/gl1999-00063.htm

Bailey, D. B., Raspa, M., Holiday, D., Bishop, E., & Olmsted, M. (2009). Functional skills of individuals with fragile x syndrome: A lifespan cross-sectional analysis. *American Journal on Intellectual and Developmental Disabilities, 114*(4), 289-303. doi:10.1352/1944-7558-114.4.289-303.

Barnes, E. F., Roberts, J., Mirrett, P., Sideris, J., & Misenheimer, J. (2006). A comparison of oral structure and oral-motor function in young males with fragile X syndrome and Down syndrome. *Journal of Speech, Language, and Hearing Research: 49*(4), 903-917. doi:49/4/903.

Barnhill, L. J., & McNelis, D. (2012). Overview of intellectual/developmental disabilities. *Focus: The Journal of Lifelong Learning in Psychiatry, 10*(3), 300-307.

Berry-Kravis, E., Doll, E., Sterling, A., Kover, S. T., Schroeder, S. M., Mathur, S., & Abbeduto, L. (2013). Development of an expressive language sampling procedure in fragile X syndrome: A pilot study. *Journal of Developmental and Behavioral Pediatrics: 34*(4), 245-251. doi:10.1097/DBP.0b013e31828742fc.

Bishop, D. V. M., & Adams, C. (1992). A prospective study of the relationship between specific language impairment, phonological disorders and reading retardation. *Journal of Child Psychology and Psychiatry, 31*: 1027–50.

Bishop, D. V. M., & Norbury, C. F. (2002). Exploring the borderlands of autistic disorder and specific language impairment: A study using standardised diagnostic instruments. *Journal of Child Psychology and Psychiatry, 43*, 917–929.

Bortolini, U., Caselli, M. C., Deevy, P., & Leonard, L. B. (2002). Specific language impairment in Italian: The first steps for a clinical marker. *International Journal of Language and Communication Disorders, 37*: 77–93.

Bray, M. (2003). The nature of dysfluency in Down's syndrome. *The Bulletin of the Royal College of Speech and Language Therapists, March 2003*, 8-9. Retrieved from http://www.stammering.org/speaking-out/articles/nature-dysfluency-downs-syndrome

Bunton, K., & Leddy, M. (2011). An evaluation of articulatory working space area in vowel production of adults with Down syndrome. *Clinical Linguistics & Phonetics, 25*(4), 321-334. doi:10.3109/02699206.2010.535647.

Chapman, R. S. (1997). Language development in children and adolescents with Down syndrome. *Mental Retardation and Developmental Disabilities Research Reviews, 3*(4), 307-312.

Clifford, S., Dissanayake, C., Bui, Q. M., Huggins, R., Taylor, A. K, &. Loesch, D. Z. (2007). Autism spectrum phenotype in males and females with fragile X full mutation and premutation. *Journal of Autism and Developmental Disorders, 37*, 738–747.

Coppens-Hofman, M. C., Terband, H. R., Maassen, B. A., van Schrojenstein Lantman-De Valk, H. M., van Zaalen-op't Hof, Y., & Snik, A. F. (2013). Dysfluencies in the speech of adults with intellectual disabilities and reported speech difficulties. *Journal of Communication Disorders, 46*(5-6), 484-494. doi:10.1016/j.jcomdis.2013.08.001

Defloor, T., Van Borsel, J., & Curfs, L. (2002). Articulation in Prader-Willi syndrome. *Journal of Communication Disorders, 35*(3), 261-282.

Dodd, B., & Thompson, L. (2001). Speech disorder in children with Down's syndrome. *Journal of Intellectual Disability Research, 45*(4), 308-316. Retrieved from https://auth.lib.unc.edu/ezproxy_auth.php?url=http://search.ebscohost.com/login.aspx?direct=true&db=psyh&AN=2001-18208-004&site=ehost-live&scope=site

Domelloff, E., Johansson, A.-M., Farooqi, A., Momelloff, M., & Ronnqvist, L, (2013), Relations among upper-limb movements and cognitive function at school age in children born preterm. *Journal of Developmental and Behavioral Pediatrics, 34*(5), 344-352.

Estigarribia, B., Martin, G. E., & Roberts, J. E. (2012). Cognitive, environmental, and linguistic predictors of syntax in fragile X syndrome and Down syndrome. *Journal of Speech, Language, and Hearing Research, 55* (6), 1600-1612.

Estigarribia, B. Martin, G. E., Roberts, J. E., Spencer, A., Gucwa, A., & Sideris, J. (2011). Narrative skill in boys with fragile X syndrome with and without autism spectrum disorder. *Applied Psycholinguistics, 32*, 359–388.

Finestack, L. H., Richmond, E. K., & Abbeduto, L. (2009). Language development in individuals with fragile X syndrome. *Topics in Language Disorders, 29*, 133-148.

Greaves-Lord, K., Eussen, M. L. J. M., Verhulst, F. C., Minderaa, R. B., Mandy, W., Hudziak, J. J., … Hartman, C. A. (2013). Empirically based phenotypic profiles of children with pervasive developmental disorders: Interpretation in the light of the DSM-5. *Journal of Autism and Developmental Disorders, 43*, 1784-1797.

Hagerman, R. J. (2002). The physical and behavioral phenotype. In R. J. Hagerman & P. J. Hagerman (Eds.), *Fragile X syndrome: Diagnosis, treatment, and research* (pp. 3-109). Baltimore, MD: Johns Hopkins University Press.

Hall, S. S., Lightbody, A. A., Hirt, M., Rezvani, A., & Reiss, A. L. (2010). Autism in fragile X syndrome: A category mistake? *Journal of the American Academy of Child and Adolescent Psychiatry, 49,* 921–933.

Harasym, J., & Langevin, M. (2012). Stuttering treatment for a school-age child with Down syndrome: A descriptive case report. *Journal of Fluency Disorders, 37*(4), 253-262. doi:http://dx.doi.org.libproxy.lib.unc.edu/10.1016/j.jfludis.2012.05.002.

Hill, P. R., Hogben, J. H., & Bishop, D. V. M. (2005). Auditory frequency discrimination in children with specific language impairment: A longitudinal study. *Journal of Speech, Language, and Hearing Research, 48,* 1136–46.

ICD (2011). *International statistical classification of diseases and related health problems.* Geneva, Switzerland: World Health Organization.

John, A. E., & Mervis, C. B. (2010). Comprehension of communicative intent behind pointing and gazing gestures by young children with Williams syndrome or Down syndrome. *Journal of Speech, Language, and Hearing Research, 53,* 950-960.

Kang, C., & Drayna, D. (2011). Genetics of speech and language disorders. *Journal of Neurodevelopmental Disorders, 12,* 145-164.

Kent, R. D., & Vorperian, H. K. (2013). Speech impairment in Down syndrome: A review. *Journal of Speech, Language, and Hearing Research: 56*(1), 178-210. doi:10.1044/1092-4388(2012/12-0148).

Kim, Y. S., Fombonne, E., Koh, Y.-J., Kim, S.-J., Cheon, K.-A., & Leventhal, B. L. (2014). A comparison of *DSM-IV* pervasive developmental disorder and *DSM-5* autism spectrum disorder prevalence in an epidemiologic sample. *Journal of the American Academy of Child and Adolescent Psychiatry, 43,* 500-508.

Kleppe, S. A., Katayama, K. M., Shipley, K. G., & Foushee, D. R. (1990). The speech and language characteristics of children with Prader-Willi syndrome. *The Journal of Speech and Hearing Disorders, 55*(2), 300-309.

Klusek, J., Martin, G. E., & Losh, M. (2014). A comparison of pragmatic language in boys with autism and fragile X syndrome. *Journal of Speech, Language, and Hearing Research,* 1-16. 10.1044/2014_JSLHR-L-13-0064.

Kover, S., & Abbeduto, L. (2010). Expressive language in males with fragile X syndrome with and without comorbid autism. *Journal of Intellectual Disability Research, 54(3),* 246–265. doi: 10.1111/j.1365-2788.2010.01255.x.

Kristoffersen, K. E. (2008). Speech and language development in cri du chat syndrome: A critical review. *Clinical Linguistics & Phonetics, 22*(6), 443-457. doi:10.1080/02699200801892108.

Laws, G., & Bishop, D. V. M. (2004). Pragmatic language impairment and social deficits in Williams syndrome: A comparison with Down's syndrome and specific language impairment. *International Journal of Language and Communication Disorders, 39,* 45-64.

Lenhoff, H. M., Wang, P. P., Greenberg, F., & Bellugi, U. (1997). Williams syndrome and the brain. *Scientific American, 277,* 68–73.

Leonard, L.B. (1998). *Children with Specific Language Impairment.* Cambridge, MA: MIT Press.

Lewis, P., Abbeduto, L., Murphy, M., Giles, N., Bruo, S., Schroeder, S., … Orsmond, G. (2006). Psychological well-being of mothers of youth with fragile X syndrome: Syndrome specificity and within-syndrome variability. *Journal of Intellectual Disability Research, 50*(12), 894-904.

Loesch, D. Z., Huggins, R. M., Bui, Q. M., Epstein, J. L., Taylor, A. K., & Hagerman, R. J. (2002). Effect of the deficits of fragile X mental retardation protein on cognitive status of fragile X males and females assessed by robust pedigree analysis. *Journal of Developmental and Behavioral Pediatrics, 23*(6), 416-423.

Mahler, L. A., & Jones, H. N. (2012). Intensive treatment of dysarthria in two adults with Down syndrome. *Developmental Neurorehabilitation, 15*(1), 44-53. doi:10.3109/17518423.2011.632784.

Majerus, S., Poncelet, M., Berault, A., Audrey, S., Zesiger, P., Sernicle, W., & Barinsinkov, K. (2010). Evidence for atypical categorical speech perception in Williams syndrome. *Journal of Neurolinguistics, 24*, 249-267.

Martin, G. E., Losh, M., Estigarribia, B., Sideris, J., & Roberts, J. (2013). Longitudinal profiles of expressive vocabulary, syntax and pragmatic language in boys with fragile X syndrome or Down syndrome. *International Journal of Language and Communication Disorders, 43*, 432-443.

Martin, G. E., Losh, M., Estigarribia, B., Sideris, J., & Roberts, J. (2013). Longitudinal profiles of expressive vocabulary, syntax, and pragmatic language in boys with fragile X syndrome or Down syndrome. *International Journal of Language and Communication Disorders, 48(4)*, 432–443. doi: 10.1111/1460-6984.12019.

McArthur G. M., & Bishop D. V. M. (2004). Which people with specific language impairment have auditory processing deficits? *Cognitive Neuropsychology, 21*, 79–94.

McLean, L. K., Brady, N. C., & McLean, J. E. (1996). Reported communication abilities of individuals with severe mental retardation. *American Journal on Mental Retardation, 100*(6), 580-591.

Mervis, C. B., & Becerra, A. M. (2007). Language and communicative development in Williams syndrome. *Mental Retardation and Developmental Disabilities Research Reviews, 13*, 3-15.

Mervis, C. B., & Velleman, S. L. (2011). Children with Williams syndrome: Language, cognitive, and behavioral characteristics and their implications for intervention. *Perspectives on Language Learning and Education, 18*(3), 98-107.

Naessm K. B., Halaas Lysterm, S. A., Hulme, C., & Melby-Lervag, M. (2011). Language and verbal short-term memory skills in children with Down syndrome: A meta-analytic review. *Research in Developmental Disabilities, 32*, 2225-2234.

Norbury C. F., & Bishop, D. V. M. (2002). Inferential processing and story recall in children with communication problems: A comparison of specific language impairment, pragmatic language impairment and high functioning autism. *International Journal of Language and Communication Disorders, 37*, 227–51.

Oakes, A., Kover, S., & Abbeduto, L. (2013). Language comprehension profiles of young adolescents with fragile X syndrome. *American Journal of Speech Language Pathology, 22(4)*, 615-26. doi: 10.1044/1058-0360(2013/12-0109).

Paul, R., & Norbury, C. (2012). *Language Disorders from infancy through adolescence: Listening, speaking, reading, writing, and communicating* (4th Ed.). St. Louis, Mo.: Elsevier.

Polisenska, K., & Kapalkova, S. (2014). Language profiles in children with Down syndrome and children with language impairment: Implications for early intervention. *Research in Developmental Disabilities, 35* (2), 373-382.

Price, J. R., Roberts, J. E., Hennon, E., Berni, M., Anderson, K., & Sideris, J. (2008). Syntactic complexity during conversation of boys with fragile X syndrome and Down syndrome. *Journal of Speech, Language, and Hearing Research, 51*, 3-15.

Price, J. R., Roberts, J. E., Vandergrift, N., & Martin, G. E. (2007). Language comprehension in boys with fragile X syndrome and boys with Down syndrome. *Journal of Intellectual Disability Research, 51*, 3-15.

Rapin, I. (1996). Historical data. In I. Rapin (Ed.), *Preschool children with inadequate communication: Developmental language disorder, autism, low IQ. Clinics in Developmental Medicine No. 139* (pp. 57–97). London: Mac Keith Press.

Reiss, A. L., & Dant, C. C. (2003). The behavioral neurogenetics of fragile X syndrome: Analyzing gene-brain-behavior relationships in child developmental psychopathologies. *Development and Psychopathology, 15*(4), 927-968.

Roberts, J., Long, S. H., Malkin, C., Barnes, E., Skinner, M., Hennon, E. A., & Anderson, K.

(2005). A comparison of phonological skills of boys with fragile X syndrome and Down syndrome. *Journal of Speech, Language, and Hearing Research, 48*(5), 980-995. doi:10.1044/1092-4388(2005/067).

Roberts, J. E., Hennon, E., Price, J., Dear, E., Anderson, K., & Vandergrift, N. (2007). Expressive language during conversational speech in boys with fragile X syndrome. *American Journal of Mental Retardation, 112*, 1–17.

Roberts, J. E., Martin, G. E., Moskowitz, L., Harris, A. A., Foreman, J., & Nelson, L. (2007). Discourse skills of boys with fragile X syndrome in comparison to boys with Down syndrome. *Journal of Speech, Language, and Hearing Research, 50*, 475-492.

Roberts, J. E., Price, J., Barnes, E., Nelson, L., Burchinal, M., Hennon, E., ... Hooper, S. R. (2007). Receptive vocabulary, expressive vocabulary, and speech production of boys with fragile X syndrome in comparison to boys with Down syndrome. *American Journal of Mental Retardation, 112*, 177-193.

Roberts, J. E., Price, J. R., & Malkin, C. (2007). Language and communication development in Down syndrome. *Mental Retardation and Developmental Disabilities Research Reviews, 13*, 26-35.

Siegel-Causey, E., & Bashinski, S. M. (1997). Enhancing initial communication and responsiveness of learners with multiple disabilities: A tri-focus framework for partners. *Focus on Autism and Other Developmental Disabilities, 12*, 105–120.

Siegel, E., & Cress, C. (2002). Overview of the emergence of early AAC behaviors. In J. Reichle, D. R. Beukelman, & J. C. Light (Eds.), *Exemplary practices for beginning communicators* (pp. 25-57). Baltimore: Paul H. Brookes.

Stansfield, J. (1990). Prevalence of stuttering and cluttering in adults with mental handicaps. *Journal of Mental Deficiency Research, 34* (Pt. 4), 287-307.

Stoel-Gammon, C. (2001). Down syndrome phonology: Developmental patterns and intervention strategies. *Down Syndrome Research and Practice, 7* (3), 93-100.

Sudhalter, V., Scarborough, H. S., & Cohen, I. L. (1991). Syntactic delay and pragmatic deviance in the language of fragile X males. *American Journal of Medical Genetics, 38*, 493-497.

Tallal, P. (2000). Experimental studies of language learning impairments: From research to remediation. In D. V. M. Bishop & L. B. Leonard (Eds.), *Specific language impairments in children: Causes, characteristics, intervention and outcome* (pp. 131-156). Hove, East Sussex: Psychology Press.

van Batenberg, T., Henrichs, J., Schenk, J., Sincer, I., deGroot, L., Hoffman, A., Jaddoe, V., Verhurst, F.C., ... Tiemeier, H. (2013). Early infant neuromotor assessment is associated with language and nonverbal function in toddlers: The generation R study. *Journal of Developmental and Behavioral Pediatrics, 34* (5), 326-334

Van Borsel, J. (1996). Articulation in Down's syndrome adolescents and adults. *European Journal of Disorders of Communication: The Journal of the College of Speech and Language Therapists, London, 31* (4), 415-444.

Van Borsel, J., & Tetnowski, J. A. (2007). Fluency disorders in genetic syndromes. *Journal of Fluency Disorders, 32* (4), 279-296. doi:S0094-730X(07)00041-1.

Van Borsel, J., & Vandermeulen, A. (2008). Cluttering in Down syndrome. *Folia Phoniatrica Et Logopaedica: Official Organ of the International Association of Logopedics and Phoniatrics (IALP), 60* (6), 312-317. doi:10.1159/000170081.

Whitehouse, A. J. O., Watt, H. J., Line, E. A., & Bishop, D. V. M. (2009). Adult psychosocial outcomes of children with specific language impairment, pragmatic language impairment and autism. *International Journal of Language and Communication Disorders, 44*, 511-528.

Wilson, C. E., Gillan, N., Spain, D., Robertson, D., Roberts, G., Murphy, C. M., ... Murphy, D. G. M. (2013). Comparison of *ICD-10R, DSM-IV-TR*, and *DSM-5* in an adult autism spectrum disorder diagnostic clinic. *Journal of*

Autism and Developmental Disorders, 43, 2515-2525.

Yairi, E. (2005). Research on incidence and prevalence of stuttering. Retrieved from http://www.stutteringhelp.org/research-incidence-and-prevalence-stuttering

Zajac, D. J., Harris, A. A., Roberts, J. E., & Martin, G. E. (2009). Direct magnitude estimation of articulation rate in boys with fragile X syndrome. *Journal of Speech, Language, and Hearing Research, 52* (5), 1370-1379. doi:10.1044/1092-4388(2009/07-0208).

Additional Readings

Booth, J. R. (2007). Brain bases of learning and language development. In D. Coch, K. W. Fischer, & G. Dawson (Eds.), *Human behavior, learning and the developing brain* (pp. 279-300). New York: Guilford Press.

Mills, D., & Conboy, B. T., (2009). Early communicative development and the social brain. In M. DeHaan & M. R. Gunnar (Eds.), *Handbook of developmental social neuroscience* (pp. 175-206). New York: Guilford Press.

Mills, D. L., & Sheehan, E. A. (2007). Experience and developmental changes in the organization of language-relevant brain activity. In D. Coch, K. W. Fischer, & G. Dawson (Eds.), *Human behavior, learning and the developing brain* (pp. 183-218). New York: Guilford Press.

Myowa-Yamakoshi, M., & Tomonaga, M. (2009). Evolutionary origins of social communication. In M. DeHaan, & M. R. Gunnar (Eds.), *Handbook of developmental social neuroscience* (pp. 207-224). New York: Guilford Press.

Peltopuro, M., Ahonen, T., Kaartinen, J., Seppala, H., & Narhi V. (2014). Borderline intellectual functioning: A systematic literature review. *Intellectual and Developmental Disabilities, 52* (6), 419-469.

Snowling, M. J., & Hayiou, T. L. (2010). Specific language impairment. In K. O. Yeates, M. D. Ris, H. G. Taylor, & B. F. Pennington (Eds.), *Pediatric neuropsychology: Research theory and practice* (pp. 363-392). New York: Guilford Press.

CHAPTER 6

Autism Spectrum Disorders

Terrence C. Bethea
Jean A. Frazier
E. Richard Blumberg
Marco O. Bertelli
Andrew C. Stanfield
Lauren R. Charlot

Research in the field of autism spectrum disorders has progressed tremendously in the past three decades. The diagnostic criteria for these disorders in the *DSM-IV-TR* were among the few developed with explicit consideration of individuals with intellectual disabilities. However, a great deal of controversy has arisen around the merging of autistic disorder, Asperger disorder, childhood disintegrative disorder, and pervasive developmental disorder not otherwise specified into a single diagnostic entity in the *DSM-5* (Hazen, McDougle, & Volkmar, 2013; Tsai & Ghazuiddin 2014). Patients, clinicians, and other stakeholders are concerned the new criteria may obscure true differences. The most prominent objection is a loss of diagnostic sensitivity to the extent that individuals lose the diagnosis and corresponding services.

The primary impetus for this change was a purported lack of validity for Asperger disorder and PDD NOS as diagnostically distinct entities. Evidence included the lack of clinical or pathophysiological data that consistently distinguished the various autism spectrum disorders (Lord et al., 2012). The defining characteristics most commonly associated with a change in diagnosis between DSM-IV-TR and DSM-5 are previous diagnosis of Asperger, previous diagnosis of PDD NOS, or IQ > 70 (McPartland, Reichow, & Volkmar, 2012; Sturmey & Dalfern 2014). Using relaxed DSM-5 criteria (typically 2 of 3 items in social communication/interaction domain) significantly improves the DSM-5's sensitivity for PDD NOS and Asperger disorder (Frazier et al., 2012). Yet in a clinical sample of youth's with DSM-IV-TR autistic disorder or PDD NOS, 1 in 6 were excluded from DSM-5 autism spectrum disorder using multiple permutations of 'relaxed' criteria (Taheri & Perry 2012). Maintaining a DSM-5 diagnosis of autism spectrum disorder appears largely a function of severity of core symptoms and presence of intellectual disability.

Research does suggest a host of genetic syndromes are associated with a subset of individuals with moderate to severe autism spectrum disorder symptoms (Rutter & Thapar, 2014). There is less clarity with regards to predisposing factors for milder autism spectrum disorder presentations. The former may be a tremendous problem given it further highlights the genetic heterogeneity that confounds the clinical diagnosis and treatment of autism spectrum disorder in individuals with intellectual disability. The latter is a relatively less significant issue given that not all individuals with milder autism spectrum disorder symptoms have intellectual disability and accordingly are beyond the scope of the *DM-ID-2*. While the *DSM-5* no longer includes the historical nomenclature, the American Psychiatric

Association explicitly allows the continued use of terms such as Asperger, PDD NOS, etc for individuals that meet prior diagnostic criteria. To maintain concordance with the *DSM-5*, this volume will transition from pervasive developmental disorder (PDD) and subsequently utilize the term autism spectrum disorder to capture the presumptive unitary nature. But we caution clinicians to be aware the International Statistical Classification of Disease (ICD-10) retains the historical terms, although this may change with the release of ICD-11.

Review of Diagnostic Criteria

Autism spectrum disorder has arguably been a diagnostic challenge from conception in part because the diagnosis captures a fairly common developmental presentation – social and communication deficits.

Since Kanner first characterized the syndrome in 1943, the concept of "early infantile autism" has become much better understood (Kanner, 1943) or more complicated. Into the 1970s, autistic disorder was thought to be the prepubescent manifestation of what would become schizophrenia in late adolescence and early adulthood. Clinicians such as Michael Rutter helped lead the field out of the wilderness by highlighting the clear distinctions between autism and other severe, chronic conditions with onset in the first two decades (Rutter, 1972). Autism spectrum disorder is now recognized as phenotypically distinct from other neuropsychiatric disorders. Yet as with schizophrenia, autism spectrum disorder presentation can be idiosyncratic or confounded by the presence of multiple comorbidities. The core features of autism spectrum disorder are impairment in social interaction and social communication (Criterion A) along with the presence of repetitive or stereotyped behaviors (Criterion B). One of the notable changes with the *DSM-5* is that impaired language development per se is no longer a core diagnostic criterion. Individuals must merely exhibit deficits in utilizing language (verbal, nonverbal) in a socially communicative manner.

Historically, symptoms of autism spectrum disorder tended to occur by toddler age with diagnosis lagging for several years until youths were entering school. But over two decades, clinicians, teachers, allied health professionals, and informed/attentive parents have begun to identify deficits much earlier, including some present by the first birthday (DeGiacomo & Fombonne, 1998; Jones et al., 2016). Early identification of social, communication and neuromotor anomalies (fine/gross motor milestones) may be critical given the success of behavioral (and possibly pharmacologic) interventions may be predicated on initiating treatment during early critical periods of development.

Summary of DSM-5 Criteria

The *DSM-5* criteria for autism spectrum disorder requires individuals to present with persistent deficits in social interaction/communication and at least two symptoms indicative of restricted, repetitive patterns of behavior, interests, or activities. Both of these domains now carry severity specifiers: Level 1 "requiring support," Level 2 "requiring substantial support," and Level 3 "requiring very substantial support." Additional specifiers include assessment of intellectual impairment, language impairment, associated somatic medical conditions, associated neurodevelopmental disorders, associated behavioral disorders, and the presence of catatonia. Symptoms must be present in early development but the *DSM-5* acknowledges that symptoms may not be fully evident in low social stress environments and may be masked or partially compensated (Criterion C).

Methodology

The literature review involved two phases. Fundamentally, the *DM-ID-2* is a companion to the *DSM-5*. An expert panel examined recently published review papers covering autism spectrum disorders as presented in the *DSM-5*. Reviews were supplemented with a manual search of high-quality journals that routinely publish research in the field of autism spectrum disorder—for example, the *Journal of the American Academy of Child and Adolescent Psychiatry*, *Journal of Autism and Developmental Disorders*, the *Journal of Child Psychology and Psychiatry*, and *Autism*. Publications from the years 1943–2016 were included.

Issues Related to Diagnosis in People with ID

The majority of the *DSM-5* criteria are behavioral descriptors well suited to individuals with impairments in social interaction and language. But some degree of impairment in these domains is fairly common in individuals with intellectual disability. Unfortunately, there's significant evidence to suggest common assessments of intelligence underestimate the cognitive abilities of individuals with autism spectrum disorder (Nader, Corchesne, Dawson, & Soulieres, 2016). To address this issue, the *DSM-5* recognizes intellectual disability as a highly comorbid condition. The *DSM-5* requires that social communication deficits exceed what would be predicted by their developmental/cognitive level (Criterion E).

Arguably, the single most confounding issue with regards to autism spectrum disorder diagnosis is how to assess intellectual disability in this population. The fundamental problem is that no one has clearly identified an assessment (or battery of assessments) that produce reliable and valid determinations of IQ in individuals with an autism spectrum disorder. Given that even nonverbal IQ scores correlate highly with language skills, it is possible, if not likely, that studies that purport to detail specific issues in the autism spectrum disorder and ID population include many individuals that perform poorly on IQ assessments but do not have strictly-defined ID.

In the context of the *DSM-5*, this may be an academic issue given that ID is not a diagnostic feature but a comorbidity. But from a clinical perspective, particularly in pediatric populations, it is important that assessments of autism spectrum disorder account for the true level of intellectual disability (if present) and that interventions are properly tailored to the abilities of the individual.

The reliable evaluation of intellectual disability in children and adults with autism spectrum disorder presents a challenge for clinicians. In this population, standardized instruments may be used to measure intellectual functioning in some individuals with mild to moderate ID, while measures of adaptive behavior may enable clinicians to assess the ability of individuals to meet environmental demands in persons with severe to profound ID. The Stanford Binet Intelligence Scale 5th Edition (SB5) may be used to measure verbal and non-verbal intellectual abilities in persons 2 years-old to adult. The Weschler Pre-School and Primary School of Intelligence (WPPSI) may be used to measure the cognitive development of children ages 2.6 to 7.7 years. This assessment includes items that may enable clinicians to assess the intellectual functioning of adults with moderate – profound intellectual disability. Presentations of milder intellectual disability, borderline intellectual functioning, or individuals that may have isolated strengths should be evaluated with standard tools such as the previously mentioned SB5 or the age-appropriate Weschler scale (WPPSI (mentioned above), Weschler Intelligence Scale for Children, Weschler Adult Intelligence Scale).

An evaluation of ID should include reliable, standardized measures of adaptive behavior, regardless of the presumed intellectual functioning of the person. The Adaptive Behavior Assessment System 3rd Edition (ABAS3) provides a comprehensive assessment of adaptive skills across the lifespan. The ABAS3 is a behavior rating scale that may be completed by parents, caregivers, and educators. It yields an assessment of adaptive skills needed for independent self-care, social interaction and the ability to meet the environmental demands of home, school, and work. The Supports Intensity Scale (SIS) provides a comprehensive assessment of a person's support needs in personal, work-related, and social activities in order to identify and describe the types and intensity of the supports an individual requires. The SIS provides information that may be used to supplement measures of adaptive behavior.

There is a growing abundance of research findings and new concepts being applied to individuals who do not meet the full criteria for autism spectrum disorder. Studies suggest a collection of personality/behavioral traits in family members of individuals with autism spectrum disorder, such as social affiliation, sensitivity to social reward, planning and cognitive inflexibility, and mild abnormalities in motor behaviors such as eye gaze, facial scanning recognition, and motor imitation ability. These autistic-like symptoms have been called the broader autistic phenotype (Piven, Palmer, Jacobi, Childress, & Arndt, 1997). Posserud, Lundervold, and Gillberg (2006) found a continuous distribution of autistic symptoms along a spectrum in a population of 7 to 9 year-old children with 2.7% of children having high scores on a symptom checklist for autistic symptoms. It is an open question as to whether there will be agreement on where 'neurotypical' ends and the autism spectrum begins. The *DSM-5* does capture a possible intermediate phenomenon; social communication disorder. Social communications disorder includes individuals with impairment in social communication but do not have sufficient symptoms to meet criteria for autism spectrum disorder. The primary distinguishing feature between social communications disorder and full criteria autism spectrum disorder is that individuals with social communications disorder do not have at least two symptoms consistent with restrictive/repetitive behaviors.

Psychiatric and Other Comorbidities in Autism Spectrum Disorder

Despite an explosion of research in the field of autism, participants in many investigations did not have ID (usually having either "high functioning autism" or Asperger syndrome; Sverd, 2003). Much of the research in autism has been aimed at elucidating pathways to the disorder or interventions aimed at core features and skill building (especially in the form of intensive early intervention). Many fewer investigations addressed the specific area of psychiatric comorbidity of people with ID and autism spectrum disorder. A number of articles provide a good overview of intervention models for the treatment of youth with autism spectrum disorder who have challenging behaviors, with most recognizing applied behavioral analysis (ABA) as having the greatest evidence base (for review see Smith & Iadarola, 2015).

Multiple studies have suggested that attention deficit/hyperactivity disorder, mood disorders, and anxiety disorders are the most common comorbidities, while first-degree relatives show a pattern of elevated risk for mood syndromes (Lainhart & Folstein, 1994; Leyfer et al., 2006). Leyfer and colleagues (2006) performed in-depth individual assessments on 109 youth with autism spectrum disorder (ages 5–17) and found phobias to be the most common comorbidity. Levy and colleagues (2010) studied a large cohort of 8-year-old children with autism spectrum disorder in a multisite investigation of psychiatric and medical comorbidity. Psychiatric disorders were documented in 10% of the sample and 16% had a neurological disorder. They noted that comorbid psychiatric, neurologic, and medical diagnoses may delay identification of autism spectrum disorder.

Only a few investigations have examined rates of psychiatric disorders in individuals with autism spectrum disorder in larger population-based studies, and the majority of these focused on children. Often, with population-based studies, recorded diagnoses are used and the youth were not directly assessed. Rosenberg, Kaufmann, Law, and Law (2011) used a national registry to review the community diagnosis of psychiatric comorbidity in 4,343 children with autism spectrum disorder. Lifetime prevalence of psychiatric disorder by age 16 in youth with autism spectrum disorder was determined to be 49% in contrast to reported rates for the general population of 37%. Having a diagnosis of Asperger syndrome or pervasive developmental disorder not otherwise specified (PDD NOS) conferred greater risk of receiving a psychiatric disorder diagnosis relative to autistic disorder.

Even fewer studies address rates of disorder in adults with autism spectrum disorder. Joshi and colleagues (2013) studied a population of clinically referred adults and also reported high rates of depression and anxiety. The most comprehensive population-based study that included some direct examination of adults with ID and autism spectrum disorder was conducted by Melville et al. (2008). Individuals in this study included over 1,000 adults with ID, 77 of whom were also diagnosed with an autism spectrum disorder. Individuals with autism spectrum disorder had a higher rate of problem behaviors than the global group with ID alone. But when individually matched with controls, people with autism spectrum disorder had similar incidence and prevalence of problem behaviors and mental health issues in general. Anxiety and affective disorders were the most frequently reported disorders. Adults with autism spectrum disorder were less likely to have recovered from mental ill health at 2-year follow-up.

A number of studies have noted higher rates of internalizing disorders among subjects with autism spectrum disorder who have either less ID or no ID when compared with individuals who have more significant cognitive challenges. Diagnoses that involve descriptions of internalizing symptoms may simply be easier to identify or may have developmentally driven variability in terms of observable or "surface features." Specifically, youth and adults with more significant developmental challenges may present more like younger children and display non-specific signs of irritability and aggression when distressed from problems such as anxiety or depression. Associated agitation and challenges to affect regulation may be viewed as evidence of bipolar disorder. Of note, studies using direct patient assessment with semi-structured interview tools reveal lower rates of psychosis and bipolar disorder and higher rates of anxiety and depression. LoVullo and Matson (2009), for example, assessed psychiatric disorders using an informant-based psychopathology tool in institutionalized adults diagnosed with autism spectrum disorder, most of whom had severe or profound ID. They reported high rates of bipolar disorder and very low rates of anxiety disorders and attention deficit/hyperactivity disorder in contrast to most other investigations reporting rates of specific psychiatric comorbidity.

Charlot and colleagues from the UMass EK Shriver Center examined psychiatric inpatients with ID with and without ASD who were diagnosed with depression. There were few differences between the inpatients with the exception that individuals with ASD had overall more symptoms of anxiety and depression (Charlot et al., 2008). Ghaziuddin and Zafar (2008) found depression and anxiety to be the most common psychiatric disorders in a clinical sample of adult outpatients with autism spectrum disorder and less attention deficit/hyperactivity disorder than generally found in studies of youth. These authors and others suggested clinicians should be cautioned that phenomenology may be affected by developmental considerations, especially expressive communication. In very young children, anxiety may be manifested by tantrums, freezing, rapid speech, and other atypical features. Individuals with autism spectrum disorder and ID may engage in anxiety-based aggression ("fight or flight"), which may be missed because of a lack of self-report of internalizing symptoms. White and colleagues (2009) emphasized that "assessment of anxiety disorders in autism spectrum disorder should be conducted using multiple informants and modalities, as children with autism spectrum disorder often do not display age typical symptoms of anxiety." Also, when agitated behavior is accompanied by poor sleep, psychomotor agitation, and aggression, there may be a tendency to overdiagnose conditions such as bipolar disorder (Charlot et al., 2008). In general, individuals with less cognitive impairment may receive certain diagnoses more because of the classification systems we employ, which relies heavily on self-report of internal states to make a diagnosis. Use of behavioral descriptions of the possible manifestations of mood symptoms when interviewing informants, and use of multiple sources for informant-based reports as well as direct observations, may increase information regarding "internalizing" symptoms.

Psychosis has been studied less frequently in people with ID but has been addressed in limited numbers of investigations with participants with autism spectrum disorder. Starling and Dossetor (2009) reviewed literature and described the difficulties inherent in differential diagnosis of psychotic disorders in individuals with autism spectrum disorder. They noted that the two disorders share many similar characteristics including perceptual abnormalities, thought disorder, catatonia, and deficiencies in reality testing. In an international investigation, van der Gaag, Caplan, van Engeland, Loman, and Buitelaar (2005) examined multiple clinical groups and found that developmental effects and verbal abilities had a significant effect on the detection and differentiation of psychotic symptoms. In these investigations, the effects of cognitive impairment and communication challenges were discussed as critical factors that may create significant diagnostic challenges when clinicians must try to differentiate developmentally driven errors in thought processes from true psychotic ideations.

As noted by Allen et al. (2001), yet another lingering question for future research is whether or not individuals with autism spectrum disorder experience separate and distinct comorbid psychiatric "syndromes" in most cases, or rather, if the clinical presentations in question are the result of shared neurological pathways and other causal mechanisms. Accurate diagnostic classification is challenging when evaluating people with cognitive challenges and is further complicated when assessing children or adults with autism spectrum disorder (with and without ID). There may be a disconnect between research regarding psychiatric comorbidities and what occurs in practice. Data from numerous surveys suggest that both people with ID and people with ID and autism spectrum disorder are increasingly treated with antipsychotic medications, regardless of diagnosis (Park et al., 2016). "Mislabeling" and confusion about the complex roots of aggressive and disruptive behaviors and affect dysregulation in patients (young and old) with autism spectrum disorder may be the most significant cause of the overuse of antipsychotic medications and of the high rate of polypharmacy in general. Mazefsky et al. (2012) found a high rate of discordance between carefully and comprehensively assessed diagnoses of autism spectrum disorder and psychiatric comorbidity and the diagnoses that the youth studied had been given. In general, these authors found evidence of teens being labeled with what appeared to be inaccurate diagnoses, numerous different diagnoses, and, probably, not the most effective treatments based on these. The "disconnect" was most pronounced unsurprisingly for youth who had some of the most negative outcomes: multiple inpatient psychiatric hospitalizations. Among this subset of the sample, most had not been diagnosed with autism spectrum disorder (with clear evidence of the syndrome). Rather they carried an oppositional defiant disorder diagnosis for which the evidence was not present.

While this is certainly a challenging population with a high rate of aggressive and disruptive behaviors, it's possible that outpatient interventions could have been more successful if their concerns had been conceptualized within the framework of their autism spectrum disorder.

Efforts to distinguish between clinical features that are representative of core aspects of autism spectrum disorder versus those suggestive of a comorbid psychiatric syndrome have been systematically attempted, using a modified version of the Kiddie-Schedule for Affective Disorders and Schizophrenia (K-SADS). Leyfer and colleagues at the University of Utah assessed rates of psychiatric disorders in samples of youth with ASD (Kaufman et al., 1997; Leyfer et al., 2006). Mazefsky et al. 2012 more recently reported on use of the modified K-SADS, that they have called the Autism Comorbidity Interview (ACI; Lainhart, Leyfer, & Folstein, 2003; Leyfer et al., 2006). The tool was developed to address concerns related to misidentifying exaggerated core features of autism spectrum disorder as symptomatic of psychiatric illness or the reverse error of labeling other psychiatric disorders as features of autism spectrum disorder.

In a similar effort to improve the accuracy of symptom identification as it contributes to a diagnosis, Charlot and colleagues from the University of Massachusetts Medical School and the EK Shriver Center published an initial validation study introducing the Mood and Anxiety Symptom Survey (MASS), (Charlot, et al., 2007). The MASS is a semi-structured interview tool in which informants report on symptoms of mood and anxiety disorders covering *DSM-TR-IV* and *DM-ID* symptom criteria. For each symptom criteria, multiple behavioral anchors are provided, including a variety of descriptions of what a person with ID might do or say if experiencing the symptom. The anchors were drawn from prior research and clinical experience of the authors. However, follow-up work or further validation of the tool has yet to be published. The methodology of providing multiple behavioral descriptions for each symptom criteria was intended to decrease problems with interpretations of terms such as "anxiety" or "depressed mood" that are rated by untrained informants in many screening tools. Unpublished data have demonstrated a moderate to high degree of convergence between diagnoses suggested by the MASS interview and those based on administration of a modified K-SADS (ACI) in a sample of adolescents with ID (restricted to anxiety and mood disorder categories).

In some investigations, it has been noted that people with ID (with and without autism spectrum disorder) may be more likely to be diagnosed with psychotic disorders when assessed by clinicians with limited training in the field. Lunsky and Bradley (2007) discussed the problem of using data from non-specialists in IDD when describing psychiatric disorders. Specifically, non-specialist evaluators reported significantly lower rates of psychotic disorders and higher rates of mood and anxiety disorders compared to the more rigorous assessments by specialists. For example, 62% of patients were given a diagnosis of a psychotic disorder by non-specialist in comparison with 26% of patients seen by clinicians with a specialization in assessment of people with IDD.

The role of contextual and psychosocial factors on the occurrence and persistence of psychopathology in youth and adults with autism spectrum disorder and ID has received little attention. Longitudinal designs may be the most critical to reveal the power of such influences, and expand our understanding of complex developmental trajectories for comorbid emotional and behavioral challenges. Simonoff and colleagues (2013) examined psychiatric symptoms using the SDQ (Strengths and Difficulties Questionnaire) and examined the stability of child, family, and other risk factors for psychopathology in a sample of 81 youth diagnosed with an autism spectrum disorder at ages 12 and 16. Lower IQ and adaptive functioning predicted higher hyperactivity and total difficulties scores. Greater emotional problems at 16 were predicted by poorer maternal mental health, family-based deprivation, and lower social class.

Nylander and colleagues (2013) examined attention deficit/hyperactivity disorder and autism spectrum disorder in a sample of adults and contrasted rates and nature of psychiatric comorbidity and psychosocial functioning for the two groups. Lifetime rates for psychiatric disorders was greater for adults with autism spectrum disorder as compared with patients without autism spectrum disorder, with major depression and "multiple anxiety disorders" being the most frequent diagnoses identified. They also noted that adults with autism spectrum disorder overall were "functionally more impaired."

Other Comorbidities

The fact that individuals with ID and autism spectrum disorder have high rates of comorbid medical problems has been established in multiple studies. Geier, Kern and Geier (2012) conducted a prospective, cross-sectional review of the health and challenging behaviors of individuals with autism spectrum disorder and found high rates of multiple problems. Among the most common were gastrointestinal problems 48%, incontinence 57%, sleep problems 57%, lethargy 26%, anxiety 74%, eating disorders 94%, and behavioral challenges 89%.

Application of Diagnostic Criteria to People with ID

Early diagnosis of autism spectrum disorder is critical to the timely initiation of evidence based practices associated with positive child outcomes. A greater awareness of autism spectrum disorder among parents and pediatricians has improved early identification. Many parents notice problems within 12-18 months after birth (Filipek, Accardo, & Ashwal, 2000). Language delays are a frequent concern by 18 months, but limited social engagement, repetitive behaviors, and sensory disturbances often emerge by 12 months. Children are often referred for medical evaluations for sensorimotor deficits that often manifest as delayed milestones.

Deficits in social skills and preverbal gestural communication are typical symptoms in children with autism spectrum disorder prior to 18 months of age (Tomanik, Pearson, & Loveland, Lane, & Shaw., 2007). A social skills deficit observed in infants and toddlers with autism spectrum disorder is a lack of joint attention (Johnson, 2008). Joint attention first appears at 8 to 10 months of age as a spontaneous behavior that indicates an infant's shared interest and enjoyment of an object or event with another person. The typically developing infant will follow a caregiver's eye gaze as the person's eyes shift from the infant to a distant object. By 10 to 12 months, the infant will respond when a caregiver points toward an object and prompts the child to "look," by looking at the object. The infant will then indicate shared interest by looking back at the caregiver and using an appropriate facial expression. Children with autism spectrum disorder typically do not respond to a shift in eye gaze or pointing, and if they do respond there is no expressed interest or looking back at the caregiver (Plauche Johnson & Myers, 2007). Deficits in joint attention appear to be a critical delay specific to children with autism spectrum disorder. Further, deficits in spontaneous shared interest and enjoyment, manifested as a lack of showing or pointing to objects, is a critical observation in the early screening of autism spectrum disorder (Cangliose & Allen, 2014)

Retrospective video analysis of young children later diagnosed with ASDs revealed that 90% of children diagnosed with autism spectrum disorder demonstrated poor eye contact, poor response to their name, and lack of showing or pointing to objects to indicate interest (Osterling & Dawson, 1994). Video analysis conducted by Baranek (1999) found that 9 to 12 month old infants later diagnosed with autism spectrum disorder found low frequency of looking at others, and failure to respond when their name was called. Baranek's study also found infants later diagnosed with autism spectrum disorder demonstrated adverse response to touch and excessive mouthing of objects. Mars, Mauk, and Dowrick (1998) used home videos of children later diagnosed with autism spectrum disorder and independent observers were able to pick out the children later diagnosed. Differences in social engagement and joint attention were the strongest differences and were evident by 30 months of age. More recently studies have shown sensorimotor impairment evident by age 6 months in youths that would meet autism spectrum disorder criteria by 24 months (Estes et al., 2015).

Pediatricians and other early childhood providers frequently utilize questionnaires to screen for autism spectrum disorder. The Modified Checklist for Autism in Toddlers (M-CHAT) is a 23 item parent report checklist that is reliable and validated for use in children 16 to 30 months of age. It was designed as a tool to screen for children who may benefit from a more thorough developmental and autism spectrum disorder assessment. The most current version of the M-CHAT is available on-line (www.mchat.org) and may be completed as part of a well-child checkup or by other professionals in early intervention programs. Children are considered at risk for autism spectrum disorder if they fail any 3 of the 23 items or 2 of 6 critical items that include lack of interest in other children, lack of pointing to objects or people, lack of showing objects to others, lack of responsiveness to name, and lack of joint attention (Kleinman et al, 2008; Robins, Fein, Barton & Green, 2001). If a child's score suggests a high risk for autism spectrum disorder, a discussion of the findings with parent/caregivers is conducted and a more thorough autism spectrum disorder evaluation is recommended.

The Childhood Autism Rating Scale (CARS2) is a more sensitive screening instrument valid for youth older than 2 years (Schopler, Reichler, & Rochen-Renner, 1998). The CARS2 is a 15-item rating scale used to identify children with autism and distinguishing them from those with developmental disabilities. It is empirically validated and provides concise, objective, and quantifiable ratings based on direct behavioral observation.

The American Academy of Pediatrics periodically publishes consensus policy on the identification and evaluation of children with autism (Plauche Johnson & Myers 2007). Expert panels usually recommend a multidisciplinary approach to diagnosing autism spectrum disorder, including professionals in speech/language, pediatrics, psychiatry or neurology, and psychology. A comprehensive history with a thorough developmental history is essential to the process of diagnosing autism spectrum disorder. A developmental neurological exam is recommended to evaluate for neurological diseases that might manifest as delayed development or loss of milestones. Examination by pediatric neurology will subsequently inform the need for further testing such as genetic screening for general chromosomal abnormalities or specific genetic syndromes such as fragile X, neurofibromatosis, tuberous sclerosis, etc.

Diagnosing autism spectrum disorder with accuracy and reliability poses a challenge to clinicians, especially when issues of differential diagnosis are considered. The task is complicated by differences in expression of symptoms across age and developmental levels and the heterogeneity of children's cognitive ability, adaptive functioning, and maladaptive behaviors. A comprehensive diagnostic evaluation includes the use of standardized assessment instruments such as the Autism Diagnostic Interview-Revised (ADI-R) and the Autism Diagnostic Observation Schedule (ADOS-2). It is, however, important to emphasize that these instruments in themselves must form only part of the full assessment. The ADI-R is a standardized, semi-structured clinical review for caregivers of children and adults. The interview contains 93 items and focuses on behaviors in three content areas or domains: quality of social interaction (e.g., emotional sharing, offering and seeking comfort, social smiling, and responding to other children); communication and language (e.g., stereotyped utterances, pronoun reversal, social usage of language); and repetitive, restricted, and stereotyped interests and behavior (e.g., unusual preoccupations, hand and finger mannerisms, unusual sensory interests). The ADI-R interview generates scores in each of the three content areas (i.e., communication and language, social interaction, and restricted, repetitive behaviors). A classification of autism is given when scores in all three content areas of communication, social interaction, and patterns of behavior meet or exceed the specified cutoffs, and onset of the disorder is evident by 36 months of age. The ADOS-2 (Lord et al., 2012) is a semi-structured assessment of communication, social interaction, and play (or imaginative use of materials) for individuals suspected of having autism or other pervasive developmental disorders. The ADOS-2 consists of five modules, each of which is appropriate for children as early as 12 months of age and adults of differing developmental and language levels, ranging from nonverbal to verbally-fluent. The ADOS-2 consists of standardized activities that allow the examiner to observe the occurrence or non-occurrence of behaviors that have been identified as indicative of autism spectrum disorder and other pervasive developmental disorders across developmental levels and chronological ages.

No routine laboratory studies have been found to be particularly beneficial. Despite recent advances in structural and functional neuroimaging (Courchesene, Campbell, & Solso, 2011), there is a dearth of evidence supporting routine imaging studies except in cases of clinical suspicions of underlying structural abnormalities. Given the complexities of making an autism spectrum disorder diagnosis as well as appropriate assessment of comorbidities, the multidisciplinary approach remains the gold-standard. Unfortunately, such evaluations are typically limited to specialty medical centers, leaving many autism spectrum disorder cases unrecognized (Bryson, Rogers, & Fombonne, 2003).

Individuals with Mild or Moderate ID

Historically, pervasive developmental disorder not otherwise specified captured two parts of the autism spectrum. The majority of this population displayed some degree of ID and mild autistic symptoms or mixed symptoms not fully meeting the diagnostic criteria for autism spectrum disorder. At the other end lie individuals with mild core ASD features (possibly partially compensated) and typically borderline or normal intelligence. Accordingly, there was a great deal of variability in how pervasive developmental disorder not otherwise specified label was utilized. Mahoney et al. (1998) found a low reliability for the diagnosis of pervasive developmental disorder not otherwise specified. Mayes reviewed 157 children with Asperger disorder and found all of them fit into the pervasive developmental disorder not otherwise specified category (Mayes, Calhoun, & Crites, 2001). In this population, Asperger disorder was indistinguishable from pervasive developmental disorder not otherwise specified (Allen et al., 2001; Myhr, 1998).

Prior, Eisenmajer, and Leekam (1998) refers to pervasive developmental disorder not otherwise specified as a "default diagnosis" clinicians use when they are not fully comfortable or confident of the presence of autism spectrum disorder due to subthreshold symptoms. She and her colleges found no clear subtypes of autism spectrum disorder in the population of individuals with mild disabilities based on performances on theory of mind, behavioral characteristics, or developmental history. Executive functioning, which plays a substantial role in core autistic symptoms, does not differentiate between high functioning autism, pervasive developmental disorder not otherwise specified, or Asperger syndrome (Verte, Geurts, Roeyers, Oosterlaan, & Sergeant, 2006). Rather, there is a continuum or spectrum of severity. Such findings arguably justify the autism spectrum disorder terminology and the use of a 'dimensional' approach to understanding this condition as opposed to the categorical approach of the past. Alternatively, the past three decades may highlight the various clinical and research disciplines' continuing inability to precisely characterize a condition with complex and diverse phenomenology.

Individuals with Severe or Profound ID

A complete absence of speech, severe repetitive behaviors, and social aloofness are common. Autism spectrum disorder diagnosis and treatment in this context are confounded by medical problems and sometimes deficits in sensory systems. Seizures, blindness, and severe sensory losses complicate the clinical picture. Numerous case reports in the literature describe genetic syndromes, severe intellectual disabilities, and a subsequent diagnosis of autism spectrum disorder (Guerin et al., 1996; Rutter & Thapar 2014). Diagnosing an autism spectrum disorder in individuals with severe sensory injury that cause communication deficits raises complex issues. Are the injuries to the sensory system the cause of communication deficits, repetitive behaviors, and/or impaired social engagement (suggestive of an autism spectrum disorder) or is this merely one of the uncommon examples where clinicians can identify the etiological insult that underlies a particular individual's autism spectrum disorder? In the past, if clinical and historical data were insufficient for an autism diagnosis, some clinicians may have utilized pervasive developmental disorder not otherwise specified. But for all individuals (and adults in particular) with potential autism spectrum disorder, the lack of a detailed developmental history (parents, caregivers, medical records) makes definitive diagnosis virtually impossible.

The *DSM-5* supports two options. Individuals with severe/profound ID and previous diagnosis of pervasive developmental disorder not otherwise specified may continue to carry that diagnosis. Alternatively, one could apply best clinical practice by gathering all available historical data and then collecting longitudinal information with tools such as Matson's Diagnostic Assessment for the Severely Handicapped (DASH) to formulate a baseline of behavioral symptoms that can then be evaluated over time. The Pervasive Developmental Disorder Behavior Inventory (Cohen, Schmidt-Lackner, Romanczyk, & Sudhalter, 2003) could be utilized in a comparable manner, given most, if not all, individuals with severe or profound ID will have full-time caregivers capable of tracking behaviors over time. If sufficient symptoms in Criterion A/B are present, these individuals will be diagnosed with autism spectrum disorder with appropriate specifiers.

Children and Adolescents with ID

With the early identification of autism spectrum disorder in children prior to age 2, questions arise regarding the stability of the diagnosis over time (Brian et al., 2015; Guthrie, Swineford, Nottke, & Wetherby, 2013; Turner & Stone 2007). Clinical features within the autism spectrum represent a heterogeneous group of children with a wide variety of symptoms and outcomes (Starr, Szatmari, Bryson, & Zwaigenbaum, 2003). There is currently no well-validated method to predict outcomes or stability of the diagnosis over time. Historically, milder manifestations such as the former Asperger disorder and higher functioning youths with pervasive developmental disorder not otherwise specified have the best outcomes but some research suggest other factors may explain differences in developmental trajectories (Lord, Bishop, & Anderson, 2015). But it is also those youths with better receptive language and higher cognitive abilities that are diagnosed later (Brian et al., 2015) and most likely to "grow out" of their autism spectrum disorder. Clinicians often witness significant remission of symptoms over time, especially with intensive behavioral and psychological interventions (Rogers, 1998). But overall cognitive functioning appears stable among individuals with intellectual disability and autism spectrum disorder with the notable caveat that cognitive assessments in this cohort (young people with autism/ID) are of questionable utility.

Summary of Limitations in Applying DSM5 Criteria to People with ID

The *DSM-5* addressed some of the concerns noted in the *DM-ID* with regards to limitations and confounders in applying *DSM-IV-TR* criteria to people with ID. For decades, researchers, clinicians, and families have advocated for a diagnostic approach that more fully captured the clinical variability seen in individuals with an autism spectrum disorder. The impairments in social and communication skills, the presence of repetitive behaviors, and the severity of social and intellectual impairments fall along a spectrum of conditions (Prior, Eisenmajer, & Leekam, 1998). Collapsing the various disorders from the *DSM-IV-TR* into autism spectrum disorder recognizes both the variability within each of the prior diagnoses but also the globally shared features. Contrary to the *DSM-IV-TR*, the *DSM5* introduces severity specifiers in the two primary symptom domains (Criterion A, B) which provide more details with regards to the intensity of symptoms and level of support needed. Further, the *DSM-5* now includes an ID specifier. For example, the label 'autism spectrum disorder **with accompanying intellectual impairment**' generates a more detailed clinical picture that did not exist in the *DSM-IV-TR*.

Nonresponse to name, lack of pointing to show interest, limited pretend play, avoiding eye contact, preference for solitary activity, presence of echolalia, emotional disturbance with minor changes in environment, intense interests, sensorimotor anomalies (stimming, fixations/reactions to sensory stimuli) are among the symptoms evident in children prior to age 2 and typically precede overt impairment in language development. In the most severe forms of autism spectrum disorder, particularly those with known genetic etiologies and severe/profound ID, the onset is early, social and communicative capacities may be completely lost, and stereotyped movements can be constant. The *DSM-5* includes three other notable specifiers '**associated with a known medical or genetic condition, or environmental factor,**' '**associated with another neurodevelopmental, mental, or behavior disorder,**' and '**with or without accompanying language impairment.**' These are advances compared to the *DSM-IV-TR* but if the diagnosing clinician fails to detail the specific underlying condition (e.g. autism spectrum disorder associated with fragile X) important clinical information may be lost if merely descriptive specifiers are utilized (e.g. autism spectrum disorder with intellectual impairment, with accompanying language impairment). As research into autism spectrum disorder continues to advance, the clinical evaluation, reporting, and characterization of patients with autism spectrum disorder will take on increased importance. But excessive "lumping" with general specifiers may obscure useful etiological or pathological demarcations and more importantly confound the development and evaluation of treatments.

On the other end of the functional spectrum will be individuals with mild impairments in social behaviors, social language, only modest, if any restrictive repetitive behaviors (beyond repetitive speech), and mild intellectual disability (or borderline intellectual functioning). These individuals will meet DSM-5 criteria for autism spectrum disorder or social communication disorder (SCD). This may become the new Asperger versus high functioning autism vs pervasive developmental disorder not otherwise specified debate. Social communication disorder may capture 'higher functioning' youths that lack current restrictive/repetitive behaviors but these behaviors are highly variable and tend to diminish over time. Reliable assessment requires a competent historian (if past), clinician for evaluation of current symptoms, and periodic monitoring. In the absence of such resources, individuals that should be diagnosed with autism spectrum disorder may not be readily identified. Although the *DSM-5* Working Group reached a consensus with regards to changes in diagnostic criteria, there remains an active debate among stakeholders about the appropriateness and impact of the new 'borderline' autism spectrum disorder category of social communication disorder (Brukner-Wertman, Laor, & Golan, 2016).

Overall, the primary limitations in utilizing DSM-5 criteria in individuals with ID are: 1) the ability of diagnosticians to disentangle behavioral and functional impairment due to autism spectrum disorder from the impairments caused by intellectual disability, 2) the lack of comprehensive, longitudinal assessment of symptoms that often vary over time, and 3) the confounding influence of other mental/behavioral health conditions that may be 'easier' to diagnose than autism spectrum disorder.

Pathogenesis

Studies have reported a wide range of differences in brain structure and function in autism spectrum disorder. These findings are extensive and are beyond the scope of this chapter. A broad caveat is that there is often little independent replication of findings in these studies which generally evaluate a small number of participants. Neuropathology studies have reported abnormalities in cell tissue throughout the brain, especially in the cerebral cortex, limbic system, brainstem, and cerebellum. Much of this literature is conflicting and lacks controls, such as matched healthy individuals. The most consistent findings in these studies are reduced numbers of Purkinje cells in the cerebellum, in the entorhinal cortex, and in the nuclei of the amygdala, especially the medially located cells (Bauman & Kemper, 2003). Differences in the organization of cortical neuronal minicolumns have also been reported (Casanova, Buxhoeveden, & Switala, 2002).

In terms of neurochemistry, serotonin dysregulation has long been suspected to be important, and cholinergic abnormalities have been found (Baumann & Kemper, 2003). Recent interest has focused on imbalances in the excitatory-inhibitory balance of the brain due to abnormal glutamatergic and GABAergic function (Nelson & Valakh, 2015). Changes to oxytocin function in the brain have also been suggested, leading to trials of intranasal oxytocin as a therapeutic intervention for autism spectrum disorder (Preti et al., 2014).

Brain imaging studies have found abnormal sizes of the amygdala, cerebellum, hippocampus, corpus callosum, and parieto-temporal lobes (Brambilla et al., 2003). More recent longitudinal studies have revealed aberrant cortical development evident in toddlers through age 5 (Schumann et al., 2010) and it has been suggested that there is a period of relative overgrowth into early postnatal years, then retarded growth or even exaggerated pruning into adolescence (Courchesne et al., 2011). Functional brain imaging studies have demonstrated changes in activation in regions of the brain associated with social and language processing, and highlighted the importance of dysconnectivity between distributed brain regions (Philip et al., 2012) with the latter being confirmed by studies of structural connectivity.

Overall, the emerging pathophysiologic data suggests early aberrant cellular structure, migration, and maturation within the brain. It is likely that the range of severity seen in autism spectrum disorder is associated with the wide range of aberrant development, greater cellular dysfunction, and diffuse network disruption.

Genetic Factors

It has long been recognized that genetic factors have an important role to play in the etiology of autism spectrum disorder. Initial evidence for this came from family history studies with heritability estimates that were extremely high. Although more recent estimates of heritability have yielded lower figures, autism spectrum disorder is still generally regarded as a highly heritable condition (Tick, Bolton, Happé, Rutter, & Rijsdijk 2016). Of course, not all genetic cases of autism spectrum disorder with a genetic cause are inherited and it is increasingly recognized that *de novo* mutations are common.

Broadly speaking the genetic mechanisms associated with autism spectrum disorder can be categorized into two main areas. The first, often referred to as polygenic inheritance, results from the accumulation of common genetic variants which are distributed throughout the population, each conferring a small increase in liability to autism spectrum disorder. Taken individually these common variants lead to little or no increase in autism spectrum disorder traits, but cumulatively (additive or synergistic) they are hypothesized to lead to the expression of autism spectrum disorder. The second mechanism involves mutations in single genes (or a few genes) that are relatively rare but have a large effect. The most well-known examples of such mutations often lead to syndromic intellectual disability and autism, and are described in more detail below. However, advances in genetic technology have led to the identification of other mutations in cases which were previously regarded as idiopathic in nature. These mutations can be very small (e.g. a single base pair), or can cover a number of contiguous genes, through copy number variation (CNV). CNVs are segments of DNA which are present in variable amounts between individuals. Within the CNV region the number of copies of a gene will therefore differ between individuals, with either fewer copies than is typical (deletion) or more copies than is typical (duplication) occurring. CNVs are found in the general population and likely represent an important source of genetic variation. However, they have been found to occur at greater frequency in the genomes of people with autism spectrum disorder (and indeed many other neuropsychiatric conditions) (Sebat et al., 2007).

It is important to note that in many cases of autism spectrum disorder, the genetic cause cannot be identified. Little weight should be given to the utility of genetic testing for polygenic factors at present. Ascribing causality is also very difficult; even when a CNV is identified, it is not clear whether it is associated with autism spectrum disorder, although examination of the function of the affected genes affected may be instructive. Even in the syndromic single gene disorders described below (which are strongly associated with autism spectrum disorder), not everyone will show autistic traits, suggesting that polygenic and environmental factors are also at play.

■ *Fragile X Syndrome*

The most common inherited cause of autism spectrum disorder, fragile X syndrome was first described in the 1940s by Martin and Bell. The condition results from a lack of expression of the FMRP protein, which in almost all cases is caused by a triplet repeat (CGG) expansion in the promotor region of the FMR1 gene on the X chromosome. People in the neurotypical population usually have up to 45 CGG repeats in this region – this is stable and does not usually change across generations. When a mutation occurs leading to a person having between 55 and 199 repeats this is referred to as a premutation. Premutation carriers do not have intellectual disability, but males may have an increase in the prevalence of autism spectrum disorder as well as a liability to a late onset neurodegenerative condition, fragile X associated tremor ataxia syndrome (FXTAS), whereas females with a premutation may experience early menopause. Further expansion of the triplet repeat occurs in the offspring of female carriers; this may lead to the offspring having more than 200 CGG repeats, thereby silencing the gene and leading to fragile X syndrome. Very rarely, fragile X syndrome may be caused by *de novo* point mutations in the presence of a typical number of CGG repeats leading to reduced or no expression of FMRP.

Fragile X syndrome presents with a number of physical features, including a long thin face, large ears, long thin digits, hyperextensible joints, and macroorchidism. Around 20% of individuals will have seizures which are usually mild, and mitral regurgitation is also common. Cognitively it is almost invariably associated with mild to severe intellectual disability in men. Around one third to two thirds of people with fragile X syndrome will display autism spectrum disorder and many also have attention deficit/hyperactivity disorder. Anxiety in response to novel or unexpected situations, sensory hypersensitivities, and gaze aversion are particularly common features. Due to the presence of two X chromosomes, females with the genetic mutation may be spared the full phenotype (as a result of random X inactivation), and indeed may be relatively unaffected.

■ *Rett Syndrome*

Rett syndrome usually results from deleterious mutations to the methyl-CpG-binding protein 2 (MeCP2) gene on the paternal X chromosome. Variant forms have been described and mutations in related genes have been associated with these, e.g. FOXG1, CDKL5, although these are increasingly regarded as separate disorders.

Rett Syndrome was a distinct diagnosis in *DSM-IV* in the pervasive developmental disorder category; for *DSM-5* it has been removed. Features of autism spectrum disorder may be apparent in girls with Rett syndrome during and after regression, but typically do not persist. Girls with Rett syndrome classically present with an initial period of apparently typical development followed by arrested development and regression of previously acquired skills across intellectual, motor, communication, and socialization domains. Abnormal hand movements, such as wringing, and breathing problems are common. Seizures often occur. Milder variants of Rett syndrome are known to occur probably through random X inactivation; boys with mutations in MeCP2 were initially thought to die in utero or very early in infancy, but some cases with less deleterious mutations have been identified in adults with intellectual disability.

■ *Tuberous Sclerosis Complex*

The individual features of tuberous sclerosis were first described in isolation in the 19th century but it was not until the early 20th century that it was recognized that these were part of the same condition. It is caused by mutations in one of the genes, TSC1 or TSC2. These code for the proteins hamartin and tuberin which complex together to help regulate cell growth and division

Tuberous sclerosis complex is a multisystem disorder characterized by the presence of benign tumors on organs throughout the body, including the brain. Skin lesions are common and include Shagreen patches, facial angiofibromas, hypomelanotic nodules and periungual fibromas. Around three quarters of individuals have seizures which often begin as focal seizures or infantile spasms. Autism, attention deficit/hyperactivity disorder, and intellectual disability each occur in around 50% of people with tuberous sclerosis complex. The condition can affect almost any organ system in the body and commonly includes cardiac rhabdomyomas, renal angiomyolipomas and cysts, pulmonary cysts, and lymphangioleiomyomatosis.

Environmental Factors

Although genetics is increasingly being indicated as the main cause of autism spectrum disorder, it does not account alone for all instances. Recent studies demonstrating differential expression of thousands of genes in peripheral cells and brain tissues of individuals with autism spectrum disorder indicate the need to look beyond genetics to uncover environment factors that contribute to the disorder. The pathogenic contribution of genetic and environment factors, their definition as risk or causative factors, and the level to which outside influences affect genetic activity are still under debate. Epigenetic mechanisms which can alter gene expression and phenotype without inducing changes in DNA sequence are more and more demonstrated to be involved in critical pathways to autism spectrum disorder.

Environmental factors may influence a person's behavior and may account for the development of symptoms in an age-dependent manner (Shishido, Aleksic, & Ozaki, 2014), which may lead to different clinical types. The environmental causative elements are commonly separated into pre-natal, peri-natal, and post-natal factors.

Prenatal Factors

Prenatal factors include infections, such as congenital rubella syndrome (secondary to rubella infection) or cytomegalovirus, inflammation indicated by C-reactive protein increase (Brown et al., 2014), and toxic substances exposure. The possible contribution of allergenic and autoimmune problems during pregnancy has been supported by the identification of circulating maternal antibodies against fetal brain proteins, which suggests the possibility of their transposition in the blood-brain barrier. Other studies have demonstrated the presence of pro-inflammatory cytokines in the fetal brain, such as tumor necrosis factor, which is preformed in maternal mast cells (Angelidou et al., 2012; Vojdani, 2008).

Most studied toxic substances are pesticides, phthalates, alcohol, and certain drugs, such as terbutaline, thalidomide, misoprostol, or valproic acid (Christensen et al., 2013).

There has been controversy for years over whether the use of common antidepressants by women during pregnancy might raise the odds of autism spectrum disorder in their children. Recently, many studies, including one with a huge sample (Sørensen et al., 2013), found no rise in the risk of autism spectrum disorder in children whose mothers used an antidepressant while pregnant; on the contrary these studies pointed out that severe untreated maternal depression may be a risk factor boosting a child's odds for autism spectrum disorder. In general, in the case of medications, any possible increased risk of autism must be balanced against a woman's medical needs. Mental health problems can likewise affect pregnancy and the health of future children.

Some researchers have recently reported strong evidence that prenatal exposure to high air pollution can up to double the chance that a child will develop autism spectrum disorder (Roberts et al., 2013). Air pollution contains many toxicants known to affect neurological function. In previous studies, metals (antimony, arsenic, cadmium, chromium, lead, mercury, manganese, nickel) (Palmer, Blanchard, & Wood, 2009; Windham, Zhang, Gunier, Croen, & Grether, 2006), styrene (Kalkbrenner et al. 2010), quinoline (Kalkbrenner et al. 2010), trichloroethylene (Windham et al. 2006), methylene chloride (Kalkbrenner et al. 2010; Windham et al. 2006), vinyl chloride (Windham et al. 2006), and diesel particulate matter (Volk, Hertz-Picciotto, Delwiche, Lurmann, & McConnell, 2011; Windham et al. 2006) have been associated with autism spectrum disorder. Arsenic, cadmium, chromium, mercury, methylene chloride, nickel, styrene, trichloroethylene, and vinyl chloride are also known or suspected mutagens.

An association between maternal metabolic conditions, particularly obesity and type 2 diabetes, and autism spectrum disorder has also been shown (Krakowiak et al., 2012). The risk increase is likely due to insulin resistance, but more research is needed to better understand how this feature can affect a child's prenatal development. Higher levels of fetal testosterone in the amniotic fluid of mothers have also been demonstrated to be associated with autism spectrum disorder (Baron-Cohen et al., 2015). It is hypothesized that testosterone pushes brain development towards improved ability to see patterns and analyze complex systems while diminishing communication and empathy, emphasizing male traits over female (Baron-Cohen et al., 2011).

Perinatal Factors

Perinatal factors are associated with obstetric conditions like low birth weight, abnormal gestation length, and birth asphyxia (Kolevzon,

Gross, & Reichenberg, 2007). Babies from gestations of less than 28 weeks have been found to have a high risk of neurological problems and those born in the 33rd gestational week to have a greater risk for autism spectrum disorder (Limperopoulos et al., 2008). There are indications that environmental factors trigger oxidative stress in individuals genetically susceptible to autism spectrum disorder, which would lead to losses in methylation and secondary neurologic deficits (Dardeno et al., 2010). Increased levels of oxidative stress markers have already been described in the cord blood of mothers who had premature births compared to those of mothers who had full term births (Joshi et al., 2008). Premature birth is associated with the formation of reactive oxygen species (Davis & Auten, 2010). Stress typically results in the release of corticotropin-releasing hormone (CRH) with elevated plasma levels being associated with premature births (Chrousos, 1995; Warren, Patrick, & Goland, 1992). CRH may stimulate the mast cells to release cytokines, which can injury the blood-brain barrier and thus increase its permeability (Esposito et al., 2001). With the increased permeability, neurotoxic molecules can reach the brain and cause an inflammatory process, which has been suggested to contributes to the pathogenesis of ASD (Theoharides, Doyle, Francis, Conti, & Kalogeromitros, 2008; Valent et al., 2012).

Postnatal Factors

Postnatal factors encompass a wide range of insults including autoimmune disease (Ashwood & van de Water, 2004), leaky gut syndrome (Johnson, 2006), viral infection, amygdala developmental failure (Schultz, 2005), oxidative stress (Kern & Jones, 2006), vitamin D deficiency (Cannell, 2007), certain foods, and heavy metal toxicity (Davidson, Myers, & Weiss, 2004). The evidence for these risk factors has not been confirmed by reliable studies.

The measles, mumps and rubella (MMR) vaccine hypothesis is probably the most extensively debated etiological hypothesis of autism spectrum disorder. Wakefield's purported causal link, based on a report of 12 children, was formally retracted by ten of Wakefield's twelve co-authors and by the journal which published the study. In January 2011, an investigation summarized the Wakefield study as deliberate fraud and manipulation of data. Over the past decade, multiple studies have been conducted to correctly assess the relationship between vaccination and autism spectrum disorder. The consensus conclusion is there is no evidence of a causal relationship (Taylor, Swerdfeger, & Eslick, 2014).

Psychosocial Factors

Individuals with milder presentations of autism spectrum disorder may not become evident until psychosocial demands exceed an individual's adaptive capacity. This may be particularly problematic for females, individuals with borderline or normal intelligence, and people with extensive/effective networks of social support.

Many people are referred to treatment for problems other than the developmental disorder per se. For example, children might be targeted for assessment in their educational settings because of social or attention problems that impact academic achievement. Major aspects of the assessment and intervention might then be conducted by educational professionals (for example, teachers, speech therapists, psychologists).

Adults, on the other hand, might present in a mental health setting for such problems as anxiety, depression, loneliness, social skill deficits, problems with dating, poor judgment, and poor problem-solving ability. Because the diagnosis of Asperger disorder was not formally available until 1994, many adults who might otherwise have been diagnosed with this disorder are still living with such inappropriate or nonspecific diagnoses as schizophrenia undifferentiated type, schizoaffective disorder, bipolar disorder with atypical features (Perlman, 2000; Ryan, 1994), atypical anxiety disorder, schizoid personality disorder (Wolff, 2000), borderline personality disorder, or possibly with less well established diagnoses as nonverbal learning disability or social communication disorder.

Application of Diagnostic Criteria

In summary, the judgment as to whether symptoms are present or not has to be set within the context of the person's overall developmental level. Diagnosing autism spectrum disorder gets more difficult as one deals with the co-occurring neurological, behavioral, and communication problems associated with severe/profound ID. The key variables may be the degree of emotional attachment, social interests, and attempts to communicate.

Attempts to diagnose autism spectrum disorder in individuals with severe/profound ID require consideration of: (1) Social deficits: Does the patient reject interaction or seek to prolong it? Does the patient actively avoid eye contact? Does the patient actively isolate him/herself from peers? (2) Need for sameness: Does the patient react catastrophically to changes in routine or environment? Does the patient have rituals and/or compulsions? (3) Stereotypy, especially toe-walking or twirling. (4) Echolalia. And (5) Splinter skills beyond tested cognitive competence.

Severity and Natural History: The intellectual, social, and communication impairments seen in autism spectrum disorder vary greatly, and adding qualifiers for the severity of impairments may promote both accuracy in diagnosis and guide treatment. Early, intensive, and targeted interventions may decrease the severity of these symptoms. Further, a label for autism spectrum disorder in remission or partial remission may capture the subset of individuals that either respond to intervention or 'grow out' of their diagnosis, a feature that appears possible for a minority of individuals with autism spectrum disorder but is not associated with intellectual disability.

Autism Spectrum Disorder

DSM-5 Diagnostic Criteria	Applying Criteria for Individuals with Mild to Profound ID
A. Persistent deficits in social communication and social interaction across multiple contexts, as manifested by the following, currently or by history:	A. No adaptation. DSM-5 explicitly requires deficits to exceed impairment consistent with level of intellectual disability.
1. Deficits in social-emotional reciprocity, ranging, from abnormal social approach and failure of normal back-and-forth conversation; to reduced sharing of interests, emotions, or affect; to failure to initiate or respond to social interactions. east two of the following:	1. No adaptation.
2. Deficits in nonverbal communicative behaviors used for social interaction, ranging, from poorly integrated verbal and nonverbal communication; to abnormalities in eye contact and body language or deficits in understanding and use of gestures; to a total lack of facial expressions and nonverbal communication.	2. No adaptation.
3. Deficits in developing, maintaining, and understanding relationships, ranging from difficulties adjusting behavior to suit various social contexts; to difficulties in sharing imaginative play or in making friends; to absence of interest in peers.	3. No adaptation.
B. Restricted, repetitive patterns of behavior, interests, or activities, as manifested by at least two of the following, currently or by history.	B. No adaptation.
1. Stereotyped or repetitive motor movements, use of objects, or speech.	1. No adaptation.
2. Insistence on sameness, inflexible adherence to routines, or ritualized patterns of verbal or nonverbal behavior.	2. No adaptation.
3. Highly restricted, fixated interests that are abnormal in intensity or focus.	3. No adaptation.
4. Hyper- or hyporeactivity to sensory input or unusual interest in sensory aspects of the environment.	4. No adaptation.
C. Symptoms must be present in the early developmental period (but may not become fully manifest until social demands exceed limited capacities, or may be masked by learned strategies in later life).	C. No adaptation.
D. Symptoms cause clinically significant impairment in social, occupational, or other important areas of current functioning.	D. No adaptation.

Autism Spectrum Disorder (continued)

DSM-5 Diagnostic Criteria	Applying Criteria for Individuals with Mild to Profound ID
E. These disturbances are not better explained by intellectual disability or global developmental delay. Intellectual disability and autism spectrum disorder frequently co-occur, to make comorbid diagnoses of autism spectrum disorder and intellectual disability, social communication should be below that expected for general developmental level.	E. No adaptation.
Specify if:	No adaptation.
With or without accompanying intellectual impairment	
With or without accompanying language impairment	
Associated with a known medical or genetic condition or environmental factor	
Associated with another neurodevelopmental, mental, or behavioral disorder	
With catatonia	

References

Allen, D. A., Steinberg, M., Dunn, M., Fein, D., Feinstein, C., Waterhouse, L., & Rapin, I. (2001). Autistic disorder versus other pervasive developmental disorders in young children: Same or different? *European Child & Adolescent Psychiatry, 10*, 67–78.

American Academy of Pediatrics. (2001). Technical report: The pediatrician's role in the diagnosis and management of autistic spectrum disorder in children. *Pediatrics, 107*, 1221–1226.

Angelidou, A., Asadi, S., Alysandratos, K. D., Karagkouni, A., Kourembanas, S., & Theoharides, T. C. (2012). Perinatal stress, brain inflammation and risk of autism-Review and proposal. *BMC Pediatrics., 12*(1), 89.

Ashwood P, & van de Water J. (2004). Is autism an autoimmune disease? *Autoimmune Review. 3*, 557–562.

Baranek, G. (1999). Autism during infancy: A retrospective video analysis of sensory-motor and social behaviors at 9-12 months of age. *Journal of Autism and Developmental Disorders, 29*(3), 213- 224.

Baron-Cohen, S., Auyeung, B., Nørgaard-Pedersen, B., Hougaard, D.M., Abdallah, M.W., Melgaard, L., … Lombardo, M.V. (2015). Elevated fetal steroidogenic activity in autism. *Molecular Psychiatry, 20*(3), 369-76.

Baron-Cohen, S., Lombardo, M.V., Auyeung, B., Ashwin, E., Chakrabarti, B., & Knickmeyer, R. (2011). Why are autism spectrum conditions more prevalent in males? *PLoS Biology, 9*(6), e1001081.

Bauman, M. L., & Kemper, T. L. (2003). The neuropathology of the autistic spectrum disorders: What have we learned? In G. Brock (Ed.), *Symposium on autism: Neuralogiclal basis and treatment possibilities* (pp. 77-108). London: John Wiley & Sons.

Brambilla, P., Hardan, A., di Nemi, S. U., Perez, J., Soares, J. C., & Bara, F. (2003). Brain anatomy and development in autism: Review of structural MRI studies. *Brain Research Bulletin, 61*, 557–569.

Brian, J., Bryson, S.E., Smith, I.M., Roberts, W., Roncadin, C., Szatmari, P., & Zwaigenbaum, L. (2015). Stability and change in autism spectrum diagnosis from age 3 to middle childhood in a high-risk sibling cohort. *Autism*, epub ahead of print.

Brown, A.S., Sourander, A., Hinkka-Yli-Salomäki, S., McKeague, I.W., Sundvall, J., & Surcel, H.M. (2014). Elevated maternal C-reactive protein and autism in a national birth cohort. *Molecular Psychiatry, 19*(2), 259-64.

Brukner-Wertman, Y., Laor, N., & Golan, O. (2016). Social (pragmatic) communication disorder and its relation to the autism spectrum: dilemmas arising from the DSM-5 classification. *Journal of Autism and Developmental Disorders, 46*(8), 2821-2829.

Bryson, S. E., Rogers, S. J., & Fombonne, E. (2003). Autism spectrum disorders: Early detection, intervention, education, and psychopharmacological management. *Canadian Journal of Psychiatry, 48*, 506–516.

Cangliose, A. & Allen, P. (2014) Screening for autism spectrum disorders in infants before 18 months of age. *Pediatric Nursing, 40(1), 33-37.*

Cannell, J.J. (2007). Autism and vitamin D. *Medical Hypotheses, 70*, 750–759.

Casanova, M.F., Buxhoeveden, D.P., Switala, A.E., & Roy, E. (2002). Minicolumnar pathology in autism. *Neurology, 58*, 428–32.

Charlot, L., Deutsch, C. K., Albert, A., Hunt, A., Connor, D. F., & McIlvane Jr, W. J. (2008). Mood and anxiety symptoms in psychiatric inpatients with autism spectrum disorder and depression. *Journal of Mental Health Research in Intellectual Disabilities, 1*(4), 238-253.

Charlot, L.R., Fox, S., Silka, V., Hurley, A., Lowry, M.A., & Pary, R. (2007). Mood disorders. In R.J. Fletcher, E. Loschen,C. Stavrakaki, & M. First (Eds.), *DM-ID: Diagnostic manual-intellectual disability: A textbook of diagnosis of mental disorders in persons with intellectual disability.* Kingston, NY: NADD Press.

Chess, S., Fernandez, P., & Korn, S. (1978). Behavioral consequences of congenital rubella. *Journal of Pediatrics, 93*(4), 699-703.

Christensen, J., Grønborg, T.K., Sørensen, M.J., Schendel, D., Parner, E.T., Pedersen, L.H., & Vestergaard, M. (2013). Prenatal valproate exposure and risk of autism spectrum disorders and childhood autism. *JAMA, 309*(16), 1696-1703.

Chrousos, G. P. (1995). The hypothalamic-pituitary-adrenal axis and immune-mediated inflammation. *New England Journal of Medicine, 18*(332), 1351-1362.

Cohen, I. L., Schmidt-Lackner, S., Romanczyk, R., & Sudhalter, V. (2003). The PDD Behavior Inventory: A rating scale for assessing response to intervention in children with pervasive developmental disorder. *Journal of Autism and Developmental Disabilities, 33*, 31–45.

Courchesne, E., Campbell, K., & Solso, S., (2011). Brain growth across the life span in autism: age-specific changes in anatomical pathology. *Brain Researech, 1380*, 138-145.

Dardeno, T. A., Chou, S. H., Moon, H. S., Chamberland, J. P., Fiorenza, C. G., & Mantzoros, C. S. (2010). Leptin in human physiology and therapeutics ((2010). *Frontiers in Neuroendocrinology, 31*(3), 377-393.

Davis, J. M., & Auten, R. L. (2010). Maturation of the antioxidant system and the effects on preterm birth. *Seminars in Fetal and Neonatal Medicine, 15*(4), 191-195.

Davidson, P.W., Myers, G.J., & Weiss, B. (2004). Mercury exposure and child development outcomes. *Pediatrics. 113*, 1023–9.

DeGiacomo, A., & Fombonne E. (1998). Parental recognition of developmental abnormalities in autism. *European Child and Adolescent Psychiatry*, 7, 131-136.

Esposito, P., Gheorghe, D., Kandere, K., Pang, X., Conally, R., Jacobson, S., & Theoharides, T. C. (2001). Acute stress increases permeability of the blood-brain-barrier through activation of brain mast cells. *Brain Research, 888*(1), 117-127.

Estes, A., Zwaigenbaum, L., Gu, H., St.John, T., Paterson, S., Elison, J.T., … Alvarez, S., Piven, J., IBIS network. (2015). Behavioral, cognitive, and adaptive development in infants with autism spectrum disorder in the first 2 years of life. *Journal of Neurodevepmental Disorders*, 7, 24.

Filipek, P. A., Accardo, P. J., & Ashwal, S. (2000). Practice parameter: Screening and diagnosis of Autism (Report of the Quality Standards Subcommittee of the American Academy of Neurology and the Child Neurology Society). *Neurology, 55*, 468–479.

Frazier, T. W., Youngstrom, E. A., Speer, L., Embacher, R., Law, P., Constantino, J., & Eng, C. (2012). Validation of proposed DSM5 criteria for autism spectrum disorder. *Journal of the American Academy of Child and Adolescent Psychiatry, 51*(1), 28.e23–40.e23.

Geier, D. A., Kern, J. K., & Geier, M. R. (2012). A prospective cross-sectional cohort assessment of health, physical, and behavioral problems in autism spectrum disorders. *Maedica*, 7(3), 193.

Ghaziuddin, M., & Zafar, S. (2008). Psychiatric comorbidity of adults with autism spectrum disorders. *Clinical Neuropsychiatry, 5*(1), 9-12.

Guerin, P., Lyon, G., Barthelemy, C., Sostak, E., Chevrollier, V., & Garreau, B. (1996). Neuropathological study of a case of autistic syndrome with severe mental retardation. *Developmental Medicine & Child Neurology, 38*, 203-211.

Guthrie, W., Swineford, L.B., Nottke, C., & Wetherby, A.M. (2013). Early diagnosis of autism spectrum disorder: stability and change in clinical diagnosis and symptom presentation. *Journal of Child Psychology and Psychiatry, 54*(5), 582-590.

Hazen, E.P., McDougle, C.J., & Volkmar, F.R. (2013). Changes in the diagnostic criteria for autism in DSM-5: Controversies and concerns. *Journal of Clinical Psychiatry, 74*(7), 739-40.

Johnson, C.P. (2008). Recognition of autism before age 2 years. *Pediatrics in Review, 29(3)*, 86-96.

Johnson, T.W. (2006). Dietary considerations in autism: identifying a reasonable approach. *Topics in Clinical Nutrition, 21*, 212–25.

Jones, E.J., Venema, K., Earl, R., Lowy, R., Barnes, K., Estes, A., … Webb, S.J. (2016). Reduced engagement with social stimuli in 6-month-old infants with later autism spectrum disorder: a longitudinal prospective study of infants at high familial risk. *Journal of Neurodevelopmental Disorders, 8*, 7.

Joshi, G., Wozniak, J., Petty, C., Martelon, M. K., Fried, R., Bolfek, A., ... Biederman, J. (2013). Psychiatric comorbidity and functioning in a clinically referred population of adults with autism spectrum disorders: a comparative study. *Journal of Autism and Developmental Disorders, 43*(6), 1314-1325.

Joshi, S. R., Mehendale, S. S., Dangat, K. D., Kilari, A. S., Yadav, H. R., & Taralekar, V. S. (2008). High maternal plasma antioxidant concentrations associated with preterm delivery. *Annals of Nutrition and Metabolism, 53*(3-4), 276-282.

Kalkbrenner, A.E., Daniels, J.L., Chen, J.C., Poole, C., Emch, M., & Morrissey, J. (2010). Perinatal exposure to hazardous air pollutants and autism spectrum disorders at age 8. *Epidemiology, 21*, 631–641.

Kanner, L. (1943). Autistic disturbances of affective contact. *Nervous Child*, 2, 217–250.

Kaufman, J., Birmaher, B., Brent, D., Rao, U. M. A., Flynn, C., Moreci, P., ... Ryan, N. (1997). Schedule for affective disorders and schizophrenia for school-age children-present and lifetime version (K-SADS-PL): initial reliability and validity data. *Journal of the American Academy of Child & Adolescent Psychiatry, 36*(7), 980-988.

Kern, J.K., & Jones, A.M.. (2006). Evidence of toxicity, oxidative stress, and neuronal insult in autism. *Journal of Toxicology and Environmental Health Part B*, 9(6), 485–99.

Kleinman, J., Robins, D., Ventola, P., Pandey, J., Boorstein, H., Esser, E., . . . Fein, D. (2008). The Modified Checklist for Autism in Toddlers: A follow-up study investigating the early detection of autism spectrum disorders. *Journal of Autism and Developmental Disorders, 38(5)*, 827-839.

Kolevzon, A., Gross, R., & Reichenberg, A. (2007). Prenatal and perinatal risk factors for autism. *Archives of Pediatric and Adolescent Medicine, 161*, 326–33.

Krakowiak, P., Walker, C.K., Bremer, A.A., Baker, A.S., Ozonoff, S., Hansen, R.L., & Hertz-Picciotto, I. (2012). Maternal metabolic conditions and risk for autism and other neurodevelopmental disorders. *Pediatrics, 129*(5), e1121-8.

Lainhart, J. E., & Folstein, S. E. (1994). Affective disorders in people with autism: A review of published cases. *Journal of Autism and Developmental Disorders, 24*(5), 587-601.

Levy, S. E., Giarelli, E., Lee, L. C., Schieve, L. A., Kirby, R. S., Cunniff, C., ... Rice, C. E. (2010). Autism spectrum disorder and co-occurring developmental, psychiatric, and medical conditions among children in multiple populations of the United States. *Journal of Developmental & Behavioral Pediatrics, 31*(4), 267-275.

Leyfer, O. T., Folstein, S. E., Bacalman, S., Davis, N. O., Dinh, E., Morgan, J., ... Lainhart,

J. E. (2006). Comorbid psychiatric disorders in children with autism: Interview development and rates of disorders. *Journal of Autism and Developmental Disorders, 36*(7), 849-861.

Limperopoulos, C., Bassan, H., Sullivan, N. R., Soul, J. S., Robertson, R. L., Jr, Moore, M., … du, Plessis. A. J. (2008). Positive screening for autism in ex-preterm infants: prevalence and risk factors. *Pediatrics*, 121(4), 758-765.

Lord, C., Bishop, S., Anderson, D. (2015). Developmental trajectories as autism phenotypes. *American Journal of Medical Genetics Part C Seminars in Medical Genetics, 169*(2), 198-208.

Lord, C., Petkova, E., Hus, V., Gan, W., Lu, F., Martin, D.M., … Risi, S. (2012). A multisite study of the clinical diagnosis of different autism spectrum disorders. *Archives in General Psychiatry, 69*(3), 306-313.

LoVullo, S. V., & Matson, J. L. (2009). Comorbid psychopathology in adults with autism spectrum disorders and intellectual disabilities. *Research in Developmental Disabilities, 30*(6), 1288-1296.

Lunsky Y, & Bradley E. (2007) Dual diagnosis or dual confusion: Limitations when utilizing non-specialist clinical data. *Journal of Developmental Disabilities*, 13(1), 185-90.

Mahoney, W., Szatmari, P., MacLean, J., Bryson, S., Bartolucci, C., Walter, S., … Zwaigenbaum, L. (1998). Reliability and accuracy of differentiating pervasive developmental disorder. *Journal of American Academy of Child and Adolescent Psychiatry, 37*, 278-285.

Mars, A., Mauk, J., Dowrick, P. (1998). Symptoms of pervasive developmental disorder as observed in prediagnostic home videos of infants and toddlers. *Journal of Pediatrics, 132*, 500-504.

Mayes, S. D., Calhoun, S. L., & Crites, D. L. (2001). Does DSM-IV-TR Asperger disorder exist? *The Journal of Abnormal Child Psychology, 29*, 263–271.

Mazefsky, C. A., Oswald, D. P., Day, T. N., Eack, S. M., Minshew, N. J., & Lainhart, J. E. (2012). ASD, a psychiatric disorder, or both? Psychiatric diagnoses in adolescents with high-functioning ASD. *Journal of Clinical Child & Adolescent Psychology, 41*(4), 516-523.

McPartland, J. C., Reichow, B., & Volkmar, F. R. (2012). Sensitivity and specificity of proposed DSM5 diagnostic criteria for autism spectrum disorder. *Journal of the American Academy of Child and Adolescent Psychiatry, 51*(4), 368–383.

Melville, C. A., Cooper, S. A., Morrison, J., Smiley, E., Allan, L., Jackson, A., ... Mantry, D. (2008). The prevalence and incidence of mental ill-health in adults with autism and intellectual disabilities. *Journal of Autism and Developmental Disorders, 38*(9), 1676-1688.

Myhr, G. (1998). Autism and other pervasive developmental disorders: Exploring the dimensional view. *The Canadian Journal of Psychiatry, 43*, 589–595.

Nader, A.M., Courchesne, V., Dawson, M., & Soulieres, I. (2016). Does WISC-IV underestimate the intelligence of autistic children? *Journal of Autism and Developmental Disorders, 46*(5), 1582-1589..

Nelson, S.B., & Valakh, V. (2015). Excitatory/inhibitory balance and circuit homeostasis in autism spectrum disorders. *Neuron*, 87(4), 684-98.

Nylander, L., Holmqvist, M., Gustafson, L., & Gillberg, C. (2013). Attention-deficit/hyperactivity disorder (ADHD) and autism spectrum disorder (ASD) in adult psychiatry. A 20-year register study. *Nordic Journal of Psychiatry, 67*(5), 344-350.

Osterling J, & Dawson G. (1994) Early recognition of children with autism: a study of first birthday home videotapes. *Journal of Autism and Developmental Disorders, 24*(3), 247-257.

Palmer, R.F., Blanchard, S., & Wood, R. (2009). Proximity to point sources of environmental mercury release as a predictor of autism prevalence. *Health Place, 15*, 18–24.

Park, S.Y., Cervesi, C., Galling, B., Molteni, S., Walyzada, F., Ameis, S.H., … Correll, C.U.

(2016). Antipsychotic use trends in youth with autism spectrum disorder and/or intellectual disability: A meta-analysis. *Journal of the American Academy of Child and Adolescent Psychiatry, 55*(6), 456-468.

Perlman, L. (2000). Adults with Asperger disorder misdiagnosed as schizophrenic. *Professional Psychology: Research and Practice, 31*, 221–225.

Philip, R.C., Dauvermann, M.R., Whalley, H.C., Baynham, K., Lawrie, S.M., & Stanfield, A.C.. (2012). A systematic review and meta-analysis of the fMRI investigation of autism spectrum disorders. *Neuroscience and Biobehavioral Reviews, 36*(2), 901-42.

Piven , J., Palmer, P., Jacobi, D., Childress, D., Arndt, S. (1997). Broader autism phenotype: evidence from a family history study of multiple-incidence autism families. *American Journal of Psychiatry, 154*, 185-190.

Plauche Johnson, C., & Myers, S.M. (2007). Identification and evaluation of children with autism spectrum disorders. *Pediatrics, 120(5)*, 1183- 1215.

Posserud, M., Lundervold, A., & Gillberg, C. (2006). Autistic features in a total population of 7-9 year-old children assessed by the ASSQ (Autistic Spectrum Screening Questionnaire). *Journal of Child Psychology and Psychiatry, 47*, 167-175.

Preti A, Melis M, Siddi S, Vellante M, Doneddu G, & Fadda R. (2014). Oxytocin and autism: a systematic review of randomized controlled trials. *Journal of Child and Adolescent Psychopharmacology, 24*(2), 54-68.

Prior, M., Eisenmajer, R., & Leekam, S. (1998). Are there subgroups with the autism spectrum? *The Journal of Child Psychological and Psychiatry, 6*, 893–902.

Roberts, A.L., Lyall, K., Hart, J.E., Laden, F., Just, A.C., Bobb, J.F., … Weisskopf MG. (2013). Perinatal air pollutant exposures and autism spectrum disorder in the children of Nurses' Health Study II participants. *Environmental Health Perspectives, 121*(8), 978-84.

Robins, D.L., Fein, D., Barton, M.L., & Green, J.A. (2001). The Modified Checklist for Autism in Toddlers: An initial study investigating the early detection of autism and pervasive developmental disorders. *Journal of Autism and Developmental Disorders, 31*, 131-144.

Rogers, S. J. (1998). Empirically supported comprehensive treatments for young children with autism. *Journal of Clinical Child Psychology, 27*, 168–179.

Rosenberg, R. E., Kaufmann, W. E., Law, J. K., & Law, P. A. (2011). Parent report of community psychiatric comorbid diagnoses in autism spectrum disorders. *Autism Research and Treatment, 2011.*

Rutter, M. (1972). Childhood schizophrenia reconsidered. *Journal of Autism and Childhood Schizophrenia*, 2, 315-337.

Rutter, M., Thapar A. (2014). Genetics of autism spectrum disorder. In F.R. Volkmar, R. Paul, K. Pelphrey, & S. Rogers (Eds), *Handbook of autism* (4th Ed). Hoboken, NJ: John Wiley.

Ryan, R. (1994). Asperger syndrome. *The Habilitative Mental Healthcare Newsletter, 13*, 1–6.

Schopler, E., Reichler, R. J., & Rochen-Renner, B. (1998). *The Childhood Autism Rating Scale (CARS)*. Los Angeles: Western Psychological Services.

Schultz, R.T. (2005). Developmental deficits in social perception in autism: The role of the amygdala and fusiform face area. *International Journal of Developmental Neuroscience, 23*(2-3), 125–41.

Schumann, C.M., Bloss, C.S., Carter-Barnes, C., Wideman, G.M., Carper, R.A., Akshoomoff, N., … Courchesne, E., (2010). Longitudinal MRI study of cortical development through early childhood in autism. *Journal of Neuroscience, 30*, 4419-4427.

Sebat, J., Lakshmi, B., Malhotra, D., Troge, J., Lese-Martin, C., Walsh, T., … Wigler, M. (2007). Strong association of de novo copy number mutations with autism. *Science.* 316(5823), 445-9. Epub 2007 Mar 15.

Shishido, E., Aleksic, B., & Ozaki, N. (2014). Copy-number variation in the pathogenesis of autism spectrum disorder. *Psychiatry and Clinical Neuroscience, 68*(2), 85-95.

Simonoff, E., Jones, C. R., Baird, G., Pickles, A., Happé, F., & Charman, T. (2013). The persistence and stability of psychiatric problems in adolescents with autism spectrum disorders. *Journal of Child Psychology and Psychiatry, 54*(2), 186-194.

Smith T, & Iadarola S. (2015). Evidence base update for autism spectrum disorder. *Journal of Clinical Child and Adolescent Psychology, 44*(6), 897-922.

Sørensen, M.J., Grønborg, T.K., Christensen, J., Parner, E.T., Vestergaard, M., Schendel, D., & Pedersen, L.H. (2013). Antidepressant exposure in pregnancy and risk of autism spectrum disorders. *Clinical Epidemiology,* 15(5),449-59.

Starling, J., & Dossetor, D. (2009). Pervasive developmental disorders and psychosis. *Current Psychiatry Reports, 11*(3), 190-196.

Starr, E., Szatmari, P., Bryson, S., & Zwaigenbaum, L. (2003). Stability and change among high-functioning children with pervasive developmental disorders: A 2-year outcome study. *Journal of Autism and Developmental Disorders, 33*, 15–22.

Sturmey, P., & Dalfern, S. (2014). The effects of DSM5 autism diagnostic criteria on number of individuals diagnosed with autism spectrum disorders: A systematic review. *Review Journal of Autism and Developmental Disorders, 1*(4), 249–252.

Sverd, J. (2003). Psychiatric disorders in individuals with pervasive developmental disorder. *Journal of Psychiatric Practice, 9*(2), 111-127.

Taheri, A, & Perry A. (2012). Exploring the proposed DSM-5 criteria in a clinical sample. *Journal of Autism and Developmental Disorders, 42*(9), 1810-7.

Taylor, L.E., Swerdfeger, A.L., & Eslick, G.D. (2014). Vaccines are not associated with autism: An evidence-based meta-analysis of case-control and cohort studies. *Vaccine, 32*(29), 3623-9.

Theoharides, T. C., Doyle, R., Francis, K., Conti, P., & Kalogeromitros, D. (2008). Novel therapeutic targets for autism. *Trends in Pharmacology, 29*(8), 375-382.

Tick, B., Bolton, P., Happé, F., Rutter, M., & Rijsdijk, F. (2016). Heritability of autism spectrum disorders: A meta-analysis of twin studies. *Journal of Child Psychology and Psychiatry, 57*(5), 585-95.

Tomanik, S.S., Pearson, D.A., Loveland, K.A., Lane, D.M., & Shaw, J.B. (2007) Improving the reliability of autism diagnoses: Examining the utility of adaptive behavior. *Journal of Autism and Developmental Disorders, 37*(5), 921-928.

Tsai, L.Y., & Ghaziuddin, M. (2014). DSM-5 ASD moves forward into the past. *Journal of Autism and Developmental Disorders. 44*(2), 321-30.

Turner, L.M., & Stone, W.L. (2007). Variability in outcome for children an ASD diagnosis at age 2. *Journal of Child Psychology and Psychiatry,. 48*(8), 793-802.

Valent, P., Akin, C., Arock, M., Brockow, K., Butterfield, J. H., Carter, M. C., … Metcalfe, D. D. (2012). Definitions, criteria and global classification of mast cell disorders with special reference to mast cell activation syndromes: A consensus proposal. *International Archives of Allergy and Immunology, 157*(3), 215-225.

van der Gaag, R. J., Caplan, R., Engeland, H. V., Loman, F., & Buitelaar, J. K. (2005). A controlled study of formal thought disorder in children with autism and multiple complex developmental disorders. *Journal of Child & Adolescent Psychopharmacology, 15*(3), 465-476.

Verte, S., Geurts, H., Roeyers, H., Oosterlaan, J., & Sergeant, J. (2006). Executive functioning in children with an autistic spectrum disorder: can we differentiate within the spectrum? *Journal of Autism and Developmental Disorders,* 36*(3), 351-72.*

Vojdani, A. (2008). Antibodies as predictors of complex autoimmune diseases and cancer. *International Journal of Immunopathology and Phamacology,* Erratum in: *International Journal of Immunopathology and Pharmacology, 21*(3), 553-566.

Volk, H.E., Hertz-Picciotto, I., Delwiche, L., Lurmann, F., & McConnell, R. (2011). Residential proximity to freeways and autism in the CHARGE study. *Environmental Health Perspectives, 119,* 873–877.

Wakefield, A.J., Murch, S.H., Anthony, A., Linnell, J., Casson, D.M., Malik, M., ... Walker-Smith, J.A. (1998). Ileal-lymphoid-nodular hyperplasia, non-specific colitis, and pervasive developmental disorder in children. *Lancet, 351,* 637–41. (RETRACTED)

Warren, W. B., Patrick, S. L., & Goland, R. S. (1992). Elevated maternal plasma corticotropinreleasing hormone levels in pregnancies complicated by preterm labor. *American Journal of Obstetrics and Gynecology, 166*(4), 1198-1204.

White, S. W., Oswald, D., Ollendick, T., & Scahill, L. (2009). Anxiety in children and adolescents with autism spectrum disorders. *Clinical Psychology Review, 29*(3), 216-229.

Windham, G.C., Zhang, L., Gunier, R., Croen, LA., & Grether, J.K. (2006). Autism spectrum disorders in relation to distribution of hazardous air pollutants in the San Francisco Bay area. *Environmental Health Perspectives, 114,* 1438–1444.

Wolff, S. (2000). Schizoid personality in childhood and Asperger syndrome. In A. Klin, F. R. Volkmar, & S. S. Sparrow (Eds.), *Asperger syndrome* (pp. 278-305). New York: Guilford Press.

CHAPTER 7

Attention-Deficit/Hyperactivity Disorder

Jessica A. Hellings
Angela M. Reiersen
L. Eugene Arnold
Alice R. Mao
Deborah A. Pearson
Michael G. Aman
Benjamin L. Handen
Jennifer L. McLaren

Attention-deficit/hyperactivity disorder (ADHD) is recognized as a separate diagnosis in the presence of comorbid autism spectrum disorder (ASD) in *DSM-5* (American Psychiatric Association, 2013). ADHD is three times more prevalent in children with intellectual disability (ID) and even more common with ID and comorbid epilepsy. The course of ADHD in individuals with ID is longer, and more disabling symptoms remain into adulthood than occurs in individuals in the general population. Although the predominantly inattentive ADHD presentation occurs most commonly in both typically developing and those with ID, hyperactive/impulsive symptoms worsen the prognosis. The hyperactive/impulsive symptoms also impair community integration and are associated with more conduct disorder and oppositional defiant disorder diagnoses and symptoms. ADHD is more prevalent in individuals with greater ID. Affect dysregulation is an important component of the disorder, which may contribute to a misdiagnosis as bipolar disorder. ADHD may be comorbid with most congenital syndromes, including fragile X and Down syndrome. Expressive language ability is not necessary for an ADHD diagnosis. Onset must be by age 12. Accommodation for developmental age may be an important diagnostic issue, but raters may unconsciously correct for it.

Attention-Deficit/Hyperactivity Disorder

Review of Diagnostic Criteria

Attention-deficit/hyperactivity disorder is a common reason for the referral of children, adolescents, and, increasingly, adults for treatment by medical professionals, including family practitioners, pediatricians, and psychiatrists (Culpepper & Mattingly, 2010; Kazdin, Siegel & Bass, 1990). Parents and caregivers of individuals with ID and ADHD are not aware of the latter disorder, they may report their children are moody, aggressive, or anxious, especially if an ASD is also present. Antipsychotics and mood stabilizers may then be inappropriately used in an attempt to control symptoms that could better respond to stimulants and other ADHD medications.

Symptoms of ADHD with inattentive presentation include inattention to tasks or play activities, inattention to details, making careless mistakes, difficulty listening and following directions, being disorganized, repeated forgetfulness, losing things, and avoiding tasks requiring sustained attention.

While ADHD-inattentive is the most prevalent presentation diagnosed in both the general population and those with ID, the hyperactive/impulsive and combined presentations are associated with more disruptive behavior and impulsive aggression

(Ahuja, Martin, Langley, & Thapar, 2013). As a result, the latter individuals are seen more commonly in tertiary referral centers, due to treatment challenges (Willcut, 2012).

Hyperactive/impulsive symptoms include fidgeting and squirming, being out of one's seat, running about or climbing inappropriately, playing noisily, and being "on the go." Talking excessively, blurting out answers, and difficulty awaiting turns are other key symptoms. In addition, impulsive aggression associated with reduced behavioral inhibition includes hitting, kicking, biting, pinching, and arguing. This is suggestive of conduct or oppositional defiant disorder, with the difference that the symptoms may respond to ADHD treatments in typically developing youth (Blader, Plizska, Jensen, Schooler, & Kafantaris, 2011; Connor, Glatt, Lopez, Jackson, & Melloni, 2002). Although affect dysregulation symptoms of irritability and moodiness are increasingly recognized as part of the ADHD symptom domain (Shaw, Stringaris, Nigg, & Leibenluft, 2014) and likely contribute to bipolar disorder over-diagnosis, affective impulsivity was not included in *DSM-5* ADHD diagnostic criteria.

Rating scales for measuring ADHD symptoms in ID include the Conners' Parent and Teacher Rating Scales, Hyperactivity Subscale of the Aberrant Behavior Checklist (Aman, Singh, Stewart, & Field, 1985), the ADHD-Rating Scale (ADHD-RS) (Zhang, Faries, Vowles, & Mickelson, 2005) which is based on *DSM-IV* criteria for ADHD, and the Swanson, Nolan and Pelham Scale, version four (SNAP-IV) (Bussing et al., 2008).

Summary of DSM-5 *Criteria*

Diagnostic criteria in *DSM-5* for attention-deficit/hyperactivity disorder (ADHD) are similar to the *DSM-IV* criteria. The same 18 symptoms as in *DSM-IV* are used, divided into the same two symptom domains of inattention and hyperactivity/impulsivity, with at least six symptoms in one domain being required for an ADHD diagnosis in children.

Changes made in *DSM-5* include: 1) ADHD is included in the neurodevelopmental disorders category, to reflect the developmental nature of the disorder. The *DSM-IV* chapter of diagnoses usually made initially in infancy, childhood or adolescence, which previously housed ADHD, now is eliminated; 2) instead of symptoms causing impairment prior to age 7 years, age of onset is prior to 12 years; 3) the symptom number requirement for the inattention domain and for the hyperactivity/impulsivity symptom domain in late adolescents and adults is five instead of six; 4) comorbid ADHD diagnosis is allowed with an ASD; 5) criterion items now have examples to facilitate application in late adolescents and adults; 6) several ADHD symptoms are required in different settings; 7) presentation specifiers that correspond directly to the prior subtypes now replace the subtypes.

DSM-5 also includes the option to diagnose "unspecified attention-deficit/hyperactivity disorder" or "other specified attention-deficit/hyperactivity disorder" in cases in which impairing and clinically significant ADHD symptoms are present, but the individual does not meet full criteria for an ADHD symptom domain. The "unspecified" category is used in situations in which the clinician chooses not to state why full criteria for ADHD are not met, and should be reserved mainly for situations in which complete information to clarify diagnosis is not available (such as emergency room settings). The "other specified" diagnosis can be used in cases in which the clinician chooses to specify why full criteria are not met.

As symptoms of inattention and hyperactivity-impulsivity are highly correlated, many individuals with six to 10 total ADHD symptoms do not meet full criteria for ADHD as a result of having slightly fewer than six inattentive symptoms along with slightly fewer than six hyperactive-impulsive symptoms. Such individuals could be described as having a mild combined form of ADHD. Although they do not meet full *DSM-5* ADHD criteria because they have an inadequate symptom count in each of the two categories, they may be more impaired and have higher comorbid psychopathology than individuals with the same number of total symptoms who meet full criteria for the predominantly inattentive or predominantly hyperactive-impulsive presentation (Reiersen & Todorov, 2013). If such individuals clearly have impairment from their ADHD symptoms, it would be reasonable to diagnose them with "other specified attention-deficit/hyperactivity disorder: subthreshold combined symptoms consistent with a mild combined form of ADHD."

Although the first printed version of *DSM-5* discouraged the use of "other specified" or "unspecified" ADHD for individuals who meet full criteria for *any* disorder in the neurodevelopmental disorders section (including ID), current consensus is that there does not appear to be any clear reason why these diagnoses should not be used in persons with ID as long as 1) they have impairing ADHD symptoms that cannot be explained by another diagnosis, and 2) they do not meet the full criteria for ADHD.

DSM-5 classifies ADHD in a new class called neurodevelopmental disorders. While conduct disorder and oppositional defiant disorder were classified in the *Diagnostic and Statistical Manual-IV* (*DSM-IV*) in the diagnostic category of "Disorders First Diagnosed in Infancy, Childhood or Adolescence" and subcategory of "Attention-Deficit and Disruptive Behavior Disorders," conduct disorder and oppositional defiant disorder are now included in a separate category, "Disruptive, Impulse Control and Conduct Disorders."

Issues Related to Diagnosis in Persons with ID

Development and Course

The prognosis socially, personally, and educationally is poorer if hyperactivity and impulsivity are present in addition to inattention. In such cases, not only is learning adversely impacted, but disruptive behavior and impulsive aggression worsen integration in general settings (Ahuja et al., 2013). While hyperactivity may diminish in the early teens, affect dysregulation and impulsive aggression often persist, hence the importance of focusing on childhood history-taking to accurately clarify ADHD as a diagnosis. Adult criteria also focus on the degree of social and occupational morbidity that are often the primary referral complaints and perhaps the source of many patients who are incorrectly labeled with chronic personality disorders.

Prevalence

The ADHD diagnosis and ADHD symptoms are three times more common overall in individuals with ID than in the general population (Baker, Neece, Fenning, Crnic, & Blacher, 2010; Neece, Baker, Blacher, & Crnic, 2011). The inattentive presentation of ADHD is most common in both the general and ID populations. Approximately one-third of children with ID have hyperactivity, inattention and impulsivity, while these ADHD symptoms occur even more commonly in ASD, being present in up to 50% (Sinzig, Morsch, Bruning, Schmidt, & Lehmkuhl, 2008).

In youth with ID, ADHD prevalence is equal in girls and boys, an important difference from the general population. However, Pearson and colleagues (2013) found a higher rate of ADHD in high-functioning school-age boys with ASD, as compared to girls. For example, in a clinical trial studying the effectiveness of psychostimulant treatment in high-functioning (mean FSIQ = 85) elementary school-age children with ASD and ADHD, the gender ratio was 3.8 boys: 1 girl.

Regulation of attention may be poorly organized or highly variable in ID, as demonstrated in some studies, versus an additional overselectivity of stimuli as occurs in ASD (Lovaas & Schreibman, 1971). Simonoff, Pickles, Wood, Gringas and Chadwick (2007) studied a population sample of 2,726 youths aged 12 to 15 years, and used a sub-sample stratified for ID, which identified 192 youths for the analysis. ID was not a predictor of profiles of ADHD symptoms or of emotional or behavioral comorbidities. Zeaman and House (1979) demonstrated that individuals with ID carrying ADHD diagnoses, even after intensive training, continued to attend to task-irrelevant stimuli and failed to show improvements. Executive function deficits commonly occurring in ADHD also occur commonly in various ID syndromes, and include abnormalities in the planning, prioritizing, and integration of neural functions (Denckla, 1996). In a study of 46 adults with ID who were compared with 92 matched controls without ID, Danielsson, Henry, Ronnberg, and Nilsson (2010) found that those with ID had significantly greater difficulty with speed of accessing lexical items and with working memory-related executive control at coding, but not with inhibition.

Presentations also vary according to the complex relationship between the many aspects of attention and executive function —arousal, selective attention, maintenance of attention, inhibition of intrusive thoughts, impulses, response inhibition of proto-imperative behaviors, set shifting/disengagement — and other facets of executive function.

Differential Diagnosis: Epilepsy and ADHD

Epilepsy occurs with a higher incidence in individuals with ID and in individuals with ASD. Furthermore, the presence of ADHD is inflated in patients with epilepsy (Dunn, Austin, & Harezlak, 2003); prevalence is three-to-five times that in the typically developing non-epileptic population (Aldenkamp, Arzimanoglou, Reijs, & Van Mil, 2006). Therefore, patients with both ID and epilepsy are more likely also to have ADHD.

In a cross-sectional study by Buelow, Austin, and Perkins (2003), female gender accompanied by low IQ posed the highest risk for inattention in 164 children with epilepsy aged 9 to 14 years. Importantly, the antiepileptic drug, phenobarbital (and thus also primidone, which is metabolized to phenobarbital and PABA) is reputed to cause reversible ADHD (Ounsted, 1955; Schain, 1979). Therefore, patients receiving phenobarbital and exhibiting ADHD warrant examination for drug-induced ADHD by careful history or by judicious substitution of phenobarbital with a newer-generation antiepileptic medication.

Other antiepileptic agents, including phenytonin, mysoline, carbamazepine, oxcarbazepine, and topiramate, may also worsen ADHD symptoms, although they sometimes are used to improve irritability and aggression.

Functional Consequences

ADHD, when comorbid with intellectual disability (ID) and/or ASD, increases impairments in the child's functioning from an early age and complicates developmental deficits associated with ID. Not all individuals with ID have attentional problems; however, if present, the latter result in a slower pace of learning and development (Ahuja et al., 2013). In addition, problems associated with the combined or hyperactive/impulsive subtypes, such as impulsive aggression, pose serious barriers to developmental progress and community integration.

Comorbidity

The *DSM-5* introduces the important change of allowing ADHD diagnosis in individuals with ASD. Studies by Frazier & coworkers in 2001, and Goldstein & Schwebach in 2004, found that a pervasive developmental disorder did not in fact alter ADHD features. In addition, *DSM-5* states that ADHD should be diagnosed if criteria are met in individuals with known genetic syndromes, such as fragile X syndrome, velocardiofacial syndrome (22q11.2 deletion syndrome), and Down syndrome. The presence of comorbid conditions changes the developmental trajectory, clinical course, and treatment responsiveness.

Rate of Response to Stimulant Therapy

Several researchers have noted that when treated with psychostimulants, the rate of clinical response among children with ID and ADHD is lower than among typically developing children with ADHD (Aman, Buican, & Arnold, 2003; Pearson et al., 2003; Aman, Farmer, Hollway, & Arnold, 2008). Lower IQ (<50 IQ) may be associated with a significantly lower response rate, although this finding has not been tested by others to confirm or disconfirm it. Greater vigilance and flexibility than usual is, therefore, warranted when prescribing to stimulant-naïve children with developmental disabilities. Stimulants may also worsen self-injury; thus, non-stimulant ADHD medications may be a more suitable choice for some individuals (Arnold et al., 2006).

Application of Diagnostic Criteria to People with ID

Expressive language ability is not required for an ADHD diagnosis; however, in its absence, the *DSM-5* criteria of "Often talks excessively" (2.f.) and "Often blurts out an answer ..." (2.g.) cannot be applied. While ADHD diagnosis requires significant impairments in at least two settings, school may not need to be one of them, especially if the student has one-to-one help and a modified curriculum. Also, for adults in cases where a developmental history is not available, clinicians may elicit the earliest history available, for example from early medical records or school records.

The *DSM-5* stipulates that the symptoms are maladaptive and excessive for developmental level. However, there are not many research studies that address this issue. In one study, age, IQ, and mental age were correlated with ADHD ratings performed by parents and teachers (Pearson & Aman, 1994). One sample was composed of a general clinical sample (n = 58) with mostly typically developing children, whereas the developmental sample (n = 55) was composed of children with developmental disabilities. Several different standardized scales of ADHD were correlated with chronological age, mental age, and IQ in these two samples. By and large, there were few significant correlations between ADHD and mental age or IQ. Most significant correlations that did emerge involved associations between ADHD scores and age (usually negative correlations, suggesting worse ADHD in younger children). The researchers suggested that most raters unconsciously correct for the child's developmental level when rating ADHD symptoms. This has important clinical implications, as it suggests that adjustments for children's mental ability are not needed when considering standardized ratings of ADHD symptoms. Consideration of the person's developmental age is an important diagnostic accommodation, but the practicalities of dealing with this issue are somewhat uncertain at this time.

General Considerations

It is vital to get to know the individual with ID and his or her circumstances in order to understand the many potential contributions to ADHD symptoms. Epilepsy must be ruled out if suspected, as well as the possible influence of parental ADHD, ID, or other psychopathology to the presenting problems. In addition, schoolwork that is too difficult for the student may result in little focus or attempt to complete it. This may occur, for example, in children with Williams syndrome, in whom verbal intelligence and social abilities often exceed performance abilities (Mervis, 2009), leading to a possible overestimation of the child's schoolwork capabilities. On the other hand, inattentive ADHD may be missed in a classroom setting with well-regulated structure and supports. Aggression occurring in adolescents and adults with ID should prompt a probe of ADHD symptoms prior to age 12 years.

Methodology

We conducted a literature review by searching PubMed, MEDLINE, Psychlit and the Cochrane Database from 2003 to present using the following terms: Intellectual disability, mental retardation, developmental disability, cognitive impairment, special needs, learning disability, attention-deficit/hyperactivity disorder, attention deficit, hyperactivity, impulsivity, inattention, inattentive problems, and hyperkinetic disorder.

Review of Research Applying to People with ID

Seventeen articles were identified pertaining to ADHD and ID with or without ASD; we excluded studies with fewer than 10 subjects.

Evaluating the Level of Evidence

Table 1. Studies of ADHD and ID.

Authors, Year	Subjects	Findings	Level of Evidence
Ahuja, Martin, Langley, & Thapar, 2013	97 children with ADHD and ID, 874 children with ADHD without ID (380 with IQ 70-84 and 494 with IQ >85) 58 children with ID without ADHD. Autism, severe ID, Tourette's, epilepsy, schizophrenia, bipolar disorder, brain damage, and neurologic or genetic disorder were excluded.	The ADHD+ID group was older than the ADHD-alone group. After covarying age and correcting for multiple tests, the only significant differences were that the ADHD+ID group had more CD diagnoses and CD symptoms. Other clinical manifestations were similar. In comparison of the ADHD+ID to ID alone, the ADHD+ID group had more males and lower IQ. After covarying sex, age, and IQ and correcting for multiple tests, The ADHD+ID group had more diagnoses of ODD and more symptoms of ODD and CD than the ID-alone group. Other differences were not significant including ADHD type, anxiety, and depression.	The samples were well-characterized and statistics reasonably done with appropriate adjustments and corrections. Sample sizes were reasonable to guard against Type 2 error. The level of evidence is strong.
Aureli, Del Beato, Sebastiani, Marimpietri, Mellilo Sechi, and Di Loreto, 2010	37 children with ADHD, 44 with ID 80 healthy volunteers, matched for ethnicity	Genotyped and compared frequencies of the BDNF gene Val66Met and 270 C/T polymorphisms. The G/A genotype of the Val66Met SNP was associated with both ADHD and ID. Also, the G allele was significantly associated with ADHD. The C/C genotype of the C270T SNP occurred significantly more frequently in ADHD and ID groups than in controls.	V
Baker, Neece, Fenning, Crnic, and Blacher, 2010	236 five year old children: 95 with ID or borderline intellectual functioning and 141 typically developing	3.21:1 ratio of ADHD in children with ID compared to typically developing peers. 38.9% of children with ID had a diagnosis of ADHD.	IV
Bigham, Daley, Hastings and Jones, 2011	28 children ages 6-12yrs	Cross-sectional study which found that parent rating scales of ADHD were positively associated with those obtained on parent interview. These associations persisted when controlling for developmental age. Observed impulsive behavior correlated more closely with developmental age differences.	IV
Burbridge et al. 2010		Presented the factor analysis for The Activity Questionnaire (TAQ) and compared the TAQ with the Repetitive Behaviour Questionnaire (RBQ) in sample of 142 individuals with ID (6-38 years of age). Scores on the TAQ were not related to level of adaptive functioning. Significant positive associations were found between Overactivity (TAQ) and Stereotyped and Restricted Preferences (RBQ); between Impulsivity (TAQ) and Stereotyped and Restricted Preferences (RBQ); and between Impulsive Speech (TAQ) and Restricted Preferences, Insistence on Sameness and Repetitive Speech (RBQ).	
Eckstein, Glick, Weill, Kay, Berger, 2011		Prevalence of ADHD among children with Down syndrome (DS) was very high, notably 43.9%. No significant correlation was found between symptoms of ADHD and level of ID. The authors concluded that children with DS are at increased risk for ADHD.	
Gligorovic and Buha Durovic, 2012	53 children with mild ID aged 10-14 years	Inhibitory control measures significantly predicted results on independent functioning, economic activity, speech and language development, and number and times domains of the AAMR-Adaptive Behavior scale –school, second edition.	IV

Table 1. Studies of ADHD and ID. (continued)

Authors, Year	Subjects	Findings	Level of Evidence
Lindblad, Gillberg, & Fernell, 2011	33 children with mild ID from a catchment of 5,671 children in 2 municipalities in Sweden	Using the 181-item Five-To-Fifteen questionnaire (FTF), index sample of 33 screened for ADHD, ASD, tic disorders, developmental coordination disorder, oppositional defiant disorder, conduct disorder, emotional disorder and learning disorders. Fourteen (42%) had diagnosed ADHD, and 5 (15%) had "subthreshold" ADHD, for a total prevalence of 18/33 (55%). Unfortunately, sex breakdowns not presented for each disorder.	
Lindblad, Svensson, Landgren, Nasic, Tideman, Gillberg, & Fernell, 2013	33 children with mild ID (including 8 who also had ADHD); 27 children with ADHD	Cross-sectional study comparing adaptive functioning (ABAS-II, completed by teachers) in children with mild ID and children with ADHD. Children in ADHD group had tendency toward lower adaptive functioning; group difference was only significant in children 12+ years old.	IV
Memisevic and Sinanovic, 2013	42 children with mild ID; 48 children with moderate ID	Examined executive functioning via the Behavior Rating Inventory of Executive Function (BRIEF) teacher version. Results: Children with ID had a significant deficit in executive function in comparison to BRIEF norms. Children with mild ID performed better than those with moderate ID.	
Neece, Baker, Blacher, and Crnic 2011	228 five year old children: 87 with ID and 141 typically developing	Longitudinal study which found ADHD was over 3 times more prevalent in children with ID. Children with ID were also diagnosed earlier with ADHD and the ADHD diagnosis was more stable; leading them to conclude that children with ID may have a longer and more persistent course of ADHD.	IV
Neece, Baker, Crnic & Blacher, 2013	30 adolescents IQ<70; 12 adolescents IQ=71-84; 100 adolescents IQ>84 (all 13 years of age)	Compared rates of ADHD in ID and TD adolescents using the Diagnostic Interview Schedule for Children. Results: 3.38:1 ratio of ADHD in adolescents with ID compared to TD peers. 40.5% of adolescents with ID had a diagnosis of ADHD (compared with 12.0% of TD peers).	IV
Oeseburg Jansen, Groothoff, Dijkstra, & Reijneveld, 2010	1044 adolescents with ID, 12-18 years, attending secondary schools in Netherlands	45% of adolescents with ID and chronic diseases had parent-rated emotional and behavioral problems on the Dutch version of the strengths and Difficulties Questionnaires compared with 17% of adolescents with ID but no chronic diseases.	IV
Owen, 2012	None	Discusses the evidence that there are shared genetic (copy number variants) and environmental risk (obstetric complications) between intellectual disability and other neurodevelopmental disorders such as ADHD. He highlights the need to think about neurodevelopmental disorders along a continuum	V

Table 2. Studies of ADHD and ASD.

Authors, Year	Subjects	Findings	Level of Evidence
Rao and Landa, 2014	153 children (age 4-8) with ASD, children who had participated in early intervention studies, low risk controls, and non-ASD children with history specific language delays	29% of the ASD group had clinically significant levels of ADHD symptoms as defined by T-score of 70 or higher on the BASC-2 Hyperactivity (n=6), Attention Problems (n=6), or both (n=6) subscales. When individuals with ASD only (n=44) were compared to those with ASD+ADHD (n=44), the group with ASD+ADHD had higher scores on ASD symptom ratings (higher scores on all subscales of the Social Responsiveness Scale) and also had lower adaptive functioning on the Vineland Adaptive Behavior Scale. Also, children with ASD+ADHD were more likely to have ID (estimated IQ<70) compared to those with ASD only (61% and 25%, respectively). This study is of some importance as is suggests that among children with ASD, the presence of high ADHD symptoms is associated with higher severity of ASD symptoms, lower adaptive functioning, and higher rates of intellectual disability.	IV
Carlsson, Norrelgen, Kjellmer, Westerlund, Gillberg, Fernell, 2013	4.5 to 6.5 year old children with Autistic Disorder (n=106), autistic-like condition (n=58), Asperger's Disorder (13) or subthreshold autistic traits (n=21) who had attended a specialized habilitation center for children with autism	Coexisting disorders considered in the study included intellectual disability (defined as IQ<70), language problems (based on testing), epilepsy, visual impairment, hearing impairment, and activity regulation problems (included severe hyperactivity, diagnosed ADHD, severe hypoactivity, severe outbursts, or severe sleeping problems). 63/198 of the children studied (32%) had severe hyperactivity or diagnosed ADHD. Of those with severe hyperactivity, 49% had ID and 62% had Autistic Disorder. The methods of this study were not ideal, and the definition of "severe hyperactivity" was somewhat vague, but the study does show that ADHD symptoms were common in individuals with ASD or ASD traits. The paper does not report the percent of individuals with ID who had ADHD or severe hyperactivity, but since 95 had ID, and 31 of the individuals with severe hyperactivity also had ID, the proportion of individuals with ID+ASD or ASD traits who had ADHD must be 31/95= 33%. Since this is about the same as the proportion of the overall ASD/ASD-trait sample who had ADHD, it does not seem that having intellectual disability in addition to ASD substantially increased risk for ADHD further compared to those with ASD or ASD traits but no ID.	V
Nylander, Holmquist, Gustavon, Gillberg, 2013	56,462 adult psychiatric patients.	ADHD was diagnosed in up to 2.7%; ASD in 1.3% of patients. Concomitant ADHD and ASD were seldom diagnosed. The authors concluded that ADHD and ASD were under-diagnosed, possibly related to DSM-IV criteria where ASD is an exclusion for ADHD, or due to decrease in ADHD symptoms with age.	

Adults with Mild to Moderate ID

It is vital that professionals ask specifically about a childhood history of ADHD diagnosis, as well as ADHD symptoms during development, including for the assessment of adults with ID and/or ASD. This important information may be overlooked in the services transition from adolescent to adult providers. The prevalence of ADHD in adults with normal intellectual functioning is between 2.9% and 16.4% (Faraone & Biederman, 2005). O'Brien, Radley, and Joyce (2000) reported an ADHD prevalence of 23% in a study of 78 community-based young adults with ID (from mild to profound ID). However, a population-based study of 1,023 adults with ID (Cooper, Smiley, Morrison, Williamson, & Allen, 2007) found a lower rate of ADHD than the previous two studies. It reported that the prevalence of ADHD in people with ID is 1.5%, although a large number of adults in this study (22.5%) were diagnosed with "problem behaviors."

The clinical presentation and course of ADHD in adults with ID differ from adults with normal intellectual functioning. Xenitidis, Paliokosta, Rose, Maltezos, and Bramham (2010) compared adults with borderline-mild ID and ADHD to adults with ADHD and normal intellectual functioning in a retrospective study. Adults with ID and ADHD manifested more severe ADHD symptoms with more hyperactive and impulsive symptoms than those with ID alone. In adults with normal intellectual functioning, they found improvement in symptoms from childhood to adulthood. However, in adults with ID and ADHD, there was little improvement in the symptoms over time. Adults with ID and ADHD were found to have more impulsive symptoms as part of their profile, while adults with normal intellectual functioning were found to have more inattentive symptoms. There was also a correlation between the severity of ID and ADHD whereby those with lower intellectual functioning were more likely to have ADHD. While clinical practitioners may be less likely to make the diagnosis of ADHD in individuals with severe or profound ID, this should be done and non-stimulant medications tried in low doses, especially in the case of accompanying self-injury.

LaMalfa, Lassi, Bertelli, Pallanti, and Albertini (2008) also found a relationship between the severity of ID and ADHD symptoms. They utilized the Conners' Adult ADHD Rating Scales screening version (CAARS-O:SV) in a study of 46 adults with ID. Almost 20% of the sample screened positive for behaviors consistent with ADHD. The severity of ID directly correlated with the subscale scores for "hyperactivity," "ADHD total," and "ADHD index" on the CAARS-O:SV. This relationship between severity of ID and higher rating scores was not found for the "inattentive" subscale.

Nylander, Holmquist, Gustavson, and Gillberg (2013) examined trends in diagnostic practice, diagnostic delay, and comorbidity regarding ADHD and ASD in adult psychiatric patients. They identified individuals diagnosed with ADHD or ASD in an adult psychiatry registry comprising 56,462 patients. ADHD was diagnosed in up to 2.7% and ASD in 1.3% of the patients. Affective disorders and psychoactive substance use-related disorders were more common in patients with ADHD, whereas psychoses and intellectual disability were more common in those with ASD. The frequency of personality disorders was equal between the two groups. Concommitant ADHD and ASD were seldom diagnosed in this study. The authors concluded that ADHD and ASD were underdiagnosed in the study group due to the possiblity that these patients were older and ADHD symptoms had diminished with age, or that clinicians followed guidelines in *DSM-IV* where ASD is an exclusion criterion for ADHD.

Rose, Bramham, Young, Paliokostas, and Xenitidis (2009) reported an increased impairment in neuropsychological functioning in adults with ID and ADHD. They examined the attentional and response inhibition tasks in 59 adults with mild ID and ADHD compared to 95 adults with ADHD and normal intellectual functioning. They found significant deficits in selective attention and response inhibition in adults with ID and ADHD when they controlled for IQ. The group concluded that adults with ID and ADHD may have a "double deficit" causing more impairment in certain areas of cognitive functioning.

In regards to treatment of patients with ID and ADHD, Jou, Handen, and Hardan (2004) retrospectively reported on 10 adults with mild to profound ID and ADHD treated with methyphendiate or amphetamine. Fifty precent of the sample responded to stimulant treatment with reductions in hyperactivity and irritability. Four out of five responders had mild intellectual disability. Mild adverse effects were noted, and the stimulants were thought to be well tolerated.

Adults with Severe or Profound ID

As discussed in the previous section, it is vital that professionals try to clarify any prior ADHD history when assessing an individual with ID who is presenting with behavior problems. Fox and Wade (1998) found that 55% of hospitalized adults with severe to profound intellectual disability met criteria for ADHD, predominantly inattentive type, while 15% met criteria for the predominantly hyperactive-impulsive type.

Summary of Limitations in Applying DSM-5 *Criteria to People with ID*

In general, individuals with ID with or without ASD are often referred for treatment of aggression, self-injury, and destructive behavior, for which there are no diagnostic categories in the *DSM-5*. It is the task of the clinician to clarify possible symptom clusters conforming as closely as possible to *DSM-5* diagnoses, especially for ADHD, which is common, in order to target treatment and assess outcomes.

Etiology and Pathogenesis

Biological Factors

In ID as well as ASD, for which a multitude of causes are likely to be identified, key brain areas necessary for information processing are impaired. These involve information processing of attention/distraction, impulse control, executive functions, and affect regulation. Key regions involved include the frontal cortex, prefrontal cortex, amygdala, and cerebellum. Apart from genetic predisposition to ID and/or ASD, factors influencing gene expression (epigenetic factors) may modify outcomes (Todd & Neuman, 2007).

Genetic Factors

Genes coding for central dopaminergic pathways may be of great importance in ADHD pathogenesis, as well as in ID and ASD. Several dopaminergic system candidate genes have been identified (Faraone, Perlis, Doyle, Smoller, Goralnick, Holmgren, & Sklar, 2005; McGough, 2005; Todd et al., 2005; Todd & Neuman, 2007). Nieoullon in 2002 suggested that dopaminergic abnormalities could underlie motor dysfunction, ADHD, and ASD. Executive function deficits occur in both ADHD and ASD, as well as in disorders with motor incoordination (Goldberg et al., 2005; Livesey, Keen, Rouse, & White, 2006; Piek, Dyck, Francis, & Conwell, 2007). Prenatal nicotine exposure in the presence of dopamine gene polymorphisms may contribute to the development of ADHD and/or ASD. While genetic inheritance of ADHD is strong, it is polygenic and in genome-wide association studies, hundreds of markers with low effect size were found to link the disorders of ADHD, specific learning disorders, ASD, schizophrenia, and epilepsy to one another.

Developmental Factors

Poor nutrition and social deprivation are other possible contributors to ADHD along with ID. Koskentausta, Ivanainen, and Almqvist (2007) described an increased risk of behavioral disturbance in individuals presenting with moderate ID and other risk factors of impaired language, living with only one biological parent, having low socioeconomic status, and poor socialization. Emerson, Moss, and Kiernan (1999) published findings that family discord and socioeconomic deprivation contributed significantly to challenging behaviors in both children with ID and typically developing children. More recently, bidirectional relationships have been described between various measures of maternal stress and severity and rates of behavior problems in offspring (Hastings, Daley, Burns, & Beck, 2006). Low levels of vitamin D (Goksugur et al., 2014) and deficiencies in omega-3 fatty acids (Antalis et al., 2006) also have been implicated. Iron deficiency (Cortese, Angriman, Lecendreux, & Konofal, 2012) and lead exposure (Nigg, Mark Knottnerus, Cavanagh, & Frederici, 2010) were more common causes identified in the typically developing population versus controls.

Attention-Deficit/Hyperactivity Disorder

DSM-5 Diagnostic Criteria	Applying Criteria for Individuals with ID
A. Either 1. or 2.: 1. Six (or more) of the following symptoms of inattention have persisted for at least 6 months to a degree that causes a direct negative impact and is inconsistent with developmental level: Note: For older adolescents and adults (age 17 and older) at least 5 symptoms are required	A. Important to take into account the person's developmental level; assess person in comparison to peers of similar developmental age and ensure that school work, tasks and activities are developmentally appropriate.
Inattention (a) Often fails to give close attention to details or makes careless mistakes in schoolwork, at work or during other activities	Inattention (a) Often fails to give close attention to details or makes careless mistakes in developmentally appropriate activities such as schoolwork, work, etc.
(b) Often has difficulty sustaining attention in tasks or play activities	(b) Often has difficulty sustaining attention in developmentally appropriate tasks or play activities
(c) Often does not listen when spoken to directly	(c) No adaptation
(d) Often does not follow through on instructions and fails to finish schoolwork, chores or duties in the workplace	(d) Often does not follow through on instructions and fails to finish developmentally appropriate schoolwork, chores or duties in the workplace
(e) Often has difficulty organizing tasks and activities	(e) Often has difficulty organizing developmentally appropriate tasks and activities
(f) Often avoids, dislikes, or is reluctant to engage in tasks that require sustained mental effort	(f) Often avoids, dislikes, or is reluctant to engage in developmentally appropriate tasks that require sustained mental effort
(g) Often loses things necessary for tasks or activities	(g) Often loses things necessary for developmentally appropriate tasks or activities
(h) Is often easily distracted by extraneous stimuli	(h) No adaptation
(i) Is often forgetful in daily activities	(i) No adaptation
2. Six (or more) of the following symptoms of hyperactivity-impulsivity have persisted for at least 6 months to a degree that causes a direct negative impact and is inconsistent with developmental level: Note: For older adolescents and adults (age 17 and older) at least 5 symptoms are required	2. Important to take into account the person's developmental level; assess person in comparison to peers of similar developmental age. Important to consider symptoms of hyperactivity and impulsivity in the context of developmentally appropriate school work, tasks and activities.
Hyperactivity-Impulsivity (a) Often fidgets with or taps hands or feet or squirms in seat	(a) No adaptation
(b) Often leaves seat in situations when remaining seated is expected	(b) No adaptation
(c) Often runs about or climbs in situations where it is inappropriate	(c) No adaptation
(d) Often unable to play or engage in leisure activities	(d) Often unable to play or engage in developmentally appropriate leisure activities
(e) Is often "on the go", acting as if "driven by a motor"	(e) No adaptation
(f) Often talks excessively	(f) Excessive noisiness
(g) Often blurts out an answer before a question has been completed	(g) No adaptation
(h) Often has difficulty waiting his or her turn	(h) No adaptation
(i) Often interrupts or intrudes on others	(i) No adaptation
B. Several inattentive or hyperactive-impulsive symptoms were present prior to 12 years old.	B. If developmental history is not available can rely on earliest history available.

Attention-Deficit/Hyperactivity Disorder (continued)

DSM-5 Diagnostic Criteria	Applying Criteria for Individuals with ID
C. Several inattentive or hyperactive-impulsive symptoms are present in 2 or more settings.	C. Several inattentive or hyperactive-impulsive symptoms are present in 2 or more settings. The 2 or more settings do not need to include school; as the school may be making significant accommodations. For example, the settings could be the supermarket, restaurant, playground, etc.
D. There is clear evidence that the symptoms interfere with social, academic or occupational functioning.	D. There must be clear evidence that symptoms of inattentive, hyperactive-impulsive symptoms are impairing functioning and not solely the ID.
E. The symptoms do not occur exclusively during the course of schizophrenia or another psychotic disorder and are not better explained by another mental disorder.	E. Other Psychosocial stressors and other diagnosis. It is important to get to know the patient and his or her circumstances.
Specify Whether Combined presentation: Both Criteria A1 and A2 are met for past 6 months Predominantly inattentive presentation: Criterion A1 but not A2 is met for past 6 months Predominantly hyperactive/impulsive presentation: Criterion A2 but not A1 is met for past 6 months	No adaptation
Specify if: In partial remission: When full criteria previously met, fewer than the full criteria have been met for the past 6 months, and the symptoms still result in impairment in social, academic or occupational functioning.	No adaptation
Specify current severity Mild: Few, if any, symptoms in excess of those required to make the diagnosis and no more than minor impairment in functioning Moderate: Symptoms or functional impairment between "mild" and "severe" are present. Severe: Many symptoms in excess of those required to make the diagnosis, or several symptoms that are particularly severe, are present, or symptoms result in marked impairment in functioning.	No adaptation

Other Specified Attention-Deficit/Hyperactivity Disorder
Unspecified Attention-Deficit/Hyperactivity Disorder

DSM-5 also provides categories for other specified attention-deficit/hyperactivity disorder, and for unspecified attention-deficit/hyperactivity disorder.

References

Ahuja, A., Martin, J., Langley, K., & Thapar, A. (2013). Intellectual disability in children with attention deficit hyperactivity disorder. *Journal of Pediatrics, 163*, 890-8

Aldenkamp, A. P., Arzimanoglou, A., Reijs, R., & Van Mil, S. (2006). Optimizing therapy of seizures in children and adolescents with ADHD. *Neurology, 67*(12 suppl 4), S49-S51.

Aman, M. G., Buican, B., & Arnold, L. E. (2003). Methylphenidate treatment in children with low IQ and ADHD: Analysis of three aggregated studies. *Journal of Child and Adolescent Psychopharmacology, 13*, 27-38.

Aman, M. G., Farmer, C. A., Hollway, J. A., & Arnold, L. E. (2008). Treatment of inattention, overactivity, and impulsiveness in autism spectrum disorders. *Child and Adolescent*

Psychiatric Clinics of North America, 12, 23-45.

Aman, M. G., Singh, N. N., Stewart, A. W., & Field, C. J. (1985). The Aberrant Behavior Checklist – A behavior rating-scale for the assessment of treatment effects. *American Journal of Mental Deficiency, 89* (5), 485-491.

American Psychiatric Association (2013). *Diagnostic and statistical manual of mental disorders (5th ed.).* Arlington, VA: American Psychiatric Association.

Antalis, C. J., Stevens, L. J., Campbell, M., Pazdro, R., Ericson, K., & Burgess, J. R. (2006). Omega-3 fatty acid status in attention-deficit/hyperactivity disorder. *Prostaglandins, Leukotrienes and Essential Fatty Acids, 75*(4-5), 299-308.

Arnold, L. E., Aman, M. G., Cook, A. M., Witwer, A. N., Hall, K. L., Thompson, S., & Ramadan, Y. (2006). Atomoxetine for hyperactivity in autism spectrum disorders: Placebo-controlled crossover pilot trial. *Journal of the American Academy of Child and Adolescent Psychiatry, 45*(10), 1196-1205.

Aureli, A., Del Beato, T., Sebastiani, P., Marimpietri, A., Melillo, C. V., Sechi, E., & Di Loreto, S. (2010). Attention-deficit hyperactivity disorder and intellectual disability: A study of association with brain-derived neurotrophic factor gene polymorphisms. *International Journal of Immunopathology and Pharmacology, 23* (3), 873-880.

Baker, B. L., Neece, C. L., Fenning, R. M., Crnic, K. A., & Blacher, J. (2010). Mental disorders in five-year-old children with or without developmental delay: Focus on ADHD. *Journal of Clinical Child and Adolescent Psychology, 39* (4), 492-505.

Bigham, K., Daley, D. M., Hastings, R. P., Jones, R. S. P. (2013). Association between parent reports of attention deficit hyperactivity disorder behaviours and child impulsivity in children with severe intellectual disability. *Journal of Intellectual Disabilities Research, 57* (2), 191-197.

Blader, J. C., Pliszka, S. R., Jensen, P. S., Schooler, N. R., & Kafantaris, V. (2010). Stimulant-responsive and stimulant-refractory aggressive behavior among children with ADHD. *Pediatrics,* Oct:126(4):e796-806. doi: 10.1542/peds.2010-0086. Epub 2010 Sep 13.

Buelow, J. M., Austin, J. K., Perkins, S. M., Shen, J., Donn, D. W., & Fastenou, P. S. (2003). Behavior and mental health problems in children with epilepsy and low IQ. *Developmental Medicine and Child Neurology, 45,* 683-692.

Burbridge, C., Oliver, C., Moss, J., Arron, K., Berg, K., Furniss, F., ... Woodcock, K. (2010). The association between repetitive behaviors, impulsivity and hyperactivity in people with intellectual disabilities. *Journal of Intellectual Disabilities Research, 54,* 1078-1092.

Bussing, R., Fernandez, M., Harwood, M., Wei Hou, Garvan, C. W., Eyberg, S. M., & Swanson, J. M. (2008). Parent and teacher SNAP-IV ratings of attention deficit hyperactivity disorder symptoms: Psychometric properties and normative ratings from a school district sample. *Assessment, 15* (3), 317-328.

Carlsson, L. H., Norrelgen, F., Kjellmer, L., Westerlund, J., Gillberg, C., & Fernell, E. (2013). Coexisting disorders and problems in preschool children with autism spectrum disorders. *Scientific World Journal.* Article ID 213979, 6 pages. http://dx.doi.org/10.1155/2013/213979

Connor, D. F., Glatt, S. J., Lopez, I. D., Jackson, D., & Melloni, R. H. Jr. (2002). Psychopharmacology and aggression. I: A meta-analysis of stimulant effects on overt/covert aggression-related behaviors in ADHD. *Journal of the Academy of Child and Adolescent Psychiatry, 41* (3), 253-261.

Cooper, S. A., Smiley, E., Morrison, J., Williamson, A., & Allan, L. (2007). Mental ill-health in adults with intellectual disabilities: Prevalence and associated factors. *The British Journal of Psychiatry: The Journal of Mental Science, 190,* 27-35. doi: 10.1192/bjp.bp.106.022483.

Cortese, S., Angriman, M., Lecendreux, M., & Konofal, E. (2012). Iron and attention deficit/hyperactivity disorder: What is the empirical evidence so far? A systematic review of the literature. *Expert Review of Neurotherapeutics, 12*(10), 1227-1240.

Culpepper, L., & Mattingly G. (2010). Challenges in identifying and managing attention-deficit/hyperactivity disorder in adults in the primary care setting: A review of the literature. *Primary Care Companion to the Journal of Clinical Psychiatry, 12*(6). doi: 10.4088/PCC.10r00951pur.

Danielsson, H., Henry, L., Ronnberg, J., & Nilsson, J. (2010). Executive functions in individuals with intellectual disabilities. *Journal of Research in Intellectual Disabilities, 31*, 1299-1304.

Denckla, M. B. (1996). A theory and model of executive function: A neuropsychological perspective. *Attention, Memory, and Executive Function.* Paul H. Brookes; Baltimore, MD. 263-277.

Dunn, D. W., Austin, J. K., & Harezlak, J. (2003). ADHD and epilepsy in childhood. *Developmental Medicine & Child Neurology, 45*(1), 50-54.

Ekstein, S., Glick, B., Weill, M., Kay, B., & Berger I. (2011). Down syndrome and attention-deficit/hyperactivity disorder (ADHD). *Journal of Child Neurology,* 26 (10), 1290-1295.

Emerson, E., Moss, S., & Kiernan, C. (1999). The relationships between challenging behaviors and psychiatric disorders in people with ID. In N. Bouras (Ed.), *Psychiatric and behavioural disorders in developmental disabilities and mental retardation* (pp. 38-48). Cambridge University Press: Cambridge, U.K.

Faraone, S. V., & Biederman, J. (2005). What is the prevalence of adult ADHD? Results of a population screen of 966 adults. *Journal of Attention Disorders, 9*, 384–391.

Faraone, S. V., Perlis, R. H., Doyle, A. E., Smoller, J. W., Goralnick, J. J., Holmgren, M. A., & Sklar, P. (2005). Molecular genetics of attention-deficit/hyperactivity disorder. *Biological Psychiatry, 57*(11), 1313-1323.

Fox, R. A., & Wade, E. J. (1998). Attention deficit hyperactivity disorder among adults with severe and profound mental retardation. *Research in Developmental Disabilities, 19* (3), 275-280.

Frazier, J. A., Biederman, J., Bellordre, C. A., Garfield, S. B., Gellar, D. A., Coffey, B. J., Faraone, S. V. (2001). Should the diagnosis of attention-deficit/hyperactivity disorder be considered in children with pervasive developmental disorder? *Journal of Attention Disorders, 4*(4), 203–211.

Gligorovic, M., & Buha Durovic, N. (2012). Inhibitory control and adaptive behaviour in children with mild intellectual disability. *Journal of Intellectual Disability Research,* doi:10.1111/jir.12000. [Epub ahead of print].

Goksugur, S. B., Tufan, A. E., Semig, M., Gunes, C., Bekdas, M., Tosun, M., & Demicioglu, F. (2014). Vitamin D status in children with attention-deficit-hyperactivity disorder. *Pediatrics International, 56*(4), 515-519.

Goldberg, M. C., Mostofsky, S. H., Cutting, L. E., Mahone, E. M., Astor, B. C., Denckla, M. B., & Landa, R. J. (2005). Subtle executive impairment in children with autism and children with ADHD. *Journal of Autism and Developmental Disorders, 35* (3), 279-293.

Goldstein, S., & Schwebach, A. S. (2004). The comorbidity of pervasive developmental disorder and attention deficit hyperactivity disorder: Results of a retrospective chart review. *Journal of Autism and Developmental Disorders. 34* (3), 329-339.

Hastings, R. P., Daley, D., Burns, C., & Beck, A. (2006). Maternal distress and expressed emotion: Cross-sectional and longitudinal relationships with behavior problems of children with intellectual disabilities. *American Journal of Mental Retardation, 111*(1), 48-61.

Jou, R., Handen, B., & Hardan, A. (2004). Psychostimulant treatment of adults with mental retardation and attention-deficit hyperactivity disorder. *Australasian Psychiatry: Bulletin of Royal Australian and New Zealand College of Psychiatrists, 12*(4), 376-379. doi:10.1111/j.1440-1665.2004.02130.x.

Kazdin, A. E., Siegel, T. C., & Bass, D. (1990). Drawing upon clinical practice to inform research on child and adolescent psychotherapy: A survey of practitioners. *Professional Psychology: Research and Practice, 21*, 189-198.

Koskentausta, T. L., Iivanainen, M., & Almqvist, F. (2007). Risk factors for psychiatric disturbance in children with intellectual disability. *Journal of Intellectual Disability Research, 2007, 51*, 43-53.

La Malfa, G., Lassi, S., Bertelli, M., Pallanti, S., & Albertini, G. (2008). Detecting attention-deficit/hyperactivity disorder (ADHD) in adults with intellectual disability: The use of Conners' Adult ADHD Rating Scales (CAARS). *Research in Developmental Disabilities, 29*(2), 158-164. doi:10.1016/j.ridd.2007.02.002.

Lindblad, I., Gillberg, C., & Fernell, E. (2011). ADHD and other associated developmental problems in child with mild mental retardation. The use of the "five-to-fifteen" questionnaire in a population-based sample. *Research in Developmental Disabilities, 32*, 2805-2809.

Lindblad, L., Svensson, L., Landgren, M., Nasic, S., Tideman, E., Gillberg, C., & Fernell, E. (2013). Mild intellectual disability and ADHD: A comparative study of school age children's adaptive abilities. *Acta Pedaitrica, 102* (10), 1027-1031.

Livesey, D. L., Keen, J., Rouse, J., & White, F. (2006). The relationship between measures of executive function, motor performance and externalising behaviour in 5- and 6-year-old children. *Human Movement Science, 25*(1), 50-64.

Lovaas, O. I., & Schreibman, L. (1971). Stimulus overselectivity of autistic children in a two stimulus situation. *Behaviour Research and Therapy, 9*(4), 305-310.

McG ough, J. J. (2005). Attention-deficit/hyperactivity disorder pharmacogenomics. *Biological Psychiatry, 57*(11), 1367-1373.

Memisevic, H. L., & Sinanovic, O. (2013). Executive functions as predictors of visual-motor integration in children with intellectual disability. *Perceptual and Motor Skills, 117*(3), 913-922.

Mervis, C. B. (2009). Language and literacy development of children with Williams syndrome. *Topics in Language Disorders, 29*(2), 149-169.

Neece, C. L., Baker, B. L., Crnic, K., Blacher, J. (2013). Examining the validity of ADHD as a diagnosis for adolescents with intellectual disabilities: Clinical presentation. *Journal of Abnormal Child Psychology, 41*(4), 597-612.

Neece, C. L., Baker, B. L., Blacher, J., & Crnic, K. A. (2011). Attention-deficit/hyperactivity disorder among children with and without intellectual disability: An examination across time. *Journal of Intellectual Disabilities Research, 55*(7), 623-635.

Nieoullon, A. (2002). Dopamine and the regulation of cognition and attention. *Progress in Neurobiology, 67*(1), 53-83.

Nigg, J. T., Mark Knottnerus, G., Cavanagh, K., & Frederici, K. (2010). Confirmation and extension of association of blood lead with attention-deficit/hyperactivity disorder (ADHD) and ADHD symptom domains at population-typical exposure levels. *Journal of Child Psychology and Psychiatry, 51*(1), 58-65.

Nylander, L., Holmqvist, M., Gustafson, L., & Gillberg, C. (2013). Attention-deficit/hyperactivity disorder (ADHD) and autism spectrum disorder (ASD) in adult psychiatry. A 20-year register study. *Nordic Journal of Psychiatry, 67*(5), 344-350.

O'Brien, G., Radley, J., & Joyce, J. (2000). Adult learning disability psychiatry services: Local implementation of national guidelines. *Hong Kong Journal of Psychiatry, 10*(4), 22-24.

Oeseburg, B., Jansen, D. E. M., Groothoff, J. W., Dijkstra, G. J., & Reijneveld, S. A., (2010). Emotional and behavioural problems in adolescents with intellectual disability with and without chronic diseases. *Journal of Intellectual Disability Research, 54*, 81-89.

Ounsted, C. (1955). The hyperkinetic syndrome in epileptic children. *Lancet, 2*, 303-311.

Owen, M. J. (2012). Intellectual disability and major psychiatric disorders: A continuum of neurodevelopmental causality. *British Journal of Psychiatry, 200*(4), 268-269.

Pearson, D. A., & Aman, M. G. (1994). Ratings of hyperactivity and developmental indices: Should clinicians correct for developmental level? *Journal of Autism and Developmental Disorders, 24*, 395-411.

Pearson, D. A., Santos, C. W., Aman, M. G., Arnold, L. E., Casat, C. D., Mansour, M., ... Cleveland, L. A. (2013). Effects of extended release methylphenidate treatment on ratings of attention-deficit/hyperactivity disorder (ADHD) and associated behavior in children with autism spectrum and ADHD symptoms. *Journal of Child and Adolescent Psychopharmacology, 23*(5), 337-351.

Pearson, D. A., Santos, C. W., Roach, J. D., Casat, C. D., Loveland, K. A., Lachar, D., ... Cleveland, L.A. (2003). Treatment effects of methylphenidate on behavioral adjustment in children with mental retardation and ADHD. *Journal of American Academy of Child and Adolescent Psychiatry, 42*(2), 209-216.

Piek, J. P., Dyck, M. J., Francis, M., & Conwell, A. (2007). Working memory, processing speed, and set-shifting in children with developmental coordination disorder and attention-deficit-hyperactivity disorder. *Developmental Medicine and Child Neurology. 49*(9), 678-683.

Rao, P. A., & Landa, R. J. (2014). Association between severity of behavioral phenotype and comorbid attention deficit hyperactivity disorder symptoms in children with autism spectrum disorders. *Autism, 18* (3), 272-80.

Reiersen, A. M., & Todorov, A. A. (2013). Exploration of ADHD subtype definitions and co-occurring psychopathology in a Missouri population-based large sibship sample. *Scandinavian Journal of Adolescent Psychiatry and Psychology, 1*(1), 3-13.

Rose, E., Bramham, J., Young, S., Paliokostas, E., & Xenitidis, K. (2009). Neuropsychological characteristics of adults with comorbid ADHD and borderline/mild intellectual disability. *Research in Developmental Disabilities, 30*(3), 496-502. doi:10.1016/j.ridd.2008.07.009; 10.1016/j.ridd.2008.07.009.

Schain, R. J. (1979). Problems with the use of conventional anticonvulsant drugs in mentally retarded individuals. *Brain and Development, 1*, 77-82.

Shaw, P., Stringaris, A., Nigg, J., & Leibenluft, E. (2014). Emotion dysregulation in attention deficit hyperactivity disorder. *American Journal of Psychiatry, 171*(3), 276-293.

Simonoff, E., Pickles, A., Wood, N., Gringras, P., & Chadwick, O. (2007). ADHD symptoms in children with mild intellectual disability. *Journal of American Academy of Child and Adolescent Psychiatry, 46*(5), 591-600.

Sinzig, J., Morsch, D., Bruning, N., Schmidt, M. H., & Lehmkuhl, G. (2008). Inhibition, flexibility, working memory and planning in autism spectrum disorders with and without comorbid ADHD symptoms. *Child and Adolescent Psychiatry and Mental Health, 2*(1), 4.

Todd, R. D., Huang, H., Smalley, S. L., Nelson, S. F., Willcutt, E. G., Pennington, B. F., ... Neuman, R.J. (2005). Collaborative analysis of DRD4 and DAT genotypes in population-defined ADHD subtypes. *Journal of Child Psychology and Psychiatry, 46*(10), 1067-1073.

Todd, R. D., & Neuman, R. J. (2007). Gene-environment interactions in the development of combined type ADHD: Evidence for a synapse-based model. *American Journal of Medical Genetics Part B-Neuropsychiatric Genetics, 144B*(8), 971-975.

Willcut, E. G. (2012). The prevalence of DSM-IV attention-deficit/hyperactivity disorder. A meta-analytic review. *Neurotherapeutics, 9*, 490-499.

Xenitidis, K., Paliokosta, E., Rose, E., Maltezos, S., & Bramham, J. (2010). ADHD symptom presentation and trajectory in adults with borderline and mild intellectual disability. *Journal of Intellectual Disability Research, 54*(7), 668-677. doi:10.1111/j.1365-2788.2010.01270.x; 10.1111/j.1365-2788.2010.01270.x.

Zeaman, D., & House, B. J. (1979). A review of attention theory. In N.R. Ellis (Ed.), *Handbook of mental deficiency* (2nd ed., pp. 63-120). Erlbaum: Hillsdale, NJ.

Zhang, S., Faries, D. E., Vowles, M., & Michelson, D. (2005). ADHD Rating Scale IV: Psychometric properties from a multinational study as a clinician-administered instrument. *International Journal of Methods in Psychiatric Research, 14*(4), 186-201.

CHAPTER 8

Specific Learning Disorders

Susan M. Havercamp
Andrea N. Witwer
Sujeet S. Jaydeokar
Jane McCarthy

A diagnosis of specific learning disorder can be made co-incident with intellectual disability but only when the learning difficulties are in excess of those usually associated with intellectual disability. Individuals with intellectual disability vary widely in their ability to do schoolwork and adapt to social demands.

The learning difficulties associated with specific learning disorder are not simply the consequence of lack of opportunity to learn, or inadequate instruction. Children with intellectual disability develop academic skills slowly such that it may not be possible to identify excessive learning difficulty until the child is older and has had more years of academic instruction.

A major national study found that approximately 5% of children in the United States had specific learning disorders. Learning deficits in one domain often co-occur with difficulties in other learning domains as well as with other disorders, especially attention-deficit hyperactivity disorder (ADHD).

The diagnosis of specific learning disorder should be established based on a compilation of the individual's history of learning difficulties and performance on curriculum-based and individual standardized tests of academic achievement. These should be interpreted within the context of the individual's medical, developmental, educational, and family histories.

There has been no empirical application of diagnostic criteria for specific learning disorders in children, adolescents, or adults with intellectual disability.

Specific learning disorders are associated with various developmental disorders causing disruption in processing of visual, auditory, and linguistic information. Risk factors for specific learning disorder include delayed language development, lower measures of verbal intelligence, poor communication environments, and slow processing that reflected genetics, the course of brain development, and interactions with environmental influences.

The underlying neurobiology of intellectual disability affects the development of complex networks and processes needed for reading, mathematics, and spelling, suggesting that intellectual disability may be a risk factor for specific learning disorder.

The lack of research and published literature limit substantial modifications of current *DSM-5* criteria for specific learning disorders in children and adults with intellectual disabilities.

Specific Learning Disorders

Review of Diagnostic Criteria

Specific learning disorders, according to the *Diagnostic and Statistical Manual-5*, are characterized by difficulties in learning and using academic skills as indicated by at least one of the following that have persisted for at least 6 months, despite the provision of extra help: (1) inaccurate or slow and effortful word reading, (2) difficulty understanding the meaning of what is read, (3) difficulty with spelling, (4) difficulty with written expression, (5) difficulty mastering number sense, number facts, or calculation, difficulty with mathematical reasoning (Criterion A). The impaired academic skills are substantially and quantifiably below those expected for the individual's chronological age, and cause significant interference with academic or occupational performance, or with activities of daily living (Criterion B). The learning difficulties begin during school-age years (Criterion C) and are not better accounted for by intellectual disabilities, uncorrected visual or auditory acuity, other mental or neurological disorders, psychosocial adversity, learning in a second language, or inadequate academic instruction (Criterion D). Specify if impairments are in reading (315.00), written expression (315.2), or mathematics (315.1).

Current severity is specified as mild, moderate, or severe:

- *Mild*

Some difficulties learning skills in one or two academic domains; individuals may be able to compensate or function well when given appropriate accommodations or supports.

- *Moderate*

Marked difficulties learning skills in one or more academic domains so that proficiency depends on intervals of intensive and specialized teaching. Accommodations or supportive services are needed at least part of the day to complete activities accurately and efficiently.

- *Severe*

Severe difficulties learning skills affecting several academic domains, so that ongoing intensive and specialized teaching is needed for most of the school day. Even with appropriate supports, individual may not be able to complete all activities efficiently.

General Description of the Disorder

Specific learning disorder is characterized by persistent difficulties learning keystone academic skills with onset during the years of formal schooling. Persistence is defined as restricted progress in learning for at least 6 months despite extra help at home or at school. Specific learning disorder disrupts the normal pattern of learning academic skills; it is not simply a consequence of lack of opportunity or inadequate instruction. Specific learning disability is evident by unexpected academic underachievement for age or avoidance of activities that require the academic skills. The learning difficulty may be restricted to one academic skill or domain. For example, the following three subtypes may be indicated: *with impairment in reading (315.00)* is characterized by difficulties in word reading accuracy, reading rate or fluency, reading comprehension; *with impairment in written expression (315.2)* is noted for difficulties with spelling accuracy, grammar and punctuation accuracy, clarity or organization of written expression; finally, *with impairment in mathematics (315.1)* may be indicated when difficulties include number sense, memorization of arithmetic facts, accurate or fluent calculation, accurate math reasoning.

Specific learning disorder is a clinical diagnosis based on a synthesis of the individual's medical, developmental, educational, and family history; the history of the learning difficulty including its previous and current manifestation; the impact of the difficulty on academic, occupational, or social functioning; previous or current school reports; portfolios of work requiring academic skills; curriculum-based assessments, and previous or current scores from individual standardized tests of academic achievement.

Summary of DSM-5 *Criteria*

A. Difficulties learning and using academic skills, as indicated by at least one of the following, which have persisted for at least 6 months despite the provision of extra help:

1. inaccurate or slow and effortful word reading
2. difficulty understanding the meaning of what is read

3. difficulties with spelling
4. difficulties with written expression
5. difficulties mastering number sense, number facts, or calculation
6. difficulties with mathematical reasoning

B. Affected academic skills are substantially and quantifiably below those expected for age and cause significant interference with academic, occupational, or daily living activities.

C. The learning difficulties begin during school age years.

D. The learning difficulties are not better accounted for by intellectual disabilities, uncorrected visual or auditory acuity, other mental or neurological disorders, psychosocial adversity, lack or proficiency in the language of academic instruction, or inadequate educational instruction.

Issues Related to Diagnosis in Persons with ID

DSM-5 stipulates that a diagnosis of specific learning disorder can be made co-incident with intellectual disability but only when the learning difficulties are in excess of those usually associated with intellectual disability. The first issue that must be considered is what usual learning difficulties are associated with various degrees of intellectual disabilities? Individuals with intellectual disability vary widely in their ability to do schoolwork and adapt to social demands (Aylward, 2002). Students with mild intellectual disabilities tend to have general, delayed development in academic skills as reflected in low achievement across content and skill areas. Many students with mild intellectual disabilities develop basic literacy skills and functional mathematics skills. For example, most students with mild intellectual disabilities learn basic computational skills and functional arithmetic skills related to money, time, and measurement (Rosenberg, Westling, & McLeskey, 2013). Most students with mild intellectual disabilities master academic skills up to about the sixth-grade level (Heward, 2010). For children with moderate intellectual impairment, the curriculum is structured around basic academics and functional skills, which include self-help and daily living skills, vocational skills, and communication training (Winzer, 2007). For this reason, it would be difficult to make a diagnosis of specific learning disorder in a child with moderate or severe intellectual impairment.

Another related issue concerns the requirement that learning difficulties persist *despite* adequate instruction and the provision of interventions that target those difficulties. The learning difficulties associated with specific learning disorder are not simply the consequence of lack of opportunity for learning or inadequate instruction. Reading instruction for students with intellectual disabilities should focus on core reading deficits of phonological awareness and phonological memory (Allor, Mathes, Roberts, Cheatham, & Otaiba, 2014; Channell, Loveall & Conners, 2013; Conners, Atwell, Renquist, & Sligh, 2001; Stanovich, Cunningham, & Freeman, 1984). Poor working memory (Hitch & McAuley,1991), phonological processing deficits (Bishop & Clarkson, 2003), and the ability to retain information encoded into the phonological loop while attending to or manipulating other information (Geary, 2010; Geary, Hoard, & Hamson, 1999) are key to understanding learning difficulties in both reading and math. With established evidence-based instruction, students with mild and moderate intellectual disability (Allor et al., 2014) and autism spectrum disorder (Hua et al., 2012) can learn basic reading skills. Unfortunately, Channell et al (2013) found that students with intellectual disabilities could not read as well as younger typically developing students matched for general verbal ability, despite having had an average of seven more years of schooling. These authors suggest that poor reading skills among students with intellectual disabilities may be due to inadequate reading instruction or that reading was simply not emphasized in the classroom.

Another issue that may limit identifying specific learning disorders in people with intellectual disability concerns measurement. Achievement tests are most sensitive in the average range of functioning (Anastasi, 1961). Students with intellectual disabilities would be expected to function well below average where the achievement test is likely to be imprecise (Anastasi, 1961). Although an IQ-achievement discrepancy is not required to make a specific learning disorder diagnosis, the lack of a strong floor on achievement tests complicates the task of demonstrating that academic skills are below expectations.

Development and Course

Many children with mild intellectual disability are not identified until they enter school and sometimes not until the second or third grade, when more difficult academic work is required (Heward, 2010). Students with mild intellectual disabilities are characterized by general delays in cognitive development that influence the acquisition of language and academic skills (Rosenberg et al. 2013). Moreover, while these students can learn much information that is part of the general education curriculum, they learn more slowly than do typical students. Similarly, specific learning disorders are typically identified in elementary school when academic difficulties become apparent. Children with intellectual disability develop academic skills slowly such that it may not be possible to identify excessive learning difficulty until the child is older and has had more years of academic instruction.

Although data is not available on the course of specific learning disorder co-incident with intellectual disability, the following findings from the general learning disability literature may be helpful. Adults with learning disabilities are likely to experience the continuation of many academic and social problems into adulthood and a prolonged period of dependence on their family (Morrison & Cosden, 1997). Adults with learning difficulty may experience personal, social, and emotional difficulties that may affect their adaptation to life tasks (Morrison & Cosden, 1997; National Joint Committee on Learning Disabilities, 1985; Shaywitz, et al. 1999). The following factors improve emotional and social adaptation in adults with learning disability: verbal skills, self-awareness of disability, and an environment that offers both practical and emotional support (Morrison & Cosden, 1997). Adults with learning disabilities often struggle with successful employment as a function of lacking academic skills and vocational skills related to specific occupations as well as occupational social skills (Elksnin & Elksnin, 2001).

Prevalence

There is a wide range in estimates of the number of people affected by learning disabilities and disorders. Some of the variation results from differences in requirements for diagnosis in different states. A major national study found that approximately 5% of children in the United States had specific learning disorders (US Department of Education, 2013). It also found that approximately 4% had both a specific learning disorder and attention-deficit hyperactivity disorder (ADHD). Other research, conducted in 2006, estimated that 4.6 million school-age children in the United States have been diagnosed with specific learning disorders (Pastor & Reuben, 2008). There is no estimate published on the prevalence of specific learning disorders among people with intellectual disabilities.

Differential Diagnosis

These differential diagnosis guidelines are provided in the *DSM-5* (APA, 2013):

■ *Intellectual Disability*

Specific learning disorder is distinguished from the learning difficulties associated with intellectual disability because the learning difficulties exceed those that would be expected given the level of intellectual impairment.

■ *Normal Variations of Academic Attainment*

In specific learning disorder, learning difficulties persist despite adequate educational opportunity, exposure to the same instruction as the peer group, and competency in the language of instruction, even if it differs from one's primary spoken language.

■ *Learning Difficulties due to Neurological or Sensory Disorders*

Specific learning disorder is distinguished from learning difficulties due to neurological or sensory disorders (e.g., pediatric stroke, traumatic brain injury, hearing impairment, vision impairment) because in these cases there are abnormal findings on neurological examination.

■ *Neurocognitive Disorders*

Unlike in neurodegenerative cognitive disorders, the clinical expression of specific learning difficulties occurs during the developmental period and the difficulties do not manifest as a marked decline from a former state.

■ *Attention-Deficit Hyperactivity Disorder*

Unlike specific learning disorder, poor academic performance associated with ADHD may not necessarily reflect specific difficulties in *learning* academic skills but rather may reflect difficulties in *performing* those skills. However, the co-occurrence of specific learning disorder and ADHD is higher than chance; if criteria for both disorders are met, both diagnoses can be given.

■ *Psychotic Disorders*

Unlike specific learning disorders, the academic and cognitive-processing difficulties associated with schizophrenia or psychosis are marked by a decline (often rapid) in these functional domains.

Functional Consequences

A lack of reading ability limits one's quality of life (Bradford, Shippen, Alberto, Houschins, & Flores, 2006) and yet only 1 in 5 students with intellectual disabilities reach minimal literacy levels (Katims, 2001). Slow development of reading skills may affect more than just one academic subject but may also delay language acquisition, general knowledge, vocabulary, and even social acceptance. Similarly, quantitative skills influence employability, wages, and on-the-job productivity above and beyond the influence of reading abilities, IQ, and a host of other factors (Rivera-Batiz, 1992).

Comorbidity

Learning difficulties in one domain often co-occur with deficits in other learning domains. Landerl & Moll (2010) found that the rates of difficulties in arithmetic, reading, or spelling were four to five times higher in samples already experiencing marked problems in one academic domain compared to the full population. These authors also found a preponderance of girls with arithmetic and reading disorder and boys with spelling disorder. The authors found evidence, through a parental questionnaire, for disorder-specific familial transmission and co-segregation of arithmetic and literacy deficits.

The largest body of literature supports a comorbid relationship between specific learning disorders and attention-deficit disorder (with or without hyperactivity). This extensive research, featuring comorbidity estimates as high as 70%, was summarized by Riccio, Gonzalez & Hynd (1994) and Maynard, Tyler & Arnold (1999). A large percentage of those who have attention-deficit hyperactivity disorder (ADHD) also have accompanying specific learning disorders, while approximately 30% of those who have specific learning disorders also have ADHD. Despite the high co-occurrence, genetic evidence suggests that the familial transmission of ADHD and specific learning disorders are independent (Faraone, et al., 1993).

A group of disorders also found frequently to be comorbid with specific learning disorders are those involving social, emotional, and/or behavioral difficulties (Arnold, 1997; Glassberg, Hooper & Mattison, 1999; Greshem, 1993; Kamphaus, Frick & Lahey, 1991). Studies suggest that anywhere from 24% to 52% of students with specific learning disorders have some form of such disorders (Rock, Fessler & Church, 1997) including conduct disorder and oppositional/ defiant disorder (DeLong, 1995; Shaywitz & Shaywitz, 1991), as well as social adjustment disorder (Lyon, 1996).

Some evidence suggests that children with specific learning disorders are at risk for developmental coordination disorder (Dewey, Kaplan, Crawford & Wilson, 2002) and depressive or dysthymic disorders (San Miguel, Forness & Kavale, 1996).

Application of Diagnostic Criteria to People with ID

General Considerations

The diagnosis of a specific learning disorder, in general, warrants a number of considerations which should also be addressed in diagnostic assessment of those with intellectual disability. Two of the most critical considerations are: 1) the need for a comprehensive assessment, and 2) the specificity of learning difficulty. As noted in *DSM-5* (APA, 2013), as well as expert consensus (Hale et al., 2010), the diagnosis of specific learning disorder should be established based on a compilation of the individual's history of learning difficulties, as wel as performance on curriculum-based and individual standardized tests of academic achievement. These should be interpreted within the context of the individual's medical, developmental, educational, and family histories. Therefore, no one point of assessment data is sufficient to confirm diagnosis. The diagnosis of specific learning disorder in those with intellectual disabilities should be made by professionals with expertise in assessing this population, who have the ability to select, administer, and interpret assessments appropriate to the individual, while maintaining standardization practices. In order to ensure accurate assessment of cognitive and academic achievement, considerations regarding attention, activity level, and sensory or motor impairments should be taken into account when selecting and administering assessments.

Establishing the specificity of the specific learning difficulty is essential when providing support for a diagnosis of specific learning disorder in intellectual disabilities. As noted in *DSM-5* criteria, the level of impairment should not be simply attributable to the individual's level of intellectual impairment. That is, specific learning disorder should be distinguished from general pervasive difficulties in learning which are associated with intellectual disabilities. Previous diagnostic criteria relied on the use of discrepancy scores, which created a significant barrier in establishing this level of specificity (see Hale et al., 2010 for comprehensive review). The revised *DSM-5* criteria take a broader assessment approach, which will enable clinicians to consider the individual's entire profile when rendering a diagnosis. However, there is a paucity of established guidelines or research in the area of learning in intellectual disabilities. While the impairment of intellectual disability often overshadows specific learning difficulties, the identification of specific learning difficulties is important in guiding intervention and educational priorities. Discrepant academic performance (as compared to other academic areas and cognitive ability) in one or two areas rather than pervasive in all areas of academic content, would support specific learning disorders which may warrant additional educational intervention.

We propose that best practices utilized in people without intellectual disability be adopted for those with intellectual disability, with particular attention to establishing evidence counter to the differential diagnosis of overall low achievement. This should be done in a method that is culturally sensitive and takes into account co-occurring health, sensory, or behavioral challenges. Scores in one or two specific areas which are deemed significant weaknesses on comparison to other areas of academic functioning may provide initial evidence for co-occurring specific learning disability. Subsequently, multiple points of standardized assessment data should be taken into account, considering discrepancies in general overall IQ versus standardized achievement test scores, as well as the individual's specific IQ and achievement test profile analyses. Relying upon an ability–achievement discrepancy as the sole means of identifying children with specific learning disorders is at odds with scientific research and with best practice (Gresham & Vellutino, 2010). As such, additional sources of information should be considered, including classroom-based/curriculum-based assessments, classroom observation, parent and teacher report, and previous evaluations. Equally important is the student's response to scientifically-based instruction, including environmental and instructional conditions (National Association of School Psychologists, 2014).

Research is needed to establish evidence-based assessment batteries and diagnostic decision-making tools. In the absence of such evidence, we propose that clinicians examine academic and cognitive profiles in detail to identify specific learning disorders in individuals with ID. Significant weaknesses in one or two areas of academic achievement (confirmed via standardized assessments, academic performance, and interview) as compared with the individual's cognitive ability and overall academic performance would support a diagnosis of specific learning disorder.

Methodology

A comprehensive search of education (i.e., Education Resources Information Center [ERIC]) and psychological (PsychInfo) databases was conducted with the following terms: "intellectual disability," "learning disability," "learning disorder," "mental retardation," "achievement."

Review of Research Applying to People with ID

While a number of studies have described the reading and mathematical abilities of those with intellectual disability, there has been no empirical application of diagnostic criteria for learning disorders in children, adolescents, or adults with intellectual disability. There is also a lack of research in regard to the application of the previous requirement of discrepancy between IQ and achievement in those with ID. Research is needed in regards to assessment and treatment of specific learning problems in individuals with ID.

Evaluating the Level of Evidence

There have been no studies that attempted to apply these diagnostic criteria to adults with mild to moderate intellectual disability (verbal).

Adults with Severe or Profound ID

There have been no studies that attempted to apply these diagnostic criteria to adults with severe or profound intellectual disability (nonverbal).

Children and Adolescents with ID

There have been no studies that attempted to apply these diagnostic criteria to children and adolescents with intellectual disability.

Summary of Limitations in Applying DSM-5 *Criteria to People with ID*

1. In order to confirm a diagnosis of specific learning disorder, a comprehensive assessment, comprised of standardized assessments of achievement and cognition will be necessary in order to interpret achievement deficits within the context of the individuals' overall cognitive and achievement abilities.
2. Confirmation that the learning difficulties persist despite adequate instruction may be a significant barrier for some. While evidence-based instruction for those with intellectual disabilities exists, this type of curriculum is not universally mandated and may not be available within the individual's educational environment.
3. Previous definitions have made diagnosing specific learning disorders in intellectual disability nearly impossible. The broader criteria in *DSM-5* should allow for wider application of criteria by clinicians and researchers in the coming years. Research is needed which explores and validates evidence-based diagnostic algorithms for establishing a diagnosis of specific learning disorder in people with intellectual disabilities. It will be critical for research in this area to establish the validity of decision making tools which assist clinicians in establishing a diagnosis of specific learning disorder versus overall low achievement commensurate with an individual's overall level of functioning.

Etiology and Pathogenesis

Specific learning disorders are associated with various developmental disorders causing disruption in processing of visual, auditory, and linguistic information. For example, we know that when it comes to difficulties with reading, disruption in any of the multiple skills required for reading, could lead to reading disorder. (Harris, 1995; Hynd, Hooper, & Takahashi, 1998; Ramus et al., 2003). There are some studies that have explored the specific etiological factors and pathogenesis of learning disorders in people with intellectual disability. However, this area needs further research; there are very few studies on mathematics disorder or spelling disorders in people with intellectual disability.

As stated earlier, it is possible to have a diagnosis of specific learning disorder in people with intellectual disability if their learning difficulty exceeds that we expect given their cognitive ability. Apart from being a possible co-morbid condition, low intelligence, along with neurological, developmental, and some genetic disorders, is considered a risk factor for specific learning disorder. Therefore, the etiology might involve factors associated with generalized deficit in measured intelligence as well as co-morbid neurological and developmental disorders (Geary, 1993; Mendez, Papasian, & Lim, 2003).

Studies suggest that risk factors include delayed language development, lower measures of verbal intelligence, poor communication environments, and slow processing reflective of genetics, the course of brain development, and interactions with environmental influences (Conner et al., 2001; Das, Mok, & Mishra, 1994; Singh & Solman, 1990). Genetic risk factors are associated with language disorders in general and to specific behavioral phenotypes associated with language development or visual motor development. Perinatal and early developmental insults also sometimes contribute to apraxia and to the developing of perceptual motor skills that impact reading and writing (Harris 1995; Tupper 1987).

Biological Factors

There has been tremendous growth in our understanding of specific learning disorders based on neuropsychological testing and the introduction of functional neurophysiological and neuro-imaging technologies. We know that children with severe and selective reading impairments in the context of otherwise normal oral language skills are likely to have a different neurobiological and genetic profile and also a different outcome from those who have more global impairments affecting all aspects of oral as well as written language (Bishop & Snowling, 2004). Studies of people with intellectual disability suggest that, apart from considerable heterogeneity of etiologies, the underlying neurobiology of intellectual disability affects the development of complex networks and processes needed for reading, mathematics, and spelling (Harris, 1995; Hynd et al., 1998; Tupper, 1987). Neuro-imaging studies consistently suggest that deficiency within a specific component of the language system (the phonologic module in the temporo-parietal-occipital brain region) underlies dyslexia (Shastry, 2007). Dyslexia could also be due to the abnormal migration and maturation of neurons during early development (Shastry, 2007).

Children with traumatic brain injury showed impairment on verbal but not visual working memory. They also had difficulties in mathematics but did not have deficits in math fact retrieval, a signature deficit of math disorders (Raghubar, Barnes, Prasad, Johnson, & Ewing-Cobbs; 2013). Although the study was not specific to people with intellectual disability, presence of right hemisphere pathology or history of traumatic brain injury should be considered as an etiological risk factor for development of specific learning disorder in people with intellectual disability.

Genetic, neuro-biological, and epidemiological evidence indicates that dyscalculia, like other learning disabilities, is a brain-based disorder. However, poor teaching and environmental deprivation have also been implicated in etiology. Dyscalculia can result from dysfunction of either hemisphere, although the left parieto-temporal area is of particular significance. Acquired lesion studies suggest that lesions in the angular gyrus intersection between the posterior-temporal, inferior occipital-parietal regions are associated with mathematical deficits (Ardila & Rosselli 2002). Dyscalculia can occur as a consequence of prematurity and low birth weight and is frequently encountered in a variety of neurological disorders, such as ADHD, epilepsy, and fragile X syndrome (Shalev, 2004); fragile X syndrome is associated with intellectual disability.

Genetic Factors

Multiple genetic influences have been implicated in specific learning disorders. Specific genotypes have not been identified for any of the specific learning disorders. Linkage mapping and related methods have been used to identify several regions of the genome likely to contain genes associated with dyslexia (Bartlett et al., 2002;

Fisher & DeFries, 2002). However, studies specific to people with ID have been very limited.

Bender, Linden, and Robinson (1991) studied children with various sex chromosome abnormalities (SCA). Study showed that while most SCA children did not have intellectual disability, most of the non-mosaic students received special education help for learning problems. The inference that specific learning disorders were genetically mediated in this group was further supported by karyotype-specific findings: 47,XXY boys tended to demonstrate lower verbal skills and a specific reading disability; 47,XXX girls, while more globally impaired, demonstrated evidence of a specific weakness in language skills; 45,X girls tended to be globally impaired, but demonstrated a contrasting specific deficit in spatial thinking skills. The presence of SCA, therefore, must be viewed as a risk factor in those with ID creating a tendency towards learning disorders and a range of phenotypic outcomes.

Although there are no specific genotypes associated with isolated mathematics disabilities, mathematical learning disorder occurs more frequently in children with specific genetic disorders like Turner syndrome, fragile X, and neurofibromatosis; a person with ID and fragile X will have significantly more risk of specific learning disorder. De Smedt, Willen, Verschaffel, and Ghesquiere (2009) reviewed mathematics disorder in children with chromosome 22q11.2 deletion syndrome/ micro-deletion syndrome; studies showed considerable difficulties in mathematics. While fact retrieval seems to be preserved, impairments in procedural calculation and word problem solving are particularly prominent. Children with 22q11.2 deletion syndrome had substantial difficulties in understanding and representing numerical quantities, possibly related to poor visual-spatial attention, which all might stem from their underlying abnormalities in the inferior parietal cortex. As 22q11.2 deletion syndrome is associated with intellectual disability, presence of deletion syndrome becomes a significant risk factor for development of specific learning disorder in people with intellectual disabilities.

Psychosocial Factors

Reading difficulties may arise from poor vision, emotional problems, decreased hearing ability, behavioral disorders, attention-deficit hyperactivity disorder, etc. (Shastry, 2007). They may result from multiple interpersonal and environmental factors, e.g. attachment, early language environment, etc. Exposure to reading may also play a role. All these factors can also affect the emergence of reading skills in children with intellectual disability (Ramus et al., 2003).

Calculation ability represents a multifactor skill, including verbal, spatial, memory, body knowledge, and executive function abilities (Ardila & Rosselli, 2002). When it came to mathematics disorder, Greiffenstein & Baker (2002) found that arithmetic difficulties in adults were associated with nonverbal reasoning and constructional problems. Overall intelligence was also lower in adults with arithmetic difficulties. Major risk factors included a lack of exposure to basic math skills, abuse contributing to brain dysfunction, and a failure to recognize mathematics disorder because of overwhelming disruptive behavioral or affective disorders.

Developmental Factors

All types of specific learning disorders involved precursor skills that were either adversely affected or underdeveloped due to deficits in brain development (Voeller, 1998). Stanovich (1985) posited that people with ID might be deficient in phonological coding and that this might impair their reading. Explicit phonological awareness and phonological coding skills were strongly linked with early reading acquisition in children without intellectual disability (Stanovich, 1985). It is clear that the ability to decode, or read single words, strongly determines overall reading ability and that poor phonological processing (i.e. processing speech sounds) underlies severe reading difficulty in a majority of cases. The concept of phonological awareness has also been associated with the acquisition of literacy in alphabetic orthographies. However, Cossu, Rossini, and Marshall (1993) posited that such skills were not essential prerequisites for reading; some children with Down syndrome could learn to read despite their failure on a set of phonological awareness tasks.

When considering what constitutes reading for people with intellectual disability, it is apparent that reading follows a developmental course and that sight recognition of words without attaching meaning (semantics) or recognizing these words in a sentence (syntactical analysis) represents early reading skills and might not predict functional literacy. Reading the word 'stop' might be a lifesaving adaptive skill, but only if the meaning is understood. Meaning could be drawn from the visual gestalt of the stop sign or the bright red color rather than from the lexigraphic or semantic meaning of the word. The developmental trajectory and neurophysiology of these functional proto-reading skills needs further study in people with severe or profound ID (Conners et al., 2001; Nummienen, Service, & Ruoppila, 2002; Shapiro, 1996).

Conners et al. (2001) examined cognitive similarities and differences between stronger and weaker decoders, all of whom had intellectual disability. Stronger decoders were significantly better than weaker decoders in language ability, phonemic awareness, and rehearsal in phonological memory, but did not have higher IQ. When age was covaried, the groups differed significantly only in rehearsal in phonological memory. It is possible that the reason the phonemic awareness measure was not as good at distinguishing the groups as the phonological rehearsal measure was because the former did not involve assembling phonological output. The authors suggested that it was the combination of poor phonological representation and poor phonological output assembly that made decoding difficult for some children with intellectual disability.

Arithmetical ability is associated with and dependent upon some verbal, visual-perceptual, visual-spatial, and memory abilities. Overall deficit in working memory was found in those with specific learning difficulties with or without intellectual disability (Maehler & Schuchardt, 2009). Acalculia can result from either a primary defect in computational abilities (primary acalculia) or a diversity of cognitive defects (language, memory, etc.) impairing normal performance in calculation tests. Generally, acalculia can be correlated with executive function defects (defects in planning and controlling the calculation sequence, impairments in understanding and solving arithmetical problems, etc.) and visual-perceptual recognition of numerical written information including defects in reading numbers and errors in reading arithmetical signs (Bishop & Snowling, 2004).

Adaptation of Diagnostic Criteria

The lack of research and published literature limit substantial modifications of current *DSM-5* criteria for specific learning disorders in children and adults with intellectual disability. *DSM* stipulates a diagnosis of specific learning disorder can be made co-incident with intellectual disability but only when the learning difficulties are in excess of those usually associated with intellectual disability. Children with mild intellectual disability might be the most likely to be recognized by teachers, but a child might fail to demonstrate learning difficulties in excess of those associated with intellectual disability because of inadequate academic instruction or because of limitations in standardized measurement threshold (floor effects). Clinicians are encouraged to consider additional sources of information including classroom or curriculum-based assessments, classroom observation, parent and teacher reports, and previous evaluations when assessing learning difficulty in children with intellectual disability.

The modified diagnostic criteria for specific learning disorder with impairment in reading (315.00), with impairment in written expression (315.2), and with impairment in mathematics (315.1) are presented together in the following table to be consistent with the *DSM-5*:

Specific Learning Disorders

DSM-5 Diagnostic Criteria	Applying Criteria for Mild-Moderate ID	Applying Criteria for Severe-Profound ID
A. Difficulties learning and using academic skills, as indicated by at least one of the following which have persisted for at least 6 months, despite the provision of extra help: 1. Inaccurate or slow and effortful word reading 2. Difficulty understanding the meaning of what is read 3. Difficulties with spelling 4. Difficulties with written expression 5. Difficulties mastering number sense, number facts or calculation 6. Difficulties with mathematical reasoning	A. No adaptation **Note**: Discrepancy between measured intelligence and academic level needs to consider the validity of the test instrument- norms on the population with intellectual disability.	A. No adaptation **Note**: No reliable measures of academic skills are available.
B. Affected academic skills are substantially and quantifiably below those expected for age and cause significant interference with academic, occupational or daily living activities as confirmed by individually administered standardized achievement measures and comprehensive clinical assessment	B. Affected academic skills are quantifiably below expectation, given cognitive ability.	B. Affected academic skills are quantifiably below expectation, given cognitive ability.
C. The learning difficulties begin during school-age years but may not become fully manifest until the demands for those affected academic skills exceed the individual's limited capacity	C. No adaptation	C. No adaptation
D. The learning difficulties are not accounted for by intellectual disabilities, uncorrected visual or auditory acuity, other mental or neurological disorders, psychosocial adversity, lack of proficiency in the language of academic institution or inadequate educational instruction.	D. No adaptation **Note**: Need to highlight that the specific learning disorders are not explained by the individual's level of cognitive ability.	D. No adaptation **Note**: Need to highlight that the specific learning disorders are not explained by the individual's level of cognitive ability.
Note: The four diagnostic criteria are to be met based on a clinical synthesis of the individual's history, school reports and psycho-educational assessment	No adaptation **Note**: Need to highlight the importance in obtaining multiple sources of information to diagnoses specific learning disorders in a person with intellectual disability.	No adaptation **Note**: Need to highlight the importance in obtaining multiple sources of information to diagnoses specific learning disorders in a person with intellectual disability.
CODING NOTE: Specify all academic domains and sub skills that are impaired Specify if: 315.00 With impairment in reading 315.2 With impairment in written expression 315.1 With impairment in mathematics	No adaptation	No adaptation

Specific Learning Disorders (continued)

DSM-5 Diagnostic Criteria	Applying Criteria for Mild-Moderate ID	Applying Criteria for Severe-Profound ID
CODING NOTE: Specify current severity: Mild: Some difficulties learning skills in one or two academic domains Moderate: Marked difficulties learning skills in one or more academic domains Severe: Severe difficulties learning skills, affecting several academic domains	With the current level of evidence an unspecified code on severity is recommended in a person with intellectual disability until further evidence is available	With the current level of evidence an unspecified code on severity is recommended in a person with intellectual disability until further evidence is available

References

Allor, J. H., Mathes, P. G., Roberts, J. K., Cheatham, J. P., & Otaiba, S. A. (2014). Is scientifically based reading instruction effective for students with below-average IQs? *Exceptional Children, 80*(3), 287–306. doi:10.1177/0014402914522208

Anastasi, A. (1961). Norms: Their nature and interpretation (pp. 76-104). In *Psychological testing (2nd edition).* New York: The Macmillan Company.

Ardila, A., & Rosselli, M. (2002) Acalculia and dyscalculia. *Neuropsychology review, 12(4)*, 179-231.

Arnold, D. H. (1997). Co-occurrence of externalizing behavior problems and emergent academic difficulties in young high-risk boys: a preliminary evaluation of patterns and mechanisms. *Journal of Applied Developmental Psychology, 18*(3), 317–330. doi:10.1016/S0193-3973(97)80003-2

Aylward, G. P. (2002). Cognitive and neuropsychological outcomes: More than IQ scores. *Mental Retardation and Developmental Disabilities Research Reviews, 8*(4), 234–240. doi:10.1002/mrdd.10043.

Bartlett, C.W., Flax, J.F., Logue, M.W., Vieland, V.J., Bassett, A.S., Tallal, P., Brzustowicz, L.M. (2002). A major susceptibility locus for specific language impairment is located on 13q21. *American Journal of Human Genetics, 71*, 45-55.

Bender, B.G., Linden, M., & Robinson, A. (1991) Cognitive and academic skills in children with sex chromosome abnormalities. *Reading and Writing: An Interdisciplinary Journal, 3*, 315-327.

Bishop, D. V. M., & Clarkson, B. (2003). Written language as a window into residual language deficits: A study of children with persistent and residual speech and language impairments. *Cortex: A Journal Devoted to the Study of the Nervous System and Behavior, 39*(2), 215–237.

Bishop, D. V. M., & Snowling, M.J. (2004). Developmental dyslexia and specific language impairment: Same or different? *Psychological Bulletin, 130(6), 858-886.*

Bradford, S., Shippen, M. E., Alberto, P., Houchins, D. E., & Flores, M. (2006). Using systematic instruction to teach decoding skills to middle school students with moderate intellectual disabilities. *Education and Training in Developmental Disabilities, 41*(4), 333–343.

Channell, M. M., Loveall, S. J., & Conners, F. A. (2013). Strengths and weaknesses in reading skills of youth with intellectual disabilities. *Research in Developmental Disabilities, 34*(2), 776–787. doi:10.1016/j.ridd.2012.10.010

Conners, F. A., Atwell, J. A., Rosenquist, C. J. & Sligh, A. C. (2001). Abilities underlying decoding differences in children with intellectual disability. *Journal of Intellectual Disability Research, 45(4)*, 292-299.

Cossu, G., Rossini, F., Marshall, J. C. (1993) When reading is acquired but phonemic awareness is not: A study of literacy in Down's syndrome. *Cognition, 46*, 129-138.

Das, J. P., Mok, M., Mishra, R. K. (1994). The role of speech processes and memory in reading disability. *Journal of General Psychology, 121(2)*, 131-146.

DeLong, R. (1995). Medical and pharmacologic treatment of learning disabilities. *Journal of Child Neurology, 10*(Suppl 1), S92–S95.

De Smedt, B., Willen, A., Verschaffel, L, & Ghesquiere, P. (2009). Mathematical learning disabilities in children with 22q11.2 deletion syndrome: A review. *Developmental Disabilities Research Reviews, 15(1)*, 4-10.

Dewey, D., Kaplan, B. J., Crawford, S. G., & Wilson, B. N. (2002). Developmental coordination disorder: Associated problems in attention, learning, and psychosocial adjustment. *Human Movement Science, 21*(5-6), 905–918.

Elksnin, N., & Elksnin, L. K. (2001). Adolescents with disabilities: The need for occupational social skills training. *Exceptionality, 9*, 91–105.

Faraone, S. V., Biederman, J., Lehman, B. K., Keenan, K., Norman, D., Seidman, L. J., ... Chen, W. J. (1993). Evidence for the independent familial transmission of attention deficit hyperactivity disorder and learning disabilities: Results from a family genetic study. *The American Journal of Psychiatry, 150*(6), 891–895.

Fisher, S. E., & DeFries, J. C. (2002) Developmental dyslexia: Genetic dissection of a complex cognitive trait. *Nature Reviews, Neuroscience, 3*, 767-780.

Fletcher, J. M., Francis, D. J., Morris, R. D., & Lyon, G. R. (2005). Evidence-based assessment of learning disabilities in children and adolescents. *Journal of Clinical Child and Adolescent Psychology, 34(3)*, 506-522.

Geary, D.C. (1993) Mathematical disabilities: Cognitive, neuropsychological and genetic components. *Psychological Bulletin, 114*, 345-362.

Geary, D. C. (2010). Mathematical disabilities: Reflections on cognitive, neuropsychological, and genetic components. *Learning and Individual Differences, 20*(2), 130. doi:10.1016/j.lindif.2009.10.008

Geary, D. C., Hoard, M. K., & Hamson, C. O. (1999). Numerical and arithmetical cognition: Patterns of functions and deficits in children at risk for a mathematical disability. *Journal of Experimental Child Psychology, 74*(3), 213–239. doi:10.1006/jecp.1999.2515

Glassberg, L. A., Hooper, S. R., & Mattison, R. E. (1999). Prevalence of learning disabilities at enrollment in special education students with behavioral disorders. *Behavioral Disorders, 25*(1), 9–21.

Greiffenstein, M. F., & Baker, W. J. (2002) Neuropsychological and psychosocial correlates of adult arithmetic deficiency. *Neuropsychology, 16(4)*, 451-458.

Gresham, F. M. (1993). Social skills and learning disabilities as a type III error: Rejoinder to Conte and Andrews. *Journal of Learning Disabilities, 26*(3), 154–158. doi:10.1177/002221949302600302

Gresham, F. M., & Vellutino, F. R. (2010). What is the role of intelligence in the identification of specific learning disabilities? Issues and clarifications. *Learning Disabilities Research & Practice, 25(4)*, 194–206.

Hale, J., Alfonso, V., Berninger, V., Bracken, B., Christo, C., Clark, E., ... Simon, J. (2010). Critical issues in response-to-intervention, comprehensive evaluation, and specific learning disabilities identification and intervention: An expert white paper consensus. *Learning Disability Quarterly, 33(3)*, 223-236

Harris, J. C. (1995). *Developmental neuropsychiatry.* New York: Oxford University Press.

Heward, W.L. (2010). Should all students with learning disabilities be educated in the regular classroom? Excerpt from *Exceptional Children: An Introduction to Special Education*, by W. L. Heward, 2006 edition, p. 212. Retrieved April 29, 2014, from http://www.education.com/reference/article/learning-disabilities-regular-class/

Hitch, G. J., & McAuley, E. (1991). Working memory in children with specific arithmetical learning difficulties. *British Journal of Psychology, 82*(3), 375–386. doi:10.1111/j.2044-8295.1991.tb02406.x

Hua, Y., Hendrickson, J. M., Therrien, W. J., Woods-Groves, S., Ries, P. S., & Shaw, J. J. (2012). Effects of combined reading and question generation on reading fluency and comprehension of three young adults with autism and intellectual disability. *Focus on Autism and Other Developmental Disabilities*, 1088357612448421. doi:10.1177/1088357612448421.

Hynd, G. W., Hooper, S. R., & Takahashi, T. (1998) Dyslexia and language-based learning disorders. In E. Coffey & R.A. Brumback (Eds), *Paediatric Neuropsychiatry.* Washington DC: American Psychiatric Association Press.

Kamphaus, R. W., Frick, P. J., & Lahey, B. B. (1991). Methodological issues and learning disabilities diagnosis in clinical populations. *Journal of Learning Disabilities*, *24*(10), 613–618. doi:10.1177/002221949102401004

Katims, D. S. (2001). Literacy assessment of students with mental retardation: An exploratory investigation. *Education and Training in Mental Retardation and Developmental Disabilities*, *36*(4), 363-72.

Landerl, K., & Moll, K. (2010). Comorbidity of learning disorders: Prevalence and familial transmission. *Journal of Child Psychology and Psychiatry, and Allied Disciplines*, *51*(3), 287–294. doi:10.1111/j.1469-7610.2009.02164.x

Lyon, G. R. (1996). Learning disabilities. *The Future of Children / Center for the Future of Children, the David and Lucile Packard Foundation*, *6*(1), 54–76.

Maehler, C., & Schuchardt, K. (2009) Working memory functioning in children with learning disabilities: Does intelligence make a difference? *Journal of Intellectual Disability Research*, *53(1)*, 3-10.

Maynard, J., Tyler, J. L., Arnold, M. (1999). Co-occurrence of attention-deficit disorder and learning disability: An overview of research. *Journal of Instructional Psychology*, *26*(3), 183.

Mendez, M. F., Papasian, N. C., & Lim, G. T. (2003) Thalamic dyscalculia. *Journal of Neuropsychiatry and Clinical Neurosciences*, *15(1)*, 115-116.

Morrison, G. M., Cosden, M. A. (1997). Risk, resilience, and adjustment of individuals with learning disabilities. *Learning Disability Quarterly*, *2*(1), 43-60.

National Association of School Psychologists. *NASP position statement: Identification of specific learning disabilities.* Retrieved from http://www.nasponline.org/about_nasp/positionpapers/Identification_of_SLD.pdf on 5/16/14.

National Joint Committee on Learning Disabilities. (1985). *Adults with learning disabilities: A call to action* (No. PS1985-00088). Rockville, MD: American Speech-Language-Hearing Association. Retrieved from http://www.asha.org/policy/PS1985-00088.htm

Numminen, H., Service, E., & Ruoppila, I. (2002). Working memory, intelligence and knowledge base in adult persons with intellectual disability. *Research Developmental Disabilities*, *23(2)*, 105-118.

Pastor, P. N., Rueben, C.A., National Health Interview Survey (U.S.), & National Center for Health Statistics (U.S.). (2008). *Diagnosed attention-deficit hyperactivity disorder and learning disability, United States, 2004-2006: Data from the National Health Interview Survey.* Hyattsville, MD: U.S. Dept. of Health and Human Services, Centers for Disease Control and Prevention, National Center for Health Statistics.

Raghubar, K. P., Barnes, M. A., Prasad, M., Johnson, C. P., & Ewing-Cobbs, L. (2013). Mathematical outcomes and working memory in children with TBI and orthopedic injury. *Journal of the International Neuropsychological Society*, *19*, 254-263.

Ramus, F., Rosen, S., Dakin, S. C., Day, B. L., Castellote, J. M., White, S., & Frith, U. (2003). Theories of developmental dyslexia: Insights from a multiple case study of dyslexic adults. *Brain*, *126*, 841-865.

Riccio, C. A., Gonzalez, J. J., & Hynd, G. W. (1994). Attention-deficit hyperactivity disorder (ADHD) and learning disabilities. *Learning Disability Quarterly, 17*(4), 311–322. doi:10.2307/1511127.

Rivera-Batiz, F. L. (1992). Quantitative literacy and the likelihood of employment among young adults in the United States. *Journal of Human Resources*, 27, 313–328.

Rock, E. E., Fessler, M. A., & Church, R. P. (1997). The concomitance of learning disabilities and emotional/behavioral disorders: A conceptual model. *Journal of Learning Disabilities, 30*(3), 245-263. doi:10.1177/002221949703000302.

Rosenberg, M. S., Westling, D. L., & McLeskey, J. (2013). *Inclusion: Effective practices for all students (2nd ed.)*. Boston: Pearson Allyn Bacon Prentice Hall.

San Miguel, S. K., Forness, S. R., & Kavale, K. A. (1996). Social skills deficits in learning disabilities: The psychiatric comorbidity hypothesis. *Learning Disability Quarterly, 19*(4), 252–261. doi:10.2307/1511211.

Shalev, R. S. (2004) Developmental dyscalculia. *Journal of Child Neurology. 19(10)*, 765-771.

Shapiro, B. K. (1996). Specific reading disability. *Mental Retardation and Developmental Disabilities Research Reviews, 2(1)*, 1-54.

Shastry, B. S. (2007) Developmental dyslexia: An update. *Journal of Human Genetics, 52(2)*, 104-109.

Shaywitz, S. E., Fletcher, J. M., Holahan, J. M., Shneider, A. E., Marchione, K. E., Stuebing, K. K., . . . Shaywitz, B. A. (1999). Persistence of dyslexia: The Connecticut longitudinal study at adolescence. *Pediatrics, 104*(6), 1351–1359.

Shaywitz, S. E., & Shaywitz, B. A. (1991). Introduction to the special series on attention deficit disorder. *Journal of Learning Disabilities, 24*(2), 68–71. doi:10.1177/002221949102400202.

Singh, N. N., & Solman, R. T. (1990). A stimulus control analysis of the picture word problem in children who are mentally retarded: The blocking effect. *Journal of Applied Behavioural Analysis, 23(4)*, 525-532.

Stanovich, K. E. (1985). Cognitive determinants of reading in mentally retarded individual. *International Review of Research in Mental Retardation, 13*, 181-214.

Stanovich, K. E., Cunningham, A. E., Freeman, D. J. (1984). Intelligence, cognitive skills, and early reading progress. *Reading Research Quarterly, 19*(3), 278–303.

Tupper, D. E. (1987). *Soft Neurological Signs*. New York: Grune and Stratton Press.

U.S. Department of Education, National Center for Education Statistics. (2013). *Digest of Education Statistics, 2012. Chapter 2: Elementary and Secondary Education*. (NCES 2014-015). Retrieved April 29, 2014, from https://nces.ed.gov/pubsearch/pubsinfo.asp?pubid=2014015.

Voeller, K. K. S. (1998). Nonverbal learning disabilities and motor skill disorders. In E. Coffey & R. A. Brumback (Eds.), *Textbook of Paediatric Neuropsychiatry*. Washington, DC: American Psychiatric Association Press.

Winzer, M. (2007). *Children with Exceptionalities in Canadian Classrooms (8th ed.)*. Chapter 6: Children with Intellectual Disabilities. New Jersey: Pearson.

CHAPTER 9

Motor Disorders

Jarrett Barnhill
Brianna Cheyne
Heidi Diepstra
Elspeth A. Bradley

Developmental co-ordination disorder, tic disorders and stereotypic movement disorder are neurodevelopmental disorders that share key functions, namely motor planning; executing multistep motor tasks; adapting behavioral goals to changing task needs and contingencies; inhibiting extraneous movements during task performance; regulating the motor expression of affective states, and combining and coordinating gross and fine motor actions. Because each unfolds during the developmental period, they emerge in tandem with other domains of higher level cognition, executive function, social communication, and emotional regulation. This section focuses on the problems created when motor disorders and intellectual disabilities co-occur.

Developmental Co-ordination Disorder

Developmental co-ordination disorder is a neurodevelopmental disorder that includes deficits in the planning, sensorimotor organization, motivation, goal directedness, regulation of motor activities and skill learning. Most of these deficits impact the development of executive motor functions which in turn influence developing cognition, emotional regulation, social behavior, and capacity to adapt communication to ongoing interactions and social skills. This section is devoted to enhancing our current understanding of the functional inter-relationships between atypical development (intellectual disabilities, ID), emerging motor skills and the role of both in late-developing psychiatric disorders.

These key issues covered in this section include:

1. The DSM-5 provides a set of generalized criteria designed for clinicians. More in depth assessments are frequently needed to fine-tune treatment and research protocols.

2. Developmental co-ordination disorder does not occur in a vacuum. It must be considered in relation to other genetic/behavioral phenotypes and other neurodevelopmental and primary psychiatric disorders (Hartman, Houwen, Scherder and Voisscher, 2010).

3. Developmental co-ordination disorder is a complex disorder that remains in a state of flux throughout the lifespan. Early changes include transitions from gross to fine motor skills, increasing complexity and hierarchical organization, and regulation of movements and the capacity to improve with practice (Ghez and Krakuer 2000a, 2000b).

4. Developmental co-ordination disorder is a lifelong process that involves incorporating new skills, while refining and adapting older, established ones. Skill acquisition requires exposure and practice to promote neuroplastic changes.

Mastery of a motor skill requires motor planning, integration of multiple brain circuits (cortical, subcortical, and cerebellar pathways), and procedural memory. Riding a bicycle, cursive writing, and playing the piano are examples of automatic, complex motor skills. (Augustyn & Zuckerman, 1998).

5. Motor development is not a linear process but one that evolves from multidirectional interactions (transactions) between developing cognitive, executive, attentional and social and motor coordination skills. These relationships underlie the linkage between developmental co-ordination disorder and other primary behavioral/psychiatric disorders. As a result, the timing of developmental insults has far reaching implications for later development (Hamilton, 2014).

6. Intellectual disability is listed in the differential diagnosis section of developmental co-ordination disorder. This creates potential problems for clinicians, especially those working with people who have moderate to profound IDD. Current procedures for diagnosing developmental co-ordination disorder may lack sufficient sensitivity (floor effects) and specificity (other complications in motor development), and meeting discrepancy criteria. As a result the clinician may have to rely on clinical judgment or assessments by experts to confirm the diagnosis in this population (American Psychiatric Association, 2013).

General Description of Developmental Co-ordination Disorder

Developmental coordination disorder replaced the Clumsy child syndrome, developmental motor coordination disorder, motor skill disorder, minimal brain dysfunction (MBD) and childhood or developmental apraxia. This streamlining however is not without problems. By de-emphasizing diversity, developmental co-ordination disorder excludes some of the richness of overlapping psychomotor functions. For example, minimal brain dysfunction originally included deficits in motor coordination, learning, affect dysregulation and hyperactivity/impulsivity. The DSM-5 tends to dissociate attention deficit/hyperactivity disorder from developmental co-ordination disorder related symptoms that comprised Minimal Brain Dysfunction (Hamilton, 2104).

Clumsiness, slowness and difficulty learning motor skills are the essence of developmental co-ordination disorder. The following represent an attempt to capture the range and breadth of this syndrome:

- Neurobiology—the development of integrated sensory-motor systems is intertwined with emerging motor coordination. The organization of both is foundational for the development of academic learning, skill training, adaptive skills, and social functioning (Hernandez and Blazer, 2006; Piek, Dawson, Smith, & Gasson 2008)
- Integrative/executive function—developmental co-ordination disorder limits the adaptability and flexibility needed to match available motor skills to novel demands, recognize the success (or failure) of task performance, terminate when the action is completed, and voluntarily shift to alternative actions when necessary (Hartman et al., 2010).
- During development, the transformation of reflexive movements, perception-motor imitation to planned voluntary activities sets the stage for joint attention; emotional communication (prosody, gesturing, pantomime, etc); emerging speech as a mode of action at a distance; and the maturation of more complex psychomotor activities (Ghez and Krakuer, 2000 a, 2000b; Hartman et al., 2010; Marlow Hennessey, Bracewood, Wolke, 2007).
- Motor skills require an increasingly complex mixtures of fine and gross motor skills. This balance shifts throughout development to accommodate the complexity of tasks and actions. The integration of fine motor skills is especially important for developing speech articulation (phonology), gestural communication, and writing. Many athletic activities, social play, and academic and occupational

skills rely on a different collection of modifiable, feedback mediated mixtures of fine/gross motor coordination (Domelloff, Johansson, Farooqi, Momelloff, & Ronnqvist, 2013; van Heugten, 2005).

- Procedural memory involves the ability to recall "how to do things"—the acquisition and retention of previously acquired motor skills. New skill learning involves nonverbal working memory and adaptive mastery through practice. The process of moving from learning new skills to those that are increasingly automatic is also essential for many cognitive and social communications needs. In these scenarios we no longer have to think about how to perform these overlearned skills (Ghez, & Krakuer, 2000a, 2000b).
- New skill learning requires exposure to training for learning new tasks. To be effective, the availability of training should match the level of individual abilities and disabilities. Difficulty mastering new motor skills is associated with many other neurodevelopmental disorders (Voeller, 1998).
- Social skill deficits, family dysfunction, and severe psychopathology, especially severe disruptive behaviors, can adversely affect access and utilization of training/habilitative resources. Such impediments can also limit inclusion into community activities. At this level, policy decisions such as the requirement for higher staffing needs have fiscal implications. The availability of appropriate services can be critical for both new training experiences and the mastery of more complex motor skills (Cairney, Hat, Faught 2005; Barnhill and Kartheiser, 2007; Barnhill and McNelis, 2012 and Leonard and Hill, 2014).

Summary of DSM-5 Criteria

The structure of the DSM-5 divides motor disorders into three distinct but interrelated neurodevelopmental syndromes: Developmental co-ordination disorder, stereotypic movement disorder and tic disorders. Developmental co-ordination disorder incorporates general symptoms: onset during the developmental period; evidence for functional impairments across multiple domains, and specifiers and exclusion criteria. The exclusion criteria provide the framework for differential diagnosis—ID is included here but will be explored in greater depth. Other exclusion criteria include primary sensory deficits (blindness) and genetic, metabolic, neurodegenerative, and acquired neurological disorders (e.g., stroke, tumor, etc.). In general, specifiers help define subtypes of developmental co-ordination disorder but are not dilated upon in the DSM-5 criteria (American Psychiatric Association, 2013).

The DSM-5 does not emphasize the inter-relatedness between emerging motor abilities and subsequent speech and language disorders, learning disabilities, or other neurodevelopmental disorders (Barnhill, de Koning, Kartheiser, 2007; Iverson, 2010; Prunty, Barnett, Wilmut, & Plumb, 2013). In addition, there is limited discussion of the role of developmental co-ordination disorder in the development of attention deficit/hyperacity disorder, autism spectrum disorder, mood disorders, anxiety disorders and schizophrenia. To understand these relationships, repeated assessments and longitudinal follow-up are necessary (Barnhill & Karthieser, 2007).

The DSM-5 does provide a broad description of developmental co-ordination disorder (phenomenology) for mental health professionals. It is less useful for researchers or experts in rehabilitation medicine and physical or occupational therapists who need more homogeneous patient samples. In addition, the DSM-5 does not address the special modifications necessary for the assessment of people with intellectual disabilities (ID) (Augustyn & Zuckerman 1998; Barnhill, McNelis, 2012; Dyck, Piek, Patrick, 2011).

Diagnostic Criteria

A. The acquisition and execution of coordinated motor skills is SUBSTANTIALLY below expected performance based on chronological age, or opportunity in skill learning and use. Clumsiness (e.g. dropping or bumping into objects), as well as slowness and inaccuracy in the performance of skills (e.g., catching an object, using scissors or cutlery, handwriting, riding a bike, or participating in sports).

B. The Motor skills deficit in Criterion A significantly and persistently interferes with activities of daily living appropriate to chronological age (e.g. self-care and self-maintenance) and impacts academic/school productivity, prevocational and vocational activities, leisure and play.

C. Onset of symptoms during the developmental period.

D. The motor skills deficits are not better explained by intellectual disability (intellectual developmental disorder), visual impairment, or neurological conditions affecting movement (cerebral palsy, muscular dystrophy, degenerative disorder)

Issues Related to Diagnosis in Person with IDD

The diagnosis of developmental co-ordination disorder in people with ID requires accommodations to address atypical neurodevelopment. For example, there will be an increased risk for diagnostic confusion created by the use of discrepancies. One source involves whether to consider chronological versus developmental age when assessing motor skill performance. This uncertainty can put the clinician in the position of relying upon clinical judgement to deal with incongruities between motor performance, chronological age and developmental age. A second issue is an outgrowth of not addressing the dimensional nature of the boundary between developmental co-ordination disorder and stereotypic movements, tic disorders (motor disorders), autism spectrum disorder as well as behavioral and psychiatric disorders. Assessment requires a thoughtful, multidisciplinary team to choreograph the many permutations of developmental co-ordination disorder in someone with ID (American Psychiatric Association, 2013; Peltopuro, Ahonen, Kaartinen, Seppala, & Narhi V, 2014: Smis-Engelsman and Hill 2012; Voeller, 1998; Landa, 2007).

Development and Course

Neuroscientists are concerned with the role of gene-environment interactions and neuroplasticity during brain development. Both are foundational to skill learning. Infant developmentalists are interested in the roles played by these brain transformations in early motor activity and emerging emotional/attachment behaviors. During early development, there appear to be critical periods or windows of opportunity during which these complex behaviors are more readily acquired (more responsive to appropriate stimulation). The disruption of time-specific gene regulation by severe psychosocial stressors and other environmental insults creates a twofold problem. The immediate effects are on emerging skills. The second and perhaps more complicated problem involves the prospect of a negative impact on late developing motor skills. These adverse effects can also include higher level executive and cognitive functions (Constantino, Todd 2000; van Heugten 2005).

The emergence of motor skills is deeply intertwined with sensory development. For example, early hand movements such as crossing the midline are linked to visual feedback for later reaching, touching and hand play. They also play a role in searching for the caregiver's face, which may be critical for visually impaired infants. Gestural communication, imitation of others, social smiling, and responding to or initiating joint attention play critical roles in the development of social, emotional, and eventual communicative skills. At the level of motor control, these behaviors move from primitive reflexes to proprioceptive guidance to visually guided reaching and manipulating objects that lay the foundation for volitional movements (Decety, & Meyer, 2009). Over time, emerging hand preference and cerebral lateralization permit increasingly precise fine motor skills. As note earlier, these neurodevelopmental changes are coordinated with unfolding higher level cognitive organization, integration of task-specific demands and rapid multi-modal sensory feedback. Deficits in these motor executive functions represent the core neurobiology of developmental co-ordination disorder (Ghez, & Krakuer, 2000b).

Many subtypes of ID are associated with atypical patterns of neuroplasticity, dendritic stabilization, interactive specialization, and myelination. Myelination accelerates the speed of neurotransmission as well as enhances the interconnection and rapid communication between various regions of the developing brain. Disruptions in developmental processes influence the basic building blocks for the hierarchical organization of sensory input, motor planning, and execution of motor and cognitive tasks. These abilities are also the foundation for top down regulation (executive functions) and ramify well beyond motor coordination. During typical development, the maturation of these brain circuits continue maturing well into the third decade. This plasticity plays a key role in the transition from behavior to verbal behaviors and then to thought experiments/planning/ and testing potential efficacy before acting. Although only partially understood, brain development in persons with IDD alters the developmental trajectory of many neural circuitries in ways that make it difficult to generalize about the impact of motor skills on other functional impairments in people with ID (Liu et al., 2014).

Prevalence

Five to six percent of school-aged children present with developmental co-ordination disorder. The majority of affected children have mild impairments. There is a distinct gender bias toward a higher male: female ratio (2-7 males: 1 female). Prematurity and low birth weight are risk factors. Children with left-handedness, mixed hand dominance, or ambidexterity have prevalence rates of developmental co-ordination disorder that are nearly five times those for controls (50% v 10%). Interestingly, left-handedness and atypical lateralization are also more common in many neurodevelopmental and some psychiatric disorders (Hamilton, 2014).

The general cutoff scores for diagnosing developmental co-ordination disorder are 1.5 to 2 standard deviations below age-stratified test scores. This translates into scores in the range of 5-20th percentiles. For older children, our best standardized test instruments tend to shift toward measurements of complex, fine motor skills (handwriting) and less on gross motor abilities. Fine motor developmental scores tend to lag in many individuals with ID and partly explain the higher developmental co-ordination disorder prevalence rates across the spectrum of ID (Smits-Engelsman, & Hill 2012).

Differential Diagnosis

The differential diagnosis of motor co-ordination disorder begins with a careful assessment of family, social, medical/neurologica,l and developmental history. The assessment/treatment team takes this data and formulates the differential diagnosis for the individual. Diagnosis is a time-limited observation that may not capture ongoing changes. Longitudinal evaluations are needed to develop a personalized developmental trajectory of motor skill development over time. Such data can help differentiate transient delays (grow out of) from those that will persist. It can also help track treatment effects. Longitudinal data can be useful for tracking psychomotor regression secondary to acquired or neurodegenerative disorders. For example, the most common scenarios involve people with borderline and mild ID who present with relatively minor neurological soft signs or a slightly delayed pace of skill acquisition. Ceiling effects may be minimal. Those with severe ID may plateau or display a ceiling effects for acquiring age-appropriate and increasingly more complex motor skills. Unfortunately the overlap between motor development, ID, other neurodevelopmental and primary neuropsychiatric disorders can complicate the differential diagnosis. Many subtle changes may go unrecognized against the backdrop of severe challenging behaviors (diagnostic overshadowing). A serious regression in psychomotor skills warrants more detailed assessment (Hamilton, 2014).

Children with transient coordination delays create problems disentangling the contributions of variations in "normal development" from those that represent risk factors for late-developing behavioral or mental disorders. For example, children with attention deficit/ hyperactivity disorder and some specific learning disorders may initially display minor neurological co-ordination deficits (neurological soft signs) that may recede with time. Others, however, can have their severe hyperactivity or impulsivity overshadow inattentiveness and learning disabilities that may have a greater negative affect than their primary symptoms on future education or employment options. Children with Tourette's disorder may find their tics or associated attention deficit/hyperactivity disorder or disruptive behaviors overshadow learning problems, fine motor deficits (hand writing), cognitive rigidity, and secondary emotional problems. Both scenarios remind us that overt behavior can overshadow underlying developmental co-ordination disorder and delay necessary, therapeutic interventions (Barnhill & Kartheiser, 2007; Hamilton, 2014).

Many neurodegenerative disorders may present with symptoms of developmental co-ordination disorder. What may start out as minor motor deficits may be followed by more severe psychomotor regression. For example, neuromuscular disorders may present with clumsiness that is frequently misattributed to developmental co-ordination disorder (muscular dystrophies). Degenerative motor disorders such as hereditary paraplegias and cerebellar ataxias may present with subtle co-ordination deficits early in their course but then regress to more severe psychomotor impairments. Several genetic syndromes present with joint laxity. Fragile X, Erhlos Danlos and other syndromes are often associated with motor complaints. Various forms of hypotonia (common in Down syndrome) can also be misattributed to clumsiness and gait disturbances. There is considerable variability in the speed of psychomotor regression. Repeated assessment and genetic studies may be needed to properly differentiate these forms psychomotor regression from DCD (Hamilton, 2014).

Functional Consequences

The functional impact of developmental co-ordination disorder reflects changing task demands and performance expectations and goals. For example, a mismatch between demands and skill levels may lead to significant distress generated by unrecognized deficits in motor co-ordination. Frustration arising from these difficulties is frequently expressed in baseline exaggeration of challenging behaviors, decreased motivation, and work avoidance.

Chronic stress may also further impede the willingness to attempt or actually learn new motor skills, as well as participation in occupational, educational, social, and recreational activities. Disruptions in social networks and disruptive behaviors can contribute to restrictions or exclusion from community-based activities.

Developmental co-ordination disorder can also contribute to mood and behavioral changes that can alert clinicians to mismatches between skill deficits and inappropriate demands and performance expectations. These changes in quality of life may overshadow the symptoms of developmental co-ordination disorder. In these circumstances the early recognition of developmental co-ordination disorder may be critical. For individuals with ID, significant scatter in the support needs/functional domains (conceptual, social, and practical domains) may suggest that motor problems underlie the variability in severity ratings. The use of these indirect measures of motor co-ordination may suggest that more formal motor testing is needed. In addition, declining quality of life may be a useful signal for psychomotor regression and mental health complications. Early recognition can help limit emerging psychosocial isolation from activities outside school or occupational settings (Cairney et al., 2005; Gillberg and Kadesjö 2003).

Comorbidity

The co-occurrence of developmental co-ordination disorder, language, and other learning disabilities underscores the key role motor coordination plays in both typical and atypical brain development. For example, many motor skills and co-ordination deficits predate the onset of other learning disorders as well as late occurring behavioral or psychiatric disorders. Unfortunately, the presence of neurological soft signs is associated with other externalizing and internalizing behavioral disorders. As a result, the predictive validity of these early motor deficits is limited. Neurological "soft signs" may play a complex role in the neurobiology of chronic schizophrenia. When present in schizophrenia spectrum disorders, soft signs may alert the clinician to an increased risk for of negative symptoms, chronicity, and limited treatment response (Barnhill, & Kartheiser, 2007; Hamilton, 2014).

From a neuropsychological perspective, subtypes of IDD with developmental co-ordination disorder are associated with higher rates of aberrant or incomplete cerebral lateralization and hand dominance. For example, clumsiness, poor dexterity, and hand dominance can complicate the learning and effective use of American Sign Language (ASL) and hand held or other electronic communication devices. In general, the deficits associated with developmental co-ordination disorder are far less severe than in cerebral palsy (static encephalopathy) but still require modifications in device selection or training. Some individuals with cerebral palsy may display hemiplegia (paralysis of the right arm), dyspraxia/motor co-ordination problems in the "unaffected" left upper extremity well as a form of dysphasia. These individuals may have difficulty comprehending and communicating via ASL. Although hemiplegia is excluded from developmental co-ordination disorder, many milder forms of hemiplegia can be misattributed to developmental co-ordination disorder (Barnhill, & Kartheiser 2007; Wisdom, Dyck. Piek, Hay, & Hallmayer 2007).

Application of Diagnostic Criteria to People with ID

A clinically significant gap between expected and observed/measured performance is a primary criteria for developmental co-ordination disorder. For people with ID, this type of discrepancy model is plagued by two problems. The first is that ID is part of the differential diagnosis of developmental co-ordination disorder. The exclusion of ID is largely based on the high probability of impaired motor coordination. The second problem area involves meeting the discrepancy requirements for developmental co-ordination disorder. The DSM-5 resolves the second problem area by incorporating more general criteria. Another alternative involves incorporating the functional deficits associated with developmental co-ordination disorder into the DSM-5 severity dimensions of ID. This combination addresses motor impairments at the level of support needs and scatter within the functional domain criteria (conceptual, social and practical). From a practical point of view, clinicians may find it more useful to address the effects on supports services rather than trying to extrapolate normative data (IQ and measures of motor skill and function) to individuals with severe ID.

From this perspective, the severity of developmental co-ordination disorder may not be easily correlated with the level of IDD. For example, many behavioral phenotypes and neurodevelopmental syndromes are associated with underlying impairments in motor co-ordination, skill learning, and mastery. Because motor coordination and skill acquisition are both developmental phenomena, it will become increasingly difficult to project outcome with any strong degree of certainty. This uncertainty generates several key questions:

- Can our developmental instruments adequately capture the many trajectories of motor skill development across the spectrum of ID (general ID population), especially deficits associated with specific syndromes or the validity of measurements among individuals with severe profound ID?
- Do we have sufficient longitudinal data to differentiate, then project whether a given coordination problem is a chronic deficit in skill development and acquisition (more likely to persist) or a developmental delay (more likely to improve over time)?
- Which is the best approach, relying upon discrepancy criteria (1.5 to 2 standard deviations from the norm on motor skill assessments) based on chronological or developmental age. The problem grows more complicated for clinicians dealing with persons with severe/profound ID. A solution may be to use the support needs/functional

domains criteria for classifying the severity of IDD. Motor disorders may have a greater impact on practical or conceptual skills.

Answers to each require more research. Assessment and treatment should be in the hands of experts in occupational and physical therapy.

General Considerations

Motor coordination involves not only the speed and accuracy of movements but also the capacity to learn and apply these skills across a broad range of social, occupational, academic, recreational, and play activities. For individuals with ID, this includes learning basic self-help skills as well. We are still early in the process of understanding the multi-directional interactions between not only these developmental disorders but also their relationships with other neurodevelopmental, behavioral, and neuropsychiatric disorders. Much of our knowledge is descriptive and devoted to fine tuning symptoms/ challenging behavior-driven diagnoses. The gap between the research in the developmental neurosciences and our clinical understanding of etiology pose major challenges for clinicians.

Methodology

Searches were conducted in health, social science, and general science-focused information resources including *MEDLINE, Cumulative Index to Nursing and Allied Health Literature* (CINAHL), the *Cochrane Database of Systematic Reviews, SocINDEX, PsycINFO, and Science Citation Index,* as well as multidisciplinary resources such as *Academic Search Complete.* Resources were searched using terms related to ID and developmental co-ordination disorder. PubMed and PsycInfo searches were conducted in an attempt to isolate published work with data regarding the co-occurrence of ID, and developmental co-ordination disorder. We consulted recent texts devoted to the gene-environmental, neurophysiological, neuropsychological, and developmental neuropsychiatric research and clinical underpinnings of developmental co-ordination disorder.

Level of Evidence

The majority of the literature fits into level 4 and 5 in the Cochrane Rating System.

Review of Research Applying to People with ID

There are several factors affecting the quality and quantity of available research for individuals with developmental co-ordination disorder and ID. One such factor involves the practice of excluding individuals with ID from many population studies. Likewise, studies that do include individuals with IDfrequently limit their cohorts to those with borderline and mild ID. In many cases this may leave clinicians in the positon of referring to specialists or when these professionals are not available, extrapolating published findings to people with severe/ profound ID (Peltopuro et al., 2014). A second limitation relates to the wide variety of etiologies associated with developmental co-ordination disorder and ID in children and adults, especially in the gray zones between developmental co-ordination disorder, ID and other neurodevelopmental disorders. This problem reflects a continuum of severity for developmental co-ordination disorder. It also frequently complicates a developmental trajectory for future skill development. For example, the variability of developmental co-ordination disorder severity within a cohort of individuals with borderline ID may be greater than the differences between those with borderline ID and a comparison group of people with moderate/severe ID. This observation suggests that the severity of developmental co-ordination disorder may show as much variability within a level of ID as it does between borderline and severe ID (declining quality of life may be a useful signal for psychomotor regression and mental health complications). Early recognition can help limit emerging psychosocial isolation form activities outside school or occupational settings (Hartman et al., 2010; Peltopuro et al., 2014).

One explanation for this conundrum arises from the variability in motor performance within each subgroup of ID. A second explanation arise from our difficulty recognizing motor disorders and differentiating it from other neurodevelopmental and psychiatric disorders. This may be a significant issue for those with severe/ profound ID. A third issue hinges on the applicability of discrepancy criteria (expected performance for a specific developmental age). Motor skill deficits may not be routinely differentiated from other neurodevelopmental disorders and both may be overshadowed by severe behavioral or psychiatric disorders. It may be prudent to assume that the boundary between developmental co-ordination disorder and other neurodevelopmental and psychiatric disorders will be difficult to disentangle or will remain relatively impenetrable. In this scenario it may be more useful to focus instead on the levels of variability within support service needs and functional domains (Vuijik, Hartman, Scherder, & Visscher, 2010).

Clinicians face another set of conundrums when trying to predict the developmental trajectory of motor skills in general, and developmental co-ordination disorder in particular. In this context, the functional or syncretic approach (combining support needs and functional criteria with more detailed, normative assessments) may strengthen our capacity to make individualized comparisons between clinical course, subtype or severity of ID, and symptoms of developmental co-ordination disorder. This model provides a more practical approach to people with severe/profound ID in three ways: more workable for those who are more difficult to assess with structured or standardized assessments; reduce the reliance on discrepancy criteria by focusing instead on changes in selected functional deficits within the functional domains criteria; and enhance the diagnostic process by combing broader scale functional data sets with more objective measures (American Psychiatric Association, 2013; Barnhill & Kartheiser, 2007; Barnhill & McNelis 2012; Gillberg & Kadesjö 2003).

We need to incorporate data on the early recognition and treatment of individuals presenting with intrauterine or perinatal complications, intrauterine toxin exposure (fetal alcohol), behavioral phenotypes, other neurodevelopmental disorders, and those at high genetic risk for major psychiatric disorders. We have a need for more longitudinal studies of developmental co-ordination disorder to keep up with the increasing sensitivity of genetic studies, the increasing number of genetic markers for neurodegenerative, neurodevelopmental, and neuropsychiatric disorders, the increasing sophistication of neurophysiological and neuroimaging technologies, and the growth of consortia that can generate much larger research cohorts (Barnhill & McNelis, 2012; Domelloff et al., 2013).

Adults with IDD

Recent studies suggest that developmental co-ordination disorder is relatively common in individuals with borderline/mild ID. It appears that there is a continuum with neuro-typicality but that their developmental trajectories may vary. How well this matches up with cognitive, occupational, adaptive skills as well as psychosocial adjustment is a more complex issue. One caveat is that milder forms of neuro-genetic disorders, specific behavioral phenotypes, and undiagnosed psychiatric disorders can impact developing motor coordination (Barnhill, & Kartheiser, 2007; Vuijik, Hartman, Scherder, & Visscher 2010). As noted earlier, developmental co-ordination disorder is often a point diagnosis — one made at a specific point in time with limited longitudinal follow-up. There are gaps in such longitudinal research across the spectrum of ID. Because skill learning continues throughout adulthood, there is a need for lifelong training and models for teaching new adaptive or occupational skills.

The nature, measurement, and patterns of improvement may be subject to ceiling effects that require differentiating a plateau in the developmental trajectory from the early stages of a neurodegenerative disorder. For example, some forms of dementia present with deficits in learning new skills but may not affect well-learned/practiced skills until much later in the course of the illness. We need more longitudinal studies that allow tracking subtle decrements in psychomotor skill learning over time. In this context, loss of motor skills may diverge from other facets of some dementias. We also need to consider the impact of schizophrenia, mood disorders, impulse control disorders, residual attention deficit/hyperactivity disorder and other co-occurring neurodevelopmental disorders (learning disabilities and autism spectrum disorder) on the course of childhood developmental co-ordination disorder (Hamilton, 2014).

There are few studies devoted to individuals with severe/profound ID. Two issues are relevant: there is a higher prevalence rate for congenital or acquired motor disorders in individuals with severe/profound ID, and the developmental trajectory of developing motor coordination is difficult to assess due to the severity of atypical brain development in severe/profound ID. A short list of these issues includes:

- New skill learning requires extended and repetitive training sessions; training may have to focus more on gross rather than fine motor skills and be taught in the area in which the skill is used.
- The style of teaching new skills may require breaking tasks down into component parts, then trying to string or sequence these together into more complex skills; even individuals with relatively good procedural memory (how to do a task) may require cueing or signaling to initiate a task, complete the task, terminate the actions, and shift sets for the next activity (perseveration).
- Perseveration and stereotypies may interfere with both learning and carrying out new skills expression.
- Introducing novel tasks may increase anxiety, stereotypies, and mannerisms that can interfere with task learning.
- Assessment tools may have limited utility in the severe/profound ID population.
- Motor coordination deficits overlap co-occurring neurological, metabolic, and genetic disorders.
- Diagnostic overshadowing by disruptive or challenging behaviors can limit training experiences.
- Greater use of multiple medications, especially antipsychotic drugs and anticonvulsants can adversely affect coordination and skill learning.

Each of these caveats accentuates the problem of recognition, differential diagnosis, assessment, and treatment needs (Barnhill, McNelis, 2012; Van Betenburg-Eddes et al., 2013).

Children with ID

One of the principle issues for children is the obvious fact that the brain is still developing and maturing. For example, the disruption between the developmental trajectories of emerging skills versus established skills and the level of ID are best illustrated by the acquisition of new fine motor skills (writing, drawing, tying shoes, buttoning, etc.). Each of these skills requires a higher degree of sequential integration of sensory processing, integration, motor planning and coordination, feedback, and adaptation as well top-down regulation (executive functions). For many children, atypical development is overshadowed by more immediate behavioral or mental health needs. In addition, developmental co-ordination disorder can also affect language development and the acquisition of academic skills. developmental co-ordination disorder may also interfere with symbolic and social play and can adversely affect more complex motor skills and cognitive development. Disruptive behaviors and psychosocial circumstances can lessen opportunities to access, utilize, and learn from new experiences.

The presence of severe/profound ID, autism spectrum disorder, and severe coordination disorders not only influences the nature and course of developmental co-ordination disorder, it also limits the availability and access to many habilitative services. Our understanding of the adverse effects of family, parental mental illness, substance abuse, abuse, and neglect on developmental co-ordination disorder is also incomplete, but researchers do note adversity during childhood has potentially lifelong consequences (Bishop 2002; Kartasidou, Varsamis, & Sampsonidou, 2012).

Summary of the Limitations in Applying DSM-5 Criteria to People with ID

The DSM-5 is not designed nor constructed to address the complex developmental issues reviewed thus far. It is a clinical instrument designed to cast a wide net and perhaps serve as starting point for referral to specialists (PT, OT, etc.). It also permits greater leeway for clinical judgment in diagnostic decision-making. For individuals with ID, meeting the criteria for developmental co-ordination disorder is a starting point for more detailed and focused assessments. Yet even though developmental co-ordination disorder is more common in the borderline/mild ID population, most referrals are for behavioral and neurodevelopmental psychiatric disorders, not motor skill deficits (Barnhill & McNelis, 2012). Subtle co-ordination deficits or neurological soft signs are frequently overlooked due to associated behavioral or psychiatric symptoms. It behooves clinician to screen for subtle deficits in motor coordination among referrals for behavioral or psychiatric interventions. The reverse process may also be true. Unrecognized developmental co-ordination disorder may be associated with more varied or treatment resistant symptoms. Developmental co-ordination disorder may also drag down performance on measures of other adaptive skills or limit opportunities for academic/occupational training and participation in sports or other social activities (Vuijik et al., 2010). People with severe/profound ID represent an even more complex problem. These complications are discussed earlier.

Etiology and Pathogenesis

In general, manual dexterity is usually classified in terms of fine motor skills, including the presence of sufficient motivation, selective attention to the task and capacity to inhibit other potentially competing brain activities, the presence of a functional, hierarchical organization that can carry out planned motor activities, and a capacity to evaluate efficacy and modify motor programs to match task demands, terminate tasks when they are completed, and shift to another task when needed. This level of integration requires reciprocating interconnections both within and between multiple brain networks. It appears that connections between the prefrontal and parietal/occipital cortices, the primary motor cortex, basal ganglia, thalamic centers, and cerebellum are critical to these developing processes. Carrying out these functions in real time requires extensive myelination of the entire system. This is a slower process that may not be completed until late adolescence. A third critical piece is the capacity to adapt neuronal networks (neuroplasticity) to learning new skills and integrating them into already established skills. Lastly, previously learned skills become habitual and "make room" for new learning as well as combine skills to generate new patterns of behavior (Ghez & Krakuer 2000a, 2000b).

Many subtypes of ID adversely affect neuron and myelin development, which interferes with the development of higher cortical functions. For example, voluntary fine motor movement moves from ideas to a general plan then to the specific movements. The coordination required by handwriting, playing the piano, manipulating puzzle pieces, or even stacking blocks necessitates the combined actions of fronto-striatal-thalamic networks in both cerebral hemispheres. Clumsiness, neurological soft signs and deficits in fine motor skills represent aberrations in these developmental processes. Although not directly causal, these interconnected circuits interact with those involved in specific learning disabilities, speech and expressive language disorders, attention deficit/hyperactivity disorder, autism spectrum disorder, and ID. This level of integration suggests a mechanism may explain the high prevalence rates of DCD among individuals with ID (Domelloff et al., 2013; Peltopuro et al., 2014). The neurobiological and psychosocial underpinnings of developmental co-ordination disorder are not completely understood, but they do interfere with the vital role played by experience and training in the development of motor coordination—the old adage: "practice makes perfect" (Bishop, 2002; Ghez & Krakuer, 2000a; Liu et al., 2014).

Biological Factors

There are many inherent problems with dissecting motor skill and co-ordination development from other neurocognitive skills. Assessment is complicated by the many subtypes of ID that constrain our capacity to routinely apply standardized test instruments or meet the discrepancy criteria outlined in the DSM-5. Brain development involves complex gene-environment interactions that are incompletely understood in many ID syndromes. These include altered neurogenesis, neuronal migration, neuroplasticity, synaptic integrity, myelination, and the emergence of increasing hemispheric and inter-hemispheric communication. This pattern of hierarchical maturation in many domains underlies the emergence of higher cortical functions (conceptual and practical domains). As noted the process is also transactional. The sequence and timing of these changes is also critical. Aberrant gene-environment interaction or insults during early infancy can have a greater impact on the maturation and linkages between cerebral, limbic, subcortical, and cerebellar network's development (Ghez, & Krakuer 2000b; Hartman Houwen, Scherder, & Visscher, 2010).

Developmental co-ordination disorder has a relatively high heritability (50% or half of the variance is related to gene activity). Unfortunately the co-occurrence of other neurodevelopmental factors interact with this genetic risk. As noted above, the timing of environmental insults has a major role in both gene expression and neuroplasticity. A partial list of these insults includes biopsychosocial events, exposure to toxins, cigarette smoking, alcohol and drug consumption, chronic maternal stress, problems with intrauterine fetal growth, and malnutrition. Unfortunately early exposure to these adverse events can have both immediate and lifelong implications for multiple lines of development (Hamilton, 2014).

Genetic Factors

Heritability reflects the degree to which genes affect the development of developmental co-ordination disorder — the percentage of the variance in a population attributable to genetic causes. Many studies suggest that as much of 50% of the variance in developmental co-ordination disorder is the result of genetic influence. Gender differences also play a role in gene expression, especially for complex neurodevelopmental disorders such as Tourette's disorder and autism spectrum disorder that involve many genes. These gene-environment interactions are due to modifications of gene activity. Although the role that these epigenetic effects play during development is essential, ongoing gene-environment interaction provides a mechanism for new skill learning to occur throughout the life span (Constantino & Todd, 2000; Hamilton, 2014).

Developmental co-ordination disorder is another example of a complex genetic disorder. Neurological soft signs are associated with a range of behavioral disorders, emotional dysregulation, impulse dyscontrol, and language disorders/specific learning disorders that are linked to external-internalizing disorders. The presence of soft signs is frequently associated with borderline-mild ID. In addition, soft signs are associated with selected behavioral phenotypes (e.g., fragile X and Williams's syndrome) that include motor co-ordination deficits. In short, the genetic analysis of developmental co-ordination disorder supports polygenic patterns of inheritance, access to environments that permit play, organized activities, and more specific skill learning. The gene-environment interactions, exposure to environmental toxins and the overlap with other neurodevelopmental and neuropsychiatric disorders place developmental co-ordination disorder among a group of complex genetic disorders. The association of developmental co-ordination disorder with autism spectrum disorder, schizophrenia, attention deficit/hyperactivity disorder, ID, and specific learning disorders is an intriguing one that needs further exploration (Wisdom et al., 2007).

Psychosocial Factors

Developmental co-ordination disorder is more frequent among infants who are small for gestational age and suffer from intrauterine growth retardation, prematurity, or have toxic exposure syndromes. For young children, prevention remains the best treatment by compensating early in their course and hopefully averting or minimizing adverse outcomes. A crucial step toward preventive strategies is developing accessible community-based programs to improve public health and prenatal care. Maternal health initiative focus on gestational issues, adequate nutrition, and reducing maternal substance abuse. For toddlers and young children, addressing food insecurity, providing supportive programs for parents and children at high risk for abuse and neglect, and support and training for young parents in basic sensory-motor stimulation are prevention strategies. These same strategies may also be helpful for children with diagnosed intellectual and other neurodevelopmental disorders. The literature suggests that long-term early psychoeducational and occupational therapy intervention beginning in infancy/preshool period and continuing throughout the developmental period are most helpful in limiting the effects of DCD on developing intellectual disorders, language/speech/phonological disorders as well as other cognitive, behavioral, and mental health disorders (Bishop 2002; Van Betenburg-Eddes et al., 2013).

Developmental Factors

It is noteworthy that severe neurological complications such as cerebral palsy (CP), epilepsy, and genetic disorders can also limit neuroplasticity or psychomotor development. The interrelationships between these disorders, developmental co-ordination disorder, and ID suggest the need to address developmental co-ordination disorder in terms of a continuum with other development disorders. For example, at the milder end are neurological soft signs; at the severe end are cerebral palsy and other motor disorders. Although excluded from developmental co-ordination disorder, it also appears that an earlier age of onset for acquired coordination disorders (stroke or traumatic brain injury) presents similar problems. Likewise, people with severe/profound ID who may not have a genetic or acquired developmental co-ordination disorder, the presence of their severe cognitive adaptive deficits can interfere with the two basic building blocks of motor coordination: skill learning and flexibility of adaptive responses. In addition, severe developmental delays during infancy can increase their vulnerability to emotional deprivation, abuse, and lack of access to early intervention programs Once again, the transactional nature of early development may lead to changes in gene regulation and activity during critical or sensitive periods for emerging and late developing skills.

Each of these topics supports the need for a thorough review of the level and nature of environmental stimulation as well as the developing child's social ecology. In short, these factors suggest that we consider the phenotype of developmental co-ordination disorder and ID from a stress diathesis perspective model (Hartman et al., 2010; Piek & Dyck, 2004).

Application of Diagnostic Criteria

The assessment of developmental coordination disorder continues to evolve as newer diagnostic technologies become available. Yet in spite of these advances, the basic clinical evaluation still depends on taking a careful past medical, developmental, and family history; detailed observation across many settings; physical/neurological examinations; evaluations by physical therapy; and, if warranted, adding psychoeducational, and neuropsychological testing to the standard evaluation. More specialized assessment instruments are usually carried out by specialists in physical and occupational therapy. Given these complexities, the diagnosis is best made by a multidisciplinary team that can address the many facets of developing motor co-ordination (Up to Date, 2014).

Developmental Coordination Disorder

DSM-5 Diagnostic Criteria	Applying Criteria for Individuals with Borderline mild/moderate IDDM-ID	Applying Criteria for Individuals with Severe profound ID	Comments-Notes
A. The acquisition and execution of coordinated motor skills is SUBSTANTIALLY below expected performance based on chronological age, or opportunity in skill learning and use. Clumsiness (e.g. dropping or bumping into objects), as well as slowness and inaccuracy or performance skills (e.g. catching an object, using scissors or cutlery, handwriting, riding a bike, or participating in sports)	No significant modifications **Note:** Performance deficits on standardized assessment instruments, neurological examination are associated with borderline ID. There is a great deal of variability in assessment scores and the level of ID	There is limited data on motor coordination skills. Testing instruments, difficulty establish 1.5-2.0 standard deviations relative to level of ID may interfere with diagnosis. Communicating, use of imitation or hand over hand assistance may be required for most skill learning. Flexibility and adaptability of learned skills may be severely limited—perseveration and difficulty accommodating existing skills to novel task demands. Presence of autism with stereotypies and severe challenging behaviors may limit exposure to training experiences.; Imbalance between fine and gross motor skills may be more prominent	motor skills must greater than that expected at any given level of ID, The applications of functional domains of support needs and scatter within cognitive, social and practical skills may be more useful than discrepancy criteria. Standardized tests like IQ tests may provide a limited view of functioning among individuals with severe/profound ID
B. The motor skills deficit in Criterion A significantly and persistently interfere with activities of daily living appropriate to chronological age (e.g. self-care and self-maintenance) and impacts academic/school productivity, prevocational and vocational activities, leisure and play.	Variability between skill level and ID is common, Breaking down complex tasks, increased number of trials, and more direct links between skill learning and the environment where the skills is to be used, more frequent rehearsals.	Breaking down many motor tasks into component parts, increased number of trials, and more direct links between skill learning and the environment where the skills is to be used, more frequent rehearsals.	
C. Onset of symptoms during the developmental period	No major adaptations, differences. Difficulties with deficit recognition may be inversely related to level of ID. **Notes:** Persistence of motor subtle motor deficits may cloud the end point for the developmental period.; These include: variability in gross/fine motor skill discrepancies may change with the complexity of task; Developmental age may not directly related to ceiling effects on motor coordination skills.	Insufficient data to establish distinct criteria changes. Difficulties with deficit recognition and measurement inversely related to level of ID. **Notes:** Persistence of motor subtle motor deficits may cloud the end point for the developmental period. These include: variability in gross/fine motor skill discrepancies may change with the complexity of task; developmental age may not directly related to ceiling effects on motor coordination skills.	

Developmental Coordination Disorder (continued)

DSM-5 Diagnostic Criteria	Applying Criteria for Individuals with Borderline mild/moderate IDDM-ID	Applying Criteria for Individuals with Severe profound ID	Comments-Notes
D. The motor skills deficits are not better explained by Intellectual Disability (Intellectual Developmental Disorder) or visual impairment, or neurological conditions affecting movement (cerebral palsy, muscular dystrophy, degenerative disorder).	Current focus on level of adaptive skills and need for supports need to be linked to measured performance. Variations in adaptive and supports needs may supplement standardized assessment.	The presence of particular deficits in adaptive skills and need for supports may be more useful than discrepancy criteria based on specific testing or assessment instruments. Higher rates of severe neurodevelopmental and neurological disorders may overshadow subtler deficits in motor learning. Medication side effects on motor coordination may be more difficult to rule out.	

Tic Disorders

Tic disorders represent a group of movement disorders associated with a range of other neurological and neurodevelopmental conditions. For example, the prevalence rates of tic disorders is higher among individuals with intellectual disabilities (ID) or autism spectrum disorder (ASD) than the general population (Canitano, & Vivanti, 2007). But those statistics can be deceptive. Tic disorders are generally underdiagnosed in most clinical settings devoted to dual diagnosis. This discrepancy is due in large part to diagnostic overshadowing by co-occurring obsessive-compulsive disorders, attention deficit/disruptive behavior and other Impulse control disorders, SIB/aggression, and autism spectrum disorders (Barnhill & Horrigan,2002). This chapter explores the problems of recognition, diagnostic overshadowing and other roadblocks to understanding the bio-psycho-sociology of tic disorders in individuals with ID.

Review of Diagnostic Criteria:

General Description

Tics are sudden, intrusive, recurrent, non-rhythmic, and for the most part involuntary movements and/or vocalizations. Tic disorders are classified based on the presence of motor or vocal tics, or both; duration (less than or more than one year since onset); and emergence during the developmental period (American Psychiatric Association, 2013). For some adults the age of onset and typology of childhood tics is more difficult to determine and the age at recognition, referral, or clinical diagnosis may be more relevant.

Tic disorders share several features with other movement disorders. These include a waxing and waning course; a tendency to intensify in response to a range of affective states and decrease during sleep. Two features of tic disorders create some confusion for clinicians: the capacity to suppress movements and vocalizations for limited periods of time, and a relative lack of awareness of their ticqueing (Robertson, 2000; Bruun, & Budman, 1993). While exploring the family history of affected children, it is not uncommon to encounter parents who do not remember their own childhood tics or appear unaware of ongoing tics. If pointed out, many will be shocked or dismiss them as harmless old habits with minimal social or functional impairment.

Tic disorders also vary widely in terms of clinical course and severity. Only a small percentage of affected young children with transient tics go on to develop persistent motor or vocal tics that are severe enough to interfere with daily activities or educational or occupational performance. For many children, the level of functional academic impairments is due mainly to co-occurring attention deficits, processing slowness, performance on multi-step academic assignments, timed tests, and developmental written language problems, and compulsive behaviors that interfere with task completion (Verte. Geurts. Roeyers, Osterlaan, Oosterlaan, & Sergeant, 2005; Murphy, Geraldi, Leckman, 2014). Social impairment correlates with the presence of these neurocognitive factors and co-occurring explosive aggression, self-injury, and socially inappropriate impulsive behaviors. The recognition of tic disorders is also overshadowed by these factors and the co-occurrence of mental health disorders (American Psychiatric Association, 2013; Fletcher et al., 2007; Zinner, 2004).

With this variability in mind, tic disorders are best conceptualized as lying on a continuum with other movement disorders. The severity of tics is determined by both genetic risk and a range psychosocial and physiological stressors. This particular pattern of stress-diathesis is consistent with other psychosomatic movement disorders. Psychosomatic disorders are defined as medical or neuropsychiatric conditions in which physical symptoms (tics in our case) are vulnerable to a range of biopsychosocial stressors (Barnhill & Hurley 2008). This aspect of tic disorders may partially explain why in spite nearly 130 years of clinical study, we still have an incomplete scientific understanding of their pathophysiology.

Summary of DSM-5 Criteria

In the DSM-5, tic disorders is assigned to motor disorders along with developmental co-ordination and stereotypic movement disorders. Tic disorders include transient tic disorders that usually appear during motor development; chronic motor and vocal tic, and Tourette disorder. Within each category, there is significant diversity and rates of associated cognitive, behavioral and psychiatric disorders. By far Tourette's disorder is the most familiar of the tic disorders (American Psychiatric Association, 2013).

- *Tourette's Disorder*

a. Both multiple motor and one or more vocal tics have been present at some time during the illness, although not necessarily concurrently.

b. The tics may wax and wane in frequency but have persisted for more than 1 year since the first tic onset.

c. Onset is before age 18 years.

d. The disturbance is not attributable to the physiological effects of a substance, or another medical condition.

- *Persistent (Chronic) Motor or Vocal Tic Disorder*

a. Single or multiple motor or vocal tics have been present during the illness, but not both motor or vocal

b. Tics may wax and wane in frequency but have persisted for more than 1 year since first tic onset.

c. Onset if before age 18 years.

d. The disturbance is not attributable to the physiological effects of a substance, or another medical condition.

Specify if:
With motor tics only
With vocal tics only

- *Provisional Tic Disorder*

a. Single or multiple motor and /or vocal tics.

b. Tics have been present for less than 1 year since tic onset.

c. Onset is before age 18 year.

d. The disturbance is not attributable to the physiological effects of a substance, or another medical condition.

e. Criteria have never been met for Tourette's Disorder or persistent motor (chronic) or vocal tic disorder

Development and Course

Preschool children are more likely to develop benign forms of transient tics that disappear after a few months. Referral is unlikely unless there are other neurodevelopmental or behavioral disorders. Children who develop persistent tics (longer than 1 year since onset) tend to follow two tracts: the motor or vocal tics wax and wane in intensity over their course;

or they develop a combination of vocal and motor tics and meet the criteria for Tourette's disorder. For most of these children tics reach a peak intensity within 5-10 years after onset. Unfortunately, this trajectory frequently collides with puberty and raises questions about the influence of gonadal hormones on severity. More recent research suggests a more complex, nuanced relationship between the neuro-endocrinology of puberty, gonadal hormone releasing factors, and other neuropeptides (oxytocin and vasopressin), and tic disorders (Barnhill & Horrigan, 2002; Shaw & Coffey, 2014).

Many children affected with persistent tic disorders display developmental changes in their typography, typology, and severity. Within 3-5 years a substantial majority start reporting premonitory or sensory tics that precede and appear to partially motivate abnormal movements. These children may also report that "feeling right" terminates their premonitory urges. Unfortunately their movements are frequently misattributed to voluntary actions, obsessive compulsive disorder, stereotypies, or other repetitive behaviors (Cohen, Simeon, Hollander, & Stein, 1997; Scahill et al., 2014). The urges associated with such "unvoluntary" can also be confused with akathisia or restless legs syndrome (Neal, & Cavanna, 2013). Finally, children with tic disorders are more likely to express a higher prevalence of sleep disorders, especially parasomnias, periodic limb movements, and restless legs syndrome. By adulthood tics may have subsided, but many of the neurobehavioral comorbidities persist. These frequently overshadow the history of childhood tics (Robertson 2000; Shaw & Coffey, 2014).

Prevalence

The prevalence rates of tic disorders vary across the life span. The gender bias (2-4 male: 1 female) remains constant in both population surveys and clinical screening. The combined rate of transient tics approaches 15-25% of the selected preschool populations. By school age these numbers drop to 1-2%, but the gender bias remains. Chronic motor and vocal tics, and Tourette's disorder dominate the statistics among elementary school children. The prevalence originally revealed 4/10,000 ratio, but the decision to eliminate coprolalia as a core criterion dramatically changed that ratio to between 0.75-1.0%. The steady decline in clinical case-ness by late adolescence and adulthood can make it difficult to do retrospective studies. Since some adults may not be aware of mild childhood tics, the cohort may be adults with persistent tics or those who have affected children. These specifiers will create a selection bias towards more severe cases (Baron-Cohen, Mortimer, Moriarity, Izaguirre, & Robertson, 1999; Shaw, & Coffey 2014,)

The gender bias for tic disorders is similar to that for other neurodevelopmental disorders. Studies suggest that tics among preschoolers are significantly more frequent among children with other neurodevelopmental disorders (Santangelo et al., 1994). Unfortunately, the lack of awareness, delayed recognition or misdiagnosis of tic disorders in children with ASD or ID introduces a selection bias into many population-based epidemiological studies (Kerserbian and Burd, 1992; Rapin, 2000; Barnhill and Horrigan, 2002).

Differential Diagnosis

Listed below is a small portion of the differential diagnosis: (Levy 2007; Robertson, 2000):

- Abnormal-movements accompanying-medical conditions
- Metabolic disorders with documented basal ganglia involvement
- Stereotypic-movement disorder
- Neurodegenerative disorders – Huntington's, Wilson's disease, neuroacanthcytosis
- Substance induced
- Genetic disorders associated with SIB (e.g. Lesch-Nyhan)
- Myoclonus/myoclonic seizures Anti-neuronal antibody syndromes, Sydenham's chorea, PANDAS, systemic lupus,
- Paroxysmal-movement disorders
- Mitochondrial disorders
- Other-hyperkinetic movement disorders

- Recent beta-hemolytic Strep and other infections that preceded the movements
- Obsessive-compulsive disorder ADHD/Tourette's disorder

This list clearly demonstrates that abnormal tic-like movements overlap many other medical/neurological or psychiatric conditions. Many children with unrecognized tics are referred to allergy specialists (sniffing, coughing) or behavioral therapists (habits, nervous mannerisms). Mental health referrals are less likely for abnormal movements, but focus instead on co-occurring hyperactivity and disruptive behaviors, anxiety/mood changes, treatment refractory of OCD, or repetitive/self-injurious behaviors (Aaron, Oliver, Moss, Berg, & Burbridge, 2011; Mills and Hedderrly, 2014; Rapin, 2000). Neurological and genetic/metabolic referrals are prompted by concerns about paroxysmal movements, myoclonus or suspected focal seizure disorders; suspicions of metabolic disorders such as Wilson's disease; or other hyperkinetic movement disorder associated with cognitive changes suggestive of neurodegenerative disorders, and/or association with PANDAS or autoimmune/auto-inflammatory movement disorders or those relate to traumatic brain disorders (Barnhill & Horrigan, 2002; Leckman et al., 2011). The presence of tic or obsessive compulsive disorders in parents and siblings or relatives, maternal smoking, and excessive vomiting during pregnancy provide useful clues but these same factors are also associated with attention deficit/hyperactivity disorder/oppositional defiant/conduct disorders and specific learning disorders (Copeland, Shanahan, Eggar, Angold, Costello, 2014; Shaw, Stringaris, Nigg, Leibenluft, 2014). As a result, the presence of tics in school-aged children warrants a careful psychological and psycho-educational assessment. The co-occurrence of tics in children with neurodevelopmental disorders such as ID or autism spectrum disorder should warrant a more focused investigation to rule out genetic/metabolic syndromes (Barry, Baird, Lancelles, Burton, & Hedderly, 2011; Robertson, 2000).

The process of differential diagnosis moves from recognition of an abnormal movement through a series of steps that involve: clarifying their involuntary nature; assessing the capacity to suppress; establishing that they follow a waxing-waning course; are subject to stress-induced exacerbation (including exposure to some medications); and are influenced by sleep. As we shall see, the presence of stereotypies/repetitive behaviors, SIB, and explosive aggressive behaviors in individuals with tic disorders can occur without ID or autism spectrum disorder. The presence these challenging behaviors in individual with ID/ASD in conjunction with other abnormal movements warrants an investigation for Tourette's disorder (Barnhill, 2011; Mills,and Hedderly, 2014; Robertson, 1992;). If the clinician is still uncertain, a referral to a movement disorder specialist can be helpful.

Functional Consequences

There are several biopsychosocial outcome scenarios:

1. Persistent tic disorders can interfere with long term adjustment. Factors associated with persistent tic disorders include: ongoing life stressors; linkage to other medical, neurological and neurodevelopmental disorders, autoimmune conditions; and a combination of environmental insults and genetic loading in both maternal and paternal lineages (Bucan & Budman, 2008; Paschou, 2013).

2. Tics go unrecognized or are overshadowed by many other neuropsychiatric states and conditions. These include psychosis, bipolar/major depressive disorder, oppositional defiant disorder/conduct disorder, explosive aggressive behaviors and self-injury. In these situations, the associated symptoms may have a greater effect on outcome than the tics per se.

3. The behavioral symptoms frequently lead to more aggressive treatments with neuroleptic/antipsychotic drugs. Their extensive use increases the risk for a variety of tardive dyskinesias and other movement disorders (Barnhill & Hurley, 2008; Zinner, 2004).

4. Long term medication treatments can contribute to the development of obesity, metabolic syndrome and other health complications, and exacerbation of neurocognitive deficits associated with tic disorders. (Levy, 2007: Zinner, 2004).

5. Neurocognitive, learning, and behavioral disorders associated with tic disorders may interfere with academic, occupational, and social adjustment. Many of these behaviors are disruptive in nature and undermine educational and occupational availability and suitability for habilitative or supportive employment resources and limit the community carrying capacity for affected individuals (Murphy et al., 2013).

6. There is a tendency for tics in Tourette's disorder to change typology and topography over time. In general, some people with tic disorders experience transitions from simple to more complex tics. More troublesome are the late-developing non-tic impairments such as deficits in sensory gating, regulatory/executive functions, motivational states, intrusive thoughts and images, repetitive or unusual sensory experiences, freezing tics associated with cataleptic or catatonic symptoms, aggressive and antisocial behaviors, and intrusive thoughts, images that are often associated with compulsive behaviors with and without insight (Bruun & Budman, 1993; Levy, 2007; Martino, Madusudan, Zis, C& avanna, 2013; Neal & Cavanna 2013)

In summary many tic disorders begin as a more clear-cut neurological syndromes but over time morph into more complex psychosomatic, neuro-psychiatric disorders. As a result referral and treatment decision making needs to change to match them.

Comorbidity

The comorbidity of tics disorders is discussed throughout this chapter. Briefly summarizing these discussions, it may be useful to subcategorize tic disorders based on their patterns of comorbidity as much as their typologies. Tics are associated with an increased risk for both internalizing and externalizing disorders. Anxiety and mood related symptoms are common in many movement disorders such as Parkinson's disease (Barnhill & Hurley, 2008; Jankovic 2007). Externalizing symptoms are in part due to a relationship with attention deficit/hyperactivity disorder and impulse control disorders. A second source of psychopathology relates to the neurocognitive deficits that accompany tic disorders in many children. As described in the section on Differential Diagnosis tic-like neurobehavioral changes arise in tandem with these deficits and can mimic or overlap many severe challenging behaviors such as SIB, stereotypies, explosive aggression, social withdrawal. Lastly the co-occurrence of mood, obsessive compulsive spectrum anxiety, disruptive and psychiatric disorders is commonplace and can overshadow accurate diagnosis (Barnhill, 2012). As emphasized earlier, relatively few patients with isolated tics are referred to mental health professionals. Most referrals are due to co-occurring behavioral or psychiatric disorders.

Application of Diagnostic Criteria to People with ID - General Considerations

There are several impediments to applying DSM-5 criteria to individuals with ID. The first has to do with the recognition of tic disorders. We have limited data on the developmental course of tic disorders in IDD or autism spectrum disorder. This is unfortunate since an understanding of how these symptom changes occur becomes crucial to our understanding their relationship to late-developing neurobehavioral comorbidities. It can be difficult to determine which disorder is the primary condition. Likewise, there are a number of other movement disorders that are difficult to diagnose in individuals with severe ID. The DSM-5 does not address the problem of diagnostic overshadowing in this population.

Perhaps it is best to view these as a continuum moving from simple motor and phonic tics towards complex compulsions often without obsession, repetitive behaviors, or mannerism. Reasonable break points will be difficult to establish with certainty for individuals with severe/profound ID but it may be helpful to get a sense of whether some repetitive behaviors (touching, counting, repetitive vocalizations, intrusive thoughts, need to line up and create symmetry) are also associated with motor or vocal tics (Barnhill and Horrigan, 2002)

Methodology

Searches were conducted in health, social science, and general science-focused information resources including *MEDLINE, Cumulative Index to Nursing and Allied Health Literature* (CINAHL), the *Cochrane Database of Systematic Reviews, SocINDEX, PsycINFO,* and *Science Citation Index, Updates, and Advances in Neurology, seminars in Neurology, and Psychiatric and Child and Adolescent Psychiatric Clinics of North America.* Resources were searched using terms related to ID and ASD. The authors are indebted to Heidi Kleipstra for developing an extensive annotated bibliography for this chapter.

Review of the Literature

The interrelationship between tic disorders, autism spectrum disorders and intellectual disorders is addressed throughout the body of this chapter. Epidemiological studies of tic disorders in autism spectrum disorder and IDD populations were originally based on population surveys dating from the early 1980's (Barnhill & Horrigan, 2002; Kerserbain & Burd, 1992; Robertson, 2000;). Two key findings were that tic disorders do occur and are probably under recognized and that prevalence rates vary relative to the age of those surveyed. School-based surveys suggest higher prevalence rates among preschool children and a gradual decrease over childhood. The recognition of tic disorders is frequently overshadowed by the presence of other movement disorders; specific challenging behaviors such as stereotypies or SIB; disruptive and other co-occurring psychiatric disorders; drug induced movement disorders (tardive dyskinesia, akathisia. dystonias), and the behavioral phenotypes genetic syndromes such as Lesch-Nyhan, and (Barnhill & Horrigan, 2002).

The differential diagnosis of tic disorders is a complex one that necessitates a thorough neuropsychiatric assessment. The task of teasing out the many neurological, metabolic, and neurodegenerative disorders is often beyond the expertise of many clinicians. As a result the biggest issue for individuals with IDD is clinical recognition of the tic disorder. Problems arise due to the following:

1. Even though transient tics are more common in preschoolers with associated developmental disorders, there is a low index of suspicion for emerging chronic tic disorders.

2. The boundaries between stereotypies, SIB, other complex repetitive behaviors and tic disorders are more difficult to detect in individuals with ID or autism spectrum disorder (Barnhill, 2011; Muehlman & Lewis, 2012; Petty, Allen, & Oliver, 2009:).

3. The boundaries between tics and neuro-inflammatory, auto-immune, and complex disorders such as catatonia is a challenge that still eludes us (Friedman 2007; Leckman et al., 2011; Neal & Cavanna, 2013; Murphy et al., 2014).

4. The genetics of complex neurodevelopmental disorders is constantly opening new perspectives on polygenic, epigenetic and perhaps genomic/gender dimorphism of tic disorders. The relationship between tic disorders, obsessive compulsive disorder, obsessive compulsive related behaviors, learning and language disorders, attention deficit/hyperactivity disorder, autism spectrum disorder, epilepsy and ID suggests that many genes with relatively small effect sizes can influence several related neurodevelopmental disorders (Browne, Gair, Jeremiah, & Grice, 2014; Nag et al., 2013).

Evaluating Level of Evidence

As noted in the introduction, there is a paucity of large population and basic research studies of tic disorders among individuals with IDD. Earlier population studies noted a higher risk among children with other developmental disorder, including IDD and autism spectrum disorder. As a result, much of the material presented in this section is extrapolations of studies done in the general population and often excluding individuals with IDD.

Adults with Mild to Moderate Intellectual Disability

Many adults with ID never were assessed or diagnosed with a tic disorder during childhood. This in part is due to the considerable diagnostic overshadowing of the tic disorder by disruptive behaviors, anxiety, obsessive compulsive related behaviors, and in severe tic disorders, stereotypies, SIB, and repetitive/ restrictive or odd social behaviors. As a general rule these symptoms have higher prevalence among individuals in institutional settings and/or present with severe-profound ID and autism spectrum disorder. The waxing-waning nature of tics can also be accompanied by a parallel intensification of challenging behaviors. When explosive aggressive behaviors are also problematic, the decision hinges on whether these are accentuated by hyperactivity or impulsivity or rise to the level of a second diagnoses such as attention deficit/hyperactivity disorder, intermittent explosive, disruptive mood dysregulation or bipolar disorders (Barnhill, 2011; Shaw, Stringaris, Nigg, Leibenluft, 2014). Other types of diagnostic overshadowing include: the presence of loud vocalizations that are often attributed to pain or proto-imperative communications; complex tics attributed to stereotypies; and explosive aggression, restlessness and sleep disturbances attributable to psychotic or mood disorders and self-injurious behaviors. These boundary issues leave the clinician in diagnostic limbo, especially if tics are not obvious or IDD and autism spectrum disorder are present (Barnhill & Horrigan, 2002).

The widespread use of neuroleptics for a range of disruptive, stereotypic, self-injurious and aggressive behaviors further complicates tic recognition. Neuroleptic treatment can suppress tics but they re-emerge during a medication taper or discontinuation. A flare-up (sudden waxing in intensity) in tics can also be misattributed to tardive dyskinesia, a relapse of severe disruptive behaviors, or a manic cycle, The co-occurrence of significant psychosocial stressors, changes in routines, or living arrangements during these times can add to the vexations. As a general rule, tardive dyskinesia is more likely to develop in patients with pre-existing movement disorders (Peltpouro, Ahonen, Kaartinen, Seppala, & Narhl, 2014). Although relatively rare, tardive Tourette's (late onset) is a form of tardive dyskinesia that adds to uncertainty. Finally, the late onset of tics or other abnormal movement usually warrants a workup to rule out neurodegenerative disorders (Mejia & Jankovic, 2005; Robertson, 2000)

Adults with Severe or Profound Intellectual Disability

Recognizing or differentiating tics can be quite difficult among individuals with severe/ profound ID. If recognized as such, vocal tics can be a useful tool in the differential diagnosis disruptive or stereotypic movement disorder (Gao & Singer, 2013; Moss, Oliver, Aaron, Burbidge, & Berg, 2009). All too often vocal tics are misattributed to attention seeking behaviors, vocal stereotypies, and as forms of communicating for nonverbal individuals. The exacerbation of vocalizations during times of distress blend with other reactions to changes in routine or environmental disruptions. The waxing-waning of such behaviors can lead to a misdiagnosis of mood disorder. The diagnosis of bipolar disorders is often given based on episodic increases in irritability, sleep disturbances, increased aggression, and hyperactivity. Differentiating the symptoms from mania can be difficult but in general tics and other movement disorders intensify during periods of depression and diminish during episodes of mania (Addington & Rapoport, 2012; Muehlmann, & Lewis, 2012).

Unless completely masked by neuroleptics, the tics and associated behaviors occur in tandem—a pattern generally opposite from classic bipolar disorder. Under these circumstance, akathisia may also intensify distress and exacerbate tics. Other psychotropics can have similar effects. The relationship between psychostimulants and tic disorders is complex, but current data do not confirm earlier claims that stimulants caused tics. Lastly, tics can be confused with myoclonus, focal epilepsy and nocturnal seizures. There is an increased frequency of parasomnias and other sleep related disorders associated with Tourette's disorders.

In short, it may be the pattern of associated behaviors that attract attention and the rest of the detective story is trying to find out if tics are present (Barnhill, 2011; Shaw and Coffey, 2014; Zinner, 2004).

Children and Adolescents with Intellectual Disability

The majority of this section is devoted to the difficulties with recognizing, diagnosing, and understanding the complex biopsychosociology of childhood onset tic disorders. These principles also to apply to children with IDD. All too often the tics are not recognized until adulthood, and it becomes a major challenge to establish "an age of onset during the developmental period," especially when the tics are not discovered until adulthood. The long term use of neuroleptics for disruptive behaviors, stereotypies, SIB, and aggression may mask co-occurring tic disorders (Barry et al., 2011; Gao & Singer, 2013). Re-emergence of tics during such a dose reduction schedule frequently uncovers the underlying tic disorder. This can be confusing when there is no documentation of childhood tics. If this occurs then the clinician needs to consider tardive or neuroleptic-induced movement disorders (Barnhill & Hurley, 2008).

Among children with IDD, secondary tic disorders are associated with infectious or autoimmune disorders, cerebrovascular or other brain insults, and genetic/metabolic disorders that emerge during the developmental period. Many of these over time will turn out to be neurodegenerative disorders in which the presence of tics is transient but may overshadow mild neurocognitive changes, psychomotor regression, and neurobehavioral changes. As the neurodegenerative changes progress, it becomes more obvious that the tics were part of the early phases of the disorder. A problem arises when neurodegenerative disorders occur in children with ID, autism spectrum disorder, epilepsy and other neuropsychiatric or severe behavioral disorders (Maski, Jeste, Spence, 2011). Frequently the process of excluding other types of movement and neurodegenerative disorders is the most important step in the differential diagnosis of Tourette's and other tic disorders. This caveat reinforces the idea that tics and other movement disorders represent final common pathways arising from many causes (Barry et al., 2011).

Summary of Limitations in Applying DSM-5 Criteria to People with ID

There are no specific accommodations in the DSM-5 criteria to capture the complex interrelationship between tic disorders, IDD/autism spectrum disorder or overlap with many neurodevelopmental and psychiatric syndromes. The leeway for clinical judgment in such situations casts a wide net and may not be useful to clinicians unfamiliar with the spectrum of movement disorders. The DSM-5 does not address the problems of delayed recognition and the role played by diagnostic overshadowing. Thirdly, there are few guidelines for differentiating complex tic disorders, obsessive compulsive related disorders, stereotypies, mannerism, nervous habits, grimacing, suggestibility of tic expression, and imitation of the movements of others (echo-phenomena). Many of these symptoms occur in catatonia and require a careful differential diagnosis (Dhossche, Getz, Gadzag, & Sienaert, 2013; Smith, Smith, Philbeick, & Kumar, 2012). Lastly, the DSM-5 does not address the boundaries between severe tic disorders and unusual repetitive behaviors and social communication difficulties associated with autism spectrum disorder. In addition, unusual experiences such as intrusive sensory experiences and bizarre movments are also observed in in children with severe traumatization and early onset psychotic disorders (American Psychiatric Association, 2013).

Etiology and Pathogenesis

Like other movement disorders tics represent a dysregulation within one or more cortico-striato-thalamic-cortical (CSTC) pathways. The CSTC networks include five distinct but interrelated neuronal networks with nodal points linking the limbic system, regions devoted to executive functions, emotional perception and patterns of responding to both internal and external stimuli, attention/impulse control and initiation, and self-appraisal and adapting social behavior to contexts. It is not surprising that Tic Disorders are associated with a wide array of other neurodevelopmental disorders as well as a behavioral and several mental disorders (Maski, Jeste, Spence, 2011: Murphy et al., 2013).

Historically clinicians lumped tics into a group hyperkinetic movement disorders associated with excessive dopamine activity (hyperdominergic state). In this model, abnormal movements result from an imbalance between dopamine/cholinergic/gaba-ergic activities within the CSTC networks. Subsequent researchers challenged this oversimplification and refocused attention on the role played by multiple neurotransmitters, neuropeptides, neuroendocrine, and auto-inflammatory/autoimmunological systems. The motivation for these reassessment arose from more detailed genetic and neurophysiological variability in tic disorders. On a more practical level, classification based on a hyperkinetic/hypotonic model that involves higher dopamine/cholinergic/gaba-ergic ratios is still a useful one (Jankovic, 2007; SRobertson, 2000; haw, & Coffey, 2014).

The incomplete integration of these cortico-striato-thalamic-cortical networks in tic disorders creates a no man's land for clinicians. Perhaps the most challenging task involve developing an understanding of brain-behavior relationships thatexplain the complex and variable typology of tics, their evolving nature (waxing/waning course and symptom changes over time), and responses to ecological factors (worsening with specific stressors). This degree of heterogeneity makes it difficult to predict the developmental trajectory for tic disorders or the risk for challenging behaviors (stereotypies, aggression, repetitive behaviors, SIB, and in some circumstances, catatonia), or mental disorders. (Barnhill & Horrigan, 2002; Muehlmann, & Lewis, 2012).

Biological Factors

Tic disorders represent the neuro-behavioral expression of multiple dysfunctional Cortico-striato-thalamic-cortical circuits. They are usually differentiated from myoclonic movements, choreas, atheotosis, tremors, and dystonias based on their non-rhythmicity, rapidity and repetitive nature of movements, worsening with stress or fragments of more complex movements, an ability to voluntarily suppress movements, and in most cases disappearance during sleep. Acquired forms of tic disorders are frequently secondary to medication effects, infectious and autoimmune disorders, vascular diseases, traumatic brain injury, and neurodegenerative disorders. Neurochemical studies of tic disorders generally focus on the dysregulation of dopamine storage, release, reuptake, and post synaptic receptor sensitivity (Meija & Jankovic 2003; Murphy et al., 2014).

More recent research expands this to include GABA, glutamate, several neuropeptides including oxytocin/vasopressin, dynorphin, cholinergic/adrenergic/nicotinergic, histaminergic and antibodies directed at DA2 receptors (Murphy et al., 2014; Shaw & Coffey 2014). Such a listing reflects the complexity of overlapping networks and circuits that utilize more than one neurotransmitter that may be acting on any of these anatomically diverse receptors. Issues related to intra-neuronal, second messenger systems, mitochondrial dysfunction, and anti-neuronal antibodies are also broadening our perspective on movement disorders (Scahill, Vaccarino, Merdcadante, Lombroso, 2008; Shaw & Coffey, 2014). Neuroimaging studies suggest aberrant gray and white matter connections, reversal of normal asymmetry, and top down regulation within the cortico-striatal networks-prefrontal cortices, basal ganglia, thalamus and limbic interconnections. Each of these may reflect an imbalance excitatory and inhibitory pathways that may play a role in autism spectrum disorder, catatonia, epilepsy, ID, and other neuropsychiatric disorders (Gao & Singer, 2013; Shaw & Coffey, 2014).

This evidence suggests that Tourette's disorders are most likely a complex group of movement disorders. It remains to be seen whether a classification system that relies upon defining subtypes based on clinical symptoms (phenomenological endophenotypes) needs fine tuning. For example, family studies suggest that having two affected parents increases the risk of a severe complex tic disorder. A second example addresses the etiology of tic disorders in terms of a final common pathway. The role of auto-immune (systemic lupus, NMDA DA2 anti-neuronal antibodies, etc.) and post infectious disorders obsessive compulsive disorder (pediatric autoimmune neuropsychiatric disorder associated with beta-hemolytic, PANDAS) in tic disorders re-iterates their multi-factorial etiology (Leckman et al., 2011; Murphy et al., 2014). As we shall see, it is more accurate to consider risk for tic disorders in probabilistic terms rather than a simple model of causality (Bucan & Broadman, 2008; Venkitaramami & Lombroso 2007).

Genetic Factors

The historical perspectives on the genetics of tic disorders began with Mendelian models of inheritance models (autosomal dominance with variance penetrance). One variation of this model was a single gene underlying multiple conditions—attention deficit/hyperactivity disorder, obsessive compulsive disorder, and other disruptive behavioral disorders. In recent years more precise molecular genetic tools, including genome wide array scans (GWAS), failed to confirm this concept but did raise the banner of a polygenic pattern of inheritance (Addington and Rapoport, 2012). But genetic researchers are finding that there are many genes affecting post-synaptic dopamine receptors, re-uptake transporter proteins, enzymes involved synthesis, vesicular dopamine release, and metabolism. None provide a definitive explanation (Melchior et al., 2013.; Moya et al., 2013). Several promising leads involve histidine de-carboxylase (production of histamine) and SLITRK1 (single nucleotide polymorphism-SNPs). In all probability tic disorders are also affected by epigenetic effects on multiple genes associated with the development of the cortico-striato-thalamic-cortical pathways. Some of these may be affecting intracellular mechanisms (second messengers, intra-nuclear, and/or intracellular pathways), effects of hormones on motor behaviors, and sensitive to environmental/ecological forces (Clarke, Lee, & Eapen, 2012; Paschou, 2013).

Markers on chromosome 16q13.1 are not only associated with an increased risk for tics disorders but also play a role in attention deficit/hyperactivity disorder/obsessive compulsive disorder, IDD, schizophrenias, and epilepsy. Other genes are involved in excessive grooming in animal models and perhaps are relevant to trichotillomania, (TTM) and perhaps other forms of obsessive compulsive spectrum disorders (Browne et al., 2014). The 16q13.1 linkage on GWAS suggests these disorders may have similar genetic markers that may play a role in their frequent co-existence in clinical samples. Although epigenetic factors are likely involved, there is little definitive evidence for genomic imprinting as an explanation for gender dimorphism (males with tics; females with obsessive compulsive disorder). Many neurodevelopmental disorders show a similar pattern of gender dimorphism (Lapidus, & Coffey, 2014; Paschou, 2013; Goodman, Grice, Shaw & Coffey, 2014).

Population, family pedigree and twin studies are still the basis of many genetic studies. These studies suggest a high degree of heritability for Tourette's and other tic disorders. But there are caveats. These studies reveal a significant heterogeneity among genetically related cohorts (e.g. monozygotic (identical) twins with Tourette's disorder). The concordance rate for monozygotic twins is less than 100% lower for children with Tourette's disorder. This concordance ratio changes when all forms of tic disorder and some obsessive compulsive related disorders are included. One explanation for this is related to multiple gene-environment interactions. Multiple vulnerability genes are switched on and off during development. Each is subject to epigenetic changes that shape phenotypic expression—severity, persistence, and risk factors for co-occurring neuropsychiatric conditions. In this sense tic disorders resemble other complex neuropsychiatric disorders, including autism, schizophrenia, epilepsy and other developmental disorders (Matthews & Grados 2011).

Psychosocial Factors

In general, comorbid IDD, autism spectrum disorder, and other psychiatric illnesses, trauma and medical comorbidities impact the course of tic disorders. For individuals with IDD, the etiology and level of functional impairment and cognitive abilities affect not only clinical course but also community access to services. Prenatal factors like excessive vomiting during early pregnancy (hyperemesis gravidarium), cigarette smoking, intra-uterine growth and viability, as well as post natal exposure to infections and brain injury can affect both the presence, severity and clinical course (Robertson, 2000; Shaw & Coffey, 2014; Shaw et al., 2014). The higher prevalence among children with other Neurodevelopmental disorders suggests that many childhood stressors affect the emergence and recurrence of tics but may not reliably predict the persistence of tics (Mills & Hedderly, 2014; Murphy et al., 2013; Zinner, 2004). The basic question: do psychosocial factors in children with ID outweigh the degree of genetic loading similar to the higher prevalence of transient tics observed in preschoolers and does this risk play a role in the development of stereotypies/SIB, habits or other repetitive patterns of behavior as well as tic disorders? A parallel question arises in relation to over exuberant dendritic branching early in development that is followed by later pruning in the regulatory and associational cortices. The early expression of transient tics may have to do with a similar pattern of over exuberance, where the risk for persistent or severe tics suggests greater gene-environmental interaction. Do these changes also affect the progression or transformation towards tic complex disorders and psychiatric comorbidities? The answers still elude us (Scotti, Schulman, Hojnsacki, 1994; Petty et al., 2009).

Developmental Factors

These issues are dilated upon throughout this chapter, but several features need re-iterating:

1. The mean age of onset is between 5-7 years old. Epidemiological or population studies suggest that tics may affect as many a 20% of preschool children (boys more so than girls). The highest rates are among children with other developmental or learning disorders. Children with IDD and autism spectrum disorder are more likely to have co-occurring tics that may go undiagnosed for years (Barnhill & Horrigan 2002; Rapin, 2000).
2. Gender plays a major role in tic disorders. Like many other neurodevelopmental disorders, males are more often affected than females. For children with a family history of tic disorders males are far more likely to develop tics, whereas female offspring are at greater risk for obsessive-compulsive disorder (Barnhill, 2011; Matthews & Grados, 2012). There are exceptions. Males who present with obsessive compulsive disorder under the age of 5 are more likely to develop tics within 5 years. This group of young males may also be resistant to standard treatments for obsessive compulsive disorder (Goodman et al., 2014).
3. The developmental trajectory for persistent tic disorders includes a worsening of tics and the emergence of sensory or premonitory tics occur around 10 years old (on or about 5 years after the onset). By late adolescence, many youth experience a waning of tic severity, while others may experience an increase in severity, increase in tic-related rituals, premonitory tics, and increasingly complex movements. A family history of tic disorders or obsessive compulsive disorder can affect the age of onset, topographical progression of tics, and severity (Goodman et al., 2014).
4. Many individuals develop premonitory urges or sensory tics that are temporarily relieved by movements. These movements can appear voluntary and resemble the urge preceding a sneeze or hiccough—the urge will continue to build until released. These "un-voluntary" movements can be confused with several subtypes of SIB as well as other repetitive behaviors (Neal & Cavanna, 2013; Scahill, Leckman, Marck, 1995; Verte et al., 2005;). More severe tic disorders are accompanied by echo-phenomena, coprolalia, and a broad range of asocial behaviors that include inappropriate touching, impulsive, aggressive, or sexual behavior, and emotional-behavioral dysregulation (Shaw et al., 2014).

Application of Diagnostic Criteria

The following modifications focus on not only adaptations of specific criteria designed to help the clinician better differentiate tics from other disorders associated with repetitive behaviors. Criteria adaptations also include notes regarding the many neurobehavioral symptoms associated with severe tic disorders that may resemble other DSM-5 disorders. For example, patients with catatonia and severe Tourette's disorder share symptoms such as periods of behavioral arrest (tics that resemble negativisms, automatic obedience, and unusual, sustained posturing), periods of cognitive freezing, echolalia and echopraxia, and sensitivity to high doses of antipsychotics (Barnhill & Horrigan, 2002). In addition stereotypies, SIB, explosive/affective/aggression, restrictive-repetitive behaviors and cognitions overlap symptoms seen in post-traumatic stress disorder, obsessive compulsive disorder, attention deficit/hyperactivity disorder and autism spectrum disorder (Barnhill, 2011; Muehlmann & Lewis, 2012). Notes are provided to help clarify the areas where diagnostic confusion is most likely to occur.

Tic Disorders

DSM-5 Diagnostic Critieria	Applying Criteria for Mild/Moderate ID	Applying Criteria for Severe/profound ID
Tourette's Disorder A. Both multiple motor and one or more vocal tics have been present at some time during the illness, although not necessarily concurrently. (A tic is a sudden, rapid, recurrent, non rhythmic, stereotyped motor movement or vocalization.)	A. No adaptation. NOTE ABOUT MOTOR TICS: 1. Sensory tics include symptoms attributed to akathisia. These may be described as a tingle, cramp, or "funny feeling" and are associated with an urge to move that is relieved with the behavior. 2. Complex tics overlap stereotypies, compulsions, and other repetitive movements. Behaviors such as counting, aligning objects, touching, need for symmetry, hoarding may be seen. Obsessions are usually lacking. 3. Self-injurious behaviors: high frequency low intensity behaviors such a nose picking, cuticle or nail pulling, manipulating minor skin wounds may lead to tissue damage. More severe SIB is more commonly associated with more severe tics, sensory phenomena, and stop when "it feels right."	A. No adaptation NOTE ABOUT MOTOR TICS: 1. Mannerisms and other repetitive behaviors associated with simple motor tics. 2. Explosive aggressive behaviors in the presence of motor tics. 3. SIB in the presence of motor tics. 4. Waxing/waning course of target behaviors.
	NOTE ABOUT PHONIC TICS: Abrupt or explosive vocalizations (coughs, grunts, barking). Exacerbation with distress Repetitive words or phrase- Imitating others (echolalia), repeating the end of ones sentences (pallilalia). Coprolalia—intrusive words without intensive affective response (to pain or anger). Continuous complex tics (humming).	NOTE ABOUT PHONIC TICS: Explosive vocalizations- exacerbated by distress. Imitative behaviors- echolalia. Waxing waning of behaviors often paralleling flare up in motor tics.

Tic Disorders (continued)

DSM-5 Diagnostic Critieria	Applying Criteria for Mild/Moderate ID	Applying Criteria for Severe/profound ID
	NOTE ABOUT SENSORY TICS – REPETITIVE BEHAVIORS: Reports of discomfort preceding tics. Improvement with motor action. Precede self-injurious behavior. Complex tics or compulsive behaviors. Do not meet the criteria for obsessive compulsive disorder.	NOTE ABOUT SENSORY TICS – REPETITIVE BEHAVIORS: Difficult to distinguish from stereotypies without subjective reports. Rule out akathisia and restless legs syndrome.
B. The tics may wax and wane in frequency but have persisted for more than 1 year since tic onset.	B. No adaptation.	B. No adaptation.
C. Onset is beforeage 18 years	C. No adaptation.	C. No adaptation. **Note:** Age of recognition and duration may be difficult to establish, especially if there are multiple genetic, neurodevelopmental, or medical conditions that may not be a direct contribution to tics (e.g. tics in individuals with fragile X or trisomy 21).
D. The disturbance is not attributable to the physiological effects of a substance (e.g., stimulants) or a general medical condition (e.g., Huntington's disease or post viral encephalitis)	D. No adaptation. **Note:** the differential diagnosis of catatonia is frequently linked to tics and other abnormal movements. For individuals with severe/profound ID or autism spectrum disorder, referral may be necessary to complete the diagnostic workup.	D. No adaptation.
Persistent (Chronic) Motor or Vocal Tc Disorder A. Single or multiple motor or vocal tics (i.e., sudden, rapid, recurrent, nonrhythmic, stereotyped motor movements or vocalizations) tics are present during the illness, but not both, motor and vocal	A. No adaptation. **Note:** See notes about motor tics, phonics tics, and sensory tics-repetitive behaviors under Tourette's disorder.	A. No adaptation. **Note:** See notes about motor tics, phonics tics, and sensory tics-repetitive behaviors under Tourette's disorder.
B. The tics may wax and wane in frequency but have persisted for more than 1 year since tic onset.	B. No adaptation.	B. No adaptation.
C. The Onset is before age 18 years.	C. No adaptation.	C. No adaptation. **Note:** Age of recognition and duration may be difficult to establish, especially if there are multiple genetic, neurodevelopmental or medical conditions that may not be a direct contribution to tics (e.g. tics in individuals with fragile X or trisomy 21).
D. The disturbance is not due to the direct physiological effects of a substance (e.g., stimulants) or a general medical condition (e.g., Huntington's disease or post viral encephalitis).	D. No adaptation.	D. No adaptation.
E. Criteria have never been met for Tourette's Disorder Specify if: With motor tics only With vocal tics only	E. No adaptation.	E. No adaptation.

Tic Disorders (continued)

DSM-5 Diagnostic Critieria	Applying Criteria for Mild/Moderate ID	Applying Criteria for Severe/profound ID
Provisional Tic Disorder		
A. Single or multiple motor and/or vocal tics (i.e., sudden, rapid, recurrent, nonrhythmic, stereotyped motor movements or vocalizations)	A. No adaptation. **Note:** See notes about motor tics, phonics tics, and sensory tics-repetitive behaviors under Tourette's Disorder.	A. No adaptation. **Note:** See notes about motor tics, phonics tics, and sensory tics-repetitive behaviors under Tourette's Disorder.
B. The tics have been present for less than 1 year since first tic onset	B. No adaptation.	B. No adaptation.
C. The onset is before age 18 years,	C. No adaptation.	C. No adaptation.
D. The disturbance is not due to the direct physiological effects of a substance (e.g., stimulants) or a general medical condition (e.g., Huntington's disease or post viral encephalitis).	D. No adaptation.	D. No adaptation. **Note:** Age of recognition and duration may be difficult to establish, especially if there are multiple genetic, neurodevelopmental or medical conditions that may not be a direct contribution to tics (e.g. tics in individuals with Fragile X or Trisomy 21).
Criteria have never been met for Tourette's Disorder or Chronic Motor or Vocal Tic Disorder	E. No adaptation.	E. No adaptation.

Other Specified Tic Disorder
Unspecified Tic Disorder

DSM-5 also provides categories for other specified tic disorder and for unspecified tic disorder.

Stereotypic Movement Disorder

This section is devoted to the diagnostic challenges associated with stereotypic movement disorder in persons with Intellectual and Developmental Disorders (ID). Perhaps the biggest challenge involves dueling heterogeneities found in ID and the many subtypes of stereotypies and self-injury. In order to accommodate such diversity, the following parameters will be explored:

1. Stereotypies are defined as "repetitive, seemingly drive, apparently purposeless behaviors"; self-injury as a form of repetitive behavior that results in tissue injury (American Psychiatric Association, 2013). Stereotypies are present in many internalizing disorders; self-injury tends to cluster among externalizing disorders, approximately 40% display both (Kurtz, Chin, Huete and Cataldo, 2012). The focus of this section is biased towards exploring the many neurodevelopmental factors that affect the frequency and intensity of self-injury.
2. The diagnostic criteria for stereotypic movement disorder begin with repetitive behaviors and then address the presence or absence of self-injury. Once this primary division is made, the focus shifts to the exclusion of many medical, neurological, and psychiatric disorders. The most complicated step involves the application of the Specifiers (subtypes). In this section we will adopt an algorithmic format as a tool that begins the process of establishing phenomenological endophenotypes. This process involves two additional steps to better fit the needs of individuals with ID. The first is establishing primary and secondary subsets of stereotypic movement disorder. Primary stereotypic movement disorder includes those cases that lack clearly defined etiologies (idiopathic). Secondary stereotypic movement disorder are related to complex genetic, medical, neurological, primary substance use or psychiatric disorders (Muthugovindan and Singer, 2009). The second process uses potential

precipitating factors (event-related/reactive) and typology (stereotypic) of self-injury. The differences between these will be explored in greater depth later in this section.

3. Environmental/ecological/psychosocial factors (including trauma related events) play key roles in the predisposition, precipitation, phenomenology, perpetuation, and treatment approaches to stereotypic movement disorder. Trauma-related ecological factors, disorganized attachment, abuse/neglect, institutionalization, family dysfunction, and other environmental events affect the developmental trajectory of stereotypic movement disorder (Barnhill & McNelis, 2011; Berger, Gelkopt, Versano-Mor, & Shpigelman, 2015; Vela, 2014).

4. Severity of stereotypic movement disorder is defined as the level of functional impairment and intensity of interventions necessary to minimize disruptions in daily activities. For example, high levels of both stereotypies and self-injury increase support needs. They also have a negative effect on the conceptual, social, practical and functional domains that are used in the DSM-5 to define the severity of ID.

5. Although not the specific focus of this section, autism spectrum disorder affects both social communication and restrictive behaviors. Both diagnostic criteria for autism spectrum disorder are also risk factors for stereotypic movement disorder. This connection may partially explain the high prevalence rates of self-injury in autism spectrum disorder. The presence of autism spectrum disorder adds to the vulnerability of people with ID and supports the higher prevalence rates of SIB in people with autism spectrum disorder plus ID than in people with ID without autism spectrum disorder (Barnhill & McNelis, 2012; Schroeder et al., 1 2014; Medeiros, Kozkoski, Beighley, Rojahn, & Matson 2014).

General Description

Stereotypic movement disorder is included among motor disorders. This category also includes motor- coordination and tic disorders (American Psychiatric Association, 2013). The combination underscores the foundational role of motor development in the maturation and organization of the central nervous system. Atypical motor development disrupts the hierarchical organization of skilled motor learning and regulation of unnecessary motor activity (tics) especially the developmental trajectory of many complex cognitive, executive and regulatory functions. The convergence of these many developmental forces underlies the emergence of stereotypies, self-injury, and other neurodevelopmental disorders (Dehaan & Gunnar, 2009; Friedman, 2007). The overlap with other neurodevelopmental disorders creates boundary issues between motivational states (purposeful v. purposeful), voluntary v. involuntary behaviors, intensity and severity of movements, risk of persistence of stereotypic movement disorder over the lifespan, and their relationship to psychiatric disorders.

Narrowing the focus to self-injury brings us to the issue of differences between event-related / reactive versus stereotypic self-injury noted in the introduction. It is apparent that many early childhood forms of self-injury may be triggered by ecologically significant events or circumstances (state-related). It also appears that event-related/reactive self-injury are more apt to occur in some psychiatric disorders (Body dysmorphic disorder, borderline personality, mood disorders, and psychotic disorder). In contrast trait-related stereotypic movement disorder is more closely linked to stereotypic forms of self-injury. The relationship between these and autism spectrum disorder, obsessive compulsive disorder-related disorders, and addiction behaviors suggests habitual behaviors. Unfortunately, there is no solid boundary separating these state and trait-related forms of self-injury. Boundaries between both are blurred even further by baseline exaggeration associated with new onset medical or psychiatric disorders and Trauma-related disorders (Barnhill, 2005; Fang, Mattheny, & Wilhelm, 2014).

Summary of DSM-5 Criteria

A. Repetitive, seemingly driven and apparently purposeless motor behavior (e.g. hand shaking or waving, body rocking, head banging, self-biting, hitting own body).

B. The repetitive motor behavior interferes with social, academic and other activities and may result in in self-injury.

C. Onset early in the developmental period.

D. Repetitive motor behavior is not attributed to the physiological effects of a substance or neurological condition and is not better explained by another neurodevelopmental or mental disorder (e.g. trichotillomania or obsessive compulsive disorder).

Specify if:

With self-injurious behavior- or behavioral that would result in an injury if preventative measures were not sued)

Without self-injurious behavior

Specify if: Associated with a known medical or neurological condition, neurodevelopmental disorder, or environmental factors (Lesch-Nyhan syndrome, ID (IDD) or intrauterine alcohol exposure.

Specify current severity:

Mild: Symptoms are easily suppressed by sensory stimulus or distraction

Moderate: Symptoms require explicit protective measures or behavioral modification

Severe: Continuous monitoring and protective measures are required to prevent serious self-injury

Issues Related to Diagnosis in People with ID

Primary repetitive behaviors represent the derailment of emerging homeostatic mechanisms for regulation of arousal states, expression of specific neurobiological and genetic disorders/behavioral phenotypes, and processes of learning and extinction. Functional behavioral analysis suggests that operant conditioning may shape these behaviors and maintain these changes over time—for example escape from demands or aversive contexts, social attention, and adverse response to withdrawal of preferred re-inforcers. The general consensus is that most self-injury has multiple motivating factors and serves multiple functions (Goldman et al. 2008).

Secondary forms of stereotypies are triggered or exacerbated by medical, neuro-toxicological, neuropsychiatric, genetic, and primary psychiatric disorders. Secondary subtypes of self-injury include Tic, Obsessive compulsive related conditions and other psychiatric disorders. Many of these are frequently under recognized or misdiagnosed in individuals with IDD (Barnhill, 2011; Barnhill and Horrigan, 2002; Robertson, Trimble, & Lees, 1989). In addition, trauma and stress related disorders challenge any simple models for self-injury among individuals with psychiatric disorders. The most complex are self-cutting by individuals with borderline personality disorder; self-mutilation in psychotic patients who are convinced that their fingers belong to the devil and need to be removed; or perceived body defects and excessive grooming individuals with body dysmorphic disorder (Barnhill, 2005), and various forms of suicidal behavior in neurotypical individuals. Sorting these out for individuals with severe-profound IDD (with and without autism spectrum disorder) can be exceedingly difficult and time consuming (Matson, Laud, & Matson, 2004; Peltpouro, Ahonen, Kaatrtinen, Seppala, & Narhl, 2014).

Other forms of self-injury are related to behavioral phenotypes such as severe self-mutilation in Lesch-Nyhan syndrome. The relentless nature of mutilating self-injury in Lesch-Nyhan syndrome as well as the use of frequent use of self-restraint provide the best example of stereotypic self-injury. (Harris, 2008). The relationship between specific behavioral phenotypes and different patterns of SIB suggests variability among biological mechanisms and "condition-ability"—vulnerability to response to syndrome-specific ways that are in part shaped by a specific genetic disorder (discussed in the chapter on behavioral phenotypes). Apparent nongenetic forms of disruptive behaviors and self-injury (e.g. fetal alcohol-related disorders) may in fact reflect more complex polygenic–environmental interactions that shape vulnerability. Many patterns of repetitive behavior resemble various forms of addiction behaviors (some habitual behaviors, obsessive compulsive disorder-related syndromes and substance use disorders). Secondary forms of event-related self- injury may occur in the context of constipation, otitis media, or medication side effects. Event-related self-injury may also play a greater role in people with severe IDD (and autism spectrum disorder) who are generally more susceptible to ecological and systemic issues such as abuse/neglect, family disorganization, social crowding, low levels of stimulation associated with institutionalization, and individualized reactions to psychosocial stressors (Coch, Dawson, & Fischer, 2007; Garcia-Villmisar & Rojahn, 2015; Vela 2014; Venkitaramani and Lombroso, 2007).

Development and Course

In most neurotypical individuals repetitive behaviors appear to be time-limited (Barry, Baird, Lascelles, Bunton, & Hedderly, 2011). Early childhood repetitive behaviors fade as higher order motor and cognitive skills come on line. Other forms of stereotypies have greater staying power. Long-lived repetitive behaviors, especially stereotypies without self-injury, seem to follow a different developmental trajectory than those with self-injury. Several decades ago researchers described the transformation of motivational forces, goal directed and communicative functions, and varying sensitivity to positive or negative contingent reinforcement. The pace of these changes suggested a relatively slow transformation from stereotypies to self-injury (Guess & Carr, 1991; Hall, Oliver, & Murphy 2001; Symons, Sperry, Dropik, & Bodfish, 2005).

Newer data suggest that the onset of stereotypies and self-injury begins during the first three years of life (mean age 20 months). Head banging and body rocking are examples of early onset stereotpies that rapidly morph into self-injury (Harris, Mahone, & Singer, 2008; Leekam et al., 2007; Tan, Salgado, & Fahn, 1997). Mild head banging, hitting, arm/hand biting, eye pressing or poking, and other topographies occur without tissue damage. Embedded in this group however are a small number of individuals who quickly progress to tissue damaging behaviors in a matter of weeks (mean duration 2 months) (Medeiros, 2013; Medeiros, Rojahn, Moore, & van Ingen, 2014; Symons et al., 2005).

Although newer models seem to contradict older ones, they are not mutually exclusive. Our understanding of the multiple pathways to self-injury is still incomplete. For example. Symons et al. (2005) address the role of the transformation of nociceptive into neuropathic pain; the complex interaction between the activation of mast cells, cytokines, and other local and central nervous system inflammatory peptides; changes in sensory maps and fields within the central nervous system and the emergence of self-injury (Symons et al., 2005). Other researchers expand on the role of sensitization and atypical forms of neuroplasticity to emerging self-injury. These models suggest that the neuroplastic changes associated with normal learning are "kidnapped" by a process that is analogous to the transformation of substance use into dependency. The remaining question is how addiction models relate to the developmental course of stereotypies and self-injury (Barnhill, 2003; Grant, Potenza, Weinstein, & Gorelek, 2011; Kraus, 2000).

Gene-environment interactions associated with repeated trauma modify pain responses as well as underlie the emergence of addiction related behaviors. The mechanism of action appears related to the effects of neuroplasticity on brain maturation (Hernandez & Blazer, 2006; Kays, Hurley, & Taber, 2012). Most individuals with ID and autism spectrum disorder start the process with impaired executive and adaptive functions. They are at risk for exaggerated stress responsiveness, fear conditioning, sensitization, habit learning (procedural memory), and resistance to extinction (Coch et al., 2007; Gonzalez and Marinez, 2014; McLaughlin, Fox, Zenneah, Nelson, 2011; Roelefs et al., 2015).

The gene-environment linkages bring together ecological factors, ongoing associative and operant conditioning, and learned patterns of stress response. Trauma-related changes bias responses to neutral or nonthreatening stimuli as well as alter the threshold and bias perception of neutral stimuli as threatening. The physiological changes contribute to exaggerated arousal, fear responses, rage, defensive aggression, or self-injury. The long term effects of gene dysregulation include disruptions on the hierarchical organization of the brain during development and limit effective responses to future psychosocial stressors. The presence of IDD and autism spectrum disorder accentuate the effects (Barnhill & McNelis 2012; McOmish & Gingrich, 2011; Rutter, 2002). The risk factors listed below are closely tied to such interactions.

Table 1- Risk Factors

genetic risk- behavioral phenotypes
impaired affect regulation,
impulse control and deficits in executive functions
disorganized attachment
behavioral phenotypes
sensitivity to physiological and psychological to ecological challenges
co-occurring aggression and disrupted pain regulation
deficits in social communication
sensory impairments
trauma and severe ecological stressors
severity of stereotypies
presence of other neurological, neurodevelopmental and neuropsychiatric disorders
Pain- nociception and neuropathy

The prevalence rates for both stereotypic movements and self-injurious behavior vary considerably. This is related in part to the reliance on retrospective studies of adults with established SIB rather than prospective studies during late infancy and early childhood (Kurtz et al. 2012). But even prospective studies may not explain the typological variability of stereotypic movement disorder. For example, do episodic/reactive differ from stereotypic forms of repetitive behaviors in terms of age of onset, clinical course, and relationship to other neurodevelopmental and psychiatric disorders (Goldman et al., 2008; Symons et al., 2005)?

Several risk factors stand out. Prevalence rates for self-injury vary inversely with the level of severity of IDD. Severity data also suggest a direct connection between severe-profound ID and higher rates of co-occurring neurological, genetic, and metabolic disorders. This data also point to a greater sensitivity between the many co-occurring features of severe/profound ID and the adverse effects of disruptive environments. Externalizing symptoms (hyperactivity, irritability, aggression, self-injury, and stereotypies) are frequently attributed to these disruptions, but externalizing symptoms are more easily recognizable than withdrawal or other internalizing symptoms. Unfortunately, this misattribution may create a selection bias in this data.

The role of psychological trauma and abuse/neglect is overlooked in the assessment of self-injury, especially when the assessment is overshadowed or biased by ongoing stressors; adverse effects of dysfunctional family or social networks; institutionalization, substance use, and behavioral and psychiatric disorders dominate the clinical presentation. This data suggests that single variable models (institutionalization) provide an incomplete picture. The institution may contribute, but the majority of institutionalized adults (68% of cases) experienced abuse and self- injury before age 5 (Furniss & Biswas, 2012; Kurtz et al., 2012; Myrbakk & von Tetzchner, 2008). Such findings suggest that the onset of self-injury preceded institutionalization. Severe self-injury might be an originating factor in seeking institutional care, yet over time the adverse effects of the institutionalized environment contribute to the severity and persistence of self-injury (Minshaw et al.; 2014; Rattaz, Michelon, and Bagdalli, 2015).

Differential Diagnosis

The diagnosis of stereotypic movement disorder requires both specific criteria and exclusion of other disorders. The differential diagnosis is largely based on these exclusion criteria.

This approach creates primary from secondary forms of self-injury. The use of the self-injury specifier subdivides stereotypic movement disorder into with and without self-injury. For example, self-injury can co-occur with tic and obsessive compulsive and related disorders. The attempt to classify self-injury in the context of severe Tourette's disorder can become complicated for people with autism spectrum disorder or severe-profound ID. In this text all diagnoses co-occur with ID (and autism spectrum disorder in many situations). The selection biases created by the ubiquitous presence of ID adds to this list of frequently unresolved issue: the high rates of co-occurrence between tic disorders and ID/autism spectrum disorder; the tendency to misattribute or fail to recognize the presence of tics in people with ID; the overlap between stereotypic movement disorder with and without self-injury and obsessive compulsive disorder and related behaviors and other neurodevelopmental disorders. In addition to diagnostic uncertainty, the various combinations of these co-occurrences may lead to greater levels of functional impairment, need for more extensive services to community support needs, and impact the determination of severity for both ID and autism spectrum disorder (Kays et al., 2012; Lanovaz, 2011; Peltpouro et al., 2014).

The mix of inclusion, exclusion and specifiers creates an apparent paradox: the presence of autism spectrum disorder is included in the differential diagnosis of stereotypic movement disorder, yet is a significant risk factor for self-injury. Self-injury is not specified among the diagnostic criteria for ASD, but is associated with higher prevalence rate of self-injury independent of ID (American Psychiatric Association, 2013). This paradox raises two questions: should stereotypic movement disorder and autism spectrum disorder be diagnosed as separate disorders, or should stereotypic movement disorder with and without autism spectrum disorder be considered as separate endophenotypes?

The differences between primitive reflexes, involuntary movements, and intentional movements are based on motivation, intent, direction, monitoring efficacy, and capacity to adjust to task contingencies. Reflexes are influenced by the state of the central nervous system but usually occur outside of conscious awareness. They occur automatically and are not associated with a sense of agency—touching a hot stove differs from turning off the stove. From a developmental perspective, reflexes during the neonatal period eventually subside or are incorporated into developing motor skills, only to re-appear when neurological injury releases them from regulatory control. Imitative behavior in neonates occurs before the movements become volitional but require levels of intermodal integration not usually associated with reflex movements (Coch et al., 2007; de Haan & Gunnar, 2009; Friedman, 2009; Muthugovindan and Singer, 2009).

Involuntary movements vary based on neurophysiology, anatomical source, and relationship to external stimuli. Some occur outside conscious awareness—seizures, myoclonic and some simple tics. Many of these movements lack intent, goal directedness, and capacity to signal or communicate. Some appear related to states of arousal, levels of environmental stimulation, or a purpose to move (Friedman, 2007). They differ from voluntary movements in terms regional patterns of cortical activation, capacity for adaptation, and instrumentality. Tics can be voluntarily suppressed for periods of time. The inability to suppress movements is more consistent with severe tic disorders, some choreas, myoclonic movements and focal seizure activity (Jankovic & Toloso, 2007).

Chronic tics are frequently accompanied by an urge to move that builds in intensity and terminates with action that restores a sense of being "just right" (Barnhill & Horrigan, 2011; Neal & Cavanna, 2013; Roberston et al., 1989). Other motor disorders are related to disinhibition or intrusion of non task-related motor activity, deficits in shifting to match new task demands, or discontinuing motor sets that are already in progress. Each of the perseverative behaviors involve a disconnection from premotor planning, execution, and accommodation. Perseveration is most often associated with frontal lobe disorders, although high dose stimulants can produce variants of this neurobehavioral disorder (Friedman, 2007; Huey et al., 2008; Lanovaz, 2011; Max, 2014).

This table provides an overview of the subtypes of stereotypic movement disorder relevant to differential diagnosis. It by no means answers these questions but does provide a summary of disorders that have stereotypy or self-injury as part of their clinical presentation.

Disorders with Stereotypies	Stereotypies-Secondary, medical	Common Topographies-Stereotypies	Disorders associated with SIB	Common-Topographies
Primary-Mannerism ID ASD Secondary Drug induced- TD, Akathisia Psychiatric Disorders Schizophrenia Catatonia Obsessive-compulsive disorder Movement Disorders Tourette's disorder Restless legs (RLS) Epilepsy	Neurodegenerative-Neuroacanthocytosis, Fronto temporal Dementias Genetic/ neurodevelopmental-Rett, Williams, Down, Fragile X syndromes Metabolic- PKU, mitochondrial disorders Vascular- stroke Sensory impairment- visual/auditory Inflammatory /autoimmune-PANDAS Encephalitides Anti-neuronal antibody syndromes Catatonia Acquired- TBI	Grimacing, oro-mandibular Rocking Nodding Finger- hand movements Flapping Stamping feet Manipulation of objects Staring Posturing Complex tics (Goldman, Wang, Salado et al, 2008; Barnhill, 2011)	Primary- ASD ID ID with ASD Severe stereotypies Aggressive behavior Affective Lability/ Irritability Impulsivity Secondary Sensory disorders Pain related- neuropathy Neurodegenerative-neuroacanthocytosis movement disorders Genetic/metabolic-Behavioral phenotypes Movement Disorders-Tourette's disorder Catatonia Psychiatric-Schizophrenia Mood/anxiety disorders Borderline Personality Body- dysmorphic disorder Acquired- Medical disorders Trauma	Bite/hit Head, Hand, Arms Legs Lips, fingers Eye poking Nail pulling Skin picking Cutting Trichotillomania Sticking objects in orifices

■ *Normal Development*

The developmental trajectory of motor development moves from primitive reflexes to actions requiring increasing reliance on voluntary motor programs, increasingly sophisticated targeting and monitoring motor, and expanded executive regulation of socially meaningful actions and gestures. Early in the process, motor overflow, repetition of emerging and newly learned motor skills are melded with maintenance of alert states, regulating over arousal, gestural communication and babbling (infant directed speech patterns or proto-language), and sustaining visual attention. Transient stereotypies appear to be interrelated with these developmental lines. They subsequently resolve or become incorporated into emerging voluntary learning of new and more sophisticated skills. Thus, early sensorimotor development plays a key role not only in the development and integration of neuronal circuitry that is critical for higher order cognitive, executive and social-emotional development (Coch et al., 2007; de Haan & Gunnar, 2009). Their persistence along with other primitive reflexes, motor overflow, and impaired motor coordination associated with deficits suggest a continuum of motor develops. These can also serve as predisposing or risk factors for other neurodevelopmental and late emerging psychiatric disrders (Lanovaz, 2011).

■ *Autism Spectrum Disorder*

Social communication deficits encompass spoken, gestural perception, interpretation and expression. The interface between these key features of autism spectrum disorder and subsequent adaptive skills, executive functions and generativity of verbal language appear as risk factors for early onset SIB. Social skill deficits, affect and impulse dysregulation, irritability, and difficulty managing psychosocial stressors serve as risk factors for a reduced threshold for event related self-injury (precipitating events). On the other hand, proneness to repetitive and restrictive behaviors, inflexibility and variable sensitivity to sensory input, and intolerance of change or ambiguous states or events affect stereotyped forms of SIB (Kays et al., 2012; Kraus, 2000). Current literature suggests that SIB in autism spectrum disorder is more closely related to restrictive-repetitive cognitions, interests and behaviors (Sayer, Oliver, Ruddick, & Wallis, 2011). Data suggests that the intensity of prodromal repetitive behaviors and affective responses to environmental change such as unexpected events, interrupting ongoing preferred activities, and task demands best predicts the emergence of SIB. Both features of autism spectrum disorder reflect deficits in top-down regulation, executive and regulatory functions central to this syndrome and accentuated by severe IDD (Rattaz et al., 2015; Richards, Oliver, Nelson, and Moss, 2012; Richman et al., 2013).

Lastly individuals with autism spectrum disorder share multiple genetic and neurodevelopmental ties to many metabolic, neurological, neurodevelopmental, and psychiatric disorders. Perhaps it is prudent to think of SIB in individuals with autism spectrum disorder as structured event complexes in which SIB is considered ecologically in terms of the company that it keeps (co-occurring behaviors, state phenomena and context variables) rather than as discrete events (Huey et al., 2008).

■ *Tic Disorders*

Many complex tics resemble stereotypies and some forms of self-injury. The differences between complex tics and stereotypic movement disorder focus on the presence of sensory tics or urges to act; electrophysiological differences in pre-movement potentials (contingent negative variation) that precede voluntary movements, and the intensification of the urge to tic during periods of suppression. (Barnhill, 2011; Barnhill & Horrigan, 2002; Neal & Cavanna 2013; Robertson, 1992; Robertson et al., 1989). This relationship is discussed earlier in this chapter.

■ *OCD and Related Disorders*

The boundary between stereotypic movement disorder and obsessive compulsive disorder related behaviors involves mostly stereotypies. In contrast to earlier classification as an anxiety disorder, obsessive compulsive disorder was defined in terms of limited repetitive behaviors that in large part served to diminish the uneasiness associated with obsessive and intrusive thoughts. The DSM-5 created a new category (obsessive compulsive and related disorders) and expanded the focus to include behaviors more closely akin to complex tics. In addition to arranging aligning, organizing, intrusive thoughts and images and need for symmetry, the DSM-5 now includes gambling (impulse dyscontrol); trichotillomania, body dysmorphic disorders (excessive grooming) and other impulsive-compulsive behaviors (Grant et al., 2011). SIB seems more closely linked to these "related-disorders"—namely tissue damage secondary to high rates of these repetitive behaviors (Barnhill 2005; Browne, Gair, Scharf, & Grice, 2014; Fang, Matthew, & Wilhelm, 2014; Murphy, Timpano, Wheaton, Greenber et al, 2010; Woods & Houghton, 2014). The diversity of obsessive compulsive- related disorders creates significant boundary problems with tic disorders; autism spectrum disorder; neurological disorders associated with repetitive movements; self-injury associated with neurodegenerative disorders, and addiction behaviors. (Huey et al., 2008; Lanovaz, 2011).

For a more complete review of these interrelationships please review Barnhill (2011).

■ *Other Neurological Conditions*

A detailed review of neurological conditions associated with stereotypic movement disorder is beyond the scope of this section. In general, stereotypic movement disorder is related to other neurodevelopmental disorders in complex ways. Stereotypies and self-injury co-occur with specific genetic phentypes, motor co-ordination disorder, tic and other movement disorders, auto-immune/auto-inflammatory disorders, focal and myoclonic forms of epilepsy, and a number of neurodegenerative disorders. The relationship between perseveration and repetitive behaviors and the role of nociceptive and neuropathic pain deserve careful assessment. All too often, SIB is attributed to pain in a generic fashion without considering its neurobiological complexity. Considering this diversity of neurological disorders associated with stereotypic movement disorder, it is useful to explore repettiive behaviors in terms of the company that it keeps—what neurological changes are associated with the presence of repetitive behaivors and self-injury (Friedman, 2007; Gal, Dysk, & Passmore, 2009; Murphy, Timpano. Wheaton, Greenberg, & Miguel, 2010).

Comorbidity

Stereotypic movement disorder is included among the neurodevelopmental disorders. Several characteristics of neurodevelopment disorders underlie their high rates of comorbidity. These are discussed in the section on motor co-ordination disorder as well as other sections of this discussion. Briefly, the age of onset impacts the developmental trajectory of most neurodevelopmental disorders. It may also influence both their severity and comorbidity with psychiatric disorders, IDD, autism spectrum disorder, and medical/neurological disorders (American Psychiatric Association, 2013; Tan, Salgado, & Fahn, 1997). These relationships create many critical decision points for clinicians –e.g. deciding if stereotypic movement disorder is the primary condition and, if so, determining if IDD/autism spectrum disorder are subsets; or that IDD/ASD are the primary conditions and self-injury or stereotypies challenging behaviors accompany both. One solution requires determining the sequence of which appeared first. Another alternative is to consider these changes as baseline exaggerations (increased frequency/severity of stereotypies or self-injury) emerging in the context of primary medical or psychiatric conditions (Fletcher, Loeschen, Stavarakaki, First, 2007). In conclusion, comorbidities are common in stereotypic movement disorder and teasing out their role often requires ongoing vigilance and longitudinal investigations.

Application of Diagnostic Criteria to People with ID

Methodology

Searches were conducted in health, social science, and general science focused information resources including *MEDLINE*, *Cumulative Index to Nursing and Allied Health Literature* (CINAHL), the *Cochrane Database of Systematic Reviews*, *SocINDEX*, *PsycINFO*, and *Science Citation Index*, as well as multidisciplinary resources such as *Academic Search Complete*. The authors are deeply indebted to Heidi Dieptsra who provided a detailed annotated bibliography that played a major role in this project.

Level of Evidence

The vast majority of studies rise to level IV and V in the Cochrane system

Review of Research for IDD

Many earlier studies were retrospective and tried to define childhood risk factors and vulnerabilities to both stereotypies and SIB. In the early 1990's, Guess, Carr and others proposed a developmental model for the transformation from childhood to chronic and persistent self-injury. Their model suggested a functional transformation that was initially linked to state regulation, physiological homeostasis, and the regulation of arousal. Over time the behaviors assumed a more direct communicative role in the expression of immediate needs, pain, or distress. The third phase of this developmental model focused on the effects of positive and negative reinforcement on these behaviors (Guess and Carr, 1991; Hall et al., 2001; Hall, Thorns, Oliver, 2003). At the time, a series of commentaries challenged several points and instead focused on a synthesis of biological-environmental forces. Since then, bio-behavioral models have moved in a different direction in the face of an expanding knowledge of gene-environment interactions and the neurobiology of neuronal neuroplasticity, sensitization, and resistance to extinction (Lanavaz, 2011; Muehlmann & Lewis, 2012).

Later retrospective studies of adults with persistent SIB concluded that a significant percentage of institutionalized adults with SIB displayed self-injury prior to age five. Researcher interest then shifted to studying the structure and developmental trajectory of self-injury in very early childhood. These studies pushed back the age of onset for self-injury into toddlerhood. The risk factors for early onset included the presence of autism, severe ID, and difficult temperaments that include negative affect/behavior dysregulation hyperactivity, impulsivity, poor affect regulation, and a low threshold for aggressive behavior (Medeiros, 2013; Minshaw et al., 2014; Muehlmann & Lewis, 2012; Shaw, Strinagaris, Nigg, & Leibenluft, 2014). (See sections on Development and Child Adolescence.)

Future studies may focus on differentiating between early onset self-injury and the stereotypic versus episodic event triggered patterns noted earlier. Along these lines, several hypotheses may need testing. It appears that the episodic/reactive variant may be more closely related to temperamental factors and primary psychiatric and trauma-related disorders. The stereotypic variant, on the other hand, appears more closely related to autism spectrum disorder, severe/profound ID, specific behavioral phenotypes, and a predisposition towards habit formation (Furniss & Biswas, 2012). Mixtures of the two subtypes may follow different pathways and partially support the developmental transformational model originated by Guess and Carr et al. The stereotypic variant may include those infants with a rapid onset and progression.

These two separate strands of research may also capture the difference between factors that initiate self-injury versus those that maintain it. Converging lines of development may leave room for neurobiological changes (neuroplasticity and sensitization); trauma-related events and disorders; and learning events that shape the development of persistence and resistance to extinction. Gene-environmental interactions may partially explain the observations of functional behavioral analysts who grapple with the conundrum of the differences between factors that initiate and sustain self-injury and the mixed pattern of antecedents and contingencies (Burbage et al., 2010; Hoch, Long, McPeak, & Rojahn, 2004).

Adults with IDD

For most adults, stereotypies are often a continuation of childhood onset movements. Subtypes of stereotypies are usually based on motivational states (voluntary v. involuntary); lack of obvious utility or apparent purpose, proposed etiology, severity, and relationship with self-injury. Symptomatic stereotypies and self-injury are associated with neurological, genetic, or primary psychiatric disorders. Epilepsy, myoclonus, tic and obsessive compulsive disorder related and other motor disorders are the most common sources of stereotypic movements (Barnhill 2011; Friedman, 2007).

Severe forms of self-injury on the other hand, include behavioral phenotypes associated with Lesch-Nyhan, Smith-Magenis (Finucane, Dirrigi, & Simon, 2001), Cornelia de Lange (Oliver, Sloneem, Hall and Arron, 2009) and co-occurring severe IDD/autism spectrum disorder (Minshaw et al., 2014; Richards et al., 2012; Tureck, Matson, & Beighley, 2013). Some forms of stereotypies may produce tissue damage secondary to their repetitive nature. These include hair twirling (Woods & Houghton 2014), nail biting or skin picking (Robertson, 1992; Robertson et al., 1989; Spendelow, 2011), and repetitive facial injury in body dysmorphic disorder (Barnhill, 2005; Fang. Mathony, & Wilhelm, 2014).

A third subgroup of stereotypic movement disorder is affected by baseline exaggeration secondary to the onset of medical, neurological, or primary psychiatric disorders. This group may display low levels of stereotypies that escalate. One measure of this regression involves significant changes in the intensity of service needs and treatments (worsening severity of IDD based on a drop in functional domain as measured in the diagnostic criteria for ID. Under these circumstances new specifiers may need to be added to the stereotypic movement disorder diagnosis.

In general, baseline exaggeration associated with the onset or relapse of medical or primary psychiatric disorders are more likely to be recognized in individuals with borderline IDD (Peltpouro et al., 2014). The linkages between recent psychosocial stressors and the exacerbation of trauma-related, mood, anxiety, schizophrenia and other psychotic disorders and personality disorder, and self-injury may also be more reliably explored (Hoch, Long, McPeak and Rojahn, 2004; van der Kolk, Perry and Herman, 1991).

Children and Adolescents with IDD

The DSM-5 placed stereotypic movement disorder among the neurodevelopmental disorders but did not dilate upon how childhood onset or even puberty influence the developmental trajectory of stereotypic movement disorder. Even the algorithmic application used in this chapter does not capture the ever-changing complexity of brain development and maturation. As a result, the diagnosis of stereotypic movement disorder is akin to a snapshot or point in time diagnosis and does not account for the evolving context of stereotypies or self-injury during childhood and adolescence. As noted earlier, a sizable percentage of individuals present with self-injury during early childhood, but other children appear to follow a different trajectory.

Under some conditions, high rates of stereotypic motor activity can also produce tissue damage: gnawing, hand mouthing, hair twirling, rubbing, nail biting, or skin picking. The examples include high frequency/low intensity behaviors that eventually result in tissue damage. Severe forms of self-injury follow a different course. In vulnerable infants, early onset self-injury may rapidly move from non-tissue damaging eye poking or pressing, head banging or hitting, and low intensity biting to relentless, stereotypic forms of severe tissue damaging behavior that involve similar topographies (Hall, Lightbody, & Reiss, 2008). There is no consistent evidence to support a prodromal period of slowly evolving self-injury. The triggers for self-injury cluster around interrupting preferred activities or removing preferred objects (frustration induced); changing routine (intolerance of change); or the need to escape nonpreferred task demands or activities (Kurtz et al., 2012; Schroeder et al., 2104).

The most common subtypes of early onset stereotypies included rocking and head banging. Early onset SIB involved head banging and hitting, eye pressing/poking, and self-biting. This group also expressed higher levels of stereotypies, aggression, and symptoms of emerging disruptive, impulsive and externalizing disorders (Kurtz, Chin, Huete, & Cataldo, 2012; Paris, 2008; Richman et al., 2013; Symons et al., 2005;).

Retrospective studies of young children with established SIB suggest that the severity of SIB is higher among patients with autism spectrum disorder plus ID than in patients with ID without autism spectrum disorder. In addition, the combination of SIB, autism spectrum disorder, and ID is associated with higher rates of co-occurring aggression, disruptive behaviors, and affective lability. These retrospective studies raise questions: Are these the same populations? Is the transition from stereotypies or proto-self-injury (onset at 22.4 months) to SIB (24 months) a different process for children who did not progress but developed later onset SIB? Does the very rapid transformation disprove other developmental model? Are there fundamental neurodevelopmental and genetic differences between children with behavioral phenotypes with later onset pattern and very early onset population? Lacking answers does not detract for the clinical reality that stereotypic movement disorder encompasses a diverse and heterogeneous group of children. (Furniss & Biswas, 2012; Gal et al., 2012; Oliver, Petty, Ruddick, Bacare-Hamilton, 2012; Rattaz et al., 2015).

The heritability of self-injury is clouded by the many atypical neurobiological and neuroplastic changes during brain development (interactive specialization). The same factors influence atypical patterns of affect regulation, reward processing, generalized biases in associative and operant conditioning, and executive functions (top down regulation). As a result of these atypical developmental lines, the neurocognitive and behavioral phenotypes of self-injurious behavior frequently include: ADHD related symptoms such as impulsivity/hyperactivity; affect dysregulation; neuroticism or negative, reactive affective states; aggression; other repetitive behaviors; sensory impairments; deficits in communication/social behavior; atypical motor development;and deficits in adaptive behaviors (Avramopulos, 2010; Barnhill, 2011; Furniss, & Biswas, 2012; Kays et al., 2012; Rutter, 2002; Tsankova, Renthal, Kumar, & Nestler, 2007).

To better understand stereotypic movement disorder during childhood, we need behavioral and neurobiological studies that integrate models of operant and associative conditioning with sensitive or critical periods during brain development and variations in attachment, temperament, level of family dysfunction, trauma-related stressors, and environmental and ecological factors. In addition, autism spectrum disorder is closely associated with self-injury across the spectrum of ID. Among younger children with autism spectrum disorder, the link to self-injury appears more closely related to the intensity of repetitive-restrictive behaviors (stereotypies). Among older children, deficits in social communication and behaviors come to play an increasing role in SIB. This shift occurs in the context of hormonal and psychosocial changes during puberty. Adolescence is also a sensitive period for complex partial seizure disorders as well as the age of onset for many primary psychiatric disorders. These age-related vulnerabilities may be a factor in the solidification of persistent stereotypic movement disorder beyond early childhood (Kurtz et al., 2012; Rattaz, Michelon, & Baghdalli, 2015).

In short, we need to approach stereotypic movement disorder along the several tracks discussed above and always consider the company that it keeps during development (Barnhill, 2011; Lanovaz, 2011;).

Limitations of DSM-5

Both the strengths and weaknesses of the DSM-5 are complex and interrelated. The first potential weakness involves a reliance on descriptive categories to define heterogeneous conditions. As noted throughout this section, stereotypic and self-injurious behaviors represent the convergence or final common pathways from many genetic, neurodevelopmental, and neurobiological sources. For example, the severity of IDD or autism spectrum disorder can make it even more difficult to determine the motivation and goal directed nature of movements with any certainty. Self-injury associated with complex tics also may lack functional utility. Motivation comes from an urge that is relieved by an action that reduces the intensity of a prodromal or sensory tic (Neal & Cavana, 2013; Robertson et al., 1989). Self-injury and stereotypies may also have intrinsic motivations but may also be maintained by an array of functional consequences such as to escape demands, to seek reinforcement, to communicate pain, to express frustration, or complex tics. We still have a limited understanding of the neurobiological transformation from contingency maintained behaviors (rewards and punishments) to habitual patters of self-injury (Hoch et al. 2004; Noll & Barrett, 2004).

In general, primary psychiatric disorders alter the quantitative and qualitative measures of stereotypies and self-injury (Fletcher, Loeschen, Stavarakaki and First, 2007). This also includes self-injury associated with parasuicidal or "cutting" behaviors in borderline personalities and delusions-that results in self-mutilation in schizophrenia. Stress can exacerbate both tics and self-injury among individuals with tic and other movement disorders (Barnhill & Horigan, 2002; Jankovic & Tolosa, 2007; see the section on tic disorders). Other medical and other neuropsychiatric disorders may contribute to the baseline exaggeration of self-injury. Successful treatment of the tic disorders may substantially attenuate self-injury to the point that the child may now participate in community programs. These and other examples are rarely included in any descriptive, categorical diagnostic system.

The most utile features of the DSM-5 criteria arise from its application as a diagnostic algorithm. This benefit may be further enhanced by integrating severity measure for stereotypic movement disorder with the functional severity domains used for conceptual, social and practical domains. Although adding new layers of complexity these applications may match up with ICD-10 guidelines.

Etiology and Pathogenesis

The pathophysiology of stereotypies and self-injury remains only partially understood. This is most likely due to the diversity of both the mechanisms that drive the behaviors and the heterogeneity of those behaviors. On the one hand, we have ample evidence that cognitive and psychological factors modulate behavioral responses to arousal states in neurotypical individuals. Managing arousal states then permits the development and eventual expression of a wide variety of coping mechanisms (de Haan and Gunnar, 2009). For individuals with IDD or autism spectrum disorder these mechanisms and coping skills are compromised, leaving the individuals more vulnerable to developing maladaptive behaviors in the face of internal and external stressors. Many neurodevelopmental and primary psychiatric disorders (e.g. obsessive compulsive disorder and related syndromes) adversely affect the development of adaptive skills and the self-regulation of impulsivity, flexibility of cognition and problem solving, and emotional responses (Garcia-Villmisa & Rojahn, 2015).

Stereotypic movement disorder with self-injury by comparison are considered to be without purposeful or goal directed movements. Instead they are attributed to automatic responses to a range of internal or external cues and contingencies. The shift from goal directed (escape demands, pain, or severe over arousal) to habitual behavior is also associated with incomplete self-regulation, limited capacity to shift sets and block the intrusion of other motor programs during an ongoing goal-directed activities (Muehlmann & Lewis, 2012; Quirk, Garcia and Gonzalez-Lima, 2006). The neurobiology of this transformation may be analogous to pre-potent patterns of responsiveness observed in attention deficit/hyperactivity disorder, tic disorders, addiction behaviors, and perseverative behaviors observed in acquired or degenerative brain disorders. The analogy breaks down when we shift from acquired disorders that appear after the developmental period. Neurodevelopmental disorders affect the emerging neuro-circuitries that underlie executive control and regulation (Furniss & Biswas, 2012; Symons et al., 2005). Degenerative disorders begin dismantling established, learned or well-practised skills (Jankovic & Toloso, 2007).

Atypical patterns of neuronal and functional brain development underlie IDD, autism spectrum disorder, other neurodevelopmental disorders, neuropsychiatric disorders in general, and stereotypic movement disorder in particular. As noted earlier, genome wide scans suggest an overlap among alleles (copy number variants and single nucleotide polymorphisms) that include most members of the group. Epigenetic changes in promoter/inhibitor regions, regulation of protein synthesis, and changes in histone/chromosome activation shape the emerging phenotype. Typical neuroanatomical development proceeds along sequential patterns of development that are sensitive to both gene actions and external events. Atypical development is associated with derailments of these processes. There may be critical or sensitive periods that are critical for emerging skills and abilities. In the long run the brain involves an integration functional and hierarchical organization of multiple regions. This interconnectedness expressed as coherence of associated brain regions undermines any simple explanation for complex behaviors. It is perhaps better to address disconnections or lack of coherence rather than anatomic systems. stereotypic movement disorder is more than the summary of its anatomical and functional parts (de Haan, & Gunner, 2009).

The missing steps involve the converge these many strands into a working model that encompasses the diversity of stereotypic behaviors and self-injury.

Biological Factors

In the DM-ID (Fletcher et al., 2007), the discussion of biological factors focused on the role of serotonin, endorphins, and several neuropeptides (Campbell et al., 1993; Sandman, Touchette, Lenjavi, Marion, & Chizc-Demet, 2003). There was a long tradition of assuming that a dopamine excess in the context of decreased serotonin activity underlay a range of repetitive behaviors. These neuropharmacological data suggested phenotypic differences in enzyme systems, transporter proteins, and second messenger systems were also major players. Since 2007, research has shifted towards dysfunctional networks of interconnected functional brain pathways. Researchers are now investigating sensitization, sensory gating, neuropathic pain, inflammatory and immune, and a more comprehensive understanding of the stress response system (sympathetic/neuroendocrine, and inflammatory components) (Schroeder et al., 2014).

The diversity of stereotypies, mannerisms, rituals, compulsive behaviors, and self-injury suggests multiple etiologies. For example, Lesch-Nyhan syndrome combines dystonia with an urge to self-mutilate regardless of severe pain. Self-restraint is a common feature that may resemble a form of suppression. When associated with Tourette's disorder, self-injury can follow a waxing and waning course that is frequently linked to the severity of associated motor tics. Distinguishing these complex tics from stereotypies or stereotypic self-injury can be a challenge (Barnhill & Horrigan 2002; Rapin, 2000; Robertson et al., 1989; Robertson, 1992). The increased risk for self-injury among persons with autism spectrum disorder is likely due to the presence of co-occurring neurological disorders and sensitivity to change as part of restrictive and repetitive behaviors, difficulties with disengagement, set shifting, and adaptive modifications of these patterns (Roelefs et al., 2015). Lastly, obsessive-compulsive and related disorders lie near this continuum and suggest that all involve a complex network of cortico-limbic-striatal pathways (Browne Gair, Scharf, & Grice, 2014; Hall et al., 2008; Murphy et al., 2010).

Gene-environment interactions, local regulation of protein synthesis and polygenic models from any complex disorders are now a part of the discussion. These newer ideas, also about the inter relatedness of stereotypic movement disorder, IDD, autism spectrum disorder, other neurodevelopmental, and psychiatric disorders, are moving towards a redefinition of the biopsychosocial model. The problems differentiating the effects these syndromes have on SIB is further complicated by the presence of IDD and the co-occurrence of the combination of genetic, neurodevelopmental, and psychiatric disorders seen in clinical practice (Garcia-Villsmar & Rojahn, 2015; Goldman et al., 2009; Lanovaz, 2011; Ousley & Cemak, 2014).

The developmental hierarchy of language and social communication play a major role in behavioral regulation, executive function, and socialization. Early appearing language deficits influence conceptual (academic), social,l and practical domains in individuals with IDD. They also influence nonverbal aspects of social communication (ASL, gestures, and prosody). The atypical development of these abilities limits the individual's capacity to verbally communicate distress. The role of communication deficits in the transformation of early childhood stereotypies into self-injury, however is less clear cut. Later in childhood, deficits in more global social skills may play a greater role in self-injury (Witwer &Lecavalier, 2008). These observations suggest that the onset of self-injury before age two may predate efficient verbal communication skills. The remaining question is whether self-injury is a means of communicating basic needs, pain, or other causes of distress (proto-imperatives). These would apply a sense of agency that serve a goal directed function that appear to contradict the habitual or stereotypic model of self-injury (Leekam et al., 2007; Petty, Allen, & Oliver, 2009). For more detailed information, see the chapter on communications disorders in this volume.

By comparison, stereotypic movement disorder is a complex behavioral disorder subject to multiple gene-environment interactions that affect learning and patterns of conditioned responses. The stereotypic/self-injury and reactive/event-related dichotomy is not universally accepted but may help avoid relying on inferences about motivational states and purposefulness or goal directedness of self-injury (Barry et al., (2011). Instead, the focus would shift to the development of cued, automatic responses to either internal or external stimuli. This transformation from goal-directed (escape demands, pain or severe over arousal) to habitual actions is consistent with dysfunctional self-regulation, interrupting established patterns of responding or shifting to alternative behaviors. These deficits are analogous to pre-potent patterns of responsiveness observed in attention deficit/hyperactivity disorder, tic disorders, addiction behaviors, and perseveration (Murphy et al., 2010). To date, we have many intriguing hypotheses and preliminary evidence, but few of these ideas fully explain these differences. The neurobiology of self-injury during infancy may differ from later onset subtypes. This idea also fits into the observations that early onset neuropsychiatric conditions tend to behave differently than those with an adult onset. If this is the case, then we might anticipate higher rates of comorbidities, treatment resistance, sensitivity to neurobiological effects of puberty, and a prolonged vulnerability to adverse biopsychosocial forces (Matson & Shoemaker, 2011).

Once established, however, many repetitive movements (including self-injury) persist for decades, and treatment becomes a lifelong process. As symptoms may wax and wane, it is difficult to assess the efficacy of behavioral or pharmacological treatments by simply phasing out the behavioral program or medication. By this stage, many of our neurotransmitter or behavioral models begin to fall by the wayside. Newer ideas involve networks of multiple neurotransmitters, neuropeptides, cytokines, and epigenetic factors (Venkitaramani & Lombros0, 2007). The focus of treatment research is shifting towards resistance to extinction (Quirk et al., 2006) and reducing the risk of relapse. Comparisons studies designed to addressichronic self-injury must also deal with their relationship to addiction behaviors (Barnhill, 2011); the effects of neuropathic pain; activation of neuro-inflammatory pathways (Mitchell and Goldstein, 2014); or the impact of chronic trauma-related models experiences (McOmish & Gingrich, 2011; Vela, 2104). In each of these scenarios the transition to chronicity involves sensitization, intracellular changes in second messenger systems, dysregulation of neuroplasticity, and epigenetic changes in gene activation. At a biopsychosocial level, chronicity translates into a multidirectional or transactional process that becomes more complex and engrained over time (Kraus, 2000).

Developmental Factors

This table includes a group of risk factors that appear throughout this narrative. The table below includes a partial list of the risk factors for stereotypies, self-injury, and the transformation from stereotypy to self-injury in some individuals.

presence of IDD and autism spectrum disorder
impaired affect regulation
impulse control and deficits in executive functions
disorganized attachment
behavioral phenotypes
sensitivity to physiological and psychological to ecological challenges
co-occurring aggression and disrupted pain regulation
deficits in social communication
sensory impairments
trauma and severe ecological stressors
severity of stereotypies
presence of other neurological, neurodevelopmental and neuropsychiatric disorders
pain—nociception and neuropathy

In earlier studies, self-injury was assumed to begin with stereotypic behavior during childhood that metamorphosed into subtypes of self-injurious behaviors (Guess & Carr, 1991). More recent studies suggest that infants and very young children show a rapid onset from proto-self injurious behaviors (hand mouthing and non-tissue damaging self-directed behaviors) that share topographies with fully developed SIB (head banging, hitting, hand biting) (Richman et al., 2015; Schroeder et al., 2014). Persistence of self-injury into adolescence and adulthood may be related to additional risk factors that suggest epigenetic forces are at work (Rattaz et al., 2015; Turek et al., 2013). It is difficult to single out the role played by age of onset, natural changes in the topography of symptoms over time, temperament, patters of dysfunctional attachment and the effects of trauma on affective aggression. These factors may also underlie the old adage that what initiates self-injury may not be the same as the forces that maintain it through time. There are many gaps in our understanding of the underlying mechanisms of this phenomenon:

1. There is evidence that self-injury begins in some young children as stereotypies. Rocking and mild head banging are examples. Overall the evidence supporting a period of evolving stereotypies is less well supported. Recent evidence supports a more rapid transformation evolution from proto-SIB to SIB in a matter of months. The relationship between emerging self-injury and early sensorimotor deficitsis often overlooked. The evidence is more definitive regarding the contribution of severe-profound IDD, autism spectrum disorders, traumatization during infancy and early childhood, and the overcrowding and reduced stimulation associated with early and prolonged exposure to institutional environments. Additional factors include hypersensitivity to sensory stimuli (including pain), sensory impairments, reduced endorphin/ oxytocin levels, neuropathic pain, dysregulation of inflammatory pathways, stress response system (hypothalamic pituitary and sympathetic/parasympathetic balance), and atypical activation of reward pathways (Muehlmann & Lewis, 2004; Lanovaz, 2011; Oliver et al., 2012; Rattez et al., 2015; Tureck et al., 2013).

2. Childhood studies suggest that not all at-risk children progress to self-injury. This finding suggests that we have an incomplete understanding of how these bio-behavioral factors lead to chronic, frequently treatment-refractory form of self-injury. It is apparent that individuals with those with reactive/impulsive (state-related) and stereotypic self-injury (more trait-related) may follow a different course. These bio-behavioral distinctions may link SIB to forms of aggressive behavior (Gardner & Griffiths, 2004: Richman et al., 2013; Schroeder et al., 2014). There is evidence that severe childhood physical and sexual abuse is a major contributor to disorganized attachment, temperamental mismatches that contribute to higher rates of neuroticism, intensity of affective and impulse dyscontrol, and neuroendocrine and sympathetic nervous system dysregulation (van de Kolk et al., 1991; Vela, 2014). Each of these factors also contributes to aggression and stress reactive self-injury (Lanovaz, 2011; Rattaz et al. 2015). This stress/reactive subgroup is also more likely to display features attributed to borderline personality disorders in neurotypical individuals (Barnhill, 2011; Peltpouro et al., , 2014). The stereotypic pattern of self-injury is analogous to that observed in selected behavioral phenotypes, and habit-addiction related behaviors (Barnhill 2003; Grant et al., 2011).

3. Behavioral phenotypes associated with Lesch-Nyhan, Smith Magenis, fragile X, Cornelia de Lange, and Prader-Willi syndrome are associated with self-injury. Comparisons between these phenotypes suggest that their developmental trajectory, severity, function, and maintenance of these disparate syndromes are by no means uniform. These behavioral phenotypes are discussed in more detail in Chapter 3.

4. Suicidal and self-injurious behavior are described in individuals with mood disorders and schizophrenias but there is limited evidence for a high rates of stereotypies prior to their onset. In childhood or very early onset schizophrenias, there are higher rates of mild autism spectrum disorder but no particular pattern of onset is clearly linked to self-injury. In general SIB in schizophrenia is associated with delusions, command hallucination, and cognitive and behavioral disorganization. There is very limited evidence to support evolving psychotic or mood disorders are clearly involved in most self-injury. Major depression, mixed bipolar states, and psychotic mood disorders are not routinely associated with self-injury. The baseline exaggeration of self-injury is, however, associated with the onset or relapse of mood and

anxiety disorders (Barnhill, 2011; Berger et al., 2015; Fletcher et al., 2007).

5. Neurodevelopmental movement disorders such as severe Tourette's disorder and neurodegenerative disorder like neuroacanthocytosis are associated with a range of self-injurious behaviors. Complex tics can resemble obsessive compulsive behaviors and stereotypies. There is a subgroup of individuals affected by these conditions that evolve over time into what appears to be a stereotypic form of self-injury. This process is akin to the evolution of addiction behaviors (Barnhill, 2003; Barnhill 2011; Grant et al., 2011). The idea of subtypes of stereotypic/repetitive behaviors evolving into severe SIB resembling the transformation of substance use to severe, self-destructive forms of addiction is intriguing but speculative.

6. A subtype of self-injury co-occurs with emotional dysregulation, neuroticism, impulsivity, aggression, and symptoms suggestive of attention deficit/hyperactivity disorder (Oliver et al., 2012; Shaw et al., 2014). Perhaps we should subtype stereotypic movement disorder applying both an algorithmic and co-occurring conditions (symptom-complex approach). This application can help distinguish complex subtypes far better than typology or motivational states or function). Classifying self-injury as converging patterns of multiple related behaviors (the company it keeps) may be useful in terms of tracking down final common pathways for stereotypic movement disorder.

Genetic Factors

The presence of specific genetic disorders (behavioral phenotypes) and the polygenic heritability of many primary psychiatric disorders limits our ability to make simple gene versus environment dichotomies. For example, there are differences between typologies and topographies in individuals with selective behavioral phenotypes. There is also a degree of variability within each behavioral phenotype (e.g. severity). Likewise, there may be a different set of genetic risk factors for stereotypies than those associated with the many forms of severe self-injury. The increased risk for self-injury among individuals with highly heritable conditions such as autism spectrum disorder, Tourette's disorder, and attention deficit/hyperactivity disorder-like conditions (Burbridge et al., 2010) suggests gene-gene and epigenetic interactions that are incompletely understood. In addition, the co-occurrence of these syndromes in the context of other movement (Freidman, 2007) and obsessive compulsive-related disorders (Barnhill, 2011; Huey et al., 2008) support the idea of variability among complex genetic disorders. It also reinforces the notion that repetitive behaviors and self-injury are best diagnosed in the context of the "company they keep."

The gene–environmental interactions in stereotypic movement disorder converge in addiction-related, neuropathic pain and inflammatory pathways (Barnhill, 2003). Evidence for a divergence comes from recent studies suggesting that self-injury emerges rapidly during infancy, often preceded by very brief period of "proto-self-injury" that transforms in a matter of months into head banging, hitting, and hand biting. Our knowledge about the relationship between age of onset for self-injury and overlapping polygene markers in autism spectrum disorder, IDD, schizophrenia, epilepsy, and other neurodevelopmental disorders is incomplete. The exploration of the role genetic factors play in both vulnerability and resilience to trauma and fear conditioning, development of executive function, and functional deficits in extinction learning are works in progress. Additional work is also needed to clarify the role of epigenetic factors in the developmental trajectory of early onset stereotypic movement disorder, and how they may differ from those associated with many behavioral phenotypes and psychiatric disorders (Avramopulos, 2010; Kays et al., 2012; Lanovaz, 2011). In stress diathesis models, age of onset, genetic loading, and their relationship to neglect, trauma, and puberty suggest additional epigenetic influences on the development of self-injury (Avramopulos, 2010; Kays et al., 2012; Tsankova et al., 2007).

Psychosocial Factors

The level of environmental stimulation, emotional support, and other ecological factors plays a critical role in most stereotypic movement disorder. Early trauma influences not only gene expression in the individual but also increases the risk that deficits in the stress response system can be passed on to subsequent offspring secondary to changes in transcription via chromatin formation (Coch et al., 2007; de Haan & Gunnar, 2009; Rutter, 2002), Each of these factor can shape pain responsiveness (nociception and neuropathic pain responses) as well as dysregulation and hyper-activation of inflammatory pathways that neuroplastic changes (sensitization) influence that influence emotional and behavioral responses that include persistent self-injury (Kraus, 2000).

These finding support a stress diathesis model for stereotypic movement disorder that can be applied across multiple developmental levels. The earlier the psychosocial stressors, the more likely they are to influence future development. This phenomenon implicates sensitive periods that are critical to sequential gene activation and brain development and maturation. The timing of severe stressors may influence the age of onset of many behavioral and psychiatric disorders by derailing the developmental trajectory of emerging skills. So can the presence of genetic risk, behavioral phenotype, and other gene-environmental interactions that underlie temperament and attachment behaviors. (Barnhill & McNelis, 2012; Gardner & Griffith, 2004; McLean & Dornbush, 2012; Myrbakk & Tetzschner, 2008).

As our understanding of stereotypies and self-injury shifts towards stress diathesis models, we will need to address gene-environment interactions and sensitive or critical periods during development (Berger et al., 2015; Gonzalez & Martinez, 2013). The vulnerability windows associated with these processes also shift during development. The balance of gene-environment interactions changes in ways that affect the individual patterns responding to later traumas and insults. In addition, the person with ID is not only affected by but also shapes the complex reciprocity of family, educational, occupational, and psychosocial ecologies (Coch et al., 2007; de Haan & Gunnar, 2007; Harris, 2008). The outcome of these transactions indirectly affects access or suitability for services, degree to which these services can be utilized, efficacy of intervention programs, and the carrying capacity of service delivery systems (Barnhill & McNelis, 2012).

These evolving insights may force us to redefine the biopsychosocial model, especially as it applies to primary and secondary forms of stereotypic movement disorder, behavioral phenotypes, and other neurodevelopmental disorders. In this sense, having a separate section for genetic, biological, and psychosocial factors is rapidly becoming an anachronism.

Applications of Diagnostic Criteria

Most referrals are for challenging behaviors without a confirmed diagnosis. Translating these complaints into accurate psychiatric diagnoses is often a very complicated task. This is especially true for individuals with severe ID (IDD), autism spectrum disorder and complex medical comorbidities. The diagnosis of stereotypic movement disorder frequently co-occurs with severe aggression, hyperactivity, impulsivity, and temperamental variations in irritability, low threshold for arousal and negative affective states (neuroticism) (Barnhill & McNelis 2012). Teasing out how these traits affect responses to environmental challenges or the effects of a co-occurring psychiatric or medical disorder often requires a multistep diagnosis. Unfortunately, most psychiatric diagnoses are snapshots that do not accommodate the ever changing nature of stereotypic movement disorder over the individual's lifetime.

Although not a part of the table of diagnostic applications, the authors suggest that an algorithmic approach to the assessment of stereotypic movement disorder is useful in two ways. One is to fine tune the diagnosis; the other is to address etiological subtypes. However, a synthesis is required:

1. Distinguishing subtypes of stereotypies: Can we reliably differentiate subtypes of

repetitive behaviors that are more likely to develop into specific subtypes of self-injury? This chapter reviews many of these vulnerability factors. The search for phenotypic subtypes is based on the presence/absence of psychiatric, neuropsychiatric, neurodevelopmental disorders; specific genetic disorders; trauma-related changes in stress responsiveness; substance use or fetal exposure syndromes; and a range psychosocial/ecological factors. An example of this approach: an individual with fragile X syndrome who presents with IDD/ mild autism spectrum disorder and a behavioral phenotype that includes gaze aversion, social anxiety, repetitive hand flapping, a complex partial seizure disorder; anxiety or panic disorder, and intense reactions to overstimulating social environments (Fletcher, Loeschen, Stavarakaki, First, 2007). This approach provides a more personalized diagnosis. This process provides an opportunity to define etiological endophenotypes based on the use of an algorithmic approach to diagnostic criteria.

2. With self-injury: Beginning with repetitive behaviors the next nodal point involves the presence/absence of self-injury. Although the DM-ID-2 is devoted to individuals with IDD, autism spectrum disorder may a greater influence on the prevalence rates for self-injury. Autism spectrum disorder exerts its influence across the spectrum of IDD. Unfortunately, self-injury is not included in the diagnostic criteria for autism spectrum disorder. This is confusing since social communication deficits and severe restrictive/repetitive behaviors are associated with self-injury and may help explain the increased prevalence rates of self-injury in autism spectrum disorder (two risk factors). In addition, stereotypic movement disorder must be considered in the context of shared genetic risks for co-occurring conditions like autism spectrum disorder, ID, other psychiatric disorders (schizophrenias and related psychotic disorders), epilepsy, and other neurodevelopmental disorders (Avramopulos, 2010; Furniss & Biswas, 2001; Garcia-Villmisar, & Rojahn, 2015).

3. Boundary issues: Problem with the differential diagnosis of stereotypic movement disorder include: the persistence of stereotypies without SIB; the early and rapid transformation from stereotypy to self-injurious behaviors; interrelationship between it and multiple medical or genetic disorders; and the role of other neurodevelopmental and psychiatric disorders. Heterogeneity brings us to the third leg of the diagnostic algorithm. The applicability of using specifiers as nodal points may be useful as a diagnostic algorithm for defining subtypes of stereotypic movement disorder. The algorithmic approach may help minimize reliance on motivation and goal directedness as diagnostic criteria and encourage relying instead on genetic, neurodegenerative, neurobiological, medical, trauma-related, neuropsychiatric, and challenging psychosocial/ ecological conditions.

4. Severity criteria: The severity of stereotypies and self-injury are linked to the severity of both IDD and autism spectrum disorder. The authors argue for the usefulness of applying the DSM-5 criteria for severity of IDD and autism spectrum disorder to the severity criteria for stereotypic movement disorder. Both applications may be useful in synthesizing and formulating the role of genetic, metabolic, medical/neurological disorders and environmental/ecological influences on the severity of stereotypic movement disorder.

Like other neurodevelopmental disorder, the nature of stereotypic movement disorder varies depending on etiology. Self-mutilation in drug-induced conditions, borderline personality disorders or chronic schizophrenia are examples. Although schizophrenia is more accurately described as a neurodevelopmenta disorder, the idea is rarely applied to our explanations of emerging self-injury during adulthood. Individuals with Borderline personality may display self-cutting during adolescence. Early in its course, self-injury appears reactive in nature but over time seems to change to a more habitual behavior. In spite of this transformation, there is no progression to stereotypic self-injury. The diverse examples reveal the complex relationship between state/trait-related repetitive behaviors. It also appears that baseline exaggeration of repetitive and self-injurious behaviors associated with co-occurring psychiatric disorders reflects not only state-trait changes but also in the balance environmental triggers. Yet we should not underestimate the power of cognitive disorganization and baseline exaggeration in the face of severe stressors, pain, trauma-related changes, and physical illness in these state changes. This vulnerability poses a major issue for individuals with severe profound ID and autism spectrum disorder (Fletcher et al., 2007). These challenges suggest that an algorithmic application to stereotypic movement disorder criteria may be an effective device for coping with this level of complexity.

Stereotypic Movement Disorder

DSM-5 Diagnostic Criteria	Applying Critieria for Mild-Moderate ID	Applying Criteria for Severe-Profound ID	Notes
A. Repetitive, seemingly driven and apparently purposeless motor behavior (e.g. hand shaking or waving, body rocking, head banging, self-biting, hitting own body)	No adaptations needed	No adaptations needed	It can be difficult to establish purposefulness of behaviors. It may be more helpful to use data from Functional Behavioral Analysis and neurological findings associated with other abnormal involuntary movements. The presence of autism spectrum disorder warrants a careful review since repetitive and restrictive behaviors are diagnostic criteria (see section on autism spectrum disorder)
B. The repetitive motor behavior interferes with social, academic and other activities and may result in in self-injury	No adaptation needed. Marked discrepancy between level of functional impairment and mild ID (IDD) may warrant a more detail assessment.	No adaptations needed.	Perhaps the best model is the functional domains: conceptual, social, and practical behaviors used to denote support service needs. The frequency, intensity, typographies, and apparent motivation/function of stereotypies and self-injury may change over time, without obvious neuropsychiatric disorders.
C. Onset early in the developmental period	No adaptation needed. Severe self-injury may warrant a more detailed medical/neurological, genetic or metabolic assessment.	No adaptations needed. Metamorphosis of stereotypies into self-injury may analogous to the relationship between language and communication and aggressive behaviors. Sensitivity to biopsychosocial stressors (baseline exaggeration) may be more obvious	As noted determining the age of onset can be complex. Some forms of SIB begin during infancy or evolve out of stereotypies. Biopsychosocial factors can influence both age of onset and course of predisposing, precipitating, perpetuating factors

DSM-5 Diagnostic Criteria	Applying Critieria for Mild-Moderate ID	Applying Criteria for Severe-Profound ID	Notes
D. Repetitive motor behavior is not attributed to the physiological effects of a substance or neurological condition and is not better explained by another neurodevelopmental or mental disorder (e.g. trichotillomania or obsessive compulsive disorder).	No adaptation needed. Behavioral phenotypes associated with self-injury should be considered in individuals with mild/moderate ID and other markers for chromosomal or genetic disorders	No Adaptation needed. Individuals with severe/ profound ID/autism spectrum disorder are more likely to have chronic SIB that may require long term behavioral or pharmacological management.	Substance-induced stereotypies may be less common in severe/ profound ID but more common in community dwelling individuals with borderline or mild ID. Akathisia, increased arousal as well as triggering psychiatric disorders associated with stereotypic movement disorder need to be explored.
Specify if: With self-injurious behavior- or behavioral that would result in an injury if preventative measures were not sued) Without self-injurious behavior Coding Note: Associated with a known medical or neurological condition, neurodevelopmental disorder, or environmental factors (Lesch-Nyhan syndrome, ID9IDD) or intrauterine alcohol exposure.	No adaptations needed.	No adaptations needed.	If possible stereotypic behaviors need to be distinguished from motor tics, obsessive compulsive behaviors, and stereotypies associated with neuro-typical development. Functional behavioral analysis may be useful for addressing subtypes based on temperament, ecological and biosocial factors that impact the valence of antecedents and may serve to maintain behaviors A similar level of analysis should be applied to SIB.
Specify current severity: Mild: Symptoms are easily suppressed by sensory stimulus or distraction Moderate: Symptoms require explicit protective measures or behavioral modification Severe: Continuous monitoring and protective measures are required to prevent serious self-injury	No adaptations needed. Marked discrepancy between level of severity and ID (IDD) may warrant more detailed assessment (e.g. severe mutilating SIB in an individual with mild ID).	No additional adaptations needed.	Severity criteria may also reflect level of ID (IDD), autism spectrum disorder, ecological factors and capacity to self-regulate stereotypy and self-injury. A transformation in level of severity over time should warrant a more detailed re-evaluation of genetic, metabolic, new medical and neurological disorders, medication side effects, and other biopsychosocial challenges. Level of antecedent pain, pain threshold, pain response to SIB, fixed typology and the presence of abnormal movementsand use of self-restraint may warrant re-examination.

Motor Disorder : Chapter Summary

Motor disorders are more common among individuals with ID (IDD). Stereotypic movements disorders (SMD), tic disorders and motor disorders to some extent unfold in a complicated ecological matrix that roughly corresponds to past learning experiences, genetic risk, and the level of functional impairment in relation to ID and autism spectrum disorders. The expression of these co-occurring phenomena influences the emergence of not only other neurodevelopmental but also affects and is affected by presence of primary psychiatric disorders. This amalgam creates a significant problem for both researchers and clinicians. In this sense the diagnosis of motor disorders in people with ID is like trying to hit a moving target that is constantly changing shape and direction in frequently unpredictable ways.

The authors attempted several new applications to the diagnosis of motor disorders. The first was the use of existing criteria sets and specifiers as both a part of the differential diagnosis but also these criteria in the development of an algorithmic approach that may help define more specific endophenotypes of Motor Disorders. This approach may be more useful to researchers than clinicians. The second step begins the search for applying existing DSM-5 criteria for the severity of ID ASD as tools for addressing the impact of motor disorders on support and intervention needs. This conceptual model needs more work but we hope that by introducing it and tentatively outlining the concepts, that it will be useful for better individualizing diagnosis and treatment planning for individuals with ID.

References

Addington, A. M., & Rapoport, J. L. (2012). Annual research review: Impact of advances in genetics in understanding developmental psychopathology. *Journal of Child Psychology and Psychiatry and Allied Disciplines, 53*(5), 510-518

American Psychiatric Association. (2013). *Diagnostic and statistical manual of mental disorders* (5th ed.). Washington, D.C: American Psychiatric Publishing.

Arron, K., Oliver, C., Moss, J., Berg, K., & Burbidge, C. (2011). The prevalence and phenomenology of self-injurious and aggressive behaviour in genetic syndromes. *Journal of Intellectual Disability Research, 55*(2), 109-120.

Augustyn, M., & Zuckerman, B. (1998). Normal brain development. In E. Coffey & R.A. Brumback (Eds.), *Textbook of pediatric neuropsychiatry* (pp. 117-138). Washington DC: American Psychiatric Association Press.

Avramopulos, D. (2010). Genetics of psychiatric disorders: methods, molecular approach. *Psychiatric Clinics of North America, 33*, 1-15.

Barnhill, L. J. (2003). Neurobiology of self-injurious behavior: Is there a relationship to addictions? *NADD Bulletin, 6(2)*, 29-37.

Barnhill, J. (2005). Body dysmorphic disorder: A subset of self-injurious behaviors. *Mental Health Aspects of Developmental Disabilities, 8*, 5-12.

Barnhill, J. (2011). Obsessive-compulsive disorders or not: Differential diagnosis of repetitive among individuals with intellectual and developmental disorder. In S. Selek (Ed.), *Different views of anxiety disorders* (pp. 37-58). Rijek Croatia: InTech.

Barnhill, J., & Hurley, A. D. (2008). Movement disorders: Things that do go bump in the night. *Mental Health Aspects of Developmental Disabilities, 11*(4), 133-137.

Barnhill, L.J., de Koning, N.D., & Kartheiser, P.H. Learning disorders. (2007). In R. Fletcher, E. Loeschen, C. Stavrakaki, M. First (Eds.), *Diagnostic manual-Intellectual disability: A textbook of mental disorders in por son with intellectual disabilities* (pp. 69-87). NADD Press: Kingston NY.

Barnhill, L. J., & Horrigan, J. P. (2002). Tourette's syndrome and autism: A search for common ground. *Mental Health Aspects of Developmental Disabilities, 5*(1), 7-15.

Barnhill, L.J., & McNelis, D. (2012). Overview of intellectual/developmental disabilities. *Focus: The Journal of Lifelong Learning in Psychiatry, 10*(3), 300-307.

Barnhill, L.J., & Kartheiser, P.H. (2007). Motor skill disorders. In R. Fletcher, E. Loeschken, C. Stavrakaki, & M. First (Eds). *Diagnostic manual-Intellectual disability: A textbook of mental disorders in person with intellectual disabilities* (pp. 89-97). NADD Press: Kingston NY.

Baron-Cohen, S. Mortimore, C. Moriatry, J. Izaguirre, J. & Robertson, M. (1999). The prevalence of Gilles de la Tourette's syndrome in children. *Journal of Child Psychology and Psychiatry, 40*(2), 213-8.

Barry, S., Baird, G., Lacselles, K., Bunton, P., & Hedderly, T. (2011). Neurodevelopmental movement disorders – An update on childhood motor stereotypies. *Developmental Medicine and Child Neurology, 53*(11), 979-985.

Berger, R., Gelkopt, M., Versano-Mor, K., & Shpigelman, C. N. (2015). Impact of exposure to potentially traumatic events in individuals with intellectual disability. *American Journal of Intelletual and Developmental Disability, 120*, 176-188.

Bishop, D.V. (2002). Motor immaturity and language impairment: Evidence for a common genetic basis. *American Journal of Medical Genetics, 114*, 56-63.

Browne, H. A., Gair, S. L., Scharf, J. M., & Grice, D. E. (2014). Genetics of obsessive-compulsive disorder and related disorders. *Psychiatric Clinics of North America, 37*(3), 319-336.

Bruun, R.D., & Budman, C.L. (1993). Natural history of Gilles de la Tourette's syndrome. In R. Kurlan (Ed.), *Handbook of Tourette's syndrome and related tic and behavioral disorders* (pp. 27-43). New York: Marcel Dekker.

Bucan, M., Brodkin, E.S., (2008). Psychiatric Diseases: Challenges in Psychiatric Genetics. In R.N. Rosenberg, D. Salvatore, H.L. Paulson, L. Ptacek, & E.J. Nestelr (Eds), *The molecular and genetic basis of neurologic and psychiatric disorders* (4th ed.) (pp. 749-758). Baltimore, MD: Lippincott, Willikams & Wilkins.

Burbridge, C., Oliver, C., Moss, J., Arron, K., Berg, K., Furniss, F., ... Woodock, K. (2010). The association between repetitive behaviors, impulsivity and hyperactivity in people with intellectual disability, *Journal of Intellectual Disability Research, 54*(12), 1078-1092.

Cairney, J., Hat, J.A., & Faught, B.E. (2005). Developmental coordination disorder, generalized efficacy toward physical activity, and participation in organized and free play activities. *Journal of Pediatrics*, 147, 515-524.

Campbell, M., Anderson, L.T., Small, A.M., Adams, P., Gonzalez, N.M., & Ernst, M. (1993). Naltrexone in autistic children: Behavioral symptoms and attentional learning. *Journal of the American Academy of Child and Adolescent Psychiatry, 32*(6), 1283-1291.

Canitano, R., & Vivanti, G. (2007). Tics and Tourette syndrome in autism spectrum disorders. *Autism, 11*(1), 19-28.

Clarke, R. A., Lee, S., & Eapen, V. (2012). Pathogenetic model for Tourette syndrome delineates overlap with related neurodevelopmental disorders including autism. *Translational Psychiatry, 2(9)*, e158.

Coch, D., Dawson, G., & Fischer, K. W. (Eds.) (2007). *Human behavior, learning and the developing brain: Atypical development.* New York: Guilford Press.

Cohen, L.J.., Simeon, D., Hollander, E., & Stein, D.J. (1997). Obsessive-compulsive spectrum disorders. In E. Hollander & D.J. Stein (Eds.), *Obsessive compulsive disorders* (pp. 47-74). New York: Marcel Dekker.

Constantino, J.N., & Todd, R.D. (2000). Genetic structure of reciprocal behavior. *American Journal of Psychiatry, 157*, 2043-2045.

Copeland, W.E., Shanahan, L., Eggar, H., Angold, A., & Costello, E.J. (2014). Adult diagnostic and functionaloutcomes of DSM-5 disruptive mood dysregulation disorder. *American Journal of Psychiatry, 171*(6), 668-674.

Decety, J., & Meyer, M. (2009). Imitation as a stepping stone to empathy. In M. De Haan, & M.R. Gunnar (Eds.), *Handbook of developmental social neuroscience* (pp142-158). New York NY: Guilford Press.

DeHaan, M., & Gunnar, M. R. (Eds.) (2009). *The handbook of developmental neurosciences*. New York: Guilford Press.

Dhossche, D.M., Getz, M., Gadzag, G., & Sienaert, P. (2013). New DSM-5 category: 'Unspecified catatonis' is a boost for pediatric catatonia: Review and case reports. *Neurospychiatry, 4*(4), 401-410.

Domelloff, E., Johansson, A,-M., Farooqi, A., Momelloff, M., & Ronnqvist, L. (2013). Relations among upper-limb movements and cognitive function at school age in children born preterm. *Journal of Developmental and Behavioral Pediatrics, 34*(5), 344-352.

Dyck, M. J., Piek, J. P., & Patrick, J. (2011). The validity of psychiatric diagnoses: The case of 'specific' developmental disorders. *Research in Developmental Disabilities, 32*(6), 2704-2713.

Fang, A., Matheny, N. L., & Wilhelm, S. (2014). Body dysmorphic disorder. *Psychiatric Clinics of North America, 37,* 287-300.

Finucane, B., Dirrigl, K. H., & Simon, E. W. (2001). Characterization of self-injurious behaviors in children and adults with Smith-Magenis syndrome. *American Journal on Mental Retardation, 106,* 52-58.

Fletcher, R., Loeschen, E., Stavrakaki, C., & First, M. (2007). *Diagnostic manual-Intellectual disabilities.* Kingston, NY: NADD Press.

Friedman, J.H. (2007). Stereotypy and catatonia. In J. Janlovic j & E. Tolosa (Eds), *Parkinson's disease and movement disorders* (5th ed.) (pp. 468-480). Baltimore: Lippincott, Williams &Wilkins.

Furniss, F., & Biswas, A. B. (2012). Recent research on aetiology, development and phenomenology of self-injurious behaviour in people with intellectual disabilities: A systematic review and implications for treatment. *Journal of Intellectual Disability Research, 56,* 453-475.

Gal, E., Dyck, M. J., & Passmore, A. (2009). The relationship between stereotyped movements and self-injurious behavior in children with developmental or sensory disabilities. *Research in Developmental Disabilities, 30,* 342-352.

Gao, S., & Singer, H. S. (2013). Complex motor stereotypies: An evolving neurobiological concept. *Future Neurology, 8*(3), 273-285.

Garcia-Villmisar, D., & Rojahn, J. (2015). Comorbid psychopathology and stress mediate the relationship between autistic traits and repetitive behaviors in adults with autism. *Journal of Intellectual Disability Research, 59,* 116-124.

Gardner, W. I., & Griffiths, D. M. (2004). Treatment of aggression and related disruptive behaviors in persons with intellectual disabilities and mental health issues. In J. L. Matson, R. B. Laud, & M. L. Matson (Eds.), *Behavioral modification for persons with developmental disorders: Treatments and supports* (pp. 279-309). Kingston, New York: NADD Press.

Ghez C, & Krakuer J (2000a). The organization of movement. In E.R. Kandel, J.H. Schwartz, & T.M. Jessell (Eds.), *The principles of neural science* (4th ed.) (pp737 755). New York, NY: McGraw-Hill.

Ghez, C., & Krakuer, J. (2000b). Voluntary movement. In E.R. Kandel, J.H. Schwartz, & T.M. Jessell (Eds), *The principles of neural science* (4th ed.) (pp 756-781) New York NY: McGraw-Hill.

Gillberg, C., & Kadesjö, B. (2003). Why bother about clumsiness? The implications of having developmental coordination disorder (DCD). *Neural Plasticity, 10*(1-2), 59-68.

Goldman, S., Wang, C., Salgado, M. W., Greene, P. E., Kim, M., & Rapin, I. (2008). Motor stereotypies in children with autism and other developmental disorders. *Developmental Medicine and Child Neurology, 5,* 30-38.

Gonzalez, P., & Marinez, K. G. (2014). The role of stress and fear in the development of mental disorders. *Psychiatric Clinics of North America, 37,* 535-546.

Goodman W.K., Grice D.E., Lapidus, K.A.B., & Coffey, B.J. (2014). Obsessive-compulsive disorder. *Psychiatric Clinics of North America 37*(3): 257-268.

Grant, J. E., Potenza, N., Weinstein, A., & Gorelik, D. A. (2011). Introduction to behavioral addictions. *American Journal of Drug and Alcohol Abuse, 38,* 243-241.

Guess, D., & Carr, E. (1991). Emergence and maintenance of stereotypy and self-injury. *American Journal of Mental Retardation, 96,* 299-319.

Hall, S., Lightbody, A.A., & Reiss, A.L. (2015). Compulsive, self-injurious, and autistic behavior in children and adoelscence with fragile X syndrome. *American Journal of Mental Retardation, 113*(1), 44-54.

Hall, S., Oliver, C., & Murphy, G. H. (2001). Early development of severe self-injurious behavior: An empirical study. *American Journal of Mental Retardation, 106,* 189-99.

Hall, S., Thorns, T., & Oliver, C., (2003). Structural and environmental characteristics of stereotyped behaviors. *American Journal of Mental Retardation, 108,* 391-402.

Hamilton, S.S. (2014). Developmental coordination disorder: Clinical features and diagnosis. *UpToDate*. Retrieved from https://www.uptodate.com/contents/developmental-coordination-disorder-clinical-features-and-diagnosis.

Harris, J. C., (2008). *Intellectual disability: Understanding its development, causes, classification, evaluation and treatment.* New York: Guilford Press.

Harris, K.M., Malone, E.M., & Singer, H.S.l. (2008). Nonautistic motor stereotypies: Clinical features and longitudinal follow up. *Pediatric Neurology, 38*, 267-272.

Hartman, E., Houwen, S., Scherder, E., & Visscher, C. (2010). On the relationship between motor performance and executive functioning on children with intellectual disabilities. *Journal of Intellectual Disability Research, 54*(5), 468- 77.

Hernandez, L.M. & Blazer, D.G. (Eds). (2006). *Genes, behavior and the social environment: Moving beyond the nature/nurture debate.* Washington, DC: National Academies Press.

Hoch, T. A., Long, K. E., McPeak, M. M., & Rojahn, J. (2004). Self-injurious behavior in mental retardation. In J. L. Matson, R. B. Laud, & M. L. Matson (Eds.), *Behavioral modification for persons with developmental disorders: Treatments and supports* (pp. 190-218). Kingston, New York: NADD Press.

Huey, E. D., Zahn, R., Kreuger, F., Moll, J., Kapogianus, D., Wassermen, E. M., & Grafman, J. (2008). A psychological and neuroanatomical model for OCD. *Journal of Neuropsychiatry and Clinical Neurosciences, 20*, 390-408.

Iverson, J.M. (2010). Developing language in a developing body: The relationship between motor development and language. *Journal of Child Language, 37*, 229-261.

Jankovic, J. (2007). Tics and Tourette's disorders in children. In J. Janlovic & E. Tolosa (Eds.), *Parkinson's disease and movement disorders* (5th ed.) (pp. 356-375). Baltimore, MD: Lippincott, Williams &Wilkins.

Jankovic, J. & Tolosa, E., (Eds), *Parkinson's disease and movement disorders.* Philadelphia: Lippincott, Wilkins & Williams.

Kartasidou, L., Varsamis, P., & Sampsonidou, A. (2012). Motor performance and rhythmic perception of children with intellectual and developmental disability and developmental coordination disorder. *International Journal of Special Education, 27*(1), 74-80.

Kays, J. L., Hurley, R. A., & Taber, K. H. (2012). The dynamic brain: Neuroplasticity and mental health. *Journal of Neuropsychiatry and Clinical Neurosciences*, 24(2), 118-124.

Kerserbian, J., & Burd, L. (1992). Epidemiology and comorbidity: The North Dakota prevalence studies of Tourette's syndrome and other developmental disorders. *Advances in Neurology, 58*, 67-74.

Kraus, J. E. (2000). Sensitization phenomena in psychiatric illness: Lessons from the Kindling model. *Journal of Neuropsychiatry and Clinical Neurosciences, 12*, 228-43.

Kurtz, P. F., Chin, M. D., Huete, J. M., & Cataldo, M. F. (2012). Identification of emerging self-injurious behavior in young children: A preliminary study. *Journal of Mental Health Research in Intellectual Disability, 5*, 260-285.

Landa, R. (2007). Early communication development and intervention for children with Autism. *Mental Retardation and Developmental Disabilities Research Reviews*, 13, 16-25.

Lanovaz, M. J. (2011). Towards a comprehensive model of stereotypy: Integrating operant and neurobiological interpretations. *Research in Developmental Disabilities, 32*, 447-455.

Leckman, J.F., King, R.A., Gilbert, D.L., Coffey, B.J., Singer, H.S., Dure IV, L.S., ... Kaplan, E. (2011). Streptococcal upper respiratory tract infections and exacerbations of tic and obsessive-compulsive symptoms: A longitudinal study. *Journal of the American Academy of Child and Adolescent Psychiatry, 50*(2), 108-118.

Leekam, S., Tandos, J., McConad, H., Meins, E.,

Parkinson, K., Wright, C., … La Couteur, A. (2007). Repetitive behaviors in typically 2-year-olds. *Journal of Child Psychology and Psychiatry, 48*, 1131-1138.

Leonard, H. C., & Hill, E. L. (2014). The impact of motor development on typical and atypical social cognition and language: A systematic review. *Child and Adolescent Mental Health*, doi:10.1111/camh.12055

Levy, R. (2007). Neurobehavioral disorders associated with basal ganglia disorders. In J. Janlovic & E. Tolosa (Eds.), *Parkinson's disease and movement disorders* (5th ed.) (pp. 23-32). Baltimore, MD: Lippincott, Williams &Wilkins.

Liu, D., Gu, X., Zhu, J., Shang, X., Han, Z., Yan, M., … Li, C.T. (2014). Medial prefrontal activity during delay periods contributes to learning of a working memory task. *Science, 346*(6208), 458-463.

Marlow N, Hennessey EM, Braceweed MA, Wolke D (2007). Motor and executive function at 6 years of age in extremely premature Infants. *Pediatrics*, 120, 793-804.

Martino, D., Madhusudan, N., Zis, P., & Cavanna, A. E. (2013). An introduction to the clinical phenomenology of Tourette syndrome. *International Review of Neurobiology, 112*, 1-33.

Maski, K.P., Jeste, S.S., & Spence, S.J. (2011). Common neurological co-morbidities in autism spectrum disorders. *Current Opinion in Pediatrics, 23*(6), 609-615.

Matson, J. L., Laud, R. B., & Matson, M. L. (Eds.) (2004). *Behavioral modification for persons with developmental disorders: Treatments and supports.* Kingston, New York, NADD Press.

Matson, J. L., & Shoemaker, M. E. (2011). Psychopathology and intellectual disability. *Current Opinions in Psychiatry, 24*, 367-b371.

Matthews, C.A., & Grados, M.A. (2011). Familiarity of Tourette syndrome, obsessive-compulsive, and attention deficit/hyperactivity disorder: Heritability analysis in large sib-pair sample. *Journal of the American Academy of Child and Adolescent Psychiatry, 50*(1), 46-54.

Max, J. E. (2014). Neuropsychiatry of pediatric traumatic brain injury. *Psychiatric Clinics of North America, 37*, 125-140.

McLaughlin, K. A., Fox, N. A., Zenneah, C. H., & Nelson, C. A. (2011). Adverse rearing environments and neural development in children: The development of frontal EEG asymmetry. *Biological Psychiatry, 70*, 1008-1015.

McLean, W. E., & Dornbush, K. (2012). Self-injury in a state wide sample of young children with developmental disabilities. *Journal of Mental Health Research in Intellectual Disability, 5*, 236-245

McOmish, C. E., & Gingrich, J. A. (2011). Stress and the baby brain. *Biological Psychiatry, 70*, 1006-1009.

Medeiros, K. (2013). The progression of severe behavior disorder in young children with intellectual and developmental disabilities. *Research in Developmental Disabilities, 34*, 3639-3647.

Medeiros, K., Kozkoski, A. M., Beighley, J. S., Rojahn, J., & Matson, J. L. (2012). The effects of developmental quotient and diagnositc criteria on challenging behaviors in toddlers with developmental disabilities. *Research in Developmental Disabilities, 33*, 1110-1116.

Medeiros, K., Rojahn, J., Moore, L. L., & van Ingen, D. J. (2014). Functional properties of behaviour problems depending on level of intellectual disability. *Journal of Intellectual Disability Research, 58*, 151-161.

Mejia, N. I., & Jankovic, J. (2005). Secondary tics and tourettism. *Revista Brasileira De Psiquiatria, 27*(1), 11-17

Melchior, L., Bertelsen, B., Debes, N. M., Groth, C., Skov, L., Mikkelsen, J. D., & Tümer, Z. (2013). Microduplication of 15q13.3 and Xq21.31 in a family with tourette syndrome and comorbidities. *American Journal of Medical Genetics, Part B: Neuropsychiatric Genetics, 162*(8), 825-831.

Mills, S., & Hedderly, T. (2014). A guide to childhood motor stereotypies, tic disorders and the Tourette spectrum for the primary care practitioner. *Ulster Medical Journal, 83*(1), 22-30.

Minshaw, N. F., Hurwitz, S., Fodstad, J. C., Biebl, S., Morriss, D. H., & McDougle, C. (2014). The association between self-injurious behaviors and autism spectrum disorders. *Psychology Research and Behavior Management, 7,* 125-136.

Mitchell, R. H. B., & Goldstein, B. I. (2014). Inflammation in children and adolescents with neuropsychiatric disorders: A systematic review. *Journal of the American Academy of Child and Adolescent Psychiatry, 53,* 274-296.

Moss, J., Oliver, C., Arron, K., Burbidge, C., & Berg, K. (2009). The prevalence and phenomenology of repetitive behavior in genetic syndromes. *Journal of Autism and Developmental Disorders, 39*(4), 572-588.

Moya, P. R., Dodman, N. H., Timpano, K. R., Rubenstein, L. M., Rana, Z., Fried, R. L., ... Wendland, J.R. (2013). Rare missense neuronal cadherin gene (CDH2) variants in specific obsessive-compulsive disorder and Tourette disorder phenotypes. *European Journal of Human Genetics, 21*(8), 850-854.

Muehlmann, A. M., & Lewis, M. H. (2012). Abnormal repetitive behaviours: Shared phenomenology and pathophysiology. *Journal of Intellectual Disability Research, 56*(5), 427-440.

Murhpy, D. L., Timpano, K. R., Wheaton, M. G., Greenberg, B. D., & Miguel, E. C. (2010). Obsessive-compuslive disorder and its related disorders: A reappraisal of obsessive-compuslvie spectrum concepts. *Dialogues in Clinical Neurosciences, 12,* 131-148.

Murphy, T.K., Geraldi, D.M., & Leckman, J.F. (2014). Pediatric acute-onset neuropsychiatric syndrome. *Psychiatric Clinics of North America, 37*(3), 353-374.

Murphy, T.K., Lewin, A.B., Storch, E.A., Stock, S., & the American Academy of Child and Adolescent Psychiatry Committee on Quality Issues (2013). Practice parameters for the assessment and treatment of children and adolescents with tic disorders. *Journal of the American Academy of Child and Adolescent Psychiatry, 52*(12), 1341-1359.

Muthugovidan, D., & Singer, H. (2009). Motor stereotypy disorders. *Current Opinion in Neurology,* 22(2), 131-136.

Myrbakk, E., & von Tetzchner, S. (2008). The prevalence of behavior problems among people with intellectual disability in community settings. *Journal of Mental Health Research in Intellectual Disabilities, 1,* 205- 220.

Nag, A., Bochukova, E. G., Kremeyer, B., Campbell, D. D., Muller, H., Valencia-Duarte, A. V., ... Ruiz-Linares, A. (2013). CNV analysis in Tourette syndrome implicates large genomic rearrangements in COL8A1 and NRXN1. *PLOS One, 8*(3).

Neal, M., & Cavanna, A. E. (2013). Not just right experiences in patients with Tourette syndrome: Complex motor tics or compulsions? *Psychiatry Research, 210*(2), 559-563.

Noll, L. M., & Barrett, R. P. (2004). Stereotyped Acts. In J. L. Matson, R. B. Laud, & M. L. Matson (Eds.), *Behavioral modification for persons with developmental disorders: Treatments and supports* (pp 219-278). Kingston, New York: NADD Press.

Oliver, C., Petty, J., Ruddick, L., & Bacarese-Hamilton, M. (2012). The association between repetitive, self-injurious and aggressive behavior in children with severe intellectual disability. *Journal of Autism and Developmental Disorders, 42,* 910-919.

Oliver, C., Sloneem, J., Hall, S., & Arron, K. (2009). Self-injurious behaviour in Cornelia de Lange syndrome: 1. Prevalence and phenomenology. *Journal of Intellectual Disability Research, 53,* 575-589.

Ousley, O., & Cemak, T. (2014). Autism spectrum disorder: Defining dimensions and subgroups. *Current Developmental Disorders Reports, 1,* 20-28.

Paris, J. (Ed). (2008). Recent research in personality disorders. *Psychiatric Clinics of North America,* 31(3), 363-566.

Paschou, P. (2013). The genetic basis of Gilles de la Tourette syndrome. *Neuroscience and Biobehavioral Reviews, 37*(6), 1026-1039.

Peltopuro, M., Ahonen, T., Kaartinen, J., Seppala, H., & Narhi, V. (2014). Borderline intellectual functioning: A systematic review of the literature. *Journal of Intellectual and Developmental Disorders, 52*(6), 419-69.

Petty, J., Allen, D., & Oliver, C. (2009). Relationship among challenging, repetitive, and communicative behaviors in children with severe intellectual disabilities. *American Journal on Intellectual and Developmental Disabilities, 114*(5), 356-368

Piek, J.P., Dawson, l., Smith, L.M., & Gasson, N. (2008). The role of early fine and gross motor development on later motor and cognitive development. *Human Movement Science, 27*, 668-681.

Piek, J. P., & Dyck, M. J. (2004). Sensory-motor deficits in children with developmental coordination disorder, attention deficit hyperactivity disorder and autistic disorder. *Human Movement Science, 23*(3-4 SPE. ISS.), 475-488.

Prunty, M.M., Barnett, A.L., Wilmut, K., & Plumb, M.S. (2013). Handwriting speed in children with developmental coordination disorder: Are they really slower? *Research in Developmental Disabilities, 34*, 2927.

Quirk, G. J., Garcia, R., & Gonzalez-Lima, F. (2006). Prefrontal mechanisms in extinction of fear conditioning. *Biological Psychiatry, 60*, 337-343.

Rapin I (2000). Autistic spectrum disorders: relevance to Tourette's Syndrome. *Advances in Neurology, 85*. 89-102.

Rattaz, C., Michelon, C., & Baghdalli, A. (2015). Symptom severity as a risk factor for self-injurious behavior in adolescents with autism spectrum disorder. *Journal of Intellectual Disability Research, 59*, 730-740.

Richards, C., Oliver, C., Nelson, L., & Moss, J. (2012). Self-injurious behaviour in individuals with autism spectrum disorder and intellectual disability. *Journal of Intellectual Disability Research, 56*, 476-489.

Richman, D. M., Barnard-Brak, L., Bosch, A., Thompson, S., Grubb, L., & Abby, L. (2013). Predictors of self-injurious behaviour exhibited by individuals with autism spectrum disorder. *Journal of Intellectual Disability Research, 57*, 429-439.

Robertson, M.M. (1992). Self-injurious behavior and Tourette's syndrome. *Advances in Neurology, 58*, 105-109.

Robertson, M.M. (2000). Tourette's syndrome, associated conditions and the complexities of treatment. *Brain*, 23, 425-63.

Robertson, M. M., Trimble, M. R., & Lees, A. A. (1989). Self-injurious behavior and Gilles de la Tourette's syndrome: A clinical study and review of the literature. *Psychological Medicine, 19*, 611-625.

Roelefs, R. L., Visser, E. M., Berger, J. C., Prins, J. B., Schrojenstein Lantman-De Valk, H. M. J., & Teunisse, J. P. (2015). Executive functioning in individuals with intellectual disabilities and autism spectrum disorders. *Journal of Intellectual Disability Research, 59*, 116-124.

Royal College of Psychiatrists. (2001). *Diagnostic criteria for psychiatric disorders for use with adults with learning disabilities/mental retardation*. London: Gaskell.

Rutter M. (2002). The interplay of nature, nurture and developmental influences. *Archives of General Psychiatry, 59*, 996-1000.

Sandman, C.A., Touchette, P., Lenjavi, M., Marion, S., & Chizc-Demet, A. (2003). B-endorphin and ACTH are dissociated after self-injury in adults with developmental disabilities. *American Journal of Mental Retardation, 108*(6), 414-424.

Santangelo, S.I., Pauls, D.L., Goldstein, J.M., Farone, S.V., Tsuang, M.T., & Leckman, J.F. (1994). Tourette's syndrome: What are the influences of gender and comorbid obsessive-compulsive disorder. *Journal of the American Academy of Child and Adolescent Psychiatry, 33*(6), 795-804.

Sayers, N., Oliver, C., Ruddick, L., & Wallis, B. (2011). Stereotyped behavior in children with autism and intellectual disability. *Journal of intellectual Disability Research, 55*, 699-709.

Scahill L.D., Leckman, J.F., & Marck, K.L. (1995). Sensory phenomena in Tourette's syndrome. *Advances in Neurology, 65*, 273-281.

Scahill, L., Dimitropoulos, A., McDougle, C. J., Aman, M. G., Feurer, I. D., McCracken, J. T.,

& Vitiello, B. (2014). Children's Yale-Brown obsessive compulsive scale in autism spectrum disorder: Component structure and correlates of symptom checklist. *Journal of the American Academy of Child and Adolescent Psychiatry, 53*(1), 97-107.

Scahill, L., Vaccarino, F.M., Mercadante, M.T., & Lombroso, P.J. (2008). Obsessive-compulsive and Tourette syndrome. In R.N. Rosenberg, D. Salvatore, H.L. Paulson, L. Ptacek, & E.J. Nestelr (Eds), *The molecular and genetic basis of neurologic and psychiatric disorders* (4th ed.) (pp. 802-816). Baltimore, MD: Lippincott, Williams & Wilkins.

Schroeder, S. R., Marquis, J. G., Reese, M., Richman, D., Mayo-Ortego, L., Oyama-Ganiko, R., … Lawrence, L. (2014). Risk factors for self-injury, aggression, stereotyped behavior among children at risk for intellectual and developmental disabilities. *American Journal of Intellectual and Developmental Disabilities, 119*, 351-370.

Scotti, J. R., Schulman, D. E., & Hojnacki, R. M. (1994). Functional analysis and unsuccessful treatment of Tourette's syndrome in a man with profound mental retardation. *Behavior Therapy, 25*(4), 721-738.

Shaw, P., Stringaris, A., Nigg, L., & Leibenluft, E. (2014). Emotional dysregulation in attention deficit hyperactivity disorder. *American Journal of Psychiatry, 171*(3), 276-293.

Shaw, Z.A., & Coffey, B.J. (2014) Tics and Tourette's syndrome. *Psychiatric Clinics of North America, 37*(3), 269-288.

Singer, H.S. (2007). Movement disorders in children. In J. Janlovic & E. Tolosa (Eds), *Parkinson's disease and movement disorders* (5th ed.) (pp. 481-503). Balitmore, MD: Lippincott, Williams &Wilkins.

Smith, J.H., Smith, V.D., Philbeick, K.L., & Kumar, N. (2012). Catatonic disorder due to general medical condition. *Journal of Neuropsychiatry and Clinical Neurosciences, 24*(2), 198-207.

Smits-Engelsman, B., & Hill, E.L. (2012). The relationship between motor coordination intelligence across the IQ range. Doi:10.1542/peds.2011-3712.

Spendelow, J. S. (2011). Assessment of behavioral and psychiatric problems in people with Prader-Willi syndrome: A review of the literature. *Journal of Policy and Practice in Intellectual Disabilities, 8*, 104-112.

Symons, F. J., Sperry, L. A., Dropik, P. L., & Bodfish, J. W. (2005). The early development of stereotypy and self-injury: A review of research methods. *Journal of Intellectual Disability Research, 49*, 144-158.

Tan, A., Salgado, M., & Fahn, S. (1997). The characterization and outcome of stereotypical movements in non-autistic children. *Movement Disorders, 12*, 47-52.

Troster, H. (1994). Prevalence and functions of stereotyped behaviors in nonhandicapped children in residential care. *Journal of Abnormal Child Psychology, 22*, 79-97.

Tsankova, N., Renthal, W., Kumar, A., & Nestler, E. J. (2007). Epigenetic regulation of psychiatric disorders. *Science: Nature Reviews, 8*, 355-367.

Tureck, K., Matson, J. L., & Beighley, J. S. (2013). An investigation of self-injurious behaviors in adults with severe intellectual disabilities. *Research in Developmental Disabilities, 34*, 2469-2474.

Van Betenburg-Eddes, T., Heinrichs, J., Schenk, J.J., Sincer, I., deGroot, L., Hofman, A., … Tiemeier, H. (2013). Early infant neuromotor assessment is associated with language and nonverbal cognitive function in toddlers: The generation R study. *Journal of Developmental and Behavioral Pediatrics, 34*(5), 326-334.

Van der Kolk, B., Perry, C., & Herman, J. P. (1991). Childhood origins of self-destructive behaviors. *American Journal of Psychiatry, 148*, 1665-1671.

Van Heugten, C. (2005). Apraxia. In P. Elsinger P (Ed.), *Neuropsychological interventions: Clinical research and practice* (pp 222-245). New York, NY: Guilford Press.

Vela, R. M. (2014). The effect of severe stress on early brain development, attachment, and emotions: A psycho-anatomical formulation. *Psychiatric Clinics of North America, 37*, 519-534.

Venkitaramani, D.V., & Lomborso, P.J. (2007). Molecular basis of genetic neuropsychiatric disorders. *Child and Adolescent Psychiatric Clinics of North America, 16*(3), 54-556.

Verté, S., Geurts, H. M., Roeyers, H., Oosterlaan, J., & Sergeant, J. A. (2005). Executive functioning in children with autism and Tourette syndrome. *Development and Psychopathology, 17*(2), 415-445.

Voeller, K.K.S. (1998). Nonverbal learning disabilities and motor skill disorders. *Textbook of pediatric neuropsychiatry* (pp 719-768). Washington, DC: American Psychiatric Association Press.

Vuijik, P.J., Hartman, E., Scherder, E., & Visscher, C. (2010). Motor performance of children with mild and borderline intellectual function. *Journal of Intellectual Disability Research,* 54(11), 955- 965.

Willemsen, S. H. (2002). The autistic spectrum: Subgroups, boundaries, and treatment. *Psychiatric Clinics of North America, 25,* 811-836.

Wisdom, S. N., Dyck, M. J., Piek, J. P., Hay, D., & Hallmayer, J. (2007). Can autism, language and coordination disorders be differentiated based on ability profiles? *European Child and Adolescent Psychiatry, 16*(3), 178-186.

Witwer, A. N., & Lecavalier, L. (2008). Psychopathology in children with intellectual disability. *Journal of Mental Health Research in Intellectual Disabilities, 1,* 75-96.

Woods, D. W., & Houghton, D. C. (2014). Diagnosis, evaluation and management of trichotillomia. *Psychiatric Clinics of North America, 37,* 301-318.

Zinner, S.H. (2004). Tourette's syndrome: Much more than tics. *Contemporary Pediatrics, 21*(8), 22-49.

CHAPTER 10

Schizophrenia and Other Psychotic Disorders

Angela Hassiotis
Lucy Fodor-Wynne
Mark H. Fleisher
Anne Desnoyers Hurley

Schizophrenia and psychotic disorders are a group of disorders characterized by several common symptoms: Delusions, hallucinations, disorganized thinking (speech), grossly disorganized or abnormal motor behavior, and negative symptoms (deficits of normal emotional responses or thought processes).

1) When diagnosing these disorders in people with ID, it is important to differentiate between psychotic symptoms and general symptoms of the ID.

2) Lack of insight into their symptoms and difficulties in communication can make diagnosing schizophrenia and psychotic disorders in this group difficult.

3) Negative symptoms may, in some cases, be underreported as they may not appear as salient as positive symptoms or may be confused with the symptoms of the ID.

4) With these diagnostic difficulties in mind, it is important to carry out an extensive and thorough examination, to gather information from a variety of sources, and to review cases regularly.

Review of Diagnostic Criteria

■ *Schizotypal (Personality Disorder)*

Schizotypal personality disorder is discussed in detail in *DSM-5* under "Personality Disorders" but is included in the chapter "Schizophrenia Spectrum and Psychotic Disorders" with a brief explanation that in the ICD-9 and ICD-10 it is a schizotypal disorder, part of the schizophrenia spectrum of disorders.

Schizotypal disorder is characterized by persistent detachment from social relationships and limited emotional expression. There may also be delusions, ideas of reference, misperceptions, illusions, and other symptoms of inappropriate or unusual behaviors outside of cultural norms that are impairing and generally begin in early adulthood.

■ *Delusional Disorder*

Delusional disorder is characterized by the presence of one or more delusions that continue for more than one month. There is also a lack of typical symptoms seen in schizophrenia (such as disorganized speech or catatonic behavior). Behavior is not markedly odd or bizarre, and normal functioning is not impaired. If there are mood episodes, they are brief relative to the delusions. Finally, the disturbance is not due to general medical condition, substance abuse, or another mental disorder. Specifiers include: A) the general theme of the delusion, or as a mixed type if no one theme predominates, or as an unspecified type; B) with bizarre content, if delusions are clearly beyond possible life experiences; C) as first, multiple, or continuous episodes, and whether the person is currently in an episode; D) severity.

■ *Brief Psychotic Disorder*

Symptoms of brief psychotic disorder are similar to those seen in schizophrenia (e.g., delusions, hallucinations), but with a duration of at least one day and less than one month. The disturbance is not due to other mental or medical conditions, or substance abuse. It is characterized by typical symptoms seen in schizophrenia, but with a duration of less than one month. Specifiers include: A) with marked stressors; B) without marked stressors; C) with post-partum onset; D) with features of catatonia; E) severity.

■ *Schizophreniform Disorder*

Schizophreniform disorder is characterized by the same symptoms and features as schizophrenia but with the symptoms lasting at least one month and less than six months. Also, functional impairment may not be present. Lastly, the disturbance is not due to a general medical condition or substance abuse. Specifiers include: A) with good prognostic features, e.g. onset of psychotic features within four weeks of change in the individual, absence of flat affect, good premorbid personality; b) without good prognostic features if two or more features from A) are not present; C) with catatonia; D) severity, in terms of the psychotic symptoms over a seven-day period.

■ *Schizoaffective Disorder*

Characterized by symptoms of psychosis and symptoms of a mood disorder (mania or depression) that occur simultaneously. Major mood disorder symptoms are present for the majority of the illness, and the disorder is not due to a general medical condition or substance abuse. Depressed mood. Delusions or hallucinations for two or more weeks in the absence of a major mood episode during the lifetime duration of the illness. Specifiers include: A) bipolar type; B) depressive type; C) with catatonia; D) first, multiple, or continuous episodes, and whether the person is currently in an episode; E) severity.

■ *Substance/Medication-Induced Psychotic Disorder*

Characterized by hallucinations and delusions that develop during or soon after substance intoxication or withdrawal or exposure to a medication, and the substance/medication is etiologically related to the disturbance. Also, the disturbance must not occur only within the course of delirium. Specifiers include: A) with onset during intoxication; B) with onset during withdrawal; C) severity.

■ *Psychotic Disorder Due to Another Medical Condition*

This disorder is characterized by prominent hallucinations or delusions that are the direct consequence of another medical condition and are not better explained by another mental disorder. The disturbance caused by these symptoms does not occur exclusively during the course of a delirium. Finally, the disturbance causes clinically significant distress or impairment in important areas of functioning. Specifiers include: A) with delusions; B) with hallucinations; C) severity.

■ *Catatonia*

There are 12 key symptoms of catatonia:

1) Stupor (i.e. no psychomotor activity)

2) Catalepsy (i.e., posture held against gravity)

3) Waxy flexibility (i.e., slight resistance to positioning by examiner)

4) Mutism (i.e., no response or very little verbal response)

5) Negativism (i.e., hostility or lack of response to instructions or external stimuli)

6) Posturing (i.e., sudden maintenance of posture against gravity)

7) Mannerism (i.e., caricature of normal behavior)

8) Stereotypy (i.e., repetitive movement such as rocking)

9) Agitation that has no external influence

10) Grimacing

11) Echolalia (i.e., mimicking speech)

12) Echopraxia (i.e., mimicking movements).

- *Catatonia Associated with Another Mental Disorder (Catatonia Specifier)*

Criteria for catatonia are met (three or more of the 12 symptoms) during the course of a mental disorder (e.g., a depressive disorder).

- *Catatonic Disorder Due to Another Medical Condition*

Three or more of the symptoms of catatonia. The disturbance is the direct consequence of another medical condition and is not better explained by another mental disorder. The disturbance does not occur exclusively in the course of a delirium. The disturbance causes distress or impairment in important areas of functioning.

Schizophrenia and Other Psychotic Disorders

General Description of the Disorders

Schizophrenia and other psychotic disorders are a group of disorders characterised by five main features. These include delusions, hallucinations, disorganized thinking (speech), grossly disorganized or abnormal motor behavior, and negative symptoms.

Delusions are fixed, false beliefs that will not be changed when patients are exposed to new, conflicting evidence. These beliefs can include a variety of themes and specifiers (e.g., grandiose, religious, persecutory).

Hallucinations are sensory experiences that do not have an external stimulus. Hallucinations are most commonly auditory, and prominent or exclusive hallucinations of other forms, such as tactile (formication) or olfactory, should expand the clinician's differential diagnoses.

Disorganized thinking is generally observed through disorganized speech, thought blocking, and derailment. For example, a patient might rapidly change topics when speaking and when asked a question, and his or her answer may be unrelated. This category of symptoms also includes "catatonic behavior," which is characterized by a marked decrease in reactivity to the environment -- for example, resistance to instruction, rigid posture, and a lack of verbal and motor response.

Grossly disorganized or abnormal motor behavior can manifest as unprovoked agitation, child-like behavior, and reacting inappropriately to the environment (e.g., laughing inappropriately).

Negative symptoms are more common across the subtypes of schizophrenia than in the other psychotic disorders. They are characterized by a withdrawal or lack of normal function. Two common negative symptoms are diminished emotional expression and avolition (a reduction in drive to fulfill goals and activities).

The *DSM-5* structures the diagnosis of schizophrenia and other psychotic disorders into several separate disorders. These are:

1) Schizotypal (personality disorder)
2) Delusional disorder
3) Brief psychotic disorder
4) Schizophreniform disorder
5) Schizophrenia
6) Schizoaffective disorder
7) Substance/medication-induced psychotic disorder
8) Psychotic disorder due to another medical condition
9) Other specified schizophrenia spectrum and other psychotic disorder
10) Unspecified schizophrenia spectrum and other psychotic disorder
11) Catatonia (including three subtypes):
    a) Catatonia associated with another mental disorder (catatonia specifier)
    b) Catatonic disorder due to another medical condition
    c) Unspecified catatonia

Issues Related to Diagnosis in Persons with ID

Development and Course

Individuals with a dual diagnosis of an intellectual disability and schizophrenia are significantly younger at first contact with mental health services compared with individuals with schizophrenia alone (Morgan, Leonard, Bourke & Jablensky, 2008). This study also found that individuals with a dual diagnosis are younger at first admission to mental health services. The authors suggest that this could be due to individuals with dual diagnosis suffering more severely with psychosis, but as they did not look specifically at this issue, conclusions cannot be drawn.

It is accepted that the presentation of symptoms of schizophrenia is similar in people with and without ID, though in lower levels of ability, where there is a lack of verbal communication, the ascertainment of the core symptoms of the disorder is in doubt. Even with verbal or other forms of communication, the lower the level of ability, the more difficult the diagnosis of these disorders. Bouras et al. (2004) found that people with ID and "schizophrenia spectrum psychoses" (according to the ICD-10 and the comprehensive psychopathological rating scale) display more negative symptoms and have a higher level of functional disability. They also found that people suffering from psychosis, with and without intellectual disability (ID), did not differ significantly on measures of reported psychopathology, but they did find the ID group to score higher in observable psychopathology. They suggest that due to the reduced communication skills in the ID group, symptoms might go unreported, bringing down the levels of reported psychopathology. They also suggest the people with ID might lack insight into their own symptoms, making it more difficult for them to report these symptoms. The researchers suggest that this higher level of observable psychopathology in the ID group might lead to stigmatization and possibly other symptoms such as depression and anxiety.

Pickard and Paschos (2005) discuss the difficulties in trying to distinguish true hallucinations from "pseudohallucinations" in people with ID. They define "pseudohallucinations" as hallucinations where the individual is aware that his/her experience is in his/her own mind and not caused by any external stimuli. The authors state that distinguishing hallucinations from pseudohallucinations is an important element in diagnosis. They present two case studies to illustrate that people with ID can present with symptoms similar to hallucinations but do not actually fit the description of true hallucinations seen in psychosis. The authors suggest that the observed response to the pseudohallucinations could be an important factor in distinguishing them from actual hallucinations that could indicate the presence of psychosis. They suggest that this observed response could be more important as a diagnostic tool in people with severe ID, from whom it may be more difficult to elicit a spoken account of their symptoms.

Higher levels of aggression have been found in people with ID and psychosis when compared to individuals with ID without psychosis (Tsiouris, Kim, Brown & Cohen, 2011). The same study also found that of the participants with ID and psychosis, younger age and more severe ID were associated with higher levels of physical aggression against others. However, the authors concluded that "impulse control, mood dysregulation and perceived threat appear to underlie most of the aggressive behaviors reported. Psychosis and depression appeared to have been over-diagnosed in persons with mild to moderate ID and underdiagnosed in persons with severe and profound ID. These findings replicate and extend findings from previous studies. The pattern of associations reported can be used as helpful indicators by professionals involved in the treatment of aggressive behaviors in persons with ID."

Bakken, Friis, Lovoll, Smeby, & Martinsen (2007) examined the types of psychotic symptoms seen in people with ID. They found that participants with ID and psychosis displayed behavioral disorganization, severely impaired global functioning, behavior suggesting hallucinations, and decreased sociability. The authors suggest that behavioral disorganization may be an indication of the presence of psychosis in people with ID, and this was verified by scores on the Psychopathology in Autism Checklist (PAC) and by qualitative case reports.

Prevalence

Cooper et al. (2007) conducted an epidemiological study of adults with ID in Scotland and found that the point prevalence of all psychotic disorders, including schizophrenia, varied between 2.6% and 4.4%, depending on the method of diagnosis used. The point prevalence was 3.4% (n = 1,023) when diagnosis was made based on the *DSM-IV-TR*.

Another study by Deb, Thomas, and Bright (2001) used the PAS-ADD and ICD-10 to diagnose psychosis. It found the levels of schizophrenia were significantly higher in the study cohort of people with ID than in the general population (4.4% with ID and 0.4% of the general population).

Morgan et al. (2008) used an algorithm written by the first author to translate all diagnoses into their ICD-9 equivalents. They looked at two cohorts, one aged 44-58 and one aged 38-43 at time of publication. They found that 5.2% of the older cohort with ID developed schizophrenia, and 4.5% of the younger cohort with ID developed schizophrenia. They also found that individuals with ID and a psychiatric diagnosis were significantly more likely to have borderline or mid-range IQ levels than individuals with just an ID and no psychiatric diagnosis. This group was also less likely to be severely affected by their ID. Among individuals with ID and a psychiatric disorder, the etiology of their ID was less likely to be genetic than the group with ID alone.

Differential Diagnosis

It can be difficult to diagnose psychotic illness in people with an ID due to many factors, such as communication problems and differing presentation of symptoms as well as cultural norms. This difficulty can be amplified by the fact that there are several other illnesses and disorders that can present with symptoms that overlap with those of psychosis. While many of these disorders are separate from schizophrenia spectrum disorders, it is important to be mindful of the fact that some could be involved in the development and course of psychosis. An example of this would be ASD, which is linked to psychosis through 22q11.2 deletion syndrome; 22q11.2 deletion syndrome is characterized by ID and has been linked to both childhood ASD (Antschel et al., 2007 [as cited in Raja & Azzoni, 2010]) and psychotic symptoms (Murphy, 2002 [as cited in Raja & Azzoni, 2010]). There are several differential diagnoses to psychosis that should be considered (Hassiotis & Sinai, 2009):

<table>
<tr><td colspan="2">Physical illnesses including: deliriums</td></tr>
<tr><td colspan="2">Epilepsy (particularly temporal lobe epilepsy)</td></tr>
<tr><td colspan="2">Traumatic brain injury</td></tr>
<tr><td colspan="2">Intracerebral conditions (e.g. space occupying lesion)</td></tr>
<tr><td colspan="2">Sleep disorders</td></tr>
<tr><td colspan="2">Infection (e.g. respiratory or urinary tract infection, meningitis)</td></tr>
<tr><td colspan="2">Endocrine causes (e.g. hyper/hypothyroidism)</td></tr>
<tr><td colspan="2">Hearing or visual impairment (e.g. individuals with Charles Bonnet syndrome who have a visual impairment may experience hallucinations or delusions)</td></tr>
<tr><td colspan="2">Causes of pain or distress (e.g. toothache, earache, constipation, menstrual pain)</td></tr>
<tr><td>Drug- or alcohol-related causes including:</td><td>Delirium tremens
Alcoholic hallucinations
Drug induced psychosis
Sensitivity to prescribed medication</td></tr>
<tr><td>Other psychiatric illness including:</td><td>Affective illness
Anxiety disorder
Post-traumatic stress disorder (PTSD)
Dementia (e.g. visual hallucinations in Lewy-body dementia)
Autistic spectrum disorder</td></tr>
<tr><td colspan="2">Other differential diagnosis (e.g. challenging behavior caused by ID or just ID itself may be diagnosed as a psychotic disorder)</td></tr>
</table>

Some of the issues with similarities of symptoms of psychotic disorders and pervasive developmental disorder (in particular, Asperger's syndrome) are discussed under the subheading below entitled "comorbidity."

Smith and Matson (2010) found that people with comorbid ID and ASD, who also had epilepsy, showed more impaired social skills than people who had only ID or ASD. Impaired social skills may be seen in psychotic disorders, which may lead to some confusion between these disorders.

Dementia in people with ID is more common than in the general population (Cooper, 1997; Strydom, Hassiotis, King, and Livingston, 2009). Dementia can often present with psychotic symptoms (Savva et al, 2009), and indeed there is some overlap in the symptoms of the disorders (e.g. abnormal speech), and so dementia may be confused with psychotic disorders in people in ID.

Social withdrawal and aggression in a person with ID may also be confused with symptoms of psychotic disorders (Hassiotis & Sinai, 2009).

Palucka, Bradley, and Lunsky (2008) highlight the importance of properly diagnosing ID and autism before making a diagnosis of schizophrenia. They suggest that due to a possible overlap between symptoms of autism and schizophrenia, patients may be given a diagnosis of schizophrenia when autism may better fit their symptoms.

Functional Consequences

Bouras et al. (2004) found that the ID group in their study showed serious impairments in social and occupational functioning on the Global Assessment of Functioning scale, compared with the scoring in the non-ID group (which showed some mild difficulty, but reasonably good function). The ID group was likely to have fewer or no friends and to have problems maintaining employment. The non-ID group was likely to have few friends for social support and to have ability, if strained, to maintain employment.

Another study by Friedlander and Donnelly (2004) found that participants with a diagnosis of psychosis not otherwise specified and moderate or severe ID were the most functionally impaired group in the study, based on the Global Assessment of Functioning scale and the Clinical Global Impression.

Comorbidity

Raja and Azzoni (2010) investigated autism spectrum disorder and schizophrenia and concluded that the comorbidity could be due to the shared neurobiology, but could also be due to a lack of experience in adult psychiatrists diagnosing ASD (i.e., patients who present with some psychotic symptoms as part of ASD are given a separate diagnosis of a psychotic disorder).

Kettunen, Lindberg, Tani, and Waris (2013) investigated comorbidity between schizophrenia and pervasive developmental disorder (PDD), particularly Asperger's syndrome in adolescents. They found that 44% (n = 18) of the adolescents with schizophrenia that they looked at fulfilled the diagnosis of PDD in childhood, even if they did not receive this diagnosis at the time. They conclude that while subjects with PDD rarely develop schizophrenia, schizophrenia patients often have a childhood diagnosis of PDD. They suggest there is not definitive agreement about the differentiation of the symptoms of psychotic disorders and the symptoms of PDD, and this is causing some confusion in diagnosis.

Application of Diagnostic Criteria to People with ID

General Considerations

There are several issues that should be considered when applying diagnostic criteria to people with ID:

1) Communication difficulties that might make the recognition of symptoms more challenging.

2) Difficulty in distinguishing normal symptoms of ID from diagnostic criteria of psychosis.

3) Symptoms of dementia, which has a higher prevalence among the ID population, can also overlap with diagnostic criteria for psychosis.

4) The impact of delays in the developmental trajectory, e.g., the presence of "imaginary

friends" in people with ID may be confused with hallucinations seen in psychosis.

Methodology

The electronic databases PsychINFO, Medline and Google Scholar were searched, using the following search terms: mental handicap, mental retardation, learning disability*, intellectual disability*, schizophrenia, schizophrenic illness, psychosis, psychotic disorder(s), schizophreniform illness, delusional disorder(s), diagnosis, psychopathology, mental disorder, and hallucination(s).

Adults with Mild to Moderate ID

Bradley, Lunsky, Palucka, and Homitidis (2011) explored the association between ID and psychiatric disorders, including psychosis. The authors suggest that the symptoms of ID may sometimes be overlooked during psychiatric assessments which, they argue, may lead to inaccurate diagnosis and incorrect treatment. They argue that patients are not regularly reviewed, and a patient may have a diagnosis for years when another diagnosis may better suit his or her symptoms. They suggest that medication is overused in this patient group and that more emphasis should be given to psychosocial therapies and good, quality care. Finally, there is a danger of misdiagnosing schizophrenia when a patient presents with positive symptoms that are caused by childhood trauma or abuse and not necessarily indicative of a psychotic disorder.

Finally, Hurley and Moore (1999) suggest that cases of erotomanic type delusional disorder in adults with ID may be underreported because it is assumed to be an immature fantasy that is a product of the cognitive limitations.

Adults with Severe or Profound ID

Cherry, Penn, Matson, and Bamburg (2000) looked at the presentation of schizophrenia in adults with severe ID by comparing their symptoms to symptoms that are seen in populations without ID. They concluded that negative symptoms were under-represented in people with ID, but positive symptoms showed similar presentation. However, the authors suggest that negative symptoms may have been underreported because they are not as "disturbing and salient" to staff. Furthermore, proxy reports of symptoms of mental disorders may generally be inaccurate, and further attempts to enhance individual communication is recommended (Di Marco and Iacono, 2007). Interviewing several people with a good knowledge of the individual and paying close attention to changes in the usual behavior may be helpful in identifying negative symptoms that may be less salient and more difficult to identify.

Children and Adolescents with ID

Lee, Moss, Friedlander, Donnelly, & Honer (2003) examined the development and stability of symptoms of early-onset schizophrenia (EOS) in children with ID. They found that EOS symptoms were unstable in their sample of 10 children. Similar to typical children and adolescents who develop EOS, the group did not recover well and remained symptomatic over two years with a decrease in cognitive abilities. At two-year follow-up, two patients were determined to not have schizophrenia. One patient fully recovered from her illness when it was determined that she instead suffered from hypothyroidism and Tourette's disorder.

The authors stress the importance of gathering information from a variety of sources when making a psychiatric diagnosis in children, especially those with an ID. They also stress the importance of reviewing symptoms frequently and the importance of looking for auditory hallucinations as an indicator of EOS, due to the pervasiveness of this symptom among the sample.

Summary of Limitations in Applying DSM-5 *Criteria to People with ID*

Generally, application of diagnostic criteria appropriate to peers of average intelligence has been shown to be restrictive and may lead to the underdiagnosis of serious and treatable mental disorders in children and adults with intellectual and developmental disabilities. The prevalence rates of psychotic disorders according to the *DSM-IV-TR* have been found to be lower than the prevalence according to the DC-LD, DCR-ICD-10, suggesting this version of the *DSM* is not as effective in diagnosing psychotic disorders in this patient group (Cooper et al., 2007). The variable presentation of communication and cognitive difficulties, the frequent lack of baseline assessment reports, the changes in caring environments and thus respondents, and the many comorbidities place significant diagnostic challenges on clinicians. Usually, the criteria have to be applied in consultations with qualified practitioners who are expert in the assessment and diagnosis of people with ID.

Etiology and Pathogenesis

Biological Factors

López et al. (2009) investigated the prevalence rates of schizophrenia in people with ID (according to the ICD-10). They found that, out of their sample of adults with schizophrenia, 3.4% had a previous diagnosis of ID. The diagnosis of ID was also linked to an increased risk of psychosis, residual schizophrenia, paranoid schizophrenia, and "persistent delusional ideas disorder." The authors suggest this evidence supports the hypothesis that schizophrenia may be caused by "alterations in neurodevelopment." This is suggested to be due to alterations in prenatal development that caused problems in social and cognitive development.

Genetic Factors

Evidence from genetic abnormalities has shown a connection between psychotic disorders and ASD. For example, 22q11.2 deletion syndrome is characterized by ID and is often comorbid with childhood ASD (Antschel et al., 2007 [as cited in Raja & Azzoni, 2010]) and psychotic symptoms (Murphy, 2002 [as cited in Raja & Azzoni, 2010]).

Prader-Willi syndrome, which is a genetic disorder characterized by abnormalities in the proximal region of chromosome 15q11-13, has also been associated with depressive psychosis. In particular, this affects individuals with maternal uniparental disomy (UPD) or imprinting abnormalities (IM). Psychosis, especially with depressive features, was identified at a prevalence of approximately 10% (Boer et al., 2002).

Finally, copy number variants (CNVs) might help to explain the relationship among schizophrenia, autism, and ID (Guilmatre et al., 2009). This study found that rare CNVs are involved in the causes of these three conditions, suggesting they may share biological pathways.

Psychosocial Factors

People with an ID and a psychotic disorder have been found to show more serious impairments in social and occupational functioning on the Global Assessment of Functioning scale, compared to mental health patients without an ID (Bouras et al., 2004). The authors also suggest that the symptoms of psychopathology may be more noticeable in people with ID, which may in turn lead to social stigmatization and withdrawal.

However, research is limited into possible psychosocial causes for psychotic disorders.

Schizophrenia and Other Psychotic Disorders

Schizophrenia

DSM-5 Diagnostic Criteria	Apply Criteria for Mild and Moderate ID	Applying Criteria for Severe and Profound ID
Please note: A significant change in behavior (for example, increased aggressive, self-injurious, or bizarre behavior) should alert the clinician to the possibility of a psychotic process. Assessment of this criterion might be especially difficult in individuals with severe or profound ID.		
A. Two (or more) of the following, each present for a significant portion of time during a 1-month period (or less if successfully treated). At least one of these must be (1), (2), or (3): (1) Delusions. (2) Hallucinations. (3) Disorganized speech (e.g., frequent derailment or incoherence). (4) Grossly disorganized or catatonic behavior. (5) Negative symptoms, (i.e., diminished emotional expression or avolition).	A. No adaptation.	A. No adaptation. **Note:** There may be self-talk, which is common and not necessarily interpreted as an expression of psychotic disorder.

Schizophrenia (continued)

DSM-5 Diagnostic Criteria	Apply Criteria for Mild and Moderate ID	Applying Criteria for Severe and Profound ID
B. For a significant portion of the time since the onset of the disturbance, level of functioning in one or more areas, such as work, interpersonal relations, or self-care are markedly below the level achieved prior to the onset (or when the onset is in childhood or adolescence, there is failure to achieve expected level of interpersonal, academic, or occupational functioning).	B. No adaptation.	B. No adaptation.
C. Continuous signs of the disturbance persist for at least 6 months. This 6-month period must include at least 1 month of symptoms (or less if successfully treated) that meet Criterion A (i.e., active-phase symptoms) and may include periods of prodromal or residual symptoms. During these prodromal or residual periods, the signs of the disturbance may be manifested by only negative symptoms or two or more symptoms listed in Criterion A present in an attenuated form (e.g., odd beliefs, unusual perceptual experiences).	C. No adaptation.	C. No adaptation.
D. Schizoaffective disorder and depressive or bipolar disorder with psychotic features have been ruled out because either (1) no major depressive or manic episodes have occurred concurrently with the active-phase symptoms, or (2) if mood episodes have occurred during active-phase symptoms, they have been present for a minority of the total duration of the active and residual periods of the illness.	D. No adaptation.	D. No adaptation.
E. The disturbance is not attributable to the physiological effects of a substance (e.g., a drug of abuse, a medication) or another medical condition.	E. No adaptation.	E. No adaptation.
F. If there is a history of autistic spectrum disorder or a communication disorder of childhood-onset, the additional diagnosis of schizophrenia is made only if prominent delusions or hallucinations, in addition to the other required symptoms of schizophrenia, are also present for at least 1 month (or less if successfully treated).	F. No adaptation.	F. No adaptation.
Specify if The following course specifiers are only to be used after a 1-year duration of the disorder and if they are not in contradiction to the diagnostic course criteria. First episode, currently in acute episode: First manifestation of the disorder meeting the defining diagnostic symptom and time criteria. An acute episode is a time period in which the symptom criteria are fulfilled. First episode, currently in partial remission: Partial remission is a period of time during which an improvement after a previous episode is maintained and in which the defining criteria of the disorder are only partially fulfilled. First episode, currently in full remission: Full remission is a period of time after a previous episode during which no disorder-specific symptoms are present. Multiple episodes, currently in acute episode: Multiple episodes may be determined after a minimum of two episodes (i.e., after a first episode, a remission and a minimum of one relapse). Multiple episodes, currently in partial remission Multiple episodes, currently in full remission Continuous: Symptoms fulfilling the diagnostic symptom criteria of the disorder are remaining for the majority of the illness course, with subthreshold symptom periods being very brief relative to the overall course. Unspecified Specify if: With catatonia Specify current severity: Severity is rated by a quantitative assessment of the primary symptoms of psychosis, including delusions, hallucinations, disorganized speech, abnormal psychomotor behavior, and negative symptoms. Each of these symptoms may be rated for its current severity (most severe in the last 7 days) on a 5-point scale ranging from 0 (not present) to 4 (present and severe). Note: Diagnosis of schizophrenia can be made without using this severity specifier.		

Schizophreniform Disorder

The criteria and adaptations for schizophreniform disorder are identical to those for schizophrenia, with the exception that criteria B on social/occupational dysfunction is not required; and that the duration criteria is for at least 1 month but less than 6 months. When the diagnosis is made without waiting for recovery, it should be qualified as "provisional."

Schizoaffective Disorder

DSM-5 Diagnostic Criteria	Applying Criteria for Mild and Moderate ID	Applying Criteria for Severe and Profound ID
A. An uninterrupted period of illness during which there is a major mood episode (major depressive or manic) concurrent with Criterion A of Schizophrenia. Note: The Major Depressive Episode must include Criterion A1.	A. No adaptation.	A. No adaptation. Please see introductory note at the top of the table.
B. Delusions or hallucinations for 2 or more weeks in the absence of a major mood episode (depressive or manic) during the lifetime duration of the illness.	B. No adaptation.	B. No adaptation. Please see introductory note at the top of the table.
C. Symptoms that meet criteria for a major mood episode are present for the majority of the total duration of the active and residual portions of the illness.	C. No adaptation.	C. No adaptation. Please see introductory note at the top of the table.
D. The disturbance is not attributable to the effects of a substance or another medical condition.	D. No adaptation.	D. No adaptation. Please see introductory note at the top of the table.
Specify whether: Bipolar type: This subtype applies if a manic episode is part of the presentation. Major depressive episodes may also occur. Depressive type: This subtype applies if only major depressive episodes are part of the presentation. Specify if: With catatonia Specify if: The following course specifiers are only to be used after a 1-year duration of the disorder and if they are not in contradiction to the diagnostic course criteria. First episode, currently in acute episode: First manifestation of the disorder meeting the defining diagnostic symptom and time criteria. An acute episode is a time period in which the symptom criteria are fulfilled. First episode, currently in partial remission: Partial remission is a period of time during which an improvement after a previous episode is maintained and in which the defining criteria of the disorder are only partially fulfilled.		

Schizoaffective Disorder (continued)

DSM-5 Diagnostic Criteria	Applying Criteria for Mild and Moderate ID	Applying Criteria for Severe and Profound ID
First episode, currently in full remission: Full remission is a period of time after a previous episode during which no disorder-specific symptoms are present. Multiple episodes, currently in acute episode: Multiple episodes may be determined after a minimum of two episodes (i.e., after a first episode, a remission and a minimum of one relapse). Multiple episodes, currently in partial remission Multiple episodes, currently in full remission Continuous: Symptoms fulfilling the diagnostic symptom criteria of the disorder are remaining for the majority of the illness course, with subthreshold symptom periods being very brief relative to the overall course. Unspecified Specify current severity: Severity is rated by a quatitative assessment of the primary symptoms of psychosis, including delusions, hallucinations, disorganized speech, abnormal psychomotor behavior, and negative symptoms. Each of these symptoms may be rated for its current severity (most severe in the last 7 days) on a 5-point scale ranging form 0 (not present) to 4 (present and severe). Note: Diagnosis of schizoaffective disorder can be made without using this severity specifier.		

Delusional Disorder

DSM-5 Criteria for Delusional Disorder	Applying Criteria for Mild and Moderate ID	Applying Criteria for Severe and Profound ID
A. The presence of one (or more) delusions with a duration of 1 month or longer.	A. No adaptation.	A. Does not apply.
B. Criterion A for schizophrenia has never been met. Note: Hallucinations, if present, are not prominent and are related to the delusional theme (e.g., the sensation of being infested with insects associated with delusions of infestation).	B. No adaptation.	B. Does not apply.
C. Apart from the impact of the delusion(s) or its ramifications, functioning is not markedly impaired and behavior is not obviously odd or bizarre.	C. No adaptation.	C. Does not apply.
D. If manic or major depressive episodes have occurred, these have been brief relative to the duration of the delusional periods.	D. No adaptation.	D. Does not apply.
E. The disturbance is not attributable to the physiological effects of a substance or another medical condition and is not better explained by another mental disorder, such as body dysmorphic disorder or obsessive-compulsive disorder.	E. No adaptation.	E. Does not apply.

Brief Psychotic Disorder

The criteria and adaptations are similar to those for schizophrenia, with the exceptions that just one of the first four symptoms listed in criteria A needs to be present; criteria B on social/occupational dysfunction is not required; and the duration criteria is for at least 1 day but less than 1 month, with eventual full return to premorbid level of functioning.

Psychotic Disorder Due to Another Medical Condition

The criteria are the same as for other mental disorders due to another medical condition, without adaptation, with the additional need for prominent hallucinations or delusions.

Substance/Medication-Induced Psychotic Disorder

The criteria are the same as for other substance/medication-induced mental disorders, without adaptation, with the additional need for presence of one or both of delusions or hallucinations.

Catatonia Associated with Another Medical Disorder (Catatonia Specifier)

DSM-5 Diagnostic Criteria	Applying Criteria for Mild and Moderate ID	Applying Criteria for Severe and Profound ID
A. The clinical picture is dominated by three (or more) of the following symptoms: 1. Stupor (i.e., no psychomotor activity; not actively relating to environment). 2. Catalepsy (i.e., passive induction of a posture held against gravity). 3. Waxy flexibility (i.e., slight, even resistance to positioning by examiner). 4. Mutism (i.e., no, or very little, verbal response [(exclude if known aphasia]). 5. Negativism (i.e., opposition or no response to instructions or external stimuli). Posturing (i.e., spontaneous and active maintenance of a posture against gravity). Mannerism (i.e. odd, circumstantial caricature of normal actions). Stereotypy (i.e., repetititve, abnormally frequent, non-goal-directed movements). Agitation, not influenced by external stimuli. Grimacing. Echolalia (i.e., mimicking another's speech). Echopraxia (i.e., mimicking another's movements). Coding note: Indicate the name of the associated mental disorder when recording the name of the condition (cataonia associated with major depressive disorder). Code first the associated mental disorder (e.g., neurodevelopmental disorder, brief psychotic disorder, schizophreniform disorder, schizophrenia, schizoaffective disorder, bipolar disorder, major depressive disorder, or other mental disorder).	A. No adaptation	**Note:** Mutism, mannerisms, stereotypies, and grimacing can be features of ID, and echolalia can be a feature of autism spectrum disorder. A history of time of onset of these symptoms may helpfully differentiate.

Catatonia Disorder Due to Another Medical Condition

The criteria are the same as for other mental disorders due to another medical condition, without adaptation, with the additional need to meet the criterion A symptoms as listed in catatonia associated with another medical disorder (catatonia specifier).

Other Specified Schizophrenia Spectrum and Other Psychotic Disorder

Unspecified Schizophrenia Spectrum and Other Psychotic Disorder

DSM-5 also provides categories for other specified schizophrenia spectrum and other psychotic disorder and for unspecified schizophrenia spectrum and other psychotic disorder.

References

American Psychiatric Association. (2013). *Diagnostic and statistical manual of mental disorders (5th Ed.)*. Arlington, VA: American Psychiatric Publishing.

Antshel, K. M, Aneja, A., Strunge, L., Peebles, J., Fremont, W. P., Stallone, K., … Kates, W. R. (2007). Autistic spectrum disorders in velocardio facial syndrome (22q11.2 deletion). *Journal of Autism and Developmental Disorders, 37,* 1776-1786. doi: 10.1007/s10803-006-0308-6

Bakken, T. L., Friis, S., Lovoll, S., Smeby, N. A., & Martinsen, H. (2007). Behavioral disorganization as an indicator of psychosis in adults with intellectual disability and autism. *Mental Health Aspects of Developmental Disabilities, 10,* 37-46.

Boer, H., Holland, A., Whittington, J., Butler, J., Webb, T., & Clarke, D. (2002). Psychotic illness in people with Prader-Willi syndrome due to chromosome 15 maternal uniparental disomy. *Lancet*, 12, 135-6.

Bouras, N., Martin, G., Leese, M., Vanstraelen, M., Holt, G., Thomas, C., … Boardman, J. (2004). Schizophrenia-spectrum psychoses in people with and without intellectual disability. *Journal of Intellectual Disability Research, 48,* 548-555. doi: 10.1111/j.1365-2788.2004.00623.x

Bradley, E., Lunsky, Y., Palucka, A., & Homitidis, S. (2011). Recognition of intellectual disabilities and autism in psychiatric inpatients diagnosed with schizophrenia and other psychotic disorders. *Advances in Mental Health and Intellectual Disabilities, 5,* 4-18. doi: 10.1108/20441281111187153

Cherry, K. E., Penn, D., Matson, J. L., & Bamburg, J. W. (2000). Characteristics of schizophrenia among persons with severe or profound mental retardation. *Psychiatric Services, 51,* 922-924. doi: 10.1176/appi.ps.51.7.922

Cooper, S.A. (1997). High prevalence of dementia amongst people with learning disabilities not attributed to Down's syndrome. *Psychological Medicine*, 27, 609-616. doi: 10.1017/S0033291796004655

Cooper, S., Smiley, E., Morrison, J., Allan, L., Williamson, A., Finlayson, J., … Mantry, D. (2007). Psychosis and adults with intellectual disabilities. *Social Psychiatry and Psychiatric Epidemiology, 42,* 530-536. doi: 10.1007/s00127-007-0197-9

Deb, S., Thomas, M., & Bright, C. (2001). Mental disorder in adults with intellectual disability: Prevalence of functional psychiatric illness among a community-based population aged between 16 and 64 years. *Journal of Intellectual Disability Research, 45,* 495-505. doi: 10.1046/j.1365-2788.2001.00374.x

Di Marco, M., & Iacono, T. (2007). Mental health assessment and intervention for people with complex communication needs associated with developmental disabilities. *Journal of Policy and Practice in Intellectual Disabilities*, 4, 40–59.

Friedlander, R. I., & Donnelly, T. (2004). Early-onset psychosis in youth with intellectual disability. *Journal of Intellectual Disability Research, 48,* 540-547. doi: 10.1111/j.1365-2788.2004.00622.x

Guilmarte, A., Dubourg, C., Mosca, A., Legallic, S., Goldenberg, A., Drouin-Garraud, V., … Champion, D. (2009). Recurrent rearrangements in synaptic and neurodevelopmental genes and shared biologic pathways in schizophrenia, autism, and mental retardation. *Archives of General Psychiatry, 66*, 947-956. doi:10.1001/archgenpsychiatry.2009.80

Hassiotis, A., & Sinai, A. (2009). Psychotic illness. In A. Hassiotis, D. A. Barron & I. Hall (Eds.), *Intellectual disability psychiatry: A practical handbook* (pp. 67-84). Chichester, England: John Wiley & Sons, Inc.

Hurley, A. D. & Moore, C. (1999). A review of erotomania in developmental disabilities and new case report. *Mental Health Aspects of Developmental Disabilities, 2*, 12-22.

Kettunen, K., Lindberg, N., Tani, P., Waris, P. (2013). The relationship between Asperger's syndrome and schizophrenia in adolescence. *European Child and Adolescent Psychiatry, 22*, 217-223. doi: 10.1007/s00787-012-0338-x

Lee, P., Moss, S., Friedlander, R., Donnelly, T., Honer, W. (2003). Early-onset schizophrenia in children with mental retardation: Diagnostic reliability and stability of clinical features. *Journal of the American Academy of Child & Adolescent Psychiatry, 42*, 162–169. doi: 10.1097/00004583-200302000-00009

López, M. N., Domínguez, A. C., Quintero, J., Rodríguez, M. M., del Moral, F., Arriero, M. A. J., … García, E. B. (2009). Mental retardation as a risk factor to develop a psychotic disorder. *Actas Españolas de Psiquiatría, 37*, 21-26.

Morgan, V. A., Leonard, H., Bourke, J., & Jablensky, A. (2008). Intellectual disability co-occurring with schizophrenia and other psychiatric illness: Population-based study. *The British Journal of Psychiatry, 193*, 364-372. doi: 10.1192/bjp.bp.107.044461

Murphy, K. C. (2002). Schizophrenia and velo-cardio-facial syndrome. *The Lancet, 359*, 426-430. doi: 10.1016/S0140-6736(02)07604-3

Palucka, A. M., Bradley, E., & Lunsky, Y. (2008). A case of unrecognized intellectual disability and autism misdiagnosed as schizophrenia: Are there lessons to be learned? *Mental Health Aspects of Developmental Disabilities, 11*, 55-60.

Pickard, M. & Paschos, D. (2005). Pseudohallucinations in people with intellectual disabilities: Two case reports. *Mental Health Aspects of Developmental Disabilities, 8*, 1-3.

Raja, M., & Azzoni, A. (2010). Autistic spectrum disorders and schizophrenia in the adult psychiatric setting: Diagnosis and comorbidity. *Psychiatria Danubina, 22*, 514-521.

Savva, G. M., Zaccai, J., Matthews, F. E., Davidson, J. E., McKeith, I., Brayne, C. (2009). Prevalence, correlates and course of behavioural and psychological symptoms of dementia in the population. *The British Journal of Psychiatry, 194*, 212-219. doi: 10.1192/Bjp.Bp.108.049619

Smith, K. R. M., & Matson, J. L. (2010). Behavior problems: Differences among intellectually disabled adults with co-morbid autism spectrum disorders and epilepsy. *Research in Developmental Disabilities, 31*, 1062-1069. doi: 10.1016/j.ridd.2010.04.003

Strydom, A., Hassiotis, A., King, M., & Livingston, G. (2009). The relationship of dementia prevalence in older adults with intellectual disability (ID) to age and severity of ID. *Psychological Medicine, 39*, 13-21. doi:10.1017/S0033291708003334

Tsiouris, J. A., Kim, S. Y., Brown, W. T., & Cohen, I. L. (2011). Association of aggressive behaviours with psychiatric disorder, age, sex and degree of intellectual disability: A large-scale survey. *Journal of Intellectual Research*, 55 (7), 636-649. doi: 10.1111/j.1365-2788.2011.01418.x

CHAPTER 11

Bipolar and Related Disorders

Robert J. Pary
Lauren R.Charlot
Sherm Fox
Jessica A. Hellings
Anne Desnoyers Hurley

DSM-5 separates bipolar and related disorders from depressive disorders. In DM-ID-2, bipolar and related disorders cover bipolar I disorder, bipolar II disorder, cyclothymic disorder, substance/medication-induced bipolar and related disorder, bipolar and related disorders due to another medical condition, other specified bipolar and related disorders, and unspecified bipolar and related disorders. DSM-5 has three modifications pertinent to the Bipolar and Related Disorders chapter.

1) Criterion A is revised to include increased energy/activity as a core symptom;
2) A person who concurrently demonstrates the full criteria for mania and depression is now diagnosed with bipolar disorder I, and the new specifier "with mixed features" instead of bipolar disorder I, mixed episode as in *DSM-IV.*
3) The third pertinent change is the introduction of the diagnostic category of disruptive mood dysregulation disorder within the depressive disorders chapter. This new diagnosis is for individuals with onset as children or adolescents who have severe, non-episodic irritability that is developmentally inappropriate. In *DSM-IV,* these persons were often diagnosed with pediatric mania.

Bipolar and Related Disorders

Review of Diagnostic Criteria

Bipolar I disorder is characterized by distinct periods of excessive elevated or irritable mood preceded or followed by sad periods that meet criteria for major depressive episode. Sleep, energy, appetite, and pursuit or lack of pursuit of pleasurable activities may all be affected.

Bipolar II disorder may be diagnosed when one or more major depressive episodes occur with distinct hypomanic periods of excessive elevated or irritable mood. A hypomanic episode is less severe than a manic one, but has similar features.

Cyclothymic disorder is a less severe mood disorder than bipolar I or II disorder, but has many similar features. There must be at least two years (one year in children or adolescents) during which the person experiences repeated periods of depressive and distinct episodes of excessive elevated or irritable mood. None of these distinct periods of mood alteration meet full criteria for a hypomanic or major depressive episode.

In **bipolar and related disorders due to another medical condition**, a medical condition or direct physiologic process causes the mood disturbance.

In **substance/medication-induced bipolar and related disorder**, the direct physiologic effects of a drug of abuse, a medication, another somatic treatment of mood disorder, or toxin exposure causes the mood disturbance.

Unspecified bipolar and related disorder is a category reserved for those instances when there are features of a bipolar disorder causing clinically significant distress and/or impairment in functioning. The symptoms, however, do not meet *full* criteria for any *specific bipolar or related disorder diagnostic group.*

Summary of DSM-5 *Criteria*

■ *Bipolar I Disorder*

In bipolar I disorder, the mood is abnormally elevated, expansive, or irritable, and energy and/or activity is increased for a minimum of one week, or any duration if hospitalization is required. Three or more additional symptoms from the following list must be present at the same time: Grandiosity, decreased need for sleep, pressured speech, flight of ideas, distractibility, increased goal-directed behaviors or psychomotor agitation, and excessive engagement in potentially harmful activities. If mood is only irritable, there must be four additional symptoms.

■ *Bipolar II Disorder*

Bipolar II disorder may be diagnosed when one or more major depressive episodes occur with a minimum of one hypomanic episode. A hypomanic episode is less severe than a manic episode, but has similar features.

■ *Cyclothymic Disorder*

Cyclothymic disorder is a less severe mood disorder than bipolar I disorder, but has many similar features. There must be at least two years during which the person experiences repeated periods of hypomania (which do not meet full criteria for a manic episode) and multiple episodes during which symptoms of depression are evident (which do not meet the full criteria for a major depressive episode).

■ *Bipolar and Related Disorders due to Another Medical Condition*

In bipolar and related disorders due to another medical condition, the mood disturbance is determined to be the direct result of a general medical condition or other physiologic process. It can be difficult at times to differentiate mood symptoms from symptoms caused directly by the associated medical condition, such as when a person with cancer appears to become depressed and has weight loss, fatigue, and difficulty sleeping. The diagnosis should not be used when mood symptoms arise and are evident only in the setting of a delirium, but is an appropriate classification for mood disturbances secondary to dementia.

■ *Substance/Medication-Induced Bipolar and Related Disorder*

A substance/medication-induced bipolar and related disorder is characterized by mood disturbance that is prominent and persistent in nature and is attributed to the direct physiologic effects of use of a drug of abuse, a medication, another somatic treatment of mood disorder, or toxin exposure.

■ *Unspecified Bipolar and Related Disorder*

Unspecified bipolar and related disorder is diagnosed when there are features of a bipolar disorder but criteria for manic, hypomanic, or major depressive episode are not met. There may be a rapid alternation between manic and depressive symptoms. This category may be used when there are recurrent hypomanic episodes, but not any depressive periods, or when a manic episode is superimposed on a psychotic disorder. Clinicians also may use this category when there are symptoms of a bipolar disorder but it is not possible to determine whether the disorder is primary or due to other chemical or medical causes.

Issues Related to Diagnosis in Persons with ID

Development and Course

It has been only in the past three decades that clinicians generally accepted the notion that a person with ID might be able to experience a mood disorder such as a bipolar disorder (Sovner & Hurley, 1983). Sovner and Hurley (1982a, 1982b) first proposed special "symptom criteria" for people with ID and mood disorders that stressed effects of developmental and cognitive disability on clinical features. Lowry &

Sovner (1992) further articulated behavioral symptoms – specific examples and descriptions of what each *DSM* symptom criteria of bipolar disorder might look like in a person with ID. These elaborations of the variations in clinical manifestations of bipolar features in people with ID form the core adaptations to *DSM-5* recommended in this chapter.

A critical goal is to improve the accuracy with which mood disorder diagnoses are made in people with ID. In pursuit of this goal, the following points are emphasized:

1) Bipolar disorders may be missed in people with ID due to differences in phenomenology. *Looking* for these differences may greatly enhance the accuracy of diagnosis in the population.

2) Developmental effects may account for many of these variations in the clinical picture, as bipolar disorders in people with ID often contain features more common in young children.

3) Most subjects in the studies reviewed in this chapter have mild ID (individuals who can be more easily assessed). Even so, *DSM-5* criteria were usually altered in these studies, often without an empirical basis.

4) Although behavioral descriptions of what people with ID might display or say can be useful, it is recommended that symptom substitutes be avoided in most cases. Aggression and other externalizing behaviors that occur in relation to bipolar disorders likely act as a "final common pathway" for underlying distress in people with ID and do not appear to be "diagnostically specific." In the case of bipolar disorders, aggression is often a behavioral manifestation of irritable mood.

5) A critical goal presently is to ensure reliability in assessment at the symptom level rather than developing new sets of criteria. The use of clear, behaviorally based descriptions of possible manifestations of each *DSM-5* symptom criterion is likely to help meet this goal.

6) Few studies of bipolar disorder in intellectual disabilities pertain to children and adolescents as subjects. Diagnosis using *DSM-5* is still based on criteria derived from adult studies in individuals without disabilities. It is critical, in order to make a reliable bipolar disorder diagnosis in youth with ID, to discern a clear time of change from previous functioning that is not merely a worsening of or fluctuation in a condition present since early childhood (American Psychiatric Association, 2013).

7) Disruptive mood dysregulation disorder has been identified as a new syndrome to capture youth who have a specific pattern of symptoms and problems that may initially appear as an "atypical" early onset bipolar disorder (American Psychiatric Association, 2013). Concerns arose that early onset bipolar disorder was being diagnosed at very high rates and that in many cases, the youth were not experiencing the same syndrome long known and well described in older adolescents and adults. Little is known as to the validity of disruptive mood dysregulation disorder as a separate and distinct syndrome in youth, and there are no specific recommended treatments as yet.

Prevalence

Although people with all levels of ID have been described with *DSM-5* bipolar disorder symptom criteria, from a systematic prospective, well controlled studies using reliable means of assessing the presence of the full *DSM-5* criteria for these disorders have not been conducted in representative samples of people with ID. People with ID have been described with symptoms of bipolar I disorder, but most related disorders have rarely been studied (e.g., bipolar II disorder or cyclothymic disorder).

Differential Diagnosis

Not everyone with bipolar-like symptoms has a bipolar disorder. This section will discuss the differential diagnoses of bipolar disorder, beginning with a new *DSM-5* category, then discussing medical disorders that are associated with bipolar symptoms. This section concludes by discussing the potential overdiagnosis of bipolar disorder.

DSM-5 introduces a new diagnostic category among depressive disorders called disruptive mood dysregulation disorder. This disorder is characterized by chronic, severe, persistent irritability that must be developmentally inappropriate. The diagnosis should not be made before age 6 years or after age 18 years.

The concept of manic symptoms being provoked by medical disorders was first developed in 1978 by Krauthammer and Klerman, who called it "secondary mania" (Krauthammer & Klerman, 1978). Over the years, a variety of medical conditions have been described as causes of manic symptoms in people who do not have ID. *DSM-IV-TR* listed these in some detail, including degenerative neurological conditions, cerebrovascular disease, metabolic conditions, endocrine conditions, autoimmune conditions, viral or other infections, and certain cancers. (American Psychiatric Association, 2013, p. 403). The authors of *DSM-5* opted not to include a concrete list, rather stating that the "listing of medical conditions that are said to be able to induce mania is never complete, and the clinician's best judgment is the essence of this diagnosis." (American Psychiatric Association, 2013, p. 146).

Incidents of some of these medical disorders causing manic symptoms in persons with ID have been described in the literature, including polycystic ovary disease (Ghaziuddin, 1989) and cluster and migraine headaches (Pary & Khan, 2002). In general, any of the medical conditions that can cause a manic syndrome in people who do not have ID can cause a similar clinical picture in persons with ID.

In addition to those medical conditions that can cause classical manic symptoms, there are multiple conditions that can cause cycles of maladaptive behavior and thus be confused with bipolar disorder in the people who have ID. Pary, Levitas, and Hurley (1999) described this issue. They listed various cyclic medical conditions, such as hay fever and inflammatory bowel diseases. In addition to these conditions, they described environmental and psychosocial causes for cyclic behavioral deterioration. They discussed the issue of evident spikes in behavioral issues being secondary to differences in recording target behaviors when relief staff worked, when there was frequent staff turnover, and when a new data system was recorded. They also described survey times as a potential cause of a dramatic escalation in target behaviors, and how this episodic flare in behaviors could be misinterpreted as bipolar disorder. In addition, they included various psychosocial stressors as potential causes of behavioral spikes misinterpreted as bipolar disorder, including having an episodically sick parent, anniversary reactions, and having a bipolar housemate. Depending on the symptomatic picture, perhaps these behavioral flares are best classified as adjustment disorders with disturbance of conduct or with mixed disturbance of emotions and conduct.

Potential Overdiagnosis of Bipolar Disorder

In recent investigations, there has been a 40-fold increase in the number of young people diagnosed and treated for bipolar disorder in the span of a decade (Blader & Carlson, 2007; Moreno et al., 2007), and "a high rate of misdiagnosis at initial presentation" (Reimherr & McClellan, 2004). The large increase in the rates of bipolar disorder reported in youth appeared to be associated with a loosening of existing criteria, but also was spurred by research suggesting that the Child Behavior Checklist-Lifetime version (CBCL) (Achenbach, 1991) showed a pattern of sub-items/scales that was characteristic of youth with bipolar disorder. The modification put forth was to forgo the usual requirement of an episodic course, and to emphasize that these youth are highly irritable (rather than grandiose), restless, inattentive, and most critically, explosively aggressive. Though the pattern was seen often in youth proposed as having bipolar disorder, other investigators eventually demonstrated that it was not specific to bipolar disorder, and was often seen in youth who met criteria for other syndromes.

Doerfler, Connor, and Toscano (2011) demonstrated that use of the CBCL pediatric bipolar disorder profile did not identify youth with a clinical diagnosis of bipolar disorder and cautioned against reliance on a checklist approach. The CBCL profile differentiates youngsters with bipolar disorder from youngsters with ADHD or other diagnoses in the aggregate, but the profile is ill-suited to identify individual youngsters with bipolar disorder (Diler et al., 2009).

Further, longitudinal studies subsequently demonstrated that youth with nonepisodic irritability do not progress to meet criteria for bipolar disorder. Rather, they appear to be at greatest risk of having a unipolar depressive disorder and anxiety disorders (Leibenluft, 2011). These patterns and related concerns, about accurate identification of psychiatric syndromes in youth who are chronically irritable with high rates of externalizing behaviors, parallel much of the research regarding the association of aggressive behavior (and irritability) in people with ID (Hollander et al., 2010). Absent research that systematically examines these differential diagnostic questions in people with ID, lessons may be learned from the child psychiatric studies on the subject. Some experts have argued strenuously that overdiagnosing or prematurely starting pharmacological treatment for bipolar disorder is neither simple nor without potential for substantial risks (Yutzy, Woofter, Abbott, Melhem, & Parrish, 2012). Strikingly, a similar worry has dominated recent reports regarding people with ID and autism spectrum disorder, often described as some of the "most medicated people" in our society (Wieland, Van Vliet, & Zitman, 2012).

Comorbidity

There is interest in determining whether certain groups of persons with intellectual disability, such as those with autistic spectrum disorder, have an increased risk for also having bipolar disorder. It is premature, however, to conclude whether or not persons with autism spectrum disorder are at greater risk. In a study of over 4,000 children with autism spectrum disorders, whose data were voluntarily submitted by families to an online United States-based research database, about 5% also had diagnoses of bipolar disorder (Rosenberg, Kaufmann, Law, & Law, 2011). In the Rosenberg et al. study, 1,170 individuals were identified as having intellectual disability, and in the remaining 3,156, presence or absence of intellectual disability was not reported. Also in the Rosenberg et al. study, the female gender was moderately protective for bipolar disorder.

No instruments exist, however, that are designed to evaluate for psychiatric comorbidities in persons with autism spectrum disorder (Mazzone, Ruta, & Reale, 2012). For example, Mazzone's group notes that a person with autism could display bursts of laughter or overactivity due to social awkwardness or impairments in social understanding, and this could be mistaken for signs of bipolar disorder.

Application of Diagnostic Criteria to People With ID

General Considerations

Symptoms of mania (i.e., inflated self-esteem or "grandiosity") may be affected by a developmental stage in ways similar to the symptoms of depression. When these symptoms are described in people with ID, content may be simplified. For example, Pary, Friedlander, and Capone (1999) described a patient who contacted car dealerships although he had no driver's license and phoned a printer to make wedding invitations although he wasn't dating.

Pressured speech may appear as increased vocalization (rate or volume) or gesturing in individuals who have limited expressive language (Pary, Levitas, & Hurley, 1999). An individual with severe ID and bipolar I disorder who was nonverbal was observed to be completely silent during depressive episodes while vocalizing almost continuously during manic periods. Denayer et al. (2012) noted that in four individuals who usually did not talk, increased babbling occurred during their manic episodes. Distractibility may manifest as changes in ability level, such as improper completion of activities of daily living or skipping from one activity to another (Pary, Freidlander, & Capone, 1999). Occasionally, one behavior can capture several manic criteria. Pary, Freidlander, and Capone (1999) described an adult with Down syndrome and mania who had such vigorous masturbation lasting most of the night that he knocked his mattress off his bed.

Review of Research Applying to People with ID

■ *Bipolar I Disorder*

Early papers on bipolar disorder in people with ID were reviewed by Sovner and Hurley (1983) and Sovner and Pary (1993). Most investigations involved small case series and single case reports of people with ID and mania. In their reviews of previously published cases in which symptoms were clearly defined, most individuals were found to meet *DSM* criteria for a manic episode. These individuals were described as presenting with characteristic mood changes (expansive mood or irritability) seen with three or four additional symptoms of a manic episode. Some variations on the typical clinical picture were noted such as the presence of aggression. Steingard and Biederman (1987), for example, described two children with pervasive development disorder diagnoses who presented with the sudden onset of dysphoric mood, sleep problems, and overactivity that co-occurred for periods of weeks. Both children also showed a high rate of aggression or self-injury during the active phase of their illness. The authors stressed the fact that their non-verbal patients could not meet *DSM* criteria, such as pressured speech or flight of ideas, but that both had family histories of manic-depressive illness, a clearly episodic course, and a total of four bipolar I disorder symptoms. The two children described by Steingard and Biederman (1987) responded to combined lithium–antipsychotic treatment.

In more recent reports, abnormal mood states seen in individuals diagnosed with bipolar disorder were correlated with aggressive behavior. In a retrospective record review of a large clinic sample of persons with ID, those diagnosed with bipolar disorder had significantly more acute anger episodes than those diagnosed with depression or anxiety (Hurley, 2008). Lowry and Sovner (1992) described two adults with severe/profound ID who both presented with symptoms of depression alternating with mania, with self-injurious behavior or assaultive behavior appearing as state-dependent features. *DSM-III-R* symptoms of depression and mania were operationally defined in measurable terms, and were carefully tracked (American Psychiatric Association, 1987). Some of the ways in which manic and depressive symptoms might be manifested by individuals with severe ID were elaborated in this article and in other reports by Sovner and Hurley (1982a, 1982b), Lowry (1997), Matson and Simraldo (1997), Levitas and Hurley (1999), Pary, Friedland and Capone (1999), and Lowry and Sovner (1990). These descriptions of possible observable manifestations of the *DSM* symptom criteria are used in the present chapter (see tables below).

Investigations describing the clinical features of mania in individuals with ID suggest that irritable mood, labile affect, overactivity, and decreased sleep are core features. Though expansive or elated mood have also been described, these symptoms were noted in fewer cases. Affective lability or "mood swings" have actually been described as features of both mania and depression in individuals with ID (Charlot, Doucette, & Mezzecappa, 1993; Tsiouris, Mann, Patti, & Sturmey, 2003). Other differences in the phenomenology of bipolar disorder have been documented. In the Charlot et al. (1993) study, rates of *DSM* symptoms of mania were reported for 14 individuals, most of whom had severe/profound ID. Irritable mood was prominent in both depression and mania but also in other psychiatric disorders among a matched comparison group. Cognitive symptoms were seen much less often in individuals with severe/profound ID. Cognitive symptoms of mania (i.e., inflated self-esteem or "grandiosity") may be affected by developmental stage in ways similar to the cognitive symptoms of depression. When these symptoms are described in people with ID, content may be simplified. For example, Pary et al. (1999) described a patient who contacted car dealerships although he had no driver's license and phoned a printer to make wedding invitations although he wasn't dating.

Pressured speech may appear as increased vocalization (rate or volume) or gesturing in individuals who have limited expressive language (Pary, Levitas, & Hurley (1999). An individual with severe ID and bipolar I disorder who was nonverbal was observed to be completely silent during depressive episodes while vocalizing almost continuously during manic periods. Distractibility may manifest as changes in ability level, such as improper completion of activities of daily living or skipping from one activity to another (Pary, Levitas, & Hurley, 1999).

Cain et al. (2003) examined the presence of *DSM-IV* criteria for bipolar I disorder in a carefully designed retrospective chart review of 166 individuals served at a specialty clinic treating adults with ID and psychiatric disorder. A total of 69 subjects were "clinically diagnosed" with a bipolar disorder. Over 50% of the subjects had a diagnosis of severe/profound ID. Raters were blind to the diagnosis. Rates of symptoms reported in individuals identified as having a bipolar I disorder were compared with those reported for people diagnosed with major depressive disorder with or without psychotic features, schizophrenia, or psychotic disorder NOS. The authors were able to differentiate between these groups, suggesting that the syndrome of bipolar I disorder can be clearly characterized in people with ID. Of note again are several of the findings. First, people with bipolar I disorder had higher rates of some symptoms of thought disorder (even when compared with people with a primary diagnosis of psychosis), including misinterpretation and obsessive fixations. Overall, the subjects with bipolar I disorder were more functionally impaired than peers with other diagnoses. Aggression, self-injurious behavior and other disruptive behaviors, and irritable mood were reported at higher rates for the subjects with bipolar disorder. About one-half of the group clinically diagnosed with bipolar I disorder did not meet *DSM-IV* criteria because of a failure to have a total of four additional non-mood symptoms, supporting earlier investigations reporting this finding.

The two patients described by Lowry and Sovner (1992) had a rapid cycling form of bipolar disorder – that is, with four or more episodes per year. Glue (1989) found that 10% of "long stay" residents with ID in a psychiatric hospital had a rapid cycling bipolar disorder. Charlot et al. (1993) found that nearly 40% of the individuals diagnosed with manic episodes had six or more episodes per year. A number of other studies reported subjects with ID and bipolar disorder had higher rates of rapid cycling when compared with data for other patient populations (Charlot, et al., 1993; Glue, 1989; Jones & Berney, 1987; King, 1999; Reid & Naylor, 1976; Sovner & Pary, 1993; Vanstraelen & Tyrer, 1999). Rapid cycling occurs in approximately 10%-20% of individuals without ID who have bipolar disorder, including about one-third of lithium non-responders (Goldberg & Harrow, 1999).

In a post hoc analysis by Vanstraelen and Tyrer (1999), data were compiled on 40 individuals with ID who had been diagnosed with rapid cycling bipolar disorder. Different methods were used to diagnose bipolar disorder in the studies reviewed. In many cases, diagnostic criteria were modified. The symptoms described were typically "observable behaviors," but pressured speech was reported for individuals who had milder cognitive disabilities. Mania was usually marked by symptoms of irritability, overactivity, sleeplessness, and "agitation." Descriptions of these patients parallel recent reports of mania in children, with and without ID (Wozniak, Biederman, & Kiely, 1995; Wozniak et al., 1997).

King (1999) described 26 outpatients with ID who were diagnosed with bipolar disorder. Patients with and without rapid cycling were compared. Of the total bipolar disorders sample, 54% had rapid cycling. Both groups manifested mood changes and aggression, but overactivity was seen at a higher rate in the rapid-cycling group. Rates of anxiety were low for both groups. King noted rapid cycling in two of three patients with a comorbid PDD, five of six individuals with seizure disorders, four of five patients with hypothyroidism, and one of five patients with obsessive compulsive disorder (OCD). Most of the individuals with severe/profound ID had rapid cycling. The participants in the King study resembled patients without ID in that they had a late age of onset of rapid cycling, included a high proportion of females, and had a high rate of thyroid dysfunction. King reportedly used Lowry's symptomatic behaviors (which were based on *DSM* criteria) to establish the diagnosis of bipolar disorder (Lowry & Sovner, 1992). In the cases reviewed by Vanstraelen & Tyrer (1999), a normal rate of thyroid dysfunction and an earlier age of onset of rapid cycling were reported. Jones and Berney (1987) and King (1999) have speculated that cerebral dysfunction may be a major factor in the increased risk of rapid cycling.

The few studies of bipolar disorder in individuals with ID that pertain to children and adolescents as subjects are mostly small case series at tertiary referral centers. Diagnosis using *DSM-5* is still based on criteria derived from adult studies in individuals without disabilities. It is critical, in order to make a reliable bipolar disorder diagnosis in youth with ID, to discern a clear time of change from previous functioning that is not merely a worsening of, or fluctuation in, a condition present since early childhood (American Psychiatric Association, 2013).

No studies addressing the phenomenology of bipolar II disorder, cyclothymic disorder or bipolar disorder NOS were identified, though a retrospective chart review of 22 cases of depression by Tsiouris (2001) did report three of 15 individuals with severe/profound ID carried a diagnosis of bipolar II disorder. Bipolar disorder NOS may be an appropriate diagnostic category for people with ID who do not meet full criteria for bipolar I disorder because of a failure to have three to four additional symptoms of mania occurring in conjunction with irritable or expansive mood.

■ *Bipolar and Related Disorders due to Another Medical Condition*

A number of medical disorders can directly provoke mood symptoms. In general, people with ID have a higher rate of comorbid medical disorders than individuals without ID (Ryan & Sunada, 1997). High rates of comorbid medical problems have been reported among psychiatric outpatients and inpatients with ID (Charlot et al., 2002; Ryan & Sunada, 1997). Thyroid disease can cause symptoms of mood disturbance; hyperthyroidism can be associated with manic-like symptoms. Polycystic ovary disease has been reported in association with symptoms of bipolar disorder in individuals with ID, possibly due to an underlying neuroendocrine abnormality (Ghaziuddin, 1989).

■ *Substance/Medication-Induced Bipolar and Related Disorder*

No studies addressing the specific question of a bipolar or related disorder being caused by a drug of abuse in persons with ID were identified. Substance abuse has been described in people with ID, but may occur less often in people who are closely supervised and do not live independently. Although the incidence may be lower than in other clinical populations, the possibility should be considered if an individual with acute onset mood disturbance might have had access to possible substances of abuse.

Substance-induced bipolar disorder can typically be distinguished from bipolar symptoms due to intoxication or withdrawal by the duration and severity of the symptoms. In people with ID, however, a potentially long-lasting "neuroleptic withdrawal syndrome" that includes features often seen in bipolar disorders such as irritability, disrupted sleep, weight loss, and agitated behavior has been described in several reports (Mikkelsen, Albert, & Upadhya, 1988). Since these agents are the most commonly prescribed psychoactive medications for people with ID (Nottestad & Linaker, 2003), and given the fact that the problem may emerge when switching from a typical or older antipsychotic medication to a newer or atypical one, clinicians should be aware of this as a possibility. Neuroleptic withdrawal-related problems might be suspected when bipolar symptoms have their onset following a rapid neuroleptic taper, switching (as described), or immediately following discontinuation of an antipsychotic medication.

Individuals with ID may also be at increased risk for experiencing neuroleptic-induced drug side effects (Gualtieri, Schroeder, Hicks, & Quade, 1986). A variety of extrapyramidal symptoms have been described, and these can also appear as tardive phenomena. In many cases, movement problems may be associated with alterations in appetite, sleep or motor behavior. Antipsychotic-induced akathisia (Van Putten, 1975) and sedative-induced disinhibition (Barron & Sandman, 1985) can be mistaken for mania.

Antidepressant-induced mania is classified as a substance-induced mood disorder, and has been described in individuals with ID in a few case reports (Akuffo, MacSweeney, & Gajwani, 1986; Khreim & Sovner, 1996). There are also reports of bipolar disorder symptoms associated with other agents. Friedman, Kastner, Plummer, Ruiz, and Henning (1992) reported cases of mania triggered by carbamazepine in individuals with ID. London (1997) reported on a case of mania triggered by olanzapine in a 16-year-old male with ID and a pervasive development disorder diagnosis.

■ *Unspecified Bipolar and Related Disorder*

Unspecified bipolar and related disorder may be used to assign a bipolar disorder diagnosis to people with ID who clearly present with features of a bipolar or related disorder, but for whom the clinical picture is particularly confusing. However, no data are available regarding this topic.

Evaluating the Level of Evidence

Adults with Mild to Moderate ID

The level of evidence for adults with mild to moderate intellectual disability is either level IV or level V, that is, well-designed observational studies, small case studies or expert opinion.

Adults with Severe or Profound ID

The diagnosis of bipolar disorder in persons with severe or profound intellectual disability is often challenging because of limited verbal and reasoning skills. One often needs to rely on behavioral observations. In clinical practice, what observations might be beneficial?

Matson Gonzalez, Terlonge, and Laud (2007) evaluated three groups of adults with either severe or profound intellectual disability, utilizing the Diagnostic Assessment for the Severely Handicapped revised (DASH-II) as well as the Parent Version of the Young Mania Rating Scale. The three groups were: 1) those with bipolar disorder who were currently manic; 2) those with an Axis I diagnosis other than bipolar disorder; and 3) those without an Axis I disorder. Compared to the group without Axis I disorders or others with non-bipolar psychopathology, those with psychomotor agitation and disturbed sleep were predictive of bipolar disorder (strength of evidence: IV). The same group designed a three-year longitudinal study and found that decreased need for sleep was the only factor of bipolar symptoms to significantly differ among the three groups (Gonzalez & Matson, 2006). Another study that utilized the DASH-II evaluated nearly 700 individuals, including over 10% with severe and nearly 80% with profound intellectual disability (Sturmey, Laud, Cooper, Matson, & Fodstad, 2010). Sturmey's group found that decreased need for sleep, restlessness, agitation, and irritability were items associated with mania. Although adults with severe/profound intellectual disability and bipolar disorder can have loud, inappropriate vocalizations, such vocalizations did not significantly differ from those in the non-bipolar psychopathology group (Matson, Terlonge, Gonzalez, & Rivet, 2006).

Children and Adolescents with ID

Few studies of bipolar disorder in individuals who have intellectual disabilities pertain to children and adolescents as subjects; those that do have mostly been small, describing case series and youth studied at tertiary referral centers. Diagnosis using *DSM-5* is still based on criteria derived from adult studies in individuals without disabilities. It is critical, in order to make a reliable bipolar disorder diagnosis in youth with ID, to discern a clear time of change from previous functioning that is not merely a worsening of, or fluctuation in, a condition present since early childhood (American Psychiatric Association, 2013).

In *DSM-5*, the cyclothymic disorder duration criterion in children and adolescents is one year, for repeated episodes of hypomania and depressive periods, in contrast to the two-year duration required for adults.

Systematic studies are lacking that address whether bipolar I and II in children also manifest more commonly as mixed, atypical, chronic or rapid cycling, as occurs in adults with ID (Olson, Helling, & Black, 2003). Jan and colleagues in 1994 and Jan and Freeman in 1995 published a case series of 10 children diagnosed with bipolar disorder, in which rapid cycling presentations were prominent. Manic periods were characterized by overactivity, increased distractibility, decreases in sleep, and increased vocalizations and aggression. This was in contrast to the depressive phases that included crying, apathy, self-injury, increased sleep, and changes in weight or appetite. Most subjects had a strong bipolar disorder family history.

In adults described with bipolar disorder and ID, irritable mood is more common than expansive or euphoric mood, and increased energy manifests as pacing or rapid rocking if the individual is non-ambulatory. Vocalizations or speech may be pressured and exhibit perseverative content if an ASD is also present. Grandiosity, hypersexual behaviors, and religiosity may be present, although as in adults, the child may consider himself/herself to have more normal abilities than he/she possesses in reality. Increased impulsivity may result in repeated, rapid flaring into aggression. Increased energy may produce repeated elopements or walking for miles, or repeated changing of clothing. Baseline repetitive behaviors may be more frenzied and rapid, for example piling up books or aligning objects.

Whether bipolar disorder is significantly different in children with autism spectrum disorder requires further study. The findings of Wozniak et al. (1997) suggested that children with bipolar disorder do not show recovery between episodes; however, these results have not been confirmed in other studies. In a British population-derived sample of 122 children with autism spectrum disorder aged 10 to 14 years, bipolar disorder was not diagnosed in any children assessed through parent interview, though nearly 30% had attention deficit hyperactivity disorder (Simonoff et al., 2008). Joshi et al. (2013) found that bipolar I disorder occurs earlier in those persons with autism spectrum disorder compared to those without.

Leyfer and colleagues (2006) studied 109 children aged 5 to 17 years with idiopathic ASD (mean full scale IQ 82.6, range 42-141), in a Boston and Salt Lake City sample using the Autism Comorbidity Interview-Present and Lifetime Version, which only collects parent information regarding the child. Lifetime prevalence rates of bipolar I disorder were 1.9%, for bipolar II disorder 0.9%, and for mixed bipolar episode 1.9%. On the other hand, major depression fulfilling *DSM-IV* criteria was diagnosed in 10%, or 24% if subsyndromal depression cases were included.

Etiology and Pathogenesis

Genetic Factors

Chromosomal microarray is considered a first-tier clinical diagnostic test for persons with unexplained intellectual disability (Miller et al., 2010). Chromosomal microarray will allow detection of copy number variations. Some of these copy number variations, either deletions or duplications, are associated with bipolar disorder (Malhotra & Sebat, 2012). For example, several individuals with a deletion on chromosome 22 (Phelan-McDermid syndrome, 22q13.3 deletion) show irritable mood, decreased need for sleep, psychomotor agitation, and increased speech (Denayer et al., 2012). The increased speech was definitely episodic because generally persons with 22q13.3 deletion do not talk. Of Denayer et al.'s seven persons with 22q13.3 deletion, four adults had bipolar disorder; the other three were 5, 6, and 17 years old and still could develop bipolar symptoms.

Another research group described two brothers with 22q13.4 deletion (Verhoeven, Egger, Willemsen, de Jeijer, & Kleefstra, 2012). The younger brother had an extreme loss of interest, social withdrawal, and anxiety. An antidepressant was prescribed but was discontinued after six months because of impulsiveness. Two years later, he became disinhibited and had compulsive rituals and disturbed sleep. His mood remained unstable until eventually responding to an antidepressant and mood stabilizer.

Early studies suggested that 22q11.2 deletion (velocardiofacial or DiGeorge syndrome) was associated with bipolar disorder (Carlson et al., 1997). A more recent review from an international consortium on the brain and behavior in

22q11.2 deletion syndrome of 1,402 participants across 15 study sites did not find an increased prevalence of bipolar disorder compared to the general population (Schneider et al., 2014). It is possible, however, that there were insufficient subjects to prove a lack of association.

Psychosocial Factors

In the general population, cognitive dysfunction is a strong predictor of psychosocial dysfunction in persons with bipolar disorder (Levy & Manove, 2012). Unfortunately, studies have not focused on individuals with pre-existing intellectual disability. Levy and Manove (2012) hypothesize several pathways that may be significant factors in persons with ID and bipolar disorder. These pathways include: 1) recurrent and intense bipolar symptoms impairing psychosocial functioning; and 2) neurotoxic effects of chronic stress leading to further executive function impairment.

In the general population, although negative life events are associated with depressive episode relapse, the evidence is less clear for negative life events to trigger manic relapses; instead, goal attainment was associated with manic recurrence (Johnson et al., 2008).

Developmental Factors

Some consider ID and neuropsychiatric disorders such as bipolar disorder to be part of a heterogeneous group of neurodevelopmental disorders caused by either genetic causes or an insult to the developing central nervous system. (Moreno-De-Luca et al., 2013). As noted above, earlier associations, such as bipolar disorder and 22q11.2 deletion, have not been replicated in larger samples.

Application of Criteria for Bipolar and Related Disorders

Manic Episode

DSM-5 Diagnostic Criteria	Applying Criteria for Mild to Profound Intellectual Disability
A. A distinct period of abnormality and persistently elevated, expansive, or irritable mood and abnormally and persistently increased goal directed activity or energy, lasting at least 1 week and present most of the day, nearly every day (or any duration if hospitalization is necessary)	A. No adaptation
B. During the period of mood disturbance and increased energy or activity, three (or more) of the following symptoms (four if the mood is only irritable) are present to a significant degree and represent a noticeable change from usual behavior.	B. For individuals who have limited expressive language skills, during the period of mood disturbance, adjust criteria to two (or more) of the symptoms listed below if present to a significant degree – three if the mood is only irritable.
1. Inflated self-esteem or grandiosity	1. No adaptation. **Note 1:** Observers may report that the individual with intellectual disability expresses: *exaggerated claims of skills or accomplishments (based on developmental profile at baseline i.e., individual claims he has a car but does not, claims skills he doesn't have such as ability to drive, states he is the director of the hospital), exaggerates social events ("I'm getting married" when not seeing anyone or not engaged), claims a relationship with a famous person, claims a relationship with a brief acquaintance, believes he is a super hero (not fantasies consistent with developmental profile).* **Note 2:** At preoperational cognitive stage of development, fantasy and reality are not distinguished. Claims may represent wishes versus mood congruent delusional beliefs.

Manic Episode (continued)

DSM-5 Diagnostic Criteria	Applying Criteria for Mild to Profound Intellectual Disability
2. Decreased need for sleep (e.g., feels rested after only 3 hours of sleep)	2. No adaptation. **Note:** Observers may report that the individual with intellectual disability sleeps 0 – 3 hours per night, goes to sleep much later than usual, wakes much earlier than usual, gets ready for the day very early. More difficulties may occur at night than previously reported. The individual may be doing usual daytime activities in the middle of the night. When sleeping less, there may be minimal signs of fatigue the next day. The individual may appear tired but cannot sleep except briefly, keeps active – seems "driven." The sleep problem resists treatment and is a departure from baseline (the individual is not disturbed by noise all night, is not sleeping during the day, and does not have a lifelong history of poor sleep).
3. More talkative than usual or pressure to keep talking	3. No adaptation. **Note 1:** Observers may report the following changes in regards to an individual with intellectual disability: increase in vocalizing, screaming, noise making, or talking; nonstop or very rapid vocalizing, etc.; asks repeated questions, doesn't wait for answers, decreased ability to listen, frequently interrupts, increase in perseverations, engages in frequent monologues, singing loudly - increases in noise making or vocalizing or screaming that is nonverbal; all symptoms are a departure from usual either because the symptoms are new or much more intense and frequent (baseline exaggeration). Note 2: Anxiety may also cause people with intellectual disability to talk fast or to talk or vocalize more.
4. Flight of ideas or subjective experience that thoughts are racing	4. No adaptation. **Note:** Observers may report that the individual with intellectual disability: jumps rapidly from topic to topic, or states thing like "My thoughts are moving fast." This must be a change from what is usual, not an individual who typically changes subjects frequently when well. The clinician must establish a baseline developmental profile from records/history.
5. Distractibility (i.e., attention too easily drawn to unimportant or irrelevant external stimuli) as reported or observed	5. No adaptation. **Note:** Observers may report that the individual with intellectual disability shows a reduced productivity at work or day program, has diminished self-care skills, appears easily distracted or cannot complete tasks he or she used to be able to finish, has shown the onset of or increase in agitated behaviors when asked to do activities that require concentration, has apparent memory problems that "come and go", has unexplained skill loss, shows an uncharacteristic inability to learn new skills as expected, has had to stop working or attending programs due to poor performance. These problems focusing attention are new and represent a change (are not life-long). The problems in concentrating or completing tasks seem mostly due to not being able to finish what is started or stay with a project and because attention is easily drawn to noise or activity going on around the person.

Manic Episode (continued)

DSM-5 Diagnostic Criteria	Applying Criteria for Mild to Profound Intellectual Disability
6. Increase in goal-directed activity (either socially, at work or school, or sexually) or psychomotor agitation i.e., purposeless non-goal-directed activity.)	6. No adaptation. **Note:** Observers may report that the individual with intellectual disability: engages in activities in a "sped up manner", rarely sits down, is up and down from seat a lot, paces, walks rapidly, seems "driven" , races around the room, has become very intrusive, is much more physically active than before, and can't even sit long enough to eat.
7. excessive involvement in pleasurable activities that have a high potential for painful consequences (e.g., engaging in unrestrained buying sprees, sexual indiscretions, or foolish business investments)	7. No adaptation. **Note:** Observers may report that the individual with intellectual disability engages *in much more sexual behavior or talk, reports more sexual activity than usual, masturbates frequently and much more than before, exposes self in public and this is usual, and is touching others in a sexual manner.*
C. The mood disturbance is sufficiently severe to cause marked impairment in social or occupational functioning or to necessitate hospitalization to prevent harm to self or others, or there are psychotic features.	C. No adaptation.
D. The episode is not attributable to the physiological effects of a substance (e.g., a drug of abuse, a medication, other treatment) or to another medical condition. **Note:** A full manic episode that emerges during antidepressant treatment (e.g. medication, electroconvulsive therapy) but persists at a fully syndromal level beyond the physiological effects of that treatment is sufficient evidence for a manic episode and, therefore, a bipolar 1 diagnosis.	D. No adaptation **Note 1:** For people with intellectual disability, residential, vocational or other program placements may be lost due to the acute mood episode. **Note 2:** For people with intellectual disability, almost any physical problem that causes pain or distress may also cause difficulty-focusing attention, sleeping, eating and psychomotor agitation. Rapid changes in medications may provoke irritability, agitation, sleep problems and withdrawal emergent motor restlessness (akathisia) that can mimic a manic episode. **Note 3:** For people with severe/profound intellectual disability, there is even less likelihood of an accurate report from the individual regarding his or her physical distress. Informants may attribute agitated behaviors to the previously diagnosed psychiatric syndrome and miss a new medical problem. There may be a tendency to diagnose bipolar syndromes in people with intellectual disability who have presented with manic like symptoms only when treated with medications such as antidepressant SSRIs.
Note: Criteria A-D constitute a manic episode. At least one lifetime manic episode is required for the diagnosis of bipolar 1 disorder.	

Hypomanic Episode

DSM-5 Diagnostic Criteria	Applying Criteria for Mild to Profound Intellectual Disability
A. A distinct period of persistently elevated, expansive or irritable mood, and abnormally and persistently increased activity or energy, lasting at least 4 consecutive days and present most of the day, nearly every day.	A. No adaptation. **Note:** Observers may report that the individual with intellectual disability has been loud, inappropriately laughing or singing, excessively giddy, silly; intrusive, getting into other's space; smiling excessively and in ways that are not appropriate to the social context. Elated mood may be alternating with irritable mood. In people with severe/profound intellectual disability, irritable mood may be more common. This must be a change from typical behavior for the person.
B. During the period of mood disturbance and increased energy and activity three (or more) of the following symptoms (four if the mood is only irritable) have persisted, represent a noticeable change from usual behavior, and have been present to a significant degree.	
1. Inflated self-esteem or grandiosity	1. No adaptation. See notes for Manic Episode above.
2. Decreased need for sleep (e.g., feels restored after only 3 hours of sleep)	2. No adaptation. See notes for Manic Episode above.
3. More talkative than usual or pressure to keep talking	3. No adaptation. See notes for Manic Episode above.
4. Flight of ideas or subjective experience that thoughts are racing	4. No adaptation. See notes for Manic Episode above.
5. Distractibility (i.e., attention too easily drawn to unimportant or irrelevant external stimuli) as reported or observed.	5. No adaptation. See notes for Manic Episode above.
6. Increase in goal-directed activity (either socially, at work or school, or sexually) or psychomotor agitation	6. No adaptation. See notes for Manic Episode above.
7. Excessive involvement in pleasurable activities that have a high potential for painful consequences (e.g., engaging in unrestrained buying sprees, sexual indiscretions, or foolish business investments)	7. No adaptation. See notes for Manic Episode above.
C. The episode is associated with an unequivocal change in functioning that is uncharacteristic of the person when not symptomatic.	C. No adaptation.
D. The disturbance in mood and the change in functioning are observable by others.	D. No adaptation.
E. The episode is not severe enough to cause marked impairment in social or occupational functioning, or to necessitate hospitalization. If there are psychotic features, the episode is, by definition, manic.	E. No adaptation. Note: Perceptions regarding the severity of the mood syndrome may be influenced by contextual factors, level of supports available to the person with intellectual disability as well as any co-occurring aggressive behavior.

Hypomanic Episode (continued)

DSM-5 Diagnostic Criteria	Applying Criteria for Mild to Profound Intellectual Disability
F. The symptoms are not due to the direct physiologic effects of a substance (e.g. a drug of abuse, medication, or other treatment). **Note:** A full hypomanic episode that emerges during antidepressant treatment (e.g. medication, electroconvulsive therapy) but persists at a fully syndromal level beyond the physiological effects of that treatment is sufficient evidence for a hypomanic episode diagnosis. However, a caution is indicated so that one or two symptoms, particularly, increased irritability, edginess, or agitation following antidepressant use) are not taken as sufficient for diagnosis of a hypomanic episode, nor necessarily indicative of a bipolar diathesis.	F. No adaptation. **Note:** For individuals with intellectual disability, extra attention should be given to medical conditions and treatments as a possible cause of changes in behavior (such as hypothyroidism)
Note: Criteria A-F constitute a hypomanic episode. Hypomanic episodes are common in bipolar 1 disorder but are not required for the diagnosis of bipolar 1 disorder.	

Major Depressive Episode

Please refer to chapter on major depressive disorders. Please see notes from major depressive disorder describing special considerations.

Bipolar I Disorder

Diagnosis of bipolar I disorder requires meeting criteria for a manic episode, which may have been preceded by and/or may be followed by hypomanic or major depressive episodes.

Bipolar II Disorder

Diagnosis of bipolar II disorder requires a current or past hypomanic episode as well as a current or past major depressive episode.

Cyclothymic Disorder

Cyclothymic disorder can be diagnosed when an adult has experienced at least 2 years of both hypomanic and depressive periods without meeting the criteria for manic, hypomanic, or major depressive episodes. In children, the duration must be a full year.

Substance/Medication-Induced Bipolar and Related Disorder

Bipolar and Related Disorder Due to Another Medical Condition

DSM-5 provides the categories of substance/medication induced bipolar and related disorder and of bipolar and related disorder due to another medical condition in recognition that a large number of substances of abuse, some prescribed medications, and several medical conditions can be associated with manic-like phenomena.

Other Specified Bipolar and Related Disorder
Unspecified Bipolar and Related Disorder

DSM-5 also provides categories for other specified bipolar and related disorder and for unspecified bipolar and related disorder.

References

Achenbach, T. M. (1991). *Manual for the Child Behavior Checklist/4–18 and 1991 Profile.* Burlington, VT: University of Vermont, Department of Psychiatry.

Akuffo, E., MacSweeney, D. A. & Gajwani, A. K. (1986). Multiple pathology in a mentally handicapped individual. *British Journal of Psychiatry*, 149, 377-378.

American Psychiatric Association (1987). *Diagnostic and statistical manual of mental disorders* (3rd ed., rev.). Washington, DC: American Psychiatric Association.

American Psychiatric Association (1994). *Diagnostic and statistical manual of mental disorders* (4th ed.). Washington, DC: American Psychiatric Association.

American Psychiatric Association (2000). *Diagnostic and statistical manual of mental Disorders* (4th ed., rev.). Washington, DC: american Psychiatric Association.

American Psychiatric Association (2013). *Diagnostic and Statistical Manual of Mental Disorders* (5th ed., rev.), Washington, DC: American Psychiatric Association.

Blader, J. C. & Carlson, G. A. (2007). Increased rates of bipolar disorder diagnoses among U.S. child, adolescent, and adult inpatients, 1996-2004. *Biologic Psychiatry*, 62(2), 107-14.

Barron, J. & Sandman, C. A. (1985). Paradoxical excitement to sedative-hypnotics in mentally retarded clients. *American Journal of Mental Deficiency*, 90, 124-129.

Cain, N. N., Davidson, P. W., Burhan, A.M., Andolsek, M. E., Baxter, J. T., Sullivan, L., ... Lam, N. (2003). Identifying bipolar disorders in individuals with intellectual disability. *Journal of Intellectual Disability Research, 47,* 31-38.

Carlson, C., Papolos D., Pandita, R. K., Faedda, G. L., Veit, S., Goldberg, R., ... Morrow, B. (1997). Molecular analysis of velo-cardio-facial syndrome patients with psychiatric disorders. *American Journal of Human Genetics, 60,* 851-9.

Charlot, L. R., Doucette, A. D. & Mezzecappa, E. (1993). Affective symptoms in institutionalized adults with mental retardation. *American Journal of Mental Retardation*, 98, 408-416.

Charlot, L. R., Abend, S., Silka, V. R., Kuropatkin, B. B., Garcia, O., Bolduc, M., & Foley, M. (2002). A short stay inpatient psychiatric unit for adults with developmental disabilities. In J. Jacobsen, J. Mulick, & S. Holburn (Eds.), *Contemporary dual diagnosis: MH/MR. service models. Volume I: Residential and day services* (pp. 35-55). Kingston, NY: NADD Press.

Denayer, A., Van Esch, H., de Ravel, T., Frijns, J-P., Van Buggenhout, G., Vogels, A., ... Swillen, A. (2012). Neuropathology in seven patients with the 22q13 deletion syndrome: Presence of bipolar disorder and progressive loss of skills. *Molecular Syndromology*, 3, 14-20.

Diler, R. S., Birmaher, B., Axelson, D,, Goldstein, B., Gill, M., Strober, M., ... Keller, M. B. (2009). The Child Behavior Checklist (CBCL) and the CBCL-bipolar phenotype are not useful in diagnosing pediatric bipolar disorder. *Journal of Child Adolescent Psychopharmacology, 19(1)*, 23-30.

Doerfler, L. A., Connor D. F, & Toscano, P. F. (2011). Aggression, ADHD symptoms, and dysphoria in children and adolescents diagnosed with bipolar disorder and ADHD. *Journal of Affective Disorder 131(1-3)*, 312-9.

Friedman, D. L., Kastner, T., Plummer, A. T., Ruiz, M. Q., & Henning, D. (1992). Adverse behavioral effects in individuals with mental retardation and mood disorders treated with carbamazepine. *American Journal of Mental Retardation, 96(5)*, 541-546.

Glue, P. (1989). Rapid cycling affective disorders in the mentally retarded. *Biological Psychiatry, 26*, 250-256.

Ghaziuddin, M. (1989). Polycystic ovary disease, manic-depressive illness and mental retardation. *Journal of Mental Deficiency Research, 33*, 335-338.

Goldberg, J. F., & Harrow, M. (1999). Poor outcome bipolar disorders. In J. F. Goldberg & M. Harrow (Eds.), *Bipolar Disorders: Clin-*

ical Course and Outcome (pp. 1-21). Washington, DC: American Psychiatric Press.

Gonzalez, M., & Matson, J. L. (2006). Mania and intellectual disability: The course of manic symptoms in persons with intellectual disability. *American Journal on Mental Retardation, 111*(5), 378-383.

Gualtieri, C. T., Schroeder, R. E., Hicks, R. E., & Quade, D. (1986). Tardive dyskinesia in young mentally retarded individuals. *Archives of General Psychiatry, 43*, 335-340.

Hollander, E., Chaplin, W., Soorya, L., Wasserman, S., Novotny, S., Rusoff, J., ... Anagnostou, E. (2010). Divalproex sodium vs. placebo for the treatment of irritability in children and adolescents with autism spectrum disorders. *Neuropsychopharmacology, 35*(4), 990–998.

Hurley, A. D. (2008). Depression in adults with intellectual disability: Symptoms and challenging behavior. *Journal of Intellectual Disability Research, 52*, 905-916.

Jan, J. E., Abroms, I. F., Freeman, R. D., Brown, G. M., Espezel, H., & Connolly, M. B. (1994). Rapid cycling in severely multidisabled children: A form of bipolar affective disorder? *Pediatric Neurology, 10*(1), 34-39.

Jan, J. E., & Freeman, R. D. (1995). Rapid cycling in severely multidisabled children. *The Habilitative Healthcare Newsletter*; *14*(2), 28-30.

Johnson, S. L., Cueller, A. K., Ruggero, C., Winett-Perlman, C., Goodnick, P., White, R., & Miller, I. (2008). Life events as predictors of mania and depression in bipolar I disorder. *Journal of Abnormal Psychology, 117*(2), 268-277.

Jones, P. M., & Berney, T. P. (1987). Early onset rapid cycling bipolar disorder. *Journal of Child Psychology and Psychiatry and Allied Disciplines, 28*, 731-738.

Joshi, G., Biederman, J., Petty, C., Goldin, R. L., Furtak, S. L., & Wozniak, J. (2013). Examining the comorbidity of bipolar disorder and autism spectrum disorders: A large controlled analysis of phenotypic and familial correlates in a referred population of youth with bipolar I disorder with and without autism spectrum disorders. *Journal of Clinical Psychiatry. 74*(6), 578-86.

King, R. (1999). Clinical implications of comorbid bipolar disorders and obsessive compulsive disorders in individuals with developmental disabilities. *The NADD Bulletin, 2*(4), 3-67.

King, R., Fay, G., & Croghan, P. (2000). Rapid cycling bipolar disorder in individuals with developmental disabilities. *Mental Retardation, 38*, 253-2261.

Khreim, I., & Sovner, R. (1996). Antidepressant-induced mania in developmentally disabled individuals. In *Proceedings of the 13th Annual Conference of NADD* (pp. 59-65). Kingston, NY: NADD Press.

Krauthammer, C., & Klerman G. L. (1978). Secondary mania: Manic syndromes associated with antecedent physical illness or drugs. *Archives of General Psychiatry, 35*(11), 1333-9.

Leibenluft, E. (2011). Severe mood dysregulation, irritability, and the diagnostic boundaries of bipolar disorder in youths. *American Journal of Psychiatry, 168*(2), 129-142.

Leyfer, O. T., Folstein, S. E., Bacalman, S, Davis, N. O., Dinh, E, Morgan, J., ... Lainhart, J. E. (2006). Comorbid psychiatric disorders in children and adolescents with autism: Interview development and rates of disorders. *Journal of Autism and Developmental Disorders, 36*, 849-861.

Levy, B., & Manove, E. (2012). Functional outcome in bipolar disorder: The big picture. *Depression Research Treatment. 2012*, 949248.

London, J. A. (1997). Mania associated with olanzapine. *Journal of the Academy of Child and Adolescent Psychiatry, 37*(2), 135-136.

Lowry, M. (1997). Unmasking mood disorders: Recognizing and measuring symptomatic behaviors. *The Habilitative Mental Healthcare Newsletter, 16*, 1-6.

Lowry, M., & Sovner, R. (1992). Severe behavior problems associated with rapid cycling bipolar disorder in two adults with profound mental retardation. *Journal of Intellectual Disabilities Research, 36*, 269-281.

Malhotra, D., & Sebat, J. (2012). CNVs: Harbinger of a rare variant revolution in psychiatric genetics. *Cell, 148*(6), 1223-1241.

Matson, J. L., Gonzalez, C., Terlonge, R. T., & Laud, R. B. (2007). What symptoms predict the diagnosis of mania in persons with severe/profound intellectual disability in clinical practice? *Journal of Intellectual Disability Research, 51(1)*, 25-31.

Matson, J. L., & Smiroldo, B. B. (1997). Validity of the mania subscale of the diagnostic assessment for the severely handicapped-II (DASH-II). *Research in Developmental Disability, 18*(3), 221-225.

Matson, J. L., Terlonge, C., Gonzalez, M. L., & Rivet, T. (2006). An evaluation of social and adaptive skills in adults with bipolar disorder and severe/profound intellectual disability. *Research in Developmental Disabilities, 27*, 681-687.

Mazzone, L., Ruta, L., & Reale, L. (2012). Psychiatric comorbidities in Asperger syndrome and high functioning autism: Diagnostic challenges. *Annals of General Psychiatry, 11*, 16-29.

Mikkelsen, E. J., Albert, L. G., & Upadhya, A. (1988). A neuroleptic withdrawal cachexia. *New England Journal of Medicine, (14)* 929, 318.

Miller, D. T., Adam, M. P., Aradhya, S., Biesecker, L. G., Brothman, A. R., Carter, N. P., ... Ledbetter, D. H. (2010). Consensus statement: Chromosomal microarray is a first-tier clinical diagnostic test for individuals with developmental disabilities or congenital anomalies. *American Journal of Human Genetics, 86*, 749-764.

Moreno, C., Laje, G., Blanco, C., Jiang, H., Schmidt, A. B., & Olfson, M. (2007). National trends in the outpatient diagnosis and treatment of bipolar disorder in youth. *Archives of General Psychiatry, 64(9)*, 1032-9.

Moreno-De-Luca, A., Myers, S. M., Challman, T. D., Moreno-De-Luca, D., Evans, D. W., & Ledbetter, D. H. (2013). Developmental brain dysfunction: Revival and expansion of old concepts based on new genetic evidence. *Lancet Neurology, 12*(4), 406-414.

Nottestad, J. A., & Linaker, O. M. (2003). Psychotropic drug use among people with intellectual disability before and after deinstitutionalization. *Journal of Intellectual Disability Research, 47*(69), 464-471.

Olson, K. M., Hellings, J. A., & Black, P. A. (2003). *Dual diagnosis: Mood disorders and developmental disabilities.* Baltimore, MD: Paul H. Brookes.

Pary, R. J., Friedlander, R., & Capone, G. T. (1999). Bipolar disorder in Down syndrome: Six cases. *Mental Health Aspects of Developmental Disabilities, 2*, 59-63.

Pary, R., & Khan, K. (2002). Cyclic behaviors in persons with developmental disabilities: Are cluster and migraine headaches being overlooked? *Mental Health Aspects of Developmental Disabilities, 5*(4), 125-129.

Pary, R. J., Levitas A. S., & Hurley A. D. (1999). Diagnosis of bipolar disorder in persons with developmental disabilities. *Mental Health Aspects of Developmental Disabilities, 2*(2), 37-49.

Reid, A. H., & Naylor, G. J. (1976). Short-cycle manic depressive psychosis in mental defectives: A clinical physiological study. *Journal of Mental Deficiency Research, 20*, 67-76.

Reimherr, J. P., & McClellan, J.M. (2004). Diagnostic challenges in children and adolescents with psychotic disorders. *Journal of Clinical Psychiatry, (65* Suppl 6), 5-11.

Rosenberg, R. E., Kaufmann, W. E., Law, J. K., & Law, P. A. (2011). Parent report of community psychiatric comorbid diagnoses in autism spectrum disorders. *Autism Research and Treatment 2011*: 405849.

Ryan, R., & Sunada, K. (1997). Medical evaluation of persons with mental retardation referred for psychiatric assessment. *General Hospital Psychiatry, 19*(4), 274-280.

Schneider, M., Debbane, M., Bassett, A. S., Chow, E. W. C., Fung, W. L. A., van den Bree, M. B. M., ... Eliez, S. (2014). Psychiatric disorders from childhood to adulthood in 22q11.2 deletion syndrome: Results from the International Consortium on Brain and Behavior in 22q11.2 Deletion Syndrome. *American Journal of Psychiatry, 171*(6), 627-639.

Simonoff, E., Pickles, A., Charman, T., Chandler, S., Loucas, T., & Baird, G. (2008). Psychiatric disorders in children with autism spectrum disorders: Prevalence, comorbidity, and associated factors in a population-based sample. *Journal of the American Academy of Child and Adolescent Psychiatry, 48*(8), 921-929.

Sovner, R., & Hurley, A. D. (1982a). Diagnosing depression in the mentally retarded. *Psychiatric Aspects of Mental Retardation Reviews, 1*, 1-3.

Sovner, R., & Hurley, A. D. (1982b). Diagnosing mania in the mentally retarded. *Psychiatric Aspects of Mental Retardation Reviews, 1*, 9-11.

Sovner, R., & Hurley, A. D. (1983). Do the mentally retarded suffer from affective illness? *Archives of General Psychiatry, 40*, 61-67.

Sovner, R., & Pary, R. J. (1993). Affective disorders in developmentally disabled persons. In J. L. Matson & R. P. Barrett (Eds.), *Psychopathology in the mentally retarded* (2nd ed.). Needham Heights, MA: Allyn & Bacon.

Steingard, R., & Biederman, J. (1987). Lithium responsive manic-like symptoms in two adults with autism and mental retardation. *Journal of the American Academy of Child and Adolescent Psychiatry, 26*, 932-935.

Sturmey, P., Laud, R. B., Cooper, C. L., Matson, J. L., & Fodstad, J. C. (2010). Mania and behavioral equivalents: A preliminary study. *Research in Developmental Disabilities, 31*, 1008-1014.

Tsiouris, J. A. (2001). The diagnosis of depression in people with severe/profound intellectual disability. *Journal of Intellectual Disability Research, 45*, 115-120.

Tsiouris, J. A., Mann, R., Patti, P. J., & Sturmey, P. (2003). Challenging behaviors should be considered as depressive equivalents in individuals with developmental disabilities. *Journal of Intellectual Disability Research, 47*(Pt. 1), 14-21.

Van Putten, T. (1975). The many faces of akathisia. *Comprehensive Psychiatry, 16*, 43-47.

Vanstraelen, M., & Tyrer, S. P. (1999). Rapid cycling bipolar disorder in people with intellectual disability: A systematic review. *Journal of Intellectual Disability Research, 43*, 349-359.

Verhoeven, W. M. A., Egger, J. I. M., Willemsen, M. H., de Leijer, G. J. M., & Kleefstra, T. (2012). Phelan-McDermid syndrome in two adult brothers: Atypical bipolar disorder as its psychopathological phenotype? *Neuropsychiatric Disease and Treatment, 8*, 175-179.

Wieland, J., Van Vliet, J. P. M., & Zitman, F. G. (2012). Challenges and advances in mental health and intellectual disabilities. *Minerva Psichiatrica, 53*(1), 29-38.

Wozniak, J., Biederman, J., & Kiely, K. (1995). Mania-like symptoms suggestive of childhood onset bipolar disorder in clinically referred children. *Journal of the American Academy of Child and Adolescent Psychiatry, 34*, 867-876.

Wozniak, J., Biederman, J., Faraone, S. V., Frazier, J., Kim, J., & Millstein, R. (1997). Mania in children with pervasive developmental disorder revisited. *Journal of the American Academy of Child and Adolescent Psychiatry, 36(11)*, 1552-1559.

Yutzy, S. H., Woofter, C. R., Abbott, C. C., Melhem, I. M., & Parish, B. S. (2012). The increasing frequency of mania and bipolar disorder. *Journal of Nervous Mental Disease, 200*(5), 380-387.

CHAPTER 12

Depressive Disorders

Lauren R. Charlot
Marc Tasse
Sherm Fox
Robert J. Pary
Betsey A. Benson
Angela Hassiotis

Three key developments of the DSM-V related to depression include (1) the separation of depressive disorders from bipolar and related disorders, (2) the addition of a new diagnostic category, disruptive mood dysregulation disorder, and (3) dropping of a bereavement exclusion for major depressive episodes. The first (separation of depressive disorders from bipolar and related disorders) stems from research demonstrating varied pathways and genetic underpinnings for unipolar depression versus bipolar disorder. The addition of disruptive mood dysregulation disorder was aimed at addressing significant concerns regarding the over diagnosis of pediatric bipolar disorder and findings suggesting youth with chronic irritable mood are more likely to have an anxiety or depressive disorder (and not bipolar disorder) as adults. Differentiation of disorders in young people with multiple comorbid conditions and ADHD has also been necessary. Further longitudinal research is required to determine the clinical course and outcomes for children with complex clinical presentations and to better characterize pathways to adult forms of disorder.

In the current chapter, most attention is given to major depressive disorder and the newly identified disruptive mood dysregulation disorder. Though the literature addressing major depressive disorder in people with ID is limited, there have been more papers regarding this specific syndrome than most others identified in DSM-5, with the possible exception of autism spectrum disorders. Much of what was concluded regarding depression in the first iteration of the DM-ID remains relevant, with a few important updates.

Key findings in this chapter include the following:

1. Depression occurs more often in people with ID than individuals without an ID. Recent epidemiological studies employ more rigorous designs, using population-based multi-stage methodologies enhancing overall utility. Depression and anxiety may co-exist or perhaps share similar but definitely overlapping/intertwining developmental pathways.
2. Depression is easier to identify in people with milder ID and more challenging to diagnose when the individual has greater cognitive impairment and communication challenges.
3. Communication challenges and the need to rely heavily on informant reports render diagnostic assessments of possible depression more difficult in our work with people with ID because mood syndrome diagnoses require reliable information regarding internal states.
4. Developmental considerations impact the phenomenology of depression in people with ID, who have features similar to mental age rather than chronological age peers. This includes frequent findings of irritable mood, motor restlessness, and the co-occurrences of conduct disturbances (ex-

ternalizing behaviors). A similar pattern has been described in children formerly labeled as "multi-complex." Many of these youth are now classified as suffering from disruptive mood dysregulation disorder (a syndrome that has not yet been studied in individuals with ID).

5. Though people with ID who are depressed present with high rates of aggressive behavior and other externalizing behavior challenges, these should not be used as "behavioral equivalents." Rather, it is important to note that depression may be missed if too much attention is paid to these referral concerns, in the absence of a broader examination of the person's mental status, mood, and biological functioning. Aggression may be best viewed as a "final common pathway" for distress in people with ID (who have few ways to demonstrate this). Aggression and other externalizing behaviors occur at high rates in association with most psychiatric disorders in people with ID and are not "diagnostically specific." Specific associations may be found, however, such as when a person with ID is depressed and aggresses to avoid activities that might otherwise be enjoyed.

6. The phenomenology of depression is generally similar in people with ID as all others, but its ascertainment differs because of the above noted concerns. Informants tend to emphasize externalizing issues and may not connect biological features with mood and behavioral ones. As in the DM-ID, examples of how a person with ID might demonstrate each depressive symptom are provided to reduce diagnostic errors related to dependence on informant reports.

7. Differential diagnosis of depression in people with ID is complicated by the need to consider how medical problems and medication side effects may influence clinical presentations (Charlot et al., 2011; Kwok & Cheung, 2007). The classic symptoms of depression can be provoked by an illness or a drug effect, so that a person who seems anhedonic, irritable, withdrawn, and slowed down may be suffering from conditions such as constipation, drug-induced Parkinson's syndromes, dental problems, or acid reflux. Medical concerns occur at higher rates in people with ID, and healthcare needs are more often missed in this population.

8. Bipolar disorder may currently be over-diagnosed in people with ID. Use of screens and checklists rather than full diagnostic criteria may play a role. For example, individuals with ID who have episodic agitation, sleep problems, and irritable or labile affect may have a wide array of factors influencing these problems, and the diagnosis of bipolar disorder may be given simply because the clinical picture is variable. Studies using more comprehensive methodologies for case ascertainment report lower rates of bipolar disorder than those using mainly screening tools or administrative data. There may be missed cases of depression because the person has co-occurring aggression and motor restlessness that is misinterpreted as mania. Suggestions for improving assessment are provided to reduce diagnostic errors, including insuring careful consideration of clinical course and history and ruling out alternative diagnoses that better explain the clinical picture. Disruptive mood dysregulation disorder and several behavioral phenotypes may become the focus of future research and changes to diagnostic practice in the population.

9. People with ID may have complex presentations and meet criteria for multiple disorders, as has been found in the general population studies to date. High rates of comorbidity between depression and anxiety in patients with ID have been reported. Also, both children and adults with ID could meet criteria outlined for the new category of disruptive mood dysregulation disorder. The implications of this are as yet unclear. Future studies might examine its utility in the population and identify people with ID who have similar developmental profiles to the target age group.

10. Risk factors for depression are somewhat similar for people with and without ID but occur more often in the lives of individuals with ID including significant life events, social disadvantage, low levels of social support, and poor self-esteem. Adult females with ID may be at greater risk for depression.

11. The biological basis of depression, though extensively investigated, has yet to yield a reli-

able biomarker or to identify structural anomalies of the brain specific to depression alone. Long-standing models that identify genetic and psychosocial risk factors remain relevant but not explanatory (i.e. diathesis-stress). A key to improved understanding may lie in the application of a developmental psychopathology approach. Findings from longitudinal studies where pathways from childhood to adult forms of illness may be elucidated may provide a robust framework (Cicchetti & Toth, 2009). In this research, the transactions between biological risk factors, environmental influences, and later adult outcomes may be clarified. Early findings suggest that the effects of the environmental context on brain development (structural and neurochemical effects) in turn have an impact on responses to later environmental influences over the course of development and may be mediated by the timing of stress. The investigation of genetic syndromes associated with ID may play a role in further defining pathways between gene action and psychopathology, as in the example of recent research regarding fragile X syndrome, a syndrome associated with anxiety, depressive disorders, autism spectrum disorder, and ID (Hagerman, Lauterborn, Au, & Berry-Kravis, 2012).

Issues Related to Diagnosis in Persons with ID

There are several important considerations when evaluating a person with ID to determine if he or she may be suffering from depression, including the following:

1. People with ID often have limited abilities to self-report internal mood states. First, the determination that an individual is experiencing alterations in mood is often highly reliant on the capacity to self-report internal states and especially to recognize and label one's feelings. Individuals with ID are often especially challenged in this regard and may not be able to describe their own emotions accurately or reliably (Costello & Bouras, 2006; Ross & Oliver, 2003). Though this is a general issue in psychiatric assessment of people with ID, it is critical to accurate identification of depression. Much of the information used to identify the presence of depression when evaluating a person with ID or ASD comes from the reports of the observations of caregivers (Charlot, Deutsch, Fletcher, & McIlvane, 2007; Costello & Bouras, 2006; Hurley, 2007). Further complicating this, caregivers, teachers, parents and other informants tend to over-report "externalizing" symptoms or behaviors and under-report internalizing ones (anxiety, depression) while dysphoric mood may cause individual's with a limited behavioral repertoire to display agitated behaviors (Charlot et al., 1993; Edelbrock, Costello, Dulcan, Kalas & Conover 1985; Moss et al, 1998). Hurtig et al. (2009) found that the self-report of adolescents with high functioning autism or Asperger's syndrome contained more references to internalizing symptoms like anxiety than those of their parents. In fact, it is well recognized in the field of child mental health that self and informant reports do not converge very well, with children who are able to self report often citing internalizing problems and informants being more likely to point to externalizing symptoms.

Mileviciute and Hartely (2015), in their investigation that employed several self and informant report measures, also verified that informants report fewer depressive symptoms than the individuals report about themselves. Individuals with ID frequently present for mental health evaluation primarily because of aggression to self, others, or property and do not usually self-refer (Hurley, 2007). Further, the tendency to focus on just the aggression may be the most critical contributing factor in the variability and inaccuracy of psychiatric diagnoses for people with ID. There is often pressure to treat aggression itself without attention to other clinical clues that might point to the identification of a mood or anxiety problem (suggesting an "internalizing" syndrome) (Tsiouris, 2010). Yet most experts agree that accurate diagnosis is key to identification of the most effective treatments. Tsiouris (2010) suggested that clinicians should be careful to resist pressures to apply a "non-specific" treatment for aggressive behaviors. Rather, it is recommended that clinicians focus on establishing whether or not a psychiatric syndrome is present and review the array of potential influences on aggression. This requires a comprehensive multidisciplinary assessment, the use of multiple sources of information, and likely more time than is usually allocated in practice with individuals who do not have an ID or ASD. It may be helpful to ask informants to describe what they have observed rather than conclusions about these observations, as informants often come with their own hypotheses (i.e. "David has been manic"). Use of detailed behavioral descriptions for informants is a cornerstone of the assessment recommendations provided here. Research suggests that when efforts are made to illicit information this way, observers can identify signs of sadness and other emotional states with some reliability. For example, it is much more helpful to ask caregivers if the patient has sad facial expressions or cries often than to simply have a checklist with an item labeled "sad mood" when evaluating patients who may not reliably self-report (Hayes, McGuire, O'Neill, Oliver & Morrison, 2011; Ross & Oliver, 2003).

2. Individuals with ID represent a highly heterogeneous population. A key issue in determining whether or not a person is experiencing a depressive disorder is to establish whether or not current behavior represents a departure from usual behavior and from what might be expected for a person of this individual's age, culture, gender, education, etc. (Costello & Bouras, 2006). In some ways, clinicians must learn the "culture" of persons with developmental syndromes. More critically, when assessing an individual with ID, the clinician must establish what is the person's neurodevelopmental profile at baseline, when functioning optimally. A similar point has recently been emphasized in regards to understanding psychopathology in youth (Carlson & Meyer, 2006) and has influenced text revisions in DSM-5. Inadvertently, clinicians who have minimal training in working with patients with ID may default to using a reference group of others of a similar age. As a result, clinicians may view certain behaviors as automatically psychopathologic, when they really need to consider whether the behavior is in fact abnormal for the person with ID (carefully considering their baseline social, cognitive, and communication challenges). Parents, siblings, and long-term caregivers as well as records of past evaluations may reveal key information regarding what is usual behavior for the individual being assessed (Charlot, et al., 2007b). Obtaining and reviewing these documents takes time but can be critical to an accurate differential diagnostic assessment.

3. The above concern (population heterogeneity) is linked to a second challenge for the diagnostician, the need to consider how symptoms of depression and mood dysregulation may present differently based on individual developmental profiles (Harris, 1998). Research has shown that typically developing children likely show some variations in terms of the nature and type of symptoms they display when depressed. One example is the finding that children with depression may present with psychomotor agitation, tantrums, and irritable mood more often than depressed adults (Cicchetti and Toth, 2009; Trad, 1987). Very young depressed children are less likely to describe suicidal ideas or hopelessness, symptoms that require a certain level of development neurologically and psychologically that supports such cognitive capacities. Individuals with ID may have neurodevelopmental and cognitive profiles that parallel peers who are younger but neuroptypical, which may affect how depression is displayed (though the core features likely remain the same) (Harris, 1998). Thus, a person who is extremely anhedonic may verbally state "I just don't care" about doing previously enjoyed activities while a child or a developmentally challenged adult with ID may simply have a "tantrum" when prompted to participate. Developmental factors may lead to individuals with ID being less likely to demonstrate certain cognitive features of these syndromes. Given expressive communication deficits and developmental considerations, clinicians may need to ask caregivers targeted questions that elicit full descriptions of clinical features to insure that a mood syndrome is not missed. Efforts should be made to illicit informant reports that provide clues to the possible presence of internalizing symptoms such as anhedonia,

sadness, and hopelessness. Clinicians are advised to avoid inadvertent misidentification of developmentally expected behaviors as signs of psychopathology when they are not and to recognize developmental influences on the specific form a symptom takes (see Hurley, 1996). It is also important to consider variability related to age of onset versus age of recognition of many symptoms and syndromes. Gene x environment transactions are multi-directional, requiring longitudinal study, and are further complicated by the presence of ID or the examination of populations with extreme or atypical baselines. Transactional or multi-directional interactions are probable influences on the emergence of depressive disorders in people with ID.

4. In patients with ID, it is particularly important that clinicians base diagnoses on the full history of the presenting problem and careful considerations of what other phenomena or conditions might better explain the clinical picture (Charlot et al., 2007b). Additional findings such as the age of onset, speed of onset, clinical course, coincidental occurrences (introductions of new medications, onset of illnesses, major life events) and family history, can enhance diagnostic accuracy in the face of diminished self-report data (Hegerl et al., 2007). When elements of the course of the disorder do not fit with what is known about the usual clinical course and history of the syndrome, alternative explanations for the clinical picture may then be more likely (rising to the top of the hypotheses about the cause of the current complaints). Reliance on checklists or a simple accounting of symptoms may be especially misleading in this patient population. As noted, missed or under treated medical problems and medication side effects may provoke a clinical picture that mimics mental illness including constipation, urinary retention and infections, reflux disease, dental pain, akathisia, extrapyramidal symptoms, sedation, seizures and numerous other physical conditions (Charlot et al, 2011 Espie et al., 2003; Gunsett, Mulick, Fernald, Martin, 1989; Kennedy, Juarez, Greenslade, Harvey, & Tally, 2007; Kwok & Cheung, 2007; Matson & Neal, 2009; O'Reilly, 1997; Valdovinos, Caruso, Roberts, Kim & Kennedy, 2005). In the study of major depressive disorder and other psychiatric syndromes, neuro-immunology and the role of inflammatory activation on brain development, neuroendocrine function and neurotransmitter activity is also a growing area of research.

5. Aggression and other externalizing behaviors may occur as "state-dependent" features of depressive episodes. A number of studies have demonstrated that individuals with ID diagnosed with depression frequently present with aggression (Charlot et al., 1993; Hurley, 2007; Meins, 1994; Reiss & Rojhan, 1993). However, some of these and other investigations suggest that the relationship is not "diagnostically specific" and do not recommend the use of "behavioral equivalents" (Allen & Davies, 2007; Charlot, 2005; Sturmey, Laud, Cooper, Matson & Fodstad, 2010; Tsiouris, Mann, Patti, & Sturmey, 2003). As suggested by Rutter (2011), for children it may be more helpful to use existing guidelines and criteria with minimal modifications and recognize that there are likely developmentally driven variations across the lifespan (Cicchetti & Toth, 2009). If a person with ID presents for evaluation, just because they have severe aggression does not mean they have an externalizing disorder (Charlot, 2005). Like neurotypical children, individuals with ID (who have a less developed or abnormal neurological and neurocognitive substrate) will often engage in negative behaviors rather than tell someone they are unhappy. A recent investigation by Hayes et al. (2011) showed that individuals with severe and profound ID with low mood were more likely to display challenging behaviors than peers who did not have mood problems. It is possible that externalizing behaviors occur in the context of mood disorders in individuals with ID related to dysphoric mood (Lowry, 1998). From a behavioral assessment perspective, Lowry (1998) noted that dysphoric mood (sadness, anxiety, irritability) may render demands more aversive and increase the person's efforts to escape them. When depressed, individuals with ID may begin to act aggressively in response to caregiver requests to attend activities in which they no longer have interest

(Lowry & Sovner, 1992). The elevated risk for aggression in this setting is "state dependent." It is important to recognize that individuals with ID by definition have abnormal brain substrates, and are less likely to be capable of regulating their dysphoric mood states because of characteristic executive deficits. In support of this perspective, Hayes et al. (2011) demonstrated that individuals with severe and profound intellectual disability with low mood were more likely to display challenging behaviors than non behavior challenged peers. Dysphoric mood (sadness, anxiety, irritability) may cause usually tolerated demands to be experienced as more aversive and increase the person's efforts to escape them (Lowry & Sovner, 1992). More recently, there have been some attempts to determine if there are subtypes of aggressive behaviors most likely associated with specific mood disorders (i.e. is self-injury more common in depressive disorders and aggression to others in mania?). Many different factors likely impact the expression of aggression by people with IDD. These include atypical brain development, temperamental tendencies, individual histories, and other contextual influences (Hunter, Wilkniss, Gardner, & Silverstein, 2008; Tsiouris, Kim, Brown, & Cohen, 2011).

Development and Course

Little is known about developmental trajectories in the evolution of psychopathology in people with ID. One longitudinal investigation found young people with ID had higher rates of symptoms and problems than peers without ID, at all ages and at each follow-up over a period of six years. However, the children with ID showed a greater reduction in problems over time (Emerson & Hatton, 2007). In a study conducted by Tonge and Enfield (2003), findings for children with ID were similar to reports regarding neurotypical individuals, in that a rise in depressive symptoms and disorders were seen in adolescence (suggesting depression is less common in younger people, with and without ID). In general, the implications are that developmental influences associated with the onset of adolescence confer elevated risk for depressive disorders (Thapar, Collishaw, Pine & Thapar, 2012).

In regards to accurate identification of a major depressive disorder, it is important to determine that symptoms are not always present and are mild most of the time, with only occasional difficult days. Symptoms must be persistent and clinically significant, interfering with the individual's ability to function. The onset should not be abrupt, as this suggests other more likely causes for the clinical picture, such as medical illness (i.e. CVA in older adults). Depressive episodes in bipolar disorder may have a more rapid onset (Hegerl et al., 2007). Abruptness of the changes may be the most relevant factor clarifying diagnosis.

The period of illness should be the same as determined in the general psychopathology literature (not one to two days periodically, but at least two weeks and usually more). For example, in one case treated by one of the chapter authors, a woman exhibited crying, loss of interest and pleasure, decreased speech, and withdrawn behavior with slowing and excessive sleep. The onset of her symptoms was abrupt, prompting more aggressive medical assessment that revealed an elevated epoxide level associated with her anti-epilepsy treatment. On a symptom checklist, she had numerous symptoms of depression, but these had been caused by a toxic metabolic encephalopathy.

Prevalence

Depression rates vary based on study methodologies, with few investigations being population based, and many using simple screens or symptom surveys as opposed to direct patient assessment or semi-structured diagnostic interview tools that are linked to a nosological system. Cooper et al. (2007a and b) conducted an epidemiological survey of adults with intellectual disabilities where screened cases were directly assessed, and rates were reported for clinical, DSM-IV-TR, and ICD-10 diagnoses. Rates were reported for a number of disorders including all mood or "affective" disorders of 6.7% based on clinical diagnosis, 5.7% based on DC-LD, 4.8% based on ICD-10-DCR, and 3.7% based on DSM-IV-TR. Using clinical judgment, 0.5% of the sample had a diagnosis of bipolar disorder (currently depressed) and 4.1% had a diagnosis of unipolar depression (currently in episode).

Dekker and Koot (2003) used the DISC and reported the rates of depression and other disorders among a group of 474 individuals with ID aged 7-20 years residing in Dutch "schools for the intellectually disabled." They found 4.4% of the population studied had a mood disorder and 25.1% a "disruptive behavior." They reported a high rate of comorbidity. Rates did not differ based on presence or absence of a pervasive developmental disorder.

White, Chant, Edwards Townsend & Waghorn (2005) conducted a population based study and reported a rate of 8% for depression in a sample of over 6,000 individuals with ID, based on ICD-10 criteria.

Leyfer and colleagues (2006) used a modified version of the The Kiddie Schedule for Affective Disorders and Schizophrenia (K-SADS) to assess a group of adolescents with ASD. Ten percent of the sample had at least one episode of major depression (based on DSM-IV criteria). About 24% were described as "sub-syndromal."

Shooshtari and colleagues (2014) conducted a population-based investigation of youth with "Developmental Disabilities" in a province in Canada, that included a matched group of children without ID. Administrative data were mined, and they reported that the youth with DD had nearly two times the rate of depressive disorder diagnoses.

There are significant discrepancies in the reported prevalence rates of depressive disorder in specific genetic conditions e.g. Down syndrome (Stavrakaki, Antochi & Emery 2004). A recent literature review on depression in individuals with a diagnosis of Down syndrome compared to other causes of intellectual disability did not support previous findings of increased prevalence of depressive disorder (Walker, Dosen, Buitelaar & Janzing, 2011). However, among the psychiatric disorders experienced by people with Down syndrome, depression is one of the most common while bipolar disorder appears to be rare.

Differential Diagnosis

Differential diagnosis of depression in people with ID requires that the clinician establish not only the presence of the symptom criteria but also that the symptoms co-occur, cause the person distress or functional impairment, are not transient, and represent a departure from usual behavior. Because some sources of potential data to aid in differential diagnostic assessment are less available when evaluating a patient with ID, it is even more important to consider the clinical course, history, and family patterns of illness, as well as the factors listed above (is the disorder severe, persistent, disruptive to this person's life etc.). In terms of accurate diagnostic assessments, it has been noted that "minor differences in the wording of probes and anchors can have a substantial influence on prevalence rates," so that studies using factor-derived screening tools are very likely to underestimate internalizing disorders such as depression (Rohde, Lewinsohn Klein, Seeley & Gau, 2012, p9). In terms of clinical work, it is also, again, highly recommended that probes are used as well as behavioral descriptions of possible manifestations of symptoms, as this is likely to help expand clinical information and increase detection of depressive disorders (Charlot et al., 2007a).

Differential diagnosis of mood disorders in people with ID has not been studied often. Adjustment disorder with depressed mood occurs in response to a specific psychosocial stressor, does not meet full criteria for a major depressive episode, and may be difficult to differentiate in people with ID. In the *DSM-5*, the bereavement exclusion has been dropped, as noted. Previously, bereavement would be diagnosed if depressive symptoms occurred after the loss of a loved one, even if the symptoms meet criteria for major depression, unless symptoms persist more than two months or the symptoms include marked functional impairment, morbid preoccupation with worthlessness, suicidal ideation, psychotic symptoms, or psychomotor retardation. Now, the clinician assesses whether the severity and symptom picture in regards to response to loss rises to the level of a major depressive episode. As with other stressful life events, the impact of personal loss may be underestimated in individuals with ID (Ghaziuddin, 1988; Stack, Haldipur & Thompson ,1987). Developmental stage could impact on the response to loss and change, and some adults with ID may respond more as children do, with significant separation anxiety or severe withdrawal (Pine et al., 2011; Trad, 1987).

Almost any form of physical distress or pain may also provoke a clinical picture that "mimics" depression, and may drive the co-occurrence of challenging behaviors as noted above. (Charlot et al., 2011).

Because people with ID (children and adults), like typically developing children, may be prone to psychomotor agitated depressions, bipolar disorder and ADHD may be a more common misdiagnosis in the setting of depression. Confusion over whether or not some youth who are irritable, explosive, and inattentive have an atypical and early onset for bipolar disorder has dominated discussions in the United States based childhood psychopathology literatures for over a decade (Leibenluft, 2011). Rates of diagnoses of bipolar disorder in children have been much higher than in other countries (i.e. United Kingdom) (Hassan, Agha, Langley & Thapar, 2011). Clearly how these disorders are defined affects case identification.

Confusion may arise when bipolar disorder is suspected for a person with ID because of mood lability, while this symptom has been identified as frequently occurring in samples of individuals with ID who are depressed (Charlot et al., 1993). Major depressive disorder is also typically episodic. As noted previously, episodic course may be seen with other factors causing apparent periods of lesser and greater challenges, (Pary, Levitas & Hurley, 1999). The critical consideration is that clinicians do not make diagnoses on the symptoms list alone, and the course of the disorder is carefully considered in the differential. The greater the definition of any disorder deviates from that applied for an established syndrome, the less confidence we can have that true variations will be found and that we can identify safe and effective treatments.

Large scale investigations have demonstrated that most people who suffer from major depressive disorder have had their first episode by early adulthood (Rohde et al., 2012). In people with ID, therefore, later onset of symptoms raises the concern that other causes of the observed symptoms should be entertained carefully.

Comorbidity

High rates of comorbidity of multiple psychiatric disorders have been described, especially between mood and anxiety disorders (Bakken et al., 2010; Charlot et.al., 2007a; Dekker & Koot, 2003). Charlot et al. (2002) found approximately 70% of inpatients met DSM criteria for more than one axis one psychiatric syndrome, with the combination of mood and anxiety disorders being most common.

Recent research regarding trauma and early life stress suggests that having a history of repeated episodes or chronic stress and trauma may predispose to more treatment resistant forms of adult psychiatric disorder, including depressive disorders (Heim & Binder, 2012). Removing the stressful factors or moving away from negative conditions can lead to significant improvement in many domains, but affective instability may be the most challenging feature of trauma-related disorders to mitigate. It is likely that for many people with ID, PTSD is a frequent comorbidity of depressive disorders.

Application of Diagnostic Criteria to People with ID

Associated Features of Depressive Disorders

In addition to the core symptom criteria described above, associated features may be seen in the context of a mood episode (i.e. catatonic features, psychotic features). Commonly associated features of depressive disorders have been described in people with ID such as psychotic symptoms, anxiety, and increases in ritualistic or obsessive-compulsive behaviors that co-vary with acute episodes of depression (Charlot et al., 2007a; Charlot, 1997; Hurley, Folstein & Lam, 2003; Marston, Perry & Roy, 1997; Tsiouris, 2001; Tsiouris et al., 2003).

Aggression and irritability are the most frequently documented "atypical" concomitants of depressive disorders in people with ID. A number of investigations have reported comorbidity of irritability, anger or aggression with depression (Charlot et al., 2007a; Charlot et al., 1993; Hurley et al., 2003; Johnson, Handen, Lubetsky, & Sacco, 1995; Lowry & Sovner, 1992; Marston et al., 1997; Meins, 1994; Reiss & Rojhan, 1993; Tsiouris, 2001). For example, Johnson et al. (1995) found that 80% of inpatient children with ID diagnosed with a mood disorder had comorbid aggression. However, a comparison group of children with other psychiatric diagnoses also displayed high rates of aggression (84%). Although commonly seen in association with mood disorders, aggression may not be specific to these syndromes in individuals with ID. Despite this, some have proposed and used such behaviors (and other symptoms and behaviors) as "substitute" symptoms for people with ID (or as "behavioral equivalents"). Others have argued that new criteria for depressive disorders are not warranted (Charlot, 2002; Charlot, 2005; Davies & Oliver, 2014; McBrian, 2003; Tsiouris, et al., 2003). Other "symptom substitutes" have been suggested for people with ID such as somatic complaints and crying (Clarke & Gomez, 1999; Davis, Judd & Herman, 1997). Somatic complaints are common developmental features seen in the setting of pre-school aged youth with depressive disorders (Bhatia & Bhatia, 2007; Cicchetti & Toth, 2009).

The relationship between mood disorder and externalizing behaviors has been somewhat controversial, with some investigators using aggression as a symptom substitute, creating special criteria for depression for people with ID. Two major reviews address the controversy in the past several years including one by Allen and Davies (2007) and most recently by Davies and Oliver (2014), with a general consensus that data simply do not support use of behavioral equivalents for diagnosing depression in people with ID. Tsiouris and colleagues (2011) concluded that depression was most likely over-diagnosed in individuals with milder ID and under-diagnosed in people with more severe cognitive challenges. There are variations in the form of aggression seen associated with different psychiatric diagnoses. However, the diagnoses were ones found in records and were not based on a direct assessment. A strength of this study was the use of a large population, including almost half of persons with ID in New York State. The study was aimed at understanding the nature and associations of sub-types of aggressive behavior, and three factors identified had the strongest associations, including perceived threat, impulse control disorder, and mood dysregulation. Of note, these variables are those frequently identified in the literature regarding outcomes of early life stress in typically developing youth who have complex clinical presentations ("multi-complex" youth) and who are at risk of adult depression in particular (Heim & Binder, 2012).

Other problems such as obsessive and compulsive symptoms, have also been reported in association with mood disorders in people with ID. Charlot (1997) found higher than expected rates of obsessive-compulsive symptoms in her sample of individuals diagnosed with major depression. Anxiety, somatic complaints, and withdrawn behavior have also been described as occurring in association with depressive disorders (Charlot, 1997; Marston et al., 1997; Meyers, 1998; Tsiouris, 2001; Tsiouris et al., 2003).

Psychotic symptoms are known to occur in the context of mood disorders and have been described in association with depression in individuals with ID (Hurley, 1996; Hurley & Moore, 1999; Meyers, 1998; Sovner & Pary, 1993; Tsiouris et al., 2003).

Review of Research Applying to People with ID

■ *Disruptive Mood Dysregulation Disorder*

There are no studies to date that address the new diagnostic category of disruptive mood dysregulation disorder in people with ID. The creation of the diagnostic category has been the subject of some controversy, and it is unclear how it may be adapted and used in the assessment of individuals with cognitive challenges. In recent years, increasing numbers of children have been diagnosed with bipolar disorder (Maj, 2013; McGough, 2014). In some cases, these children with unstable mood clearly met current diagnostic criteria for bipolar disorder, and in others the diagnosis was unclear (Axelson et.al.,

2011). The syndrome of disruptive mood dysregulation disorder was first defined to capture the symptomatology of children whose diagnostic status with respect to bipolar disorder was uncertain. These children had nonepisodic irritability and the hyperarousal symptoms characteristic of mania but lacked the well-demarcated periods of elevated or irritable mood characteristic of bipolar disorder. Levels of impairment are comparable between youths with bipolar disorder and those with severe mood dysregulation (Copeland, Angold, Costello & Egger 2013; Leibenluft, Cohen, Gorrindo, Brook, & Pine, 2006; McGough, 2014). An emerging literature compares children with severe mood dysregulation and those with bipolar disorder in longitudinal course, family history, and pathophysiology. Longitudinal data in both clinical and community samples indicate that nonepisodic irritability in youths is common and is associated with an elevated risk for anxiety and unipolar depressive disorders, but not bipolar disorder, in adulthood (Copeland et al., 2013; Leibenluft et al., 2006). Data also suggest that youths with severe mood dysregulation have lower familial rates of bipolar disorder than do those with bipolar disorder (Leibenluf et al., 2006). While youths in both patient groups have deficits in face emotion labeling and experience more frustration than do normally developing children, the brain mechanisms mediating these pathophysiologic abnormalities appear to differ between the two patient groups.

Findings that disruptive mood dysregulation disorder occurs mainly in younger children is significant for work with people with ID, as many have similar developmental profiles to these children. Also, many people with ID have been diagnosed with bipolar disorder based on a similar expansion of the diagnostic criteria to include people with chronic irritability, over-arousal, and explosive behaviors (LoVullo & Matson, 2009). Capacities for affective regulation and executive controls over behavioral impulses clearly differ for children at one or another point in their developmental trajectory (Pine et al., 2011). The same is likely true for people with ID (youth and adults) but based on unique and sometimes uneven developmental profiles, especially in autism spectrum disorders (Goldstein, Beers, Siegel & Minshew, 2001).

Individuals with a history of disruptive mood dsyregulation disorder also had higher rates for health problems, lower educational achievement, were more likely to be poor, and had more police contact (Copeland et al., 2013). These findings might be replicated in the future, in a study in which individuals with ID are included.

■ *Major Depressive Disorder*

Research regarding major depressive disorder in people with ID has shown that these individuals do present with symptoms of depression, including mood symptoms. A number of studies suggest that sad mood may be reported but also described by others (Charlot et al., 2007a; Charlot et al., 1993; Charlot et al., 2007b; Charlot et al., 2008; Clarke & Gomez, 1999; Meyers, 1998; Sovner & Hurley, 1983; Tsiouris et al., 2003). Several reports note frequent occurrence of irritable mood among individuals with ID who have been clinically diagnosed with depression (Charlot, 1997; Charlot et al., 1993; Reiss & Rojhan, 1993; Tsiouris et al., 2003). These findings parallel studies on the nature of depression in young children (Cicchetti & Toth, 2009; Rutter, 1988).

Hurley (2007) investigated outpatients with ID diagnosed with depression (n = 85), bipolar disorder (n = 70), or anxiety disorders (n = 30) and controls that were not diagnosed with a psychiatric syndrome (n = 27). She found that anhedonia, sad mood, and crying were key symptomatic features of depression in the sample. Hurley described the co-occurrence of aggression and other challenging behaviors in the outpatients with depression as being atypical features of depression but emphasized these were not "diagnostically specific." Also, of note, many patients with ID and depression in the study failed to meet DSM-IV-TR or DM-ID criteria for major depression due to having too few symptoms identified. She speculated that this might have been due to a lack of expressive communication skills or to caregivers failing to observe and report symptoms that may have been evident.

In a study by Tsiouris et al. (2003), 93 people with ID were assessed, and 33 were diagnosed with depression. The sample was further subdivided into depressed and non-depressed subjects, and a number of comparisons were then made. A variety of measures were used, and DSM-IV diagnostic criteria were applied. The sample included people who lived in community care situations or with their family as compared with a number of reports that included a large number of subjects from institutional settings (i.e. Charlot, 1997; Charlot et. al., 1993). It was unclear whether all of the people had been referred for psychiatric evaluation, and 40% were diagnosed with Down syndrome. Of note is the fact that nearly half of the subjects had severe/profound ID.

There are no details regarding the rates of specific psychiatric diagnoses of the "non-depressed" subjects in the investigation by Tsiouris and colleagues (2003), although it was noted that people diagnosed with schizoaffective disorder, manic episode, ocd, or psychotic disorder NOS were placed in this category. Irritability and aggression occurred at similar rates in the depressed and non-depressed group. However, this may not be surprising depending on how many of the people in the non-depressed group had other mood disorders. Aggression actually occurred at fairly low rates in both groups (depressed = 17% and non-depressed = 28%), compared to other clinically referred samples (Hurley et al., 2003).

In the Tsiouris et al. (2003) study, the eight most frequently reported symptoms (from the total of 30 listed) for subjects diagnosed with depression were as follows: anxiety (86%), depressed affect (66%), irritability (66%), loss of interest (54%), social isolation (54%), lack of emotion (49%), sleep disturbance (49%), and loss of confidence (49%). Significant associations were reported between group membership and 13 symptoms including: depressed affect, tearfulness, loss of interest, lack of emotion, sleep disturbance, diurnal variation, psychomotor retardation, loss of appetite, weight loss, loss of confidence, lack of energy, social isolation, and constipation. Factor analyses yielded a strong single factor resolution which contained the items of depressed affect, loss of interest, loss of energy, psychomotor retardation, and lack of emotional response. To validate the five-symptom depression scale, the authors divided the subjects into three groups including not depressed, mildly depressed (in remission), and depressed. Mean scores for this five-factor scale were highly significantly different for the three groups, suggesting that depression could be differentiated from other conditions (similar to findings reported by Cain et al., 2003, in regards to bipolar disorder). Challenging behaviors (a number of behaviors including aggression and self-injury but also running away, screaming, and stereotyped behavior) did not show any significant correlation with this five–point scale.

Withdrawn behavior appears to be common in individuals with ID who have been diagnosed with depression (Charlot, 1997; Charlot et al., 1993; Marston et al., 1997). Charlot (1997) suggested that withdrawn behavior may be a correlate or manifestation of anhedonia as informants in her investigations described individuals with suspected depression and ID as retreating from others due to their decreased interest in things that were previously enjoyed. Psychomotor agitation may be more common than psychomotor retardation, but some individuals show a combination of both (i.e., the person is withdrawn and underactive at times, and then becomes restless or agitated in response to demands) (Charlot, 1997; Charlot, et al., 1993; Meins, 1994). Several investigations noted depressed appearance, withdrawal, and somatic complaints to be commonly described symptoms (Charlot, 1997; Charlot, et al., 1993; Lowry, 1998; Meins, 1994; Reiss & Rojhn, 1993). Charlot et al. (1993) found that withdrawal, fatigue, decreased appetite, and presence of an episodic pattern differentiated individuals with mood disorders from peers who had other psychiatric diagnoses.

Individuals with adequate expressive language skills and more mild cognitive deficits have been noted to present with suicidal ideation, as well as symptoms of guilt and hopelessness (Benson & Laman, 1988; Charlot, 1997; Davis, Judd, & Herrman, 1997; Hurley, 2007; Hurley, 1998; Pawlarcyzk & Bekwith, 1987;

Sovner & Hurley, 1983; Sovner & Pary, 1993; Sternlicht, Pustel, & Duetsch, 1970; Walters, Barrett, Knapp & Borden, 1995).

In an unusual approach to studying depressive symptoms, Mayville, Matson, Laud, Cooper & Kuhn (2005) examined the relationship between patterns of eating and psychiatric symptoms. Individuals studied who met criteria for a depressive disorder had lower levels of food intake (Mayville et al., 2005). As noted by Hurley (2007), identifying symptoms that can be observed and measured can be helpful when trying to diagnose depression in a person who has limited communication skills.

■ *Bereavement*

Little has been written regarding pathologic or complicated bereavement in people with ID, though a very comprehensive review paper by Dodd, Dowling and Hollins (2005) summarizes key findings and considerations. They note that people with ID are living longer, so that it is more common for them to be in a family home, intensifying the impact of the loss. Further, in many of these situations, the person loses a parent or caregiver and then also has the stress of immediately needing to move. Degree of cognitive impairment (or developmental profile) has an impact on whether or not the person with ID may understand that death is irreversible. Despite this observation, people with ID may show grief responses from the simple absence of someone with whom they had been close. As Dodd and colleagues emphasize, in the instance of grief and loss, people with ID are more like everyone else than not. Consistent with recent concerns raised about dropping of the bereavement exclusion criteria for the diagnosis of major depressive disorder, the authors note that at times normal grieving can be inadvertently and inappropriately treated (as if it were a sign of psychopathology) in people with ID.

Similar to findings in youth, grief reactions of people with ID may also be associated with disturbed behavior, adding to the risk that the reaction will be seen as reflecting psychiatric syndromes. This then may trigger a potentially unnecessary medical intervention, or even prevent implementation of more important grief counseling strategies. In aiding individuals with ID to cope with losses (and to prevent development of psychiatric sequelae), interventions may need to be adapted to meet the needs of the person with his/her unique developmental profile of skills and challenges. Further research will be required to define the boundaries between a normal grief reaction and one that has persisted or evolved into the clinical syndrome of depression in people with ID. Dodd and colleagues (2005) suggest that clinicians should assess symptoms "carefully...with a view to accurately describing the specific symptoms of traumatic grief in this population" (p. 542). Perhaps addressing attachment and separation as developmental issues germane to ID would be a solution.

In terms of the DSM-5 dropping the bereavement exclusion for major depressive disorder, some argue that for people with ID a similar concern may arise (or already be in operation) where routine responses to stress that are developmentally driven (so appear more primitive in some adults with ID) may be viewed as requiring medication rather than more basic supportive care.

■ *Persistent Depressive Disorder (Formerly Dysthymia)*

Few studies address "dysthymia" or persistent depressive disorder in people with ID. In one report, two individuals had histories of what appeared to be dysthymia and both eventually experienced major depressive episodes. Symptoms described included the following: depressed mood, hypochondriasis, social withdrawal, reduced interest, reduced concentration, irritability, wish to die, hysterical symptoms, agitation, absconding from hospital, poor appetite, low energy, and paranoid ideas. Vegetative symptoms were primarily evident only during major depressive episodes. Jancar and Gunaratne (1994) speculated that dysthymia might be missed in people with ID.

A second investigation out of Italy from 1999 used the Kiddie-Schedule for Schizophrenia and Affective Disorders or K-SADs (Puig-Antich & Chambers, 1983) to examine the phenomenology of outpatients with ID after establishing that these individuals were capable of responding to the semi-structured interview questions (Masi, Mucci, Favilla, & Poli, 1999). The authors excluded outpatients with "double depression," or those who met criteria for both dysthymia and major depressive disorder, and individuals meeting criteria for a major personality disorder or psychosis. The investigation is especially significant for its examination of developmental effects. The final study groups consisted of twelve individuals with ID (mean age about 16 years) and two subsets of children and teens with typical developmental histories aged 7-11 and 12-18 years. The authors found that the K-SADs was a useful diagnostic tool and provides a clinical profile of depressive symptoms. Parent and child responses were more concordant for the youth with ID than previously found in studies of neurotypical youth, though the subjects reported more depressed mood than parents, who did note poor self-image at high rates. A profile emerged for the subjects with ID that included high rates of the symptoms of depressed mood, irritability, excessive guilt, and low self-image. Of note, the subjects with ID showed a profile more similar to that found in the younger subjects without ID. There was a high rate of comorbid generalized anxiety disorder.

■ *Premenstrual Dysphoric Disorder*

Few studies address the occurrence of premenstrual dysphoric disorder in populations of people with ID. One investigation of "period pain" and premenstrual mood disorder in youth with Down syndrome and autism spectrum disorder concluded that individuals studied who had Down syndrome or autism spectrum disorder were more likely to have pain than neurotypical peers, but also were more likely to demonstrate this primarily through behavioral changes (Burke, Kalpakjian, Smith & Quint, 2010). Another investigation including adolescents with Down syndrome, cerebral palsy and autism spectrum disorder found subjects with autism spectrum disorder were the most likely to have mood problems associated with menses and were also more likely to display menses associated challenging behaviors (Kaminer et al., 1988). Hamilton and colleagues (2011) studied 10-25 year olds with ASD and noted premenstrual syndrome and dysmenorrhea symptoms were "frequent" and "severe" (Hamilton, Marshal & Murray, 2011). All authors note a paucity of research on this topic and the need for more investigation (Kyrkou, 2005).

■ *Depressive Disorder Due to Another Medical Condition*

A number of medical disorders can directly provoke depressive symptoms and can play a role for people with ID (i.e. hypothyroidism). In general, people with ID have a higher rate of comorbid medical disorders than individuals without ID and are at risk for these problems being missed or under-treated (Kerr et al., 2003; Kwok & Cheung, 2007). High rates of comorbid medical problems have been reported among psychiatric inpatients with ID (Charlot et al., 2011).

In studies of individuals with Down syndrome, dementia shares many symptoms with depression, such as apathy, psychomotor slowing, decreased ability to perform activities of daily living, anhedonia, sleep disturbance, appetite disturbance, and decreased memory and concentration (Burt, Loveland & Lewis, 1992). Differential diagnosis can be particularly complicated in people with ID, and in some cases, these conditions co-exist.

More generally, as described above, people with ID are likely to display altered mood and behavior when ill from any kind of a health issue or medication side effect. It is not uncommon for people with neurodevelopmental disorders to be withdrawn, refuse activities, and seem moody or irritable when experiencing pain or physical distress. Cooper et al. (2007a), for example, found that people with ID identified with psychiatric syndromes in a general population study had a greater number of medical contacts in the 12-month period prior to the study.

Individuals with ID or who have structural brain anomalies may be at increased risk for experiencing neuroleptic-induced drug side effects (Gualtieri, Schroeder, Hicks & Quade, 1986). Cognitive impairment has been identified as a risk factor for drug induced movement disorders (Bhidayasiri & Boonyawairoj, 2010).

A variety of extrapyramidal symptoms have been described, and these can also appear as tardive phenomena. In many cases, movement problems may be associated with alterations in mood, appetite, sleep, or motor behavior (Peluso, Lewis, Barnes & Jones, 2012).

A potentially long lasting "neuroleptic withdrawal syndrome" that includes features often seen in depressive disorders such as irritability, disrupted sleep, weight loss, and agitated behavior has been described in several reports (Mikkelsen, Albert, & Upadhya, 1988). Since these agents are the most commonly prescribed psychoactive medications for people with ID (Davies & Olvier, 2014; Lott et al. 2004; Nøttestad & Linaker, 2003), and given the fact that the problem may emerge when switching from a typical or older antipsychotic medication to a newer or atypical one, clinicians should be aware of this as a possibility (Peluso et al., 2012). Neuroleptic withdrawal-related problems might be suspected when depressive symptoms including irritability, poor sleep and appetite, and motor restlessness have their onset following a rapid neuroleptic taper, switching (as described), or immediately following discontinuation of an antipsychotic medication.

■ *Substance/Medication-Induced-Depressive Disorder*

Few studies address the specific question of a depressive disorder caused by a drug of abuse in persons with ID. As noted elsewhere, persons with intellectual disability "suffer disproportionately" from substance use problems when compared to typically developing peers (Chapman & Wu, 2012). While fewer persons with ID use alcohol and recreational drugs than the general population, the likelihood of misuse is relatively high (McGillicuddy, 2006). More research is needed to determine whether individuals with ID and major depression are at greater risk for a substance use disorder. Chaplin, Gilvarry and Tsakanikos (2011) conducted a retrospective review of 115 adults with ID. Psychiatric disorders were divided into schizophrenia spectrum, affective disorders, personality disorders, and autism spectrum. Alcohol was most frequently used followed by cannabis and then cocaine. Nicotine was not included. Among adults with ID, only those with a diagnosis of schizophrenia spectrum were significantly more likely to have occasional or continuous/heavy use. Another study, however, suggests that mood symptoms may be associated with substance misuse in persons with ID. To, Neirynck, Vanderplasschen, Vanheule and Vandevelde (2014) sent a questionnaire to caregivers in northern Belgium. There were 104 persons with ID identified who either used or misused substances. Again, alcohol was the most common substance, followed by cannabis and then cocaine. Also, nicotine was not included in the study. Those who misused substances were significantly more likely to have mood changes or suicidal ideation.

Adults with Mild to Moderate Intellectual Disability

Most of the studies reviewed in this chapter involved people with mild/moderate ID though a few had mixed samples (usually a much smaller number of subjects had severe/profound ID). Sample selection techniques and the methods used to establish cases varied widely. In many cases, raters were not blind to diagnosis, reviews were retrospective, or there were other problems with reliability and validity. Despite all of these concerns, there were some consistent findings including the fact that people with mild/moderate ID show the full range of mood symptoms as described in DSM-IV-TR. Although some variations in surface features are reported, the core syndromes seem to be much the same as described in people without ID. Rates for aggression or other comorbid externalizing behavior problems appear to be somewhat lower for people with mild/moderate ID when compared with people with severe/profound ID. In people with very mild cognitive impairments, a combination of self and informant reports about symptoms and history may be used. The general consensus appears to be that people with very mild cognitive disabilities and good expressive language skills can be assessed with minimal adjustments to diagnostic criteria, clinical interviews, and self-report questionnaires. However, clinicians should be cautious and make this determination based on a solid understanding of the developmental level and skills of the individual being assessed. Individuals with moderate ID are often grouped with people with mild ID but may have significantly less ability to report cognitive symptoms of depression if one considers the relationship between these and typical skills associated with developmental level (Harris, 1998).

Adults with Severe or Profound Intellectual Disability

As for people with mild/moderate ID, studies including subjects with severe/profound ID have not used clearly established, reliable, and validated means to determine if individuals met DSM or other specific criteria for a depressive disorder. The application of widely varying techniques to establish cases, sample selection problems, failure to perform evaluations blind to diagnosis, and a host of other methodological weaknesses have been noted. Despite these concerns, some general findings have been reported.

Cognitive symptoms of depression are not typically described in people with little or no verbal abilities (e.g., with severe or profound ID). Symptoms of hopelessness, feelings of guilt, and expressing thoughts about death or a wish to die are not accessible or may not be possible, due to complexity of cognitive functioning (Charlot, 1997; Charlot, et. al, 1993; Clarke & Gomez, 1999; Meins, 1994).

Ross & Oliver (2003) reviewed studies of mood disorders in people with ID in which at least some of the subjects assessed had severe/profound ID diagnoses. They concluded that most of these studies still had a larger proportion of subjects with mild/moderate ID, with the exception of the Charlot et al. (1993) study in which approximately 73% of subjects had a severe/profound ID. This study had a number of methodological problems, in particular because the manner of identifying the presence or absence of given DSM-III-R symptoms was not clearly explained. However, these authors found that subjects did display symptoms of mood disorders according to multiple informants interviewed and that people with severe/profound ID who failed to meet criteria did so because of a failure to meet cognitive criteria. By virtue of this, some of the subjects with severe/profound ID had only 3 additional mood symptoms, apart from the core mood symptom. Cain et al. (2003) made a similar observation. Meins (1994) also concluded that people with ID (including some who had severe/profound ID) typically met basic criteria but sometimes had fewer than a total of five symptoms of depression.

Ross & Oliver (2003) found that most investigations of mood disorders in people with severe/profound ID modified DSM-III-R criteria, and the assessment tools used to identify the presence of mood symptoms posed some special problems. These authors expressed particular concern about the reliability and validity of techniques used to establish the presence (or absence) of diagnostic criteria such as the evaluation of irritable mood, suicidal tendencies, guilt, and hopelessness. Even on the DASH-II, an informant-based psychiatric assessment tool developed specifically for use with people with severe/profound ID, some of the items cannot be assessed in people who do not have speech (Matson, Gardner, Coe & Sovner, 1991). When rating scales or screening tools were used, such terms were not clearly operationally defined. In a more recent investigation, Hayes and colleagues (2011) studied a series of institutional residents with severe to profound ID and were able to gain information regarding observed indicators of low mood based on informant reports. The authors used the MIPQ (Mood Interest and Pleasure Questionnaire), an informant-based instrument that employs behavioral descriptions of depressed mood and anhedonia specifically designed for use with persons with more severe cognitive challenges. Challenging behaviors were associated with low mood. The authors point out that low mood may occur related to either medical issues or medication side effects, and such influences might also provoke challenging behaviors, suggesting that future investigations should examine such relationships.

In people with severe/profound ID, it may be even more critical that clinicians recognize that externalizing behaviors may not be specific to mood disorders. Rates of aggression in general are higher in people with severe/profound ID and were reported at higher rates for these individuals when compared with persons with mild ID also diagnosed with a mood disorder (Charlot, 1997; Meins, 1994). Hayes and colleagues (2011), for example, demonstrated that individuals with severe and profound intellectual disability with low mood were more likely to display challenging behaviors than non behavior challenged peers.

Sovner & Pary (1993) summarized some of the challenges in assessing people with more severe levels of cognitive disability:

> For patients who are nonverbal due to the severity of their disabilities or presence of a pervasive developmental disorder, the major diagnostic task is to detect syndrome-specific affective behavior against a background of nonspecific behavioral responses triggered by a multiplicity of physiological, psychological, and social stimuli. A low 'signal to noise ratio' makes it difficult, if not impossible, to elicit full DSM-III-R criteria for depression and mania in individuals with greater than moderate handicaps. (p.102)

Ross & Oliver (2003) concluded that there may be merit to an approach in which external and universally accepted signs of positive mood can be observed and measured reliably and that the reverse may also be possible (to observe and measure behavioral signs of negative affect). The application of this approach to the assessment of DSM-5 depressive disorders symptoms criteria in people with ID, however, has not been systematically investigated. Sovner & Hurley (1983) suggested that clinicians can focus on certain critical features of mood disorders in people with severe/profound ID that can be observed (and even measured), and do not require reliance on the individual's ability to self-report. Alterations in patterns of eating/weight, sleep, and motor activity can be reliably reported by others. Familiar informants often provide what appear to be accurate reports about mood. Multiple informants interviewed separately will often agree that a person with severe/profound ID has been, for example, smiling less, crying, or refusing activities that were once preferred or clearly enjoyed.

In general, people with severe/profound ID are less likely to meet full criteria because they cannot meet cognitive criteria for the various mood disorder diagnoses, as emphasized by Hurley and others (Hurley, 2007; Charlot et al., 1993; Meins, 1994).

Children and Adolescents with Intellectual Disability

Major depressive disorder occurs at similar rates in adolescents as in adults in general population studies, with youth demonstrating significant comorbidity, between 30 and 80% (Rohde et al., 2012). When there is an earlier onset, the form taken may be more severe (Rohde et al., 2012). As noted previously, many youth with symptoms of disruptive mood dysregulation disorder eventually develop a depressive disorder (Leibenluft, 2011). A few studies have examined the nature of depressive disorders in youth with ID. Matson, Barrett and Helsel (1988) examined depression in seven clinically diagnosed children with ID, comparing these inpatients with ID to a non-referred group of children without ID and to other inpatients with ID who had different psychiatric problems. DSM symptoms of depression were found at high rates in the children who had received this diagnosis, and cutoff scores from standard childhood depression rating instruments correlated highly with the diagnosis. A retrospective study of 50 children and adolescent inpatients with mood disorders and ID found depressed appearance, withdrawal, and somatic complaints to be common symptoms that differentiated children with ID and mood disorders from peers with other psychiatric diagnoses (Johnson et al., 1995). These authors also noted a high comorbidity of externalizing behavior problems, commenting on the consistency of their finding with research regarding depressed children without ID. However, the comparison group of youth with ID with other psychiatric disorders also had high rates of challenging behaviors.

Reiss and Rojhan (1993) conducted the first large study of depression in people with ID that included a substantial number of children. These authors used a two-step procedure to select subjects, starting with large and more representative groups than some of the other investigations (that were mainly composed of clinically-referred subjects). Reiss and Rojhan did not report on the application of DSM criteria, but used a factor-derived scale cut–off score to identify individuals as depressed or not depressed. The scales, however, did include a number of DSM-III-R symptom criteria (though not all). The authors found that the risk of aggression was four times greater for their subjects who were classified as depressed. Measures of "anger" also correlated highly with sad mood and aggression, suggesting a possible connection among these three factors.

More recent research has added to the research base examining depressive disorders in youth with ID. An Australian longitudinal study provides critical information about the course and emergence of depressive symptoms in youth. Findings included that depressive sub scale items from the DBC (Developmental Behaviour Checklist) were significantly higher at time points (with 8-9 years of follow-up) where the subjects had entered adolescence as compared with younger age points, similar to findings in the general child psychopathology literature. Emerson (2003) and later Emerson and Hatton (2007) contrasted children with and without ID and did not find that depression occurred any more often in the youth with ID, though overall psychopathology was greater in the group with ID. Of note the overall rate of any psychiatric disorder of 36% is similar to that reported for adults with ID. Dekker and Koot (2003) found rates of depression in youth to be about 4.4 %, a rate similar though slightly higher to that reported for non-ID youth (Cooper et al., 2007a; Rohde et al., 2012).

In typically developing youth, risk for depression includes being female, having a family history of depression, past childhood abuse or neglect, stressful life events, and chronic illness (Bhatia & Bhatia, 2007). All of these factors are elevated in youth and adults with ID (see psychosocial risk factors section of this chapter). A recent review of the research in childhood maltreatment found that having a history of abuse in childhood significantly increases the risk of later having recurrent depressive episodes (Nanni, Uher, & Danese, 2012), suggesting that people with ID may be at particular risk for depression as adults. Experts in childhood psychopathology emphasize the fact that depression phenomenology may vary based on developmental influences (age or stage), noting that, "some children and adolescents may have difficulty identifying and describing internal mood states" (p. 73). They describe children under the age of 7 (who may share much in common with many adults with ID) as presenting with irritability and having "angry, hostile behavior." As suggested, findings regarding developmental influences on depressive phenomenology in typically developing youth may aid in diagnostic assessment of both younger and older people with ID (because they share developmental features that influence surface manifestations).

Bhatia and Bhatia (2007), for example, note that under-diagnosis of depression is a greater risk in youth under the age of 7 years. The same concern may be raised in regards to both children and adults with ID with severe or profound ID, who, as Tsiouris and colleagues (2011) suggested, may be at greatest risk of having a depression missed.

Summary of Limitations in Applying DSM-IV-TR Criteria to People with ID

Some experts have argued that existing diagnostic systems are inadequate to meet the unique needs of individuals with ID (Dosen, 2005). In general, as noted in other sub-sections of this chapter, use of DSM criteria for diagnosing depressive disorders is seen as useful and realistic for most people with mild ID and many with more severe cognitive challenges. Dosen urged a process-oriented approach, rather than a symptom-based procedure, to develop case formulations. He described a developmental framework, providing guidance as to the various ways developmental features may impact clinical phenomena. Though DSM-5 as it was finally operationalized remains much the same as its preceding iterations, one advance has been the recognition that contextual influences such as developmental profile or age and gender may significantly impact at least how disorders are manifested, if not their pathogenesis. In terms of the latter, longitudinal investigations have shown that complex transactions occur between early experience, brain development, and later behavioral patterns (Rutter, 2011). Timing of stressful experiences is important, and there may be variable outcomes when traumatic events occur in younger versus older children, for example. Depressive disorders, possibly more than most others, are often preceded by stressful life events for people with and without ID. Rutter (2011) has emphasized that there are also highly variable outcomes from discrete stressful or traumatic events, and ongoing or chronic adversity. Significant recovery is possible when adverse environments change, and positive supports and experiences replace them. Vulnerabilities likely play a role in how well people bounce back after adversities and, therefore, who develops depression and who does not. Individuals with ID may be at great risk for depressive disorders, and the rates reported to date may be low because of the imitations to using categorical classifications, in general, and, in particular, their use with a population with highly complex challenges in medical, neurological, and psychosocial domains.

As DSM-5 emerged, there has been some disappointment with regards to early hopes of finding biomarkers and structural neurological problems that would help demarcate syndromes. As noted above, shared pathways have been the norm with minimal findings of specificity for DSM categorical diagnoses reported to date. The DSM-5 does embrace the need for more consideration of developmental effects on disorder development as well as phenomenology, and there is a deeper understanding that direct genotype to phenotype explanations of specific syndromes are highly unlikely (King, Veenstra-VanderWeele & Lord, 2013). As argued by many experts, a blended model of categorical and dimensional approaches to the characterization of psychopathology seems required, to develop case formulations from which effective treatments may be designed.

As noted above, findings from prevalence and epidemiologic research regarding psychiatric syndromes in populations of individuals with ID show widely varying rates depending on methods applied. A lesson might be taken from childhood psychopathology studies suggesting that investigations (and clinical practices) where lists of symptoms dominate the process of case identification tend to lack specificity and lack utility in the search for biomarkers and efforts to elucidate unique pathways for specific disorders. In contrast, studies in which the process includes much more attention to clinical course and history of symptom evolution, contextual and developmental influences, family history, treatment responses, and in general, applies a more "gestalt" approach yield much greater predictive power (Cicchetti & Toth, 2009).

The risk of under-selection of true cases may have been of the most concern to advocates for people with ID, who were thought not even capable of suffering from depressive syndromes as recently as the 1980's (Sovner & Hurley, 1983) However, more recent trends suggest people with ID may be over-diagnosed with disorders such as bipolar disorder and other psychotic disorders, while depression and anxiety may be missed. This contention is most supported by the observation that population-based studies using multi-stage methodologies find higher rates of anxiety and depression, and lower rates for bipolar disorder and psychosis, when compared to less rigorous investigations. It is unclear how this translates into daily clinical practices, but the extraordinarily high rates of prescriptions of antipsychotic medications given to people with ID suggests that either depressive disorders are missed, or that treatment focus is on reducing comorbid aggression, or both (Lott et al., 2004; Matson & Neal, 2009; Sheehan et al., 2015).

Critically, because "people with ID" are a highly heterogeneous population, investigations of groups of people with specific genetic anomalies holds the most promise for future treatment development (i.e. options that target the basic underlying deviations in protein function such as some of the research in fragile X syndrome). These studies may also play a key role in elucidating pathogenesis of symptoms or disorders (King et al., 2013).

Etiology and Pathogenesis

Biological Factors

Some authors have suggested that abnormalities in serotonin pathways may play a role in the development of depressive disorders in people with ID, based on case reports of improvement following treatment with SSRIs (Davis et al., 1997; Sovner, Fox, Lowry & Lowry, 1993) and on the co-occurrence of impulsive aggression, obsessive-compulsive symptoms, and depression (Charlot, 1997). As stated earlier, the biological basis of depression, though extensively investigated, has yet to yield a reliable biomarker or to identify structural anomalies of the brain specific to depression alone. In neurotypical individuals, multiple neurotransmitter/receptor systems have been implicated, perhaps acting in concert, including serotonin, dopamine, norepinephrine, glutamate, and mu and kappa opioid systems. Mitochondrial dysfunction may play a role (Rezin, Amboni, Zugno, Quevedo & Streck, 2009). As noted by Kupfer, Frank and Phillips (2012) there are several categories of peripheral hormone-type factors that may be involved in the development of depression: neurotrophic factors and other growth factors (including BDNF, vascular endothelial growth factor, and insulin-like growth factor-1); proinflammatory cytokines (including interleukin-1 , interleukin-6, and tumour necrosis factor-); and impaired regulation of the hypothalamic-pituitary-adrenocortical (HPA) axis. In one example they sited, serum BDNF is decreased in individuals with major depression, and antidepressant treatment reverses this decrease (Brunoni, Lopes, & Fregni, 2008; Sen, Duman & Sanacora 2008). To the knowledge of this chapter's authors, these issues have not been specifically explored in individuals with ID.

Age is a risk factor in depressive disorders in people without ID. Rates reported for major depressive disorder increase markedly after puberty (Geller & Luby, 1997). There has been very limited study of the topic regarding individuals with ID (Smiley, 2005). Female gender has also been identified as a risk factor in the general psychiatric literature and was also confirmed in reports regarding people with ID. The DSM-5 states that females without ID experience 1.5 to 3 fold higher rates than males without ID for prevalence of major depression beginning in early adolescence. In a study utilizing structured interviews of adults with ID and their caregivers (Lunsky, 2003), females with ID reported statistically significantly higher levels of depressive symptoms than did males with ID.

Sleep disorder or sleep problems may occur at very high rates in people with ID and especially in persons with severe/profound ID (Harris, 1998). Individuals with ID appear to be at risk for elevated rates of a variety of medical problems including thyroid disease, which may cause symptoms of depression (Hendrick, Altshuler, Gitlin, Delrahim & Hammen, 2000). People with Down syndrome have higher than usual rates of hypothyroidism (some estimates suggest as high as 35%), suffer from depression at elevated rates, and rarely present with mania (Pary, Strauss, & White, 1996).

Seizure disorders have been reported at high rates in individuals with ID (Espie et al., 2003; Harris, 1998) . Some individuals have mood changes secondary to seizure foci in specific brain areas that make them more vulnerable to develop a mood disorder (Tisher et al., 1996). Rates for depressive and other mood syndromes have ranged between 7 to nearly 30% among individuals with ID and epilepsy. Of note, some individuals show reduced signs of depression and irritability after a period of low seizure frequency, only when they finally have another seizure. Turky, Felce, Jones, and Kerr (2011) contrasted psychiatric disorders among two groups of individuals with ID (n = 45 each) with and without comorbid epilepsy, matched for level of cognitive challenges, and found much higher rates of depressive disorders in the epilepsy/ID group.

A link between a temporal lobe focus in epilepsy and depression has been reported (Sanchez-Gistau et al., 2010). Smith and Matson (2010) found that institutionalized adults with ID, autism spectrum disorder, and epilepsy had the highest rates of challenging behavior as compared with peers without the three comorbidities, but they did not report associations with specific psychiatric disorder diagnoses. On the other hand, in a study of 318 community based adults with ID, Cooper and van der Speck (2009) found no statistically significant difference in rates of mental ill health and problem behavior between persons who had epilepsy and those who did not.

Depressive symptoms can occur in relation to decreased stimulation associated with onset or increased severity of sensory impairment (e.g., vision or hearing loss). Sensory impairments occur at elevated rates among persons with ID (Harris, 1998) and may occur at high rates in people without ID when compared with other outpatients (Hurley et al., 2003). Depression may also occur if deteriorating vision or hearing leads to a loss of ability to function and a loss of independence.

The ways in which brain damage causes increased risk of psychiatric disorder are not well understood. Effects may be direct (based on disruptions to certain pathways) or indirect (causing affected individuals to be more vulnerable to stressful circumstances) (Harris, 1998). People with cerebral palsy (which occurs at high rates among people with ID) may be at greater risk for depression and may have specific problems in regulating affective states (Harris, 1998).

In a retrospective chart review of patients with and without ID in one out-patient clinic (Hurley et al., 2003) depressive disorder was the most likely diagnosis in those with mild ID and was found at a statistically significant higher rate than in individuals with moderate/severe ID. Depression has been reported to occur more in people with mild or moderate ID as compared with severe or profound ID (Cooper et al., 2007a; Holden & Gitlesen, 2004). The discrepancies may relate not to the degree of global brain impairment, but more so to methodological differences in case ascertainment.

Genetic Factors

There are data suggesting increased rates of depressive disorders in the first degree relatives of probands with ID diagnosed with depression, though most have identified elevated rates of mood disorders in the family members of individuals with bipolar disorder. Dosen (1984) found that 29% of the depressed children he studied had a family history of major psychiatric disorder. In the Lainhart and Folstein (1994) report, 50% of the 17 cases had a family history of mood disorders or suicidalty. Although obtaining a family history can be helpful in any psychiatric evaluation, it may be especially useful in clarifying a confusing diagnostic picture when assessing an individual with ID.

A number of syndromes that cause ID have also been found to confer increased risk of various "behavioral phenotypes," or for specific psychiatric syndromes, including depressive disorders. Those with some association with depressive syndromes include Tubersouys sclerosis, 22 q11 deletion syndrome, Neurofibramatosis (NF1), Prader-Willi Syndrome (PWS), Phenylketo-nuria (PKU), Myotonic dystrophy type 1, Rubenstein Taybi syndrome (RTS) (Boustany, 2010; Brumm, Bilder & Waisbren, 2010; Cassidy & Driscoll, 2009; Jolin, Weller & Weller, 2011; Maalouf, Hatoum, Atwi & Boustany 2010; Muzykewicz, Newberry, Danforth, Halpern & Thiele, 2007; Verhoeven, Tuinier, Kuijpers, Egger & Brunnerd, 2010; Winblad, Jensen, Mansson, Samuelsson & Lindberg, 2010). See Chapter 3 for details regarding behavioral phenotypes with impact on depressive and other psychiatric disorders.

Psychosocial Factors

There is an extensive literature that links significant life events and subsequent psychiatric disorder in the general population. Children with ID were found to experience a greater number of adverse life events than individuals without disability (Hatton & Emerson, 2004). For children with ID, life events were found to be associated with emotional and behavioral problems (Taggart, Taylor & McCrum-Gardner, 2010) and with the occurrence of psychiatric disorder, emotional disorder, or conduct disorder (Hatton & Emerson, 2004). For adults with ID, research findings support the association of prior significant life events and psychopathology, in general (Cooper et al., 2007b; Hamilton, Sutherland & Iacono, 2005; Tsakanikos, Bouras, Costello & Holt, 2007). It has been suggested that the experience of a traumatic event has a more significant impact on subsequent mental ill-health than the life events typically surveyed (Martorell et al., 2009).

There is a link between significant life events and depression, specifically in the general population (Paykel et al., 1969). Some evidence indicated that the type of life event was important, such that events largely viewed as negative, including personal losses, were more likely to have occurred prior to a depression diagnosis than other events (Paykel et al., 1969). For adults with ID, several studies substantiated a correlation between the number of prior significant life events and the PAS-ADD Affective/ Neurotic subscale score (Moss et al., 1998) both in an inpatient setting and in the community (Hamilton et al., 2005; Hastings, Hatton, Taylor & Maddison, 2004; Owen et al., 2004).

Research on the psychosocial correlates of depression in individuals with ID has more often focused on the number of depressive symptoms obtained from self-report or informant report than through study of diagnosed individuals. However, studies with diagnostic groups also substantiate an association between the number of prior life events and a depression diagnosis (Cooper et al., 2007a; Esbensen & Benson, 2006). In the Esbensen and Benson study (2006) the total number of significant life events and the number of events perceived as negative, but not events viewed as positive, were associated with the diagnosis in adults with ID. An association between the number of life events and subsequent diagnosis of depression was also found in children with pervasive developmental disorder in an inpatient setting (Ghaziuddin, Alessi & Greden, 1995).

Whereas significant life events refers to discrete happenings such as change in residence, death of a loved one, or losing a job, the concept of daily hassles refers to other environmental factors that can also cause distress such as hearing an argument or disagreeing with a peer. Lunsky and Bramston (2006) found a significant correlation between depressive symptoms and scores on a Lifestress Inventory in adults with ID. The association between significant life events and subsequent depression has primarily been studied retrospectively which limits the interpretation of the association to correlation, not causation. Longitudinal studies are required to further explore the nature of the relationship and to gauge the relative impact of other factors (Hulbert-Williams & Hastings, 2008; Hulbert-Williams et al., 2014).

Social support has been viewed as a potential buffer against the impact of significant life events on mental health. McGillivray and McCabe (2007) found that the quality and frequency of social support provided to adults with ID was a significant regression model predictor of depression symptoms based on Beck Depression scores. Perceived social support was negatively associated with self-reported depression symptoms in adults with Down syndrome (Ailey, Miller, Heller & Smith, 2006). Lack of social support has also been found to be associated with suicidal ideation in adults with ID (Lunsky, 2004). Social strain, the experience of interpersonal conflict, may potentiate the impact of significant life events on mental health. Social strain and problems getting along with family members were associated with depressive symptoms in adults with ID (Lunsky, 2003; Lunsky & Benson, 2001). Adults with ID diagnosed with depression had more stressful social interactions than did non-depressed individuals (Hartley & MacLean, 2009).

Low self-esteem, loneliness, automatic negative thoughts, and downward social comparison have each been found to be associated with depressive symptoms in adults with mild to moderate ID (Ailey et al., 2006; McGillivray & McCabe, 2007). Hartley and McClean (2009) found that adults with mild ID diagnosed with depression had a more negative attributional style and used more avoidant and less active coping strategies than did non-depressed individuals. The authors suggested that these mechanisms may support the maintenance of depressed mood in adults with ID.

Disruptive Mood Dysregulation Disorder

DSM-5 Diagnostic Criteria	Applying Criteria for Mild to Profound ID
A. Severe recurrent temper outbursts manifested verbally (e.g., verbal rages) and/or behaviorally (e.g., physical aggression toward people or property) that are grossly out of proportion in intensity or duration to the situation or provocation.	A. No adaptation
B. The temper outbursts are inconsistent with developmental level.	B. Consider person's developmental profile, degree and type of intellectual challenges. Some adults with IDD may meet criteria for this disorder when considering developmental profile rather than chronological age.
C. The temper outbursts occur, on average, three or more times per week.	C. No adaptation.
D. The mood between temper outbursts is persistently irritable or angry most of the day, nearly every day, and is observable by others (e.g., parents, teachers, peers).	D. No adaptation.
E. Criteria A-D have been present for 12 or more months. Throughout that time, the individual has had a bad period last 3 or more consecutive months without all of the symptoms in Criteria A-D.	E. No adaptation.
F. Criteria A-D are present in at least two or more settings (e.g., at home, at school, with peers) and are severe in at least one of these.	F. No adaptation.
G. The diagnosis should not be made for the first time before age 6 years or after age 18.	G. No adaptation.
H. By history or observation, the age at onset of Criteria A-E is before 10 years.	H. No adaptation.
I. There has never been a distinct period lasting more than 1 day during which the full symptom criteria, except duration, for a manic or hypomanic episode have been met. **Note:** Developmentally appropriate mood elevation, such as occurs in the context of a highly positive event or its anticipation, should not be considered as a symptom of mania or hypomania.	I. No adaptation.
J. The behaviors do not occur exclusively during an episode of major depressive disorder and are not better explained by another mental disorder. **Note:** This diagnosis cannot coexist with oppositional defiant disorder, intermittent explosive disorder, or bipolar disorder, though it can coexist with others, including major depressive disorder, ADHD, conduct disorder, and substance use disorders. Individuals whose symptoms meet criteria for both disruptive mood dysregulation disorder and oppositional defiant disorder should only be given the diagnosis of disruptive mood dysregulation disorder. If an individual has ever experienced a manic or hypomanic episode, the diagnosis of disruptive mood dysregulation disorder should not be assigned.	J. No adaptation.
K. The symptoms are not attributable to the physiological effects of a substance or to other medical or neurological condition.	K. No adaptation.

Major Depressive Disorder

DSM-5 Diagnostic Criteria	Applying Criteria for Mild to Profound ID
A. Five (or more) of the following symptoms have been present during the same 2-week period and represent a change from previous functioning; at least one of the symptoms is either (1) depressed mood or (2) loss of interest or pleasure. **Note:** Do not include symptoms that are clearly attributable to another medical condition.	A. Four (or more) symptoms have been present during the same 2-week period and represent a change from previous functioning: At least one of the symptoms is either (1) depressed mood, (2) loss of interest or pleasure, or (3) irritable mood. **Note:** Do not include symptoms that are clearly attributable to another medical condition.
1. Depressed mood most of the day, nearly every day, as indicated by either subjective report (e.g., feels sad or empty) or observation made by others (e.g., appears tearful). (Note: In children and adolescents, can be irritable mood.	1. Depressed or irritable mood most of the day, nearly every day, as indicated by either subjective report or observation made by others. **Note:** In people with ID, depressed mood may be described by others in one or more of the following ways, that constitutes a change from what is usually observed in this individual: sad facial expression, flat affect or absence of emotional expression, rarely smiles or laughs, cries or appears tearful. **Note:** Observers may describe individuals with ID who are irritable as: appearing grouchy or having an angry facial expression, having the onset of (or increase in) agitated behaviors (assaults, self-injurious behavior, spitting, yelling, swearing disruptive or destructive behaviors) accompanied by angry affect.
2. Markedly diminished interest or pleasure in all, or almost all, activities most of the day, nearly every day (as indicated by either subjective account or observation).	2. No adaptation. **Note:** Observers may report the individual with ID: refuses preferred activities, appears withdrawn, spends excessive time alone (more time than before), participates but shows no signs of enjoyment, becomes aggressive in response to request to participate in activities he or she used to like, has lost response to reinforcers, finds previously motivating events or objects no longer motivating, avoids social activities, aggresses or becomes agitated when prompted to attend social activities once enjoyed.
3. Significant weight loss when not dieting or weight gain (e.g., a change of more than 5 percent of body weight in a month), or decrease or increase in appetite nearly every day. (Note: In children, consider failure to make expected weight gains.)	3. No adaptation. **Note:** Observers may report the individual with ID: is eating to excess, is obsessing about food, is stealing food, is refusing meals, has experienced recent weight loss or gain, exhibits agitated behaviors emerge during meal times or in relation to food (throws food on the floor, screams when meal arrives).
4. Insomnia or hypersomnia nearly every day.	4. No adaptation. **Note**: Observers may report the individual with ID: has difficulty falling asleep, awakens in the early morning, sleeps excessively, has shown a recent increase in problem behaviors late at night, very early in the morning, takes frequent naps, falls asleep during the day, is up and down all night, sleeps very little at night and seems tired.
5. Psychomotor agitation or retardation nearly every day (observable by others, not merely subjective feelings of restlessness or being slowed down).	5. No adaptation. **Note:** Observers may report the individual with ID: rarely sits down, is up and down from seat a lot, paces, walks rapidly, fidgets, has slowed movements, has decreased or stopped talking, vocalizes much more or less than usual, is much less physically active than before.

Major Depressive Disorder (continued)

DSM-5 Diagnostic Criteria	Applying Criteria for Mild to Profound ID
6. Fatigue or loss of energy nearly every day.	6. No adaptation. **Note:** Observers may report the individual with ID: appears tired or reports feeling tired, refuses or becomes agitated about activities that require physical effort, spends excessive amounts of time just sitting, or excessive amounts of time lying down, has dark circles under eyes.
7. Feelings of worthlessness or excessive or inappropriate guilt (which may be delusional) nearly every day (not merely self-reproach or guilt about being sick).	7. No adaptation. **Note:** Observers may report the individual with ID: makes negative self-statements; identifies self as a "bad" person; often expects punishment, without a history of harsh treatment; blames self for problems inappropriately; unrealistically fears caretakers will be angry or rejecting, even after minor transgressions; excessively seeks reassurances that he or she is accepted as a good person, or makes other negative self-statements at a high frequency (and this is a change from baseline). **Note:** People with Severe/Profound ID do not function at cognitive levels consistent with the capacity to experience or express feelings of guilt or worthlessness.
8. Diminished ability to think or concentrate, or indecisiveness, nearly every day (either by subjective account or as observed by others).	8. No adaptation. **Note:** Observers may report the individual with ID: shows a reduced productivity at work or day program, has diminished self care skills, appears easily distracted or can't complete tasks he or she used to be able to finish, has shown the onset of or increase in agitated behaviors when asked to do activities that require concentration, has apparent memory problems that "come and go", has unexplained skill loss, shows an uncharacteristic inability to learn new skills as expected, or has had to stop working or attending programs due to poor performance.
9. Recurrent thoughts of death (not just fear of dying), recurrent suicidal ideation without a specific plan, or a suicide attempt or a specific plan for committing suicide.	9. No adaptation. **Note:** Observers may report the individual with Mild/Moderate ID: often talks about death or people who have died or has other morbid preoccupations, has frequent unrealistic or unfounded physical complaints and fears of illness or death, makes threats to kill or harm self or has actually attempted suicide (unconventional means such as running in front of cars or jumping from windows may be impulsive acts, but may be suicidal in nature).
B. The symptoms cause clinically significant distress or impairment in social, occupational or other important areas of functioning.	B. No adaptation. **Note:** Individuals with ID may lose residential placements, jobs, vocational or other day programs due to apparent skill loss or associated disruptive behaviors, or there may be significant stress in the family or caretaking situation.

Major Depressive Disorder (continued)

DSM-5 Diagnostic Criteria	Applying Criteria for Mild to Profound ID
C. The episode is not attributable to the physiological effects of a substance or to another medical condition. **Note:** Criteria A–C represent a major depressive episode. **Note:** Responses to a significant loss (e.g., bereavement, financial ruin, losses from a natural disaster, a serious medical illness or disability) may include the feelings of intense sadness, rumination about the loss, insomnia, poor appetite, and weight loss noted in Criterion A, which may resemble a depressive episode. Although such symptoms may be understandable or considered appropriate to the loss, the presence of a major depressive episode in addition to the normal response to a significant loss should also be carefully considered. This decision inevitably requires the exercise of clinical judgment based on the individual's history and the cultural norms for the expression of distress in the context of loss.[1]	C.No adaptation. **Note:** For people with ID, almost any physical problem that causes pain or distress may also cause difficulty focusing attention, sleeping, eating and psychomotor agitation. In addition to direct causes for mood problems (problems in thyroid functions), infections, common medical problems may provoke symptoms that look like depression. These medical problems include: UTIs, otitis media, cellulites, fungal infections of the skin etc.), constipation, GERD, migraine headaches, or a variety of medication induced movement disorders (akathisia, other EPS), or other drug side effects (lethargy, sedation, delirium).
D. The occurrence of the major depressive episode is not better explained by schizoaffective disorder, schizophrenia, schizophreniform disorder, delusional disorder, or other specified and unspecified schizophrenia spectrum and other psychotic disorders.	D. No adaptation.
E. There has never been a manic episode or a hypomanic episode. **Note:** This exclusion does not apply if all of the manic-like or hypomanic-like episodes are substance-induced or are attributable to the physiological effects of another medical condition.	E. No adaptation.

Persistent Depressive Disorder (Dysthymia)

DSM-5 Diagnostic Criteria	Applying Criteria for Mild to Profound ID
This disorder represents a consolidation of DSM-IV-defined chronic major depressive disorder and dysthymic disorder. A. Depressed mood for most of the day, for more days than not, as indicated by either subjective account or observation by others, for at least 2 years. Note: In children and adolescents, mood can be irritable and duration must be at least 1 year.	A. Depressed or irritable mood for most of the day, for more days than not, as indicated by either subjective account or observation by others, for at least 2 years.

[1] In distinguishing grief from a major depressive episode (MDE), it is useful to consider that in grief the predominant affect is feelings of emptiness and loss, while in MDE it is persistent depressed mood and the inability to anticipate happiness or pleasure. The dysphoria in grief is likely to decrease in intensity over days to weeks and occurs in waves, the so-called pangs of grief. These waves tend to be associated with thoughts or reminders of the deceased. The depressed mood of MDE is more persistent and not tied to specific thoughts or preoccupations. The pain of grief may be accompanied by positive emotions and humor that are uncharacteristic of the pervasive unhappiness and misery characteristic of MDE. The thought content associated with grief generally features a preoccupation with thoughts and memories of the deceased, rather than the self-critical or pessimistic ruminations seen in MDE. In grief, self-esteem is generally preserved, whereas in MDE feelings of worthlessness and self-loathing are common. If self-derogatory ideation is present in grief, it typically involves perceived failings vis-à-vis the deceased (e.g., not visiting frequently enough, not telling the deceased how much he or she was loved). If a bereaved individual thinks about death and dying, such thoughts are generally focused on the deceased and possibly about "joining" the deceased, whereas in MDE such thoughts are focused on ending one's own life because of feeling worthless, undeserving of life, or unable to cope with the pain of depression.

Persistent Depressive Disorder (Dysthymia) [continued]

DSM-5 Diagnostic Criteria	Applying Criteria for Mild to Profound ID
B. Presence, while depressed, of two (or more) of the following: 1. Poor appetite or overeating. 2. Insomnia or hypersomnia. 3. Low energy or fatigue. 4. Low self-esteem. 5. Poor concentration or difficulty making decisions. 6. Feelings of hopelessness.	B. No adaptation. **Note:** See notes for Major Depressive Episode. People with mild ID may be particularly vulnerable to problems with self-esteem in relation to a strong desire to be "normal" and a sense of hopelessness that the usual accomplishments/events of adulthood will not be forthcoming (i.e. getting a driver's license, buying a car, having one's own apartment, dating, marrying or having children). This may be more pronounced when the person with ID has close ties to siblings or friends without ID who begin to have such experiences when the person with ID does not. **Note:** People with Severe/Profound ID are unlikely to experience or express the cognitive symptoms of dysthymia. Chronic problems with attention can often be attributed to the same factors that caused the ID. It is important to establish that chronic symptoms of crying, sad appearance, with alterations in patterns of eating, sleeping and motor activity are not due to untreated or ineffectively treated Major Depressive Disorder.
C. During the 2-year period (1 year for children or adolescents) of the disturbance, the individual has never been without the symptoms in Criteria A and B for more than 2 months at a time.	C. No adapation.
D. Criteria for a major depressive disorder may be continuously present for 2 years.	D. No adapatation.
E. There has never been a manic episode or a hypomanic episode, and criteria have never been met for cyclothymic disorder.	E. No adaptation.
F. The disturbance is not better explained by a persistent schizoaffective disorder, schizophrenia, delusional disorder, or other specified or unspecified schizophrenia spectrum and other psychotic disorder.	F. No adaptation. **Note:** Differential diagnosis of depression with psychotic features versus various syndromes dominated by psychosis, but containing mood features, may be challenging, even in many people with mild ID. It is important to consider developmental profile of skills and challenges and how this affects cognition. People with ID may function similar to young children and may be operating cognitively and emotionally with developmental profile such that reality-fantasy distinctions are poor and it is common to use fantasy to cope with stress, to engage in self-talk, or to express odd or intense fears. **Note:** People with Severe/Profound ID usually cannot be diagnosed with psychotic features. Avoid labels of psychosis based on person seems "bizarre" due to the lack of any valid measures of the meaning of unusual behaviors in people with greater central nervous system impairment and more severe cognitive disabilities.
G. The symptoms are not attributable to the physiological effects of a substance (e.g., a drug of abuse, a medication) or another medical condition (e.g. hypothyroidism).	G. No adaptation. **Note:** For people with ID, almost any physical problem that causes pain or distress may also cause difficulty focusing attention, sleeping, eating and psychomotor agitation. In addition to direct causes for mood problems (problems in thyroid functions), infections, common medical problems may provoke symptoms that look like depression. These medical problems include: UTIs, otitis media, cellulites, fungal infections of the skin etc.), constipation, GERD, migraine headaches, or a variety of medication induced movement disorders (akathisia, other EPS), or other drug side effects (lethargy, sedation, delirium).

Persistent Depressive Disorder (Dysthymia) [continued]

DSM-5 Diagnostic Criteria	Applying Criteria for Mild to Profound ID
H. The symptoms cause clinically significant distress or impairment in social, occupational, or other important areas of functioning. **Note:** Because the criteria for a major depressive episode include four symptoms that are absent from the symptom list for persistent depressive disorder (dysthymia), a very limited number of individuals will have depressive symptoms that have persisted longer than 2 years but will not meet criteria for persistent depressive disorder. If full criteria for a major depressive episode have been met at some point during the current episode of illness, they should be given a diagnosis of major depressive disorder. Otherwise, a diagnosis of other specified depressive disorder or unspecified depressive disorder is warranted.	H. No adaptation. **Note:** Individuals with ID may lose residential placements, jobs, vocational or other day programs due to apparent skill loss or associated disruptive behaviors, or there may be significant stress in the family or caretaking situation. **Note:** For people with ID, almost any physical problem that causes pain or distress may also cause difficulty focusing attention, sleeping eating and psychomotor agitation. **Note:** For people with Severe/Profound ID, there is even less likelihood of an accurate report from the individual of a source of physical distress.

Premenstrual Dysphoric Disorder

DSM-5 Criteria	Adapted Criteria Mild to Profound ID
A. In the majority of menstrual cycles, at least five symptoms must be present in the final week before the onset of menses, start to improve within a few days after the onset of menses, and become minimal or absent in the week postmenses.	A. No adaptation.
B. One (or more) of the following symptoms must be present: 1. Marked affective lability (e.g., mood swings; feeling suddenly sad or tearful, or increased sensitivity to rejection). 2. Marked irritability or anger or increased interpersonal conflicts. 3. Marked depressed mood, feelings of hopelessness, or self-deprecating thoughts. 4. Marked anxiety, tension, and/or feelings of being keyed up or on edge.	B. No adaptation.
C. One (or more) of the following symptoms must additionally be present, to reach a total of five symptoms when combined with symptoms from Criterion B above. 1. Decreased interest in usual activities (e.g., work, school, friends, hobbies). 2. Subjective difficulty in concentration. 3. Lethargy, easy fatigability, or marked lack of energy. 4. Marked change in appetite; overeating; or specific food cravings. 5. Hypersomnia or insomnia. 6. A sense of being overwhelmed or out of control. 7. Physical symptoms such as breast tenderness or swelling, joint or muscle pain, a sensation of "bloating," or weight gain. **Note:** The symptoms in Criteria A–C must have been met for most menstrual cycles that occurred in the preceding year.	C. No adaptation. **Interests Note:** Observers may report the individual with ID: refuses preferred activities, appears withdrawn, spends excessive time alone (more time than before), participates but shows no signs of enjoyment, becomes aggressive in response to request to participate in activities he or she used to like, has lost response to reinforcers, finds previously motivating events or objects no longer motivating, avoids social activities, aggresses or becomes agitated when prompted to attend social activities once enjoyed.

Premenstrual Dysphoric Disorder (continued)

DSM-5 Criteria	Adapted Criteria Mild to Profound ID
	Concentration Note: Observers may report the individual with ID: onset of difficulty concentrating may be observed as a reduction in productivity at work or day program, has diminished self care skills, appears easily distracted or can't complete tasks he or she used to be able to finish, has shown the onset of or increase in agitated behaviors when asked to do activities that require concentration, has apparent memory problems that "come and go", has unexplained skill loss, shows an uncharacteristic inability to learn new skills as expected, or has had to stop working or attending programs due to poor performance.
	Energy Note: Observers may report the individual with ID: appears tired or reports feeling tired, refuses or becomes agitated about activities that require physical effort, spends excessive amounts of time just sitting, or excessive amounts of time lying down, has dark circles under eyes.
	Appetite Note: Observers may report the individual with ID: is eating to excess, is obsessing about food, is stealing food, is refusing meals, has experienced recent weight loss or gain, exhibits agitated behaviors emerge during meal times or in relation to food (throws food on the floor, screams when meal arrives).
	Sleep Note: Observers may report the individual with ID: has difficulty falling asleep, awakens in the early morning, sleeps excessively, has shown a recent increase in problem behaviors late at night, very early in the morning, takes frequent naps, falls asleep during the day, is up and down all night, sleeps very little at night and seems tired.
	Pain Note: Individuals with ID can experience pain but may have difficulty expressing their pain or pain level in an effective manner. Intensity of pain is subjective and abstract. Look for behaviors of touching around pain area or increased irritability and motor agitation or stereotyped behaviors that may be signs of increased physical discomfort.
D. The symptoms are associated with clinically significant distress or interference with work, school, usual social activities, or relationships with others (e.g., avoidance of social activities; decreased productivity and efficiency at work, school, or home).	D. No adaptation. **Note:** Individuals with ID may lose residential placements, jobs, vocational or other day programs due to apparent skill loss or associated disruptive behaviors, or there may be significant stress in the family or caretaking situation. **Note:** For people with ID, almost any physical problem that causes pain or distress may also cause difficulty focusing attention, sleeping eating and psychomotor agitation. **Note:** For people with Severe/Profound ID, there is even less likelihood of an accurate report from the individual of a source of physical distress.
E. The disturbance is not merely an exacerbation of the symptoms of another disorder, such as major depressive disorder, panic disorder, persistent depressive disorder (dysthymia), or a personality disorder (although it may co-occur with any of these disorders).	E. No adaptation.
F. Criterion A should be confirmed by prospective daily ratings during at least two symptomatic cycles. (Note: The diagnosis may be made provisionally prior to this confirmation.)	F. No adaptation.
G. The symptoms are not attributable to the physiological effects of a substance (e.g., a drug of abuse, a medication, other treatment) or another medical condition (e.g., hyperthyroidism).	G. No adaptation.

Substance/Medication-Induced Depressive Disorder

DSM-5 criteria for substance/medication-induced depressive disorder are the same as for other mental disorders, without adaptation, with the additional need for a prominent and persistent disturbance in mood.

Depressive Disorder Due to Another Medical Condition

DSM-5 criteria for depressive disorder due to another medical condition are the same as for other mental disorders due to another medical condition without adaptation, with the additional need for a prominent and persistent disturbance in mood or markedly decreased interest in almost all activities.

Other Specified Depressive Disorder
Unspecified Depressive Disorder

DSM-5 also provides categories for other specified depressive disorder and for unspecified depressive disorder.

References

Allen, D., & Davies, D. (2007). Challenging behaviour and psychiatric disorder in intellectual disability. *Current Opinion in Psychiatry, 20*(5), 450-455.

Ailey, S. H., Miller, A. M., Heller, T., & Smith, E. V. (2006). Evaluating an interpersonal model of depression among adults with Down syndrome. *Research and Theory for Nursing Practice: An International Journal, 20*(3), 229-246.

Axelson, D. A., Birmaher, B., Findling, R. L., Fristad, M. A., Kowatch, R. A., Youngstrom, E. A., ... Diler, R. S. (2011). Concerns regarding the inclusion of temper dysregulation disorder with dysphoria in the Diagnostic and Statistical Manual of Mental Disorders. *The Journal of Clinical psychiatry, 72*(9), 1257.

Bakken, T. L., Helverschou, S. B., Eilertsen, D. E., Heggelund, T., Myrbakk, E., & Martinsen, H. (2010). Psychiatric disorders in adolescents and adults with autism and intellectual disability: A representative study in one county in Norway. *Research in Developmental Disabilities, 31*(6), 1669-1677.

Benson, B. A., & Laman, D.S. (1988). Suicidal tendencies of mentally retarded adults in community settings. *Australia and New Zealand Journal of Developmental Disabilities, 14*, 49-54.

Bhidayasiri, R., & Boonyawairoj, S. (2010). Spectrum of tardive syndromes: clinical recognition and management. *Post-Graduate Medical Journal. doi:10.1136/pgmj.2010.103234*

Bhatia, S. K., & Bhatia, S. C. (2007). Childhood and adolescent depression. *American Family Physician, 75*(1), 73-80.

Boustany, R.N. (2010) Psychiatric comorbidities in common genetic disorders with physical disability. *Pediatric Health, 4*(6), 591–601.

Brumm, V.L., Bilder, D. & Waisbren, S.E. (2010) Psychiatric symptoms and disorders in phenylketonuria. *Molecular Genetics and Metabolism, 99*, 559-563

Brunoni, A. R., Lopes, M., & Fregni, F. (2008). A systematic review and meta-analysis of clinical studies on major depression and BDNF levels: implications for the role of neuroplasticity in depression. *International Journal of Neuropsychopharmacology, 11*(8), 1169-1180.

Burke, L. M., Kalpakjian, C. Z., Smith, Y. R., & Quint, E. H. (2010). Gynecologic issues of adolescents with Down syndrome, autism, and cerebral palsy. *Journal of Pediatric and Adolescent Gynecology, 23*(1), 11-15.

Burt, D.B., Loveland, K.A., & Lewis, K.R. (1992). Depression and the onset of dementia in adults with mental retardation. *American Journal of Mental Retardation*, 96, 502-511.

Cain, N. N., Davidson, P. W., Burhan, A.M., Andolsek, M. E., Baxter, J. T., Sullivan, L., ... Lam, N. (2003). Identifying bipolar disorders in individuals with intellectual disability. *Journal of Intellectual Disability Research, 47,* 31-38.

Carlson, G. A., & Meyer, S. E. (2006). Phenomenology and diagnosis of bipolar disorder in children, adolescents, and adults: complexities and developmental issues. *Development and Psychopathology, 18*(04), 939-969.

Cassidy, S.B. & Driscoll, D.J. (2009) Prader–Willi syndrome. *European Journal of Human Genetics, 17*(1), 3–13.

Chaplin, E., Gilvarry, C., & Tsakanikos, E. (2011). Recreational substance use patterns and co-morbid psychopathology in adults with intellectual disability. *Research in Developmental Disabilities, 32*(6), 2981-2986.

Chapman, S. L. C., & Wu, L. T. (2012). Substance abuse among individuals with intellectual disabilities. *Research in Developmental Disabilities, 33*(4), 1147-1156.

Charlot, L.R. (1997). Irritability, aggression, and depression in adults with mental retardation: A developmental perspective. *Psychiatric Annals, 27,* 190-197.

Charlot, L.R. (2002). Mission impossible: Developing an accurate classification of psychiatric disorders in individuals with developmental disabilities. *Mental Health Aspects of Developmental Disabilities, 6 (1), 26-33.*

Charlot, L. R. (2005) Use of behavioral equivalents for symptoms of mood disorders. In P. Sturmey (Ed.), *Mood disorders and people with mental retardation.* Kinston, NY: NADD Press.

Charlot, L., Abend, S., Ravin, P., Mastis, K., Hunt, A., & Deutsch, C. (2011). Non-psychiatric health problems among psychiatric inpatients with intellectual disabilities. *Journal of Intellectual Disability Research, 55*(2), 199-209.

Charlot, L., Deutsch, C., Alberts, A., Hunt, A., Connors, D., & McIlvane, W. (2008). Mood and anxiety symptoms in psychiatric inpatients with autism spectrum disorder and depression. *Journal of Mental Health Research in Intellectual Disabilities, 1,* 238-253.

Charlot, L., Deutsch, C.K., Fletcher, K., & McIlvane, W.J. (2007a). Validation of the mood and anxiety semi-structured (mass) interview for patients with intellectual disabilities. *Journal of Intellectual Disability Research, 51*(10), 821-834.

Charlot L.R., Fox, S., Silka, V.R., Hurley, A., Lowry, M., Pary, R. (2007b). Mood disorders in individuals with intellectual disabilities. In R. Fletcher, E. Loschen, C. Stavrakaki, M. First (Eds.), *Diagnostic manual-Intellectual disability (DM-ID): A textbook of diagnosis of mental disorders in persons with intellectual disability* (pp. 271-316). Kingston NY: NADD Press.

Charlot, L.R., Doucette, A.D. & Mezzecappa, E. (1993). Affective symptoms in institutionalized adults with mental retardation. *American Journal of Mental Retardation, 98,* 408-416.

Charlot, L.R., Abend, S., Silka, V.R., Kuropatkin, B.B., Garcia, O., Bolduc, M., & Foley, M. (2002). A short stay inpatient psychiatric unit for adults with developmental disabilities. In J. Jacobsen (Ed.), *Model programs for individuals with developmental disabilities and psychiatric disorders.* Kingston, NY: the NADD.

Cicchetti, D., & Toth, S. L. (2009). The past achievements and future promises of developmental psychopathology: The coming of age of a discipline. *Journal of Child Psychology and Psychiatry, 50*(1-2), 16-25.

Clarke, D.J. & Gomez, G.A. (1999). Utility of the DCR-10 criteria in the diagnosis of depression associated with intellectual disability. *Journal of Intellectual Disability Research, 43*(5), 413-420.

Cooper, S. A., Smiley, E., Morrison, J., Williamson, A., & Allan, L. (2007a). An epidemiological investigation of affective disorders with a population-based cohort of 1023 adults with intellectual disabilities. *Psychological Medicine, 37*(06), 873-882.

Cooper, S. A., Smiley, E., Morrison, J., Williamson, A., & Allan, L. (2007b). Mental ill-health in adults with intellectual disabilities: prevalence and associated factors. *British Journal of Psychiatry, 190*, 27-35.

Cooper, S.A. & van der Speck, R. (2009) Epidemiology of mental ill health in adults with intellectual disability. *Current Opinion in Psychiatry, 22*, 431-436

Copeland, W. E., Angold, A., Costello, E. J., & Egger, H. (2013). Prevalence, comorbidity, and correlates of DSM-5 proposed disruptive mood dysregulation disorder. *American Journal of Psychiatry, 170*(2), 173-179.

Costello, H., & Bouras, N. (2006). Assessment of mental health problems in people with intellectual disabilities. *Israel Journal of Psychiatry and Related Sciences, 43*(4), 241.

Davies, L. E., & Oliver, C. (2014). The purported association between depression, aggression, and self-injury in people with intellectual disability: a critical review of the literature. *American Journal on Intellectual and Developmental Disabilities, 119*(5), 452-471.

Davis, J.P., Judd, F.K., & Herrman, H. (1997). Depression in adults with intellectual disability part 1: A review and part 2: A pilot study. *Australia and New Zealand Journal of Psychiatry, 31*, 232-251.

Dekker, M. C., & Koot, H. M. (2003). DSM-IV disorders in children with borderline to moderate intellectual disability. I: Prevalence and impact. *Journal of the American Academy of Child & Adolescent Psychiatry, 42*(8), 915-922.

Dodd, P., Dowling, S., & Hollins, S. (2005). A review of the emotional, psychiatric and behavioural responses to bereavement in people with intellectual disabilities. *Journal of Intellectual Disability Research, 49*(7), 537-543.

Dosen,A.(1984) Depresive conditions in mentally handicapped children. *Acta Paedopsychiatra, 50*, 29-40.

Dosen, A. (2005). Applying the developmental perspective in the psychiatric assessment and diagnosis of persons with intellectual disability: part II–diagnosis. *Journal of Intellectual Disability Research, 49*(1), 9-15.

Edelbrock, C., Costello, A. J., Dulcan, M. K., Kalas, R., & Conover, N. C. (1985). Age differences in the reliability of the psychiatric interview of the child. *Child Development*, 265-275. Hoboken, NJ: Wiley.

Emerson, E. (2003). Prevalence of psychiatric disorders in children and adolescents with and without intellectual disability. *Journal of Intellectual Disability Research, 47*(1), 51-58.

Emerson, E., & Hatton, C. (2007). Mental health of children and adolescents with intellectual disabilities in Britain. *The British Journal of Psychiatry, 191*(6), 493-499.

Esbensen, A. J., & Benson, B. A. (2006). A prospective analysis of life events, problem behaviours and depression in adults with intellectual disability. *Journal of Intellectual Disability Research, 50*(4), 248-258.

Espie, C.A., Watkins, J., Curtuice, L., Espie, A., Duncan, R., Ryan, J.A., ... Sterrick, M. (2003). Psychopathology in people with epilepsy and intellectual disability; an investigation of potential explanatory variables. *Journal of Neurology, Neurosurgery &Psychiatry, 74*(11), 1485-1492.

Geller, B. & Luby, J. (1997) Child & adolescent bipolar disorder: Review of the last ten years. *Journal of the American Academy of Child & Adolescent Psychiatry, 36*, 1168-1176.

Ghaziuddin, M. (1988). Behavioral disorder in the mentally handicapped: The role of life events. *British Journal of Psychiatry, 183*, 683-686.

Ghaziuddin, M., Alessi, N. & Greden, J. F. (1995). Life events and depression in children with pervasive developmental disorders. *Journal of Autism and Developmental Disorders, 25*(5), 495-502.

Goldstein, G., Beers, S. R., Siegel, D. J., & Minshew, N. J. (2001). A comparison of WAIS-R profiles in adults with high-functioning autism or differing subtypes of learning disability. *Applied Neuropsychology, 8*(3), 148-154.

Gualtieri, C. T., Schroeder, R.E., Hicks, R.E., & Quade, D. (1986). Tardive dyskinesia in young mentally retarded individuals. *Archives of General Psychiatry, 43*, 335-340.

Gunsett R., Mulick J., Fernald W., & Martin J. (1989). Brief report: indications for medical screening prior to behavioral programming for severely and profoundly mentally retarded clients. *Journal of Autism and Developmental Disorders, 19*, 167-172.

Hagerman, R., Lauterborn, J., Au, J., & Berry-Kravis, E. (2012). Fragile X syndrome and targeted treatment trials. In *Modeling fragile X syndrome* (pp. 297-335). Berlin: Springer.

Hamilton, A., Marshal, M. P., & Murray, P. J. (2011). Autism spectrum disorders and menstruation. *Journal of Adolescent Health, 49*(4), 443-445.

Hamilton, D., Sutherland, G., & Iacono, T. (2005). Further examination of relationships between life events and psychiatric symptoms in adults with intellectual disability. *Journal of Intellectual Disability Research, 49* (11), 839-844.

Harris, J. (1998). *Developmental neuropsychiatry Volume II: Assessment, diagnosis, and treatment of developmental disorders* (pp. 91-126). New York: Oxford

Hartley, S. L., & MacLean, W. E. (2009). Depression in adults with mild intellectual disability: Role of stress, attributions, and coping. *American Journal of Intellectual and Developmental Disabilities, 114* (3), 147-160.

Hassan, A., Agha, S. S., Langley, K., & Thapar, A. (2011). Prevalence of bipolar disorder in children and adolescents with attention-deficit hyperactivity disorder. *The British Journal of Psychiatry, 198*(3), 195-198.

Hastings, R. P., Hatton, C., Taylor, J. L., & Maddison, C. (2004). Life events and psychiatric symptoms in adults with intellectual disabilities. *Journal of Intellectual Disability Research, 48*, 42-46.

Hatton, C., & Emerson, E. (2004). The relationship between life events and psychopathology amongst children with intellectual disabilities. *Journal of Applied Research in Intellectual Disabilities, 17*, 109-117.

Hayes, S., McGuire, B., O'Neill, M., Oliver, C. & Morrison, T. (2011) Low mood and challenging behaviour in people with severe and profound intellectual disabilities. *Journal of Intellectual Disability Research, 55*, 182-189.

Heim, C., & Binder, E. B. (2012). Current research trends in early life stress and depression: Review of human studies on sensitive periods, gene–environment interactions, and epigenetics. *Experimental Neurology, 233*(1), 102-111.

Hegerl, U., Bottner, A. C., Mergl, R., Holtschmidt-Taeschner, B., Seemueller, F., Scheunemann, W., ... Born, C. (2007). Speed of onset of depressive episodes: a clinical criterion helpful for separating uni-from bipolar affective disorders. *Neuropsychiatrie: Klinik, Diagnostik, Therapie und Rehabilitation: Organ der Gesellschaft Osterreichischer Nervenarzte und Psychiater, 22*(2), 92-99.

Hendrick, V., Altshuler, L. L., Gitlin, M. D., Delrahim, M. S., & Hammen, C. (2000). Gender and bipolar illness. *Journal of Clinical Psychiatry, 61*(5), 393-396.

Holden, B., & Gitlesen, J. P. (2004). The association between severity of intellectual disability and psychiatric symptomatology. *Journal of Intellectual Disability Research, 48*(6), 556-562.

Hulbert-Williams, L., & Hastings, R. P. (2008). Life events as a risk factor for psychological problems in individuals with intellectual disabilities: a critical review. *Journal of Intellectual Disability Research, 52*, 883-895.

Hulbert-Williams, L., Hastings, R., Owen, D. M., Burns, L., Day, J., Mulligan, M. J., & Noone, S. J. (2014). Exposure to life events as a risk factor for psychological problems in adults with intellectual disabilities: a longitudinal design. *Journal of Intellectual Disability Research, 58*, 48-60.

Hunter, R. H., Wilkniss, S., Gardner, W. I., & Silverstein, S. M. (2008). The multimodal functional model-advancing case formulation beyond the "diagnose and treat" paradigm: Improving outcomes and reducing aggression and the use of control procedures in psychiatric care. *Psychological Services, 5*(1), 11.

Hurley, A. D. (1996). The misdiagnosis of hallucinations and delusions in persons with mental retardation: A neurodevelopmental perspective. *Seminars in Clinical Neuropsychiatry, 1*, 122-133.

Hurley, A. D. (1998). Two cases of suicide attempt by patients with Down syndrome. *Psychiatric Services*, 49, 1618-1619.

Hurley, A.D. (2007). Depression in adults with intellectual disability: Symptoms and challenging behaviour. *Journal of Intellectual Disability Research*, 52, 905-916.

Hurley, A., Folstein, M., & Lam, N. (2003). Patients with and without intellectual disability seeing outpatient psychiatric services: diagnosis and prescribing pattern. *Journal of Intellectual Disabilities Research, 47*(1),39-50

Hurley, A. D. & Moore, C. (1999). A review of erotomania in developmental disabilities and new case report. *Mental Health Aspects of Developmental Disabilities, 2*, 12-21.

Hurtig, T., Kuusikko, S., Mattila, M. L., Haapsamo, H., Ebeling, H., Jussila, K., ... Moilanen, I. (2009). Multi-informant reports of psychiatric symptoms among high-functioning adolescents with Asperger syndrome or autism. *Autism, 13*(6), 583-598.

Jancar, J. & Gunaratne, I. J. (1994). Dysthymia and mental handicap. *British Journal of Psychiatry*, 164, 691-693.

Johnson, C. R., Handen, B. L., Lubetsky, M.J. & Sacco, K.A. (1995). Affective disorders in hospitalized children and adolescents with mental retardation: A retrospective study. *Research in Developmental Disabilities, 16*(3), 221-231.

Jolin, E.M., Weller, R.A., & Weller, E.B. (2011) Occurrence of affective disorders compared to other psychiatric disorders in children and adolescents with 22q11.2 deletion syndrome. *Journal of Affective Disorders, 136*(3), 222-228.

Kaminer, Y., Feinstein, C., Barrett, R. P., Tylenda, B., & Hole, W. (1988). Menstrually related mood disorder in developmentally disabled adolescents: Review and current status. *Child Psychiatry and Human Development, 18*(4), 239-249.

Kennedy, C., Juarez, A.P., Greenslade, K., Harvey, M.T., & Tally, B. (2007). Children with severe developmental disabilities and behavioral disorders have increased special healthcare needs. *Developmental Medicine and Child Neurology, 49*, 926-930.

Kerr, A. M., McCulloch, D., Oliver, K., McLean, B., Coleman, E., Law, T., ... Prescott, R. J. (2003). Medical needs of people with intellectual disability require regular reassessment, and the provision of client and carer-held reports. *Journal of Intellectual Disability Research, 47*(2), 134-145.

King, B. H., Veenstra-VanderWeele, J., & Lord, C. (2013). DSM-5 and autism: Kicking the tires and making the grade. *Journal of the American Academy of Child & Adolescent Psychiatry, 52*(5), 454-457.

Kwok, H., & Cheung, P. (2007). Co-morbidity of psychiatric disorder and medical illness in people with intellectual disabilities. *Current Opinion in Psychiatry, 20*(5), 443-449.

Kupfer, D. J., Frank, E., & Phillips, M. L. (2012). Major depressive disorder: new clinical, neurobiological, and treatment perspectives. *The Lancet, 379*(9820), 1045-1055.

Kyrkou, M. (2005). Health issues and quality of life in women with intellectual disability. *Journal of Intellectual Disability Research, 49*(10), 770-772.

Lainhart, J. E. & Folstein, S. E. (1994). Affective disorders in autism. *Journal of Autism and Developmental Disorders, 24*, 587-601.

Leibenluft, E. (2011). Severe mood dysregulation, irritability, and the diagnostic boundaries of bipolar disorder in youths. *American Journal of Psychiatry, 168*(2), 129-142.

Leibenluft, E., Cohen, P., Gorrindo, T., Brook, J. S., & Pine, D. S. (2006). Chronic Versus Episodic Irritability in Youth: A community-based, longitudinal study of clinical and diagnostic associations. *Journal of Child & Adolescent Psychopharmacology, 16*(4), 456-466.

Leyfer, O.T., Folstein, S.E., Bacalman, S. Davis, N.O., Dinh, E., Morgan, J., ... Lainhart, J.E. (2006). Comorbid psychiatric disorders in children withautism: Interview development and rates of disorders. *Journal of Autism and Developmental Disorders, 36*, 849-861.

Lott, I. T., McGregor, M., Engelman, L., Touchette, P., Tournay, A., Sandman, C., ... Walsh, D. (2004). Longitudinal prescribing patterns for psychoactive medications in community based individuals with developmental disabilities: Utilization of pharmacy records. *Journal of Intellectual Disability Research, 48*, 563-571.

LoVullo, S. V., & Matson, J. L. (2009). Comorbid psychopathology in adults with autism spectrum disorders and intellectual disabilities. *Research in Developmental Disabilities, 30*(6), 1288-1296.

Lowry, M. (1998). Assessment and treatment of mood disorders in persons with developmental disabilities. *Journal of Developmental and Physical Disabilities, 10*(4), 387-406.

Lowry, M. & Sovner, R. (1992). Severe behavior problems associated with rapid cycling bipolar disorder in two adults with profound mental retardation. *Journal of Intellectual Disabilities Research, 36*, 269-281.

Lunsky, Y. (2003) Depressive symptoms in ID: does gender play a role? *Journal of Intellectual Disabilities Research, 47*(6), 417-427

Lunsky, Y. (2004). Suicidality in a clinical and community sample of adults with mental retardation. *Research in Developmental Disabilities, 25*, 231-243.

Lunsky, Y., & Benson, B. A. (2001). Association between perceived social support and strain, and positive and negative outcome for adults with mild intellectual disability. *Journal of Intellectual Disability Research, 45*, 106-114.

Lunsky, Y., & Bramston, P. (2006). A preliminary study of perceived stress in adults with intellectual disabilities according to self-report and informant ratings. *Journal of Intellectual & Developmental Disability, 31*(1), 20-27.

Maalouf, F.T., Hatoum, C., Atwi, M., Boustany, R.N. (2010). Psychiatric comorbidities in common genetic disorders with physical disability. *Pediatric Health, 4*(6), 591–601.

Maj, M. (2013). “Clinical judgment” and the DSM-5 diagnosis of major depression. *World Psychiatry, 12*(2), 89.

Marston, G. M., Perry, D. W. & Roy, A. (1997). Manifestations of depression in people with intellectual disability. *Journal of Intellectual Disability Research, 41*(6), 476-480.

Martorell, A., Tsakanikos, E., Pereda, A., Gutierrez-Recacha, P., Bouras, N., & Ayuso-Mateos, J. L. (2009). Mental health in adults with mild and moderate intellectual disabilities: The role of recent life events and traumatic experiences across the life span. *Journal of Nervous and Mental Disease, 197*(3), 182-185.

Masi, G., Mucci, M., Favilla, L., & Poli, P. (1999). Dysthymic disorder in adolescents with intellectual disability. *Journal of Intellectual Disability Research, 43*(2), 80-87.

Matson, J. L. & Barrett, L. P., & Helsel, ,W.J. (1988). Depression in mentally retarded children. *Research in Developmental Disabilities, 9*, 39-46.

Matson, J. L., Gardner, W. I., Coe, D. A., & Sovner, R. (1991). A scale for evaluating emotional disorders in severely and profoundly mentally retarded persons: development of the diagnostic assessment of the severely handicapped (DASH) scale. *British Journal of Psychiatry, 159*, 404-409.

Matson, J.L. & Neal, D. (2009) Psychotropic medication use for challenging behaviors in persons with intellectual disabilities: an overview. *Research in Developmental Disabilities, 30*, 572-86.

Mayville, S. B., Matson, J. L., Laud, R. B., Cooper, C., & Kuhn, D. E. (2005). The relationship between depression and feeding disorder symptoms among persons with severe and profound mental retardation. *Journal of Developmental and Physical Disabilities, 17*(3), 213-224.

McBrian, J. A. (2003). Assessment and diagnosis of depression in people with intellectual disability. *Journal of Intellectual Disability Research, 47*(1),1-13.

McGough, J. J. (2014). Chronic Non-Episodic Irritability in Childhood: Current and Future Challenges. *American Journal of Psychiatry, 171*(6), 607-610.

McGillicuddy, N. B. (2006). A review of substance use research among those with mental retardation. *Mental Retardation and Developmental Disabilities Research Reviews, 12*(1), 41-47.

McGillivray, J. A., & McCabe, M. P. (2007). Early detection of depression and associated risk factors in adults with mild/moderate intellectual disability. *Research in Developmental Disabilities, 28*, 59-70.

Meyers, B. A. (1998). Major depression in persons with moderate to profound mental retardation: Clinical presentation and case illustrations. *Mental Health Aspects of Developmental Disabilities, 1*(3), 57-68.

Meins, W. (1994). Symptoms of major depression in mentally retarded adults. *Journal of Intellectual Disabilities Research, 39*, 41-45.

Mikkelsen, E. J., Albert, L. G., & Upadhya, A. (1988) A neuroleptic withdrawal cachexia. *New England Journal of Medicine*, (14) 929, 318

Mileviciute, I., & Hartley, S. L. (2015). Self-reported versus informant-reported depressive symptoms in adults with mild intellectual disability. *Journal of Intellectual Disability Research, 59*(2), 158-169.

Moss, S., Prosser, H., Costello, H., Simpson, N., Patel, P., Rowe, S., Turner, S., & Hatton, C. (1998). Reliability and validity of the APS-ADD checklist for detecting psychiatric disorders in adults with intellectual disability. *Journal of Intellectual Disability Research, 42*, 173-183.

Muzykewicz, D.A., Newberry, P., Danforth, N., Halpern, E., & Thiele, E (2007). Psychiatric comorbid conditions in a clinic population of 241 patients with tuberous sclerosis complex. *Epilepsy & Behavior, 11*(4), 506-517.

Nanni, V., Uher, R., & Danese, A. (2012). Childhood maltreatment predicts unfavorable course of illness and treatment outcome in depression: A meta-analysis. *American Journal of Psychiatry, 169*(2), 141-151.

Nøttestad, J. A., & Linaker, O. M. (2003). Psychotropic drug use among people with intellectual disability before and after deinstitutionalization. *Journal of Intellectual Disability Research, 47*(6), 464-471.

O'Reilly, M. (1997). Functional analysis of episodic self-injury correlated with recurrent otitis media. *Journal of Applied Behavioral Analysis, 30*(1), 165-167.

Owen, D. M., Hastings, R. P., Noone, S. J., Chinn, J., Harman, K., Roberts, J., & Taylor, K. (2004). Life events as correlates of problem behavior and mental health in a residential population of adults with developmental disabilities. *Research in Developmental Disabilities, 25*, 309-320.

Pary, R.J., Levitas A.S. & Hurley A.D. (1999). Diagnosis of bipolar disorder in persons with developmental disabilities. *Mental Health Aspects of Developmental Disabilities, 2*(2), 37-49.

Pary, R.J., Strauss, D., & White, J.F. (1996). A population survey of bipolar disorder in persons with and without Down syndrome. *Down Syndrome Quarterly, 1*, 1-4.

Paykel, E.S., Myers, J. K., Dienelt, M., Klerman, G. L., Lindenthal, J., & Pepper, M. (1969). Life events and depression: A controlled study. *Archives of General Psychiatry, 21*, 753-760.

Pawlarcyzk, D. & Beckwith, B. (1987). Depressive symptoms displayed by persons with mental retardation: A review. *Mental Retardation, 25*(6), 323-330.

Peluso, M. J., Lewis, S. W., Barnes, T. R., & Jones, P. B. (2012). Extrapyramidal motor side-effects of first-and second-generation antipsychotic drugs. *The British Journal of Psychiatry, 200*(5), 387-392.

Pine, D. S., Costello, E. J., Dahl, R., James, R., Leckman, J., Leibenluft, E., Klein, R.,

Rapoport, J., Shaffer, D., Taylor, E., & Zeanah, C. (2011). Increasing the developmental focus in DSM-V: Broad issues and specific potential applications in anxiety. *The conceptual evolution of DSM-5*, 305-626.

Puig-Antich, J., & Chambers, W. J. (1983). Schedule for affective disorders and schizophrenia for school-age children (6–18 years). Pittsburgh: Western Psychiatric Institute.

Reiss, S. & Rojhan, J. (1993). Joint occurrence of depression and aggression in children and adults with mental retardation. *Journal of Intellectual Disabilities Research, 37*, 287-294.

Rezin, G.T., Amboni, G., Zugno, A.I., Quevedo, J., Streck,E. (2009). Mitochondrial dysfunction and psychiatric disorders. *Neurochemical Research. 34*, 1021-1029

Rohde, P., Lewinsohn, P. M., Klein, D. N., Seeley, J. R., & Gau, J. M. (2012). Key characteristics of major depressive disorder occurring in childhood, adolescence, emerging adulthood, and adulthood. *Clinical Psychological Science*, 2167702612457599.

Ross, E. & Oliver, C. (2003). The Assessment of mood in adults who have severe or profound mental retardation. *Clinical Psychology Review, 23*, 225-245.

Rutter, M. (1988). Depressive disorders. In M. Rutter, A.H. Tuma & I.S. Lann (Eds.), *Assessment and diagnosis in child psychopathology* (pp. 347-376). New York: Gilford Press.

Rutter, M. (2011). Research Review: Child psychiatric diagnosis and classification: concepts, findings, challenges and potential. *Journal of Child Psychology and Psychiatry, 52*, 647-660.

Sanchez-Gistau, V., Pintor, L., Sugranyes, G., Baillés, E., Carreño, M., Donaire, A., ... & Rumia, J. (2010). Prevalence of interictal psychiatric disorders in patients with refractory temporal and extratemporal lobe epilepsy in Spain. A comparative study. *Epilepsia, 51*(7), 1309-1313.

Sen, S., Duman, R., & Sanacora, G. (2008). Serum brain-derived neurotrophic factor, depression, and antidepressant medications: meta-analyses and implications. *Biological Psychiatry, 64*(6), 527-532.

Sheehan, R., Hassiotis, A., Walters, K., Osborn, D., Strydom, A., & Horsfall, L. (2015). Mental illness, challenging behaviour, and psychotropic drug prescribing in people with intellectual disability: UK population based cohort study. *British Journal of Medicine, 351, h4326.*

Shooshtari, S., Brownell, M., Dik, N., Chateau, D., Yu, C. T., Mills, R. S., Burchill, C., & Wetzel, M. (2014). A population-based longitudinal study of depression in children with developmental disabilities in Manitoba. *Journal of Mental Health Research in Intellectual Disabilities, 7*(3), 191-207.

Smiley, E. (2005). Epidemiology of mental health problems in adults with learning disability: an update. *Advances in Psychiatric Treatment, 11*(3), 214-222.

Smith, K. R., & Matson, J. L. (2010). Psychopathology: Differences among adults with intellectually disabled, comorbid autism spectrum disorders and epilepsy. *Research in Developmental Disabilities, 31*(3), 743-749.

Sovner, R., Fox, C.J., Lowry, M.J. & Lowry, M.A. (1993). Fluoxetine treatment of depression and associated self-injury in two adults with mental retardation. *Journal of Intellectual Disability Research, 37*, 301-311.

Sovner, R. & Hurley, A.D. (1983). Do the mentally retarded suffer from affective illness? *Archives of General Psychiatry, 40*, 61-67.

Sovner, R. & Pary, R.J. (1993). Affective disorders in developmentally disabled persons. In J.L. Matson & R.P. Barrett (Eds.), *Psychopathology in the mentally retarded* (2nd ed.). Needham Heights, MA: Allyn & Bacon.

Stack, L.S., Haldipur, C.V., & Thompson, M. (1987). Stressful life events and psychiatric hospitalization of mentally retarded patients. *American Journal of Psychiatry, 144*(5), 661-663.

Stavrakaki, C., Antochi, R., & Emery, P. (2004). Obsessive compulsive disorder in adults with Down syndrome and other developmental disability. *Psychiatry Annals, 34*, 196-200.

Sternlicht, M., Pustel, G., & Duetsch, M. (1970). Suicidal tendencies among institutionalized retardates. *Journal of Mental Subnormality, 16*, 93-102.

Sturmey, P., Laud, R.B., Cooper, C.L., Matson, J.L. & Fodstad, J.C. (2010) Challenging behaviors should not be considered depressive equivalents in individuals with Intellectual Disabilities II: A replication study. *Research in Developmental Disabilities, 31*, 1002-1007.

Taggart, L., Taylor, D., & McCrum-Gardner, E. (2010). Individual, life events, family and socio-economic factors associated with young people with intellectual disability and with and without behavioural/emotional problems. *Journal of Intellectual Disabilities, 14*(4), 267-288.

Thapar, A., Collishaw, S., Pine, D. S., & Thapar, A. K. (2012). Depression in adolescence. *The Lancet, 379*(9820), 1056-1067.

Tisher, P.W., Holzer, J.C., Greenberg, M., Benjamin, S., Devinsly, O. & Bear, D.M. (1996). Psychiatric presentations of epilepsy. *Harvard Review of Psychiatry. 11*(12), 219-228.

To, W. T., Neirynck, S., Vanderplasschen, W., Vanheule, S., & Vandevelde, S. (2014). Substance use and misuse in persons with intellectual disabilities (ID): Results of a survey in ID and addiction services in Flanders. *Research in Developmental Disabilities, 35*(1), 1-9.

Tonge, B. J., & Einfeld, S. L. (2003). Psychopathology and intellectual disability: The Australian child to adult longitudinal study. *International review of research in mental retardation, 26*, 61-91.

Trad, P. V. (1987). *Infant and childhood depression: Developmental factors.* New York: John Wiley & Sons. 309 - 341.

Tsakanikos, E., Bouras, N., Costello, H., & Holt, G. (2007). Multiple exposure to life events and clinical psychopathology in adults with intellectual disability. *Social Psychiatry and Psychiatric Epidemiology, 42*, 24-28.

Tsiouris, J. A. (2001). Diagnosis of depression in people with severe/profound intellectual disability. *Journal of Intellectual Disability Research, 45*(2), 115-120.

Tsiouris J. A. (2010) Pharmacotherapy for aggressive behaviours in persons with intellectual disabilities: treatment or mistreatment? *Journal of Intellectual Disability Research, 54*, 1–16.

Tsiouris, J. A., Kim, S. Y., Brown, W. T., & Cohen, I. L. (2011). Association of aggressive behaviours with psychiatric disorders, age, sex and degree of intellectual disability: a large-scale survey. *Journal of Intellectual Disability Research, 55*(7), 636-649.

Tsiouris, J. A., Mann, R., Patti, P.J. & Sturmey, P. (2003). Challenging behaviours should not be considered as depressive equivalents in individuals with intellectual disability. *Journal of Intellectual Disability Research, 47*, 14-21.

Turky, A., Felce, D., Jones, G., & Kerr, M. (2011). A prospective case control study of psychiatric disorders in adults with epilepsy and intellectual disability. *Epilepsia, 52*(7), 1223-1230.

Valdovinos, M. G., Caruso, M., Roberts, C., Kim, G., & Kennedy, C. H. (2005). Medical and behavioral symptoms as potential medication side effects in adults with developmental disabilities. *American Journal of Mental Retardation, 110*, 164-170.

Verhoeven, W. M. A., Tuinier, B. S., Kuijpers, H. J. H., Egger, J. I. M., & Brunnerd, C. H. G. (2010). Psychiatric profile in Rubinstein-Taybi syndrome: A review and case report. *Psychopathology, 43*,63–68

Walker, J. C., Dosen, A., Buitelaar, J. K., & Janzing, J. G. E. (2011). Depression in Down syndrome: A review of the literature. *Research in developmental disabilities, 32*(5), 1432-1440.

Walters, A.S., Barrett, R.P., Knapp, L.G. & Borden, M.C. (1995). Suicidal behavior in children and adolescents with mental retardation. *Research in Developmental Disabilities, 16*(2), 85-96.

White, P., Chant, D., Edwards, N., Townsend, C., & Waghorn, G. (2005). Prevalence of intellectual disability and comorbid mental illness in an Australian community sample. *Australian and New Zealand Journal of Psychiatry, 39*(5), 395-400.

Winblad, S., Jensen, C., Mansson, J., Samuelsson, L., & Lindberg, C. (2010). Depression in myotonic dystrophy type 1: clinical and neuronal correlates. *Behavior and Brain Functions, 6*(25), 1–7.

CHAPTER 13

Anxiety Disorders

Sherva Elizabeth Cooray
Tim Andrews
Nicola M. Bailey
John Devapriam
Jennifer L. McLaren
Kiran N. Purandare
Sujeet S. Jaydeokar
Marc J. Tassé
Anusha Wijeratne

1. The DSM-5 includes eleven subcategories of anxiety disorders namely: separation anxiety disorder, selective mutism , specific phobia, social anxiety disorder (social phobia), panic disorder, panic attack (specifier), agoraphobia, generalized anxiety disorder, substance/medication-induced anxiety disorder, anxiety disorder due to another medical condition, other specified anxiety disorder and unspecified anxiety disorder.
2. The DSM-5 adopts a developmental approach and examination of disorders across the lifespan, including children and older adults with assurances that the diagnostic criteria for anxiety disorders are applicable to all age, gender, and cultural groups.
3. The anxiety disorders in the DSM-5 has been rearranged into separate groupings of classical anxiety disorders which now also includes selective mutism and separation anxiety disorder.
4. These changes are underpinned by systematic literature reviews, reanalysis of available data, and evaluation of results following the DSM-5 principles.
5. Diagnosis-specific and cross-cutting dimensional anxiety scales have been developed to supplement categorical diagnosis which appears to facilitate assessment of severity and course of treatment.
6. It was also assured that the criteria are applicable to all age, gender, and cultural groups.
7. Nevertheless, the diagnostic criteria rely heavily on adequate cognitive function and communication which are compromised to varying degrees in people with intellectual disability (ID). Consequently, diagnosis of AD in this population is difficult, especially in those with more severe degrees of ID.
8. The literature in this population is mainly confined to case reports with the exception of a few. We evaluate the validity and applicability of anxiety disorder criteria in people with ID and highlight the dearth of empirical evidence.
9. Using strategies such as behavioral equivalents, we explore and suggest recommendations to address these shortcomings within the context of best available evidence.
10. It is envisaged that this would facilitate diagnosis of anxiety disorder in people with ID, more robust research in the future, and enhance the evidence base.

Review of Diagnostic Criteria

General Description of the Disorder

The *DSM-5* categories are designed to permit differentiation among several different forms of anxiety disorder (for example, panic disorder, social phobia, generalized anxiety), though one person may be diagnosed with multiple anxiety disorders. In contrast with DSM-IV, the classification of panic disorder and agoraphobia has been radically simplified and both conditions can now be separately coded in DSM-5. Overlap between these disorders is signified by a comorbid double diagnosis.

a) Separation Anxiety Disorder

Formerly classified under Disorders Usually First Diagnosed in Infancy, Childhood, or Adolescence, the onset before the age of 18 requirements has been removed in DSM-5. To meet the criteria for this disorder, fear, anxiety, or avoidance must last at least 4 weeks in children and adolescents and typically 6 months or more in adults. With regard to the differential diagnosis, distinctions are now drawn between separation anxiety disorder and some personality disorders such as dependent personality disorder and borderline personality disorder.

b) Selective Mutism

This was included under "Disorders Usually First Diagnosed in Infancy, Childhood, or Adolescence" in DSM-IV-TR and is now subsumed within the general category of DSM-5 anxiety disorders. Selective mutism is a condition wherein a child, adolescent, or adult will only speak to a select few people. Failure to speak has significant consequences on achievement in academic or occupational settings or otherwise interferes with normal social communication.

c) Specific Phobia

People suffering from this condition are fearful or anxious about or avoidant of circumscribed objects or situations. The fear, anxiety, or avoidance is almost always immediately induced by the phobic situation and of a degree that is persistent and out of proportion to the actual risk posed. There are various types of specific phobias: animal; natural environment; blood-injection-injury; situational; and other situations. The age specifier in DSM-IV-TR has been eliminated. Consequently, unlike previously, the 6-months duration of symptoms is no longer a stringent requirement but rather a guideline.

d) Social Anxiety Disorder (Social Phobia)

The individual is fearful or anxious about or avoidant of social interactions and situations that involve the possibility of being scrutinized. Included are social interactions such as meeting unfamiliar people, situations in which the individual may be observed eating or drinking, and situations in which the individual performs in front of others. Cognitively, this involves being negatively evaluated by others, by being embarrassed, humiliated, or rejected, or offending others.

The DSM-5 requires that "the fear or anxiety is out of proportion to the actual threat posed by the social situation and to the sociocultural context." The subtypes of social anxiety disorder have changed: where DSM-IV-TR specified "generalized" social anxiety disorder (when fears include most social situations), DSM-5 specifies "performance only" social anxiety (when fear is restricted to speaking or performing in public). The duration criterion provides a guideline of "the persistent fear, anxiety, or avoidance" as, typically lasting for six months or more.

e) Panic Disorder

In panic disorder, the individual experiences recurrent unexpected panic attacks and is persistently concerned or worried about having more panic attacks or changes his or her behavior in maladaptive ways because of the panic attacks (e.g., avoidance of exercise or of unfamiliar locations). Panic attacks are abrupt surges of intense fear/discomfort that reach a climax within minutes, accompanied by physical and/or cognitive symptoms. Limited-symptom panic attacks include fewer than four symptoms. Panic attacks may be expected, such as in response to a typically feared object or situation, or unexpected, meaning that the panic attack occurs for no apparent reason. Panic attacks function as a marker and prognostic factor for severity of diagnosis, course, and comorbidity across an array of disorders, including, but not limited to, the anxiety disorders (e.g., substance use, depressive, and psychotic disorders). Consequently, panic attack may be used as a descriptive specifier for any anxiety disorder as well as other mental disorders. This should be noted within the diagnosis (e.g., social anxiety disorder with panic attacks). The DSM-5 also clarifies that culture-specific symptoms are not considered symptoms of a panic attack.

f) Agoraphobia

Involves marked fear or anxiety regarding two or more of the following situations: (i) using public transportation; (ii) being in open spaces; (iii) being in enclosed places; (iv) standing in line or being in a crowd; and (v) being outside of the home alone. The individual fears or avoids these situations due to thoughts that escape might be difficult or help might not be available in the event of developing panic-like symptoms or other incapacitating or embarrassing symptoms. It is also required that the agoraphobic situations almost always provoke fear or anxiety. The situations are actively avoided, require the presence of a companion, or are endured with intense fear or anxiety. Also, the fear or anxiety is out of proportion to the actual danger posed by the agoraphobic situations and to the sociocultural context. The fear, anxiety, or avoidance is persistent, typically lasting for six months or more, is not better explained by the symptoms of another mental disorder, and causes significant distress or impairment in social, occupational, or other important areas of functioning. Agoraphobia no longer requires individuals over age 18 to recognize that their anxiety is excessive or unreasonable. In DSM-5, agoraphobia is diagnosed regardless of the presence of panic disorder. When both disorders are present, each is diagnosed separately.

g) Generalized Anxiety Disorder

Generalized anxiety disorder is characterized by excessive, uncontrollable, and often irrational worry. The core features being persistent and excessive anxiety and worry about various domains, including work and school performance that the individual finds difficult to control. In addition, the individual experiences physical symptoms, including restlessness or feeling keyed up or on edge; being easily fatigued; difficulty concentrating or mind going blank; irritability; muscle tension; and sleep disturbance. The DSM-5 makes a categorical distinction between sub-threshold and threshold cases of generalized anxiety disorder with emerging evidence that these criteria lend themselves to making both categorical decisions about cases as well as being indices of a continuum of severity. (Hobbs, Anderson, Slade, & Andrews, 2014)

h) Substance/Medication-Induced Anxiety Disorder

Substance/medication-induced anxiety disorder involves anxiety due to substance intoxication or withdrawal or to a medication treatment. Disorder-specific scales are available to better characterize the severity of each anxiety disorder and to capture change in severity over time. For ease of use, particularly for individuals with more than one anxiety disorder, these scales have been developed to have the same format (but different focus) across the anxiety disorders, with ratings of behavioral symptoms, cognitive ideation symptoms, and physical symptoms relevant to each disorder.

i) Anxiety Disorder Due to Another Medical Condition

The anxiety symptoms are attributed to the physiological consequence of another medical condition (e.g., pheochromocytoma, hyperthyroidism). The individual's anxiety and worry are judged, based on history, laboratory findings, or physical examination.

j) Other Specified Anxiety Disorder

k) Unspecified Anxiety Disorder

l) Unspecified Anxiety Disorder

Summary of DSM-5 Criteria

The DSM-5 (American Psychiatric Association, 2013) defines anxiety as "The apprehensive anticipation of future danger or misfortune accompanied by a feeling of worry, distress, and/or somatic symptoms of tension. The focus of anticipated danger may be internal or externa.l.

Eleven types of anxiety disorders are described in the *DSM-5*. Additionally, all anxiety disorder diagnoses include a qualifying criterion of severity; that is, the anxiety must be of a sufficient degree of severity to interfere significantly with the person's social, occupational, or other areas of functioning.

The *DSM-5* categories are designed to permit differentiation among several different forms of anxiety disorder (for example, panic disorder, social phobia, generalized anxiety), though one person may be diagnosed with multiple anxiety disorders.

A panic attack (not codable) is considered a descriptive specifier for both anxiety disorders and other mental health disorders. A panic attack signifies a discrete period of intense apprehension, fearfulness, or terror, often associated with feelings of impending doom. During such an attack, such symptoms as shortness of breath, palpitations, chest pain or discomfort, choking or smothering sensations, and a fear of "going crazy" or of losing control are present.

The codable types of anxiety disorders include separation anxiety disorder, selective mutism, specific phobia (wherein the coding procedure is based on the phobic stimulus – for example, animal, natural environment, blood-injection injury, situational, or other) social anxiety disorder (also known as social phobia), panic disorder, agoraphobia, generalized anxiety disorder, substance/medication-induced anxiety disorder (wherein the coding procedure is based on the specific substance involved—for example, alcohol, caffeine, cannabis, opioid, or a hallucinogen), anxiety disorder due to another medical condition (wherein the coding procedure notes include the name of the other medical condition in the name of the mental disorder – for example, anxiety disorder due to hyperthyroidism). An anxiety disorder that does not meet criteria for a specific disorder can be coded as other specified anxiety disorder

Issues Related to Diagnosis in Persons with ID

All the disorders in the anxiety disorders section of DSM-5 (with the exception of selective mutism) use the terms fear, anxiety, or worry. **Fear** is defined as "the emotional response to real or perceived danger," whereas **anxiety** is the "anticipation of future threat." **Worry** is defined as "apprehensive expectation" within the description of diagnostic features of generalized anxiety disorder, and this is further clarified in the glossary of technical terms as being "unpleasant or uncomfortable thoughts that cannot be consciously controlled by trying to turn the attention to other subjects. [It] is often persistent, repetitive and out of proportion to the topic worried about." It can be seen that some ability to recognize and describe one's own emotions and would be necessary in order to meet criteria containing these terms, with the cognitive component being less for fear than for anxiety or worry. People with severe and profound intellectual disability will find it difficult or impossible to describe these terms, and even people who function at the lower end of the moderate intellectual disability range may have difficulties describing the cognitive aspects of worry. Matson and his colleagues (Matson, Smiroldo, Hamilton, & Baglio, 1997) noted from a study investigating anxiety symptoms in individuals with severe and profound intellectual disability that worry, fear of particular stimulus, and avoidance were not able to be reliably assessed in this group. However, Forte, Jahoda, and Dagnan (2011) demonstrated that with visual prompts, young adults with mild to moderate intellectual disability were able to describe worries and rate time spent worrying and distress caused, although explicit reference is not made to whether a subjective description was obtained of worries feeling out of control. In a study investigating the presentation of depression, people with anxiety disorders were reported to have significantly more fearfulness compared with people with depression, whereas people with depression were reported to have significantly more withdrawal, sadness, crying, anhedonia, aggression, and impulsivity than individuals with anxiety (Hurley, 2008). Interestingly, crying was only reported in 1 of the 30 individuals in the anxiety group. The presence of fear can often be observed through facial expression or other physiological or behavioral manifestations in individuals who are unable to self-report, (Matson et al., 1997; Pruijssers, van Meijel, Maaskant, Nijssen, & van Achtenberg, 2014; Stavrakaki & Mintsioulis, 1997). This is taken into account for children in DSM-5 by allowing fear or anxiety to be expressed by "crying, tantrums, freezing or clinging" in the criteria for specific phobia or "crying, tantrums, freezing or clinging, shrinking or failing to speak" in social anxiety disorder. However, there is no reference in the text to the use of this modifier in adults with intellectual disability who are functioning at a similar developmental level. It is interesting to note that anxiety disorders which are typically first diagnosed in childhood include behavioral manifestations in their criteria. (In separation anxiety, disorder half of features of excessive fear and anxiety concerning separation are behavioral, and selective mutism is entirely behaviorally defined.) Facial expressions of children with severe and profound intellectual disability may be more subtle and have been shown to be recognized more frequently by parents compared with adults inexperienced in the care of children with intellectual disability (Adams & Oliver, 2011). Behaviors associated with anxiety have been described in children with fragile X syndrome and mild to moderate intellectual disability (Sullivan, Hooper, & Hatton, 2007) such as arguing, performing repetitive acts, and avoiding difficult tasks. Moreover, informants have been shown to describe behavioral symptoms of anxiety in people with intellectual disabilities and autism, although they seem to recognize the severity of physiological signs less well (Helverschou & Martinsen, 2011). In older adults with intellectual disability, rates of ICD -10 anxiety disorders were less than in a general population comparison group, but rates of anxiety symptoms were similar in both. The authors suggested that this could be explained by informants finding it difficult to recognize both physiological and cognitive symptoms in people with more severe intellectual disability (Hermans, Beekman, & Evenhuis, 2013). Charlot and her colleagues derived behavioral descriptors of DSM-IV symptoms of anxiety with good correlation with diagnoses made clinically (Charlot, Deutsch, Hunt, Fletcher, & McLivane, 2007).

Avoidance or requiring the presence of a companion may be problematic in people with intellectual disability. People with intellectual disability may not be given the opportunity to make or demonstrate choices of this sort or, if they do, may not express the reasons for them. Moreover, some individuals may be accompanied whenever in the community by reason of their adaptive functioning, e.g. poor road crossing skills, thereby masking his or her phobic symptoms. With regard to agoraphobia, the individual has to be able to give a reason for their avoidance as being 'because of thoughts that escape might be difficult, or help might not be available.' People with more severe intellectual disability are unlikely to be able to express cognitions of such complexity. A similar difficulty arises with respect to the concepts of derealization, depersonalization, fear of losing control or "going crazy," or fear of dying in the criteria for panic disorder (or panic specifier for other disorders). This effectively reduces the pool of possible symptoms for people with severe and profound intellectual disability making it more difficult for this group to reach the criterion threshold. Similarly, in generalized anxiety disorder, the need for 3 of 6 additional symptoms 2 of which are unlikely to be described by people with profound intellectual disability (poor concentration or mind going blank; muscle tension). However, the remaining 4 additional symptoms can possibly be observed by others at least if more marked (restlessness, being easily fatigued, irritability, and sleep disturbance). Again, there is a modifier for children that only one of these additional features is required, but no reference is made in the text to this being appropriate for individuals with intellectual disability of similar functional ability.

It can be seen that there are considerable difficulties in applying DSM-5 criteria for anxiety disorders in individuals with intellectual disability. However, despite the reliance on cognitive symptoms in some diagnostic criteria, the revision of the criterion in DSM-IV-TR specific phobia and social phobia of "the person recognizes that the fear is excessive or unreasonable" to "the fear or anxiety is out of proportion" in DSM-5 represents a considerable improvement, thus enabling it to be applied across the intellect

Development and Course

Anxiety disorders are complex and probably develop from a combination of genetic, environmental, psychological, and developmental factors.

There is general consensus that anxiety disorders are characterized by a pronounced dysfunction of systems underpinning stress regulation and fear responses (Mineka & Zinbarg, 1996; Rosen & Schulkin, 1998).

Course

The course of anxiety disorders is chronic and manifests itself in residual symptoms and mild impairment in social roles even after many years and is frequently complicated with depression. The best predictors are severity and duration of symptoms, as well as comorbidity with depression. According to Angst and Vollrath (1991), prognosis varied across disorders, with favorable remittance rates for panic disorder without agoraphobia and generalized anxiety disorder; gradually declining for social phobia and for panic disorder with agoraphobia. Those with multiple anxiety disorder showed a more chronic course than pure anxiety disorders. Both baseline duration and severity were course predictors. Avoidance behavior symptoms predicted the outcome better than anxiety arousal symptoms (Hendricks, Spijker, Licht, Beekman, & Penninx, 2013). In anxiety disorders, symptom remission is accompanied by improvements in functioning, but significant functional impairments may persist because of co-morbid disorders, lower functioning prior to the onset of the anxiety disorder, or residual sub-threshold anxiety symptoms (Iancu et al., 2014)

Prevalence

The prevalence of anxiety disorders in the general population is high with 12-month estimates of 18.1%; (Kessler et al., 2005). A World Health Organization Collaborative Study, (Sartorius et al., 1996) estimated that 10% of primary care patients have current anxiety disorders (generalized anxiety disorder 7.9%, panic disorder=1.1%, and agoraphobia +/- PD = 1.5%). In adolescents in the United States, the 12-month prevalence is 1.6% (Kessler, Petukhova, Sampson, Zaslavsky, & Wittchen, 2012).

All types of anxiety disorders have been well recognized in people with intellectual disability (Bailey & Andrews, 2003; McNally & Ascher, 1987). According to some studies (King, De Antonio, McCracken, Forness & Ackerland, 1994; Raghavan, 1998; Deb, Thomas, & Bright, 2001a), anxiety disorders are reported to be as common as or more common in individuals with ID than in the general population. Bailey and Andrews (2003) carried out a comprehensive review of literature and concluded that despite their uncertain prevalence, the use of modified diagnostic criteria may aid further research in this area.

A cross-sectional observational study by Deb, Thomas, and Bright (2001a, 2001b) in a community sample of those with mild ID, using *ICD-10* criteria and the Diagnostic Assessment for the

Severely Handicapped scale (DASH; Matson, Gardner, Coe, & Sovner, 1991) in individuals with severe ID, revealed a prevalence rate of 2.2% for generalized anxiety disorder. They also found a significantly higher rate of phobic disorder in the study cohort when compared with the general population.

White, Chant, Edwards, Townsend, and Waghorn (2005), assessed the prevalence of ID and mental illness in an Australian community sample and reported the prevalence of anxiety disorder in ID was 14%.

Cooper, Smiley, Morrison, Williamson, and Allan (2007) conducted a large population-based study (N=1,023) to determine the point prevalence of mental illness in adults with ID using a combination of diagnostic criteria and clinical diagnosis. The prevalence of anxiety disorder (excluding specific phobia) was reported as 3.8% (clinical diagnosis), 3.1% (DC-LD criteria), 2.8% (ICD-10 DCR) and 2.4% (DSM-IV-TR). Within the anxiety disorder category, 1.7% had a generalised anxiety disorder, 0.7% had agoraphobia, 0.3% social phobia, 0.5% adjustment disorder, 0.3% post-traumatic stress disorder, 0.2% panic disorder, and 0.2% mixed anxiety and depression. The point prevalence in those with a mild ID (6.0%) was higher than those with a moderate-profound ID (2.4%). There was a greater prevalence of anxiety disorder in females (4.3%) than males (3.4%).

Verhoeven and Tuinier (1997) proposed that anxiety disorders were probably under-diagnosed in this population. The phenomenon of diagnostic overshadowing (Jopp & Keys, 2001; Reiss, Levitan, & Szyszko, 1982) can also result in the under-reporting of anxiety disorders.

Cooper (1997) found higher rates of anxiety disorders in the elderly when compared with younger age groups. Among people with self-injurious behavior, anxiety disorders were identified as being more prevalent than in those without such behavior. It is not clear whether this finding relates specifically to the presence of self-injurious behavior or whether it is because this group contained more individuals with profound intellectual disability (Moss, Moss, Emerson, & Kiernan, 2000).

Repetitive behaviors, stereotypies, and self-injurious behaviors are reportedly common in persons with severe/profound ID (Schroeder, 1989).

Differential Diagnosis

The differential diagnosis of anxiety disorder includes mental disorders such as schizophrenia, manic episode, depressive disorder, adjustment disorder, and physical or organic states that present as anxiety (for example, substance intoxication or withdrawal, dementia, or multiple sclerosis). Depressive symptoms are frequently associated with anxiety, sometimes making it impossible to determine which the primary disorder is (Cameron, 1985). Overlap of syndromes probably also occurs with other primary psychiatric disorders, especially somatoform disorders, adjustment disorder with anxious mood, and several personality disorders.

Differential diagnosis among the anxiety disorders can hence be very difficult, and the high comorbidity with mood disorders, unexplained physical symptoms, and medical disorders makes the precise assessment complicated. Nevertheless, anxiety disorders differ from one another in the types of objects or situations that induce fear, anxiety, or avoidance behavior and the associated cognitive ideation. Thus, while the anxiety disorders tend to be highly comorbid with each other, they can be differentiated by close examination of the types of situations that are feared or avoided and the content of the associated thoughts or beliefs (American Psychiatric Association, 2013). For example, phobic disorders (exogenous anxiety) are characterized by anxiety reliably elicited by specific environmental stimuli. Panic attacks and generalized anxiety (endogenous anxiety) involve symptoms of anxiety not associated only with specific eliciting stimuli. While both panic disorder and generalized anxiety usually have some level of persistent anxiety, panic disorder differs from generalized anxiety disorder by the presence of discrete attacks.

Primary anxiety can also be confused with several medical syndromes, especially when the medical disorder has not been recognized. Nevertheless, medical causes of anxiety may be qualitatively different from primary anxiety disorders, especially the psychic anxiety component.

Functional Consequences

Anxiety disorders are similar to major depression and chronic diseases such as diabetes in functional impairment. They markedly compromise quality of life and psychosocial functioning with significant impairment in individuals with sub threshold forms (Mendlowicz & Stein, 2000). Anxiety disorders are independently associated with several physical conditions in the community, and this comorbidity is significantly associated with poor quality of life and disability (Sareen et al., 2006). Anxiety disorders increase risk of hypertension, coronary heart disease, and death in myocardial infarction.

Most with anxiety disorders present with somatic symptoms mimicking physical illness resulting in fruitless evaluations and missed psychiatric diagnosis (Katon, Vitiliano, Russo, Jones, & Anderson, 1986). Patients and physicians regard anxiety as an expected consequence of illness. Consequently, potentially treatable disorders are overlooked (Sensky, 1989).

Comorbidity

A high level of comorbidity has been reported in the general population of people suffering from an anxiety disorder (Brown et al., 2001). This comorbidity is particularly evident in generalized anxiety disorder. Community studies in the general population indicate that comorbid conditions—for example, depressive disorder and anxiety disorder—commonly occur together. In individuals with ID, it can be extremely difficult at the primary-care level to distinguish between the two, either because (a) the person complains of both emotions as having equal severity, or (b) there are so few associated symptoms that it is impossible to make a syndromic diagnosis. Empirical evidence on comorbidity in people with ID is minimal. However, an observational study by Masi, Favilla, and Mucci (2000) of adolescents with ID revealed a high level of comorbidity with depressive disorders. Charlot, Deutsch, Hunt, Connor, and McIlvane (2008) also found high rates of co-morbid anxiety disorders as well as externalizing behaviors in an inpatient population with depression.

Among people with self-injurious behavior, anxiety disorders were identified as being more prevalent than in those without such behavior (Moss et al., 2000). However, it was not clear whether this finding related specifically to the presence of self-injurious behavior or whether it was because this group contained more individuals with profound ID. Anxiety disorders were associated with having a chronic physical condition. Multivariate logistic regression showed that the presence of a chronic physical condition, deviant anxiety, and self-absorbed behaviors were the strongest predictors of anxiety disorders (Dekker & Koot; 2003). However, it was not clear whether this association indicated co-morbidity or had causal link. While studying demographic features in 283 patients with somatoform disorders, co-morbid illness were seen in 24.8% of patients and included mood disorder, anxiety disorder, and personality disorder, as well as borderline intellectual functioning and mental retardation (Kuwabara, Van Voorhees, Gollan, & Alexander, 2007).

There were two studies (see Cohan, Chavira, & Stein., 2006; Kristensen, 2000) indicating links between selective mutism and anxiety disorders. Kristensen (2000) assessed the co-morbidity of developmental disorder/delay in children with selective mutism and assessed other co-morbid symptoms such as anxiety, enuresis, and encopresis. Results showed that of the children with selective mutism, 68.5% met the criteria for a diagnosis reflecting developmental disorder/delay compared with 13.0% in the control group; the criteria for any anxiety diagnosis were met by 74.1% in the selective mutism group compared to 7.4% in the control group. In the selective mutism group, 46.3% of the children met the criteria for both an anxiety diagnosis and a diagnosis reflecting developmental disorder/delay versus 0.9% in the controls. Predisposition to anxiety interacted with factors such as communication disorders that resulted in mutism, thus explaining high level of co-morbidity (Cohan et al., 2006).

As expected, there was a strong link between the diagnosis of anxiety disorder and co-morbid diagnosis of autism spectrum disorders. Anxiety was three times as common in people with autism spectrum disorder and ID (Gillott & Standen; 2007). In a study by Skokauskas and Gallagher (2012), almost half (46.2%) the autism spectrum disorder group met Child Behavior Checklist/DSM criteria for clinically significant anxiety problems. In an inpatient group with depression, anxiety disorders were reported in 62% of individuals with autism spectrum disorder and 38% of those without ASD (Charlot et al., 2008). Weisbrot, Gadow, DeVincent, and Pomero (2005) found that association of anxiety symptoms with psychotic symptoms suggested high co-morbidity and some overlap in causal mechanism in pervasive developmental disorders.

Application of Diagnostic Criteria to People with ID

General Considerations

We have approached this by using the modifications in DM-ID as a starting point. In going through the diagnostic criteria for each anxiety disorder in the DSM-5 and comparing with DM-ID, a few general points were apparent.

1. We have split the moderate and mild groups, since our opinion (based on clinical experience) is that diagnoses become difficult even in moderate intellectual disability if there is too much reliance on complex cognitive phenomena with fewer adaptations relevant in this group than expected. This is the case for anxiety disorders.

2. All references to fear should state that fear can be observed by an informant rather than subjectively described/self-reported for people with severe/profound ID and where relevant to those with moderate ID as well.

3. There should be consistency both within anxiety disorders (e.g., in making reference to anchor points to define time scales this should be in all disorders not just panic disorder as in DM-ID modifications. We are not sure this is necessary in any case, since we do not think there is an expectation for timescales to be self-reported in the DSM-IV-TR or DSM-5 criteria) and modifications elsewhere in DM-ID-2 (e.g., if poor concentration can be observed for depressive disorder, this should also be the case in anxiety disorders).

4. Based on clinical opinion but not on empirical evidence, it is reasonable to surmise that in people with lower end moderate to profound ID, generalized anxiety will be virtually impossible to diagnose. This is because the likelihood of eliciting the cognitive quality of worry, particularly "being difficult to control" would not be viable in this group. As such, the DSM-5 criteria in generalized anxiety disorder cannot be adequately modified to accommodate this. Given this situation, an optional stipulation such as "observed fear" and anxiety and not requiring "difficult to control" is desirable in this population.

Methodology

We carried out a literature review and evaluation within the context of the strength of evidence (Cochrane Convention) on anxiety disorders and intellectual disability using Preferred Reporting Items for Systematic reviews and Meta-Analyses guidelines (PRISMA; Liberati et al., 2009).

This involved a comprehensive electronic literature search of MEDLINE, Cochrane Library, PsychLit, EMBASE, and CINAHL as well as grey literature, hand search, and personal communication. However, as methodological reviews differ from systematic reviews in several ways, (Bertens et al., 2013-PLOS Med) not all items of the PRISMA guidelines were applicable. The systematic review highlighted considerable variability in research design, clinical setting, person selection, with an overall paucity of robust evidence-based high quality studies.

Review of Research Applying to People with ID

One of the largest literature reviews on anxiety disorders in persons with ID was done by Bailey and Andrews (2003) who undertook a major review of Medline, PsychINFO (English language up to 2000) and hand searches. This returned 202 electronic and 28 hand searched articles out of which 49 relevant articles were included. The sample included people with intellectual disability and anxiety disorders but excluded acute stress reaction, adjustment disorders and post-traumatic stress disorder and non-intellectual disability studies. The different diagnostic and rating scales used were PIMRA, DSM, DCLD, SCID, BAT (Behavior Approach Test), Fear Survey Schedule, Compatible Behavior Checklist and Trait Anxiety Scale. The key findings were that adapted diagnostic criteria such as DCLD may prevent overshadowing due to hierarchical approach and prompting clinician to account for symptoms in a structural way. DCLD also accounted for behavioral presentation of anxiety to be taken into account and in specific phobia does not expect individual to recognize that the fear is unreasonable and excessive. In persons with ID, assessment of impact on social functioning plays a key role in diagnosing obsessive compulsive disorder.

Waisbren and Levy (1991) described in a case report, the presence of an anxiety disorder in someone with phenylketonuria using the Trait Anxiety Scale as a diagnostic tool. It is important to consider the age appropriateness of certain type of fears and anxieties as they may be developmentally appropriate (Duff, La Rocca, & Lizzert, 1981; Pickersgill, Valentine, May, and Brewin, 1994; Sternlicht, 1979). The issue of diagnostic overshadowing whereby symptoms of anxiety are attributed to intellectual disability itself is present (Levitan & Reiss, 1983) but the effect is small (White et al., 1995).

Khreim and Mikkelson (1997) suggested that increased weightage should be given to behavioral equivalents of anxiety in people with ID as internal subjective experience can be difficult to communicate and that excessive and uncontrollable worry of general anxiety disorder may have a different presentation in people with ID. Ellison (1997) in a case report described how generalized anxiety disorder observational symptoms were used instead of subjective description as patient could not speak (DCLD allows for this) and how symptoms of de-personalization and de-realization may not be diagnosable in persons with ID. Matson et al. (1991) and Chiodos and Maddux (1985) reported improvement in symptoms of social phobia in people with ID with behavioral and psychological treatments. They also observed that such symptoms can occur as part of fragile X syndrome and therefore constituting diagnostic overshadowing. Jackson (1983) recommended Behavior Approach Test, Fear Survey Schedules, electronic and cardiac rate measurements to support the diagnosis of specific phobias.

Diagnosing obsessive compulsive disorder in people with ID is difficult (Bodfish et al., 1995; Khreim & Mikkelson, 1997). Vitiello, Spreat, and Behar (1989) found that inter-rater reliability in distinguishing compulsions from stereotypies and tics (obsessive compulsive disorder/autism spectrum disorder) is good. Bodfish et al. (1995) used Compatible Behavior Checklist (CBC) and demonstrated good reliability and validity. Obsessive compulsive disorder is thought to be under-diagnosed in persons with ID and often termed "autistic traits" (Fitzgerald, Stewart, Tawile, & Rosenberg, 1999). Cognitive thoughts and compulsive behaviors as in the three C's of cleaning, counting, and checking may be relevant for people with ID (McDougal et al., 1995). Compulsions are easy to observe, but cognitive aspects like resistance are difficult to elicit in people with ID, and this was accounted for in DSM-III-R (Bodfish et al., 1995).

In a study evaluating the use of the PAS-ADD, Costello, Moss, Prosser, and Hatton (1997) reported that the greatest reliability weakness was in relation to symptoms of anxiety (due to difficulty in getting information on autonomic symptoms from people with ID and descriptions of panic and phobic anxiety demand a high level of verbal and intellectual ability). Moss, Ibbotson, and Prosser (1997) found that reporting of neurotic and depressive symptoms was positively and significantly related to IQ.

In a survey on the utility of DM-ID, Fletcher et al. (2009) found that greater specificity was elicited for anxiety and mood disorders compared to psychotic disorders and PDD.

Evaluating Level of Evidence The evidence available has been graded according to the Cochrane Convention as below. As can be seen, most of the evidence falls at the Type V level.

Type I Evidence: Good systematic review and Meta-analysis including at least one randomized controlled trial – nil.

Type II Evidence: Randomized controlled trial – nil.

Type III Evidence: Well-designed interventional studies – nil.

Type IV Evidence: Well-designed observational studies – Bailey et al., (2003), Fletcher et al. (2009).

Type V Evidence: Expert opinion, influential reports and studies – Barak et al., (1995); Bodfish et al., (1995); Costello et al. (1997), Duff et al. (1981); Ellison (1997); Jackson (1983); Khreim and Mikkelson (1997); Levitan & Reiss (1983); Chiodos and Maddux (1985); Matson et al. (1991); Moss et al. (1997); Pickersgill et al. (1994); Reiss and Benson (1984); Vitiello et al. (1989); Sternlicht (1979); Waisbren & Levy (1991); White et al. (1995).

Adults with Mild to Moderate Intellectual Disability

Fletcher and his colleagues (2009) reported on a survey of the utility of DM-ID involving 63 clinicians and 845 patients that they found that the DM-ID was rated as "easy" or "very easy" to use in over 68% of 845 responses. The positive response to DM-ID did not vary significantly across levels of ID, and the DM-ID helped avoid the "NOS" category, resulting in more specific diagnosis. Greater specificity was elicited for anxiety and mood disorders compared to psychotic disorders and PDD.

Adults with Severe or Profound Intellectual Disability

It is generally accepted that most diagnostic criteria need adaptation for use in adults with severe or profound intellectual disability. The use of behavioral equivalents is suggested.

Children and Adolescents with Intellectual Disability

There are no current studies looking at utility of diagnostic criteria in anxiety disorders in children with ID.

Summary of Limitations in Applying DSM-5 Criteria to People with ID

The DSM-5 adopts a developmental approach and examination of disorders across the lifespan, including children and older adults with assurances that the diagnostic criteria for anxiety disorders are applicable to all ages, gender, and cultural groups. The anxiety disorders in the DSM-5 have been rearranged into separate groupings of classical anxiety disorders which now also include selective mutism and separation anxiety disorder. Nevertheless, the diagnostic criteria rely heavily on adequate cognitive function and communication which are compromised to varying degrees in people with intellectual disability. Consequently, diagnosis of anxiety disorders in this population is difficult, especially in those with more severe degrees of ID. With a few exceptions, the literature in this population is mainly confined to case reports which highlights the dearth of empirical evidence with relation to the validity and applicability of anxiety disorder criteria in people with ID. Using strategies such as behavioral equivalents is recommended to address these shortcomings within the context of best available evidence.

Etiology and Pathogenesis

Biological Factors

Neuroimaging techniques such as high-resolution magnetic resonance imaging, functional magnetic resonance imaging, positron emission tomography, or single photon emission tomography have contributed greatly to the identification of the structural and functional neuroanatomy of anxiety disorders. There is now a consensus on the crucial role of the amygdala, anterior cingulate cortex, and insula in the pathophysiology of anxiety disorders (Damsa, Kosel, & Moussally, 2009), and all three have been referred to as the "fear network" (Holzschneider & Mulert, 2011). Dysregulation of the body's response to stress mediated via the hypothalamic-pituitary-adrenal (HPA) axis is seen in almost all anxiety disorders (Faravelli et al., 2012).

Abnormalities in neurotransmitter systems in the brain have been implicated in the etiology of anxiety disorders. There is also emerging evidence that a relative deficiency in GABA neurotransmission, can be augmented by agents acting on different components of the GABA system (Nemeroff, 2003).

Dysregulation of central serotonin (5-hydroxytryptamine, 5-HT) systems have been implicated in the pathophysiology and treatment of anxiety disorder (Heisler, Zhou, Bajwa, Hsu, & Tecott, 2007). Other neurotransmitters that have been linked with anxiety disorders include corticotrophin –releasing hormone (CRH) and cholecystokinin (Coplan & Lydiard, 1998).

Studies in humans have revealed that serotonin-related genetic variants interact with early-life stress to regulate stress-induced cortisol responsiveness and activate the neural circuits involved in mood and anxiety disorders. Emerging data demonstrate that early-life adversity induces epigenetic modifications in serotonin-related genes. Finally, recent findings reveal that selective serotonin reuptake inhibitors can reinstate juvenile-like forms of neural plasticity, thus allowing the erasure of long-lasting fear memories. (Dayer, 2014). It has also been demonstrated that antenatal maternal anxiety is related to HPA-axis dysregulation and self-reported depressive symptoms in adolescence: prospective study on the fetal origins of depressed mood.

Genetic Factors

Although our understanding of the etiology of anxiety disorders is incomplete, there is compelling evidence that familial and genetic factors are established risk factors (Smoller, Blocks, & Young, 2009). Despite their moderate to strong heritabilities, the search for candidate genes has been limited as a consequence of methodological shortcomings (e.g., the use of clinically defined but neurobiologically heterogeneous categorical phenotypes). However, studies to date consistently demonstrate strong genetic effects on the responsiveness of the fear circuit, particularly of genetic variants previously discussed as potential susceptibility variants for anxiety (e.g., the COMT 158val allele or the 5-HTTLPR short allele; Domschke & Dannlowski, 2010).

Twin studies found heritability of 0.43 for panic disorder and 0.32 for generalized anxiety disorder (Hettema, Neale, & Kendler, 2001). Panic disorder, generalized anxiety disorder, and phobias, all have significant familial aggregation. For panic disorder, generalized anxiety disorder, and probably phobias, genes largely explain this familial aggregation (Hettema et al., 2001).

Genetic causes of ID associated with anxiety include fragile-X syndrome and social anxiety, Williams syndrome with anxiety (Einfeld, Tonge, & Rees, 2001) and phobias (Dykens, 2003). There is a strong association between Williams syndrome and anxiety disorders. Children with Williams syndrome had a significantly higher prevalence of specific phobia, generalized anxiety disorder, and separation anxiety; the elevated prevalence rates of anxiety disorders in children with Williams syndrome suggested a connection between the deletion found in Williams syndrome and anxiety disorders. Leyfer, Woodruff-Borden, Klein-Tasman, Fricke, & Mervis (2008) reported that the odds ratio of a child with Williams syndrome having an anxiety disorder increased with age and with the severity of maternal anxiety. Dykens (2003) in her study also found that generalized and anticipatory anxiety were found in 51% to 60% of the sample with Williams syndrome; specific phobia was more prevalent, with 96% showing persistent and marked fears and 84% avoiding their fears, or enduring them with distress.

Psychosocial Factors

Traditionally the classical attachment theory has been a core construct in psychological models of anxiety. It has been hypothesized that exposure to anxiety and stress in the prenatal environment may result in susceptibility to psychopathology, such as anxiety disorders and/or depression, in humans (Van den Bergh, Van Calster, Smits, Van Huffel, & Lagae, 2007). Children and adults with intellectual disability are negatively affected by the experience of life events in the same way persons from the general population are affected. Using the life events section of the PAS-ADD, Hastings and his colleagues (2004) found that 46% of individuals from a large community-based sample reported having experienced at least one life event such as moving residence, serious illness, death, etc. in the last 12 months. The presence of such life events increased the probability of the person being diagnosed with a psychiatric disorder (Hastings, Hatton, Taylor, & Maddison, 2004; Hubbert-Williams et al., 2013). Scott and Havercamp (2014) studied the relationship between stress and mental health in a large sample of 10,627 adults with intellectual disability. They found that 39% of their sample reported experiencing at least one stressful life event in the past year. The presence of a stressor was positively correlated with the presence of a psychiatric disorder, and, in fact, for every additional stressor reported, the likelihood of having a psychiatric diagnosis was increased by 20% (Scott & Havercamp, 2014).

Anxiety disorders have been perceived as a manifestation of interpersonal conflict, a conditioned response learned over time, and/or existence of dysfunctional thought patterns, for example, the overestimation of the amount of danger in a given situation.

Developmental Factors

Nolte, Guiney, Fonagy, Mayes, and Luyten (2011) have cogently argued for an integrated model of contemporary attachment theory which has the potential to integrate neurobiological and behavioral findings within a multidisciplinary developmental framework. This relates to the influence of attachment relationships on the development of stress regulation strategies and the role those relationships play in the development and maintenance of anxiety disorders, particularly the neurobiological alterations that underpin them. Early attachment experiences are conceptualized as the key organizer of a complex interplay between genetic, environmental, and epigenetic contributions to the development of anxiety disorders – a multifactorial etiology resulting from dysfunctional co-regulation of fear and stress states. Nolte and colleagues (2011) also suggest that attachment experiences further influence the development of anxiety as potential moderators of risk factors, differentially impacting on genetic vulnerability and relevant neurobiological pathways.

Separation Anxiety Disorder

DSM 5 Diagnostic Criteria	Applying Criteria for Mild ID	Applying Criteria for Moderate ID	Applying Criteria for Severe to Profound ID
A. Developmentally inappropriate and excessive fear or anxiety concerning separation from those to whom the individual is attached, as evidenced by at least three of the following:	A. No adaptation	A. No adaptation	A. **Note:** fear can be observed rather than subjectively described)
1. Recurrent excessive distress when anticipating or experiencing separation from home or from major attachment figures.			
2. Persistent and excessive worry about losing major attachment figures or about possible harm to them, such as illness, injury, disasters, or death.			
3. Persistent and excessive worry about experiencing an untoward event (e.g., getting lost, being kidnapped, having an accident, becoming ill) that causes separation from a major attachment figure.			
4. Persistent reluctance or refusal to go out, away from home, to school, to work, or elsewhere because of fear of separation.			
5. Persistent and excessive fear of or reluctance about being alone or without major attachment figures at home or in other settings.			

Separation Anxiety Disorder (continued)

DSM 5 Diagnostic Criteria	Applying Criteria for Mild ID	Applying Criteria for Moderate ID	Applying Criteria for Severe to Profound ID
6. Persistent reluctance or refusal to sleep away from home or to go to sleep without being near a major attachment figure.			
7. Repeated nightmares involving the theme of separation.			
8. Repeated complaints of physical symptoms (e.g., headaches, stomachaches, nausea, vomiting) when separation from major attachment figures occurs or is anticipated.			
B. The fear, anxiety, or avoidance is persistent, lasting at least 4 weeks in children and adolescents and typically 6 months or more in adults.	B. No adaptation	B. No adaptation	B. No adaptation
C. The disturbance causes clinically significant distress or impairment in social, academic, occupational, or other important areas of functioning.	C. No adaptation	C. No adaptation	C. No adaptation
D. The disturbance is not better explained by another mental disorder, such as refusing to leave home because of excessive resistance to change in autism spectrum disorder; delusions or hallucinations concerning separation in psychotic disorders; refusal to go outside without a trusted companion in agoraphobia; worries about ill health or other harm befalling significant others in generalized anxiety disorder; or concerns about having an illness in illness anxiety disorder.	D. No adaptation	D. No adaptation	D. No adaptation

Selective Mutism

DSM 5 Diagnostic Criteria	Applying Criteria for Mild ID	Applying Criteria for Moderate ID	Applying Criteria for Severe to Profound ID
A. Consistent failure to speak in specific social situations in which there is an expectation for speaking (e.g., at school) despite speaking in other situations.	A. No adaptation	A. No adaptation	A. No adaptation
B. The disturbance interferes with educational or occupational achievement or with social communication.	B. No adaptation	B. No adaptation	B. No adaptation
C. The duration of the disturbance is at least 1 month (not limited to the first month of school).	C. No adaptation	C. No adaptation	C. No adaptation
D. The failure to speak is not attributable to a lack of knowledge of, or comfort with, the spoken language required in the social situation.	D. No adaptation	D. No adaptation	D. No adaptation
E. The disturbance is not better explained by a communication disorder (e.g., childhood-onset fluency disorder) and does not occur exclusively during the course of autism spectrum disorder, schizophrenia, or another psychotic disorder.	E. No adaptation	E. No adaptation	E. No adaptation

Specific Phobia

DSM 5 Diagnostic Criteria	Applying Criteria for Mild ID	Applying Criteria for Moderate ID	Applying Criteria for Severe to Profound ID
A. Marked fear or anxiety about a specific object or situation (e.g., flying, heights, animals, receiving an injection, seeing blood). **Note:** In children, the fear or anxiety may be expressed by crying, tantrums, freezing, or clinging.	A. No adaptation	A. No adaptation	A. Note: fear can be observed rather than subjectively described e.g. fear or anxiety may be expressed by crying, tantrums, freezing or clinging
B. The phobic object or situation almost always provokes immediate fear or anxiety.	B. No adaptation	B. No adaptation	B. Fear can be observed rather than subjectively described
C. The phobic object or situation is actively avoided or endured with intense fear or anxiety.	C. No adaptation	C. No adaptation	C. Fear can be observed rather than subjectively described
D. The fear or anxiety is out of proportion to the actual danger posed by the specific object or situation and to the sociocultural context.	D. No adaptation	D. No adaptation	D. Fear can be observed rather than subjectively described
E. The fear, anxiety, or avoidance is persistent, typically lasting for 6 months or more.	E. No adaptation	E. No adaptation	E. Fear can be observed rather than subjectively described
F. The fear, anxiety, or avoidance causes clinically significant distress or impairment in social, occupational, or other important areas of functioning.	F. No adaptation	F. No adaptation	F. Fear can be observed rather than subjectively described
G. The disturbance is not better explained by the symptoms of another mental disorder, including fear, anxiety, and avoidance of situations associated with panic-like symptoms or other incapacitating symptoms (as in agoraphobia); objects or situations related to obsessions (as in obsessive-compulsive disorder); reminders of traumatic events (as in posttraumatic stress disorder); separation from home or attachment figures (as in separation anxiety disorder); or social situations (as in social anxiety disorder).	G. No adaptation	G. No adaptation	G. No adaptation

Social Anxiety Disorder

DSM 5 Diagnostic Criteria	Applying Criteria for Mild ID	Applying Criteria for Moderate ID	Applying Criteria for Severe to Profound ID
A. Marked fear or anxiety about one or more social situations in which the individual is exposed to possible scrutiny by others. Examples include social interactions (e.g., having a conversation, meeting unfamiliar people), being observed (e.g., eating or drinking), and performing in front of others (e.g., giving a speech). **Note**: In children, the anxiety must occur in peer settings and not just during interactions with adults.	A. No adaptation	A. Anxiety occurs in peer settings	A. Fear can be observed rather than subjectively described, or expressed by crying, tantrums, freezing, clinging, shrinking, failure to speak in social situations. Anxiety occurs in peer settings.

Social Anxiety Disorder (continued)

DSM 5 Diagnostic Criteria	Applying Criteria for Mild ID	Applying Criteria for Moderate ID	Applying Criteria for Severe to Profound ID
B. The individual fears that he or she will act in a way or show anxiety symptoms that will be negatively evaluated (i.e., will be humiliating or embarrassing; will lead to rejection or offend others).	B. No adaptation	B. No adaptation	B. Fear can be observed rather than subjectively described, or expressed by crying, tantrums, freezing, clinging, shrinking, failure to speak in social situations.
C. The social situations almost always provoke fear or anxiety. **Note**: In children, the fear or anxiety may be expressed by crying, tantrums, freezing, clinging, shrinking, or failing to speak in social situations.	C. No adaptation	C. No adaptation	
D. The social situations are avoided or endured with intense fear or anxiety.	D. No adaptation	D. No adaptation	
E. The fear or anxiety is out of proportion to the actual threat posed by the social situation and to the sociocultural context.	E. No adaptation	E. No adaptation	
F. The fear, anxiety, or avoidance is persistent, typically lasting for 6 months or more.	F. No adaptation	F. No adaptation	
G. The fear, anxiety, or avoidance causes clinically significant distress or impairment in social, occupational, or other important areas of functioning.	G. No adaptation	G. No adaptation	
H. The fear, anxiety, or avoidance is not attributable to the physiological effects of a substance (e.g., a drug of abuse, a medication) or another medical condition.	H. No adaptation	H. No adaptation	
I. The fear, anxiety, or avoidance is not better explained by the symptoms of another mental disorder, such as panic disorder, body dysmorphic disorder, or autism spectrum disorder.	I. No adaptation	I. No adaptation	
J. If another medical condition (e.g., Parkinson's disease, obesity, disfigurement from burns or injury) is present, the fear, anxiety, or avoidance is clearly unrelated or is excessive.	J. No adaptation	J. No adaptation	

Panic Disorder

DSM 5 Diagnostic Criteria	Applying Criteria for Mild ID	Applying Criteria for Moderate ID	Applying Criteria for Severe to Profound ID
A. Recurrent unexpected panic attacks. A panic attack is an abrupt surge of intense fear or intense discomfort that reaches a peak within minutes, and during which time four (or more) of the following symptoms occur: **Note:** The abrupt surge can occur from a calm state or an anxious state. 1. Palpitations, pounding heart, or accelerated heart rate. 2. Sweating. 3. Trembling or shaking. 4. Sensations of shortness of breath or smothering. 5. Feelings of choking. 6. Chest pain or discomfort. 7. Nausea or abdominal distress. 8. Feeling dizzy, unsteady, light-headed, or faint. 9. Chills or heat sensations. 10. Paresthesias (numbness or tingling sensations). 11. Derealization (feelings of unreality) or depersonalization (being detached from oneself). 12. Fear of losing control or "going crazy." 13. Fear of dying. **Note:** Culture-specific symptoms (e.g., tinnitus, neck soreness, headache, uncontrollable screaming or crying) may be seen. Such symptoms should not count as one of the four required symptoms.	A. No adaptation	A. A panic attack is an abrupt surge of intense fear or intense discomfort, which can be either be observed or reported, that reaches a peak within minutes, and during which time 4 or more of the following symptoms occur (then adaptation as for panic attack)	A. A panic attack is an abrupt surge of intense fear or intense discomfort, which can be either be observed or reported, that reaches a peak within minutes, and during which time 3 or more of the following symptoms occur. (then adaptation as for panic attack)
B. At least one of the attacks has been followed by 1 month (or more) of one or both of the following:	B. Note: the person may have difficulties with temporal sequencing. To identify one month of time use time frame or anchor events	B. Note: the person may have difficulties with temporal sequencing. To identify one month of time use time frame or anchor events, or description of time frame from informant report	B. Use description of time frame by informant report
1. Persistent concern or worry about additional panic attacks or their consequences (e.g., losing control, having a heart attack, "going crazy").	1. No adaptation	1. No adaptation	1. Usually cannot be described
2. A significant maladaptive change in behavior related to the attacks (e.g., behaviors designed to avoid having panic attacks, such as avoidance of exercise or unfamiliar situations).	2. No adaptation	2. No adaptation	2. No adaptation

Panic Disorder (continued)

DSM 5 Diagnostic Criteria	Applying Criteria for Mild ID	Applying Criteria for Moderate ID	Applying Criteria for Severe to Profound ID
C. The disturbance is not attributable to the physiological effects of a substance (e.g., a drug of abuse, a medication) or another medical condition (e.g., hyperthyroidism, cardiopulmonary disorders). D. The disturbance is not better explained by another mental disorder (e.g., the panic attacks do not occur only in response to feared social situations, as in social anxiety disorder; in response to circumscribed phobic objects or situations, as in specific phobia; in response to obsessions, as in obsessive-compulsive disorder; in response to reminders of traumatic events, as in posttraumatic stress disorder; or in response to separation from attachment figures, as in separation anxiety disorder).	No adaptation	No adaptation	No adaptation

Panic Attack Specifier

DSM 5 Diagnostic Criteria	Applying Criteria for Mild ID	Applying Criteria for Moderate ID	Applying Criteria for Severe to Profound ID
Note: Symptoms are presented for the purpose of identifying a panic attack; however, panic attack is not a mental disorder and cannot be coded. Panic attacks can occur in the context of any anxiety disorder as well as other mental disorders (e.g., depressive disorders, posttraumatic stress disorder, substance use disorders) and some medical conditions (e.g., cardiac, respiratory, vestibular, gastrointestinal). When the presence of a panic attack is identified, it should be noted as a specifier (e.g., "posttraumatic stress disorder with panic attacks"). For panic disorder, the presence of panic attack is contained within the criteria for the disorder and panic attack is not used as a specifier.	No adaptation	No adaptation	No adaptation
An abrupt surge of intense fear or intense discomfort that reaches a peak within minutes, and during which time four (or more) of the following symptoms occur: **Note:** The abrupt surge can occur from a calm state or an anxious state.	No adaptation	an abrupt surge of intense fear or intense discomfort, which can be either be observed or reported, that reaches a peak within minutes, and during which time 4 or more of the following symptoms occur	an abrupt surge of intense fear or intense discomfort, which can be either be observed or reported, that reaches a peak within minutes, and during which time 3 or more of the following symptoms occur.
1. Palpitations, pounding heart, or accelerated heart rate.	1. No adaptation	1. No adaptation	1. Pounding, racing heart beats might be identified by taking pulse or listening with stethoscope
2. Sweating.	2. No adaptation	2. May be observed or self-reported	2. May be observed or self-reported
3. Trembling or shaking.	3. No adaptation	3. May be observed or self-reported	3. May be observed or reported

Panic Attack Specifier (continued)

DSM 5 Diagnostic Criteria	Applying Criteria for Mild ID	Applying Criteria for Moderate ID	Applying Criteria for Severe to Profound ID
4. Sensations of shortness of breath or smothering.	4. No adaptation	4. May be observed or self-reported	4. May be observed if the person is gasping for breath, over breathing/hyper-ventilating. Smothering sensations cannot usually be detected
5. Feelings of choking.	5. No adaptation	5. No adaptation	5. Consider that sensation of choking may be present if coughing, or clutching throat.
6. Chest pain or discomfort.	6. No adaptation	6. No adaptation	6. Consider that chest pain may be present if clutching or rubbing chest
7. Nausea or abdominal distress.	7. No adaptation	7. No adaptation	7. Nausea could be observed as retching or vomiting
8. Feeling dizzy, unsteady, light-headed, or faint.	8. No adaptation	8. No adaptation	8. Dizziness and unsteadiness could be observed as seeing the person 'going grey', staggering or collapsing
9. Chills or heat sensations.	9. No adaptation	9. No adaptation	9. Flushing may be observed
10. Paresthesias (numbness or tingling sensations).	10. No adaptation	10. No adaptation	10. Cannot be detected
11. Derealization (feelings of unreality) or depersonalization (being detached from oneself).	11. No adaptation	11. Difficult to detect	11. Cannot be detected
12. Fear of losing control or "going crazy."	12. No adaptation	12. No adaptation	12. Cannot be detected
13. Fear of dying. **Note:** Culture-specific symptoms (e.g., tinnitus, neck soreness, headache, uncontrollable screaming or crying) may be seen. Such symptoms should not count as one of the four required symptoms.	13. No adaptation	13. No adaptation	13. Cannot be detected

Agoraphobia

DSM 5 Diagnostic Criteria	Applying Criteria for Mild ID	Applying Criteria for Moderate ID	Applying Criteria for Severe to Profound ID
A. Marked fear or anxiety about two (or more) of the following five situations: 1. Using public transportation (e.g., automobiles, buses, trains, ships, planes). 2. Being in open spaces (e.g., parking lots, marketplaces, bridges). 3. Being in enclosed places (e.g., shops, theaters, cinemas). 4. Standing in line or being in a crowd. 5. Being outside of the home alone.	A. No adaptation	A. No adaptation	A. **Note:** fear can be observed rather than subjectively described

Agoraphobia (continued)

DSM 5 Diagnostic Criteria	Applying Criteria for Mild ID	Applying Criteria for Moderate ID	Applying Criteria for Severe to Profound ID
B. The individual fears or avoids these situations because of thoughts that escape might be difficult or help might not be available in the event of developing panic-like symptoms or other incapacitating or embarrassing symptoms (e.g., fear of falling in the elderly; fear of incontinence).	B. No adaptation	B. No adaptation	B. Not required in persons with profound intellectual disability
C. The agoraphobic situations almost always provoke fear or anxiety.	C. No adaptation	C. No adaptation	C. No adaptation
D. The agoraphobic situations are actively avoided, require the presence of a companion, or are endured with intense fear or anxiety.	D. No adaptation	D. No adaptation **Note:** avoidance of situations may not be prominent if limited opportunities to make choices. **Note:** establish the reason for requiring a companion is related to fear of situation.	D. No adaptation **Note:** avoidance of situations may not be prominent if limited opportunities to make choices. **Note:** establish the reason for requiring a companion is related to fear of situation.
E. The fear or anxiety is out of proportion to the actual danger posed by the agoraphobic situations and to the sociocultural context.	E. No adaptation	E. No adaptation	E. No adaptation
F. The fear, anxiety, or avoidance is persistent, typically lasting for 6 months or more.	F. No adaptation	F. No adaptation	F. No adaptation
G. The fear, anxiety, or avoidance causes clinically significant distress or impairment in social, occupational, or other important areas of functioning.	G. No adaptation	G. No adaptation	G. No adaptation
H. If another medical condition (e.g., inflammatory bowel disease, Parkinson's disease) is present, the fear, anxiety, or avoidance is clearly excessive.	H. No adaptation	H. No adaptation	H. No adaptation
I. The fear, anxiety, or avoidance is not better explained by the symptoms of another mental disorder—for example, the symptoms are not confined to specific phobia, situational type; do not involve only social situations (as in social anxiety disorder); and are not related exclusively to obsessions (as in obsessive-compulsive disorder), perceived defects or flaws in physical appearance (as in body dysmorphic disorder), reminders of traumatic events (as in posttraumatic stress disorder), or fear of separation (as in separation anxiety disorder).	I. No adaptation	I. No adaptation	I. No adaptation
Note: Agoraphobia is diagnosed irrespective of the presence of panic disorder. If an individual's presentation meets criteria for panic disorder and agoraphobia, both diagnoses should be assigned.			

Generalized Anxiety Disorder

DSM 5 Diagnostic Criteria	Applying Criteria for Mild ID	Applying Criteria for Moderate ID	Applying Criteria for Severe to Profound ID
A. Excessive anxiety and worry (apprehensive expectation), occurring more days than not for at least 6 months, about a number of events or activities (such as work or school performance).	A. No adaptation	A. No adaptation	A. **Note:** fear or anxiety can be observed rather than subjectively described
B. The individual finds it difficult to control the worry.	B. No adaptation	B. No adaptation	B. Not required in persons with profound intellectual disability
C. The anxiety and worry are associated with three (or more) of the following six symptoms (with at least some symptoms having been present for more days than not for the past 6 months): **Note:** Only one item is required in children. 1. Restlessness or feeling keyed up or on edge. 2. Being easily fatigued. 3. Difficulty concentrating or mind going blank. 4. Irritability. 5. Muscle tension. 6. Sleep disturbance (difficulty falling or staying asleep, or restless, unsatisfying sleep).	C. No adaptation	C. No adaptation	C. Only one item is required in persons with severe and profound intellectual disability
D. The anxiety, worry, or physical symptoms cause clinically significant distress or impairment in social, occupational, or other important areas of functioning.	D. No adaptation	D. No adaptation	D. No adaptation
E. The disturbance is not attributable to the physiological effects of a substance (e.g., a drug of abuse, a medication) or another medical condition (e.g., hyperthyroidism).	E. No adaptation	E. No adaptation	E. No adaptation
F. The disturbance is not better explained by another mental disorder (e.g., anxiety or worry about having panic attacks in panic disorder, negative evaluation in social anxiety disorder [social phobia], contamination or other obsessions in obsessive-compulsive disorder, separation from attachment figures in separation anxiety disorder, reminders of traumatic events in posttraumatic stress disorder, gaining weight in anorexia nervosa, physical complaints in somatic symptom disorder, perceived appearance flaws in body dysmorphic disorder, having a serious illness in illness anxiety disorder, or the content of delusional beliefs in schizophrenia or delusional disorder).	F. No adaptation	F. No adaptation	F. No adaptation

Anxiety Due to Another Medical Condition

The criteria are the same as for other mental disorders due to another medical condition, without adaptation, with the additional need for panic attacks or anxiety.

Substance/Medication-Induced Anxiety Disorder

The criteria are the same as for other substance/medication-induced mental disorders, without adaptation, with the additional need for presence of panic attacks or anxiety.

Other Specified Anxiety Disorder
Unspecified Anxiety Disorder

DSM-5 also includes categories for other specified anxiety disorder and for unspecified anxiety disorder.

References

Adams, D. & Oliver, C. (2011). The expression and assessment of emotions and internal states in individuals with severe or profound intellectual disability. *Clinical Psychology Review, 31(3)*, 293-306.

American Psychiatric Association. (2013). *Diagnostic and statistical manual of mental disorders (5th edition)*. Washington, DC: American Psychiatric Press.

Angst, J., & Vollrath, M. (1991). The natural history of anxiety disorders. *Acta Psychiatrica Scandinavica, 84*, 446–452.

Bailey, N. M. & Andrews, T. M. (2003). Diagnostic criteria for psychiatric disorder for use with adults with learning disabilities/mental retardation (DC-LD) and the diagnosis of anxiety disorders: A review. *Journal of Intellectual Disability Research, 47, suppl. 1*, 50-61.

Barak, Y., Ring, A., Levy, D., Granek, I., Szor, H., & Elizur, A. (1995). Disabling compulsions in 11 mentally retarded adults: An open trial of clomipramine SR. *Journal of Clinical Psychiatry, 56*(10), 459-461.

Bertens, L.C.M., Broekhuizen, B.D.L., Naaktgeboren, C.A., Rutten, F.H., Hoes, A.W., van Mourik, Y., … Reitsma, J.B.. (2013). Use of expert panels to define the reference standard in diagnostic research: A systematic review of published methods and reporting. *PLoS Medicine 10(10)*, e1001531. doi:10.1371/journal.pmed.1001531

Bodfish, J.W., Crawford, T.W., Powell, S.B., Parker, D.E., Golden, R.N., & Lewis, M.H. (1995). Compulsions in adults with mental retardation: Prevalence, phenomenology and comorbidity with stereotypy and self injury. *American Journal of Mental Retardation, 100*, 183-192.

Brown, T.A., Campbell, L.A., Lehman, C.L., Grisham, J.R., & Mancill, R.B. (2001). Current and lifetime comorbidity of the DSM-IV anxiety and mood disorders in a large clinical sample. *Journal of Abnormal Psychology 110(4)*, 585–599.

Cameron, O. G. (1985). The differential diagnosis of anxiety: Psychiatric and medical disorders *Psychiatric Clinics of North America, 8*(1), 3-23.

Charlot, L., Deutsch, C.K., Hunt, A.A., Connor, D.F., & McIlvane Jr., W.J. (2008). Mood and anxiety symptoms in psychiatric in-patients with autism spectrum disorder and depression. *Journal of Mental Health Research in Intellectual Disabilities, 1*(4), 238-253.

Charlot, L., Deutsch, C., Hunt, A. Fletcher, K., & McLivane, W. (2007). Validation of the mood and anxiety semi-structured (MASS) interview for patients with intellectual disabilities. *Journal of Intellectual Disability Research, 51*(10), 821-834.

Chiodos, J., & Maddux, J.E. (1985). A cognitive and behavioral approach to anxiety management of retarded individuals: Two case studies. *Journal of Child and Adolescent Psychotherapy, 2*, 16-20.

Cohan, S.L., Chavira, D.A., & Stein, M.B. (2006). Practitioner review: Psychosocial interventions for children with selective mutism: A critical evaluation of the literature from 1990-2005. *Journal of Child Psychology and Psychiatry, 47*, 1085-1097.

Cooper, S.-A., Smiley, E., Morrison, J., Allan, L., & Williamson, A. (2007). Prevalence of and associations with mental ill health in adults with intellectual disabilities. *British Journal of Psychiatry, 190*, 27–35.

Coplan, J.D., & Lydiard, R.B. (1998). Brain circuits in panic disorder. *Biological Psychiatry, 44*(12), 1264-1276.

Costello, H., Moss, S., Prosser, H., & Hatton, C. (1997). Reliability of the ICD 10 version of psychiatric assessment schedule for adults with developmental disability (PAS-ADD). *Social Psychiatry and Psychiatric Epidemiology, 32*(6), 339-43.

Dayer, A. (2014) Serotonin-related pathways and developmental plasticity): Relevance for psychiatric disorders. *Dialogues in Clinical Neuroscience, 16(1)*.

Damsa, C., Kosel, M., & Moussally, J. (2009). Current status of brain imaging in anxiety disorders. *Current Opinions in Psychiatry, 22*, 96-110.

Deb, S., Thomas, M., & Bright, C. (2001a). Mental disorder in adults who have intellectual disability. 1: Prevalence of functional psychiatric illness among a 16-64 years old community-based population. *Journal of Intellectual Disability Research, 45*(Pt. 6), 495-505.

Deb, S., Thomas, M., & Bright, C. (2006). Mental disorder in adults who have intellectual disability. 2: The rate of behavior disorders among a 16-64 years old community-based population. *Journal of Intellectual Disability Research*, 45(Pt. 6), 506-14/

Dekker, D., Marielle, C., & Koot, H. M. (2003). DSM-IV disorders in children with borderline to moderate intellectual disability. II: Child and family predictors. *Journal of the American Academy of Child & Adolescent Psychiatry. 42(8)*, 923-931.

Domschke, K., & Dannlowski, U. (2010). Imaging genetics of anxiety disorders. *NeuroImage, 53(3)*, 822–83.

Duff, R., La Rocca, J., & Lizzert, A. (1981). A comparison of fears of mildly retarded adults with children of their mental age and chronological age matched controls. *Journal of Behaviour Therapy and Experimental Psychiatry*, 12, 121-124.

Dykens, E. M. (2003). Anxiety, fears, and phobias in persons with Williams syndrome. *Developmental Neuropsychology, 23*, 291–316.

Einfeld, S. L., Tonge, B.J., & Rees, V.W. (2001). Longitudinal course of behavioural and emotional problems in Williams syndrome. *American Journal of Mental Retardation, 106*, 73–81.

Ellison, D.M. (1997). Compliance training decreases maladaptive behaviors in two people. *Behavioral Interventions, 12*(4), 183-194.

Faravelli, C., Lo Sauro, C., Lelli, L., Pietrini, F., Lazzeretti, L.., Godini, L., … Ricca, V. (2012). The role of life events and HPA axis in anxiety disorders: A review. *Current Pharmaceutical Design, 18(35)*, 5663-5674.

Fitzgerald, K.D., Stewart, C.M.< Tawile, V., & Rosenberg, d. (1999). Risperidone augmentation of serotonin reuptake inhibitor treatment of paediatric OCD. *Journal of Child and Adolescent Psychopharmacology, 9*, 115-123.

Fletcher, R.J., Havercamp, S.M., Ruedrich, S.L., Benson, B.A., Barnhill, L.J., Cooper, S.A., & Stavrakaki, C. (2009) Clinical usefulness of the diagnostic manual-intellectual disability for mental disorders in persons with intellectual disability: Results form a brief field survey. *Journal of Clinical Psychiatry, 70*(7), 967-974.

Forte, M., Jahoda, A., & Dagnan, D. (2011). An anxious time? Exploring the nature of worries experienced by young people with a mild to moderate intellectual disability as they make the transition to adulthood. *The British Journal of Clinical Psychology / the British Psychological Society, 50 (4)*, 398-411.

Gillot, A., & Standen, P.J. (2007). Levels of anxiety and sources of stress in adults with autism. *Journal of Intellectual Disabilities, 11*(4), 359-370.

Hastings, R. P., Hatton, C., Taylor, J. L., & Maddison, C. (2004). Life events and psychiatric symptoms in adults with intellectual disabilities. *Journal of Intellectual Disabilities Research, 48*, 42-46.

Heisler, L.K., Zhou, L., Bajwa, P., Hsu, J., & Tecott, L.H. (2007). Serotonin 5-HT(2C) receptors regulate anxiety-like behavior. *Genes, Brains and Behavior, 6*(5), 491-496.

Helverschou, S. B. & Martinsen, H. (2011). Anxiety in people diagnosed with autism and intellectual disability: Recognition and phenomenology. *Research in Autism Spectrum Disorders, 5 (1)*, 377-387.

Hendriks, S. M., Spijker, J., Licht, C.M., Beekman, A.T., & Penninx, B.W. (2013). Two-year course of anxiety disorders: different across disorders or dimensions? *Acta Psychiatrica Scandinavica, 128(3)*, 212-221

Hermans, H., Beekman, A. T. F., & Evenhuis, H. M. (2013). Prevalence of depression and anxiety in older users of formal Dutch intellectual disability services. *Journal of Affective Disorders. 144*, 94-100.

Hettema, J. M., Neale, M. C., & Kendler, K. S. (2001). A review and meta-analysis of the genetic epidemiology of anxiety disorders. *American Journal of Psychiatry, 158*, 1568-1578.

Hobbs, M.J., Anderson, T.M., Slade, T., & Andrews, G. (2014). Structure of the DSM-5 generalized anxiety disorder criteria among a large community sample of worriers. *Journal of Affective Disorders, 57*, 18-24.

Holzschneider, K. & Mulert, C. (2011). Neuroimaging in Anxiety Disorders. *Dialogues in Clinical Neuroscience, 13(4)*, 453–461.

Hulbert-Williams, L., Hastings, R., Owen, D. M., Burns, L., Day, J., Mulligan, J., & Noone, S. J. (2014). Exposure to life events as a risk factor for psychological problems in adults with intellectual disabilities: a longitudinal design. *Journal of Intellectual Disability Research, 58*(1), 48-60.

Hurley, A. D. (2008). Depression in adults with intellectual disability: symptoms and challenging behaviour. *Journal of Intellectual Disability Research, 52(11)*, 905-916.

Iancu, *S.* C., Batelaan, N.M., Zweekhorst, M.B.M., Bunders, J.F.G., Veltman, D.J.B., Pennix, W.J.H., & van Balkom, A.J. (2014). Trajectories of functioning after remission from anxiety disorders: 2-year course and outcome predictors. *Psychological Medicine, 44(3)*, 593-605.

Jackson, H. (1983). Current trends in the treatment of phobias in autistic and mentally retarded persons. *Australia and New Zealand Journal of Developmental Disabilities, 9*(4), 191-208.

Jopp, D.A., & Keyes, C.B. (2001). Diagnostic overshadowing reviewed and reconsidered. *American Journal on Mental Retardation, 106*(5), 416-433.

Katon, W., Vitiliano, P.P., Russo, J., Jones, M., & Anderson, K. (1986). Panic disorder: Epidemiology in primary care. *Journal of Family Practice, 23*, 233-239.

Kessler, R. C., Berglund, P., Demler, O., Jin, R., Merikangas, K.R., & Walters, E.E. (2005). Prevalence, severity, and comorbidity of 12-month DSM-IV disorders in the National Comorbidity Survey Replication. *Archives of General Psychiatry, 62(6)*, 617-627.

Kessler, R.C., Petukhova, M., Sampson, NA.A., Zaslavsky, A.M., & Wittchen, H-U. (2012). Twelve-month and lifetime prevalence and lifetime morbid risk of anxiety and mood disorders in the United States. *International Journal of Methods in Psychiatric Research, 21*(3), 169-184.

King, B.H., DeAntonio, C., McCracken, J.T., Forness, S.R., & Ackerland, V. (1994). Psychiatric consultation in severe and profound mental retardation. *American Journal of Psychiatry, 151*(12), 1802-1808.

Kreim, I., & Mikkelson, E. (1997). Anxiety disorders in adults with mental retardation. *Psychiatric Annals, 27*, 271-281.

Kristensen, H. (2000). Selective mutism and comorbidity with developmental disorder/delay, anxiety disorder, and elimination disorder. *American Academy of Child & Adolescent Psychiatry, 39*(2), 249-256.

Kuwabara, S.A., Van Voorhees, B.W., Gollan, J.K., & Alexander, C. (2007). A qualitative exploration of depression in emerging adulthood: Disorder, development, and social context. *General Hospital Psychiatry, 29*, 317-324.

Levitan, G.W., & Reiss, S. (1983). Generality of diagnostic overshadowing across disciplines. *Applied Research in Mental Retardation, 4*, 59-64.

Leyfer, O.T., Woodruff-Borden, J., Klein-Tasman, B.P., Fricke, J.S., & Mervis, C.B. (2008). Prevalence of psychiatric disorders in 4 to 16-year-olds with Williams syndrome. *American Journal of Medical Genetics, 141B*(6), 615-622.

Liberati, A, Altman, D., Tetzlaff, J., Mulrow, C., Gotzsche, P.C., Ioannidis, J.P.A., …Moher, D. (2009). The PRISMA statement for reporting systematic reviews and meta-analyses of studies that evaluate healthcare interventions: explanation and elaboration. *British Medical Journal, 62(6)*, 617-627.

Masi, G., Favilla, L., & Mucci, M. (2000). Generalized anxiety disorder in adolescents and young adults with mild mental retardation. *Psychiatry, 63*(1), 54-64.

Matson, J.L., Gardner, W.I., Coe, D.A., & Sovner, R. (1991). A scale for evaluating emotional disorders in severely and profoundly mentally retarded persons. Development of the Diagnostic Assessment for the Severely Handicapped (DASH) scale. *British Journal of Psychiatry, 159*, 404-409.

Matson, J. L., Smiroldo, B. B., Hamilton, M., & Baglio, C.S. (1997). Do anxiety disorders exist in people with severe and profound mental retardation? *Research in Developmental Disabilities 1*, 39-44.

McDougle, C.J., Kresch, L.E., Goodman, W.K., Naylor, S.T., Volkmar, F.R., Cohen, D.J., & Price, L.H. (1995). A case controlled study of repetitive thoughts and behavior in adults with autistic disorder and obsessive compulsive disorder. *American Journal of Psychiatry, 152*, 772-777.

McNally, R.J., & Ascher, L.M. (1987). Anxiety disorders in mentally retarded people. In L. Michelson & L.M. Ascher (Eds.), *Anxiety and stress disorders: Cognitive behavioral assessment and treatment* (pp. 379-394). New York: Guilford Press.

Mendlowicz, M. V. & Stein, M. B. (2000). Quality of life in individuals with anxiety disorders. *American Journal of Psychiatry, 157(5)*, 669-682.

Mineka, S. & Zinbarg, R. (1996). Conditioning and ethological models of anxiety disorders: stress-in-dynamic-context anxiety models. Perspectives on anxiety, panic, and fear. *Nebraska Symposium on Motivation 43*, 135–211.

Moss, S., Ibbotson, B., Prosser, H. (1997). Validity of the PAS-ADD for detecting psychiatric symptoms in adults with learning disability (mental retardation). *Social Psychiatry and Psychiatric Epidemiology, 32*, 344-354.

Moss, S.C., Moss, S., Emerson, E., & Kiernan, C. (2000). Psychiatric symptoms in adults with learning disability and challenging behavior. *British Journal of Psychiatry, 177*, 452-456.

Nemeroff, C. B. (2003). The role of GABA in the pathophysiology and treatment of ADs. *Psychopharmacology Bulletin, 37 (4)*, 133–146

Nolte, T., Guiney, J., Fonagy, P., Mayes, L.C., & Luyten, P. (2011). Interpersonal stress regulation and the development of anxiety disorders: An attachment-based developmental framework. *Frontiers in Behavioral Neuroscience, 5*, 55.

Pickersgill, M.J. Valentine, J.D., May, R., & Brewin, C.R. (1994). Fears in mental retardation. Part 1. Types of fears reported by men and women with and without mental retardation. *Advances in Behavior Research Therapy, 16*, 277-296.

Pruijssers, A.C., van Meijel, B., Maaskant, M., Nijssen, W., & van Achtenberg, T. (2014). The relationship between challenging behaviour and anxiety in adults with intellectual disabilities: A literature review. *Journal of Intellectual Disability Research, 58 (2)*, 162-171.

Raghavan, R. (1998). Anxiety disorders in people with learning disabilities: A review of the literature. *Journal of Learning Disabilitiesi for Nursing, Health and Social Care, 2*(1), 3-9.

Reiss, S., & Benson, B.A. (1984). Awareness of negative social conditions among mentally retarded, emotionally disturbed outpatients. *American Journal of Psychiatry, 141*(1), 88-90.

Reiss, S., Levitan, G.W., & Szyszko, J. (1982). Emotional disturbance and mental retardation: Diagnostic overshadowing. *American Journal of Mental Deficiency. 86*(6), 567-574.

Rosen, J. B. & Schulkin, J. (1998). From normal fear to pathological anxiety. *Psychological Review 105*(2), 325-350.

Royal College of Psychiatrists (2001). *Diagnostic criteria for use with adults with learning disabilities (DC-LD)*. London: Gaskell Press.

Sareen, J., Jacobi, F., Cox, B.J., Belik, S.L., Clara, I., & Stein, M.B. (2006). Disability and poor quality of life associated with comorbid anxiety disorders and physical conditions. *Arch Intern Med, 166(19)*, 2109-2116.

Sartorius, N., Ustun, T. B., Lecrubier, Y., Wittchen, H. V. (1996). Depression comorbid with anxiety: Results from the WHO study on psychological disorders in primary health care. *British Journal of Psychiatry, 168(Suppl 30)*, 38-43.

Schroeder, S. R. (1989). Abnormal stereotyped behaviors. In *Treatments of Psychiatric Disorders: A Task Force Report.* Washington, DC: American Psychiatric Association Press.

Scott, H. M., & Havercamp, S. M. (2014). Mental health for people with intellectual disability: The impact of stress and social support. *American Journal on Intellectual and Developmental Disabilities, 119*, 552-564.

Sensky, T. (1989). Cognitive therapy with patients with chronic physical illness. *Psychotherapy and Psychosomatics, 52*(1-3), 26-32.

Skokauskas, N., & Gallagher, L. (2012). Mental health aspects of autistic spectrum disorders in children. *Journal of Intellectual Disability Research, 56*(3), 248-257.

Smoller, J. W., Blocks, S.R., & Young, M.M. (2009). Genetics of anxiety disorders: the complex road from DSM to DNA. *Anxiety and Depression, 26(11)*, 965–975.

Stavrakaki, C. & Mintsioulis, G. (1997). Implications of a clinical study of anxiety disorders in persons with mental retardation. *Psychiatric Annals 27*, 182 -189.

Sternlight, M. (1979). Fears of institutionalized mentally retarded adults. *Journal of Psychology, 101*, 57-71.

Sullivan, K., Hooper, S., & Hatton, D. (2007). Behavioural equivalents of anxiety in children with fragile X syndrome: Parent and teacher report. *Journal of Intellectual Disability Research, 51(1)*, 54-65.

Van den Bergh, B. R. H., Van Calster, B., Smits, T., Van Huffel, S., & Lagae, L. (2007). Antenatal maternal anxiety is related to HPA-axis dysregulation and self-reported depressive symptoms in adolescence: A prospective study on the fetal origins of depressed mood. *Neuropsychopharmacology,* 33(3), 536–545.

Verhoeven, W.M.A., & Tuinier, S. (1997). Neuropsychiatric consultation in mentally retarded patients: A clinical report. *European Psychiatry, 12*, 242-248.

Vitiello, B., Spreat, S., & Behar, D. (1989). Obsessive-compulsive disorder in mentally retarded patients. *Journal of Nervous Mental Disease, 177*(4), 232-236.

Waisbren, S.E., & Levy, H.L. (1991). Agorophobia in phenylketonuria. *Journal of Inherited Metabolic Diseases, 14*(5), 755-764.

Weisbrot, D.M., Gadow, K.D., DeVincent, C.J., & Pomero, J. (2005). The presentation of anxiety in children with pervasive developmental disorders. *Journal of Child and Adolescence Psychopharmacology, 15*(3), 477-496.

White, M.J., Nichols, C.N., Cook, R.S., Spengler, P.M., Walker, B.S., & Look, K.K. (1995). Diagnostic overshadowing and mental retardation : A meta-analysis. *American Journal of Mental Retardation, 100*(3), 293-298.

White, P., Chant, D., Edwards, N., Townsend, C., & Waghorn, G. (2005). Prevalence of intellectual disability and comorbid mental illness in an Australian community sample. *Australian and New Zealand Journal of Psychiatry, 39(5)*, 395-400.

World Health Organization (1993). *The ICD 10 Classification of Mental and behavioural Disorders: Diagnostic criteria for research.* Geneva: Author.

CHAPTER 14

Obsessive-Compulsive and Related Disorders

Julie P. Gentile
Betsey A. Benson
Allison E. Cowan
Mark H. Fleisher
Paulette Marie Gillig

Changes in Classification

The fifth edition of the *Diagnostic and Statistical Manual of Mental Disorders (DSM-5)* includes a new chapter on obsessive-compulsive and related disorders to reflect the increasing evidence of the set of disorders' affiliation with one another, and their distinction from other anxiety disorders. There is similarity among the set of disorders across symptoms, neurobiological networks, genetics, course of illness, and treatment response.

Disorders in this new chapter of the *DSM* include previously identified disorders such as obsessive-compulsive disorder (OCD), body dysmorphic disorder, and trichotillomania (hair-pulling disorder). In addition, new disorders also have been identified: Hoarding disorder and excoriation (skin-picking) disorder. Substance/medication-induced obsessive-compulsive and related disorder and obsessive-compulsive and related disorder due to another medical condition are also included. The descriptions of this set of related disorders should allow clinicians to more accurately diagnose and treat individuals suffering from obsessive thoughts, compulsive behaviors, preoccupations, and repetitive behaviors. The set of disorders included in this newly established chapter are inter-related with regard to diagnostic validators and have enough similarities to group them together but enough important differences to exist as distinct disorders.

The increasing literature base describing the topics of hoarding and of skin-picking (excoriation) is sufficient to qualify these disorders as separate entities within the chapter. Trichotillomania (hair-pulling disorder) has been moved from "impulse-control disorders not elsewhere classified" in the *DSM-IV* to Obsessive-Compulsive and Related Disorders in the *DSM-5*. The *DSM-IV* specifier "with obsessive-compulsive symptoms" was moved from anxiety disorders to the new category of obsessive-compulsive and related disorders. All of the disorders with a cognitive component (OCD, hoarding disorder, and body dysmorphic disorder) have an "insight" specifier for rating patients' insight into their disorder-related beliefs.

Obsessive-Compulsive Disorder

Review of Diagnostic Criteria

Obsessive-compulsive disorder (OCD), an anxiety disorder, is characterized by the presence of obsessions, compulsions, or both. Obsessions and compulsions are commonly associated with intellectual disability (Matson & Dempsey, 2009). Prevalence rates of OCD in individuals with intellectual disability have been established in the range of 1.1%-2.7% (Deb, Thomas, & Bright, 2001; Vitiello, Spreat, & Behar, 1989). This section describes the assessment issues related to the diagnosis of OCD, reviews the relevant literature for children and adults, and describes how to apply criteria for varying degrees of cognitive deficits. More accurate diagnosis of this important anxiety disorder will lead to effective treatment interventions.

According to the *Diagnostic and Statistical Manual Fifth Edition* (*DSM-5*), the features of OCD are recurrent obsessions and compulsions that are time-consuming (specifically more than one hour daily) or causing clinically significant distress or impairment in important areas of functioning (American Psychiatric Association, 2013). According to the *DSM-5* an individual must experience obsessions (defined as persistent ideas, thoughts, impulses, or images) as intrusive and unwanted at some point during the illness; the individual must attempt to ignore or suppress the obsessions to neutralize them with some other thought or action. In individuals with intellectual disability, it may be less likely that the obsessions are ego-dystonic, especially if more severe cognitive deficits are present. Anxiety or distress occurs in most individuals but is not required to make the diagnosis. The compulsions are repetitive behaviors that the individual feels driven to perform; the behaviors or mental acts are aimed at preventing or reducing anxiety or distress or preventing some dreaded event or situation, although in reality they are not connected to the event they are designed to prevent. If there are co-occurring psychiatric disorders, the content of the obsessions or compulsions are not restricted to symptoms of the co-occurring disorder. The obsessive and compulsive signs and symptoms cannot be the direct physiological effect of a substance or of a general medical condition.

Issues Related to Diagnosis in Persons with ID

Deb, Thomas, et al. (2001) established the prevalence for OCD in individuals with intellectual disability to be between 1.1-2.7% from a review of published work. Persons with intellectual disability sometimes do not appear anxious or complain of symptoms of anxiety, and for these individuals it is important to document observable compulsions when making the diagnosis. This is especially true in individuals with severe or profound intellectual disability (Deb, Thomas, et al., 2001; Vitiello et al., 1999).

Diagnosis in individuals with intellectual disability who have repetitive behaviors and repetitive speech or other vocalizations is complicated by a decrease in self-report of internal conflicts or anxiety. Historically this has led to heavy reliance on observable and behavioral data. Diagnosis is also complicated by potential co-occurring stereotypies, tics, dyskinesias, athetosis, dystonias, akathisia, self-injury, or self-stimulatory behavior, at times combined with obsessions and compulsive behaviors (Fletcher, Loschen, Stavrakaki, & First, 2007).

There is a lack of consensus regarding the significance of some behaviors that creates uncertainty in clinical settings. However, the efficacy of serotonin agents and behavioral interventions for symptoms of OCD has been demonstrated, and there are consensus recommendations for first-line treatments for OCD in individuals with intellectual disability (Deb, Matthews, Holt, & Bouras, 2001; Fletcher et al., 2007).

Application of Diagnostic Criteria to People with ID

Specific issues related to individuals with intellectual disability (Fletcher et al., 2007) include:

1. Limited expressive language skills decrease self-report or the use of scales or inventories.

2. Sensory impairments may further restrict the range of obsessive-compulsive phenomena.

3. The presence of anxiety is no longer required for the diagnosis. The elimination of the criterion of anxiety facilitates making the diagnosis in individuals with intellectual disability that previously was complicated by the fact that these persons may not experience their symptoms as anxiety producing or may not be able to identify or communicate symptoms of anxiety to clinicians.

4. Obsessions in the general population are experienced as intrusive or unwanted; this description may not apply to some individu-

als with intellectual disability depending on their ability to identify and/or communicate this concept.

5. Compulsions that require abstract thought may not be possible (i.e. contamination or safety issues) and counting skills may be absent in individuals with intellectual disability.
6. Individuals in the general population attempt to ignore or suppress the obsessions or to neutralize them with some other thought or action; this description may not apply to some individuals with intellectual disability depending on their ability to understand and conceptualize the act of suppression of obsessions.
7. Compulsions in the general population are aimed at preventing or reducing anxiety or distress; individuals with intellectual disability may not be able to articulate the aims of their behaviors or mental acts.
8. Individuals with intellectual disability may be unaware of societal disapproval, and therefore this knowledge may not serve to reduce the behaviors as it would in the general population.
9. Hoarding and skin picking are now distinguished as individual disorders but are included as disorders related to OCD; symptoms in these categories should be diagnosed accordingly.
10. Aggression may be the presenting issue of concern in the individual with intellectual disability; a careful history should be taken to determine, for example, if the etiology of the aggression is an attempt by a caregiver to remove an obstacle or due to a caregiver attempting to prevent a compulsive act, in which case the diagnosis of OCD should be considered.

Methodology

Pubmed and Medline were searched utilizing the following key words: Obsessive compulsive, behavioral syndromes, developmental disability, intellectual disability, obsessive compulsive disorder, skin picking, picking, impulse control disorder, trichotillomania, hair pulling, hoarding, excoriation, mental retardation, assessment, diagnosis, obsessions, compulsions, rituals, repetitive behavior, and genetics. The full text of relevant articles was reviewed in addition to related articles.

Review of Research Applying to People with ID

The *Diagnostic and Statistical Manual (DSM) III* (American Psychiatric Association, 1980) placed emphasis on behavioral and phenomenologically based criteria with less emphasis on subjective symptoms and inner conflicts requiring self-report. With the *DSM-IV* and now the *DSM-5*, there has been a conceptual shift that facilitates the diagnosis in individuals with limited cognitive and/or language skills.

The *DSM-IV* stated that "differentiating between self-stimulatory stereotypic behavior and compulsions can be difficult in non-verbal individuals who cannot describe obsessional thoughts and identify compulsions as obsessions" (American Psychiatric Association, 2000; Szymanski & King 1999). Barnhill (1999) criticized the categorical and phenomenological approach of the *DSM-IV*, questioning its applicability to individuals with intellectual disability, and argued that accurate diagnosis required careful evaluation of the setting (clues to specific triggers, level of complexity of the environment, demands for novelty, and requirements for adaptation), set (individual's temperament, intensity of physiological arousal, an individual's threshold for repetitive stereotypic behavior, and genetic vulnerability), and behavioral repertoire of the individual.

Specific modifications to the *DSM-IV* criteria for OCD were suggested, including (1) a description of physiological arousal, fear responses, reactions to novelty, and threshold for repetitive and stereotypic behavior, (2) an observational approach reflecting the state of the individuals and level of reactivity, adaptivity, and proneness to repetitive behavior, and (3) more emphasis on observation of attachment behaviors that might intensify in stressful situations in individuals with severe/profound intellectual disability, particularly in situations which would be perceived as a loss or disruption. Barnhill also noted that prevalence rates of OCD are affected by higher rates of language impairment, brain dysfunction (especially working memory and deficits that impede sense of task completion), seizure disorders, and sensory impairments.

Experts around the globe agree that there should be an emphasis on behavioral, generally observable components of the disorder of OCD. Deb, Matthews, et al. (2001) established best practice guidelines for the assessment and diagnosis of health problems in adults with intellectual disability. These guidelines include obsessions and compulsions, defined as "repetitive, unpleasant, excessive and unreasonable" thoughts and behaviors originating in the mind of the individual who must attempt to resist thinking the thought or carrying out the behavior. The guidelines stated that it may be difficult to identify obsessions because the individual with intellectual disability may be unable to recognize the thoughts as coming from his/her own mind and resistance may not occur. Compulsive behavior needs to be distinguished from stereotyped behavior and movement disorders caused by underlying brain damage.

Gothelf et al. (2008) reported that there appear to be common etiological and pathophysiological pathways for OCD and autism spectrum disorders. This was established in previously published reviews of Bejerot (2006, 2007) and Gross-Isseroff, Hermesh, and Weizman (2001). Variants of the serotonin transporter gene are associated with both OCD and autism spectrum disorders neuroimaging shows abnormal frontal-striatal pathways in both conditions, and improvement with use of serotonin agents and anti-dopaminergic agents (Raush et al. 2001). Matson and Dempsey (2009) discuss the debate about whether obsessions and compulsions constitute core features of both autism and intellectual disability or are phenomena seen with both disorders. Accurate diagnosis and appropriate treatment interventions based on this determination are vital issues in individuals with intellectual disability because these symptoms represent a high likelihood of morbidity for individuals.

Adults with Mild to Moderate ID

Clinical presentation and assessment in mild intellectual disability is similar to the general population with the exception of the relative lack of subjective reporting from individuals with limited expressive language skills and variations in the level of insight into the symptoms.

In moderate intellectual disability, the presentation of OCD depends on the degree of disability and on expressive language skill development; if little or no speech, the individual may present with excessive repetitive behaviors which may be difficult to distinguish from self-injurious and other ritualistic or self-stimulatory behaviors (Fletcher et al., 2007). The individual with moderate intellectual disability may not resist the compulsive behaviors or seek corrective solutions depending on the level of insight.

Adults with Severe or Profound ID

Absence of subjective obsessions and compulsions does not rule out OCD in this group; the lack of abstract thinking and limited or no language skills make collateral and observational data necessary for most individuals with severe or profound intellectual disability. In the general population, one of the most common compulsive behaviors includes acts of hand washing, cleaning, showering, etc. The dependency needs in individuals with severe/profound intellectual disability necessitate involvement of caregivers that prevents independent decision making surrounding such issues.

The criterion that the symptoms "cause marked distress" may not apply to individuals with severe or profound intellectual disability because they may 1) lack social awareness about the level of appropriateness of behavior so may not feel distress, and 2) lack judgment to evaluate how unsafe or unacceptable behaviors are and therefore do not feel distress about them, or 3) lack language skills to report subjective feelings of distress.

The diagnostic requirement from the *DSM-5* that OCD should be diagnosed if the obsessions or compulsions take "more than one hour a day" may not be applicable in individuals with intellectual disability. The symptoms must be excessive (take more than one hour daily) and also significantly interfere with his/her routine, relationships, or social activities. Individuals with severe or profound intellectual disability may spend more time than is typical to complete their daily routine and often have caregivers involved in the process. If there are compulsions that do not interfere with a daily routine, the criterion of excessive time should be suspended if the symptoms have minimal disruption in the individual's life. Non-problematic routines are not unusual in individuals with severe/profound intellectual disability.

Children and Adolescents with ID

Children may not have language skills to describe their thoughts. It may be difficult to define the etiology of the behaviors; recognition that compulsive behaviors are unreasonable does not apply to children or adolescents with mild or moderate intellectual disability as they lack sufficient cognitive skills to evaluate themselves and to make these judgments.

Symptoms can be disruptive and interfere with overall functioning; in addition children and adolescents with intellectual disability may be greatly preoccupied with the symptoms. Attempts by interested others to reduce, discourage, or stop the compulsions will increase anxiety and often manifest as aggression and other behavioral responses (Fletcher et al., 2007). Children and adolescents with intellectual disability and co-occurring OCD usually present with ordering, checking, and cleaning rituals; the symptoms are typically identified by parents or caregivers and are more likely to occur in home environments. Typical toddlers and preschoolers may have rituals; typical older children often utilize strict rules about how games or activities should be conducted. Children with and without intellectual disability may not utilize these strict rules, depending on the individual's developmental age and expressive language skills.

Etiology and Pathogenesis

Biological Factors

Bokor and Anderson (2014) reported that the biological underpinnings of OCD involve the orbitofrontal cortex, anterior cingulate gyrus, and _basal ganglia_. Overall, 30T30TOCD_ is thought to be due to a malfunction in the cortico-striato-thalamo-cortical circuit in the brain. Neurotransmitters implicated in _OCD_ include serotonin, dopamine, and glutamate. Opiates and neuropeptides (vasopressin in some animal models) are also useful models as well as differences between various forms of perseveration and obsessions/compulsions (Rojas-Corrales, Gilbert-Rahola, & Mico, 2007; Marazziti, Baroni, & Catena Dell'Osso, 2010).

Genetic Factors

Individuals with intellectual disability have increased prevalence of compulsive like behavior, which has been documented in Prader-Willi syndrome, Down syndrome, fragile X syndrome, Cornelia de Lange, and Williams syndrome (Fletcher et al., 2007). Hall Lightbody, & Reiss (2008) studied compulsive, self-injurious, and autistic behaviors in children and adolescents with fragile X syndrome; compulsive behavior was found in 72% of males and 55% of females. Potential biological markers in individuals with fragile X syndrome include decreased levels of fragile X mental retardation protein (FMRP) and cortisol.

Jacob, Landeros-Weisenberg, & Leckman (2009) studied obsessive-compulsive disorder and its association to various genetic disorders. The behavioral phenotype of fragile X syndrome includes obsessive-compulsive behaviors. A study of individuals with the premutation but without age-related fragile X tremor/ataxia syndrome reported higher levels of OC symptoms. In men only, elevated FMR1 mRNA, rather that CGG repeat size or percent of FMRP expression, was significantly associated with increased OC symptoms and psychotic episodes regardless of FXTAS symptoms. Bourgeois et al. (2009) reported that premutation expansions are frequent in the general population; approximately 1 per 113-259 females and 1 per 260-800 males. Late onset neurodegenerative disorder and FXTAS can occur in these individuals. The psychopathology of FXTAS often includes dementia and may include both frontal lobe and subcortical features.

Gross-Isseroff et al. (2001) discussed repetitive and stereotyped behavior patterns in individuals with autism spectrum disorders; these can be similar to the compulsive symptoms of OCD. McDougle et al. (1995) reported that obsessive thoughts with aggressive, contamination, religious, symmetry, or somatic content were found to be more typical of autism; compulsive behaviors such as ordering, tapping, and rubbing have been identified as being more closely identified with OCD. Autism and OCD may co-occur and the distinction of the two symptom sets is a diagnostic challenge for most clinicians.

Jacob et al. (2009) reported that OC behaviors are associated with Prader-Willi syndrome and other disorders exhibiting alterations in the 15q11-q13 region. Individuals with Prader-Willi syndrome typically have mild or moderate intellectual disability; the OC behaviors often seen in Prader-Willi syndrome include hoarding, ordering/arranging items, requiring symmetry and exactness, routinized behavior, and verbal perseveration, among others. Zarcone et al. (2007) reported that individuals who have Prader-Willi syndrome with the long type I (TI) 15q deletion had increased compulsions surrounding personal cleanliness which were more difficult to interrupt while those with the short type II (TII) 15q deletion were more likely to exhibit symptoms in the symmetry and ordering domain.

Dimitropoulos, Blackford, Walden, and Thompson (2006) reported that children with Prader-Willi syndrome exhibited both food- and non-food-related compulsions. They found that children with Prader-Willi syndrome exhibited more severe ritualistic behavior than typically developing children but not other children with developmental delays. They concluded that there may be a common neurobiological mechanism linking hyperphagia and non-food-related compulsivity. Matson and Dempsey (2009) discussed the high prevalence of obsessive-compulsive behaviors in persons with Prader-Willi syndrome. There may be a relationship between OCD and genetic syndromes or addiction behaviors, but more research is needed.

Psychosocial Factors

Gothelf et al. (2008) reported that struggles with limitations in adaptive functioning with independence issues during adolescence increases the vulnerability of individuals with intellectual disability to develop anxiety disorders such as OCD. Psychosocial factors that may affect individuals depending on the level of intellectual disability include low self-esteem, deficits in problem solving, dependency needs, and social stigma.

Obsessive-Compulsive Disorder

DSM-5 Diagnostic Criteria	Applying Criteria for Mild to Moderate Intellectual Disability	Applying Criteria for Severe to Profound Intellectual Disability
A. Presence of obsessions, compulsions, or both	A. No adaptation	A. No adaptation
Obsessions are defined by (1) and (2): 1. Recurrent and persistent thoughts, urges, or images that are experienced, at some time during the disturbance, as intrusive and unwanted, and that in most individuals cause marked anxiety or distress. 2. The individual attempts to ignore or suppress such thoughts, urges, or images, or to neutralize them with some other thought or action (i.e. by performing a compulsion).	Obsessions are defined by (1) and (2) 1. No adaptation. Note: Recurrent and persistent thoughts, urges, or images may not be experienced as intrusive and unwanted depending on the cognitive functioning of the individual. 2. No adaptation. **Note**: The individual may or may not (due to cognitive deficits) attempt to ignore or suppress such thoughts, urges, or images, or to neutralize them with some other thought or action.	Obsessions are defined by (1) and (2): 1. No adaptation. **Note:** Recurrent and persistent thoughts, urges, or images may not be experienced as intrusive and unwanted depending on the cognitive functioning of the individual. 2. No adaptation. **Note:** The individual may or may not (due to cognitive deficits) attempt to ignore or suppress such thoughts, urges, or images, or to neutralize them with some other thought or action. The individual may be unable to report wanting to ignore, suppress, or neutralize the obsessions.

Obsessive-Compulsive Disorder (continued)

DSM-5 Diagnostic Criteria	Applying Criteria for Mild to Moderate Intellectual Disability	Applying Criteria for Severe to Profound Intellectual Disability
Compulsions are defined by (1) and (2): 1. Repetitive behaviors (e.g. hand washing, ordering, checking) or mental acts (e.g. praying, counting, repeating words silently) that the individual feels driven to perform in response to an obsession or according to rules that must be applied rigidly. 2. The behaviors or mental acts are aimed at preventing or reducing anxiety or distress, or preventing some dreaded event or situation; however, these behaviors or mental acts are not connected in a realistic way with what they are designed to neutralize or prevent, or are clearly excessive. Note: Young children may not be able to articulate the aims of these behaviors or mental acts.	Compulsions are defined by (1) and (2): 1. No adaptation. **Note:** Repetitive behaviors or mental acts may be difficult to elicit due to cognitive deficits and limited expressive language skills. Consider ordering, telling, asking, or repetitive physical acts (e.g. rubbing) as compulsions. 2. No adaptation. **Note:** The function of the compulsive behavior may not be ascertainable due to cognitive deficits and limited expressive language skills; recognition of excessiveness or intent of the behaviors may not be present.	Compulsions are defined by (1) and (2): 1. No adaptation. **Note:** Absence of compulsions that require abstract thinking does not rule out OCD; observe individuals for compulsions requiring simple thinking, such as fixed sequences or arrangements, excessive ordering, and filling/emptying. 2. No adaptation. **Note:** The function of the compulsive behavior may not be ascertainable due to cognitive deficits and limited expressive language skills. The criteria regarding intent of the behavior does not apply to children, and does not apply to individuals with severe/profound intellectual disability.
B. The obsessions or compulsions are time-consuming (e.g. take more than 1 hour per day) or cause clinically significant distress or impairment in social, occupational, or other important areas of functioning.	B. No adaptation. **Note:** Distress may not occur and/or may not be ascertainable. Intense preoccupation may be observed or drive to perform the compulsion may be observed. Challenging behavior, especially aggression, and self-injurious behavior, may occur if the individual is prevented from completing the compulsion.	B. No adaptation. **Note:** Distress may not occur and/or may not be ascertainable. Intense preoccupation, strong urges to engage in compulsive activity may be observed. Aggression, especially directed toward caregivers who impede the completion of the compulsion, may be seen.
Specify if: Good Insight, Fair Insight, Poor Insight or Absent/Delusional Beliefs	The various specifiers for rating patient's insight into disorder-related beliefs (e.g. good, fair, poor or absent/delusional beliefs) should be applied in the context of the cognitive and developmental functioning of the individual.	The various specifiers for rating patient's insight into disorder-related beliefs (e.g. good, fair, poor or absent/delusional beliefs) should be applied in the context of the cognitive and developmental functioning of the individual.
C. The obsessive-compulsive symptoms are not attributable to the physiological effects of a substance (e.g., a drug of abuse, a medication) or another medical condition.	C. The various specifiers for rating patient's insight into disorder-related beliefs (e.g. good, fair, poor or absent/delusional beliefs) should be applied in the context of the cognitive and developmental functioning of the individual.	C. The various specifiers for rating patient's insight into disorder-related beliefs (e.g. good, fair, poor or absent/delusional beliefs) should be applied in the context of the cognitive and developmental functioning of the individual.

Obsessive-Compulsive Disorder (continued)

DSM-5 Diagnostic Criteria	Applying Criteria for Mild to Moderate Intellectual Disability	Applying Criteria for Severe to Profound Intellectual Disability
D. The disturbance is not better explained by the symptoms of another mental disorder (e.g., excessive worries, as in generalized anxiety disorder; preoccupation with appearance, as in body dysmorphic disorder; difficulty discarding or parting with possessions, as in hoarding disorder; hair pulling, as in trichotillomania [hair-pulling disorder]; skin picking, as in excoriation [skin-picking] disorder; stereotypes, as in stereotype movement disorder; ritualized eating behavior, as in eating disorders; preoccupation with having an illness, as in illness anxiety disorder; sexual urges or fantasies, as in paraphilic disorders; impulses, as in disruptive, impulse-control, and conduct disorders; guilty ruminations, as in major depressive disorder,; thought insertions or delusional preoccupations, asa in schizophrenia spectrum and other psychotic disorders; or repetitive patterns of behavior, as in autism spectrum disorder).	D. The various specifiers for rating patient's insight into disorder-related beliefs (e.g. good, fair, poor or absent/delusional beliefs) should be applied in the context of the cognitive and developmental functioning of the individual.	D. The various specifiers for rating patient's insight into disorder-related beliefs (e.g. good, fair, poor or absent/delusional beliefs) should be applied in the context of the cognitive and developmental functioning of the individual.

Hoarding Disorder

Review of Diagnostic Criteria

Hoarding disorder is a new diagnosis within *DSM-5*, although it is subsumed under the general category of obsessive-compulsive and related disorders.

Summary of DSM-5 *Criteria*

Hoarding disorder is characterized by a persistent difficulty discarding or parting with possessions, regardless of their actual value. This difficulty is due to strong urges to save items and/or distress associated with discarding them. As a result, accumulation of a large number of possessions occurs, which clutters active living areas of the home or workplace to the extent that their intended use is no longer possible.

The symptoms of hoarding disorder cause clinically significant distress or impairment in social, occupational, or other important areas of functioning (including maintaining a safe environment for self and others).

Issues Related to Diagnosis in Persons with ID

The diagnosis of hoarding disorder is not made in the context of cognitive deficits in dementia, restricted interests in autism spectrum disorder, or food storing as seen in Prader-Willi syndrome. The diagnosis of hoarding disorder is not made when hoarding symptoms are due to a general medical condition such as brain injury (more common in individuals with intellectual disability) or cerebrovascular disease. For this reason, persons with intellectual disability may demonstrate hoarding behavior but some should not be diagnosed with hoarding disorder, according to the current *DSM-5* criteria.

Several distinct differences exist between the symptom descriptions of hoarding disorder and obsessive-compulsive disorder. In contrast to hoarding behavior that can occur as one compulsive behavior in OCD, thoughts related to hoarding in persons with hoarding disorder are not experienced as intrusive, but rather part of the normal stream of thought (Ayers, Saxena,

Golshan, & Wetherell, 2010; Frost & Gross, 1993; Frost, Steketee, & Tolin, 2012; Kyrois, Frost, & Steketee, 2004; Landau, Iervolino, Pertusa, Santo, & Mataix-Cols, 2011; Lochner et al., 2005; Mataix-Cols et al., 2010; Pertusa et al., 2008; Pertusa et al., 2010; Samuels et al., 2012; Samuels et al., 2007; Steketee & Frost, 2003; Torres et al., 2012; Wheaton, Timpano, Lasalle-Ricci, & Murphy, 2008). In hoarding disorder, thoughts about hoarding are not repetitive and are not associated with rituals (Frost & Gross, 1993; Kyrios et al., 2004), and they are seldom experienced as distressing or unpleasant unless this is related to the resulting clutter (Frost & Gross, 1993). Persons with hoarding disorder resist any effort to discard any possessions and can experience grief or anger when this is forced upon them (Frost, Krause, & Steketee, 1996). Hoarding symptoms usually worsen over the course of an individual's life (Grisham, Frost, Steketee, Kim, & Hood, 2006), and disability may occur late in the course of the disorder.

Hoarding disorder may be associated with higher rates of depression than found in other OCD comparison groups (Landau et al, 2011). An increased incidence of hoarding behavior has been observed in patients with anxiety disorders, especially social phobia (Frost, Steketee, & Tolin, 2011). Anxiety disorders and depressive disorders occur commonly among persons with intellectual disability and may place them at higher risk for hoarding behavior.

The dopaminergic system apparently plays a crucial role in hoarding behavior (Alonso et al, 2008; Grisham & Baldwin, 2015; Grisham and Norberg, 2010; Kalsbeek, DeBruin, Feenstra, Matthijssen & Uylings, 1988; Kelley & Stinus, 1985; Pertusa et al., 2010). There is evidence that hoarding behavior is related to a dysfunction in the anterior cingulate cortex and its connections to the limbic system. Lesions that are most associated with the sudden onset of hoarding behavior after brain trauma have been in the medial prefrontal region adjacent to the anterior cingulate cortex. Functional MRI studies also suggest that hoarding may also be related to dysfunction in the precentral gyrus and the superior frontal gyrus (Grisham & Baldwin, 2015). Individuals with intellectual disability are often more susceptible to developing tardive dyskinesia and so may also have cortico-limbic dysfunctions that involve the anterior cingulate and medial prefrontal areas of the brain. If so, they may be at a higher risk for dysfunction within the dopamine system, but this has not been systematically studied.

Some authors (e.g. Fontenelle, Oostermeijier, Harrison, Pantelis, & Yucel, 2011) have argued that obsessive-compulsive disorder symptoms, including hoarding behavior, might respond to medications that are effective in drug addiction management, such as topiramate. In addition, although serotonin-reuptake inhibitors (SSRIs) have not been successful in the management of the particular problem of hoarding behavior among patients with obsessive-compulsive disorders, there has been some improvement with selective serotonin-norepinephrine reuptake inhibitors (SNRIs; Grisham & Baldwin, 2015).

Hoarding disorder patients in typical populations have relatively higher rates of attention-deficit hyperactivity disorder (ADHD) than do other populations (Hartl, Duffany, Allen, Steketee, & Frost, 2005; Sheppard et al, 2010), especially inattentive type (Sheppard et al., 2010; Tolin, Villavicencio, Umbach, & Kurtz, 2011). ADHD is more prevalent in persons with intellectual disability, which may increase their risk. Hoarding behavior may co-occur with skin picking, which has a higher prevalence rate in individuals with intellectual disability. In typical populations, hoarding symptoms usually begin in childhood or adolescence, but also may first emerge in the context of dementia, for which some patients with intellectual disability are at higher risk, particularly individuals with Down syndrome. According to the exclusion criteria, hoarding disorder should not be diagnosed when hoarding is related to dementia or acquired brain injury.

Review of Research Applying to People with ID

There is some evidence that hoarding disorder may be neurobiologically distinct from OCD in terms of resting state brain network and brain activity during hoarding (Saxena,

2008a; Saxena, 2008b; Pertusa, Frost, & Mataix-Cols, 2010; An et al, 2009). Hoarding disorder shows a unique pattern of resting state brain function that may not overlap with non-hoarding OCD (Saxena & Maidment, 2004). Persons with hoarding disorder typically have a resting state brain network apparently mediated by front-limbic circuits involving the cingulate cortex, ventromedial prefrontal cortex, and limbic structures. Neurotropic factors also may contribute to the genetic susceptibility to OCD in general, and specific gene changes may contribute to hoarding behavior (Alonso et al., 2008), although genetic results have been inconsistent (Samuels et al., 2007). These specific genetic susceptibilities and how they manifest themselves in individuals with intellectual disability have not been studied.

Both OCD and hoarding disorder patients in general populations have disturbed implicit memory function (Blom et al., 2011; Mataix-Cols, Pertusa, & Snowdon, 2011). Baseline implicit memory capabilities would be expected to vary among the intellectual disability population and may affect individuals with intellectual disability differently, which could potentially increase their risk for hoarding disorder, although this has not been studied systematically. Subcortical limbic structures and the ventromedial prefrontal cortex are implicated in hoarding disorder, which suggests that the dopaminergic system plays a crucial role in hoarding behavior (Alonso et al, 2008; Grisham and Norberg, 2010; Kalsbeek et al., 1988; Kelley & Stinus, 1985; Pertusa et al., 2010).

Most studies of treatment of hoarding disorder in typical populations have emphasized cognitive-behavioral methods, which may not be suitable for all persons with intellectual disability. Pharmacotherapy and behavior therapy do not work as well for persons with hoarding disorder as for OCD in the general population, and treatment of persons with intellectual disability has not been systematically studied (Matais-Cols et al, 2010; Saxena 2011). There is some very limited support for using a form of behavioral therapy to treat hoarding disorder in persons with intellectual disability (Ayllon, 1963; Testa et al., 2011; Van Houten & Rolider, 1988). One recent small study (n = 3) of the effects of individualized reinforcement-based and item return procedures on persons with severe intellectual disability (Berry & Schell, 2006) found reductions in hoarding behavior when adequate reinforcers could be individually identified for the given participants in the study using the Reinforcement Assessment for Individuals with Severe Disabilities tool (RAISD; Fisher, Piazza, Bowman, & Amari, 1996).

Hoarding symptoms may first emerge in the context of dementia, for which some patients with intellectual disability are at higher risk. Hoarding disorder would not be diagnosed in this case, because dementia is an exclusion criterion for the diagnosis. In individuals with dementia the hoarding behavior may have less emotional context, may consist of very inappropriate objects (e.g. decaying food), may be variable in expression, and also may be accompanied by other symptoms of loss of impulse control and executive function (Anderson, Demasio, & Damasio, 2005; Hwang, Tsai, Yan, Liu, & Lirng, 1998).

Some patients from typical populations who have suffered acquired brain injury damage have otherwise normal functioning except for the development of hoarding symptoms. Hoarding disorder would not be diagnosed in these cases due to acquired brain damage being an exclusion criterion. However, the neuroradiological findings in these situations may be informative. Functional MRI imaging of such individuals who develop hoarding behavior in the context of acquired brain damage has implicated damage to the ventromedial prefrontal cortex, extending to the anterior cingulate cortex. (Anderson et al., 2005; Cohen, Angladette, Benoit, & Pierrot-Deseilligny, 1999; Hahm, Kang, Cheong, & Na, 2001; Volle, Beato, Levy, & Dubois, 2002). These fMRI findings resemble areas damaged in fronto-temporal dementia (Mendez & Shapira, 2008), which also is associated with hoarding behavior. Patients with intellectual disability who have limitations in these brain areas may be at a high risk for hoarding behavior, although if there is documented brain injury, or the presence of dementia, a diagnosis of hoarding disorder is excluded by the *DSM-5*. It has been proposed that the behavior of hoarding may be related to damage, which disrupts a subcortically driven mechanism that normally allows an individual to adjust acquiring objects to appropriate context (Anderson et al, 2005; Tolin, Kiehl, Worhunsky, Book, & Maltby, 2009).

Adaptation of Diagnostic Criteria

The diagnosis of hoarding disorder is excluded in the context of cognitive deficits in dementia, restricted interests in ASD, or food storing as seen in Prader-Willi syndrome. Otherwise, hoarding disorder can be diagnosed in the intellectual disability population.

One of the criteria for the diagnosis of hoarding disorder in typical populations requires that the individual have strong urges to save items and/or distress associated with discarding them (Grisham et al., 2009). The assessment of these feeling states may require more behavioral observation in persons who cannot describe their thoughts and emotions to the examiner. Also, individuals with intellectual disability may value objects that are not considered important to other persons and may resist parting with specific objects for reasons other than hoarding. Finally, some individuals with intellectual disability may not discard items because of the inability to determine what constitutes a "safe environment for self and others," and so this diagnostic criterion may not apply. Hoarding disorder can present a particularly difficult problem for persons with intellectual disability, because it can interfere with relationships and affect community placement (Berry & Schell, 2006).

Most studies of treatment of hoarding disorder in typical populations have emphasized cognitive-behavioral methods (Frost, 2010), which may not be suitable for all persons with intellectual disability. A modified behavioral approach has shown some promise. Pharmacotherapy and behavior therapy do not work as well for persons with hoarding disorder as for OCD, and no treatment of persons with intellectual disability and hoarding disorder has been systematically studied (Mataix-Cols et al, 2010).

Hoarding Disorder

DSM-5 Diagnostic Criteria	Applying Criteria for Mild to Moderate Intellectual Disability	Applying Criteria for Severe to Profound Intellectual Disability
A. Persistent difficulty discarding or parting with possessions, regardless of their actual value.	A. No adaptation. **Note:** Realistic "value" of the possessions to the individual should be interpreted in terms of the objective and subjective function as well as developmental levels of the individual with intellectual disability	A. No adaptation. **Note:** Realistic "value" of the possessions to the individual should be interpreted in terms of the objective and subjective function and developmental levels of the individual with intellectual disability
B. This difficulty is due to a perceived need to save the items and to distress associated with discarding them.	B. No adaptation. **Note:** The individual's insight into the consequences of accumulating objects or of discarding them may be limited. Expressions of grief and distress may require behavioral observation in individuals who have limitation with verbal expression of emotions	B. Unable to determine in most individuals in this category **Note:** Recurrent and persistent thoughts, impulses, or images may not be experienced as intrusive or inappropriate nor cause marked anxiety or distress; delusional beliefs, if present and organized into a system, may not be possible to determine due to cognitive and communicative deficits; distress also may occur when a fixed pattern of arrangement of clutter is altered.

Hoarding Disorder (continued)

DSM-5 Diagnostic Criteria	Applying Criteria for Mild to Moderate Intellectual Disability	Applying Criteria for Severe to Profound Intellectual Disability
C. The difficulty discarding possessions results in the accumulation of possessions that congest and clutter active living areas and substantially compromises their intended use. If living areas are uncluttered, it is only because of the interventions of third parties (e.g., family members, cleaners, authorities).	C. No adaptation. **Note:** The individual's ability to understand health consequences of clutter and storage limitations should be taken into consideration.	C. No adaptation. **Note:** The individual's ability to understand health consequences of clutter and storage limitations should be taken into consideration. The individual may not have the ability to take the initiative to discard objects.
D. The hoarding causes clinically significant distress or impairment in social, occupational, or other important areas of functioning (including maintaining a safe environment for self and others).	D. No adaptation.	D. Unable to determine in some individuals in this category. **Note:** Baseline areas of functioning may already be limited. Changes in behavior need to be interpreted as compared with baseline for the individual.
E. The hoarding is not attributable to another medical condition (e.g, brain injury, cerebrovascular disease, Prader-Willi syndrome).		
F. The hoarding is not better explained by the symptoms of another mental disorder (e.g., obsessions in obsessive-compulsive disorder, decreased energy in major depressive disorder, delusions in schizophrenia or another psychotic disorder, cognitive deficits in major neurocognitive disorder, restricted interests in autism spectrum disorder).	F. No adaptation. **Note:** Prader-Willi, dementia and other syndromes involving hoarding behavior that are sometimes seen in autism are diagnosed elsewhere and do not require an additional hoarding disorder diagnosis.	F. No adaptation. **Note:** Prader-Willi, dementia and other syndromes involving hoarding behavior that are sometimes seen in autism are diagnosed elsewhere and do not require an additional hoarding disorder diagnosis.
Specify if: With excessive acquisition: If difficulty discarding possessions is accompanied by excessive acquisition of items that are not needed or for which there is no available space.	**Note:** The specifier should be applied in the context of the cognitive and developmental functioning of the individual	**Note:** The specifier should be applied in the context of the cognitive and developmental functioning of the individual
Specify if: With good or fair insight: The individual recognizes that hoarding-related beliefs and behaviors (pertaining to difficulty discarding items, clutter, or excessive acquisition) are problematic. With poor insight: The individual is mostly convinced that hoarding-related beliefs and behaviors (pertaining to difficulty discarding items, clutter, or excessive acquisition) are not problematic despite evidence to the contrary. With absent insight/delusional beliefs: The individual is completely convinced that hoarding-related beliefs and behaviors (pertaining to difficulty discarding items, clutter, or excessive acquisition) are not problematic despite evidence to the contrary.	**Note:** The various specifiers for rating patient's insight into disorder-related beliefs (e.g. good, fair, poor or absent/delusional beliefs) should be applied in the context of the cognitive and developmental functioning of the individual.	**Note:** The various specifiers for rating patient's insight into disorder-related beliefs (e.g. good, fair, poor or absent/delusional beliefs) should be applied in the context of the cognitive and developmental functioning of the individual.

Excoriation (Skin-Picking) Disorder

Excoriation (skin-picking) disorder is characterized by the recurrent picking of one's own skin, which causes tissue damage (Grant & Odlaug, 2009; Keuthen et al. 2010). Prevalence rates in the general population are 1.2-5.4%, with almost 63% of respondents exhibiting some form of skin-picking that does not reach a level of clinical significance (Hayes, Storch, & Berlanga, 2009; Keuthen et al., 2010; Monzani et al., 2012). Comprehensive research on the prevalence of excoriation disorder in individuals with intellectual disability is limited; however, specific syndromes including Prader-Willi syndrome, fragile X syndrome and Smith-Magenis syndrome have been shown to have significantly higher rates of skin-picking than the general population (Didden, Korzilius, & Curfs, 2007; Edelman et al., 2007; Hiraiwa et al., 2007; Symons et al., 2003). This section describes the assessment issues related to the diagnosis of the excoriation disorder, reviews the relevant literature for children and adults, and recommends modifications to the existing criteria for varying degrees of cognitive deficits.

Review of Diagnostic Criteria

The primary features of excoriation disorder are recurrent skin-picking that results in skin lesions, with repeated attempts to decrease or stop skin-picking, and with resulting clinically significant distress or impairment in other areas of functioning (American Psychiatric Association, 2013). The skin-picking also must not be caused by a symptom of another mental illness (e.g. delusions of parasitosis) or physical illness (e.g., pruritus caused by liver failure, generalized peripheral neuropathies).

Issues Related to Diagnosis in Persons with ID

Excoriation disorder was previously categorized as an impulse-control disorder not otherwise specified and was first included as its own separate disorder only in the most recent *DSM* (APA, 2000). Individuals with intellectual disability who have self-soothing behaviors such as rubbing or tapping themselves may complicate diagnosis, as may individuals with sensory-integration disorders who prefer the sensation of scratching. Individuals most often pick their face, arms, trunk, hands, and legs.

In individuals with intellectual disability, self-report and communication of attempts to decrease or stop skin-picking may be limited due to limited expressive language skills. In part due to inadequate clinical data and in part due to the recent distinction of this disorder from others, there is a lack of consensus regarding phenomenological and behavioral dimensions that create uncertainty in clinical settings.

Application of Diagnostic Criteria to People with ID

Criterion A states that recurrent skin-picking results in skin lesions. While excoriation in people with disabilities can be easily observed, the reason for the skin-picking can be more difficult to determine. Sensory-integration variations and self-stimulating behaviors occur more in individuals with intellectual disability that may cause overlap of symptoms. Self-injurious behaviors also confound diagnosis.

Specific issues related to individuals with intellectual disability (Fletcher et al., 2007) include:

1. Limited expressive language skills decrease self-report and limit the uses of psychometrics.
2. Sensory integration issues may lead an individual to desire more intense stimulation that skin-picking provides.
3. Repetitive behaviors such as rubbing or scratching may not be related to skin-picking.

Criterion B states that individuals must attempt to decrease or stop skin-picking; this may not apply to some individuals with intellectual disability depending on their ability to implement or communicate this concept. Criterion C states that the picking causes clinically significant distress, but individuals with intellectual disability may lack awareness of the impact or ramifications of the disorder. The disorder may limit the individual's social or occupational functioning if the consequences of skin-picking, such as an open wound, would disallow participation in activities (at swimming pools, failure to meet health and safety standards in workshops, etc.). In contrast to hoarding disorder, the presence of a genetic syndrome such as Prader-Willi syndrome does not exclude the additional diagnosis of excoriation disorder.

Review of Research Applying to People with ID

Because excoriation disorder is a new classification related to OCD, research in individuals with intellectual disability remains limited. Research in individuals without intellectual disability shows that this disorder exists across age cohorts and across cultures (Grant et al., 2012), that most people experienced increased tension before and relief after picking (Arnold et al, 1998) but that it was not necessary for the diagnosis, and that a vast preponderance of individuals with the disorder were women (Grant, Odlaug, Hampshire, Schreiber, & Chamberlain, 2013; Lochner, Grant, Odlaug, & Stein, 2012).

Adults with Mild to Moderate ID

Individuals with mild intellectual disability are similar to the general population in that they may or may not seek treatment for this disorder. Just as persons without intellectual disability may present without the characteristic of awareness while picking, so may an individual with intellectual disability. Variations in the level of distress and impaired functioning are expected in connection with an individual's ability to communicate and form abstract thought.

Clinical presentation in individuals with moderate intellectual disability depends on the communication ability of the individual. It may be difficult if there is a lack of expressive language skills to differentiate self-injury and sensory issues from skin-picking.

Adults with Severe or Profound ID

Observational data and information from caregivers is needed to make the diagnosis of excoriation disorder. Criteria that require an individual to attempt to decrease a behavior do not apply as issues related to communication ability and cognitive function.

Children and Adolescents with ID

As with OCD, children may not have language skills to describe their thoughts; parent and caregiver report may be needed for this diagnosis. Children may have the ability to decrease picking depending on their developmental stage.

Summary of Limitations in Applying DSM-5 *Criteria to People with ID*

1. The diagnostic criterion requiring repeated attempts to decrease or stop skin-picking may not apply to individuals with intellectual disability as they may not understand the ramifications of skin-picking or be aware of the behavior.

2. The diagnostic requirement that skin-picking causes clinically significant distress or impairment may not apply to individuals with intellectual disability and is less likely with more significant cognitive deficits.

Etiology and Pathogenesis

Biological Factors

White matter brain abnormalities in the anterior cingulate cortex and white matter in proximity of the left temporo-parietal junction were found in individuals with Excoriation Disorder (Grant et al 2013). Skin-picking has been shown to have a genetic basis, including a twin study, and a mouse study showed a connection between excessive grooming, increased anxiety-like behaviors, and cortico-striatal synaptic defects that improved with fluoxetine (Monzani et al., 2012; Welch et al., 2007).

Skin picking has been proposed as a part of a familial OCD spectrum (Bienvenu et al 2000). Individuals with OCD are more likely than controls to have a grooming disorder (like trichotillomania or skin-picking) (Bienvenu et al, 2012). Individuals with 'psychogenic excoriation' were more likely than controls (45.2% vs 3.7%) to be diagnosed with OCD as well (Calikusu, Yucel, Polat, & Baykal, 2003).

Skin-picking remains a diagnosis of exclusion. Care should be taken to exclude other possible factors that may cause an individual to pick or scratch his or her skin. Powers (2005) notes that pain, boredom, allergic dermatitis, dental pain, oral disease, perineal discomforts, and impaction can all cause symptoms that mimic excoriation disorder.

Genetic Factors

The most well researched of the genetic syndromes in which excoriation disorder occurs is Prader-Willi syndrome. Dykens and Kasari (1997) showed that children with Prader-Willi were many times more likely (95%) to have skin picking than matched children with Down syndrome (20%) or non-specific intellectual disability (26%). Didden et al (2007) found that 86% of individuals with Prader-Willi syndrome exhibit excoriation, including 37% reporting mild skin-picking, 36% moderate, and 25% severe. Symons, Butler, Sanders, Feurer, & Thompson (1999) reported 81% of subjects with self-injury with the most prevalent presentation skin-picking. Additionally, individuals with the 15q11-q13 deletion self-injured significantly more sites on the body that those with maternal disomy 15.

Symons et al. (2003) reported that in a survey of boys with fragile X syndrome, 34% engaged in picking or pulling of the skin or hair and 19% exhibited skin rubbing or scratching. Hall et al. (2008) found 22.3% of boys and 13.8% of girls with fragile X syndrome rubbed or scratched at skin; in addition 3% of both boys and girls reported pulling hair or skin and 20% exhibited compulsive grooming.

A systematic review of case studies noted three individuals with ASD who were participants in treatment for skin-picking (Lang et al., 2010), but there remains a lack of research on this specific area.

Smith-Magenis syndrome is usually characterized by a 17p deletion, developmental delay and intellectual disability, a distinctive behavioral phenotype, and sleep disturbance (27). A certain subset showed 54-100% prevalence for skin-picking.

Psychosocial Factors

Individuals with excoriation disorder often report shame or embarrassment with skin picking (Arnold, Auchenback, & McElroy, 2001). It would stand to reason that individuals would engage in skin-picking when they are experiencing more psychosocial stressors. Additionally, given that individuals with intellectual disability have limited adaptive functioning, skin picking may be utilized as a coping technique.

Excoriation Disorder

DSM-5 Diagnostic Criteria	Applying Criteria for Mild to Moderate Intellectual Disability	Applying Criteria for Severe to Profound Intellectual Disability
A. Recurrent skin picking resulting in skin lesions.	A. No adaptation.	A. No adaptation.
B. Repeated attempts to decrease or stop skin picking.	B. No adaptation. **Note:** Repeated attempts to decrease or stop skin picking may not be possible due to cognitive and communicative deficits.	B. No adaptation. **Note:** Repeated attempts to decrease or stop skin picking may not be possible due to cognitive and communicative deficits. The individual may make no to decrease or stop skin picking.
C. The skin picking causes clinically significant distress or impairment in social, occupational, or other important areas of functioning.	C. No adaptation. **Note:** The skin picking may or may not cause clinically significant distress or impairment in social, occupational, or other important areas of functioning. Distress may not occur or may not be ascertainable. Consider occupational limitations like an individual not being able to work due to open sores or inability to keep from picking. Also consider medical complications such as infection, scarring, and irritation.	C. No adaptation. **Note:** The skin picking may not cause clinically significant distress or impairment in social, occupational, or other important areas of functioning. Distress may not occur or may not be ascertainable. Consider occupational limitations like an individual not being able to work due to open sores or inability to keep from picking. Also consider medical complications such as infection, scarring, and irritation.

Excoriation Disorder (continued)

DSM-5 Diagnostic Criteria	Applying Criteria for Mild to Moderate Intellectual Disability	Applying Criteria for Severe to Profound Intellectual Disability
D. The skin picking is not attributable to the physiological effects of a substance (e.g., cocaine) or another medical condition (e.g., scabies).	D. No adaptation.	D. No adaptation.
E. The skin picking is not better explained by symptoms of another mental disorder (e.g., delusions or tactile hallucinations in a psychotic disorder, attempts to improve a perceived defect or flaw in appearance in body dysmorphic disorder, stereotypies in stereotypic movement disorder, or intention to harm oneself in a nonsuicidal self-injury.	E. No adaptation.	E. No adaptation.

Trichotillomania (Hair-Pulling Disorder)

Review of Diagnostic Criteria

The diagnostic criteria for trichotillomania (TTM) include persistent hair pulling leading to hair loss, with repeated attempts to stop, resulting in significant distress and functional limitations. It cannot be better accounted for by a medical condition or other mental health disorder such as body dysmorphic disorder. Previously, trichotillomania was classified as an impulse-control disorder. In the *DSM-5*, TTM is included with OCD to recognize the similarities with other OC-spectrum disorders. Other changes in diagnostic criteria include the removal of the requirements that the hair loss be noticeable by others and that the patient report a sense of tension prior to pulling and relief after the hair is removed.

Hair pulling can occur from any part of the body, although it frequently involves the head, eyebrows, or eye lashes (Harrison & Franklin, 2012). Manipulation of the hair with the fingers prior to and following hair pulling often occurs. Pulled hair may be put in the mouth and may be swallowed, which can cause significant gastrointestinal complications.

Development and Course

Hair-pulling disorder in the general population is reported to develop in either one of two age ranges, either early onset, prior to age 6 years, or during adolescence. The information available on the development and course of trichotillomania in persons with ID comes from case studies in which a history of the disorder was obtained. The retrospective reports from family members indicate a range of ages that trichotillomania started between the age of eighteen months and nine years and it tends to persist (Barmann & Vitali, 1982; Ghazuiddin, Tsai, & Ghazuiddin, 1991).

For the general population, there have been clinical distinctions made in terms of the style of hair pulling to distinguish between "automatic" pulling that takes place outside of awareness and "focused" pulling which seems to be related to affective and cognitive antecedents. Many individuals with TTM engage in both types (Franklin, Zagrabbe, & Benavides, 2011).

Prevalence

Information on the prevalence of trichotillomania in persons with ID is rather limited. This is because it is infrequently reported as a separate disorder in epidemiological studies and instead it is grouped with impulse control disorders, self-injurious behaviors, or OCD behaviors. *The Behavior Problems Inventory* (Rojahn, Matson, Lott, Esbensen, & Smalls, 2001) and the *Diagnostic Assessment for the Severely Handicapped – Second Edition* (*DASH-II*) are rating scales for the assessment of individuals with developmental disabilities that include hair pulling as a separate item (Sevin, Matson, Williams, & Kirkpatrick-Sanchez, 1995).

The results of two large scale community surveys of self-injurious behavior in individuals with developmental disability indicated that approximately .2-.3% engage in hair pulling (Griffin et al., 1987; Rojahn, 1986). More females than males were reported to engage in the behavior (Griffin et al., 1987). The rate of hair pulling in institutional populations is reported to be greater than in community samples and was 2% in one study (Singh, 1977) and 4% in another (Horovitz et al., 2011).

Hair pulling is reported to be more frequent among some diagnostic groups. For example, 16% of parents of children and adolescents with Prader-Willi syndrome reported trichotillomania. Most of these individuals also engaged in skin picking (Wigren & Hansen, 2003). Among children aged 10-14 years with ASD, the prevalence was 3.9% based on parent report (Simonoff et al., 2008).

Functional Consequences

Trichotillomania has significant consequences on the appearance of the individual which can have negative effects on relationships with others. Individuals with mild cognitive deficits who engage in hair pulling may take several measures to hide the disorder, including wearing a hat or other hair covering. Individuals may be teased and avoid activities with others as a result. TTM can have negative effects on family dynamics and increase stress in family interactions. Trichotillomania occupies the individual's hands and thereby interferes with engaging in other more adaptive behavior.

Comorbidity

Trichotillomania has been considered a form of self-injury, a stereotypic movement disorder, an impulse-control disorder, or an obsessive-compulsive behavior depending on the classification system in use at the time. Skin picking and nail biting frequently occur along with hair pulling and are sometimes referred to collectively as body-focused repetitive behavior disorders. TTM may occur in conjunction with Tourette's disorder (Bodfish & Lewis, 2002).

Application of Diagnostic Criteria to People with ID

General Considerations

The removal of the requirement that trichotillomania requires a tension-release cycle leading up to and following hair pulling (*DSM-IV-TR*) is beneficial for the diagnosis with persons with ID since it was difficult to establish in the ID population.

The current requirement of repeated attempts to stop hair pulling is problematic for the diagnosis in persons with ID. Family members, teachers, and caregivers may have tried to interrupt or prevent the individual from hair pulling. The person with ID may not have the requisite awareness to identify the hair pulling as a problem or to initiate action to change the behavior. Individuals with ID who use expressive language skills might request assistance with managing the behavior, however.

Review of Research Applying to People with ID

Research in this area is limited to a few case reports about the behavioral assessment and treatment of trichotillomania with persons with ID. There is one case report concerning an open label medication report of the use of haloperidol with a child that was reported to be successful (Ghazuiddin et al., 1991). Several case studies reported on the functional analysis of trichotillomania and concluded that the function was primarily automatic reinforcement through tactile stimulation (Miltenberger, Long, Rapp, Lumley, & Elliott, 1998; Rapp et al, 2000) and sometimes secondarily reinforced by attention or escape from demands (Steege, Wacker, Berg, Cigrand, & Cooper, 1989). The importance of completing a functional assessment prior to behavioral intervention has been emphasized. Several different behavioral interventions have been successful in treating persons with TTM and intellectual disability including response interruption, response prevention, competing response, and habit reversal training.

Etiology and Pathogenesis

There is some evidence of a familial link in TTM in the general population. The heritability estimate of TTM from a twin study was 76 percent (Novak, Keuthen, Stewart, & Pauls, 2009). A study of gene encoding of SLITRK1 on chromosome 13, which has also been investigated for an association with Tourette's disorder, detected polymorphisms specific to TTM cases compared to non-TTM controls (Zuchner et al., 2006). Neuropsychological and neuroimaging studies have yielded mixed findings.

Trichotillomania (hair-pulling disorder)

The criteria for trichotillomania are the same as for excoriation disorder, except that criterion A is "recurrent pulling out of one' hair, resulting in hair loss," and B-E relate to hair pulling.

Obsessive-compulsive and Related Disorders Due to Another Medical Condition

The criteria are the same as for other mental disorders due to another medical condition, without adaptation, with the additional need for obsessions, compulsions, preoccupations with appearance, hoarding, skin-picking, hair pulling, other body-focused repetitive behaviors, or other symptoms characteristic of the obsessive-compulsive and related disorders.

Substance/Medication-induced Obsessive Compulsive and Related Disorder

The criteria are the same as for other substance/medication-induced mental disorders, without adaptation, with the additional need for obsessions, compulsions, skin-pricking, hair pulling, other body-focussed repetitive behaviors, or other symptoms characteristic of the obsessive-compulsive and related disorders.

Other Specified Obsessive Compulsive and Related Disorders Unspecified Obsessive Compulsive and Related Disorders

DSM-5 also provides categories for other specified obsessive compulsive and related disorders and for unspecified obsessive compulsive and related disorders.

References

Alonso, P., Gratacòs, M., Menchón, J.M., Segalàs, C., González, J.R., Labad, J., ... Estivill, X. (2008). Genetic susceptibility to obsessive-compulsive hoarding: The contribution of neurotrophic tyrosine kinase receptor type 3 gene. *Genes Brain and Behavior, 7,* 778-85.

American Psychiatric Association (1980) *Diagnostic and statistical manual of mental disorders* (3rd edition) Washington DC: Author.

American Psychiatric Association (2000) *Diagnostic and statistical manual of mental disorders* (4.th. edition, text revision). Washington DC: Author.

American Psychiatric Association. (2013). Obsessive-compulsive and related disorders. In *Diagnostic and statistical manual of mental disorders* (5th Ed.) (pp. 235-264). Washington, DC: Author.. doi:10.1176/appi.books.9780890425596.744053.

An, S.K., Mataix-Cols, D., Lawrence, N.S., Wooderson, S., Giampietro, V., Speckens, A., ... Phillips, M.L. (2009). To discard or not to discard: The neural basis of hoarding symptoms in obsessive-compulsive disorder. *Molecular Psychiatry, 14,* 318-331.

Anderson, S.W., Demasio, H., & Damasio, A.R (2005). A neural basis for collecting behaviour in humans. *Brain,* 128, 201-212,

Arnold, L. M., Auchenbach, M. B., & McElroy, S. L. (2001). Psychogenic excoriation. *CNS Drugs, 15*(5), 351-359.

Arnold, L. M., McElroy, S. L., Mutasim, D. F., Dwight, M. M., Lamerson, C. L., & Morris, E. M. (1998). Characteristics of 34 adults with psychogenic excoriation. *The Journal of Clinical Psychiatry, 59*(10), 509-514.

Ayers, C.R., Saxena, S., Golshan, S., & Wetherell, J.L. (2010). Age at onset and clinical features of late life compulsive hoarding. *International Journal of Geriatric Psychiatry, 2*, 142-149.

Ayllon, T. (1963). Intensive treatment of psychotic behavior by stimulus satiation and food reinforcement. *Behaviour Research and Therapy, I*, 53-61.

Barmann, B. C., & Vitali, D. L. (1982). Facial screening to eliminate trichotillomania in developmentally disabled persons. *Behavior Therapy*, 13, 735-742.

Barnhill, L. J. (1999). Diagnosis and treatment of anxiety disorders in persons with developmental disabilities. *NADD Bulletin, 2*, 136-141.

Bejerot, S. (2006). Autism spectrum disorders, autistic traits and personality disorders in obsessive compulsive disorder. In: R. Gross-Isseroff & A. Weizman (Eds.), *Obsessive compulsive disorder and comorbidity* (pp. 59-102). Hauppauge, NY: Nova Science.

Bejerot, S. (2007). An autistic dimension: A proposed subtype of obsessive compulsive disorder. *Autism*, 11, 101-110.

Berry, C.L, & Schell, R.M. (2006). Reducing hoarding behavior with individualized reinforcement and item return. *Behavioral Interventions, 21*: 123-135.

Bienvenu, O. J., Samuels, J. F., Riddle, M. A., Hoehn-Saric, R., Liang, K., Cullen, B. A., & Nestadt, G. (2000). The relationship of obsessive–compulsive disorder to possible spectrum disorders: Results from a family study. *Biological Psychiatry, 48*(4), 287-293.

Bienvenu, O., Samuels, J., Wuyek, L., Liang, K., Wang, Y., Grados, M., & Rasmussen, S. (2012). Is obsessive–compulsive disorder an anxiety disorder, and what, if any, are spectrum conditions? A family study perspective. *Psychological Medicine, 42*(1), 1.

Blom, R.M., Samuels, J.F., Grados, M.A., Chen, Y., Bienvenu, O.J., Riddle, M.A., ... Nestadt, G. (2011). Cognitive functioning in compulsive hoarding. *Journal of Anxiety Disorders, 25*, 1139-1144.

Bodfish, J. W., & Lewis, M. H. (2002). Self-injury and comorbid behaviors in developmental, neurological, psychiatric, and genetic disorders. In S.R. Schroeder, S. L. Oster-Granite, & T. Thompson (Eds.), Self-injurious behavior (pp. 23-39). Washington, DC: American Psychological Association.

Bokor, G. & Anderson, P.D. (2014). Obsessive-compulsive disorder. *Journal of Pharmacy Practice. 27*(2), 116-30. doi: 10.1177/0897190014521996. Epub 2014 Feb 27.BIOLOGICAL

Bourgeois, J., Coffey, S., Rivera, S.M., Hessl, D., Gane, L., Tassone, F., ... Hagerman R. (2009). Fragile X premutation disorders – Expanding the psychiatric perspective. *Journal of Clinical Psychiatry, 70*(6), 852-862.

Çalıkuşu, C., Yücel, B., Polat, A., & Baykal, C. (2003). The relation of psychogenic excoriation with psychiatric disorders: A comparative study. *Comprehensive Psychiatry, 44*(3), 256-261. doi:http://dx.doi.org/10.1016/S0010-440X(03)00041-5

Charlot, L., Fox, S., & Friedlander, R. (2002). Obsessional slowness in Down's syndrome. *Journal of Intellectual Disability Research. 46*(6), 517–524. DOI: 10.1046/j.1365-2788.2002.00419.x

Cohen, L., Angladette, L., Benoit, N., & Pierrot-Deseiligny, C. (1999). The man who borrowed cars. *Lancet, 353*, 34.

Deb, S., Matthews, T., Holt, G., & Bouras, N. (Eds.) (2001). *Practice guidelines for the assessment and diagnosis of mental health problems in adults with intellectual disability.* Brighton, UK: Pavilion Publishing.

Deb, S., Thomas, M., & Bright, C. (2001). Mental disorder in adults with intellectual disability. 1: Prevalence of functional psychiatric illness among a community-based population aged between 16 and 64 years. *Journal of Intellectual Disability Research. 45*,(6), 495–505.

Didden, R., Korzilius, H., & Curfs, L.M.G. (2007). Skin-picking in individuals with Prader-Willi syndrome: Prevalence, functional assessment, and its comorbidity with compulsive and self-injurious behaviours. *Journal of Applied Research in Intellectual Disabilities, 20*(5), 409-419.

Dimitropoulos, A., Blackford, J., Walden, T., Thompson, T. (2006). Compulsive behavior in Prader-Willi syndrome: Examining severity in early childhood. *Research in Developmental Disabilities, 27*, 190-202.

Dykens, E. M., & Kasari, C. (1997). Maladaptive behavior in children with Prader-Willi syndrome, Down syndrome, and nonspecific mental retardation. *American Journal on Mental Retardation,*_ _*102*(3), 228-237.

Edelman, E.A., Girirajan, S., Finucane, B., Patel, P.I., Lupski, J.R., Smith, A.C., & Elsea, S.H. (2007). Gender, genotype, and phenotype differences in Smith–Magenis syndrome: A meta-analysis of 105 cases. *Clinical Genetics, 71*(6), 540-550.

Fisher, W.W., Piazza, C.C., Bowman, L.G., & Amari, A. (1996). Integrating caregiver report with a systematic choice assessment. *American Journal on Mental Retardation, 101*, 5-25.

Fletcher, R., Loschen, E., Stavrakaki, C., & First, M. (Eds.). (2007). *Diagnostic manual-Intellectual disability (DM-ID): A textbook of diagnosis of mental disorders in persons with intellectual disability.* Kingston, NY: NADD Press.

Fontenelle, L.F., Oostermeijier, S., Harrison, B.J., Pantelis, C., & Yucel, M. (2011). OCD, ICD and drug addiction: Common features and potential treatments. *Drugs, 71*(7), 827-840.

Franklin, M. E., Zagrabbe, K., & Benavides, K. L. (2011). Trichotillomania and its treatment: A review and recommendations. *Expert Review of Neurotherapeutics*, 11(8), 1165-1174.

Frost, R.O. (2010). Treatment of hoarding. *Expert Review of Neurotherapeutics, 10*, 251-61.

Frost, R.O., & Gross, R.C. (1993). The hoarding of possessions. *Behaviour Research and Therapy, 31*, 367-381.

Frost, R.O., & Hartl, T.L. (1996). A cognitive-behavioral model of compulsive hoarding. *Behaviour Research and Therapy, 34*, 341-350.

Frost, R.O., & Hristova, V. J. (2011). Assessment of hoarding. *Clinical Psychology, 67*, 456-66.

Frost, R.O., Krause, M.S., & Steketee, G. (1996). Hoarding and obsessive-compulsive symptoms. *Behavior Modification, 20*, 116-132. Doi:10.1177/01454455960201006

Frost, R.O., Steketee, G., & Tolin, D.F. (2011). Comorbidity in hoarding disorder. *Depression and Anxiety, 28*, 876-84.

Frost, R.O., Steketee, G., & Tolin, D.F. (2012). Diagnosis and assessment of hoarding disorder. *Annual Review of Clinical Psychology, 8*, 219-42.

Ghazuiddin, M., Tsai, L. Y., & Ghazuiddin, N. (1991). Brief report: Haloperidol treatment of trichotillomania in a boy with autism and mental retardation. *Journal of Autism and Developmental Disorders*, 21(3), 365-371.

Gothelf, D., Goraly, O., Avni, S., Stawski, M., Hartmann, I., Basel-Vanagaite, L. & Apter, A. (2008). Psychiatric morbidity with focus on obsessive compulsive disorder in an Israeli cohort and adolescents with mild to moderate mental retardation. *Journal Neural Transmission, 115*, 929-936 DOI 10.1007/s00702-008-0037-4

Grant, J. E., & Odlaug, B.L. (2009). Update on pathological skin picking. *Current Psychiatry Reports*_, _*11*(4), 283-288.

Grant, J. E., Odlaug, B. L., Chamberlain, S. R., Keuthen, N. J., Lochner, C., & Stein, D. J. (2012). Skin picking disorder. *American Journal of Psychiatry, 169*(11), 1143-1149.

Grant, J. E., Odlaug, B. L., Hampshire, A., Schreiber, L. R., & Chamberlain, S. R. (2013). White matter abnormalities in skin picking disorder: A diffusion tensor imaging study.

Neuropsychopharmacology, 38(5), 763-769.

Griffin, J. C., Ricketts, R. W., Williams, D. E., Locke, B. J., Altmeyer, B. K., & Stark, M. T. (1987). A community survey of self-injurious behavior among developmentally disabled children and adolescents. *Hospital and Community Psychiatry*, 38 (9), 959-963.

Grisham, J.R., & Baldwin, P.A. (2015). Neuropsychological and neurophysiological insights into hoarding disorder. *Neuropsychiatric Disease and Treatment, 11*, 951-962.

Grisham, J.R., Frost, R.O., Steketee, G., Kim, H.J., & Hood, S. (2006). Age of onset of compulsive hoarding. *Journal of Anxiety Disorders, 20*, 675-686.

Grisham, J.R., Frost, R.O., Steketee, G., Kim, H.J., Tarkoff, A., & Hood, S. J. (2009), Formation of attachment to possessions in compulsive hoarding. *Anxiety Disorders, 23*, 357-61.

Grisham, J.R., & Norberg, M.M. (2010). Compulsive hoarding: current controversies and new directions. *Dialogues in Clinical Neurosciences, 12*, 233-40.

Gross-Isseroff, R., Hermesh, H., & Weizman, A. (2001). Obsessive compulsive behavior in autism – Towards an autistic-obsessive compulsive syndrome? *World Journal of Biological Psychiatry, 2*, 193-197.

Hahm, D.S., Kang, Y., Cheong, S.S., Na, D.L. (2001). A compulsive collecting behavior following an A-com aneurysmal rupture. *Neurology, 56*(3), 398-400.

Hall, S.S., Lightbody, A.A., & Reiss, A.L (2008). Compulsive, self-injurious, and autistic behavior in children and adolescents with fragile X syndrome. *American Journal on Mental Retardation, 113*(1), 44-53.

Harkin, B., & Kessler, K. (2011). The role of working memory in compulsive checking and OCD: A systematic classification of 58 experimental findings. *Clinical Psychology Review, 31*(6), 1004-21. Doi: 10.1016/j.cpr.2011.06.004. Epub 2011 Jun 22.

Harrison, J. P., & Franklin, M. E. (2012). Pediatric trichotillomania. *Current Psychiatry Research*, 14, 188-196.

Hartl, T.L., Duffany, S.R., Allen, G.J., Steketee, G., & Frost, R.O. (2005). Relationships among compulsive hoarding, trauma, and attention-deficit/hyperactivity disorder. *Behaviour Research and Therapy, 43*, 269-76.

Hayes, S. L., Storch, E.A., & Berlanga, L. (2009). Skin picking behaviors: An examination of the prevalence and severity in a community sample. *Journal of Anxiety Disorders, 23*(3), 314-319.

Hiraiwa, R. Maegaki, Y., Oka, A., & Ohno, K. (2007). Behavioral and psychiatric disorders in Prader-Willi syndrome: A population study in Japan. *Brain and Development*., *29*(9), 535-542.

Horovitz, M., Matson, J.L., Sipes, M., Shoemaker, M., Belva, B., & Bamburg (2011). Incidence and trends in psychopathology symptoms over time in adults with severe to profound intellectual disability. *Research in Developmental Disabilities*, 32, 685-692.

Hwang, J.P., Tsai, S.J., Yang, C.H., Liu, K.M. & Lirng, J.F. (1998). Hoarding behavior in dementia. A preliminary report. *American Journal of Geriatric Psychiatry, 6*, 285-289.

Jacob, S., Landeros-Weisenberger, Leckman, J.F. (2009). Autism spectrum and obsessive-compulsive disorders: OC behaviors, phenotypes and genetics. *Autism Research, 2*, 293-311.

Kalsbeek, A., De Bruin, J.P., Feenstra, M.G., Matthijssen, M.A., & Uylings, H.B. (1988). Neonatal thermal lesions of the mesolimbocortical dopaminergic projection decrease food-hoarding behavior. *Brain Research, 475*, 80-90.

Kelley, A.E., & Stinus, L. (1985). Disappearance of hoarding behavior after 6-hydroxydopamine lesions of the mesolimbic dopamine neurons and its reinstatement with L-dopa. *Behavioral Neuroscience, 3*, 531-545.

Keuthen, N.J., Koran, L.M., Aboujaoude, E., Large, M.D., & Serpe, R.T. (2010). The prevalence of pathologic skin picking in US adults. *Comprehensive Psychiatry*., *51.2*, 183-186.

Kyrios, M., Frost, R.O., & Steketee, G. (2004). Cognitions in compulsive buying and acquisition. *Cognitive Therapy and Research, 28*, 241-258.

Lambrecq, V., Rotge, J.Y., Jaafari, N., Aouizerate, B., Langbour, N., Bioulac, B, … Guehl D. (2013). Differential role of visuo-spatial working memory in the propensity toward uncertainty in patients with obsessive compulsive disorder and in healthy subjects. *Psychological Medicine*, 31, 1-12.

Landau, D., Iervolino, A.C., Pertusa, A., Santo, S., & Mataix-Cols, D. (2011). Stressful life events and material deprivation in hoarding disorder. *Journal of Anxiety Disorders, 25*, 192-202.

Lang, R., Didden, R., Machalicek, W., Rispoli, M., Sigafoos, J., Lancioni, G. … Kang, S. (2010). Behavioral treatment of chronic skin-picking in individuals with developmental disabilities: A systematic review. *Research in Developmental Disabilities, 31*(2), 304-315.

Lochner, C., Grant, J. E., Odlaug, B. L., & Stein, D. J. (2012). DSM-5 field survey: Skin picking disorder. *Annals of Clinical Psychiatry: Journal of the American Academy of Clinical Psychiatrists, 24*, 300-304.

Lochner, C., Kinnear, C.J., Hemmings, S.M., Seller, C., Niehaus, D.J., Knowles, J.A., … Stein, D.J. (2005). Hoarding in obsessive-compulsive disorder: Clinical and genetic correlates. *Journal of Clinical Psychiatry, 66*, 1158-1160.

Marazziti, D., Consoli, G., Baroni, S., & Catena Dell'Osso, M. (2010). Past, present and future drugs for the treatment of obsessive-compulsive disorder. *Current Medicinal Chemistry, 17*(29), 3410-3421. Review. PMID: 20712565

Mataix-Cols, D., Frost, R.O., Pertusa, A., Clark, L.A., Saxena, S., Leckman, J.F., … Wilhelm, S. (2010). Hoarding disorder: A new diagnosis for DDM-V? *Depression and Anxiety, 27*, 556-572.

Mataix-Cols, D., Pertusa, A., & Snowdon, J. (2011). Neuropsychological and neural correlates of hoarding: a practice-friendly review. *Journal of Clinical Psychology, 67*, 467-76.

Matson, J.L., & Dempsey, T. (2009). The nature and treatment of compulsions, obsessions, and rituals in people with developmental disabilities. *Research in Developmental Disabilities, 30*, 603-611.

McDougle, C.J., Kresch, L.E., Goodman, W.K., Naylor, S.T., Volkmar, F.R., Cohen, D.J., & Price, L.H. (1995). A case-control study of repetitive thoughts and behavior in adults with autistic disorder and obsessive-compulsive disorder. *American Journal of Psychiatry, 152*, 772-777.

Mendez, M.F., & Shapira, J.S. (2008). The spectrum of recurrent thoughts and behaviors in frontotemporal dementia. *CNS Spectrums, 13*, 202-208.

Miltenberger, R. G., Long, E. S., Rapp, J. T., Lumley, V., Elliott, A. J. (1998). Evaluating the function of hair pulling: A preliminary investigation. *Behavior Therapy*, 29, 211-219.

Monzani, B., Rijskijk, F., Cherkas, L., Harris, J., Keuthen, N., & Mataix,-Cols, D. (2012). Prevalence and heritability of skin picking in an adult community sample: A twin study. *American Journal of Medical Genetics Part B: Neuropsychiatric Genetics*.., *.159*(5), 605-610.

Novak, C. E., Keuthen, J. J., Stewart, S. I., & Pauls, D. L. (2009). A twin concordance study of trichotillomania. *American Journal of Medical Genetics*, 150, 944-949.

Pertusa, A., Frost, R.O., & Mataix-Cols, D. (2010). When hoarding is a symptom of OCD: A case series and implications for DSM-V. *Behaviour Research and Therapy, 48*(10), 1012-1020. 10.1016/j.brat.2010.07.003

Pertusa, A., Fullana, M.A., Singh, S., Alonso, P., Menchon, J.M., & Mataix-Cols, D. (2008). Compulsive hoarding: OCD symptom, distinct clinical syndrome, or both? *American Journal of Psychiatry.*

Powers, R. E., (2005) Medical assessment and management of skin-picking and scratching self-injurious behavior (SIB) in the person with mental retardation and developmental disabilities (MR/DD). DDMED8, Bureau of Geriatric Psychiatry.

Rapp, J.T., Miltenberger, R.G., Galensky, T.L., Ellingson, S.A., Stricker, J., Garlinghouse, M., & Long, E.S. (2000). Treatment of hair pulling and hair manipulation maintained by digital-tactile stimulation. *Behavior Therapy, 31*, 381-393.

Raush, S.L., Whalen, P.J., Curran, T., Shin, L.M., Coffey, B.J., Savage, C.R.,...Jenike, M.A. (2001). Probing striato-thalamic function in obsessive-compulsive disorder and Tourette syndrome using neuroimaging methods. *Advances in Neurology, 85*, 207-224.

Rojahn, J. (1986). Self-injurious and stereotypic behavior of noninstitutionalized mentally retarded people: Prevalence and classification. *American Journal of Mental Deficiency*, 91(3), 268-276.

Rojahn, J., Matson, J. L., Lott, D., Esbensen, A. J., & Smalls, Y. (2001). The Behavior Problems Inventory: An instrument for the assessment of self-injury, stereotyped behavior and aggression/destruction in individuals with developmental disabilities. *Journal of Autism and Developmental Disorders, 31*, 577-588.

Rojas-Corrales, M.O., Gibert-Rahola, J., & Mico, J.A. (2007). Role of atypical opiates in OCD. Experimental approach through the study of 5HT (2A/C) receptor-mediated behavior. *Psychopharmacology* (Berl). *190*(2), 221-231. Epub 2006 Nov 11.

Samuels, J., Bienvenu, O.J., Grados, M.A., Cullen, B., Riddle, M.A., Liang, K.Y., & Nestadt, G. (2008). Prevalence and correlates of hoarding behavior in a community-based sample. *Behaviour Research and Therapy, 46*(7), 836-844.

Samuels, J., Shugart, Y.Y., Grados, M.A., Willour, V.L., Bienvenu, O.J., Greenberg, B.D., ... Nestadt G (2007). Significant linkage to compulsive hoarding on chromosome 14 in families with obsessive-compulsive disorder: Results from the OCD Collaborative Genetics Study. *American Journal of Psychiatry, 164*, 493-9.

Saxena, S. (2008a). Neurobiology and treatment of compulsive hoarding. *CNS Spectrums, 13*, 29-36.

Saxena, S. (2008b). Recent advances in compulsive hoarding. *Current Psychiatry Reports, 10*, 297-303.

Saxena, S. (2011). Pharmacotherapy of compulsive hoarding. *Journal of Clinical Psychology, 67*, 477-84.

Saxena, S., & Maidment, K.M. (2004). Treatment of compulsive hoarding. *Journal of Clinical Psychology, 60*, 1143-1154.

Sevin, J. A., Matson, J., L., Williams, D., & Kirkpatrick-Sanchez, S. (1995). Reliability of emotional problems with the Diagnostic Assessment for the Severely Handicapped. *British Journal of Clinical Psychology*, 34, 93-94.

Sheppard, B., Shavira, D., Azzam, A., Grados, M.A., Umana, P., Garrido, H., & Mathews, C.A. (2010). ADHD prevalence and association with hoarding behaviors in childhood onset OCD. *Depression and Anxiety, 27*, 667-674.

Simonoff, E., Pickles, A., Charman, T., Chandler, S., Loucas, T., & Baird, G. (2008). Psychiatric disorders in children with autism spectrum disorders: Prevalence, comorbidity, and associated factors in a population-derived sample. *Journal of the American Academy of Child and Adolescent Psychiatry*, 47 (9), 921-929.

Singh, N. N. (1977). Prevalence of self-injury in institutionalized retarded children. *New Zealand Medical Journal*, 86, 325-327.

Steege, M.W., Wacker, D.P., Berg, W.K., Cigrand, K.K., & Cooper, L.J. (1989). The use of behavioral assessment to prescribe and evaluate treatments for severely handicapped children. *Journal of Applied Behavior Analysis, 22*, 23-33.

Steketee G & Frost R (2003). Compulsive hoarding: Current status of the research. *Clinical Psychology Review*, 23, 905-927.

Steketee, G., Frost, R.O., Tolin, D.F., Rasmussen, J., & Brown, T.A. (2010). Waitlist-controlled trial of cognitive behavior therapy for hoarding disorder. *Depression and Anxiety, 27*, 476-484.

Symons, F.J., Butler, M. G., Sanders, M. D., Feurer, I. D., & Thompson T. (1999). Self-injurious behavior and Prader-Willi Syndrome: Behavioral forms and body locations. *American Journal on Mental Retardation, 104*(3), 260-269.

Symons, F.J., Clark, R.D., Hatton, D.D., Skinner, M., & Bailey, B.D. (2003). Self-injurious behavior in young boys with fragile X syndrome. *American Journal of Medical Genetics Part A, 118*(2), 115-121.

Szymanski, L., & King, B.H. (1999). Practice parameters for the assessment and treatment of children, adolescents, and adults with mental retardation and comorbid mental disorders. *Journal of American Academy of Child and Adolescent Psychiatry, 38*(Suppl. 12), 5S-31S.

Testa, R., Pantelis, C., & Fontenelle, L.F. (2011). Hoarding behaviors in children with learning disabilities. *Journal of Child Neurology, 26*, 574-9.

Tolin, D.F., Kiehl, K.A., Worhunsky, P., Book, G.A., & Maltby, N. (2009). An exploratory study of the neural mechanisms of decision making in compulsive hoarding. *Psychological Medicine, 39*, 325-36.

Tolin, D.F., Stevens, M.C., Villavicencio, A.L., Norberg, M.M., Calhoun, V.D., Frost, R.O., … Pearlson, G.D. (2012). Neural mechanisms of decision making in hoarding disorder. *Archives of General Psychiatry, 69*, 832-41.

Tolin, D.F., Villavicencio, A., Umbach, A., & Kurtz, M.M. (2011). Neuropsychological functioning in hoarding disorder. *Psychiatry Research, 189*, 413-8.

Torres, A.R., Fontenelle, L.F., Ferrão, Y.A., do Rosário, M.C., Torresan, R.C., Miguel, E.C., & Shavitt, R.G. (2012). Clinical features of obsessive-compulsive disorder with hoarding symptoms: A multicenter study. *Journal of Psychiatry Research, 46*, 724-32.

Van Houton, R., & Rolider, A. (1988). Recreating the scene: An effective way to provide delayed punishment for inappropriate motor behavior. *Journal of Applied Behavior Analysis, 21*, 18-192.

Vitiello, B., Spreat, S., & Behar, D. (1989). Obsessive-compulsive disorder in mentally retarded patients. *Journal of Nervous and Mental Disorder, 177*, 232-236.

Volle, E., Beato, R., Levy, R., & Dubois, B. (2002). Forced collectionism after orbitofrontal damage. *Neurology, 58*(3), 488-490.

Welch, J. M., Lu, J., Rodriguiz, R. M., Trotta, N. C., Peca, J., Ding, J., Luo, J. (2007). Cortico-striatal synaptic defects and OCD-like behaviours in Sapap3-mutant mice. *Nature, 448*(7156), 894-900.

Wheaton, M., Timpano, K.R., Lasalle-Ricci, V.H. & Murphy, D. (2008). Characterizing the hoarding phenotype in individuals with OCD: Associations with comorbidity, severity and gender. *Journal of Anxiety Disorders, 22*, 243-252.

Wigren, M., & Hansen, S. (2003). Rituals and compulsivity in Prader-Willi syndrome: profile and stability. *Journal of Intellectual Disability Research*, 47(6), 428-438.

Zarcone, J., Napolitano, D., Peterson, C., Breidbord, J., Ferraioli, S. Caruso-Anderson, M., … Thompson, L. (2007). The relationship between compulsive behavior and academic achievement across the three genetic subtypes of Prader-Willi syndrome. *Journal of Intellectual Disability Research, 51*, 478-487.

Zuchner, S., Cuccaro, M. L., Tran-Viet, K. N., Cope, H., Krishnan, R. R., & Pericak-Vance, M. A. (2006). SLITRK1 mutations in trichotillomania. *Molecular Psychiatry*, 11, 887-889.

CHAPTER 15

Trauma- and Stressor-Related Disorders

Jane McCarthy
Roberto A. Blanco
Valerie L. Gaus
Nancy J. Razza
Daniel J. Tomasulo

Trauma- and stressor-related disorders include disorders in which exposure to a traumatic or stressful event is listed explicitly as a diagnostic criterion. This is a new chapter within DSM-5 and includes reactive attachment disorder, disinhibited social engagement disorder, posttraumatic stress disorder (PTSD), acute stress disorder, and adjustment disorders. Within *DM-ID* these disorders were described in separate chapters, but, in keeping with *DSM-5*, they are bought together to reflect the increased understanding in the variation of expressing psychological distress when an individual is exposed to a traumatic or stressful event. The inclusion of reactive attachment disorders and disinhibited social engagement disorder, which develop early in life due to lack or absence of adequate caregiving, shows a recognition in the importance of early experiences on the later development of an individual including those with intellectual disability (ID).

Reactive attachment disorder has been redefined to include the formerly inhibited subtype of reactive attachment disorder in the *DSM-IV*. Reactive attachment disorder diagnoses are often associated with numerous co-morbid diagnoses and developmental delays independent of other disabilities. Disinhibited social engagement disorder is a new diagnosis which is defined as the formerly disinhibited subtype of reactive attachment disorder in the *DSM-IV*. Just like reactive attachment disorder, disinhibited social engagement disorder diagnoses are often associated with numerous co-morbid diagnoses and developmental delays independent of other disabilities. The prevalence of both reactive attachment disorder and disinhibited social engagement disorder and the genetic, psychosocial, and developmental risks for development of these disorders in individuals with ID are just beginning to be elucidated.

The evidence throughout the chapter was evaluated using the following hierarchy:

Type I Evidence
Good systematic review and meta-analysis including at least one randomized controlled trial
Type II Evidence
Randomized controlled trial
Type III Evidence
Well-designed interventional studies
Type IV Evidence
Well-designed observational studies
Type V Evidence
Expert opinion, influential reports and studies

Reactive Attachment Disorder

General Description of the Disorder

Reactive attachment disorder is a disorder that stems from inadequate attachment in early life to a primary attachment figure and results in the inability to seek or respond to comfort from caregivers.

Individuals with reactive attachment disorder have a pattern of behavior that is emotionally withdrawn and does not express much positive affect. Reactive attachment disorder, as it is currently defined and conceptualized in the *DSM-5*, is similar to the inhibited subtype of Reactive Attachment Disorder from previous editions of the Diagnostic and Statistical Manual of Mental Disorders.

Reactive Attachment Disorder is a disorder characterized by the inability to seek or respond to comfort from caregivers due to a childhood history of insufficient care from early primary caregivers. In the *DSM-IV-TR*, reactive attachment disorder was subdivided into inhibited and disinhibited subtypes depending on whether the disordered attachment behavior was internalized or externalized. In the *DSM-5*, the subtypes no longer exist. The "inhibited" subtype of reactive attachment disorder is now simply "reactive attachment disorder." The "disinhibited" subtype of reactive attachment disorder is now "disinhibited social engagement disorder."

Reactive attachment disorder is the developmental consequence and social deficit that results from an inability to form a secure attachment with a primary caregiver. It is often diagnosed in very early childhood and most diagnoses should be made prior to school age. John Bowlby's twentieth century studies into the importance of mother-infant interactions revealed the importance of adequate early attachment in the global development of the child (Blacher, 1984). An attachment figure represents the home base from which all further learning and exploration of the world can take place. Humans are naturally social beings and attachment figures can either soothe or exacerbate distressed feelings depending on their quality and on the relational fit with the individual (Schuengel, Claisien de Schipper, Sterkenburg, & Kaf, 2013).

Ainsworth further delineated the stages of attachment through a process of differentiating people from things at 3 months to identifying preferred attachment figures for comfort and proximity at 6 to 8 months to full trust between child and caregiver by age four or five years (Blacher, 1984). If these stages of attachment are interrupted for whatever reason, disrupted attachment behavior will result. Ainsworth's research also resulted in an objective test of childhood attachment called "the strange situation." The strange situation delineated children's attachment responses in one of four categories: (1) secure attachment, (2) anxious-avoidant insecure attachment, (3) anxious-ambivalent/resistant insecure attachment, and (4) disorganized/disoriented attachment.

The main characteristics of reactive attachment disorder include social withdrawal resulting from poor caregiving and, therefore, poor attachment in early childhood. Children with reactive attachment disorder do not seek comforting nor do they respond to the normal techniques used with children to calm them when distressed. They are unable to respond positively to the normal social cues which demonstrate warmth and caring, presumably due to the lack of having had this in their past. Individuals with reactive attachment disorder are often found in settings of extreme insufficiencies of care commonly associated with nutritional deficits and lack of the basic physical necessities. However, the proximal cause of Reactive Attachment Disorder is a lack of an adequate primary attachment figure, such as a mother, which is necessary for early childhood emotional and cognitive development. Examples of possible causes include the primary attachment figure being inadequate, frequent changes in primary attachment figures due to their placement in foster system, multiple non-primary caregivers who the child does not attach to, or inadequate access for the child to a primary caregiver such as what occurs at understaffed orphanages or institutional settings. This is especially true if no consistent attachment figure is present prior to 2 years of age (Bos, Zeanah, Fox, Drury, & Nelson, 2011).

In the past, reactive attachment disorder was divided into subtypes, namely inhibited and disinhibited types. Reactive Attachment Disorder in its current form consists of mainly the inhibited subtype which is more often a result of victimization physically and/or sexually, rather than the neglect and deprivation which more commonly is related to disinhibited social engagement disorder. Limitations to the classification of Reactive Attachment Disorder and Disinhibited Social Engagement Disorder are that some individuals present with symptoms of both disorders (Raaska et al., 2011).

Summary of DSM-5 Criteria

The *DSM-5* criteria for Reactive Attachment Disorder include the following (American Psychiatric Association, 2013): Behavior exhibited by a child in which a child is inhibited and emotionally withdrawn toward adult caregivers. This may be manifested by rarely or minimally seeking comfort when distressed and rarely or minimally responding to comfort when distressed. In addition, children with Reactive Attachment Disorder often have minimal social and emotional responsiveness to others, limited positive affect, and episodes of unexplained irritability, sadness, or fearfulness that are evident even during nonthreatening interactions with adult caregivers.

The child also has experienced a pattern of extremes of insufficient care such as social neglect or deprivation in the form of persistent lack of having basic emotional needs met, repeated changes of primary caregivers that limit opportunities to form stable attachments (e.g. multiple placements in foster care), or rearing in unusual settings that severely limit opportunities to form selective attachments (e.g. large orphanage with high child-to-staff ratios) which is the cause of disturbed behavior. The symptoms are not due to autism spectrum disorder. The disturbance begins before age 5 and the child has a developmental age of at least 9 months.

Specifiers:

- Persistent – Present for longer than 12 months
- Severe – Child exhibits all symptoms at high levels

Issues Related to Diagnosis in Persons with ID

Despite the frequency of pathogenic care and risk for neglect or abuse in the ID community, it is difficult to diagnose individuals who have ID with reactive attachment disorder. This is due to a variety of reasons including congenital and genetic factors that influence an individual's ability to attach and the lack of research which is available pertaining to reactive attachment disorder and intellectual disability.

In addition, reactive attachment disorder is typically diagnosed in young children and fairly rare, even in populations of children that have been severely neglected or maltreated. The adaptive deficits related to intellectual disability can be a possible confounder in the diagnosis and make symptoms due to reactive attachment disorder more difficult to distinguish. In addition, due to slower rates of development and differing levels of language and cognition, it is often difficult to distinguish when an individual has reached the 9 month developmental threshold in order to diagnose reactive attachment disorder.

Recent studies have indicated that a more promising and reliable area of inquiry would be in the attachment-related behaviors and relationships rather than in looking at the diagnosis of reactive attachment disorder in individuals with intellectual disability (Schuengel et al., 2013).

Disordered attachment in individuals with intellectual disability is a result of multiple variables. The attachment relationship is a dynamic relationship based on the delicate give-and-take between mother and infant. Thus, reactive attachment disorder can be related to innate variables within the child such as adaptive and cognitive relative deficits and strengths, parental variables such as lack of attunement or psychopathology, parent-child relational issues such as failure to understand or misinterpreting non-verbal communication and limited availability for or quality of contact, and environmental stressors such as financial or parental conflict (Blacher, 1984). Individuals with communication or cognitive deficits may have a lower threshold for considering situations frightening and without solution. Research on individuals with Down syndrome showed similar attachment behaviors compared with typically developing children when reunited with a primary caregiver after separation. However, affective responding was delayed and not as robust as in typically-developing children and so was more likely to be missed by a caregiver (Schuengel et al., 2013). In addition, if not securely attached, individuals with Down syndrome were more likely to have disorganized attachment styles which are more often associated with pathology.

Deficits in social skills are shared with autism spectrum disorders or in individuals with primary sensory deficits. However, proximity to inadequate attachment figures as an etiology often distinguishes reactive attachment disorder from autism spectrum disorder. In addition, improvement in social skills and communication often takes place in Reactive Attachment Disorder after placement in an adequate, nurturing environment at an early age.

Since the typical interaction between caregiver and child can be disrupted or altered by intellectual disability, some caregivers will need to change their interactional style to compensate for deficits that may be present. Disabilities in hearing, sight, cognitive ability, or ability to understand or express language are common in individuals with intellectual disability and may necessitate a change in interactional style from the caregiver in order to nurture or comfort in ways that the child can understand (Blacher, 1984). In addition, caregivers may need guidance in attachment behaviors in individuals with ID which may be more subtle and less complex than the individuals who do not have ID (Blacher, 1984).

Research on the attachment behaviors in individuals with intellectual disability has shown that attachment behaviors happen in the same general sequence but that in individuals with ID, normal attachment developmental milestones may be delayed by months or years (Berry, Gunn, & Andrews, 1980; Cicchetti & Serafica, 1981). However, most individuals with Intellectual Disability will be securely attached to primary caregivers despite the increased risk of disordered attachment.

Because social neglect can be caused by or associated with risks for developmental delays, reactive attachment disorder frequently co-occurs with developmental delay. Another confounder is that mild forms of ID are not usually diagnosed until the school-age years, often after a diagnosis of Reactive Attachment Disorder. Severe or Profound forms of intellectual disability are more easily diagnosed at an early age. However, individuals with ID who do not have reactive attachment disorder will exhibit positive emotional responsiveness commensurate with developmental level, whereas, individuals with reactive attachment disorder will not. Individuals with autism and individuals with reactive attachment disorder can show stereotypies of movement likely related to the possible cognitive delays that can accompany both.

There are instruments to assess the attachment behaviors of individuals with intellectual disabilities. One such instrument is the Secure Base Safe Haven Observation List (SBSHO) to assess attachment behavior in young individuals with moderate to severe intellectual disability. The survey is rated by professional caregivers in group home settings and allows staff to screen individuals for difficulties in attachment behaviors with individual professional caregivers (Schuengel et al., 2013). In addition, the Manchester Attachment Scale (MAST) also assesses general attachment behaviors in adults with intellectual disability. The scale is also intended to be filled out by professional caregivers. While screens filled out by professional caregivers have shown good validity, parent-reported assessments of child attachment behavior have not. In addition, the reliability of attachment semi structured interviews with caregivers is well validated and can be used in individuals with mild to moderate intellectual disability as well. Another tool is the Relationship Problems Questionnaire which is an 18 item questionnaire used for parents and care givers or teachers and has been used to elucidate disordered attachment behaviors. Finally, a clinical observation of attachment has been developed for clinical practice which bears many similarities to the strange situation procedure. Using this tool may necessitate a change in procedure in individuals with intellectual disability (Schuengel et al., 2013).

Diagnostic evaluation of individuals should include a thorough history of attachment relationships, the development of attachment behaviors, and charting of early life experiences and care-giving environments for clues as to disrupted relationships neglect or evidence of abuse. In addition, individuals should undergo structured or semi structured observations of attachment in the clinical setting. Tools such as those outlined above may be useful in clarifying symptoms and in elucidating a primary diagnosis.

Development and Course

Reactive attachment disorder results from the inability to attach to a caregiver prior to 9 months of age due to multiple causes with resultant pathological withdrawal and negativity. The diagnosis is able to be made after this critical window of attachment from a developmental perspective. However, it is unclear if biology dictates a time-related window for primary attachment or if delayed developmental trajectories, such as those in ID, allow for recovery of attachment-related function with time. Due to possible delays in attention (including delays in joint attention), communication, and cognition, achieving the 9 month developmental age equivalent in individuals who have an intellectual disability can be delayed significantly. Because attachment signals can be misinterpreted or missed by the individual or attachment figure, this may be part of the higher relative rates in the ID community. It is noted that the rates of reactive attachment disorder often diminish as children age. This observation suggests some improvement in the numerous factors related to the security of attachments and functioning or other maturational factors. Individuals with intellectual disability are more likely to be exposed to pathogenic care environments from an earlier age. It is noted that rates of reactive attachment disorder are increased as related to amount of adversity experienced during childhood (Minnis, Fleming, & Cooper, 2010).

Risk factors for the development of reactive attachment disorder and subsequent difficulties are not created equal. Evidence from numerous studies has shown that caregiving in large institutional settings or orphanages may be the highest risk location for development of RAD and other developmental delays, especially in relation to cognitive development (Bos et al., 2011). In addition, while foster placement and subsequent adoption is preferred to the large institutional setting for development, the more foster placements a child undergoes, the higher risk for the development of reactive attachment disorder and other symptoms. In addition, the younger a child is at the time of adoption, the lower the likelihood of development of reactive attachment disorder symptoms and the more likely that reactive attachment disorder symptoms are to remit (Bos et al., 2011). In fact, 24 months of age may be a demarcation point which determines improved security attachments. This may relate to a critical time effect of brain maturation prior to 2 years of age. Preliminary evidence has shown that early entry into high-quality, stable foster care in lieu of institutionalization can have dramatic effects on rates of reactive attachment disorder and increase positive affect in individuals (Bos et al., 2011).

Prevalence

In individuals with borderline intellectual functioning or mild intellectual disability referred for psychiatric consultation, 42% exhibited symptoms of disordered attachment overall, 16% showed symptoms of reactive attachment disorder, and 11% showed symptoms of both reactive attachment disorder and disinhibited social engagement disorder (Giltaij, Sterkenburg, & Schuengel, 2013). Individuals in this study were aged 5 to 11 and had borderline or mild intellectual disability with IQs ranging between 50 and 85 and a mean IQ of 71.7 (Giltaij et al., 2013).

This data differs from previous studies on the DSM-IV diagnosis of reactive attachment disorder. In the studies, reactive attachment disorder had a 56% prevalence in the deprived institutional setting in Romania. In a sample of toddlers in foster care with a history of maltreatment, rates of DSM-IV reactive attachment disorder were 38%. In a group of toddlers and young children in foster care, rates of DSM-IV reactive attachment disorder were 18% (Giltaij et al., 2013).

In individuals with Down syndrome, 50% of children and parents are able to build secure attachment relationships which is lower than in children without disabilities (Van Ijzendoorn, Scheungel, & Bakermans-Kranenburg, 1999).

Differential Diagnosis

Autism spectrum disorders are frequently difficult to differentiate from reactive attachment disorder. This is because both disorders have as their main characteristics deficits in the social realm of behavior and functioning. In addition, these aberrant social behaviors are generalized for both disorders and not limited to social interactions with caregivers (Giltaij et al., 2013). Some notable differences between reactive attachment disorder and autism include individuals with reactive attachment disorder having a normal capacity for social reciprocity, the remission of social symptoms once placed in a nurturing environment in RAD, the lack of abnormal quality of communication in reactive attachment disorder, the reactivity of cognitive deficits in response to environmental changes, and the lack of repetitive behaviors with RAD. RAD and autism are distinct entities and instruments are available to assist clinicians in differentiating between the two. Examples of these instruments include the disturbance of attachment interview (DAI) and the AUTI-revised scale (AUTI-R) which measures autism symptoms (Giltaij et al., 2013).

In addition to autism, reactive attachment disorder can also be confused with PTSD or complex trauma. These diagnoses can often be comorbid given the common etiological factors involved in trauma related symptoms and attachment related symptoms. Other internalizing behaviors such as depression and anxiety can also be mistaken for reactive attachment disorder. In infants with reactive attachment disorder, care should be given to make sure that infants are not suffering from common medical illnesses early in life. Failure to thrive, otitis media and other infections, pain related symptoms, endocrine abnormalities, and GERD could all present with social withdrawal that may mimic RAD (Guedeney, Foucault, Bougen, Larroque, & Mentre, 2008).

Functional Consequences

Individuals with intellectual disability are in significant need of adequate attachment relationships for improved functional outcomes. Limitations in capabilities from developmental delay mean that attachment figures often play a larger role in increasing the adaptive capabilities of individuals with intellectual disability. There is significant data showing that non-ID individuals with reactive attachment disorder show delays in multiple areas of development and functioning. These include delays in learning (Raaska et al., 2011), communication, daily living skills, and socialization (Becker-Weidman, 2009), expressive and receptive language and coping skills (Oztop & Uslu, 2007), and other psychosocial difficulties (Guedeney et al., 2008). It is likely that these delays would be significantly exacerbated in individuals with reactive attachment disorder and intellectual disability due to the increased dependence on caregivers. In addition, attachment-related behaviors can be quite problematic in the context of professional caregiving in and out of group home settings due to differential attunement of caregiver and individual preferences. In some studies, attachment-related behaviors like crying or acting out when a preferred staff member leaves or following staff members has been the most problematic behavior noted (Schuengel et al., 2013).

In addition, due to multiple deficits in ADLs, individuals with intellectual disability are more likely to depend on caregivers for a long period of time. A diagnosis of reactive attachment disorder can thus limit functional capacity in terms of causing disordered behaviors in these relationships. Individuals with RAD may be more apt to misinterpret benign cues and lead to maladaptive behaviors or an increase in aggressive or destructive behaviors. In a study of attachment style and ID, individuals who were more insecurely attached, were also more likely to refuse medications (Larson Alim, & Tsakanikos, 2011)

Comorbidity

Comorbidity in RAD is the rule rather than the exception. The reasoning behind this is the multiple areas of functioning affected by attachment failure. Attachment is critical in learning, communication, socialization, affect regulation, and general living skills. Attachment-related difficulties can stunt development in a number of critical areas with diverse and long-lasting sequelae as a result.

In addition, individuals raised in settings with poorer attachment figures are more likely to be victims of sexual or physical abuse and may develop post-traumatic stress disorder, depression, and anxiety. In addition to the internalizing symptoms, individuals with reactive attachment disorder can also exhibit externalizing behaviors and diagnoses such as ADHD, disruptive behavior disorder, and conduct disorder. Early trauma, neglect, and poor attachment can lead to increased rates of substance abuse disorders, bipolar disorder, psychotic illnesses, and personality disorders as individuals develop and age (Becker-Weidman, 2009). Risk-taking behaviors may also put these individuals at increased risk for sexually-transmitted diseases. In contrast to the positive effects of placement in high quality foster care on reactive attachment disorder, placement out of an institution does not have as robust effects on comorbid psychiatric diagnoses, especially in relation to externalizing disorders (Bos et al., 2011). In females with internalizing symptoms, placement in foster care from institutions significantly decreased these symptoms. The effects on males with regard to internalizing symptoms were not as robust.

Disinhibited Social Engagement Disorder

General Description of the Disorder

Disinhibited social engagement disorder is similar to the previous disinhibited type of reactive attachment disorder from previous editions of the *Diagnostic and Statistical Manual*. Main features of disinhibited social engagement disorder include inappropriate and developmentally inappropriate sociability with adult strangers, which is the result of a disrupted attachment with a primary caregiver in early childhood.

Disinhibited social engagement disorder is a recently added diagnosis to DSM-5 which encompasses the Disinhibited form of reactive attachment disorder from previous editions of the *Diagnostic and Statistical Manual of Mental Disorders*. The disorder stems from disordered attachment patterns related to inadequate caregiving early in childhood. Due to this poor attachment, children with disinhibited social engagement disorder indiscriminately interact with unfamiliar adults in a way that is not developmentally appropriate. This is exhibited through inappropriate closeness with unfamiliar adults (i.e. sitting on their laps, walking away with them, or holding hands) in childhood in a way that is not developmentally or culturally appropriate. In addition, they often explore or move away from familiar adults at young ages without the "check-in" or glance back with them which is typical of adequately attached children. As children age, behaviors related to disinhibited social engagement disorder can develop and change. However, DSM criteria are aimed at young children and those with a developmental level of at least 9 months who have had inadequate caregiving and subsequent disinhibited social behaviors.

Summary of DSM-5 criteria

The *DSM-5* criteria for disinhibited social engagement disorder includes the following (American Psychiatric Association, 2013):

Behavior exhibited by a child in which a child actively engages with unfamiliar adults without developmentally appropriate reticence in approach. In addition, children show overly familiar or physical behavior with strangers or a willingness to go off with an unfamiliar adult which is not solely due to impulsivity. The child has experienced a pattern of extremes of insufficient care such as social neglect or deprivation in the form of persistent lack of having basic emotional needs met, repeated changes of primary caregivers that limit opportunities to form stable attachments (e.g. multiple placements in foster care), or rearing in unusual settings that severely limits opportunities to form selective attachments (e.g. large orphanage with high child-to-staff ratios) which is the cause of disturbed behavior. The child must be a developmental age of at least 9 months.

Specifiers:

- Persistent – Present for longer than 12 months
- Severe – Child exhibits all symptoms at high levels

Similar to reactive attachment disorder, disinhibited social engagement disorder develops in the context of a lack of a consistent, responsive caregiver in early life. Environmental factors that can lead to the development of disinhibited social engagement disorder include placement in an institutional setting at an early age, a history of foster care placement, and lack of adequate caregiving due to caregiver drug or alcohol abuse, caregiver mental health difficulties, or caregiver disruption (Follan et al., 2011).

In contrast to reactive attachment disorder, disinhibited social engagement disorder often persists throughout childhood and often is expressed differently at different developmental stages. The indiscriminate interaction with adults as a toddler progresses to attention-seeking, intrusiveness and acting-out behaviors during preschool. In the school age child, an individual with a history of disinhibited social engagement disorder will express inauthentic emotions and an inability to empathize with others. In adolescence, indiscriminate interactions with others can lead to superficial relationships with peers, significant risk-taking in order to be accepted, and conflicts with others. This behavior often places these individuals at increased risk for negative outcomes from predators at all ages.

Individuals with disinhibited social engagement disorder can only be diagnosed after they have reached a developmental age of 9 months. This is due to the need to have adequate time and opportunity for attachment and the cognitive faculties to exhibit attachment-related behaviors prior to assessing whether attachment-related behaviors are adequate or inadequate. Adequate attachment in infants can be observed between 4 and 6 months of age; however, stranger anxiety does not peak until between 7 to 8 months when infants have the cognitive and intellectual abilities to become more aware of their surroundings. Having adequate stranger anxiety is a critical component in the exclusion or diagnosis of disinhibited social engagement disorder.

There is strong evidence that indicates that individuals with institutional placement have an increased early care risk compared with children in foster care or raised in their family. In addition, the severity of disinhibited social behaviors has been associated with the length of time spent in institutional care and is inversely related to the innate characteristic of the level of inhibitory control (Bruce, Tarullo, & Gunnar, 2009).

In addition, where physical or sexual abuse can increase the risk of reactive attachment disorder, it is thought that neglect and emotional deprivation can lead to increased risk of DSED. Disruptive social behaviors may be adaptive in the setting of deprivation and neglect or frequent changes of caregivers as being able to quickly form relationships might result in a powerful caregiving figure favoring that child in relation to other children and therefore decrease the levels of physical and emotional deprivation (Chisholme, Carter, Ames, & Morrison, 1995). Other researchers have conjectured that disinhibited social behavior may be a way to control an otherwise unpredictable situation (Follan et al., 2011) or that, similar to ADHD, it results from delay in cortical development.

Issues Related to Diagnosis in Persons with ID

The risks inherent in individuals with disinhibited social engagement disorder are magnified in individuals with intellectual disability, as indiscriminate association with strangers is likely to put with ID at more risk for predation. Individuals with ID are more likely to be abused than the general population, and disinhibited social engagement disorder symptoms can only increase this risk. Given this, individuals with ID and disinhibited social engagement disorder will need closer supervision and protection from potentially abusive situations.

Because of the complexities of development and attachment behaviors and the limitations of adequate diagnostic tools in individuals with ID, there is very limited data regarding the validity of the diagnosis of disinhibited social engagement disorder. Most studies provide a descriptive and quantitative difference in attachment behaviors and relationships in individuals with ID.

In addition, because attachment-related behaviors are associated with levels of adaptive ability in individuals with ID, attachment behaviors in individuals with ID need to be considered in the context of judgement and cognitive faculties. Individuals with ID and poor judgement can also appear to have disinhibited social engagement disorder when they do not.

Development and Course

Individuals with disinhibited social engagement disorder, need to have a developmental age of 9 months in order to have adequate stranger anxiety to distinguish disinhibited behavior from normal behavior. This can cause challenges in diagnosing the illness in individuals with intellectual disability, as it can be difficult to assess when the achievement of a 9 month developmental age has occurred due to differing rates of development in cognitive, emotional, and attentional spheres.

The development of disinhibited social engagement disorder is complex and multifactorial. In individuals with ID, attenuated forms of attachment behaviors due to limited reciprocal interactions and signaling of needs can make attachments more difficult. In addition, grief and depression are significant factors in caregivers which should be taken into account as well.

As noted above, disinhibited social engagement disorder can change through development and persist into adulthood. Disinhibited social engagement disorder is also more resistant to change and therefore, is thought to develop before reactive attachment disorder and before 24 months of age.

Prevalence

In individuals with borderline intellectual functioning or mild intellectual disability referred for psychiatric consultation, 42% exhibited symptoms of disordered attachment overall, 37% showed symptoms of disinhibited social engagement disorder, and 11% showed symptoms of both reactive attachment disorder and disinhibited social engagement disorder (Giltiaj et al., 2013). Individuals in this study were aged 5 to 11 and had borderline or mild intellectual disability with IQs ranging between 50 and 85 and a mean IQ of 71.7 (Giltaij et al., 2013).

Differential Diagnosis

Due to the difficulty in differentiating between DSED and ADHD due to the overlap in individual's poor inhibitory control, studies have attempted to examine whether the two diagnoses are able to be discerned in an outpatient setting. In addition, a traumatic history can often worsen ADHD symptoms significantly. Symptoms that are shared by both diagnoses include inattention, impulsivity, and hyperactivity (Dahmen, Herpertz-Dahlmann, Konrad, 2012). Symptoms most likely to be able to discriminate disinhibited social engagement disorder from ADHD in typically developing children are "cuddliness with strangers" and "comfort seeking with strangers" (Dahmen et al., 2012; Follan et al., 2011). These, in addition to contextual clues, are keys to discriminating disinhibited social enagaement disorder from other externalizing and "acting out" behaviors.

In addition to attention deficit, hyperactivity disorder, disinhibited social engagement disorder can also be confused with post-traumatic stress disorder or complex trauma. These can often also be comorbid diagnoses given the common etiological factors involved in trauma-related symptoms and attachment-related symptoms. Other internalizing behaviors such as depression and anxiety can also be mistaken for disinhibited social engagement disorder. On the other hand, extroversion can also be confused with disinhibited social engagement disorder, but etiological factors of inadequate attachment are missing in extroversion. In addition, the pattern of non-adaptive behavior is not persistent or as severe in extroversion.

Functional Consequences

Individuals with intellectual disability are at high risk for traumatic incidents in general, and studies have shown high rates of sexual or physical trauma and predation which often go undiagnosed. DSED presumably raises the risk of traumatic predation due to the individual's willingness to go with strangers. Judgment which may be related to emotional and cognitive development can be impaired and work synergistically to increase the risk of and opportunity for sexual or physical abuse.

Comorbidity

Individuals with disinhibited social engagement disorder can often have accompanying developmental delays. This is due to the lack of developmental progress in multiple areas that goes along with physical neglect and deprivation, but also with the emotional attachment that is necessary for normal development. This may affect a child's language and ability to communicate, attention span and ability to focus, and other cognitive delays. Co-morbidity with a number of other conditions such as attention deficit/hyperactivity disorder, post-traumatic stress disorder, depression, and anxiety are also very common. Early trauma or neglect can also predispose to the development of more serious psychiatric illness such as bipolar disorder and schizophrenia. Poor impulse control can lead to increased risk for substance abuse later in life.

Posttraumatic Stress Disorder (PTSD)

General Description of the Disorder

PTSD is a chronic disorder which develops in response to traumatic exposure. It is considered to be cyclic and progressive, with symptoms that compromise functioning across biological, psychological, and social domains.

Summary of DSM-5 Criteria

Key to PTSD's revision in the DSM-5 is that it is no longer conceptualized as an anxiety disorder; it is now in a category called *Trauma-and Stressor-Related Disorders*. Further, DSM-IV had required the presence of a specific type of initial emotional reaction, -- such as intense fear, helplessness, or horror, -- in response to the traumatic stressor, but this initial reaction is no longer a criterion in DSM-5. Such initial reactions have not been found to predict the development of core PTSD symptoms (Wakefield, 2013). Another important change in DSM-5 is that the core symptoms have been expanded from three to four categories: re-experiencing; avoidance; persistent negative alterations in mood and cognition; and arousal.

For children age 6 and younger, the A criterion, i.e., the criterion regarding traumatic exposure, includes three options: In addition to directly experiencing the trauma or observing the trauma, the criterion can also be met by the child's learning that a parent or caregiver has experienced trauma. For children age 6 and younger, the criterion concerning intrusive memories might also be met by the child's displaying repetitive play patterns reflective of the trauma; these may *or may not* be associated with expressions of distress. Trauma-specific reenactments may occur during play. Also, the child may experience recurrent distressing dreams, the content of which may not appear to resemble the traumatic event.

It has been reported that the DSM-5 task force put considerable effort into clarifying the nature of traumatic stressors to cement the distinction between PTSD and more general emotional reactions to negative events (Wakefield, 2013). Specifying what constitutes a traumatic stressor so extreme that it is likely to cause pathological reactions in any exposed individual has been controversial ever since the diagnosis of PTSD was introduced (Smith, 2011). The original point of creating the diagnosis of PTSD was to acknowledge the idea that some experiences are beyond the coping capacity of normal psychological processes. However, while there are undeniable limits to the human capacity for stress tolerance, the development of symptoms of PTSD seems to be far more strongly related to preexisting individual variables than originally thought (Breslau, Troost, Bohnert, & Luo, 2013; McNally, 2009). These predisposing variables have been demonstrated to include such factors as prior trauma exposure; parental psychopathology and/or addictions; female gender; and, importantly for our work, intellectual functioning/IQ (Breslau, Troost, et al., 2012; Breslau, Chen, & Luo, 2013; Koenen et al., 2009).

Issues Related to Diagnosis in Persons with ID

With respect to diagnosis, research supports three important points: 1) that people with ID seem to be more vulnerable to the development of PTSD than members of the general population; 2) that people with ID are more often exposed to conditions known to contribute to the development of PTSD, such as interpersonal abuse and violence; and 3) that for people with only mild ID, the presentation of PTSD is similar to that seen in members of the general population, while for people with more severe ID, the presentation may be complicated by differing symptoms. The research related to these findings is detailed in the next section.

Acute Stress Disorder

General Description of the Disorder

Acute stress disorder is characterized by symptoms similar to those of posttraumatic stress disorder that occurs immediately following exposure to one or more traumatic events. The symptoms last from 3 days to 1 month and include intrusion symptoms, negative mood, dissociative symptoms, and avoidance and arousal symptoms. The clinical presentation typically involves an anxiety response that includes some form of re-experiencing or reactivity to a traumatic event.

Summary of DSM-5 criteria

For a diagnosis within DSM-5 the individual must have exposure to actual or threatened death, serious injury, or sexual violation either through direct experience of traumatic event, being a witness in person, learning that the event(s) occurred to a close family member or close friend, or experiencing repeated or extreme exposure to aversive details. The individual must experience intrusion symptoms such as distressing memories, dissociative reactions (e.g. flashbacks), and intense or prolonged psychological distress. Persistent negative mood and dissociative symptoms such as inability to remember an important aspect of the traumatic event can be presenting symptoms for the diagnostic criteria of negative alterations in cognitions and mood. Avoidance symptoms such as efforts to avoid distressing memories and arousal symptoms such as sleep disturbance, irritability, hyper vigilance and an exaggerated startle response are symptoms that can begin or worsen after the traumatic event.

These symptoms of post-traumatic stress disorder can cause clinical significant distress or impairment in functioning but should not be attributable to substance misuse or another medical condition such as mild traumatic brain injury.

Issues Related to Diagnosis in Persons with ID

There is no literature describing the presentation of acute stressor disorders in people with intellectual disability, while there is no evidence to say presentation is significantly different, one may observe a more behavioral presentation with evidence of distress and decline in functioning.

Development and Course

Acute stress disorder cannot be diagnosed until 3 days after a traumatic event. About half of individuals who develop PTSD initially present with acute stressor disorder but there is no evidence to say this is any different for people with ID.

Prevalence

Acute stress disorder is identified in 20% of cases following traumatic events, but higher rates of 20% to 50% are reported following interpersonal traumatic events including assault, rape, and witnessing a mass shooting. There is no literature of prevalence in persons with intellectual disability.

Differential Diagnosis

An adjustment disorder would be considered if the response to Criterion A event does not meet the criteria of an acute stress disorder or when the symptom pattern of acute stress disorder occurs in response to a stressor that does not meet Criterion A. An acute stressor disorder is distinguished from PTSD if symptoms persist for more than a month and meet the criteria for PTSD. Traumatic brain injury may overlap with neurocognitive symptoms but symptoms of acute stressor disorder persist for only one month

Functional Consequences

Impaired functioning in social, interpersonal, or occupational domains is recognized and occurs in people with ID in relation to the experiencing of a traumatic event (Wigham, Hatton & Taylor, 2011).

Comorbidity

Due to short course, no comorbidity is reported but there is recognition that panic attacks, anxiety, and depressive symptoms may be observed in those presenting with an acute stressor disorder.

Adjustment Disorders

General Description of the Disorder

Adjustment Disorders involve the development of clinically significant emotional or behavioral symptoms in response to an identifiable psychosocial stressor or stressors. The stressor may be a single event or multiple events or circumstances and may be recurrent or continuous. This definition incorporates an extremely valuable diagnostic concept, suggesting that environmental stressors, so common in the lives of persons with ID, might be a critical source of psychopathology, which could otherwise be mistaken for other behavioral or mental health disorders. So simply put in the DSM-5, "When bad things happen, most people get upset….the diagnosis should only be made when the magnitude of the distress…exceeds what would normally be expected…" (American Psychiatric Association, 2013, p. 289). Also noted in *DSM-5* is the fact that what is normally expected may vary in different cultures, so clinicians serving people with ID must take into consideration that the world of a person with ID is a culture (e.g., residential setting) within a broader culture (geographic region, ethnic community etc.).

Summary of DSM-5 Criteria

Adjustment disorders as a group are emotional or behavioral responses to identifiable environmental stressors, developing within three months of the onset of the stressor, consisting either of marked distress that is out of proportion to the severity or intensity of the stressor in excess of what would be expected, given the nature of the stressor, or of significant impairment of functioning, not meeting the criteria for another specific disorder, not merely an exacerbation of a preexisting disorder, and not part of normal bereavement. Adjustment disorder can be diagnosed in the presence of another disorder if the latter does not account for the pattern of symptoms occurring in response to the stressor. An adjustment disorder must resolve within six months of the termination of the stressor (or its consequences), but symptoms might persist for longer than six months if they occur in response to a chronic stressor or to a stressor that has enduring consequences. A subtype must be specified, and they are defined by the predominating symptoms as follows:

- **Adjustment disorder with depressed mood**, characterized by low mood, tearfulness, or feelings of hopelessness
- **Adjustment disorder with anxiety**, characterized by nervousness, worry, jitteriness, or separation anxiety
- **Adjustment disorder with mixed anxiety and depressed mood**, characterized by a combination of anxiety and depressed mood as defined above
- **Adjustment disorder with disturbances of conduct**, characterized by disturbance of conduct, such as truancy, vandalism, reckless driving, fighting, defaulting on legal responsibilities, etc.
- **Adjustment disorder with mixed disturbances of emotions and conduct**, characterized by both emotional symptoms (depressed mood, anxiety) and disturbance of conduct
- **Adjustment disorder, unspecified**, characterized by maladaptive reactions that are not classifiable as one of the specific subtypes of adjustment disorder

Issues Related to Diagnosis in Persons with ID

The clinician should modify existing diagnostic criteria for application individuals with ID, especially for application to individuals with severe or profound ID. To use this diagnostic category accurately and with benefit to the patient, the clinician should be very familiar with the subculture of ID (Aman, 1991). The important clinical features of adjustment disorder are delineated in the preceding sections and in the *DSM-5*. The flexibility of cultural context noted in the foregoing section enables the clinician to consider the diagnosis in relation to the stressors typical of the lives of people with ID.

Development and Course

Several *DSM-5* clinical criteria present challenges when the clinician attempts to diagnose adjustment disorder in a patient with ID. First, symptoms must develop "within 3 months of the onset of the stressor." Therefore, the stressor must be identifiable; in the case of a patient with ID, there must be a reliable source for history. It is important to be aware of the expected sources of stress in the lives of people with ID, and of the significance to a person with ID of "stressors" (for example, the change of vocational supervisor) that would be considered innocuous in the lives of persons without ID (Levitas & Gilson, 2001). In general, a stressor can be anything in the life of a person with ID that is beyond the person's power to resolve alone (Levitas & Gilson, 2001). The clinician must, therefore, be aware of the details of changes in the life of the patient.

Prevalence

Raitasuo, Talminien, and Salokangas (1999) concluded that Adjustment Disorder was probably under diagnosed in individuals with ID, but their observations were regarded as equivocal, requiring further research to assess the effects of stressors. The patient database of the Division of Prevention and Treatment of Developmental Disorders, Department of Psychiatry, UMDNJ/SOM, yielded 64 patients with a diagnosis of an Adjustment Disorder in the first 2,144 patients—a rate of 3% (Levitas, 2002). A study of outpatients that compared rates of adjustment disorder in those with normal intelligence to those with Mild ID to those whose ID ranged from moderate to profound yielded the respective rates of 2% (normal intelligence), 1% (mild ID), and 2%t (moderate to profound ID) (Hurley, Folstein, & Lam, 2003). Nehama, Dakar, Stawski & Szor (2006) found especially high rates of adjustment disorder in a sample of people with mild to moderate ID in a vocational rehabilitation center; 24% had adjustment disorder as a primary diagnosis.

Differential Diagnosis

The diagnosis should not be used if the disturbance meets the criteria for another specific disorder (for example, a specific anxiety or mood disorder) or is "merely an exacerbation of a preexisting mental disorder." A person's limited life routines or limited behavioral repertoire can make it difficult to distinguish an episode of adjustment disorder from the exacerbation of a preexisting disorder. This is particularly true for people with Severe or Profound ID. A limited behavioral repertoire might lead one to assume that an exacerbation of symptoms of these developmental disorders does not merit a diagnosis of an adjustment disorder, despite a clear relation to a stressor. On the contrary, an exacerbation of symptoms that represents the individual's typical responses to stress can be a sign of an adjustment disorder as long as the pattern of behavior is a change from baseline levels of functioning and results in impairment of the individual's usual functioning level.

The diagnosis of an adjustment disorder does not apply when the symptoms represent bereavement. Bereavement is a normal process, but one for which many people with ID might have little or no preparation. The death of a family member or a caregiver might be not only a symbolic loss, but also the loss of a person active in the care of and advocacy for the patient (Levitas & Gilson, 2001). It is, therefore, difficult to define what would constitute normal grief expression in a person with ID. It might be prudent to consider that the loss of favored staff, housemates, and friends are losses that cause significant grief to people with ID. Conventional responses to loss might be undetectable in a person with autistic spectrum disorder—except as, for example, catastrophic reactions to the cessation of routine or of scheduled parental visits. When a grief reaction is judged to be severe and persistent, then the diagnosis of "other specified trauma-and-stressor-related disorder" is made, with the "persistent complex bereavement disorder" specification.

Functional Consequences

The clinical significance of the reaction is indicated either by "marked distress that is out of proportion to the severity or intensity of the stressor" considering the context and cultural factors that may influence an individual's reaction to that stressor or by causing "significant impairment in social, occupational or other important areas of functioning." It is important to be aware of signs of distress in a patient with ID and, on the basis of cognitive or adaptive testing, of the patient's actual (as opposed to presumed) level of function. Recognition of the patient's depressed mood and anxiety, as expressed in changes in his or her autonomy and interpersonal relations, is crucial to recognition of the subtypes of adjustment disorder.

Comorbidity

An adjustment disorder can be diagnosed in the presence of another disorder if the latter does not account for the pattern of symptoms that have occurred in response to the stressor. This criterion presumes either accurate earlier diagnosis or a source of history that makes possible a diagnosis of conditions that existed before the onset of the adjustment disorder (e.g., co-morbid with autism, ID, anxiety disorder, etc.).

Reactive Attachment Disorder

General Considerations

Because of the complexities of development and attachment behaviors and the limitations of adequate diagnostic tools for individuals with ID, there is very limited data regarding the validity of the diagnosis of reactive attachment disorder. Most studies provide a descriptive and quantitative difference in attachment behaviors and relationships in individuals with ID.

In addition, because attachment-related behaviors are associated with levels of adaptive ability in individuals with ID, attachment behaviors in individuals with ID need to be considered in the context of social situation (Schuengel et al., 2013). The interplay between the adequacy of placement in relation to adaptive needs and caregiving and peer-related interactions should be taken into account. Social environments should be stable, low discord environments, that are patient-centered with a focus on stimulation, relationship-building, and positive support.

Most individuals with ID are securely attached with their primary caregivers, even though they may display atypical attachment behaviors. Reactive Attachment Disorder can only be diagnosed once individuals reach a development level of 7-9 months, regardless of age (American Psychiatric Association, 2013). This is the earliest that normal attachment behaviors can be observed. In individuals with ID, this can often be difficult to determine.

Parental or caregiving education on attachment behaviors through increased sensitization to attachment behaviors can often improve outcomes. Individuals with more severe forms of ID rely heavily on caregivers, so caregiver psychopathology is likely to be more problematic and lead to lower adaptive and developmental goals achieved.

There is no longitudinal data following reactive attachment disorder in its current form into adolescence or adulthood, but numerous studies have shown some remission of symptoms over time, especially with early placement into improved care settings such as out of institutions and into more permanent placements with stable and identifiable attachment figures.

Methodology

A literature search was performed which focused on normal attachment, attachment disorders including RAD, ID and variations of the nomenclature along with learning disability. PUBMED and MEDLINE were the primary resources used.

Review Research Applying to People with ID

In the FINADO study which explored symptoms of reactive attachment disorder and learning difficulties in internationally adopted children in Finland, reactive attachment disorder symptoms at the time of adoption were associated with learning difficulties at school, age 8, years later (Raaska et al., 2011). In addition, it was found that the younger the age at adoption the lower the risk of learning difficulties. Also, greater than one placement before adoption led to higher risk of learning difficulties. Reactive attachment disorder symptoms were also associated with higher levels of disability, higher numbers and types of placements before adoption, and older age and arrival from an international orphanage. Overall, 33% of international adoptees had some learning difficulties which is three times the average rate in non-institutionalized, non-adopted individuals. In addition, 12.7% of the international adoptees had severe learning difficulties which is six times the rate of in non-adopted individuals. Overall reactive attachment disorder symptoms increase the risk of learning difficulties, with an odds ratio of 4:6 and increase the risk of severe learning difficulties with an odds ratio of 7:4 even after adjustment for other risk factors.

In a study of 57 children who were adopted or in the foster care system with diagnoses of reactive attachment disorder and complex trauma, developmental delay was found in all domains and subdomains of communication, daily living skills, and socialization as evaluated through the Vineland-II (Becker-Weidman, 2009). In addition, while the chronological age of study subjects was 9.9 years, the developmental age for these subjects was 4.4 years. Overall, older children showed more disturbed socialization and adaptive behavioral functioning than younger children. Children with reactive attachment disorder and complex trauma showed more impairment than the emotional/behavioral disturbance sample in the Vineland-II manual. The study has implications for treatment, as increasing age in this population increases the severity of disturbances in socialization and adaptive functioning. In addition, delays in receptive and expressive language need to be kept in mind when considering treatment regimens (Becker-Weidman, 2009).

One possible mechanism in the myriad effects of disorganized attachment may be through the effect of maltreatment and neglect on joint attention. Early in development, joint attention allows us to imitate, learn the context of different objects, and give meanings to our surroundings. Without this, language development, social competence, cognitive development, and curiosity can be stunted or delayed. In a study examining attachment and joint attention in a population at high risk for developmental delay, infants with disorganized attachment initiated joint attention with the experimenter significantly less than secure or other insecure toddlers (Claussen, Mundy, Mallik, & Willoughby, 2002). This study examined 56 high-risk infants prenatally exposed to cocaine. 52% of these infants lived with their mothers who were receiving or had received substance abuse treatment, 36% lived with relatives, and 12% lived with foster or adoptive mothers. Infants with disorganized attachment were less likely to engage in face-to-face attention with caregivers and less likely to engage in coordinated joint attention. This pattern of behavior was generalized not only to the caregiver-infant relationship but also to the infant-tester relationship. Infants in this study responded fairly well to contextual clues; however, they did not initiate joint attention as would be expected. While deficits in joint attention can also be seen in autism spectrum disorders, individuals with Autism would not be able to identify the contextual social clues in order to initiate joint attention (Claussen et al., 2002).

In a cross-sectional study of 640 children attending a child health screening center in France, withdrawal behavior in infants between 14 and 18 months old was associated with parent-reported psychological difficulties ($p<0.0001$) and developmental delay ($p<0.0001$). Withdrawal behavior was also associated with being a boy ($p<0.01$), living in high-risk conditions for disturbed attachment such as in a joint custody situation or with a foster family ($p<0.08$), being adopted ($p<0.0005$), or being a twin ($p<0.01$). In addition, withdrawn infants were more likely to be cared for at home. Disordered withdrawal behavior was not associated with SES, ethnic origin, birth rank, or with the number of days spent in the hospital after birth (Guedeney et al., 2008).

In 15 infant-mother dyads with depressed mothers, there were significant delays in expressive (p<0.03), receptive (p<0.05), and overall communication (p<0.03) when compared to non-depressed infant-mother dyads. In addition, there were significant delays in the infants of depressed mothers in coping skills as measured by the Vineland (p<0.03), total scales of development (p<0.05), and increased levels of psychosocial stressor severity (p<0.01). Infants of depressed mothers were more likely to have relationship disorders (p<0.01) and problematic attachment behaviors (Oztop & Uslu, 2007).

The Bucharest early intervention project is the first randomized, controlled trial of foster care as an intervention for institutionalized children. As previously outlined, institutionalization puts children at the highest risk for attachment related difficulties and developmental delays. This is likely due to relative social isolation, low creativity from regimentation, high child-to-caregiver ratios, low psychosocial investment by caregivers, and low levels of stimulation for children (Bos et al., 2011). Previous studies have shown that institutional placement leads to lower levels of emotional regulation, lower levels of attention, higher levels of hyperactivity, high levels of anxiety, and an increased rate of attachment disorders.

This study randomized 136 children to usual care which consisted of continued institutional placement versus foster placement. The average age of foster care placement was 22 months. Baseline attachment, attachment disorder, and emotional reactivity were assessed with follow-ups at 30, 42, and 54 months of age. At baseline, 19% of institutionalized children were securely attached versus a control group that had never been institutionalized at 74% secure attachment. High levels of reactive attachment disorder were found in the institutionalized group. At 42 months of age, 49% of children in foster care had developed secure attachments, and there were significant decreases in the rates of reactive attachment disorder at 30, 42, and 54 months. This is in contrast to the institutionalized group where 18% of children at 42 months had secure attachments. Foster parents were recruited and screened prior to placement and received significant training, monitoring, and support. This is not typical of all foster programs, and because of this results may not be reproducible in other countries or settings. However, it does offer the possibility that reactive attachment disorder symptoms can be improved with time and placement in settings with adequate, stable attachment figures. In individuals whose RAD symptoms don't improve or worsen, impairments in other domains develop over time and can be associated with both internalization and externalization.

As above, differentiating reactive attachment disorder from autism spectrum disorder can be quite challenging in the clinical setting. However, in a study of 102 children aged 5 to 11 with borderline or mild intellectual disability, reactive attachment disorder and autism were able to be clearly delineated using screening instruments (Giltaij et al., 2013).

Evaluating Level of Evidence

The research reviewed has been evaluated according to criteria specified in the Cochrane Library as described earlier in the chapter. There was no Type I and Type II evidence around people with ID. A majority of the research reviewed for this section consists of type IV to V evidence.

Adults with Mild to Moderate Intellectual Disability

No studies were found relating to adults with mild to moderate ID.

Adults with Severe or Profound Intellectual Disability

In a review of 50 adults with ID with reactive attachment disorder and disinhibited social engagement disorder, it was found that symptoms of disordered attachment were associated with early childhood adversity and inversely related to age. As such, the more childhood adversity an individual faced, the more symptoms of disordered attachment were described. Similar to individuals who do not have ID, these symptoms diminished with age. This age-related effect may be related to brain maturational changes which diminish the effect of lack of nurturing early in development similar to the way that trauma-related symptoms can diminish with time or an altered or blunted response to stress hormones. The majority of this sample consisted of individuals with severe or profound intellectual disability individuals (Minnis et al., 2010). In this study, researchers were able to identify reactive attachment symptoms in the intellectually disabled population using the Relationship Problems Questionnaire (Minnis et al., 2010)

In general, training group home caregivers in responsiveness and harmonious interactions decreased conflictual interactions (Schuengel et al., 2013).

Children and Adolescents with Intellectual Disability

It has been shown that rates of reactive attachment disorder are higher in children with borderline to mild intellectual disability than in children who do not have ID. This risk is independent of other modifying factors (Giltaij et al., 2013). One possible explanation for this is that cognitive and development delays can be additive and form a positive feedback loop whereas poor cognitive function limits early joint attention which can further limit typical development and adaptive skills and so forth (Claussen et al., 2002). In addition, this process can delay the development of certain skills within critical development periods along with delaying critical milestones in sensory and cognitive processes. These skills that are slow to develop can limit attachment-related behaviors prior to age 2 and onward (Bos et al., 2011).

Because attachment is interactional in nature and attachment-related behaviors are often more subtle in children and adolescents with ID, parent or attachment-figure training on identifying and responding to often-missed attachment-related behaviors in infants and children who have ID can likely improve outcomes and prevent some reactive attachment disorder symptoms prior to their development.

Limitations in Applying DSM-5 Criteria to People with ID

Adults and children with intellectual disability can show signs and symptoms of disordered attachment or reactive attachment disorder even with a secure attachment pattern (Minnis et al., 2010). This is due to the complexities of social behavior in individuals with ID. Therefore, behaviors alone should not be used to diagnose reactive attachment disorder in individuals with ID. There must also have been evidence for neglect, maltreatment, multiple changes of primary providers, or inadequate primary providers in the patient's early years. In addition, the majority of individuals who do not have ID do not go on to develop reactive attachment disorder. The same is also likely true for individuals with ID, although the exact interplay of inadequate caretaking and cognitive and adaptive variables in intellectual disability has not been elucidated. This likely relates to the variable relative strengths and weaknesses in this population.

In addition, independent of the phenotype of attachment-related pathology, attachment may develop differently in parent-infant dyads with children with severe ID as synchrony and attunement can often be disturbed. This can affect attachment-related developmental milestones early on and then affect attachment-related milestones downstream of this.

A possible confounder in the diagnosis of reactive attachment disorder in individuals with ID is autism spectrum disorder. While autistic spectrum disorder and reactive attachment disorder do not co-exist on strict DSM criteria, there can be similarities in the ability for individuals with autism and reactive attachment disorder to create social relationships. In addition to deficits in social reciprocity, young children with both conditions can have impairments in cognition, ability to communicate and use language, and dampened emotional responsiveness to what would typically lead to positive emotions (American Psychiatric Association, 2013). However, the presence or absence of neglect in early childhood and repetitive or restricted interests or behaviors are often used to distinguish the two disorders, especially in individuals with ID.

Disinhibited Social Engagement Disorder

General Considerations

Individuals with no signs of insecure attachment can also present with disinhibited social engagement disorder and disinhibited social behaviors. In addition, the majority of individuals who have been severely neglected do not go on to develop disinhibited social engagement disorder. Even in high-risk populations who've suffered severe neglect, rates are reported to be approximately 20% of individuals (American Psychiatric Association, 2013). There is evidence for disinhibited social engagement disorder's persistence in childhood and adolescence (Minnis et al., 2010).

Methodology

A literature search was performed which focused on normal attachment, attachment disorders including disinhibited social engagement disorder, ID and variations of the nomenclature along with LD. Reactive attachment disorder was included due to disinhibited social engagement disorder's history of being RAD, disinhibited type. PUBMED, MEDLINE, and Google Scholar were the primary resources used. In addition, references in included papers were also searched for inclusion.

Review of Research Applying to People with ID

Because most studies have not delineated populations according to the new diagnosis of disinhibited social engagement disorder vs. reactive attachment disorder, definite conclusions regarding this diagnosis are difficult to make compared with reactive attachment disorder. There were fewer studies related to DSED given its relative newness as a distinct diagnosis and the fact that most studies with the *DSM-IV* reactive attachment disorder diagnosis did not separate inhibited from disinhibited subtypes of reactive attachment disorder.

However, in the recent Bucharest early intervention project, disinhibited subtypes of reactive attachment disorder were delineated. Details of this study are outlined in the section on Reactive Attachment Disorder. Results from the foster placement on disinhibited social engagement disorder were significantly less dramatic than on RAD. Decreased disinhibited social engagement symptoms were not as robust and noted at 42 months instead of 30 months as with individuals with RAD (Bos et al., 2011). This is consistent with other studies which have outlined similar persistence of symptoms into childhood and adolescence.

In addition, Rutter and colleagues (2009) found an association between disinhibited attachment styles and mild cognitive delay in a sample of adoptees from Romania.

Evaluating Level of Evidence

The research reviewed has been evaluated according to criteria specified in the Cochrane Library as described earlier in the chapter. There was no Type I and Type II evidence around people with ID. A majority of the research reviewed for this section consists of type IV to V evidence.

Adults with Mild to Moderate Intellectual Disability

No studies were found relating to adults with mild to moderate ID.

Adults with Severe or Profound Intellectual Disability

In a review of 50 individuals who have ID with reactive attachment disorder and disinhibited social engagement disorder, it was found that symptoms of disordered attachment were associated with early childhood adversity and inversely related to age. As such, the more childhood adversity an individual faced, the more symptoms of disordered attachment were described. Similar to individuals who do not have ID, these symptoms diminished with age. The majority of this sample consisted of individuals with severe or profound intellectually disabilitys (Minnis et al., 2010). In this study, researchers were able to identify reactive attachment symptoms in individuals with intellectual disability using the Relationship Problems Questionnaire

Children and Adolescents with Intellectual Disability

Post-institutionalized children are more likely than domestic adoptions to have disinhibited social behavior. This is likely due to the negative consequences of institutionalization. In children and adolescents, disinhibited social engagement disorder is felt to be closely related to ADHD and its biology and development.

Studies have shown that Disinhibited Social Engagement Disorder is associated with decreased inhibitory control abilities of children. Disinhibited social behaviors have not been related to cognitive ability on a consistent basis (Bruce et al., 2009).

Limitations in Applying DSM-5 Criteria to People with ID

Indiscriminately going with strangers can be a sign of poor judgment associated with developmental delays and is not necessarily a sign of disinhibited social engagement disorder. In order to make a diagnosis of disinhibited social engagement disorder in an individual with ID, the individual must have a history of neglect or disordered or disrupted attachment. Due to cognitive and social deficits independent of attachment in individual with ID, assessment of danger and typical social engagement may not be similarly present despite a history of adequate attachment with a primary caregiver.

Posttraumatic Stress Disorder

General Considerations

For adults with only mild intellectual disabilities, symptom presentation tends to be similar to that seen in people without ID. Individuals who are able to self-report can and should be interviewed by the clinician to assess as fully as possible the individual's subjective experience of his or her symptoms. Similarly, the interview can be used to help clarify the patient's perception of the traumatic event or events.

It is often useful to have a caregiver participate in part of the initial interview. Be sure to see the patient alone, however, for at least a portion of the time. Caregivers can be of particular value with patients who have more severe ID. It is good practice, however, to get the patient's perspective on the traumatic events as well as the caregiver's. Bear in mind that events not commonly viewed as traumatic, such as a move to a new residence or a bus accident, can lead to post traumatic symptoms in some individuals. It is important to ask the patient how he or she felt about the events he/she is describing, and to search for behavioral changes such as aggression, self-injury, or withdrawn/isolative behavior. In some cases, caregivers have reported "noncompliance" as a problem, noting that the patient refused to go to program or on trips. In at least some of those cases, the noncompliant behavior was determined to be an effort to avoid stimuli associated with traumatic events.

In some adults with more severe ID, trauma-specific reenactments may be displayed in much the same way as seen in traumatized children. In general, the lower the developmental level, the greater the likelihood of behavioral rather than verbal expressions of distress. When an adult with ID acts out traumatic experience behaviorally, it can look quite bizarre and be quite distressing or even threatening to those who observe it. It can take considerable assessment time and observations to distinguish psychotic symptoms from trauma-specific reenactments.

Up until 2014, there has been no standardized measure for assessing PTSD in people with ID. However, Hall, Jobson, and Langdon (2014) recently revised the Impact of Event Scale for use with people with ID, creating the Impact of Event Scale-Intellectual Disabilities (IES-IDs). Preliminary research suggests that the IES-IDs has good psychometric properties, but further study is needed to examine factor structure.

Methodology

The literature reviewed in this section was identified via computer searches of PsychINFO, PubMed/Medline, and Google Scholar. We employed variations on search terms for ID as well as for PTSD, along with: *trauma, abuse, diagnosis, dual diagnosis, psychopathology, and IQ.*

Review Research Applying to People with ID

In a 2013 study, Wieland, Wardenaar, Dautovic, & Zitman compared 45 patients with ID and PTSD with 45 patients who do not have ID with PTSD matched for age and gender. The authors reported that they found small differences on three subscales of the BSI: obsession-compulsion, psychoticism, and depression. They concluded, however, that the presentation of PTSD in people with ID compared to those who do not have ID was non-significant. Note that the patients with ID in this sample had only mild ID or borderline intellectual functioning.

In 2010, Mevissen and de Jongh published a review of the literature on prevalence, assessment, and treatment of PTSD in people with ID. The authors identified and reviewed 18 articles. They concluded that there is support for the idea that lower developmental and cognitive-developmental level increases the risk of developing PTSD and increases the risk of more severe symptomatology. They also concluded that empirically validated tools for assessment of PTSD in people with ID are still lacking, that prevalence rates vary dramatically across the few available studies, and that empirically validated treatment protocols have yet to be developed. Importantly, however, they conclude that the literature indicates that many established therapeutic modalities used for the treatment of PTSD in the general population have been used successfully with patients who also have ID.

In a large-sample (n=1,037) longitudinal study, tracking subjects from birth to age 32, Koenen, et al. (2009) tested the hypothesis that low childhood IQ is associated with increased risk and increased severity of adult psychopathology. The authors concluded that lower cognitive reserve, as determined by childhood IQ, is an antecedent of several psychiatric disorders and also predicts greater symptom persistence and comorbidity. Regarding posttraumatic stress disorder specifically, the authors found that lower IQ appeared to increase the risk of posttraumatic stress disorder and that higher IQ appeared to reduce that risk. The effects of childhood IQ on adult posttraumatic stress disorder in this study approached, but did not meet, significance, due to the small number of subjects who developed posttraumatic stress disorder in this sample.

Wigham et al. (2011) conducted a literature review on the effects of trauma on people with ID. Fifteen articles were selected and reviewed. The authors concluded that research has been hampered by inconsistent definitions of trauma and an absence of a standardized instrument to measure the effects of trauma on people with ID. The review is useful, nevertheless, in that it finds that certain symptoms may be present in people with ID following trauma exposure that do not typically show up in patients with PTSD who do not have ID. Those symptoms include stereotyped behavior, challenging aggressive behavior, and reduced self-care. They also note that flashbacks may be expressed as current experiences; these can give the appearance of psychotic symptoms, possibly resulting in misdiagnosis.

Breslau and colleagues (Breslau, Chen, & Luo, 2013; Breslau, Lucia, Alvarado, 2006) have looked at the role of intelligence in the development of PTSD. In their 2006 study, Breslau et al. examined a sample of 823 children from birth to age 17. It was found that higher IQ, specifically an IQ of 115 or higher at age 6, was associated with a significantly reduced risk of exposure to traumatic events, as well as to the development of PTSD if exposed. Children with an IQ score greater than 115 at age 6 were at far lower risk for the development of PTSD than children at or below the population mean. Although males were more often exposed to traumatic events, females' risk of PTSD following traumatic exposure was approximately twice that of males, a pattern that has been reported in other studies. In their 2013 study, Breslau, Chen et al. examined whether lower IQ played a bigger role among victims of lower magnitude traumas than among victims of more extreme traumas. In fact, low IQ was found to be associated with PTSD development whether the type of trauma was of high or low magnitude. For a child with an IQ score at age 6 one standard deviation lower (generally, 15 points lower) than a comparison child, there was an increased relative risk ratio of developing PTSD from either high or low magnitude trauma of 50%.

Sequeira, Howlin, and Hollins (2003)—in their well-designed case-control comparison with methodology that included standardized criteria for determining sexual abuse (and, thus, group assignment), standardized measures of symptomatology and psychopathology, and statistical analysis of the differences—compared differences in measures of mental disturbance in adults with ID, evaluating a group of known abuse survivors against a control group with no suspected or reported abuse. Of the 54 subjects in each, the known survivor and comparison group ranges in intellectual disability (ID) were noted; 16 in each group were people with severe or profound ID, 14 had moderate ID, and 24 had mild ID, but there was no analysis reported for differences between these three levels of distinction. The group was analyzed as a whole and the percentage of people meeting the criteria for PTSD was significantly higher in the abused group. The researchers found 19 of the 54 abused individuals met the criteria for PTSD, as opposed to only 2 of the 54 individuals in the comparison groups. Individuals with ID, at any level of severity, who experienced abuse demonstrated more severe behavior problems than did those in the comparison group. The largest differences were found for aggressive and agitated behavior, including aggression toward others, self-injury, temper outbursts, and sudden mood change. The abused group also showed significantly more symptoms of social withdrawal.

In a study on the effect of abuse on men and women with severe intellectual disability in the United Kingdom (Rowsell, Clare, & Murphy, 2013), family members and caregivers evaluated levels of functioning with a repeated measures design. They used a structured interview to identify level of functioning prior to the abuse, after the abuse, and at the time of the study. Survivors experienced multiple forms of abuse, usually over extended periods of time, and were found to have sharp increases in frequency and intensity on a range of emotional, physiological, and behavioral symptoms of psychological distress.

Evaluating Level of Evidence

The research reviewed has been evaluated according to criteria specified in the Cochrane Library as described earlier in the chapter. However, randomized control trials and other intervention studies are infrequent in research aimed at understanding how diagnostic criteria presents in samples of the population. A majority of the research reviewed for this section consists of observational studies of groups of people who have experienced certain conditions, represent certain key categories, and are observed for the presentation of sets of symptoms.

Adults with Mild to Moderate Intellectual Disability

Adults with mild to moderate ID often present with symptom pictures very similar to that of nondisabled persons. The A criterion, i.e., the traumatic event or events, may not fit the strictest definition. Care should be taken to assess the patient as well as to gather information from related parties who know the patient well.

Adults with Severe or Profound Intellectual Disability

In addition to the points noted above, recall that at lower intellectual/developmental levels, behavioral, rather than verbal, expression is more likely to be present. Behavioral symptoms may include trauma-specific reenactments, which can be mistaken for psychosis, as well as increased aggression, self-injurious behavior, agitation, and refusal to participate in activities.

Children and Adolescents with Intellectual Disability

In addition to research support for the higher than average rates of PTSD in people with ID, there is a considerable body of research documenting that people with ID, as children and as adults, experience significantly higher rates of interpersonal trauma, such as physical and sexual abuse, than do members of the general population (Hershkowitz, Lamb, & Horowitz, 2007; Sobsey, 2005; Spencer et al., 2005; Strand, Benzein, & Saveman, 2004; and Sullivan & Knutson, 2000).

Soylu, Alpaslan, Ayaz, Esenyel, & Oruc (2013) conducted an evaluation of sexually abused children and adolescents ages 6-16 in Turkey. The sample included youths with and without intellectual disabilities. They compared 102 children with ID (mild: 87%, moderate: 11.8%, and severe: 1%) with 154 who did not have ID on the psychological impact of sexual abuse. Those with ID experienced abuse that was more severe (penetration) and more frequent. There was no difference between the 2 groups in the rates of PTSD or MDD (major depressive disorder), the two most commonly occurring post-abuse disorders. There was, however, a significantly higher rate of CD (conduct disorder) in the ID group.

Limitations in Applying DSM-5 Criteria to People with ID

As previously noted, events not ordinarily considered traumatic have been observed to result in symptoms of PTSD in some people with ID. The assessment needs to consider a rather broad definition of trauma with respect to the A criterion. In addition, because information often comes through the report of third parties, care must be taken to evaluate the patient's perspective on his or her experience, in addition to the perspective of the caregiver. Finally, it is critical to consider the patient's intellectual/developmental level during the assessment, bearing in mind that the lower the intellectual/developmental level, the more likely that symptoms will be expressed behaviorally, such as through trauma-specific reenactments, physical aggression, self-injurious behavior, and/or refusal to engage in activities, as opposed to verbal reports of subjective experiences, such as reporting recurrent, unwanted memories, nightmares, flashbacks, or negative mood states.

Acute Stress Disorder

General Considerations

Acute stress disorder is characterized by symptoms similar to those of PTSD that occur immediately after one or more traumatic event and last less than a month

Methodology

An electronic and manual literature search was performed to identify all empirical studies on acute stress disorder and people with intellectual disabilities. The literature search was from 2002 to April 2014. The five databases used were: CINAHL, EMBASE, MEDLINE, Psych Info and Cochrane Library.

The search terms used were acute stress disorder, mental retardation, learning disability, learning difficulty, and developmental disability. The inclusion criteria were broad including assessment, etiology, diagnosis, treatment, and interventions.

Review Research Applying to People with ID

There is very little research on acute stress disorder presenting in those with ID reported in the literature. Most of the evidence is from studies of PTSD with no reference to the first month of presentation when an acute stress disorder would be present.

Evaluating Level of Evidence

There is no Type I to Type II evidence available on acute stress disorder in persons with intellectual disability and evidence reported is Type III to V on PTSD.

Adults with Mild to Moderate Intellectual Disability

Over a lifetime a significant number of adults with mild to moderate ID, up to 75%, will experience a traumatic event significantly increasing their risk of a psychiatric disordered (Martorell et al., 2009). No studies were found relating acute stressor disorder to adults with mild to moderate ID.

Adults with Severe or Profound Intellectual Disability

Reports on those with severe ID show that they experience similarly traumatic events to the wider population (Mevissen, Lievegoed, Seubert, & de Jongh, 2012). No studies were found relating acute stressor disorder to adults with severe to profound intellectual disability.

Children and Adolescents with Intellectual Disability

The most frequently experienced events in young people with mild to borderline intellectual disability were death or serious injury in a person or a pet, witnessing an accident or a fire and being confronted with bullying (Mervissen & de Jongh, 2010). No studies were found relating acute stress disorder to children and adolescents with intellectual disability.

Limitations in Applying DSM-5 Criteria to People with ID

Acute stress disorder was introduced to identify people who, shortly after trauma exposure, are at high risk for PTSD. People with acute stress disorder are at risk of posttraumatic stress disorder but not everyone who is found to have PTSD initially shows an acute stress disorder (Bryant, Friedman, Spiegel, Ursano, & Strain, 2010). The review of the literature by Bryant and colleagues (2010) did not include people with intellectual disability, but there is no evidence to say that an acute stressor disorder is not also a risk for PTSD in people with intellectual disability.

Adjustment Disorders

General Considerations

The existing *DSM-5* criteria are applicable to people with ID, assuming that one has sufficient clinician knowledge of the subculture of ID, as suggested by Aman (1991) in regards to the DSM-IV criteria. The concept of adjustment disorder can be useful for clinicians treating people with ID, affording the opportunity to remove or ameliorate noxious elements in their lives. Knowledge of the events in the lives of people with ID that can precipitate a crisis and a mental health consultation can result in an accurate diagnosis and a more rapid therapeutic resolution. As per the *DSM- 5* criteria, an adjustment disorder must resolve within 6 months of the termination of the stressor (or its consequences). The symptoms might persist for a prolonged period (that is, longer than 6 months) if they occur in response to a chronic stressor (for example, a chronic disabling general medical condition) or to a stressor that has enduring consequences. It could be argued that the ID itself is a chronic stressor under this definition (although, as a *DSM-5* diagnostic category, it is not considered a "general medical condition"). The consequences of accepting this argument would be to consider every person with ID to have an adjustment disorder, that ID is a "stressor" that can never be integrated into a successful life, and that it is a constant and unending source of distress and disability in the same way that, for example, juvenile rheumatoid arthritis is. Such an argument strains the definition of adjustment disorder without adding anything useful to the understanding or mental health care of people with ID. It is assumed that relief from the stressor will result in relief from the mental health symptoms, an assumption impossible to make about an irreversible condition that affects life and development from the earliest days of life. It may be more useful to consider the ID not as a stressor in and of itself, but as a set of vulnerabilities that lead to more stressful events and/or cause difficulty as an affected individual interfaces with the environment. As suggested by Levitas & Gilson (2001), ID and its consequences can render an individual more prone to disturbance by certain types of stressors, most prominently those calling for novel responses or for responses requiring more than accustomed or attained levels of autonomy.

The *DSM-5* provides a further description of stressors: "The stressor may be a single event (e.g., termination of a romantic relationship), or there may be multiple stressors (e.g., marked business difficulties and marital problems). Stressors may be recurrent (e.g., associated with seasonal business crises) or continuous (e.g., living in a crime-ridden neighborhood). Stressors may affect a single individual, an entire family, or a larger group or community (e.g., as in a natural disaster). Some stressors may accompany specific developmental events (e.g., going to school, leaving parental home, getting married, becoming a parent, failing to attain occupational goals, retirement)." For people with ID, because each novel life event might demand more autonomous responses than the individual is able to readily demonstrate, the stressor does not accompany, but rather it consists of, the developmental event (Levitas & Gilson, 2001).

A stressor might go unnoticed by caregivers, or it might be unreported by a person with ID who does not want to "rock the boat" or disappoint caregiver expectations. The clinician must bear in mind the fact that many stressors in the lives of a person with ID are beyond the power of the person to change. For example, a stressful job or a threatening roommate might only be escaped after prolonged negotiation with caregivers and a caregiving bureaucracy, a process stressful in itself for a person inexperienced with self-advocacy or thwarted by an inadequate caregiving system. It is a process that might be experienced as more stressful than the precipitating stressor. In addition, moderate to severe levels of personnel turnover among those who work with the individual can be a recurrent stressor.

Methodology

An electronic database search was conducted in PsycNET using keywords "intellectual disability," "autistic disorder," and "adjustment disorders" from 2005-2014.

Research Applying to People with ID

There were very few studies that that appeared in the search which focused on adjustment disorder in people with intellectual disability or autistic disorders. Those that did appear did not use DSM-5 criteria, but rather ICD 10 or DSM-IV-TR, though there is very little difference in the criteria in these different manuals. In one study, Tsakanikos, Bouras, Costello & Holt (2007) looked at a clinical sample of people with ID and used regression analysis to demonstrate that ID is associated with a general increased psychological vulnerability to life events, with adjustment disorder being more likely for people with ID exposed to *multiple* events (but not as closely associated with *single* life events).

Evaluating Level of Evidence

Only Type IV and Type V evidence is available in the study of adjustment disorders in samples of people with intellectual disability or autistic disorders.

Adults with Mild to Moderate Intellectual Disability

Only one study, cited earlier, by Tsakanikos et al. (2007), looked at the risk of various ICD 10-defined mental health disorders in relation to single or multiple life events in a sample of adults with ID.

Adults with Severe or Profound Intellectual Disability

No studies have been found to date.

Children and Adolescents with Intellectual Disability

No studies have been found to date.

Limitations in Applying DSM-5 Criteria to People with ID

People with ID, due to restricted lifestyles and difficulty communicating distress, may experience stressors that are not detected by caregivers or helpers. Therefore, the timing of the onset of the stressor may be unknown. In addition, what is stressful for a person with ID may not be the same as for people in the same culture who do not have ID, so the cultural considerations outlined in DSM-5 must be applied flexibly as the world of people with ID and their caregivers must be considered a culture and community unto itself. The chronic stress that is characteristic of the life of a person with ID may make the time constraints outlined in DSM-5 difficult to apply for these individuals.

Reactive Attachment Disorder

Reactive attachment disorder develops in young children who have suffered neglect, abuse, or inadequate attachment to primary caregivers at an early age. However, only 10% of the people without ID who have suffered this go on to develop symptoms of reactive attachment disorder.

Biological Factors

The hypothalamic-pituitary-adrenal (HPA) axis regulates the body's response to stress through its effect on hormones and the sympathetic nervous system. Numerous studies indicate impaired HPA response to stress in individuals with a history of neglect or abuse. Toddlers with disorganized attachments may have altered stress reactivity as measured by elevated cortisol levels during 'the Strange Situation' as previously described. The toddlers with altered cortisol and stress reactivity were the disorganized/disoriented (D) group and so cortisol dysregulation may be a mediating factor in limited or increased emotional reactivity in relation to caregiver interactions in individuals with disordered attachment (Hertsgaard, Gunnar, Erickson, & Nachmias, 1995). In addition, excessive cortisol release has been noted to cause permanent damage to the hippocampus which may also mediate RAD's effect on memory, learning, and development (Becker-Weidman, 2009). Excessive cortisol may affect the hippocampus preferentially due to its elevated concentration of cortisol receptors. Studies indicate that excessive cortisol can damage or suppress the production of hippocampal neurons. Excessive Cortisol can also decrease amygdala volumes into adulthood and areas of the prefrontal cortex. Cortisol can mediate its effects through alterations of the GABA receptors in the Amygdala. GABA is a primarily inhibitory neurotransmitter and so may limit its ability to attenuate activity in the AMYGDALA and possibly emotional valence (Corbin, 2007). Also individuals with a history of severe early neglect have higher baseline levels of cortisol many years later, which can lead to affective illness or dysregulation (Bos et al., 2011). Alterations in the sympathetic nervous system through HPA-axis dysregulation affects autonomic reactivity including heart rate and general arousal which may mediate affective states and anxiety levels to potentially stressful situations.

Studies with institutionalized children have shown lower levels of vasopressin overall and lower levels of oxytocin after interacting with primary caregivers. Oxytocin is a hormone which is known to be highly involved in attachment behaviors and pair bonding as well as in social interactions (Bos et al., 2011). Oxytocin maintains different functions regarding bonding in males and females. Vasopressin is also associated with attachment behaviors and Vasopressin receptors have been found to be highly concentrated in the lateral septum and amygdala in humans. These areas are closely linked to areas associated with reward, memory, and affect regulation (Corbin, 2007).

Boys are more likely to develop symptoms of reactive attachment disorder than girls, in general. However, it has been noted that girls are more likely to present with symptoms of reactive attachment disorder than disinhibited social engagement disorder (Minnis et al., 2007). Some unidentified biological factor may be at play which is protective for girls. Boys are also more likely to have pathologic withdrawal behavior in infancy (Guedeney et al., 2008).

Genetic Factors

In a large-scale twin study on 13,472 twins aged 8 years, attachment-related behaviors were found to be distinct. Large differences were found in monozygotic and dizygotic twins in terms of development of reactive attachment disorder which points to a strong genetic explanation. In addition, the reactive attachment disorder symptoms were related to parental negativity and harshness. Variance in RAD in males was explained by additive genetic effects, whereas the variance in females was explained mainly by environmental effects. This points to a possible protective effect in females. Researchers are interested in exploring X-linked genes for possible protective effects (Minnis et al., 2007). Genes for Neuropeptide Y, MAO-A, COMT, HTTPr polymorphisms are being explored along with genes for the HPA axis as possibly implicated in the development of numerous psychiatric illnesses after trauma or neglect early in life. Face-to-face interactions have been shown to affect gene expression at an early age. This may be the mechanism by which gene expression is altered by early neglect or lack of appropriate attachment-figure stimulation (Corbin, 2007).

Psychosocial Factors

Risk factors relate to the etiology of reactive attachment disorder symptoms and include institutionalization in facilities with large staff-to-individual ratios or where there is rapid turnover in primary caregivers. In addition, inadequate caretaking with severe emotional or physical neglect is a risk factor for developing reactive attachment disorder. As above, foster placement is, in general, preferred to institutionalization. However, not all foster settings are equally good, and the lesser degree of placement disruptions diminishes the risk of development of reactive attachment disorder.

Overall, however, it has been shown that Institutionalization may be the most problematic environment in relation to attachment. Other environments where neglect, physical or sexual abuse, or inattentive parenting take place will increase the risk of reactive attachment disorder.

The early parent-infant relationship is the secure base from which all development proceeds. Infants with mothers who are depressed or engaged in substance abuse are at high risk for disordered attachment behaviors (Oztop &

Uslu, 2007). Depressed mothers are more likely to have negative, critical, coercive, and intrusive behaviors. They're more likely to be irritable and unable to engage children with high needs. These caregivers are unable to provide the optimal conditions for play, stimulation, and positive affect needed for attachment and optimal general development (Oztop & Uslu, 2007). In addition, they are more likely to miss the subtler attachment responses of their children who have and compromise the attachment-related milestones related to dyadic synchrony and attachment.

Developmental Factors

It is likely that the younger a child is at adoption or placement in a stable care home, the lower risk for the development of reactive attachment disorder. Research has shown that longer periods in institutions, with their lack of stimulation, trusted care figures, and consistent human stimulation, accompany larger deficits in cognition and socioemotional development (Bos et al., 2011).

Typically-developing infants as young as two months old have the interactional skills to engage caregiving figures. These skills include making eye contact, vocalizing, using facial expressions, and using body and head movements to interact (Guedeney et al., 2008). The lack of these developmental skills in individuals with ID can inhibit joint attention, attachment, and subsequent developmental milestones. Numerous studies show that early attachment predicts both later socioemotional development and language skills. Effects on cognition are not as consistent. Some studies have shown limited effects and associations between cognition and attachment. Others have shown no effects. However, cumulative context risk accounted for a lot of the variance in the effects of attachment on development and language (Belsky & Pasco Fearon, 2002). This is consistent with other studies' results showing accumulation of risk factors for poor attachment resulting in poorer general outcomes on development and language from preschool through adulthood (Belsky & Pasco Fearon, 2002).

Disinhibited Social Engagement Disorder

Evidence tends to point to an etiology of very early social neglect beginning in the first months of life; neglect after age 2 is felt to be non-contributory to the development of the disorder. This leads to the hypothesis of a critical period of attachment (between birth and age 2) that is necessary for some individuals to be able to adequately interact and form an attachment with a chosen primary attachment figure necessary for typical social interaction.

Bowlby's work in 1982 formulated an etiology of emotional deprivation rather than physical deprivation as the cause of disinhibited social engagement disorder. Further studies have supported this theory in reactive attachment disorder and disinhibited social engagement disorder. Studies have shown that primary caregiver consistency may be an important preventative measure in institutions to decrease the development of disinhibited social engagement disorder and disinhibited social behavior (Smyke, Dunitrescu, & Zeanah, 2002). In addition, after placement in adequate or markedly improved social settings of attachment, prognosis only modestly improves and in many cases, the disorder persists despite a significant improvement in environment.

Biological Factors

Given that the majority of children exposed to serious social neglect do not develop disinhibited social engagement disorder, there must be some type of neurobiological vulnerability which distinguishes who gets the disorder and who does not. In general, boys do tend to develop disinhibited social engagement disorder more commonly than girls (Minnis et al., 2007).

Research on cortical sensitivity is similar in children with disinhibited social engagement disorder and in children with reactive attachment disorder. However, post-institutionalized children have higher cortisol levels when interacting with their biological mother in comparison to the cortisol level when interacting with unfamiliar adults. This may indicate a stress mechanism whereby individuals with disinhibited social engagement disorder are more likely to follow an unfamiliar adult rather than stay with the primary caregiver (Bos et al., 2011).

In addition, EEG studies on individuals with the disinhibited symptoms were more likely to have a decrease in alpha wave relative power and an increase in theta waves among institutionalized children in frontotemporal and occipital regions. This pattern is similar to EEG findings on individuals with ADHD and may be a common mechanism related to delayed cortical maturation. These EEG findings predicted hyperactivity and impulsivity at 54 months of age (Bos et al., 2011). Attachment is also mediated by right hemisphere cortical and subcortical connections to the limbic and autonomic systems, especially in infancy. This exerts inhibitory control over approach to novel and emotionally-charged stimuli and may be damaged in disinhibited social engagement disorder in particular (Corbin, 2007).

Genetic Factors

Individuals with a variety of congenital illnesses can present with symptoms of Disinhibited Social Engagement Disorder. For example, individuals with Williams Syndrome can be overly social and friendly on initial meeting with strangers (Järvinen, Korenberg, & Bellugi, 2013). In fact, the recommendation for individuals with Williams syndrome is that they undergo safety training to help them identify strangers. The disinhibited social behavior of individuals with Williams Syndrome has come under more interest from a genetic perspective.

In addition, twin studies have indicated that genetic variance can account for the differences in propensities to be diagnosed with DESD in both males and females (Minnis et al., 2007). Studies have also found an association between the Dopamine D4 Receptor Gene and disorganized attachment (Minnis et al., 2007).

Psychosocial Factors

Some studies have shown that children who exhibit disinhibited social behavior can have reasonable attachment. In addition, other studies have related disinhibited social behavior to a lack of awareness of social cues (O'Connor et al., 1999), a decrease in ability to interpret social cues (Wismer Fries & Pollack, 2004), and a decrease in an awareness of theory of the mind (Tarullo , Bruce, & Gunnar, 2007). However, some of the most consistent data has surrounded the inhibitory control abilities of the child. For this reason, ADHD is high on the differential diagnosis for Disinhibited Social Engagement Disorder. In typically developing children, cognitive ability, emotional abilities, and attachment-related behavior in the session were not related to disinhibited social behaviors (Bruce et al., 2009).

In multiple studies, disinhibited social engagement behaviors are much more difficult to extinguish than reactive attachment disorder behaviors (Bos et al., 2011; Rutter, Kreppner, & Sonuga-Barke, 2009). In contrast to RAD, DSED behaviors persist longer and have lower levels of remission after placement in foster care after institutionalization (Bos et al., 2011).

Developmental Factors

Disinhibited social engagement disorder behavior results from a failure to develop committed intimate relationships and the subsequent stress that this causes individuals. Because of the difficulty in achieving remission with placement or improvement of social situation, researchers have postulated that critical periods in brain development, especially in the cortex, may have passed. Evidence for this may be related to the biological similarities in EEG between attention deficit hyperactivity disorder and disinhibited social engagement disorder (Bos et al., 2011). However, it is also possible that disinhibited behaviors can be adaptive in early infancy in getting needs met in environments of deprivation or with multiple caregivers. Disinhibition in this way could facilitate a child getting away from negative caretakers and meeting new positive caretakers. More research, however, needs to be undertaken to completely elucidate this phenomenon (Rutter et al., 2009).

Posttraumatic Stress Disorder

Biological and Genetic Factors

Research indicates that risk for posttraumatic stress disorder (PTSD) is shaped by the interaction between genetic vulnerability and early caregiving experiences (Feldman, Vengrober, & Ebstein, 2014). Repeated exposure to traumatic events during the first years of life, when critical brain structures are maturing, carries an even greater risk for psychopathology. In a prospective, longitudinal study, Feldman et al. (2014) found that genetic risk, as determined by genetic liability along the axis of vasopressin–oxytocin (OT) interacted with maternal caregiving, with both factors contributing significantly to posttraumatic stress disorder risk. The authors found that repeated trauma exposure during the first years of life markedly increased the propensity to develop psychiatric disorders by middle childhood and that children experiencing less supportive parenting demonstrated greater susceptibility to developing psychiatric disorders in middle childhood. Among exposed children, chronicity of posttraumatic stress disorder was related to both genetic risk and parenting behavior so that greater genetic risk and less supportive parenting differentiated children with chronic posttraumatic stress disorder from those with early posttraumatic stress disorder who recovered by middle childhood. Similarly, for exposed children, both genetic risk and parenting contributed to child symptomatology in the four post-traumatic symptom clusters in young children (re-experiencing, avoidance, hyperarousal, fears-and-aggressions) as well as to the degree of developmental regression.

Psychosocial Factors

Research suggests that psychosocial factors play an important role in the relative risk of PTSD development. These factors, as noted in the research above and in the *DSM-5*, include: lower socioeconomic status, prior trauma exposure, preexisting psychological disorders, parental psychopathology, lower educational level, lower intelligence, and inadequate social and/or familial support. Also, females develop PTSD at higher rates than males.

Developmental Factors

While the DSM5 notes that younger age increases the risk of developing posttraumatic stress disorder following trauma exposure, we can add that lower developmental level, not simply lower chronological age, appears to increase PTSD risk.

Acute Stress Disorder

Biological Factors

Females are at greater risk for developing an acute stress disorder which may be linked to differences between genders in neurobiological differences in stress responses. There are no recognized genetic risk factors.

Psychosocial Factors

Risk factors in the wider population are prior mental disorder, higher levels of negative affect and an avoidant coping style. There is no evidence of these risk factors for people with intellectual disability.

Developmental Factors

A history of previous trauma is a risk factor in the wider population. There is no evidence of this for people with intellectual disability.

Adjustment Disorders

Biological Factors

There is no evidence to date for any biological pre-disposition to adjustment disorder.

Genetic Factors

There is no evidence to date for any genetic risk factor for adjustment disorder.

Psychosocial Factors

As stated in DSM-5, individuals who have lives that are disadvantaged or marked by high rates of stressful events are more likely to be at higher risk for adjustment disorders. As described earlier, people with ID are more likely to be living in circumstances in which environmental stressors are of higher frequency and higher intensity.

Developmental Factors

In a study by Tsakanikos et al. (2007), a recent history of multiple life events in a sample of people with ID referred for mental health treatment was associated with a diagnosis of adjustment disorder but was also associated with personality disorder and depression diagnoses.

Applying Criteria

Reactive Attachment Disorder

The following factors should be considered in

the differential diagnosis and should raise the clinician's index of suspicion for attachment-related problems. They do not rise to the level of specific diagnostic criteria:

1. Changes in attachment behaviors unrelated to primary mental disorder, response to pain, or recent medical illness.
2. Disturbances in attachment behaviors more severe than severity ratings for autism spectrum or level of ID. Attachment behaviors are markedly inconsistent with social and emotional level and interactions expected for the developmental age.
3. Aloofness or failure to form attachment to primary caregivers; lack of interest in social contact, friends, or proximity seeking with caregivers, especially in times of distress.
4. Displays inconsistent proximity seeking; marked ambivalence; withdrawal from, or aggressive behaviors directed at, caregivers.
5. Episodes of unexplained sadness, irritability, or fearfulness with adult caregivers not associated with trauma or transition.
6. Failure to display "reunion behaviors."

Care-giver related behaviors:

1. Gross disregard for temperamental and psychological needs for attachment – including a consistent inability or unwillingness to respond to the individual's signals of distress or to recognize or respond to fear, fatigue, hunger, or pain cues – or imperviousness to, or overtly rejecting, attempts at social or emotional contact.
2. Gross disregard for environmental enrichment, social contact with others, excessive confinement, and habilitative needs.
3. Caregiver is overwhelmed by needs of individual and unable to manage in current living arrangement due to mental disorders, substance abuse, or severity of the individual's challenging behaviors.
4. A history of placement with numerous caregivers at an early age – including institutionalization, foster care, adoption – or a history of significant neglect or abuse.

Application of Diagnostic Criteria-for Reactive Attachment Disorder

Reactive Attachment Disorder

DSM-5 Diagnostic Criteria	Applying Criteria for Mild and Moderate ID	Applying Criteria for Severe and Profound ID
A. A consistent pattern of inhibited, emotionally withdrawn behavior toward adult caregivers, manifested by both of the following:	A. Markedly inhibited, emotionally withdrawn behavior toward adult caregivers, manifested by both of the following when compared to children of similar measured intelligence or adaptive skills:	A. Same as criteria for Mild ID. **Note:** Attachment behaviors in children with sensory impairments should be compared with those children with similar disabilities.
1. The child rarely or minimally seeks comfort when distressed.	1. The child rarely or minimally seeks comfort when distressed in a developmentally appropriate fashion including agitated, impaired or aggressive behaviors with distress.	1. Same as adaptations for Mild ID.
2. The child rarely or minimally responds to comfort when distressed.	2. The child rarely or minimally responds to comfort when distressed including refusing comforting or becoming, agitated, aggressive or destructive with comforting in a maladaptive way.	2. Same as adaptations for Mild ID.

Reactive Attachment Disorder (continued)

DSM-5 Diagnostic Criteria	Applying Criteria for Mild and Moderate ID	Applying Criteria for Severe and Profound ID
B. A persistent social and emotional disturbance characterized by at least two of the following:	B. No adaptation **Note:** When compared to other individuals of similar levels of measured intelligence and adaptive skills:	B. No adaptation.
1. Minimal social and emotional responsiveness to others	1. No adaptation **Note:** History of abuse or neglect during infancy, childhood, and later caregivers	1. No adaptation. **Note**: History of abuse or neglect during infancy, childhood and later caregivers
2. Limited positive affect	2. Limited positive affect despite appropriate environmental setting for adaptive functioning and positive supports	2. Same as adaptations for Mild ID.
3. Episodes of unexplained irritability, sadness, or fearfulness that are evident even during nonthreatening interactions with adult caregivers.	3. Episodes of unexplained irritability, sadness, or fearfulness that are evident even during nonthreatening interactions with adult caregivers - Not during times of transition or with traumatic reminders.	3. Same as adaptations for Mild ID.
C. The child has experienced a pattern of extremes of insufficient care as evidenced by at least one of the following: 1. Social neglect or deprivation in the form of persistent lack of having basic emotional needs for comfort, stimulation, and affection met by caregiving adults. 2. Repeated changes of primary caregiver that limit opportunities to form stable attachments (e.g., frequent changes in foster care) 3. Rearing in unusual settings that severely limit opportunities to form selective attachments (e.g. institutions with high child to caregiver ratios).	C. No adaptation.	C. No adaptation.
D. The care in criterion C is presumed to be responsible for the disturbed behavior in criterion A (e.g., the disturbances in Criterion A began following the lack of adequate care in Criterion C).	D. No adaptations.	D. No adaptations.
E. The criteria are not met for autism spectrum disorder.	E. Autism spectrum disorder and reactive attachment disorder are able to be distinguished through the quality of communication, presence or absence of repetitive behaviors or interests, etc.	E Same as adaptations for Mild ID.
F. The disturbance is evident before age 5.	F. No adaptations.	F. No adaptations.
G. The child has a developmental age of at least 9 months.	G. No adaptations.	G. No adaptations.

Reactive Attachment Disorder (continued)

DSM-5 Diagnostic Criteria	Applying Criteria for Mild and Moderate ID	Applying Criteria for Severe and Profound ID
Specify if: Persistent: the disorder has been present for more than 12 months. Specify current severity: Reactive attachment disorder specified as severe when a child exhibits all symptoms of the disorder, with each symptom manifesting at relatively high levels	No adaptations.	No adaptations.

Disinhibited Social Engagement Disorder

The following factors should be considered in the differential diagnosis and should raise the clinician's index of suspicion for attachment related problems. They do not rise to the level of specific diagnostic criteria:

1. Changes in attachment behaviors unrelated to primary mental disorder, response to pain, or recent medical illness.
2. Disturbances in attachment behaviors more severe than severity ratings for PDD or level of ID. Attachment behaviors are markedly inconsistent with social and emotional level and interactions expected for the developmental age.
3. In times of distress, turning indiscriminately to no preferred caregivers.
4. Displays inconsistent proximity seeking; marked ambivalence; withdrawal from, or aggressive behaviors directed at, caregivers.
5. No checking in with adult caregivers after venturing away or absence of asking to leave a current situation, even in an unfamiliar setting.
6. Failure to display "reunion behaviors."

Caregiver-related behaviors:

1. Gross disregard for temperamental and psychological needs for attachment – including a consistent inability or unwillingness to respond to the individual's signals of distress or to recognize or respond to fear, fatigue, hunger, or pain cues – or imperviousness to, or overtly rejecting of, attempts at social or emotional contact.
2. Gross disregard for environmental enrichment, social contact with others, excessive confinement, and habilitative needs.
3. Caregiver is overwhelmed by needs of individual and unable to manage in current living arrangement due to mental disorders, substance abuse, or severity of the individual's challenging behaviors.
4. A history of placement with numerous caregivers at an early age – including institutionalization, foster care, adoption – or a history of significant neglect or abuse.

Application of Criteria for-Disinhibited Social Engagement Disorder

Disinhibited Social Engagement Disorder

DSM-5 Diagnostic Criteria	Applying Criteria for Mild and Moderate ID	Applying Criteria for Severe and Profound ID
A. A pattern of behavior in which a child actively approaches and interacts with unfamiliar adults and exhibits at least two of the following:	A. A pattern of behavior in which a child actively approaches and interacts with unfamiliar adults and exhibits at least two of the following when compared to children of similar measured intelligence or adaptive skills:	A. Same as criteria for Mild ID. **Note:** Attachment behaviors in children with sensory impairments should be compared with those children with similar disabilities.
1. Reduced or absent reticence in approaching and interacting with unfamiliar adults.	1. Reduced or absent reticence in approaching and interacting with unfamiliar adults. When compared to children of similar measured intelligence or adaptive skills:	1. Same as adaptations for Mild ID.
2. Overly familiar verbal or physical behavior (that is not consistent with culturally sanctioned and with age-appropriate social boundaries) 3. Diminished or absent checking back with adult caregiver after venturing away, even in unfamiliar settings. 4. Willingness to go off with an unfamiliar adult with minimal or no hesitation.	2. Overly familiar verbal or physical behavior (that is not consistent with culturally sanctioned and with age-appropriate or developmentally-appropriate social boundaries) 3. No adaptations 4. Willingness to go off with an unfamiliar adult with minimal or no hesitation that is not due to lapses in judgment due to cognitive, emotional, or adaptive deficits.	2. Same as criteria for Mild ID. 3. No adaptations 4. Same as criteria for Mild ID.
B. The behaviors in Criterion A are not limited to impulsivity (as in attention – deficit/hyperactivity disorder) but include socially disinhibited behavior.	B. No adaptation **Note:** When compared to other individuals of similar levels of measured intelligence and adaptive skills:	B. No adaptation.
C. The child has experienced a pattern of extremes of insufficient care as evidence by at least one of the following:	C. No adaptation **Note:** History of abuse or neglect during infancy, childhood, and later caregivers	C. No adaptation. **Note:** History of abuse or neglect during infancy, childhood and later caregivers
1. Social neglect or deprivation in the form of persistent lack of having basic emotional needs for comfort, stimulation, and affection met by caregiving adults.	1. No adaptation	1. No adaptation. For all of these, brain development, processing maternal cues and pattern of response may complicate things for parents with of infants with SPID or ASD. This brings up the idea of interactive specialization of areas related to attachment and intermodal integration as issues. These may be issues of transaction not unidirectional influences
2. Repeated changes of primary caregivers that limit opportunities to form stable attachments (e.g. frequent changes in foster care).	2. No adaptation.	2. No adaptation.

Disinhibited Social Engagement Disorder (continued)

DSM-5 Diagnostic Criteria	Applying Criteria for Mild and Moderate ID	Applying Criteria for Severe and Profound ID
3. Rearing and unusual settings that severely limit opportunities to form selective attachments (e.g. institutions with high child-to-caregiver ratios).	3. No adaptation.	3. No adaptation.
D. The caring criterion C is presumed to be responsible for the disturbed behavior in criterion A (e.g. the disturbances in criterion A began following the pathogenic care in criterion C)	D. No adaptations.	D. No adaptations.
E. The child has a developmental age of at least 9 months	E. No adaptations.	E. No adaptations.
Speciffy if: Persistent: the disorder has been present for more than 12 months. Specify current severity: Disinhibited social engagement disorder is specified as severe when the child exhibits all symptoms of the disorder, with each symptom manifesting at relatively high levels.		

Posttraumatic Stress Disorder

DSM-5 Diagnostic Criteria	Applying Criteria for Mild-Moderate ID	Applying Criteria for Severe-Profound ID
Note: The following criteria apply to adults, adolescents and children older than 6 years		
A. Exposure to actual or threatened death, serious injury or sexual violation in one (or more) of the following ways:	A. The person has been exposed to a traumatic event they have experienced as being traumatic. This can include exposure to actual or threatened death, serious injury or sexual violation in one (or more) of the following ways, but may also be activated by less serious events. (See note below)	A. The person has been exposed to a traumatic event they have experienced as being traumatic. This can include exposure to actual or threatened death, serious injury or sexual violation in one (or more) of the following ways, but may also be activated by less serious events. (See note for Mild-Moderate ID)

Posttraumatic Stress Disorder (continued)

DSM-5 Diagnostic Criteria	Applying Criteria for Mild-Moderate ID	Applying Criteria for Severe-Profound ID
1.Directly experiencing the traumatic event(s). 2.Witnessing in person the event(s) as it occurred to others. 3.Learning that the traumatic event(s) occurred to a close family member or close friend. In cases of actual or threatened death of a family member or friend, the event(s) must have been violent or accidental. 4. Experiencing repeated or extreme exposure to aversive details of the traumatic event(s) (e.g., first responders collecting human remains; police officers repeatedly exposed to details of child abuse). **Note:** Criterion A4 does not apply to exposure through electronic media, television, movies, or pictures, unless this exposure of work related.	No adaptation.as to the 4 criteria, but the threshold is often lowered for vulnerability and consequent activation of these conditions. In assessing for traumatic exposure in people with ID, take note that events such as developmental milestones, residential placement, and even adult, consensual sexual experiences and ending of romantic relationships have led to posttraumatic reactions in some individuals with ID. It appears that the range of potentially traumatizing events is greater for individuals with a lower developmental age, though no hard data is available that would merit clear-cut distinctions for criteria between Mild-Moderate ID and Severe/Profound ID. What composes a traumatic reaction is determined by how the event was interpreted by the individual. Typically the lower the developmental age, the lower the threshold for what qualifies as traumatic.	1.- 4. Read section under Modified Criteria for Mild/Moderate ID
B. Presence of one (or more) of the following intrusion symptoms associated with the traumatic event(s), beginning after the traumatic event(s) occurred:	B. No modification	B. No modification.
1. Recurrent, involuntary, and intrusive memories of the traumatic event(s). **Note:** In children older than 6 years, repetitive play may occur in which themes or aspects of the traumatic event(s) are expressed	1. No modification	1. Behavioral acting out of traumatic experiences is more common for individuals with greater cognitive impairments. Some cases of self-injurious behavior may in fact be symptomatic of traumatic exposure.
2. Recurrent distressing dreams in which the content and/or affect of the dream are related to the traumatic event(s). **Note:** In children there may be frightening dreams without recognizable content.	2. No modification	2. Frightening dreams without recognizable content appear to be more common in individuals with greater cognitive impairments.
3. Dissociative reactions (e.g., flashbacks) in which the individual feels or acts as if were recurring. (Such reactions may occur on continuum with the most extreme expression being a complete loss of awareness of present surroundings. **Note:** In children, trauma-specific reenactment may occur in play.	3. Trauma-specific enactments have been observed in adults with Moderate to Severe ID. These episodes require judicious assessment in that they can appear to be symptoms of psychosis in adults.	3. Read section under Modified Criteria for Mild/Moderate ID
4. Intense or prolonged psychological distress at exposure to internal or external cues that symbolize or resemble an aspect of the traumatic event(s).	4. No modification. There is considerable evidence; however, of increased likelihood of disorganized or agitated behavior in individuals with greater levels of impairment and this can be a manifestation of the reaction.	4.No modification, however disorganized or agitated behavior appears to be quite common for individuals with greater cognitive impairments who have experienced trauma.

Posttraumatic Stress Disorder (continued)

DSM-5 Diagnostic Criteria	Applying Criteria for Mild-Moderate ID	Applying Criteria for Severe-Profound ID
5. Marked physiologic reactions to internal or external cues that symbolize or resemble an aspect of the traumatic event.	5. No modification.	5.No modification
C. Persistent avoidance of stimuli associated with the traumatic event(s), beginning after the traumatic event(s) occurred, as evidenced by one or both of the following:	C. No modification. However as lower developmental age results in lower and broader thresholds for activation of traumatic reactions it also lowers and broadens the threshold for avoidance of stimuli.	C. Read section under Modified Criteria for Mild/Moderate ID
1. Avoidance of or efforts to avoid distressing memories, thoughts, or feelings about or closely associated with the traumatic event(s).		
2. Avoidance of or efforts to avoid external reminders (people, places, conversations, activities, objects, situations) that arouse distressing memories, thoughts, or feelings about or closely associated with the traumatic event(s)..		
D: Negative alterations in cognitions and mood associated with the traumatic event(s), beginning or worsening after the traumatic event(s) occurred, as evidenced by two (or more) of the following	D. No modification	D. No modification.
1. Inability to recall key features of the traumatic event (usually dissociative amnesia; not due to head injury, alcohol, or drugs).	1. No modification. Note, however, problems with recall may appear to be solely a function of the individual's cognitive impairment and require careful assessment	1. Read section under Applying Criteria for Mild/Moderate ID.
2. Persistent and exaggerated negative beliefs and expectations about oneself, others, or the world (e.g., "I am bad," "No one can be trusted," "The world is completely dangerous," :My whole nerous system is permanently ruined"). 3. Persistent distorted cognitions about cause or consequences of the traumatic event(s) that lead the individual to blame himself/herself or others 4. Persistent negative emotional state (e.g., fear, horror, anger, guilt, or shame).	2.-4. No modification. Note, however, that avoidance behaviors may be reported by caregivers as "noncompliance", especially for individuals with more severe cognitive impairment who cannot adequately verbalizing their posttraumatic desire to avoid activities, places or people that arouse recollections of the trauma.	2.-4. Read section under Applying Criteria for Mild/Moderate ID
5. . Markedly diminished interest in or participation in significant activities.	5.No modification.	5.No modification
6. Feelings of detachment or estrangement from others.	6. No modification.	6.No modification, although diminished participation may be reported by caregivers as "noncompliance".

Posttraumatic Stress Disorder (continued)

DSM-5 Diagnostic Criteria	Applying Criteria for Mild-Moderate ID	Applying Criteria for Severe-Profound ID
7. Persistent inability to experience positive emotions (e.g., inability to experience happiness, satisfaction, or loving feelings).	7. Some people with ID appear to show evidence of this symptom in the same way that members of the general population do. However, it is important to note that many non-traumatized people with ID do not have normative expectations regarding their futures. For those with greater levels of cognitive impairment, a cognitive inability to think abstractly may prevent them from developing a set of ideas about the future. For less impaired individuals who can consider future projections, the understanding that they are fundamentally different from peers and siblings (e.g., in not being able to drive, or to go to college) may lead them to believe that their futures will not be normative. A reduced sense of personal efficacy, common in people with ID, is at the core of these beliefs regarding the future. There may be a risk of false positives on this criterion.	7.This criterion may be of limited utility in assessing posttraumatic states in individuals with greater degrees of cognitive impairment. Normative expectations for the future may not be present in many members of this subgroup, even in the absence of traumatic exposure, owing to the severity of the disability.
E: Marked alterations in arousal and reactivity associated with the traumatic event(s), beginning or worsening after the traumatic event(s) occurred, as evidenced by two (or more) of the following	E. No modification	E. No modification
1. Irritable behavior and angry outbursts (with little or no provocation) typically expressed as verbal or physical aggression toward people or objects. 2. Reckless or self-destructive behavior 3. Hypervigilance 4. Exaggerated startle response. 5. Problems in concentration. 6. Sleep disturbance (e.g., difficulty falling or staying asleep or restless sleep).		
F. Duration of disturbance (Criteria B, C, D, and E) is more than 1 month.	F. No modification	F. No modification
G. The disturbance causes clinically significant distress or impairment in social, occupational, or other important areas of functioning.	G. No modification	G. No modification
H. The disturbance is not attributable to the physiological effects of a substance (e.g., medication, alcohol) or another medical condition.	H. No modification	H. No modification

Posttraumatic Stress Disorder (continued)

DSM-5 Diagnostic Criteria	Applying Criteria for Mild-Moderate ID	Applying Criteria for Severe-Profound ID
Specify whether: With dissociative symptoms: The individual's symptoms meet the criteria for post-traumatic stress disorder, and in addition, in response to the stressor, the individual experiences persistent or recurrent symptoms of either of the following: 1. Depersonalization: Persistent or recurrent experiences of feeling detached from and as if one were an outside observer of, one's mental processes or body (e.g., feeling as though one were in a dream; feeling a sense of unreality of self or body or of time moving slowly). 2. Derealization: Persistent or recurrent experiences of unreality of surroundings (e.g., the world around the individual is experienced as unreal, dreamlike, distant, or distorted). **Note:** To use this subtype, the dissociative symptoms must not be attributable to the physiological effects of a substance (e.g., blackouts, behavior during alcohol intoxication) or another medical condition (e.g., complex partial seizures). .	Behavioral acting out of traumatic experiences is more common for individuals with greater cognitive impairments. Some cases of self-injurious behavior may in fact be symptomatic of traumatic exposure. There is considerable evidence; however, of increased likelihood of disorganized or agitated behavior in individuals with greater levels of impairment and this can be a manifestation of the reaction. Unusual intra-psychic emotional states as depersonalization and derealization combined with a lack of ability to verbalize these states can often result in acting out of the trauma, self injury, disorganized, agitated, or aggressive behavior.	Read section under Modified Criteria for Mild/Moderate ID
Specify if: With delayed expression: If the full diagnostic criteria are not met until at least 6 months after the event (although the onset and expression of some symptoms may be immediate).	No modification	No modification
Posttraumatic Stress Disorder for Children 6 Years and Younger A. In children 6 years and younger, exposure to actual or threatened death, serious injury, or sexual violence in one (or more) of the following ways: 1. Directly experiencing the traumatic event(s). 2. Witnessing in person, the event(s) as it occurred to others, especially primary caregivers. Note: Witnessing does not include events that are witnessed only in electronic media, television, movies, or pictures. 3. Learning that the traumatic event(s) occurred to a parent or caregiving figure.	No adaptation. **Note:** Typically the lower the developmental age, the lower the threshold that qualifies as traumatic	No adaptation **Note:** Typically the lower the developmental age, the lower the threshold that qualifies as traumatic
B. Presence of one (or more) of the following intrusion symptoms associated with the traumatic event(s), beginning after the traumatic event(s) occurred:	No modification	No modification **Note:** Read section for children older than 6 years

Posttraumatic Stress Disorder (continued)

DSM-5 Diagnostic Criteria	Applying Criteria for Mild-Moderate ID	Applying Criteria for Severe-Profound ID
1. Recurrent, involuntary, and intrusive distressing memories of the traumatic event(s). Note: Spontaneous and intrusive memories may not necessarily appear distressing and may be expressed as play reenactment. 2. Recurrent distressing dreams in which the content and/or affect of the dream are related to the traumatic event(s). 3. Dissociative reactions (e.g., flashbacks) in which the child feels or acts as if the traumatic event(s) were recurring. (Such reactions may occur on a continuum, with the most extreme expression being a complete loss of awareness of present surroundings.) Such trauma-specific reenactment may occur in play. 4. Intense or prolonged psychological distress at exposure to internal or external cues that symbolize or resemble an aspect of the traumatic event(s). 5. Marked physiological reactions to reminders of the traumatic event(s).		
C. One (or more) of the following symptoms, representing either persistent avoidance of stimuli associated with the traumatic event(s) or negative alterations in cognitions and mood associated with the traumatic event(s), must be present, beginning after the event(s) or worsening after the event(s): Persistent Avoidance of Stimuli 1. Avoidance of or efforts to avoid activities, places, or physical reminders that arouse recollections of the traumatic event(s). 2. Avoidance of or efforts to avoid people, conversations, or interpersonal situations that arouse recollections of the traumatic event(s).	No adaptation **Note:** Read section for children older than 6 years	No adaptation **Note:** Read section for children older than 6 years
Negative Alterations in Cognitions: 3. Substantially increased frequency of negative emotional states (e.g., fear, guilt, sadness, shame, confusion). 4. Markedly diminished interest or participation in significant activities, including constriction of play. 5. Socially withdrawn behavior 6. Persistent reduction in expression of positive emotions.	No adaptation	No adaptation

Posttraumatic Stress Disorder (continued)

DSM-5 Diagnostic Criteria	Applying Criteria for Mild-Moderate ID	Applying Criteria for Severe-Profound ID
D. Alterations in arousal and reactivity associated with the traumatic event(s), beginning or worsening after the traumatic event(s) occurred, as evidenced by two (or more) of the following: 1. Irritable behavior and angry outbursts (with little or no provocation) typically expressed as verbal or physical aggression toward people or objects (including extreme temper tantrums). 2. Hypervigilance. 3. exaggerated startle response. 4. Problems with concentration. 5. Sleep disturbance (e.g., difficulty falling or staying asleep or restless sleep).	No adaptation **Note:** children with ID need to show alterations in arousal are linked to traumatic experiences	No adaptation **Note:** children with ID need to show alterations in arousal are linked to traumatic experiences
E. The duration of the disturbance is more than 1 month.	No adaptation	No adaptation
F. The disturbance causes clinically significant distress or impairment in relationships with parents, siblings, peers, or other caregivers or with school behavior.	No adaptation	No adaptation
G. The disturbance is not attributable to the physiological effects of a substance (e.g., medication or alcohol) or another medical condition.	No adaptation	No adaptation
Specify whether: With dissociative symptoms: The individual's symptoms meet the criteria for post-traumatic stress disorder, and the individual experiences persistent or recurrent symptoms of either of the following:	No adaptation **Note:** Read section for children older than 6 years	No adaptation **Note:** Read section for children older than 6 years
1. Depersonalization: Persistent or recurrent experiences of feeling detached from, and as if one were an outside observer of, one's mental processes or body (e.g., feeling as though one were in a dream; feeling a sense of unreality of self or body or of time moving slowly).	No adaptation **Note:** Read section for children older than 6 years	No adaptation **Note:** Read section for children older than 6 years
2. Derealization: Persistent or recurrent experiences of unreality of surroundings (e.g., the world around the individual is experienced as unreal, dreamlike, distant, or distorted). **Note:** To use this subtype, the dissociative symptoms must not be attributable to the physiological effects of a substance (e.g., blackouts) or another medical condition (e.g., complex partial seizures).	No adaptation **Note:** Read section for children older than 6 years	No adaptation **Note:** Read section for children older than 6 years
Specify if: With delayed expression: If the full diagnostic criteria are not met until at least 6 months after the event (although the onset and expression of some symptoms may be immediate).	No adaptation	No adaptation

Acute Stressor Disorder

DSM-5 Diagnostic Criteria	Applying Criteria for Mild-Moderate ID	Applying Criteria for Severe-Profound ID
		Note: Symptoms and signs may only be observed.
A.Exposure to actual or threatened death, serious injury or sexual violation in one (or more) of the following ways:	A. No Adaptation **Note:** A wider range of events may lead to an acute stress reaction in people with ID	A. No adaptation. **Note:** A wider range of events may lead to an acute stress reaction in people with ID
1.Directly experiencing the traumatic event(s) 2.Witnessing in person the event(s) 3.Learning that the event(s) occurred to a close family or close friend. Note: In cases of actual or threatened death of a family member or friend, the event(s) must have been violent or accidental. 4. Experiencing repeated or extreme exposure to aversive details of the traumatic event(s) (e.g., first responders collecting human remains, police officers repeatedly exposed to details of child abuse). **Note:** This does not apply to exposure through electronic media, television, movies or pictures, unless this exposure is work related.		
B. Presence of nine (or more) of the following symptoms from any of the five categories of intrusion, negative mood, dissociation, avoidance, and arousal, beginning or worsening after the traumatic event(s) occurred:	B. No adaptation	B. No adaptation
Intrusion symptoms 1. Recurrent, involuntary and intrusive distressing memories of the traumatic event(s). Note: In children, repetitive play may occur in which themes or aspects of the traumatic event(s) are expressed. 2. Recurrent distressing dreams in which the content and/or affect of the dream are related to the event(s). Note: In children, there may be frightening dreams without recognizable content. 3. Dissociative reactions (e.g. flashbacks), in which the individual feels or acts as if the traumatic event(s) were recurring. (Such reactions may occur on a continuum, with the most extreme expression being a complete loss of awareness of present surroundings.) Note: In children, trauma-specific reenactment may occur in play. 4. Intense or prolonged psychological distress or marked physiological reactions in response to internal or external cues that symbolize or resemble an aspect of the traumatic event(s).	1. No adaptation 2. Frightening dreams without recognizable content may occur 3. No adaptation 4. No adaptation	1. Behavioral acting out of distressing memories may be present e.g. self-injurious behavior. 2. Frightening dreams without recognizable content may occur 3. Trauma-specific enactments may be observed in those with moderate to severe ID 4. Disorganized agitated behavior may be more common.
Negative mood 5. Persistent inability to experience positive emotions (e.g., inability to experience happiness, satisfaction, or living feelings).	5. No adaptation	5. No adaptation

Acute Stressor Disorder (continued)

DSM-5 Diagnostic Criteria	Applying Criteria for Mild-Moderate ID	Applying Criteria for Severe-Profound ID
Dissociative symptoms 6. An altered sense of the reality of one's surroundings or oneself (e.g., seeing oneself from another's perspective, being in a daze, time slowing). 7. Inability to remember an important aspect of the traumatic event(s) (typically due to dissociative amnesia and not to other factors such as head injury, alcohol, or drugs).	No adaptation	No adaptation although people with moderate to severe ID may not be able to verbalize these experiences
Avoidance symptoms 8. Efforts to avoid distressing memories, thoughts or feelings about or closely associated with the traumatic event(s). 9. Efforts to avoid external reminders (people, places, conversations, activities, objects, situations) that arouse distressing memories, thoughts, or feelings about or closely associated with the traumatic event(s).	No adaptation	No adaptation although may be reported by caregivers as 'noncompliance' or 'oppositional' behaviors as those with moderate to severe ID may not be able to verbalizes their desire to avoid activities, places or people that are reminders of the traumatic experiences(s)
Arousal symptoms 10. Sleep disturbance (e.g., difficulty falling or staying asleep, restless sleep). 11. Irritable behavior and angry outbursts (with little or no provocation), typically expressed as verbal or physical aggression toward people or objects. 12. Hypervigilance. 13. Problems with concentration. 14. Exaggerated startle response.	No adaptation **Note:** People with ID need to show alterations in arousal are linked to the traumatic experience(s)	No adaptation **Note:** People with ID need to show alterations in arousal are linked to the traumatic experience(s)
C. Duration of the disturbance (symptoms in Criterion B) is 3 days to 1 month after trauma exposure **Note:** Symptoms typically begin immediately after the trauma, but persistence for at least 3 days and up to a month is needed to meet disorder criteria.	C. No adaptation	C. No adaptation
D. The disturbance causes clinically significant distress or impairment in social, occupational, or other important areas of functioning	D. No adaptation **Note:** People with ID need to show evidence show a change in function prior to the traumatic experience (s)	D. No adaptation **Note:** People with ID need to show evidence show a change in function prior to the traumatic experience (s)
E. The disturbance is not attributable to the physiological effects of a substance (e.g., d medication or alcohol) or another medical condition (e.g., mild traumatic brain injury) and is not better explained by brief psychotic disorder.	E. No adaptation	E. No adaptation

Adjustment Disorder

DSM-5 Diagnostic Criteria	Applying Criteria for Mild to Moderate ID	Applying Criteria for Severe to Profound ID
A. The development of emotional or behavioral symptoms in response to an identifiable stressor(s) occurring within 3 months of the onset of the stressor(s).	A. No adaptation. **Note:** Stressors in the lives of persons with Mild/Moderate ID can include any need for an increase in autonomous functioning (move to new home or away from family, loss or change status of important caregiver, promotion to educational, vocational or residential placement beyond one's level of comfort, onset of illness).	A. No adaptation. **Note:** Stressors in the lives of persons with Severe/Profound ID can include any need for an increase in autonomous functioning (move to new home or away from family, loss or change status of important caregiver, promotion to educational, vocational or residential placement beyond one's level of comfort, onset of illness).
B. These symtoms or behaviors are clinically significant, as evidenced by one or both of the following: 1. Marked distress that is out of proportion to the severity or intensity of the stressor, taking into account the external context and the cultural factors that might influence symptom severity and presentation 2. Significant impairment in social, occupational, or other important areas of functioning.	B. Anxiety and depression may manifest in persons with Mild/Moderate ID as they would in persons without ID, but also as clinging, apparent loss of skills, withdrawal, or irritability.	B. Anxiety and depression may manifest in persons with Severe/Profound ID as they would in persons without ID, but also as clinging, apparent loss of skills, withdrawal, irritability, aggression, self-injury, destructiveness, and loss of earlier compliance with routines of care.
C. The stress-related disturbance does not meet the criteria for another mental disorder and is not merely an exacerbation of a preexisting mental disorder.	C. A clear history of a stressor and the differences from previous patterns seen in pre-existing disorders must be noted.	C. A clear history of a stressor and the differences from previous patterns seen in pre-existing disorders must be noted. Assessment must be made for such disorders, as they may not have been diagnosed prior to the current mental health contact. It should not be assumed from the limited behavioral repertoire that exacerbations of symptoms of Severe/Profound ID do not merit diagnosis of an Adjustment Disorder despite clear relation to a stressor.
D. The symptoms do not represent normal bereavement.	D. In many persons with moderate intellectual disability, bereavement may take the form of anger and irritability, with resulting disturbance of conduct; in this situation, other specified trauma-and-stressor-related disorder: "persistent complex bereavement disorder" should be diagnosed, as the phenomena of normal bereavement may be significantly surpassed. In addition, loss of housemates, friends, favored staff, and even routines may be causes of grief.	D. In many persons with severe/profound ID, bereavement may take the form of anger and irritability, with resulting disturbance of conduct; in this situation, other specified trauma-and-stressor-related disorder: "persistent complex bereavement disorder" should be diagnosed, as the phenomena of normal bereavement may be significantly surpassed. Bereavement may occur in response to loss, not only by death, but also due to promotion, retirement or transfer, of important caregivers. In addition, loss of housemates, friends, favored staff, and even routines may be causes of grief.

Adjustment Disorder (continued)

DSM-5 Diagnostic Criteria	Applying Criteria for Mild to Moderate ID	Applying Criteria for Severe to Profound ID
E. Once the stressor or its consequences have terminated, the symptoms do not persist for more than an additional 6 months.	E. An Adjustment Disorder must resolve within 6 months of the termination of the stressor (or its consequences). However, the symptoms may persist for a prolonged period (i.e. longer than 6 months) if they occur in response to a chronic stressor (e.g. a chronic disabling general medical condition, **unrelieved inappropriate educational, residential or vocational placement, repeated caregiver turnover, unrelieved peer problem exposure, other experiences beyond the capacity of the individual to resolve independently**) or to a stressor that has enduring consequences.	E. An Adjustment Disorder must resolve within 6 months of the termination of the stressor (or its consequences). However, the symptoms may persist for a prolonged period (i.e. longer than 6 months) if they occur in response to a chronic stressor (e.g. a chronic disabling general medical condition, **unrelieved inappropriate educational, residential or vocational placement, repeated caregiver turnover, unrelieved peer problem exposure, other experiences beyond the capacity of the individual to resolve independently**) or to a stressor that has enduring consequences.
Specify *whether:* **With Depressed Mood**: Low mood, tearfulness, or feelings of hopelessness are predominant.	Depression may manifest in persons with mild/ moderate ID as it would in persons without ID, but also as clinging, apparent loss of skills, withdrawal, or irritability.	Depression may manifest in persons with severe/ profound ID as clinging, apparent loss of skills, withdrawal, or irritability.
With anxiety: Nervousness, worry, jitteriness, or separation anxiety is predominant.	Anxiety may manifest in persons with mild/ moderate ID as it would in persons without ID, but also as clinging, apparent loss of skills, irritability or anger.	Anxiety may manifest in persons with severe/ profound ID as clinging, apparent loss of skills, irritability, aggression, self-injury (including changes in the patterns of the latter).
With mixed anxiety and depressed mood: A combination of depression and anxiety is predominant.	See above.	See above.
With disturbance of conduct: Disturbance of conduct is predominant.	*Adjustment disorder with disturbance of conduct* is characterized by violation of the rights of others or of major age appropriate societal norms and rules (e.g. truancy, vandalism, reckless driving, fighting, defaulting on legal responsibilities **self-injury, threats, and aggression and property destruction). For people with ID, this may also be observed as in increase in the frequency or severity of pre-existing maladaptive behavioral repertoires.**	*Adjustment disorder with disturbance of conduct* is characterized by violation of the rights of others or of major age appropriate societal norms and rules (e.g. truancy, vandalism, reckless driving, fighting, defaulting on legal responsibilities**: self-injury, threats, aggression and property destruction, and changes in existing patterns of any or all of these). For people with ID, this may also be observed as in increase in the frequency or severity of pre-existing maladaptive behavioral repertoires.**).
With mixed disturbance of emotions and conduct: Both emotional symptoms (e.g., depression, anxiety) and a disturbance of conduct are predominant.	See above.	See above.
Unspecified: For maladaptive reactions that are not classifiable as one of the specific subtypes of adjustment disorder.	No adaptation.	No adaptation.

References

Aman, M.G. (1991). Review and evaluation of instruments for assessing emotional and behavioural disorders. *Austalia and New Zealand Journal of Developmental Disabilities, 17*(2), 127-145

American Psychiatric Association. (2013). *Diagnostic and statistical manual of mental disorders* (5th Ed.). Arlington, VA: American Psychiatric Publishing

Aupperle, R. L., Melrose, A. J., Stein, M. B., & Paulus, M. P. (2012). Executive function and PTSD: Disengaging from trauma. *Neuropharmacology, 62*(2), 686-694.

Becker-Weidman, A. (2009). Effects of early maltreatment on development: A descriptive study using the Vineland Adaptive Behavior Scales-II. *Child Welfare, 88*, 137-161.

Belsky, J., & Pasco Fearon, R.M. (2002). Infant-mother attachment security, contextual risk, and early development: Amoderational analysis. *Development and Psychopathology* 14: 293-310.

Berry, P., Gunn, P., & Andrews, R. (1980). Behavior of Down syndrome infants in the strange situation. *American Journal of Mental Deficiency, 85*, 213-218.

Blacher, J. (1984). Attachment and severely handicapped children: Implications for intervention. *Developmental and Behavioral Pediatrics*, 5(4), 178-183.

Bos, K., Zeanah, C.H., Fox, N.A., Drury, S.S., McLaughlin, K.A., & Nelson, C.A. (2011). Psychiatric outcomes in young children with a history of institutionalization. *Harvard Review of Psychiatry, 19*, 15-24.

Bowlby, J. (Ed.). (1982). *Attachment and loss (volume 1 Attachment)* (2nd ed.). New York, NY: Basic Books.

Breslau, N., Chen, Q., & Luo, Z. (2013). The role of intelligence in posttraumatic stress disorder: Does it vary by trauma severity? *PLoS ONE, 8*(6).

Breslau, N., Lucia, V.C., & Alvarado, G.F. (2006). Intelligence and other predisposing factors in exposure to trauma and posttraumatic stress disorder: A follow-up study at age 17 years. *Archives of General Psychiatry, 63*(11), 1238-1245.

Breslau, N., Troost, J. P., Bohnert, K., & Luo, Z. (2013). Influence of predispositions on post-traumatic stress disorder: does it vary by trauma severity? *Psychological Medicine, 43*(2), 381.

Bruce, J., Tarullo, A., & Gunnar, M. (2009). Disinhibited social behavior among internationally adopted children. *Development and Psychopathology,* 21, 157-171.

Bryant, R.A., Friedman, J.J., Spiegel, D., Ursano, R., & Strain, J. (2010). A review of acute stressor disorder in DSM-5. *Depression and Anxiety, 28*(9), 802-817.

Chisholme, K., Carter, M.C., Ames, E.W., & Morrison, S.J. (1995). Attachment security and indiscriminate friendly behavior in children adopted from Romanian orphagees. *Development and Psychopathology,* 7, 283-294.

Cicchetti, D. & Serafica, F.C. (1981). Interplay among behavioral systems: Illustrations from the study of attachment, affiliation, and wariness in young children with Down's syndrome. *Developmental Psychology,* 17, 36-49.

Claussen, A.H., Mundy, P.C., Mallik, S.A., & Willoughby, J.C. (2002). Joint attention and disorganized attachment status in infants at risk. *Development and Psychopathology,* 14, 279-291.

Corbin, J.R. (2007). Reactive attachment disorder: A biopsychosocial disturbance of attachment. *Child & Adolescent Social Work Journal,* 24, 539-552.

Dahmen, B., Putz, V., Herpertz-Dahlmann, B., & Konrad, K. (2012). Early pathogenic care and the development of ADHD-like symptoms. *Biological Child and Adolescent Psychiatry,* 119, 1023-1036.

D'Andrea, W., Ford, J., Stolbach, B., Spinazzola, J., & van der Kolk, B. A. (2012). Understanding interpersonal trauma in children: Why we need a developmentally appropriate trauma diagnosis. *American Journal of Orthopsychiatry, 82*(2), 187-200.

Daud, A., & Rydelius, P. A. (2009). Comorbidity/overlapping between ADHD and PTSD in relation to IQ among children of traumatized/non-traumatized parents. *Journal of Attention Disorders, 13*(2), 188-196.

Feldman, R., Vengrober, A., & Ebstein, R. P. (2014). Affiliation buffers stress: Cumulative genetic risk in oxytocin–vasopressin genes combines with early caregiving to predict PTSD in war-exposed young children. *Translational psychiatry, 4*(3), e370.

Follan, M., Anderson, S., Huline-Dickens, S., Lidstone, E., Young, D., Brown, G., & Minnis, H. (2011). Discrimination between attention deficit hyperactivity disorder and reactive attachment disorder in school aged children. *Research in Developmental Disabilities, 32*, 520-526.

Gardner, W. I., Griffiths, D. M., & Hamlin, J. (2012). Biopsychosocial features influencing aggression: A multimodal assessment and therapy approach. In J. K. Luiselli (Ed.), *The handbook of high-risk challenging behaviors: Assessment and intervention* (pp. 83–102). Towson, MD: Brookes.

Giltaij, H.P., Sterkenburg, P.S., & Schuengel, C. (2013). Psychiatric diagnostic screening of social maladaptive behavior in children with mild intellectual disability: Differentiating disordered attachment and pervasive developmental disorder behavior. *Journal of Intellectual Disability Research*, 1-12.

Guedeney, A., Foucault, C., Bougen, E., Larroque, B., & Mentre, F. (2008). Screening for risk factors of relational withdrawal behavior in infants aged 14-18 months. *European Psychiatry*, 23, 150-155.

Hall, J.C., Jobson, L., & Langdon, P.E. (2014). Measuring symptoms of post-traumatic stress disorder in people with intellectual disabilities: The development and psychometric properties of the Impact of Event Scale-Intellectual Disabilities (IES-IDs). *British Journal of Clinical Psychology, 53*(3), 315-552.

Hershkowitz, I., Lamb, M.E., & Horowitz, D. (2007). Vicitmization of children with disabilities. *American Journal of Orthopsychiatry, 77*(4), 629-635.

Hertsgaard, L., Gunnar, M., Erickson, M.F., & Nachmias, M. (1995). Adrenocorticol responses to the Strange situation in infants with disorganized/disoriented attachment relationships. *Child Development, 66*, 1100-1106.

Hulbert-Williams, L., Hastings, R., Owen, D. M., Burns, L., Day, J., Mulligan, J., & Noone, S. J. (2013). Exposure to life events as a risk factor for psychological problems in adults with intellectual disabilities: A longitudinal design. *Journal of Intellectual Disabilities Research, 58*(1), 48-60.

Hurley, A.D., Folstein, M.F., & Lam, N. (2003). Patients with and without intellectual disability seeking outpatient psychiatric services: Diagnosing and prescribing pattern. *Journal of Intellectual Disability Research, 47*, 39-50.

Järvinen, A., Korenberg, J.R., & Bellugi, U. (2013). The social phenotype of Williams syndrome. *Current Opinion in Neurobiology, 23*(3), 414-422.

Koenen, K. C., Moffitt, T. E., Roberts, A. L., Martin, L. T., Kubzansky, L., Harrington, H., ... Caspi, A. (2009). Childhood IQ and adult mental disorders: A test of the cognitive reserve hypothesis. *The American Journal of Psychiatry, 166*(1).

Kremen, W. S., Koenen, K. C., Afari, N., & Lyons, M. J. (2012). Twin studies of posttraumatic stress disorder: Differentiating vulnerability factors from sequelae. *Neuropharmacology, 62*(2), 647-653.

Larson, F., Alim, N., & Tsakanikos, E. (2011). Attachment style and mental health in adults with intellectual disability: Self-reports and reports by carers. *Advances in Mental Health and Intellectual Disabilities, 5*, 15-23.

Levitas, A. (2003). Unpublished data. Stratford NJ: Department of Psychiatry (UMDNJ/SOM, 40 East Laurel Road #200, Stratford, NJ 08084-1504; data available upon request).

Levitas, A., & Gilson, S.F. (2001). Predictable crises in the lives of people with mental retardation. *Mental Health Aspects of Developmental Disabilities, 4*, 89-100.

Martorell, A., Tsakanikos, E., Pereda, A., Gutierrez-Recacha, P. Bouras, N., & Ayuso-Mateos, J.L. (2009). Mental health in adults with mild and moderate intellectual disabilities: The role of recent life events and traumatic experiences across the life span. *Journal of Nervous and Mental Disease, 197*(3), 182-186.

McNally, R. J. (2009). Can we fix PTSD in DSM-V? *Depression and Anxiety, 26*(7), 597-600.

Mevissen, L., & de Jongh, A. (2010). PTSD and its treatment in people with intellectual disabilities: A review of the literature. *Clinical Psychology Review, 30*(3), 308-316.

Mevissen, L., Lievegoed, R., & De Jongh, A. (2011). EMDR treatment in people with mild ID and PTSD: 4 cases. *Psychiatric Quarterly, 82*(1), 43-57.

Minnis, H., Fleming, G., & Cooper, S-A. (2010). Reactive attachment disorder symptoms in adults with intellectual disabilities. *Journal of Applied Research in Intellectual Disabilities*, 23, 398-403.

Minnis, H., Reekie, J., Young, D., O'Connor, T., Ronald, A., Grayand, A., & Plomin, R. (2007). Genetic, environmental and gender influences on attachment disorder behaviors. *British Journal of Psychiatry, 190*, 490-495.

Nehama, Y, Dakar, Z., Stawski, M., & Szor, H. (2006). An alternative model for psychiatric service delivery for people with intellectual disabilities in a vocational rehabilitation center. *Israel Journal of Psychiatry and Related Sciences, 43*(4), 285-92.

O'Connor, T.G., Bredenkamp, D., Rutter, M., & the English and Romanian Adoptees Study Team. (1999). Attachment disturbances and disorders in children exposed to early severe deprivation. *Infant Mental Health Journal, 20*, 10-29.

Oztop, D., & Uslu, R. (2007). Behavioral, interactional, and developmental symptomatology in toddlers of depressed mothers: a preliminary clinical study within the DC:0-3 framework. *Turkish Journal of Pediatrics, 49*, 171-178.

Raaska, H., Elovainio, M., Sinkkonen, J., Matomaki, J., Makipaa, S., & Lapinleimu, H. (2011). Internationally adopted children in Finland: Parental evaluations of symptoms of reactive attachment disorder and learning difficulties. *Child: Care, Health and Development* 38: 697-705.

Raitasuo, S., Talminen, S., & Salokangas, R.K.R. (1999). Characteristics of people with intellectual disability admitted for psychiatric inpatient treatment. *Journal of Intellectual Disability Research*, 43(2), 112-118.

Razza, N.J., & Tomasulo, D.J. (2005). *Healing trauma: The power of group treatment for people with intellectual disabilities.* Washington, DC: American Psychological Association.

Reid, K. A., Smiley, E., & Cooper, S. A. (2011). Prevalence and associations of anxiety disorders in adults with intellectual disabilities. *Journal of Intellectual Disability Research, 55*(2), 172.

Rowsell, A.C., Clare, I.C.H., & Murphy, H. (2013). The psychological impact of abuse on men and women with severe intellectual disabilities. *Journal of Applied Research in Intellectual Disabilities, 26*, 257-270.

Rutter, M., Kreppner, J., & Sonuga-Barke, E. (2009). Emanuel Miller Lecture: Attachment insecurity, disinhibited attachment, and attachment disorders: Where do research findings leave the concepts? *Journal of Child Psychology and Psychiatry*, 50, 529-543.

Saigh, P. A., Yasik, A. E., Oberfield, R. A., Halamandaris, P. V., & Bremner, J. D. (2006). The intellectual performance of traumatized children and adolescents with or without posttraumatic stress disorder. *Journal of Abnormal Psychology, 115*(2), 332-340.

Sar, V. (2011). Developmental trauma, complex PTSD, and the current proposal of DSM-5. *European Journal of Psychotraumatology, 2*, 5622

Schafer, I., & Fisher, H. L. (2011). Childhood trauma and psychosis-what is the evidence?

Dialogues in Clinical Neuroscience, 13(3), 360-365.

Schuengel, C., Claisien de Schipper, J., Sterkenburg, P.S., & Kaf, S. (2013). Attachment, Intellectual disabilities and mental health: Research, assessment and intervention. *Journal of Applied Research in Intellectual Disabilities*, 26, 34-46.

Sequeira, H., Howlin, P., & Hollins, S. (2003). Psychological disturbance associated with sexual abuse in people with learning disabilities: case control study. *The British Journal of Psychiatry*, 183, 451-456

Siegel, D.J. (2007). *The mindful brain in psychotherapy: How neural plasticity and mirror neurons contribute to emotional well-being.* New York: Norton.

Smith, D. M. (2011). Diagnosing liability: The legal history of posttraumatic stress disorder. *Temple Law Review, 84*, 1.

Smyke, A.T., Dunitrescu, A., & Zeanah, C.H. (2002). Attachment disturbances in young children. The continuum of caretaking casualty. *Journal of the Academy of Child & Adolescent Psychiatry*, 41, 972-982.

Sobsey, D. (2005). Violence and disability. In W.M. Nehring (Ed.) *Health promotion for persons with intellectual/developmental disabilities: The state of scientific evidence.* Washington, DC: American Association on Mental Retardation.

Soylu, N., Alpaslan, A.H., Ayaz, M, Esenyel, S., & Oruc, M. (2013). Psychiatric disorders and characteristics of abuse in sexually abused children and adolescents with and without intellectual disabilities. *Research in Developmental Disabilities, 34*, 4334-4342.

Spencer, N., Devereux, E., Wallace, A., Sundrum, R., Shenoy, M. Bacchus, C., & Logan, S. (2005). Disabling conditions and registration for child abuse and neglect: A population-based study. *Pediatrics, 116*(3), 609-614.

Strand, M., Benzein, E., & Saveman, B.I. (2004). Violence in the care of adult persons with intellectual disabilities. *Journal of Clinical Nursing, 13*(4), 506-514.

Sullivan, P.M. & Knutson, J.F. (2000). Maltreatment and disabilities: A population-based epidemiological study. *Child Abuse and Neglect, 24*(10), 1257-1273.

Tarullo, A.R., Bruce, J., & Gunnar, M.R. (2007). False belief and emotion understanding in post-institutionalized children. *Social Development* 16: 57-78.

Tsakanikos, E., Bouras, N., Costello, H, & Holt, G. (2007). Multiple exposure to life events and clinical psychopathology in adults with intellectual disability. *Social Psychiatry and Psychiatric Epidemiology, 42* (1), 24-28.

Twamley, E. W., Allard, C. B., Thorp, S. R., Norman, S. B., Cissell, S. H., Berardi, K. H., & Stein, M. B. (2009). Cognitive impairment and functioning in PTSD related to intimate partner violence. *Journal of the International Neuropsychological Society, 15*(6), 879-887.

Van Ijzendoorn, M.H., Scheungel, C., & Bakermans-Kranenburg, M.J. (1999). Disorganized attachment in early childhood: Meta-analysis of precursors, concomitants & sequelae. *Development and Psychology, 11*, 225-249.

Vasterling, J. J. (2009). The influence of pre-deployment neurocognitive functioning on post-deployment PTSD symptom outcomes among Iraq-deployed army soldiers. *Journal of the International Neuropsychological Society, 15*, 840-852.

Wakefield, J. C. (2013). DSM-5: An overview of changes and controversies. *Clinical Social Work Journal*, 1-16.

Wieland, J., Wardenaar, K. J., Dautovic, E., & Zitman, F. G. (2013). Characteristics of post-traumatic stress disorder in patients with an intellectual disability. *European Psychiatry, 28*(1), 1.

Wigham, S., Hatton, C., & Taylor, J.L. (2011). The effects of traumatizing life events on people with intellectual disabilities: A systematic review. *Journal of Mental Health Research in Intellectual Disabilities, 4*(1), 19-39.

Wismer Fries, A.B. & Pollack, S.D. (2004). Emotion understanding in post institutionalized Eastern Europe Children. *Development and Psychopathology*, 16, 355-369.

CHAPTER 16

Dissociative Disorders

Alya Reeve
Tim Andrews
Eve Loren Wedeen
Dora Wang

This chapter presents a brief review of the DSM-5 criteria for dissociative identity disorder and its subtypes, as adapted in recognition of populations with intellectual and/or developmental disabilities (IDD). From this review, the chapter moves into a summary of the DSM-5 criteria, then discusses the presentation and diagnosis in populations with IDD. Suggestions regarding applying diagnostic criteria for persons with IDD, along with adaptations of assessment techniques, are included under methodology and summarized in a table.

Review of Diagnostic Criteria

General Description of the Dissociative Disorders.

Dissociative disorders are characterized by disruptions in an individual's maintenance of consciousness in a continuous or integrated manner. Symptoms may manifest as fractures in memory, attention, physical ability, bodily representation, and perception. Symptoms of dissociation are frequently seen in trauma-related disorders but can persist independent of trauma or develop unrelated to a known traumatic event.

DSM-5 organizes the dissociative disorders into five categories: problems of forming a cohesive personal identity; problems of maintaining a coherent sense of personal memory; problems in maintaining connection to one's sense of self or external surroundings; the last two categories include partial constellations of symptoms or ones that are induced under particular circumstances only.

Summary of DSM-5 Criteria

- *Dissociative Identity Disorder*

A. Disruption of identity characterized by two or more distinct personality states, which may be described in some cultures as an experience of possession. The disruption in identity involves marked discontinuity in sense of self and sense of agency, accompanied by related alterations in affect, behavior, consciousness, memory, perception, cognition, and/or sensory-motor functioning. These signs and symptoms may be observed by others or reported by the individual.

B. Recurrent gaps in the recall of everyday events, important personal information, and/or traumatic events that are inconsistent with ordinary forgetting.

C. The symptoms cause clinically significant distress or impairment in social, occupational, or other important areas of functioning.

D. The disturbance is not a normal part of a broadly accepted cultural or religious practice. Note: in children, the symptoms are not better explained by imaginary playmates or other fantasy play.

E. The symptoms are not attributable to the physiological effects of a substance (e.g. blackouts or chaotic behavior during alcohol intoxication) or another medical condition (e.g. complex partial seizures).

- *Dissociative Amnesia*

A. An inability to recall important autobiographical information, usually of a traumatic or stressful nature, that is inconsistent with ordinary forgetting.

B. The symptoms cause clinically significant distress or impairment in social, occupational, or other important areas of functioning.

C. The disturbance is not attributable to the physiological effects of a substance (e.g. alcohol or other drug of abuse, a medication) or a neurological or other medical condition (e.g. partial complex seizures, transient global amnesia, sequelae of a closed head injury/traumatic brain injury, other neurological condition).

D. The disturbance is not better explained by dissociative identity disorder, post-traumatic stress disorder, acute stress disorder, somatic symptom disorder, or major or mild neurocognitive disorder.

- *Dissociative Amnesia with Dissociative Fugue*

Apparently purposeful travel or bewildered wandering that is associated with amnesia for identity or for other important autobiographical information.

- *Depersonalization/Derealization Disorder*

A. The presence of persistent or recurrent experiences of depersonalization, derealization, or both:

1. Depersonalization: Experiences of unreality, detachment, or being an outside observer with respect to one's thoughts, feeling, sensations, body, or actions (e.g. perceptual alterations, distorted sense of time, unreal or absent self, emotional and/or physical numbing).

2. Derealization: Experiences of unreality or detachment with respect to surrounding (e.g. individuals or objects are experienced as unreal, dreamlike, foggy, lifeless, or visually distorted).B. During the depersonalization or derealization experiences, reality testing remains intact.C. The symptoms cause clinically significant distress or impairment in social, occupational, or other important areas of functioning.

D. The disturbance is not attributable to the physiological effects of a substance (e.g. a drug of abuse, medications) or another medical condition (e.g., seizures).

E. The disturbance is not better explained by another mental disorder, such as schizophrenia, panic disorder, major depressive disorder, acute stress disorder, post-traumatic stress disorder, or another dissociative disorder.

- *Other Specified Dissociative Disorder*

This category applies to presentations in which symptoms characteristic of a dissociative disorder that cause clinically significant distress or impairment in social, occupational, or other important areas of functioning predominate but do not meet the full criteria for any of the disorders in the dissociative disorders diagnostic class. Examples include:

1. Chronic and recurrent syndromes of mixed dissociative symptoms: This category includes identity disturbance associated with less-than-marked discontinuities in sense of self and agency, or alterations of identity or episodes of possession in an individual who reports no dissociative amnesia.

2. Identity disturbance due to prolonged and intense coercive persuasion (e.g., brainwashing, thought reform, indoctrination while captive, torture, long-term political imprisonment, and recruitment by sects/cults or by terror organizations).

3. Acute dissociative reactions to stressful events: This category is for acute, transient conditions that typically last less than one

month, and sometimes only a few hours or days. These conditions are characterized by constriction of consciousness; depersonalization; derealization; perceptual disturbances (e.g., time slowing, macropsia) micro-amnesias; transient stupor; and/or alterations in sensory-motor functioning (e.g., analgesia, paralysis).

4. Dissociative trance: This condition is characterized by an acute narrowing or complete loss of awareness of immediate surroundings that manifests as profound unresponsiveness or insensitivity to environmental stimuli. The unresponsiveness may be accompanied by minor stereotyped behaviors (e.g., finger movements) of which the individual is unaware and/or that he or she cannot control, as well as transient paralysis or loss of consciousness. The dissociative trance is not a normal part of a broadly accepted collective cultural or religious practice.

- *Unspecified Dissociative Disorders*

The unspecified dissociative disorder category is used in situations in which the clinician chooses not to specify the reason that the criteria are not met for a specific dissociative disorder, and includes presentations for which there is insufficient information to make a more specific diagnosis (e.g., in emergency room settings).

Issues Related to Diagnosis in Persons with ID

Development and Course

Dissociation commonly follows a situation of overwhelming psychological challenge such as trauma. Two prominent theories underscore scholarship in this area, the post traumatic model and the social cognitive model (Boysen & VanBergen, 2013). Events perceived as threatening are not always recalled, particularly if the occurrence was in early childhood (Reed-Gavish, 2013). As a person becomes older, it is easy to rely upon this method for handling significant stressors. Since this is an internal method for compartmentalizing and coping with difficult situations, a person is usually older before dissociative symptoms are more readily visible to others (Fairley, Jones, McGuire & Stevenson, 1995; Fotheringham & Thompson, 1994).

When interviewing or attempting to assess a person with IDD, it is important not to rely on verbal communication as the best or only way of assessment. Many individuals with IDD have limitations in cognitive abstraction and demonstrate concrete thinking patterns of a young child. Thus their comprehension will demonstrate a concreteness of thinking similar to that developmental stage. People with IDD have wide ranges of abilities and need to be properly assessed for their developmental level of comprehension in different settings or circumstances. A concreteness of understanding about social interactions may coexist with poor or good abstraction about time or events; some concepts may have verbal expressions and others may be better expressed in pictures, stories, or pantomime, for example.

The course of dissociative disorders is to improve with supportive treatment. While much of the literature uses phrases such as integration of different personalities or recovery of lost time, the experience of many individuals who have dissociated is that these internal psychological experiences remain segregated, but more readily accessible in a functional manner. Thus, the lost time in dissociative amnesia is never fully experienced as re-integrated, but there is an awareness of the time for which amnesia occurred and available recall for those events. In Dissociative Identity Disorder the different personae have varying responsibilities to deal with certain emotions, challenges, or actions and may become more readily accessible to assist in seamless daily functioning (Forrest, 2001).

Prevalence

The prevalence of dissociative disorders has not been reliably studied. There is no data (Paris, 2012). Dissociative disorders are relatively rare in the general population, estimated at 1.5%. As with other mental illness diagnoses, real data about prevalence is needed to determine whether dissociative disorders occur at roughly the same rate (similar to schizophrenia) or at increased rates (such as PTSD)

(McAllister, 2000). There is no indication from anecdotal experience to think that dissociative disorders occur at a reduced rate among people with IDD (Rossini, Schwartz & Braun, 1996).

Differential Diagnosis

Dissociation occurs in many other psychiatric illnesses. It is a major symptom of post-traumatic stress disorder, borderline personality disorder, anxiety disorders, depressive disorders, and trauma spectrum disorders (Pope, Barry, Bodkin & Hudson, 2006). Attention deficit disorders, early symptoms of dementia, and encoding problems associated with clinical and sub-clinical seizure disorders can mask as problems in accounting for continuous awareness of reality or loss of memory. The differential diagnostic criteria are well delineated in DSM-5; these criteria are applicable to people with IDD with minor adaptations for communication style and cognitive functioning. People with IDD may manifest their experiences differently, such as by talking to their different alters. Some symptoms are not suggestive of dissociation such as maintaining imaginary playmates appropriate to their developmental stage; people with autism frequently will speak about themselves in the third person. These differences in interacting in the world are neither predictive of, nor protective from, having dissociative experiences or disorders.

Functional Consequences

The greatest detriment to people with ID is that dissociation is attributed to responding to internal stimuli, to talking to imaginary people, to hearing voices, to erratic changes in mood or willful disregard for commitments or consequences of decisions – in a word, to overt misdiagnosis. Misattribution of symptoms then leads to mistakes in therapeutic approaches. People will receive excess doses or even medications that are ineffective. Wrong therapy can be as lethal as inappropriate or over-use of antipsychotic medications, with irreversible side effects of developing tardive dyskinesia or even neuroleptic malignant syndrome. Many individuals with dissociative disorders are punished for their responses because they appear to be impulsive and ignoring the rules that have been established for their safety or the safety of others around them. When professionals and caregivers lack the context in which to understand, a person's behavior is open to grave mis-interpretation and mis-representation. People with IDD often lack sufficient access to ways to build social skills (van Duiji, Kleijn & de Jong, 2013). Providing training and rehearsal of social skills may aid these individuals to better identify and avoid potential situations of abuse or ambiguous demands that may lead to abuse. Thus, as discussed further in Methodology, the examiner must be alert to the veracity of information provided to them for consideration.

Comorbidity

Dissociative disorders exist alongside intellectual disability, other psychiatric illnesses or adjustment disorders, and chronic medical conditions (Fujii, Suzuki, Sato, Murakami & Takahashi, should be identified so that treatment can be tailored and supported to meet the therapeutic needs of the individual and his or her caregivers can be informed about effective ways to support the individual (Rossini et al, 1996).

Application of Diagnostic Criteria to People with ID

General Considerations

In general, psychiatric disorders occur at an increased rate in populations with intellectual and/or developmental disabilities (IDD) compared to the general population, at an estimated increase of two-to-three-fold greater. This is thought, in part, to be due to the vulnerability of this population, which is often dependent upon the care and attitudes of others. It is also a reflection of primary underlying developmental disorders in the development of the central nervous system.

Methodology

The assessment for dissociative disorders involves ascertainment of history and direct observation of the patient, including observation of body language. Corroborative information from observers other than the patient, is important, as the individual's recollections, by definition of the disorder, may exclude non-sequiturs of memory or awareness. Requesting written or drawn depictions of experiences, and descriptions of sequences of events in multiple locations, may aid in diagnosis. Art therapy is a validated method for understanding an individual's experiences of confusion and trauma, as well as a means of therapeutic resolution (International Society for the Study of Trauma and Dissociation, 2011; Malchiodi, 1994; Mills, 1995; Murphy, 1994, Thompson, 2011; Uttley et al 2015).

Review of Research Pertaining to People with ID

A comprehensive literature search was conducted using the terms: dissociation, multiple personality, dissociative identity disorder, dissociative amnesia, and intellectual disability. The search was limited to publications in the past 20 years, in human subjects. Of the 750 initial articles, 157 were judged as relevant to DSM-5 criteria. There is a paucity of literature about this condition in people with IDD (Boysen & VanBergen, 2013; McAllister, 2000; Pope et al., 2006; Rossini et al., 1996).

Evaluating Level of Evidence.

The level of evidence for diagnosis and treatment of dissociative disorders in people with IDD remains at Cochrane level V, the level of opinion and case reports (Boon & Draijer, 1993; Fairley et al., 1995; Fotheringham & Thompson, 1994; Pope et al, 2006; Xiao et al, 2006;). Among these, only two articles provided case descriptions of single examples and therapeutic strategies. One review article highlighted the need to evaluate the comorbidity of attention deficit disorders as affecting encoding of memories and attentiveness to immediate surroundings.

Adults with Mild, Moderate, Severe or Profound Intellectual Disabilities

The evaluation of individuals with IDD requires adaptation of usual methods, to accommodate limitations in cognition and communication abilities (Rossini et al., 1996). The degree of intellectual disability, whether mild, moderate, severe, or profound, does not predict the tendency for dissociation.

Children and Adolescents with Intellectual Disability.

The diagnosis of a dissociative disorder should be made with caution in children and adolescents with IDD, given that they are still developing and maturing. In many cases, an accurate diagnosis might only be achieved in adulthood. Concrete thinking is typical for children, as well as people with IDD.

Limitations in Applying DSM-5 Criteria to People with ID.

In summary, clinicians should be aware of the possibility of dissociative disorders in this population and adapt their assessment methods to accommodate this population's limitations in cognition and verbal expression.

Etiology and Pathogenesis

Much of the literature about dissociative disorders continues to address the validity of this diagnosis. There is little known or investigated regarding the etiology and pathogenesis of dissociative experiences or how these could be prevented, especially in vulnerable populations (Boon & Draijer, 1993; Boysen & VanBergen, 2013; Chodoff, 1997; Modestin, 1992; Reed-Gavish, 2013).

Dissociative Identity Disorder

DSM-5 Diagnostic Criteria	Applying Criteria for Individuals with Intellectual Disability
A. Disruption of identity characterized by two or more distinct personality states, which may be described in some cultures as an experience of possession. The disruption in identity involves marked discontinuity in sense of self and sense of agency, accompanied by related changes in affect, behavior, consciousness, memory, perception, cognition, and/or sensory-motor function. These signs and symptoms may be observed by others or reported by the individual.	A. Include non-verbal expressions of self-awareness and cues to altered states of the self.

Dissociative Identity Disorder (continued)

DSM-5 Diagnostic Criteria	Applying Criteria for Individuals with Intellectual Disability
B. Recurrent gaps in recall of everyday events, important personal information, and/or traumatic events that are inconsistent with ordinary forgetting.	B. Need to recognize any pre-existing cognitive impairments for types of memory (specific to the individual's strengths, limitations, and abilities).
C. The symptoms cause clinically significant distress or impairment in social, occupational, or other important areas of functioning.	C. No adaptation.
D. The disturbance is not part of a broadly accepted cultural or religious practice. **Note:** In children, the symptoms are not better explained by imaginary playmates or other fantasy play.	D. No adaptation.
E. The symptoms are not attributable to physiological effects of a substance (e.g., blackouts or chaotic behavior during alcohol intoxication) or another medical condition (e.g., complex partial seizures).	E. No adaptation.

Dissociative Amnesia

DSM-5 Diagnostic Criteria	Applying Criteria for Individuals with Intellectual Disability
A. The inability to recall important autobiographical information, usually of traumatic or stressful nature, that is inconsistent with ordinary forgetting. **Note:** Dissociative amnesia most often consists of localized or selective amnesia for a specific event or events; or generalized amnesia for identity and life history.	A. Recognize the individual's expression(s) of autobiographical information in their usual state of functioning (baseline).
B. The symptoms cause clinically significant distress or impairment in social, occupational, or other important areas of functioning.	B. No adaptation.
C. The disturbance is not attributable to physiological effects of a substance (e.g. alcohol or other drug of abuse, a medication) or a neurological or other medical condition (e.g., partial complex seizures, transient global amnesia, sequelae of a closed head injury/traumatic brain injury, other neurological condition.	C. No adaptation.
D. The disturbance is not better explained by dissociative identity disorder, posttraumatic stress disorder, acute stress disorder, somatic symptom disorder, or major or mild neurocognitive disorder.	D. No adaptation.
Dissociative Amnesia with Dissociative Fugue Apparently purposeful travel or bewildered wandering that is associated with amnesia for identity or other important autobiographical information.	No adaptation.

Depersonalization/Derealization Disorder

DSM-5 Diagnostic Criteria	Applying Criteria for Individuals with Intellectual Disability
A. The presence of persistent or recurrent experiences of depersonalization, derealization, or both: 1. Depersonalitzation: Experiences of unreality, detachment, or being an outside observer with respect to one's thoughts, feelings, sensations, body, or actions (e.g., perceptual alterations, distorted sense of time, unreal or absent self, emotional and/or physical numbing. 2. Derealization: Experiences of unreality or detachment with respect to surroundings (e.g., individuals or objects are experienced as unreal, dreamlike, foggy, lifeless, or visually distorted).	A. Include use of non-verbal assessment techniques. It may be normal to discuss one's experiences in the 3rd person.
B. During the depersonalization or derealization experiences, reality testing remains intact.	B. No adaptation.
C. The symptoms cause clinically significant distress or impairment in social, occupational, or other important areas of functioning.	C. No adaptation.
D. The disturbance is not attributable to physiological effects of a substance or another medical condition.	D. No adaptation.
E. The disturbance is not better explained by schizophrenia, panic disorder, major depressive disorder, acute stress disorder, posttraumatic stress disorder, or another dissociative disorder.	E. No adaptation.

Other Specified Dissociative Disorder
Unspecified Dissociative Disorder

DSM-5 also provides criteria for other specified dissociative disorder and for unspecified dissociative disorder.

References

Boon, S., & Draijer, N. (1993, Mar). Multiple personality disorder in the Netherlands: A clinical investigation of 71 patients. *American Journal of Psychiatry, 150*(3), 489-94.

Boysen, G.A., & VanBergen, A. (2013, Jan). A review of published research on adult dissociative identity disorder 2000-2010. *Journal of Nervous and Mental Disease, 201*(1), 5-11.

Chodoff, P. (1997, Aug). Turkish dissociative identity disorder. *American Journal of Psychiatry, 154*(8), 1179.

Fairley, M., Jones, R.C., McGuire, B.E., & Stevenson, J. (1995, Mar). Multiple personality disorder in an intellectually disabled man: A case report. *Austalian and. New Zealand Journal of Psychiatry, 29*(1), 146-9.

Forrest, K.A. (2001, Sep). Toward an etiology of dissociative identity disorder: A neurodevelopment approach. *Conciousness and Cognition, 10*(3), 259-93.

Fotheringham, J.B., & Thompson, F. (1994, Mar). Case report of a person with Down's syndrome and multiple personality disorder. *Canadian Journal of Psychiatry, 39*(2), 116-9.

Fujii, Y., Suzuki, K., Sato, T., Murakami, Y., & Takahashi, T. (1998, Jun). Multiple personality disorder in Japan. *Psychiatry and Clinical Neurosciences, 52*(3), 299-302.

International Society for the Study of Trauma and Dissociation. (2011). Guidelines for treating dissociative identity disorder in adults, third revision. *Journal of Trauma and Dissociation, 12*(2), 115-87.

Malchiodi, C.A. (1994). Introduction to special section on sexual abuse and dissociative disorder. *Art Therapy: Journal of the American Art Therapy Association, 11*(1), 34-36.

McAllister, M.M. (2000). Dissociative identity disorder: a literature review. *Journal of Psychiatric and Mental Health Nursing, 7*(1), 25-33.

Mills, A. (1995). Outpatient art therapy with multiple personality disorder: A survey of current practice. *Art Therapy: Journal of the American Art Therapy Association,* 12(4), 253-56.

Modestin, J. (1992, Jan). Multiple personality disorder in Switzerland. *American Journal of Psychiatry, 149*(1), 88-92.

Murphy, P.S. (1994). The contribution of art therapy to the dissociative disorders. *Art Therapy: Journal of the American Art Therapy Association, 11*(1), 43-7.

Paris, J. (2012). The rise and fall of dissociative identity disorder. *Journal of Nervous and Mental Diseases, 200*(12), 1076-9.

Pope, H.G. Jr, Barry, S., Bodkin, A., & Hudson, J.I. (2006). Tracking scientific interest in the dissociative disorders: A study of scientific publication output 1984-2003. *Psychotherapy and Psychosomatics, 75*(1), 19-24.

Reed-Gavish, M. (2013). Cognitive abuse within the incestuous family as a factor in the development of dissociative identity disorder. *Journal of Child Sexual Abuse, 22*(4), 444-61.

Rossini, E.D., Schwartz, D.R., & Braun, B.G. (1996 May). Intellectual functioning of inpatients with dissociative identity disorder and dissociative disorder not otherwise specified. Cognitive and neuropsychological aspects. *Journal of Nervous and Mental Diseases, 184*(5), 289-94.

Thompson, G. (2011). Multiplicity and self-identity: trauma and integration in Shirley Mason's art. *Art Therapy: Journal of the American Art Therapy Association, 28*(1), 39-42.

Uttley, L., Scope, A., Stevenson, M., Rawdin, A., Taylor Buck, E., Sutton, A., … Wood C. (2015, March). Systematic review and economic modeling of the clinical effectiveness and cost-effectiveness of art therapy among people with non-psychotic mental health disorders. *Health Technology Assessment, 19*(18), 1-148.

van Duijl, M., Kleijn, W., & de Jong, J. (2013). Are symptoms of spirit possessed patients covered by the DSM-IV or DSM-5 criteria for possession trance disorder? A mice-method explorative study in Uganda. *Social Psychiatry Psychiatric Epidemiology, 48*(9), 1417-30.

Xiao, Z., Yan, H., Wang, Z., Zou, Z., Xu, Y., Chen, J., … Keyes BB. (2006). Trauma and dissociation in China. *American Journal of Psychiatry, 163*(8), 1388-91.

CHAPTER 17

Somatic Symptom and Related Disorders

Marco O. Bertelli
Bruce J. Tonge
Avril V. Brereton

Somatic symptom and related disorders is a new category of the DSM-5 (American Psychiatric Association, 2013), which includes somatic symptom disorder and the other disorders with prominent somatic symptoms. These are: illness anxiety disorder, conversion disorder (functional neurological symptom disorder), psychological factors affecting other medical conditions, factitious disorder, other specified somatic symptom and related disorder, and unspecified somatic symptom and related disorder. All of the disorders in this category are characterized by the prominence of somatic symptoms associated with significant distress and impairment in daily life.

Somatic symptom disorder entails manifestations of psychological distress presenting as medically unexplained disabling physical symptoms. Illness anxiety disorder is characterized by a preoccupation with having or acquiring a serious, undiagnosed medical illness. Conversion disorder has a core feature of neurological symptoms, which are found, after specific assessment, to be incompatible with neurological illnesses. Psychological factors affecting other medical conditions embody the presence of one or more clinically significant psychological or behavioral factors that negatively impact on a medical condition by increasing the risk for suffering, death, or disability. Factitious disorders are deliberately created or an exaggeration of physical or psychological symptoms to achieve a sick role.

Individuals with disorders with prominent somatic symptoms are encountered in primary care and other medical settings more commonly than in psychiatric and other mental health contexts. They might be linked to developmental disadvantage or recent psychological stress. A co-occurrence with depression and anxiety is common and differential diagnosis, though difficult in persons with ID, may have helpful treatment implications.

The DSM-5 diagnostic criteria are generally applicable to persons with ID with minor adaptation, if they have some language or communication ability. Nevertheless, as for all the other psychiatric disorders, it is necessary to obtain collateral information on the environmental context and daily routines and lifestyle, problem behaviors, attachment behavior, interpersonal relationships, reaction to stress, help-seeking behavior, and communicative ability.

Review of DSM-5 Diagnostic Criteria and Innovations

The most relevant changes to the DSM-IV (American Psychiatric Association 1994, 2000) criteria were made to clarify the boundaries of different disorders within the group, to eliminate overlap across them, and to better reflect the complex interface between mental and physical health. Because patients suffering from somatic symptom and related disorders are not primarily seen in psychiatric settings but in general medical settings, the new criteria clarify confusing terms and reduce the number of disorders and sub-categories to make the diagnoses more useful to non-psychiatric medical and care providers.

Somatization disorder, hypochondriasis, pain disorder, and undifferentiated somatoform disorder have been removed and merged, but not completely, into the somatic symptom disorder.

Somatic symptom disorder is characterized by persistent somatic symptoms that are either very distressing or result in significant disruption of functioning, as well as excessive and disproportionate thoughts, feelings and behaviors regarding those symptoms. A key change in the DSM-5 criteria is that it de-emphasizes the centrality of medically unexplained symptoms in favor of the persistence of disproportionate thoughts, feelings, and behaviors related to these symptoms. The somatic symptom disorder criteria no longer have the DSM-IV somatization disorder requirements of a specific number of complaints from among four symptom groups; however, somatic symptoms must be significantly distressing or disruptive to daily life and must be accompanied by excessive thoughts, feelings, or behaviors. Furthermore, somatic symptoms are no longer required to be medically unexplained to make a diagnosis of somatic symptom disorder, which means that symptoms may or may not be associated with another medical condition. The DSM-5 text description that accompanies the criteria for somatic symptom disorder points out that it is not appropriate to diagnose individuals with a mental disorder solely because a medical cause cannot be demonstrated and that more proportionate attention in the diagnostic process should be addressed to the rest of the criteria.

The DSM-5 narrative text for somatic symptom disorder also specifies that patients with physical conditions can experience disproportionate and excessive thoughts, feelings, and behaviors related to their illness, and that they can be diagnosed with somatic symptom disorder and access treatment for these symptoms. When co-occurring with a medical illness, somatic symptom disorder is more difficult to identify, especially without clinical training and experience.

Psychological symptoms enhance predictive validity and clinical utility of the somatic symptom disorder diagnostic criteria in comparison to DSM-IV somatoform disorders. Furthermore, the change in emphasis from medically unexplained symptoms to persistence of disproportionate thoughts, feelings, and behaviors attenuates the mind-body separation of the previous DSM edition, reduces the likelihood that the individual will regard the diagnosis as pejorative, and encourages clinicians to make a comprehensive assessment and use dimensional judgment.

DSM-5 criteria for somatic symptom disorder eliminate overlap and confusion from previous editions and encourage comprehensive assessment of patients for precise diagnosis and holistic care.

To ensure that the new criteria would indeed help clinicians better identify individuals who need care; clinical researchers tested the somatic symptom disorder criteria in actual clinical practices during the DSM-5 field trials. The diagnosis of somatic symptom disorder was found to be very reliable in these field tests. It was also found that the DSM-5 diagnosis identified more psychologically impaired patients than its DSM-IV precursor (Voigt et al., 2012).

One study indicated that at a one year follow-up mental functioning can be better predicted by the DSM-5 than by DSM-IV criteria (Voigt et al., 2013).

In DSM-5, the DSM-IV-TR category of pain disorder has become a qualifier of somatic symptom disorder. Only a few individuals with chronic pain would be more appropriately diagnosed as having "psychological factors affecting other medical conditions" or an adjustment disorder. This change was determined by the appreciation of the lack of evidence supporting the previous criteria of distinguishing pain associated solely with psychological factors from pain associated solely with medical diseases or injuries, or pain associated with both.

The change is also justified given the research demonstrating that psychological factors may influence and be influenced by all kinds of pain. The clinical experience of the authors of the present chapter confirms that most individuals with chronic pain report a complex interaction of somatic, psychological, and environmental causes and perpetuating factors.

Illness Anxiety Disorder replaces the DSM-IV diagnosis of hypochondriasis, which has been eliminated as a disorder. One of the main reasons for this elimination was the stigma surrounding the term, due in turn to the public's misperception of the disorder. Many people incorrectly characterize hypochondriacs as individuals who intentionally fake illness for gain. This stigmatization was found to considerably limit an effective therapeutic relationship.

Illness anxiety disorder is characterized by high health anxiety without somatic symptoms. Those in whom health anxiety is better explained by an anxiety disorder, such as generalized anxiety disorder, have to be diagnosed with this primary disorder.

Conversion Disorder (Functional Neurological Symptom Disorder) has been set with new criteria to increase the importance of the neurological examination and diminish that of the presence of relevant psychological factors at the time of diagnosis.

Conversion disorder (functional neurological symptom disorder) is characterized by the presence of at least one symptom of altered voluntary motor or sensory function with evidence of incompatibility between the symptom and recognized neurological or medical conditions.

Factitious Disorders are characterized by feigned physical or psychological symptoms that are produced intentionally to achieve the role of a sick, impaired, or injured person and are associated with deceptive behavior, even in the absence of external rewards. Patients with factitious disorders frequently report a history of multiple and extensive contact with hospitals.

Psychological factors affecting other medical conditions was formerly included in the DSM-IV-TR chapter "Other Conditions That May Be a Focus of Clinical Attention." Factitious disorder is placed among the somatic symptom and related disorders because it is most often encountered in medical settings and because somatic symptoms are predominant within the cluster of symptoms. The variants of psychological factors affecting other medical conditions have been removed in favor of the stem diagnosis.

Summary of DSM-5 Criteria

Somatic symptom disorder presents with multiple, current, somatic symptoms that are distressing or result in significant impairment in daily functioning (Criterion A). Although any one somatic symptom may not be continuously present, the state of being symptomatic is lasting (Criterion C). Symptoms of somatic symptom disorder may be specific (e.g., localized pain) or relatively nonspecific (e.g., fatigue). Excessive and persistent thoughts about the seriousness of one's symptom, high levels of anxiety about the symptoms, and considerable time and energy being devoted to symptoms or health concerns are typical features of this disorder (Criterion B). Individuals with somatic symptom disorder experience distress that is mainly focused on somatic symptoms and their meaning. They usually give inconsistent and exaggerated descriptions of their illnesses, and they seek treatment from a variety of practitioners and clinics, resulting in multiple medical procedures and treatments.

In children the presence of a single prominent symptom is more frequent than in adults.

Moreover, in older individuals who present with many somatic symptoms the co-occurrence of a depressive disorder is common.

The disorder is often associated with an impairment of health-related quality of life. Cognitive features associated with somatic symptom disorder consist of thoughts focused on somatic symptoms, attribution of usual bodily sensations to physical illness, preoccupation about illness, and apprehension that any activity involving use of the body may cause injuries. The behavioral features related to the disorder may involve repetitive examination of the body for abnormalities, repeated seeking of medical help, and limitation of physical activity.

There may be cultural differences in the pattern and type of symptoms experienced, but the relationship between somatic symptoms and depression seems similar across the world. Description of symptoms, explanatory models, and medical treatments vary among cultural groups.

The main differential diagnosis is a general medical condition, but a somatic symptom disorder and a medical illness can co-occur. The presence of somatic symptoms without a medical explanation is not sufficient to make the diagnosis of somatic symptom disorder. For example, the symptoms of disorders like irritable bowel syndrome or fibromyalgia would not necessarily satisfy the diagnostic criterion of somatic symptom disorder (Criterion B). On the contrary, having disabling somatic symptoms and worry in the setting of a clear medical condition (e.g., diabetes) meets the criteria for the diagnosis of somatic symptom disorder.

Somatic symptoms are often a feature of illness anxiety disorder, depressive disorders, conversion disorder (functional neurological symptom disorder) and symptoms of somatic symptom disorder need also to be differentiated from those of delusional disorder and body dysmorphic disorder.

Another differential diagnosis is obsessive-compulsive disorder. The distinction can be made on the basis that those with somatic symptom disorder do not manifest the characteristic compulsive behaviors aimed at decreasing anxiety due to obsessive thoughts.

Co-morbidity occurs most frequently with anxiety and depressive disorders.

Conversion disorder (functional neurological symptom disorder) presents with pseudo-neurological symptoms manifesting as altered voluntary motor or sensory symptoms (Criterion A) that are not consistent with a medical or neurological condition (Criterion B) and are not better explained by another medical or mental illness (Criterion C). The symptom or deficit produces significant distress or impairment in daily activities and in socio-occupational functioning (Criterion D). Conversion disorder may present with one or more symptoms of different types. For example, motor symptoms of weakness, paralysis, or abnormal gait or movements; and sensory symptoms of altered, reduced, or even absent skin sensation, vision, hearing. To make a diagnosis of conversion disorder, the results of medical investigations have to clearly show incompatibility with neurological illness or nerve function. There are also other associated features that support this diagnosis, such as a history of multiple analogous somatic symptoms, psychological or physical stress or trauma, or dissociative symptoms (depersonalization, derealization, or dissociative amnesia) particularly at the onset of the symptom.

The diagnosis does not require a definite decision that the symptom are not feigned and for secondary gain, as assessment of intention can be difficult, but clear evidence of a personal gain or malingering motivation would justify the differential diagnosis of factitious disorder. Preoccupying somatic symptom thoughts and behaviors seen in somatic symptom disorder are not characteristic of conversion disorder. Conversion disorder may coexist with a neurological disease, and it also may be diagnosed in addition to somatic symptom disorder. The differential diagnosis for conversion disorder includes neurological disorders, somatic symptom disorder, factitious disorder, dissociative disorders, depressive disorders, body dysmorphic disorder, and panic disorder.

Comorbidity commonly occurs with anxiety disorder, depressive disorders, and personality disorders, whereas psychosis and substance use disordr are uncommon.

Illness anxiety disorder is defined by preoccupying fears of having a serious, undiagnosed medical illness based on a misinterpretation of minor bodily symptoms or signs (criterion A). If somatic symptoms are present, they are only mild in intensity (Criterion B). Worry about illness has been for at least 6 months but the specific illness may change over that period (Criterion E). The preoccupation is accompanied by substantial anxiety about health (Criterion C) and the concerns about undiagnosed disease do not respond to suitable medical reassurance, negative diagnostic tests, or benign course.

Illness concerns become a central characteristic of the person's identity and self-image. People with the disorder often examine themselves repeatedly (Criterion D), research their suspected disease excessively (e.g., on the Internet), and continuously seek reassurance from family, friends, or physicians.

Individuals with illness anxiety disorder commonly report high rates of utilization of medical services, often seek the advice of many health professionals, and in general are unsatisfied with their medical care.

The onset of the disorder is generally thought to be in early and middle adulthood. It produces considerable functional impairment by reducing physical activity and quality of life, interfering with family and social relationships, and impairing occupational performance.

The main differential diagnosis is a general medical condition for example involving neurological or endocrine conditions or hidden malignancies. The presence of symptoms attributable to a medical condition does not exclude a coexisting illness anxiety disorder when concerns related to the medical condition are disproportionate to its gravity. Individuals with generalized anxiety disorders may report preoccupations involving health but in illness anxiety disorder disabling health-related fears are more constant and enduring. Intrusive thoughts about having an illness may also be symptomatic of an obsessive-compulsive disorder if the anxious thoughts are focused on a fear of acquiring an illness in the future, whereas in illness anxiety disorder the concerns are usually centered on having an illness.

Adjustment disorder, somatic symptom disorder, and major depressive disorder are other differential diagnoses. Concerns and fears about diseases may be present also in psychotic disorders, but in this case, somatic delusions are more bizarre whereas the concerns that can be seen in illness anxiety disorder, despite not based on the reality, are believable.

Little is known about which conditions are likely to be co-morbid with illness anxiety disorder, but it is suggested that people with illness anxiety disorder may have an elevated risk of also suffering from somatic symptom disorder and personality disorders.

Psychological factors affecting other medical conditions are conditions defined by the presence of one or more clinically relevant psychological or behavioral factors that do not meet criteria for another mental illness, such as psychological distress, patterns of personal interaction, coping styles, maladaptive health behaviors, and poor adherence to medical advice, that adversely affects an existing medical condition (Criterion A) thus increasing the risk of suffering, disability, or death. The factors are additional to well-established health risks for the person. They adversely affect an illness by influencing its course or treatment or underlying pathophysiology, thus leading to an exacerbation of symptoms or the need for medical attention (Criterion B). These psychological factors are not better explained by another mental illness such as a depression (Criterion C).

These factors can range from acute to chronic, can occur across the lifespan and may be related to a life stage or stress such as caring for a sick relative. The psychological disturbance can be associated with any medical condition including those characterized by explicit pathophysiology, functional syndromes, or idiopathic medical symptoms. To make the diagnosis it is necessary that the psychological factor has a clinically relevant and evident effect on the medical condition. Therefore, there must be reasonable evidence to suggest a temporal relationship, even though it may often not be possible to demonstrate clear causality or the mechanism underlying the association between the psychological factors and the medical condition.

The main differential diagnosis is "mental disorder due to another medical condition" where there is also a temporal association between symptoms of a mental illness and those of a medical condition, but in this case the medical condition is determined to be causing the mental disorder. In contrast, for "psychological factors affecting other medical conditions," the psychological or behavioral factors are judged to only be affecting the course of the medical condition. Abnormal psychological or behavioral factors that develop in response to a medical condition should be diagnosed as an adjustment disorder. However, the psychological response to an illness and then the effect of that response back on the medical illness can be an interaction that makes the distinction between the two conditions arbitrary. In the case where a person has an existing mental illness that adversely affects or causes a medical illness then it is sufficient to diagnose that mental illness and the medical condition. "Psychological factors affecting other medical conditions" should be diagnosed only when the psychological traits or behaviors do not meet criteria for another mental illness diagnosis. A somatic symptom disorder can also be a differential diagnosis where the emphasis is on maladaptive thoughts, feelings, and behaviors in contrast to "psychological factors affecting other medical conditions" where the emphasis is on the exacerbation of the medical condition. An illness anxiety disorder is another differential diagnosis that is defined by high illness anxiety that is disruptive to daily life but with minimal somatic symptoms and in most cases no serious disease is present. In contrast for those with "psychological factors affecting other medical conditions" anxiety may represent a significant psychological factor but the clinical concern is the unfavorable effects on an existing medical condition.

Factitious disorder is categorized in the DSM 5 into two types: factitious disorder imposed on self and factious disorder imposed on another. Falsification of physical or psychological signs or symptoms or a combination of these occurs in factitious disorder. It may also include self-injury, for example cutting the skin to produce blood to mix with urine to fabricate renal disease. There are no obvious rewards like money or time off of work to explain why the individual is deceiving others. To make the diagnosis, it is necessary to rule out delusions or other evidence of psychosis. Factitious disorder can occur as a single episode or be a recurrent pattern.

One example of factitious disorder is to mimic behavior that is typical of a mental illness, such as schizophrenia. The person may appear confused, make absurd statements, and report hallucinations (the experience of sensing things that are not there; for example, hearing voices).

Another example is deceptively claiming to have symptoms related to a physical illness, such as chest pain, stomach problems, or fever. In the past this was referred to as Munchausen syndrome, named for Baron von Munchausen, an 18th century German officer who was known for embellishing the stories of his life and experiences.

Factitious disorder imposed on another was formerly called factitious disorder by proxy or Munchausen syndrome by proxy. Individuals with this disorder produce or fabricate symptoms of illness in another under their care such as children, elderly adults, disabled persons, or pets. It most often occurs in mothers, although it can occur in fathers, who intentionally harm their children in order to receive attention. The diagnosis is not given to the victim, but rather to the perpetrator.

A person with a factitious disorder intentionally presents to medical services with signs or symptoms (criterion A) of a physical disorder or a psychological illness. For example, he or she might fabricate complaints of acute abdominal pain, falsify a sign (for example, tamper with a thermometer), self-inflict a wound, or feign a medical condition (for example, an epileptic seizure). This behavior places the person in a sick role (criterion B), but he or she is not seeking any external gain, such as financial compensation (criterion C).

The person usually presents to a hospital or clinic in a dramatic manner and gives an elaborate, fabricated, but often inconsistent account of his or her symptoms ("pseudologia fantastica"). The person might travel widely seeking hospital admission but usually demands discharge against medical advice when challenged about the contrived nature of the symptoms.

A person with psychological signs and symptoms might present with weeping, ideas of suicide, hallucinations, or memory loss. These symptoms are based on the person's perception of a mental illness, which might not relate to any specific diagnostic category if the person is unsophisticated. Munchausen's syndrome, which manifests as repeated hospitalization, peregrination (traveling), and pseudologia fantastica, is the most severe form of this disorder.

Other specified somatic symptom and related disorders include presentations characterized by symptoms of somatic symptom and related disorders which do not fully satisfy the criteria of any specific disorder, although they cause impairment in individual functioning or significant distress. Specific disorders within this category are identified by specific reasons for not fully accomplishing criteria of any disorder in the somatic symptom and related disorders group.

For duration less than 6 months, clinicians have to diagnose a 'brief somatic symptom disorder' or a 'brief illness anxiety disorder.' For lack of excessive health-related behaviors clinicians have to diagnose an 'illness anxiety disorder without excessive health-related behaviors'.

The category also includes 'pseudocyesis', which is characterized by a belief of being pregnant without objective signs, laboratory, and instrumental findings of pregnancy.

Unspecified somatic symptom and related disorders include presentations characterized by symptoms of somatic symptom and related disorders associated with impairment in individual functioning or significant distress, which do not fully satisfy the criteria of any specific disorder, not even 'other specified somatic symptom and related disorders'. Clinicians should generally avoid using this category if the only reason is the unavailability of information for a more specific diagnosis.

Issues Related to Diagnosis in People with ID

Somatic symptom disorder. The research on specific issues that impact upon the diagnosis of a somatic symptom disorder in persons with ID is lacking, and the strength of evidence in this field is quite low, around IV-V. In general, the DSM diagnosis of this group of conditions requires that the individual can verbally communicate the symptoms, and this requirement limits the diagnosis of somatization to individuals with ID who have language ability. Nevertheless, the DM-ID is based on the appraisal that persons with ID may present behavioural signs and symptoms of psychiatric disorders and communicate non-verbally. It is possible that persons with more severe ID and no functional language might present signs and symptoms of somatization with behavioral changes, baseline behavior exaggerations, or postural changes or positions, for example, to indicate persistent back pain or pseudo-neurological loss of sensation in a limb for which no medical cause could be found. The use of specific symptom and behavior observation records kept over time by caregivers or family members is usually necessary to better understand and describe pain as well as other somatic symptoms.

Paradoxically, it might be more straightforward to confirm the diagnosis of conversion disorder or somatic symptom disorder in a person with ID and some verbal skills, such as a person with mild ID, than it would in a person without ID, as the former is more likely to be medically naïve, unsophisticated, and liable to give an inconsistent history and implausible symptoms. In this case, an integrative history from a caretaker or a relative is a critical element to make a reliable diagnosis.

A crucial element in the diagnosis of a somatic symptom disorder is to determine that there is no medical issue that could fully account for the presentation. In comparison with the general population, persons with ID are more likely to have reduced or inconsistent access to medical services (Disability Rights Commission, 2006) and general medical practitioners often lack skills in dealing with an individual with ID (Wullink, Veldhuijzen, Lantman-de Valk, Metsemaker, & Dinant, 2009). Therefore, it is possible that the symptoms will be considered simply as a medical condition without adequate investigation or will be regarded simply as a consequence of the ID. For the same reason, it is likely that there are an unknown number of persons with ID who suffer from somatic symptom disorder who are not referred to mental health services and therefore remain undiagnosed.

The diagnosis of a somatic symptom disorder requires the presence of "significant disruption of daily life." It is essential, therefore, to obtain a reliable account of the individual's usual or pre-morbid level of emotional and behavioral adjustment. For example, a person with moderate ID might always have been irritable and easily upset in response to minor frustrations or changes in routine. This person's most meaningful activities might be an afternoon walk with other members of the residential unit and helping to set the table for meals. A loss of interest or ability to participate in these activities would be a significant impairment and would meet this criterion.

The most difficult, and at times probably insurmountable, problem in the diagnosis of a somatic symptom disorder in a person with ID is to differentiate the presenting signs and symptoms from another mental disorder, particularly a mood disorder or an anxiety disorder. In an individual with ID, it might be necessary to rely on such vegetative or behavioral symptoms as loss of interest or energy, or refusal to eat, in diagnosing a mood disorder, but these symptoms can also be present in a somatic symptom disorder.

In a person with ID, such subjective symptoms of anxiety as worry, fearful thoughts, and palpitations can be difficult to assess, because their diagnosis relies on self-report; on the other hand, somatic symptoms that can be observed, such as sweating, trembling, shaking, and agitation, can be reliably diagnosed (Masi, Favilla, & Mucci., 2000; Matson, Smiroldo, Hamilton, & Baglio, 1997). Individuals with ID are also more likely to have altered sensory responsiveness particularly those who also have an ASD who may show hypo- or hypersensitivity to pain (Andrasik & Rime, 2009, Baldridge & Andrasik 2010).There might be a genetic predisposition to experiencing somatic symptoms for some people with ID as there is some evidence that individuals with Prader Willi syndrome (Skokanskas Sweeney, Meehan, & Gallagher, 2012) and velo-cardio-facial syndrome(Antshel et al., 2007) are more likely to have somatization symptoms than others with ID or the general population.

It is also difficult to assess whether a symptom such as pain is "not intentionally produced or feigned" for some gain, for example, assuming a sick role, obtaining medical attention, or receiving some external reward, such as compensation or avoiding a duty. It is likely that a person with ID who is receiving some form of daily care and supervision, for example, in a community residential unit, might quickly receive some form of secondary gain, such as extra attention or avoidance of domestic chores, if he or she develops nausea or pain as one of the symptoms of a somatic symptom disorder.

A person with ID is also at increased risk of experiencing stressful life events, traumatic experiences, denigration, and inconsistent, conflicted, or abusive care (Greenbaum & Auerbach, 1998)and homelessness(Van Straaten et al. 2014) all of which predicate anxiety disorders and stress disorder such as posttraumatic stress disorder. These same psychological traumas are also risk factors for somatic symptom disorders and are also recognized as risk and prognostic factors in conversion disorder. The clinician must gain, if possible, an understanding from the person with ID, supplemented by information from caretakers, of any psychological stresses that might be experienced by the individual being assessed.

A person with ID is likely to have a limited capacity to influence and deal with environmental changes or events (Greenbaum & Auerbach, 1998). Therefore, a diagnostic assessment requires an adequate understanding of the person's past emotional and behavioral adjustment and response to change, conflict, and even daily life events (Glick, 1998). For example, the loss of a regular caregiver, the closure of a specific day program, or even the change in the route of the daily bus to a day program might be experienced as most stressful by a person with ID.

In the general population, unexplained or multiple somatic symptoms are strongly associated with depressive and anxiety disorders. Predictors of psychiatric co-morbidity include recent stress, lower self-rated health, and higher somatic symptom severity, as well as high healthcare utilization, difficult patient encounters as perceived by the physician, and chronic medical disorders (Kroenke, 2003).

The diagnosis of an anxiety or a mood disorder takes precedence over that of a somatic symptom disorder. Therefore, in situations of diagnostic uncertainty, particularly in persons with more severe levels of ID and poor communication skills, it would be more appropriate to make a diagnosis of a mood or an anxiety disorder rather than of a somatic symptom disorder if the profile of somatic symptoms and observed behaviors suggests either a mood or an anxiety disorder, on the one hand, or a somatic symptom disorder, on the other hand.

Illness anxiety disorder. The main problem in making this diagnosis in people with ID and some capacity to communicate is that they are likely to have a limited and simplistic understanding of illness together with poor insight and be unable to recognize that their fears regarding illness or death are unreasonable. It is even more difficult if not impossible to make this diagnosis in those with more severe levels of ID and little or no language but it is possible that a distressing experience of pain and illness might predicate an excessive emotional response to reminders of this experience or another illness justifying the diagnosis of an illness anxiety disorder. A careful history of previous medical illness and its circumstances and the person's response can help diagnosis.

Conversion disorder. A major diagnostic issue in individuals with ID is the differentiation of epileptic seizures from "non epileptic seizures". Individuals with recurrent or refractory epileptic seizures are at risk of also having non-epileptic seizures and this risk is probably further increased in those with ID (Barnhill 2007, Duncan & Oto 2008, Rawat et al. 2015). Current psycho-social stress and cultural factors might increase the likelihood of non-epileptic seizures (Chudleigh et al. 2013, Duncan & Oto 2008, Rawat et al. 2015). There might be a genetic neuro-developmental basis, related to altered activation of brain frontal inhibitory structures, in some cases of conversion disorder and non-epileptic seizures, for example as has been identified as a risk in individuals with fragile X syndrome (Seritan et al., 2009)

Factitious disorders. The critical diagnostic issue is to determine if the psychological symptoms or physical signs are produced intentionally in the absence of any obvious reward. It is possible that people with mild ID might be more obvious or naïve in disclosing their intentions. For those with more severe levels of ID, it is likely that intention can be inferred only from the content of the behavior and detailed observation by caregivers. People with ID are unlikely to have much, if any, knowledge of a specific psychological disorder, such as depression, but they might in a naïve and incoherent manner produce such symptoms as wailing, memory loss, or auditory hallucinations, particularly if they have seen others with these symptoms, for example, in a television show.

Similarly, the enacting of a physical disorder is likely to be inconsistent and naïve. Careful observation and documentation of the context and consequences of illness symptoms and self-injurious behavior, such as biting a wrist wound, would be necessary to determine whether the primary intention of the behavior was to seek an obvious reward such as care and attention. In such a circumstance the behavior might be malingering or if the person has anxiety about his/her health then diagnosis of illness anxiety disorder would be appropriate. The clinician's ability to differentiate secondary gain from a primary intentional production of symptoms or malingering depends upon a clear account by an observer of the chronology of the development of symptoms and their environmental content, as well as the response of others to the symptoms and an understanding of any gain received by the individual from his or her own perspective. For example, being isolated and put to bed in a quiet bedroom because of nausea and headache might be a substantial gain to a person with autism and moderate ID when noisy building renovations are underway in the living rooms of their residential unit.

A critical issue in diagnosis is making a differentiation from malingering, in which the goal of the behavior is to achieve an external reward or outcome. This diagnostic distinction can create difficulties for the clinician and again underlines the necessity to gather a comprehensive description of the context and consequences of the symptoms. For example, a young man with ID who makes himself vomit and misses the bus to the day program, but then who enjoys the day listening to his favorite music at his residence, is malingering. In contrast, the young man who induces vomiting until he is in a situation of constant supervision and care in bed is more likely to have a factitious disorder.

Münchausen's syndrome is a form of factitious disorder imposed on the self. There is a case report of Münchausen's syndrome in an individual with probably mild ID (Morgan, Roy, Houldey, & Miller, 2001). It is unlikely, however, that a person with a Moderate or more severe level of ID would have sufficient sophistication to be able to plan, fabricate, and pursue the behaviors required to create this chronic disorder. As a note of caution to clinicians treating people with ID, there is a reported case of Munchausen's syndrome, where the individual feigned "symptoms of mental handicap as well as suicidal ideas and symptoms of bereavement and psychosis" (Craddock & Brown 1993).There is also an unpublished case known to the author (BT) of Münchausen's syndrome by proxy, (factitious disorder imposed on another) involving a child with ID. A mother presented her son as severely intellectually disabled to the hospital, seeking treatment for a range of serious but fabricated disorders, including epilepsy, encopresis, and diabetes, all of which subsequently proved to be fabricated. During the admission, it became apparent when the boy was separated from his mother, that he was not as severely delayed as was thought. When attempts were made to investigate his cognitive ability, the mother discharged him and disappeared, only to subsequently present him to another hospital in another part of the country.

Application of Diagnostic Criteria to People with ID

In general, the *DSM-5* criteria for somatic symptom and related disorders are applicable to people with Mild to Moderate levels of ID who have functional language. Some of the diagnostic criteria, however, have observable, behavioral manifestations, such as pain, altered motor or sensory function, and excessive behavioral response to a medical condition. The symptoms are frequently associated with stressful events. To determine what might constitute a stressful event for a person with ID, the clinician must understand the context of the individual's environment, the individual's comprehension of events, and the history of the individual's reaction to stress, coping skills, and experience of earlier traumatic events.

Persons with ID are more likely to be suggestible and to lack sophistication. They therefore might be vulnerable not only to the influences of their wider culture but also to the social pressures of their immediate care environment. Behavior that is syntonic with the social and cultural context must be differentiated from psychopathology.

The diagnostic criteria for all of these conditions require a determination that the presenting symptoms and signs are not fully explained by a medical condition or the use of a substance. Persons with ID are at increased risk of suffering chronic medical conditions and are often not able to communicate their symptoms accurately (Beange, McElduff, & Baker, 1995). For example, undiagnosed or treated osteoporosis or musculoskeletal and joint disorders (Whitefield & Russell, 1996) and chronic dental caries and gum disease (Beange et al., 1995) are common causes of chronic pain in individuals with ID. Chronic constipation is frequently a cause of discomfort and behavioral disturbance. Gastro-esophageal reflux with associated recurrent vomiting and dental erosions is commonly found in persons with ID, particularly those who are relatively immobile or who have spastic quadriplegia (Bohmer, 1996).

Epilepsy is the single most common chronic medical condition associated with ID. Pre- or post-ictal phenomena or behavioral symptoms of partial epilepsy (temporal lobe) seizures might produce such symptoms as behavioral disturbance, altered sensation, derealization, visual hallucinations, fugue-like states, and amnesia (Coulter, 1993).

A thorough physical examination, health review, and appropriate laboratory investigations are, therefore, essential components in the assessment of symptoms and signs that might be due to a somatic disorder.

The relative risk of substance abuse in persons with ID is not known, but persons with mild ID are likely to be at risk, given their vulnerability to social pressure and their relative lack of understanding of the effects of substances. For example, tobacco use is a significant health problem for people with ID (Tracy & Hosken, 1997). Alcohol and solvent abuse are also recognized as problems for individuals with mild ID. Caffeine ingestion can be a problem for individuals with more severe levels of ID who are in care (O'Connor & Davis, 1999). Investigation regarding the use of both legal and illicit substances, particularly those that are readily available, such as caffeine, solvents tobacco, and alcohol, is a necessary component of a psychiatric diagnostic assessment.

he identification of a possible psychologically traumatic event or stress and the determination of the significance of resulting impairment in social life and daily activities will be facilitated by knowledge of the individual's usual behavior, emotional adjustment, response to change, and daily routine. Necessary elements of the diagnostic process are a comprehensive history from caregivers and other informants, supplemented, if possible, by the use of behavior observation charts and structured checklists, such as the Aberrant Behaviour Checklist (Aman & Singh, 1986) or the Developmental Behaviour Checklist for children and adolescents (Einfeld & Tonge, 2002) or adults (Mohr, Tonge & Einfeld 2004)

Methodology

The literature review included searches of the PsycINFO and Medline databases from 1966 to the present with the keywords *somatic symptom, factitious disorders, somatoform disorders, somatization, conversion, Briquet's syndrome, hysteria, malingering, pain disorder, hypochondriasis, pseudocyesis, Münchausen's syndrome, Ganser syndrome, Psychogenic fugue, intellectual disability, intellectual developmental disorders, mental retardation, learning disability,* and *mental handicap.* This search revealed 1379 and 220 citations respectively. On close inspection 74 articles were relevant and only 6 of these were published since 2013 when the DSM-5 was published.

Review of Research Applying to People with ID

Somatic symptom disorder. There were no definitive case reports found in the literature but publications before 2013 report on somatic symptoms and somatization in people with ID. For example, there is a case study of a man with moderate ID and somatic symptoms of globus pharyngeus which meet criteria for a somatic symptom disorder (Piacentino, Politi, Moscariello, Meutti, & Biondi, 2010). A study of 75 individuals with Prader Willi syndrome matched to IQ, sex and age found significantly more somatic symptoms scored on the Child Behaviour Checklist than the control group (Skokauskas et al., 2012).

Empirical studies of somatic symptoms have been facilitated by the use of checklists such as the Psychopathology Inventory for Mentally Retarded Adults (PIMRA) (Matson, 1988). The PIMRA is a structured diagnostic checklist completed by clinicians or caregivers, which includes a "Somatoform Disorder Scale."

A study of 652 individuals, aged 14–74 years with a range of ID from mild to severe, living in the community or in residential facilities, confirmed the factorial validity of the Somatoform Disorders Scale of the PIMRA (Balboni, Battagliese, & Pedrabissi, 2000). Another study of 431 young people with mild to moderate ID in schools or day-care centers also confirmed the factorial validity of the Somatoform Disorders Scale of the PIMRA and found no age or level of ID effects.

It is reasonable to conclude that the PIMRA is likely to detect somatization symptoms in adults with ID, but diagnostic sensitivity and specificity in relation to the DSM-5 diagnosis of somatic symptom disorder have yet to be determined. A high Somatoform Disorders Scale score on the PIMRA might possibly indicate another diagnosis, such as depression or anxiety or illness anxiety disorder, rather than fulfill the clinical criteria for a somatic symptom disorder somatic symptom disorder. It is clear, however, that the use of robust taxonometric instruments such as the PIMRA offers a promising approach to future studies of somatic symptom and related disorders in persons with ID.

An indication that somatic symptom disorder might be more prevalent in persons with ID than in the general population has been provided by Fink (1995) in a study of 56 individuals with persistent somatization compared with 57 other frequent users of non-psychiatric inpatient hospital services in Denmark. All of these patients had been admitted to hospital on ten or more occasions over an 8-year period. The definition of somatization as a medically unexplained symptom that leads the person to seek medical help is consistent with *DSM-5* criteria for somatic symptom disorder or illness anxiety disorder. Although this study has relatively small numbers, 16% of the persistent somatizers had ID compared with 3.5% of the other patients. Age, gender, and level of ID characteristics of these individuals were not described. Comorbidity with anxiety (54%), depression (30%), phobias (18%), and psychosis (20%) was notable.

Illness anxiety disorder. This category has replaced the diagnosis of hypochondriasis of which there were some case studies of adults with ID in the older literature. For example, there is a case of an adult man with moderate ID who suffered from a persistent and solitary hypochondriacal anxious delusion that his teeth were becoming smaller (Brooke, Collacut, & Bhaumik, 1996). Another man with mild ID and "dermatitis artifacta" was reported to suffer a persistent isolated hypochondriacal delusion that it was due to an HIV infection (Pumar, & Icaro, 2013). However, because these two cases were judged by the authors to be experiencing delusions, the diagnosis would probably be that of a delusional disorder and would not meet criteria for an illness anxiety disorder.

Conversion disorder Only one study since the publication of the DSM-5 was located. This study of 44 children with non-epileptic seizures living in Bangladesh found that 34 of these had a conversion disorder and of those 23% also had ID (Rawat et al., 2015).

There is an older literature where cases probably would meet diagnostic criteria. For example, a description of pseudo-seizures in a 13-year-old with "educable" ID meets the criteria for conversion disorder (Lachenmeyer, Olson, & Madelyn, 1990). This girl had a history of epilepsy, but these "seizures" were manifested as different non-seizurelike body movements, were not associated with EEG abnormalities, and gained attention and care from nurses and teachers.

Factitious disorders. There are a few unambiguous case reports in the literature. Morgan et al. (2001) describe an intriguing case of Münchausen's syndrome in a 30-year-old man with probably mild ID, which meets the criteria for a factitious disorder. The unusual feature of this case was that the individual did not disappear when confronted with his fabricated symptoms but was able to be successfully treated over 2 years.

Heger (1998) reports a man with ID presenting with deliberately manufactured urinary tract symptoms that met the criteria for a factitious disorder. Feigned symptoms and behavior of a person with ID were also part of the presentation of an intellectually able adult with Münchausen's syndrome reported by Craddock & Brown (1993). A case report of severe self-injurious behavior (SIB) causing intraoral injuries in a 4-year-old girl with autism suggests that the SIB was a means of seeking attention (Medina, Sogbe, Gomez-Rey, & Mata, 2003). There is no clear evidence in the literature on SIB in persons with ID that the purpose, at least in some cases of SIB, is to seek a sick person role. Further study of SIB is required to determine if some cases might be defined as a factitious disorder. There is a case report of the successful use of non-contingent rewards in the treatment of a man with ID who probably had a Factitious disorder (HagopianLeBlanc, & Maglieri, 2000).

Evaluating the Level of Evidence Using the Cochrane Method

The foregoing review of research indicates that several well-designed cohort studies (Type

IV evidence), which although they were prior to the publication of DSM- 5 are of symptoms consistent with somatic symptom disorder (Fink, 1995; Balboni et al., 2000). Other literature based on case reports provides Type V evidence for illness anxiety disorder, Conversion disorder and factitious disorder within the somatic symptom and related disorders group.

Adults with Mild to Moderate ID

The foregoing literature review mostly relates to adults with mild to moderate ID and supports the conclusion that the diagnoses of somatic symptom and related disorders can be made in these adults. The case reports provide face validity for these diagnoses. The cohort study of persons with ID using the PIMRA questionnaire suggests that somatization symptoms can be reliably observed by clinicians or caregivers (Balboni et al., 2000). However, there is no evidence in the literature of the level of clinician agreement for these diagnoses. Therefore, the reliability of these diagnoses remains unknown.

Adults with Severe or Profound ID

Symptoms that might be consistent with a somatic symptom disorder or illness anxiety disorder or Other Specified or Unspecified somatic symptom and related disorders can be observed in persons with severe ID (Balboni et al., 2000). Therefore, there is li somatic symptom and related disorders mited evidence that the diagnosis of a somatic symptom and related disorders might be possible in a person with more severe levels of ID. The PIMRA questionnaire cohort study of persons with ID demonstrated that somatic symptoms could be assessed in individuals with severe ID and some level of language and communication ability. However, it is increasingly difficult, if not impossible to make a somatic symptom and related disorders diagnosis in a person with no language and Severe or Profound ID.

There is no evidence in the literature of the successful application of diagnostic criteria for Factitious Disorder in persons with Severe or Profound ID.

Children and Adolescents with ID

There are no reports in the recent literature of children with ID who have somatic symptom and related disorders. Earlier studies such as the PIMRA study included some adolescents with ID who had somatic symptoms that might be consistent with a somatic symptom and related disorders (Balboni et al., 2000).

The Australian 15 year longitudinal study of emotional and behavioral disorders in children and adolescents with ID (Einfeld & Tonge, 1996a, 1996b; Tonge & Einfeld, 2000, 2003) indicates that parents and caregivers, using the Developmental Behaviour Checklist, are able to reliably report somatic symptoms in children. These parental reports of somatic symptoms might indicate the possibility of a somatic symptom and related disorders but are not diagnostic. This study indicates that about 12–14% of this representative sample of children with ID had somatic symptoms, and this prevalence remained stable as the individuals moved through adolescence into young adult life. Children with Williams syndrome were 2.7 times more likely than the epidemiological sample of children with ID to have somatic symptoms, but children with Down Syndrome were 5 times less likely to have somatic symptoms. As the children in this study moved into young adult life, the frequency of somatic symptoms decreased in those with Williams syndrome (34% to 23%) but increased in those with Prader Willi syndrome (15% to 36%), Fragile X syndrome (11% to 17%), autism (15% to 18%) and Down syndrome (3% to 10%). The reporting of somatic symptoms was associated with increased total psychopathology scores and subscale scores for depression, anxiety, disruptive or antisocial behavior, self-absorption, and communication disturbance independently of age, gender, and IQ level.

These studies suggest that it is possible to reliably observe somatic symptoms in children and adolescents with from mild to severe ID. These symptoms are not necessarily diagnostic of a somatic symptom and related disorders, however, and might occur in other disorders, such as anxiety disorders. There are no studies that confirm that a reliable and valid diagnosis of somatic symptom and related disorders can be made in children and adolescents with ID.

There are no studies to date that have attempted to modify *DSM-5* diagnostic criteria for specific application to children and adolescents in general or for those with ID.

The *DSM 5* does specify some modifications for children in general as follows:

(i) **Somatic Symptoms Disorder.** In children, somatic symptom disorder presents more frequently with a single prominent symptom, which is often represented by recurrent abdominal pain, headache, fatigue, and nausea. The presence of somatic complaints in younger children is "rarely" associated with concern about illness. The parents' response to the symptoms is likely to influence the level of distress in the child and determine and time off school and medical intervention (p. 313).

(ii) **Illness Anxiety Disorder.** This disorder is "thought to be rare in Children" (p. 316).

(iii) **Conversion Disorder.** It is suggested that the prognosis for children may be better than for adolescents and adults (p. 320)

(iv) **Psychological Factor Affecting Other medical Conditions.** The symptoms and history should be corroborated by parents and teachers.

Until there is evidence to the contrary, however, it is reasonable to apply the diagnostic criteria for somatic symptom and related disorders to children and adolescents with ID, provided the individuals have sufficient language and communication ability to convey and demonstrate their symptoms and distress and provided the individuals' pre-morbid developmental level, abilities, history, and information is obtained from parents, and teachers, and behavior are taken into account.

Summary of Limitations in Applying DSM-5 Criteria to People with ID

Somatic symptoms disorders. There is a modest case report literature and some limited cohort surveys to confirm that the diagnostic criteria for this group of disorders can be ascertained in adults with ID, although probably not in those without some language and communication ability. The applicability of the diagnostic criteria to children has not been established, although somatoform symptoms can be reliably observed.

Illness anxiety disorder. There is a modest case report literature and some limited cohort surveys that indicate that adults with ID can be overanxious about their health. Given that this new diagnosis is similar to the previous diagnosis of hypochondriasis the earlier case report and survey literature is relevant and confirms that the diagnostic criteria for this disorder can be ascertained in adults with ID who have sufficient language and communication ability. However, the diagnosis of illness anxiety disorder is unlikely to be possible in those with more severe ID and limited or no communication ability. The applicability of the diagnostic criteria to children has not been established. Earlier case report literature suggests it can be can be reliably observed in adolescents but it is rare in children

Conversion disorder. There is a modest case report literature and some limited cohort surveys to confirm that the diagnostic criteria for this group of disorders can be ascertained in adults with ID. Careful neurological examination, laboratory investigations, and clinical history from caretakers will be necessary to make the diagnosis in those with more severe levels of ID who have limited or no language and communication ability. The applicability of the diagnostic criteria to children has been described in a few case reports and cohort surveys. A comprehensive developmental and clinical history from parents, neurological examination and appropriate laboratory investigations are essential to make the diagnosis.

Psychological factor affecting other medical conditions. There is a modest case report literature to confirm that the diagnostic criteria for this group of disorders can be ascertained in adults with ID. Careful clinical observation, appropriate medical investigations, and history from caretakers is necessary in those without some language and communication ability. The applicability of the diagnostic criteria to children has not been established. Developmental history from the parents and appropriate medical assessment is necessary to make a diagnosis.

Factitious disorders. It is possible to diagnose factitious disorders in adults with ID, but probably not in those with more severe levels of ID who have limited or no language. There is no evidence of the applicability of the diagnostic criteria in children and adolescents with ID.

Other specified somatic symptoms and related disorder. There are no specific studies in the literature but cohort studies using symptom questionnaires indicate that somatic symptoms are relatively common in adults and children with ID. There are case reports of pseudocyesis in women with ID and language ability. It is likely that this diagnosis might be more applicable to individuals with ID and somatic symptoms when communication difficulties, particularly in those with more severe levels of ID, make the diagnosis of other specified somatic symptoms and related disorder problematic.

Unspecified somatic symptom and related disorder. There is no literature on this diagnosis applied to people with ID. The DSM-5 cautions against the use of this category unless there are "decidedly unusual situations where there is insufficient information to make a more specific diagnosis" (p. 327). Paradoxically this might make this a relevant diagnosis for people with ID and somatic symptoms, particularly for those with limited or no communication skills. However, it remains absolutely necessary to ensure that a full history from caretakers and medical examination and appropriate laboratory investigations are conducted to ensure that better alternative medical and /or psychiatric diagnoses are excluded in order to ensure the welfare of the patient and to avoid diagnostic overshadowing.

Etiology and Pathogenesis

There is a paucity of information on causative and contributing factors in the development of somatic symptom disorder, factitious disorder, illness anxiety disorder and others somatic symptom and related disorders.

Risk Factors

Somatoform symptoms are probably more prevalent in persons with ID than in the general community (Fink, 1995). The Australian longitudinal follow-up study of an epidemiological sample of young people with ID found that 12-14% of the young people had somatic symptoms (Einfeld & Tonge, 1996a, 1996b; Tonge & Einfeld, 2000, 2003)

Biological Factors

The experience of a serious or chronic medical illness in childhood might give an individual with ID some knowledge of disease symptoms and the psychopathological rewards of medical and nursing care and might predispose them to an overanxious and fearful response to illness and medical treatment. These experiences which are likely to be more common in people with an ID who have an increased risk of suffering a chronic medical condition might influence the development of a somatic symptom and related disorder.

Alcohol or substance use might be an associated factor. In the inpatient study of persistent somatic symptoms by Fink (1995), 48% of the sample had an alcohol or substance use disorder, but it is not known if this association was causal.

There might also be a genetic predisposition to somatic symptoms inherent in some genetic causes of ID as a manifestation of a behavioral phenotype, such fragile X syndrome (Seritan et al., 2009) with conversion disorders and Prader Willi syndrome with somatic symptoms (Skokauskas et al., 2012).

The 14-year longitudinal follow-up study of young people with ID in Australia (Einfeld & Tonge, 1996a, 1996b; Tonge & Einfeld, 2000, 2003) found that young people with Williams syndrome had 3 times the frequency of caregiver-reported somatic symptoms than those in the comparison epidemiological sample of young people with ID and 36% of adolescents with Prader Willi syndrome had somatic symptoms. On the other hand, children and adolescents with ID in the epidemiological sample were 4 times more likely to have Somatic symptoms than were children with Down syndrome.

These findings are consistent with the evidence that young people with Williams syndrome are likely to suffer from anxiety (Einfeld, Tonge, & Rees, 2001; Einfeld, Tonge, Turner,

Parmenter, & Smith, 1999; Tonge & Einfeld, 2003) and that children with Down syndrome are relatively less likely to suffer emotional and behavioral problems than are other children with ID (Einfeld et al., 1999; Tonge & Einfeld, 2003).

Psychological Factors

Psychological stress, conflict, or a traumatic experience might act as a precipitant or sustaining factor in somatic symptom and related disorders. For example, current stressful life events were a significant risk for non-epileptic seizures (conversion disorder) in a New Zealand cohort study of adults with and without ID but a past history of sexual abuse was a risk factor only in the non-ID group, not the ID group (Duncan & Oto 2008). Persons with ID are likely to be more vulnerable to the effects of adverse life events due to their limited knowledge and comprehension and due to the increased likelihood of traumatic experiences, such as abuse, bullying and stigmatisation. For example, a study of 84 adults with mild ID living in supported accommodation found that over half of them reported social strain or the experience of upsetting social interaction. Social strain significantly predicted both somatic complaints and depressive symptoms six months later, independent of gender and the perceived degree of social support (Lunsky & Benson, 2001).

The presence of another psychopathological disorder, particularly depression and anxiety, is probably a common association with somatic symptoms that would meet criteria for a somatic symptom and related disorder (Fink, 1995). There is no evidence, however, that these associated co-morbid conditions are either antecedent or consequential.

Application of Diagnostic Criteria
Somatic Symptoms Disorder

DSM - 5 Diagnostic Criteria	Applying Criteria for Mild/Moderate ID	Applying Criteria for Severe/Profound ID
A. One or more somatic symptoms that are distressing or result in significant disruption of daily life.	A. One or more somatic symptoms that are distressing or result in significant disruption of daily life or result in treatment being sought or significant impairment in social, occupational, or other important areas of common behaviors and functioning, including daily living skills, usual activities, and routines.	A. One or more somatic symptoms that result in significant disruption of daily life or result in treatment being sought or significant impairment in social, occupational, or other important areas of common behaviors and functioning, including daily living skills, usual activities, and routines.
	Note: A person with ID might not complain verbally but might demonstrate through behavior that he or she has pain or other bodily symptoms. The individual with ID might not have the independence or capacity to seek medical treatment; however, the symptoms and behavior will gain the attention of caregivers. It is usually another person who seeks treatment for the individual with ID, and that person's motivation and timing might complicate the diagnostic assessment.	
Specify if: with predominant pain (previously pain disorder). This specifier is for individuals whose somatic symptoms predominantly involve pain.	No adaptation.	**Note:** In persons with little or no language and communication ability, it is usually very difficult to assess this specifier. Nevertheless, people sometimes communicate that they feel pain in a part of the body by indicating it or touching it with their own hand or somebody else's hand.

Somatic Symptoms Disorder (continued)

DSM - 5 Diagnostic Criteria	Applying Criteria for Mild/Moderate ID	Applying Criteria for Severe/Profound ID
B. Excessive thoughts, feelings, or behaviors related to the somatic symptoms or associated health concerns as manifested by at least one of the following:	B. No adaptation.	B. Excessive behavior related to the somatic symptoms or associated health concerns as manifested by at least one of the following:
1. Disproportionate and persistent thoughts about the seriousness of one's symptoms.	1. No adaptation.	**Note:** In persons with little or no language and communication ability, it is usually not possible to assess this specifier. Nevertheless, preoccupations may be expressed as behavioral changes, with the person appearing to be frightened, agitated, or distressed.
2. Persistently high level of anxiety about health or symptoms.	2. No adaptation.	**Note:** In persons with little or no language and communication ability, anxiety may be observed rather than self-reported. Commonly the person appears to be frightened, agitated, or distressed.
3. Excessive time and energy devoted to these symptoms or health concerns.	3. No adaptation.	No adaptation.
C. Although any one somatic symptom may not be continuously present, the state of being symptomatic is persistent (typically more than 6 months).	C. No adaptation.	C. No adaptation.
Specify if: Persistent: a persistent course is characterized by severe symptoms, marked impairment, and long duration (more than 6 months).	No adaptation.	No adaptation.
Specify current severity: Mild: Only one of the symptoms specified in Criterion B is fulfilled. Moderate: Two or more of the symptoms specified in Criterion B are fulfilled. Severe: Two or more of the symptoms specified in Criterion B are fulfilled, plus there are multiple somatic complaints (or one very severe somatic symptom).	No adaptation.	Specify current severity: Mild/Moderate: only the symptoms 1 or 2 specified in Criterion B are fulfilled. Severe: all the symptoms specified in Criterion B are fulfilled, plus there are behavioural signs (see above) of multiple somatic complaints (or one very severe somatic symptom behaviour).

Illness Anxiety Disorder

DSM - 5 Diagnostic Criteria	Applying Criteria for Mild/Moderate ID	Applying Criteria for Severe/ Profound ID
A. Preoccupation with having or acquiring a serious illness.	A. No adaptation. **Note:** A person has more limited ability to verbally communicate his or her concern and preoccupation, but this might manifest as repetitive behavior, such as checking in a mirror or pointing at a minor skin blemish, or preoccupation with medical equipment such as a thermometer or bandage.	**Note:** In persons with little or no language and communication ability, it is usually not possible to identify this symptom. Nevertheless, preoccupation may be expressed as behavioral changes directed at a bodily abnormality such as a bruise or skin blemish or medical equipment such as a thermometer or bandage, and with the person appearing to be frightened, agitated or distressed.
B. Somatic symptoms are not present or, if present, are only mild in intensity. If another medical condition is present or there is a high risk for developing a medical condition (e.g., strong family history is present), the preoccupation is clearly excessive or disproportionate.	B. No adaptation. **Note:** Limited or distorted knowledge and comprehension can complicate the process of reassuring a person with ID. Simple language, the use of visual means of communication, the involvement of relatives or caregivers, and the provision of physical comfort might help to confirm if reassurance is possible.	**Note.** Somatic symptoms may result in significant disruption of daily life or in treatment being sought or significant changes in social, occupational, or other important areas of common behaviors and functioning, including daily living skills, usual activities, and routines.
C. There is a high level of anxiety about health, and the individual is easily alarmed about personal health status.	C. No adaptation. **Note:** In comparison with neurotypical individuals, persons with ID are likely to have progressively less insight as the level of ID increases. However, it might be possible to comment on the current level of insight relative to the individual's premorbid level of understanding about serious illness.	**Note:** In persons with little or no language and communication ability, it is usually not possible to identify this symptom. Nevertheless, anxiety and preoccupation may be expressed as behavioral changes, with the person appearing to be frightened, agitated or distressed.
D. The individual performs excessive health-related behaviors (e.g. repeatedly checks his or her body for signs of illness) or exhibits maladaptive avoidance (e.g., avoids doctors appointments and hospitals).	D. No adaptation.	D. No adaptation.
E. Illness preoccupation has been present for at least 6 months, but the specific illness that is feared may change over that period of time.	E. Since there is a likelihood of frequent atypical presentation and difficulties in early identification, the length of illness preoccupation can be lower than 6 months, but still should be present for a period of at least 3 months.	E. Since the difficulties in early identification, the length of illness preoccupation can be lower than 6 months, but still present for a period of at least 3 months.
F. The illness-related preoccupation is not better explained by another medical disorder, such as somatic symptom disorder, panic disorder, generalized anxiety disorder, body dysmorphic disorder, obsessive-compulsive disorder, or delusional disorder, somatic type.	F. No adaptation.	F. No adaptation. **Note:** See A.
Specify whether: Care-seeking type: medical care, including physician visits or undergoing tests and procedures, is frequently used. Care-avoidant type: medical care is rarely used.	No adaptation.	No adaptation. **Note:** See A.

Conversion Disorder (Functional Neurological Symptom Disorder)

DSM - 5 Diagnostic Criteria	Applying Criteria for Mild/Moderate ID	Applying Criteria for Severe/ Profound ID
A. One or more symptoms of altered voluntary motor or sensory function.	A. No adaptation. **Note:** A person with ID might not complain verbally but might demonstrate through behavior that he or she has a bodily symptom. The individual with ID might not have the independence or capacity to seek medical treatment; however, the symptoms and behavior will gain the attention of caregivers.	A. No adaptation. **Note:** Persons with little or no language and communication ability, demonstrate through behavior that they have a bodily symptom. Individual with severe ID have not the independence or capacity to seek medical treatment; however, the symptoms and behavior usually gain the attention of caregivers.
B. Clinical findings provide evidence of incompatibility between the symptom and recognized neurological or medical conditions.	B. No adaptation.	B. No adaptation.
C. The symptom or deficit is not better explained by another medical or mental disorder.	C. No adaptation.	C. No adaptation.
D. The symptom or deficit causes clinically significant distress or impairment in social, occupational, or other important areas of functioning or warrants medical evaluation. Specify symptom type: with weakness or paralysis with abnormal movement (e.g. tremor, dystonic movement, myoclonus, gait disorder) with swallowing symptoms with speech symptom (e.g. dysphonia, slurred speech) with attacks or seizures with anaesthesia or sensory loss with special sensory symptom (e.g. visual, olfactory, or hearing disturbance) with mixed symptoms.	D. No adaptation.	D. No adaptation.
Specify if: Acute episode: symptoms present for less than 6 months. Persistent: Symptoms occurring for 6 months or more.	Since there is a likelihood of frequent atypical presentation and difficulties in early identification, the length of illness preoccupation can be lower than 6 months, but still present for period of at least 3 months.	Since the difficulties in early identification, the length of illness preoccupation can be lower than 6 months, but still present for a period of at least 3 months.
Specify if: With psychological stressor (specify stressor) Without psychological stressor	No adaptation but a history from parents or caretakers is necessary	No adaptation but a history from parents or caretakers is necessary

Factitious Disorder Imposed on Self

DSM - 5 Diagnostic Criteria	Applying Criteria for Mild to Moderate ID	Applying Criteria for Severe to Profound ID
A. Falsification of physical or psychological signs or symptoms, or induction of injury or disease, associated with identified deception.	A. No adaptation **Note:** It might be difficult to assess intention and motivation in persons with limited language and communication ability. However, if the repeated consequence of symptoms that are shown not to have a medical cause is the achievement of a sick role, then the criterion is indicated.	A. **Note:** In persons with little or no language and communication ability, it is usually not possible to assess this criterion.
B. The individual presents himself or herself to others as ill, impaired, or injured.	B. No adaptation. **Note:** See A.	B. **Note:** See A.
C. The deceptive behavior is evident even in the absence of obvious external rewards.	C. The deceptive behavior is evident even in the absence of external rewards (such as economic gain, avoiding legal responsibility, achieving a favorite activity, avoiding a disliked activity, or improving well-being).	C. **Note:** See A.
D. The behavior is not better explained by another mental disorder, such as delusional disorder or another psychotic disorder.	D. No adaptation.	D. **Note:** See A.
Specify: Single episode Recurrent episodes (two or more events of falsification of illness and/or induction of injury)	No adaptation.	**Note:** See A.

Factitious Disorder Imposed on Another

DSM - 5 Diagnostic Criteria	Applying Criteria for Mild to Moderate ID	Applying Criteria for Severe to Profound ID
A. Falsification of physical or psychological signs or symptoms, or induction of injury or disease, in another, associated with identified deception.	A. No adaptation **Note:** Diagnosis is possible only in those individuals with mild ID who are able to have another person under their care. It might be difficult to assess intention and motivation in persons with limited language and communication ability. However, if the repeated consequence of symptoms that are shown not to have a medical cause is the achievement of a sick role, then the criterion is indicated.	A. **Note:** In persons with little or no language and communication ability who are not likely to be responsible for the care of another it is not possible to make tis diagnosis.
B. The individual presents another individual (victim) to others as ill, impaired, or injured.	B. No adaptation. **Note**: See A.	B. **Note:** See A.
C. The deceptive behavior is evident even in the absence of obvious external rewards.	C. The deceptive behavior is evident even in the absence of external rewards (such as economic gain, avoiding legal responsibility, achieving a favorite activity, avoiding a disliked activity, or improving well-being).	C. **Note:** See A.

Factitious Disorder Imposed on Another (continued)

DSM - 5 Diagnostic Criteria	Applying Criteria for Mild to Moderate ID	Applying Criteria for Severe to Profound ID
D. The behavior is not better explained by another mental disorder, such as delusional disorder or another psychotic disorder.	D. No adaptation.	D. **Note:** See A.
Specify: Single episode Recurrent episodes (two or more events of falsification of illness and/or induction of injury)	No adaptation.	**Note:** See A.

Other Specified Somatic Symptom and Related Disorder
Unspecified Somatic Symptom and Related Disorder

DSM-5 also includes categories for other specified somatic symptom and related disorder and for unspecified somatic symptom and related disorder.

References

Aman, M., & Singh, N. (1986). *Aberrant behaviour checklist: Manual.* New York: Slosson Educational Publications.

American Psychiatric Association. (2013). *Diagnostic and statistical manual of mental disorders (DSM 5)* (5th ed.). Washington, DC: American Psychiatric Association.

American Psychiatric Association. (1994). *Diagnostic and statistical manual of mental disorders (DSM-IV)* (4th ed.). Washington, DC: American Psychiatric Association.

American Psychiatric Association. (2000). *Diagnostic and statistical manual of mental disorders (DSM-IV-TR)* (4th ed.). Text revision. Washington, DC: American Psychiatric Association.

Andrasik, F. & Rime, C. (2009). Pain assessment. In J.L. Matson, F. Andrasik, & M.L. Matson (Eds.), *Assessing childhood psychopathology and developmental disabilities.* (pp. 445-470). New York, NY, Springer Science + Business Media,. doi:10.1007/978-0-387-09528-8_15.

Antshel, K. M., Faraone, S.V., Fremont, W., Monuteaux, M., Kates, W. R., Doyle, A., ... Biederman, J. (2007). Comparing ADHD in velocardiofacial syndrome to idiopathic ADHD: A preliminary study. *Journal of Attention Disorders, 11,* 64-73. doi:10.1177/108705470729939

Balboni, G., Battagliese, G., & Pedrabissi, L. (2000). The psychopathology inventory for mentally retarded adults: Factor structure and comparisons between subjects with or without dual diagnosis. *Research in Developmental Disabilities,* 21(4), 311–321.

Baldridge, K.H., & Andrasik, F.K. (2010) Pain assessment in people with intellectual or developmental disabilities. *American Journal of Nursing,* 110(12), 28-35

Barnhill, Jarrett. (2007). Body dysmorphic disorder in people with intellectual disability: A bio-psycho-social approach. *Mental Health Aspects of Developmental Disabilities, 10*(1), 1-12. Retrieved from http://ovidsp.ovid.com/ovidweb.cgi?T=JS&PAGE=reference&D=-psyc5&NEWS=N&AN=2008-03321-001.

Beange, H., McElduff, A., & Baker, W. (1995). Medical disorders of adults with mental retardation: A population study. *American Journal of Mental Retardation, 99,* 595–604.

Bohmer, C. (1996). *Gastro-esophageal reflux disease in intellectually disabled individuals.* Amsterdam: VU University Press.

Brooke, S., Collacott, R.A., & Bhaumik, S. (1996) Monosymptomatic hypochondriacal psychosis in a man with learning disabilities. *Journal of Intellectual Disability Research, 40*(1), 71-4.

Coulter, D. (1993). Epilepsy and mental retardation: An overview. *American Journal of Mental Retardation*, 98 (suppl.), 1–11.

Craddock, N., & Brown, N. (1993). Munchausen syndrome presenting as mental handicap. *Mental Handicap Research*, 6(2), 184–190.

Chudleigh, C., Kozlowska, K., Kothur, K., Davies, F., Baxter, H., Landini, A., Hazell, P., & Baslet, G. (2013) Managing non-epileptic seizures and psychogenic dystonia in an adolescent girl with preterm brain injury. *Harvard Review of Psychiatry*, 21(3), 163-74.

Disability Rights Commission (2006) *Equal treatment: Closing the gap. A formal investigation into the physical health inequalities experienced by people with learning disabilities and/or mental health problems.* London: Disability Rights Commission.

Duncan, R., & Oto, M. (2008) Psychogenic nonepileptic seizures in patients with learning disability: Comparison with patients with no learning disability. *Epilepsy and Behaviour, 12*, 183-186.

Einfeld, S. L., & Tonge, B. J. (1996a). Population prevalence of behavioural and emotional disturbance in children and adolescents with mental retardation: I. Rationale and methods. *Journal of Intellectual Disability Research*, 40(2), 91–98.

Einfeld, S. L., & Tonge, B. J. (1996b). Population prevalence of behavioural and emotional disturbance in children and adolescents with mental retardation: II. Epidemiological findings. *Journal of Intellectual Disability Research, 40*(2), 99–109.

Einfeld, S. L., & Tonge, B. J. (2002). *Manual for the developmental checklist* (2nd ed., Primary carer version [*DBC-P*] and teacher version [*DBC-T*]). Melbourne and Sydney: Monash University Centre for Developmental Psychiatry and Psychology and School of Psychiatry, University of New South Wales.

Einfeld, S. L., Tonge, B. J., & Rees, V. W. (2001). Longitudinal course of behavioural and emotional problems in Williams syndrome. *American Journal of Mental Retardation*, 106(1), 73–81.

Einfeld, S. L., Tonge, B. J., Turner, G., Parmenter, T., & Smith, A. (1999). Longitudinal course of behavioural and emotional problems of young persons with Prader-Willi, fragile X, Williams and Down syndromes. *Journal of Intellectual & Developmental Disability*, 24(4), 349–354.

Fink, P. (1995). Psychiatric illness in patients with persistent somatisation. *British Journal of Psychiatry*, 166, 93–99.

Glick, M. (1998). A developmental approach to psychopathology in people with mild mental retardation. In J. A. Burack, R. M. Hodapp, & E. Zigler (Eds.), *Handbook of mental retardation and development* (pp. 563–580). Cambridge, England: Cambridge University Press.

Greenbaum, C. W., & Auerbach, J. G. (1998). The environment of the child with mental retardation: Risk, vulnerability and resilience. In A. Burack, R. M. Hodapp, & E. Zigler (Eds.), *Handbook of mental retardation and development* (pp. 583–605). Cambridge, England: Cambridge University Press.

Hagopian, L.P., LeBlanc, L.A., & Maglieri, K.A. (2000) Noncontingent attention for the treatment of excessive medical complaints in a medically fragile man with mental retardation. *Research on Developmental Disabilities, 21*(3), 215-21.

Heger, S. (1998). Factitious disorder in a mentally retarded patient in urology. *Psychiatrische Praxis, 24*(4), 206.

Kroenke, K. (2003). Patients presenting with somatic complaints: epidemiology, psychiatric comorbidity and management. *International Journal of Methods in Psychiatric Research, 12*(1), 34-43.

Lachenmeyer, J. R., Olson, M. E., & Madelyn, E. (1990). Behaviour medication in the treatment of pseudoseizures: A case report. *Behavioural Psychotherapy, 18*(1), 73–78.

Lunsky, Y., & Benson, B. A. (2001). Association between perceived social support and strain, and positive and negative outcome for adults with mild intellectual disability. *Journal of Intellectual Disability Research*, *45*(2), 106–114.

Masi, G., Favilla, L., & Mucci, M. (2000). Generalized anxiety disorder in adolescents and young adults with mild retardation. *Psychiatry, 63(1)*, 54-4.

Matson, J. L. (1988). *The PIMRA manual.* Orland Park, IL: International Diagnostic Systems, Inc.

Matson, J. L., Smiroldo, B. B., Hamilton, & Baglio, C. S. (1997). Do anxiety disorders exist in persons with severe and profound mental retardation? *Research in Developmental Disabilities*, 18(1), 39–44.

Medina, A. C., Sogbe, R., Gomez-Rey, A. M., & Mata, M. (2003). Factitial oral lesions in an autistic paediatric patient. *International Journal of Paediatric Dentistry*, 13(2), 130–137.

Mohr, C., Tonge, B., & Einfeld, S. (2004), *Manual for the developmental behaviour checklist-adult version.* Melbourne and Sydney: Monash University Centre for Developmental Psychiatry and Psychology and School of Psychiatry, University of New South Wales.

Morgan, C. N., Roy, A., Houldey, L., & Miller, D. (2001). Munchausen's syndrome in learning disability. *Journal of Intellectual Disabilities*, 5(3), 259–265.

O'Conner, W., & Davis, R. (1999). Challenging behaviour. In N. Lennox, & J. Diggins (Eds.), *People with developmental and intellectual disabilities: Management guidelines* (pp. 73–85). Melbourne, Australia: Therapeutic Guidelines Ltd.

Piacentino, D., Politi, R., Moscariello, M.M., Meuti, V., & Biondi, M. (2010) Mental retardation and somatoform disorder with globus pharyngeus: a case study of comorbidity. *Rivista di Psichiatria*, 45(5), 334-339. Italian.

Pumar, M. I., & Kumar, R. (2013). Dermatitis artefacta in an intellectually disabled man with monosymptomatic hypochondriacal delusion of HIV infection. *Australian and New Zealand Journal of Psychiatry, 47*, 974-975. doi:10.1177/0004867413488219

Rawat, V.S., Dhiman, V., Sinha, S., Vijay Sagar, K.J., Thippeswamy, H., Chaturvedi, S.K., … Satishchandra, P. (2015) Co-morbidities and outcome of childhood psychogenic non-epileptic seizures--an observational study. *Seizure*, 25, 95-8.

Seritan, A.L., Schneider, A., Olichney, J.M., Leehey, M.A., Akins, R.S., & Hagerman, R.J. (2009) Conversion disorder in women with the FMR1 premutation. *American Journal of Medical Genetics, 149A*(11), 2501–2506.

Skokauskas, N., Sweeny, E., Meehan, J., & Gallagher, L. (2012) Mental health problems in children with prader-willi syndrome. *Journal of the Canadian Academy of Child and Adolescent Psychiatry, 21*(3), 194-203

Tonge, B. J., & Einfeld, S. L. (2000). The trajectory of psychiatric disorders in young people with intellectual disabilities. *Australian and New Zealand Journal of Psychiatry*, 34, 80–84.

Tonge, B. J., & Einfeld, S. L. (2003). Psychopathology and intellectual disability: The Australian child to adult longitudinal study. In L. M. Glidden (Ed.), *International review of research in mental retardation* (Vol. 27, pp. 61–91). San Diego, CA: Academic Press.

Tracy, J., & Hosken, R. (1997). The importance of smoking with education and preventative health strategies for people with intellectual disability. *Journal of Intellectual Disability Research*, 41(5), 416–421.

Van Straaten, B., Schrijvers, C.T., Van der Laan, J., Boersma, S.N., Rodenburg, G., Wolf, J.R.L.M., & Van de Mheen, D. (2014) Intellectual disability among Dutch homeless people: Prevalence and related psychosocial problems. *PLoS One.* 2014 Jan 21; 9(1):e86112. doi: 10.1371/journal.pone.0086112

Voigt, K., Wollburg, E., Weinmann, N., Herzog, A., Meyer, B., Langs, G., & Löwe, B. (2012) Predictive validity and clinical utility of DSM-5 somatic symptom disorder--Comparison with DSM-IV somatoform disorders and additional criteria for consideration. *Journal of Psychosomatic Research, 73*(5), 345-350.

Voigt, K., Wollburg, E., Weinmann, N., Herzog, A., Meyer, B., Langs, G., & Löwe B (2013) Predictive validity and clinical utility of DSM-5 somatic symptom disorder: Prospective 1-year follow-up study. *Journal of Psychosomatic Research*, *75*(4), 358-361.

Whitefield, M., & Russell, O. (1996). Assessing general practitioner's care of adult patients with learning disability: Case control study. *Quality Health Care*, *5*, 31–35.

Wullink, M., Veldhuijzen, W., Lantman-de Valk, H.M., Metsemakers, J.F., & Dinant, G.J. (2009) Doctor-patient communication with people with intellectual disability: a qualitative study. *BMC Family Practice*, *17*, 10:82.

CHAPTER 18

Feeding and Eating Disorders

Nellieke de Koning
Frank Moreland
Julie P. Gentile
Pieter Troost

DSM-5 has brought feeding and eating disorders formerly classified as disorders of infancy or early childhood (pica, rumination disorder, avoidant/restrictive food intake disorder) together with the eating disorders of anorexia nervosa and bulimia nervosa. The relocation of disorders formerly classified as childhood disorders to feeding and eating disorders serves to emphasize the occurrence of these disorders across the lifespan. Binge-eating disorder, included in the "criteria sets and axes provided for further study" in *DSM-IV-TR,* is also now included in the *DSM-5* feeding and eating disorder chapter. There is also a category of other specified feeding or eating disorders and of unspecified feeding or eating disorder; these two categories are not, of course, operationalized.

The literature for all of these conditions is limited (Jones & Samuel, 2010), and findings from studies previously conducted with institutionalized populations of people with intellectual disabilities are not likely to be generalizable to people living in the community today.

The disorders included in this chapter are considered in turn.

Pica

General Description of the Disorder

Pica, the eating of nonnutritive substances, can cause serious medical complications and cause significant mortality. The prevalence of the disorder is relatively high, not only in children but also in adults with intellectual disabilities. Management of the condition will depend on any underlying causes.

The essential feature of pica is the eating of nonnutritive substances. People with pica persist with this behavior beyond infancy. The incidence of indiscriminate eating declines between 1 and 4 years of age from 35% to 6% (Rutter & Taylor, 2002).

Pica can have serious, life-threatening health consequences. For families living in older homes, pica has been associated with the risk of lead poisoning because children may ingest paint flakes (Rutter & Taylor, 2002). Other serious physical complications are bowel obstructions, which may necessitate surgical resolution, parasitic infestation and aspiration. Pica can result in significant mortality (Gravestock, 2000).

A number of causes of pica have been suggested, including nutritional deficiencies (mainly iron and zinc); general developmental delay; such caregiver behaviors as deprivation or neglect; or more general deprivation of the home environment (Rutter & Taylor, 2002).

Summary of DSM-5 *Criteria*

The *DSM-5* criteria for pica focus on developmentally inappropriate and persistent eating of nonnutritive substances. The criteria include developmental level, since mouthing and sometimes eating of nonnutritive substances is relatively common before the ages of 18-24 months.

If eating nonnutritive substances occurs concurrently with the course of another mental disorder — for example, ID, pervasive developmental disorder, schizophrenia, or borderline personality disorder — a separate diagnosis of pica is made only if the eating behavior is sufficiently severe to warrant clinical attention. Due to the potentially serious health ramifications, a single episode might warrant a diagnosis.

Excluded is the eating of dirt or any other seemingly nonnutritive substance if in the context of a culturally accepted practice.

The criteria allow for pica in remission to also be coded.

Issues Related to Diagnosis in Persons with ID

Intellectual disability is a predisposing factor for pica (Szymanski & King, 1999), with the prevalence increasing with the severity of the intellectual disabilities. Pica has been reported to be as high as 15% in adults with severe and profound intellectual disabilities.

The level of intellectual disability affects the way people are able to discriminate between food and nonnutritive substances. People with more severe levels of intellectual disabilities might ingest objects that they think are food items. In addition, people with intellectual disabilities might ingest objects to communicate an emotional need, lacking the skills to communicate their need in another way (Moreland & Henderson, 2003).

Application of Diagnostic Criteria to People with ID

Pica is confirmed in people with intellectual disabilities by parents or staff observing the ingestion itself, by the presence of foreign objects in the person's feces, or through diagnostic imaging such as an X-ray or MRI. Close supervision might be needed to notice the behavior and to protect the patient from ingesting dangerous items. Mouthing and sometimes eating nonnutritive substances is seen more frequently at a younger developmental age. In the assessment procedure, a good estimation should be made of the developmental level of the individual. There are many interventions to minimize the chance of ingestions (McAdams, Sherman, Sheldon, & Napolitano, 2004).

Methodology

MEDLINE was searched (November 2006-January 2014) using the key words "pica and mental retardation," "pica and developmental disability," and "pica and neurobiology." The full text of relevant articles was studied, and related articles were screened. Recent books on child psychiatry and neuropsychiatry were also screened for information on etiology, diagnostic criteria, and management strategies of pica.

Review of Research Applying to People with ID

Recent research on this topic is limited. New diagnostic criteria applicable to adults with intellectual disabilities were developed in the *Diagnostic Criteria for Psychiatric Disorders for Use with Adults with Learning Disabilities/Mental Retardation (DC-LD)* by the Royal College of Psychiatrists (2001). A review of the literature along with expert consensus led to the development of *DC-LD* (Cooper, Melville, & Eindfeld, 2003; Gravestock, 2003). No studies that attempted to apply *DSM-5* diagnostic criteria to people with intellectual disabilities were found.

Summary of Limitations in Applying **DSM-5** *Criteria to People with ID*

In the application of the *DSM-5* criteria, the diagnosis of pica, and the severity of its health consequences, can be easily overlooked if the disorder occurs during the course of another mental disorder (including intellectual disability) or when the eating behavior is seen as developmentally appropriate.

The *DSM-5* criteria do not account for singular episodes or significant time intervals between ingestions. The desire to ingest nonnutritive substances might exist in a latent form, but actual ingestions may be suppressed due to the interventions of others or the lack of access to the items. Therefore, the circumstances surrounding an ingestion should be reviewed carefully. Singular episodes of ingestions, or long intervals in between episodes, should not exclude the diagnosis of pica, and the criteria do have an "in remission" option.

The *DSM-5* criteria do not take into account etiological factors (genetic syndromes, nutrient deficiencies) and comorbidity issues. Etiological factors and comorbidity issues, however, are of major importance in management and treatment strategies.

Etiology and Pathogenesis

Prevalence rates of pica are higher in people with more severe levels of intellectual disabilities, younger adults, males, and people with weight problems (Gravestock, 2000). Pica is also more frequently seen in people with comorbid behavioral problems, autism (O'Brien & Whitehouse, 1990; Parry-Jones & Parry-Jones, 1992), depressive disorder, or personality disorder (Gravestock, 2000).

Biological Factors

In some cases, vitamin or mineral deficiencies (for example, zinc or iron) have been reported, but usually no biological abnormalities are found. There is no apparent correlation between the substances ingested and specific dietary deficiencies (Parry-Jones & Parry-Jones, 1992). Whenever trace mineral evaluations indicate that a person has a mineral deficiency, however, nutritional supplements should be in the treatment package (McAdams et al., 2004).

Pica is occasionally seen in pregnant females (Parry-Jones & Parry-Jones, 1992). Nicotine dependence might play a role in specific forms of pica, such as the eating of cigarette butts (Gravestock, 2000; Moreland & Henderson, 2003).

Serotonin and dopamine neurotransmission theories exist (Gravestock, 2000). Some cases of pica can be conceptualized as lying within an obsessive-compulsive spectrum of symptoms and disorders. These people might respond to treatment with a serotonin re-uptake inhibitor (Stein, Bouwer, & Van Heerden, 1996).

Pica is seen in some genetic syndromes. Prader-Willi syndrome is characterized by marked hypotonia, feeding difficulties, and failure to thrive in the first 6 months, then between 1 and 4 years of age, hyperphagia and sometimes pica can develop. The Kleine-Levin syndrome is characterized by periods of extreme somnolence alternated with megaphagia, mental changes, and behavioral symptoms. The cause of this syndrome is still unknown. Pica can be one of the behavioral symptoms.

Psychosocial Factors

Poverty, psychosocial or environmental deprivation, and lack of parental (or staff) supervision increase the risk for pica (Gravestock, 2000; Matson, et al., 2005; Moreland & Henderson, 2003). Several behavioral interventions, close supervision, and environmental enrichment are suggested treatment strategies (Gravestock, 2000; Kern, Starosta, & Adelman, 2006).

Developmental Factors

Prevalence rates of pica are higher in people with more severe levels of intellectual disability, autism, and personality disorders (Gravestock, 2000).

Adaptation of Diagnostic Criteria

Pica can cause serious health problems and should be diagnosed and treated in an early phase. Modifications of the *DSM-5* criteria for people with intellectual disabilities are needed.

Pica

DSM-5 Diagnostic Criteria	Applying Criteria for Mild-Profound ID
A. Persistent eating of non-nutritive, non-food substances over a period of at least 1 month.	A. Persistent eating of non-nutritive, non-food substances over a period of at least 1 month, not due to people with severe or profound ID just being hungry and unable to differentiate between prepared and unprepared, raw or discarded food.
B. The eating of non-nutritive, non-food substances is inappropriate to the developmental level of the individual.	B. No adaptations necessary.

Pica (continued)

DSM-5 Diagnostic Criteria	Applying Criteria for Mild-Profound ID
C. The eating behavior is not part of a culturally supported or socially normative practice.	C. No adaptations necessary.
D. If the eating behaviour occurs in the context of another mental disorder (e.g. intellectual disabilities, autism spectrum disorder, schizophrenia), or medical condition (including pregnancy), it is sufficiently severe to warrant additionally clinical attention.	D. No adaptations necessary.

Rumination Disorder

General Description of the Disorder

Rumination is defined as the chewing and re-swallowing or expulsion of regurgitated stomach contents. Rumination can be subtle, difficult to observe, and often continues unreported and untreated. Rumination disorder is more prevalent in individuals with intellectual disabilities compared to the general population (Fletcher, Loschen, Stavrakaki, & First, 2007; Hartmann, Becker, Hampton, & Bryant-Waugh, 2012). The disorder can occur across the lifespan into adulthood. Early diagnosis is critical because of the potential for serious medical complications such as weight loss, dehydration, and gastrointestinal pathology. Behavioral interventions and treatment are effective and therefore should be instituted at the time of diagnosis to improve prognosis and outcomes (American Psychiatric Association, 2013; Fletcher et al., 2007; Hartmann et al., 2012).

Rumination disorder consists of voluntary regurgitation of partially digested food with minimal effort, and in certain individuals there is pleasure derived from this behavior (American Psychiatric Association, 2013; Fletcher et al., 2007). Prevalence is unknown for several reasons; many clinicians do not inquire about this symptom set, and often regurgitation is a covert behavior. In addition, there are various classification systems utilized across the globe and a variety of terms used including regurgitation disorder and rumination syndrome.

Regurgitation is voluntary or volitional, which is a distinguishing factor from vomiting or gastro-esophageal reflux disease (American Psychiatric Association, 2013; Fletcher et al., 2007; Hartmann et al., 2012). There is no nausea or other associated medical symptoms with regurgitation. There are various presentations with regurgitation, and individuals may cough, place fingers in his or her mouth, or utilize tongue or abdominal muscle movements or contractions to facilitate the behavior. To distinguish self-induced vomiting from regurgitation can be difficult.

When infants regurgitate, they may arch the back with repetitive movements (Fletcher et al., 2007; Hartmann et al., 2012). There may be associated behavioral patterns, and co-occurring intellectual disabilities should be investigated and identified at the first sign of suspected regurgitation. Diagnosis of rumination disorder should only be made if the individual experiences consequences that require additional clinical intervention.

Summary of DSM-5 *Criteria*

Relatively minor changes were made in the diagnostic criteria of rumination disorder in the *DSM-5*. The changes had two intended goals: First, to improve clinical application to individuals across the lifespan, and second, to eliminate obscurity in the description of the diagnostic criteria (American Psychiatric Association, 2013).

The core feature of rumination disorder is voluntary, repetitive regurgitation of food (American Psychiatric Association, 2013; Fletcher et al., 2007). In the *DSM-IV-TR*, it was required that the individual both regurgitate and re-chew food to qualify for the diagnosis. This has been eliminated in the *DSM-5* because it is known that some individuals re-swallow or spit out the food rather than re-chew. The *DSM-5* includes a broader range of spitting, chewing, and swallowing patterns in the diagnostic criteria for rumination disorder to accommodate the variation among individuals (American Psychiatric

Association, 2013; Fletcher et al., 2007). In addition, the *DSM-IV* requirement that the regurgitation must follow a period of normal functioning no longer exists in the *DSM-5*; this was thought to be a vague and complicating factor that was difficult to verify. The diagnosis can co-occur with a medical condition, with the provision that the regurgitation is not entirely explained by the identified medical condition. Finally, the diagnosis should not be made if the regurgitation is part of other feeding and eating disorders, as in anorexia nervosa or bulimia nervosa, for example. The exception is with pica, which may co-occur with rumination disorder.

Issues Related to Diagnosis in Persons with ID

Suspicion of and testing for intellectual disabilities should be considered at first presentation of regurgitation if not previously identified, because rumination disorder is seen more frequently in persons with intellectual disabilities compared to the general population. If the disorder occurs exclusively during the course of intellectual disabilities or autism, the symptoms must be significant enough to warrant additional clinical attention (Fletcher et al., 2013). Individuals with intellectual disabilities who present with regurgitation should be screened for anxiety disorders, in particular generalized anxiety disorder. Self-stimulatory or self-soothing behavior should also be considered in individuals with intellectual disabilities.

Individuals with intellectual disabilities often have limited expressive language skills, and therefore general medical conditions must be considered as the cause or increase of symptoms. Swallowing difficulty, pyloric stenosis, and gastro-esophageal reflux disease may be mistaken for rumination disorder.

Application of Diagnostic Criteria to People with ID

Rumination disorder can be diagnosed in persons with intellectual disabilities based on subjective information from the patient or objective collateral data from caregivers (Fletcher et al., 2007; Hartmann et al., 2012). Due to the potential for serious medical consequences of rumination disorder, it is vital to alert caregivers to monitor weight, hydration, and nutritional status. As the cognitive deficits become more significant, the nutritional dependency needs of the individual increase considerably and should be taken into consideration.

Methodology

PubMed was searched utilizing these key words: behavioral syndrome, developmental disability, intellectual disability, rumination disorder, rumination syndrome, mental retardation, assessment, treatment, diagnosis, pharmacology, regurgitation, repetitive behavior, prevalence, etiology, and genetics. The full text of relevant articles was reviewed in addition to related articles.

Review of Research Applying to People with ID

Gupta, Kaila, and Gupta (2012) concluded that rumination is frequently confused with intractable vomiting in adults and that misdiagnosis leads to delay in appropriate management.

Chial, Camilleri, Williams, Litzinger, and Perrault (2003) studied rumination syndrome in children with respect to the importance of early and accurate diagnosis. The study reported that weight loss was found in 42.2% and other common symptoms included abdominal pain, constipation, nausea, and diarrhea. Average length of time prior to diagnosis was over two years, with 46% having been hospitalized and 11% having undergone surgery for evaluation and/or management of symptoms; 54% showed reflux/regurgitation as measured by esophageal pH testing. The authors concluded that the diagnosis is often delayed and associated with significant morbidity. Excessive diagnostic testing was deemed unnecessary but may be viewed differently in the intellectual disabilities population since it is typical for there to be a lack of subjective data (Chial et al., 2003).

Rajindrajith, Devanarayana, and Cirspus Perera (2012) found that the most common presenting symptoms were abdominal pain, bloating, and weight loss (19.1%, 17.3%, and 11.8% respectively). In this study, there was no clear relationship between rumination and exposure to stressful events. School absenteeism was seen in 11.8% of affected children.

Birmingham and Firoz (2006) and O'Brien, Bruce, and Camilleri (1995) describe the typical clinical features of rumination as follows:

1) Repetitive regurgitation of gastric contents occurring within minutes of a meal;
2) Episodes that often persist for 1 to 2 hours;
3) Regurgitated material that usually consists of partially recognizable food;
4) Regurgitation that is effortless or preceded by a sensation of belching;
5) The absence of retching or nausea before regurgitation;
6) A conscious decision made to swallow or eject the material once it is present in the oropharynx; the choice may depend on the social situation;
7) The long-term nature of the behavior.

With regard to the conscious decision to swallow or eject the material, this may differ in the intellectually disabled population, especially in the severe/profound level of cognitive impairment. Reviews by several authors of assessment and treatment of rumination disorder in children and adults have produced similar findings (Drossman et al., 2006; Nichols & Bryant-Waugh, 2008; Papadopoulos & Mimidis, 2007; Uher & Rutter, 2012).

Etiology and Pathogenesis

Following are potential risk factors for rumination disorder:

- Intellectual disabilities, especially the more severe the level;
- Males;
- Younger age groups (in children, more equal gender distribution is possible);
- Institutional settings;
- May co-occur with pica, autism, anorexia nervosa, bulimia nervosa, generalized anxiety disorder, and other anxiety disorders.

Biological Factors

Rumination disorder is associated with gastric, sensory, and motor dysfunction (Fletcher et al., 2007; Hartmann et al., 2012). Associated medical issues may include nutritional deficits, electrolyte imbalance, dehydration, esophageal ulceration, halitosis, dental caries and eroded dentition, starvation, and in severe cases death, depending on the severity of the condition.

Rumination disorder should be suspected when consumption of non-food items is suspected or confirmed; i.e. with a finding of a bezoar or elevated lead level (Fletcher et al., 2007; Hartmann et al., 2012). It is important to broach the topic with patients and collateral data sources in a nonjudgmental manner, and to include education regarding potential medical consequences with individuals as well as caregivers.

No specific genetic syndromes are associated with rumination disorder.

Psychosocial Factors

Precipitating factors include anxiety and depression in primary caregiver; environments with under- and over-stimulation are documented factors for OCD. Social undesirability is an important factor (Fletcher et al., 2007; Hartmann et al., 2012), but may be less applicable as the level of cognitive impairment becomes more severe.

Adaptation of Diagnostic Criteria

Potential medical complications seen in individuals with co-occurring intellectual disabilities and rumination disorder and associated morbidity and mortality make it imperative to diagnose and treat the disorder as early as possible. The changes made to the *DSM-5* criteria for rumination disorder help clinicians recognize the symptoms in the early stages and define the condition as occurring across the lifespan. Minor revisions in the diagnostic criteria serve to increase clinical utility and lead to effective behavioral, psychiatric, and medical treatment interventions.

People with intellectual disabilities are often dependent on their caregivers for an adequate diet. The Criterion B adaptation is to ensure the clinician is cognizant of potential undiagnosed medical conditions, and rules out inadequate diet and insufficient care.

Rumination Disorder

DSM-5 Diagnostic Criteria	Applying Criteria for Mild- Profound ID
A. Repeated regurgitation and rechewing of food for a period of at least 1 month. Regurgitated food may be re-chewed, re-swallowed, or spit out.	A. No adaptations necessary.
B. The repeated regurgitation is not attributable to an associated gastrointestinal or other general medical condition (e.g. esophageal reflux, pyloric stenosis).	B. The behavior is not due to an associated gastrointestinal or other general medical condition (e.g. esophageal reflux, pyloric stenosis), or an inadequate diet or insufficient care.
C. The eating disturbance does not occur exclusively during the course of Anorexia Nervosa, Bulimia Nervosa Binge-eating disorder, or avoidant/restrictive food intake disorder.	C. No adaptations necessary.
D. If the symptoms occur in the context of another mental disorder (e.g. intellectual disability or another neurodevelopmental disorder) they are sufficiently severe to warrant additional clinical attention.	D. No adaptations necessary.

Avoidant/Restrictive Food Intake Disorder

General Description of the Disorder

Avoidant/restrictive food intake disorder replaces the non-specific category of feeding disorder of infancy or early childhood and, in addition, explicitly includes adolescent and adult cases presenting with psychologically motivated inadequate food intake for reasons related to the physical properties or feared consequences of eating specific types of food, other than effects on body weight and shape.

Avoidant/restrictive food intake disorder overlaps with anorexia nervosa in terms of restrictive food intake and the resulting underweight, but differs in psychopathology and motives for restrictive eating. These include avoiding types of food of specific color or texture or limiting food intake to a small number of specific "safe" types of food because of perceived health consequences.

Since there is a vast normal variation in eating habits, differentiation from normality is important. As a rule, avoidant/restrictive food intake disorder should only be diagnosed when the restrictive/avoidant eating is a cause of inadequate nutrition that may be associated with delayed growth in children, weakness, anemia or other medical consequences in any age group, or inadequate development of the fetus in pregnant women. Dietary practices that are endorsed by large groups of people, such as vegetarianism or religious fasting, do not constitute a basis for diagnosing avoidant/restrictive food intake disorder (Rutter & Uher, 2012).

Avoidant/restrictive food intake disorder might be caused by immature biological regulatory mechanisms. Parent-child interaction problems can contribute to, or exacerbate, an infant's feeding problem (Rutter & Taylor, 2002).

Summary of DSM-5 Criteria

The main diagnostic feature of avoidant/restrictive food intake disorder is avoidance or restriction of food intake with malnutrition but no body image disturbance or fear of weight gain. One or more of the following key features must be present: Significant weight loss, significant nutritional deficiency (or related health impact), dependence on enteral feeding or oral nutritional supplements, or marked interference with psychosocial functioning.

DSM-5 criteria require an eating or feeding disturbance, as manifested by persistent failure to meet appropriate nutritional and/or energy needs. The disturbance must neither be better explained by lack of available food or by an associated culturally sanctioned practice, nor occur exclusively during the course of anorexia nervosa or bulimia nervosa. It must not be due to, or better explained by, a concurrent medical condition.

Issues Related to Diagnosis in Persons with ID

People with intellectual disabilities are at risk of developing the *DSM-IV* diagnosis feeding disorder of infancy or early childhood (Gravestock, 2003; Szymanski & King, 1999). Among a sample of adults with intellectual disabilities living in communities, 1.3% rejected or refused food on a daily basis (Hove, 2004). In a population of children with intellectual disabilities, eating/feeding problems proved prevalent across all levels, but certain categories of problems (i.e., skills and aspiration risk) are more prevalent among the group falling within the severe/profound range of ID (Gal & Hardal-Nasser, 2011).

In people with intellectual disabilities, physical and dental health problems and difficulties with eating, chewing, or swallowing are more often seen and may directly impact on food choice and the ability to eat well unaided (Kuhn & Matson, 2004; Sullivan et al., 2002). Also, digestive problems such as gastro-esophageal reflux disorder and bowel function problems such as constipation and diarrhea may deter people from eating.

Structural brain damage or dysfunction such as epilepsy, seen in some people with intellectual disabilities, has been linked to appetite, metabolic and weight changes, hypersensory impairments, and the need for assistance with eating, and a loss of eating independence may reduce enjoyment at mealtimes, which may present as resistance against food (Crawley, 2007). Feeding problems are also frequently seen in specific genetic syndromes associated with intellectual disabilities.

It is important to realize that it might be difficult for people with more severe intellectual disabilities to communicate whether they like or dislike the particular food (Kuhn & Matson, 2004). People with intellectual disabilities may have peculiar eating preferences, which can cause malnutrition.

Often a combination of a medical condition and eating disorders is seen. Moreover, when the medical condition is treated successfully, concurrent psychological factors continue or may even worsen (Bazyk, 1990; Handen, Mandell, & Russo, 1986). In this population, selective food refusal may develop into severe and even life-threatening situations of total food refusal. A selective food preference is not always overtly apparent but may become manifest by atypical symptoms such as food refusal, agitation, temper tantrums, a turning away of the head or keeping lips sealed while being fed, spitting, throwing with cutlery, or vomiting during or after the meal. Often, individuals with ID show signs of agitation or oppositional behavior when activities take place related to preparing meals (Luiselli, 1994). Adults may particularly be creative in their refusal of food. Behaviors such as extreme auto-mutilation, vomiting in the face of caretakers, masturbation, compulsive singing, and apathy are observed during food refusal treatments.

Application of Diagnostic Criteria to People with ID

General Considerations

The *DSM-5* criteria are in part dependent on the information given by the client. Clients with more severe forms of ID often cannot communicate which aspects of food are aversive (e.g., appearance, texture, or taste), and symptoms of avoidant/restrictive food intake disorder in this population may easily be overlooked. Therefore, special attention is needed for atypical manifestations of avoidant/restrictive food intake disorder and medical indicators that may refer to avoidant/restrictive food intake disorder as a result of an inadequate diet: Failure to thrive, aberrant BMI, and medical symptoms of malnutrition. In the case of some known chromosomal abnormalities, such as Down syndrome and Turner syndrome, adapted growth charts are available and should be used when evaluating failure to achieve expected weight gain.

Moreover, clients with more severe intellectual disabilities are dependent on their caregivers for an adequate diet and good care. It is important to pay attention to the fact that the feeding problems are not caused by an inadequate diet or by insufficient care.

Methodology

MEDLINE was searched (1980-February 2014) using the keywords "feeding disorder and mental retardation," "feeding disorder and intellectual disability," "feeding disorder and behavioral syndrome," and "ARFID-avoidant/

restrictive food intake disorder." The full text of relevant articles (addressing the diagnostic classification of feeding disorder of infancy or early childhood and avoidant/restrictive food intake disorder) was studied, and related articles were screened. Recent books on child psychiatry, neuropsychiatry, and behavioral phenotypes were also screened for information on etiology, diagnostic criteria, and management of strategies for treating feeding disorder of infancy or early childhood or ARFID.

Review of Research Applying to People with ID

Studies that have attempted to apply diagnostic criteria to people with intellectual disabilities are scarce. New diagnostic criteria applicable to adults with intellectual disabilities were developed in the *Diagnostic Criteria for Psychiatric Disorders for Use with Adults with Learning Disabilities/Mental Retardation (DC-LD)* by the Royal College of Psychiatrists (2001). A review of the literature along with expert consensus led to the development of *DC-LD*. The new diagnostic criteria and classification were piloted with 52 field investigators drawing on 709 clinical cases. Of these cases, only 14 individuals met the criteria for eating disorders. Validity was measured by comparing the criteria providing *DC-ID* diagnosis with the "gold standard" of clinical judgment of learning-disabilities psychiatrists (Cooper, Melville, & Eindfeld, 2003).

No studies that attempted to apply *DSM-5* diagnostic criteria to people with intellectual disabilities were found.

Summary of Limitations in Applying **DSM-5** *Criteria to People with ID*

Explications of criteria such as "avoidance based on the sensory characteristics of food" and "concern about aversive consequences of eating" are not always applicable in diagnosing clients with more severe forms of intellectual disabilities, because of limitations in expressing motives for restrictive food intake.

Special attention should be paid to inadequate diet as a result of insufficient care, as clients with intellectual disabilities often are dependent on caregivers.

Etiology and Pathogenesis

The disorder is more frequently seen in people with more severe levels of intellectual disabilities. The disorder is equally common in males and females.

Biological Factors

A number of biological regulatory systems are involved in the development of rooting and sucking reflexes: The development of oral-motor control (mouth opening, sucking, lip movements, chewing, and swallowing); taste perception; the biological rhythmicity in hunger and appetite; food preferences; and gastric regulation (biological immaturity can lead to reflux). Children who have experienced prolonged supplementary feeding often exhibit food refusal and gagging when textured food is offered (Rutter et al., 2010).

Genetic Syndromes

Several genetic syndromes are linked, often characterized by a general medical condition that is associated with feeding problems. A diagnosis of avoidant/restrictive food intake disorder should only be made if the degree of disturbance is of greater severity than would be expected on the basis of the medical condition alone.

In people with Down syndrome, oral motor functions are often impaired, resulting in feeding difficulties (Kuhn & Matson, 2004). Also, in individuals with Joubert syndrome feeding difficulties occur. In Joubert syndrome the cerebellar vermis, which controls balance and coordination, is absent and underdeveloped. The syndrome is characterized by ataxia, hypotonia, and abnormal eye movements (O'Brien, 2002).

Prader-Willi syndrome is characterized by marked hypotonia and failure to thrive in the first 6 months, and these infants usually have extreme feeding difficulties up to 6 months of age (O'Brien, 2002). Between 1 and 4 years of age, hyperphagia develops. Feeding difficulties also occur in the neonatal period in Costello syndrome, a rare genetic condition known to involve developmental delay (Galéra et al., 2006).

The primary behavioral manifestation of Lesch-Nyhan syndrome is self-injury. Motor disability and feeding difficulties also occur (O'Brien, 2002). The Smith-Lemli-Opitz syndrome is a metabolic disorder in which there is abnormal metabolism of cholesterol. It is characterized by multiple malformations and a distinct behavioral phenotype with features of autistic disorder and ID. There are major feeding difficulties, and gastrostomy feeding is often required (O'Brien, 2002).

In Sotos syndrome, accelerated growth begins prenatally and is prominent for the first 5 years of life. Early feeding problems, jaundice, and hypotonia are seen in infants with Sotos syndrome (O'Brien, 2002).

Willem Bueren syndrome (idiopathic infantile hypercalcaemia) is a developmental disorder involving vascular, connective tissue and the nervous system. In infants, low birth weight, cardiac murmur, and feeding problems can be detected (O'Brien, 2002).

Psychosocial Factors

Some children may have small appetites. If caregivers put too much pressure on the children in their care to eat, the feeding problems might increase. In some children, food refusal can be seen as a component of separation anxiety disorder. The disorder might be intensified if the caregivers are anxious about the child's weight or growth (Gravestock, 2000; Rutter et al., 2010). Other factors associated with avoidant/restrictive food intake disorder are parental psychopathology and child abuse or neglect.

Often, a combination of medical conditions and eating disorders is seen in clients with intellectual disabilities. Even when medical conditions are successfully treated, psychological factors may continue to play a role and can even lead to life-threatening situations such as total food refusal (Bazyk 1990; Handen et al., 1986).

Adaptation of Diagnostic Criteria

Clients with more severe forms of intellectual disabilities often cannot communicate which aspects of food are aversive (e.g., appearance, texture, or taste), and symptoms of avoidant/restrictive food intake disorder in this population may easily be overlooked. Therefore, special attention is needed for atypical manifestations of avoidant/restrictive food intake disorder such as food refusal, agitation, temper tantrums, a turning away of the head or keeping lips sealed while being fed, spitting, throwing with cutlery, or vomiting during or after the meal.

The B criterion in the *DSM-5* states that the feeding disturbance is not better explained by a lack of available food or by an associated culturally sanctioned practice. For people with intellectual disabilities, that should be amended to include that the disturbance is not due to an inadequate diet or insufficient care.

DSM-5 allows for "in remission" to be specified.

Avoidant/Restrictive Food Intake Disorder

DSM-5 Diagnostic Criteria	Applying Criteria for Mild to Profound ID
A. An eating or feeding disturbance (e.g., apparent lack of interest in eating or food; avoidance based on the sensory characteristics of food; concern about aversive consequences of eating) as manifested by persistent failure to meet appropriate nutritional and/or energy needs, associated with one or more of the following: 1. significant weight loss (or failure to achieve expected weight gain, or faltering growth in children) 2. significant nutritional deficiency 3.dependence on enteral feeding or oral nutritional supplements 4.marked interference in psychosocial functioning.	A. An eating or feeding disturbance (e.g., apparent lack of interest in eating or food; avoidance based on the sensory characteristics of food; concern about aversive consequences of eating; atypical manifestations such as food refusal, turning away of the head or keeping lips sealed while being fed, vomiting during or after the meal) as manifested by persistent failure to meet appropriate nutritional and/or energy needs, associated with one or more of the following: 1. significant weight loss (or failure to achieve expected weight gain, or faltering growth in children) 2. significant nutritional deficiency 3.dependence on enteral feeding or oral nutritional supplements 4.marked interference in psychosocial functioning.
B. The disturbance is not better explained by lack of available food or by an associated culturally sanctioned practice.	B. The disturbance is not better explained by lack of available food, an inadequate diet, insufficient care, or by an associated culturally sanctioned practice.

Avoidant/Restrictive Food Intake Disorder (continued)

DSM-5 Diagnostic Criteria	Applying Criteria for Mild to Profound ID
C. The eating disturbance does not occur exclusively during the course of anorexia nervosa or bulimia nervosa, and there is no evidence of disturbance in the way in which one's body weight or shape is experienced.	C. No adaptation necessary
D. The eating disturbance is not attributable to a concurrent medical condition or not better explained by another mental disorder. When the eating disturbance occurs in the context of another condition or disorder, the severity of the eating disturbance exceeds that routinely associated with the condition or disorder and warrants additional clinical attention.	D. No adaptation necessary.

Anorexia Nervosa

General Description of the Disorder

Anorexia nervosa is characterized by maintaining a body weight that is below a minimal normal level for developmental stage, a fear of gaining weight, and a distorted body image (Call, Walsh, & Attia, 2013). It primarily affects adolescent girls and young women (Hock, 2006) and is seen in people with intellectual disabilities (Hove, 2004). Assessment can be challenging as people with intellectual disabilities usually have limited verbal skills. It is critical to rule out somatic disorders, medication side effects, and insufficient care as a cause of weight loss and to treat comorbid psychiatric disorders. *DSM-5* criteria can be applied without adaptations to individuals with anorexia nervosa and mild intellectual disability. A minor adaptation is suggested for individuals with moderate to profound intellectual disabilities.

Review of Diagnostic Criteria

A significant number of individuals with anorexia nervosa did not fit in the *DSM-IV* category (American Psychiatric Association, 2013b) and received a diagnosis of "eating disorder not otherwise specified." A goal of the *DSM-5* was for more people experiencing eating disorders to have a diagnosis with greater clinical utility that accurately describes symptoms and behaviors (American Psychiatric Association, 2013a).

Some important changes made in the diagnostic criteria of anorexia nervosa in the *DSM-5* are:

- Criterion A no longer includes the word "refusal" in terms of weight maintenance, as this can be difficult to assess. "Restriction of energy intake" is described instead.
- "Amenorrhea" is deleted, as it was not a useful criterion for men, premenarchal females, females taking oral contraceptives, and post-menopausal women.
- The level of severity is included in *DSM-5*.

Summary of DSM-5 *Criteria*

The category requires restriction of energy intake, leading to a significantly low body weight in the context of age, sex, developmental trajectory, and physical health. "Significantly low weight" is defined as a weight that is less than minimally normal or, for children and adolescents, less than that minimally expected. It also requires intense fear of gaining weight or of becoming fat, or persistent behavior that interferes with weight gain, even though at a significantly low weight, plus disturbance in the way in which one's body weight or shape is experienced, undue influence of body weight or shape on self-evaluation, or persistent lack of recognition of the seriousness of the current low body weight.

DSM-5 allows specifiers of restricting type and binge-eating/purging type, and also a specifier on severity (based on current BMI or, for children and adolescents, on BMI percentile) and the need for supervision.

Issues Related to Diagnosis in Persons with ID

One study (Hove, 2004) reports a high prevalence of anorexia nervosa in people with intellectual disabilities (1.6%), higher than that reported in the general population (Hook, 2006). However, this staff-completed questionnaire study of 311 adults did not require disturbed body image to be present, contrary to the DSM definition of the condition, so these figures are not directly comparable. This important criterion of the classification of anorexia nervosa requires a cognitive component. It can be challenging to assess information about the fear of gaining weight or a distorted body image in people with intellectual disabilities (Dymek & le Grange, 2002). Observer input from people who know the person well can give important additional information.

As individuals with intellectual disabilities often have limited expressive language skills, it is important to first rule out somatic disorders, medication side effects, and insufficient care as a cause of food refusal or weight loss. It can be difficult to differentiate anorexia nervosa from depression, obsessive compulsive disorder, social phobia (fear of eating in public), or schizophrenia (delusions), as it is challenging to understand the underlying cognitions of food refusal in people with intellectual disabilities.

There is a statistically significant comorbidity of the anxiety and affective disorders with anorexia nervosa in the general population (Halmi et al., 1991) and a low incidence of anorexia with comorbid psychotic disorders (Dymek & le Grange, 2002; Halmi et al., 1991). The prevalence of comorbidity of anxiety and affective disorders in people with anorexia nervosa and intellectual disabilities is unknown.

Application of Diagnostic Criteria to People with ID

Methodology

Few studies are available for anorexia nervosa in people with intellectual disabilities. A search of the literature was performed using PubMed, utilizing the search terms "intellectual disability and anorexia" and "mental retardation and anorexia." Ninety-two articles were retrieved. The full text of relevant articles was reviewed in addition to related articles.

Although eating disorders may be seen in people with intellectual disabilities more frequently than in the general population (Gravestock, 2000), little research has been done. Most of the studies were prevalence studies or case reports (Fletcher, Loschen, Stavrakaki, & First, 2007). Few reviews applying to people with intellectual disabilities have been reported. Gravestock (2000) reviewed 17 published studies and concluded that eating disorders are more frequently seen in individuals with ID than in the general population. Gravestock found that 5%-43% of adults with intellectual disability are significantly underweight (BMI < 17), and that 35%-72% of adults with severe or profound intellectual disability are significantly underweight. Communication problems and body image assessment difficulties in adults with intellectual disabilities were highlighted.

Summary of Limitations in Applying **DSM-5** *Criteria to People with ID*

Assessment of anorexia nervosa is complicated by communication problems in people with intellectual disabilities. As individuals with intellectual disabilities often have limited expressive language skills, it is challenging to rule out somatic disorders or other psychiatric or behavior disorders as a cause of weight loss.

Although the "fear of gaining weight" can be difficult to assess, the additional *DSM-5* criterion "persistent behavior that interferes with weight gain" is more useful in people with intellectual disabilities.

The C criterion in *DSM-5* focuses on a distorted body image or the lack of recognition of the seriousness of the low body weight. This can be more difficult to assess in people with moderate to profound intellectual disabilities, as it asks for reflective cognitive capacities.

Etiology and Pathogenesis

Anorexia nervosa in adults with intellectual disabilities is related to prior dieting, family psychopathology and conflicts, identity problems, bereavement, sexual issues, and regression (Gravestock, 2000). There have been several case reports of anorexia nervosa in individuals with Down syndrome (Cotrell & Crisp, 1984; Holt, Bouras, & Watson, 1988; Morgan, 1989; Raitasuo & Virtanen, 1998; Szymanski & Biederman, 1984). Anorexia nervosa might develop following insufficient treatment of depression in individuals with Down syndrome (Raitasuo & Virtanen, 1998). Single case reports describe anorexia nervosa as a comorbid disorder in Prader-Willi syndrome, possibly associated with other psychopathology (Counts, 2001) and in phenylketonuria (Clarke & Yapa, 1991).

Adaptation of Diagnostic Criteria

DSM-5 criteria can be applied to any individual with intellectual disabilities who has the ability to communicate about disturbance of body image or reflect on the seriousness of low body weight. This includes most individuals with mild or moderate intellectual disabilities. These criteria can usually not be applied to individuals with severe or profound intellectual disabilities. Non-verbal communication and the additional observations of family and caretakers can be useful additional information in making an accurate assessment.

Anorexia Nervosa

DSM-5 Diagnostic Criteria	Applying Criteria for Mild-Profound ID
A. Restriction of energy intake relative to requirements, leading to a significantly low body weight in the context of age, sex, developmental trajectory, and physical health. *Significantly low weight* is defined as a weight that is less than minimally normal or, for children and adolescents, less than that minimally expected.	A. No adaptations necessary
B. Intense fear of gaining weight or of becoming fat, or persistent behavior that interferes with weight gain, even though at a significantly low weight.	B. No adaptations necessary
C. Disturbance in the way in which one's body weight or shape is experienced, undue influence of body weight or shape on self-evaluation, or persistent lack of recognition of the seriousness of the current low body weight.	C. No adaptations necessary for individuals with mild intellectual disabilities. For individuals with moderate to profound intellectual disabilities additional observations from care givers and family will be necessary.

Bulimia Nervosa

General Description of the Disorder

Bulimia nervosa is characterized by severe recurrent episodes of binge eating and associated inappropriate behaviors and cognitive distortions. The criteria in *DSM-5* have not changed from those presented in *DSM-IV-TR*, other than the requirement for binging being an average occurrence of at least once per week for three months, rather than the twice per week specified in *DSM-IV-TR*. There have also been changes in the specifiers that can be used.

Summary of DSM-5 *Criteria*

Excessive, or binge, eating is associated with a sense of a lack of control of eating and recurrent inappropriate compensatory mechanisms (usually occurring in secrecy or inconspicuously) to prevent weight gain, such as self-induced vomiting, excessive exercise, and misuse of drugs such as laxatives and diuretics. Self-evaluation is unduly influenced by body shape and weight. The binge eating and inappropriate compensatory mechanisms must occur on average at least once per week for three months, and not be exclusively during periods of anorexia nervosa.

DSM-5 specifiers for bulimia nervosa include "in partial remission" and "in full remission," with severity ¾ based on the frequency of recurrent inappropriate compensatory mechanisms ¾ being "mild," "moderate," "severe," or "extreme."

Issues Related to Diagnosis in Persons with ID

Careful observation is needed for caregivers to be aware of secretive inappropriate behaviors, and an individual's self-perception of body shape and weight can be difficult to elicit, even in people with mild intellectual disabilities. The use of pictures may be helpful to evaluate body image. Weight and weight changes are easier to measure and record, but weight can be normal as well as overweight or underweight in people with bulimia nervosa. Given the high level of comorbidities in people with intellectual disabilities, it is important to eliminate these as a cause of the disturbed eating and associated behaviors.

Application of Diagnostic Criteria to People with ID

There are very few studies of bulimia nervosa in people with intellectual disabilities to inform the application or adaptation of diagnostic criteria for this population.

Methodology

The literature review was updated in October 2015. Only one new article was identified since the publication and literature review for the *DM-ID* first edition (Jones & Samuel, 2010). Few articles had originally been identified on eating disorders, with one specifically on bulimia nervosa in a person with Prader-Willi syndrome, highlighting the very limited evidence base on this condition for people with intellectual disabilities. Several other articles were found on abnormal eating in Prader-Willi syndrome but not of relevance to this specific chapter of *DM-ID*.

Review of Research Applying to People with ID

The existing literature reports a very wide prevalence range for eating disorders in people with intellectual disabilities, due to environmental, service, sampling, definitional, and other methodological factors between studies (Gravestock, 2000). With regard specifically to bulimia nervosa, Hove (2004) reported bulimia nervosa in 1.3% of 311 adults with intellectual disabilities on whom staff completed a questionnaire, with the disorder occurring equally in men and women. Bulimia was defined as the presence of binge eating, with self-induced vomiting, and compulsive eating, and hence does not meet DSM criteria. An individual case report has also been reported (Gallucci Anersen, Hackerman, & Mondimore, 2003).

Evaluating the Level of Evidence

The evidence on this disorder in people with intellectual disabilities is severely limited. The study reported by Hove (2004) did not include an evaluation of body image. No literature was found regarding children or young people.

Summary of Limitations in Applying DSM-5 *Criteria to People with ID*

The main limitation is the ability of individuals to communicate their views on and self-evaluation of body shape and weight. Accessible assessment methods are required such as the use of pictures, but assessments may remain limited.

Etiology and Pathogenesis

Very little information is available on etiology. Gilmour, Skuse, and Pembrey (2001) described a small group of individuals with mild intellectual disabilities and short stature who exhibited hyperphagia when in high-stress living conditions and who did not have Prader-Willi syndrome.

Adaptation of Diagnostic Criteria

DSM-5 criteria can be applied directly to anyone who can describe self-image. There is too little evidence to conclude whether this item should be modified for people who cannot report on body image and weight.

Bulimia Nervosa

DSM-IV Diagnostic Criteria	Applying Criteria for Mild to Profound ID
A. Recurrent episodes of binge eating. An episode of binge eating is characterized by both of the following: 1. Eating, in a discrete period of time (e.g., within any 2-hour period), an amount of food that is definitely larger than most people would eat during a similar period of time and under similar circumstances 2. A sense of lack of control over eating during the episode (e.g., a feeling that one cannot stop eating or control what or how much one is eating)	A. No adaptation necessary.

Bulimia Nervosa (continued)

DSM-IV Diagnostic Criteria	Applying Criteria for Mild to Profound ID
B. Recurrent inappropriate compensatory behavior in order to prevent weight gain, such as self-induced vomiting; misuse of laxatives, diuretics, or other medications; fasting; or excessive exercise.	B. No adaptation necessary.
C. The binge eating and inappropriate compensatory behaviors both occur, on average, at least once a week for 3 months.	C. No adaptation necessary.
D. Self-evaluation is unduly influenced by body shape and weight.	D. No adaptation indicated, in the absence of an evidence base.
The disturbance does not occur exclusively during episodes of Anorexia Nervosa.	No adaptation necessary.

Binge-Eating Disorder

General Description of the Disorder

Binge-eating disorder has been introduced into the main chapters of DSM for the first time. It shares in common the binge eating seen in bulimia nervosa but is not accompanied by the recurrent inappropriate compensatory behavior seen in bulimia, and does not require self-evaluation to be unduly influenced by body shape and weight. It does require marked distress to be associated with the binge eating.

Summary of DSM-5 *Criteria*

Excessive, or binge, eating is associated with a sense of a lack of control of eating. It is associated with eating more rapidly than normal, eating until uncomfortably full, eating large amounts when not hungry, eating alone to avoid embarrassment of eating large amounts, and a sense of self-disgust or guilt. The condition needs to cause marked distress to be recorded and with binges occurring at least once a week for three months and not exclusively during the course of bulimia nervosa or anorexia nervosa. Distinct from bulimia, it is not associated with recurrent inappropriate compensatory behaviors.

DSM-5 specifiers for binge eating disorder include "in partial remission" and "in full remission," with severity – based on the frequency of episodes of binge eating – being "mild," "moderate," "severe," or "extreme."

Issues Related to Diagnosis in Persons with ID

It may be difficult to elicit a feeling of self-disgust, depression, or guilt after binges in people with intellectual disabilities, but this is one of five items, of which three are needed. Availability of food in a communal setting should be considered when considering this diagnosis. There is a lack of evidence to further inform our knowledge on issues related to diagnosis in people with intellectual disabilities.

Application of Diagnostic Criteria to People with ID

There is a lack of studies to inform the application or adaptation of diagnostic criteria for this population.

Methodology

The literature review was updated in October 2015. Only one relevant article was found.

Review of Research Applying to People with ID

Hove (2004) described staff reports of binge eating in 19.0% of 133 adults with intellectual disabilities. However, this was defined as "eating fast, bolting one's food, and excessive eating ... symptoms present at least twice a week for the preceding 3 months," so the criteria is not in keeping with *DSM-5* criteria for this disorder.

Summary of Limitations in Applying DSM-5 *Criteria to People with ID*

The main limitation is the ability of individuals to communicate their experiences and views.

Etiology and Pathogenesis

Very little information is available on etiology.

Binge-Eating Disorder

In the absence of evidence to the contrary, *DSM-5* criteria should be applied directly without adaptation. Further research on this condition in people with intellectual disabilities is much needed.

Other Specified Feeding or Eating Disorder
Unspecified Feeding or Eating Disorder

DSM-5 also provides categories for other specified feeding or eating disorder and for unspecified feeding or eating disorder.

References

American Psychiatric Association (2000). *Diagnostic and statistical manual of mental disorders (4th Ed.).* Arlington, VA: American Psychiatric Association.

American Psychiatric Association (2013a). Feeding and eating disorders (fact sheet). Retrieved from http://www.dsm5.org/Documents/Eating%20Disorders%20Fact%20Sheet.pdf.

American Psychiatric Association (2013b). Feeding and eating disorders. In *Diagnostic and statistical manual of mental disorders (5th Ed.).* Doi:10.1176/appi.books.9780890425596.744053.

Amor, D. J. (2002). Morbid obesity and hyperphagia in the WAGR syndrome. *Clinical Dysmorphology, 11,* 73–74.

Ayoob, K. T., Kaminer, R. K., & Zawel, J. (1994). Chronic overeating without obesity in children with developmental disabilities: Description of a new syndrome. *Mental Retardation, 32,* 194–199.

Bazyk, S. (1990). Factors associated with the transition to oral feeding in infants fed by nasogastric tubes. *American Journal of Occupational Therapy, 44*(12), 1070-1078.

Birmingham, C. L., & Firoz, T. (2006). Rumination in eating disorders: Literature review. *Eating and Weight Disorders, 11,* e85-e89.

Call, C., Walsh, B. T., & Attia, E. (2013). From *DSM-IV* to *DSM-5*: Changes to eating disorder diagnosis. *Current Opinions in Psychiatry, 26,* 532-6.

Chial, H. J., Camilleri, M., Williams, D. E., Litzinger, K., & Perrault, J. (2003). Rumination syndrome in children and adolescents: Diagnosis, treatment, and prognosis. *Pediatrics, 111*(1), 158-62.

Clarke, D. J., & Yapa, P. (1991). Phenylketonuria and anorexia nervosa. *Journal of Mental Deficiency Research, 35,* 165–170.

Cooper, S-A., Melville, C. A., & Einfeld, S. L. (2003). Psychiatric diagnosis, intellectual disabilities and diagnostic criteria for psychiatric disorders for use with adults with learning disabilities/mental retardation (DC-LD). *Journal of Intellectual Disability Research, 47,* 3-15.

Cotrell, R., & Crisp, A. H. (1984). Anorexia nervosa in a Down's syndrome patient: A case report. *British Journal of Psychiatry, 145,* 195-196.

Counts, D. (2001). An adult with Prader-Willi syndrome and anorexia nervosa: A case report. *International Journal of Eating Disorders, 30,* 231–233.

Crawley, H. (2007). *Eating well: Children and adults with learning disabilities.* The Caroline Walker Trust. *www.cwt.org.uk*

Drossman, D. A., Corazziari, E., Delvaux, M., Spiller, R. C., Talley, N. J., Thompson, W. G., & Whitehead, W. E. (2006). *Rome III: The functional gastrointestinal disorders (3rd Ed.).* McLean, VA: Degnon.

Dymek, M., & le Grange, D. (2002). Anorexia nervosa with comorbid psychosis and borderline mental retardation: A case report. *International Journal of Eating Disorders, 31* (4), 478-482.

Fletcher, R., Loschen, E., Stavrakaki, C., & First, M. (Eds.) (2007). *Diagnostic manual-intellectual disability (DM-ID): A textbook of diagnosis of mental disorders in persons with intellectual disability.* Kingston, NY: NADD Press.

Fox, R., Karan, O. C., & Rotatori, A. F. (1981). Regression including anorexia nervosa in a Down's syndrome adult: A seven year follow up. *Journal of Behavioral Therapy & Experimental Psychiatry, 12,* 351–354.

Gal, E., Hardal-Nasser, R., Engel-Yeger, B. (2011). The relationship between the severity of eating problems and intellectual developmental deficit level. *Research in Developmental Disability, 32*(5), 1464-1469.

Galéra, C., Delrue, M. A., Goizet, C., Etchegoyhen, K., Taupiac, E., Sigaudy, S., ... Lacombe, D. (2006). Behavioral and temperamental features of children with Costello syndrome. *American Journal of Medical Genetics, 140A*(9), 968-974.

Gallucci, G., Andersen, A. E., Hackerman, F., & Mondimore, F. M. (2003). Eating and feeding difficulties in patients with intellectual and developmental disabilities: Four cases. *Mental Health Aspects of Developmental Disabilities, 6*, 114–119.

Gilmour, J., Skuse, D., & Pembrey, M. (2001). Hyperphagic short stature and Prader-Willi syndrome: A comparison of behavioural phenotypes, genotypes, and indices of stress. *British Journal of Psychiatry, 179*, 129–137.

Gravestock, S. (2000). Eating disorders in adults with intellectual disability. *Journal of Intellectual Disability Research, 44*, 625–637.

Gravestock, S. (2000). Eating disorders in people with intellectual disabilities. Review. *Journal of International Disability Research, 44*(6), 625-37.

Gravestock, S. (2003) Diagnosis and classification of eating disorders in adults with intellectual disability: The *Diagnostic Criteria for Psychiatric Disorders for Use with Adults with Learning Disabilities/Mental Retardation (DC-LD)* approach. *Journal of Intellectual Disability Research, 47*, 72-83.

Gupta, R., Kaila, M., & Gupta, J. B. (2012). Adult rumination syndrome: Differentiation from psychogenic intractable vomiting. *Indian Journal of Psychiatry, 54*(3), 283-285. Doi: 10.4103/0019-5545.102434.

Halmi, K. A., Eckert, E., Marchi, P., Sampugnaro, V., Apple, R., & Cohen, J. (1991). Comorbidity of psychiatric disorders in anorexia nervosa. *Archives of General Psychiatry, 48*(8), 712-718.

Handen, B. L., Mandell, F., & Russo, D. C. (1986). Feeding induction in children who refuse to eat. *American Journal of Diseases of Children, 140*(1), 52-54.

Hartmann, A. S., Becker, A. E., Hampton, C., & Bryant-Waugh, R. (2012). Rumination disorder in *DSM-5*. *Psychiatric Annals, 42*(11), 426-430. Doi: 10.3928/00485713-20121105-09.

Heal, M., & O'Hara, J. (1993). The music therapy of an anorectic mentally handicapped adult. *British Journal of Medical Psychology, 66*, 33–41.

Hoek, H. W. (2006). Incidence, prevalence and mortality of anorexia nervosa and other eating disorders. *Current Opinions in Psychiatry, 19*(4), 389-394.

Holt, G. M., Bouras, N., & Watson, J. P. (1988). Down's syndrome and eating disorders: A case study. *British Journal of Psychiatry, 152*, 847–848.

Hove, O. (2004). Prevalence of eating disorders in adults with mental retardation living in the community. *American Journal of Mental Retardation, 109*(6), 505-506.

Hurley, A. D., & Sovner, R. (1979). Anorexia nervosa and intellectual disability: A case report. *Journal of Clinical Psychiatry, 40*, 480–482.

Jones, C. J., & Samuel, J. (2010). The diagnosis of eating disorders in adults with learning disabilities: Conceptualization and implications for clinical practice. *European Eating Disorders Review, 18*, 352-366.

Keng, W. T., Cole, T., Pilz, D., & Portcous, M. E. (2002). Food aversion and facial dysmorphism — A newly described syndrome? *Clinical Dysmorphology, 11*, 249–253.

Kern, L., Starosta, K., & Adelman, B. E. (2006). Reducing pica by teaching children to exchange inedible items for edibles. *Behavior Modification, 30*, 135–158.

Kuhn, D. E., & Matson, J. L. (2004). Assessment of feeding and mealtime behavior problems in persons with mental retardation. *Behavior Modification, 28*(5), 638-648.

Luiselli, J. K. (1994). Oral feeding treatment of children with chronic food refusal and multiple developmental disabilities. *American Journal of Mental Retardation, 98*(5), 646-655.

Matson, J. L., Mayville, S. B., Kuhn, D., Sturmey, P., Laud, R., & Cooper, C. (2005). The behavioral function of feeding problems as assessed by the questions about behavioural function (QABF). *Research in Developmental Disabilities, 26*, 399-408.

McAdams, D. B., Sherman, J. A., Sheldon, J. B., & Napolitano, D. A. (2004). Behavioural interventions to reduce the pica of persons with developmental disabilities. *Behavior Modification*, 26, 45-72.

Mohl, P. C., & McMahon, T. (1980). Anorexia nervosa associated with mental retardation and schizoaffective disorder. *Psychosomatics, 21*, 602–603.

Moreland, F., & Henderson, M. (2003). Interagency multidisciplinary approach to PICA in adults with ID. *Proceedings NADD 204 annual conference.* Kingston, NY: NADD Press.

Morgan. J. R. (1989). A case of Down's syndrome, Insulinoma and anorexia. *Journal of Mental Deficiency Research, 33*, 185-187.

Nicholls, D., & Bryant-Waugh, R. (2008). Eating disorders of infancy and childhood: Definition, symptomatology, epidemiology and co-morbidity. *Child and Adolescent Psychiatric Clinics of North America, 18*(1), 17–30. Doi:10.1016/j.chc.2008.07.008.

O'Brien, G., & Whitehouse, A. M. (1990). A psychiatric study of deviant eating behaviour among mentally handicapped adults. *British Journal of Psychiatry, 157*, 281-284.

O'Brien, G. (Ed.) (2002). *Behavioural phenotypes in clinical practice.* Cambridge, UK: Cambridge University Press.

O'Brien, M. D., Bruce, B. K. & Camilleri, M. (1995). The rumination syndrome: Clinical features rather than manometric diagnosis. *Gastroenterology, 108*, 1024-1029.

Papadopoulos, V., & Mimidis, K. (2007). The rumination syndrome in adults: A review of the pathophysiology, diagnosis and treatment. *Journal of Postgraduate Medicine, 53*(3), 203-206. Doi:10.4103/0022-3859.33868._

Parry-Jones, B. & Parry-Jones, W. L. L. (1992). Pica: Symptom or eating disorder? A historical assessment. *British Journal of Psychiatry, 160*, 341-345.

Rader, K., Braun-Scharm, H., Linn, M., & Martinius, J. (1992). Anorectic reactions in low intelligence. *Zeitschrift für Kinder- und Jugendpsychiatrie, 20*, 54–61.

Rader, K., Specht, F., & Reister, M. (1989). Anorexia nervosa and Down syndrome. *Praxis der Kinderpsychologie und Kinderpsychiatrie, 38*, 343–346.

Raitasuo, S., & Virtanen, H. (1998). Anorexia nervosa, major depression and OCD in a Down's syndrome patient. *International Journal of Eating Disorders, 23*, 107-109.

Raitasuo, S., Virtamen, H., & Raitasuo, J. (1998). Anorexia nervosa, major depression, and obsessive-compulsive disorder in a Down's syndrome patient. *International Journal of Eating Disorders, 28*, 107–109.

Rajindrajith, S., Devanarayana, N. M., & Cirspus Perera, B. J. (2012). Rumination syndrome in children and adolescents: A school survey assessing prevalence and symptomatology. *BioMed Central Gastroenterology, 12*, 163. Doi: 10.1186/1471-230X-12-163.

Royal College of Psychiatrists (2001). *Diagnostic criteria for psychiatric disorders for use with adults with learning disabilities/mental retardation (DC-LD).* London: Gaskell Press.

Rutter, M., Bishop, D., Pine, D., Scott, S., Stevenson, J., Taylor, E., & Thapar, A. (2010). *Rutter's child and adolescent psychiatry (5th Ed.).* Oxford, UK: Blackwell Publishing.

Rutter, M., & Taylor, E. (Eds.) (2002). *Child and adolescent psychiatry.* Oxford, UK: Blackwell Publishing.

Sarimski, K. (1996). Specific eating and sleeping problems in Prader-Willi and Williams-Beuren syndrome. *Child Care Health Development, 22*, 143–150.

Stein, D. J., Bouwer, C., & van Heerden, B. (1996). Pica and the obsessive-compulsive spectrum disorders. *South African Medical Journal, 86*(12 Suppl.), 1586-8, 1591-2.

Sullivan, P. B., Juszczak, E., Lambert, B. R., Rose, M., Ford-Adams, M. E., & Johnson, A. (2002). Impact of feeding problems on nutritional intake and growth: Oxford feeding study II. *Developmental Medicine and Child Neurology, 44*(7), 461-467.

Szymanski, L., & King, B. H. (1999). Practice parameters for the assessment and treatment of children, adolescents, and adults with mental retardation and comorbid mental disorders. American Academy of Child and Adolescent Psychiatry Working Group on Quality Issues. *Journal of the American Academy of Child and Adolescent Psychiatry, 38*(12 Suppl.), 5S-31S.

Szymanski, L. S., & Biederman, J. (1984). Depression and anorexia nervosa of persons with Down syndrome. *American Journal on Mental Deficiency, 89*, 246–251.

Uher, R., & Rutter, M. (2012). Classification of feeding and eating disorders: Review of evidence and proposals for ICD-11. *World Psychiatry, 11*(2), 80–92. Doi:10.1016/j.wpsyc.2012.05.005.

CHAPTER 19

Elimination Disorders

Sarah M. Lytle
Stephen L. Ruedrich
Kristin L. Kaelber
Edwin J. Mikkelsen

Elimination disorders include enuresis and encopresis, disorders related to incontinence of urine and stool, respectively. Diagnostic criteria include consideration of (1) the age (or equivalent developmental level) of the individual, (2) frequency and duration of incontinence, and (3) lack of a direct effect of a substance or medical condition. Enuresis and encopresis may occur as separate disorders or may co-occur. In addition, these disorders may be primary or secondary, the latter being when the individual has had a period of time during which he or she has been continent.

Enuresis

Review of Diagnostic Criteria

In the *Diagnostic and Statistical Manual of Mental Disorders, 5th Edition* (*DSM-5*), enuresis is defined as involuntary or intentional voiding that occurs at least twice a week for three months and causes significant distress or impairment in functioning. It is divided into subtypes including nocturnal only, diurnal only, or nocturnal and diurnal (American Psychiatric Association, 2013). These subtypes are based on incontinence during the daytime, nighttime, or daytime and nighttime, respectively. Primary enuresis occurs when an individual has had no period of urinary continence. Secondary enuresis occurs when an individual has had a period of urinary continence, after which he or she becomes enuretic.

Enuresis is included in the elimination disorders section of the *DSM-5* and includes nocturnal, diurnal, and a combination of both subtypes.

Summary of* DSM-5 *Criteria

A. Repeated voiding of urine into bed or clothes, whether involuntary or intentional.

B. The behavior is clinically significant, as manifested by either frequency of at least twice a week for at least three consecutive months or the presence of clinically significant distress or impairment in social, academic (occupational), or other important areas of functioning.

C. Chronological age is at least 5 years or equivalent developmental level.

D. The behavior is not attributable to the physiological effects of a substance (e.g., a diuretic, an antipsychotic medication) or another medical condition (e.g., diabetes, spina bifida, a seizure disorder).

The *DSM-5* also identifies three subtypes:

(1) Nocturnal only refers to passage of urine during nighttime sleep. This is sometimes referred to as monosymptomatic enuresis and is the most common subtype.

(2) Diurnal only refers to passage of urine during waking hours and occurs in the absence of nocturnal enuresis. It is sometimes referred to as urinary incontinence. The *DSM-5* distinguishes two subtypes: Those with "urge incontinence" who have detrusor muscle instability and sudden urges to urinate, and those with "voiding postponement" who delay voiding until incontinence results.

(3) Nocturnal and diurnal, which is a combination of the nocturnal and diurnal subtypes. It is also referred to as non-monosymptomatic enuresis.

Issues Related to Diagnosis in Persons with ID

Development and Course

By definition, enuresis occurs in individuals who have a chronological age of at least 5 years. Individuals younger than 5 years of age cannot be diagnosed with enuresis. In individuals with ID, the criterion is based on developmental age, such that a 20-year-old individual with ID must have a developmental age of at least 5 years of age to be diagnosed with enuresis.

Prevalence

The prevalence of enuresis varies between individuals who are neurotypical and those with ID. A cohort study reported rates of daytime urinary incontinence in neurotypical first-graders of 6.3% and in fourth-graders of 4.3%, and reported nocturnal enuresis in the same groups at rates of 7.1% and 2.7%, respectively (Soderstrom, Hoelcke, Alenius, Soderling, & Hjern, 2004). Enuresis occurs more frequently in males as compared to females with about twice as many boys having enuresis (Chiozza, et al., 1998; Yeung, Sreddher, Sinhoe, Sit, & Lau, 2006).

There have been a number of studies examining the prevalence of enuresis in persons with ID; however, it should be noted that many studies failed to report a well-defined developmental level, making interpretation of the data difficult. Individuals with ID have higher rates of enuresis than those without ID with reported rates of between 23% and 86% (Van Laeke, 2008). One study of 7-year-old children with ID ranging from mild to profound reported that 38% had nocturnal enuresis and 39% had diurnal enuresis (von Wendt, Simila, Niskann, & Jarvelin, 1990). In this study, 20% of 20-year-old individuals with ID had nocturnal enuresis, and 20% had diurnal enuresis. Individuals with more severe ID were more likely to be enuretic.

A parental questionnaire-based study of 357 individuals ages 4-52 years (mean age 17.9 +/- 9.5) with Prader-Willi and fragile X syndrome (two genetically identifiable causes of ID) compared rates and types of incontinence in these individuals (Equit, Piro-Hussong, Niemczyk, Curfs, & von Gontard, 2013). Although individual levels of ID were not established in this study, results indicated that 29.3% of individuals with Prader-Willi and 48.8% of those with fragile X had one elimination disorder, with nocturnal enuresis being most common (25.9%). Incontinence did decline as individuals aged with 54.1% of children, 37.9% of teens, 25.9% of young adults, and 20% of adults having at least one elimination disorder. It was noted that individuals with fragile X syndrome (typically associated with moderate ID) as compared to individuals with Prader-Willi syndrome (associated with mild ID) were more likely to have an elimination disorder.

These data demonstrate overall higher rates of elimination disorders in individuals with ID as compared to neurotypical persons. In addition, they suggest that the likelihood of having enuresis increases with increasing severity of ID. However, the ability of an individual to communicate his/her need for access to facilities, need for assistance, and privacy in toileting functions may influence the apparent frequency of urinary incontinence.

Differential Diagnosis

Enuresis is most commonly idiopathic but is often associated with fecal incontinence and constipation (Caldwell, Deshpande, & von Gontard, 2013). Incontinence due to underlying medical causes (including but not limited to diabetes, spina bifida, seizure disorder, and urinary tract infection) does not meet the criteria for enuresis.

Functional Consequences

As is true with other *DSM-5* disorders, the ability to express distress may be difficult for persons with ID, so levels of impairment and/or the presence of "clinically significant distress" may have to be determined or estimated by the caregiver.

Nocturnal enuresis in some neurotypical individuals may lead to poorer sleep quality as a result of sleep disruption including increased nighttime awakening, greater sleep latency, and subjective fatigue before sleep and after awakening (Cohen-Zrubavel, Kushnir, Kushnir, & Sadeh, 2011). Disrupted sleep or loss of sleep may have a variety of consequences, including reduction or prevention of brain activities required for brain maturation, effect on regulation, memory and learning, and cognitive function deficits and disruptions in behavior regulation as a result of daytime sleepiness (see Sadeh, 2007, for a review).

While one article reported no differences in emotional or behavioral traits among neurotypical primary enuretics, former enuretics, and children with no prior history of enuresis (Wille & Anveden, 1995), most suggest potential negative effects. One study suggested that neurotypical children who had nocturnal enuresis at age 9 had poorer peer relationships as teenagers, even if they were no longer enuretic (Bottomley, 2011). In addition, emotional and financial stress, parental guilt and feelings of helplessness, or parental intolerance may result (Bottomley, 2011). Enuresis may affect an individual's social interactions, peer relationships, and self-esteem and lead to a lower perceived quality of life, as well as increased behavioral problems particularly in older children (Caldwell et al., 2013; Redsell & Coller, 2001).

There are no specific data on functional consequences of elimination disorders in individuals with ID. It seems likely, however, that sleep disruption, familial stress, social/peer relationships, and behavioral problems would be consequences in individuals with ID as well.

Comorbidity

There are no published data specifically addressing medical issues comorbid with enuresis in individuals with ID. Enuresis can occur in patients with comorbid medical conditions including, but not limited to, constipation and neurogenic bladder. In addition, it has been associated with a variety of factors in neurotypical children including lower socioeconomic status, sexual abuse, co-sleeping (Ma et al., 2014); conduct disorder, attention-deficit hyperactivity disorder (ADHD) (Mellon et al.,2013); and obstructive sleep apnea (OSA) (Bascom et al., 2011). Parent-reported psychological problems occur more in neurotypical children with daytime wetting than in those without, and include higher reported rates of difficulty with attention and oppositional and defiant behavior (Joinson, Heron, Butler, von Gontard, & the Avon Longitudinal Study of Parents and Children Study Team, 2006).

■ *ADHD*

Evidence in neurotypical children suggests that there is a strong association between nocturnal enuresis and ADHD. One study showed that children with ADHD were twice as likely to have enuresis as those without ADHD (Mellon et al., 2013). Another reported an adjusted odds ratio of 2.88 (1.26-6.57) for enuresis comorbid with ADHD as compared to enuresis without ADHD (Shreeram, He, Kalaydjian, Brothers, & Merikangas, 2009). There has been no causal relationship established for the two disorders. Screening and treatment for ADHD in neurotypical and persons with ID and enuresis, and vice versa, are strongly recommended, although it is unclear if treating ADHD can lead to resolution or reduction in symptoms of enuresis.

■ *Obstructive Sleep Apnea*

Nocturnal enuresis has been reported in 8%-57% of neurotypical children with OSA caused by adenotonsillar hypertrophy (Brooks & Topol, 2003; Wang, Elkins, & Keech, 1998). Resolution of enuresis may occur in patients who are treated for their OSA with about half of those individuals with nocturnal enuresis showing a decline in or complete resolution of symptoms after tonsillectomy and adenoidectomy (Kovacevic et al., 2013; Thottman, Madgy, & Abdulhamid, 2013). Diurnal urinary incontinence was resolved in 17% of children after the same type of surgery (Kovacevic et al., 2013). Due to this association, it is strongly recommended that both neurotypical individuals and persons who have ID, with enuresis, be screened for obstructive sleep apnea, and vice versa.

Application of Diagnostic Criteria to People with ID

General Considerations

The *DSM-5* criteria for enuresis includes that the individual's chronological or developmental age must be at least 5 years. Therefore, an individual with ID whose developmental age is less than 5 years should not be diagnosed with enuresis. In theory, then, persons with profound ID should not be diagnosed with enuresis, based on strict *DSM-5* criteria, because they likely have not reached a developmental age of 5 years. Traditionally, an individual's "intelligence quotient" was obtained by dividing his/her mental age by his/her chronological age, and multiplying by 100 (Tasse 2012). See formula below:

Mental age ÷ chronological age x 100 = IQ

However, the concept of "mental age" (or developmental age) has been largely replaced by a multi-dimensional approach to the classification of persons with ID, which incorporates assessment of intellectual ability, adaptive behavior skills, and needed environmental supports (American Psychiatric Association 2013). Because individuals often have very disparate intellectual and adaptive abilities, there cannot be a direct correlation between ID severity level and attainment of specific developmental tasks such as urinary or fecal continence.

Methodology

The literature review included a search within the PubMed database for all studies published in the 20 years leading up to and including May 2014. A hand search of the reference sections of the retrieved papers was also conducted. In addition, the *DSM-5* and the prior edition of the *NADD DM-ID* were used as references.

Review of Research Applying to People with ID

The previous edition of the *NADD DM-ID* provided a review of articles published prior to January 2004 (Tasse Barnhill, Havercamp, & Reeve, 2007). The majority of these articles had strength of evidence III. The authors' conclusions based on this review were that individuals with mild ID can obtain continence by age 5, but that individuals with ID may need greater assistance in obtaining continence. They also noted that persons with profound ID could be successfully taught toilet training (Tasse et al., 2007).

Only a few studies of individuals with ID and enuresis have been published since then (Equit et al., 2013; Joinson et al., 2006; von Gontard, Didden, Sinnema, & Curfs, 2010). These are summarized below:

A study of greater than 6,000 children in which parents completed a questionnaire indicated that bed-wetting was associated with lower Wechsler Intelligence Scale for Children-Third Edition IQ scores compared to controls (Joinson et al., 2007).

Individuals with Prader-Willi syndrome (which is often associated with ID) were noted to have a high percentage of lower urinary tract symptoms: Straining, interrupted stream, urgency, and postponement (von Gontard et al., 2010).

Individuals with fragile X syndrome (typically associated with moderate ID) as compared to individuals with Prader-Willi syndrome (associated with mild ID) were more likely to have an elimination disorder (Equit et al., 2013).

Evaluating the Level of Evidence

There are no studies that examine the validity of *DSM-5* diagnostic criteria for enuresis in individuals with ID. As described above, there are a number of studies examining prevalence, modifying factors, and treatment strategies for individuals with ID. The diagnosis of enuresis is one of the few *DSM-5* diagnoses that requires a particular developmental level as part of the criteria necessary for making the diagnosis. As such, modifications of criteria for persons with ID would default to the individual's developmental level.

Adults with Mild to Moderate ID

All *DSM-5* diagnostic criteria are applicable to adults with mild to moderate ID; however, the individual must have a chronological or developmental age greater than 5. No modifications or adjustments are recommended for these individuals.

Adults with Severe or Profound ID

All *DSM-5* diagnostic criteria are applicable to adults with severe ID; however, the individual must have a chronological or developmental age greater than 5. No modifications or adjustments are recommended for these individuals. As mentioned above, individuals with profound ID cannot be diagnosed with enuresis based on strict *DSM-5* criteria as they will not have reached a developmental age of 5 years.

Children and Adolescents with ID

All *DSM-5* diagnostic criteria are applicable to children or adolescents with ID. No modifications or adjustments are needed for these individuals; however, the individual must have a chronological or developmental age greater than 5.

Summary of Limitations in Applying DSM-5 *Criteria to People with ID*

Individuals with a developmental age of less than 5 cannot be diagnosed with enuresis. Therefore, the developmental age should be ascertained or estimated prior to making this diagnosis.

Etiology and Pathogenesis

Biological Factors

A number of mechanisms, which are not exclusive of each other, have been proposed to explain nocturnal and diurnal enuresis. Nocturnal enuresis may be caused by excessive nocturnal urine production due to abnormally low levels of vasopressin, leading to decreased ability to concentrate urine during sleep (Butler & Holland, 2000; Rittig, Knudsen, Norgaard, Pedersen, & Djurhuus, 1989). Some have proposed that individuals with nocturnal enuresis are "deep sleepers" and therefore do not awaken in response to bladder sensations (Butler & Holland, 2000; Neveus, 2003). Neurotypical children with enuresis have been noted to be more difficult to arouse than non-enuretic children (Wolfish, Pivik, & Busby, 1997). Enuresis may also be due to delayed development of areas of the central nervous system involved in micturition control, particularly the prefrontal cortex, which is a key area for inhibition function (Lei et al., 2012; Von Gontard, Schmelzer, Seifen, & Pukrop, 2001). It may also be due to overactivity of the bladder detrusor muscle (Yeung, Chiu, & Sit, 1999).

In addition to these possible etiologies of enuresis, many medications, including some of those used in the treatment of individuals with *DSM-5* diagnoses (i.e., risperidone, olanzapine, sodium valproate), can have enuresis as an adverse effect (Cheng, Lin, & Lu, 2013; Dada, Oluwole, Adegun, & Tareo, 2012; Herguner & Mukaddes, 2007).

Genetic Factors

Enuresis has been shown to have a strong heritable component, and a family history of enuresis may be predictive of the age when a neurotypical individual obtains nocturnal bladder control (Fergusson, Horwood, & Shannon, 1986). Children with a mother or father who had nocturnal enuresis are 3.83 or 1.85 times, respectively, more likely to have nocturnal enuresis. Children with a mother or father who had daytime urinary incontinence are 3.28 or 10.1 times, respectively, to have daytime urinary incontinence (von Gontard, Heron, & Johnson, 2011). As described previously, genetic syndromes associated with high rates of ID have high rates of enuresis.

Psychosocial Factors

Neurotypical children with enuresis and/or voiding dysfunction have been found to be at an increased risk of psychosocial difficulties as compared to children without these issues (Wolfe-Christensen, Veentra, Kovacevic, Elder, & Lakshmanan, 2012). In addition, children with enuresis have been noted to have daytime sleepiness, bedtime resistance, and sleep anxiety (Abou-Khadra, Amin, Ahmen, 2013).

Developmental Factors

Neurotypical children typically master controlled urination and defecation between the ages of 2 and 4. However, some typically developing children will not master one or the other of these until they are much older and, conversely, some patients with ID will master them earlier than their developmentally equivalent age would predict. It is also interesting to consider how some persons with profound ID can obtain bowel and bladder continence, when based on their developmental level it would not be expected.

Enuresis

DSM-5 Diagnostic Criteria	Applying Criteria for Mild to Moderate ID	Applying Criteria for Severe to Profound ID
A. Repeated voiding of urine into bed or clothes, whether involuntary or intentional.	A. No adaptation	A. No adaptation for severe. Diagnosis likely excluded for profound.
B. The behavior is clinically significant as manifested by either frequency of at least twice a week for at least 3 consecutive months or the presence of clinically significant distress or impairment in social, academic (occupational), or other important areas of functioning.	B. No adaptation	B. No adaptation for severe. Diagnosis likely excluded for profound.
C. Chronological age is at least 5 years (or equivalent developmental level).	C. Developmental age of at least 5 years old.	C. Developmental age of at least 5 years old.
D. The behavior is not attributable to the physiological effects of a substance (eg. diuretic, an antipsychotic medication) or another medical condition (eg. diabetes, spina bifida, a seizure disorder).	D. No adaptation	D. No adaptation for severe. Diagnosis likely excluded for profound.

Encopresis

Review of Diagnostic Criteria

In the *DSM-5* (American Psychiatric Association 2013), encopresis is defined as repeated voluntary or involuntary passage of feces at least once a month for three months into inappropriate places that causes significant distress or impairment in functioning. It is divided into two subtypes: Encopresis with constipation and overflow incontinence, and encopresis without constipation and overflow incontinence. Primary encopresis occurs when an individual has not had a period of stool continence. Secondary encopresis occurs when an individual has had a period of stool continence, after which he or she becomes encopretic.

Encopresis is included in the elimination disorders section of the *DSM-5* and includes encopresis with constipation and overflow incontinence and encopresis without constipation and overflow incontinence.

Summary of DSM-5 *Criteria*

A. Repeated passage of feces into inappropriate places (e.g., clothing, floor), whether involuntary or intentional.

B. At least one event occurs each month for at least three months.

C. Chronological age is at least 4 years old or equivalent developmental level.

D. The behavior is not attributable to the physiological effects of a substance (e.g., laxatives) or another medical condition, except through a mechanism involving constipation.

The *DSM-5* also identifies two subtypes:

(1) With constipation and overflow incontinence in which there is evidence of constipation on physical examination or by history. It is noted in the *DSM-5* that feces in this subtype are often poorly formed, and leakage may be infrequent to continuous, usually during the day and rarely during sleep. During toileting only a part of the feces is passed, and this type of incontinence generally resolves after constipation is treated.

(2) Without constipation and overflow incontinence in which there is no evidence of constipation on physical examination or by history. It is noted in the *DSM-5* that feces are generally of normal form and consistency and that soiling is not continuous, but is intermittent.

Issues Related to Diagnosis in Persons with ID

Development and Course

By definition, encopresis occurs in individuals who have a chronological age of at least 4 years. Individuals younger than 4 years of age cannot be diagnosed with encopresis. In individuals with ID, the criterion is based on developmental age, such that a 20-year-old individual with ID must have a developmental age of at least 4 years of age to be diagnosed with encopresis.

Prevalence

The prevalence of encopresis varies between neurotypical individuals and persons with ID, with prevalence rates of 1% to 9.8% reported in neurotypical individuals. A cohort study reported rates of fecal incontinence in first-graders of 9.8% and in fourth-graders of 5.6% (Soderstrom, Hoelcke, Alenius, Soderling, & Hjern, 2004). Prevalence of encopresis was noted to be 4.1% and 1.6% in 5-6-year-olds and 11-12-year-olds, respectively (van der Wal, Benninga, & Hirasing, 2005). Males are more likely to have encopresis than females (Heron, Joinson, Croudace, & von Gontard, 2008; Joinson et al., 2006).

Individuals with ID have higher reported rates of encopresis than those without ID. However, it should be noted that many studies fail to report a well-defined developmental level, making interpretation of the data difficult. One study of 7-year-old and 20-year-old individuals with ID noted that 30.5% and 19%, respectively, had fecal incontinence. Individuals with more severe ID were more likely to have encopresis than those with milder ID (von Wendt et al., 1990). In another study, 20.5% of children who soiled frequently (more than once a week) were developmentally delayed (WISC-III IQ <70 or having been issued a statement of special educational needs) (Joinson et al., 2006).

The ability of an individual to communicate his/her need for access to facilities, need for assistance, and privacy in toileting functions may influence the apparent frequency of fecal incontinence.

Differential Diagnosis

Up to 90% of chronic encopresis is considered functional, meaning that there is no identifiable underlying organic cause (Har & Croffie, 2010). However, the differential diagnosis for encopresis is extensive and includes (but is not limited to) constipation, abnormal anorectal innervation, spinal cord lesion or damage, having a history of imperforate anus, ectopic anus or anal stenosis, ultra-short segment Hirschsprung disease, neuronal intestinal dysplasia, visceral myopathy or neuropathy, cystic fibrosis, endocrine tumors, celiac disease, laxative abuse, and medications (Har & Croffie, 2010).

Functional Consequences

As is true with other *DSM-5* disorders, the ability to express distress may be difficult for persons with ID, so levels of impairment and/or the presence of "clinically significant distress" may have to be determined or estimated by the caregiver.

Functional consequences of encopresis may be related to psychological or medical outcomes. Neurotypical children with encopresis, as compared to children without encopresis, may be more likely to have attention and social problems, more disruptive behavior, poorer school performance, and more anxiety and depression symptoms (Cox, Morris, Borowitz, & Sutphen, 2002; Johnston & Wright, 1993, Young, Brennen, Baker, & Baker, 1995). A 10-year follow-up study of children with functional (not caused by an organic defect) encopresis reported that 46% remained constipated, 25% continued to have constipation, and 56% had recurrent abdominal pain (Avez-Couturier et al., 2009).

Comorbidity

There are few studies examining conditions comorbid with encopresis, and none were found for individuals with ID. Up to 40% of neurotypical individuals with encopresis have comorbid enuresis (Har & Croffie, 2010). Soderstrom et al. (2004) reported a strong association between daytime urinary incontinence and fecal incontinence (adjusted odds ratio [OR] 7.2), but not between nocturnal enuresis and fecal incontinence (OR 1.2). It has also been noted that children with ADHD are more likely to have functional encopresis due to distractibility and inattention to toileting (Har & Croffie, 2010). Johnston and Wright (1993) reported that 23.4% of neurotypical individuals with encopresis they studied also had ADHD.

Application of Diagnostic Criteria to People with ID

General Considerations

The *DSM-5* criteria for encopresis include that the individual's chronological or developmental age must be at least 4 years. Therefore, an individual with ID whose developmental age is less than 4 years should not be diagnosed with encopresis. In theory, then, a person with profound ID should not be diagnosed with encopresis, based on strict *DSM-5* criteria, because he or she has not reached a developmental age of 4 years.

Methodology

The literature review included a search within the PubMed database for all studies published in the 20 years leading up to and including May 2014. A hand search of the reference sections of the retrieved papers was also conducted. In addition, the *DSM-5* and the prior edition of the *NADD DM-ID* were used as references.

Review of Research Applying to People with ID

The previous edition of the *NADD DM-ID* provided a review of articles published prior to January, 2004. The majority of these articles had strength of evidence III. The authors' conclusions based on this review were that persons with mild ID were capable of obtaining bowel continence by a developmental age of 4 years. They also noted that toilet training of individuals with profound ID was possible (Tasse et al., 2007).

There are limited studies of individuals with ID and encopresis, one of which is reviewed below.

A study of greater than 6,000 children in which parents completed a questionnaire indicated that wetting and soiling that co-occurred were associated with lower Wechsler Intelligence Scale for Children-Third Edition IQ scores than soiling, daytime wetting, or bed-wetting alone (Joinson et al., 2007).

Evaluating the Level of Evidence

There are no studies examining the validity of *DSM-5* diagnostic criteria for encopresis in individuals with ID. As described above, there are a number of studies examining prevalence, modifying factors, and treatment strategies for individuals with ID. The diagnosis of encopresis is one of the few *DSM-5* diagnoses that requires a particular developmental level as part of the criteria necessary for making the diagnosis. As such, modifications of criteria for persons with ID would default to the individual's developmental level.

Adults with Mild to Moderate ID

All *DSM-5* diagnostic criteria are applicable to adults with mild to moderate ID; however, the individual must have a chronological or developmental age of at least 4. No modifications or adjustments are needed for these individuals.

Adults with Severe or Profound ID

All *DSM-5* diagnostic criteria are applicable to adults with severe ID; however, the individual must have a chronological or developmental age of at least 4. No modifications or adjustments are needed for these individuals. Persons with profound ID cannot be diagnosed with encopresis based on strict *DSM-5* criteria as they will not have reached a developmental age of 4 years.

Children and Adolescents with ID

All *DSM-5* diagnostic criteria are applicable to children or adolescents with ID. No modifications or adjustments are needed for these individuals; however, the person must have a chronological or developmental age of at least 4.

Summary of Limitations in Applying DSM-5 *Criteria to People with ID*

Individuals with a developmental age of less than 4 cannot be diagnosed with encopresis. Therefore, the developmental age should be ascertained or estimated prior to making this diagnosis.

Etiology and Pathogenesis

Biological Factors

There is little published regarding mechanisms or biological factors that may explain encopresis. However, some studies suggest that a greater number of individuals with encopresis have issues related to external anal sphincter relaxation during stooling as compared to a control group (Catto-Smith, Nolan, & Coffey, 1998; Sentovich et al., 1998,).

Genetic Factors

No studies were found examining heritability or genetic factors associated with encopresis in individuals with ID. However, encopresis may occur as a result of disorders such as Hirschsprung's disease, cystic fibrosis or hypothyroidism.

Psychosocial Factors

A variety of psychosocial factors may contribute to the development or maintenance of encopresis. These can include: A history of painful passages of stool, leading to fear of defecation and withholding behaviors; difficulty with toilet training; fears (i.e., falling in the toilet or being flushed away); and factors related to the environment such as teasing, sanitary conditions, or restrictions as to when and for how long an individual can use the bathroom. One study noted that neurotypical children who had encopresis were significantly more likely to have parent-reported emotional and behavioral problems, and significantly more likely to have child-reported bullying (both as the aggressor and the victim), self-worth problems, and antisocial activities (Joinson et al., 2006). There is no data related to psychosocial factors in individuals with ID.

Developmental Factors

Neurotypical children typically master controlled urination and defecation between the ages of 2 and 4. However, some typically developing children will not master one or the other of these until they are much older and, conversely, some patients with ID will master them earlier than their developmentally equivalent age would predict. It is also interesting to consider how some persons with profound ID can obtain bowel and bladder continence, when based on their developmental level it would not be expected.

Encopresis

DSM-5 Diagnostic Criteria	Applying Criteria for Mild to Moderate ID	Applying Criteria for Severe to Profound ID
A. Repeated passage of feces into inappropriate places (e.g., clothing, floor), whether involuntary or intentional.	A. No adaptation	A. No adaptation for severe. Diagnosis likely excluded for profound.
B. At least one event occurs each month for at least three months.	B. No adaptation	B. No adaptation for severe. Diagnosis likely excluded for profound.
C. Chronological age is at least 4 years old (or equivalent developmental level).	C. Developmental age of at least 4 four years.	C. Developmental age of at least 4 four years.
D. The behavior is not attributable to the physiological effects of a substance (e.g., laxatives) or another medical condition, except through a mechanism involving constipation.	D. No adaptation	D. No adaptation for severe. Diagnosis likely excluded for profound.

Other Specified Elimination Disorder
Unspecified Elimination Disorder

DSM-5 also provides categories for other specified elimination disorder and for unspecified elimination disorder.

References

Abou-Khadra, M. K., Amin, O. R., & Ahmen, D. (2013). Association between sleep and behavioral problems among children with enuresis. *Journal of Paediatrics and Child Health, 49*, E160-E166.

American Psychiatric Association (2013). *Diagnostic and statistical manual of mental disorders (5th ed,)*. Washington, DC: Author.

Avez-Couturier, J., Michaud, L., Cuiseet, J. M., Lamblin, M. D., Dolhem, P., Turck, D.,… Gottrand, F. (2009). Encopresis revealing myotonic dystrophy in two children. *Archives de Péediatrie*; *16*, 430-4.

Bascom, A., Penney, T., Metcalfe, M., Knox, A., Witmans, M., Uweira, T., & Metcalfe, P. D. (2011). High risk of sleep disordered breathing in the enuresis population. *The Journal of Urology, 186*, 1710-3.

Bottomley, G. (2011). Treating nocturnal enuresis in children in primary care. *The Practitioner, 255*, 23-26.

Brooks, L. J., & Topol, H. (2003). Enuresis in children with sleep apnea. *Journal of Pediatrics, 142*(5), 515-518.

Butler, R. J., & Holland, P. (2000). The three systems: A conceptual way of understanding nocturnal enuresis. *Scandinavian Journal of Urology and Nephrology, 34*, 270-277.

Caldwell, P. H. Y., Deshpande, A. V., & Von Gontard, A. (2013). Management of nocturnal enuresis. *The BMJ, 347*, f6259.

Catto-Smith, A. G., Nolan, T. M., Coffey, C. M. (1998). Clinical significance of anismus in encopresis. *Journal of Gastroenterology and Hepatology 1998, 13*(9), 955-960.

Cheng, W., Lin, X., & Lu, D. (2013). Sodium valproate-induced enuresis in a pediatric bipolar patient. *Neuropsychiatric Disease and Treatment, 9*, 1671-1672.

Chiozza, M. L., Bernardinelli, L., Caione, P., Del Gado, R., Ferrara, P., Giogi, P.L., ... Vertucci, P. (1998). An Italian epidemiological multicenter study of nocturnal enuresis. *British Journal of Urology, 81*, 86-89.

Cohen-Zrubavel, V., Kushnir, B., Kushnir, J., & Sadeh, A. (2011). Sleep and sleepiness in children with nocturnal enuresis. *Sleep, 34*, 191-194.

Cox, D. J., Morris, J. B., Borowitz, S. M., & Sutphen, J. L. (2002). Psychological differences between children with and without chronic encopresis. *Journal of Pediatric Psychology, 27*(7), 585-591.

Dada, M. U., Oluwole, L. O., Adegun, P. T., & Tareo, P. O. (2012). Olanzapine as a cause of urinary incontinence: A case report. *Iranian Journal of Psychiatry, 7*(3), 146-148.

Equit, M., Piro-Hussong, A., Niemczyk, J., Curfs, L., von Gontard, A. (2013). Elimination disorders in persons with Prader-Willi and fragile-X syndromes. *Neurourology and Urodynamics, 32*, 986-992.

Fergusson, D. M., Horwood, L. J., & Shannon, F. T. (1986). Factors related to the age of attainment of nocturnal bladder control: An 8-year longitudinal study. *Pediatrics, 78*: 884-890.

Har, A., & Croffie, J. (2010). Encopresis. *Pediatrics in Review, 31*(9), 368-374.

Herguner, S., & Mukaddes, N. M. (2007). Risperidone-induced enuresis in two children with autistic disorder. *Journal of Child and Adolescent Psychopharamacology, 17*(4), 527-530.

Heron, J., Joinson, C., Croudace, T., & von Gontard, A. (2008). Trajectories of daytime wetting and soiling in a United Kingdom 4 to 9-year-old population birth cohort study. *Journal of Urology, 179*, 1970-1975.

Johnston, B. D., & Wright, J. A. (1993). Attentional dysfunction in children with encopresis. *Journal of Developmental and Behavioral Pediatrics, 14*, 381-385.

Joinson, C., Heron, J., Butler, U., von Gontard, A., & the Avon Longitudinal Study of Parents and Children Study Team. (2006). Psychological differences between children with and without soiling problems. *Pediatrics, 117*, 1575-1584.

Joinson, C., Heron, J., Butler, R., Von Gontard, A., Butler, U., Emond, A., & Golding, J. (2007). A United Kingdom population-based study of intellectual capacities in children with and without soiling, daytime wetting, and bed-wetting. *Pediatrics, 120*, e308-316.

Kovacevic, L., Jurewicz, M., Dabaja, A., Thomas, R., Diaz, M., Madgy, D., & Lakshmanan, Y. (2013). Enuretic children with obstructive sleep apnea syndrome: Should they see otolaryngology first? *Journal of Pediatric Urology, 9*, 145-50.

Lei, D., Ma, J., Shen, X., Du, X., Shen, G., Liu, W., Xu, Y., & Gengying, L. (2012). Changes in the brain microstructure of children with primary monosymptomatic nocturnal enuresis: A diffusion tensor imaging study. *PLOS ONE, 7*(2), e31023.

Ma, J., Li, S., Jian, F., Jin, X., Shen, X., & Li, F. (2014). Co-sleeping and childhood enuresis in China. *Journal of Developmental & Behavioral Pediatrics, 35*, 44-49.

Mellon, M. W., Natchev, B. E., Slavic, K. K., Coligan, R. C., Weaver, A. L., Voigt, R. G., & Barbaresi, W. J. (2013). Incidence of enuresis and encopresis among children with attention- deficit/hyperactivity disorder in a population-based birth cohort. *Academic Pediatrics; 13*: 322-327.

Neveus, T. (2003). The role of sleep and arousal in nocturnal enuresis. *Acta Paediatrica, 92*, 1118-1123.

Redsell, S. A., & Coller, J. (2001). Bedwetting, behavior and self-esteem: A review of the literature. *Child Care, Health and Development, 27*(2), 149-162.

Rittig, S., Knudsen, U. B., Norgaard, J. P., Pedersen, E. B., & Djurhuus, J. C. (1989). Abnormal diurnal rhythm of plasma vasopressin and urinary output in patients with enuresis. *American Journal of Physiology: Renal, Fluid and Electrolyte Physiology, 25*, F664-F671.

Sadeh, A. (2007). Consequences of sleep loss or sleep disruption in children. *Sleep Medicine Clinics, 2*, 513-520.

Sentovich, S. M., Kaufman, S. S., Cali, R. L., Falk, P. M., Blatchford, G. J., Antonson, D. L., ... Christensen, M. A. (1998). Pudendal nerve function in normal and encopretic children. *Journal of Pediatric Gastroenterology and Nutrition, 26*(1), 70-72.

Shreeram, S., He, J., Kalaydjian, A., Brothers, S., & Merikangas, K. R. (2009). Prevalence of enuresis and its association with attention-deficit/hyperactivity disorder among U.S. children: Results from a nationally representative sample. *Journal of the American Academy of Child and Adolescent Psychiatry, 48*(1), 35-41.

Soderstrom, U., Hoelcke, M., Alenius, L., Soderling, A.-C., Hjern, A. (2004). Urinary and faecal incontinence: A population-based study. *Acta Paediatrica, 93*, 386-389.

Tasse, M. J., Barnhill, L. J., Havercamp, S. M., & Reeve, A. (2007) Elimination disorders. In R. Fletcher, E. Loschen, C. Stavrakaki, & M. First (Eds.), *Diagnostic manual — Intellectual disability. A textbook of diagnosis of mental disorders in persons with intellectual disability* (pp. 173-182). Kingston, NY: NADD Press.

Thottman, P. J., Kovacevic, L., Madgy, D., & Abdulhamid, I. (2013). Sleep architecture parameters that predict postoperative resolution of nocturnal enuresis in children with obstructive sleep apnea. *Annals of Otology, Rhinology and Laryngology, 122*(11), 690-694.

Van der Wal, M. F., Benninga, M. A., & Hirasing, R. A. (2005). The prevalence of encopresis in a multicultural population. *Journal of Pediatric Gastroenterology and Nutrition, 40*: 345-348.

Van Laecke, E. (2008). Elimination disorders in people with intellectual disability. *Journal of Intellectual Disability Research, 52*:810.

Von Gontard, A., Schmelzer, D., Seifen, S., & Pukrop, R. (2001). Central nervous system involvement in nocturnal enuresis: Evidence of general neuromotor delay and specific brainstem dysfunction. *The Journal of Urology, 166*, 2448-2451.

Von Gontard, A., Didden, R., Sinnema, M., & Curfs, M. (2010). Urinary incontinence in persons with Prader-Willi syndrome. *BJU International, 106*, 1758-1762.

Von Gontard, A., Heron, J., & Johnson, C. (2011). Family history of nocturnal enuresis and urinary incontinence: Results from a large epidemiological study. *The Journal of Urology, 185*, 2303-2307.

Von Wendt, L., Simila, S., Niskann, P., & Jarvelin, M. R. (1990). Development of bowel and bladder control in the mentally retarded. *Developmental Medicine and Child Neurology, 32*, 515-518.

Wang, R. C., Elkins, T. P., & Keech, D. (1998). Accuracy of clinical evaluation in pediatric obstructive sleep apnea. *Otolaryngology — Head and Neck Surgery, 118*, 69-73.

Wille, S., & Anveden, I. (1995). Social and behavioural perspectives in enuretics, former enuretics and non-enuretic controls. *Acta Paediatrica, 84*, 37-40.

Wolfe-Christensen, C., Veenstra, A., Kovacevic, L., Elder, J., & Lakshmanan, Y. (2012). Psychosocial difficulties in children referred to pediatric urology: A closer look. *Urology, 80*, 907-913.

Wolfish, N. M., Pivik, R. T., & Busby, K. A. (1997). Elevated sleep arousal thresholds in enuretic boys: Clinical implication. *Acta Paediatrica, 86*, 381-384.

Yeung, C. K., Chiu, H. N., & Sit, F. K. Y. (1999). Bladder dysfunction in children with refractory monosymptomatic primary nocturnal enuresis. *The Journal of Urology, 162*: 1049-1055.

Yeung, C. K., Sreddhar, B., Sihoe, J. D. Y., Sit, F. K. Y, & Lau, J. (2006). Differences in characteristics of nocturnal enuresis between children and adolescents: A critical appraisal from a large epidemiological study. *BJU International, 97*, 1069-1073.

Young, M. H., Brennen, L. C., Baker, R. D., & Baker, S. S. (1995). Functional encopresis: Symptom reduction and behavioral improvement. *Developmental and Behavioral Pediatrics*, 16(4), 226-232.

CHAPTER 20

Sleep Wake Disorders

Jarrett Barnhill
Takahiro Soda
Ann Poindexter
Jill A. Hollway

This chapter explores sleep disorders in people with intellectual disabilities (ID). The biggest challenge facing clinicians in this arena involves integrating sleep physiology and sleep disorders with the diverse neurobiology of people with ID. In order to accommodate this level of heterogeneity this chapter takes a developmental psychosomatic approach to sleep disorders. This model incorporates the convergence of genetic, medical/neurological disorders, and psychosocial forces. The developmental piece addresses the problem of changes in sleep that accompany each new phase of the life cycle (Barnhill, 2006; Moline, Broch, & Zak, 2004). Unfortunately, our knowledge of these developmental trajectories in people with ID is still incomplete.

People with ID have an overabundance of risk factors for developing sleep disorders. A short list includes: vulnerability to psychosocial stressors-based deficits in cognitive and adaptive skills; higher rates of sensory impairments, co-morbid disturbances in brain development, epilepsy, and inadequate sleep hygiene; and higher prevalence rates for traumatization (psychological, physical, and sexual abuse), polypharmacy, and medical and psychiatric disorders (Ghanizadeh & Faghih, 2011; Judd & Sateia, 2015). Our biggest obstacle to diagnosis in many cases remains our difficulty recognizing the clinical manifestations of various sleep disorders across the broad spectrum of neurodevelopmental disorders.

In many clinical settings, sleep disturbances are most frequently misattributed to a few disorders—insomnia or sleep apneas. The first goal of this chapter is to expand our awareness of the diversity of sleep disorders by upgrading clinical knowledge. A secondary goal is to raise the clinical index of suspicion and enhance clinical decision-making. The third goal is to provide a basic awareness of which patients warrant referral to specialists and the information to make such a referral.

General Description of Sleep Disorders

Sleep is a reversible change in level of conscious awareness, cognition, and volitional activities. Sleep involves thalamic, brain stem, limbic, paralimbic, and cortical networks that help regulate sleep-wake homeostasis, as well as circadian and sleep-cycle rhythms (McLaughlin Crabtree & Williams, 2009). Homeostatic mechanisms evoke the urge to sleep and sequentially switches off conscious awareness, sustaining the state of sleep and then reversing the process. Neuro-biologically, the initiation and maintenance of sleep requires a choreographed release of adenosine, delta sleep peptide, multiple neuropeptides, immune regulation, and the reduction of the neurotransmitter networks responsible for sustaining prolonged wakefulness (Markov & Goldman, 2006; Nofzinger, 2005).

When there is insufficient sleep there is a build-up of "sleep debt" that is generally compensated for by slow wave or rapid eye movement (REM) sleep rebound. These compensatory strategies or attempts to "make-up" lost sleep time are only partially successful. Shortages of slow wave sleep and REM sleep have many consequences for both the integrity of sleep (arousals) and day-time functioning. People with chronic insomnia, sleep arousal disorders/movement disorders/ apneas, delayed sleep phase, circadian sleep rhythm and chronic insufficient sleep disorders accrue a sleep debt that is not easily repaid (Judd & Sateia, 2015). In addition to many health consequences, there are considerable economic and psychological costs associated with chronic sleep deprivation. Decreased concentration, productivity, and proneness to accidents and injuries are frequently the result of the effects of sleep deprivation on cognitive, behavioral, attentional, occupational, executive functional, and motor skills (Carskadon, 2004; Durmer & Dinges, 2005; O'Brien, 2009).

Sleep is also a rhythmic phenomenon. Daily sleep wake cycles (circadian rhythms) are the most noticeable. Humans are readily entrained to day-night cycles. Light-dark entrainment (primary cues or zeitgebers) plays a major role in organizing and regulating sleep-wake cycles. The anterior, suprachiasmic, and periventricular hypothalamic nuclei are actively involved in setting these circadian rhythms. Melatonin signals the suprachiasmic nuclei to changes in day-night fluctuations. For diurnal primates, light is essential to suppressing melatonin. Darkness (dim light onset) releases melatonin and signals sleep onset. Additional circadian changes involve hormone and temperature rhythms. Disturbance in the complex interaction between light, melatonin synthesis and excretion, and regulation of sleep onset are major contributors to circadian rhythm disorders and some forms of insomnia (Aldrich, 1999; Bruni et al., 2015; Rechtschaffen & Siegal, 2000; Shneerson, 2000c).

Sleep is also characterized by recurring cycles of intrinsic neurophysiological rhythms that include variations in EEG frequencies, muscle tone, body temperature, and hormone excretion. These rhythmic changes occur in 90-120 minute cycles that accompany transitions from drowsiness to slow wave and REM sleep. In addition to arousal and homeostatic mechanisms, the dysregulation and instability of circadian and sleep cycle rhythms occur in parasomnias, sleep related movement and breathing disorders, and other disturbances in sleep architecture (Hirshkowitz, 2004; Markov & Goldman, 2006). Disruptions in intrinsic sleep cycles also affect the restorative properties of sleep. These rhythms include:

a. Stage I, which represents the neurophysiological process of disengagement. Accompanying it are rhythmic sleep movements, sleep starts, and manifestations of restless legs syndrome (Erman, 2006). Other factors that influence sleep onset include improper sleep environments, over stimulation prior to bedtime, medication or drug effects (Judd & Sateia, 2015), poor sleep hygiene, and psychiatric disorders such as anxiety disorders that affect sleep onset (Becker, 2006; Mellman, 2006). Most people affected by these problems will complain about difficulty falling or returning to sleep.

b. Stage II, which represents a shift in thalamic activity that results in characteristic EEG changes. During this phase of sleep individuals are still reactive to external events. Disruptions in phase II sleep are seen in individuals with periodic limb movements of sleep, and they may also complain about insomnia. With periodic limb movements bed partners are more likely to experience significant distress than the patient. Restless legs syndrome and periodic limb movements of sleep are often co-existing conditions (Barnhill, 2006; Erman, 2006; Judd & Sateia, 2015).

c. Stage III-IV, or slow wave sleep, are essential to normal cognitive functioning. Disturbances in slow wave sleep can occur secondary to sleep deprivation, alcohol and other drugs (Mahowald, 2004), as well as aging and some degenerative disorders (Bhatt, Podder, & Chokroverty, 2005; Cooke & Ancoli-Israel, 2006; Neikrug & Ancoli-Israel, 2015). Neuromuscular disorders can also disrupt slow wave sleep by decreasing upper airway patency (leading to sleep breathing disorders). Involvement of chest wall movement can result in both hypoventilation and apnea/hypoxemia (Culebras, 2005). During childhood the most common problems with slow wave sleep involve breakdowns in the integrity and stability of stage IV sleep. Parasomnias (night terrors and somnambulism occur out of slow wave sleep (Zucconi & Bruni, 2001). Seizures are also more likely to occur out of this sleep phase (Bazil, 2002; Zucconi & Bruni, 2001). Aging, mood disorders, and dementias have the greatest effects on stage IV sleep (Cooke & Ancoli-Israel, 2006). Disruptions in slow wave sleep leave the individual tired, "sleepy," and result in significant cognitive and emotional changes. Fibromyalgia and other pain disorders may also disrupt the integrity of slow wave sleep (via alpha intrusions, which cause the patient to wake or to be aroused into lighter level of sleep) (Breau & Camfield, 2011; Roehrs & Roth, 2005; Vatthauer et al., 2015). The relationship between pain and sleep disorders is most likely multi-directional and best fits the psychosomatic model.

d. REM or paradoxical sleep represents an arousal transition from slow wave sleep. It is associated with multiple physiological changes that are expressed during dreaming and nightmares (Aldrich, 1999). During REM sleep the respiratory pump (diaphragm) is not affected by generalized muscle paralysis. Sleep related breathing disorders associated with REM sleep arise from damage to the phrenic nerve and/or weakness or paralysis of the diaphragm. This mechanism differs from the mechanism of nonREM breathing disorders or obstructive sleep apnea, that affects upper airway patency (Culebras, 2005). Narcolepsy is the product of a malfunctioning network that normally suppresses sleep and REM activity during wakefulness. Narcolepsy is associated with sleep attacks, and variable levels of cataplexy (muscle weakness while awake), sleep paralysis, and hallucinations (Aldrich, 1999; Wise, 2004). REM related behavior disorder represents dreaming without paralysis. In some circumstances violent behavior can occur. REM related behavior disorder is associated with many neurodegenerative disorders that affect the brainstem and midbrain (Bhatt et al., 2005). Many medications suppress REM sleep and may result in significant REM rebound when they are discontinued (Neikrug & Ancoli-Israel, 2015; Rechtschaffen & Siegal, 2000).

Summary of DSM-5 Criteria

The DSM-5 has three basic requirements for diagnosis of sleep-wake disorders: quantitative and qualitative changes in sleep, severity, and impact on many facets of daily function. The designation of medical, psychiatric, and substance use specifiers are helpful for differentiating primary from secondary sleep disorders—those associated with co-occurring medical/neurological, psychiatric and behavioral disorders as well as the effect of pharmaceuticals on particular aspects of sleep physiology and daytime alertness. These criteria can also be applied as diagnostic algorithms and as a useful starting point in the search for specific phenomenological and neurophysiological endophenotypes.

The diagnoses of most sleep disorders are based on history, medical/neurological examination, and clinical presentation. Definitive diagnosis often requires combinations of polysomnography (PSG), Multiple Sleep Latency Test (MSLT), actigraphy, measurements of hypoxia (low oxygen levels), hypercapnia (elevated carbon dioxide), biochemical markers (CSF hypocretin, neuroendocrine measurements), specific neuroimaging, and genetic testing (Avidan, 2005; Shneerson, 2000a).

Ten major variants of sleep disorders are discussed in the DSM-5. See table 1 below for a more comprehensive outline of specifiers, differential diagnosis, and common neurophysiological and genetic subtypes:

1. **Insomnia disorder** is the most frequently encountered and diverse of the sleep disorders. The diagnostic criteria include: prolonged sleep latency (problems falling sleep), difficulty maintaining major sleep, and sleep-related difficulties with daytime attention, con-

centration, memory, cognition, and executive function. The differential diagnosis includes not only other primary sleep disorders but also an extensive list of psychiatric, medical, neurological, and pharmacological co-occurring conditions.

2. **Hypersomnolence disorder** is characterized by excessive sleepiness (hypersomnolence) despite a baseline sleep period lasting at least seven hours. Total sleep time and naps are described as nonrestorative and are frequently associated with disturbances in motor or cognitive activities upon awakening. To meet criteria, hypersomnia must occur at least three times per week, for a minimum of three months. The main sleep cycle must be more than 10 continuous hours. Daytime sleepiness interferes with social, academic, or occupational demands.

3. **Narcolepsy** includes repeated irresistible attacks of refreshing sleep, cataplexy (spells of sudden, bilateral, reversible loss of muscle tone lasting for seconds to minutes, usually precipitated by intense emotion), or recurrent intrusions of elements of rapid eye movement sleep into the transition between sleep and wakefulness, as manifested by paralysis of voluntary muscles or dreamlike hallucinations. Episodes usually result in unintended sleep in inappropriate situations. Low-stimulation, low-activity situations make the degree of sleepiness more severe. Episodes usually last 10-20 minutes but may be longer if uninterrupted.

4. **Breathing-related sleep disorder** includes three relatively distinct disorders: obstructive sleep apnea hypopnea, central sleep apnea, and sleep-related hypoventilation. They are associated with daytime sleepiness and fatigue. Obstructive sleep apnea hypopnea includes at least five obstructive apneas per hour of sleep and may be nocturnal breathing disturbances such as snoring, snorting/gasping, or breathing pauses during sleep. Central sleep apnea may include Cheyne-Stokes breathing, where the depth of breathing oscillates relative of oxygen and carbon dioxide levels. This contrasts with sleep-related hypoventilation in which respiratory drive is uncoupled from declining oxygen and rising carbon dioxide levels. Combined forms are common among persons with chronic sleep related breathing disorder (Culebras, 2005; Judd & Sateia, 2015).

5. **Circadian rhythm sleep disorder** (formerly sleep-wake schedule disorder) is a persistent or recurring pattern of disrupted sleep that arises due to disruption in the circadian timing system and a disconnection between the circadian sleep-wake system and external demands regarding the timing and duration of sleep. Zeitgeber's or sleep cues are entrained during infancy. Light is the most powerful zeitgeber for setting the time for sleep onset. This effect may not apply to people with some forms of blindness. Seasonal variations in circadian rhythms are also related to rapid variation in photoperiod (Fahey & Zee, 2006; Ivanenko & Gururaj, 2009; Markov & Goldman, 2006).

6. **Non-rapid eye movement (nonREM) sleep arousal disorders** include recurrent episodes of intrusive arousals from stage III-IV sleep with incomplete awakening from sleep. Most occur during the first third of the major sleep episode and include sleep walking and sleep terrors, which aren't better explained by drug use, medication, or coexisting mental and medical disorders (American Psychiatric Association, 2013).

7. **Nightmare disorder** involves repeated, severe anxiety dreams during REM sleep. Most occur later in the sleep wake cycle as the duration and intensity of REM cycles increase. There are significant relationships between acute trauma, Post-traumatic stress disorders, and anxiety-related dreams (Charuvastra & Cloitre, 2009; Sadech, 1996).

8. **Rapid-Eye Movement (REM) Sleep Behavior Disorder** involves recurring behaviors during REM sleep. There is a malfunction in the normal muscle atony associated with REM sleep. The behaviors can include vocalizations and/or complex motor behaviors. Aggression can occur during these episodes.

Like nightmares, they tend to occur well into the sleep cycle and are more frequent during the later portions of the sleep period. REM sleep behavior disorders are associated with vascular disorders and may be prodromal to some synucleopathies (neurodegenerative movement disorders) (Bhatt et al., 2005).

9. **Restless-legs syndrome** includes an urge for leg movements in the face of uncomfortable and unpleasant sensations in the lower extremity. Symptoms are more intense in the evening and delay sleep onset. Chronic and some forms hereditary restless legs syndrome may also spill over into daytime and resemble akathisia. restless legs syndrome co-occurs with periodic limb movements of sleep in more than 70% of affected individuals (Judd & Sateia, 2015; Rama & Kushida, 2004).

10. **Substance/medication-Induced sleep disorder** is directly associated with medications that affect homeostatic and circadian sleep rhythms. They can be due to increased arousal that directly interfere with sleep onset, disrupts nonREM or REM sleep or during withdrawal states (Qureshi & Lee-Chiong, 2004).

As noted, sleep disorders are also subclassified based on specifiers, exclusion of secondary causes, and the level of functional impairment criteria (see applications table). Some have specific levels of impairment (sleep-related breathing disorders and AHI index). Other sleep disorders have more generic markers like sleep initiation. All require substantial interference with daily activities. Perhaps the most vexing feature of sleep disorder is their co-occurrence with each other. For example, restless legs syndrome co-occurs with periodic limb movements of sleep, and breathing related sleep disorders frequently co-occur (Aldrich, 1999; Bloomfield & Shatkin, 2009; Judd & Sateia, 2015). Children with sleep disorders are particularly prone to the overlap between restless legs syndrome and periodic limb movements of sleep. This observation suggests that developmental changes in sleep regulation are in play. In addition sleep stage transitions (e.g. nonREM to Stage II or REM sleep) underlie parasomnias, narcolepsy and REM parasomnias (Erman, 2006; Markov & Goldman, 2006; Wise, 2004).

The table is designed to compact the DSM-5 criteria. It is by no means all-inclusive or definitive but is useful when applying DSM-5 criteria to people with co-occurring IDD.

Table 1: (American Psychiatric Association, 2013)

Type of sleep disorder	DSM-5 Specifiers	Differential DX	Laboratory findings	Other
Insomnia	With mental disorders, With other medical disorders, With other sleep disorders Severity/subtypes Episodic >1mo< 3 mos. Persistent >3 mos Recurrent 2 episodes within 1 yr.	Normal Sleep- short cycle sleepers, Situational/acute, Delayed sleep phase restless legs syndrome/ periodic limb movements of sleep Sleep related breathing disorders Narcolepsy, Parasomnias Substance/ medical/ medication related, epilepsy	Increase in sleep latency Inc. time awake in bed (dec, sleep efficiency Inc. high frequency EEG (arousal); Inc, cortisol, sympathetic nervous system arousal,	Daytime sleepiness, fatigue without sleepiness. Hyper-activity, poor concen-tration, irritability, cognitive and executive dysfunction
Hypersomnolence	With mental, medical, and other sleep disorders Severity sub-types Acute, subacute, persistent (>3mos)	Normal sleep cycle- late cycle sleeper, breathing related disorder, circadian rhythm disorders, parasomnia, other medication-related, mental and medical disorders	Short sleep latency, increased sleep efficiency, automatic behaviors, PSG- normal sleep phase	

Table 1: (American Psychiatric Association, 2013) (continued)

Type of sleep disorder	DSM-5 Specifiers	Differential DX	Laboratory findings	Other
Narcolepsy	With Hypocretin 1 deficiency, without hypocretin deficiency, 2 specific autosomal dominant genetic disorders, due to medical disorders	Hypersomnias, sleep deprivation, SRBD, major depressive disorder, conversion disorder, seizure disorders movement disorders schizophrenia	MSLT- sleep attacks with short REM latency, cataplexy (loss of muscle tone) in response to emotional events, sleep paralysis, hypnogogic/hypnopompic hallucinations, hypocretin- regulating arousal; appetite stimulation, HLA markers- ? autoimmune disorder	Full tetrad -relatively rare, amphet-amine use/abuse, cocaine withdrawal, psychotic symptoms other than sleep-related hallucination
Breathing related Disorders- obstructive type	Upper airway, mixed type. Severity based on number of apnea-hypoxia events per hour.	Snoring without hypoxia, insomnia, panic attacks, opiate use, Cheyne stokes secondary to brain stem lesions, other sleep disorders	PSG- Apnea noted, measured by AHI <15/hr –mild 15-30 moderate >30 severe >5 associated with hypertension, risk for cardiovascular diseases p02- oxygen desaturation, mixed central and sleep related may also have inc. pC02	Risks from sedative hypnotics, alcohol. Risk for cardio-vascular, morning headaches, type II diabetes and cognitive deficits, treatment refractory mood disorders
Breathing-related central apnea	Hypo-alveolar (pump failure), idiopathic, Cheyne Stokes, comorbid sleep-related and medical etiology	Other causes for hypo-ventillation; other sleep related breathing disorder	Autonomic dysfunction (orthostasis), blunted C02 response, decreased respiratory drive polycythemia; pC02>55 p02 < 85, gene markers related to development of autonomic nervous system, significant cognitive changes	Often co-occurs with chronic sleep related breathing disorders, some medications can reduce central C02 response. Hig C02 and panic attacks
Circadian rhythm disorders	Delayed, advanced, irregular sleep-wake cycle, shift work/jet lag	Normal sleep phase shifts secondary to aging. Environmental factors, severe visual impairment in irregular sleep-wake cycle	Advance- late onset melatonin release, late AM awakening, fatigue, youth problem, sleep-phase advance, aging, mood and anxiety disorders. Total sleep time, efficiency may be stable. Clock (PER2) gene, melanopsin receptors, retino-hypothalamic tract	Mania with apparent sleep phase delay without fatigue, reduction in total sleep time, without com-pen-sation, late weekend awakenings
Parasomnias, REM and Non-REM related	REM related sleep disorder, nonREM related-sleep walking, eating, sexual behavior, sleep terror	REM related- lack of muscle atonia, “acting on dreams	Brain stem lesions (locus coeruleus), R/O nocturnal seizures- usually frontal lobe partial seizure; worsened by alcoholand many antidepressants. Synucleopathies (Parkinsons, Lewy body dementia- REM parasomnia may precede by decades.	
Nightmare disorders	REM related NonREM	BRSD, parasomnias REM-related behavior disorder.	Glutamate and cholinergic interaction, sympathetic over-arousal. NonREM related onset, more common in children; PSG sleep arousal out of III IV stages;	PTSD- increased frequency and severity of nightmares; limited anticipatory arousal/anxiety

Table 1: (American Psychiatric Association, 2013) (continued)

Type of sleep disorder	DSM-5 Specifiers	Differential DX	Laboratory findings	Other
Restless legs/ Periodic limb movement	Parasomnias SRBD Dissociative state, panic disorder, Drug related Night eating disorder	Sleep onset- akathisia like discomfort Renal failure, low iron storage (ferritin), pregnancy, aging, thyroid disorders	Akathisia like, Decreased dopamine synthesis and availability	Distinguish from aging; anti-psychotics, SSRIs and other meds may increase severity.
Substance related	Direct drug effect on sleep cycle, withdrawal, relationship to other psychiatric disorders	Other medical conditions, parasomnias, REM and nonREM related,	Sympathetic over-arousal, suppression of sleep phases reversed during abstinence;	May be more likely among community based individuals

Issues Related to Diagnosis in IDD

The recognition of sleep disorders can be the most challenging part of the diagnostic process. Yet, confirming the suspicion still requires the clinician to translate referral complaints; draw conclusions from the available sleep data; tease out the connections between sleep changes and daytime behaviors; and then complete the assessment and differential diagnosis. Listed below are a few additional challenges that require more detective work:

1. Deficits in self-reporting by many persons with IDD create the need to draw upon reports from multiple sources.
2. Limited clinician understanding of the interaction between sleep physiology, atypical brain development, and the many phenotypes of sleep disorders.
3. Adapting this data across the spectrum of ID- from people with borderline ID to severe-profound IDD.
4. Training deficits—many clinicians are not trained in gathering sleep histories; applying direct observations about sleep related behaviors; re-framing sleep data in terms of circadian or sleep cycle disruptions; and especially applying data from polysomnography, MSLT, and actinography to a differential diagnosis.

Boyle et al. (2010) provided an extensive epidemiological review of sleep related disorders in IDD. Their findings question some long standing assumptions about previous findings about the prevalence rates of insomnias to ID. They argue that some published studies may overestimate true prevalence rates. Exceptions may include the impact of epilepsy and other health related changes associated with the severity of ID and co-occurrence with treatment refractory epilepsy and other health, mental health, and behavior disorders. It seems that many studies had small sample sizes, selection biases towards clinical patients, and methodological shortcomings. In clinical settings, referrals for sleep disorders can be impeded by inadequate staff training, low index of suspicion or high threshold for sleep disorder, or problems teasing out the effects of the many health-related complications associated with severe/profound ID. They concluded with a call for more research.

There is a need for more research devoted to the interactions between developmental variations in sleep physiology associated with the level of ID and co-occurring neurodevelopmental disorders (including autism spectrum disorders). The underlying causes are linked to multi-directional interaction between atypical brain development and enhanced vulnerability to psychosocial and ecological factors (psychosomatic aspects). Yet even after resolving these issues, the clinician still must synthesize this complex data set and match it up with DSM-5 criteria. In most clinical situations the DSM-5 criteria are readily applicable.

Development and Course

Even though sleep is an essential physiological process, most sleep habits are not innate; they are learned. During infancy and early childhood we are entrained to light/dark cycles and environmental cues for sleep onset (zeitgebers). The most powerful zeitgeber is the day-night cycle (Bruni et al., 2015). During infancy, entrainment programs the inherent circadian biological rhythms to match the pattern of nighttime sleep and daytime alertness. This process unfolds over the first six months of infancy and parallels early cortical development. Most parents welcome the entrainment of nocturnal sleep organization or "settling in" (McLaughlin Crabtree & Williams, 2009).

During early infancy, the patterns of sleep are dominated by "active sleep" (a variant of REM sleep). Active sleep is characterized by a short latency to REM-like activity but without atonia or muscle paralysis noted in later REM sleep. These transitional phenomena are closely related to brain stem activity. By 3-6 months, the presence of nonREM sleep becomes the dominant pattern of sleep as sleep spindles, K complexes, and slow wave activity take up much of the sleep cycle. These changes in sleep architecture are associated with cortical maturation and maturing thalamo-cortical circuits (Markov & Goldman, 2006; McLaughlin Crabtree & Williams, 2009).

Slow wave sleep dominates the sleep wake cycles of older infants and toddlers. They spend nearly 50% of their sleep in active sleep associated with nonREM activity. This percentage decreases during the first year of life and approaches adult levels during early childhood. The relative predominance of slow wave sleep may overlap the rise of parasomnias and nightmares during preschool. Decreases in slow wave sleep and the maturation of cortical regulatory functions may explain the age-related decline in parasomnias (Aldrich, 1999; Markov & Goldman, 2006).

Slow wave sleep begins a second decline with aging. With advancing age, there are also changes in REM latency and density; sleep efficiency declines. In addition, sleep becomes more fragmented and less restorative, and daytime napping resurfaces. Several physiological changes underlie these phenomena: melatonin production declines, access and sensitivity to light and other zeitgebers wane, sleep phase advances, and perhaps most significantly, pain and chronic illnesses accentuate each (Cooke & Ancoli-Israel, 2006).

Many psychosocial changes affect sleep onset and efficiency -social isolation, limited exercise, more generalized decline in physical activity, loss of work or activity organizers (social zeitgebers) and chronic insomnia, depression and anxiety increase in frequency (Charuvastra & Cloitre, 2009; Giannotti & Cortesi, 2009; Maaskant, van de Wouw, van Wijck, Evenhuis, & Echteld, 2013; K. J. Reid, Chang, & Zee, 2004). Minor cognitive impairment and frank dementias disrupt sleep wake cycles, architecture and sleep phase. There is also evidence that chronic insomnia and depression negatively affect the course of many forms of dementia (Bhatt et al., 2005; Neikrug & Ancoli-Israel, 2015).

Prevalence

The heterogeneity of both ID and sleep disorders may explain the wide range of prevalence rates for sleep disorders. Other factors include selection biases (clinic versus community patients) and small sample sizes (Boyle et al., 2010). In addition, studies of people with ID tend to focus more on insomnia than other primary sleep disorders. As a result, several basic questions remain unanswered: What is the relationship between the severity of ID, autism spectrum disorder and sleep disorders? Are the data on subtypes of sleep disorders present in specific behavioral phenotypes transposable to people with more complicated genetic, metabolic, neurological, and neuropsychiatric disorders? Do studies that focus on borderline/mild ID also apply to severe/profound ID? Are current studies biased towards chronic insomnia because of difficulties recognizing and misdiagnosing other sleep disorders?

Based on changes throughout the life cycle, sleep disorders should also be considered neurodevelopmental disorders. The prevalence rates of specific sleep disorders may change secondary to brain maturation and development and changing environmental expectations and demands. These changes influence and are influenced by the timing of gene-environmental interactions. For example, during infancy entraining sleep to day night cycles, sleeping through the night and the waning of daytime napping are major milestones (McLaughlin Crabtree & Williams, 2009; Shneerson, 2000c).

Disruptions in the process of entrainment occur in the context of difficult temperament, anxious or disorganized attachment behaviors, parental exhaustion, inexperience, psychosocial stressors and anxieties, conflicts over sleeping arrangements, and disagreements over management based on the dueling opinions of grandparents, other parents and multiple expert opinions related to sleep management and hygiene. Family dynamics and psychopathology play dual roles. They increase the risk for maternal depression and pass on the attributional style and genetic risk for sleep disorders and mental disorders (Giannotti & Cortesi, 2009; Ivanenko & Gururaj, 2009; Krahn, 2005).

The table below addresses published prevalence rates for children and adults that expand beyond insomnia to include other sleep disorders.

TABLE 2:

Sleep disorder	Children and Youth	Adults	Notes
Insomnia disorder	20% of children 3 subtypes: Sleep onset-associative 25-30% Cued onset 25-30% Adult-like 4-11% Sleep phase delay (K. J. Reid et al., 2004)	9-17% chronic plus short term sleep phase advance	Adults-best review meta-analysis by (Boyle et al., 2010) Children—children subtypes gradually supplanted by adult type
Hypersomnolence	4%- less common except in sleep deprivation- usually present as disruptive behaviors (Kotagal, 2009)	Insufficient sleep- 37% of population < 7 hrs sleep/night	Periodic hypersomnia- Kleine-Levin males predominate, 1-2 week long periods, hypersomnia, hyperphagia, irritability (Kotagal, 2009)
Narcolepsy Hypocretin deficiency Nl hypocretin- without cataplexy Autosomal dominant forms-deafness, ataxia and obesity, Type II DM	1/3 onset at age 16 0.02-0.05% (Erman, 2006; Wise, 2004)	Rare- 0.5% HLA DQA1( )01:02 DQB1( )06:02 haplotypes, most common (Ollila et al., 2015; (Shneerson, 2000b)	Idiopathic hypersomnia may be prodromal to narcolepsy; Probably underDx due to partial expression in many (Meltzer & Mindell, 2006)
Breathing related Central Mixed Hypoventilation Hypercapnia plus or minus hypoxia	2% Obstructive type- oropharyngeal abnormalities; obesity Apnea/hypoxia index- snoring plus drop in oxygen levels (p02)	Severity shapes prevalence males>females Mild—9-28%--related to hypertension Moderate--5-15% Severe—1- 7%	COPD, spinal cord injuries, TBI, in children- cystic fibrosis
Circadian sleep wake Non 24 hr sleep-wake cycle Irregular sleep wake	Sleep phase delay—7-16% of young males; gene markers; male predominance;10% of all insomnia; Blindness; severe ID, autism spectrum disorder with irregular sleep wake cycle (Ivanenko & Gururaj, 2009)	7-16% Gene marker for melatonin synthesis and receptor; Blind from birth- hypersensitive melatonin receptors (Fahey & Zee, 2006).	Maturation of homoestatic/ circadian system Severe/profound ID, traumatic brain injury, autism spectrum disorder in Irregular sleep-wake disorder (Johnson, Giannotti, & Cortesi, 2009)

TABLE 2 (continued)

Sleep disorder	Children and Youth	Adults	Notes
nonREM parasomnia Bruxism (7-15% in children) sleep walking Sleep-eating disorder- female predominant)	higher levels of slow wave sleep in children; Sleepwalking—1 5% with one lifetime episode; 1-6% with multiple events Confusional—17% with periodic recurrence Sleep terrors—6% (Bloomfield & Shatkin, 2009)	Higher rates of psychopathology in adults with parasomnias; continuous vs. recurrent Confusional—4.2 % Night terrors—1-2% (Plante & Wilkelman 2006)	Reduction in frequency from late adolescence Higher rates in ADHD, Tourette's disorder Many nocturnal epilepsies occur during slow wave sleep - differential diagnosis can require video PSG. (Neikrug & Ancoli-Israel, 2015; Nofzinger, 2005)
Nightmare	Remembered dream- content changes during development 87-96% children with occasional bad dream (Judd & Sateia, 2015)	Become less common except trauma or psychiatric disorders (Mellman, 2006)	Trauma-related disorders, especially post traumatic stress disorder with re-enactment dreams (Charuvastra & Cloitre, 2009)
REM parasomnia	Rare, 0.38-0.5% Relationship to frontal lobe seizure and movement disorders- usually in slow wave sleep not REM (Plante & Winkelman, 2006)	Older males (>50 yo) Alcohol use and withdrawal, cerebrovascular and neurodegenerative disorders may trigger REM	Antidepressants may increase risk of REM behavior disorders
Restless legs/Periodic limb movements	1-2% Commonly both occur; greater heritability/environment ratio (Bloomfield & Shatkin, 2009)	5-19% Older males, linked to motor and neurocognitive disorders, disorders More frequent in females (pregnancy, Fe deficient, (Erman, 2006)	Differentiate—Fe deficiency, akathisia, nocturnal movement disorders
Substance induced	Youth abuse a rage of drugs Community placed IDD more likely Prescription drug effects. (Gromov & Gromov, 2009)	Opiate induced hypersomnia; rates vary- substance (stimulants); withdrawal (ETOH) (Judd & Sateia, 2015)	

Differential Diagnosis

The diagnosis of sleep disorders requires a thorough, careful sleep history and basic medical evaluation (Greenberg et al., 1996; Pary, Tobias, Webb, & Lippmann, 1996). The variations in sleep physiology in people with ID can present a challenge in interpreting polysomnography, due to instability of phasic shifts - sleep-wake transitions—during sleep (Buckley et al., 2010; Carroll, Bliwise, & Dement, 1989; Johnson et al., 2009). The differential diagnoses of sleep disorders can be more complex for individuals with severe-profound ID. This is in large part due to their limited capacity for self-reporting and monitoring as well as the higher prevalence rates for medical, neurological, and neuropsychiatric disorders. Both factors suggest the need for a high index of suspicion and a systematic investigation for sleep disorders.

Table 3: Diagnostic data necessary to assess sleep disorders (Barnhill, 2006)

Traditional sleep chart; charting total sleep time over time; onset of sleep problem; pattern of sleep latency, nighttime awakenings, morning arousals; duration of sleep problem; bedtime—specifically recent changes or seasonal variations; pattern of late evening feeding habits; customary rituals prior to bedtime;
snoring or excessive motor activity during sleep;
ease of awakening in AM; behaviors on awakening- level of consciousness, organization, and complexity of behavior;
irresistible sleep attacks—falling asleep at work or during preferred activities, sleep related hallucinations, difficulty with movement upon awakening, periods of muscle weakness or persistent head nodding; staring, reduced eye blinking, automatism (micro-sleeps); changes in daytime target behaviors
environment for sleeping; level of physical activity;
age and gender;
presence of psychiatric or neurological diagnoses, including seizure type, severity and frequency; medical diagnosis—e.g. reflux disease, anemia, renal insufficiency; current medications—compare any changes in medicines to time line of the sleep disturbance; caffeine, nicotine, and other medications that may activate increases arousal; past interventions;
family history of sleep disorder;

More specific diagnostic information can be elicited by using current rating instruments. The Stanford Sleepiness Scale (Hoddes, Zarcone, Smythe, Phillips, & Dement, 1973) and the Sleep Disturbance Questionaire (Espie, Inglis, Harvey, & Tessier, 2000; Espie & Tweedie, 1991) are useful for individuals with ID. Polysomnography, video PSG, actigraphy to assess sleep related movements, sleep related breathing, parasomnias, and REM and other sleep rhythm disorders. The Multi-Sleep Latency Test provides more specific information about narcolepsy and other hypersomnias (Carskadon et al., 1986). Unfortunately, such studies are either not practical or inaccessible/unavailable for many people. Those with severe-profound ID or severe disruptive or destructive behaviors are unlikely to tolerate neurophysiological sleep studies.

Column 3 in table 1 outlines the most common co-morbid conditions. Table 3 lists the disorders subject to the differential diagnoses. From this data several points emerge with regards to sleep disorders: a high rate of co-occurrence among primary sleep disorders; significant permeability in the boundaries between various subtypes of sleep disorders; and high rates of comorbidity with other neurodevelopmental, metabolic, genetic and medical/neurological conditions. These circumstances suggest that our understanding of sleep physiology and the forces that appear to lower the threshold for sleep disorders in people with ID is still incomplete (Aldrich, 1999; Hirshkowitz, 2004; Neikrug & Ancoli-Israel, 2015).

Atypical neurodevelopmental trajectories influence the emergence of sleep phases/rhythms (sleep architecture) during childhood and regression during old age (Judd & Sateia, 2015; Neikrug & Ancoli-Israel, 2015). Both genes and the environment have effects on homeostatic mechanisms (sleep onset and pressure), circadian rhythms (adenosine, delta sleep peptides, gaba-ergic function and melatonin synthesis, secretion, and metabolism), entrainment process to day night cycles (zeitgebers) and the timing of disrupted sleep patterns and sleep cycles (e.g. REM v. nonREM parasomnias). Many behavioral phenotypes are associated with sleep disorders. These trait phenomena may present unique opportunities to study the relationship between specific gene markers and patterns of sleep disorders (Barnhill, 2006; Ghanizadeh & Faghih, 2011; Shneerson, 2000a). People with autism spectrum disorder, both with and without ID, present with many sleep issues. Some appear unique to the neurophysiology of autism spectrum disorder. Others, like the high rates of insomnia due to sleep hygiene and psychophysiological conditioning, are also problematic for many individuals with autism spectrum disorder (Baker & Richdale, 2015; Buckley et al., 2010; Hare, Jones, & Evershed, 2006; Johnson et al., 2009). Lastly the high prevalence rates of psychiatric disorders, trauma, neurodegenerative disorders, and other psychosocial stressors in people with ID make it difficult to differentiate from some primary sleep disorders (Charuvastra & Cloitre, 2009).

Functional Consequences

Even though we are a predominantly diurnal species, we must entrain our sleep-wake cycles for night time sleep (McLaughlin Crabtree & Williams, 2009). A breakdown in the process or maintenance of entrained zeitgebers contributes to erratic sleep patterns and disturbs the balance between these homeostatic needs and circadian rhythms (Hirshkowitz, 2004; Markov & Goldman, 2006). This imbalance can result in significant disturbances in the transition from wakefulness, difficulty initiating sleep, maintenance of sleep and increased problems returning to sleep after brief awakenings (Barnhill, 2006; Judd & Sateia, 2015; Markov & Goldman, 2006).

There are compensatory mechanisms to deal with brief periods of disrupted sleep. Unfortunately these mechanisms (rebound increase in slow wave sleep and REM sleep) are less effective for chronic insomnia or insufficient sleep (Becker, 2006; O'Brien, 2009; Shneerson, 2000b). Over time chronic insomnia disrupts normal alertness and arousal and produces an intrusive and often irresistible urge to sleep (drowsiness) as well as micro-sleep events (catnaps) and sleep automatisms (similar to road hypnosis). Daytime hypersomnolence is commonly related to insufficient sleep, chronic insomnia, sleep related breathing, arousal, movement, and insufficient sleep disorders.

Excessive daytime sleepiness can also result from over sedation, nocturnal seizures, and other medical/neurological disorders (Brown, 1996; Carskadon, 2004; Durmer & Dinges, 2005). In this context, clinicians may misattribute medication side effects to narcolepsy, irregular and other sleep-wake cycle disorders, circadian sleep phase delay of advancement, REM and non REM sleep behavior disorders, depression in bipolar disorder, seizure activity or post-ictal seizures, and conversion disorders (Cooke & Ancoli-Israel, 2006; Peterson & Benca, 2006).

Sleep disturbances are the result of dysfunctional sleep induction (aberrant conditioned sleep cues and rituals); insufficient downregulation of cortical arousal; disruption of sleep rhythms; or inefficient transition gating to prevent the intrusion of pathological arousal states. Insomnia can result from a single or combination of these problems. Conditioned psychophysiological difficulties and dysfunctional bedtime rituals also contribute to difficulty falling asleep (G. J. Reid, Huntley, & Lewin, 2009).

Sleep-phase shifts, restless legs syndrome, sleep related breathing disorders, and parasomnias are also associated with insomnias. In restless legs syndrome, the creeping sense of discomfort in the extremities is abated by movement or standing up. Sleep onset can be delayed for several hours (Erman, 2006). Many children with attention deficit hyperactivity disorder and tic disorders describe a similar feeling of discomfort and need to move (O'Brien, 2009). restless legs syndrome can be related to thyroid disorders, anemia, caffeine and nicotine sensitivity, and multiple medications (Judd & Sateia, 2015). restless legs syndrome is also similar to the neuroleptic side effect, akathisia. restless legs syndrome and akathisia may be difficult to differentiate in clients with severe ID and difficulties in sleep initiation (Barnhill, 2006). Periodic limb movements of sleep is commonly associated with restless legs syndrome and is characterized by rhythmic movements during stage II sleep that result in brief arousal and disrupted sleep. These arousal states lead to inefficient sleep, resulting in nonrestorative sleep, daytime fatigue and sleepiness (Bloomfield & Shatkin, 2009). Disrupted sleep secondary to sleep apneas generally causes excessive daytime fatigue,e and sleepiness. Left unchecked, chronic insomnia has been associated with an increased risk for mood disorders and poor social/occupational performance (Barnhill, 2006; Becker, 2006; Benson, 2006; Krahn, 2005).

There is growing evidence for the negative effects of sleep deprivation on normal growth, cognitive development, behavior, and general health of children. The adverse effects of chronic sleep deprivation differ symptomatically in children. In contrast to adults, where mental slowing, poor concentration, lethargy, fatigue, and increased daytime somnolence are prominent, children with chronic sleep disturbances more frequently present with hyperactivity, irritability, and impaired learning (Hare et al., 2006; O'Brien, 2009).

Adults with ID may respond to sleep loss with increases in irritability, hyperactivity, aggression, and SIB, rather than with fatigue or excessive daytime sleepiness (Durmer & Dinges, 2005; Grigg-Damberger & Ralls, 2013; O'Brien, 2009). People with ID and autism spectrum disorder may also be vulnerable to cyclical and seasonal changes in sleep duration. These changes are hypothesized to represent sensitivity to rapidly changing photoperiods associated with the effects sunlight on longer rhythms (Judd & Sateia, 2015; Rechtschaffen & Siegal, 2000). The effects of sensitivities to photoperiod shifts underlies seasonal affective disorders, onset of mania, worsening of panic attacks, and relapse in the schizophrenias (Benson, 2006). Long term insomnia, untreated sleep related breathing disorders, and mood disorders can accelerate the course of immunological, neurocognitive, and neurodegenerative disorders (Provini, Lombardi, & Lugaresi, 2005).

Comorbidity

Insomnia is the most common sleep disorder among the general population and people with IDD. Yet for many with ID, diagnosing insomnia remains a challenge. The task requires teasing out the nuances of disrupted sleep onset and maintenance disorders. This process requires a working knowledge of sleep homeostasis, circadian rhythms, sleep architecture, and the many environmental and psychological impediments to sleep. Because of the role played by medical and neurological disorders in insomnia, it is useful to classify it in terms of primary and secondary subtypes by also listing co-occurring sleep disorders, medical/neurological, psychiatric, and pharmacological in the diagnosis. The table below is designed to connect various patterns of insomnia to primary psychiatric disorders and ID:

Table 4. Comorbidities

Primary Psychiatric Disorders	Difficulty Falling Asleep	Awakening—middle insomnia	Early morning awakening	Daytime sleepiness
Depression can be linked to difficulty falling asleep, early morning awakening, middle insomnia, daytime sleepiness	Past sleep patterns: Usual bedtime Duration of sleep Time of awakening Evidence of sleep phase delay Risk factors for Restless Legs Pain (Roehrs & Roth, 2005)	Past sleep patterns: Time of bedtime (phase advance) Time and duration of awakening Documented sleep, nocturnal panic, mood, or seizure disorder Behaviors associated with awakening Associated medical conditions	Past pattern of sleep: Timing of awakening Duration of sleep prior to awakening Behaviors associated with awakening Efficacy of sleep—short cycle or phase advance may not experience fatigue or continued sleepiness	Past history of daytime somnolence: Obesity, OSAS, behavioral phenotype like Prader-Willi REM instability- other symptoms of narcolepsy Most recent seizure of AED regimen Level of environmental stimulation Medical status

Table 4. Comorbidities (continued)

Primary Psychiatric Disorders	Difficulty Falling Asleep	Awakening—middle insomnia	Early morning awakening	Daytime sleepiness
Bipolar and psychotic Disorders (Fahey & Zee, 2006; Krahn, 2005; Peterson & Benca, 2006) Schizophrenia (Benson, 2006)	Phase advance —short REM latency Acute phase, decreased sleep; effects of anti-psychotic drugs on Sleep wake cycle.	Associated with more severe forms of depres-sion- melancholia	Melancholia	Atypical, seasonal, and bipolar depressed illness; depression may be the underlying cause of daytime fatigue in individuals with sleep related breathing dis-orders
Anxiety Disorders (Charuvastra & Cloitre, 2009; Judd & Sateia, 2015; Krahn, 2005; Mell-man, 2006)	Increased arousal state Comorbidity with bipolar disorder	Less common, although parasomnias may recur during times of distress	Nightmares may occur, especially severe in post- traumatic stress disorder	Over sedation, Alcohol use/abuse Bipolar disorder, de-pressed phase
Seizure Disorder (Zucconi & Bruni, 2001)	Fear of seizures during sleep Anticonvulsant effects Comorbid psychiatric disorder	>Nocturnal seizures during slow wave sleep >Arousal disorders	Comorbid depression Early morning sei-zures- myoclonus followed by tonic clon-ic generalized seizures	Atypical Absence Post-ictal state Medication side effects Comorbid primary sleep disorder
Degenerative disorders	Sun downing, nocturnal agitation Medication side effects Lack of light exposure and daytime activities	Phase advance Frequent awakenings Severe phase advance Comorbid mood disorder	REM related Behavior disorders Phase advance Severe mood disorder	Sleep deprivation Boredom Thyroid and other endo-crine changes

Application of Diagnostic Criteria to People with ID

Review of Research Applying to People with IDD

Sleep disturbances in people with developmental disabilities may be the result of immature or dysfunctional sleep networks, primary psychiatric disorders, visual impairments, and psychosocial factors associated with decreased adaptability, attachment disorder, and poor sleep related hygiene (Barnhill, 2006).

Many people with severe ID produce ill-timed or insufficient melatonin and sleep inducing peptides to initiate sleep. Others may not suppress melatonin production during daylight hours that disrupt circadian rhythms and in some circumstances produce behavioral activation. Many display aberrant sleep rhythms such as slow wave/REM sleep fragmentation restless legs syndrome, sensitivity to medication side effects, nocturnal epilepsy, or other physiological problems with sleep onset. For example, people with Rett, Down, Prader Willi (Kaplan, Fredrickson, & Richardson, 1991), Smith-Magenis, and Cornelia de Lange syndromes and those with orofacial and upper airway anomalies are prone to obstructive sleep apneas and disrupted sleep (Angriman, Caravale, Novelli, Ferri, & Bruni, 2015; Rajan et al., 2012). Rather than excessive daytime somnolence, irritability, hyperactivity, increased aggression or SIB may result. Individuals with severe visual impairments lack melanopsin receptors and a dysfunction pattern of dim-light onset release of melatonin (Bruni et al., 2015; Grigg-Damberger & Ralls, 2013).

More recent studies focus on sleep disorders among individuals with specific behavioral phenotypes and autism spectrum disorder. The value of behavioral phenotypes arises from three sources: heritability of many sleep disorders; significant gene X environmental interactions associated with entrainment by light and other social zeitgebers, and the relative fewer genes involved in behavioral phenotypes. As expected among heterogeneous neurodevelopmental disorders, people with autism spectrum disorder present a complex array of both sleep onset, circadian rhythm, variability in sleep architecture and arousal phenomena. One subtype bears special attention: the relationship between regressive subtype of autism spectrum disorder and REM related parasomnias (Buckley et al., 2010). This presence of REM behavior disorders may bear a relationship to the integration of cortical, mesencephalic, and pontine regulation of motor generators and perhaps the increase in atypical cortical neurons and head circumference associated with this group (Judd & Sateia, 2015; Markov & Goldman, 2006).

Sleep disruption and fragmentation are frequent occurrences in people with severe and profound intellectual disability (Brylewski & Wiggs, 1998; Poindexter & Bihm, 1994). (Shibagaki, Kiyono, & Matsuno (1985) studied the development of night-time sleep of a group of 79 children and adolescents with intellectual disability and found patterns similar to those previously found for age-matched neurotypical controls. This same group (Shibagaki, Kiyono, & Takeuchi, 1985) compared sleep patterns in 23 children with cerebral palsy and intellectual disability to 39 children with intellectual disability and no cerebral palsy. Their results suggest an increased rate of abnormal sleep physiology in people with ID plus cerebral palsy. The convergence of diverse pathophysiologies suggests that most sleep disorders are final common pathways for several excitatory/inhibitory brain networks.

In longitudinal studies circadian rhythm changes associated with severe visual impairment and insomnias were common (Khan et al., 2011). Okawa and group (1987) studied four congenitally blind children with intellectual disability (Okawa et al., 1987). They note Circadian rhythm disturbances in all four. They suggested that the social deficits associated with severe ID interfered with the adoption and use of alternative zeitgebers (social time cues). A number of single and small group case studies have also been reported, including a discussion of parental report of sleep problems in children with autism (Gail Williams, Sears, & Allard, 2004; Schreck & Mulick, 2000) and sleep-related breathing disorders in adults with Down syndrome (Resta et al., 2003).

More recent meta-analyses based on large community-based samples suggest a more complex relationship between insomnia and ID (van de Wouw, Evenhuis, & Echteld, 2012). Data from sleep studies of multiple behavioral phenotypes support a diverse picture of sleep disturbances associated with specific genetic disorders. More complex genetic disorders such as many neuropsychiatric disorders suggest that multiple genes and more diverse gene-environment interactions are responsible. The complex nature of secondary disorders suggests a multi directional relationship between primary and secondary sleep disorders.

In addition, sleep disorders provide another example of a stress-diathesis model. This model encompasses the complex interplay of gene expression and regulation, ongoing brain development, changing attachment needs, entrainment to environmental zeitgebers, unfolding temperament, and the effects psychosocial demands on circadian rhythms and sleep architecture (Markov & Goldman, 2006; Rechtschaffen & Siegal, 2000).

Adults with Intellectual Disability

Many sleep disorders appear to be neurodevelopmental disorders. Most studies, however, do not support a linear relationship between the prevalence rates for specific sleep disorders and developmental age (see Prevalence and Development). But as we have seen sleep disorders like insomnia are intertwined with the underlying neurobiology of sleep disorders (Boyle et al., 2010; Esposito & Carotenuto, 2014). This apparent paradox suggests that the relationship between sleep disorders and ID is a multifaceted one. Insomnia is a frequent problem for individuals with ID, autism spectrum disorder and other neurodevelopmental disorders, post traumatic stress disorder, comorbid psychiatric or neurological disorders (Bhatt et al., 2005) and in some behavioral phenotypes (Angriman et al., 2015). Secondary forms of insomnia are also associated with pain-related disorders (Breau & Camfield, 2011). People with severe ID, autism spectrum disorder, and insomnia have overlapping sleep disorders that either remain unrecognized or confused with seizure activity or severe psychiatric disorders (Baker & Richdale, 2015; Neikrug & Ancoli-Israel, 2015). Insufficient sleep, sleep phase changes, and sleep related disorders may present with increased irritability, agitation, and hyperactive and aggressive/self-injurious behaviors instead of daytime somnolence (Maaskant et al., 2013).

The prevalence rates of sleep related breathing, central and hypoventilation disorders, REM related parasomnias, restless legs syndrome, and periodic limb movements tend to increase with age. Chronic pulmonary (e.g. COPD), cardiovascular, cerebrovascular, and neuromuscular disease serve as primary risk factors for secondary central apnea and hypoventilation sleep disorders. Circadian rhythm and sleep cycle changes are associated with aging, neurodegenerative disorders, and dementias. These effects can be overshadowed by the effects of aging on sleep in individuals with ID (Cooke & Ancoli-Israel, 2006; Morgenthaler et al., 2007).

Declines in vision and hearing, decreased sensitivity to external zietgebers (light) and marked reductions in slow wave sleep and REM sleep associated with aging among neurotypical adults can be confused with psychiatric disorders or more serious neurodegenerative disorders. Blindness and severe visual impairment are more commonly associated with irregular sleep wake cycle disorder. Non-24-hour sleep wake cycle disorders are more diverse. Non-24-hour sleep rhythms, are observed in patients with IDD and/or autism spectrum disorder, sensory impairments and mood disorders (mania in particular). Fragmented sleep is also associated with autism spectrum disorder, traumatic brain injury, and dementias. REM-related movement disorder is associated with synucleopathies (neurodegenerative disorders like Parkinson's disease and progressive supranuclear palsy), dementias, and vascular disorders. For individuals with synucleopathies, REM related movements may occur decades before the onset of the neurodegenerative disorder (Maaskant et al., 2013; Provini et al., 2005).

The types of psychosocial and health related stressors associated with insomnias change during the life cycle. The power of alternative zietgebers (social schedules, activities, TV schedules) to serve as organizers of circadian and sleep rhythms wane and increase the risk of non-24-hour sleep rhythm disturbances. Perhaps more importantly, increasing medical complication and polypharmacy regimens can mimic many primary sleep disorders as well as contribute to delirium and cognitive decline (Carskadon, 2004; K. J. Reid et al., 2004).

Children with Intellectual Disability

The developmental trajectory of sleep physiology is driven by brain maturation and the integration of the neuronal networks associated with sleep mechanics. For example, circadian rhythms and sleep architecture change during both infant development and aging. In this sense many sleep disorders are also developmental. For example, primary nonREM parasomnias reach their peak in early childhood when slow wave sleep is predominant but then wane as slow wave sleep declines in late adolescence and all but disappear in the elderly (Cooke & Ancoli-Israel, 2006; McLaughlin Crabtree & Williams, 2009; Plante & Winkelman, 2006). By adulthood, most nonREM parasomnias are more likely due to co-occurring stressors or medical/psychiatric disorders (secondary parasomnia). Others like restless legs syndrome and periodic limb movements of sleep display a high degree of heritability. Early onset restless legs syndrome may be more likely to occur in families suggesting the greater impact of genetic mechanisms (primary restless legs syndrome). restless legs syndrome onset among older people may reflect emerging neurodegenerative or known secondary cases (Bloomfield & Shatkin, 2009; Erman, 2006; Neikrug & Ancoli-Israel, 2015; Rama & Kushida, 2004).

But there is a rub. Most sleep disorders are the result of complex gene-environmental interactions and the boundaries between syndromes are semi-permeable. The impact of atypical development associated with IDD and autism spectrum disorder on this developmental trajectory is not well understood. The exception may be selected behavioral phenotypes where at least some gene-environment and atypical brain maturation are relatively well established (Angriman et al., 2015).

Prevalence rates for sleep-wake cycle disorders are affected by the instability of transitions between sleep stages (nonREM to REM and back again). The predominance of slow wave sleep in early childhood overlaps the emergence of nonREM paramsonnia. Sleep phase instability (especially during transitions) and traumatic experiences also influence the prevalence rates for nightmares. By adolescence, primary parasomnias and nightmares subside, but they are "replaced" by sleep phase delay, narcolepsy, persistent enuresis, chronic sleep deprivation due to psychosocial and academic demands, insomnia, substance use, and the increasing prevalence of primary psychiatric disorders (Bloomfield & Shatkin, 2009; Plante & Winkelman, 2006).

Recent epidemiological studies suggest higher rates of complex sleep disorders is associated with tic disorders (Barnhill, 2006) and traumatization (Charuvastra & Cloitre, 2009; Johnson et al., 2009). Early traumatic brain injuries and other neurodevelopmental disorders such as IDD and autism spectrum disorder may have higher rates of complicated sleep disorders (Grigg-Damberger & Ralls, 2013). Other sources of sleep disruptions include nocturnal movement disorders, complex, treatment refractory seizure disorders, periodic limb movements, and restless legs/akathisia-like insomnia secondary to medication side effects. In children, hypoventilation disorders may be more likely associated with genetic (cystic fibrosis), neuromuscular, and central nervous system problems (Zucconi & Bruni, 2001). The presence of IDD, autism, attention deficit hyperactivity disorder, and other neurodevelopmental disorders has both quantitative and qualitative influences on sleep. Insomnia, irregular sleep wake cycles, fragmentation of sleep, and REM related parasomnias are not uncommon in children with autism spectrum disorder and IDD (Grigg-Damberger & Ralls, 2013; Johnson et al., 2009).

Summary of Limitations in Applying DSM or ICD Criteria to People with ID

The DSM-5 criteria are applicable to people with ID. The major stumbling block is recognition and differential diagnosis of disordered sleep.

Etiology and Pathogenesis

Biological Factors

Sleep onset is a complex process. In addition to diurnal patterns of sleep-activity, we experience a growing urge to sleep. Recent studies suggest that over the course of the day, the accumulation of sleep related factors (adenosine, 5-HT, melatonin, and other sleep-related peptides) begin to override declining arousal (orexins/hypocretin, histamine, cholinergic, and other peptides). The suprachiasmic nuclei and periventricular nuclei of the hypothalamus also regulate sleep onset and organization of normal phasic changes in sleep cycles. By late childhood the synchronization of sleep and daytime activities is relatively stable. This may not be the case for persons with IDD or autism spectrum disorder. The experience of sleepiness is a balance of these factors. Emerging slow wave (theta) activity on EEG suggests drowsiness. Adequate sleep restarts this cycle by reversing the balance in the homeostatic mechanisms (Aldrich, 1999; Hirshkowitz, 2004; Judd & Sateia, 2015; Markov & Goldman, 2006; Shneerson, 2000c).

Normal sleep is a progressive repetition of roughly 90-120 minute phase changes in EEG rhythms, endocrine activity, body temperature, and brain activity. Normal sleep begins with drowsiness and a gradual slowing of EEG frequencies. The appearance of "k" complexes and sleep spindles herald stage II sleep and changing levels of thalamic activation. Later in the sleep cycle, the EEG rhythm slows and is dominated by increasing amounts of delta activity (0-3 cycles per second). This shift in the percentage of delta waves differentiates Stages III and IV sleep. The normal 90-120 minute sleep cycle culminates in a paradoxical state of EEG arousal, increased REM activity, increased brain activity, and muscle paralysis-REM sleep.

REM sleep is associated with dreaming (Judd & Sateia, 2015; Rechtschaffen & Siegal, 2000; Shneerson, 2000c).

These typical sleep stages are accompanied by phasic changes in heart rate, respiration, and dramatic changes in EMG activity (muscle tone). There are significant metabolic and endocrine changes throughout the sleep cycle. Most hormones show sleep-related changes in excretion- prolactin, growth hormone, vasopressin, gonadotropins, and cortisol display phasic changes in excretion rates during sleep. The pattern and timing of their release gives each sleep phase a neurobiological signature. For example, growth hormone is released early in the evening when slow wave (Stage III-IV) sleep predominates. Prolactin, cortisol, and other hormones are released during REM sleep. Gonadotropin release changes to a pattern of pulsatile release during puberty (McLaughlin Crabtree & Williams, 2009; Shneerson, 2000b).

Circadian rhythms result from synchronization of phasic hormone release, body temperature fluctuations, drug action, and metabolism. Normal sleep and circadian rhythms require the co-ordination of cortical, hypothalamic, and ascending reticular activating system in the brain stem. The suprachiasmic nuclei and periventricular nuclei in the anterior hypothalamus organize and synchronize these circadian rhythms. These hypothalamic nuclei also work in tandem with several brainstem nuclei to regulate sleep onset and the phasic changes associated with normal sleep (Judd & Sateia, 2015; Rechtschaffen & Siegal, 2000).

The process of entrainment involves synchronizing the suprachiasmic nuclei/periventricular nuclei to specific zeitgebers- diurnal changes associated with day-night cycles. The process of settling in during infancy is an example of the role of entrainment in choreographing hypothalamic, brain stem reticular activiating system and cortical systems to fit day-night sleep wake cycles. Without entrainment of suprachiasmic nuclei/periventricular nuclei activity (especially light of sufficient intensity), normal diurnal sleep-wake cycles become desynchronized (free running) with variations in day-night rhythms. This pattern is encountered in many individuals with autism spectrum disorder and some forms of blindness (Khan et al., 2011; Morgenthaler et al., 2007).

Melatonin is produced from l-trypophan by the pineal gland. The synthesis of melatonin depends on the availability of tryptophan, integrity of the tryptophan hydroxylase and hydroxyindole acetic methyl-transferase (rate limiting step), and the effects of light on these enzyme systems. In humans, melatonin is involved in a complex dance with day-night cycles. Light impacts the retina, suprachiasmic nuclei, and the pineal gland where melatonin is synthesized. This complex interaction plays a key role in the phasic shifts in sleep-wake cycles (Bruni et al., 2015; Judd & Sateia, 2015).

Disruption in this cyclical pattern of melatonin activity plays a role in sleep phase disorders and perhaps some forms of psychopathology. Melatonin production is impaired in many with intellectual disabilities and autism (Chen, Mullegama, Alaimo, & Elsea, 2015; Johnson et al., 2009). Sleep in these individuals tends to be fragmented, and erratic, and the transition between cycles can be difficult to tease out. Some people with autism spectrum disorder or who are visually impaired appear to run on an irregular sleep wake cycle that is not entrained to light. For these individuals, sleep rhythms are out of sync with day-night zeitgebers and many rely on social cues (wake up time or regular schedules) to entrain sleep onset (Baker & Richdale, 2015; Fahey & Zee, 2006). These compensatory changes are vulnerable to environmental challenges and are frequently associated with significant levels of externalizing and disruptive behavior.

There is no clear cut evidence that insufficient melatonin is directly responsible for disruptive behavior in individuals with severe developmental disabilities. It is apparent, however, that clients with autism, severe/profound ID, and visual impairment do not produce sufficient amounts of melatonin; it may be secreted during the day rather than at night or is rapidly metabolized. Defects in melatonin receptors may also be present and may explain why some individuals do not respond to melatonin. These individuals have sleep disturbances and desynchronization of circadian rhythms involved in hormone production, body temperature, and sleep maintenance (Ivanenko & Gururaj, 2009; Judd & Sateia, 2015; Markov & Goldman, 2006; Rechtschaffen & Siegal, 2000). Their behavior (diurnal agitation, aggression, hyperactivity, and increased SIB) may be more directly related to sleep deprivation (Espie & Tweedie, 1991).

Genetic Factors

Many sleep disorders are related to genetic variations in the synthesis and metabolism of melatonin, sleep related peptides, GABA, and dopamine. These familial forms of restless leg syndrome tend to be more severe and begin earlier in life (Ollila et al., 2015). Alzheimer's, Parkinson's, cerebrovascular disease and some hereditary neurodegenerative disorders are risk factors or directly affect the rates of central apneas, parasomnias and nocturnal movement disorders, and REM behavior disorder (Bhatt et al., 2005; Neikrug & Ancoli-Israel, 2015). The list is a bit more complicated for persons with IDD. For example, some individuals with autism spectrum disorder and Smith-Magenis syndrome may show a reversal of melatonin synthesis and release (Chen et al., 2015). For persons with Angelman's syndrome and complicated epilepsy, anticonvulsants, dysfunctional GABA receptors, problems with arousal, and nocturnal seizures can all disrupt sleep (Ehlen et al., 2015). Nocturnal frontal lobe seizures are associated with nicotinic cholinergic receptors and require differentiation for parasomnias and REM related behaviors (Bazil, 2002; Provini et al., 2005).

Body structural changes of the mid-face, often seen with Down syndrome, as well as obesity, such as seen with Prader-Willi syndrome, may be associated with breathing disorders (obstructive sleep apnea) (Angriman et al., 2015). While these structural changes have been assumed to cause sleep problems in individuals with Down syndrome, other studies show central apnea (hypotonia and respiratory drive) in this group as well (Aldrich, 1999; Dahlqvist, Rask, Rosenqvist, Sahlin, & Franklin, 2003). While researchers have identified distinct behavioral phenotypes among individuals with intellectual disability, Harvey and Kennedy (2002) found evidence for the presence of polysomnographic phenotypes in these individuals. Differences in sleep architecture have been identified in people with autism, Down syndrome, and fragile X syndrome (Kronk et al., 2010). There appears to be a correlation between the severity of ID and total sleep time, frequency of awakenings REM frequency and density, less time spent in rapid eye movement sleep, and the stability in sleep architecture (Angriman et al., 2015). Smith-Magenis syndrome, often associated with intellectual disability, has sleep disorder as a primary symptom. This in part relates to inversion of melatonin production (De Leersnyder et al., 2003). There are behavioral consequences to reduced nocturnal sleep as well as melatonin production during daylight (Chen et al., 2015; De Leersnyder et al., 2003). Children with Rett syndrome (Ellaway, Peat, Leonard, & Christodoulou, 2001) lack age-related decrease in total and daytime sleep time seen in normal children. Those children with co-occurring seizure disorders displayed fewer episodes of slow wave sleep (Ammanuel et al., 2015); as noted earlier, many nocturnal seizures arise from slow wave sleep. Sleep disturbances are frequently seen in people with Angelman syndrome. In a study of fifteen children with this syndrome, important abnormalities of sleep polysomnographic patterns were found as compared to normal individuals (Miano et al., 2004). The impact of GABA receptor defects and UBE3A play a role in both aberrant sleep homeostasis and the physiology of sleep onset but also increase seizure activity and complicate its management (Ehlen et al., 2015).

Studies of sleep disorders in people with specific behavioral phenotypes are one way of simplifying the gene-environmental factors that shape atypical sleep physiology. There are trends that also suggest syndrome specific patterns of disrupted sleep or melatonin excretion. For example, people with Cornelia de Lange syndrome illustrate two phenomena: higher prevalence rates of insomnia and circadian rhythm disorders during childhood but a gradual reduction in this problem by adulthood (Rajan et al., 2012; Stavinoha et al., 2011). These findings return to an idea addressed earlier, namely our limited understanding of the neurodevelopmental trajectory of many ID syndromes and how these might influence disordered sleep physiology during development.

Psychosocial Factors

Adequate sleep is crucial to normal daytime functioning. Unfortunately, most people in industrialized societies sleep far less than our ancestors did 100 years ago. Societal changes that contribute to insufficient sleep include: high stress levels associated with work or academic demands; time in natural and artificial light exposure; late evening use of computers, TV watching and other electronic devices; obesity; fixed bedtimes in residential programs that disregard sleep phase and lifelong sleep patterns; large scale use of pharmaceuticals that impact sleep wake cycles; and many other psychosocial or cultural factors. In many industrializing countries, the psychosocial meaning of time changes. For example, the culture of work becomes one in which time becomes money or people work on click-time rather than by suntime. These shifts replace traditional work attitudes and time management. In those societies, work expectations affect the amount of sleep by disrupting zeitgebers (sun or light) that once set circadian sleep-wake cycles. The increasing emphasis on productivity and creativity in the workplace by cutting down our total sleep time may not be the best solution.

Inadequate sleep has obvious consequences for cognition, motor performance, attention, memory, and most complex executive skills (Aldrich, 1999; Cooke & Ancoli-Israel, 2006; Shneerson, 2000a).

Sleep deprivation increases the urge to sleep and increases sleep debt compensatory demands. Compensatory sleep catchup begins with increased slow wave sleep first, then REM sleep. Extended periods of weekend sleep in adolescents and those with delayed sleep phase disorders are examples. But these mechanisms are not completely effective in settling or restoring the adequate sleep state. Both acute and chronic sleep deprivation affect daytime alertness, attention-vigilance, judgment, problem solving, and other forms of cognition (Giannotti & Cortesi, 2009; Hare et al., 2006; O'Brien, 2009). Deprivation also contributes to daytime sleepiness, and eventual intrusion of fragments of sleep into waking hours (automatic behaviors) (Judd & Sateia, 2015). Children and many adults with intellectual disability may not experience fatigue or sleepiness but instead display increased hyperactivity, irritability, increases in disruptive or stereotypic behaviors, and self-injurious or aggressive behaviors (Barnhill, 2006).

Sleep deprivation can also adversely affect the level of functional impairments and support needs for people with chronic sleep disorders. Neurocognitive and adaptive deficits secondary to sleep deprivation affect the severity of functional impairments (conceptual, social, and practical domains). As we have observed, social, technological, choice of occupations and cultural attitudes have contributed to reduced sleep times and the widespread problems of insufficient sleep. In most industrialized societies, the introduction of electric lights (melatonin excretion, sleep phase changes) and wage economies (shift jobs, work pressure) affect sleep. Declines in mood, concentration, attention, memory, and motor performance affect both unsupervised and supportive employment, and increased levels of disruptive behaviors can limit community-based activities. Lastly, sleep deprivation can lower the threshold for parasomnia (rebound stage III-IV sleep) and sleep disorders to both insomnia and circadian rhythms (Giannotti & Cortesi, 2009).

Under normal circumstances there is a balance between homeostatic and circadian sleep zeitgebers. When this balance is disrupted there are adverse effects on sleep wake cycles that ultimately have negative psychosocial consequences. Without sufficient sleep we feel tired, lethargic, irritable, drowsy, or become increasingly inattentive. Even minor fluctuations in our usual sleep time or efficiency can have an adverse effect on a wide range of higher cognitive functions such as alertness, concentration, and decision-making that can lead to an increased risk for serious accidents (Aldrich, 1999; Shneerson, 2000b). For the most part, the same set of psychosocial and environmental issues is common to neurotypical and IDD populations. Their impact on a person with IDD, however, may vary depending on the level of the IDD and the presence of other risk factors for disrupted sleep. The negative consequences of relative sleep deprivation may degrade the quality of life for many, and increase the rates of disruptive and destructive behaviors (Johnson et al., 2009).

Developmental Factors

The organization of sleep architecture changes during development. Infants display high levels of "active sleep" that is analogous to REM activity with motor paralysis. Over the first six months of age, there is an increase in slow wave sleep, reduction in "active sleep" and the emergence of characteristic REM sleep, and reduction in total sleep time (McLaughlin Crabtree & Williams, 2009). By adulthood, most individuals face slow declines in slow wave sleep and REM sleep. By the time most reach their 60's, slow wave sleep is disappearing, and Stages I and II and REM sleep predominate (Ayalon, Liu, & Ancoli-Israel, 2004). The changes may be accelerated or distorted by the increased burden of medical disorders, and the emergence of chronic depression and dementias among the elderly (Cooke & Ancoli-Israel, 2006; Moline et al., 2004; Neikrug & Ancoli-Israel, 2015). We still lack longitudinal data on the developmental trajectory of brain "aging" in many ID subpopulations. We have neuroimaging and autopsy data on brain aging and dementia in Down syndrome but more limited information for the remaining and more heterogeneous ID population. The presence of Alzheimer's dementia is not alone among neurocognitive disorders in disrupting and disorganizing sleep physiology. For example, there are few studies addressing the relationship between emerging tauopathies, synucleopathies, cerebrovascular disease and REM parasomnias (REM behavior disorders) in people with ID (Neikrug & Ancoli-Israel, 2015; Resta et al., 2003).

Application of Diagnostic Criteria

Insomnia Disorder
Hypersomnolence Disorder
Narcolepsy
Obstructive Sleep Apnea Hypopnea
Central Sleep Apnea
Sleep-Related Hypoventilation
Circadian Rhythm Sleep-Wake Disorders
Non-Rapid Eye Movement Sleep Arousal Disorders
Nightmare Disorder
Rapid Eye Movement Sleep Behavior Disorder
Restless Legs Syndrome

The DSM-5 provides a workable set of criteria that require little modification. It remains critical for clinicians to collect sufficient information to facilitate the recognition of sleep disturbances and initiate a differential diagnosis. Since most individuals with severe-profound ID cannot report significant sleep disruptions, diagnoses are suspected based on observational and available sleep data

Primary insomnia, parasomnias, nightmares and sleep related breathing disorders are by far the most common sleep disorders among individuals with ID(IDD). Table 2 is devoted to the process of differential diagnosis and provisional diagnosis. In most cases, referral to specialists in sleep disorders is needed for a final or definitive diagnosis. The authors felt that the text explains the nuances of sleep disorders and along with Table 2 provides sufficient information for most clinical needs. We opted to not provided a table since the DSM-5 criteria are sufficient and do not require significant adaptations.

Substance/Medication-Induced Sleep Disorder

The criteria are the same as for other substance/medication-induced mental disorders, without adaptation, with the additional need for presence of a prominent and severe disturbance in sleep.

Other Specified Insomnia Disorder
Unspecified Insomnia Disorder
Other Specified Hypersomnolence Disorder
Unspecified Hypersomnolence Disorder
Other Specified Sleep-Wake Disorder
Unspecified Sleep-Wake Disorder

DSM-5 also provides categories for other specified insomnia disorder, unspecified insomnia disorder, other specified hypersomnolence disorder, unspecified hypersomnolence disorder, other specified sleep-wake disorder, and unspecified sleep-wake disorder.

References:

Aldrich, M. S. (1999). *Sleep medicine.* New York: Oxford University Press.

American Psychiatric Association. (2013). *Diagnostic and statistical manual of mental disorders: DSM-5* (5th ed.). Washington, D.C.: American Psychiatric Association.

Ammanuel, S., Chan, W. C., Adler, D. A., Lakshamanan, B. M., Gupta, S. S., Ewen, J. B., . . . Kadam, S. D. (2015). Heightened delta power during slow-wave-sleep in patients with Rett Syndrome associated with poor sleep efficiency. *PLoS One, 10*(10), e0138113. doi:10.1371/journal.pone.0138113

Angriman, M., Caravale, B., Novelli, L., Ferri, R., & Bruni, O. (2015). Sleep in children with neurodevelopmental disabilities. *Neuropediatrics, 46*(3), 199-210. doi:10.1055/s-0035-1550151

Avidan, A. Y. (2005). Sleep in the geriatric patient population. *Seminars in Neurology, 25*(1), 52-63. doi:10.1055/s-2005-867076

Ayalon, L., Liu, L., & Ancoli-Israel, S. (2004). Diagnosing and treating sleep disorders in the older adult. *Medical Clinics of North America, 88*(3), 737-750, ix-x. doi:10.1016/j.mcna.2004.01.005

Baker, E. K., & Richdale, A. L. (2015). Sleep patterns in adults with a diagnosis of high-functioning autism spectrum disorder. *Sleep, 38*(11), 1765-1774. doi:10.5665/sleep.5160

Barnhill, L. J. (2006). The assessment and differential diagnosis of insomnia in people with developmental disabilities. *Mental Health Aspects of Developmental Disabilities, 9*(4), 10.

Bazil, C. W. (2002). Sleep and epilepsy. *Seminars in Neurology, 22*(3), 321-327. doi:10.1055/s-2002-36651

Becker, P. M. (2006). Insomnia: Prevalence, impact, pathogenesis, differential diagnosis, and evaluation. *Psychiatric Clinics of North America, 29*(4), 855-870; abstract vii. doi:10.1016/j.psc.2006.08.001

Benson, K. L. (2006). Sleep in schizophrenia: impairments, correlates, and treatment. *Psychiatric Clinics of North America, 29*(4), 1033-1045; abstract ix-x. doi:10.1016/j.psc.2006.08.002

Bhatt, M. H., Podder, N., & Chokroverty, S. (2005). Sleep and neurodegenerative diseases. *Seminars in Neurology, 25*(1), 39-51. doi:10.1055/s-2005-867072

Bloomfield, E. R., & Shatkin, J. P. (2009). Parasomnias and movement disorders in children and adolescents. *Child and Adolescent Psychiatric Clinics of North America, 18*(4), 947-965. doi:10.1016/j.chc.2009.04.010

Boyle, A., Melville, C. A., Morrison, J., Allan, L., Smiley, E., Espie, C. A., & Cooper, S. A. (2010). A cohort study of the prevalence of sleep problems in adults with intellectual disabilities. *Journal of Sleep Research, 19*(1 Pt 1), 42-53. doi:10.1111/j.1365-2869.2009.00788.x

Breau, L. M., & Camfield, C. S. (2011). Pain disrupts sleep in children and youth with intellectual and developmental disabilities. *Research in Devevelopmental Disabilies, 32*(6), 2829-2840. doi:10.1016/j.ridd.2011.05.023

Brown, L. W. (1996). Sleep and epilepsy. *Child and Adolescent Psychiatric Clinics of North America, 5*(3), 701-714.

Bruni, O., Alonso-Alconada, D., Besag, F., Biran, V., Braam, W., Cortese, S., . . . Curatolo, P. (2015). Current role of melatonin in pediatric neurology: clinical recommendations. *European Journal of Paediatric Neurology, 19*(2), 122-133. doi:10.1016/j.ejpn.2014.12.007

Brylewski, J. E., & Wiggs, L. (1998). A questionnaire survey of sleep and night-time behaviour in a community-based sample of adults with intellectual disability. *Journal of Intellectual Disability Research, 42 (Pt 2)*, 154-162. Retrieved from http://www.ncbi.nlm.nih.gov/pubmed/9617699

Buckley, A. W., Rodriguez, A. J., Jennison, K., Buckley, J., Thurm, A., Sato, S., & Swedo, S. (2010). Rapid eye movement sleep percentage in children with autism compared with children with developmental delay and typical development. *Archives of Pediatric and Adolescent Medicine, 164*(11), 1032-1037. doi:10.1001/archpediatrics.2010.202

Carroll, J. S., Bliwise, D. L., & Dement, W. C. (1989). A method for checking interobserver reliability in observational sleep studies. *Sleep, 12*(4), 363-367. Retrieved from http://www.ncbi.nlm.nih.gov/pubmed/2762690

Carskadon, M. A. (2004). Sleep deprivation: Health consequences and societal impact. *Medical Clinics of North America, 88*(3), 767-776. doi:10.1016/j.mcna.2004.03.001

Carskadon, M. A., Dement, W. C., Mitler, M. M., Roth, T., Westbrook, P. R., & Keenan, S. (1986). Guidelines for the multiple sleep latency test (MSLT): A standard measure of sleepiness. *Sleep, 9*(4), 519-524. Retrieved from http://www.ncbi.nlm.nih.gov/pubmed/3809866

Charuvastra, A., & Cloitre, M. (2009). Safe enough to sleep: sleep disruptions associated with trauma, posttraumatic stress, and anxiety in children and adolescents. *Child and Adolescent Psychiatric Clinics of North America, 18*(4), 877-891. doi:10.1016/j.chc.2009.04.002

Chen, L., Mullegama, S. V., Alaimo, J. T., & Elsea, S. H. (2015). Smith-Magenis syndrome and its circadian influence on development, behavior, and obesity - own experience. *Developmental Period Medicine, 19*(2), 149-156. Retrieved from http://www.ncbi.nlm.nih.gov/pubmed/26384114

Cooke, J. R., & Ancoli-Israel, S. (2006). Sleep and its disorders in older adults. *Psychiatric Clinics of North America, 29*(4), 1077-1093; abstract x-xi. doi:10.1016/j.psc.2006.08.003

Culebras, A. (2005). Sleep disorders and neuromuscular disease. *Seminars in Neurology, 25*(1), 33-38. doi:10.1055/s-2005-867071

Dahlqvist, A., Rask, E., Rosenqvist, C. J., Sahlin, C., & Franklin, K. A. (2003). Sleep apnea and Down's syndrome. *Acta Otolaryngol, 123*(9), 1094-1097. Retrieved from http://www.ncbi.nlm.nih.gov/pubmed/14710914

De Leersnyder, H., de Blois, M. C., Bresson, J. L., Sidi, D., Claustrat, B., & Munnich, A. (2003). [Inversion of the circadian melatonin rhythm in Smith-Magenis syndrome]. *Revue Neurologique (Paris), 159*(11 Suppl), 6S21-26. Retrieved from http://www.ncbi.nlm.nih.gov/pubmed/14646795

Durmer, J. S., & Dinges, D. F. (2005). Neurocognitive consequences of sleep deprivation. *Seminars in Neurology, 25*(1), 117-129. doi:10.1055/s-2005-867080

Ehlen, J. C., Jones, K. A., Pinckney, L., Gray, C. L., Burette, S., Weinberg, R. J., . . . DeBruyne, J. P. (2015). Maternal Ube3a loss disrupts sleep homeostasis but leaves circadian rhythmicity largely intact. *Journal of Neuroscience, 35*(40), 13587-13598. doi:10.1523/JNEUROSCI.2194-15.2015

Ellaway, C., Peat, J., Leonard, H., & Christodoulou, J. (2001). Sleep dysfunction in Rett syndrome: Lack of age related decrease in sleep duration. *Brain Development, 23 Suppl 1*, S101-103. Retrieved from http://www.ncbi.nlm.nih.gov/pubmed/11738852

Erman, M. K. (2006). Selected sleep disorders: restless legs syndrome and periodic limb movement disorder, sleep apnea syndrome, and narcolepsy. *Psychiatric Clinics of North America, 29*(4), 947-967; abstract viii-ix. doi:10.1016/j.psc.2006.09.007

Espie, C. A., Inglis, S. J., Harvey, L., & Tessier, S. (2000). Insomniacs' attributions. psychometric properties of the dysfunctional beliefs and attitudes about sleep scale and the sleep disturbance questionnaire. *Journal of Psychosomatic Research, 48*(2), 141-148. Retrieved from http://www.ncbi.nlm.nih.gov/pubmed/10719130

Espie, C. A., & Tweedie, F. M. (1991). Sleep patterns and sleep problems amongst people with mental handicap. *Journal of Mental Deficiency Research, 35 (Pt 1)*, 25-36. Retrieved from http://www.ncbi.nlm.nih.gov/pubmed/2038024

Esposito, M., & Carotenuto, M. (2014). Intellectual disabilities and power spectra analysis during sleep: A new perspective on borderline intellectual functioning. *Journal of Intellectual Disability Research, 58*(5), 421-429. doi:10.1111/jir.12036

Fahey, C. D., & Zee, P. C. (2006). Circadian rhythm sleep disorders and phototherapy. *Psychiatric Clinics of North America, 29*(4), 989-1007; abstract ix. doi:10.1016/j.psc.2006.09.009

Gail Williams, P., Sears, L. L., & Allard, A. (2004). Sleep problems in children with autism. *Journal of Sleep Research, 13*(3), 265-268. doi:10.1111/j.1365-2869.2004.00405.x

Ghanizadeh, A., & Faghih, M. (2011). The impact of general medical condition on sleep in children with mental retardation. *Sleep and Breathing, 15*(1), 57-62. doi:10.1007/s11325-009-0312-0

Giannotti, F., & Cortesi, F. (2009). Family and cultural influences on sleep development. *Child and Adolescent Psychiatric Clinics of North America, 18*(4), 849-861. doi:10.1016/j.chc.2009.04.003

Greenberg, F., Lewis, R. A., Potocki, L., Glaze, D., Parke, J., Killian, J., . . . Lupski, J. R. (1996). Multi-disciplinary clinical study of Smith-Magenis syndrome (deletion 17p11.2). *American Journal of Medical Genetics, 62*(3), 247-254. doi:10.1002/(SICI)1096-8628(19960329)62:3<247::AID-AJMG9>3.0.CO;2-Q

Grigg-Damberger, M., & Ralls, F. (2013). Treatment strategies for complex behavioral insomnia in children with neurodevelopmental disorders. *Current Opinions in Pulmonary Medicine, 19*(6), 616-625. doi:10.1097/MCP.0b013e328365ab89

Gromov, I., & Gromov, D. (2009). Sleep and substance use and abuse in adolescents. *Child and Adolescent Psychiatric Clinics of North America, 18*(4), 929-946. doi:10.1016/j.chc.2009.04.004

Hare, D. J., Jones, S., & Evershed, K. (2006). Objective investigation of the sleep-wake cycle in adults with intellectual disabilities and autistic spectrum disorders. *Journal of Intellectual Disability Research, 50*(Pt 10), 701-710. doi:10.1111/j.1365-2788.2006.00830.x

Harvey, M. T., & Kennedy, C. H. (2002). Polysomnographic phenotypes in developmental disabilities. *International Journal of Developmental Neuroscience, 20*(3-5), 443-448. Retrieved from http://www.ncbi.nlm.nih.gov/pubmed/12175885

Hirshkowitz, M. (2004). Normal human sleep: an overview. *Medical Clinics of North America, 88*(3), 551-565, vii. doi:10.1016/j.mcna.2004.01.001

Hoddes, E., Zarcone, V., Smythe, H., Phillips, R., & Dement, W. C. (1973). Quantification of sleepiness: A new approach. *Psychophysiology, 10*(4), 431-436. Retrieved from http://www.ncbi.nlm.nih.gov/pubmed/4719486

Ivanenko, A., & Gururaj, B. R. (2009). Classification and epidemiology of sleep disorders. *Child and Adolescent Psychiatric Clinics of North America, 18*(4), 839-848. doi:10.1016/j.chc.2009.04.005

Johnson, K. P., Giannotti, F., & Cortesi, F. (2009). Sleep patterns in autism spectrum disorders. *Child and Adolescent Psychiatric Clinics of North America, 18*(4), 917-928. doi:10.1016/j.chc.2009.04.001

Judd, B. G., & Sateia, M. J. (2015, May 06, 2015). Classification of sleep disorders. Retrieved from http://www.uptodate.com/home

Kaplan, J., Fredrickson, P. A., & Richardson, J. W. (1991). Sleep and breathing in patients with the Prader-Willi syndrome. *Mayo Clinic Proceedings, 66*(11), 1124-1126. Retrieved from http://www.ncbi.nlm.nih.gov/pubmed/1943244

Khan, S. A., Heussler, H., McGuire, T., Dakin, C., Pache, D., Norris, R., . . . Charles, B. (2011). Therapeutic options in the management of sleep disorders in visually impaired children: A systematic review. *Clinical Therapeutics, 33*(2), 168-181. doi:10.1016/j.clinthera.2011.03.002

Kotagal, S. (2009). Hypersomnia in children: interface with psychiatric disorders. *Child and Adolescent Psychiatric Clinics of North America, 18*(4), 967-977. doi:10.1016/j.chc.2009.04.006

Krahn, L. E. (2005). Psychiatric disorders associated with disturbed sleep. *Seminars in Neurology, 25*(1), 90-96. doi:10.1055/s-2005-867077

Kronk, R., Bishop, E. E., Raspa, M., Bickel, J. O., Mandel, D. A., & Bailey, D. B., Jr. (2010). Prevalence, nature, and correlates of sleep problems among children with fragile X syndrome based on a large scale parent survey. *Sleep, 33*(5), 679-687. Retrieved from http://www.ncbi.nlm.nih.gov/pubmed/20469810

Maaskant, M., van de Wouw, E., van Wijck, R., Evenhuis, H. M., & Echteld, M. A. (2013). Circadian sleep-wake rhythm of older adults with intellectual disabilities. *Research in Developmental Disability, 34*(4), 1144-1151. doi:10.1016/j.ridd.2012.12.009

Mahowald, M. W. (2004). Parasomnias. *Medical Clinics of North Americ, 88*(3), 669-678 ix. doi:10.1016/j.mcna.2004.01.003

Markov, D., & Goldman, M. (2006). Normal sleep and circadian rhythms: neurobiologic mechanisms underlying sleep and wakefulness. *Psychiatric Clinics of North America, 29*(4), 841-853; abstract vii. doi:10.1016/j.psc.2006.09.008

McLaughlin Crabtree, V., & Williams, N. A. (2009). Normal sleep in children and adolescents. *Child and Adolescent Psychiatric Clinics of North America, 18*(4), 799-811. doi:10.1016/j.chc.2009.04.013

Mellman, T. A. (2006). Sleep and anxiety disorders. *Psychiatric Clinics of North America, 29*(4), 1047-1058; abstract x. doi:10.1016/j.psc.2006.08.005

Meltzer, L. J., & Mindell, J. A. (2006). Sleep and sleep disorders in children and adolescents. *Psychiatric Clinics of North America, 29*(4), 1059-1076; abstract x. doi:10.1016/j.psc.2006.08.004

Miano, S., Bruni, O., Leuzzi, V., Elia, M., Verrillo, E., & Ferri, R. (2004). Sleep polygraphy in Angelman syndrome. *Clinical Neurophysiology, 115*(4), 938-945. doi:10.1016/j.clinph.2003.11.004

Moline, M. L., Broch, L., & Zak, R. (2004). Sleep in women across the life cycle from adulthood through menopause. *Medical Clinics of North America, 88*(3), 705-736, ix. doi:10.1016/j.mcna.2004.01.009

Morgenthaler, T. I., Lee-Chiong, T., Alessi, C., Friedman, L., Aurora, R. N., Boehlecke, B., . . . Standards of Practice Committee of the American Academy of Sleep, M. (2007). Practice parameters for the clinical evaluation and treatment of circadian rhythm sleep disorders. An American Academy of Sleep Medicine report. *Sleep, 30*(11), 1445-1459. Retrieved from http://www.ncbi.nlm.nih.gov/pubmed/18041479

Neikrug, A. B., & Ancoli-Israel, S. (2015, 8/27/2015). Sleep wake disturbances and sleep disorders in patients with dementia. Retrieved from http://www.uptodate.com/home

Nofzinger, E. A. (2005). Functional neuroimaging of sleep. *Seminars in Neurology, 25*(1), 9-18. doi:10.1055/s-2005-867070

O'Brien, L. M. (2009). The neurocognitive effects of sleep disruption in children and adolescents. *Child and Adolescent Psychiatric Clinics of North America, 18*(4), 813-823. doi:10.1016/j.chc.2009.04.008

Okawa, M., Nanami, T., Wada, S., Shimizu, T., Hishikawa, Y., Sasaki, H., . . . Takahashi, K. (1987). Four congenitally blind children with circadian sleep-wake rhythm disorder. *Sleep, 10*(2), 101-110. Retrieved from http://www.ncbi.nlm.nih.gov/pubmed/3589322

Ollila, H. M., Ravel, J. M., Han, F., Faraco, J., Lin, L., Zheng, X., . . . Mignot, E. (2015). HLA-DPB1 and HLA class I confer risk of and protection from narcolepsy. *American Journal of Human Genetics, 96*(1), 136-146. doi:10.1016/j.ajhg.2014.12.010

Pary, R., Tobias, C. R., Webb, W. K., & Lippmann, S. B. (1996). Treatment of insomnia. Getting to the root of sleeping problems. *Postgraduate Medicine, 100*(5), 195-198, 201-110. Retrieved from http://www.ncbi.nlm.nih.gov/pubmed/8917333

Peterson, M. J., & Benca, R. M. (2006). Sleep in mood disorders. *Psychiatric Clinics of North America, 29*(4), 1009-1032; abstract ix. doi:10.1016/j.psc.2006.09.003

Plante, D. T., & Winkelman, J. W. (2006). Parasomnias. *Psychiatric Clinics of North America, 29*(4), 969-987; abstract ix. doi:10.1016/j.psc.2006.08.006

Poindexter, A. R., & Bihm, E. M. (1994). Incidence of short-sleep patterns in institutionalized individuals with profound mental retardation. *American Journal of Mental Retardation, 98*(6), 776-780. Retrieved from http://www.ncbi.nlm.nih.gov/pubmed/8054205

Provini, F., Lombardi, C., & Lugaresi, E. (2005). Insomnia in neurological diseases. *Seminars in Neurology, 25*(1), 81-89. doi:10.1055/s-2005-867074

Qureshi, A., & Lee-Chiong, T., Jr. (2004). Medications and their effects on sleep. *Medical Clinics of North America, 88*(3), 751-766, x. doi:10.1016/j.mcna.2004.01.007

Rajan, R., Benke, J. R., Kline, A. D., Levy, H. P., Kimball, A., Mettel, T. L., . . . Ishman, S. L. (2012). Insomnia in Cornelia de Lange syndrome. *International Journal of Pediatric Otorhinolaryngology, 76*(7), 972-975. doi:10.1016/j.ijporl.2012.03.008

Rama, A. N., & Kushida, C. A. (2004). Restless legs syndrome and periodic limb movement disorder. *Medical Clinics of North America, 88*(3), 653-667, viii. doi:10.1016/j.mcna.2004.01.004

Rechtschaffen, A., & Siegal, J. (2000). Sleep and dreaming. In J. H. S. E.R. Kandel, & T.M. Jessell (Eds.), *Principles of neural science* (4th ed., pp. 936-946). New York: McGraw-Hill, Health Professions Division.

Reid, G. J., Huntley, E. D., & Lewin, D. S. (2009). Insomnias of childhood and adolescence. *Child and Adolescent Psychiatric Clinics of North America, 18*(4), 979-1000. doi:10.1016/j.chc.2009.06.002

Reid, K. J., Chang, A. M., & Zee, P. C. (2004). Circadian rhythm sleep disorders. *Medical Clinics of North America, 88*(3), 631-651, viii. doi:10.1016/j.mcna.2004.01.010

Resta, O., Barbaro, M. P., Giliberti, T., Caratozzolo, G., Cagnazzo, M. G., Scarpelli, F., & Nocerino, M. C. (2003). Sleep related breathing disorders in adults with Down syndrome. *Downs Syndrome Research and Practice, 8*(3), 115-119. Retrieved from http://www.ncbi.nlm.nih.gov/pubmed/14502839

Roehrs, T., & Roth, T. (2005). Sleep and pain: interaction of two vital functions. *Seminars in Neurology, 25*(1), 106-116. doi:10.1055/s-2005-867079

Sadech, A. (1996). Stress, trauma, and sleep in children. *Child and Adolescent Psychiatric Clinics of North America, 5*(3), 685-670.

Schreck, K. A., & Mulick, J. A. (2000). Parental report of sleep problems in children with autism. *Journal of Autism and Developmental Disorders, 30*(2), 127-135. Retrieved from http://www.ncbi.nlm.nih.gov/pubmed/10832777

Shibagaki, M., Kiyono, S., & Matsuno, Y. (1985). Nocturnal sleep of severely mentally retarded children and adolescents: ontogeny of sleep patterns. *American Journal of Mental Deficiency, 90*(2), 212-216. Retrieved from http://www.ncbi.nlm.nih.gov/pubmed/4050881

Shibagaki, M., Kiyono, S., & Takeuchi, T. (1985). Nocturnal sleep in mentally retarded infants with cerebral palsy. *Electroencephalography and Clinical Neurophysiology, 61*(6), 465-471. Retrieved from http://www.ncbi.nlm.nih.gov/pubmed/2415320

Shneerson, J. (2000a). Assessment of sleep disorders *Handbook of sleep medicine* (pp. 59-69). Oxford; Malden, MA: Blackwell Science.

Shneerson, J. (2000b). Insomnia. *Handbook of sleep medicine* (pp. 78-109). Oxford ; Malden, MA: Blackwell Science.

Shneerson, J. (2000c). Physiological basis of sleep and wakefulness *Handbook of sleep medicine* (pp. 16-32). Oxford ; Malden, MA: Blackwell Science.

Stavinoha, R. C., Kline, A. D., Levy, H. P., Kimball, A., Mettel, T. L., & Ishman, S. L. (2011). Characterization of sleep disturbance in Cornelia de Lange Syndrome. *International Journal of Pediatric Otorhinolaryngology, 75*(2), 215-218. doi:10.1016/j.ijporl.2010.11.003

van de Wouw, E., Evenhuis, H. M., & Echteld, M. A. (2012). Prevalence, associated factors and treatment of sleep problems in adults with intellectual disability: a systematic review. *Research in Developmental Disabilities, 33*(4), 1310-1332. doi:10.1016/j.ridd.2012.03.003

Vatthauer, K. E., Craggs, J. G., Robinson, M. E., Staud, R., Berry, R. B., Perlstein, W. M., & McCrae, C. S. (2015). Sleep is associated with task-negative brain activity in fibromyalgia participants with comorbid chronic insomnia. *Journal of Pain Research, 8*, 819-827. doi:10.2147/JPR.S87501

Wise, M. S. (2004). Narcolepsy and other disorders of excessive sleepiness. *Medical Clinics of North America, 88*(3), 597-610, vii-viii. doi:10.1016/j.mcna.2004.02.001

Zucconi, M., & Bruni, O. (2001). Sleep disorders in children with neurologic diseases. *Seminars in Pediatric Neurology, 8*(4), 258-275. Retrieved from http://www.ncbi.nlm.nih.gov/pubmed/11768788

CHAPTER 21

Sexual Dysfunction

Georgina Parkes
Peter E. Langdon
Claire Reynolds
Daniel Wilson

In this chapter, we consider how diagnostic criteria for sexual dysfunctions can be used with people who have intellectual disabilities (ID), considering that very little is known about the prevalence of sexual dysfunctions amongst this population. The existing literature suggests that a lack of socio-sexual knowledge, poor support systems, mental health problems, and psychotropic medications are likely to be prominent etiological factors for the development of sexual dysfunction amongst people with ID. However, while people with ID experience atypical development within the cognitive, emotional, and social domains, their physical and sexual development is sometimes typical. Clinicians need to be aware of the impact of this dysynchronous development.

Within this chapter, the relevant biological, genetic, and psycho-social factors, including developmental factors, are reviewed. People with ID may experience extreme negative reactions to normal sexual behavior which results in concealment and, for some, suppression of sexuality, or, for others, antisocial behaviors. They are vulnerable to victimization, including sexual abuse, and may conform to the wishes of those around them. Clinicians need to conduct their assessmenttaking into account cognitive, developmental, and psychosocial factors which may impact upon presentation and course, and remain involved whilst mainstream services are accessed.

Sexual Dysfunction

Review of Diagnostic Criteria

The diagnostic criteria for sexual dysfunctions underwent a number of important changes with the publication of the DSM-5, reducing the number of disorders from eleven to seven, with one further diagnosis being applied to both sexes; namely, substance/medication induced sexual dysfunction. Most notably, within DSM-5, sexual dysfunctions appear in a separate chapter, while in the DSM-IV they were grouped as part of sexual and gender identity disorders. Other changes include replacing male orgasmic disorder with delayed ejaculation, while both vaginismus and dyspareunia are now described as genito-pelvic pain/penetration disorder. Male hypoactive sexual desire disorder appears separately, while sexual interest/arousal disorder replaces female hypoactive desire dysfunction and arousal dysfunction. Further changes include grouping together substance/medication induced sexual dysfunction which is no longer subclassified as male or female. Finally, sexual dysfunction not otherwise specified (NOS) is replaced by other specified sexual dysfunction and unspecified sexual dysfunction within DSM-5 (American Psychiatric Association, 2013).

General Description of Sexual Dysfunction

Sexual dysfunctions are a heterogeneous set of dysfunctions characterised by a clinically significant disturbance in a person's ability to respond sexually or to experience sexual pleasure; with the exception of substance/medication induced sexual dysfunction, they must be present for at least six months and be associated with substantial distress. An individual can have several dysfunctions at the same time. If the presenting problem is associated with a lack of sexual stimulation, a diagnosis would not be made. These dysfunctions are characterised by subtypes: *lifelong vs. acquired*, or *generalised vs. situational*. The subtypes can help to determine the etiology of a given dysfunction, as well as which treatments may be helpful for it. Additional severity criteria, namely *mild*, *moderate*, or *severe* are also used. Other important factors are to be considered which include partner factors, relationship factors, individual vulnerability factors, stressors/ life events, psychiatric comorbidity, cultural or religious factors, and as medical factors. Where it is the case that the etiology of the difficulty can be best explained by another mental health problem, then a diagnosis of a sexual dysfunction should not be made (American Psychiatric Association, 2013).

Within DSM-5, reference is made to the potential role that a lack of sexual knowledge may play within the development of some sexual dysfunctions. DSM-5 states "these cases may include, but are not limited to, conditions in which a lack of knowledge about effective simulation prevents the experience of arousal or orgasm." There are clear implications for people with ID who may have poor sociosexual knowledge which may inadvertently lead to symptoms akin or related to sexual dysfunction.

The sexual dysfunctions are described as: delayed ejaculation, erectile dysfunction (ED), female orgasmic disorder, female sexual interest/arousal disorder, genito-pelvic pain/ penetration disorder, male hypoactive sexual desire disorder, premature (early) ejaculation, substance/medication induced sexual dysfunction, other specified sexual dysfunction, and unspecified sexual dysfunction.

Summary of DSM-5 Criteria

Below is a brief description of the sexual dysfunctions, taken from DSM-5 (American Psychiatric Association, 2013).

■ *Delayed Ejaculation*

This is described as a marked delay or inability to achieve ejaculation during almost all instances of sexual activity with another person for at least six months. It can be associated with difficulties in conception and psychological distress, but prevalence in the general population is largely unknown. It increases with aging, and differential diagnoses of medical causes (e.g. retrograde ejaculation), including the role of substances and medication, need to be explored. Further, it is important to consider whether there is a psychological cause to the problem by considering whether there are any specific circumstances associated with successful ejaculation (e.g. paraphilic arousal, or ritualised sexual activity).

■ *Erectile Disorder*

At least one of three symptoms must be experienced for a period of no less than six months: difficulties with either 1) obtaining, or 2) maintaining erections, or 3) a marked decrease in erectile stiffness. These difficulties are often associated with low self-esteem and low self-confidence, but should not be better explained by a nonsexual mental health problem or substantial relationship difficulties. Consider whether nocturnal erections occur which may help identify the etiology. Cultural factors must also be taken into consideration. Again, prevalence within general population is largely unknown, although it is thought to increase with age. There is some evidence that this problem is associated with having sex with an unknown partner, substance misuse, and peer pressure. It can be an acquired disorder associated with medical conditions (e.g. cardiovascular disease, diabetes, spinal injury) and comorbid mental illnesses, particularly major depressive disorders, anxiety disorders, including neurotic personality traits. Alexithymia has been noted to be common in men with erectile dysfunction thought to have a psychological etiology.

■ *Female Orgasmic Disorder*

An absence, or a marked delay, infrequency, or reduced intensity of orgasmic sensations on almost all occasions during the previous six months. If orgasm is experienced through clitoral stimulation, but not vaginal penetration, the diagnosis is not made. Additionally, if there is inadequate sexual stimulation, then the diagnosis should be avoided. Causes are often multifactorial or unknown. Reported prevalence is 10% to 42% in the general population, but often these figures have been calculated without considering distress, so fewer may reach diagnostic threshold. It has been estimated that 10% of women never achieve orgasm in their lifetime. It is postulated that there may be a significant genetic contribution to orgasmic function in women. Reported rates of successful orgasm tend to be higher during masturbation than during sexual activity with a partner. There is an association with psychosocial problems, including relationship problems, and cultural factors are important to consider, as rates vary according to geographical region. There is also an association with vulvovaginal atrophy, but an association with menopause is unclear. It is important to consider interpersonal factors, including relationship problems, as well as other mental health problems, such as depression.

■ *Female Sexual Interest/Arousal Disorder*

This is characterised by a lack of or reduction in sexual interest and arousal presenting with at least three of the following six criteria for at least six months: 1) a reduction or lack of interest in sexual activities, 2) a reduction or absence of sexual thoughts and fantasy, 3) a reduction or absence of the initiation of sexual activity or response to a partner's attempt to initiate sexual activity, 4) a reduction or absence in sexual pleasure or excitement during sex activities, 5) a lack or reduction in sexual interest or arousal to stimuli that are associated with sexual activities, and 6) a reduction or absence of sensations during sexual activities. A lower desire for sexual activity than a partner is not sufficient for diagnosis, and relationship difficulties are important to consider. Prevalence is unknown in the general population. It is associated with depression, thyroid problems, anxiety, urinary incontinence, arthritis and irritable bowel syndrome. A thorough assessment of a person's beliefs and preferences is also indicated.

■ *Genito-pelvic Pain/Penetration Disorder*

This is defined as difficulties with vaginal penetration, vulvovaginal or pelvic pain when attempting to penetrate or during intercourse, fear and anxiety associated with vulvovaginal and pelvic pain, and tense pelvic floor muscles upon attempted penetration during at least the previous six months. Diagnosis can be made on one symptom dimension, but all four should be assessed. Difficulty having intercourse is commonly with a partner, but it can also be the inability to undergo a medical examination, or insert a tampon, etc. Marked pain can be either superficial or pelvic, and therefore may not be experienced until deeper penetration. Typically, the pain will be reproduced during examination. Genito-pelvic pain/penetration disorder may occur with other sexual dysfunctions, and the condition may lead to avoidance of sexual activity or intimate situations. Prevalence in the general population is unknown, but approximately 15% of North American women report recurrent pain on intercourse. Sexual and physical abuse has been considered to be a predictor of this disorder, but this is controversial. Cultural factors should be considered as there is some evidence that the prevalence may be higher in some non-Western countries. Onset can be preceded by vaginal infections, and even when resolved symptoms can persist, and it is important to consider somatic symptoms. Currently, within DSM-5, this diagnosis is only given to women, even though there is evidence that men can experience genito-pelvic pain. Other medical conditions must be considered such as lichen sclerosis, endometriosis, and pelvic inflammatory disease. Menopausal symptoms, vaginal dryness and age are common predictors.

■ *Male Hypoactive Sexual Desire Disorder*

This is defined as reduced or absent sexual fantasy or desire for sexual activities for a period of not less than six months. It is important to consider whether such issues can be accounted for by differences between partners. A reduced frequency in the initiation of sexual activities may be preferential, rather than a symptom akin to hypoactive sexual desire disorder. Difficulties with reduced fantasy and desire may also be associated with difficulties with erections or ejaculation and reduced frequency of masturbation. There is a correlation with reduced fantasy/desire and age. Mental health problems, including depression and anxiety, are related, as is alcohol abuse. Attitudes toward sex and sexuality are relevant, as is sexual knowledge and early trauma. Issues such as hyper-prolactinemia and hypogonadism must be considered along with other endocrinological factors.

■ *Premature (Early) Ejaculation*

This means ejaculation within 1 minute of penetration which is persistent and unwanted for at least six months. Within DSM-5, this is confined to vaginal penetration, and specific comment is made that no time limits have been set for other sexual activities which would include manual stimulation, oral and anal sex, and well as other sexual activities. However, DSM-5 also recommends that the duration of 1 minute can be applied to men who are not exclusively heterosexual and within different sexual activities. The prevalence of concerns about premature ejaculation has been estimated to be in the region of 20 to 30%, while the application of the time cut-off reduces this to 1 to 3%. Younger men may experience premature ejaculation early in life which dissipates with time, while some men may acquire the problem. There may be a relationship between anxiety disorders, self-esteem, and premature ejaculation; cultural and religious factors need to be assessed.

■ *Substance/Medication-induced Sexual Dysfunction*

This is defined as a sexual dysfunction that has developed during or after substance misuse, stopping substance misuse, or following the introduction of medication. The symptoms must be produced by the substance or medication. The difficulties must not be associated with delirium. Psychotropic medications are associated with sexual dysfunction including antidepressants, opioids, and antipsychotics.

■ *Other Specified Sexual Dysfunction*

This diagnosis is reserved for people who present with sexual dysfunction that does not meet the diagnostic criteria of any of the other sexual dysfunctions. The rationale as to why the diagnostic criteria for other disorders are not met must be justified.

■ *Unspecified Sexual Dysfunction*

This diagnosis is similar to *other specified sexual dysfunction* because the diagnostic criteria of specified sexual dysfunctions are not met, but in this instance, a rationale as to why the diagnostic criteria are not met is not given. This may be because of insufficient clinical information.

Issues Related to Diagnosis in Persons with ID

There are several important factors to consider when attempting to use the current diagnostic criteria for sexual dysfunctions with people who have ID. These include societal attitudes and socio-sexual knowledge; the role of support staff; distress; mental health problems; abuse; and medication.

For many people with ID, their support staff are an integral part of their everyday lives. There is some evidence to suggest that support staff have increasingly liberal views toward sexual expression by people with ID (Herzog et al., 2005; Isojarvi, Repo, Pakarinen, Lukkarinen, & Myllylä, 1995; Morrell et al., 2005; Stimmel & Gutierrez, 2006), although the view that some individuals should be subject to sterilization remains (Aunos & Feldman, 2002). Löfgren-Mårtenson (2004) reported that younger people with ID appear to have intercourse infrequently, and parents and staff members were seen to be regulating socio-sexual activities. There is some evidence that older carers and parents may have more conservative attitudes about sexual expression than younger carers (Aunos & Feldman, 2002; Cuskelly & Bryde, 2004).

Support staff are "gatekeepers" for people with ID. This means that they often make decisions on behalf of people with ID and regulate all aspects of their lives, including access to knowledge, as well as opportunities for social and sexual encounters. As such, the person and the carer's own attitudes, including their cultural beliefs, are very important to consider when deciding whether someone with ID is experiencing a sexual dysfunction.

Distress is an important criterion within DSM-5. For a diagnosis of a sexual dysfunction the presence of substantial distress is required. However, for people with ID, who may have poor socio-sexual knowledge and reduced opportunities for sexual expression, it is sometimes unclear how distress is experienced. It can be hidden or may present as general irritability, in which case distress associated with sexual dysfunction would not be obvious. There may be concern from carers that increasing socio-sexual knowledge and understanding of sexual dysfunction may lead to an increase in distress, or increased sexual expression, which some may wish to avoid.

There is an elevated prevalence and incidence of mental health problems amongst people with ID (Herzog et al., 2005; Isojarvi et al., 1995; Morrell et al., 2005; Stimmel & Gutierrez, 2006). There is also a relationship between mental health problems, including substance misuse, and sexual dysfunction (Herzog et al., 2005; Isojarvi et al., Morrell et al., 2005; Stimmel & Gutierrez, 2006). It has been estimated that between 1.2% and 27% of people with ID have mental health problems that are not adequately treated (Balogh, Ouellette-Kuntz, Bourne, Lunsky, & Colantonio, 2008) which has implications for our understanding of sexual dysfunction amongst people with ID. While in some cases, people with ID may have a genetic vulnerability leading to an increased risk of developing mental health problems, there remains evidence that people with ID can experience substantial traumatic events, including both sexual and physical abuse (Herzog et al., 2005; Isojarvi et al., 1995; Morrell et al., 2005; Stimmel & Gutierrez, 2006). Together, these factors, including a history of traumatic events, are likely to lead to an increased vulnerability to the development of sexual dysfunction amongst populations of people with ID.

Accessible information for people with ID is sparse. Clinicians should routinely enquire about sexual symptoms before prescription of antipsychotics and again at follow up.

Healthcare professionals need to be aware of these needs. Men may find masturbation important, even if they do not have a sexual partner, and erectile dysfunction would be problematic. Asking about sexual needs could be included in the annual health check, to which all people with ID are entitled within primary care. Words for anatomy may need to be adapted to those easier to say and understand. Treatment of underlying physical causes should be obtainable and counselling should be done by a trained person experienced in working with people with ID. Joint working with ID staff and sexual health professionals is highly recommended, and prescription medication for erectile dysfunction may be appropriate but needs to be explained properly.

Development and Course

Another important factor to consider in children, adolescents, and adults with ID is that problems may arise due to lack of basic knowledge about their anatomy and sex education. For family and paid carer alike, it can be difficult to talk about sex, and it is not necessarily something any of us do openly. This can inhibit recognition of difficulties and almost lead to a feeling of relief that the person with ID is "asexual" and this does not need to be addressed, when in fact a person may have a sexual dysfunction requiring treatment.

People with ID may present with sexual dysfunctions much later in life than the general population. People may have been dissuaded from expressing their feelings by social, institutional, family, or peer pressure. Other important factors include the attitudes of gatekeepers who may have previously responded to requests or conversations about sex with negative reactions. Difficulty expressing sexual needs or having a poorly formed sense of self identity may also play a role.

Prevalence

There is very little data on the prevalence of sexual dysfunctions in people with ID. In the general population, there have been global studies that have reported rates of sexual dysfunction at 38% in women and 29% in men (Laumann et al., 2005; Moreira et al., 2005; reveiwed in Bhugra & Colombini, 2013). Rates vary across cultures; however, often the reported prevalence remains high. For example, another study reviewed in Bhugra and Colombini (2013) reported that the lifetime prevalence is approximately 50% for married couples, and 97.5% for gay men, with 52.5% having current concerns. As healthcare systems around the world improve, people with ID will have increased life expectancies, and as many sexual dysfunctions are associated with increasing age (e.g. erectile dysfunction), these may grow more prevalent amongst people with ID, bearing in mind that we know little about the genuine prevalence of sexual dysfunctions amongst people with ID.

However, most people in the general population do not seek professional help; this is reported to be as low as one in five of those with dysfunctions. Given this difficulty of the general population to seek help, people with ID are likely to seek help even less, and their problems are likely to remain secret and hidden.

Differential Diagnosis

The differential diagnosis is similar to DSM-5 and includes the following:

Depression
Anxiety
Schizophrenia
Interpersonal problems
Relationship issues
Stress
Low self esteem
Affairs
Religious conflict
Issues around child bearing
Differences in cultural expectations
Physical illness

Functional Consequences

Erectile and other sexual dysfunctions are likely to be a hidden problem for men with ID (Parkes & Keoghan 2007). Some men with ID overcompensate, behaving in a more stereotypical male, or even aggressive, way while others maintain a "childlike" self-image, which carers may encourage.

These overcompensating behaviors can be aggressive and potentially criminal in nature, such as masturbating in public places within a shared home, possibly due to a lack of understanding, or previous sexual abuse, or even boredom. An individual's anxiety levels can be high if they are unable to express themselves or are excessively sheltered (in a misguided attempt to protect them) and are treated like a child by family or professional carers. Some may develop psychiatric symptoms such as depression or anxiety, although these can remit when the core sexual dysfunction is addressed.

There are particular difficulties with homosexual expression and ID, as early attempts at disclosure may lead to negative, oppressive, or even catastrophic reactions by family or carers, prompting subsequent social conformity, denial, and considerable internal distress or an internal agreement that they become asexual. They may have difficulty establishing intimacy with others and consequently lack any fulfilling or meaningful sexual or non-sexual relationships.

A true exploration of a person's self-concept and sexual identity, as well as understanding of basic concepts around anatomy and sex education should happen as soon as possible.

For women, issues can be around low fertility, being unable to have children and subsequent feelings of loss or of being less of a woman. Again difficulties can be hidden; depression can be common as well as low self-esteem.

Comorbidity

Sexual dysfunction can co-occur with any mental illness but is commonly seen as a consequence of treatment for mental illness, as antipsychotic, antiepileptic, and antidepressant medication can produce sexual dysfunctions. Sometimes these side effects can be treated separately, for example treating erectile dysfunctions with sildenafil (Parkes & Keoghan (2007) if the continuation of the psychotropic medication is deemed necessary in terms of risk assessment. Person-centred planning is important in all these cases.

Sexual dysfunction can also be a consequence of a mental disorder:

ASD
Depression
Sexual abuse and trauma
Generalized anxiety disorder
Problems with identity, including sexual and self-concept
Social phobia
Psychotic disorders

Application of Diagnostic Criteria to People with ID

There has been no known research looking at applying the diagnostic criteria to people with ID and sexual dysfunctions.

General Considerations

Longer assessments are required in people with ID as their self-concept needs to be explored for reasons described above. Lack of sexual knowledge needs to be addressed, and a medication history taken.

Methodology

A literature search was conducted in peer-reviewed psychiatric, nursing, and social health care journals from the years 1966 to December 2014. The sources searched were MEDLINE, AMED, CINAHL, British Nursing Index, EMBASE, PsycINFO, Health Business Elite and HMIC using the terms learning disab*, learning difficulty, Mental retard*, mental handicap, intellectual disab*, Disabled person, Developmental disab*, Retard*, Mental, were combined with Sexual dysfunction, Disorders of desire, Hypoactive sexual desire disorder, Sexual aversion disorder, Lack/loss of sexual desire, Sexual aversion/lack of sexual enjoyment, Excessive sexual drive, Disorders of arousal, Vaginal dryness, Impotence, Female sexual arousal disorder, Male erectile disorder, Failure of genital response, Disorders of orgasm (delay, absence, premature ejaculation), Female orgasmic disorder, Male orgasmic disorder, Premature ejaculation, Orgasmic dysfunction, Premature ejaculation, Disorders of sexual pain, Vaginismus, Substance-induced dysfunction, Subnormal and sexual dysfunction, female orgasmic disorder, female arousal disorder, dyspareunia.

In addition to searching computerised databases, we used the ancestry method and contacted researchers with an interest in this area.

Review Research Applying to People with ID

The above searches revealed 6 papers of interest, Giami (1987), Lambert (2001), Kaplan (2004), Parkes & Keoghan (2007), Greydanus & Omar (2008), Taylor Gomez (2012). These were expert opinion pieces and relevant summaries of the literature but not systematic literature reviews.

Giami (1987) is mainly an opinion piece around sexuality and perceived attitudes towards people with disability. He describes a survey which he undertook in 1983, where people without ID were surveyed; the sexuality of those with ID was denied, and families still regarded their adult offspring as children. Only a minority of parents accepted masturbation. Same sex relationships, sexual intercourse was even more denied. Contraception was discussed, and he talked about females with ID having sterilization on the pretext of a minor abdominal operations.

Lambert (2001) is a review of literature regarding epilepsy and sexual functioning. No methodology is mentioned. It discusses that many of the papers excluded people with ID. One paper reviewed did find a positive correlation between higher IQ and having had intercourse at all (Fenwick et al., 1985; reviewed in Lambert, 2001). They surveyed men with mean IQ of 74 (range 34 to 115). Many difficulties were described in this group; 35% had never experienced spontaneous erections on waking, 48% had never had an orgasm, with 64% never having one in the past year. Only 21% had ever had intercourse. Another paper reviewed by Lambert (Gebhard, 1973) assessed the sexual functioning of men with ID who didn't have epilepsy and found 93% masturbated with an average frequency of once a week. Indicating, possibly, that the previous sexual dysfunctioning described in Fenwick et al. was more likely to be related to epilepsy and anti-epileptic drugs(AEDs) than to IQ.

Kaplan (2004) reviews the literature relating to AEDs. He cites 134 papers but no methodology is discussed. The paper reviews the sexual dysfunctional side effects of AEDs. He also discusses epilepsy and other neurological conditions and their association with a reduction in libido, arousal, and sexual activity as well as impaired fertility. AEDs also cause depression, weight gain, and obesity and decrease sexual activity.

Parkes and Keoghan (2007) provide some background information but no systematic review. They report on a case of a man with ID who experienced erectile dysfunction as a side-effect of medication. Due to his offending behavior, and a relapse after a reduction in medication, he was then prescribed sildenafil to good effect which increased his compliance with the rest of his treatment plan.

Greydanus and Omar (2008) discuss normal adolescent development of sexuality and the impact of having a disability and/or a chronic illness on this development. 199 papers are reviewed, but again no methodology is stated. They report on the difficulties adolescents have emancipating themselves from their parents and how much more difficult that is with a disability and the challenge of developing a positive and secure self-image. The authors also discuss parents' wish to overprotect and the guilt they may experience over having a disabled child.

Having a disability may lead to rejection or criticism from peers and increase stress which in itself may have a negative impact on the disability and chronic illness. A lot of adolescents dwell on body image and those with disability may have to tolerate real deviations from the ideal desired body image. They also mention the increased risk of sexual abuse and incest in this group.

Taylor Gomez (2012) reviews 63 papers, but again no methodology is described. She discusses the history of suffering people with ID have had to contend with (such as forced sterilization) and the misconceptions they continue to face around sexuality. For example, people with ID are thought of in extremes whether as asexual or hypersexual. They face problems when marrying or wanting to marry. There is a discussion around how services respond by sometimes being restrictive or aversive. Ideas about more inclusive ways of supporting people with ID are discussed.

Evaluating the Level of Evidence

The current literature consists of Type V evidence only.

Adults with Mild to Moderate ID

Adults with mild to moderate ID present with similar issues to that of the general population, but in particular issues of secrecy, especially around disclosing homosexuality, lack of sexual knowledge, and basic anatomy differ from the general population. They are more likely to be viewed as asexual or hyper-sexual. They may have real life body image difficulties to contend with impacting on self-esteem. They are also at higher risk of sexual abuse than the general population.

Adults with Severe or Profound ID

In this population normal sexual behavior such as intercourse in the general population is not expected as capacity to consent would be an issue, making it a crime for the person who does have capacity. Sexual consent would not be possible in this group. Because of this sexual dysfunctions may be less likely to be thought of and assessed. Masturbation would be typical for some; however they would need support to ensure it is carried out in appropriate situations, e.g. in their bedroom, in private.

Excessive masturbation or inappropriate sexual behavior towards others can be around self-stimulation (sensory stimulation), boredom, and/or sexual abuse.

Children and Adolescents with ID

Children with Intellectual Disabilities

In cases of sexualized behavior in children with ID, considerations to make are: high vulnerability to abuse, boredom and self-stimulation, sensory needs, and lack of awareness. Also this may be due to sexual exploration, as in children in the general population.

Adolescents with Intellectual Disabilities

Adolescents with mild ID go through the same psychological developmental stages as typically developing adolescents, although there may be a developmental lag (reviewed in Greydanus

& Omar, 2008). Adolescents with ID are often aware of their disabilities and may have difficulty emancipating themselves from their parents and establishing a secure self-image. They can have the same sex drives and desire for coital behavior as their typically developing counterparts, but this is not always accepted. Parents often worry about dating, sexual abuse, pregnancy, and infections, but adolescents require education to avoid these concerns. Parents may not always accept that their adolescent children with ID have legal rights to such information and can be judged competent to handle sexual intimacy. This needs to be balanced against the need to protect those with ID from sexual exploitation. Parents who have a disabled child may mourn the loss of a perfect child and experience guilt associated with having a disabled child, seeking to protect them from life's difficulties; overprotection may encourage dependence and reduce transition through normal emancipation life stages.

Adolescents with an ID may have difficulties with their self-image which may then impact on sexual development. Stress from attempting to negotiate sexual development can exacerbate the effects of disability or chronic illness. Rejection or criticism from peers for being different can also be experienced. All adolescents can become preoccupied with body image, especially with the onset of secondary sex characteristic development; those with developmental disability also have to tolerate real abnormalities and deviations from society's desired body image. Timing of puberty can change with disability which can affect development of intimacy.

Some disorders or medications are associated with a delay in maturation, or cause hypogonadism. Others can cause precocious puberty, where sexual issues and experimentation may occur. Some disorders may be associated with physical characteristics that are judged to be unattractive which may affect developing self-esteem. Inadvertently, difficulties with self-esteem and self-concept may lead to risky sexual behaviors amongst some individuals as well as supressing them.

Young women with ID are at higher risk of being sexually abused (evidence summarised in Greydanus & Omar, 2008). Sex education and gynaecological care (including smear tests, tests for sexually transmitted infections, and Human Papilloma Virus vaccinations) are important and may provide an opportunity for disclosure of abuse, as well as providing routine medical care, and should be offered to those with ID. Contraception should be discussed with young women who are sexually active and those who have questions; different contraceptive options have different issues (ease of use or side effects) which should be considered.

As discussed earlier, sexual dysfunction may arise due to lack of proper education, and during adolescence, sexual expression and reproductive capacity should be addressed by informed professionals. This helps correct misconceptions and encourages healthy sexual functioning. Physical deformities including paraplegia, amputations, ostomies or abnormal genitalia may interfere with sexual expression, and require special counselling. Many may feel inadequate compared to "normal" peers which can lead to dysfunctions. Chronic illness may mean enjoyment of sexuality is limited even if physical functioning is normal.

As part of their generalized developmental delay, adolescents with intellectual disability progress more slowly through the different developmental stages later in life. Adolescence as a psychological life stage may be both delayed and also prolonged. However, their bodies often go through the development of secondary sexual characteristics and hormone surges at similar ages as those without such delay. Basic sex education and body awareness in young people with ID is often lacking. This can lead to distorted views of sexual identity and roles as discussed elsewhere in this chapter.

Limitations in Applying DSM-5 Criteria to People with ID

People with ID may be less likely to complain of sexual dysfunction. There are low rates of people coming forward with problems despite the risk factors already discussed. The DSM-5 criteria apply to people with ID as they are but are limited in that people may not have the knowledge, awareness, support, or understanding to be able to identify that they have a problem and seek help and thus a diagnosis. People with ID may present with other features such as mental illness, anxiety, challenging behavior, and aggression, all can cause sexual dysfunctions or be caused by sexual dysfunctions. It is, therefore, important a thorough assessment is undertaken.

Etiology and Pathogenesis

Sexual dysfunction in people with ID would be broadly similar in etiology as in the general population, which is to say, as a consequence of a multifactorial developmental process in which biological, genetic, psychological, social, and cultural factors play a role. In addition, and particularly in relation to people with ID, concrete thinking, sexual abuse, chronic illness, neurological conditions including epilepsy are more common and are associated with sexual dysfunctions.

Biological Factors

The prescribing of psychotropic medications to people with ID is exceptionally high. Tsiouris, Kim, Brown, Pettinger, & Cohen (2013) surveyed 4049 adults with ID in the state of New York, reporting that 58% were prescribed one or more psychotropic medications, including antipsychotics, antidepressants, mood stabilizers, and anxiolytics. Medication was often prescribed in order to treat challenging behaviors.

Many of these medications are associated with sexual dysfunction, including antidepressants (Herzog et al., 2005; Isojarvi et al., 1995; Morrell et al., 2005; Stimmel & Gutierrez, 2006), antipsychotics, bearing in mind that some of the newer antipsychotics have less of an impact upon sexual functioning, (Herzog et al., 2005; Isojarvi et al., 1995; Morrell et al., 2005; Stimmel & Gutierrez, 2006), anticonvulsants (Herzog et al., 2005; Isojarvi et al., 1995; Morrell et al., 2005; Stimmel & Gutierrez, 2006), and mood stabilisers (La Torre et al., 2014).

There is also a population of people with ID who are prescribed androgen-depleting medications, as well as antidepressants and antipsychotics, as a consequence of inappropriate sexual behavior. Sajith, Morgan, & Clarke, (2008) reviewed the literature in this area, drawing attention to the possibility that these medications may be prescribed because they are a potentially easy option, but nevertheless lead to a reduction in sexual expression and the development of substance/medication-induced sexual dysfunction.

Considering that people with ID are more likely to be prescribed psychotropic medications, it would be anticipated that there would be an increased rate of substance/medication-induced sexual dysfunction amongst people with ID, although there is currently no associated prevalence data.

Women with epilepsy, especially those on anti-eplieptic drugs, (AEDs), are at increased risk of endocrine dysfunction and infertility; men with epilepsy may also be affected. Stigma may be an issue as well as impaired libido, sexual function, and menstrual cycle abnormalities. People with severe neurological conditions can experience impaired social functioning and have lower marriage rates, decreased libido, decreased incidence of reproductive sexual activity, and impaired fertility. AEDs can be sedating and may decrease wake-time activities including sexual activity and contribute to feelings of listlessness and depression. Some AEDs are associated with weight gain which may decrease physical activity, increase obesity, and impair social pairing and sexual activity. Sexual arousal, functioning, and fertility have been shown to be impaired in epilepsy. In focal temporal lobe epilepsy genital blood flow was impaired in arousal. In 5/6 men with focal epilepsy who had erectile complaints, one study revealed impaired nocturnal erectile function. Many women with epilepsy experience vaginismus, lack of lubrication and dyspareunia despite normal libido. Endogenous sex hormone levels may be affected by AEDs which are also metabolized in the P-450 cytochromes in the liver (as are sex hormones) (reviewed in Kaplan, 2004).

AEDS are also used as mood stabilizers in other disorders and may have similar effects in non-epileptic patients.

Sexual disorders including hypo-sexuality are common in people with epilepsy (reviewed in Lambert, 2001). Epilepsy is much more common in those with ID although many studies excluded those with ID. Sexual disorders can be directly related to the seizure (ictal) and/or unrelated to the seizures (inter-ictal); the most common is hypo sexuality which occurs inter-ictally. There are many studies in men with epilepsy, but less involving women.

Causes of sexual dysfunction in epilepsy include reduced desire and impairment of functioning, with a likely neurophysiological basis. The same neurological deficit which has caused epilepsy can also be responsible for causing a sexual dysfunction (for example, dementia, cerebrovascular disorders, and brain injury, especially those involving frontal or temporal lobes). However, many studies exclude people with these types of neurological disorders, and, therefore, information and evidence is limited by this.

One study found a positive correlation between having a higher IQ and having had sexual intercourse (Fenwick et al., 1985.) as discussed earlier in this chapter. One third who were sexually active had difficulty achieving and maintaining an erection, a quarter were anxious about sexual activity causing a fit, and 8.3% reported they had had a fit during intercourse or masturbation.

Seizures and AEDs can affect the hypothalamic-pituitary-gonadal axis in both sexes which causes changes to hormones and sexuality. Testosterone levels can affect sexual activity, as can high prolactin levels and luteinizing hormone in men. In women with epilepsy a higher (25-33% vs. 10%) rate of menstrual disorders is seen, compared to those without.

AEDs are also linked with hypo-sexuality. Carbamazepine has shown sexual side effects in people without epilepsy. Lowered androgen and increased estrogen levels have been shown in men on AEDs, and low semen volume, low sperm count, abnormal morphology and low motility were seen. Phenytoin and valproate have been shown to affect semen and sperm. AEDS that are liver-enzyme inducing have been linked to elevated testosterone and sex hormone binding globulin. There is an increased level of psychiatric disorders seen in epilepsy and as discussed before psychotropic medication is linked to sexual dysfunction.

Psychosocial effects are seen in those with epilepsy, i.e. reduced friendships and relationships. A study found people with epilepsy identified sexual relationships as an area of concern (Chaplin, Yepez, Shorvon, & Floyd, 1990).

Psychotropic medication can also cause side effects such as hyper-prolactinaemia, weight gain, and sexual dysfunction. People with ID are also at higher risk of developing movement disorders from extended use of antipsychotics.

Parkinson's can affect arousal, orgasm, and low sexual desire in women, and in men erectile dysfunction, sexual dissatisfaction and premature ejaculation (reviewed in Taylor Gomez, 2012). Concomitant depression and antidepressants can make it worse. In multiple sclerosis, sexual dysfunction is reported due to pain, numbness, fatigue, coordination problems, and body self-image. Spinal cord injury or dysfunction causes similar problems. People with serious mental illness in one study who had been living in institutional and or community housing found problems with sexual isolation – reasons included limited access to potential partners, sexual dysfunction, and in the main, medication side effects, history of abuse, fearing disease or pregnancy, moral or religious doubts, and sexually restrictive cultures (Taylor Gomez, 2012). All these issues will also affect people with ID.

Genetic Factors

People with ID are more likely than the general population to have genetic syndromes. These can have specific features that are linked to sexual dysfunction including the following:

Downs syndrome is associated with hypogonadism.

Prader Willi syndrome is associated with small penis-size, hypogonadism in males, and delayed puberty in females.

Keinfelter's syndrome (47 XXY or more than one X chromosome in males) is associated with reduced body hair, smaller genitals, decreased libido, and increased breast tissue. It is also associated with reading difficulties and some speech problems, although IQ can be normal (Eunice Kennedy Schriver National Institute of Child Health and Human Development, 2013).

Turner's syndrome (45 X) is associated with amenorrhea, lack of breast tissue, and infertility.

Fragile X syndrome is associated with macro-orchidism and premature menopause.

Psychosocial Factors

People with ID have historically been subject to sexual segregation (summarised in Taylor Gomez, 2012), confinement, marital prohibition, and legally-sanctioned sterilisation. There are misconceptions and fallacies, as previously discussed, around sexuality of people with ID; they may be regarded as asexual, or hypersexual. Today having an ID can mean lack of privacy, lack of education, limited economic independence, being tested on deficits not strengths, being "other" or "captive of care," having to be grateful and compliant, being at higher risk of abuse, and having no means of communicating. Social barriers also exist: being poor, having a low level of education and many people often enter their adult lives with few qualifications and little or nothing to do in the way of occupation or activity. Their social networks are often limited.

Services can respond to sexuality differently; they can be restrictive or aversive and not offer ways for expression or privacy. There can be a fear that talking about sex will lead to abuse or to encourage people to sexually offend. False assumptions can be made such as that people with autism will not be able to connect in deep relationships. Less support has been found for homosexual relationships and sexual intercourse as opposed to masturbation in general.

People with ID may not have any viable means of communication to convey their needs and desires. Poor life experiences lead to limited knowledge of the body, sexuality and sexual expression. Sexual dysfunction in people with ID can present to clinical services as challenging behavior or irritability. People with ID want to experience dating, intimacy, and sexual interaction but feel unsure how to meet people and talk to them (reviewed in Taylor Gomez 2012). The right to take risks is not as accepted as it is in the general population.

People with a disability are perceived as sexually undesirable or less desirable than non-disabled people – which leads to the person's perceptions of him- or herself being sexually incompetent. There is a lack of positive role models as well as education and information.

Developmental Factors

People with ID usually develop physically at the same rate as typically developing adults, but their social, emotional and psychosexual development can be dysynchronous as previously discussed.

A key criterion may be related to their level of sexual knowledge and understanding. They may also need support to meet potential partners and spend time alone with them, facilitated by either family or paid carers.

It is impossible to discuss sex, sexuality, or sexual dysfunction without considering the history of societal attitudes toward people with ID. Historically, people with ID were stopped from having sexual lives in order to prevent them from reproducing "to protect society" (Oliver, Anthony, Leimkuhl, & Skillman, 2002). Such developments led to sterilization programs for people with ID. Sterilization often took place without the consent of the individual, continuing well into the 20th century (Stansfield, Holland, & Clare, 2007), as well as today.

As part of this culture, people with ID have not been taught appropriate socio-sexual knowledge. Often, people with ID have been desexualized, and sexual behaviors have been supressed or punished (Craft, 1987). There is evidence that people with ID do not have age-appropriate sexual knowledge (Herzog et al., 2005; Isojarvi et al. 1995; Morrell et al., 2005; Stimmel & Gutierrez, 2006), and as such they may not be able to recognize whether they are experiencing difficulties with sexual functioning. Similarly, this attitude is likely to have affected the discussion and understanding of sexual dysfunction in people with ID.

More recently there has begun to be a change in attitude. However, opportunity for sexual expression has to be balanced with protection from exploitation. Some males and females can become victims of offenders resulting in them being groomed for abuse or into prostitution or sex work. Assessing capacity to engage in relationships is key and is made more difficult when the relationship is abusive.

In less extreme cases, sex can be viewed negatively by carers and as wrong by people with ID themselves, leading to feelings of guilt or shame.

Application of Diagnostic Criteria

Diagnostic criteria remains as in DSM-5. No modifications.

References

American Psychiatric Association. (2013). *Diagnostic and statistical manual of mental disorders* (5th ed.). Washington, DC: American Psychiatric Publishing.

Aunos, M., & Feldman, A. A. (2002). Attitudes towards sexuality, sterilization and parenting rights of persons with intellectual disabilities. *Journal of Applied Research in Intellectual Disabilities, 15*(4), 285-296.

Balogh, R., Ouellette-Kuntz, H., Bourne, L., Lunsky, Y., & Colantonio, A. (2008). Organizing health care services for persons with an intellectual disability. *Cochrane Database of Systematic Reviews*, 4, 1-41.

Bhugra, D., & Colombini, G. (2013). Sexual dysfunction: Classification and assessment. *Advances in Psychiatric Treatment, 19*, 48-55.

Chaplin, J. E., Yepez, R., Shorvon, S.,& Floyd, M.(1990). A quantitative approach to measuring the social effects of epilepsy. *Neuroepiedmiology, 9*, 151-158.

Craft, A. (1987). *Mental handicap and sexuality: Issues and perspectives.* Kent: Costello.

Cuskelly, M., & Bryde, R. (2004). Attitudes towards the sexuality of adults with an intellectual disability: parents, support staff, and a community sample. *Journal of Intellectual and Developmental Disability, 29*(3), 255-264.

Eunice Kennedy Shriver National Institute of Child Health and Human Development. (2013). What are common symptoms of Klinefelter syndrome (KS)? Retrieved from https://www.nichd.nih.gov/health/topics/klinefelter/conditioninfo/Pages/symptoms.aspx#17.

Fenwick, P. B., Toone, B. K., Wheeler, M. J., Nanjee, M. N., Grant , R., & Brown, D. (1985). Sexual behaviour in a centre for epilepsy. *Acta Scandinavia*; *71*, 428-435

Gebhard, P. H., (1973). Sexual behaviour of the mentally retarded. In F. De La Cruz & G.D. LaVeck (Eds.), *Human sexuality and the mentally retarded* (pp. 29-49). New York Brunner/Mazel.

Giami, A., (1987). Coping with the sexuality of the diabled: A comparison of the physically disabled and the mentally retarded. *International Journal of Rehabilitation Research, 10*(1), 41-48.

Greydanus, D. E., & Omar H. A. (2008). Sexuality issues and gynecologic care of adolescents with developmental disabilities. *Pediatric Cliniccs of North America, 55*(6), 1315-1335.

Herzog, A., Drislane, F., Schomer, D., Pennell, P., Bromfield, E., Dworetzky, B., . . . Frye, C. (2005). Differential effects of antiepileptic drugs on sexual function and hormones in men with epilepsy. *Neurology, 65*(7), 1016-1020.

Isojarvi, J. I., Repo, M., Pakarinen, A. J., Lukkarinen, O., & Myllylä, V. V. (1995). Carbamazepine, phenytoin, sex hormones, and sexual function in men with epilepsy. *Epilepsia, 36*(4), 366-370.

Kaplan, P. W. (2004). Reporductive health effects and teratogenicity of antiepileptic drugs. *Neurology, 63*(10), S13-23

La Torre, A., Giupponi, G., Duffy, D., Pompili, M., Grözinger, M., Kapfhammer, H., & Conca, A. (2014). Sexual dysfunction related to psychotropic drugs: A critical review. Part III: Mood stabilizers and anxiolytic drugs. *Pharmacopsychiatry, 47*(1), 1-6.

Lambert, M. V. (2001). Seizures, hormones and sexuality. *Seizure.* 10, 319-340.

Laumman, E., O., Nicolosi, A., Glasser, D.B., Palik, A., Gingell, C., Moriira, E.D., & Wang, T. (2005). Sexual problems among women and men aged 40-80: Prevalence and correlates identified in the global study of sexual attitudes and behaviors. *International Journal of Impotence Research, 17,* 39-57.

Löfgren-Mårtenson, L. (2004). "May I?" About sexuality and love in the new generation with intellectual disabilities. *Sexuality and Disability, 22*(3), 197-207.

Moreira, E.D., Brock, D.,B., Glasser, D.B., Nicolosi, A., Laumann, E.O., Paik, A., ... Gingell, C. (2005). Help-seeking behavior for sexual problems: The global study of sexual attitudes and behaviors. *International Journal of Clinical Practice, 59*(1), 6-16.

Morrell, M. J., Flynn, K. L., Doñe, S., Flaster, E., Kalayjian, L., & Pack, A. M. (2005). Sexual dysfunction, sex steroid hormone abnormalities, and depression in women with epilepsy treated with antiepileptic drugs. *Epilepsy & Behavior, 6*(3), 360-365.

Oliver, M. N., Anthony, A., Leimkuhl, T. T., & Skillman, G. D. (2002). Attitudes toward acceptable socio-sexual behaviors for persons with mental retardation: Implications for normalization and community integration. *Education and Training in Mental Retardation and Developmental Disabilities, 193*-201.

Parkes, N., & Keoghan, S. (2007). Erectile dysfunction: Meeting the needs of men with learning disabilities. *Nursing Standard. 21*(31), 35-41.

Sajith, S., Morgan, C., & Clarke, D. (2008). Pharmacological management of inappropriate sexual behaviours: A review of its evidence, rationale and scope in relation to men with intellectual disabilities. *Journal of Intellectual Disability Research, 52*(12), 1078-1090.

Stansfield, A. J., Holland, A. J., & Clare, I. C. (2007). The sterilisation of people with intellectual disabilities in England and Wales during the period 1988 to 1999. *Journal of Intellectual Disability Research, 51*(8), 569-579.

Stimmel, G. L., & Gutierrez, M. A. (2006). Sexual dysfunction and psychotropic medications. *CNS Spectrums, 11*(S9), 24-30.

Taylor Gomez M. (2012). The s words: Sexuality, sensuality, sexual expression and people with intellectual disabilitiy. *Sexuality and Disability, 30*(2), 237-245.

Tsiouris, J. A., Kim, S.-Y., Brown, W. T., Pettinger, J., & Cohen, I. L. (2013). Prevalence of psychotropic drug use in adults with intellectual disability: Positive and negative findings from a large scale study. *Journal of Autism and Developmental Disorders, 43*(3), 719-731.

CHAPTER 22

Gender Dysphoria

Georgina Parkes
James Barratt
Nigel Beail
Sonika Bhasin
Walter Pierre Bouman
Annelou L.C. de Vries
Daniel Wilson

In this chapter we consider how the diagnostic criteria for gender dysphoria can be used with people who have ID who present with the phenomena of gender incongruence and those who present with cross-gender identification. A review of the literature found very little data to indicate prevalence in people with ID and also very little research literature. What there is suggests that issues related to diagnosis may include more emphasis on behavior and developmental factors requiring the use of both the diagnostic criteria for children and adults combined. In the general population, gender dysphoria manifests differently in different age groups. However, people with ID are developmentally delayed cognitively, emotionally, and socially, but physical and sexual development is usually typical. So clinicians need to be aware of the impact of dyssynchronous development in the development and course of gender dysphoria in people who have ID.

Biological, genetic, psycho-social, and developmental factors are reviewed. The literature suggests that people with ID may confuse cross dressing and sexual orientation with being or wanting to be the other gender. They may lack basic sex education and experience extreme negative reactions to their behavior which results in concealment. They are vulnerable to victimization such as sexual harm, may conform to the wishes of those around them, and may not have access to role models. No recommendations for modifications to the criteria are made, but clinicians need to conduct their assessment taking into account the cognitive, developmental, and psychosocial factors which may impact on presentation and course.

Review of Diagnostic Criteria

The diagnostic criteria for gender dysphoria underwent a number of important changes with the publication of the *DSM-5*. For other reviews of the diagnostic changes from the DSM-IV to the DSM-5, see also Cohen-Kettenis & Pfäfflin (2010), Drescher, Cohen-Kettenis & Winter (2012), and Zucker (2010).

The first change concerns the name of the diagnosis. In the *DSM-5* the diagnostic name "gender identity disorders" has been replaced with "gender dysphoria" as one overarching diagnosis. Replacing "disorder" with "dysphoria" in the diagnostic terminology is not only more appropriate and consistent with familiar clinical sexology terminology, it also removes the connotation that the patient is "disordered." This change of terminology reduces stigma attached to a unique diagnosis that is used by mental health professionals but for which treatment often involves endocrinologists, surgeons, and other clinical professionals.

The second change is the inclusion of separate, developmentally appropriate criteria sets for children (gender dysphoria in children) and another for adolescents and adults (gender dysphoria in adolescents and adults). Moreover, a time criterion has been incorporated stating that clinical symptoms of gender dysphoria must be of at least 6 months' duration. For both groups, the criteria include a specifier, which indicates whether the individual's condition is related to a disorder of sex development such as congenital adrenal hyperplasia; this modification is in contrast to *DSM-IV* in which the presence of a disorder of sex development or intersex condition was an exclusionary criterion for the diagnosis of gender identity disorder. The criteria for adolescents and adults also include a specifier to indicate whether the individual has transitioned to full-time living in the desired gender. The specifier on the basis of sexual orientation is removed in the *DSM-5* because the distinction is no longer considered clinically useful.

Furthermore, two new categories have been created namely "other specified gender dysphoria" and "unspecified gender dysphoria" replacing "gender identity disorder not otherwise specified."

The third change involves creating a new diagnostic class of gender dysphoria in DSM-5 – and a chapter unto itself - not only highlighting the uniqueness of gender dysphoria as a diagnostic entity, but also firmly separating gender dysphoria from sexual dysfunctions and paraphillic disorders.

General Description of Gender Dysphoria

Gender dysphoria is a new diagnostic class in *DSM-5* and reflects a change in conceptualisation of the condition's defining features by emphasising the phenomenon of "gender incongruence" rather than cross-gender identification per se. Gender incongruence refers to people whose gender identity feels incongruent with their physical bodies. Gender dysphoria consists of specific gender dysphoria in children; gender dysphoria in adolescents or adults; other specified gender dysphoria; and unspecified gender dysphoria.

Summary of the DSM-5 Criteria

The general DSM-5 criteria for gender dysphoria include a "marked incongruence between one's experienced/expressed gender and assigned gender, of at least 6 months' duration" causing "clinically significant distress or impairment in social, school (for children)/occupational (for adolescents and adults), or other important areas of functioning" (p.452). The criteria can be applied to those with a physical index condition by coding the disorder of sex development as well as gender dysphoria.

The criteria differ for children compared to criteria for adults and adolescents. For children, criterion A1 "(a strong desire to be of the other gender or an insistence that he or she is the other gender…)" is now necessary but not sufficient to make the diagnosis. This modification makes the diagnosis more restrictive and conservative, and minimizes pathological gender variance or gender non-conforming. In children, the symptoms can further include a strong preference for cross-dressing, cross-gender roles in fantasy play, or toys, games, and activities usually associated with the other assigned gender. Children may express a strong desire for the primary and/or secondary sex characteristics that match their experienced gender. Furthermore, children may show an aversion to their genitalia and to stereotypical activities and clothes associated with their assigned gender. In earlier editions of the DSM it was assumed that some children may not be verbal or self-conscious enough as to express their desire explicitly; this is no longer the case in DSM-5.

By adolescence and throughout adult life, there is often a strong desire to get rid of one's primary and/or secondary sex characteristics of the other gender. There is a strong desire to be, live as, and be treated as the other sex. Many people with gender dysphoria indicate they have what they state are typical feelings and reactions of the other gender.

Other specified gender dysphoria meets symptoms criteria for gender dysphoria, but the duration is less than 6 months.

Unspecified gender dysphoria is used in situations in which the clinician chooses not to specify the reason that criteria are not met for gender dysphoria, and it includes presentations in which there is insufficient information to make a more specific diagnosis.

In the DSM-5 the criteria for adults and adolescents have been broadened and acknowledge that a dichotomous division in two gender categories, male or female, does not reflect the experience of many individuals who feel they are somewhere on a more continuous gender spectrum. They may identify as "shemale," "hemale," "third gender," "pan-/poly-/or omnigendered," "gender fluid," instead of male or female or even transsexual (Bockting, 2008). On the internet, there is extensive information, and many different "gender queer" communities meet online, and new terminologies seem to emerge almost every day. It can be that for individuals with an intellectual disability, this protean terminology is confusing.

For some individuals, however, cross-dressing and the accompanied sexual arousal in adolescence is just a stage in the development to a full cross-gender identification. As there is usually no childhood history of cross-gender behavior in these cases, it is often referred to as late-onset gender dysphoria and accompanied by a sexual attraction opposite to one's sex assigned at birth. Subtyping of gender dysphoria according to sexual attraction has been controversial; according to age of onset, less so. There is no research that specifically addresses this subject in adolescents or adults with an intellectual disability.

Issues Related to Diagnosis in Persons with ID

Presentation in people with ID is more often in terms of behavioral issues or cross dressing than seen in general with adolescents and adults. People with ID are more frequently brought to the attention of clinicians by staff rather than as a self-referral. Aggressive and sometimes offending behaviors can be a mode of presentation to clinicians.

The networks supporting people with ID may identify their cross dressing as a problem or challenging behavior. Stigma, bullying, and victimization are reasons why help is sought.

People with ID often have a less developed sense of their own identity and can be unduly influenced by groups or individuals. This can affect the development of gender dysphoria. Others may present after sexual assault or abuse, with a wish to escape their abused selves manifesting itself in a very concrete way, wanting to become someone else.

Development and Course

Expression of gender dysphoria varies with age in those without ID. In the DSM-5 this is represented by differences between the criteria for children and those for adolescents and adults. More importantly, whilst gender dysphoria presenting after puberty very rarely remits, most childhood gender dysphoria will have faded by early adolescence. Children may show explicit cross-gender behaviour at a young age and can express the wish to be the other gender as soon as they can talk. They may like cross dressing, show non-stereotypical gendered play and have favourite friends of the opposite gender. Some ask for genitals other than the ones they are born with. However, various studies of children referred to gender identity clinics have shown that only 15% (12-27%) still show full cross-gender identification in adolescence or adulthood and subsequently undergo gender reassignment. The majority will thus develop a gender identity in keeping with their natal sex, although a higher percentage than would be expected in the general population will turn out to have a non-heterosexual sexual orientation (Drummond, Bradley, Peterson-Badali & Zucker, 2008; Wallien & Cohen-Kettenis, 2008). The persistence of gender dysphoria into adolescence is more likely if the gender dysphoria had been extreme in childhood (Wallien & Cohen-Kettenis, 2008). Whether the above holds true for children with an intellectual disability is not studied.

Normative gender identity develops in stages (gender labelling, gender stability, and gender constancy) and the cognitive understanding of *gender constancy* develops for most children along with developing a core sense of self as male or female that is confluent with their natal sex (for a review see (Ruble, Martin, & Berenbaum, 2006). There are indications that in children with gender dysphoria, this learning process seems delayed (Zucker et al., 1996). Whether a delayed general development leads to an increased change of developing gender dysphoria is unproven but suspected. There are case reports but there are no population-wide prevalence studies devoted to this (see for an overview Parkes & Hall, 2006). However, although we know that children with autism and intellectual disability are able to develop a gender identity, one study showed that their level of understanding with regard to gender constancy is related to their cognitive and language development as well as their social and self-help skills (Abelson, 1981).

Another complication in children with an intellectual delay may arise due to their concrete and rigid thinking. The cognitive limitations may lead these children to mistakenly think that because they show cross-gender behavior, they really *are* the opposite gender. For these children it seems important to explain to them that *gender role behavior* and *gender identity* are two different things.

This understanding can be a reason gender dysphoria may remit as a person moves through developmental levels. People with ID have the same developmental process, but the stages can be much later, and there may need to be some structured professional input to move it along.

In adults and adolescents in general, this condition features an early identification with a gender different to sex assigned at birth, and this continues throughout life. If treatment is not available there may be psychological and emotional problems including mental illness and suicidal feelings. By contrast, outcomes are favorable if there is an appropriate treatment.

In the general population, a small proportion of born male patients who initially self-identity as gay, with a liking for wearing female clothing, come to identify as more female, as time passes. Eventually, the female social role dominates, with a desire for bodily alteration. Objects of sexual attraction tend to be heterosexual males throughout.

In professional experience and in the literature, there are reports of natal males with ID who self-identify as gay, have an interest in wearing female clothing, and who eventually declare a desire to live as a woman. However, rather than those described above in the general population, in these men with ID, the desire has its basis in their negative self concept of being identified as a gay men. The declared desire to change sex seems based on their assumption that to have an intimate relationship with a man they have to become female (Parkes, Hall, & Wilson, 2009; Wilson 2006). Through individual counselling, people presenting in this way have been able to develop a more positive sexual identity with no desire to live as a woman.

In the general population, there are also women who identify more with the male gender, and again, as time passes, their degree of masculinity grows, with a desire for bodily alteration and a male social gender role. Objects of attraction throughout tend to be feminine females or, rarely, gay males. These have been seen clinically by the authors in large gender identity clinic services. For people with ID, all presentations are seen – from those who have experienced gender dysphoria from a very early age and who go on to live in the opposite gender role to transvestites who in late life become more gender dysphoric (dual role transvestism, evolving into transsexualism) and live as the opposite gender role seeking genital reconstructive surgery (GRS). (For case example and literature review see Parkes and Hall, 2006.)

Gender dysphoric people with ID often present much later in life than typically developing gender dysphoric peers. Patients may have been dissuaded from expressing their feelings by social, institutional, or peer pressure. Other factors also play a part in that they may need help or support to buy clothes, including those of the other gender, which they may either not have felt able to voice their desire or have had such requests met with strong negative reactions. Difficulty expressing their sexual and gender needs or being aware of sense of self identity may play a role.

Prevalence

Very little data on the prevalence of gender dysphoria and ID exist. Parkes and Hall (2006) reviewed the published literature from 1966 to 2004 and found only 9 case reports and one survey. The survey was of children and adolescents attending a UK gender identity clinic (Di Ceglie, Freedman, McPherson, & Richardson, 2002). Of 124 patients seen, 10 (8%) had a diagnosis of ID. Another children's clinic based study was carried out in the Netherlands by de Vries, Noes, Cohen-Kettenis, van Berckelaer-Onnes, & Doreleijers (2010). Unpublished data supplied by the authors showed that 3 (1.6%) out of 190 children with gender dysphoria had an IQ of 70 or less. One clinic report from North America looked at 32 adults with ID and found 4 (12.5%) has Gender Dysphoria (Bedard et al. (2010). The number of people with ID and gender dysphoria across these studies exceeds what would be expected. However, these are clinic-based studies and the numbers are small, so these data should be treated with caution. All the people in these reports had mild or moderate ID. Children with severe and profound ID were excluded from assessment of intellectual functioning in the de Vries et al. unpublished data, suggesting the true rate of ID would have been higher.

Differential Diagnosis

The differential diagnosis is similar to DSM-5 and includes the following:
transvestic disorder
body dysmorphic disorder
psychotic disorders/schizophrenia
non conformity with gender roles
autistic spectrum disorders
with additional:
gender constancy developmental lag
internalized homophobia

Functional Consequences

People with ID often present to services with the functional consequences of gender dysphoria rather than the gender dysphoria per se. These can be aggressive or offending behaviors, such as stealing underwear or clothes, especially if living in institutional or restrictive situations. They may become depressed or suicidal if they are unable to express themselves by living as the gender they feel they are. Some may develop psychiatric symptoms, although this generally remits once the gender dysphoria is adequately treated.

People with ID may cross dress without great social success by wearing inappropriate clothes and make-up, which can lead to further stigmatizing, bullying, and victimization. Early attempts at disclosure may lead to negative, oppressive, or even catastrophic reactions, prompting subsequent social conformity, denial, and considerable internal distress. They may have difficulty establishing intimacy with others and consequently lack fulfilling or meaningful sexual or non-sexual relationships.

A true exploration of a person's self concept should happen as soon as possible, individually, and ahead of accessing support networks, particularly lay or informal since the particularly accepting and non-judgmental nature of such groups may cause people with ID, who are lonely and have poor sense of self identity, to make a change of gender role as the price of acceptance.

Comorbidity

Gender dysphoria can co-occur with any mental illness, but is commonly seen with:
autism spectrum disorder
depression and suicidality prior to gender dysphoria being addressed
sexual abuse and trauma
generalised anxiety disorder
Ppoblems with identity, including sexual and self concept
social phobia
psychotic disorders

Application of Diagnostic Criteria to People with ID

Parkes et al.'s (2009) retrospective case notes review used DSM-IV criteria as the basis for the proforma for data collection and found three people with ID who met the criteria for diagnosis of gender identity disorder, which is now termed gender dysphoria. Bedard et al. (2010) used two gender identity questionnaires, one of which met diagnostic criteria gender identity disorder according to DSM-IV. The study found four people with ID who met criteria for gender identity disorder.

General Considerations

Longer assessments are needed in people with ID as their self concept needs to be explored for reasons described above along with an assessment of whether there is a developmental lag in gender constancy. Co-morbid autism spectrum disorder would need to be screened for given the high rates of autism spectrum disorder in this population.

High rates of childhood sexual abuse and sexual assault as adults were seen in both Bedard et al. (2010) and Parkes et al (2009) studies. Care, sensitivity and time to develop trusting relationships are needed in assessments in order to elicit and discuss sexual abuse. Assessment would also need to look at whether the change in identity is sought as a means of escape or as a way to feel better by very concretely becoming someone other than a person (themselves) who they may see as damaged or as a victim.

Methodology

A literature search was conducted in peer-reviewed psychiatric, nursing and social health care journals from the years 2005 to 2013, given that a literature review was published reviewing the years 1966 to 2004 (Parkes & Hall, 2006). The sources searched were MEDLINE, AMED, CINAHL, British Nursing Index, EMBASE, PsycINFO, Health Business Elite, and HMIC, using the terms *learning disability, disabled person, intellectual disability, developmental disability, retardation, mental handicap, mental, subnormal* and *transsex*, gender, transgender,* and *cross-dress.* In addition to searching computerised databases, we followed-up on references from relevant articles and contacted researchers with an interest in this area.

Results of literature search:

The computerized database revealed a total of 4 papers of interest.

Follow up of authors working in this field revealed 2 papers of interest.

Review Research Applying to People with ID

Parkes and Hall (2006) found that many of the people described in the case reports were of borderline intellectual functioning. In one of the case reports one person began cross dressing when moving out of a long stay institution and had more freedom to express himself; another individual was allowed to express cross-dressing behavior in private and aggression stopped. Another individual met a woman with whom he developed a relationship and, thereafter, stopped cross-dressing. Three people reported that sexual abuse as an adult directly preceded cross dressing.

Parkes Hall and Wilson (2009) surveyed the case notes of 13 patients (12 had ID and one had borderline ID with autism) presenting at an organization in the UK offering counselling for sexual and gender needs. Three people met the criteria for gender identity disorder (DSM IV); of these one stated escaping trauma, rape as an adult, as a reason for wanting to become someone else. Three others self identified as gay; they seemed to be experiencing peer and social pressures and wanted to have gender reassignment as a solution to this. One person in addition wanted to be both male and female. There were high rates of childhood sexual abuse of 62% (8). Two people met criteria for fetishistic transvestism and one stated using cross dressing as a way of escaping anger. In three others, motivation was unknown with too little information available.

Wilson (2006) provides an expert opinion paper whose concepts have been discussed elsewhere in this chapter, along with the other three papers.

Evaluating the Level of Evidence

The current literature consists of Type IV and Type V evidence.

Adults with Mild to Moderate ID

One study described above (Parkes Hall and Wilson 2009) applied DSM-IV criteria to the case notes of those presenting with cross dressing and gender dysphoria in the United Kingdom. Three people met these criteria. This shows that gender dysphoria, as it is now classified, is a valid diagnosis in people with ID. However, care must be taken as a declared desire to change social gender role can have other origins, such as escape from oneself, the lack of a fulfilling sexual relationship, or peer pressure to not be gay.

For this group, presentation is more concrete than for an adult and adolescent group without ID and is more similar to that described in children with gender dysphoria in DSM-5.

Adults with Severe or Profound ID

There are no case reports or information in the literature about this population. While there is nothing to suggest that people with severe or profound ID do not develop gender dysphoria, it is possible that as their dependency on others is so pronounced they have more difficulties expressing their needs, this being a reason they have not presented to services.

Children and Adolescents with ID

Children with Intellectual Disability

In every child who is assessed for gender dysphoria it is essential to take account of a developmental perspective and this is even more important in children with an intellectual disability. In clinical practice, gender dysphoria presents in many ways. Some gender dysphoric children are very open and verbally fluent about how they feel while others are shy or are so sensitive to what gender stereotypical behavior is expected of them that they hardly dare to do or say otherwise, or do so only at certain times and under certain circumstances (Meyer-Bahlburg, 2002).

In children with intellectual disabilities, who may have difficulties in expressing and verbalizing in general, the latter might especially be true, making it harder to give a child the diagnosis of gender dysphoria. Probably cross gender behavior is more easily accepted in girls than in boys, and consequently parents of gender dysphoric boys more often seek help. There is the impression that in individuals with an intellectual disability, it is mostly males with cross gender behavior and identification who come to clinical attention (Parkes & Hall, 2006).

Adolescents with Intellectual Disability

As part of their generalized developmental delay, adolescents with intellectual disability progress more slowly through the different developmental stages later in life. Adolescence as a psychological life stage may be both delayed and also prolonged. However, their bodies go through the development of secondary sexual characteristics and hormone surges at the same age as those without such delay (Parkes & Hall, 2006). In DSM-5, the same criteria of gender dysphoria apply to adolescents and adults but when physical and psychological development are not in line with each other, as be the case of adolescents with an intellectual disability it is imperative that a developmental perspective is taken into account at assessment.

The development of secondary sexual characteristics can be extremely stressful for gender dysphoric individuals. There is an impression that cross gender identification in adolescence is unlikely to remit, at least in adolescents referred to gender identity clinics.

This does not seem to be true, though, for adolescents with a development delay. Apart from physical puberty, the changes in social environment that come with adolescence and the discovery of sexuality are important factors related to whether there is an increase or decrease of early childhood gender variance (Steensma, Biemond, Boer, & Cohen-Kettenis, 2011). Careful assessment, along with explanation and providing the necessary knowledge, is essential. Some adolescents with intellectual disability confuse gender identity and sexual orientation. They might think that if they have cross gender behavior combined with romantic feelings for same sex partners, this means that they should *be* the other gender.

Other sexual experiences and feelings might arise that give the individual the impression that he or she is transgender. There is research that suggests individuals with intellectual delay show more atypical sexual behaviors (Hellemans, Colson, Verbraeken, Vermeiren, & Deboutte, 2007) and transvestic fetishism is among them. Such transvestic cross-dressing can lead the intellectually delayed individual to think that he or she is cross-gender identifying.

Basic sex education of young people with ID is often lacking. Moreover in most people with ID basic body awareness is also lacking. This lack of knowledge and awareness may lead to distorted views of sexual identifies and roles.

Limitations in Applying DSM-5 Criteria to People with ID

1. People with ID may confuse cross dressing with being another gender.

2. People with ID may confuse sexual orientation with wanting to be another gender.
3. People with ID may see becoming another gender as a concrete way of reducing the risk of further sexual trauma or achieving a more empowered life.
4. Experiencing early extremely negative reactions in response to a tentative disclosure may lead to prolonged concealment thereafter and a late and abrupt change of social gender role – often soon after the death of a parent or other carer.
5. Lack of basic sex education may contribute to any of the above.
6. Poor self concept may contribute to any of the above.
7. Vulnerability to conformism may cause a reluctance to declare gender dysphoria or paradoxically, may cause a lonely but not gender dysphoric person to change gender role to achieve membership of a non-judgemental and accepting gender dysphoric circle of acquaintances.
8. Some gender dysphoric people with ID may not have access to accounts of or by people who have successfully changed social gender role and so lack positive role models.

Etiology and Pathogenesis

Gender dysphoria in people with ID would be broadly similar in etiology as in the general population which is to say as a consequence of a multi-factorial developmental process in which biological as well as psychological, social, and cultural factors play a role. There is a growing body of evidence which shows that key biological factors are involved in the development of gender dysphoria (e.g. Garcia-Faulgueras & Swaab, 2008; Gomez-Gil et al.,2010; Gomez-Gil et al., 2011 Kruijver et al., 2000; Rametti et al., 2011; Simon et al.; 2013' Zhou, Hoffman, Gooren, & Swaab, 1995). It is also well established that psychological, social and cultural factors play a role (e.g. Cohen-Kettenis & Gooren, 1999; Veale, Clarke, & Lomax, 2010a, 2010b).

In addition, and particularly in relation to people with ID, concrete thinking, developmental lag, and sexual abuse and assault have been directly linked with development of gender dysphoria.

Biological Factors

Biological research on gender dysphoria has focused on neuroanatomical (Garcia-Falgueras & Swaab, 2008; Kruijver et al., 2000; Zhou et al., 1995), hormonal (Swaab, 2007) and genetic influences. Port-mortem anatomical studies have shown that some subcortical structures are feminized in trans women. Similarly, structural imaging studies have shown that certain brain regions and structures in trans people are closer of that of subjects with the same gender identity than to that of subjects with the same biological sex (Rametti et al., 2011; Simon et al., 2013; Yokota, Kawamura, & Kameya, 2005). Notwithstanding these neuroanatomical differences, most of these findings are limited because the practical or functional significance is unknown.

The main mechanism postulated for the development of gender identity claims a direct effect [or lack] of testosterone on the developing human brain as seen in certain conditions; for instance, people with intersex and related conditions who have been exposed to prenatal androgen levels which are at variance to either their genotype (male or female sex chromosomes) or their assigned brain gender. These individuals are much more likely to change from the gender they were assigned at birth than persons without these conditions (Cohen-Kettenis, 2005; Dessens, Slijper, & Drop, 2005; Mazur, 2005; Meyer-Bahlburg, 2005). Similarly, increased androgen exposure in utero may contribute to the development with autism spectrum disorder more often than in the general population (de Vries et al., 2010; Pasterski, Gilligan, & Curtis, 2014); this could be one explanation for the increased rate of gender dysphoria that seems to be found in people with ID. There may be common biological factors in the etiology of gender dysphoria and ID, but more specific data in this area are lacking. There are no studies which specifically research structural imaging and/or hormones in people with gender dysphoria and ID.

Genetic Factors

The literature on genetic determinants of gender dysphoria is very limited and has been derived from familial, twin, molecular, and chromosomal studies (Bentz et al., 2007; Bentz et al., 2008; Garden & Rothery, 1992; Gómez -Gil et al., 2010; Henningsoon et al., 2005; Hyde & Kenna, 1977; Sadeghi & Fakhari, 2000; Segal, 2006; Ujike et al., 2009). A number of chromosomal abnormalities have been reported in people with gender dysphoria (Buhrich, Barr, & Lam-Po-Tang, 1978; Haberman, Hollingsworth, Falek, & Michael, 1975; Snaith, Penhale, & Horsfield, 1991; Taneja, Ammini, Mohapatra, Saxena, & Kucheria, 1992; Turan et al, 2000). In all cases, sex chromosomes were involved. The most common association with the disomy-Y (47,XYY). However, due to the relatively high prevalence of sex chromosome aneuploidy in the population (1 in 800-1000 male newborns for XYY; 1 in 1000 female newborns (Grumbach, Hughes, & Conte, 2003) these cases only represent a random association with gender dysphoria. Conversely, Hengstschläger et al., (2003) analysed G-banded karyotypes of 30 trans female and 31 trans males and found no chromosomal abnormalities in these individuals apart from one balanced translocation 46,XY. People with ID are more likely than the general population to have genetic syndromes. However, at present there is no evidence for a genetic association between gender dysphoria and ID (Hengstschläger et al., 2003)

Psychosocial Factors

Psychosocial factors that have been theorized to influence the development of gender dysphoria have been summarized elsewhere (Veale et al., 2010a).

There is evidence that a poor or absent parental relationship, being an adoptee, having older brothers, childhood abuse, and parental encouragement to express a child's desired gender rather than their assigned gender at birth are more common amongst people with Gender Dysphoria (Cohen-Kettenis & Arrindell, 1990; Gehring & Knudson, 2005; Grossman, Drossman, & Salter, 2006; Veale et al., 2010a, 2010b; Zucker & Bradley, 1995; Zucker at al., 1997; Zucker & Bradley, 1998). Sexual abuse and assault has been reported to have a higher incidence amongst people with ID. Reports on children and adults with ID and gender dysphoria who present clinically have also been noted to have high rates of sexual abuse. It remains unclear whether these are a cause or effect of gender dysphoria. It is likely than any psychosocial variables which play a causative role in the development of gender dysphoria are complex and interact with biological etiological factors. Studies on the prevalence of gender dysphoria in individuals with ID have not been carried out.

Developmentally Factors

People with ID usually develop physically at the same rate as typically developing adults, but their social, emotional, and psychosexual development is dyssynchronous as previously discussed. A key criterion for the way in which adults with ID express their gender dysphoria may also be related to their level of sexual knowledge and understanding. In typically developing adults expressions of anatomic dysphoria are more common once secondary sex characteristic have developed. However, an adult with ID may feel discomfort in his or her assigned gender role but may not present with anatomic dysphoria. Here a wish to have the genitalia of the experienced gender will be dependent on knowledge of what this is.

Further they may also need support to fulfill their desire to cross dress (Parkes, Hall, & Wilson, 2009). Thus it may be that psycho-sexual education needs to be part of an assessment process to inform the clients about anatomy and to enable them to look at gender roles more loosely.

It may also be that the person who has ID confuses feeling of attraction and arousal for someone of the same sex with the idea that they themselves, instead of being gay or bisexual, may be of the other gender. Thus any assessment process may need to also include help for the person to come to terms with his/her sexuality.

Application of Diagnostic Criteria

Gender Dysphoria in Children

DSM-5 Diagnostic Criteria	Applying Criteria for Individuals with IDD
A. A marked incongruence between one's experienced/expressed gender and assigned gender, of at least 6 months duration, as manifested by at least six of the following(one of which must be Criterion A1): 1. A strong desire to be of the other gender or an insistence that one is the other gender (or some alternative gender different from one's assigned gender). 2. In boys (assigned gender), A strong preference for cross-dressing or simulating female attire; or in girls (assigned gender), a strong preference for wearing only typical masculine clothing and a strong resistance to the wearing of typical feminine clothing. 3. A strong preference for cross-gender roles in make-believe play or fantasy play. 4. A strong preference for the toys, games, or activities stereotypically used or engaged in by the other gender. 5. A strong preference for playmates of the other gender. 6. In boys (assigned gender), a strong rejection of typically masculine toys, games, and activities and a strong avoidance of rough-and-tumble play; or in girls (assigned gender), a strong rejection of typically feminine toys, games, and activities. 7. A strong dislike of one's sexual anatomy. 8. A strong desire for the primary and/or secondary sex characteristics that match one's experienced gender. B The condition is associated with clinically significant distress or impairment in social, school, or other important areas of functioning. Specify if: With a disorder of sex development (e.g., a congenital adrenogenital disorder such as 255.2 [E34.5] androgen insensitivity syndrome). Coding note: Code the disorder of sex development as well as gender dysphoria.	No modification

Gender Dysphoria in Adolescents and Adults

DSM-5 Diagnostic Criteria	Applying Criteria for Individuals with IDD
A. A marked incongruence between one's experienced/expressed gender and primary and/or secondary sex characteristics (or in young adolescents, the anticipated secondary sex characteristics). 1. A marked incongruence between one's experienced/expressed gender and primary and/or secondary sex characteristics (or in young adolescents, a desire to prevent the development of the anticipated secondary sex characteristics). 2. A strong desire to be rid of one's primary and/or secondary sex characteristics because of a marked incongruence with one's experienced /expressed gender (or in young adolescents, a desire to prevent the development of the anticipated secondary sex characteristics). 3. A strong desire for the primary and/or secondary sex characteristics of the other gender. 4. A strong desire to be of the other gender (or some alternative gender different from one's assigned gender). 5. A strong desire to be treated as the other gender (or some alternative gender different from one's assigned gender). 6. A strong conviction that one has the typical feelings and reactions of the other gender (or some alternative gender different from one's assigned gender).	No modifications

References

Abelson, A.G. (1981). The development of gender identity in the autistic child. *Child Care and Health Development*, 7(6), 347-356.

American Psychiatric Association (2013). *Diagnostic and statistical manual of mental disorder* (5th ed.). Washington D.C.: APA.

Andreazza, T.S., Costa, A.B., Massuda, R., Salvador, J., Silveira, E.M., Piccon, F., ... Belmonte-de-Abreu, P. (2014). Discordant transsexualism in male monozygotic twins: Neuroanatomical and psychological differences. *Archives of Sexual Behavior*, 43, 399-405.

Bao, A. & Swaab, D.F. (2011). Sexual differentiation of the human brain: Relation to gender identity, sexual orientation and neuropsychiatric disorders. *Frontiers in Neuroendocrinology*, 32, 214-226.

Bedard C; Zhang H; Zucker KJ. (2010) Gender identity and sexual orientation in people with developmental disabilities. *Sexuality & Disability*, (28/3) 165-175.

Bentz, E.K., Schneeberger, C., Hefler, L.A., Van Trotsenburg, M., Kaufmann, U., Huber, J.C., Tempfer, C.B. (2007). A common polymorphism of the SRD5A2 gene and transsexualism. *Reproductive Science*, 14, 705-709.

Bentz, E.K., Hefler, L.A., Kaufmann, U., Huber, J.C., Kolbus, A., & Tempfer, C.B. (2008). A polymorphism of the CYP17 gene related to sex steroid metabolism is associated with female-to-male and transsexualism but not male-to-female transsexualism. *Fertility and Sterility, 90*, 56-59.

Bockting, W. O. (2008). Psychotherapy and the real-life experience: From gender dichotomy to gender diversity. *Sexologies, 17*, 211-224.

Buhrich, N., Barr, R. & Lam-Po-Tang, P.R.L.C. (1978). Two transsexuals with 47 XYY karyotype. *British Journal of Psychiatry*, 133, 77-81.

Cohen-Kettenis, P. T. (2005). Gender Change in 46,XY Persons with 5-Reductase-2 Deficiency and 17-Hydroxysteroid Dehydrogenase-3 Deficiency. *Archives of Sexual Behavior*, 34, 399-410.

Cohen-Kettenis, P. T. & Arrindell, W.A. (1990). Perceived parental rearing style, parental divorce and transsexualism: A controlled study. *Psychological Medicine*, 20, 613-620.

Cohen-Kettenis, P. T., & Gooren, L. J. G. (1999). Transsexualism: A review of etiology diagnosis and treatment. *Journal of Psychosomatic Research, 46* (4), 315-333.

Cohen-Kettenis, P.T. & Pfäfflin, F. (2010). The DSM diagnostic criteria for gender identity disorder in adolescents and adults. *Archives of Sexual Behavior*, 39, 499-513.

Dessens, A.B., Cohen-Kettenis, P.T., Mellenbergh, G.J., Van de Poll, N., Koppe, J.G., & Boer, K. (1999). Prenatal exposure to anticonvulsants and psychosexual development. *Archives of Sexual Behavior*, 28, 31-44.

Dessens, A.B., Slijper, F.M.E., Drop, S.L.S. (2005). Gender dysphoria and gender change in chromosomal females with congenital adrenal hyperplasia. *Archives of Sexual Behavior*, 34, 389-397.

de Vries, A. L., & Cohen-Kettenis, P. T. (2012). Clinical management of gender dysphoria in children and adolescents: The Dutch approach. *Journal of Homosexuality, 59*(3), 301-320.

de Vries, A. L., Noens, I. L., Cohen-Kettenis, P. T., van Berckelaer-Onnes, I. A., & Doreleijers, T. A. (2010). Autism spectrum disorders in gender dysphoric children and adolescents. [Research Support, Non-U.S. Gov't]. *Journal of Autism and Developmental Disorders, 40*(8), 930-936.

Di Ceglie D., Freedman D., McPherson S., Richardson P. (2002) Children and adolescents referred to a specialist gender identity development service: clinical features and demographic characteristics. *The International Journal of Transgenderism, 6*, 1.

Drescher, J., Cohen-Kettenis, P. & Winter, S. (2012). Minding the body: Situating gender identity diagnoses in the ICD-11. *International Review of Psychiatry*, 24(6), 568-577.

Drummond, K. D., Bradley, S. J., Peterson-Badali, M., & Zucker, K. J. (2008). A follow-up study of girls with gender identity disorder. *Developmental Psychology, 44*(1), 34-45.

Garcia-Falgueras, A. & Swaab, D.F. (2008). A sex difference in the hypothalamic uncinate nucleus: Relationship to gender identity. *Brain*, 131, 3132-3146.

Garden, G.M. & Rothery, D.J. (1992). A female monozygotic twin pair discordant for transsexualism. Some theoretical implications. *British Journal of Psychiatry*, 161, 852-854.

Gehring, D. & Knudson, G. (2005). Prevalence of childhood trauma in a clinical population of transsexual people. *International Journal of Transgenderism*, 8, 23-30.

Gómez-Gil, E., Esteva, I., Carrasco, R., Cruz Almaraz, M., Pasaro, E., Salamero, M., & Guillamon, A. (2011). Birth order and ratio of brothers to sisters in Spanish transsexuals. *Archives of Sexual Behavior*, 40, 505-510.

Gómez-Gil, E., Esteva, I., Cruz Almaraz, M., Pasaro, E., Segovia, S., & Guillamon, A. (2010). Familiality of gender identity disorder in non-twin siblings. *Archives of Sexual Behavior*, 39, 546-552.

Grossman, A. H., Drossman,, A. R., & Salter, N.P. (2006). Male-to-female transgender youth: gender expression milestones, gender atypicality, victimization, and parent's responses. *Journal of GLBT Family Studies*, 2, 71-92.

Grumbach, M.M., Hughes, I.A., & Conte, F.A. (2003). Disorders of sex differentiation. In P.R. Larsen, H.M. kronenberg, S. Melmed & K.S. Polonsky (Eds.), *Williams textbook of endocrinology* (10th ed., pp. 842-1002). Philadelphia: Saunders.

Haberman, M., Hollingsworth, F., Falek, A. & Michael, R.P. (1975). Gender identity confusion, schizophrenia and 47 XYY karyotype: A case report. *Psychoneuroendocrinology*, 1, 207-209.

Hellemans, H., Colson, K., Verbraeken, C., Vermeiren, R., & Deboutte, D. (2007). Sexual behavior in high-functioning male adolescents and young adults with autism spectrum disorder. *Journal of Autism and Developmental Disorders*, 37(2), 260-269.

Hengstschläger, M., Van Trotsenburg, M., Repa, C., Marton, E., Huber, J.C. & Bernaschek, H. (2003). Sex chromosome aberrations and transsexualism. *Fertility and Sterility*, 79, 639-640.

Henningsson, S., Westberg, L., Nilsson, S., Lundström, B., Ekselius, L., Bodlund, O., ... Landén, M. (2005). Sex steroid related genes and male to female transsexualism. *Psychoneuroendocrinology*, 30(7), 657-664.

Hyde, C. & Kenna, J.C. (1977). A male MZ twin pair, concordant for transsexualism, discordant for schizophrenia. *Acta Psychiatrica Scandinavica*, 56, 265-273.

Knickmeyer. R.C. & Baron-Cohen, S. (2006). Fetal testosterone and sex differences in typical social development and in autism. *Journal of Child Neurology, 21*, 825-845.

Kruijver, F.M.P., Zhou, J.N., Pool, C.W., Hofman, M.A., Gooren, L.J.G., & Swaab, D.F. (2000). Male-to-female transsexuals have female neuron numbers in a limbic nucleus. *Journal of Clinical Endocrinology and Metabolism*, 85, 2034-2041.

Mazur, T. (2005). Gender Dysphoria and Gender Change in Androgen Insensitivity or Micropenis. *Archives of Sexual Behavior*, 34, 411-421.

Meyer-Bahlburg, H. F. (2002). Gender identity disorder in young boys: A parent-and peer-based treatment protocol. *Clinical Child Psychology and Psychiatry, 7*(3), 360-376.

Meyer-Bahlburg, H.F... (2005). Gender identity outcome in female-raised 46,XY persons with penile agenesis, cloacal exstrophy of the bladder, or penile ablation. *Archives of Sexual Behavior, 34*, 423-438.

Ngun, T.C., Ghahramani, N., Sani, N., Si, NBocklandt, S., Vilain, E. (2011). The genetics of sex differences in brain and behavior. *Frontiers in Neuroendocrinology*, 32, 227-246.

Parkes, G., & Hall, I. (2006). Gender dysphoria and cross-dressing in people with intellectual disability: a literature review. *Mental Retardation, 44*(4), 260-271.

Parkes, G., & Hall, I. (2009). Cross dressing and gender dysphoria in people with learning disabilities: A descriptive study. *British*

Journal of Learning Disabilities, 37(2), 151-156.

Pasterski, V., Gilligan, L. & Curtis, R. (2014). Traits of autism spectrum disorders in adults with gender dysphoria. *Archives of Sexual Behavior*, 43, 387-393.

Rametti, G., Carrillo, B., Gomez-Gil, E., Junque, C., Zubiarre-Elorza, L., Segovia, S., ... Guillamon, A. (2011). The microstructure of white matter in male to female transsexuals before cross-sex hormonal treatment. A DTI study. *Journal of Psychiatric Research*, 45, 949-954.

Ruble, D. N., Martin, C. L., & Berenbaum, S. A. (2006). Gender Development. In W. Damon (Series Ed.) & N. Eisenberg (Vol. Ed.), *Handbook of child psychology: Vol. 3. Social, emotional, and personality development* (6th ed., pp. 858-932). New York: Wiley.

Sadeghi, M. & Fakhrai, A. (2000). Transsexualism in female monzygotic twins. A case report. *Australian and New Zealand Journal of Psychiatry, 34*, 862-864.

Sato, T., Matsumoto, T., Kawano, H, Wanatabe, T., Uematsu, Y., Sekine, K., ... Kato, S. (2004). Brain masculinisation requires androgen receptor function. *Proceedings of the National Academy of Sciences in the United States of America*, 101, 1673-1678.

Savic, I., Garcia-Falgueras, A. & Swaab, D.F. (2010). Sexual differentiation of the human brain in relation to gender identity and sexual orientation. *Progress in Brain Research*, 186, 41-62.

Segal, N.L. (2006). Two monozygotic twin pairs discordant for female-to-male transsexualism. *Archives of Sexual Behavior*, 35, 347-358.

Simon, L., Kozák, L.R., Simon, V., Czobor, P., Unoka, Z., Szab,, A., Csukly, G. (2013). regional grey matter structure differences between transsexuals and healthy controls – A voxel based morphometry study. *PloSOne*, 8(12): e83947. doi:10.1371/journal.pone.0083947.

Snaith, R.P., Penhale, S. & Horsfield, P. (1991). Male-to-female transsexual with XYY karyotype. *Lancet*, 337, 557-558.

Steensma, T. D., Biemond, R., Boer, F. D., & Cohen-Kettenis, P. T. (2011). Desisting and persisting gender dysphoria after childhood: A qualitative follow-up study. *Clinical Child Psychology and Psychiatry.*

Swaab, D.F. (2007). Sexual differentiation of the brain and behavior. *Best Practice & Research Clinical Endocrinology & Metabolism*, 21(3), 431-444.

Taneja, N., Ammini, A.C., , Mohapatra, I., Saxena, S. & Kucheria, K. (1992). A transsexual male with 47,XYY karyotype. *British Journal of Psychiatry*, 161, 698-699.

Turan, M.T., Eşel, E., Dündar, M., Candemir, Z., Baştürk, B, M., Sofuoğlu, S., & Özkul, Y. (2000). Female-to-male transsexual with 47,XYY karyotype. *Biological Psychiatry*, 48, 1116-1117.

Ujike, H., Otani, K., Nakatsuka, M., Ishii, K., Sasaki, A., Oishi, T., ... Kuroda, S. (2009). Association study of gender identity disorder and sex hormone-related genes. *Progress in Neuro-Psychopharmacology and Biological Psychiatry*, 33, 1241-1244.

Veale, J.F., Clarke, D.E., & Lomax, T.C. (2010a). Biological and psychosocial correlates of adult gender-variant identities: A review. *Personality and Individual Differences*, 48, 357-366.

Veale, J.F., Clarke, D.E., & Lomax, T.C. (2010b). Biological and psychosocial correlates of adult gender-variant identities: New findings. *Personality and Individual Differences*, 49, 252-257.

Wallien, M. S., & Cohen-Kettenis, P. T. (2008). Psychosexual outcome of gender-dysphoric children. *Journal of the American Acadamy of Child and Adolescent Psychiatry*, 47(12), 1413-1423.

Wilson, D. (2006). Gender identity, cross-dressing and gender reassignment and people with learning disabilities. *Tizard Learning Disability Review*, 11, 2, 4-15, 1359-5474, April.

Yokota, Y., Kawamura, Y., Kameya, Y. (2005). Callosal shapes at the midsagittal plane: MRI differences of normal males, normal females, and GID. In: Proceedings of the

2005 IEEE, Engineering in Medicine and Biology 27th Annual Conference, p.3055e8.

Zhou, J. N., Hofman, M. A., Gooren, L. J., & Swaab, D. F. (1995). A sex difference in the human brain and its relation to transsexuality. *Nature, 378,* 68-70.

Zucker, K.J. (2010). The DSM diagnostic criteria for gender identity disorder in children. *Archives of Sexual Behavior,* 39, 477-498.

Zucker, K.J., & Bradley, S.J. (1995). *Gender identity disorder and psychosocial problems in children and adolescents.* New York: Guildford Press.

Zucker, K.J. & Bradley, S.J. (1998). Adoptee overrepresentation among clinic-referred boys with gender identity disorder. *Canadian Journal of Psychiatry, 43,* 1040-1043.

Zucker, K. J., Bradley, S. J., Oliver, G., Blake, J., Fleming, S., & Hood, J. (1996). Psychosexual development of women with congenital adrenal hyperplasia. *Hormones and Behavior, 30*(4), 300-318.

Zucker, K.J., Green, R., Coates, S., Zuger, B., Cohen-Kettenis, P.T., Mansueto Zecca, G., ... Blachard, R. (1997). Sibling sex ratio of boys with gender identity disorder. *Journal of Child Psychology and Psychiatry, 38*(5), 543-551.

CHAPTER 23

Disruptive, Impulse-Control, and Conduct Disorders

Shoumitro Deb
Terrence C. Bethea
Susan M. Havercamp
Arthur Rifkin
Lisa Underwood

This chapter describes the new category of disruptive, impulse-control, and conduct disorders in *DSM-5* as it applies to people with intellectual disability.

Changes in Classification

In *DSM-IV-TR* and *DM-ID*, oppositional defiant disorder and conduct disorder were included in the attention deficit hyperactivity disorder and disruptive behavior disorder category. In *DSM-IV-TR* and *DM-ID*, impulse-control disorders included intermittent explosive disorder, kleptomania, and pyromania. These are now classified as disruptive, impulse-control, and conduct disorders. Also included in this category are oppositional defiant disorder, conduct disorder (both previously classified as disorders usually first diagnosed in infancy, childhood, or adolescence), and antisocial personality disorder.

Trichotillomania and pathological gambling were also included in impulse-control disorders not elsewhere classified. However, these disorders are now in the *DSM-5* and *DM-ID-2* chapters on obsessive-compulsive & related disorders and substance-related & addictive disorders, respectively. Habit disorders such as finger sucking, body rocking, and bruxism are classified as stereotypic movement disorders and are included among motor disorders in the neurodevelopmental disorders sections of *DSM-5* and *DM-ID-2*. Antisocial personality disorder is included in *DSM-5* both under the disruptive, impulse-control, and conduct disorder category and the personality disorder category. In *DM-ID-2*, this will be covered within the personality disorder chapter.

Disruptive, Impulse-Control, and Conduct Disorders

Review of Diagnostic Criteria

Disruptive, impulse-control, and conduct disorders are characterized by impairment in the ability to control emotions and behaviors to an extent that the resulting behaviors have a clinically significant impact on an individual and her/his interactions with others or society. There are six specified disruptive, impulse-control, and conduct disorders: (a) antisocial personality disorder, (b) conduct disorder, (c) intermittent explosive disorder, (d) kleptomania, (e) pyromania, and (f) oppositional defiant disorder.

Diagnoses of other specified or unspecified disruptive, impulse-control, and conduct disorders may be given when an individual has symptoms that are characteristic of the specific disorders listed above but do not meet the full diagnostic criteria. These diagnoses may be used for individuals with presentations in which there is insufficient information to make a more specific diagnosis.

Summary of DSM-5 *Criteria*

In order to meet diagnostic criteria for disruptive, impulse-control, and conduct disorders, there should be evidence that an individual presents with behaviors that violate the rights of others (e.g., aggression, destruction of property) and/or bring the individual into significant conflict with societal norms or authority figures.

Other Specified Disruptive, Impulse-Control, and Conduct Disorders

According to *DSM-5*, this category should be used when "the clinician chooses to communicate the specific reason that the presentation does not meet the criteria for any specific disruptive, impulse-control, and conduct disorder." The reason that no specific disorder has been diagnosed should be stated. The example given in *DSM-5* is "recurrent behavioral outbursts of insufficient frequency." Applying a diagnosis of other specified or unspecified disruptive, impulse-control, and conduct disorder may be useful in circumstances where there appears to be a clinical benefit in providing treatment to an individual with intellectual disability whose symptoms do not meet the full diagnostic criteria for any specific disruptive, impulse-control, and conduct disorder.

Unspecified Disruptive, Impulse-Control, and Conduct Disorders

The unspecified disorders category is used when a clinician does not specify the reason that the criteria are not met for a specific disruptive, impulse-control, and conduct disorder.

Issues Related to Diagnosis in Persons with ID

There are a number of difficulties in applying the oppositional defiant disorder, intermittent explosive disorder, and conduct disorder diagnosis in individuals with intellectual disability. First in the intellectual disability literature, these diagnostic categories are rarely used and instead broader terms to describe behavior such as challenging behavior, behavior problem, disturbed behavior, problem behavior, maladaptive behavior, behavioral disorder, etc. have been used.

The term used in the introduction section of this chapter is "problem behavior," as this was used in the UK Royal College of Psychiatrists' publication (2001) and the World Psychiatric Association's publication (Deb et al., 2009). In the World Psychiatric Association's report (Deb et al., 2009) problem behavior is defined as a "socially unacceptable behavior that causes distress, harm or disadvantage to the persons themselves or to other people, and usually requires some intervention." The examples of problem behavior include (a) verbal aggression, (b) physical aggression to others, property and/or self, (c) screaming, shouting, (d) indiscriminate wandering, (e) objectionable personal habits including smearing of feces and pica etc., (f) antisocial behavior including taking others' possession without permission etc., and (g) stereotyped movement not caused by neurological disorder etc.

Development and Course

DSM-5 reports that disruptive, impulse-control, and conduct disorders usually develop in childhood or adolescence. There is no evidence or reason to suggest that this might be different for individuals with intellectual disability. However, for individuals with intellectual disability there may be a higher likelihood that symptoms remain unrecognized or are misinterpreted until adulthood because of the difficulties encountered when assessing and diagnosing psychiatric and behavioral disorders in this group, particularly among children and adolescents.

Comorbidity

Among the general population who do not have an intellectual disability, disruptive, impulse-control, and conduct disorders are known to commonly occur with each other, substance use disorders and attention deficit hyperactivity disorder (American Psychiatric Association, 2013).

Application of Diagnostic Criteria to People with ID

General Considerations

The *DSM-5* acknowledges that many of the behaviors associated with disruptive, impulse-control, and conduct disorders are present in the general population and that when formulating a diagnosis "the frequency, persistence, pervasiveness across situations, and impairment associated with the behaviors... [should] be considered relative to what is normative for a person's age, gender, and culture." For individuals with intellectual disability, attention should also be paid to what is considered normative relative to an individual's developmental level.

One of the reasons for which diagnoses such as oppositional defiant disorder and conduct disorder are rarely used in intellectual disability literature is that by definition, these disorders assume that the person is behaving with intent, which is difficult to determine in most cases of problem behavior in intellectual disability. The other difficulty is to determine the criterion that these behaviors are inappropriate for their age, as in intellectual disability, the chronological age does not correspond to the developmental age. Also a diagnosis of intermittent explosive disorder cannot be made before 6 years of age or equivalent developmental level according to *DSM-5* criteria, which makes this diagnosis null and void for individuals with severe and profound intellectual disability and also for most with less severe intellectual disability. Although categorized under childhood onset disorders in *DSM-IV-TR*, due to the emphasis on lifespan disorders in *DSM-5*, oppositional defiant disorder and conduct disorder are no longer classified under childhood onset disorders. Nevertheless these disorders by and large have onset during childhood in most cases. Whereas oppositional defiant disorder/intermittent explosive disorder/conduct disorder diagnoses are occasionally used for children and adolescents with intellectual disability, they are very rarely used for adults with intellectual disability.

Another problem in applying this diagnostic category is the overlap with the diagnostic category of "disruptive mood dysregulation disorders" (DMDD). In order to provide a diagnostic category for youths with chronic severe irritability and aggression, *DSM-5* has created this new category under "depressive disorders." Although theoretically DMDD is distinguishable from oppositional defiant disorder and conduct disorder on the basis of severity, it is not so easy in practice to apply this distinction. Lochman et al. (2015) highlighted the potential pitfalls of this diagnosis. DMDD is defined primarily by two features: a) frequent severe temper outburst, and b) persistent irritability evident every day for most of the day. Unlike severe mood dysregulation diagnosis, DMDD excludes hyperarousal (e.g., insomnia, agitation, distractibility, racing thoughts) from the essential criteria. There is considerable debate whether or not to include DMDD in the forthcoming revision of ICD-10 as a separate diagnostic category or use this as a specifier of oppositional defiant disorder (Lochman et al., 2015). Lochman et al. (2015) also highlighted the practice of misdiagnosing severe chronic irritability as a bipolar disorder, which may lead to use of inappropriate medication.

Therefore, the way oppositional defiant disorder, intermittent explosive disorder, and conduct disorder have been defined in *DSM-5* makes it impossible for these diagnoses to apply in people with severe and profound intellectual disability and even difficult in most cases of mild to moderate intellectual disability; yet problem behavior is common in intellectual disability. This means that there should be a way to incorporate problem behavior within the diagnostic formulation for individuals with intellectual disability. A broader symptomatic diagnosis of problem behavior could also be used in this context. There are many reasons for which an individual with intellectual disability manifests problem behavior, and the management of problem behavior will require a thorough assessment of causes and effects of the individual's behavior. Therefore, it is recommended here that a formulation based on the causes and effects of problem behavior must be established first before initiating any intervention. In practice, it is not always easy to distinguish among oppositional defiant disorder, intermittent explosive disorder, and conduct disorder, although in *DSM-5* oppositional defiant disorder is described as a milder form of conduct disorder and intermittent explosive disorder is seen as a behavior for which the explicit intent is absent.

In assessing problem behavior, the types of problem behavior should be described along with severity ratings (mild, moderate, severe) and frequency ratings (low, medium, high). As a diagnosis of disruptive, impulse-control, and conduct disorders cannot be made in most cases of people with intellectual disability, particularly for those who have severe and profound intellectual disability, we recommend that in practice clinicians make a diagnosis of "problem behavior" outside the *DSM-5* framework and describe the frequency and severity of these behaviors. As the definition of severity and frequency would vary depending on many factors such as the type of behavior and perception of the person reporting the behavior, neither "severity" nor "frequency" is defined here and is left with the clinicians to define under each specific circumstance. As an assessment of the causes and effects is at the heart of the management of problem behavior, a guide for assessment is presented in this introductory section and subsequent sections on oppositional defiant disorder, intermittent explosive disorder, and conduct disorder.

Etiology and Pathogenesis

In this section biopsychosocial etiopathogenesis is combined with assessment of problem behavior because of the overlap between them and the importance of assessment in the management of problem behavior. Important aspects include an assessment of the (a) behavior, (b) person showing the behavior, (c) cause(s) of the behavior, (d) reaction to and consequences of the behavior, and (e) environment and the risks involved with the behavior.

Using the biopsychosocial model, assessment may be carried out under four broad headings, namely Behavior, Medical, Psychological/Psychiatric, and Social (BMPS).

An important area of assessment of problem behavior includes the assessment of the individuals with intellectual disability themselves. This should include an assessment of (a) their strengths and abilities, opportunities, and resources available to them, (b) their mental and physical health needs, educational/vocational needs, and the impact of disabilities, service, and resource gaps in their lives, (c) their likes, dislikes, and preferences and how they express these, (d) their history such as social, developmental, psychological, and history of their use of services, and (e) difficulties in developing fulfilling relationships, etc. Therefore, the formulation for the management of problem behavior should be person-centered. In this context, it is helpful to have a description of the individual's current and past weekly routines.

Behavior (B)

Assessment of the actual behavior should include (a) the person's history of problem behavior, (b) baseline behavior prior to the onset of problem behavior, (c) the onset of the behavior(s) to describe whether they appeared gradually over time or relatively abruptly, perhaps precipitated by an acute event, (d) the frequency, severity, and duration of the behavior(s), (e) the nature, content, and context of the behavior as some behavior may occur in certain circumstances/settings but not in others, (e) associated behaviors, and (f) the impact of the behavior(s) on the person's life, others' lives, and the environment. The behavior(s) may lead to reduced quality of life for the individual and her/his caregiver. The behavior(s) may lead to reduced access to services including education, day service, and employment opportunity, and may lead to a threatened or actual loss of placement in a residential setting or day placement. The behavior(s) may lead to reduced social activities including leisure activities, access to friends, etc. In severe cases the individual may end up being physically restrained, medicated, or taken to a hospital or police station. All these scenarios may subsequently have their impact on the individuals, their behavior, and their caregivers. For example, some of these outcomes may work as perpetuating factors for the ongoing behavior(s). These outcomes may be seen as inappropriate or excessive and the individuals or their caregivers may perceive them as punishments.

Assessment of risk including (a) risk to others, (b) risk to the individual, (c) risk to the environment, and (d) other risks form an important part of the formulation. Clinicians should use the right methods of risk assessment, take note of previous risk assessments, review risks on a regular basis, and keep records of reviewing the reduction of risks.

The behavior must be described in terms that are (a) clear, specific, and unambiguous, (b) measurable (by observation, self-report or observer rating), and (c) capable of future replication.

Medical and Organic Factors (M)

Assessment of medical and organic factors should include:

(a) Chronic physical conditions such as headaches, toothaches, pain in other parts of the body, etc., which may manifest as problem behavior. Some individuals with intellectual disability, particularly those with autistic features, may have an impaired response to pain, either hypersensitive or hyposensitive (Nader, Oberlander, Chamber, & Craig, 2004).

(b) Medical conditions such as acid reflux, which is common in intellectual disability, recurrent chest infection, heart/lungs/kidney/endocrine disease, etc.

(c) Epilepsy as there is a special relationship between epilepsy and problem behavior in individuals with intellectual disability (Deb, 2007).

(d) Other neurological conditions such as limb spasticity in cerebral palsy.

(e) Genetic conditions such as Lesch-Nyhan syndrome, fragile X syndrome, Prader-Willi syndrome, etc. These are associated with a higher prevalence of problem behavior.

(f) Sensory impairment such as hearing and visual impairment that may lead to problem behavior through frustration. But impairment in sensory processing, as is known to affect individuals with autism spectrum disorder and intellectual disability, may also lead to problem behavior, particularly if caregivers are not aware of these difficulties.

(g) Communication problems, as it is often said that problem behavior is a form of communication for many people with intellectual disability as the only way they can express their distress is through problem behavior. However, other forms of communication difficulties, such as a discrepancy between expressive and comprehensive speech skills and impaired social communication skills, may also cause confusion and lead to problem behavior.

(h) Physical disabilities such as paralysis may cause frustration and lead to problem behavior.

(i) Illicit drug- and alcohol-related factors, although this is not known to be a major problem in individuals with intellectual disability, could affect a number of individuals with borderline intelligence.

(j) Some prescribed drugs could cause adverse events that may lead to problem behavior.

Psychological/Psychiatric Factors (P)

This could include an assessment of psychiatric disorders as well as neuropsychological and other psychological factors. Psychiatric disorders such as depression, bipolar disorder, schizophrenia and other psychoses, and anxiety-related disorders may lead to problem behavior among individuals with intellectual disability. However, it is not always easy to diagnose psychiatric disorders in this population (Deb, Matthews, Holt, & Bouras, 2001). Autism spectrum disorder and attention deficit hyperactivity disorder are also common comorbidities of intellectual disability and are associated with a higher rate of problem behavior. Therefore, it is important to investigate for these conditions because the management of problem behavior may vary depending on the presence or absence of any psychiatric disorder. Clinicians should look for evidence of persistent enduring abnormalities of personality that are contributing to difficulties in interpersonal, occupational, and social domains (e.g. paranoid, psychopathic). However, clinicians should be careful in using a diagnosis such as a personality disorder, which may simply be a way of describing problem behavior in people with mild to moderate intellectual disability, whereas the same behavior among individuals with severe and profound intellectual disability may not attract a diagnosis of a personality disorder. Further description of this condition is provided in the personality disorder chapter.

Clinicians should also look for other contributory psychological and emotional factors such as bereavement; psychological trauma; physical, sexual, and emotional abuse; new, ongoing, or recurrent stress; and relationship difficulty leading to loss of self-esteem and isolation that may perpetuate problem behavior. There are important neuropsychological factors such as (a) impaired intelligence, (b) impaired memory, (c) impaired or abnormal communication skills, (d) impaired executive function, (e) impaired frontal lobe function such as apathy and lack of initiative, and (f) lower threshold of stress tolerance etc., which should all be considered when clinicians are assessing problem behavior to formulate a management plan.

Impairment in executive function may take the form of lack of planning ability, ability to think in abstract terms, multi-tasking abilities, and sense of judgment. A lack or impairment of these functions is likely to cause stress and inability to address problems in day-to-day life and, as a result, may lead to problem behavior. Many people with intellectual disability are likely to show impairment in their executive function. This impairment may remain subtle and undetected, and indeed there are practical difficulties in reliably assessing these aspects of cognitive function in most people with intellectual disability. However, in the absence of an understanding of this process, the potential for problem behavior may increase.

Many people with intellectual disability may appear lazy to their caregivers, and more and more demands may be placed on them in order to rectify these behaviors. However, the caregivers may not realize that these behaviors are caused by the impaired function of the pre-frontal cortex and the individual may not therefore have any control over these behaviors. This simple understanding on the part of the caregiver may help immensely in the management of such problem behaviors.

Individuals with intellectual disability may have a lowered tolerance of stress, and this may lead to problem behavior. The lower threshold could be caused by many factors including (a) the cognitive factors that are discussed above, (b) a lack of social support, (c) a lack of self-esteem, (d) poor self-image, (e) learned maladaptive behavior from the past, (f) a lack of psychological and social reserve, including the inability to use advanced psychological defenses as opposed to using more primitive psychological defenses, and (g) an inability to think in abstract terms. All these areas need careful consideration in the assessment. In this context, an assessment of the person's developmental history is also imperative.

Social Factors (S)

Assessment of environmental factors including description of daily activities, educational activities, occupational and leisure activities, relationships and friendships with others including family members and authority figures, and change in the environment are all important factors for consideration in the formulation of management of problem behavior. Such factors may play a major role in predisposing to, precipitating, and perpetuating problem behavior. Some individuals may perceive their environment as too demanding. For example, individuals may not want to carry out certain activities that are required of them and are seen as necessary for their personal welfare by the care staff. Similarly some individuals may find the lack of space around them, other people around them, and lots of activities/noise around them overwhelming and stressful. It is important to keep in mind that certain activities that may not seem demanding to a person who does not have intellectual disability may be perceived as demanding by some individuals with intellectual disability. Similarly some individuals may perceive their environment as under-stimulating and lacking in appropriate activities. Both under- and over-stimulation in the environment may lead to problem behavior.

Personalities of other people around the individual, including those of care staff, are likely to affect the individual's behavior. Similarly the way an individual with intellectual disability is managed also will have an impact on her/his behavior. The lack of respect for the individual with intellectual disability may be evident and can lead to problem behavior. The lack of support from others including caregivers and other residents in a house may lead to problem behavior. Similarly a confrontational attitude on the part of the care staff is likely to perpetuate problem behavior. Although these are important causes for problem behavior and must be considered during assessment, these issues have to be handled with sensitivity and caution to avoid any conflict with the caregivers or the individual with intellectual disability.

Clinicians should also assess whether the individual has experienced any significant life events in the recent or distant past (e.g. loss, change). This should include any history of ongoing or past sexual, emotional, and physical abuse. The individual may not feel part of an inclusive service or wider community or experience stigmatization and discrimination. He or she may also lack appropriate social exposure and support. All these should be considered carefully.

An important area to assess is whether the caregivers are adequately supported (including having had adequate training) and whether they are fully involved in the formulation and provision of care. The need for support for stress and fatigue amongst caregivers should be assessed carefully. Absence of these supports may help perpetuate problem behavior by creating a vicious cycle.

Other important areas to assess are the organizational settings, systems, and processes in place to support the individual with intellectual disability and her/his caregivers, and the need to address the possible absence of adequate support.

Review of Research Applying to People with ID

In this introductory section, literature-based evidence on prevalence of problem behavior in general and their risk factors are presented with particular emphasis on adults with intellectual disability. In the following sections, prevalence and risk factors for oppositional defiant disorder, intermittent explosive disorder, and conduct disorder are presented with particular emphasis on children and adolescents with intellectual disability.

Methodology

Searches of the following databases were carried out from 1980 to January 2014: Embase, Global Health, Health Management Information Consortium, International Pharmaceutical Abstracts, MEDLINE, PsycINFO, CINAHL, ASSIA, Cochrane Database, and Social Policy & Practice. Search terms for intellectual disability were combined with different terms for problem behavior. Cross references were used from other articles.

Prevalence

Studies have found that the prevalence of broader problem behaviors among people with ID may be as high as 60% (Ballinger, Ballinger, Reid, & McQueen, 1991; Cooper, Smiley, Morrison, Williamson, & Allan, 2007; Corbett, 1979; Deb, Thomas, & Bright, 2001; Holden & Gitlesen, 2006; Hove & Havik, 2008; Lund, 1985; O'Brien, 2003). None of these studies reported specific rates of disruptive, impulse-control, and conduct disorders. However, it has been estimated that 21-29% of individuals with intellectual disability have impulse-control disorder (Bertelli et al., 2012; King, DeAntonio, McCracken, Forness, & Ackerland, 1994; Tsiouris, Kim, Brown, & Cohen, 2011). Estimated rates for disruptive behavior disorders (e.g. conduct disorder and oppositional defiant disorder) range from 0.5 to 25% (Dekker & Koot, 2003; Emerson, 2003; Emerson & Hatton, 2007).

There is some evidence that, among individuals with intellectual disability, rates of impulse-control disorder vary according to individual characteristics (such as gender or age) and are higher among offenders and those with mild intellectual disability (Bertelli et al., 2012; Tsiouris et al., 2011; Yamada, 2010).

Impairments in impulse control have been found to be associated with aggressive behavior in children and adults with intellectual disability and borderline intellectual functioning (Rojahn, Matson, Naglieri, & Mayville, 2004; Tsiouris et al., 2011; Van Nieuwenhuijzen, Orobio De Castro, Van Aken, & Matthys, 2009). Tsiouris et al. (2011) quoted prevalence of aggressive behavior between 30% and 60% according to various studies. Lunsky, Lake, Balogh, Weiss, & Morris (2013) quoted in their paper findings of a Quebec-based study that reported a prevalence rate of 51.8% for aggressive behavior in a large community sample of adults with intellectual disability over a 12-month period. In a recent total-population-based study in Sweden, Lundqvist (2013) reported problem behavior (self-injury, stereotyped, and aggressive/destructive behavior) among 62% (n = 915) of individuals with intellectual disability, and in 18.7% of cases these behaviors were identified as challenging; the prevalence was 80.3 per 100,000 in the base population. The authors found that the most pronounced risk markers for aggressive behavior were severity of intellectual disability, autism, night sleep disturbances, sensory hypersensitivity, communication dysfunction, social deficits, psychiatric involvement, and psychotropic medication. Protective markers were Down syndrome and to some extent cerebral palsy.

Jones, Cooper, Smiley, Allan, Williamson, & Morrison (2008) and Hemmings, Deb, Chaplin, Hardy, & Mukherjee (2013) reviewed the prevalence studies of problem behavior in intellectual disability, particularly among adults. Their findings have been summarized here. The overall prevalence of problem behavior reported in individuals with intellectual disability varies between 6% and 60%. The reported rate of aggression varies between 7% and 23% with self-injurious behavior (SIB) varying between 3% and 24%. Severe problem behavior was found among 18% of individuals in the form of aggression, destructiveness, and SIB. The reasons for this wide discrepancy lay principally in case detection and case definition difficulties. Some of the older studies included only hospital inpatients, giving an artificially high prevalence rate. Similarly, clinic-based studies are also likely to obtain a higher prevalence than community-based population studies. Even community-based population studies typically only assess people known to health or social services, who are likely to have a higher rate of psychopathology and/or problem behaviors. Studies to date have not identified all the individuals with intellectual disability in the general population, and this case detection problem will tend to hamper the determination of the true prevalence of problem behavior. The problem of case definition lies in the fact that there is no universally accepted definition of problem behavior and so prevalence rates have been reported on the basis of the rating scales used, which have differed among studies. Similarly, the method of assessment of problem behavior has varied widely, for example from direct observation to observer-rated reporting.

The rate of different types of problem behavior also varies depending on the definition and method used. For example, Deb, Thomas, & Bright (2001) reported aggression in 23%, destructiveness in 12%, self-injurious behavior in 24%, temper tantrum in 36%, over-activity in 26%, screaming/shouting in 29%, scattering objects aimlessly in 11%, wandering in 8%, nighttime disturbance in 18%, objectionable personal habits in 20%, antisocial behavior in 11%, sexual delinquency in 4%, and attention-seeking behavior in 38% of 120 randomly selected adults with intellectual disability within a population of 75,600 people aged between 16 and 64 years in South Wales, UK. In another study, Smith et al. (1996) gathered data on 2,202 people with intellectual disability from a comprehensive register of individuals with intellectual disability in Leicestershire, UK, with approximately 32%, 31%, 26%, and 12% of the population having had profound, severe, moderate or mild, or borderline intellectual disability, respectively. Among the findings, 1,407 individuals (64%) had at least one current problem behavior, and 867 (39%) had a problem behavior that was either severe or frequent (>3 times weekly). The authors reported aggressive behavior among 21.6%, self-injurious behavior in 17.4%, destructiveness in 17.2%, over-activity in 14.3%, and screaming among 22% of the individuals studied.

Risk factors

McClintock, Hall, & Oliver (2003), Jones et al. (2008), and Hemmings et al. (2013) have reviewed different risk factors for problem behavior, particularly in adults with intellectual disability, which has been summarized in this section. In the subsequent sections risk factors associated with oppositional defiant disorder, intermittent explosive disorder, and conduct disorder, particularly in children and adolescents with intellectual disability, will be presented.

■ *Age*

It is difficult to ascertain a true association between age and the rate and type of problem behavior as no long-term longitudinal cohort study assessing problem behavior from childhood to adulthood exists. The overall rate and severity of problem behavior may increase from childhood to adolescence and young adulthood, with a subsequent decline in late adulthood to old age (Bouras & Drummond, 1992; Collacott, Cooper, & Branford, 1998; Lowe et al., 2007; Tyrer et al., 2006). However, other studies have failed to show any statistically significant association between age and the overall prevalence rate of problem behavior (Jones et al., 2008).

■ *Gender*

Some studies reported no significant relationship between gender and the rate and severity of problem behavior (e.g. Lowe et al., 2007). However, Bouras and Drummond (1992) found self-injurious behavior was more common in women, whereas antisocial and socially inappropriate behavior were more common in men. Some researchers (Jones et al., 2008) have found a higher rate of problem behavior in women, whereas others (McClintock et al., 2003; Tyrer et al., 2006) found aggression to be significantly associated with male gender. However, Deb et al. (2001) found a statistically significant association between severe problem behavior and self-injurious behavior and female gender. Emerson et al. (1997) also found an association between female gender and self-injurious behavior.

■ *Degree of Intellectual Disability*

Increasing severity of intellectual disability has been reported to be associated with a higher rate of problem behavior (Jones et al., 2008). Most studies have reported an association between self-injurious behavior and severity of intellectual disability and/or impaired speech/receptive and expressive communication and/or social impairments and lower ability (e.g. Lowe et al., 2007). There may be a difference in the type of problem behavior reported in individuals with different severity of intellectual disability. For example, Emerson et al. (2001) reported an association between mild intellectual disability and verbal aggression, meanness, and cruelty, and between severe intellectual disability and physical aggression and temper tantrums.

■ *Autism Spectrum Disorder*

It has been frequently reported that individuals with intellectual disability and comorbid autism spectrum disorder have a higher rate of problem behavior than people with intellectual disability who do not have an associated diagnosis of autism spectrum disorder (e.g. Bhaumik, Branford, McGuther, & Thorp, 1997; Matson & Cervantes, 2014; McCarthy et al., 2010; Visser, Berger, Prins, Van Schrojenstein Lantman-De Valk, & Teunisse, 2014).

■ *Genetics*

Behavioral, social, linguistic, or cognitive aspects of a syndrome may be so striking and characteristic as to prompt a diagnosis. Examples include the severe self-injury associated with Lesch-Nyhan syndrome and the combination of appetite abnormality, ritualistic behaviors, sleep abnormalities, skin-picking, repetitive speech, and vulnerability to psychiatric disorder associated with Prader-Willi syndrome. Such patterns of vulnerability to particular emotional or behavioral problems or peculiarities associated with biologically determined syndromes have been called behavioral phenotypes.

Environmental factors may interact with a genetically determined vulnerability to a behavior to determine whether or not it occurs in a given setting. Knowledge of the nature of this interaction may be important in order to determine effective treatment or management strategies (Clarke & Deb, 2009).

Charlot and Beasley (2013) highlighted in their review paper current US-based research on behavioral phenotype, particularly in association with fragile X syndrome, velo-cardio-facial syndrome and fetal alcohol syndrome. An association between problem behavior and some genetic syndromes that lead to intellectual disability has been reported in the literature (see review by Deb, 1997a, Deb, 1998; Arron, Oliver, Moss, Berg, & Burbidge, 2011). Arron et al. (2011) found aggressive behavior and self-injurious behavior among 45% of individuals with Angelman syndrome, 77% of cri du chat syndrome, 70% of Cornelia de Lange syndrome, 51% of fragile X syndrome, 52% of Prader-Willi syndrome, 64% of Lowe syndrome, and 93% of Smith Magenis syndrome. Some other intellectual disability syndromes that have association with aggression and other problem behaviors include Rett, Joubert, Aicardi, FG, and possibly Smith-Lemli-Opitz syndromes, untreated phenylketonuria, and tuberous sclerosis. This list is by no means exhaustive.

Conversely, research has demonstrated that those with Down syndrome are less likely to exhibit physically aggressive behavior (Collacott, Cooper, Branford, & McGrother, 1998; Esbensen, Seltzer, & Krauss, 2008; Tyrer et al, 2006).

■ *Neurodevelopmental and Neurobiological*

Unwin (2014) in her thesis quoted that further investigations of the determinants of aggressive behavior have attempted to isolate specific genetic conditions and have reported that monoamine oxidase was associated with aggressive behaviors in adults with intellectual disability, suggesting that a common variant in the monoamine oxidase gene may be responsible (May et al., 2009). May, Lightfoot, Srour, Knwolchuk, & Kennedy (2010) also hypothesized that serotonin transporter polymorphisms in adult males with intellectual disability may relate to aggressive behavior; however, they conclude that the relationships between genes and behaviors are likely to be complex, with multiple genes and environmental interactions involved. However, Willner (2014) argued that the role in aggression of the neurotransmitters serotonin, dopamine, and gamma-aminobutyric acid (GABA) is no longer as clear as it once appeared. Indeed RCT based evidence does not always support a role of dopaminergic (antipsychotics), seretonergic (SSRI anti-depressants and also new generation antipsychotics) and GABA-ergic (mood stabilizers) drugs in ameliorating problem behavior/aggression in ID (see review by Deb, 2016).

Unwin (2014) also quoted in her thesis that researchers have implicated an organic cause in the form of neurological damage in the absence of a specified genetic condition (Davison & Neale, 1974). Allen (2000) suggests that such damage may be linked to neuro-cognitive sequelae, such as poor impulse control, impaired memory, and reduced attention span, all features of intellectual disability that may predispose aggressive behavior. Such factors are also related to psychiatric illnesses with a significant biological origin (for example, depression or psychosis). Some suggested that aggressive behaviors may be the direct manifestation of psychiatric disorders, considered as behavioral equivalents, especially in those with severe or profound intellectual disability (Clarke & Gomez, 1999; Marston, Perry, & Roy, 1997). However, others have challenged this position and the relationship continues to be questioned, particularly in relation to specific psychiatric disorders such as depression (Allen & Davies, 2007; Deb et al, 2001; Matson & Mayville, 2001; Sturmey, Laud, Cooper, Matson, & Fodstad, 2010a, b; Tsiouris, Mann, Pattie, & Sturmey, 2003; Tsiouris, 2001). Others have suggested that psychiatric illness may provide a motivational basis for aggressive behavior (Holden & Gitlesen, 2008; Carr, Reeve, & Magito-McLaughlin, 1996; Lowry & Sovner, 1992).

Proactive aggression is seen as part of a cold, calculated act, whereas reactive aggression is seen as part of a "fight or flight" reaction, which is likely to affect individuals with a more severe degree of intellectual disability (Matlock & Aman, 2014). This distinction is not always easy in the general population, and it is even more difficult to apply in the context of intellectual disability (Matlock & Aman, 2014). However, there may be different neural substrates responsible for different types of aggression. For example, overactivation of amygdala and underactivation of ventro-medial pre-frontal cortex has been suggested as a possible neural mechanism in the causation of reactive aggression (Siever, 2008).

■ *Epilepsy*

Mental health symptoms could be observed in the pre-ictal, ictal, post-ictal, and inter-ictal phases. In certain types of seizures, particularly those associated with complex partial seizures, certain psychological and behavioral symptoms could be manifested during the "ictal" phase. The inter-ictal psychopathology has been the subject of research over many years, and the findings in this area to some extent still remain controversial. In particular, the relationship between aggressive behavior and epilepsy remains controversial (Geschwind, 1975 quoted in Deb, 2007).

There have been six controlled studies of problem behavior and psychopathology among adults with intellectual disability, with and without epilepsy (Chung & Cassidy, 2001; Deb, 1997b; Espie, Gillies, & Montgomery, 1990; Matson, Bamburg, Mayville, & Khan, 1999; Tyrer et al., 2006). Overall, no significant difference is observed in the rate of problem behavior between the epilepsy and the non-epilepsy groups. Further non-controlled studies have supported that finding (Deb & Joyce, 1998; Deb, Thomas et al., 2001; Espie et al., 2003). Deb and Hunter (1991) reported a significantly higher rate of problem behavior among the subgroups of individuals with epilepsy who showed generalized epileptiform EEG changes, who received one anti-epileptic drug at a time, and those who received carbamazepine. However, some recent studies and particularly the ones involving children have shown a possible relationship between problem behavior and active epilepsy (see review by Kerr, Gil-Nagel, Glynn, Mula, Thompson, & Zuberi, 2013) and also when intellectual disability is associated with autism spectrum disorders (Smith & Matson, 2010).

Some studies have shown an increased rate of psychopathology in general but not necessarily problem behavior among children with epilipsy in the general population and also with intellectual disability (Jones et al., 2007; Rutter, Tizard, Yule, Graham, & Whitmore, 1976). However, some have shown that problem behavior started in children before the onset of epilepsy (Austin et al., 2001), perhaps supporting the hypothesis proposed by Deb & Hunter (1991) that although multi-factorial in origin, the underlying brain damage that causes the intellectual disability rather than the epilepsy per se is a stronger determinant of psychopathology, particularly problem behaviors in individuals with intellectual disability as both epilepsy and problem behaviors are common in this population.

■ *Physical Disability*

Evidence suggests that problem behavior is less common in those with physical disability (Jones et al., 2008). Collacott, Cooper, and Brandford (1998) have shown an association between self-injurious behavior and hearing impairment and also immobility.

■ *Life Events*

In a recent systematic review, Wigham, Hatton, & Taylor (2011) summarized findings from 15 studies. There is also a more recent publication by the same authors on this subject (Wigham, Taylor, & Hatton, 2014). Most of these studies reported an association between life events and problem behavior. The types of life events described in the summarized studies included sexual abuse, general life events, bereavement, and abuse. The description of problem behaviors included aggression, self-injurious behavior, irritability, "acting out," hyperactivity, inappropriate or unusual statements, destructive behavior, conduct disorders, adjustment disorders, stereotypical behavior, and inappropriate speech.

Oppositional Defiant Disorder

Review of Diagnostic Criteria

The essential feature of oppositional defiant disorder is a recurrent pattern of angry/irritable mood, with defiant/disobedient and hostile/vindictive behavior towards at least one individual who is not a sibling.

Summary of DSM-5 *Criteria*

DSM-5 provides a list of eight symptoms for oppositional defiant disorder across three categories. Diagnosis requires the presence of four or more symptoms lasting at least six months.

This criterion is met only if the behavior occurs more frequently than is typically observed in individuals of comparable age and developmental level. Specifically, children younger than 5 years old must present with symptoms on most days, while individuals 5 and older must have issues at least weekly to meet the minimum frequency criteria. In addition, the disturbance in behavior has to cause clinically significant impairment in social, academic, or occupational functioning.

Issues Related to Diagnosis in Persons with ID

Problem behaviors are quite prevalent in individuals with intellectual disability, many of which, on face value, are the same behaviors listed in the diagnostic criteria for oppositional defiant disorder. Often, individuals with intellectual disability have inadequate cognitive, social, and coping skills to effectively navigate daily psychosocial stressors. They are going to be more easily frustrated and might feel more intimidated by peer and authority figures alike, particularly given that the locus of control in their lives is often outside their control. Therefore, it is quite common for this frustration to manifest as insufficient self-regulation of mood coincident with argumentative/defiant behaviors. The behavior should indicate a pervasive pattern of irritable, argumentative, or vindictive behavior towards others. There is a danger that this disorder will be over-diagnosed if clinicians simply use the criteria as a checklist of symptoms to tick off rather than carefully scrutinizing why these behaviors have been identified as a problem.

The symptoms of oppositional defiant disorder are considered to be within the physical and mental capacity of a 4-year-old to perform (Quay, 1999). Therefore, most individuals with severe or profound intellectual disability would lack the necessary verbal and cognitive skills to meet some of the criteria (for example, "often blames others for his or her mistakes or misbehavior," "often argues with adults," "is spiteful or vindictive" etc.).

For oppositional defiant disorder, an adequate level of verbal skills would be necessary in order to blame others for one's mistakes or to argue with adults or an authority figure. The criterion that the behavior "is often spiteful or vindictive" would require verbal skills to ascertain a deliberate desire to hurt. For the criterion "actively defies or refuses to comply with requests from authority figures or rules," the clinician would need to determine if the individual with intellectual disability was capable of comprehending the request and/or capable of carrying it out.

DSM-5 addresses intellectual disability in the context of developmental level and other factors (gender, culture) where the frequency and intensity of the behaviors are significantly greater than those commonly observed. In essence, an individual with intellectual disability must have symptom severity well outside the range of the typical intellectual disability youth to receive the additional diagnosis of oppositional defiant disorder. Further, the clinician has to take into consideration that transient oppositional behavior is very common among preschool children and adolescents and should exercise caution when evaluating individuals in these developmental periods. The clinician should apply all these guidelines when considering each of the behaviors listed in the oppositional defiant disorder diagnostic category.

Application of Diagnostic Criteria to People with ID

There is little guidance in the *DSM-5* about assessing for developmental appropriateness. Many of the behaviors could mimic other mental disorders, and many individuals with intellectual disability might be living in situations that are far from ideal. It is thus incumbent on the clinician to conduct a comprehensive assessment of all relevant factors, including physical and mental health status, quality of the environment, possible sources of stress, and possible abuse (see assessment schedule in the Introduction section).

Children and adults alike communicate something about their internal difficulties through their observable behavior and their interactions with the environment. Standardized direct observation is the most empirical method for identifying the nature of behaviors, the relevant contextual factors, and the clinically relevant interactions that might be occurring. In addition, interviews should be conducted, not only with informants but also with the person her/himself whenever possible. Such interviews might not always be appropriate for young children, however, because children often cannot describe their internal experience and history reliably.

The clinician should consider the following questions:

- The nature of the problematic behaviors must be explored in detail, including the circumstances in which they occur, the precipitants, and the amount of control the individual seems to have over them. What are the current disruptive behaviors being displayed? Clarify the referral question. For whom are these behaviors most distressing? Where and when do they occur? Define them in each area of the individual's life. Are they developmentally appropriate or inappropriate? With respect to people with intellectual disability, assess developmental appropriateness according to both chronological age and developmental age.

- What happened prior to the current assessment that might be relevant to the individual's disruptive behavior? Obtain a careful biopsychosocial history, to chart onset, course, and contributing risk factors. However, a common confound is that many details of retrospectively obtained histories might prove to be inaccurate when compared with prospective information. For individuals with intellectual disability who have been in institutional care, a careful review of social services records will be vital. In particular, it will be important in the gathering of information to document not only evidence of behaviors but also evidence of intent. Look for evidence of planned aggression and variation in behavior in different environments.

- What strengths and weaknesses does the individual present that might account for or contribute to the disruptive behaviors? Complete a psychoeducational assessment, if one has not been completed already, to detect the nature of cognitive processing deficits including executive function and social cognition. What other diagnoses might account for the disruptive behaviors? Anxiety disorders, autism spectrum disorder, posttraumatic stress disorder following abuse experiences, reactive attachment disorders, and disturbed behavior associated with histories of neglect can mimic symptoms associated with disruptive behavior.

- How has the individual's behavior affected the social environment and vice versa? What systematic factors contribute to or maintain the disruptive behavior? What has the individual been referred for and by whom? Evaluate the reliability of the referral and informant sources as reporters of the child's disruptive behavior.

A diagnosis of oppositional defiant disorder often lends the impression that the responsibility for the problem lies mainly within the child her/himself, rather than an interaction between the child and the social environment or with other systemic factors.

Methodology

The literature was searched using MEDLINE and PsychLit on terms relating to *mental retardation, intellectual disability, developmental disability, learning disability, special needs, cognitive impairment, oppositional defiant disorder, oppositional disorder, disobedient, challenging behavior*, and *problem behavior.*

Review of Research Applying to People with ID

Some studies have explored challenging behavior, and within this constellation of behaviors are included noncompliance, temper tantrums, and verbal aggression, but few assessments included specific comorbid diagnoses such as oppositional defiant disorder. Jacobson (1982) reported behavioral information on 30,000 individuals with intellectual disability. Of relevance, he reported that "blaming others" was less prominent among individuals with more severe levels of intellectual disability. This finding is not surprising, given that it has been established that an adequate level of verbal ability is needed to meet some of the criteria.

Emerson et al. (1997) reported on the prevalence of challenging behavior in adults and children with intellectual disability. Of interest are the reported rates among children with intellectual disability, which included verbal aggression among 62.7%, generalized noncompliance among 86.6% (with a significant difference reported between adults and children), and temper tantrums among 59.8%. These results raise concerns about the difficulty clinicians will encounter when trying to differentiate what is associated with challenging behavior and what is associated more with a pattern of negativistic, defiant, and hostile behavior. Emerson and Hatton (2007) reported oppositional defiant disorder among 13.3% of youths with intellectual disability compared with 2.3% in typically developing youths.

In a recent study Christensen, Baker, & Blacher (2013) compared rates of oppositional defiant disorder among children with intellectual disability (n = 49), children with borderline intellectual functioning (n = 20), and typically developing children (n = 115). The authors administered the Diagnostic Interview Schedule for Children (DISC) to mothers at child ages 5, 6, 7, 8, and 9 years. Using the combined variables that indicate whether criteria for oppositional defiant disorder were "ever met," the authors found oppositional defiant disorder to be present among 50.4% of typically developing children compared with 70.5% of the borderline intellectual functioning children and 73.5% of the children with intellectual disability. This difference was not statistically significant. The point prevalence of oppositional defiant disorder was between 21%-29% among the typically developing group across ages, compared with 35%-44% among the borderline intellectual functioning group and 39%-48% among the intellectual disability group. The authors also reported that the comorbidity of oppositional defiant disorder with other disorders, particularly attention deficit hyperactivity disorder, was raised for children with intellectual disability. There were no group differences in gender, age of onset, or stability of oppositional defiant disorder, and all three groups endorsed symptoms of oppositional defiant disorder with the same relative frequency.

Evaluating the Level of Evidence Using the Cochrane Method

The majority of studies on oppositional defiant disorder comorbid with intellectual disability represent convenience samples of Type V evidence. One notable exception is Christensen et al. (2013), which is Type IV.

Adaptation of Diagnostic Criteria

In general, it is important for clinicians to think clearly about the function of the behaviors they are questioning, how the behaviors affect the social environment and vice versa, and whether they represent a clear pattern of angry, argumentative, defiant, and at times vindictive behaviors that are more markedly present than is typically observed. The diagnosis of oppositional defiant disorder *cannot* be consistently applied to individuals with severe or profound intellectual disability, given that at least four of the behaviors require an adequate level of verbal ability.

The adapted criteria are presented in relation to mild to moderate intellectual disability. Generally, it is easier to apply the criteria to individuals with mild intellectual disability; however, developmental profiles can be variable, and this assumption cannot, therefore, always be guaranteed. For example, there will be situations where an individual with mild intellectual disability might have difficulty verbalizing her or his thoughts and feelings. Therefore, the issue of intent might be more difficult to ascertain even in comparison to someone with an even lower cognitive/adaptive functioning.

Oppositional Defiant Disorder

DSM-5 Diagnostic Criteria	Applying Criteria for Mild to Moderate Intellectual Disability
A. Pattern of angry/irritable mood, argumentative/defiant behavior or vindictiveness lasting at least 6 months, during which four (or more) of the following are present:	A. No adaptation.
1. Often loses temper	(1) No adaptation. **Note**: The clinician needs to rule out any other reasons for the behavior, such as a mood disorder, psychotic disorder and substance use etc. (see discussion on etiology and assessment of oppositional defiant disorder and problem behavior)
2. Often touchy or easily annoyed	(2) No adaptation.
3. Often angry and resentful	(3) No adaptation.
4. Often argues with authority figures or, for children and adolescents, with adults	(4) No adaptation.
5. Often actively defies or refuses to comply with requests from authority figures or with rules	(5) No adaptation. **Note**: The clinician needs to complete a language and cognitive assessment to rule out comprehension and specific cognitive difficulties that might otherwise explain the noncompliance.
6. Often deliberately annoys others	(6) No adaptation. **Note**: Assessment of intent is required.
7. Often blames others for his or her mistakes or misbehavior	(7) No adaptation.
8. Spiteful or vindictive at least twice within the past 6 months	(8) No adaptation. **Note**: The behavior requires evidence of intent to hurt.
Note: Consider a criterion met only if the behavior occurs more frequently than is typically observed in individuals of comparable age and developmental level.	**Note**: An assessment of developmental age is required.
B. The disturbance in behavior is associated with distress in the individual or others in the immediate social context. Further it causes clinically significant impairment in social, academic, or occupational functioning.	B. No adaptation.
C. The behaviors do not occur exclusively during the course of a psychotic disorder, mood disorder or substance use.	C. No adaptation.

Intermittent Explosive Disorder

Review of Diagnostic Criteria

Individuals with intellectual disability are at risk for impulsive and aggressive behavior.

The risk factors that predict intermittent explosive disorder among people without disability are present at high rates among people with intellectual disability (physical and emotional trauma, autonomic hyperarousal, brain injury/abnormality, seizure disorder, etc.).

Although many intermittent explosive disorder diagnostic features are observable and relatively objective, the diagnosis does require a developmental level equivalent to a 6-year-old, which limits its application to the intellectual disability population.

Intermittent explosive disorder is characterized by recurrent impulsive aggressive outbursts that are grossly out of proportion to any provocation or psychosocial stressor. Explosive episodes may be frequent and less severe (non-injurious) and less frequent but involving severe aggressive behavior, such as destruction of property or physical assault with injury against an animal or person. An important qualifier is that the aggressive outbursts are impulsive in nature and not premeditated or instrumental. The recurrent aggressive outbursts cause marked distress or impairment in occupational or interpersonal functioning or are associated with social, financial, or legal consequences. Intermittent explosive disorder is characterized by more intense impulsive aggression as compared with the outbursts associated with attention deficit hyperactivity disorder, oppositional defiant disorder, conduct disorder, antisocial personality disorder, and borderline personality disorder. Intermittent explosive disorder should not be diagnosed in children younger than 6 or in children aged 6-18 if aggression occurs in the context of an adjustment disorder. Intermittent explosive disorder should not be diagnosed in people with disruptive mood dysregulation disorder, or whose impulsive aggressive outbursts are attributable to another medical condition or to the physiological effects of a substance.

Summary of DSM-5 *Criteria*

DSM-5 provides six criteria for intermittent explosive disorder, each of which must be present for a diagnosis. These criteria require recurrent impulsive aggressive behavioral outbursts with a magnitude that is grossly out of proportion to the provocation or to any precipitating psychosocial stressor. Criteria are met only if outbursts are impulsive, rather than premeditated, and must cause significant distress or impairment. Chronological or developmental equivalent must be 6 years of age, and the behavior is not better explained by another mental disorder. For children 6-18 years, aggressive behavior that occurs as part of an adjustment disorder should not be considered for this diagnosis. Intellectual disability can be diagnosed concurrent with attention deficit hyperactivity disorder, conduct disorder, oppositional defiant disorder, or autism spectrum disorder when recurrent impulsive aggressive outbursts are in excess of those usually seen in these disorders.

Issues Related to Diagnosis in Persons with ID

One difficulty in applying intermittent explosive disorder diagnostic criteria to people with intellectual disability is that certain features of intellectual disability may make impulsive aggression more likely. For example, people with intellectual disability have less control over their impulses generally. In addition, intellectual disability is associated with fewer communication and self-calming skills that could be used to mitigate aggressive outbursts. Lacking communication skills, many people with intellectual disability may use aggression and other destructive behavior instrumentally. Although instrumental aggression is excluded from consideration for an intermittent explosive disorder diagnosis, it may be difficult to be sure of the instrumental nature of behavior in people with significant intellectual and communication impairment. Aggressive acts that appear unplanned and that persist without positive or negative reinforcement (i.e., is dysfunctional) may meet Criterion C. In people with intellectual disability, impulsive aggression could be correlated with seizure disorders, developmental brain abnormalities, and environmental factors and with severity of intellectual disability. Impulse control disorders may lead to aggressive behavior. Siever (2008) proposed that neurobiological characteristics such as over-arousal, low frustration tolerance, impulsivity, mood dysregulation, and impaired cortical control of an amygdala hypersensitive to stimuli that are linked to violence in people without intellectual disability may show similar correlation between impulse control and aggression in people with intellectual disability. Another difficulty in making a diagnosis of intermittent explosive disorder in children and adults with intellectual disability is criteria E, that the chronological age must be at least 6 years (or equivalent developmental level). This criterion impacts individuals functioning with moderate to profound intellectual impairment. These factors complicate the evaluation of impulsive aggression as clinically it is not always easy to determine the developmental age of a person with intellectual disability.

The most difficult issue concerning impulse control disorders is the question of whether or not aggressive behavior represents a true disorder. In people with intellectual disability, the extreme heterogeneity of impulsive aggression is magnified by the differences between mild versus profound intellectual impairment. One solution to the problem of accurate psychiatric diagnosis was proposed by Robins and Guze (1970) who suggested that data collection focus on measuring groups of symptoms rather than syndromes. To be valid, a syndrome requires not only symptoms that are consistently observed together, but that also follow a predictable course and display a common pathophysiology and response to treatment. Since few mental disorders have clear biological uniformity, clinicians rely on observable descriptions of symptoms that are then compared with established criteria. Unfortunately, impulse control disorders lack this degree of internal consistency, especially for individuals with intellectual disability. Therefore, a symptomatic description of behaviors rather than using a rigid difficult to apply *DSM-5* criteria-based diagnosis may be a better way forward for the clinicians to understand and manage behavior problems in general and intermittent explosive disorder in particular.

Associated Features Supporting Diagnosis

Mood disorders, psychotic disorders, anxiety disorders, and substance use disorders may be associated with intermittent explosive disorder, although onset of these disorders occurs typically later in life than that of intermittent explosive disorder.

Development and Course

The onset of recurrent, problematic impulsive aggressive behavior is most common in late childhood or adolescence (Kessler et al., 2006) and rarely begins for the first time after age 40 years. The core features of intermittent explosive disorder typically are persistent and continue for many years. The course of the disorder may be episodic, with recurring periods of impulsive aggressive outbursts. It also appears to be quite common regardless of the presence or absence of attention deficit hyperactivity disorder or disruptive impulse control and conduct disorder or oppositional defiant disorder.

In an adult (>18 years) sample, age was not related to verbal aggression towards others; however, verbal aggression, and physical aggression against others, objects, and self were all significantly decreased as age increased about one Standard Deviation (14 years) (Tsiouris, Kim, Brown, & Cohen, 2011; Tenneij, Didden, Stolker & Koot, 2009). Belden, Thomson, & Luby (2008) found in preschool children without intellectual disability that the frequency and severity of tantrums and self-injurious behavior were higher in sample with depressive and disruptive characteristics than in controls, confirming that mood dysregulation, anxiety, fear, hyper-arousal, impulsivity, and brain immaturity play primary roles in the initiation, maintenance, and exacerbation of aggressive behavior.

Prevalence

One-year prevalence data for intermittent explosive disorder in the US is about 2.7% (narrow definition) (American Psychiatric Association, 2013). Intermittent explosive disorder is more prevalent among younger individuals (e.g., younger than 35-40 years), compared with older individuals (older than 50 years) and in individuals with a high school education or less (American Psychiatric Association, 2013). McLaughlin et al., (2012) found that 7.8% of adolescents (age 13-17) met *DSM-IV* criteria for lifetime intermittent explosive disorder. Intermittent explosive disorder was significantly (63.9%) comorbid with mood, anxiety, and substance disorders. Coccaro, Schmidt, Samuels, & Nestadt (2004) reported a lifetime prevalence rate of 11% and a one-month prevalence of 2.3% in a community sample of adults with intellectual disability. These prevalence rates depend on the definition used for intermittent explosive disorder. Lifetime prevalence can be 7.3% and 12-month to 3.9% (Kessler et al., 2006) when a broad definition of intermittent explosive disorder is used (three or more attacks occurring over a lifetime).

Risk and Prognostic Factors

- *Environmental*

Individuals with a history of physical and emotional trauma during the first two decades of life are at increased risk for intermittent explosive disorder (Nickerson, Aderka, Bryant, & Hofmann, 2012). Exposure to trauma, especially interpersonal trauma, in childhood is related to development of intermittent explosive disorder over and above the impact of trauma severity, post-traumatic stress disorder, and generalized anxiety disorder. Ghaziuddin (1988) reported an association between life events and aggressive outbursts in adults with intellectual disability, which may suggest a connection between explosive aggression and hyperarousal provoked by specific conditioned fear experiences.

- *Genetic and Physiological*

First degree relatives of individuals with intermittent explosive disorder are at increased risk for intermittent explosive disorder, and twin studies have demonstrated a substantial genetic influence of impulsive aggression (Coccaro, 2010). In a blinded, controlled, family history study of intermittent explosive disorder by research criteria (intermittent explosive disorder-IR), which include the essence of *DSM-IV* intermittent explosive disorder criteria but are more precise and valid, Coccaro (2010) found familial risk in first degree relatives of intermittent explosive disorder to have significantly elevated morbid risk of intermittent explosive disorder compared with controls.

Adults with intermittent explosive disorder are more likely than controls to be younger, male, unmarried, white, have less than college education, to smoke, to abuse alcohol and other drugs, to have a history of depression, and to be obese (McCloskey, Kleabir, Berman, Chen, & Coccaro, 2010). Individuals with intermittent explosive disorder were more likely to report having had an accident or injury requiring treatment, though these incidents were unrelated to fighting. Individuals with intermittent explosive disorder were more likely to have heart disease, hypertension, stroke, diabetes, arthritis, neck/back pain, headaches, ulcer, and other chronic pain.

Research provides neurobiological support for the presence of serotonergic abnormalities, globally and in the brain, specifically in areas of the limbic system (anterior cingulate gyrus) and orbitofrontal cortex in individuals with intermittent explosive disorder (Coccaro, Lee, & Kavoussi, 2010). Amygdala responses to anger stimuli during functional magnetic resonance imaging scanning are greater in individuals with intermittent explosive disorder compared with healthy individuals. Coccaro and colleagues (2010), in a study of serotonin, aggression, suicidality, and impulsivity, found inverse correlation between serotonin response and a composite measure of aggression. Individuals with intermittent explosive disorder demonstrated a reduction in residual peak delta prolactin and a highly selective agent for serotonin d-Fenfluramine (d-FEN) PRL [d-FEN]-R values in aggressive and suicidal participants and an increase among healthy controls. Similarly, Angoa-Perez et al. (2012) found that deletion of brain serotonin leads to a robust phenotype of behavior disinhibition including compulsive and motor impulsive behaviors and extreme impulsive aggression in mice.

Haller & Kruk (2006) suggested that hyperarousal plays an important role in sudden outbursts characteristic of intermittent explosive disorder accompanied by excessive autonomic arousal and affective reactions. The sympathetic tone, adrenaline production, cortisol stress responses, and autonomic reaction are all increased. These hyperarousal-driven forms of aggressive behavior appear to have strong emotional and autonomic hyperarousal and high social impact. However, it is difficult to ascertain whether hyperarousal is caused by the intermittent explosive disorder or is the cause for the intermittent explosive disorder.

- *Culture-Related Diagnostic Issues*

The lower prevalence of intermittent explosive disorder in some regions (Asia, Middle East) or countries (Romania, Nigeria) compared with the USA suggests that information about recurrent problematic impulsive aggressive behavior either is not elicited on questioning or is less likely to be present because of cultural factors (American Psychiatric Association, 2013).

- *Gender-Related Diagnostic Issues*

According to some studies, the prevalence of intermittent explosive disorder is greater in males than females (odds 1.4: 2.3); however, other studies have found no gender difference (American Psychiatric Association, 2013).

Differential Diagnosis

A diagnosis of intermittent explosive disorder should not be made if Criteria A1 and A2 are only met during an episode of another mental disorder (major depression, bipolar disorder, psychotic disorder etc.) or when impulsive aggressive outbursts are attributable to another medical condition or to the physiological effects of a substance or medication. This diagnosis should also not be made, especially in children and adolescents aged 6-18 years, when the impulsive aggressive outbursts occur in the context of an adjustment disorder.

Other examples in which recurrent problematic impulsive aggressive outbursts may, or may not, be diagnosed as intermittent explosive disorder, include the following:

- *Disruptive Mood Dysregulation Disorder (DMDD)*

In contrast to intermittent explosive disorder, disruptive mood dysregulation disorder is characterized by persistently negative mood state (irritability, anger) most of the day nearly every day, between impulsive aggressive outbursts. A diagnosis of disruptive mood dysregulation disorder can only be made when the recurrent problematic impulsive aggressive outbursts start before age 10 years. Finally, a diagnosis of disruptive mood dysregulation disorder should not be made for the first time after age 18 years. Otherwise, these diagnoses are mutually exclusive.

- *Antisocial Personality Disorder or Borderline Personality Disorder*

Antisocial personality disorder and borderline personality disorder are often associated with recurrent problematic impulsive, aggressive outbursts. However, the severity of impulsive aggression in personality disorders is lower than in intermittent explosive disorder. Further discussion on personality disorder is presented in the relevant chapter.

- *Delirium, Major Neurocognitive Disorder, and Aggressive Type Personality Change due to Another Medical Condition*

A diagnosis of intermittent explosive disorder should not be made if outbursts are the result of the physiological effects of another diagnosable medical condition (e.g., brain injury associated with change in personality characterized by aggressive outbursts, complex partial epilepsy). Nonspecific abnormalities detected on neurological examination (e.g., soft signs) and nonspecific electroencephalographic changes are compatible with a diagnosis of intermittent explosive disorder unless another condition better explains behavior.

- *Substance Intoxication or Substance Withdrawal*

A diagnosis of intermittent explosive disorder should not be made when impulsive aggression is nearly always associated with intoxication or withdrawal from substances including alcohol. However, when a sufficient number of outbursts also occur in the absence of substance intoxication or withdrawal, and these warrant independent clinical attention, a diagnosis of intermittent explosive disorder may be given.

- *Attention Deficit Hyperactivity Disorder, Oppositional Defiant Disorder, Conduct Disorder, Autism Spectrum Disorder*

Impulsive aggression can occur with many childhood-onset conditions but the nature of the outburst is different and typically lower than intermittent explosive disorder. In oppositional defiant disorder, outbursts are usually limited to temper tantrums and verbal arguments with authority figures, while intermittent explosive disorder outbursts are in response to a broader array of provocation and include physical assault. In conduct disorder, aggression is proactive and predatory. If Criteria A thorough E are also met, and the impulsive aggressive outbursts warrant independent clinical attention, a diagnosis of intermittent explosive disorder may be given.

Functional Consequences of Intermittent Explosive Disorder

Social (e.g., loss of friends or relatives, marital instability, etc.), occupational (e.g., demotion, loss of employment), financial (e.g., due to value of objects destroyed, loss of wages from occupational consequences), and legal (e.g., civil suits as a result of aggressive behavior against person or property, criminal charges for assault) problems often develop as a result of intermittent explosive disorder (American Psychiatric Association, 2013).

Comorbidity

Depressive disorders, anxiety disorders, and substance use disorders are common comorbidities of intermittent explosive disorder. In addition, individuals with antisocial personality disorder or borderline personality disorder and individuals with a history of disruptive behavior (attention deficit hyperactivity disorder, conduct disorder, oppositional defiant disorder) are at greater risk for comorbid intermittent explosive disorder. In a study of adults receiving outpatient treatment for bipolar disorder, 6.5% of participants were found to have intermittent explosive disorder (Karakus & Tamam, 2011). McCloskey, Ben-Zeev, Lee, Coccaro, (2008) reported suicidal attempts among 12.5% and self-injurious behavior among 16% of adults with intermittent explosive disorder.

Application of Diagnostic Criteria to People with ID

General Considerations

A multidisciplinary assessment is needed to confirm a diagnosis of intermittent explosive disorder in an individual with intellectual disability. The multidisciplinary team may include a psychiatrist, a psychologist or behavior specialist, a speech and language therapist, a nurse, an occupational therapist, a social worker, and a neurologist where necessary. Caregivers and other close informants such as teachers should also contribute to the discussion. Individual with intellectual disability should also take part in the discussion where necessary and appropriate. A thorough physical and mental state examination is necessary to exclude any medical and psychiatric cause of aggressive behavior. A neurologist may assist in the diagnosis and management of epilepsy and other neurological disorders which may be contributing to the aggressive behavior. The psychologist or behavior specialist/nurse may help in gathering data on the nature, frequency, target, and impact (damage or injury) of aggression and carrying out a functional assessment of the behavior. Interviewing a close informant or eye witness to the aggressive episodes is needed to form an impression on the intensity of provocation, psychosocial stressors that may contribute to the behavior and possible instrumental gains from the aggressive behavior. Finally, any history of abuse or trauma should be discussed in the context of identifying stimuli that may trigger an aggressive fear response.

Methodology

A literature search was performed using the Pubmed database and the EBSCOhost Online Research Database service accessed via The Ohio State University's online library catalog.

Review of Research Applying to People with ID

The first consideration that must be addressed regarding the evidence base for intermittent explosive disorder in people with intellectual disability is that the evidence base is very thin. No studies were found that attempted to apply *DSM* criteria for intermittent explosive disorder in intellectual disability. As only a few studies reported on intermittent explosive disorder in intellectual disability, literature on aggression in intellectual disability and on impulse control disorders in intellectual disability was reviewed. It is important to consider impulsive aggression as a function of age, gender, and severity of intellectual disability.

▪ *Prevalence and Course*

Tsiouris et al. (2011) conducted a large (n = 4069) survey of adults receiving developmental disability services in New York State. They found that only 17% of their sample did not show any aggressive behavior. Psychiatric diagnoses were made in 59% of the population, with impulse control disorders being the most prevalent category representing 21% of the sample. Emerson et al. (2001) reported a total population study of challenging behavior in children and adults with intellectual disability in two areas of England. Overall, 16.5% of the population was reported to have challenging behavior to the extent that it was considered by informants to constitute a serious management problem. Of these, 64% were reported to show demanding aggression. Cooper et al. (2009) conducted a prevalence and remission rate study of aggression in adults with intellectual disability in Scotland in UK. They found that 9.8% of adults had aggressive behavior at baseline and the two year remission rate was 27.7%. Cooper et al. (2009) found that aggression was highly associated with attention deficit hyperactivity disorder.

Although only recurrent impulsive aggressive outbursts are considered in a diagnosis of intermittent explosive disorder, individuals may present both impulsive and instrumental aggressive behavior. *DSM-5* does allow the concurrent diagnosis of intermittent explosive disorder and conduct disorder, for example.

▪ *Determinants*

Although some studies have found aggression to be more common among men (McClintock et al., 2003; Tsiouris et al., 2011) others found no gender difference (McMillan, Hastings, & Coldwell, 2004; Tenneij, Didden, Stolker, & Koot, 2009) and one study found aggression to be more common among women (Cooper et al., 2009). Similarly, mixed findings have been reported on the association between aggression and severity of intellectual disability. Some studies have found aggression to be more and others less common (Cooper et al., 2009; McClintock, et al., 2003) as intellectual disability becomes more severe. Davidson et al. (1999) did not find an association between aggression and severity of intellectual disability. Tsiouris et al. (2011) examined the type of aggressive behavior and found that the frequency of verbal aggression and property destruction decreased as IQ decreases but physical aggression increases as IQ decreases. Tsiouris et al. (2011) found higher prevalence of impulse control disorder diagnoses among adults with mild intellectual disability (27%) and lowest among adults with profound intellectual disability (15%). Age was not often examined as a function of aggression or impulsivity and findings vary. Tenneij et al. (2009) found no association between aggression and age while Tsiouris et al. (2011) found that age was not related to verbal aggression but that physical aggression tended to decrease with age in adults with intellectual disability.

Evaluating the Level of Evidence

The overall level of evidence on intermittent explosive disorder diagnosis in children and adults with intellectual disability is Type IV Evidence. Precious few studies speak to this issue and those that do are well designed observational studies.

Adults with Mild to Moderate ID

No research applied *DSM-IV* criteria of intermittent explosive disorder to individuals with mild to moderate intellectual disability.

Adults with Severe or Profound ID

No research applied *DSM-IV* criteria of intermittent explosive disorder to individuals with severe or profound intellectual disability.

Children and Adolescents with ID

No research applied *DSM-IV* criteria of intermittent explosive disorder to children or adolescents with intellectual disability.

Summary of Limitations in Applying DSM-5 *Criteria to People with ID*

The first criterion for a diagnosis of intermittent explosive disorder, recurrent impulsive aggressive behavioral outbursts, is objective, directly observable, and easily applied to individuals at all levels of intellectual disability. Criterion B requires a determination that the aggressive act was out of proportion to the provocation which may be difficult to evaluate in individuals with limited expressive communication and requires an understanding of the individual's developmental level. What seems like an egregious provocation to an 8-year old may not even irritate an older, more mature, person. The impact of impulsive aggression must take into account the life circumstance of the individual; the impact on community inclusion and the service delivery system (e.g., aggression causes loss of residential placement) should be considered as well as occupational, interpersonal, financial, and legal consequences. An important criterion for diagnosing intermittent explosive disorder in intellectual disability is Criterion E, which requires a minimum developmental age of 6 years. This criterion precludes a diagnosis of intermittent explosive disorder in severe and profound intellectual disability and requires a careful developmental assessment in individuals with less severe cognitive impairment.

Etiology and Pathogenesis

Biological Factors

Although biological factors of intermittent explosive disorder have been explored, no research addressed biological etiology of intermittent explosive disorder in intellectual disability.

Genetic Factors

No research was found addressing genetic factors of intermittent explosive disorder in intellectual disability.

Psychosocial Factors

Although no research spoke directly to the diagnosis of intermittent explosive disorder in intellectual disability, Emerson & Hatton (2007) examined social determinants of mental health in children and adolescents with intellectual disability and found that intellectual disability conferred significant social disadvantage including exposure to negative life events, single parent family, poor family functioning, mother with suspected mental health disorder, income poverty, which constitute risk factors for higher risk of mental health problems (36% in intellectual disability versus 8% in non-intellectual disability group). In fact, controlling for social/environmental risk resulted in a 50% reduction in attributable risks for emotional disorder, a 38% reduction for conduct disorder, and a 33% reduction for hyperactivity.

Developmental Factors

No research was found addressing developmental factors impacting intermittent explosive disorder in intellectual disability.

Intermittent Explosive Disorder

DSM-5 Diagnostic Criteria	Applying Criteria for Mild-Moderate Intellectual Disability	Applying Criteria for Severe/Profound Intellectual Disability
A. Recurrent impulsive aggressive behavioral outbursts including: 1. Verbal aggression or physical aggression toward property, animals, or other individuals, occurring twice weekly, on average, for a period of three months. 2. Three behavioral outbursts involving damage or destruction of property and/or physical assault involving physical injury against animals or other individuals occurring in a 12 month period.	No adaptation.	Diagnosis cannot be made.

B. The magnitude of outbursts is grossly out of proportion to the provocation or to any precipitating psychosocial stressor.	**Note**: The clinician should consider what may constitute a psychosocial stressor for a person with intellectual disability which may not be the same as for a person without intellectual disability.	Diagnosis cannot be made.
C. The recurrent aggressive outbursts are impulsive, not premeditated or instrumental.	**Note**: The clinician should assess the premeditated or instrumental nature of the outburst in the context of the person's cognitive development.	Diagnosis cannot be made.
D. The recurrent aggressive outbursts cause either marked distress in the individual or impairment in occupational or interpersonal functioning, or are associated with financial or legal consequences.	**Note**: The impact of the outburst on social inclusion/service delivery system should also be considered.	Diagnosis cannot be made.
E. Chronological age is at least 6 years (or equivalent developmental level).	**Note**: Consideration of chronological or developmental age is required for diagnosis	This criterion all but precludes an IED diagnosis in severe/profound ID.
F. The recurrent aggressive outbursts are not better explained by another mental disorder and are not attributable to another medical condition or to the physiological effects of a substance. For children ages 6-18 years, aggressive behavior that occurs as part of an adjustment disorder should not be considered for this diagnosis.	**Note**: The clinician should consider the difficulty that may be faced in diagnosing mental disorder in a person with intellectual disability.	Diagnosis cannot be made.

Conduct Disorder

Review of Diagnostic Criteria

The essential feature of conduct disorder is a repetitive and persistent pattern of behavior that violates the basic rights of others or that breaks major age-appropriate societal norms or rules.

Summary of DSM-5 *Criteria*

Included in the *DSM-5* criteria for conduct disorder are behaviors that are grouped into four major categories:

- Aggression to people or animals
- Destruction of property
- Deceitfulness or theft
- Serious violations of rules

DSM-5 provides a list of 15 symptoms under these four groups. Diagnosis requires the presence of three or more of the symptoms during the preceding 12 months, with at least one symptom being present during the preceding six months. As with all psychiatric conditions, the presentation must cause clinically significant impairment in social, academic, or occupational functioning (Criterion B).

Two subtypes can be specified, based on the age of onset of at least one symptom: Childhood-Onset Type (onset prior to age 10 years) and Adolescent-Onset Type (no symptoms prior to age 10 years). Unspecified-Onset captures individuals that meet criteria for conduct disorder but there is insufficient information to determine onset of symptoms.

Issues Related to Diagnosis in Persons with ID

A core concern in making the diagnosis of conduct disorder is the implied assumption in the general criteria that the person *understands* the basic rights of others and appropriate social norms. This certainly cannot be assumed in people with intellectual disability (Enfield & Tonge, 1991). The four categories of behaviors to be rated in conduct disorder cannot be viewed as equivalent in the case of people with intellectual disability. There are numerous cases of people with intellectual disability showing aggression towards people or animals and destroying property, but there are far fewer cases where deceitfulness or serious violation of rules is present. Clearly, the difference is in the nature of the *intent*. Aggression and destruction can occur simply because the person is frustrated and does not have any other available outlet, as happens in many cases of challenging behaviors. Serious violation of rules could also occur in the absence of intent, either because the person does not understand the rules or because the person does not appreciate the consequences of her or his actions. Deceit, however, is by definition an intended act.

DSM-5 requires that the behavior be "age-inappropriate" but provides no guidelines for the clinician to make this dichotomous assessment. For clinicians making the diagnosis in children (or adults) with intellectual disability, the matter is even more problematic. Traditionally, clinicians working with individuals with intellectual disability have adjusted for developmental age when considering the "appropriateness" of a given behavior. The issue is important given that in neurotypical children and adolescents behaviors such as threatening, cruelty to animals, attention-demanding, physical attacks, temper tantrums, and disobedience at home tend to decline with age. But by definition, youths and adults with intellectual disability are functioning at a level much lower than their chronological age.

Instead of designing an elaborate system for adjusting for developmental age, it is better that the clinician examines all the behaviors and try to understand the significance of them in the context of pursuing evidence of intent. Overall, the problems of determining the level of understanding of societal rules and intent make the application of conduct disorder diagnoses very difficult in this population. Even individuals with borderline intellectual functioning (Full Scale IQ in 70s) are often considered at the margins of culpability for their behavior. As we progress through the various levels of intellectual disability, the validity and reliability of a conduct disorder diagnosis becomes ever the more questionable. Whatever the severity of the intellectual disability, however, it is of critical importance to establish beyond doubt that intent was present before making the diagnosis.

Application of Diagnostic Criteria to People with ID

The assessment recommendations that were made in the oppositional defiant disorder section of this chapter apply equally to conduct disorder. In particular, the clinician should focus specifically on how the individual's behavior is affected by the social environment and vice versa, and what systemic factors contribute to or maintain the behaviors. A diagnosis of conduct disorder often lends the impression that the responsibility for the problem lies mainly within the individual her/himself, rather than an interaction between the individual and the social environment or with other systemic factors.

Methodology

A review of the literature was conducted, searching MEDLINE and PsychLit on terms relating to *mental retardation*, *intellectual disability*, *developmental disability*, *learning disability*, *special needs*, *cognitive impairment*, *conduct disorder*, *disruptive behavior disorder*, *challenging behavior*, *problem behavior* and *behavior problems*.

Review of Research Applying to People with ID

There is very little research looking at conduct disorder in people with intellectual disability. No studies have been published with regards to the application of *DSM-5* criteria. One major issue is that challenging behaviors are prevalent in this population, and a large proportion of the studies deal with nonspecific aggressive or disruptive behaviors. In some studies, the term *conduct disorder* is loosely applied to any behavioral problem where conduct is a concern. This must be taken into consideration when evaluating studies of prevalence. Overall, there is a clear need to clarify and tighten the criteria for this population (which is also true for the general population).

- *Prevalence of Conduct Disorder Relative to the General Population*

Youth with intellectual disability exhibit higher rates of aggression and conduct problems compared with controls (Koller, Richardson, Katz, & McLaren, 1982). School-specific studies reveal children in special education classes displaying higher rates of aggressive and antisocial behavior compared with students in mainstream classes (Cullinan, Epstein, Matson, & Rosemier, 1984). Emerson (2003) reviewed the prevalence of mental disorders in children and adolescents with and without intellectual disability. The study was a secondary analysis of the 1999 Office for National Statistics Survey of the Mental Health of Children and Adolescent in Great Britain. The presence of mental disorders was detected using the Developmental and Well Being Assessment, which involves (a) two structured interviews, one with the primary caregiver and the other with the child, (b) a questionnaire used with the child's teacher, and (c) a computer-assisted diagnostic rating system that provides diagnoses against the *DSM-IV* and the *ICD-10*.

The results indicated that the prevalence of any diagnosed *ICD-10* disorder, conduct disorder, anxiety disorder, hyperkinesis or pervasive developmental disorder was significantly greater among children with intellectual disability than it was among their peers who do not have intellectual disability. In particular, the conduct disorder group made up 25% of the intellectual disability group (compared with 4.2% in the non-intellectual disability group) and included oppositional defiant disorder (13.3%), unsocialized conduct disorder (3.4%), socialized conduct disorder (3.8%), and other conduct disorder (4.9%). In considering the results of Emerson's study, there is, however, a question about the validity of the Development and Wellbeing Assessment for assessing mental disorders in children and adolescents with intellectual disability.

Jacobson (1982) summarized information about problem behavior and mental impairment in a population of over 30,000 individuals receiving developmental disabilities services in the USA. There were 29 behaviors selected for the report, grouped into four main categories: cognitive, affective, major, and minor. Of interest is the category of major behaviors, including violent, destructive, and antisocial acts, which not only pose a serious barrier to community placement and maintenance but are also generally legally proscribed. A breakdown by intellectual level and age of the percentage of cases for which each behavior was reported indicated that physical assault upon others and property destruction increased with the increase in the severity of the intellectual disability. Property theft and fire setting were also associated with the more severe levels of intellectual disability.

- *Family Factors*

There is some evidence that family factors play a prominent role in the occurrence of conduct problems in children and adolescents with intellectual disability. Richardson, Koller, and Katz (1985) found significantly more behavioral disturbances among people with intellectual disability, as well as a significant effect of stability of upbringing – a greater behavioral disturbance being associated with unstable upbringing. When conditions of upbringing were held constant, however, there was no difference in behavioral disturbance between groups with or without intellectual disability. This latter finding might be due to the relatively high levels of family problems and instability resulting from the stress of bringing up a child with an intellectual disability. Unfortunately, intellectual disability is not protective against common family level risk factors such as parental neglect, rejection, inconsistent child-rearing practices, harsh discipline, abuse, instability in caregivers, parental criminality, and familial psychopathology.

- *Gender*

As in the general population, highly significant gender differences are typically reported for aggression and conduct problems in youth with intellectual disability, with males outnumbering females 2:1 or more (Benson, 1995; Borthwick-Duffy, 1994).

- *Age*

Quay and Gredler (1981) reported that conduct disorder was more commonly diagnosed in younger individuals (9–17 years) than in older ones (18–26 years). In large-scale surveys that include community residents, the rate of conduct problems is greater in children older than 10 years with the 15–19-year age range deemed particularly critical (Harris, 1993). But phenomenology is confounded by the clinical continuity between conduct disorder which is essentially a "pediatric" disorder and antisocial personality disorder which by definition is an adult condition (Blair, Leifenluft & Pine 2013).

- *Severity Level of Intellectual Disability*

Conventional wisdom is that higher rates of aggression appear in individuals with more severe levels of intellectual disability. There is limited consistency across studies and much of the data are confounded by a failure to distinguish intended actions from outbursts. Notably, the form of aggressive behavior differs depending on the severity level of intellectual disability (Benson & Aman, 1999). For instance, Davidson et al. (1994) reported that aggressive individuals who destroyed property but were not aggressive toward people tended to be higher functioning.

Studies that have not clearly distinguished the level of intention when making diagnoses tend to report high rates of conduct disorder in lower-functioning individuals. Thus, Meyers (1987) looked at conduct disorder in adolescents with developmental disabilities who were being seen in a clinic for a mental health problem and reported that 25 of 56 individuals (44%) who had been categorized in the conduct disorder group had moderate to profound intellectual disability. Meyers (1987) thus concluded that there was *more* conduct disorder among individuals with more severe levels of intellectual disability than among those with a less severe level of intellectual disability.

Apart from a number of methodological problems with this study, this finding highlights the danger of applying these criteria solely on the basis of observed behaviors and the consequent need to tighten diagnostic criteria for this population. People with profound intellectual disability are unlikely to have the degree of intent that is necessary to make a diagnosis of conduct disorder, and the same probably applies to the majority of those with severe intellectual disability. In fact, it remains an open question whether any of these criteria can be reliably applied to individuals with any level of intellectual disability.

Evaluating the Level of Evidence Using the Cochrane Method

The vast majority of studies utilize convenience samples. Accordingly, virtually all reports are Type V evidence.

Summary of Limitations in Applying DSM5 *Criteria to People with ID*

Different informants contribute different strengths to an assessment (Loeber, Burke, Lahey, Winters, & Zera, 2000), so it is recommended that a variety of informants be utilized to collect information. If concerns about behaviors are voiced, it will be useful to ask for examples and evidence of such symptoms. Gathering information from social services, physicians, allied health professionals and schools, if possible, will also assist in the collaboration and reliability of information.

It is important when using multiple informants to be on guard for possible systematic bias. Unfortunately, correlation between different informants on disruptive behavior disorder has been found to be low. Angold, Erkanli, Costello, & Rutter (1996) raised concerns about the relatively low precision of parent and child reports of age of onset of disruptive behavior problems, a finding that has implications for determining the sub-classification of conduct disorder according to age of onset. The findings of Moffitt & Caspi (2001) further confound age of onset, given that estimates are often two years later than actual onset.

In the general population, children are essential informants regarding the diagnosis of conduct disorder, because their covert acts are not always noticed by adults. Although interviewing children with mild or moderate intellectual disability is possible, there is no evidence suggesting that they are reliable reporters. This problem refers not only to the verbal limitations but also to the conceptual difficulties involved in communicating about covert disruptive behaviors.

General Considerations

- *Focus of the Interviews and Observations*

The data collection should focus on obtaining the most direct information regarding current behaviors. Information on previous disruptive behavior should be collected to determine onset, course and predisposing factors for the individual's behavior. Whether current or past, each of the disturbed behaviors is assessed along the following dimensions; (a) frequency and intensity of the behavior for a determination of clinical impairment (Kazdin, 1995), (b) repetitiveness and chronicity to indicate the onset and stability over time, and (c) developmental appropriateness.

- *Determining Age Appropriateness*

Information regarding onset, duration, and identifiable difficulties across developmental levels is a fundamental part of differential diagnosis because of the need to determine that the behaviors are actually inappropriate for the person's age. The determination of age appropriateness relies on an understanding of both normal developmental patterns and the patterns presented in youth with disturbed behavior. In individuals with intellectual disability, the notion of "age appropriate" can be very problematic. For example, one might be reluctant to assign the label "stealing" to a child for whom it is unclear whether she or he has a concept of personal ownership.

- *Evaluating Interactions Between Behaviors and Environments.*

After the severity, course, and developmental inappropriateness of the disruptive behaviors have been evaluated, the assessment should consider whether there are significant interactions between the child's behavior and the environment. Behaviors that are inconsistent across settings suggest environmental dependency. The behaviors may even be *generated* by external factors rather than by the person's conduct alone. Such interactions would thus weigh against a diagnosis of conduct disorder.

An additional strength of making assessments across multiple settings is that multiple informants are likely to be used, thus somewhat mitigating reporting bias.

Application of Diagnostic Criteria

In general, it is important for the clinician to accurately assess the function of the behaviors and how they can ascribe evidence of intent to harm (malice). The diagnosis will be difficult if not impossible to make (with a high degree of certainty) in individuals with severe or profound intellectual disability, because the basic premise of this disorder is that the person understands the basic rights of others and appropriate social norms and then acts with the clear intent of violating them. The application of criteria are presented in relation to mild intellectual disability only. However, developmental profiles can be variable, and this assumption cannot always be guaranteed. Some individuals with mild intellectual disability might have difficulty verbalizing their thoughts and feelings. Therefore, the issue of intent might be more difficult to ascertain than in someone whose level of intellectual disability is actually lower.

Conduct Disorder

DSM-5 Diagnostic Criteria	Applying Criteria for Individuals with Mild intellectual disability
A. Repetitive and persistent pattern of behavior in which the basic rights of others or major age-appropriate societal norms or rules are violated, as manifested by the presence of three (or more) of the following criteria in the past 12 months, with at least one criterion present in the past 6 months:	A. No adaptation. **Note:** The clinician should assess age appropriateness of the behavior and ascertain that the individual understands societal rules and norms.
Aggression to People and Animals 1. Often bullies, threatens, or intimidates others.	1. No adaptation.
2. Often initiates physical fights.	2. No adaptation.

Conduct Disorder (continued)

DSM-5 Diagnostic Criteria	Applying Criteria for Individuals with Mild intellectual disability
3. Has used a weapon that can cause serious physical harm to others (e.g., bat, brick, broken bottle, knife, gun).	3. No adaptation.
4. Has been physically cruel to people.	4. No adaptation. **Note:** It is important to ascertain that the individual displaying the behavior has understood the significance and impact of her or his actions.
5. Has been physically cruel to animals.	5. No adaptation. **Note:** It is important to ascertain that the individual displaying the behavior has understood the significance and impact of her or his actions.
6. Has stolen while confronting a victim (e.g., mugging, purse snatching, extortion, armed robbery).	6. No adaptation.
7. Has forced someone into sexual activity.	7. No adaptation. **Note:** The clinician should ascertain that the person with intellectual disability understands normal societal rules about sexual behavior.
Destruction of Property 8. Has deliberately engaged in fire setting with the intention of causing serious damage.	8. No adaptation. **Note:** Clinician should assess intent.
9. Has deliberately destroyed others' property (other than by fire setting).	9. No adaptation. **Note:** Clinician should assess intent.
Deceitfulness or Theft 10. Has broken into someone else's house, building, or car.	10. No adaptation.
11. Often lies to obtain goods or favors or to avoid obligations (i.e., "cons" others).	11. No adaptation. **Note:** It is important to establish that the individual understands concept of ownership.
12.. Has stolen items of nontrivial value without confronting a victim (e.g., shoplifting, but without breaking and entering; forgery).	12. No adaptation. **Note:** It is important to establish that the individual understands concept of ownership.
Serious Violations of Rules 13. Often stays out at night despite parental prohibitions, beginning before age 13 years.	13. No adaptation. **Note:** It is important to carefully examine the home environment and the reasons why the individual is staying out at night. For example, if there is evidence of inadequate supervision, neglect, or abuse, the relevance of this behavior to the diagnosis should be questioned.
14. Has run away from home overnight at least twice while living in parental or parental surrogate home (or once without returning for a lengthy period).	14. No adaptation. **Note:** It is important to carefully examine the home environment and the reasons why the individual is running away. For example, if there is evidence of inadequate care, neglect, or abuse, the relevance of this behavior to the diagnosis should be questioned.

Conduct Disorder (continued)

DSM-5 Diagnostic Criteria	Applying Criteria for Individuals with Mild intellectual disability
15. Is often truant from school, beginning before age 13 years.	15. No adaptation. **Note:** Careful examination of school environment is necessary to rule out any reasonable cause such as distress due to bullying etc.
B. The disturbance in behavior causes clinically significant impairment in social, academic, or occupational functioning.	B. No adaptation.
C. If the individual is 18 years or older, criteria are not met for Antisocial Personality Disorder.	C. No adaptation.
Code based on age at onset: **Conduct Disorder, Childhood-Onset Type:** onset of at least one criterion characteristic of Conduct Disorder prior to age 10 years **Conduct Disorder, Adolescent-Onset Type:** absence of any criteria characteristic of Conduct Disorder prior to age 10 years **Conduct Disorder, Unspecified Onset:** age at onset is not known	No adaptation.
Specify severity: **Mild:** few if any conduct problems in excess of those required to make the diagnosis and conduct problems cause only minor harm to others **Moderate:** number of conduct problems and effect on others intermediate between "mild" and "severe" **Severe:** many conduct problems in excess of those required to make the diagnosis or conduct problems cause considerable harm to others	No adaptation.

Pyromania

Review of Diagnostic Criteria

Pyromania is diagnosed when a person repeatedly sets fires deliberately to relieve arousal or obtain pleasure from or relief of unpleasant tension upon watching the fire.

Summary of DSM-5 *Criteria*

The fire-setting must be repetitive, deliberate, and for the purpose of attraction to fire which provides pleasure or relief of tension and is not done for some other purpose or due to another mental disorder.

Issues Related to Diagnosis in Persons with ID

Only a small proportion of persons with an intellectual disability who set fires can be diagnosed with pyromania since most cases of fire-setting occur for reasons that would exclude the diagnosis, such as understandable reasons or on the basis of comorbidity.

The diagnosis of pyromania requires understanding of the person's motivation and the ability to make a differential diagnosis to distinguish pyromania from other disorders. This is not possible with persons with severe and profound intellectual disability. No data exist to determine if intellectual disability affects the prevalence, course, or influence of comorbidity of pyromania.

Application of Diagnostic Criteria to People with ID

General Considerations

Intellectual disability might cause difficulty in assessing motivation and the presence of tension and relief of tension. In the case of severe or profound intellectual disability such assessments would be very difficult. *DSM-5* excludes the diagnosis of pyromania in the presence of impaired judgment.

Methodology

The review of the literature used the PubMed database and references in relevant articles.

Review of Research Applying to People with ID

There are no studies or reports of pyromania in intellectual disability as defined in *DSM-III, IV* or *5*. Reports identify individuals as fire-setters or arsonists in forensic settings, not in a community sample. Pyromania is a small subgroup of fire-setters. Chaplin (2006), Lindsay et al. (2012), Lindsay & Taylor (2010), Read & Read (2008), and Taylor & Lindsay (2006) have reviewed evidence of fire-setting in the context of intellectual disability. Others have described cases of people with intellectual disability who committed arson (Dickens et al., 1996). It is not clear whether or not fire-setting is more or less prevalent among people with intellectual disability than in the general population who do not have intellectual disability. However, Jacobson (1982) reported an association between the rate of fire-settings and an increasing severity of intellectual disability. Taylor, Thorne, Robertson, & Avery (2002) and Taylor, Robertson, Thorne, Belshaw, & Watson (2006) showed that group intervention could be effective for women with intellectual disability who set fires.

Evaluating the Level of Evidence

Not applicable.

Adults with Mild to Moderate ID

Not applicable.

Adults with Severe or Profound ID

Not applicable.

Children and Adolescents with ID

Not applicable.

Summary of Limitations in Applying DSM-5 *Criteria to People with ID*

DSM-5 requires tension or affective arousal before the act, and pleasure, gratification or relief of tension after the act. Persons with severe or profound intellectual disability may be difficult to assess for these symptoms. Similarly, the observer would have difficulty assessing whether the act came from certain motives or psychopathology. *DSM5* criteria exclude persons with impaired judgment due to intellectual disability. This would exclude all persons with severe and profound intellectual disability.

Etiology and Pathogenesis

There is no information about the etiopathogenesis of pyromania in persons with intellectual disability.

Pyromania

DSM-5 Diagnostic Criteria	Applying Criteria for Mild-Moderate Intellectual Disability	Applying Criteria for Severe/Profound Intellectual Disability
A. Deliberate and purposeful fire setting on more than one occasion.	A. No modification.	**Note**: Diagnosis cannot made.
B. Tension or affective arousal before the act.	B. No modification.	**Note**: Diagnosis cannot made.
C. Fascination with, interest in, curiosity about, or attraction to fire and its situational contexts (e.g., paraphernalia, uses, consequences).	C. No modification. **Note**: Exclude abnormal rituals and interests associated with Autism Spectrum Disorder.	**Note**: Diagnosis cannot be made.
D. Pleasure, gratification, or relief when setting fires or when witnessing or participating in their aftermath.	D. No modification. **Note**: It may be difficult to ascertain the exact inner feelings of a person with intellectual disability.	**Note**: Diagnosis cannot be made.

E. The fire setting is not done for monetary gain, as an expression of sociopolitical ideology, to conceal criminal activity, to express anger or vengeance, to improve one's living circumstances, in response to a delusion or hallucination, or as a result of impaired judgment (e.g., in major neurocognitive disorder, intellectual disability (intellectual developmental disorder), substance intoxication).	E. No modification.	**Note**: Diagnosis cannot be made.
F. The fire setting is not better explained by conduct disorder, a manic episode, or anti-social personality disorder.	F. No modification.	**Note**: Diagnosis cannot be made.

Kleptomania

Review of Diagnostic Criteria

The critical diagnostic issues involve determining the motivation and conditions for the repetitive stealing.

The most important features of the disorder are excluding persons who steal repetitively for understandable reasons, but only to alleviate tension and achieve gratification.

Summary of DSM-5 *Criteria*

Diagnosis of kleptomania requires repetitive stealing not due to the need for personal use, monetary value, anger, vengeance, or in response to delusions, hallucinations or other mental disorders. The stealing is done to alleviate tension.

Issues Related to Diagnosis in Persons with ID

Kleptomania involves stealing without concern for personal use, monetary value or to express anger, and is not due to psychosis or other mental disorders.

It may be difficult to determine whether these conditions are met in mild and moderate intellectual disability, and is not possible in profound and severe intellectual disability.

The diagnosis of kleptomania requires assessment of motives, intentions, presence of tension and gratification, and the understanding of ownership. Depending on the severity of the intellectual disability, these features may be difficult or impossible to determine.

Development and Course

No information is available about this in the literature.

Prevalence

The prevalence is unknown, although stealing without meeting criteria for kleptomania seems common.

Differential Diagnosis

No data are available concerning symptoms of stealing in other common diagnoses in intellectual disability. Stealing might be seen in mania, conduct disorder or antisocial personality disorder.

Functional Consequences

Kleptomania would severely interfere with social adaptation.

Comorbidity

No data are available.

Application of Diagnostic Criteria to People with ID

General Considerations

The diagnosis of kleptomania requires ascertainment of motives and the presence of tension and gratification upon stealing. Some persons with intellectual disability will have difficulty describing these measures due to poor verbal skills, lack of understanding of what these measures mean, and even, inability to understand the concept of ownership and personal property.

Methodology

PubMed was used to search the literature.

Review of Research Applying to People with ID

There is no research literature concerning kleptomania in intellectual disability and no epidemiological studies or treatment studies.

Orihuela-Flores, Deriaz, & Carminati (2010) described a case of intellectual disability and kleptomania in the context of naltrexone treatment to improve compulsive and dissocial disorders. Jacobson (1982) reported an increased rate of property theft associated with increased severity of intellectual disability.

Evaluating the Level of Evidence

There is no evidence to any level of evidence using the Cochrane Convention.

Adults with Mild to Moderate ID

There are no studies applying criteria for this population, or any evidence that the *DSM-IV-5* criteria are reliable or valid.

Adults with Severe or Profound ID

Likewise, there are no studies or reports about the reliability or validity of diagnostic criteria in this population.

Children and Adolescents with ID

In this category as well no studies or reports have evaluated the reliability or validity of diagnostic criteria in the population.

Etiology and Pathogenesis

There are no data to provide understanding of the etiology or pathogenesis of kleptomania in persons with intellectual disability, including biological, genetic, psychosocial and developmental factors.

Kleptomania

DSM-5 Diagnostic Criteria	Applying Criteria for Mild-Moderate Intellectual Disability	Applying Criteria for Severe-Profound Intellectual Disability
A. Recurrent failure to resist impulses to steal objects that are not needed for personal use or for their monetary value.	A. No modification. **Note**: Assess that the individual understands the sense of ownership and normal societal rules regarding possession.	**Note**: Diagnosis cannot be made.
B. Increasing sense of tension immediately before committing the theft.	B. No modification. **Note**: The difficulty of assessing inner feelings of a person with intellectual disability should be considered.	**Note**: Diagnosis cannot be made.
C. Pleasure, gratification, or relief at the time of committing the theft.	C. No modification. **Note**: The difficulty of assessing inner feelings of a person with intellectual disability should be considered.	**Note**: Diagnosis cannot be made.
D. The stealing is not committed to express anger or vengeance and is not in response to a delusion or a hallucination.	D. No modification.	**Note**: Diagnosis cannot be made.
E. The stealing is not better explained by conduct disorder, a manic episode, or antisocial personality disorder.	E. No modification.	**Note**: Diagnosis cannot be made.

Other Specified Dissociative Disorder
Unspecified Dissociative Disorder

DSM-5 also provides categories for other specified dissociative disorder and for unspecified dissciative disorder.

References

Allen, D. (2000). Recent research on physical aggression in persons with intellectual disability: An overview. *Journal of Intellectual Disability Research, 25*(1), 41-57.

Allen, D., & Davies, D. (2007). Challenging behaviour and psychiatric disorder in intellectual disability. *Current Opinion in Psychiatry, 20*, 250-255.

American Psychiatric Association. (2013). *Diagnostic and statistical manual of mental disorders* (5th ed.). Arlington, VA: American Psychiatric Publishing.

Angoa-Perez, M., Kane, M. J., Briggs, D. I., Sykes, C. E., Shah, M. M., Francescutti, D. M., ... Kuhn, D. M. (2012). Genetic depletion of brain 5HT reveals a common molecular pathway mediating compulsivity and impulsivity. *Journal of Neurochemistry, 121*(6), 974–984. doi:10.1111/j.1471-4159.2012.07739.x

Angold, A., Erkanli, A., Costello, E. J., & Rutter, M. (1996). Precision, reliability and accuracy in dating symptom onsets in child and adolescent psychopathology. *Journal of Child Psychology and Psychiatry, 37*, 657–664.

Arron, K., Oliver, C., Moss, J., Berg, K., & Burbidge, C. (2011). The prevalence and phenomenology of self-injurious and aggressive behaviour in genetic syndromes. *Journal of Intellectual Disability Research, 55* (2), 109-120.

Austin, J. K., Harezlak, J., Dunn, D. W., Huster, G. A., Rose, D. F., & Ambrosius, W. T. (2001). Behavior problems in children before recognized seizures. *Pediatrics, 107*, 115-122.

Ballinger, B., Ballinger, C., Reid, A., & McQueen, E. (1991). The psychiatric symptoms, diagnosis, and care needs of 100 mentally handicapped patients. *British Journal of Psychiatry, 158*, 251–254.

Belden, A. C., Thomson, N. R., & Luby, J. L. (2008). Temper tantrums in healthy versus depressed and disruptive preschoolers: Defining tantrum behaviors associated with clinical problems. *The Journal of Pediatrics, 152*(1), 117–122. doi:10.1016/j.jpeds.2007.06.030

Benson, B. A. (1995). Behavior disorders and mental retardation: Associations with age, sex, and level of functioning in an outpatient clinic sample. *Applied Research in Mental Retardation, 6*, 79–85.

Benson, B. A., & Aman, M. A. (1999). Disruptive behavior disorders in children with mental retardation. In H. C. Quay & A. E. Hogan (Eds.), *Handbook of Disruptive Behavior Disorders*. 559-578, New York, Kluwer Academic/Plenum Publishers.

Bhaumik, S., Branford, D., McGrother, C., & Thorp, C. (1997). Autistic traits in adults with learning disabilities. *British Journal of Psychiatry, 170*, 502-506.

Blair, J.R., Leibenluft, E., Pine, D.S., (2013). Conduct disorder and callous-unemotional traits in youth. *The New England Journal of Medicine*, 371(23), 2207-2216.

Borthwick-Duffy, S. (1994). Prevalence of destructive behaviors: A study of aggression, self-injury and property destruction. In T. Thompson & D. B. Gray (Eds.), *Destructive behavior in developmental disabilities*, 3-23, Thousand Oaks, CA: Sage.

Bouras, N., & Drummond, C. (1992). Behavior and psychiatric disorders of people with mental handicaps living in the community. *Journal of Intellectual Disability Research, 36*, 349–357.

Carr, E. G., Reeve, C. E., & Magito-McLaughlin, D. (1996). Contextual influences on problem behaviour in people with development disabilities. In L. K. Koegel, R. L. Koegel, & G. Dunlap (Eds.), *Positive behavioural support: including people with difficult behaviour in the Community*. Baltimore: Brookes.

Chaplin, E. H. (2006). Forensic aspects in people with intellectual disabilities. *Current Opinion in Psychiatry, 19*(5), 486-491.

Charolt, L. & Beasley, J. B. (2013). Intellectual disabilities and mental health: United States-based research. *Journal of Mental Health Research in Intellectual Disabilities*, 6, 74-105.

Christensen L., Baker B. L., Blacher J. (2013). Oppositional defiant disorder in children with intellectual disability. *Journal of Mental Health Research in Intellectual Disabilities*, 6, 225-244.

Chung, M. C., & Cassidy, G. A. (2001). A preliminary report on the relationship between challenging behaviour and epilepsy in learning disability. *European Journal of Psychiatry, 15*, 23-32.

Clarke, D. J., & Deb, S. (2009). Syndromes causing intellectual disability. In M. G. Gelder, N. Andreasen, J. J. López-Ibor Jr., J. R. Geddes (Eds.), *New Oxford textbook of psychiatry* (2nd ed.), (chapter 10.4 pp. 1838-1848). Oxford: Oxford University Press.

Clarke, D. J., & Gomez, G. A. (1999). Utility of modified DCR-10 criteria in the diagnosis of depression associated with intellectual disability. *Journal of Intellectual Disability Research, 43*(5), 413-420.

Coccaro, E. F. (2010). A family history study of intermittent explosive disorder. *Journal of Psychiatric Research, 44*(15), 1101–1105. doi:10.1016/j.jpsychires.2010.04.006.

Coccaro, E. F., Lee, R., & Kavoussi, R. J. (2010). Aggression, suicidality, and intermittent explosive disorder: Serotonergic correlates in personality disorder and healthy control subjects. *Neuropsychopharmacology, 35*(2), 435–444. doi:10.1038/npp.2009.148

Coccaro, E. F., Schmidt, C. A., Samuels, J. F., & Nestadt, G. (2004). Lifetime and 1-month prevalence rates of intermittent explosive disorder in a community sample. *The Journal of Clinical Psychiatry, 65*(6), 820–824.

Collacott, R. A., Cooper, S-A., & Branford, D. (1998a). Epidemiology of self-injurious behvior in adults with learning disabilities. *British Journal of Psychiatry, 173*, 428-432.

Collacott, R. A., Cooper, S-A., Brandford, D., & McGrother, C. (1998b). Behaviour phenotype for Down's syndrome. *British Journal of Psychiatry, 172*, 85-89.

Cooper, S.-A., Smiley, E., Jackson, A., Finlayson, J., Allan, L., Mantry, D., & Morrison, J. (2009). Adults with intellectual disabilities: Prevalence, incidence and remission of aggressive behavior and related factors. *Journal of Intellectual Disability Research, 53*(3), 217–232. doi:10.1111/j.1365-2788.2008.01127.x

Cooper, S. A., Smiley, E., Morrison, J., Williamson, A., & Allan, L. (2007). Mental ill-health in adults with intellectual disabilities: Prevalence and associated factors. *British Journal of Psychiatry, 190*, 27-35.

Corbett, J. (1979). Psychiatric morbidity and mental retardation. In R. Snaith (Ed.), *Psychiatric illness and mental handicap*. London: Gaskell.

Cullinan, D., Epstein, M. H., Matson, J. L., & Rosemier, R. A. (1984). Behavior problems of mentally retarded and nonretarded adolescent pupils. *School Psychology Review, 13*, 381–384.

Davidson, P. W., Cain, N. N., Sloane-Reeves, J. E., Van Speybroech, A., Segal, J., Gitkin, J., Quijano, L.E.,…Goldstein, E. (1994). Characteristics of community-based individuals with mental retardation and aggressive behavioral disorders. *American Journal of Mental Retardation, 98*, 704–716.

Davidson, P. W., Houser, K. D., Cain, N. N., Sloane-Reeves, J., Quijano, L., Matons, L., …Ladrigan, P. M. (1999). Characteristics of older adults with intellectual disabilities referred for crisis intervention. *Journal of Intellectual Disability Research, 43*(1), 38–46.

Davison, G. C., & Neale, J. M. (1974). *Abnormal psychology: An experimental clinical approach*. New York: Wiley.

Deb, S. (1997a). Behavioural phenotypes. In S. G. Read (Ed.), *Psychiatry in learning disability* (93-116). London: W. B. Saunders.

Deb, S. (1997b). Mental disorder in adults with mental retardation and epilepsy. *Comprehensive Psychiatry, 38*(3), 179-184.

Deb, S. (1998). Self-injurious behaviour as part of genetic syndromes. *British Journal of Psychiatry, 172*, 385-388.

Deb, S. (2007). Mental health and epilepsy among adults with intellectual disabilities. In N. Bouras, & G. Holt (Eds.) *Psychiatric and behavioral disorders in intellectual and developmental disabilities* (pp. 238-

251). Cambridge: Cambridge University Press, Cambridge.

Deb, S. (2016). Psychopharmacology. In:N.N. Singh (Ed.), *Handbook of evidence-based practices in intellectual and developmental disabilities, evidence-based practices in behavioral health* (pp. 347-381). Cam, Switzerland: Springer International Publishing.

Deb, S., & Hunter, D. (1991). Psychopathology of people with mental handicap and epilepsy. I: Maladaptive behavior. *British Journal of Psychiatry, 159*, 822-826.

Deb, S. & Joyce, J. (1998). Psychiatric illness and behavioral problems in adults with learning disability and epilepsy. *Behavioral Neurology, 11*, 125–129.

Deb S., Kwok H., Bertelli M., Salvador-Carulla L., Bradley E., Torr J. & Barnhill J. (2009). International guide to prescribing psychotropic medication for the management of problem behaviors in adults with intellectual disabilities. *World Psychiatry, 8*(3), 181-186.

Deb S., Matthews T., Holt G. & Bouras N. (Eds.) (2001a). Practice guidelines for the assessment and diagnosis of mental health problems in adults with intellectual disability. *European Association for Mental Health in Mental Retardation* (EAMHMR), Pavilion Press, London. www.iassid.org

Deb, S., Thomas, M., & Bright, C. (2001b). Mental disorder in adults with intellectual disability. 2: The rate of behavior disorders among a community-based population aged between 16 and 64 years. *Journal of Intellectual Disability Research, 45*(6), 506-514. doi: 10.1046/j.1365-2788.2001.00373.x

Dekker, M. C., & Koot, H. M. (2003). DSM-IV disorders in children with borderline to moderate intellectual disability. I: Prevalence and impact. *Journal of the American Academy of Child and Adolescent Psychiatry, 42*(8), 915-922.

Dickens, G., Sugarman, P., Ahmad, F., Edgar, S., Hofberg, K., & Tewari, S. (2008). Characteristics of low IQ arsonists at psychiatric assessment. *Medicine, Science and the Law, 48*(3), 217-220.

Emerson, E. (2003). Prevalence of psychiatric disorders in children and adolescents with and without intellectual disability. *Journal of Intellectual Disability Research, 47*(1), 51-58. doi: http://dx.doi.org/10.1046/j.1365-2788.2003.00464.x.

Emerson, E., Alborz, A., Reeves, D., Mason, H., Swarbrick, R., Kiernan, C., & Mason, L. (1997). The HARC challenging behavior project. Report 2: The prevalence of challenging behavior. Manchester, UK: Hester Adrian Research Centre, University of Manchester.

Emerson, E., & Hatton, C. (2007). Mental health of children and adolescents with intellectual disabilities in Britain. *The British Journal of Psychiatry, 191*, 493–499. doi:10.1192/bjp.bp.107.038729.

Emerson, E., Kiernan, C., Alborz, A., Reeves, D., Mason, H., Swarbrick, R., Hatton, C. (2001). Predicting the persistence of severe self-injurious behavior. *Research in Developmental Disabilities, 22*(1), 67–75.

Enfield, S. L., & Tonge, B. J. (1991). Psychometric and clinical assessment of psychopathology in developmentally disabled children. *Australia and New Zealand Journal of Developmental Disabilities, 17*, 147–154.

Esbensen, A. J., Seltzer, M. M., & Kruass, M. W. (2008). Stability and change in health, functional abilities, and behaviour problems among adults with and without Down syndrome. *American Journal on Mental Retardation, 113*(4), 263-277.

Espie, C. A., Gillies, J. B., Montgomery, J. M. (1990). Antiepileptic polypharmacy, psychosocial behaviour and locus of control orientation among mentally handicapped adults living in the community. *Journal of Mental Deficiency Research, 34*, 351-360.

Espie, C. A., Watkins, J., Curtice, L., Espie, A., Duncan, R., Ryan, J. A.,...Sterrick, M. (2003). Psychopathology in people with epilepsy and intellectual disability; an investigation of potential explanatory variables. *Journal of Neurology Neurosurgery and Psychiatry, 74*, 1485-1492.

Geschwind, N. (1975). The clinical setting of aggression in temporal lobe epilepsy. In

Neural Basis of Violence and Aggression, ed. W. S. Fields and W. H. Sweet, 273-281. St. Louis, MI: Warren H. Green.

Ghaziuddin, M. (1988). Behavioural disorder in the mentally handicapped: The role of life events. *British Journal of Psychiatry, 152*, 683-686.

Haller, J., & Kruk, M. R. (2006). Normal and abnormal aggression: Human disorders and novel laboratory models. *Neuroscience and Biobehavioral Reviews, 30*(3), 292–303. doi:10.1016/j.neubiorev.2005.01.005

Harris, P. (1993). The nature and extent of aggressive behavior amongst people with learning difficulties (mental handicap) in a single health district. *Journal of Intellectual Disability Research, 37*, 221–242.

Hemmings, C., Deb, S., Chaplin, E., Hardy, S., & Mukherjee, R. (2013). Research for people with intellectual disabilities and mental health problems: A view from the UK. *Journal of Mental Health Research in Intellectual Disability, 6*(2),127-158. http://dx.doi.org/10.1080/19315864.2012.708100

Holden, B., & Gitlesen, J. (2006). A total population study of challenging behavior in the county of Hedmark, Norway: Prevalence, and risk markers. *Research in Developmental Disabilities, 27*(4), 456-465. doi: 10.1016/j.ridd.2005.06.001

Holden, B., & Gitlesen, J. P. (2008). The relationship between psychiatric symptomatology and motivation of challenging behaviour: A preliminary study. *Research in Developmental Disabilities, 29*, 408-413.

Hove, O., & Havik, O. (2008). Mental disorders and problem behavior in a community sample of adults with intellectual disability: Three-month prevalence and comorbidity. *Journal of Mental Health Research in Intellectual Disabilities, 1*(4), 223-237. doi: 10.1080/19315860802269198

Jacobson, J. W. (1982). Problem behavioral and psychiatric impairment within a developmentally disabled population, I: Behavior frequency. *Applied Research in Mental Retardation, 3*, 121–139.

Jones, S., Cooper, S-A., Smiley, E., Allan, L., Williamson, A. & Morrison, J. (2008). Prevalence of, and factors associated with, problem behaviors in adults with intellectual disabilities. *Journal of Nervous and Mental Disease, 196*, 678–86.

Jones, J. E., Watson, R., Sheth, R., Caplan, R., Koehn, M., Seidenberg, M., & Hermann, B. (2007). Psychiatric comorbidity n children with new onset epilepsy. *Developmental Medicine & Child Neurology, 49*, 493-497.

Karakus, G., & Tamam, L. (2011). Impulse control disorder comorbidity among patients with bipolar I disorder. *Comprehensive Psychiatry, 52*(4), 378–385. doi:10.1016/j.comppsych.2010.08.004

Kazdin, A. E., (1995). *Conduct disorders in childhood and adolescence*. Thousand Oaks, CA: Sage.

Kazdin, A. E., Seigel, T. C., & Bass, D. (1990). Drawing upon clinical practice to inform research on child and adolescent psychotherapy: A survey of practitioners. *Professional Psychology: Research and Practice, 21*, 189–198.

Kerr, M., Gil-Nagel, A., Glynn, M., Mula, M., Thmpson, R., & Zuberi, S. M. (2013). Treatment of behavior problems in intellectually disabled adult patients with epilepsy. *Epilepsia, 54*(S1), 34-40.

Kessler, R. C., Coccaro, E. F., Fava, M., Jaeger, S., Jin, R., & Walters, E. (2006). The prevalence and correlates of DSM-IV Intermittent Explosive disorder in the National Comorbidity Survey Replication. *Archives of General Psychiatry, 63*(6), 669–678. doi:10.1001/archpsyc.63.6.669

King, B. H., DeAntonio, C., McCracken, J., Forness, S., & Ackerland, V. (1994). Psychiatric consultation in severe and profound mental retardation. *American Journal of Psychiatry, 151*, 1802–1808.

Koller, H., Richardson, S. A., Katz, M., & McLaren, J. (1982). Behavior disturbance in childhood and the early adult years in populations who were and were not mentally retarded. *American Journal of Mental Deficiency, 87*, 386–395.

Lindsay, W. R., Carson, D., Holland, A. J., Michie, A. M., Taylor, J. L., Bambrick, M.,..., Steptoe, L. (2012). A comparison of sex offenders and other types of offenders referred to intellectual disability forensic services. *Psychiatry, Psychology and Law, 19*(4), 566-576.

Lindsay, W. R., & Taylor, J. L. (2010). Understanding and treating offenders with learning disabilities: A review of recent developments. *Journal of Learning Disabilities and Offending Behavior, 1*(1), 5-16.

Lochman, J. E., Evans, S. C., Burke, J. D., Roberts, M. C., Fite, P. J., Reed, G. M., de la Pena, F. R.,...Garralda, M.E (2015). An empirically based alternative to DSM-5's disruptive mood dysregulation disorder for ICD-11. *World Psychiatry, 14*(1), 30-33.

Loeber, R., Burke, J. D., Lahey, B. B., Winters, A., & Zera, M. (2000). Oppositional defiant disorder and conduct disorder: A review of the past 10 years, Part 1. *Journal of the American Academy of Child and Adolescent Psychiatry, 39*, 1468–1484.

Lowe, K., Allen, D., Jones, E., Brophy, S., Moore, K., & James, W. (2007). Challenging behaviors: Prevalence and topographies. *Journal of Intellectual Disability Research, 51*, 625–636.

Lowry, M. A., & Sovner, R. (1992). Severe behaviour problems associated with rapid cycling bipolar disorder in two adults with profound mental retardation. *Journal of Intellectual Disability Research, 36*, 269-281.

Lund, J. (1985). The prevalence of psychiatric morbidity in mentally retarded adults. *Acta Psychiatrica Scandinavica, 72*, 563–570.

Lundqvist, L-O. (2013). Prevalence and risk markers of behavior problems among adults with intellectual disabilities: a total population study in Örebro County, Sweden. *Research in Developmental Disabilities, 34*, 1346-1356.

Lunsky, Y., Lake, J. K., Balogh, R., Weiss, J., & Morris, S. (2013). A review of Canadian mental health research on intellectual and developmental disabilities. *Journal of Mental Health Research in Intellectual Disabilities, 6*(2), 106-126.

Marston, G. M., Perry, D. W., & Roy, A. (1997). Manifestations of depression in people with intellectual disabilities. *Journal of Intellectual Disability Research, 41*(6), 476-80.

Matlock, S. T., & Aman, M. G. (2014). Psychometric characteristics of the adult scale of hostility and aggression: Reactive/proactive (A-SHARP) and relation to psychiatric features of adults with developmental disabilities. *Research in Developmental Disabilities, 35*, 3199-3207.

Matson, J., Bamburg, J. W., Mayville, E. A., & Khan, I. (1999). Seizure disorders in people with intellectual disability: an analysis of differences in social functioning, adaptive functioning and maladaptive behaviours. *Journal of Intellectual Disability Research, 43*(6), 531-539

Matson, J. L., & Cervantes, P. E. (2014). Assessing aggresssion in persons with autism spectrum disorders: An overview. *Research in Developmental Disabilities, 35*, 3269-3275.

Matson, J. L., & Mayville, E. A. (2001). The relationship of functional variables and psychopathology to aggressive behaviour in person with severe and profound mental retardation. *Journal of Psychopathology and Behaviour Assessment, 23*, 3-9.

May, M. E., Lightfoot, D. A., Srour, A., Kowalchuk, R. K., & Kennedy, C. H. (2010). Associations between serotonin transporter polymorphisms and problems behaviour in adult males with intellectual disabilities. *Brain Research, 1375*, 97-103.

May, M. E., Srour, A., Hedges, L. K., Lightfoot, D. A., Phillips, J. A., Blakeley, R. D., & Kennedy, C. H. (2009). Monoamine oxidase A promoter gene associated with problem behaviour in adults with intellectual/developmental disabilities. *American Journal of Intellectual and Developmental Disability, 144*(4), 269-273.

McCarthy, J., Hemmings, C., Kravariti, E., Dworzynski, K., Holt, G., Bouras, N., & Tsakanikos, E. (2010). Challenging behavior and co-morbid psychopathology in adults with intellectual disability and autism spectrum disorders. *Research in Developmental Disabilities, 31*, 362-366.

McClintock, K., Hall, S., & Oliver, C. (2003). Risk markers associated with challenging behaviors in people with intellectual disabilities: A meta-analytic study. *Journal of Intellectual Disability Research, 47*(6), 405–416.

McCloskey, M. S., Ben-Zeev, D., Lee, R., & Coccaro, E. F. (2008). Prevalence of suicidal and self-injurious behavior among subjects with intermittent explosive disorder. *Psychiatry Research, 158*(2), 248–250. doi:10.1016/j.psychres.2007.09.011

McCloskey, M. S., Kleabir, K., Berman, M. E., Chen, E. Y., & Coccaro, E. F. (2010). Unhealthy aggression: Intermittent explosive disorder and adverse physical health outcomes. *Health Psychology: Official Journal of the Division of Health Psychology, American Psychological Association, 29*(3), 324–332. doi:10.1037/a0019072

McLaughlin, K. A., Green, J. G., Hwang, I., Sampson, N. A., Zaslavsky, A. M., & Kessler, R. C. (2012). Intermittent explosive disorder in the National Comorbidity Survey Replication Adolescent Supplement. *Archives of General Psychiatry, 69*(11), 1131–1139. doi:10.1001/archgenpsychiatry.2012.592

McMillan, D., Hastings, R. P., & Coldwell, J. (2004). Clinical and actuarial prediction of physical violence in a forensic intellectual disability hospital: A longitudinal study. *Journal of Applied Research in Intellectual Disabilities, 17*(4), 255–265. doi:10.1111/j.1468-3148.2004.00213.x

Meyers, B. (1987). Conduct disorders of adolescents with developmental disabilities. *Mental Retardation, 25*, 335–340.

Moffitt, T. E., & Caspi, A (2001). Childhood predictors differentiate life-course persistent and adolescence-limited antisocial pathways among males and females. *Developmental Psychopathology*, 13(2), 355-375.

Murphy, G. H., & Clare, I. C. H. (1996). Analysis of motivation in people with mild learning disabilities (mental handicap) who set fires. *Psychology, Crime & Law, 2*(3), 153-164.

Nader, R., Oberlander, T. F., Chamber, C. T., & Craig, K. D. (2004). Expression of pain in children with autism. *Clinical Journal of Pain, 20*(2), 88-97.

Nickerson, A., Aderka, I. M., Bryant, R. A., & Hofmann, S. G. (2012). The relationship between childhood exposure to trauma and intermittent explosive disorder. *Psychiatry Research, 197*(1-2), 128–134. doi:10.1016/j.psychres.2012.01.012

O'Brien, G. (2003). The classification of problem behavior in diagnostic criteria for psychiatric disorders for use with adults with learning disabilities/mental retardation (DC-LD). *Journal of Intellectual Disability Research, 47*(Supplement 1), 32-37.

Orihuela-Flores, M., Deriaz, N., & Carminati, G. G. (2010). Naltrexone in adults with intellectual disability improves compulsive and dissocial disorders: A case report. *Progress in Neuro Psychopharmacology & Biological Psychiatry, 34*(6), 1137-1138.

Quay, H. C. (1999). Classification of the disruptive behavior disorders. In H. C. Quay & A. E. Hogan (Eds.), *Handbook of Disruptive Disorders* (pp 3-21). New York: Kluwer Academic/Plenum Publishers.

Quay, H. C., & Gredler, Y. (1981). Dimensions of problem behavior in institutionalized retardates. *Journal of Abnormal Child Psychology, 9*, 523–528.

Read, F., & Read, E. (2008). Learning disability and serious crime-arson. *Mental Health and Learning Disabilities Research and Practice, 2*, 210-223.

Richardson, S. A., Koller, H., & Katz, M. (1985). Relationship of upbringing to later behavior disturbance of mildly mentally retarded young people. *American Journal of Mental Deficiency, 90*, 1–8.

Robins, E., & Guze, S. B. (1970). Establishment of diagnostic validity in psychiatric illness: Its application to schizophrenia. *American Journal of Psychiatry, 126*(7), 983–987.

Rojahn, J., Matson, J. L., Naglieri, J. A., & Mayville, E. (2004). Relationships between psychiatric conditions and behavior problems among adults with mental retardation. *American Journal on Mental Retardation, 109*(1), 21-33+77.

Royal College of Psychiatrists. (2001). *Diagnostic criteria for psychiatric disorders for use with adults with learning disabilities/mental retardation (DC-LD).* Occasional paper OP 48. London: Gaskell.

Rutter, M., Tizard, J., Yule, W., Graham, P., & Whitmore, K. (1976). Research report: Isle of Wight studies, 1964–1974. *Psychological Medicine, 6*(2), 313–332.

Siever, L. J. (2008). Neurobiology of aggression and violence. *American Journal of Psychiatry, 165*(4), 429–442.

Smith, S., Branford, D., Collacott, R. A., Cooper, S-A. & McGrother, C. (1996). Prevalence and cluster typology of maladaptive behaviors in a geographically defined population of adults with learning disabilities. *British Journal of Psychiatry, 169*, 219–227.

Smith, K. R. M., & Matson, J. L. (2010). Behavior problems: Differences among intellectually disabled adults with co-morbid autism spectrum disorders and epilepsy. *Research in Developmental Disabilities, 31*, 1062-1069.

Sturmey, P., Laud, R. B., Cooper, C. L., Matson, J. L., & Fodstad, J. (2010a). Mania and behavioral equivalents: A preliminary study. *Research in Developmental Disabilities, 31*(5), 1008-1014.

Sturmey, P., Laud, R. B., Cooper, C. L., Matson, J. L., & Fodstad, J. C. (2010b). Challenging behaviors should not be considered depressive equivalents in individuals with intellectual disabilities. *Research in Developmental Disabilities, 31*(5), 1002-1007.

Taylor, J. L., & Lindsay, W. R. (2007). Developments in the treatment and management of offenders with intellectual disabilities. *Issues in Forensic Psychology, 6*, 23-31.

Taylor, J. L., Robertson, A., Thorne, I., Belshaw, T., & Watson, A. (2006). Responses of female fire-setters with mild and borderline intellectual disabilities to a group intervention. *Journal of Applied Research in Intellectual Disabilities, 19*(2), 179-190.

Taylor, J. L., Thorne, I., Robertson, A., & Avery, G. (2002). Evaluation of a group intervention for convicted arsonists with mild and borderline intellectual disabilities. *Criminal Behavior and Mental Health, 12*(4), 282-293.

Tenneij, N. H., Didden, R., Stolker, J. J., & Koot, H. M. (2009). Markers for aggression in inpatient treatment facilities for adults with mild to borderline intellectual disability. *Research in Developmental Disabilities, 30*(6), 1248–1257.

Tsiouris, J. A. (2001). Diagnosis of depression in people with severe/profound intellectual disability. *Journal of Intellectual Disability Research, 45*, 115-120.

Tsiouris, J. A., Kim, S. Y., Brown, W. T., & Cohen, I. L. (2011). Association of aggressive behaviours with psychiatric disorders, age, sex and degree of intellectual disability: a large-scale survey. *Journal of Intellectual Disability Research, 55*(7), 636–649.

Tsiouris, J. A., Mann, R., Pattie, P. J., Sturmey, P. (2003). Challenging behaviours should not be considered as depressive equivalents in individuals with intellectual disability. *Journal of Intellectual Disability Research, 47*(1), 14-21.

Tyrer, F., McGrother, C. W., Thorp, C. F., Donaldson, M., Bhaumik, S., Watson, J. M., & Hollin, C. (2006). Physical aggression towards others in adults with learning disabilities: prevalence and associated factors. *Journal of Intellectual Disability Research, 50*, 295–304.

Unwin, G. L. (2014). A longitudinal observational study of aggressive behaviour in adults with intellectual disabilities. PhD Thesis, University of Birmingham, UK.

Van Nieuwenhuijzen, M., Orobio De Castro, B., Van Aken, M. A. G., & Matthys, W. (2009). Impulse control and aggressive response generation as predictors of aggressive behavior in children with mild intellectual disabilities and borderline intelligence. *Journal of Intellectual Disability Research, 53*(3), 233-242.

Visser, E. M., Berger, H. J. C., Prins, J. B., Van Schrojenstein Lantman-De Valk, H., M., J., & Teunisse, J. P. (2014). Shifting impairment and aggression in intellectual disability and Autism Spectrum Disorder. *Research in Developmental Disabilities, 35*, 2137-2147.

Wigham, S., Hatton, C., & Taylor, J. L. (2011). The effects of traumatizing life events on people with intellectual disabilities: a systematic review. *Journal of Mental Health Research in Intellectual Disabilities, 4*, 19-39.

Wigham, S., Taylor, J. L., & Hatton, C. (2014). A prospective study of the relationship between adverse life events and trauma in adults with mild to moderte intellectual disabilities. *Journal of Intellectual Disability Research, 58*(12), 1131-1140.

Willner, P. (2014) The neurobiology of aggression: implications for the pharmacotherapy of aggressive challenging behavior by people with intellectual disabilities. *Journal of Intellectual Disability Research,* Online Early (retrieved on 13.11.2014), doi: 10.1111/jir.12120.

Yamada, M. (2010). Comparisons of psychopathology between intellectually disabled sexual offenders and intellectually disabled nonoffenders. [Dissertation Abstract]. *Dissertation Abstracts International: Section B: The Sciences and Engineering, 70*(12-B).

CHAPTER 24

Substance-Related and Addictive Disorders

Edwin J. Mikkelsen
Joanne E.L. VanDerNagel
William R. Lindsay

The primary differences between the substance-related and addictive disorders category between DSM-IV and DSM-5 are conceptual in nature. The principal change is the combination of the categories of "substance dependence" and "substance abuse" as a single disorder that occurs on a continuum and is termed a "use disorder," prefixed by the relevant substance, e.g., "alcohol use disorder." In addition, there are criteria for "substance intoxication," and for "substance withdrawal." The DSM-5 has also identified distinct related categories of "substance-induced disorders," which share phenomenology with psychiatric disorders described in other chapters.

Although substance use disorder (SUD) can definitely be diagnosed in individuals with intellectual disabilities (ID), the prevalence in the ID group as a whole is lower than it is in the general population. This is primarily due to issues of access, especially among those with more severe disabilities. Thus, the criteria will usually be only met by individuals who function in the borderline-to-mild range of disabilities.

This chapter also includes the non-substance-related "gambling disorder." The rationale for its inclusion here is the overlap between the addictive behavioral patterns that contribute to both substance use disorder and gambling disorder.

Review of Diagnostic Criteria

General Description of the Disorder

Substance-related and addictive disorders in the DSM-5 encompass several diagnoses related to (excessive) use of psychoactive substances, as well as gambling disorders.

The DSM-5 criteria identify ten classes of substances that are commonly found to have addictive potential for a large number of the general population. Though ten separate classes of drugs (with distinct effects) are distinguished, all types of substances, as well as gambling behaviors, activate the brain reward system in such an intense way that normal activities may be neglected.

These substances are: alcohol; caffeine; cannabis; hallucinogens (phencyclidine or other hallucinogens); inhalants; opiods; sedatives, hypnotics, and anxiolytics; stimulants (amphetamine-type substances, cocaine, or other or unspecified type); tobacco; and other (or unknown) substances. Specific criteria are provided for each of these substances.

The DSM-5 text also identifies a number of substance-induced psychiatric disorders that derive from the abuse of these substances.

Gambling disorder is discussed with substance abuse disorders, as there are a number of over-lapping characteristics. The first of these is the addictive nature of the disorder. Much as the substance abuse disorder progresses to the ingestion of increasing amounts of the drug, the individual who is addicted to gambling will be compelled to extend increasing amounts of financial resources and time. There is also a compulsive aspect to both disorders.

Summary of DSM-5 Criteria

■ *Substance Use Disorder*

"Substance use disorder" is defined for each class of substance, except for caffeine, by 11 criteria related to: 1) impaired control over quantity and duration of substance use (criteria 1-4); 2) social impairment due to substance use (criteria 5-7); 3) risky use (criteria 8-9); and 4) tolerance and withdrawal (10-11). For hallucinogens and inhalants the number of criteria is 10, since no withdrawal syndrome is established for these groups. SUD severity is rated to be mild (two to three symptoms); moderate (four to five symptoms), or severe (six or more symptoms), but can fluctuate across time.

Specifiers for each of the SUDs provide an option to indicate if the disorder is in early remission, in sustained remission, or if the person is in a controlled environment; and additionally for opiods and tobacco, whether the person is on maintenance therapy. There is also a severity specifier; Mild, Moderate, or Severe.

■ *Intoxication and Withdrawal*

The categories of "substance intoxication" and "substance withdrawal" are related to the direct use of the substance. For all classes of substances, specific substance-induced disorders that derive from the use of these substances are described; substance intoxication (not for tobacco), substance withdrawal (not for hallucinogens and inhalants).

While the criteria provided for SUD for each of the nine substances are broadly similar, there are obviously some differences in the criteria for substance intoxication and substance withdrawal, due to the specific and differing physiological effects of these substances.

The coding of the substance intoxications (cannabis; opiod; sedative, hypnotic and anxiolytics; and stimulants), plus alcohol withdrawal, also provides the option to specify whether the disorder includes perceptual disturbances.

■ *Substance-Induced Mental Disorder*

In addition to SUD, intoxication and withdrawal, there are ten distinct "substance/medication-induced mental disorders", which include the following: psychotic disorders, bipolar and related disorders, depressive disorder, anxiety disorder, obsessive-compulsive and related disorders, sleep disorder, sexual dysfunction, delirium, and neuro-cognitive disorder. These substance-induced mental disorders are diagnosed instead of intoxication or withdrawal when the symptoms are sufficiently severe to warrant independent clinical attention; they resemble the disorders as described in other chapters in DSM-5, and are listed there as well. Naturally, the diagnoses of these disorders require not only the documentation of the symptoms of the specific psychiatric disorder, but also that they occur in the context of severe intoxication and/or withdrawal from a substance capable of producing these symptoms.

■ *Other Disorders*

There is also an "unspecified substance-related disorder" for each substance. Additionally, within the hallucinogen-related disorders, there is a category for "hallucinogen persisting perception disorder."

The diagnostic criteria for gambling disorder are categorized into two domains. The first of these relates to the behavioral characteristics of the disorder, which include the mental preoccupation with gambling, along with the mental distress that results from attempts to suppress these impulses. The criteria in this domain also discuss the negative interpersonal and vocational consequences of the behavior. The second criteria further specifies that the gambling behavior "is not better explained by a manic episode." In addition, this section clarifies the diagnostic modifiers of "episodic" versus "persistent." Additional guidance is provided regarding the classification of the disorder as being in "early" or "sustained" remission for those individuals who previously met the full criteria. The final classification of severity is divided into the following three broad categories: mild (4-5 criteria present); moderate (6-7 criteria); and severe (8-9 criteria).

Issues Related to Diagnosis in Persons with ID

Development and Course

The development and course of SUDs in individuals with ID usually follows the same as those in the general population. Substance use typically begins in early adolescence, though this may be delayed in those with IDD. Substance use need not be a problem in and of itself, and the use of several types of substances is, in fact, associated with many social conventions. However, prolonged and increasing exposure to several types of substances may lead to a physiological need for the substance to prevent withdrawal symptoms, as well as tolerance; i.e., the need to take more of the substance to reach the desired effect. Prolonged substance use is also associated with persisting changes in brain circuits related to motivation and reward, as well as inhibitory control and salience. This leads to reinforcement of substance use taking behavior, even when this leads to clinical impairment. This mechanism also holds true for those substances in which physiological dependence (tolerance and withdrawal symptoms) is small. Individuals with pre-existing impairment of self-control, as can be the case for those with IDD, can be more vulnerable to progression to SUD. Changes in brain circuitry in SUD may persist for years; thus, SUD often are chronic conditions.

The substance use-induced behaviors usually develop more precipitously following prolonged, excessive use of the substance.

Prevalence

A large study (Slayter, 2010a), which utilized Medicaid claims data, indicated that 2.6% of the individuals with ID engaged in substance use that would qualify for a diagnosis of substance abuse. However, the true prevalence of SUD in individuals with ID is almost impossible to accurately determine. One of the reasons for this is that individuals who function in the mild range of intellectual disability and have been assimilated into the general population, without being identified, and who also have a SUD, will not be included in those calculations. In fact, adaptive problems in this group may be wrongfully ascribed to the SUD, instead of to the ID.

Another reason is the lack of recognition of SUD. Though information on substance use and its consequences should be relatively easy to ascertain for those who are receiving active services, unfortunately, this is not always the case. Many persons with ID have access to substance use without their caregivers knowing. Depending on the level of autonomy of the individual, substance use may occur secretively, signs of substance use may be missed, and symptoms of SUD may have attributed to other causes (e.g., other psychiatric conditions, behavioral problems). To add to this, those with SUD often do not seek help themselves. The cases identified with SUD, therefore, are probably the tip of the iceberg.

Thirdly, investigations based on differing measuring methodologies provide a wide range of prevalence rates (Deb & Bright, 2008; Strain, Buccino, Brooner, Schmidt, & Bigelow, 1993), and the same is true for different methods of sampling strategies (VanDerNagel et al., 2014). Lack of validated questionnaires further hinders research into epidemiology of SUD among ID (VanDerNagel, Kemma, & Didden, 2013).

Last, but not least, the prevalence of SUD in ID depends highly on sample characteristics. Studies suggest that those with mild or borderline ID, psychiatric co-morbidity, and forensic or severe behavioral problems are especially at risk for developing SUD. On the other hand, both SUD (with the exception of nicotine dependence and caffeine withdrawal) and gambling disorder are extremely rare in individuals with severe-to-profound ID, primarily due to lack of access. However, in this group, the issue of poisoning through abuse by another individual or the prescription of anxiolytic agents by providers is possible.

Though, as stated before, it is difficult to provide overall prevalence rates, data suggest that all types of substances are used in this group (To,

Neirynck, Vanderplasschen, Vanheule, & Vandevelde, 2014; VanDerNagel, Kiewik, Buitelaar, & DeJung, 2011). While alcohol is the main substance used and misused in both individuals with and without ID, percentages of alcohol use and misuse seem to be lower among those with ID and a large proportion of individuals with ID are teetotalers (i.e., they do not use any substances; Simpson, 2012; VanDerNagel et al., 2011). In a Dutch survey, the prevalence of the use and misuse of cannabis and other illicit drugs among individuals with ID, on the other hand, seemed relatively high compared to that in individuals without ID (VanDerNagel et al., 2011).

Lindsay, Tinsley, & Emara (2013) have extensively reviewed the published literature regarding the prevalence of substance use by individuals with ID. A brief summary of the significant results derived from the relevant investigations they described are as follows:

- A survey of 329 individuals indicated that alcohol use was reported by less than 5% (Rimmer, Braddock, & Marks, 1999). Although another survey study reported that approximately 40% drank alcohol with females drinking less than males (Lawrenson, Lindsay, & Walker, 1995).
- The review of a sample of 122 individuals with ID indicated that 39% had consumed alcohol, while 4% had used illegal drugs. However, approximately half of these who drank consumed alcohol at problematic levels (McGillicuddy & Blane, 1999).
- A study which compared a sample of 95 individuals with ID (age 11-15) with a data base of over 4,000 adolescents without ID reported that the rate of reported alcohol consumption for those with ID was 12%, as compared to 23% for the control sample (Emerson & Turnbull, 2005).

A subset of studies investigated the use of alcohol by individuals with ID who also commit criminal offenses (Lindsay et al., 2013). Their extensive review of the published literature indicates that the consumption of alcohol and other substances is clearly a risk factor in the commission of crimes by individuals with ID, although the rates reported in the studies they reviewed varied considerably. This risk relates to both substance use that occurs on the day of the criminal activity, as well as a past history of substance use in offender populations.

A separate issue is the prevalence of comorbid substance use occurring in individuals with both ID and a diagnosable psychiatric disorder (Sinclair, 2004). A review of this literature again indicated a wide range of prevalence rates (7%-20%). These rates are higher than the 7.6% rate of comorbid substance use in individuals who have a comorbid mental illness, but do not have an intellectual disability (Quintero, 2011).

Differential Diagnosis

The diagnosis for SUD is primarily related to impaired control over quantity and duration of substance use, social impairment due to substance use, risky use, and tolerance and withdrawal. When this information is available, diagnosis of SUD is relatively straightforward. However, SUD is probably under-diagnosed (see previous section), and signs and symptoms of SUD may wrongfully be misattributed to behavioral problems, psychiatric disorders, or the ID itself. On the other hand, ID among persons with SUD (e.g., among patients of addiction facilities) probably is under-diagnosed as well.

The differential diagnosis for the ten categories of substance-induced disorders would consist of the differential diagnostic factors for those disorders, plus the confirmed diagnosis of substance use disorder.

Differential diagnosis of substance-induced disorders concerns primarily the corresponding disorders as described in other chapters in *DSM-5*, as well as their differential diagnosis. The major defining criterion for substance-induced disorders is that they develop in the context of severe intoxication and/or withdrawal from a substance capable of producing these symptoms.

Functional Consequences

The functional consequences of SUD are amplified by the degree of the indivdual's ID. In a reciprocal fashion, the substance use disorder negatively impacts the ability of the individual with ID to function at his or her optimal level. These consequences can subside when substance use is stopped, but in other cases substance use can lead to lasting cognitive and physical damage.

Comorbidity

Substance use disorder is associated with both physical and psychiatric comorbidity. Both direct effects on mind and body of the substances taken, as well as route of administration (orally, by inhalation, intravenously), and environment and conditions of substance use (unfavorable housing conditions, violence, and trauma) contribute to this. In addition, psychiatric disorder (and to a lesser extent, physical illness) in some cases predispose to SUD. Lastly, SUD and other psychiatric conditions share social risk factors and genetic vulnerability.

This association between SUD and psychiatric and physical co-morbidity calls for scrutiny in the diagnostic process, especially since SUD symptoms, as well as intoxication and withdrawal, may mask other conditions.

Please note: both 'legal' and 'illegal' substances are associated with severe comorbidity when taken in excess.

Application of Diagnostic Criteria to People with ID

General Considerations

The application of the diagnostic criteria of SUD to individuals with mild-to-moderate ID is relatively straightforward, assuming that one has access to accurate information concerning the four groups of criteria (impaired control; social impairment due to substance use; risky use; and tolerance and withdrawal). However, it may be difficult to obtain reliable information about several criteria that include difficult to observe or interpret behavior.

Any diagnostic ambiguity in the substance-induced psychiatric disorders is similar to those for the non-substance-induced disorders, as discussed elsewhere in this manual. Naturally, the connection between the substance use and the psychiatric disorder has to be established.

Methodology

The methodology for this review was primarily based on the review of the related literature, as identified by literature searches of recognized databases using search terms related to diagnosis of substance abuse, mental retardation, intellectual disability, and substance-induced psychiatric disorders.

Review Research Applying to People with ID

The literature concerning this subject is primarily related to descriptions of service models. The issue of the diagnostic criteria is not consistently defined in this literature. However, the articles related to prevalence do include diagnostic criteria. The literature related to the prevalence of substance abuse in individuals with ID is discussed above.

Jackson (2013) has provided an overview of the general underlying principles in the development of programmatic treatment models. An interesting observation in this regard is the focus on behavioral analysis and the maintenance of behaviors by operant conditioning and related environmental factors. While this is an important facet of treatment, biological and interpersonal aspects of addiction should also be considered. The supervision that is inherent in these treatment programs also greatly increases abstinence, which is an important component of the recovery process.

In their review of the literature of substance use by individuals with ID, Lindsay et al. (2013) noted "There is very little information on the treatment of alcohol problems in people with ID." Many of the published articles are in the form of program descriptions, without rigorous follow-up studies that would shed light on the variables related to success or failure.

Evaluating Level of Evidence

The quality of evidence was assessed by the degree to which specific diagnostic criteria were identified and then applied to the study subjects in a consistent manner.

Overall, in terms of scientific rigor, the quality of the research in this area would have to be classified as relatively low-to-moderate. This is, in large part, due to the methodological issues described above, which make it almost impossible to capture a truly representative population-based sample. The exception to this would be the prevalence studies, such as the Medicaid claims study by Slayter (2010b). The relatively narrow design of that study made it possible to fully define all of the parameters of the investigation.

Adults with Mild-to-Moderate ID

The applications of the diagnostic criteria to individuals with mild-to-moderate ID are relatively straightforward, unless there are specific comorbid deficits in expressive speech. This observation also holds true for the substance-induced psychiatric disorders.

Adults with Severe-to-Profound ID

It is almost impossible to apply the diagnostic criteria for substance abuse to individuals with severe-to-profound degrees of ID. The reason for this is the number of criteria that require access to the individual's internal thoughts and motivation via the spoken word. Many of the individuals who function at these intellectual levels have either no or very limited expressive abilities.

Children and Adolescents with ID

As with the general population, children with mild-to-moderate deficits would be unlikely to develop SUDs or substance-induced disorders, due primarily to lack of access. However, adolescents may have the same issues with access as seen in the general population. The primary difference would be in the ability for those with ID to obtain substances through illicit sources, which would likely be more available to those with average or greater intellectual abilities, due to the greater extent of their social networks.

3.8 Summary of Limitations in Applying DSM-5 Criteria to People with ID

There are relatively few limitations in the application of these diagnoses to individuals with mild-to-moderate ID, as the criteria are straightforward and objective. The symptoms and signs of intoxication and withdrawal are more difficult, as these signs and symptoms may be obscured or missed because of the individual's developmental and intellectual deficits. The diagnosis of specific substance-induced mental disorders, however, is more difficult, as outlined in the relevant chapters, and the ambiguity in applying these diagnoses to individuals with ID is compounded by the added variable of the SUD.

Etiology and Pathogenesis

Biological Factors

The same biological factors that are operative in the general population would also apply to individuals with ID. However, there is the added burden of the ID and any related physical deficits which may make the individual more vulnerable.

Recent research in the area in the general population include endocrine factors, such as cortisol/corticotrophin ratio, neurotrophic factor, degree of frontal lobe function, and hyper-arousal of the anterior cingulate area, as well as concomitant psychiatric disorders, i.e., depression (Sinha, 2011).

Another line of research relates to disruptions in brain regions involved in the motivational, reward, and inhibitory control process (Koob, 2013), caused by (prolonged) substance use. These are characterized by changes in both implicit, automatic processes (e.g., attention, evaluation of environmental cues, and approach/avoidance behavior) and explicit, controlled processes, such as executive control and motivation (Field & Cox, 2008; Van Duijvenbode, VanDerNagel, & Didden, 2013). As a result of these changes, patients with SUD have poorer control over (substance taking) behavior. Thus, though different types of substances have different pharmacological effects, they share functional changes in the nervous system when used repeatedly (Van Duijvenbode et al. – submitted. Research into feasibility and usefulness of measurements of (changes in) such processes among persons with ID and SUD is ongoing (e.g., VanDuijvenbode et al., 2013).

Genetic Factors

Individuals with ID would be expected to inherit a genetic predisposition to SUD at the same rate as the general population, unless there was a genetic basis for their ID, which made them more vulnerable.

For example, the National Institute on Drug Abuse has indicated that "40%-60% of individuals predisposed to addiction can be attributed to genetics." Complete genome analyses are being utilized in an attempt to identify the specific genes.

Psychosocial Factors

The same psychosocial stressors that have been identified in the general population also apply to people with ID. However, individuals with ID are more likely to experience psychosocial stressors, e.g., related to poverty and limited social connections.

Lack of awareness of SU risks among individuals with ID, lack of recognition by staff members of risky SU, as well as limited access to preventative interventions and SU treatment, may further contribute to the progression of SUD among individuals with ID.

Developmental Factors

Individuals with ID have developmental delays commensurate with their intellectual level. To the extent that these developmental delays negatively impact the individuals' judgment and ability to delay gratification, they would increase the individual's susceptibility to addictive substances.

To the extent that these developmental delays have a negative impact on the individual's self-image, it may increase their susceptibility to join social groups where SUD is more common and, thus, increase their vulnerability.

Application of Diagnostic Criteria

It is not clear that diagnostic modifications are required.

DSM-5 SUBSTANCE-RELATED AND ADDICTIVE DISORDERS

Substance Use Disorder

Substance use disorder in *DSM-5* combines the *DSM-IV* categories of substance abuse and substance dependence into a single disorder measured on a continuum from mild to severe. Ten classes of substances are included in *DSM-5* (see Table 4.1). Each specific substance (other than caffeine, which cannot be diagnosed as a substance use disorder) is addressed as a separate use disorder (e.g., alcohol use disorder, stimulant use disorder, etc.), but nearly all substances are diagnosed based on the same overarching criteria. Mild substance use disorder in *DSM-5* requires two to three symptoms from a list of 11; moderate substance use disorder requires four to five symptoms; severe substance use disorder requires six or more symptoms (see Table 4.2).

Addictive Disorders

Gambling disorder is the only addictive disorder included in *DSM-5* as a diagnosable condition (Table 4.1). Internet gaming disorder is included in Section III of the manual. Disorders listed there require further research before their consideration as formal disorders.

10 Classes of Substances in *DSM-5*	Addictive Disorders
Alcohol	Gambling
Caffeine	
Cannabis	
Hallucinogens (PCP & others)	
Inhalants	
Opiods	
Sedatives, hypnotics, and anxiolytics	
Stimulants	
Tobacco	
Other	

Substance Classes and Addictive Disorders in *DSM-5*

DSM-5 Diagnostic Criteria for Substance Use Disorders	Adapted Criteria for ID (Mild to Profound)
Using larger amounts or using for a longer time than intended	No adaptation required
Persistent desire or unsuccessful attempts to cut down or control use	No adaptation required **Note:** Lack of access may make it difficult to assess this criteria
Great deal of time is spent obtaining, using, or recovering	No adaptation required
Craving or a strong desire or urge to use	No adaptation required **Note:** This may be difficult to assess depending on the individual's verbal abilities
Failure to fulfill major roles at work, school, or home	This criteria will need to be modified to reflect the individual's functional level
Persistent social or interpersonal problems caused by substance use	No adaptation required
Important social, occupational, recreational activities given up or reduced	No adaptation required
Use in physically hazardous situations	No adaptation required
Use despite physical or psychological problems caused by use	No adaptation required **Note:** Class may be limited by supervision before it reaches this point
Tolerance	No adaptation required **Note:** Environmental supervision may prevent substance use before it reaches the point of tolerance
Withdrawal (not documented after repeated use of PCP, inhalants, hallucinogens)	No adaptation required **Note:** May be mistaken for aberrant behavior if substance use is not recognized

Severity Criteria

Mild: 2-3 symptoms

Moderate: 4-5 symptoms

Severe: 6 or more symptoms

Diagnostic Criteria and Severity Index for Substance-Induced

Disorders in *DSM-5*

Substance-Induced Disorders In DSM-5	Adapted Criteria for ID (Mild to Profound)
Intoxication Withdrawal Psychotic Disorder Bipolar Disorder Depressive Disorder Anxiety Disorder Sleep Disorder Delirium Neurocognitive Sexual Dysfunction	The criteria for the substance-induced disorders are identical to those described in the chapters of this book, which relate to each specific disorder.

Substance-Induced Disorders in *DSM-5*

Gambling Disorder

Diagnostic Criteria

Persistent and recurrent problematic gambling behavior leading to clinically significant impairment or distress, as indicated by the individual exhibiting four (or more) of the following, in a 12-month period:

Gambling Disorder

DSM-5 Diagnostic Criteria	Applying Criteria for Mild to Profound ID
A. Persistent and recurrent problematic gambling behavior leading to clinically significant impairment or distress, as indicated by the individual exhibiting four (or more) of the following in a twelve month period:	A. No adaptation required.
1. Needs to gamble with increasing amounts of money in order to achieve the desired excitement	1. No adaptation required **Note:** Access to money may be limited
2. Is restless or irritable when attempting to cut down or stop gambling	2. No adaptation required
3. Has made repeated unsuccessful efforts to control, cut back, or stop gambling	3. No adaptation required **Note:** May not have had access to treatment
4. Is often preoccupied with gambling (e.g., having persistent thoughts of reliving past gambling experiences, handicapping or planning the next venture, thinking of ways to get money with which to gamble)	4. No adaptation required
5. Often gambles when feeling distressed (e.g., helpless, guilty anxious, depressed)	5. No adaptation required **Note:** May not have access to gambling at those times
6. After losing money gambling, often returns another day to get even ("chasing" one's losses)	6. No adaptation required **Note:** May not have access to necessary resources
7. Lies to conceal the extent of involvement with gambling	7. No adaptation required
8. Has jeopardized or lost a significant relationship, job, or educational or career opportunity because of gambling	8. No adaptation required

Gambling Disorder (continued)

DSM-5 Diagnostic Criteria	Applying Criteria for Mild to Profound ID
9. Relies on others to provide money to relieve desperate financial situations caused by gambling.	9. No adaptation required
B. The gambling behavior is not better explained by a manic episode	B. No adaptation required.
Specify if: **Episodic:** Meeting diagnostic criteria more than one time point, with symptoms subsiding between periods of Gambling Disorder for at least several months. **Persistent:** Experiencing continuous symptoms to meet diagnostic criteria for multiple years. Specify if: **In early remission**: After full criteria for gambling disorder were previously met, none of the criteria for gambling disorder have been met for at least three months, but less than 12 months. **In sustained remission**: After full criteria for gambling disorder were previously met, none of the criteria for gambling disorder have been met during a period of 12 months or longer. Specify current severity criteria: **Mild:** 4-5 criteria met **Moderate**: 6-7 criteria met **Severe**: 8-9 criteria met	

References

American Psychiatric Association. (2013). *Diagnostic and statistical manual of mental disorders* (5th ed.). Arlington, VA: American Psychiatric Publishing.

Deb, S. & Bright, T.C. (2008). Mental disorder in adults with intellectual disability 1: Prevalence of functional psychiatric illness among a community-based population aged between 16 and 64 years. *Journal of Intellectual Disabilities*, 45(6), 495-505.

Emerson, E. & Turnbull, L. (2005). Self-reported smoking and alcohol use among adolescents with intellectual disabilities. *Journal of Intellectual Disabilities*, 9, 58-69.

Field, M. & Cox, W.M. (2008). Attentional bias in addictive behaviors: A review of its development, causes, and consequences. *Drug Alcohol Dependent.* Sep 1; 97(1-2):1-20.

Jackson, K. (2013). Substance abuse in people with intellectual and developmental disabilities – breaking down treatment barriers. *Social Work Today*, 13(5), 26.

Koob, G. (2013). Addiction is a reward deficit and stress surfeit disorder. *Front Psychiatry, 1*, 4-72.

Lawrenson, H., Lindsay, W.R., & Walker, P. (1995). The pattern of alcohol consumption within a sample of mentally handicapped people in Tayside. *Mental Handicap Research*, 8, 54-59.

Lindsay, W.R., Tinsley, S. & Emara, M. (2013). Alcohol use and offending in people with intellectual disability. In M. McMurran (Ed.), *Alcohol-related violence: Prevention and treatment* (pp. 285-302). Hoboken, NJ: John Wiley & Sons.

McGillicuddy, N.B. & Blane, H.T. (1999). Substance use in individuals with mental retardation. *Addictive Behavior*, 24, 869-878.

Quintero, M. (2011). Substance abuse in people with intellectual disabilities. *Social Work Today*, 11(4), 26.

Rimmer, J.H., Braddock, D. & Marks, B. (1995). Health characteristics and behavior of adults with mental retardation residing in three living arrangements. *Research in Developmental Disabilities*, 16, 489-499.

Simpson, M. (2012). Alcohol and intellectual disability: Personal problem or cultural exclusion? *Journal of Intellectual Disability Research*, 16, 183-192.

Sinclair, T.J. (2004). Meeting the needs of persons with mental retardation within a twelve-step program of recovery. *NADD Bulletin*, 7(6), 103-105.

Sinha, R. (2011). New findings on biological factors predicting addiction relapse vulnerability. *Current Psychiatry Reports*, 13(5), 398-405.

Slayter, E.M. (2010a). Demographic and clinical characteristics of people with intellectual disabilities with and without substance abuse disorders in a Medicaid population. *Intellectual and Developmental Disabilities*, 48(6), 417-431.

Slayter, E.M. (2010b). Not immune: Access to substance abuse treatment among Medicaid covered youth with mental retardation. *Journal of Disability Policy Studies*, 20, 195-204.

Strain, E.C., Buccino, D.L., Brooner, R.K., Schmidt, C.W., & Bigelow, G.E. (1993). The triply diagnosed: Patients with major mental illness, cognitive impairment, and substance abuse. *Journal of Nervous Mental Disease, 181*(9), 585-587.

To, W.T., Neirynck, S., Vanderplasschen, W., Vanheule, S., & Vandevelde, S. (2014). Substance use and misuse in persons with intellectual disabilities (ID): Results of a survey in ID and addiction services in Flanders. *Research in Developmental Disabilities*, 35, 1-9.

VanDerNagel, J.E.L., Kiewik, M., Postel, M.G., Dijk, M. v.Didden, R., Buitelaar, J.K., & DeJong, C.A.J. (2014). Capture recapture estimation of the prevalence of mild intellectual disability and substance use disorder. *Research in Developmental Disabilities*, 35, 808-813.

VanDerNagel, J.E.L., Kemna, L.E.M., Didden, R. (2013). Substance use among persons with mild intellectual disability: Approaches to screening and interviewing. *NADD Bulletin*, 16(5), 87-92.

VanDerNagel, J.E.L., Kiewik, M., Buitelaar, J.K., & DeJong, C.A.J. (2011a). Staff perspectives of substance use and misuse among adults with intellectual disabilities enrolled in Dutch disability services. *Journal of Policy and Practice in Intellectual Disabilities*, 8, 143-149.

VanDuijvenbode, N., VanDerNagel, J.E.L., & Didden, R. (2014). The road ahead: New developments in the field of substance use in individuals with intellectual disability. Paper presented at the NADD 31st Annual Conference, San Antonio, November, 2014.

INTERNET RESOURCES

Genome wide analyses are being used to identify novel candidate genes that increase the risk for addiction. *National Institute on Drug Abuse*.

http://www.drugabuse.gov/publications/addiction-science/genes-environment-comorbidity/genome-wide-analysis-are-being-used-to-identify-novel-candidate-

http://www.dsm5.org/Documents/Substance%20Use%20Disorder%20Fact%20Sheet.pdf

DSM-5: http://www.dsm5.org Psychiatry.org: http://www.psychiatry.org/practice/dsm

CHAPTER 25

Neurocognitive Disorders

André Strydom
Mark H. Fleisher
Shoumitro Deb
Howard Ring
Lucille Esralew
Karen Dodd
Tamara al Janab
Jullian Trollor
Sarah L. Whitwham

DSM-5 replaced the terminology of the dementias with a characterization of these neurodegenerative disorders as neurocognitive disorders. Throughout this chapter, the term "dementia" is avoided and the presentation and diagnosis of the neurocognitive disorders are discussed. In this chapter, we review the diagnosis of the disorders and consider how they are applied. We then go on to examine the etiology and pathology and to suggest changes necessary to the diagnostic criteria for the disorders in people with intellectual disabilities.

Neurocognitive Disorders

Review of Diagnostic Criteria

The disorders in this section concern a clinically significant acquired deficit in cognition that results in a significant decline from a previous level of functioning. They include delirium, major neurocognitive disorder (dementia), and mild neurocognitive disorder. The underlying etiology varies among individuals, but in the case of major neurocognitive disorder (dementia), several subtypes have been recognised.

Delirium is commonly seen in general medical hospitals (American Psychiatric Association, 2006). The essential feature of delirium is an acquired and usually acute disturbance of consciousness accompanied by a change in cognition. The disturbance develops over a short period of time, tends to fluctuate during the course of the day, and is usually a consequence of a medical condition, substance intoxication or withdrawal, or a medication at toxic or even therapeutic doses.

The essential feature of a major neurocognitive disorder is the development of multiple cognitive deficits that are severe enough to cause impairment in daily functioning and represent a decline from a previous level of functioning.

Summary of DSM-5 Criteria

The neurocognitive disorders (known as Dementia, Delirium, Amnestic, and Other Cognitive Disorders in *DSM-IV-TR*) comprise delirium, and major and mild neurocognitive disorder (NCD), divided into etiological subtypes. *DSM-5* introduces the terms "major" and "mild neurocognitive disorder" to indicate severity of the impairment. The term "dementia" is avoided in the *DSM-5* criteria but may still be used where physicians and patients are accustomed to this term. The term "neurocognitive disorder" is often preferred, especially for conditions affecting younger adults. Neurocognitive disorder is also seen as broader and encompasses disorders included under "Amnestic Disorders" in *DSM-IV-TR*.

Delirium

Review of Diagnostic Criteria

A disturbance in attention, awareness, and cognition/perception that develops over a short period of time (less than a few days) and is likely a direct physiological consequence of another medical condition or substance or is due to multiple etiologies and not better explained by a developing or established neurocognitive disorder. The clinician should specify if the delirium is acute or persistent and if the individual is hyper-/hypoactive or has a mixed level of activity. In hospital settings, delirium usually lasts about a week, but it may have a more prolonged course in some individuals. The hyperactive state may be more common (or more frequently recognized) and is typically associated with substance- or medication-related delirium. The hypoactive state is more commonly recognized in older adults. Delirium is frequently accompanied by disturbances in the sleep-wake cycle and emotional/behavioral disturbances. There is additionally often generalized slowing on electroencephalography (EEG) recordings (or, occasionally, abnormally fast activity) although EEG is insufficiently sensitive or specific enough for diagnostic use for delirium.

Delirium should be specified according to its etiological sub-type:

- *Substance-Intoxication Delirium*

This diagnosis should be made instead of substance intoxication when a disturbance in attention and awareness that has developed over a short period of time predominates in the clinical presentation and the disturbance is sufficiently severe to warrant clinical attention. Coding is done for specific substance intoxication-related delirium.

- *Substance-Withdrawal Delirium*

Symptoms as above, but etiology of the condition is related to substance withdrawal rather than substance use. Coding is done for specific substance withdrawal-related delirium.

- *Medication-Induced Delirium*

A disturbance in attention, awareness and cognition that develops as a consequence of a medication taken as prescribed. Specific medication category should be coded for.

- *Delirium due to Another Medical Condition*

There is evidence that the disturbance may be attributable to another medical condition. The name of the other medical condition should be included in the name of the delirium (e.g. 293.0 [F05]: delirium due to hepatic encephalopathy). The other medical condition should also be coded and listed separately immediately before the delirium.

- *Delirium due to Multiple Etiologies*

There is evidence that the disturbance may be attributable to multiple etiologies. Multiple separate codes should be used in the same style as delirium due to another medical condition.

There are also categories for other specified delirium and unspecified delirium. Other specified delirium should be used when it is clinically significant but doesn't otherwise meet the full criteria for delirium (e.g., attenuated delirium syndrome). The clinician should specify the reason that the presentation does not meet the criteria for the general diagnosis of delirium. Unspecified delirium can be used when the clinician is unable to specify the reason the presentation does not meet the criteria for the general diagnosis of delirium, such as when there is insufficient information available about the patient or the patient is previously unknown.

Major and Mild Neurocognitive Disorders

Review of Diagnostic Criteria

Major Neurocognitive disorder can be distinguished from mild Neurocognitive disorder by the severity of the cognitive decline and the impact the symptoms have on the individual's ability to carry out his or her daily living activities.

To meet the diagnostic criteria for an Neurocognitive disorder, individuals must present with significant (major Neurocognitive disorder) or modest (mild Neurocognitive disorder) cognitive decline in one or more domains (including complex attention, executive function, learning and memory, language, perceptual-motor, or social cognition). There should be prior concern that there has been a significant (major) or mild (mild) decline in cognitive function, which is evidenced by substantial (major) or modest (mild) impairment in cognitive performance (preferably evidenced by a standardized cognitive test). The deficits should not occur exclusively in the context of delirium and should not be better explained by another mental disorder. For a diagnosis of mild neurocognitive disorder, the cognitive decline should not interfere with everyday life. For major neurocognitive disorder, the symptoms must interfere with independence in everyday activities. The clinician must specify the severity of the symptoms for major neurocognitive disorder and whether there are any behavioral disturbances with both mild and major neurocognitive disorder. In addition to cognitive decline, psychosis, mood disturbances, agitation, apathy, and other behavioral symptoms are frequently observed.

The neurocognitive disorders are sub-classified according to etiology/pathology as follows, and several include the option to specify whether or not they occur with behavioral disturbance:

- *Alzheimer's Disease*

Mild or major neurocognitive disorder due to Alzheimer's disease is diagnosed where there is gradual progression of cognitive deficits in one or more domains (for major Neurocognitive disorder, two or more domains must be impaired) and the symptoms are not better explained by cerebrovascular disease, another neurodegenerative disorder, the use of a substance, or another mental, neurological, or systemic disorder. Criteria needs to be met also for either probable or possible Alzheimer's disease as follows: Major Neurocognitive disorder due to probable Alzheimer's disease may be diagnosed where there is evidence of the presence of a known pathogenic mutation, or there is clear evidence of a steadily progressive decline in learning and memory and at least one other cognitive domain and no evidence of mixed etiology; otherwise possible Alzheimer's disease should be diagnosed.

Mild Neurocognitive disorder due to Alzheimer's disease may be diagnosed as *probable* if there is evidence of the presence of a known pathogenic mutation from genetic testing or family history. If no such evidence is available, *possible* Alzheimer's disease may be diagnosed if there is a clear evidence of decline in learning and memory, the cognitive decline is steadily progressive and gradual, and there is no evidence of mixed etiology

Psychological and behavioral manifestations of Alzheimer's disease are very commonly observed in patients upon presentation and, even at the mild stage, depression and/or apathy are often seen, and coding includes the presence of behavioral disturbance. Common behavioral/psychological features in major Neurocognitive disorder due to Alzheimer's disease are psychosis, irritability, agitation, combativeness, and wandering in the moderately severe stage with gait disturbance, dysphagia, incontinence, myoclonus, and seizures frequently being observed in the later stages. Cortical atrophy, amyloid-predominant neuritic plaques, and tau-predominant neurofibrillary tangles are characteristic of Alzheimer's disease and may be observed through neuroimaging or through *post mortem* histopathology. Coding is done for the certainty of the presence of Alzheimer's disease.

- *Frontotemporal Lobar Degeneration*

Major or mild frontotemporal neurocognitive disorder is diagnosed when there is either a progressive behavioral problem (including three or more symptoms including behavioral disinhibition, apathy or inertia, loss of sympathy or empathy, perseverative, stereotyped or ritualistic behavior, and hyperorality or dietary changes) or a progressive language problem (a prominent decline in language ability, speech production, word-finding, grammar, or word-comprehension).

The language variant of frontotemporal lobar degeneration comprises three types: semantic, agrammatic/nonfluent, and logopenic. The cognitive deficit is relatively sparing of learning and memory and perceptual-motor function and should not be better explained by cerebrovascular disease, another neurodegenerative disorder, the use of a substance, or another mental, neurological, or systemic disorder.

If there is evidence of known pathogenic mutation from either family history or genetic testing or there is evidence of disproportionate involvement of the frontal and/or temporal lobes from neuroimaging, a diagnosis of *probable* frontotemporal lobar degeneration can be made. *Possible* frontotemporal lobar degeneration should be diagnosed otherwise. Patients may present with both the behavioral and the language variant of frontotemporal lobar degeneration concurrently, and coding includes a system for indicating the presence of behavioral disturbance. Extrapyramidal features, features of motor neurone disease, or visual hallucinations may be apparent in some cases.

■ *Lewy Body Disease*

Major or mild neurocognitive disorder with Lewy bodies should be diagnosed in individuals presenting with the following core diagnostic features: Fluctuating cognition with pronounced variations in attention and alertness; recurrent vivid visual hallucinations; spontaneous features of Parkinsonism (with onset after the development of cognitive decline). Suggestive diagnostic features are fulfilling the criteria for REM sleep behavior disorder and severe neuroleptic sensitivity.

For *probable* major or mild neurocognitive disorder with Lewy bodies, the individual must present with two core features, or one suggestive feature and with one or more core features. For *possible* major or mild neurocognitive disorder with Lewy bodies, the individual has only one core feature, or one or more suggestive features. The symptoms should not be better explained by cerebrovascular disease, another neurodegenerative disease, the effects of a substance, or another mental, neurological, or systemic disorder.

A diagnosis of mild neurocognitive disorder with Lewy bodies should be made when the cognitive and functional symptoms presenting are not sufficiently severe to warrant a diagnosis of a major disorder. People with neurocognitive disorder with Lewy bodies frequently report repeated falls and syncope and transient loss of consciousness. Dysfunction of the autonomic nervous system and features of psychosis may also be observed. Coding is done for the certainty of the presence of major or mild neurocognitive disorder with Lewy bodies and the presence/absence of behavioral disturbances.

■ *Vascular Disease*

Major or mild vascular neurocognitive disorder should be diagnosed in individuals whose clinical features are consistent with a vascular etiology (suggested by cognitive deficits with an onset following a cerebrovascular event or decline in complex attention (including processing speed) and frontal-executive functioning, and where there is evidence of cerebrovascular disease from physical examination, history, and/or neuroimaging.

Probable vascular neurocognitive disorder should be diagnosed if one of the following is present (otherwise *possible* vascular neurocognitive disorder should be diagnosed): Cerebrovascular disease is supported by neuroimaging, the symptoms are temporally related to a cerebrovascular event, or both clinical and genetic evidence of cerebrovascular disease is present. Personality and mood changes, lack of initiative, depression, and emotional lability are often present. In older adults with progressive small vessel ischemic disease, depression, psychomotor slowing and executive dysfunction are common. Coding is done for the certainty of the presence of vascular neurocognitive disorder and the presence/absence of behavioral disturbances.

■ *Traumatic Brain Injury*

Major or mild neurocogntive disorder due to traumatic brain injury should be diagnosed in individuals where there is evidence of a traumatic brain injury and loss of consciousness, post-traumatic amnesia, disorientation and confusion, or other neurological signs. The disorder must present immediately after the brain injury or immediately after regaining consciousness and must persist beyond the acute post-injury period. Individuals frequently present with emotional and behavioral disturbances. Coding is done for behavioral disturbances, skull fracture and loss of consciousness, and the severity of the neurocognitive disorder should be rated, but not the severity of the underlying traumatic brain injury.

■ *Substance/Medication Use*

Substance- or medication-induced major or minor neurocognitive disorder should be diagnosed in individuals presenting with neurocognitive impairments that do not occur exclusively during the course of delirium and persist beyond the ordinary course of intoxication and (acute) withdrawal. The substance and/or medication must be capable of producing the deficits and the temporal course of the symptoms should be consistent with substance and/or medication use. Coding is done for substance, abstinence or intoxication state, and severity and persistence can be specified.

■ *HIV Infection*

Major or mild neurocognitive disorder due to HIV infection should be diagnosed in individuals presenting with cognitive impairments and documented infection with HIV. The symptoms should not be attributable to any other medical condition and should not be explained by another mental disorder. Major or mild Neurocognitive disorder is more common in individuals testing HIV positive who had had prior episodes of severe immunosuppression, high viral loads in the cerebrospinal fluid, and anemia and hypoalbuminemia. Coding is done for behavioral disturbances.

■ *Prion Disease*

Major or mild neurocognitive disorder due to prion disease should be diagnosed in individuals with progressive neurocognitive deficits with motor features of prion disease (such as myoclonus or ataxia) or biomarker evidence and where the symptoms cannot be explained by another medical or mental disorder. Coding is done for the presence/absence of behavioral disturbances.

■ *Parkinson's Disease*

Major or mild neurocognitive disorder due to Parkinson's disease should be diagnosed in individuals presenting with progressive cognitive deficits with established Parkinson's disease and where the symptoms are not better explained by another diagnosis. Other features commonly observed in individuals with neurocognitive disorder due to Parkinson's disease include apathy, mood disturbances, psychotic symptoms, personality changes and sleep problems. Coding is done for the presence/absence of behavioral disturbances.

■ *Huntington's Disease*

Major or mild neurocognitive disorder due to Huntington's disease should be diagnosed in individuals presenting with progressive cognitive deficits with established Huntington's disease (or at risk from family history) and where the symptoms are not better explained by another diagnosis. Other features commonly observed in individuals with Neurocognitive disorder due to Huntington's disease include mood disturbances, obsessive-compulsive symptoms, apathy, and, occasionally, psychotic symptoms. Coding is done for the presence/absence of behavioral disturbances.

■ *Another Medical Condition*

A number of medical conditions can cause neurocognitive impairments. Individuals diagnosed with major or mild neurocognitive disorder due to another medical condition should present with evidence (through history, physical examination, etc.) that the deficits are a pathophysiological consequence of another medical condition (excluding those already covered in the section in the *DSM-5*).

■ *Multiple Etiologies*

The diagnosis is as above although the etiology is presumed to arise from multiple conditions and/or events, excluding substance use.

There is also an unspecified neurocognitive disorder category, to classify neurocognitive disorders where there is insufficient information and/or the precise etiology of the deficits cannot be determined and the criteria for other neurocognitive disorders in the *DSM-5* cannot be fulfilled.

Issues Related to Diagnosis in Persons with ID

Most of what we know about the course of neurocognitive disorders in individuals with intellectual disability comes from the study of individuals with Down syndrome and probable Alzheimer's-type dementia. Individuals with Down syndrome often present with an early onset form of Alzheimer's-type disease, with clinical manifestation of dementia in this population often preceding by more than two decades its appearance among individuals with non-Down syndrome intellectual disability or the general population (Strydom, Hassiotis, King, & Livingston, 2009).

Development and Course

Neurocognitive disorders generally have a progressive and unremitting course (although there are exceptions such as vascular dementia and dementia as a result of head injury) as opposed to other conditions that may affect cognition and function such as depression and delirium but which may resolve with timely and targeted treatment. Given that cognitive and functional decline occurs as an overlay upon pre-existing deficits associated with developmental disability, it is important to consider all factors that may complicate both the presentation and the course of the disorder including depression, sensory loss, and other co-morbid psychiatric or medical illness (McCarron, Gill, McCallion, & Begley, 2005, p. 200).

There are few stage-based comparisons of the disorder across developmental subtypes. The disorder is often assumed to be more rapidly progressive among individuals with Down syndrome than the advancement of dementia among those with non-Down syndrome intellectual disability or within the general population, though data on progression is limited (Dodd, Bhaumik, & Benbow, 2009).

Early Stage and Late Stage Symptoms of Neurocognitive Disorder in Down Syndrome

An IASSID dementia and aging work group reviewed the literature published between 1997 and 2008 (Strydom et al., 2009) and described a range of early symptoms of Alzheimer's disease in Down syndrome including memory changes, maladaptive behaviors, decreased social engagement, and neurological signs.

Memory and language skills have been noted to be early cognitive changes (e.g. Devenny, Krinsky-McHale, Sersen, & Silverman, 2000); personality and behavior changes and erosion of social skills are early non-cognitive changes (Adams & Oliver, 2010; Ball et al., 2006; Ball, Holland, Treppner, Watson, & Huppert, 2008; Ball, Holland, Watson, & Huppert, 2010; Holland, Hon, Huppert, & Stevens, 2000; Oliver, Kalsy, McQuillan, & Hall, 2011). Physical changes and functional skills loss can also appear early in the course of the condition. Early compromise of complex activities of daily living may include decline in ability to maintain personal hygiene, housekeeping, and work skills; later progression involves dyspraxia and decline of basic self-help skills such as toileting, dressing, and eating (Dalton & Fedor, 1998; Evenhuis, 1997). An increase in maladaptive behaviors may be evident representing increased impulsivity and personality changes (Kannabiran & Deb, 2010).

Early personality and behavioral changes and cognitive decline associated with frontal lobe degeneration may precede full clinical manifestation of dementia in individuals with Down syndrome (Holland et al., 2000). This initial presentation is considered to be an important difference compared with the general population (Deb, 2003; (Deb, Hare, & Prior, 2007). Individuals are reported to display uncharacteristic apathy, lack of motivation, and stubbornness. Frontal presentation may also include psychiatric symptoms among individuals with no known previous history of mental illness. The preponderance of frontal lobe symptoms reported for the Down syndrome population, which includes neuropsychological findings such as deficits in executive function, has led some researchers to refer to a "frontal-temporal like dementia" (Kannabiran & Deb, 2010). Two types of behavioral problems are manifest in dementia in Down syndrome: Behavioral excesses such as irritability, aggression or self-injury, and then behavioral deficits that would include slowness, apathy, loss of interest, and lessened social engagement (Oliver et al., 2011)

Late stage symptoms of neurocognitive disorders in Down syndrome are characterised by the individual's lack of response to the environment, loss of mobility, loss of communication skills, incontinence, seizures and may include Parkinsonian features (Strydom et al., 2009; Visser et al., 1997).

Cognitive Changes

Memory and other cognitive deficits do sometimes occur in Down syndrome in advance of formal clinical diagnosis of neurocognitive disorder and may be present before the person meets the clinical criteria for dementia (Devenny et al., 2000; Devenny, Zimmerli, Kittler, & Krinsky-McHale, 2002; Krinsky-McHale, Devenny, & Silverman, 2002). Cognitive decline during early and middle stage dementia involves progressively more areas of cognitive functioning, starting with complex cognitive functions, followed by visual organization as well as verbal memory before affecting semantic and short-term memory (Devenny et al., 2000). Dyspraxia tends to occur at a later stage (Crayton, Oliver, Holland, Bradbury, & Hall, 1998; Patti, 1999). Executive functions, visual organization and verbal memory appear to usually decline before semantic memory and short-term memory (Kittler, Krinsky-McHale, & Devenny, 2006).

Physical Changes

Reduced speech and deterioration in gait may be early symptoms of dementia in Down syndrome (V. P. Prasher, 1995). First time adult onset of seizures among individuals with Down syndrome with no previous history of epilepsy may be a marker for neurocognitive disorder (Kannabiran & Deb, 2010). Neurological changes noted among early presenting symptoms include late onset myoclonic epilepsy in Down syndrome (LOMEDS); this is characterized by myoclonic jerks upon awakening and generalized tonic-clonic seizures and generalized spikes in waves on EKGs (Möller, Hamer, Oertel, & Rosenow, 2001). Incontinence may be among early physiological signs of neurocognitive change.

McCarron et al. (2005) have proposed that there is an increased risk of health comorbidities among individuals with Down syndrome and dementia. Observed medical problems include respiratory problems, gastrointestinal problems, vision, hearing, and weight loss which may further complicate the course of a neurocognitive disorder. Additional physiological signs may include rigidity, postural abnormalities, and pathological grasping and sucking reflexes.

Neurocognitive Disorder Among Individuals with Non-Down Syndrome ID

We do not know the extent to which descriptions of the development and course of neurocognitive disorder based upon Down syndrome are generalizable to adults with intellectual disability who do not have Down syndrome who manifest cognitive and adaptive skills changes.

According to the IASSID workgroup, individuals with non-Down syndrome intellectual disability and dementia display a general deterioration of function and behavioral or emotional changes (Strydom et al., 2009). Further study is required regarding subtypes of developmental disorder and subtypes of neurocognitive disorder.

Generally, the course for those with non-Down syndrome intellectual disability of moderate or more severe disability is similar to those with Down syndrome, but it has been suggested that the course of neurocognitive disorder for individuals with mild intellectual disability is similar to the general population (Dodd et al., 2009). Memory problems and other changes may be observed in early stages, and symptoms of depression, lack of energy, low mood, disturbed sleep, persecutory delusions, and auditory hallucinations or delusions may also be apparent. Observed changes in physical status include urinary and fecal incontinence and gait disturbance (Cooper, 1997; Cooper & Prasher, 1998).

Course of Neurocognitive Disorder

Although it is known that anatomical brain changes precede clinical presentation, it is on the basis of observed behavioral change that neurocognitive disorder is diagnosed. Reported observed changes that bring individuals to the attention of practitioners include changes in daily living skills, work habits, and memory.

Description of the progression of neurocognitive disorder is complicated by several factors including when during the course of the disorder individuals receive a formal diagnosis. Given the difficulties with early recognition, an individual may progress to advanced stages of dementia before receiving formal diagnosis. Changes in behavior may not be considered as possible signs of dementia in a population with pre-existing neurobehavioral problems.

Determination of the trajectory of decline depends upon the point at which significant change is identified and whether or not change is effectively tracked over time. Perception of decline and how decline is manifest depends upon such factors as premorbid level of intellectual disability and patterns of cognitive abilities, sensory and mood problems as well as environmental demands placed upon the person (Aylward, Burt, Thorpe, Lai, & Dalton, 1997; Strydom et al., 2009).

A variety of factors impede establishing a reliable pre-morbid baseline which is needed in order to track the progression of symptoms. Careful assessment of baseline functioning would help in differentiating among delirium, dementia, and depression and therefore aid in the description of the course of change in cognitive and adaptive skills. We currently lack the tools to reliably and directly assess individuals on the lower end of the range of intellectual functioning.

There are insufficient data on the extent to which patient characteristics such as pre-morbid severity of intellectual ability, pre-morbid cognitive and adaptive skills, or co-morbid psychiatric illness may influence trajectory of neurocognitive decline (Dodd et al., 2009). However, the presence of neurocognitive disorder and the severity of intellectual disability are significant predictors of decline in adaptive skills (Deb, Prior, & Bhaumik, 2007). It has also been suggested that the residential setting in which care is delivered and other environmental factors may also influence outcomes (Courtenay, Jokinen, & Strydom, 2010).

More research is needed with regards to the natural history of cognition and adaptive skills in aging adults with intellectual disability across levels of intellectual impairment and types of developmental disorder to allow for clearer distinction between normative and non-normative changes in function as individuals age. Further research is required to determine the extent to which subtype of dementia, level of intellectual disability, type of developmental disorder, or caregiving factors may influence the course of dementia.

Prevalence and Incidence

Major Neurocognitive Disorder in People With Down Syndrome

Several of studies have confirmed that dementia is frequent in older adults with Down syndrome. Prevalence appears to increase sharply in this group between ages 40 and 60. Prevalence estimates have ranged from 1.4% in those with Down syndrome under 40 (Tyrrell et al., 2001) to 40% in the 50-59 age group (Holland, Hon, Huppert, Stevens, & Watson, 1998). Coppus and colleagues (2006) found that up to the age of 60 the prevalence of dementia doubled with each 5-year interval (from >49 to 60 years). Studies have varied in their findings beyond the age of 60. Some studies have found that prevalence continues to increase, with most individuals eventually diagnosed with dementia (major neurocognitive disorder) (Tyrrell et al., 2001; Visser et al., 1997); whilst others (Coppus et al., 2006) described a decrease in prevalence to 25.6% at ages 60 and over due to the increased mortality associated with neurocognitive disorder.

Incidence increased steadily with increasing age, from 2.5 per 100 person years in those aged <50 to 13.31 per 100 person years in those aged 60 and older (Coppus et al., 2006).

Major Neurocognitive Disorder in People With ID Without Down Syndrome

Estimates of the prevalence and incidence of dementia in people with intellectual disabilities (without Down syndrome) are lower than in the Down syndrome population but may be higher than the general population average.

Cooper (1997) found a prevalence rate of 20% in people aged 65 years and over. Later Strydom and colleagues (2007) found a similar prevalence rate of 18.3% among those aged 65 and older. Alzheimer's disease was found to be the most common type of dementia and had a prevalence of 12%, three times greater than comparable general older adult population rates. One study has, however, found dementia rates comparable to the general population in the over 65 age group (Zigman et al., 2004) though this group later reanalyzed their data due to diagnostic issues and adjusted their estimate to a slightly higher rate (Zigman, 2013). This group also found an incidence rate for Alzheimer's disease to be 8 cases over 3 years in a cohort of approximately 100 participants over the age of 65. Strydom, Chan, King, Hassiotis, & Livingston (2013) found an overall incidence rate for those aged 60 of 54.6/1000 person years with the highest incidence rate in the age group 70–74 years.

Differential Diagnosis and Comorbidity

Any condition that affects cognitive functioning should be considered in the differential diagnosis of a neurocognitive disorder – the possibilities to consider has been reviewed elsewhere (Knopman et al., 2001). It is particularly important to exclude common comorbidities in intellectual disability such as hearing or vision loss, thyroid function disorders (particular in individuals with Down syndrome; (Määttä, Kaski, Taanila, Keinänen-Kiukaanniemi, & Iivanainen, 2006; Määttä et al., 2011), and mental health concerns such as depression – see the section below on general considerations for more detail.

Functional Consequences

Overall, the natural history of the disorder involves a progressive loss of skills, increased loss of independence and increased dependence upon others for personal assistance and maintenance of daily routine. Later stages of dementia among individuals with Down syndrome are associated with dyspraxia and extensive loss of self-help skills (Prasher, 1995), as well as the development of neurological symptoms such as problems with swallowing, myoclonic jerks and seizures.

Neurocognitive decline and its functional implications impact upon caregiving and health care practices including the level of supervision at which an individual needs to stay safe, staffing to provide personal assistance, and planning including allocation of resources and environmental modifications.

Application of Diagnostic Criteria to People with ID

General Considerations

Due to generally better access to medical and social care and healthier lifestyles, people with intellectual disability are living longer and therefore increasingly at risk of age-related disorders such as neurocognitive disorders. Although neurocognitive disorders are more common in this population, a number of factors make diagnosis of neurocognitive disorders in adults with intellectual disability difficult (for reviews see (Evans et al., 2013; Moran, Rafii, Keller, Singh, & Janicki, 2013; Strydom et al., 2010).

The main difficulties include that 1) baseline functioning varies widely between individuals, making it difficult to interpret change and to apply screening approaches across the population; 2) individuals with intellectual disability may be unable to answer questions about their memory or higher cognitive functioning; 3) there are many other treatable conditions that could explain an apparent decline in cognitive and functional abilities, including medical co-morbidities, mental health problems, and behavioral responses to stress or change in environment, and 4) in many geographic areas, there is a relative paucity of qualified healthcare providers for this population relative to the general population (Moran et al., 2013). The diagnosis of dementia in people with intellectual disability is further hampered by the lack of reliable and standardized diagnostic tools and procedures, especially in the early stages of decline. Furthermore, the use of investigations such as neuroimaging and lumbar puncture is limited by its acceptability in this population, as well as the complexities of interpreting results.

As previously discussed, the presentation of major neurocognitive disorders may differ in people with intellectual disability compared to the general population. Memory loss may not be prominent in the early stages. Cognitive changes are frequently present, but they may be difficult to evaluate because of limitations in the individual's language, communication, and functional abilities. In contrast to the general population, people with intellectual disability may experience a predominance of changes in functioning (i.e. activities of daily living and work habits) early in the course (Aylward et al., 1997; Strydom et al., 2010). Functional abilities can be influenced by many different factors and are more dependent on disability level and comorbidity than dementia (Lin et al., 2014). Behavioral problems, such as behavioral excesses (e.g. restlessness, aggression) or deficits (e.g. withdrawal, inactivity), may also be an early sign associated with neurocognitive disorders (Adams et al., 2008, p. 200; Oliver et al., 2011).

Neurological symptoms associated with dementia such as epileptic seizures and depth perception difficulties may occur more often than in the general population, particularly in those with Down syndrome (Lott & Dierssen, 2010; McCarron, McCallion, Reilly, & Mulryan, 2014). Sensory deficits (particularly hearing loss) are also associated with cognitive decline or dementia in Down syndrome (Lott & Dierssen, 2010; McCarron et al., 2014). Therefore, the assessment and identification of dementia should take into account a nuanced consideration of functional abilities, cognitive status, behavioral indicators, and clinical factors.

There is no universal test for dementia that can be used for older people with intellectual disability who are showing deterioration in function, though an assessment of cognitive function is recommended (Moran et al., 2013). Furthermore, the standard tests used on the general population are inappropriate for people with intellectual disability and different types of assessment tools are required for those with mild intellectual disability compared to those with more severe intellectual disability. The options for formal assessment in this population have been reviewed elsewhere (Zeilinger, Stiehl, & Weber, 2013) and include proxy-rated (i.e. caregiver-rated) dementia screening questionnaires (e.g. Dementia Questionnaire for people with Mental Retardation or Learning disabilities - also referred to as DMR or DLD; (Evenhuis, 1997); Dementia Screening Questionnaire for Individuals with Intellectual disabilities, DSQIID (Deb, Hare, Prior, & Bhaumik, 2007, p. 200); The Adaptive Behavior Questionnare, ABDQ ; (Prasher, Farooq, & Holder, 2004)), several cognitive functioning test batteries completed with the person (e.g. Burt-Aylward battery [Burt & Aylward, 2000]; NAID [Crayton et al., 1998]), and proxy ratings of adaptive ability or everyday functioning (e.g. Vineland Adaptive behavior scale, (Sparrow, 2011) or dementia symptoms (e.g. CAMDEX-DS informant interview, (Ball et al., 2004). Although proxy report has limitations, this remains the most feasible option to track change over time from all individuals with intellectual disabilities regardless of their ability.

Ultimately diagnosis of a neurocognitive disorder requires the exclusion of other conditions that may be implicated in either apparent or actual cognitive or functional decline. A comprehensive medical history (Moran et al., 2013) and a physical work-up should therefore be conducted as part of any assessment (Dodd et al., 2009). The impact of sensory losses such as impaired sight and hearing should be considered (Haveman et al., 2010; Haveman et al., 2011). People with Down syndrome often experience the effects of premature aging including cataracts (Evenhuis, 1997; Evenhuis, Theunissen, Denkers, Verschuure, & Kemme, 2001) and presbyacusis (Haveman et al., 2010), which can impact on function.

A recent Finnish population-based study of case records of older people with Down syndrome also found that thyroid disease was common (Määttä et al., 2006; Määttä et al., 2011), which should be excluded as the cause of cognitive decline. Seizures may also be common in this population, but it needs to be established whether this preceded the onset of decline, as seizures often develop with Alzheimer's-type dementia in individuals with Down syndrome and affect the progression of the disorder (Lott et al., 2012).

Other physical causes of cognitive decline including vitamin deficiencies, electrolyte imbalances, chronic diseases including central nervous system manifestations of untreated coeliac disease, occult malignancies, and central nervous system conditions such as tumors, inflammatory conditions, hydrocephalus, and infections such as neuro-syphilis should be excluded. Mental health conditions such as depression are common in older individuals with intellectual disability regardless of etiology of the intellectual disability (Cooper, Smiley, Morrison, Williamson, & Allan, 2007) and affect functional and cognitive abilities in people with intellectual disability (Hermans & Evenhuis, 2013). A psychiatric and life events examination is therefore also recommended as part of a comprehensive work-up for neurocognitive disorders.

Methodology

We undertook a comprehensive literature search across several databases (EMBASE, Medline, Cinahl) using all equivalent terms for intellectual disability (e.g. mental retardation and learning disabilities) and combining these with terms for neurocognitive disorders (dementia, Alzheimer's disease). Additionally, we completed searches using terms for other types of neurocognitive disorders, including fronto-temporal dementia, Lewy body dementia, and vascular dementia. We also completed searches for delirium and mild neurocognitive disorder and equivalent terms (e.g. mild cognitive impairment).

Searches were limited to English and the time frame 2008-February 2014 because a comprehensive series of reviews included the literature prior to that date (Haveman et al., 2010; Strydom et al., 2010; Torr, Strydom, Patti, & Jokinen, 2010), and we also consulted the reference lists of these reviews.

Review of Research Applying to People with ID

No research studies were identified concerning the application or modification of criteria for delirium in individuals with intellectual disability.

A small number of studies have considered the diagnostic issues related to mild neurocognitive disorder (similar to but not exactly the same as mild cognitive impairment) and associated symptoms in individuals with intellectual disability. While there is generally an emphasis on earlier detection of underlying disease, this presents challenges in individuals with intellectual disability. One approach has been to identify adults with intellectual disability who show declines in excess of "normal aging," which may be viewed as a prodromal stage of dementia, particularly in older adults with Down syndrome. Using this type of approach, several groups found that the prodromal signs of Alzheimer's disease in older adults with Down syndrome often included signs of frontal lobe dysfunction such as emotional changes, behavioral problems and frontal release signs (Ball et al., 2006; NelsonOrme, Osann, & Lott, 2001; Urv, Zigman, & Silverman, 2010; Urv, Zigman, Silverman, & MacLean, 2008).

In adults with intellectual disability without Down syndrome, informants tended to report general deterioration of functioning more than memory or other cognitive changes (Strydom et al., 2007). However, in individuals who can complete cognitive testing, change in cognitive functioning (particularly episodic memory) has been observed in adults with Down syndrome several years before clinical diagnosis of dementia (Crayton et al., 1998; Devenny et al., 2002; Krinsky-McHale et al., 2002). Nevertheless, changes in behavior and personality now form the basis of several caregiver-reported screening tools for dementia, particularly for individuals with Down syndrome (Oliver et al., 2011; Deb et al., 2007; Whitwham, McBrien, & Broom, 2011).

Strydom, Chan, Fenton, et al. (2013) defined mild cognitive impairment as individuals who had previously screened positive for possible dementia on the Dementia Questionnaire for People with Intellectual Disability screening tool (DMR; Evenhuis, 1992), or because of concerns about decline in functioning or memory, and explored its predictive value for dementia diagnoses two years later using ICD-10 and *DSM-IV* criteria. Only 13% of those with mild cognitive impairment were diagnosed with dementia after follow-up of approximately 2.9 years, which was not much different than that of a "normal" state. This compares to an annual dementia conversion rate of 5-10% for mild cognitive impairment reported in the general population (Petersen, 2011).

Silverman, Zigman, Krinsky-McHale, Ryan, and Schupf (2013) defined mild cognitive impairment as those showing cognitive decline larger than expected with aging but having insufficient "breadth or severity" to be considered dementia and applied this to their study of dementia in older adults with intellectual disability without Down syndrome. Although they identified dementia or mild cognitive impairment in more than 20% of their sample, they had difficulty designating the majority of these with certainty to a specific category. In their review of the literature on mild cognitive impairment in intellectual disability, Krinsky-McHale & Silverman (2013) emphasized the need for empirically based assessment methods and classification criteria for mild cognitive impairment.

Several studies were identified which applied ICD-10 and *DSM-IV* dementia criteria for major neurocognitive disorder (dementia) in individuals with intellectual disability. Clinical judgment, based on ICD-10 criteria, resulted in more adults with Down syndrome diagnosed with dementia than methods based on test batteries (Diana B. Burt et al., 2005). DSM IV criteria showed substantial inter-rater reliability (Kappa = 0.68) (Strydom, Chan, Fenton, et al., 2013) and were found to diagnose more people with dementia than ICD-10 criteria (A. Strydom et al., 2007). However, diagnostic instability may be more common in individuals with intellectual disability compared to the general population, affecting the predictive validity of diagnoses. *DSM-IV* criteria diagnosed a few false positive cases with dementia because of the extent of pre-existing cognitive deficits, but cases were occasionally missed when caregivers did not report memory loss in those who did not have sequential cognitive test data. Sensitivity and specificity for either dying or being re-diagnosed with dementia after approximately 2.9 years after a *DSM-IV* diagnosis of dementia was 0.28 and 0.95, respectively (Andre Strydom, Chan, Fenton, et al., 2013).

The challenges in diagnosing dementia in this population included variable quality of informant reports with poor judging of indicators of early and intermediary dementia (Herron & Priest, 2013), difficulties in the assessment of those with moderate and severe intellectual disability (Bell, Turnbull, & Bruce Kidd, 2009), or sensory impairments (Moran et al., 2013), and difficulties in interpreting periods of plateau in vascular dementia and the floor effect in advanced dementia when longitudinal information is not available.

DSM-5 criteria for major neurocognitive disorder could improve the ability to diagnose dementia in individuals with intellectual disabilities. The hierarchical approach to subtyping (i.e. requiring that criteria for major or mild neurocognitive disorder are met before applying criteria for neurocognitive disorder subtypes such as Alzheimer's disease, frontotemporal lobar degeneration, vascular disease, and Lewy body disease) could be helpful. The de-emphasis of a central focus on memory deficits (*DSM-IV*) in favor of the broader inclusion of six possible cognitive domains, as well emphasis on "decline" from a previous level of performance (criterion A) rather than "impairment," are important changes. Coupled with the option for cognitive decline to be reported by the individual, a knowledgeable informant, or a clinician (A1), these changes should improve predictive validity of the criteria.

However, some aspects of the criteria may prove difficult in their application to people with an intellectual disability, particularly those with more severe disabilities or those with communication difficulties. Firstly, it is important to distinguish neurocognitive disorder from premorbid cognitive impairment or impairments due to non-degenerative or stable conditions such as brain injury. Secondly, the requirement that evidence of cognitive decline be documented by standardized neuropsychiatric testing or another quantified clinical assessment (A2) is particularly difficult in the context of intellectual disability. For people in whom standardized neuropsychological assessment or other quantified assessment is not feasible, it is suggested that caregiver ratings of cognitive functioning should be sufficient to meet this criterion (level of evidence: IV). A limitation of this approach is that some people with intellectual disability may already be performing at the floor of such instruments. Furthermore, criterion B suggests that the cognitive deficits should be severe enough to interfere with independence in daily activities – however, individuals with intellectual disability will by definition already have limitations in functioning, and it should therefore be clarified that a significant change from pre-existing ability in everyday functioning is required (Moran et al., 2013).

The diagnostic criteria for mild neurocognitive disorder requires modest cognitive decline from previous level of function in at least one of six possible cognitive domains. The presence of cognitive decline is determined by a combination of the concern of an individual, informant or clinician, together with modest impairment in performance in comparison to prior or expected results or clinical assessment. There is a specific requirement that cognitive deficits do not result in additional supports being required by the individual.

The existing literature in people with intellectual disability highlights the difficulty in identifying cognitive deficits of such fine granularity from pre-existing cognitive deficits, and highlights the poor predictive validity of mild cognitive impairment definitions in people with intellectual disability. There may be several reasons for changes in cognitive function in individuals with intellectual disability who may be particularly sensitive to the cognitive effects of physical illness, environmental disturbance, changes in support, or mental illness and stress. These factors need to be considered in addition to the possibility of mild neurocognitive disorder. However, most clinicians working with older individuals with Down syndrome will recognize the value in being able to apply a diagnosis of mild neurocognitive disorder when symptoms of Alzheimer's disease are recognized early, i.e. before it has a significant impact on the person's level of functioning. On the flipside, there is a risk of overdiagnosis, and there is not sufficient evidence that people with this diagnosis will progress to major neurocognitive disorder.

In the absence of evidence for the *DSM-5* diagnostic criteria of mild neurocognitive disorders, we suggest that this diagnostic category should be used with caution in individuals with intellectual disabilities, and further research to help identify biomarkers and neurocognitive tests that improve the predictive validity of mild neurocognitive diagnosis will be useful.

Evaluating the Level of Evidence

There is limited evidence on the use of diagnostic criteria for dementia (major neurocognitive disorder) in this population and extremely limited evidence for the use of criteria for mild cognitive impairment and mild neurocognitive disorder.

Adults with ID

Most of the existing studies on dementia criteria in individuals with intellectual disability have been with adults with mild to moderate intellectual disability. Jamieson-Craig, Scior, Chan, Fenton, & Strydom (2010) examined retrospective caregiver reports of early symptoms of dementia in adults with intellectual disability and found that reports of change in memory were a better indicator for possible dementia in those with mild intellectual disability, while in those with more severe intellectual disability decline in everyday functioning was a more reliable indicator of possible dementia. In general, caution is advised when applying dementia criteria in people with more severe intellectual disability.

Children and Adolescents with ID

We have not found any studies that have applied diagnostic criteria for delirium or dementia in children and adolescents with intellectual disability.

Summary of Limitations in Applying DSM-5 *Criteria to People with ID*

Several limitations in applying the criteria for neurocognitive disorders in individuals with intellectual disability are apparent:

1. Difficulty in objectively defining cognitive impairment and decline in a population with pre-morbid deficits (very difficult when cognitive deficits are more subtle). This is the main concern with applying the criteria for mild neurocognitive disorder, which does not

require functional decline to be present and could thus result in over-diagnosis in this population. However, this label may be useful to identify individuals at high risk for future decline, particularly in research settings, as long as it is not prematurely concluded that all persons with more subtle cognitive decline will progress to full-blown dementia.

2. Formal neuropsychological testing:
   a. People with intellectual disability contrast with the general population where clinicians may have greater control over factors which "optimize" cognitive test performance, whereas clinicians working with this population have to deal with considerable unpredictability (factors include contextual issues, emotional states, sensory problems, medical status, medications etc.).
   b. Limited range of tests suitable for this population, especially for those with more severe intellectual disability.
   c. Individuals may have a wide range of baseline abilities across different domains, and there is considerable between-individual variation.
3. Questionnaire-based assessment of cognitive functioning completed with or by caregivers.
   a. Questions often do not map well onto specific cognitive domains.
   b. The "context" is not considered, e.g. whether a task is regularly ignored because the person is unwilling to do it rather than unable to do it, or the familiarity of the person with his/her caregivers.
4. Questionnaires do not discriminate between "physical" and "cognitive" reasons for functional impairments.
5. Reliability of informant reports of impairment or decline is also occasionally an issue, particularly when information is obtained from different caregivers at different times.

Etiology and Pathogenesis

Biological Factors for Delirium

Delirium is always caused by an underlying medical condition or combination of conditions but may be exacerbated in the context of functional impairment, immobility, a history of falls, low levels of activity, and use of illicit drugs and medications with psychoactive properties (particularly alcohol and anticholinergic drugs) (American Psychiatric Association, 2013).

Genetic Factors for Major and Mild Neurocognitive Disorders

The amyloid cascade hypothesis remains the most prominent etiological theory for Alzheimer's disease and is of much interest in Down syndrome, as the APP gene on chromosome 21 is strongly implicated in the development of Alzheimer's neuropathology in these patients. Recent advances in Positron Emission Tomography (PET) imaging using new ligands have enabled researchers to show deposition of cerebral amyloid and tau in people with Down syndrome (Nelson et al., 2005) supporting the role of these proteins in the development of Alzheimer's disease in Down syndrome. ApoE4 is a strong risk factor for Alzheimer's disease in the general population, and also relevant in Down syndrome (Prasher, Chowdhury, Rowe, & Bain, 1997). Oxidative stress is also thought to play a role in the pathophysiology of Alzheimer's disease and is particularly of interest in Down syndrome, as the dosage sensitive superoxide dismutase gene (SOD1) is located on chromosome 21. However, a randomized controlled trial of antioxidant supplementation in people with Down syndrome and dementia had disappointing results (Lott et al., 2011). Nevertheless, understanding the link between Down syndrome and Alzheimer's disease would contribute substantially to our understanding of the disease in general.

Little attention has been paid to the risk of dementia in other specific intellectual disability syndromes. Several intellectual disability syndromes have neurocognitive decline as a common characteristic — these include Cockayne syndrome, Rett syndrome, and Sanfilippo syndrome. Cockayne syndrome (progeria-like syndrome), a rare autosomal recessive disorder, is characterized by premature aging, including neurodegeneration and dementia (Rapin et al., 2006). Sanfilippo syndrome, or mucopolysaccharidosis III, is a lysosomal storage disease caused by the impaired degradation of heparan sulfate and characterized by severe central nervous system degeneration. There are several types, depending on the genetic origin of the disease. Although most people with the disease die during childhood, those with type B disease (i.e. affecting alpha-N-acetylglucosaminidase) may survive into adulthood. A very high proportion of adults with Sanfilippo syndrome type B developed dementia (Moog et al., 2007; Skandar, Schoonbrood-Lenssen, Van den Akker, & Maaskant, 2005).

There are controversial findings in the literature regarding whether or not severity of intellectual disability acts as a risk factor for dementia (see review by Evans et al., 2013).

Traumatic brain injury may increase the risk of major or mild neurocognitive disorder due to Alzheimer's disease in the general population (Fleminger, Oliver, Lovestone, Rabe-Hesketh, & Giora, 2003). Age is the strongest risk factor for Alzheimer's disease, and in the case of people with Down syndrome the effect of age is independent of severity of intellectual disabilities and gender (Strydom et al., 2009). Multiple vascular risk factors influence risk for Alzheimer's disease and may act by increasing cerebrovascular pathology or also through direct effect on Alzheimer's disease pathology (see review by Deb & McHugh, 2010). A positive family history of Alzheimer's disease and inactive lifestyle may also act as risk factors (Deb, 2003).

Coppus et al. (2012) showed that in individuals with Down syndrome, higher levels of plasma A 40 and A 42 were associated with increased risk of dementia. Others have failed to show this association with dementia but showed A 40 level to be associated with cognitive decline in people with Down syndrome (Head et al., 2011). On the other hand (Matsuoka et al., 2009) showed that the ratio of A 42 to A 40 rather than absolute levels of the peptides is important to the pathophysiology of Alzheimer's disease in genetically vulnerable population such as people with Down syndrome. Other factors such as the raised mean corpuscular volume (MCV) of red blood cells (RBC) (Prasher, Uppal, Parveen, Adams, & Haque, 2013), impaired balance between excitatory and inhibitory neurotransmitter system, particularly involving GABAA system (Rissman & Mobley, 2011), and higher levels of macrophage inflammatory protein-1 (MIP-1) (Carta et al. cited in Kannabiran & Deb, 2010) have been implicated as risk factors but further proof is required to confirm these findings.

Use of certain medications particularly those with anticholinergic properties may enhance the expression of neurocognitive disorder. A number of medication classes have been reported to be associated with possible worsening of cognitive function in people with dementia. These include antihistamines, especially first generation (diphenhydramine, hydroxyzine, promethazine), bladder agents (oxybutynin, tolterodine), certain pain medications (meperidine, propoxiphene), tricyclic antidepressants, certain antipsychotics (chlorpromazine, clozapine, pimozide) ,and benzodiazepines (see review by Moran et al., 2013).

Psychosocial Factors

Esbensen, Mailick, & Silverman (2013) found that higher initial maternal and paternal levels of depressive symptoms and lower initial levels of paternal relationship quality were significant predictors of a higher likelihood of a dementia diagnosis in the adults with Down syndrome ten years later. Furthermore, lower initial levels of maternal positive psychological well-being predicted a higher likelihood of developing dementia in adults with Down syndrome ten years later, but the effect was only marginally significant.

Poorer overall physical health and depression were shown to be associated with an increased rate of dementia in people with intellectual disability (Evenhuis, 1997). However, it is not clear to what extent other known risk factors for dementia in the non- intellectual disability general population such as lack of engagement in mentally stimulating leisure and social activities, poor educational achievement, emotional trauma and associated post-traumatic stress disorder, poor diet, and lack of exercise also have a role in individuals with intellectual disability.

Neurocognitive Disorders

Delirium

DSM-5 Diagnostic Criteria	Applying Criteria for Mild-Profound ID
A. A disturbance in attention (i.e., reduced ability to direct, focus, sustain, and shift attention) and awareness (reduced orientation to the environment).	A. Needs to be interpreted as a change from baseline levels of attention and awareness
B. The disturbance develops over a short period of time (usually hours to a few days), represents a change from baseline attention and awareness, and tends to fluctuate during the course of the day.	B. No change
C. An additional disturbance in cognition (e.g., memory deficit, disorientation, language, visuospatial ability, or perception).	C. Needs to be interpreted as a change from baseline cognitive ability
D. These cognitive disturbances are not better explained by another preexisting, established, or evolving neurocognitive disorder and do not occur in the context of a severely reduced level of arousal, such as coma.	D. No change
E. There is evidence from the history, physical examination, or laboratory findings that the disturbance is a direct physiological consequence of another medical condition, substance intoxication or withdrawal (i.e., due to a drug of abuse or to a medication), or exposure to a toxin, or is due to multiple etiologies.	E. No change
Substance intoxication delirium: This diagnosis should be made instead of substance intoxication when the symptoms in criteria A and C predominate in the clinical picture and they are sufficiently severe to warrant clinical attention.	No change
Substance withdrawal delirium: This diagnosis should be made instead of substance withdrawal when the symptoms in criteria A and C predominate in the clinical picture and they are sufficiently severe to warrant clinical attention.	No change
Other specified delirium: as for delirium but symptoms do not meet the full criteria but cause clinically significant distress or impairment. **Note:** The clinician must specify the reason the delirium does not meet the full criteria.	No change
Unspecified delirium: as for delirium but symptoms do not meet the full criteria but cause clinically significant distress or impairment. **Note:** The clinician does not specify the reason the delirium does not meet the full criteria.	No change

Major Neurocognitive Disorder

DSM-5 Diagnostic Criteria	Applying Criteria for Mild-Profound ID
A. Evidence of significant cognitive decline from a previous level of performance in one or more cognitive domains (complex attention, executive function, learning and memory, language, perceptual-motor, or social cognition) based on: 1. Concern of the individual, a knowledgeable informant, or the clinician that there has been a significant decline in cognitive function; and 2. A substantial impairment in cognitive performance, preferably documented by standardized neuropsychological testing or, in its absence, another quantified clinical assessment.	A. Take care to determine previous level of performance and change in performance need to be clearly established Neuropsychological tools should have been designed for individuals with an intellectual disability and/or validated in this population; including proxy-rated tools of cognitive performance
B. The cognitive deficits interfere with independence in everyday activities (i.e., at a minimum, requiring assistance with complex instrumental activities of daily living such as paying bills or managing medications).	B. Needs to be a change from previous level of functioning (i.e. measured against the person's own premorbid baseline)
C. The cognitive deficits do not occur exclusively in the context of a delirium.	C. No change
D. The cognitive deficits are not better explained by another mental disorder (e.g., major depressive disorder, schizophrenia).	D. No change

Mild Neurocognitive Disorder

DSM-5 mild neurocognitive disorder has the same criteria as for major neurocognitive disorder, except that the cognitive decline is modest/mild and does not interfere with capacity for independence in everyday activities.

The reliability and validity of this diagnosis in individuals with ID has not been established and we advise caution in using this diagnosis.

Major or Mild Neurocognitive Disorder Due to Alzheimer's Disease

DSM-5 Diagnostic Criteria	Applying Criteria for Mild-Profound ID
A. The criteria are met for major or mild neurocognitive disorder	A. No change, but see concerns about mild neurocognitive change
B. There is insidious onset and gradual progression of impairment in one or more cognitive domains (for major neurocognitive disorder, at least two domains must be impaired).	B. No change, but see comments above about change from previous level of performance
C. Criteria are met for either probable or possible Alzheimer's disease as follows: **For major neurocognitive disorder:** Probable Alzheimer's disease is diagnosed if either of the following is present; otherwise, possible Alzheimer's disease should be diagnosed: 1. Evidence of a causative Alzheimer's disease genetic mutation from family history or genetic testing. 2. All three of the following are present: a. Clear evidence of decline in memory and learning and at least one other cognitive domain (based on detailed history or serial neuropsychological testing). b. Steadily progressive, gradual decline in cognition, without extended plateaus. c. No evidence of mixed etiology (i.e., absence of other neurodegenerative or cerebrovascular disease, or another neurological, mental, or systemic disease or condition likely contributing to cognitive decline). **For mild neurocognitive disorder:** Probable Alzheimer's disease is diagnosed if there is evidence of a causative Alzheimer's disease genetic mutation from either genetic testing or family history. Possible Alzheimer's disease is diagnosed if there is no evidence of a causative Alzheimer's disease genetic mutation from either genetic testing or family history, and all three of the following are present: 1. Clear evidence of decline in memory and learning. 2. Steady progressive, gradual decline in cognition, without extended plateaus. 3. No evidence of mixed etiology (i.e., absence of other neurodegenerative or cerebrovascular disease, or another neurological or systemic disease or condition likely contributing to cognitive decline).	C. No change
D. The disturbance is not better explained by cerebrovascular disease, another neurodegenerative disease, the effects of a substance, or another mental, neurological, or systemic disorder.	D. No change

Major or Mild Frontotemporal Neurocognitive Disorder

No change from DSM-5 criteria, but see concerns about mild neurocognitive change.

Major or Mild Neurocognitive Disorder with Lewy Bodies

DSM-5 Diagnostic Criteria	Applying Criteria for Mild-Profound ID
A. The criteria are met for major or mild neurocognitive disorder.	A. No change, but see concerns about mild neurocognitive change
B. The disorder has an insidious and gradual progression	B. No Change
C. The disorder meets a combination of core diagnostic features and suggestive diagnostic features for either probable or possible neurocognitive disorder with Lewy bodies. For probable major or mild neurocognitive disorder with Lewy bodies, the individual has two core features, or one suggestive feature with one or more core features. For possible major or mild neurocognitive disorder with Lewy bodies, the individual has only one core feature, or one or more suggestive features. 1. Core diagnostic features: a. Fluctuating cognition with pronounced variations in attention and alertness. b. Recurrent visual hallucinations that are well-formed and detailed. c. Spontaneous features of Parkinsonism, with onset subsequent to the development of cognitive decline 2. Suggestive diagnostic features: a. Meets criteria for rapid eye movement sleep behavior disorder b. Severe neuroleptic sensitivity	C. No Change
D. The disturbance is not better explained by cerebrovascular disease, another neurodegenerative disease, the effects of a substance, or another mental, neurological, or systemic disorder.	D. No Change

Major or Mild Vascular Neurocognitive Disorder

DSM-5 Diagnostic Criteria	Applying Criteria for Mild-Profound ID
A. The criteria are met for major or mild neurocognitive disorder	A. No change, but see concerns about mild neurocognitive change
B. The clinical features are consistent with a vascular etiology, as suggested by either of the following: 1. Onset of the cognitive deficits is temporally related to one or more cerebrovascular events. 2. Evidence for decline is prominent in complex attention (including processing speed) and fronto-executive function.	B. No Change
C. There is evidence of the presence of cerebrovascular disease from history, physical examination, and/or neuroimaging considered sufficient to account for the neurocognitive deficits.	C. No Change
D. The symptoms are not better explained by another brain disease or systemic disorder.	D. No Change

Major or Mild Vascular Neurocognitive Disorder (continue)

DSM-5 Diagnostic Criteria	Applying Criteria for Mild-Profound ID
Probable vascular neurocognitive disorder is diagnosed if one of the following is present; otherwise possible vascular neurocognitive disorder should be diagnosed: 1. Clinical criteria are supported by neuroimaging evidence of significant parenchymal injury attributed to cerebrovascular disease (neuroimaging-supported). 2. The neurocognitive syndrome is temporally related to one or more documented cerebrovascular events. 3. Both clinical and genetic (e.g., cerebral autosomal dominant arteriopathy with subcortical infarcts and leukoencephalopathy) evidence of cerebrovascular disease is present. Possible vascular neurocognitive disorder is diagnosed if the clinical criteria are met but neuroimaging is not available and the temporal relationship of the neurocognitive syndrome with one or more cerebrovascular events is not established.	

Major or Mild Neurocognitive Disorder Due to Traumatic Brain Injury

DSM-5 Diagnostic Criteria	Applying Criteria for Mild-Profound ID
A. The criteria are met for major or mild neurocognitive disorder	A. No change, but see concerns about mild neurocognitive change
B. There is evidence of a traumatic brain injury – that is, an impact to the head or other mechanisms of rapid movement or displacement of the brain within the skull, with one or more of the following: 1. Loss of consciousness 2. Posttraumatic amnesia 3. Disorientation and confusion 4. Neurological signs (e.g. neuroimaging demonstrating injury; a new onset of seizures; a marked worsening of a pre-existing seizure disorder; visual field cuts; anosmia; hemiparesis	B. No Change
C. The neurocognitive disorder presents immediately after the occurrence of the traumatic brain injury or immediately after recovery of consciousness and persists past the acute post-injury period.	C. No Change

Substance-/Medication-induced Major or Mild Neurocognitive Disorder

DSM-5 criteria for substance-medication-induced neurocognitive disorder are the same as for other mental disorders, without adaptation, with the additional need for presence of the criteria for major or mild neurocognitive disorder.

Major or Mild Neurocognitive Disorder Due to HIV Infection

Major or Mild Neurocognitive Disorder Due to Prion Disease

Major or Mild Neurocognitive Disorder Due to Parkinson's Disease

Major or Mild Neurocognitive Disorder Due to Huntington's Disease

Major or Mild Neurocognitive Disorder Due to Another Medical Condition

Major or Mild Neurocognitive Disorder Due to Multiple Etiologies

Unspecified Neurocognitive Disorder

DSM-5 also provides criteria for major and mild neurocognitive disorders due to HIV, prion disease, Parkinson's disease, Huntington's disease, or multiple etiologies. No modifications are suggested to these criteria. There is also a category for unspecified neurocognitive disorder.

References

Adams, D., & Oliver, C. (2010). The relationship between acquired impairments of executive function and behaviour change in adults with Down syndrome. *Journal of Intellectual Disability Research, 54*(5), 393–405. doi:10.1111/j.1365-2788.2010.01271.x

Adams, D., Oliver, C., Kalsy, S., Peters, S., Broquard, M., Basra, T. ... McQuillan, S. (2008). Behavioural characteristics associated with dementia assessment referrals in adults with Down syndrome. *Journal of Intellectual Disability Research, 52*(4), 358–368. doi:10.1111/j.1365-2788.2007.01036.x

American Psychiatric Association. (2013). *Diagnostic and statistical manual of mental disorders* (5th ed.). Washington, D.C: American Psychiatric Publishing.

American Psychiatric Association. (2006). *American Psychiatric Association practice guidelines for the treatment of psychiatric disorders: Compendium 2006.* Washington, DC: American Psychiatric Pubishing.

Aylward, E. H., Burt, D. B., Thorpe, L. U., Lai, F., & Dalton, A. (1997). Diagnosis of dementia in individuals with intellectual disability. *Journal of Intellectual Disability Research, 41*(2), 152–164. doi:10.1111/j.1365-2788.1997.tb00692.x

Ball, S. L., Holland, A. J., Hon, J., Huppert, F. A., Treppner, P., & Watson, P. C. (2006). Personality and behaviour changes mark the early stages of Alzheimer's disease in adults with Down's syndrome: findings from a prospective population-based study. *International Journal of Geriatric Psychiatry, 21*(7), 661–673. doi:10.1002/gps.1545

Ball, S. L., Holland, A. J., Huppert, F. A., Treppner, P., Watson, P., & Hon, J. (2004). The modified CAMDEX informant interview is a valid and reliable tool for use in the diagnosis of dementia in adults with Down's syndrome. *Journal of Intellectual Disability Research, 48*(6), 611–620. doi:10.1111/j.1365-2788.2004.00630.x

Ball, S. L., Holland, A. J., Treppner, P., Watson, P. C., & Huppert, F. A. (2008). Executive dysfunction and its association with personality and behaviour changes in the development of Alzheimer's disease in adults with Down syndrome and mild to moderate learning disabilities. *The British Journal of Clinical Psychology, 47*(Pt 1), 1–29. doi:10.1348/014466507X230967

Ball, S. L., Holland, A. J., Watson, P. C., & Huppert, F. A. (2010). Theoretical exploration of the neural bases of behavioural disinhibition, apathy and executive dysfunction in preclinical Alzheimer's disease in people with Down's syndrome: potential involvement of multiple frontal-subcortical neuronal circuits. *Journal of Intellectual Disability Research, 54*(4), 320–336. doi:10.1111/j.1365-2788.2010.01261.x

Bell, D. M., Turnbull, A., & Bruce Kidd, W. (2009). Differential diagnosis of dementia in the field of learning disabilities: A case study. *British Journal of Learning Disabilities, 37*(1), 56–65. doi:10.1111/j.1468-3156.2008.00524.x

Burt, D. B., & Aylward, E. H. (2000). Test battery for the diagnosis of dementia in individuals with intellectual disability. Working group for the establishment of criteria for the diagnosis of dementia in individuals with intellectual disability. *Journal of Intellectual Disability Research, 44 (Pt 2)*, 175–180.

Burt, D. B., Primeaux-Hart, S., Loveland, K. A., Cleveland, L. A., Lewis, K. R., Lesser, J., & Pearson, P. L. (2005). Tests and medical conditions associated with dementia diagnosis. *Journal of Policy and Practice in Intellectual Disabilities, 2*(1), 47–56. doi:10.1111/j.1741-1130.2005.00007.x

Cooper, S.-A. (1997). High prevalence of dementia among people with learning disabilities not attributable to Down's syndrome. *Psychological Medicine, 27*(03), 609–616. doi:10.1017/S0033291796004655

Cooper, S.-A., & Prasher, V. P. (1998). Maladaptive behaviours and symptoms of dementia in adults with Down's syndrome compared with adults with intellectual disability of other aetiologies. *Journal of Intellectual Disability Research, 42*(4), 293–300. doi:10.1046/j.1365-2788.1998.00135.x

Cooper, S.-A., Smiley, E., Morrison, J., Williamson, A., & Allan, L. (2007). Mental ill-health in adults with intellectual disabilities: Prevalence and associated factors. *The British Journal of Psychiatry: The Journal of Mental Science, 190*, 27–35. doi:10.1192/bjp.bp.106.022483

Coppus, A., Evenhuis, H., Verberne, G.-J., Visser, F., Van Gool, P., Eikelenboom, P., & Van Duijin, C. (2006). Dementia and mortality in persons with Down's syndrome. *Journal of Intellectual Disability Research, 50*(10), 768–777. doi:10.1111/j.1365-2788.2006.00842.x

Coppus, A. M. W., Schuur, M., Vergeer, J., Janssens, A. C. J. W., Oostra, B. A., Verbeek, M. M., … M, C. (2012). Plasma amyloid and the risk of Alzheimer's disease in Down syndrome. *Neurobiology of Aging, 33*(9), 1988–1994. doi:10.1016/j.neurobiolaging.2011.08.007

Courtenay, K., Jokinen, N. S., & Strydom, A. (2010). Caregiving and adults with intellectual disabilities affected by dementia. *Journal of Policy and Practice in Intellectual Disabilities, 7*(1), 26–33. doi:10.1111/j.1741-1130.2010.00244.x

Crayton, L., Oliver, C., Holland, A., Bradbury, J., & Hall, S. (1998). The neuropsychological assessment of age related cognitive deficits in adults with Down's syndrome. *Journal of Applied Research in Intellectual Disabilities, 11*(3), 255–272. doi:10.1111/j.1468-3148.1998.tb00066.x

Dalton, A. J., & Fedor, B. L. (1998). Onset of dyspraxia in aging persons with Down syndrome: Longitudinal studies. *Journal of Intellectual and Developmental Disability, 23*(1), 13–24. doi:10.1080/13668259800033551

Deb, S. (2003). Dementia in people with an intellectual disability. *Reviews in Clinical Gerontology, 13*(2), 137–144. doi:10.1017/S095925980301325X

Deb, S., Hare, M., & Prior, L. (2007). Symptoms of dementia among adults with Down's syndrome: A qualitative study. *Journal of Intellectual Disability Research, 51*(Pt 9), 726–739. doi:10.1111/j.1365-2788.2007.00956.x

Deb, S., Hare, M., Prior, L., & Bhaumik, S. (2007). Dementia screening questionnaire for individuals with intellectual disabilities. *The British Journal of Psychiatry, 190*(5), 440–444. doi:10.1192/bjp.bp.106.024984

Deb, S., & McHugh, R. (2010). Dementia among persons with Down syndrome. *International Review of Research in Mental Retardation, 39*, 221–255. doi:10.1016/S0074-7750(10)39008-2

Devenny, D. A., Krinsky-McHale, S. J., Sersen, G., & Silverman, W. P. (2000). Sequence of cognitive decline in dementia in adults with Down's syndrome. *Journal of Intellectual Disability Research, 44 (Pt 6)*, 654–665.

Devenny, D. A., Zimmerli, E. J., Kittler, P., & Krinsky-McHale, S. J. (2002). Cued recall in early-stage dementia in adults with Down's syndrome. *Journal of Intellectual Disability Research, 46*(6), 472–483. doi:10.1046/j.1365-2788.2002.00417.x

Dodd, K., Bhaumik, S., & Benbow, S. M. (2009, September). Dementia and people with learning disabilities: Guidance on the assessment, diagnosis, treatment and support of people with learning disabilities who develop dementia. British Psychological Society.

Esbensen, A. J., Mailick, M. R., & Silverman, W. (2013). Long-term Impact of parental well-being on adult outcomes and dementia status in individuals with Down syndrome. *American Journal on Intellectual and Developmental Disabilities, 118*(4), 294–309. doi:10.1352/1944-7558-118.4.294

Evans, E., Bhardwaj, A., Brodaty, H., Sachdev, P., Draper, B., & Trollor, J. N. (2013). Dementia in people with intellectual disability: Insights and challenges in epidemiological research with an at-risk population. *International Review of Psychiatry, 25*(6), 755–763. doi:10.3109/09540261.2013.866938

Evenhuis, H. M. (1992). Evaluation of a screening instrument for dementia in ageing mentally retarded persons. *Journal of Intellectual Disability Research, 36 (Pt 4)*, 337–347.

Evenhuis, H. M. (1997). The natural history of dementia in ageing people with intellectual disability. *Journal of Intellectual Disability Research, 41 (Pt 1)*, 92–96.

Evenhuis, H. M., Theunissen, M., Denkers, I., Verschuure, H., & Kemme, H. (2001). Prevalence of visual and hearing impairment in a Dutch institutionalized population with intellectual disability. *Journal of Intellectual Disability Research, 45*(5), 457–464. doi:10.1046/j.1365-2788.2001.00350.x

Fleminger, S., Oliver, D. L., Lovestone, S., Rabe-Hesketh, S., & Giora, A. (2003). Head injury as a risk factor for Alzheimer's disease: The evidence 10 years on; a partial replication. *Journal of Neurology, Neurosurgery, and Psychiatry, 74*(7), 857–862.

Haveman, M., Heller, T., Lee, L., Maaskant, M., Shooshtari, S., & Strydom, A. (2010). Major health risks in aging persons with intellectual disabilities: An overview of recent studies. *Journal of Policy and Practice in Intellectual Disabilities, 7*(1), 59–69. doi:10.1111/j.1741-1130.2010.00248.x

Haveman, M., Perry, J., Salvador-Carulla, L., Walsh, P. N., Kerr, M., Van Schrojenstein Lantman-de Valk, H., … Weber, G. (2011). Ageing and health status in adults with intellectual disabilities: Results of the European POMONA II study. *Journal of Intellectual & Developmental Disability, 36*(1), 49–60. doi:10.3109/13668250.2010.549464

Head, E., Doran, E., Nistor, M., Hill, M., Schmitt, F. A., Haier, R. J., & Lott, I. T. (2011). Plasma amyloid- as a function of age, level of intellectual disability, and presence of dementia in Down syndrome. *Journal of Alzheimer's Disease, 23*(3), 399–409. doi:10.3233/JAD-2010-101335

Hermans, H., & Evenhuis, H. M. (2013). Factors associated with depression and anxiety in older adults with intellectual disabilities: Results of the healthy ageing and intellectual disabilities study. *International Journal of Geriatric Psychiatry, 28*(7), 691–699. doi:10.1002/gps.3872

Herron, D. L., & Priest, H. M. (2013). Support workers' knowledge about dementia: A vignette study. *Advances in Mental Health and Intellectual Disabilities, 7*(1), 27–39. doi:10.1108/20441281311294675

Holland, A. J., Hon, J., Huppert, F. A., & Stevens, F. (2000). Incidence and course of dementia in people with Down's syndrome: Findings from a population-based study. *Journal of Intellectual Disability Research, 44 (Pt 2)*, 138–146.

Holland, A. J., Hon, J., Huppert, F. A., Stevens, F., & Watson, P. (1998). Population-based study of the prevalence and presentation of dementia in adults with Down's syndrome. *The British Journal of Psychiatry, 172*(6), 493–498. doi:10.1192/bjp.172.6.493

Jamieson-Craig, R., Scior, K., Chan, T., Fenton, C., & Strydom, A. (2010). Reliance on carer reports of early symptoms of dementia among adults with intellectual disabilities. *Journal of Policy and Practice in Intellectual Disabilities, 7*(1), 34–41. doi:10.1111/j.1741-1130.2010.00245.x

Kannabiran, M., & Deb, S. (2010). Diseases of the nervous system II: Neurodegenerative diseases including dementias. In J. O'Hara, J. McCarthy, & N. Bouras (Eds.), *Intellectual disability and ill health* (pp. 203-213). Cambridge University Press. Retrieved from http://dx.doi.org/10.1017/CBO9780511770715.021

Kittler, P., Krinsky-McHale, S. J., & Devenny, D. A. (2006). Verbal intrusions precede memory decline in adults with Down syndrome. *Journal of Intellectual Disability Research: JIDR, 50*(Pt 1), 1–10. doi:10.1111/j.1365-2788.2005.00715.x

Knopman, D. S., DeKosky, S. T., Cummings, J. L., Chui, H., Corey–Bloom, J., Relkin, N., … Stevens, J. C. (2001). Practice parameter:

Diagnosis of dementia (an evidence-based review). Report of the Quality Standards Subcommittee of the American Academy of Neurology. *Neurology, 56*(9), 1143–1153. doi:10.1212/WNL.56.9.1143

Krinsky-McHale, S. J., Devenny, D. A., & Silverman, W. P. (2002). Changes in explicit memory associated with early dementia in adults with Down's syndrome. *Journal of Intellectual Disability Research, 46*(Pt 3), 198–208.

Krinsky-McHale, S. J., & Silverman, W. (2013). Dementia and mild cognitive impairment in adults with intellectual disability: Issues of diagnosis. *Developmental Disabilities Research Reviews, 18*(1), 31–42. doi:10.1002/ddrr.1126

Lin, J.-D., Lin, L.-P., Hsia, Y.-C., Hsu, S.-W., Wu, C.-L., & Chu, C. M. (2014). A national survey of caregivers' perspective of early symptoms of dementia among adults with an intellectual disability based on the DSQIID scale. *Research in Autism Spectrum Disorders, 8*(3), 275–280. doi:10.1016/j.rasd.2013.12.010

Lott, I. T., & Dierssen, M. (2010). Cognitive deficits and associated neurological complications in individuals with Down's syndrome. *Lancet Neurology, 9*(6), 623–633. doi:10.1016/S1474-4422(10)70112-5

Lott, I. T., Doran, E., Nguyen, V. Q., Tournay, A., Head, E., & Gillen, D. L. (2011). Down syndrome and dementia: A randomized, controlled trial of antioxidant supplementation. *American Journal of Medical Genetics Part A, 155*(8), 1939–1948. doi:10.1002/ajmg.a.34114

Lott, I. T., Doran, E., Nguyen, V. Q., Tournay, A., Movsesyan, N., & Gillen, D. L. (2012). Down syndrome and dementia: Seizures and cognitive decline. *Journal of Alzheimer's Disease, 29*(1), 177–185. doi:10.3233/JAD-2012-111613

Määttä, T., Kaski, M., Taanila, A., Keinänen-Kiukaanniemi, S., & Iivanainen, M. (2006a). Sensory impairments and health concerns related to the degree of intellectual disability in people with Down syndrome. *Down Syndrome Research and Practice, 11*(2), 78–83. doi:10.3104/reports.317

Määttä, T., Määttä, J., Tervo-Määttä, T., Taanila, A., Kaski, M., & Iivanainen, M. (2011). Healthcare and guidelines: A population-based survey of recorded medical problems and health surveillance for people with Down syndrome. *Journal of Intellectual and Developmental Disability, 36*(2), 118–126. doi:10.1080/13668250.2011.570253

Matsuoka, Y., Andrews, H. F., Becker, A. G., Gray, A. J., Mehta, P. D., Sano, M. C., ... Aisen, P. S. (2009). The relationship of plasma Abeta levels to dementia in aging individuals with Down syndrome. *Alzheimer's disease and Associated Disorders, 23*(4), 315–318. doi:10.1097/WAD.0b013e3181aba61e

McCarron, M., Gill, M., McCallion, P., & Begley, C. (2005). Health co-morbidities in ageing persons with Down syndrome and Alzheimer's dementia. *Journal of Intellectual Disability Research: JIDR, 49*(Pt 7), 560–566. doi:10.1111/j.1365-2788.2005.00704.x

McCarron, M., McCallion, P., Reilly, E., & Mulryan, N. (2014). A prospective 14-year longitudinal follow-up of dementia in persons with Down syndrome. *Journal of Intellectual Disability Research: JIDR, 58*(1), 61–70. doi:10.1111/jir.12074

Möller, J. C., Hamer, H. M., Oertel, W. H., & Rosenow, F. (2001). Late-onset myoclonic epilepsy in Down's syndrome (LOMEDS). *Seizure—European Journal of Epilepsy, 10*(4), 303–306. doi:10.1053/seiz.2000.0500

Moog, U., van Mierlo, I., van Schrojenstein Lantman-de Valk, H. M. J., Spaapen, L., Maaskant, M. A., & Curfs, L. M. G. (2007). Is Sanfilippo type B in your mind when you see adults with mental retardation and behavioral problems? *American Journal of Medical Genetics Part C: Seminars in Medical Genetics, 145C*(3), 293–301. doi:10.1002/ajmg.c.30142

Moran, J. A., Rafii, M. S., Keller, S. M., Singh, B. K., & Janicki, M. P. (2013). The national task group on intellectual disabilities and dementia practices consensus recommendations for the evaluation and management of dementia in adults with intellectual disabilities. *Mayo Clinic Proceedings, 88*(8), 831–840. doi:10.1016/j.mayocp.2013.04.024

Nelson, L. D., Orme, D., Osann, K., & Lott, I. T. (2001). Neurological changes and emotional functioning in adults with Down syndrome. *Journal of Intellectual Disability Research, 45*(5), 450–456. doi:10.1046/j.1365-2788.2001.00379.x

Nelson, L., Johnson, J. K., Freedman, M., Lott, I., Groot, J., Chang, M., … Head, E. (2005). Learning and memory as a function of age in Down syndrome: A study using animal-based tasks. *Progress in Neuro-Psychopharmacology and Biological Psychiatry, 29*(3), 443–453. doi:10.1016/j.pnpbp.2004.12.009

Oliver, C., Kalsy, S., McQuillan, S., & Hall, S. (2011). Behavioural excesses and deficits associated with dementia in adults who have Down syndrome. *Journal of Applied Research in Intellectual Disabilities, 24*(3), 208–216. doi:10.1111/j.1468-3148.2010.00604.x

Patti, D. (1999). Cognitive changes in memory precede those in praxis in aging persons with Down syndrome. *Journal of Intellectual & Developmental Disability, 24*, 169–187.

Petersen, R. C. (2011). Mild cognitive impairment. *New England Journal of Medicine, 364*(23), 2227–2234. doi:10.1056/NEJMcp0910237

Prasher, V. (1995). End-stage dementia in adults with Down syndrome. *International Journal of Geriatric Psychiatry, 10*(12), 1067–1069. doi:10.1002/gps.930101213

Prasher, V., Farooq, A., & Holder, R. (2004). The Adaptive Behaviour Dementia Questionnaire (ABDQ): Screening questionnaire for dementia in Alzheimer's disease in adults with Down syndrome. *Research in Developmental Disabilities, 25*(4), 385–397. doi:10.1016/j.ridd.2003.12.002

Prasher, V. P. (1995). Age-specific prevalence, thyroid dysfunction and depressive symptomatology in adults with down syndrome and dementia. *International Journal of Geriatric Psychiatry, 10*(1), 25–31. doi:10.1002/gps.930100106

Prasher, V. P., Chowdhury, T. A., Rowe, B. R., & Bain, S. C. (1997). ApoE genotype and Alzheimer's disease in adults with Down syndrome: Meta-analysis. *American Journal on Mental Retardation, 102*(2), 103–110.

Prasher, V. P., Uppal, H., Parveen, S., Adams, C., & Haque, S. (2013). Ten year serial mean corpuscular volume—A peripheral marker for Alzheimer's disease in Down syndrome. *International Journal of Geriatric Psychiatry, 28*(10), 1097–1098. doi:10.1002/gps.3956

Rapin, I., Weidenheim, K., Lindenbaum, Y., Rosenbaum, P., Merchant, S. N., Krishna, S., & Dickson, D. W. (2006). Cockayne syndrome in adults: Review with clinical and pathologic study of a new case. *Journal of Child Neurology, 21*(11), 991–1006. doi:10.1177/08830738060210110101

Rissman, R. A., & Mobley, W. C. (2011). Implication for treatment: GABAA receptors in aging, Down syndrome and Alzheimer's disease. *Journal of Neurochemistry, 117*(4), 613–622. doi:10.1111/j.1471-4159.2011.07237.x

Silverman, W. P., Zigman, W. B., Krinsky-McHale, S. J., Ryan, R., & Schupf, N. (2013). Intellectual disability, mild cognitive impairment, and risk for dementia. *Journal of Policy and Practice in Intellectual Disabilities, 10*(3). doi:10.1111/jppi.12042

Skandar, A., Schoonbrood-Lenssen, A., Van den Akker, M., & Maaskant, M. (2005). Verouderingskenmerken bij mensen met het syndroom van Sanfilippo. *Tijdschrift Voor Artsen Voor Verstandelijk Gehandicapten, 23*(4), 3–5.

Sparrow, S. S. (2011). Vineland Adaptive Behavior Scales. In J. S. Kreutzer, J. DeLuca, & B. Caplan (Eds.), *Encyclopedia of clinical neuropsychology* (pp. 2618–2621). Springer New York. Retrieved from http://link.springer.com/referenceworkentry/10.1007/978-0-387-79948-3_1602

Strydom, A., Chan, T., Fenton, C., Jamieson-Craig, R., Livingston, G., & Hassiotis, A. (2013). Validity of criteria for dementia in older people with intellectual disability. *The American Journal of Geriatric Psychiatry, 21*(3), 279–288. doi:10.1016/j.jagp.2012.11.017

Strydom, A., Chan, T., King, M., Hassiotis, A., & Livingston, G. (2013). Incidence of dementia in older adults with intellectual disabilities. *Research in Developmental Disabilities, 34*(6), 1881–1885. doi:10.1016/j.ridd.2013.02.021

Strydom, A., Hassiotis, A., King, M., & Livingston, G. (2009). The relationship of dementia prevalence in older adults with intellectual disability (ID) to age and severity of ID. *Psychological Medicine, 39*(01), 13–21. doi:10.1017/S0033291708003334

Strydom, A., Livingston, G., King, M., & Hassiotis, A. (2007). Prevalence of dementia in intellectual disability using different diagnostic criteria. *The British Journal of Psychiatry, 191*(2), 150–157. doi:10.1192/bjp.bp.106.028845

Strydom, A., Shooshtari, S., Lee, L., Raykar, V., Torr, J., Tsiouris, J., ... Maaskant, M. (2010). Dementia in older adults with intellectual disabilities—Epidemiology, presentation, and diagnosis. *Journal of Policy and Practice in Intellectual Disabilities, 7*(2), 96–110. doi:10.1111/j.1741-1130.2010.00253.x

Torr, J., Strydom, A., Patti, P., & Jokinen, N. (2010). Aging in Down syndrome: Morbidity and mortality. *Journal of Policy and Practice in Intellectual Disabilities, 7*(1), 70–81. doi:10.1111/j.1741-1130.2010.00249.x

Tyrrell, J., Cosgrave, M., McCarron, M., McPherson, J., Calvert, J., Kelly, A., ... Lawlor, B. A. (2001). Dementia in people with Down's syndrome. *International Journal of Geriatric Psychiatry, 16*(12), 1168–1174. doi:10.1002/gps.502

Urv, T. K., Zigman, W. B., & Silverman, W. (2010). Psychiatric symptoms in adults with Down syndrome and Alzheimer's disease. *American Journal on Intellectual and Developmental Disabilities, 115*(4), 265–276. doi:10.1352/1944-7558-115.4.265

Urv, T. K., Zigman, W. B., Silverman, W., & MacLean, J., William E. (2008). Maladaptive behaviors related to dementia status in adults with Down syndrome. *American Journal on Mental Retardation, 113*(2), 73–86. doi:10.1352/0895-8017(2008)113[73:MBRTDS]2.0.CO;2

Visser, F. E., Aldenkamp, A. P., van Huffelen, A. C., Kuilman, M., Overweg, J., & van Wijk, J. (1997). Prospective study of the prevalence of Alzheimer's-type dementia in institutionalized individuals with Down syndrome. *American Journal on Mental Retardation, 101*(4), 400–412.

Whitwham, S., McBrien, J., & Broom, W. (2011). Should we refer for a dementia assessment? A checklist to help know when to be concerned about dementia in adults with Down syndrome and other intellectual disabilities. *British Journal of Learning Disabilities, 39*(1), 17–21. doi:10.1111/j.1468-3156.2009.00606.x

Zeilinger, E. L., Stiehl, K. A. M., & Weber, G. (2013). A systematic review on assessment instruments for dementia in persons with intellectual disabilities. *Research in Developmental Disabilities, 34*(11), 3962–3977. doi:10.1016/j.ridd.2013.08.013

Zigman, W. B. (2013). Atypical aging in Down syndrome. *Developmental Disabilities Research Reviews, 18*(1), 51–67. doi:10.1002/ddrr.1128

Zigman, W. B., Schupf, N., Devenny, D. A., Miezejeski, C., Ryan, R., Urv, T. K., ... Silverman, W. (2004). Incidence and prevalence of dementia in elderly adults with mental retardation without Down syndrome. *American Journal on Mental Retardation, 109*(2), 126–141. doi:10.1352/0895-8017(2004)109<126:IAPODI>2.0.CO;2

CHAPTER 26

Personality Disorders

William R. Lindsay
Lawrence A. Dana
Regi T. Alexander
Dorothy M. Griffiths
Steve Wilkinson

This chapter may represent something of a pivotal point in the diagnosis of mental disorders according to *DSM-5*, because on the one hand it has changed very little in the consideration of personality disorder and on the other it has changed fundamentally. As an introduction it is necessary to review the technical and ideological discussions prior to the publication of *DSM-5* leading to two systems for the diagnosis of personality disorder. One ideological principle in the considerations of *DSM-5* was that there is a dimensional continuum between normality and psychopathology. Categories of mental illness are almost always fuzzy around the edges with no precise distinction between mental illness and normality and so the principle that there is a fundamental difference between pathology and normality was questioned. This was particularly true in relation to personality disorder in that (as we shall review later) there is an abundance of research suggesting that abnormal personality traits lie at the extreme of a continuum from normal adaptive to maladaptive personality.

It is in this context that a plan was made to change completely the diagnosis of personality disorder. It has always been acknowledged that personality variables are "fuzzy". Variables are considered as fuzzy when they define concepts or classes without sharp boundaries in which there is a gradual shift from membership of one classification to membership of another (Acton, 1998). A fuzzy variable is, therefore, one that is an imperfect measure of that concept. In personality terms, people differ on a continuum of trait concepts such as dominant-submissive. A few of us are likely to be extremely dominant or extremely submissive but most of us fall somewhere in between the extremes. Similarly, the boundary between normal personality and personality disorder is not clear. It is difficult to estimate where normal personality becomes pathological and maladaptive. Most of us have interpersonal difficulties as a result of "personality clashes", some of us have serious interpersonal difficulties, and it can be difficult for the clinician to judge when interpersonal difficulties are so great that they become a pervasive disorder of personality.

For these reasons, a dimensional approach to the diagnosis of personality disorder was proposed for *DSM-5*. In the end, the proposals were too radical to be adopted, and, instead, personality disorder was chosen as "a poster child" by the *DSM-5* task force to evaluate the advantages of a dimensional system as a replacement for categorical psychiatric diagnosis (Paris, 2013). The main proposals for DSM 5 are essentially unchanged from DSM IV and there is little need to change the previous recommendations outlined in *DM-ID* (Lindsay, Dana, Dosen, Gabriel, & Young, 2007). However, the alternative system will also be reviewed in this chapter, and it is fundamentally different from the previous diagnostic approach.

Introduction

Personality is reflected in behavior and experience that occur consistently across a variety of situations and throughout the individual's lifetime. A persistently disrupted personality can be classified under the 11 categories of personality disorder. There are 10 personality disorders including paranoid personality disorder, schizoid personality disorder, schizotypal personality disorder; antisocial personality disorder, borderline personality disorder, histrionic personality disorder, narcisstic personality disorder; avoidant personality disorder, dependent personality disorder, and obsessive-compulsive personality disorder. Where the person has a maladaptive personality but does not fulfil the traits for any single personality disorder, it is possible to diagnose personality disorder not otherwise specified. Each diagnosis was arrived at through expert opinion (Paris 2013) and the current authors have considered them in the light of existing research, and a range of modifications are proposed for the diagnostic criteria. These modifications include considerations of the cultural framework within which people with ID are likely to have developed, an increased use of behavioral observation, and an increased use of informant information.

Review of Diagnostic Criteria

The *DSM-IV-TR* and *DSM-5* define personality disorder as "an enduring pattern of inner experience and behavior that deviates markedly from the expectations of the individual's culture," that is "inflexible and pervasive," that "its onset can be traced back at least to adolescence or early adulthood," that "is stable and of long duration," and that "leads to clinically significant distress or impairment" (American Psychiatric Association, 2013, pp. 646-647). There are six criteria for a diagnosis of personality disorder, two of which are exclusion criteria:

- that the behaviors or symptoms are not better accounted for by another mental disorder,
- that they are not due to substance abuse or a medical condition.

The inclusion criteria are as follows:

- that there is a significant deficit in two of the four areas of cognition, affectivity, interpersonal functioning, and impulse control;
- that the deficits occur across a broad range of personal and social situations;
- that the deficits occur across occupational and other important areas of functioning; and
- that the deficits are stable and of long duration, with an onset traced back at least to adolescence or early adulthood.

Livesley (2001), while noting that the term *personality* has received dozens of definitions, writes that there is a consensus concerning the fundamental elements and concepts. Personality is reflected in behavior, interaction, and forms of experience (cognition, perception, and emotion) that occur regularly and consistently across a variety of situations and throughout the individual's lifetime. Personality is also coherent. Individual traits and attributes form an integrated system that characterizes the qualities of any given individual. Given such an ubiquitous definition of personality, it follows that disorders of personality are similarly ubiquitous. The themes underlying definitions of personality are reflected in the diagnosis of personality disorder. Antisocial or aberrant individual traits make up an abnormality of personality or disrupt the coherence of personality. Some polemic exists, however, between those writings that employ a categorical description of personality disorder and those that employ a dimensional system. The *DSM-5* contains categorical descriptions of personality disorders, whereby individuals have or do not have the constellation of traits described within each disorder. Others (see later) argue that Personality Disorders represent a constellation of traits, which lie in dimensions from normal to extreme and are thus best represented within a dimensional system. The alternative system for diagnosis of personality disorder in DSM-5 is described in the second section of this chapter

Livesley (2001) notes five main variants of the concept of personality: that personality disorder is a less serious form of major mental disorders; that it represents deficits in the development of personality; that it is a specific form of personality organization; that it represents social deviance and a failure of socialization; and, finally, that it is an extreme of the normal variation of personality. The *DSM-IV-TR* specifically recommends that diagnosis not be made if the observed pattern of personality is better accounted for as a manifestation or consequence of another mental disorder. However, Livesley's other four concepts for personality disorder are relevant in the consideration of the diagnosis. This general conceptual framework is important when one is reviewing the diagnosis of an individual client.

Summary of DSM-5 Criteria

As previously mentioned, there are 10 specific personality disorders and 1 nonspecific personality disorder.

- **Paranoid personality disorder** describes a pattern of suspiciousness and distrust.
- **Schizoid personality disorder** constitutes a pattern of detachment from social relationships and a restricted range of emotional expression.
- **Schizotypal personality disorder** constitutes acute discomfort in close relationships and such eccentricities of behavior as superstitions, feelings of magical control, idiosyncratic speech, and an unkempt manner of dress. Individuals with this disorder might report perceptual alterations without holding delusional conviction about them.
- **Antisocial personality disorder** features a notable lack of empathy, callousness, cynicism, and contemptuousness for the feelings and rights of others.
- **Borderline personality disorder** features an instability of interpersonal relationships and significant impulsivity. It might feature anger toward caregivers or close friends if they are seen as neglectful or abandoning. Individuals with this disorder display impulsivity in at least two of the following areas: spending, sex, substance abuse, reckless driving, and binge eating.
- **Histrionic personality disorder** features excessive emotionality and attention seeking. Individuals like to be the center of attention, can be sexually provocative and theatrical, display shallow and shifting emotions, and are suggestible.
- **Narcissistic personality disorder** features grandiosity, a preoccupation with fantasies of success, and the belief that he or she is special. The individual will lack empathy, show arrogance, and yet be envious of others and exploitative.
- **Avoidant personality disorder** features social avoidance and inhibition, preoccupation with rejection, and hypersensitivity.
- **Dependent personality disorder** is characterized by a fear of separation or loss of support, a need for reassurance, and a need for others to assume responsibility.
- **Obsessive-compulsive personality disorder** is characterized by a preoccupation with perfectionism and orderliness. The individual is over-conscientious and stubborn.
- **Personality disorder not otherwise specified**. Here there might be features of more than one personality disorder, and these features do not meet the full criteria for any specific disorder. This diagnosis can also be used when two or three criteria are pervasive; the examples given in the *DSM-IV TR* are depressive personality disorder and passive-aggressive personality disorder.

Issues Related to Diagnosis in People with Intellectual and Developmental Disabilities (IDD)

In our consideration of issues related to IDD, we have been particularly aware of the possibility of special circumstances surrounding the developmental processes of individuals with intellectual and developmental disabilities. Because of the IDD, individuals are likely to experience a delayed development that may result in an immature or a less completely developed personality, which will have traits or features of personality disorder. Such a developmental delay sets up cultural expectations in people with IDD that might differ from normal expectations. For example, such individuals are less likely to be expected to show normal progress at school. A nosological diagnostic system, such as the *DSM-5*, intrinsically holds an acceptable range of cultural development as a framework that might be insufficient for the purposes of establishing a diagnosis of personality disorder in an individual with IDD. We must, therefore, keep in mind more general works on personality structure that employ a developmental approach, such as that of Zigler and his colleagues (Zigler, Bennet-Gates, Hodapp, & Heinrich, 2002) (Strength of evidence: III) (see "Application of Diagnostic Criteria to People with ID"). However, we are also aware that we run the risk of falling into the twin traps of, on the one hand, declaring that individuals with IDD are immune from some personality disorders or, on the other hand, suggesting that these individuals present in ways grossly divergent from individuals without IDD. Therefore, we do not wish to set a precedent for other demographic groups.

We have, therefore, given much thought to the issue of special considerations regarding diagnosis. Much of this thought has revolved around the cultural expectations and experience of individuals with IDD, and some of this is related to features of intellectual disability itself. In relation to the latter, the concept of empathy appears in some of the diagnostic classifications for personality disorder. We will discuss this more extensively later in relation to the alternative diagnostic system, but empathy involves a perspective taking process, and perspective taking is a developmental skill. This has been well established by developmental psychology. If an individual has developmental delay to the extent of developmental impairment, it is likely that the perspective taking abilities are correspondingly impaired. As a result, they are likely to have significant impairments in perspective taking and, by extension, empathic ability. This should be considered during assessment as a possible feature of IDD rather than a feature of personality disorder.

Some individuals could have had extensive institutional experience and might have adapted to institutional life by developing behavioral and cognitive patterns that are consistent with personality disorder. For example, an individual might have adapted to institutional social norms by developing dependent features or aspects of antisocial personality disorder as a result of oppositional behavior. (The philosophical and political evidence for this has determined much of the development of services over the past few decades (Edgerton 1967, 1973). It is axiomatic that personality is a result of biological substrates, psychosocial factors, experience, and environmental circumstances. If the environmental circumstances have produced distorted experiences or distorted cultural expectations, then an individual might adapt in ways that result in personality disorder. Such a possibility has implications for etiology, clarifying whether the condition was genetic or was due to life experience. We feel, however, that an unusual personal history does not exclude someone from a diagnosis of personality disorder. The diagnosis is made, or not made, on the basis of whether the person's behavior, cognition, and attitudes meet or do not meet the criteria set.

The only caveat would be the issue of the persistent nature of personality disorder. Since the personality disorder might be a result of adaptation or learning, the diagnosis might be made on a provisional basis—the provision being the possibility that the behaviors and attitudes might change as a function of the person now living in a more normal environment.

One major condition of the personality disorder criteria is the notion that the traits are enduring and exist across environments. If there is a reasonable expectation that a previously institutionalized person can be resocialized through combined social learning, treatment, and contingency management techniques, then we caution the reader to reassess the individual annually during any training or treatment process. All of the foregoing considerations hold for other special considerations—for example, if the person has been treated as an infant throughout the developmental years or if the individual has had few opportunities to learn social norms.

Some of the issues in diagnosis of personality disorder are not specific to IDD. Perhaps the main issue is differentiating the traits of personality disorder from other major mental disorders. If an individual has IDD, the differentiation can be even more difficult to make because of the linguistic and cognitive limitations involved. A second difficulty is the relationship between behavioral disorder, personality disorder, and mental illness. If one includes the diagnosis of behavioral disturbance in mental illness, the incidence of mental illness in the population increases dramatically (Lund, 1985). Behavior disorder, however, might be an enduring characteristic of a personality disorder, or, alternatively, it might be a feature of a behavior phenotype. A further consideration is the confusion that can arise because of the developmental delay itself. One might, therefore, have difficulty in separating the immaturity resulting from developmental delay from the immaturity as a criterion for Personality Disorder. We are reminded, nevertheless, of our earlier assertion that the diagnosis of personality disorder is made, or not made, simply on the basis of whether the person's behavior meets the criteria set. It is well documented that, because of diagnostic masking, certain mental illnesses can have alternative manifestations in this client group. Some behavioral disturbance might, therefore, be symptomatic of mental illness. Similarly, personality disorders are likely to be presented as behavioral disturbance as well as cognitive and linguistic manifestations (Sovner & Hurley 1986).

Finally, there is the problem of whether it is even possible to consider personality disorder in someone with severe or profound IDD. In the end, consistent with the DC-LD (Royal College of Psychiatrists, 2001), we suggest that, in general, individuals with severe or profound IDD do not have sufficiently well developed or mature personalities for a reliable diagnosis to be made.

Several authors (Alexander & Cooray, 2003; Reid, Lindsay, Law, & Sturmey, 2004) have noted the lack of reliable diagnostic instruments and the high variation in prevalence of personality disorder across studies. It is also the case that most individuals with IDD do not have sufficient reading skills to fill out a self-report personality questionnaire. There have been considerable developments in the use of self-report inventories for a range of psychological problems (Dagnan & Lindsay, 2004; Finlay & Lyons, 2001), and these inventories have now extended to personality questionnaires (see literature review below). Alexander and Cooray (2003) make a strong recommendation for greater use of behavioral observation and informant information in making a diagnosis of personality disorder. One might, therefore, have to rely more heavily on informant information than one might have to in the mainstream population.

Issues Related to Specific Criteria

Several items, across diagnoses, refer to intimate and sexual relationships. Individuals with IDD might have had protected upbringings and relatively restricted exposure to intimate sexual relationships. Therefore, any assessment should recognize a relative shift in this culture toward less experience of such relationships. Put simply, if one has never been allowed to have sexual experiences, it is difficult to have an interest in them. Also, if one has had a sheltered upbringing with no encouragement to learn how to develop close friendships and understand the nature of a confidante, one is unlikely to be able to do it at present (Craft & Craft, 1978; Edgerton 1967, 1973; Griffiths et al. in this volume).

Dependency and fear of failure are referred to against several features of personality disorder. Studies have found that it is not uncommon for people with IDD to experience repeated failure and negative self-evaluation in relation to nondisabled peers. You should bear this fact in mind as another cultural experience, and you should make any judgments against this framework (Dagnan & Sandhu, 1999; Dagnan & Waring, 2004; Lindsay, Stenfert Kroese, & Drew, 2004). The IDD itself can also have an effect on the individual's ability to take personal responsibility.

Issues related to the ability to make decisions are relevant when considering several criteria. Individuals with IDD might have limited opportunities to practice increasingly complex decision making and, as a result, might demonstrate such difficulties in adult life. At the extreme, an individual with IDD might have been treated as an infant all of his or her life and might have been sheltered from situations that require decisions. Again, we make this point not because it represents an exclusion criterion but because it sets a cultural context for consideration in the diagnosis of avoidant personality disorder and because it might also constitute a crucial etiological factor. Perhaps one could consider a provisional diagnosis pending a remediation program for the development of skills and decision making. As with other diagnoses, any provisional judgment should be revisited annually. There is also evidence concerning deficits in decision-making ability and the remediation of decision-making deficits (Arscott, Dagnan, & Stenfert Kroese, 1999).

Anger and aggression are considered to be behavioral equivalents across a range of different types of diagnoses. Anger has been reported as a frequent problem across different types of ID services (Novaco & Taylor, 2004; Taylor, Novaco, Gillmer, & Thorne, 2002). Although anger, aggression, and irritability are common features in a range of personality disorders, they should not be considered a defining characteristic in the absence of other diagnostic features.

Several criteria within diagnoses require fairly sophisticated verbal skills and, even if one is making assessments with an informant, these issues would be difficult for clients to express. You should, therefore, keep in mind the intellectual limitations and linguistic limitations of the individual when considering such issues as identity disturbance or chronic feelings of emptiness (Expert opinion of the authors).

People with IDD might have limitations with regard to understanding things in perspective and abstract thinking, specifically because of the intellectual deficit. Several items within the personality disorder diagnoses are related to empathy, remorse, and other understanding-in-perspective abilities (Jervis & Baker, 2004). Understanding things in perspective becomes more difficult as intellectual limitations increase, so the lack of understanding-in-perspective abilities might be absolute in some individuals with moderate or severe IDD. Our position on this factor, as indicated above, has become clearer and indeed strengthened on the basis of research by Joliffe and Farrington (2004). They studied 349 offenders and found that ability to demonstrate empathy was directly related to IQ. Those participants of lower intellectual ability showed greater deficits in empathy. Such a lack may not be due to personality disorder but to the IDD itself.

Finally, issues of being easily led, being dependent, and, in particular, suggestibility are invoked against a number of the criteria. It is well documented that individuals with IDD have, in general, a heightened propensity toward suggestibility. Again, this is a cultural factor that you should take into account when assessing these issues (Beail, 2002; Gudjonsson, 1997).

Application of Diagnostic Criteria to People with IDD

The application of diagnostic criteria should take into account the issues related to diagnosis summarized in the preceding section. The DC-LD (Royal College of Psychiatrists, 2001) stipulates that a diagnosis should take account of the developmental delay in the formation of personality. It is argued there that personality continues to develop in an individual with IDD throughout adolescence, and a diagnosis of personality disorder should not be considered until the individual is 21 years old. In considering diagnosis of personality disorder for people with IDD in relation to the *DSM-5* criteria, we are entirely in agreement with this position and endorse the view that a reliable diagnosis cannot be considered under the age of 21 years. In general, it is more difficult to apply diagnostic criteria as the severity of the IDD increases with a corresponding impoverishment of intellectual, linguistic, and adaptive behavior function. As we have indicated, diagnosis should not normally be considered in individuals with severe or profound IDD.

In "Issues Related to Diagnosis in People with IDD," we have outlined a number of general considerations regarding the diagnosis of personality disorder in individuals with IDD. The most significant of these are the importance of considering the cultural context in which one is making the diagnosis. People with IDD are subject to developmental delay and might also experience restricted upbringing, repeated incidents of failure, negative self-evaluation compared with non-impaired peers, and limitations in intimate sexual relationships. All of these issues are personal characteristics that are considered in the diagnosis of personality disorder.

A second general consideration is that acknowledged by Alexander and Cooray (2003) and Reid et al. (2004) when they note the importance of informant information when making a diagnosis of personality disorder. Developments in self-report methods for this client group have not extended to personality questionnaires, and therefore behavioral observation and informant information are correspondingly more important. In "Issues Related to Diagnosis in People with IDD," we outlined a number of specific issues in relation to the cultural framework for a diagnosis—for example, increased propensity toward suggestibility.

Methodology

We conducted the current literature review with the help of the following databases: Medline, Embase, and Psychlink. We also used the normal university library sources.

Review of Research Applying to People with IDD

The extensive research on personality, personality disorders, and the integration of the two (Bender, Moray & Skodal, 2011; Blackburn, 1993, 2000; Hopwood, Wright, Ansell, & Pincus, 2011; Livesley & Jackson, 1991; Miller et al., 2010; Widiger & Costa, 2012) has not extended to the field of IDD. A five-factor model has emerged from a wealth of research investigating personality structure (Costa & McCrae, 1985; Digman, 1990; Goldberg, 1990) with the "big five" factors being extraversion, neuroticism, openness, agreeableness, and conscientiousness. There has been a significant amount of recent research investigating the relationship between personality traits and Personality Disorders as defined in the *DSM-IV-TR* (Miller et al., 2010; Hopwood et al., 2011; Widiger & Costa, 2012). Work that attempts to integrate these taxonomic systems has provided a range of insights into the relationship between personality structure and personality disorders, both in terms of finite classification and the dimensions of moderate to extreme personality classifications. It is only recently that preliminary reports using the five factor model for people with intellectual disabilities have started to appear (Lindsay, Rzpecka, & Law 2007).

Our knowledge regarding the relationship between personality, personality disorder, and psychopathology in people with ID has begun to develop at a much better rate than was the case for the previous edition of this chapter. We have mentioned in previous sections that there is a greater prevalence of a range of mental illnesses within this client population. Given the widespread acceptance of a comorbidity of disorders (Blackburn, 2000; Oldham et al., 1995;) it is likely that a similar comorbidity, or coexistence of disorders, is present in people with IDD.

Early studies on personality disorder and people with IDD noted that, similar to studies on the general population and personality disorder there was likely to be co-morbidity with other mental disorders and illnesses (Blackburn 2000; Earl 1961). One of the first systematic investigations into personality disorder and IDD was conducted by Corbett (1979) in a sample of 402 participants. He identified a prevalence rate of 25.4% of which almost half was immature and unstable personality disorder. The extent to which one can separate the effects of developmental delay as a result of IDD from immature and unstable personality illustrates some of the difficulties inherent in the diagnosis of personality disorder. Eaton and Menolascino (1982) reported a prevalence rate of 27% for personality disorder in a community based sample of 115 people with IDD in an institutional setting. Ballinger & Reid (1987) used the Standardised Assessment of Personality

(SAP; Mann, Jenkins, Cutting, & Cowan 1981) and reported a prevalence rate of severe personality disorder in 22% of 100 individuals with mild or moderate IDD. These authors along with Gostasson (1987) also commented on the difficulty in applying diagnostic criteria for personality disorder to individuals with severe and profound IDD. Early studies established that personality disorder could be assessed and was prevalent to some extent in this population. They identified some of the difficulties concerning co-morbidity and diagnosis in more severe levels of IDD and pointed out some confusion with immaturity and dependence.

Ten years on, as ICD-10 (World Health Organisation 1990) and DSM-IV (American Psychiatric Association 1990) were published, there were further studies on personality disorder and IDD. Khan, Cowan & Roy (1997) also used the SAP and reported that 50% of their sample had personality abnormalities and 31% had a degree of impairment sufficient to warrant a diagnosis of personality disorder. Of those diagnosed, the specific disorders were as follows: schizoid 10%, impulsive 7%, paranoid 5%, dependent 3%, dissocial 3%, histrionic 1%, anxious 1%, and anankastic 1%. Goldberg, Gitta & Puddephatt (1995) reported very high levels of personality disorder in samples of people with IDD. They used DSM III-R diagnostic criteria and two other screening measures for mental health symptomotology. They found abnormal personality traits in 57% of individuals in an institutional sample and 91% of individuals in a community sample. Flynn, Matthews & Hollins (2002) studied a hospital inpatient sample of 36 cases and reported that 92% were diagnosed with personality disorder using ICD 10 criteria. On the other hand, working with the same ICD 10 criteria, Naik, Gangadharan and Alexander (2002) found personality disorder in 7% of a community sample while Alexander, Piachaud, Odebiyi & Gangadharan (2002) found it in 58% of a sample of patients referred to a forensic hospital.

A turning point in research on personality disorder and IDD came with Alexander and Cooray's (2003) review of studies. They noted that there was a lack of reliable diagnostic instruments, the use of different diagnostic systems (ICD-10 and DSM-IV), a confusion of definition and personality theory, and difficulty in distinguishing personality disorder from other problems integral to IDD such as communication problems, sensory disorders, and developmental delay. They concluded that "the variation in the co-occurrence of personality disorder in learning disability, with prevalence ranging from less than 1% to 91% in a community setting and 22% to 92% in hospital settings, is very great and too large to be explained by real differences" (p. s28). They recommended tighter diagnostic criteria and greater use of behavioral observation and informant information. Reid et al. (2004) made similar recommendations and made initial attempts to integrate mainstream work on personality with the small amount of work available investigating personality disorder and ID. These authors used the NEO-PI assessments of the five factor personality structure (Costa & McCrae, 1985). This is one of the most widely accepted assessments for personality with considerable empirical support. It has also been one of the bases for the alternative model to assess personality disorder in DSM-5 (reviewed later). In a series of case illustrations, Reid et al. (2004) found that those individuals who scored high on psychopathy (Psychopathy Checklist Revised, Hare 1993) had low scores on the agreeableness and conscientiousness scale of the NEO-PI. This finding is similar to that reported in mainstream personality research (Blackburn, 2000).

Lindsay et al. (2006) employed the recommendations made by Alexander & Cooray (2003) in a study of 164 males with IDD in three forensic settings—high secure, medium/low secure, and community forensic services. They employed four independently rated measures of personality disorder: a DSM IV criteria checklist completed firstly from file review, secondly by a clinician and thirdly from nurse observations, and finally the SAP completed by care staff. A consensus rating was derived from the four assessments and a total prevalence of personality disorder in this forensic sample was 39.5%. They reported that the ratings had high levels of reliability. As would be expected in a forensic population, antisocial personality disorder was the largest category at 22% of cases and rates of personality disorder across the other categories were between 1 and 3%. It should be noted that care was taken in these guidelines to avoid the confusion first mentioned by Corbett (1979), that of confusing developmental delay with immature or dependent personality disorder, and there were no cases with dependent personality disorder in the entire sample. It is also interesting that a previous more general file review of mental disorder in this sample (Hogue et al 2006) had found personality disorder recorded at 22.6% in the case files. By far the highest level of under recording was in the community forensic sample which was 1.4% in the case files and 33% in the carefully organized assessment study. These authors noted that even the highest figures found in this forensic IDD sample were lower than the figures of over 90% in studies on community samples reviewed by Alexander and Cooray (2003).

Lindsay, Rzepecka, et al. (2007) then reported a factor analysis of the personality disorder categories. In mainstream personality disorder research, Blackburn, Logan, Renwick, Donnelly (2005) had previously investigated higher order dimensions with 168 male forensic psychiatric patients and found two higher order factors that appeared to underlie personality structure. They labelled these two factors as "acting out" and "anxious-inhibited" which was similar to higher order structures identified by Morey (1988). In a similar confirmatory factor analysis on offenders with IDD, Lindsay, Rzepecka, et al. (2007) produced a two factor solution similar to that found previously with an "avoidant/inhibition" factor with high loadings from schizotypal personality disorder, avoidant personality disorder, obsessive compulsive personality disorder, and a lower loading from schizoid personality disorder, and an "acting out" factor with high loadings from borderline, narcissistic, and paranoid personality disorder with a smaller loading from antisocial personality disorder. Therefore the higher order dimensions of personality disorder in this study (Lindsay, Rzepecka, et al., 2007) on forensic participants with IDD were similar to those found on populations with mental disorder found in other studies (Blackburn et al., 2005; Krueger et al., 2007; Morey, 1988).

Alexander, Crouch, Haltstead, & Pichaud (2006) reported on the outcome of 65 patients with ID treated in medium secure forensic hospital settings. They found that the main associations with reconviction were a previous offense of theft or burglary, age of less than 27 years, and a presence of a personality disorder. This relationship between personality disorder and crime has been shown repeatedly with mainstream offending populations (Fazel & Danesh, 2002; Monahan et al., 2001). Indeed, one of the main reasons promoting the study of personality disorder has been, on the one hand, the predictive relationship between anti social personality disorder and crime while on the other, the predictive relationship between borderline personality disorder and psychiatric patient status (Widiger & Frances, 1985). Using the same population as Lindsay et al. (2006), Morrissey, Mooney, Hogue, Lindsay, & Taylor (2007) found that the PCL-R was significantly associated with negative treatment progress in terms of a move to more restricted treatment conditions. The PCL-R is strongly associated with antisocial personality disorder. These authors have consistently made the caution that the construct of personality disorder is a highly devaluing label and should be used very carefully with the population of people with IDD who are already highly devalued.

Most of the more recent work on personality disorder and IDD has been done on forensic populations. Alexander et al. (2010) compared the progress of 138 patients with IDD in a secure setting over a six year period, 77 with a dissocial or emotionally unstable personality disorder (ICD-10) and 61 without. They found that previous histories of aggression and violence were no different in the two groups but convictions for violent offenses and compulsory detentions were significantly more common in the group with personality disorder. However, there were no clinically significant differences in terms of outcome for the groups, and the authors concluded that patients with personality disorder and ID could be successfully treated in a general service for people with ID and a range of mental disorders. In a further comparison, Alexander, Chester, Gray, & Snowdenl (2012) compared the progress of three groups following treatment in a secure hospital system, one with ID, a second with ID and personality disorder, and a third with personality disorder only. The two groups with ID appeared to follow similar treatment and management trajectories while the group with personality disorder followed a very different trajectory. Both ID groups had lower rates of post release conviction and lower rates of violent re-offenses at two year follow up.

Three small treatment studies have used an adapted version of Dialectical Behaviour Therapy (DBT) in small groups of people with IDD. Sakdalan, Shaw & Collier (2010) used a thirteen week program with six participants, and although the sample size was very small,they found significant improvements on dynamic risk assessment. Morrissey & Ingamells (2011) developed a longer sixty session DBT program and reported anecdotal improvements in 4 out of 6 participants, twelve months following treatment. Mason (2007) reported a single case where assessment of personality and personality disorder guided successful treatment.

The Assessment of Personality and People with IDD

Since the authors of DSM-5 have considered carefully the relationship between normal personality and personality disorder we will now review the assessment of personality in people with IDD. Research on personality has a long history both in terms of the understanding of human functioning and with respect to applications focused on clinical problems. Over the last 50 years, two structural models have become well established: the Five Factor Model (FFM) of Personality and the Circumplex Model of Interpersonal Behavior. Beginning with Cattell (1946), factor models were developed and refined with five robust factors emerging most consistently (Goldberg 1981; McCrae & Costa 1987; Norman 1963). These factors are extraversion/introversion, agreeableness, conscientiousness, neuroticism and openness to experience. Circumplex models of personality have emerged from a different research context, generally focusing on clinical utility with eight octant variables ordered in a circle around the underlying co-ordinates of dominance/submissiveness and hostility/nurturance. While the FFM is a comprehensive statistical summary of personality traits, the circumplex model has emerged from a conceptualization of interpersonal relationships and interactions. An individual's responses on circumplex assessment will place him/her within one of the octants on the circle.

Researchers have found that the interpersonal circumplex is defined by the two FFM dimensions of extraversion and agreeableness (McCrae & Costa, 1989) and concluded that these two models of personality appear to complement each other in describing the structure of personality and understanding interpersonal behaviour (McCrae & Costa, 1989; Trapnell &Wiggins, 1990). Lindsay et al. (2009) evaluated the applicability of the circumplex model in a sample of 123 offenders with IDD. They found that the measures and resulting factor structure conformed to the circumplex structure.

The Five Factor Model (FFM) of personality assumes a trait theory perspective, in that individual differences characterize a person, and these, in turn, will influence thoughts, feelings, and behaviors (McCrae & Costa, 1991). The development of this model has been ongoing for the last four decades, and the five dimensions are thought to be fully comprehensive and generally agreed to be the basic dimensions of 'normal' personality (Emmons, 1995). Neuroticism (N) is the most consistent domain and runs on a continuum from neurotic to stable. A tendency to feel negative affect, for example, fear, guilt, or anger, is at the core of N. Extraversion (E) runs on a continuum from extraversion to introversion. E is sometimes known as the 'sociable' domain; however, it also includes factors such as sensation-seeking and assertiveness, which do not necessarily have a sociable component.

Openness (O) refers to the individual's openness to experience and covers a wide range of attributes including intellect, imagination, and values. The Agreeableness (A) domain focuses most strongly on interpersonal abilities and needs and runs on a continuum from agreeable to disagreeable. Conscientiousness (C) reflects determination, strong will, and a sense of duty and is also related to some aspects of N such as impulsivity and self-control factors (Costa & McCrae, 1995; Piedmont & Weinstein, 1993).

The NEO-PI-R is the most widely accepted and evaluated questionnaire measuring the FFM (Berry et al., 2001) which is the model employed for the alternative diagnostic system in *DSM-5*. The 241 questions of the NEO-PI-R thoroughly identify the five domains and also the 30 facets which are the defining features of the domains. The six facets of each domain are grounded in psychological theory and ensure that the domain is widely covered and that they highlight key individual differences. N's facets are anxiety, anger, hostility, depression, selfconsciousness, impulsiveness, and vulnerability. The facets identified with E are warmth, gregariousness, assertiveness, activity, excitement seeking, and positive emotions. O's facets were recognized as being fantasy, aesthetics, feelings, actions, ideas, and values. Trust, straightforwardness, altruism, compliance, modesty, and tender-mindedness are facets of A. Finally, C's facets have been identified as competence, order, dutifulness, achievement, striving, self-discipline, and deliberation. It has been suggested (Roepke, McAdams, Lindamer, Patterson, & Jeste, 2001) that personality profiles are fairly stable over time, and there is little difference in the profiles of adults aged 50–84 and 85–100. After some criticism regarding the lack of validity scales within the NEO-PI-R (for example, Schinka, Kinder, & Kremer, 1997), Costa and McCrae (1995) included an observer rating (form R) to be taken in addition to the self-rating (form S), which they believe reveals the validity of the responses. This also provides a strength for the present research study in that there is a check on the self-ratings and also allows comparisons of both sets of results.

The NEO-PI-R has had many clinical implications in applied settings. McCrae and Costa (1991) showed how the inventory can be used in a counselling setting in order to aid diagnosis and treatment. It can give indications in terms of emotional stability, willingness to change, and other factors related to the potential success of the counselling. Similarly, Harkness, Bagby, Joffe, and Levitt (2002) related personality dimensions of the NEO-PI-R to depression, suggesting that it could identify those who would be more adaptable to treatment and could highlight those patients who might need a different approach. The NEO-PI-R has also been related to mood, with findings indicating that A and C are not related to mood at all, while E is positively associated with positive affectivity, and N is negatively associated with positive affectivity. Quirk, Christiansen, Wagner, and McNulty (2003) found scores for the NEO-PI-R to be useful in clinical settings, with the facet level being of more practical use than the domain level. Furthermore, the NEO-PI-R has been used to obtain profiles of anxiety traits in patients with panic disorder (Foot & Koszycki, 2004), to examine personality and ease of adjustment into residential settings for patients with Alzheimer's disease (Brandt et al., 1998), and to examine differences in personality for individuals with post-traumatic stress disorder (Talbert, Braswell, Albrecht, Hyer, & Boudewyns, 1993). NEO-PI-R has also been linked with IQ in that O correlates with the Wechsler Adult Intelligence Scale-Revised, full scale IQ (WAIS-R FSIQ), verbal IQ (VIQ) and performance IQ (PIQ) (Holland, Dollinger, Holland, & MacDonald, 1995).

Lindsay, Rzpecka and Law (2007) adapted and simplified the language of the NEO-PI to be suitable for people with IDD. They first tested that the adapted assessment produced results with normally able participants, very similar to the full questionnaire. They then used the self and observer versions to assess its applicability for the client group with 40 participants with IDD and carers who knew the person well. They found that there were consistent differences between self and observer ratings with people with IDD rating themselves as significantly more agreeable, more extraverted, and more conscientious than observers. The difference was an average of 10 percentile points in introversion where the self ratings were 5 percentiles above the mean, and the observer mean were 5 percentiles below the mean. There was a difference of 10 percentile points for the A factor and 19 percentile points for the C factor, and in both factors observers rated the participant lower in agreeableness and conscientiousness than the people with IDD did themselves.

Given the extent of work on these various models of personality in mainstream literature, it is something of a surprise that research in the field of personality and IDD has developed from an entirely different standpoint. The standpoint of all previous work has been, on the one hand, developmental, reviewing the way in which developmental experiences form personality characteristics in individuals with IDD and, on the other, the personality factors behind the way in which people with ID are motivated to interact with their environment. Therefore, in a series of studies with children, Switzky and colleagues (Switzky, 2001; Switzky & Haywood, 1991, 1992,) concluded that motivational orientation (intrinsic vs. extrinsic) was a central concept in personality development in individuals with IDD. In another model, Reiss and Havercamp (1997, 1998) outlined 16 basic values that provide motivation for all individuals including people with IDD and in a factor analytic study found a factor solution that conformed to the basic values in their theoretical construction. Reiss and Havercamp (1997, 1998) also found that people with and without IDD showed the same motivational profiles in relation to achieving these basic values. They specified these basis values as social contact, curiosity, honor, family, independence, power, order, idealism, status, vengeance, romance, exercise, acceptance, tranquillity, eating, and saving.

A further personality approach based on a developmental perspective is that of Zigler and colleagues (Zigler, 2001; Zigler & Bennett-Gates, 1999; Zigler et al., 2002) who have derived an alternative personality structure describing seven traits as follows: positive reaction tendency ('heightened motivation . . . to both interact with and be dependent upon a supportive adult'), negative reaction tendency ('initial wariness shown when interacting with strange adults'), expectancy of success ('the degree to which one expects to succeed or fail when presented a new task'), outer directedness ('tendency . . . to look to others for the cues to solutions of difficult or ambiguous tasks'), efficacy motivation ('the pleasure derived from tackling and solving difficult problems'), obedience, and curiosity/creativity. Their assessment, the EZPQ, is a psychometrically well developed instrument with good evidence of reliability and validity. However, it is clear that there are significant differences between the personality structure developed through the work of Zigler and colleagues, and the structures, previously described, developed within mainstream personality research.

We have reviewed these systems of personality assessment because normal personality has been a focus for the *DSM-5* alternative system of classification. As mentioned, *DSM-5* has emphasized the primary assessment system – the FFM. While there is little research on this system in people with IDD, it is the case that there is a wealth of disparate research on personality and one research paper substantiating the use of the FFM with this population, with appropriate adjustments.

Psychiatric Disorders, Personality Disorder, and Personality

Over the last two decades there has been a steady clinical and research interest in the relationship between the assessment of psychiatric disorders in clinical settings, the assessment of personality disorders, and their relationship to normal personality dimensions (Caperton, Edens, & Johnson 2004; Edens, 2009; Quirk et al., 2003; Reynolds & Clark, 2001). High levels of neuroticism and low levels of extroversion feature strongly in a variety of psychiatric populations (Zuuckerman, 1999). As an example, Quirk et al. (2003) examined the relationship between assessed psychiatric problems, personality features, and personality disorder in 1,342 in patients. Neuroticism scores were strongly related to anxiety disorders and borderline personality disorder while introversion was related to post traumatic stress disorder and borderline personality disorder. The strongest relationships to emerge in this field are between coercive personality characteristics and acting out personality disorders (antisocial, narcissistic, aggressive) (Morey et al 2003, Edens 2009); neurotic personality characteristics and several psychiatric disorders such as depression, paranoia, social introversion, anger, obsessivness and schizophrenia (Caperton et al., 2004; Morey et al., 2003; Reynolds & Clark, 2001); externalising psychopathology and anti social and paranoid traits and finally internalising psychopathology and borderline personality disorder traits (Edens 2009; Morey et al., 2003).

Lindsay et al. (2010) studied these relationships using a forensic sample of 212 male participants with IDD. They previously established the validity of two circumplex assessments of normal personality (described earlier) and used these to study the relationship between personality, personality disorder, and risk using validated risk assessments. The findings suggested an orderly convergence of emotional problems, personality, and risk. Externalising emotional problems had a significant relationship with antisocial personality disorder and narcissistic personality disorder while internalizing emotional problems correlated significantly with avoidant personality disorder. There were similar strong relationships between externalizing emotional problems and dominant personality characteristics and significant negative correlations between externalizing emotional problems and nurturant personality dimensions. There was a strong relationship between narcissistic personality disorder and dominant personality characteristics and further negative statistical relationships between avoidant personality disorder and dominant personality characteristics and negative correlations between antisocial personality disorder and nurturant personality characteristics.

All of this research has been conducted on people with moderate and mild IDD. It does show an emerging literature on the reliability and validity of a personality disorder diagnosis with this client group and also demonstrates an orderly relationship between personality disorder, underlying personality constructs, and emotional difficulties. There is, however, a paucity of research in the field, and it is an obvious drawback that most of the recent studies have come from two principal research groups (Alexander & Lindsay).

Adults with Mild to Moderate IDD

Most of the foregoing research has been conducted with individuals who have Mild or moderate IDD or low borderline IQ.

Adults with Severe or Profound IDD

Very little work has been done on adults with severe or profound ID. There are some comments in the literature regarding individuals with this level of intellectual ability. For example, in their study of 430 outpatients with ID, Naik et al. (2002) noted that the vast majority fell into the categories of mild IDD or borderline ID. They wrote "although a significant proportion of people with moderate or severe learning disability may satisfy many criteria for personality disorders, a definitive diagnosis may not be possible due to the inability to elicit information about their inner mood states, experiences or belief systems. Indeed, if diagnostic criteria are applied in such a way that an overwhelming majority of those with learning disability satisfy the criteria for personality disorders, it is not of much clinical use, either for the management of the individual patient or the planning of services" (p. 98). It is the opinion of the authors that, in general, the development of personality will be immature or impaired to such an extent that diagnosis of personality disorder is impossible in people with severe or profound IDD.

Children and Adolescents with IDD

There is no data to support making a diagnosis of personality disorder in a person of general developmental delay who is younger than 21 years of age. The DC-LD (Royal College of Psychiatrists, 2001) states that because of the general developmental delay in individuals with IDD, personality, consistent with other attributes, continues to develop throughout adolescence. We are similarly of the opinion that because of this developmental delay, a diagnosis of personality disorder should not be considered until the individual is 21 years old.

Summary of Limitations in Applying* DSM-5 *Criteria to People with ID

- Any diagnosis of personality disorder should take into account personal characteristics in the context of a normal cultural framework. People with IDD are likely to have developed within a cultural framework that might be somewhat different from the norm. Before considering a diagnosis, therefore, assessors should be familiar with the population of clients with IDD.
- People with IDD are less likely to show normal progress at school, resulting in educational delays commensurate with their IDD.
- The IDD itself is likely to present some features that are the same as those of personality disorder. The principle example is lack of empathic responding that may be a feature of IDD rather than personality disorder (see elsewhere for description).
- The IDD is likely to have contributed to delayed development and a degree of immaturity.
- Institutional experience is pervasive among this client group, and adaptation to institutional life should be taken into account when considering a diagnosis.
- Many individuals with IDD have experienced a protected upbringing, giving them a reduced access to opportunities to learn social norms, community skills, and so on. This fact should also be considered when making a diagnosis.
- There is some evidence that people with IDD are more likely than are mainstream groups to have experienced stigma, the fear of failure, and negative self-evaluation.
- Recent authors have noted that different methods and criteria for making a diagnosis could have produced widely differing prevalence rates of Personality Disorder across studies.
- Along with other authors, the current committee recommends the use of behavioral observation and informant information, collected in a standardized manner, as a primary information source in making a diagnosis.

Etiology and Pathogenesis

Risk Factors

The committee considers that those issues which are salient in the population of people with IDD, and which contribute to the cultural shift in the population, can also be considered as risk factors when they impinge on the individual to such an extent that they produce a disorder in the development of personality and individual characteristics. We have mentioned that the experience of institutionalization is common in this client group. Institutionalization in itself constitutes an unusual environment in which to be brought up and can be considered a risk factor for the development of unusual personal characteristics. There has certainly been an association with sexual abuse (Thompson & Brown, 1997) and aggression (Taylor, 2002). In addition, it is human nature to adapt to one's living circumstances, and individuals might have adapted to institutional life in ways that are functional for that type of upbringing but that would be considered distorted when the individual is in mainstream society. Again, this can be considered a risk factor and at its extremes could manifest as personality disorder.

Authors have also made the observation that some people with IDD might have been brought up in relatively protected environments that reduced their opportunity for exposure to normal life experiences, community hazards, and social learning. Again, such an upbringing might contribute to the cultural context in which you could make a diagnosis, but, at its more extreme levels, the upbringing could be a risk factor for the development of personality disorders; individuals might be less socially skilled, less willing to engage in social and community activities, and more likely to show dependency in personal and social situations. The IDD itself might contribute to the individual experiencing fear of failure and negative self-evaluation in relation to more able peers. A history of such experiences can certainly contribute to the development of the individual's personality and can be considered a risk factor. Similarly, the repeated experience of stigma at the hands of peer groups or other members of society—a stigma specifically directed at the individual's intellectual limitations and social deficits—can also be considered a risk factor in this client group.

Biological Factors

There is some evidence that persistent sexual and physical abuse in childhood produces neurological substrates that are different from normal (Sapolsky, 1997). There is no reason why these effects should not also be seen in people with IDD. The extent to which these neurological changes are related to personality disorder is less clear. Apart from this information, which in itself is speculative, there is no research relating neurological substrates or biochemical processes to personality disorder in people with IDD.

Psychosocial Factors

All of the risk factors just mentioned are clearly psychosocial factors considered in the etiology of personality disorder. It is worth reiterating that these factors might be apparent to some extent in most individuals with IDD and that they might contribute to the cultural context in which a diagnosis is made. It is toward the extremes of these considerations that you might invoke the concept of personality disorder in an individual with IDD.

Genetic Syndromes

There are no specific links between personality disorder and genetic syndromes in this client group.

Application of Diagnostic Criteria

Previously we have reviewed a number of special considerations for people with IDD, including the effects of institutionalization, the consequences of being treated as an infant throughout formative years, developmental delay, and immaturity. As we have stated, we do not wish to declare that individuals with IDD are immune from some personality disorders or to suggest that they present in grossly divergent ways from the mainstream population. The DC-LD manual (Royal College of Psychiatrists, 2001) has suggested that a diagnosis of schizoid, "anxious" (avoidant), or dependent personality disorders should usually be avoided, because it is difficult to differentiate their diagnostic criteria from the underlying developmental disabilities. "Difficult" is not "impossible," however, but one should carefully consider the context of the population of individuals with IDD when determining whether a specific person has, for example, extreme traits that would constitute a dependent personality disorder.

So little research has been done in this field that it is worthwhile reiterating some of the cautions we have expressed throughout the chapter on the diagnosis of personality disorder in this population. The primary "special consideration" is that of developmental delay. One should be wary about considering any delayed development of personality as indicative of any disorder in the development of personality. Moreover, one should consider the issues around institutionalization, repeated scholastic and adaptive "failure" as a result of an individual's being slower than his or her peers, and the well-documented higher incidence of sexual and physical abuse in people with IDD (Sequeira & Hollins, 2003). One should also consider the interesting finding that the work on personality in this population reveals an alternative set of statistical factors when compared with the work on the mainstream population. These factors would be considered etiological, however, and might not change the diagnosis of personality disorder.

Table 1: Application of Criteria for DSM-5 main system Paranoid Personality Disorder

DSM-5 Diagnostic Criteria	Applying Criteria for Individuals with ID
A. A pervasive distrust and suspiciousness of others such that their motives are interpreted as malevolent, beginning by early adulthood and present in a variety of contexts, as indicated by four (or more) of the following:	A. No adaptation
(1) Suspects without sufficient basis that others are exploiting, harming, or deceiving him or her.	(1) No adaptation.
(2) Is preoccupied with unjustified doubts about the loyalty or trustworthiness of friends or associates.	(2) No adaptation. **Note:** Some of these criteria require a considerable degree of abstract thinking and ability to understand things in perspective, which are more difficult as intellectual limitations increase. They are, therefore, more likely to be seen in an individual who has borderline ID than an individual with a moderate level of ID.
(3) Is reluctant to confide in others because of an unwarranted fear that the information will be used maliciously against him or her.	(3) No adaptation. **Note:** as above.
(4) Reads hidden, demeaning, or threatening meanings into benign remarks or events.	(4) No adaptation.
(5) Persistently bears grudges—i.e., is unforgiving of insults, injuries, or slights.	(5) No adaptation. **Note**: In certain populations of people with ID, hot-headedness and temper are frequent problems. The clinician should not be overly influenced by such a tendency and should attend to other criteria that constitute the disorder.
(6) Perceives attacks on his or her character or reputation that are not apparent to others, and is quick to react angrily or to counterattack.	(6) No adaptation. **Note:** as above.
(7) Has recurrent suspicions, without justification, regarding the fidelity of a spouse or sexual partner.	(7) No adaptation. **Note:** Persons with ID may have lifelong restrictions on intimacy and sexuality.
B. Does not occur exclusively during the course of schizophrenia, a bipolar disorder or depressive disorder with psychotic features, or another psychotic disorder and is not attributable to the physiological effects of another medical condition. **Note:** If criteria are met prior to the onset of schizophrenia, add "premorbid," i.e., "paranoid personality disorder (premorbid)."	B. No adaptation

Schizoid Personality Disorder

DSM-5 Diagnostic Criteria	Applying Criteria for Individuals with ID
A. Pervasive pattern of detachment from social relationships and a restricted range of expression of emotions in interpersonal settings, beginning by early adulthood and present in a variety of contexts, as indicated by four (or more) of the following:	A. No adaptation
(1) Neither desires nor enjoys close relationships, including being part of a family.	(1) No adaptation.
(2) Almost always chooses solitary activities.	(2) No adaptation.

Schizoid Personality Disorder (continued)

DSM-5 Diagnostic Criteria	Applying Criteria for Individuals with ID
(3) Has little, if any, interest in having sexual experiences with another person.	(3) No adaptation. **Note:** This item should be considered in the light of the fact that people with ID may have lifelong restrictions on intimacy and sexuality.
(4) Takes pleasure in few, if any, activities.	(4) No adaptation.
(5) Lacks close friends or confidants other than first-degree relatives.	(5) No adaptation.
(6) Appears indifferent to praise or criticism of others.	(6) No adaptation.
(7) Shows emotional coldness, detachment, or flattened affectivity.	(7) No adaptation. **Note:** Diagnosis of autistic spectrum disorder or Asperger's syndrome should be differentiated and coded as such.
B. Does not occur exclusively during the course of schizophrenia, a bipolar disorder or depressive disorder with psychotic features, another psychotic disorder, or autism spectrum disorder and is not attributable to the physiological effects of another medical condition. **Note:** If criteria are met prior to the onset of schizophrenia, add "premorbid," i.e., "schizoid personality disorder (premorbid)."	B. No adaptation.

Schizotypal Personality Disorder

DSM-5 Diagnostic Criteria	Applying Criteria for Individuals with ID
A. Pervasive pattern of social relationships and interpersonal deficits marked by acute discomfort with, and reduced capacity for, close relationships as well as by cognitive or perceptual distortions and eccentricities of the following:	**Note:** Diagnosis of autistic spectrum disorder or Asperger's syndrome should be differentiated and coded as such.
(1) Ideas of reference (excluding delusions of reference)	(1) No adaptation.
(2) Odd beliefs or magical thinking that influences behavior and is inconsistent with subcultural norms (e.g., superstitiousness, belief in clairvoyance, telepathy, or "sixth sense"; in children and adolescents, bizarre fantasies or preoccupations)	(2) No adaptation. **Note:** Many of these criteria involve styles of thinking—e.g., magical thinking, styles of speech and unusual behavior. The clinician should be especially aware of the client group as a whole, and consider these characteristics in relation to cultural patterns that are acceptable among peers who have ID. Many individuals with ID have communication difficulties because of congenital organic dysfunction. Any deviation in relation to these items should be outside that which one would expect within this population.
(3) Unusual perceptual experiences, including bodily illusions	(3) No adaptation. **Note:** As above
(4) Odd thinking and speech (e.g., vague, circumstantial, metaphorical, overelaborate, or stereotyped)	(4) **Note:** As above
(5) Suspiciousness or paranoid ideation	(5) No adaptation.
(6) Inappropriate or a constricted affect	(6) No adaptation.
(7) Behavior or appearance that is odd, eccentric, or peculiar.	(7) No adaptation. **Note:** As above.
(8) Lack of close friends or confidants other than first-degree relatives.	(8) No adaptation.

Schizotypal Personality Disorder (continued)

DSM-5 Diagnostic Criteria	Applying Criteria for Individuals with ID
(9) Excessive social anxiety that does not diminish with familiarity and tends to be associated with paranoid fears rather judgments about self	(9) No adaptation.
B. Does not occur exclusively during the course of schizophrenia, a bipolar disorder or depressive disorder with psychotic features, another psychotic disorder, or autism spectrum disorder and is not attributable to the physiological effects of another medical condition. **Note:** If criteria are met prior to the onset of schizophrenia, add "premorbid," i.e., "Schizoid personality disorder (premorbid."	B. No adaptation.

Antisocial Personality Disorder

DSM-5 Diagnostic Criteria	Applying Criteria for Individuals with ID
A. A pervasive pattern of disregard for and violation of the rights of others, occurring since age 15 years, as indicated by three (or more) of the following:	A. There is a pervasive pattern of disregard for and violation of the rights of others occurring since age 18 years, as indicated by three (or more) of the following:
(1) Failure to conform to social norms with respect to lawful behaviors, as indicated by repeatedly performing acts that are grounds for arrest	(1) No adaptation. **Note:** This item assumes that the individual has the ability to develop an understanding of the laws and mores of society. Such an assumption is increasingly problematic with an increasing level of ID. This ability might be absent in an individual with a moderate or more severe level of ID.
(2) Deceitfulness, indicated by repeated lying, use of aliases conning others for personal profit or pleasure	(2) No adaptation.
(3) Impulsitivity or failure to plan ahead	(3) No adaptation. **Note:** The clinician should make sure that the individual has the intellectual ability to make conceptual leaps from the present to the future for the purposes of planning ahead.
(4) Irritability and aggressiveness, as indicated by repeated physical fights or assaults.	(4) No adaptation.
(5) Reckless disregard for the safety of others	(5) No adaptation.
(6) Consistent irresponsibility, as indicated by repeated failure to sustain consistent work behavior or honor financial obligations	(6) No adaptation. **Note:** Sustaining work behavior assumes that the individual has a functional ability to do so. Such an ability should first be established.
(7) Lack of remorse as indicated by being indifferent or rationalizing having hurt, mistreated, or stolen from another.	(7) No adaptation. **Note:** The suitability of this criterion requires that the individual has a well-developed ability to understand things in perspective, allowing him or her to understand the feelings of others and to regret actions Such an ability becomes increasingly unlikely in individuals with increasing severities of ID.
B. The individual is at least age 18 years.	B. The individual is at least age 21 years.
C. There is evidence of Conduct Disorder with onset before age 15 years.	C. There is evidence of Conduct Disorder with onset before age 18 years.
D. The occurrence of antisocial behavior is not exclusively during the course of schizophrenia or bipolar disorder	D. No adaptation

Borderline Personality Disorder

DSM-5 Diagnostic Criteria	Applying Criteria for Individuals with ID
A pervasive pattern of instability of interpersonal relationships, self-image, and affects and marked impulsivity beginning by early adulthood and present in a variety of contexts, as indicated by five (or more) of the following:	No adaptation
(1) Frantic efforts to avoid real or imagined abandonment. Note: Do not include suicidal or self-mutilating behavior covered in Criterion 5.	(1) People with ID are generally more reliant on caregivers than are other sections of the population. You should take this cultural difference into account when considering this criterion.
(2) A pattern of unstable and intense interpersonal relationships characterized by alternating between extremes of idealization and devaluation	(2) No adaptation. **Note:** As above.
(3) Identity disturbance: markedly and persistently unstable self-image or sense of self	(3) No adaptation. **Note:** Because it might require fairly overt, fairly sophisticated verbal skills, it may be difficult for an individual with ID to express identity disturbance. Making such an assessment with an informant requires sensitive and sophisticated judgment.
(4) Impulsivity in at least two areas that are potentially self-damaging (e.g., spending, sex, substance abuse, reckless driving, binge eating). Note: Do not include suicidal or self-mutilating behavior covered in Criterion5.	(4) No adaptation.
(5) Recurrent suicidal behavior, gestures, threats, or self-mutilating behavior	(5) No adaptation. **Note:** Self-injury is a frequent well-documented problem in this client group. There are numerous reasons for self-injurious behavior that should be discounted before consideration of a diagnosis of borderline personality disorder.
(6) Attentive instability due to a marked reactivity of mood (e.g., intense episodic dysphoria, irritability, or anxiety usually lasting a few hours and only rarely more than a few days)	(6) No adaptation.
(7) Chronic feelings of emptiness	(7) **Note:** Because it might require sophisticated verbal skills, expression of chronic feelings of emptiness may be difficult for an individual with ID. Making such an assessment with an informant requires sensitive and sophisticated judgment.
(8) Inappropriate, intense anger or difficulty controlling anger (e.g., frequent displays of temper, constant anger, recurrent physical fights)	(8) No adaptation. **Note:** Anger problems are documented frequently with this client group. Further obvious causes of anger in this client group should be considered.
(9) Transient stress-related paranoid ideation or severe dissociative symptoms	(9) No adaptation.

Histrionic Personality Disorder

DSM-5 Diagnostic Criteria	Applying Criteria for Individuals with ID
A pervasive pattern of excessive emotionality and attention seeking, beginning by early adulthood and present in a variety of contexts, as indicated by five (or more) of the following:	Symptom count may be reduced to 4 of 6 due to issues with symptoms 7 and 8 (see below).
(1)Is uncomfortable in situations where he or she is not the center of attention	(1)No adaptation. **Note:** An individual with ID might show discomfort by being agitated, intrusive, or self-abusive, or by engaging in other problematic behaviors
(2) Interaction with others is often characterized by inappropriate sexually seductive or provocative behavior	(2) No adaptation. **Note:** First establish that the person understands appropriate sexual behavior.
(3) Displays rapidly shifting and shallow expressions of emotions	(3) No adaptation.
(4) Consistently uses physical appearance to draw attention to self	(4) No adaptation.
(5) Has a style of speech that is excessively impressionistic and lacking in detail	(5) No adaptation. Make this consideration with an understanding of the communication difficulties and the styles of speech prevalent in the population of individuals with ID.
(6) Shows self-dramatization, theatrical and exaggerated expressions of emotion	(6) Using these criteria requires that the individual with ID understands the normal expression of emotion in the general population.
(7) Is suggestible (8) Considers relationships to be more intimate than they actually are	(7) & (8) These criteria are pervasive well-documented problems in the population of individuals with ID. They should not normally be considered in the diagnosis. Given that these items are likely to be discounted, we would recommend that four or more of the remaining six criteria are prevalent.

Narcissistic Personality Disorder

DSM-5 Diagnostic Criteria	Applying Criteria for Individuals with ID
A pervasive pattern of grandiosity (in fantasy or behavior), need for admiration, and lack of empathy, beginning by early adulthood and present in a variety of contexts, as indicated by five (or more) of the following:	No adaptation.
(1) Has a grandiose sense of self-importance (e.g., exaggerates achievements and talents, expects to be recognized as superior without commensurate achievements)	(1) No adaptation. **Note:** Because of their experience with repeated failure or with an exaggerated reinforcement of such minor achievements as drawing a picture, people with ID might naturally exaggerate minor achievements and talents. The criterion should apply only if such manifestations are outside the cultural expectations of what is expected of an individual with ID—e.g., if the individual acts as though he or she is a member of the staff.
(2) Is preoccupied with fantasies of unlimited success, power, brilliance, beauty, or ideal love. (3) Believes that he or she is "special" and unique, and can only be understood by, or with other special or high-status people (or institutions)	(2 & 3) **Note:** A sufficient degree of developmental maturation is specifically important for these criteria to apply. Narcissistic forms of thinking are common in young children, and functional maturation for these criteria should be of at least 8–10 years. A diagnosis of Narcissistic Personality Disorder cannot be made in individuals with an IQ less than 50.
(4) Requires excessive admiration.	(4) No adaptation.

Narcissistic Personality Disorder (continued)

DSM-5 Diagnostic Criteria	Applying Criteria for Individuals with ID
(5) Has a sense of entitlement, i.e., unreasonable expectations of especially favorable treatment or automatic compliance with his or her expectations	(5) No adaptation.
(6) Is interpersonally exploitative, i.e., taking advantage of others to achieve his or her own ends	(6) No adaptation.
(7) Lacks empathy; is unwilling to recognize or identify with the feelings and needs of others	(7) **Note:** For these criteria to apply, the individual must be able to understand things in perspective and realize that interpersonal relationships require reciprocity.
(8) Is often envious of others or believes others are envious of him or her.	(8) No adaptation
(9) Shows arrogant, haughty behavior or attitudes	(9) No adaptation

Avoidant Personality Disorder

DSM-5 Diagnostic Criteria	Applying Criteria for Individuals with ID
A pervasive pattern of social inhibition, feelings of inadequacy, and hypersensitivity to negative evaluation, beginning by early adulthood and present in a variety of contexts, as indicated by four (or more) of the following:	**General Note:** People with ID might have a greater incidence than do people in general of avoiding situations, of unwillingness to get involved with people, and of social inhibition, because of repeated experiences of criticism and failure. Some adjustment might therefore be made to allow a diagnosis of Avoidant Personality Disorder in the context of the culture of individuals with ID.
(1) Avoids occupational activities that involve significant interpersonal contact, because of fears of criticism, disapproval, or rejection	(1) No adaptation
(2) Is unwilling to get involved with people unless certain of being liked.	(2) No adaptation
(3) Shows restraint within intimate relationships because of the fear of being shamed or ridiculed	(3) No adaptation
(4) Is preoccupied with being criticized or rejected in social situations	(4) No adaptation
(5) Is inhibited in new interpersonal situations because of feelings of inadequacy	(5) No adaptation
(6) Views himself or herself as socially inept, personally unappealing, or inferior to others	(6) No adaptation
(7) Is unusually reluctant to take personal risks or to engage in any new activities because they prove embarrassing	(7) No adaptation

Dependent Personality Disorder

Dependent personality disorder cannot be diagnosed in people with IDD.

The Alternative DSM-5 Model for Personality Disorders

Categorical diagnosis makes a clear differentiation between normal and abnormal: you either have it or you do not. For many conditions, this is an obvious position to take: you either have a broken leg or you do not. For many other conditions, however, the differentiation is less obvious, with personality disorders being a good example. The notion of a dimension in classification is more familiar to those of us working in intellectual and developmental disabilities than in any other area of diagnosis. Intellectual disability itself is on the dimension from normal intelligence, to a condition that can be classified, but even here there are "fuzzy" areas. With

IQ, even the best standardised measure has an error range that must be taken into account. This is normally around 8-10 IQ points with 3-5 points below the identified score and 5-7 points above the identified score. Therefore 67 to 75 IQ points represents the "fuzzy" area between intellectual disability and borderline intelligence. There is nothing wrong with "fuzzy" variables; they are well known to science and to research in personality (Acton, 1998; Acton & Revelle 2002;, Lindsay et al., 2009).

The notion of dimensionality was seriously considered for DSM-5 but eventually rejected as too radical a change. However, huge support has been given to the field of personality disorder to test these ideas. In DSM-IV (and still in the main guidelines for DSM-5) the task for clinicians is to identify which personality disorder traits the person is demonstrating and to assign a specific categorical diagnosis. Where one specific category cannot be assigned, but the clinician considers that there are a sufficient number of traits for maladaptive personality functioning, then 'other specified personality disorder' or 'unspecified personality disorder' can be used as a classification. There has been a long and occasionally acrimonious debate on the utility of this diagnostic system and the major criticisms are as follows. Firstly, the categories of personality disorder diagnosis have no research foundation. They were largely pulled together through committee consensus. Secondly, there is considerable overlap between the personality disorder categories, and, indeed, this overlap is built into the diagnostic traits. For example, while paranoid personality disorder has 8 traits related to suspiciousness and mistrust, schizotypal personality disorder also has a trait related to social anxiety associated with paranoid fears, and borderline personality disorder has a trait related to transient, stress related paranoid ideation. Antisocial personality disorder has items related to impulsivity, irritability and aggressiveness while borderline personality disorder also has impulsivity, and frequent displays of temper and anger. Both narcissistic personality disorder and antisocial personality have a lack of empathy (or the related concept remorse) as important traits. Therefore, overlap in categories is integral to the system. A third difficulty was the number of maladaptive traits within each classification and the fact that only a certain number were required to be met. Therefore, two patients having the same personality disorder diagnosis could have a different trait profile fostering heterogeneity within each category. This is clearly seen in schizotypal PD where one patient may have a predominance of traits typified by odd beliefs, unusual perceptual experiences, ideas of reference, and eccentric behavior while another may be characterized with suspiciousness and paranoid ideation, constricted affect, excessive social anxiety, and a lack of close friends. Clearly, these two descriptions are at odds, but both fall within the same classification. Finally, authors have pointed out that about half of those patients who meet the criteria for personality disorder have to be ascribed as personality disorder not otherwise specified (Paris 2013a; Zimmerman, Rothschild, & Chelminski, 2005) suggesting that the classificatory system is inadequate for up to 50% of those for whom a classification of personality disorder is appropriate. This constitutes the background for developing the new proposals.

The alternative system consists of a staged diagnostic process:

- The first stage is recognising a new general definition of personality disorder that reviews deficits and core components of self and interpersonal personality functioning.
- The second stage is based on an assessment of global personality functioning which is represented by five levels of severity in self and interpersonal functioning ranging from normal functioning to extreme deficits.
- Once deficits in personality functioning have been established, the third stage consists of identifying whether or not the person conforms to any particular personality disorder. Six personality disorder types have been retained from the original ten in DSM-IV (and retained in the primary diagnostic system in DSM-V). The six retained personality disor-

der types are antisocial personality disorder, borderline personality disorder, narcissistic personality disorder, schizotypal personality disorder, avoidant personality disorder and obsessive compulsive personality disorder.

- The final stage is to identify maladaptive traits along five broad higher order personality domains that correspond to the five factor model. Therefore, the first stage refers to general personality function and the last two stages examine specific personality disorders and traits. We will now describe these stages in more detail with specific reference to intellectual and developmental disabilities.

The first stage is to recognize the core components of personality functioning that are split into self and interpersonal dimensions. Hopwood et al. (2011) conducted a prospective study on 605 patients with personality disorders and found that those personality traits loading most highly on a severity dimension of personality disorder were preoccupation with social rejection, fear of social ineptness, feelings of inadequacy, anger, identity disturbance, and paranoid ideation. They interpreted these items as being consistent with disturbances in the views of oneself and of other people. These 2 dimensions – self and interpersonal – have been investigated extensively (Bender, Morey & Skodol 2011) and have been incorporated as the main dimensions for the initial conception of personality disorder in the alternative DSM-5.

The elements for rating level of personality functioning can be seen in the table below and, when they are rated 0-4, constitute the Level of Personality Functioning Scale (LPFS). They are as follows:

- Self 1. Identity: Experience of oneself as unique, with clear boundaries between self and others; stability of self-esteem and accuracy of self appraisal; capacity for, and ability to regulate, a range of emotional experience. (American Psychiatric Association, 2013, p. 762)
- Self 2: Self direction: The pursuit of coherent and meaningful short term and life goals; utilisation of constructive and pro-social internal standards of behaviour; ability to self reflect productively. (American Psychiatric Association, 2013, p. 762)
- Interpersonal 1: Empathy: Comprehension and appreciation of others' experiences and motivations; tolerance of differing perspectives; understanding the effects of one's own behaviour on others. (American Psychiatric Association, 2013, p. 762)
- Interpersonal 2: Intimacy: Depth and duration of connection with others; desire and capacity for closeness; mutuality of regard reflected in interpersonal behaviour. (American Psychiatric Association, 2013, p. 762)

Generalized severity of personality functioning has been found to be the best single predictor of personality pathology. Hopwood et al. (2011) found that "generalised severity (of personality dysfunction) is the most important single predictor of concurrent and prospective dysfunction" (p.305). Therefore, there is a considerable amount of evidence supporting the conceptualisation of personality disorder in this way and for the clinical utility of evaluating severity. The degrees of disturbance in self and interpersonal dimensions are then continuously distributed from normal/no impairment through mild impairment, moderate impairment, serious impairment and extreme impairment. In order to make the judgements on severity of personality functioning, the DSM-5 details a five point scale for each of the personality elements (self identity, self direction, interpersonal empathy, interpersonal intimacy). DSM-5 contains good descriptions of personality functioning at each point in the scale. In general, a rating of 0 (no impairment) or 1 (some impairment) would indicate that the individual is below the threshold for any consideration of personality disorder. A rating of 2, 3 or 4 (moderate, severe and extreme impairment respectively) indicate increasing degrees of personality dysfunction when diagnosis of personality disorder should be considered. Some of the descriptions of these graduations can be seen in Table 2. These are the first two stages of the diagnosis of personality disorder in the alternative system.

In applying these elements, there are a number of important considerations.

Life goal setting

The intellectual disability itself may limit the person's ability to plan life goals in a coherent manner. Many individuals with IDD have not been afforded the opportunity to goal set. This has been traditionally something others have done for them and imposed on them. Thus, failure to do so may be a lack of exposure that may require some teaching or support. However, they should be able to do this with support so difficulties may not represent maladaptive personality features.

Empathy

Empathy requires perspective taking and perspective taking is a developmental skill. Because people with IDD have, by definition, developmental delay, their perspective taking abilities are likely to be compromised. This difficulty in perspective taking with subsequent implications for perspective taking skills such as empathy and remorse should be considered carefully as a consequence of IDD rather than personality disorder.

When an individual with IDD also has autism spectrum disorder, this will be an additional consideration for the assessor. A lack of empathic response is a feature of autism spectrum disorder and when a lack of empathy is the primary feature of personality dysfunction, and diagnosis of autism spectrum disorder should be reviewed before diagnosis of personality disorder.

People with IDD have often been brought up in relatively punitive environments (Griffiths et al., 2013) and have learned that any empathic or remorseful response related to an admission of guilt might be met with fault finding and punishment. As a result, they may be reluctant to acknowledge another person's feelings in situations of conflict.

Relationships

Often individuals with IDD have been sheltered from relationships or have lived within a system, where relationships changed frequently or have been severed by system changes (moves, change of staff, etc.), so that long term relationships are not typically the problem of the person with IDD but the social systems that have supported them.

Only 58% of individuals are reported to have friends (Smith & Melda, 201 4).

People with ID in general have fewer close relationships. Any relationship that ends, therefore, could be one of a very few relationships—or even the *only* close relationship—that the individual has. As a result, the individual might indeed feel a greater urgency to develop new relationships; this might, however, be an isolated issue related to IDD rather than Personality Disorder.

Self-esteem

People with IDD tend towards reduced self esteem and this general trend should be considered by the assessor. She/he should gauge the extent to which reduced self esteem exists relative to the well functioning population of individuals with IDD.

Identity

People with IDD tend towards reduced self esteem and this general trend should be considered by the assessor. She/he should gauge the extent to which reduced self esteem exists relative to the well functioning population of individuals with IDD.

Self-direction

If the individual is under guardianship or some other legal order, he or she might be prevented from assuming responsibility for short term planning. This criterion applies only to the extent to which a person with IDD can realistically be expected to assume such responsibility.

Individuals with IDD routinely require some support in organizing domestic finances, in planning for holidays, or in organizing educational or occupational-opportunities, and such a need for support should not be considered a criterion of personality disorder.

People with IDD might have had limited opportunities to practice increasingly complex decision making, and, as a result, they might demonstrate such difficulties in adult life.

You should consider only a provisional diagnosis of personality disorder pending the results of a remediation program for the development of decision-making skills.

Table 2: Application of Criteria for DSM 5 Alternative Model. Level of Severity of Personality Impairment.

Elements of Global Personality Functioning	
Normal functioning	
Self – 1. Identity. 0 – little or no impairment; 1 – some impairment The person has an intact or relatively intact sense of self with clear or reasonably clear boundaries between self and others. The person's self esteem is intact but can be diminished at times when they may be over critical of the self. The person can generally tolerate strong emotions with some distress and occasional restriction in range.	No modification
Self – 2. Self direction. 0 – little or no impairment 1 – some impairment Within reasonable limits, the individual can set goals based on their capacities. He or she can set reasonable standards for achieving these goals and can reflect on the internal experiences constructively. They may set some inappropriate personal standards that limit a sense of fulfilment without causing excessive distress	**Note:** The intellectual disability itself may limit the person's ability to plan life goals in a coherent manner, and some will not have had the opportunity to learn this, hence the importance of basing this on their capabilities.
Interpersonal – 1. Empathy 0 – little or no impairment 1 – some impairment The person can understand others' experiences and motivations even when disagreeing and they are aware of the effects of their own actions. This may be somewhat compromised with unreasonable expectations of others or a wish to control situations. The individual may be inconsistent in their awareness of the effects of their behaviour or disregard their knowledge of the effect. These slight impairments do not cause significant interpersonal distress.	**Note:** Empathy should be judged in keeping with the persons developmental level, and also take account of whether the parson has, and extent of a person's autism.
Interpersonal – 2. Intimacy. 0 – little or no impairment 1 – some impairment The person has an ability to maintain relationships, is able to cooperate with and respond to others and has a desire to engage in caring, reciprocal relationships. The person may be inhibited in the intimacy by some unrealistic standards on a limited ability to respect or respond to others and this may present some limitations on the depth and satisfaction of relationships. Any slight impairments will not cause significant interpersonal distress.	**Note:** This should be considered within the person's context: often individuals with IDD have been sheltered from relationships, or have lived within a system, where relationships changed frequently.
Increasing personality pathology	

Table 2: Application of Criteria for DSM 5 Alternative Model. Level of Severity of Personality Impairment.(continued)

Elements of Global Personality Functioning	
Self – 1. Identity.( ) 2 – moderate impairment 3 – severe impairment 4 – extreme impairment The person has an excessive dependence on others; vulnerable self esteem and a wish for approval. They may have a sense of inferiority with lowered or compensatory inflated self-esteem. Threats to self-esteem may produce strong emotions such as anger or shame. With more severe impairment these tendencies increase to a lack or complete absence of identity, feelings of emptiness and poor boundaries between self and others. Self-esteem is increasingly fragile and emotions either shifting rapidly or chronically set (e.g. despair, jealousy resentment). The person has significant distortions and confusion in self appraisal with very poorly regulated emotion.	**Note:** People with IDD tend towards reduced self esteem and this general trend should be considered by the assessor. She/he should gauge the extent to which reduced self esteem exists relative to the well functioning population of individuals with IDD.
Self – 2. Self direction. 2 – moderate impairment 3 – severe impairment 4 – extreme impairment Personal goals are increasingly related to gaining external approval. Personal standards become increasingly unrealistic (either high or low) with a poor capacity for self reflection. With increasing impairment, there will be difficulty in setting and achieving personal goals, vague or incoherent personal standards and increasing difficulty in gaining any personal fulfilment. The person will have increasing difficulty in reflecting on their own experience.	**Note:** the criterion applies only to the extent to which the person can realistically be expected to assume such responsibility.
Interpersonal – 1. Empathy 2 – moderate impairment 3 – severe impairment 4 – extreme impairment An ability to understand others' thoughts and feelings is increasingly limited particularly in relation to vulnerability and suffering. The person has an increasing difficulty in understanding others points of view and opinions. A lack of awareness of the effect of his or her actions with decreasing attention to the perspective of others. Is likely to feel threatened by others' opinions if they differ from one's own.	**Note:** Empathy should be judged in keeping with the person's developmental level, and also take account of whether the person has, and extent of, a person's autism.
Interpersonal – 2. Intimacy 2 – moderate impairment 3 – severe impairment 4 – extreme impairment The capacity to form relationships becomes increasingly compromised by a requirement for intimacy or expectation of abandonment. Feelings may alternate between rejection and the need for closeness. There will be a decreasing respect for mutuality in relationships with other people viewed only in terms of how they affect the self. Cooperation increasingly disrupted to the extent that it is absent. Social interaction is increasingly regarded as a means of fulfilling basic needs or avoiding distress.	**Note:** This should be considered within the person's context: often individuals with IDD have been sheltered from relationships, or have lived within a system, where relationships changed frequently.

Table 2 contains criteria that are considerably truncated and we recommend that readers refer to the extensive guidance in the DSM 5, pp. 775-778.

Stages 3 & 4 of Diagnosis.

The next step in diagnosis is to consider whether the personality disturbance matches one of six diagnostic types. These are antisocial personality disorder, borderline personality disorder, avoidant personality disorder, obsessive compulsive personality disorder, schizotypal personality disorder, and narcissistic personality disorder. There are changes to the descriptions of these disorders in Table 3. These changes reflect the emphasis on understanding the associated maladaptive personality traits. As in table 1, these diagnostic types are not suitable for people with severe and profound intellectual disabilities, and the higher age cut off of 21 should be applied. The diagnosis of personality disorder in an individual with IDD cannot be made through an interview alone. Behavioral observation and informant interviews are crucial for obtaining the appropriate information required for any judgment.

Four personality disorders were eliminated from the alternative system. Paris (2013a) writes that two of them – paranoid personality disorder and dependent personality disorder – were eliminated because of their overly narrow focus as they describe individual dysfunctional traits rather than a range of pathological personality characteristics. Both traits have been retained in other personality disorder categories. For example, the trait of suspiciousness is included in schizotypal personality disorder while mistrust is associated with borderline personality disorder. Dependence is associated with bordeline personality disorder. Neither histrionic nor schizoid personality disorder have emerged from research findings apart from being associated with other personality disorders. It is, however, essential to remember that the traits associated with these personality disorders (paranoid, dependant, dramatic and so on) are retained in the overall system. It can be seen in table 3 that the remaining six personality disorders have signifiers in the items most associated with severity: preoccupation with social rejection, fear of social ineptness, fear of inadequacy, anger, identity disturbance, and paranoid ideation.

Thus far, the system seems relatively straight forward and has parallels with the ICD-10 system where the assessor is required first to consider whether the person has sufficient dysfunction to be considered for a general diagnosis of personality disorder and then to allocate one or more specific types of dysfunction such as dissocial personality disorder, anankastic personality disorder, impulsive personality disorder, emotional type and impulsive type. The alternative DSM-5 gives information on the central focus for generalized personality disturbance in terms of self and interpersonal dimensions and provides anchored descriptions for degrees of severity. Table 2 gives guidance on the way this severity should be considered for individuals with IDD.

The final stage in classification of personality disorder seems to us more technical and time consuming for individual clinicians. It pertains to the category of personality disorder trait specified and conforms to the Five Factor Model of personality describing dysfunctional traits in terms of the facets that are associated to each factor. As we have described, the five factors that emerge consistently in personality research are neuroticism, extraversion, openness to experience, agreeableness, and conscientiousness. The description for the alternative DSM-5 is the pathological correlate of each dimension as follows: negative affectivity versus emotional stability (neuroticism), detachment v extraversion, antagonism v agreeableness, disinhibition v conscientiousness, and psychotocism v lucidity. It can be seen that the only one that does not conform to the five factors is psychotocism although it does have some aspects of lack of openness to experience. These have been incorporated into the personality disorder Trait Specified category in table 3.

This next stage in classification involves a decision on whether the personality disorder characteristics conform to any of the 6 retained personality disorder categories.

While the nomenclature of the categories is the same, some characteristics have been altered significantly to conform to the known research on the 5 factor model of personality and the traits subsumed within these 5 factors. One major change to note is that antisocial personality disorder no longer requires the presence of conduct disorder as a child.

Each category includes descriptions of impairments to the global severity components as well as the maladaptive personality traits.

Table 3: Description of DSM-5 Personality Disorders with Application of Criteria for IDD.

Antisocial Personality Disorder - Global Severity Indicators	
Identity; Self-direction; Empathy; Intimacy	Refer to table 2
Traits	
1.Manipulativeness	No modification
2. Callousness	**Note:** Where this refers to apparent indifference the assessor should consider whether the lack of empathic response/callousness is a function of the IDD itself. If a person with IDD engages in behavior in which there is "negative empathy"—such as enjoying the obvious pain or fear caused by this person's actions, then no modifications are necessary.
3. Deceitfulness	The assessor should consider whether the person is being actively deceitful or has not remembered because of memory problems.
4. Hostility	No adaptation **Note:** anger and hostility problems are documented frequently with this client group. For the obvious causes of anger in this client group should be considered.
5. Risk taking	The assessor should appraise whether or not the client has the intellectual ability to understand the risks that they are taking.
6. Impulsivity	No adaptation **Note:** the clinician should make sure that the individual has the intellectual ability to make conceptual leaps from the present to the future for the purposes of planning ahead.
7. Irresponsibility	No adaptation **Note:** sustaining some activities e.g. work or some leisure pursuits assumes that the individual has a functional ability to do so. Such an ability should first be established.
Avoidant PD - Global Severity Indicators	
Identity; Self-direction; Empathy; Intimacy	Refer to table 2
Traits	
1.Anxiousness 2. Withdrawal 3. Anhedonia 4. Intimacy	No adaptation No adaptation. No adaptation. No adaptation
Borderline PD - Global Severity Indicators	
Identity; Self-direction; Empathy; Intimacy	Refer to table 2
Traits	
1.Emotional lability	No adaptation
2. Anxiousness	No adaptation

Table 3: Description of DSM-5 Personality Disorders with Application of Criteria for IDD. (continued)

Antisocial Personality Disorder - Global Severity Indicators	
3. Separation insecurity	People with IDD are generally more reliant on caregivers than are other sections of the population. The clinician should take this cultural context into account when considering this criterion.
4. Depressivity	Self injury is a frequent, well-documented problem in this client group. There are numerous reasons for self injurious behavior that should be discounted before depression, impulse control or risk-taking are considered as features of borderline personality disorder.
5. Impulsivity	No adaptation. Note the caveat mentioned above concerning the ability to plan being a requirement for impulse control.
6. Risk taking	The assessor should appraise whether or not the client has the intellectual ability to understand the risks that they are taking
7. Hostility	No adaptation. Note, mentioned above, that anger and hostility has been recorded frequently in this client group and are not necessarily a result of personality disorder.
Narcissistic PD - Global Severity Indicators	
Identity; Self-direction; Empathy; Intimacy	Refer to table 2
Traits	
1.Grandiosity	No adaptation. **Note 1:** because of experience of repeated failure or exaggerated reinforcement of main achievements, people with IDD might naturally exaggerate minor achievements and talents. The criterion should only apply if such manifestations are outside the cultural expectations e.g. if the individual acts as though he/she is a member of staff. **Note 2:** a sufficient degree of developmental maturation is specifically important in relation to grandiosity. Narcissistic forms of thinking are common in young children and functional maturation for these criteria should be at least 8-10 years.
2. Attention seeking	No adaptation
Obsessive Compulsive PD - Global Severity Indicators	
Identity; Self-direction; Empathy; Intimacy	Refer to table 2
Traits	
1.Rigid perfectionism 2. perseveration 3. Intimacy avoidance 4. Restricted affectivity	See chapter 20 for discussion of obsessive-compulsive disorder.
Schizotypal PD - Global Severity Indicators	
Identity; Self-direction; Empathy; Intimacy	Refer to table 2
Traits	

Table 3: Description of DSM-5 Personality Disorders with Application of Criteria for IDD. (continued)

Antisocial Personality Disorder - Global Severity Indicators	
1.Cognitive and perceptual dysregulation 2. Unusual beliefs and experiences 3. Eccentricity 4. Restricted affectivity 5. Withdrawal 6. Suspiciousness	No adaptation **Note:** many of these personality traits involve styles of thinking e.g. magical thinking, styles of speech and unusual behavior. The clinician should be aware of the client group as a whole and consider these characteristics in relation to cultural patterns that may be acceptable among peers with IDD. Many individuals with IDD have communication difficulties because of congenital organic dysfunction. Any deviation in relation to these personality traits should be outside that which one would expect within this population.
Personality Disorder – Trait Specified	
Moderate or greater impairment in two or more areas of Global Severity Indicators	Refer to table 2
Impairment in one or more personality trait domains corresponding to the 5 factors of personality as follows:	
1.Negative Affectivity. This trait domain reflects the polar opposites to the FFM Neuroticism factor. The traits to be considered are emotional lability, anxiousness, separation insecurity, submissiveness, hostility, perseveration, depressivity, and suspiciousness. Very high evaluations are relevant for most traits but some e.g., very low anxiousness can also be relevant.	1.Traits included in Negative Affectivity Separation insecurity – BPD trait 3 above Submissiveness – If the person is under a legal order, he or she might be prevented from assuming responsibility. Individuals with ID routinely require some support in organizing finances, planning holidays, or in organizing educational or occupational opportunities, and such a need for support should not be considered submissiveness. Hostility – Note: anger and hostility problems are documented frequently with this client group. For the obvious causes of anger in this client group should be considered. Depressivity – Self injury is a frequent, well-documented problem in this client group. There are numerous reasons for self injurious behavior that should be discounted before depression, impulse control, or risk-taking are considered as features of borderline personality disorder. Perseveration - General issues related to the ways of thinking and culture in the population of individuals with ID are relevant. Once an individual develops a successful way to function in a particular area, he or she is likely to stick to it precisely because it is successful. Inflexibility might therefore be related to successful problem solving rather than perseveration.
2. Detatchment. This trait domain reflects the polar opposites to the FFM Extraversion factor. Traits comprise withdrawal, intimacy avoidance, anhedonism, depressivity, restricted affect and suspiciousness, Both very low levels and very high levels of each trait should be evaluated. E.g. very high levels of extraversion (opposite of withdrawal) are associated with Narcisism (in combination with other traits).	2.Traits included in Detatchment Withdrawal – no adaptation Intimacy avoidance – This should be considered within the person's context: often individuals with IDD have been sheltered from relationships, or have lived within a system, where relationships changed frequently. Anhedonism – no adaptation Depressivity – Self injury is a frequent, well-documented problem in this client group. There are numerous reasons for self injurious behavior that should be discounted before depression, impulse control or risk-taking are considered as features of borderline personality disorder. Restricted affect – no adaptation Suspiciousness – no adaptation

Table 3: Description of DSM-5 Personality Disorders with Application of Criteria for IDD. (continued)

Antisocial Personality Disorder - Global Severity Indicators	
3.Antagonism. This trait domain reflects the polar opposites to the FFM Agreeableness factor. Traits comprise manipulativeness, deceitfulness, grandiosity, attention seeking, and callousness. Very high levels of traits should be considered in relation to PD Trait Specified.	3.Traits included in Antagonism Manipulativemess – no adaptation Deceitfulness – no adaptation Grandiosity – **Note 1:** because of experience of repeated failure or exaggerated reinforcement of main achievements, people with IDD might naturally exaggerate minor achievements and talents. The criterion should only apply if such manifestations and outside the cultural expectations e.g. if the individual acts as though he/she is a member of staff. **Note 2:** a sufficient degree of developmental maturation is specifically important in relation to grandiosity. Narcissistic forms of thinking are common in young children and functional maturation for these criteria should be at least 8-10 years. Attention seeking – no adaptation Callousness – Where this refers to apparent indifference, the assessor should consider whether the lack of empathic response/callousness is a function of the IDD itself. If a person with IDD engages in behavior in which there is "negative empathy"--such as enjoying the obvious pain or fear caused by this person's actions, then no modifications are necessary.
4.Disinhibition. This trait domain reflects the polar opposites to the FFM Conscientiousness factor. Traits comprise irresponsibility, impulsivity, distractibility, risk taking, and lack of rigid perfectionism. Generally very high levels of each trait should be considered.	4. Traits included in Disinhibition. Irresponsibility – sustaining some activities e.g. work or some leisure pursuits assumes that the individual has a functional ability to do so. Such an ability should first be established. Impulsivity –**Note:** the clinician should make sure that the individual has the intellectual ability to make conceptual leaps from the present to the future for the purposes of planning ahead. Distractibility – People with iDD are likely to have poorer concentration as a feature of the intellectual limitations. This trait should be evaluated in that context. Risk Taking – The assessor should appraise whether or not the client has the intellectual ability to understand the risks that they are taking
5.Psychoticism. This trait domain reflects the polar opposites to the FFM Openness/Lucidity factor. Traits comprise unusual beliefs or experiences, eccentricity and cognitive/perceptual dysregulation.	Unusual beliefs – Any deviation in relation to this personality trait should be outside that which one would expect within this population.

Strengths and Weaknesses of the Alternate System

The first strength of the alternative system is that it reflects the available research on personality. This has been a repeated criticism over the past two decades. It can also serve as an aid to treatment and management of the individual. A good differential diagnosis should serve as both a pathway to a treatment plan and also suggest that there is or is not potential e.g. for self harm or problematic behaviors. In the case of the DSM-IV and previous manuals the diagnoses for personality disorders simply told the referring clinician what he/she already knew. It is more helpful for services and agencies who are providing treatment if a diagnostic system directs the clinician to a treatment option. For example, the alternate system specifies trait deficits that can be incorporated into a treatment approach or be included as treatment targets. It allows the therapist to involve the client in treatment by specifying and discussing these details. In most clinical disciplines, diagnosis drives treatment, and the alternative personality disorder diagnostic system easily leads to treatment choices by pointing out the specific areas of deficiency within the patient and also a baseline statement suggesting severity as well. This supports the clinician to specify clinically useful data that has functional value to those trying to help these people (or protect any potential victims).

However, it is a serious deficit that any system that combines normal and abnormal functioning has the potential to fall into the trap of overdiagnosis. Where there is a threshold as normal functioning graduates to abnormal functioning, it is important that the threshold is as clear as possible. In the case of personality disorder, where the threshold between normal and abnormal functioning can be very subjective, there is the danger of conflating difficulties with personality functioning and personality disorder leading to diagnostic inflation. This has been described in relation to personality disorder and other disorders in DSM-5 by Frances (2013) when he wrote "the new suggestions (DSM-5) all share the common problems of greatly expanding the reach of mental disorders at the expense of normality" (p 101). In turn, there is a danger of diagnosing many (Frances suggests "millions" or "tens of millions") false positives across a range of diagnoses. In the case of personality disorder this has the potential for considerable harm since personality disorder is incorporated into many recent legislative frameworks as a basis for compulsory detention. This is clearly a considerable drawback to the extent of an abuse, and clinicians should be very careful about personality disorder diagnosis under this alternative system. Alexander and Cooray (2003) foresaw this problem in relation to IDD and personality disorder several years ago when they noted the wide disparity in prevalence reported by different studies which were reviewing essentially similar populations of people with IDD. In fact, because of the problems with emotional recognition, poor perspective taking, dependence on others, unusual communication styles, and so on that are features of the IDD itself, most people with IDD are likely to have unusual personality features when compared to the general population. To diagnose all of them with personality disorder would be an obvious nonsense since severe personality disorder is associated with experiences such as criminality, self harm, suicidal ideation, severe disruptions in relationships, and bizarre ways of thinking that most people do not have.

A second difficulty is one that would be the case with any new system. Clinicians have been used to a categorical diagnostic system and the alternative system has complexities and is difficult to learn. As Paris (2013b) suggested "it is safe to assume that busy clinicians, who have been ignoring the precise instructions of the DSM system for the last three decades, would never have carried out these procedures."

Conclusions

We have outlined the two systems for the diagnosis of personality disorder in people with IDD, reflecting the main diagnostic system and the alternative diagnostic system contained in the DSM-5. In fact, in contrast to commentators reflecting on the complexity of the alternative system (Frances, 2013; Paris 2013b), we feel that the alternate system is not overly complex until the clinician is required to consider each individual maladaptive trait. There are additional consideration to be made for people with intellectual disabilities. The first stages in the diagnostic process seem fairly straightforward. The new system also has fairly direct references across to the previous system with the six retained personality disorders and their description in terms of traits described in the Five Factor Model.

There are also strengths in the new system in that it is very idiomatic to the extent that it can provide treatment and management targets for services. The main drawback, and it is a very serious drawback, is that by drawing a dimension between normal personality and personality disorder that is the significant pitfall for overdiagnosis with the corresponding danger of classifying unusual but essentially normal personality in the category of personality disorder.

References

Acton G. S. (1998). Classification of psychopathology: The nature of language. *The Journal of Mind & Behaviour 19*, 243–56.

Acton, G.S., & Revelle, W. (2002). Interpersonal personality measures show circumplex structure based on new psychometric criteria. *Journal of Personality Assessment, 79*, 456-481.

Alexander, R., & Cooray, S. (2003). Diagnosis of personality disorders in learning disability. *British Journal of Psychiatry, 182 (Suppl. 44)*, S28–S31.

Alexander R. T., Piachaud J., Odebiyi L. & Gangadharan S. K. (2002). Referrals to a forensic service in the psychiatry of learning disability. *British Journal of Forensic Practice 4, 29-33*

Alexander, R.T., Chester, V., Gray, N.S. & Snowden, R.J. (2012). Patients with personality disorders and intellectual disability – Closer to personality disorders or intellectual disability? A three-way comparison. *Journal of Forensic Psychiatry and Psychology*, 23(4) 435-451.

Alexander, R.T., Crouch, K., Halstead, S., & Pichaud, J. (2006). Long-term outcome from a medium secure service for people with intellectual disability. *Journal of Intellectual Disability Research, 50*, 305-315.

Alexander, R.T., Green, F.N., O'Mahony, B., Gunaratna, I.J., Gangadharan, S.K. & Hoare, S. (2010). Personality disorders in offenders with intellectual disability: A comparison of clinical, forensic and outcome variables and implications for service provision. *Journal of Intellectual Disability Research*, 54 (7) 650–658.

Alexander R.T., Piachaud J., Odebiyi L. & Gangadharan S. K. (2002) Referrals to a forensic service in the psychiatry of learning disability. *British Journal of Forensic Practice, 4*, 29–33.

American Psychiatric Association. (1994). *Diagnostic and statistical manual of mental disorders* (4th ed.). Washington, DC: Author.

American Psychiatric Association. (2013). *Diagnostic and statistical manual of mental disorders* (5th ed.). Washington, DC: American Psychiatric Publishing.

Arscott, K., Dagnan, D., & Stenfert Kroese, B. (1999). Assessing the ability of people with a learning disability to give informed consent to treatment. *Psychological Medicine, 29*, 1367–1375.

Ballinger, B. R., & Reid, A. H. (1987). A standardised assessment of personality in mental handicap. *British Journal of Psychiatry, 150*, 108–109.

Beail, N. (2002). Interrogative suggestibility, memory, and intellectual disability. *Journal of Applied Research in Intellectual Disabilities, 15*, 129–137.

Bender, D.S. Morey, LC. & Skodol, A.E. (2011). Toward a model for assessing level of personality functioning in DSM-5, Part I: A review of theory and methods. *Journal of Personality Assessment, 93*, 332–346.

Berry, D.T.R., Bagby, M.R., Smerz, J., Rinaldo, J.C., Caldwell-Andrews, A., & Baer, R.A. (2001). Effectiveness of the NEO-PI-R research validity scales for discriminating analog malingering and genuine psychopathology. *Journal of Personality Assessment, 76*(3), 496–517.

Blackburn, R. (1993). *The psychology of criminal behaviour: Theory, research and practice.* Chichester, UK: Wiley.

Blackburn, R. (2000). Classification and assessment of personality disorders in mentally disordered offenders: A psychological perspective. *Criminal Behaviour & Mental Health, 10*, (Special Suppl.), S8–S32.

Blackburn, R., & Coid, J. W. (1998). Psychopathy and the dimensions of personality disorder in violent offenders. *Personality & Individual Differences, 25*, 129–145.

Blackburn, R., Logan, C., Renwick, S.J.D., & Donnelly, J.P. (2005). Higher order dimensions of personality disorder: Hierarchical and relationships with the five factor model, the interpersonal circle and psychopathy. *Journal of PersonalityDisorders, 19*, 597–623.

Brandt, J., Campondonico, J.R., Rich, J.B., Baker, L., Steele, C., & Ruff, T. (1998). Adjustment to residential placement in Alzheimer's disease patients: Does premorbid personality matter? *International Journal of Geriatric Psychiatry, 13*(8), 509–516.)

Caperton, J.D., Edens, J.F., & Johnson, J.K. (2004). Predicting sex offender institutional adjustment and treatment compliance using the Personality Assessment Inventory. *Psychological assessment, 16*, 187–191.

Cattell R. B. (1946) Confirmation and clarification ofprimary personality factors. *Psychometrika* 12, 197–220.

Clark, L. A. (1990). Towards a consensual set of symptom clusters for assessment of personality disorder. In J. Butcher, & C. Spielberger (Eds.), *Advances in personality assessment* (Vol. 8, pp. 243–266). Hillsdale, NJ: Lawrence Erlbaum.

Clark, L. A., Livesley, W. J., Schroeder, M. L., Morey, L., & Watson, D. (1996). Convergence of two systems for assessing personality disorder. *Psychological Assessment, 8*, 294–303.

Corbett, J. A. (1979). *Psychiatric illness in mental handicap.* London: Gaskell Press.

Costa, P. T., Jr., & McCrae, R. R. (1985) *The NEO personality inventory.* Odessa, FL: Psychological Assessment Resources.

Costa, P.T. Jr., & McCrae, R.R. (1995). Domains and facets: Hierarchical personality assessment using the revised NEO Personality Inventory. *Journal of Personality Assessment, 64*(1), 21–50.

Craft, M., & Craft, A (1978). *Sex and the mentally handicapped.* London: Routledge & Kegan Paul.

Dagnan, D., & Lindsay, W. R. (2004). Research paradigms in cognitive therapy. In E. Emerson, C. Hatton, T. Thompson, & T. Parmenter (Eds.), *International handbook of applied research in intellectual disabilities.* Chichester, UK: Wiley & Sons.

Dagnan, D., & Sandhu, S. (1999). Social comparison, self-esteem and depression in people with learning disabilities. *Journal of Intellectual Disability Research, 43*, 372–379.

Dagnan, D., & Waring, M. (2004). Linking stigma to psychological distress: Testing a social-cognitive model of the experience of people with intellectual disabilities, *Clinical Psychology & Psychotherapy, 11(4)*, 247-254.

Digman, J.M. (1990). Personality structure: Emergence of the five factor model. *Annual Review of Psychology, 41*, 441-477.

Earl, C.J.C. (1961). *Subnormal personalities: Their clinical investigation and assessment.* London: Bailliere, Tindall & Cox.

Eaton, I.F., & Menolascino, F.J. (1982). Psychiatric disorders in the mentally retarded: Types problems and challenges. *American Journal of Psychiatry, 139*, 1297-1303.

Edens, J.F. (2009). Interpersonal characteristics of male criminal offenders: Personality, psychopathological and behavioural correlates. *Psychological Assessment, 21*, 89–98.

Edgerton, R. (1967). *The cloak of competence.* Berkeley, CA: University of California Press.

Edgerton, R. (1973). Sociocultural research considerations. In F. F. De La Cruz & G. G. La Veck (Eds.), *Human sexuality and the mentally retarded* (pp. 240–249). New York: Brunner/Maze.

Emmons, R.A. (1995). Levels and domains in personality: An introduction. *Journal of Personality, 63*(3),342–364.

Fazel, S., & Danesh, J. (2002). Serious mental disorder among 23,000 prisoners: systematic review of 62 surveys. *Lancet*, 16, 545–550.

Finlay, W. M., & Lyons, E. (2001). Methodological issues in interviewing and using self-report questionnaires with people with mental retardation. *Psychological Assessment, 13*, 319–335.

Flynn, A., Mathews, H., & Hollins, S. (2002). Validity of the diagnosis of personality disorder in adults with learning disability and severe behaviour problems. *British Journal of Psychiatry, 180*, 543–546.

Foot, M., & Koszycki, D. (2004). Gender differences in anxiety-related traits in patients with panic disorder. *Depression & Anxiety, 20*(3), 123–131

Francis, A. (2013) the DSM in Philosophyland: Curiouser and Curiouser. In J. Paris & J.

Phillips (Eds). *Making the DSM 5: Concepts and controversies.* Ch7, p95-104. Springer: New York

Goldberg, L.R. (1981). Language and individual differences: The search for universals in personality lexicons. In L. Wheeler (Ed), *Review of personality and social psychology* (Vol. 2, pp. 141-165). Beverley Hills, CA: Sage.

Goldberg, L. R. (1990). An alternative "description of personality." The big five factor structure. *Journal of Personality & Social Psychology, 59,* 1216–1229.

Goldberg, B., Gitta, M. Z., & Puddephatt, A. (1995). Personality and trait disturbance in an adult mental retardation population: Significance for psychiatric management. *Journal of Intellectual Disability Research, 39,* 284–294.

Gostasson, R. (1987). Psychiatric illness among the mildly mentally retarded. *Journal of Medical Science, 44* (Suppl.), 115–124.

Griffiths et al 2013

Gudjonsson, G. H. (1997). *Gudjonsson Suggestibility Scales.* Hove, Sussex, UK: Psychology Press.

Harkness, K.L., Bagby, R.M., Joffe, R.T., & Levitt, A. (2002). Major depression, chronic minor depression and the five factor model of personality. *European Journal of Personality, 16*(4), 271–282.

Hare, R.D. (1993). *The Hare psychopathy checklist–revised.* Toronto: Multi Health Systems.

Hogue, T.E., Steptoe, L., Taylor, J.L., Lindsay, W.R., Mooney, P. & Pinkney, L. (2006). A comparison of offenders with intellectual disability across three levels of security. *Criminal Behaviour and Mental Health, 16,* 13–28.

Holland, D.C., Dollinger, S.J., Holland, C.J., & MacDonald, D.A. (1995). The relationships between psychometric intelligence and the Five Factor Model of personality in a rehabilitation sample. *Journal of Clinical Psychology, 51*(1), 79–89.

Hopwood, J.H., Wright, A.G., Ansell, E, A. & Pincus A.L. (2011). The interpersonal core of personality pathology *Journal of Personality Disorders, 27,* 270-95

Jervis, N., & Baker, M. (2004). Clinical and research implications of an investigation into theory of mind (TOM) task performance in children and adults with non-specific intellectual disabilities. *Journal of Applied Research in Intellectual Disabilities, 17,* 49–58

Jolliffe, D., & Farrington, D.P. (2004). Empathy and offending: A significant review and meta-analysis. *Aggression & Violent Behaviour, 9,* 441-476.

Khan, A., Cowan, C., & Roy, A. (1997). Personality disorders in people with learning disabilities: A community survey. *Journal of Intellectual Disability Research, 41,* 324–330.

Krueger, R. F., Skodol, A. E., Livesley, W. J., Shrout, P. E., & Huang, Y. (2007). Synthesizing dimensional and categorical approaches to personality disorders: Refining the research agenda for DSM-V Axis II. *International Journal of Methods in Psychiatric Research, 16,* 65–73.

Lindsay, W.R., Dana, L., Dosen, A., Gabriel, S., & Young, S. (2005), Personality Disorders. In R Fletcher, E. Loshen, C. Stavrakaki, & M. First (Eds.), *Diagnostic manual – Intellectual disability (DM-ID): A textbook of diagnosis of mental disorders in persons with intellectual disability.* Kingston, NY: NADD Press.

Lindsay, W. R., Hogue, T., Taylor, J.T., Steptoe, L., Mooney, P., Johnston, S., ... Smith, A. H.W. (2006), Two studies on the prevalence and validity of personality disorder in three forensic learning disability samples. *Journal of Forensic Psychiatry and Psychology 17,* 485–506.

Lindsay, W. R., Rzepecka, H., & Law, J. (2007). An exploratory study into the use of the five factor model of personality with people with intellectual disabilities. *Clinical Psychology and Psychotherapy, 14,* 428–37.

Lindsay, W. R., Stenfert Kroese, B., & Drew, P. (2004) Cognitive-behavioral approaches to depression in people with learning disabilities. In P. Sturmey (Ed.), *Mood disor-*

ders and people with mental retardation Kingston, NY: NADD Press.

Lindsay, W.R., Steptoe, L., Hogue, T.E., Mooney, P., Taylor, J.L., & Morrisey, C. (2009). Structure, fit and coherence of two circumplex assessments of personality in a population with intellectual disabilities. *Journal of Intellectual Disability Research, 53*, 329–337.

Lindsay, W.R., Taylor, J., Hogue, T., Steproe. L., Mooney P., & Morrisey, C. (2010). The relationship between assessed emotion, personality, personality disorder and risk. *Psychiatry, Psychology and Law*, 17, 385 – 397.

Livesley, W. J. (1986). Trait and behavioral prototypes of personality disorder. *American Journal of Psychiatry, 143*, 728–732.

Livesley, W. J. (2001). Conceptual and taxonomic issues. In W. J. Livesley (Ed.), *Handbook of personality disorders: Theory, research and treatment* (pp. 3–38). New York: Guilford Press.

Livesley, W. J., & Jackson, D. N. (1991). Construct validity and the classification of personality disorders. In J. Oldham (Ed.), *DSM-III-R Axis II: Perspectives on validity* (pp. 3–22). Washington DC: American Psychiatric Association.

Livesley, W. J., Jackson, D. N., & Schroeder, M. L. (1992). Factorial structure of traits delineating personality disorders in clinical and general population samples. *Journal of Abnormal Psychology, 101*, 432–440.

Lund, J. (1985). The prevalence of psychiatric morbidity in mentally retarded adults. *Acta Psychiatrica Scandinavica, 72*, 563–570.

Mann, A. H., Jenkins, R., Cutting, J. C., & Cowan, P. J. (1981). The development and use of a assessment of abnormal personality. *Psychological Medicine, 11*, 839–847

Mason, J. (2007). Personality assessment in offenders with mild and moderate intellectual disabilities. *The British Journal of Forensic Practice*, 9 (1) 31-39.

McCrae R. R. & Costa P.T. Jr. (1987). Validation of the five factor model of personality across instruments and observers. *Journal of Personality & Social Psychology* 52, 81–90.

McCrae R. R. & Costa P.T. Jr (1989) The structure of interpersonal traits: Wiggins' circumplex and the five factor model. *Journal of Personality & Social Psychology*, 56, 586–95.

McCrae, R.R., & Costa, P.T., Jr. (1991). The NEO Personality inventory: Using the five factor model in counselling. *Journal of Counselling & Development, 69*(4), 367–373.

Miller, J., Maples, J., Few, L., Morse, J., Yaggi, K. & Pilkonis, P. (2010). Using clinician rated five factor model data to school at the DSM IV personality disorders. *Journal of Personality Assessment*, 92, 269-305

Monahan, J., Steadman, H., Silver, E., Appelbaum, P., Robbins, T., Mulvey, E., ... Banks, S. (2001). *Re-thinking risk assessment: The MacArthur study of mental disorder and violence.* New York: Oxford University Press.

Morey, L.C. (1988). The categorical representation of personality disorder: A cluster analysis of DSM III-R personality features. *Journal of Abnormal Psychology, 97*, 314-321.

Morrissey, C., Mooney, P., Hogue, T., Lindsay, W.R., & Taylor, J.L. (2007). Predictive validity of psychopathy in offenders with intellectual disabilities in a high security hospital: Treatment progress. *Journal of Intellectual and Developmental Disabilities, 32*, 125–133

Morrissey, C., & Ingamells, B. (2011). Adapted dialectical behaviour therapy for mal e offenders with intellectual disability in a high secure environment: six years on. *Journal of Learning Disabilities and Offending Behaviour, 2*, 11-17

Naik, B. I., Gangadharan, S. K., & Alexander, R. T. (2002). Personality disorders in learning disability—The clinical experience. *British Journal of Developmental Disabilities, 48*, 95–100.

Norman W.T. (1963) Toward an adequate taxonomy of personality attributes: replicated factor structure in peer nomination personality ratings. *Journal of Abnormal & Social Psychology*, 66, 574–83.

Novaco, R. W., & Taylor, J. L. (2004). Assessment of anger and aggression in offenders with developmental disabilities. *Psychological Assessment, 16*, 42–50.

Oldham, J. M., Skodol, A. E., Kellman, H. D., Hyler, S. E., Doidge, N., Rosnick, L., ... Gallander, P.E. (1995). Comorbidity of axis I and II disorders. *American Journal of Psychiatry, 152*, 571–580.

Paris, J. (2013a). *The ideology behind DSM 5.* In J. Paris & J. Phillips (Eds), *Making the DSM 5: Concepts and controversies*, (pp. 39-46). New York: Springer.

Paris, J. (2013b). *The intelligent clinician's guide to the DSM 5.* Oxford University press: Oxford

Piedmont, R.L., & Weinstein, H.P. (1993). A psychometric evaluation of the new NEO-PI-R facet scales for agreeableness and conscientiousness. *Journal of Personality Assessment, 60*(2), 302–318.

Quirk, S.W., Christiansen, N.D., Wagner, S.H., & McNulty, J.L. (2003). On the usefulness of normal measures of personality for clinical assessment: Evidence of the incremental validity of the revised NEO personality inventory. *Psychological Assessment, 15*, 311–325.

Reynolds, S.K., & Clark, L.A. (2001). Predicting dimensions of personality from domains and facets of the five factor model. *Journal of Personality, 69*, 199–222.

Reid, A. H., & Ballinger, B. R. (1987). Personality disorder in mental handicap. *Psychological Medicine, 17*, 983–987.

Reid, A. H., Lindsay, W. R., Law, J., & Sturmey, P. (2004). The relationship of offending behaviour and personality disorder in people with developmental disabilities. In W. R. Lindsay, J. L. Taylor, & P. Sturmey (Eds.), *Offenders with developmental disabilities* (pp. 289–303). Chichester, UK: Wiley & Sons.

Reiss S. & Havercamp S. H. (1997) The sensitivity theoryof motivation: why functional analysis is not enough.*American Journal of Mental Retardation*, 101, 553–66.

Reiss S. & Havercamp S. H. (1998) Towards a comprehensiveassessment of functional motivation: factorstructure of the Reiss profiles. *Psychological Assessment*, 10, 97–106.

Roepke, S., McAdams, L.A., Lindamer, L.A., Patterson, T.L., & Jeste, D.V. (2001). Personality profiles among normal aged individuals as measured by the NEO-PI-R. *Aging & Mental Health, 5*(2), 159– 165.

Royal College of Psychiatrists. (2001). *Diagnostic criteria in learning disability (DC-LD).* London: Gaskell.

Sapolsky, R. M. (1997). Stress and glucocorticoid response. *Science, 275*, 1662–1663.

Sakdalan, J., Shaw, J., &Collier, V. (2010). Staying in the here-and-now: A pilot study on the use of dialectic behaviour therapy for forensic clients with intellectual disability. *Journal of Intellectual Disability Research, 54*(6), 568-572.

Schinka, J.A., Kinder, B.N., & Kremer, T. (1997). Research validity scales for the NEO-PI-R: Development and validation. *Journal of Personality Assessment, 68*(1), 127–138.

Sequeira, H., & Hollins, S. A. (2003). Clinical effects of sexual abuse on people with learning disability. *British Journal of Psychiatry, 182*, 13–19.

Smith, D., & Melda (2014). *Trends in outcomes achieved for persons with intellectual and developmental disabilities: Findings from 20 years of personal outcomes measures data.* Towson, MD: Council on Quality and Leadership.

Sovner, R., & Hurley, A. D. (1986). Four factors affecting the diagnosis of psychiatric disorders in mentally retarded persons. *Psychiatric Aspects of Mental Retardation Reviews, 5*, 45–49.

Switzky, H. N. (2001). *Personality and motivational differences in persons with mental retardation.* Mahwah, NJ: Lawrence, Erlbaum Associates.

Switzky, H. N., & Haywood, H. C. (1991). Self reinforcement schedules in persons with mild mental retardation. Effects of motivational orientation and instructional demands. *Journal of Mental Deficiency Research*, 35, 221–30.

Switzky, H. N., & Haywood H. C. (1992). Self reinforcement schedules in young children: Effects of motivational orientation and instructional demands. *Learning & Individual Differences, 4*, 59–71.

Talbert, F.S., Braswell, L.C., Albrecht, J.W., Hyer, L.A., & Boudewyns, P.A. (1993). NEO-PI profiles in PTSD as a function of trauma level. *Journal of Clinical Psychology, 49*(5), 663–669.

Taylor, J. L. (2002). A review of the assessment and treatment of anger and aggression in offenders with intellectual disability. *Journal of Intellectual Disability Research, 46* (Suppl.1), 57–73.

Taylor, J. L., Novaco, R. W., Gillmer, B., & Thorne, I. (2002). Cognitive behavioural treatment of anger intensity among offenders with intellectual disabilities. *Journal of Applied Research in Intellectual Disabilities, 15*, 151–165.

Thompson, D., & Brown, H. (1997). Men with intellectual disabilities who sexually abuse: A review of the literature. *Journal of Applied Research in Intellectual Disabilities, 10*, 140–158.

Trapnell, P. D., & Wiggins J. S. (1990). Extension of the interpersonal adjective scales to include the big five dimensions of personality. *Journal of Personality & Social Psychology, 59*, 781–90.

Widiger, T., & Costa P. (2012). Integrating the normal and abnormal personality structure: the five factor model. *Journal of Personality, 80*, 1471-1506.

Widiger, T.A., & Frances, A.J. (1985). The DSM-III personality disorders: Perspectives from psychology. *Archives of General Psychiatry, 42*, 615-623.

World Health Organization. (1990). *International statistical classification of disease and related health problems* (10th ed.). Retrieved from http://apps.who.int/classifications/icd10/browse/2010/en-/R41.8

Young, S. (2004). Diagnosis of personality disorder (PD) and pervasive developmental disorder (PDD) in individuals with intellectual disability, in a maximum secure setting. *Journal of Intellectual Disability Research, 48*, 465.

Zigler, E., Bennett-Gates, D., Hodapp, R., & Henrich, C. C. (2002). Assessing personality traits of individuals with mental retardation. *American Journal on Mental Retardation, 107*, 181–193.

Zigler, E. (2001). Looking back 40 years and still seeing the person with mental retardation as a whole person. In H.N. Switzky (Ed.), *Personality and motivational differences in persons with mental retardation* (pp. 3–55). Mahway, NJ: Lawrence, Erlbaum Associates.

Zigler, E., & Bennett-Gates D. (1999). *Personality development in individuals with mental retardation.* Boston, MA: Cambridge University Press.

Zigler, E., Bennett-Gates, D., Hodapp, R., & Henrich, C. C. (2002). Assessing personality traits of individuals with mental retardation. *American Journal on Mental Retardation, 107*, 181–93.

Zimmerman, M., Rothschild, L., & Chelminski, I. (2005), The prevalence of DSM IV personality disorders in psychiatric outpatients. *American Journal of psychiatry, 162*, 1911-1918.

Zuckerman, M. (1999). *The vulnerability to psychopathology: A biosocial model.* Washington, DC: American Psychological Association

CHAPTER 27

Paraphilia[1]

Dorothy M. Griffiths
J. Paul Fedoroff
Deborah A. Richards
William R. Lindsay

Although the DSM-5 criteria remains largely applicable to persons with intellectual disabilities, special consideration and assessment of the persons' learning history and knowledge is needed in order to ensure that the exhibited behavior is not an artifact of institutional learning or a lack of learning about socially appropriate sexual relations, public-private, consent, or a symptom of abuse, medical discomfort, or a genetic syndrome.

Review of Diagnostic Criteria

The term *paraphilia* is derived from the Greek words meaning *beside* and (brotherly) *love*. The definition has changed over the years and differs from society to society. For example, homosexuality used to be classified as a pathologic sexual deviation but was excluded from the *Diagnostic and Statistical Manual* (DSM) of the APA in 1980. The DSM-5 defines paraphilia as a sexual interest that is intense, persistent, and in some cases preferential. The only sexual interests considered non-paraphilic are genital stimulation or fondling with a partner who is consenting, phenotypically normal, and physically mature. The DSM-5 identifies a *paraphilic disorder* as a paraphilia that causes distress either to the individual or someone else. Paraphilic disorders cause harm directly or indirectly to the person or a direct or indirect victim. As such, a paraphilia, denoting an unconventional interest or preference, is not sufficient to be a paraphilic disorder and as such may not require clinical intervention. Paraphilic interests are not sexual orientations.

General Description of the Disorder

The DSM-5 divides paraphilias into *anomalous activity preferences*, such as the so-called courtship disorders and algolagnic disorders and those that represent *anomalous target preferences*. The *courtship disorders* include spying on others in private activities (voyeuristic disorders), exposing genitals (exhibitionistic disorder), and touching or rubbing against a non-consenting individual (frotteuristic disorders). *Algolagnic disorders* include disorders that involve undergoing humiliation, bondage, or suffering (sexual masochism disorder) or inflicting humiliation, bondage, or suffering (sexual sadism disorder). The second group, *anomalous target preferences*, represents disorders that involve sexual interests that target children (pedophilic disorder), non-genital body parts (fetishistic disorders), or sexually arousing cross-dressing (transvestic disorders). Although the eight paraphilic disorders listed in the DSM-5 are far from exhaustive, they represent some of the most well-known paraphilic disorders.

[1] Adapted from Griffiths, D., Fedoroff, P., Richards, D., Cox-Lindenbaum, D., Langevin, R., Linsday, W. D., Hucker, S., & Goldman, M. (2007). Gender and sexual disorders. In R. Fletcher, E. Loschen, C. Stavrakaki, C., & M. First (Eds.). *Diagnostic manual -- Intellectual disability (DM-ID): A textbook of diagnosis of mental disorders in persons with intellectual disability.* (pp. 411-459). Kingston, NY: NADD Press.

The DSM-5 notes that:

> "Some paraphilias primarily concern the individual's erotic activities, and others primarily concern the individual's erotic targets. Examples of the former would include intense and persistent interests in spanking, whipping, cutting, binding, or strangulating another person, or an interest in these activities that equals or exceeds the individual's interest in copulation or equivalent interaction with another person. Examples of the latter would include intense or preferential sexual interest in children, corpses, or amputees (as a class), as well as intense or preferential interest in nonhuman animals, such as horses or dogs, or in inanimate objects, such as shoes or articles made of rubber." (American Psychiatric Association, 2013,p. 685)

Summary of DSM-5 Criteria

The DSM-5 adopts a definition of "paraphilia" based on what it is not. It states that anything is paraphilic that "denotes any intense and persistent sexual interest other than sexual interest in genital stimulation or preparatory fondling with phenotypically normal, physically mature, consenting human partners" (American Psychiatric Association, 2013, p. 685). There are eight specific paraphilias listed meaning that most of the over 100 known paraphilias (Fedoroff, 2010) fall under the categories of other specified paraphilic disorder (302.89) or "unspecified paraphilic disorder (3012.9). Other specified paraphilic disorders are simply ones not listed in the DSM-5. Unspecified paraphilic disorders are ones in which "...the clinician chooses *not* to specify the reason that the criteria are not met...and includes presentations in which there is insufficient information to make a more specific diagnosis" (American Psychiatric association, 2013, p. 705; italics in original). The text is silent on why a clinician would ever chose to assign a paraphilic label without specifying why, but the term "unspecified paraphilic disorder" makes this possible.

The DSM-5 also divides paraphilias into "paraphilias" and "paraphilic disorders." Paraphilic disorders are defined as, "... a paraphilia that is currently causing distress or impairment to the individual or a paraphilia whose satisfaction has entailed personal harm, or risk of harm, to others (pp. 685-686). This distinction is problematic primarily due to the fact that the stigma due to being ascertained as having pedophilia is likely the same as being diagnosed with as having pedophilic disorder even though the criteria are different (e.g. Fedoroff, 2011). It is of particular concern for individuals with intellectual disabilities since behaviors in this group are more easily mislabeled, (Griffiths, Hingsburger, Hoath, & Ioannou, 2013), and it is easy for their behaviors to be considered harmful.

The eight specific paraphilias described in the DSM-5 are the following (listed in the order they occur in the DSM-5): voyeuristic disorder (observing an unsuspecting person), exhibitionistic disorder (exposing genitals to an unsuspecting person); frotteuristic disorder (touching or rubbing a non-consenting person), sexual masochism disorder (being humiliated, beaten, bound or otherwise made to suffer), sexual sadism disorder (sexual arousal from the psychological or physical suffering of another person), pedophilic disorder (sexual activity with a prepubescent child or children (generally age 13 or younger), fetishistic disorder (sexual arousal from either the use of nonliving objects or a highly specific focus on non-genital body part(s)), transvestic disorder (sexual arousal from cross-dressing). Sexual masochism disorder also includes a subspecifier: asphyxiophilia (sexual arousal related to restriction of breathing).

Each of the DSM-5 paraphilic disorders has two main criteria. Category A criteria are as follows:

"Over a period of at least 6 months, recurrent and intense sexual arousal from..." (the paraphilic interest or act).

The category B criteria are as follows:

"The individual has acted on these sexual urges with a non-consenting person, or the sexual urges or fantasies cause clinically significant distress or impairment in social, occupational, or other important areas of functioning."

In the DSM-5, determination of "sexual masochism disorder," "fetishistic disorder," and "transvestic disorder" do not require non-consent. Pedophilic disorder retains the grammatically incorrect criteria of "intense sexually arousing fantasies" and does not explicitly state that sex with a child is by definition non-consensual.

Issues Related to Diagnosis in Persons with ID

The diagnosis of a *paraphila* may be more challenging in patients with intellectual disabilities because of difficulties arising from procedures used to assess sexual interest.

Several authors have recognized that although sex offenders with intellectual disabilities present with problems similar to nondisabled offenders, there are important differences that mandate assessment and service provisions that require modification to account for specific needs (Day, 1997; Murphy, Coleman & Haynes, 1983; Nezu, Nezu & Dudek, 1998). These differences include deficits in sociosexual skills and knowledge, decreased past and current opportunities for sexual behavior, past sexual victimization, difficulties in understanding future consequences, and specific difficulties recognizing and expressing emotions.

Within the population of people with intellectual disabilities and problematic sexual interests, there is a higher incidence of reported sexual abuse (Gilby, Wolf, & Goldberg, 1989; Griffiths, Quinsey, & Hingsburger, 1989; Sobsey, 1994), poor self-esteem (Lackey & Knopp, 1989), lack of sociosexual knowledge and experience (Hingsburger, 1987; McCarthy & Thompson, 1998), poor social problem-solving skills (Hingsburger, 1987), and knowledge of the law that pertains to sexual offenses (Craig, 2010). All of these factors may contribute to the false diagnosis of a paraphilia. Comprehensive clinical evaluation of the complex factors that could be influencing problematic sexual behaviors in people with intellectual disabilities is required to distinguish *paraphilias* from sexually inappropriate behavior that may superficially *look like* paraphilias but which lacks the recurring and pathological use of problematic sexual fantasies, urges, or behaviors. Non-paraphilic behaviors can be differentiated from *paraphilic behaviors* by the fact that non-paraphilic behaviors are not primarily sexually motivated and do not constitute the person's persistent, preferred, and recurring sexual behaviors. Non-paraphilic sexual behaviors usually begin at a later stage in development and are often sporadic.

Although some individuals with specific syndromes may exhibit sexual behaviors that are ostensibly characteristic of known paraphilias, there are many contributing factors to problematic sexual behaviors by people with intellectual disabilities. Lack of adequate understanding of acceptable social and sexual interactions may cause individuals to behave in ways that give rise to concern. Limited social contact with the opposite gender due to same sex residences may lead heterosexual individuals to express themselves sexually with individuals of the same sex. Lack of privacy in residences increases the risk that the individual will express his/her sexuality publicly.

Development and Course

The DSM-5 provides a brief description of the development and course of each of the paraphilias that are listed in the DSM-5. For all eight paraphilias the DSM-5 opines that first awareness of the paraphilic interest usually occurs "during adolescence or early adulthood." Exceptions to this observation include sexual masochism (childhood), fetishistic disorder (prior to adolescence), and transvestic disorder (childhood) (pp. 695,701, and 703, respectively). The DSM-5 designates a minimum age of 18 for the diagnosis of voyeurism and 16 for pedophilia because "...there is substantial difficulty in differentiating (voyeurism or pedophilia) from age-appropriate puberty-related sexual curiosity and activity" (p 688 and p. 699, respectively). All the paraphilias listed in the DSM-5 have a sub-specifier of "in full remission," with the exception of pedophilia. The DSM-5 states, "Pedophilia per se appears to be a lifelong condition" (p. 699). Unlike all the other paraphilias, only pedophilia does not have any subspecifiers indicating it is in remission. However, the DSM-5 notes that the course of all the paraphilias, including pedophilia, "may fluctuate."

Prevalence

It is difficult to establish the true prevalence of sexual deviance amongst individuals with intellectual disabilities because study samples typically consist of people who have come to attention due to incarceration or hospitalization, varying methods of identification of intellectual disability were used, and problems establishing who to include in the samples (Lindsay, 2002; Lindsay, Hastings, Griffiths, & Hayes, 2007). Murphy, Coleman, and Abel (1983) found that sexual arousal patterns and cognitive distortions were reported among persons with intellectual disabilities. Research on the incidence of sexual offense committed by persons with intellectual disabilities has indicated a range from 3-4% to 43-51% (Mohr, Turner & Jerry, 1964; Selling, 1953, respectively). Other research has documented a rate ranging from 15 to 33% of charged sexual offenders who are intellectually disabled (Shapiro, 1986; Steiner, 1984). In 1991, Hayes reported a 3.7 % rate of conviction for people with intellectual disability.

Griffiths, Watson, Lewis, and Stoner (2004) cautioned that most research data are based on prison data or arrest/conviction rates and as such may not be indicative of an over representation of higher rates of sexual offences among this population but instead represent higher rates of arrest, confession, and conviction (Murphy, Coleman & Haynes, 1983; Santamour & West, 1978). People with intellectual disabilities are more likely to be apprehended, confess to the crime, incriminate themselves, be led by the interviewer, plead guilty, waive their rights without full comprehension of the process, be less likely to plea bargain or appeal judgment, less likely to see the implications of their statements, and be less likely to afford appropriate legal defense (Abel & Rouleau, 1990; Brown & Courtless, 1971; McGee & Menolascino, 1992; Moschella, 1982; Murphy, et al, 1983; Satamour & West, 1978).

Day (1994) provided a rival hypothesis: namely that incidence data for sexual offenses underestimates the actual offense rates because people with intellectual disabilities are diverted from the criminal justice system into residential care facilities for the intellectually disabled or mentally ill. Thus, existing research clearly indicates that people with intellectual disabilities are overrepresented among those committing crimes, including those of a sexual nature (Langevin, 1992; Shapiro, 1986; Steiner, 1984). However, it is unclear whether the frequency of sexually inappropriate behavior is elevated in this population compared to the nondisabled population. Nonetheless, Day (1994) has argued that *paraphilias* are rare among persons with intellectual disabilities (Day, 1994).

Sexual offense rates do not take into account other factors that may relate to the experiences of persons with intellectual disabilities that may contribute to the commission of an offense that may be not related to the presence of paraphilia. Lindsay (2002) in a review of the research and literature on sex offenders with intellectual disabilities concluded there is no clear evidence that there is either an over or under representation of people with intellectual disabilities who sexually offend. This represents the current state of research evidence on incidence.

Differential Diagnosis

In 1990, Knight and Prentky proposed six different types of sexual aggressors: 1) opportunistic, 2) non-sadistic sexual, 3) pervasively angry, 4) vindictive, 5) overt sadistic, and 6) muted sadistic. However, Day (1994) argued that there are only two categories of sexual aggression for people who have an intellectual disability. These consist of (a) individuals who commit sex offences only and (b) those who commit a range of offenses, including those of a sexual nature. He observed that the latter group demonstrates a higher incidence of sociopathic personality disorder, brain damage, family dysfunction, and other problematic sexual behaviors (Day, 1994). It was found that the latter were at a higher risk for violence and reoffense (Day, 1994; MacEachran, 1979). The higher risk posed by sex offenders who have an intellectual disability has also been identified as: more sociopathic, having been socially deprived, more brain damaged, and having lengthier histories of antisocial behavior, being more under-socialized, having poorer impulse control, and being more likely to commit serious sexual offenses than the lower risk individuals who committed sexual offenses only. Day (1994) found that high risk sex offenders who have an intellectual disability have also been reported to be more persistent sex offenders, and the nature of their crimes are described as more serious than that of the low risk sex offenders who have an intellectual disability Age at first conviction and age at first sexual offense were also variables that predicted the group into which the offender would fall. The younger the age at first sexual offense and at first conviction, the more likely the individual would fall into the category "sexual offenses and other crimes" (Day, 1994). This group is more specific and persistent in their sexual offenses, and members are less sexually naive.

Gilby et al. (1989) reported that sexual aggressors with intellectual disabilities generally commit less serious assault offenses, but more inappropriate behaviors such as public masturbation, exhibitionism, and voyeurism. In contrast to the non-disabled sample that targeted mostly females, aggressors with intellectual disabilities offended equally against males and females (Gilby et al., 1989; Griffiths, Quinsey & Hingsburger, 1989). In addition, people with intellectual disabilities appeared to have far fewer victims.

Some researchers have found that sex offenders with an intellectual disability have a larger proportion of male victims, albeit the majority of their victims, as in the case of non-intellectually disabled offenders, are female (Brown & Stein, 1997; Gilby et al., 1989; Murrey, Briggs, & Davis, 1992). Others have found that the numbers of male and female victims are equivalent (Brown & Stein, 1997; Day, 1994; Gilby et al., 1989; Griffiths, Hingsburger & Christian, 1985; Klimecki, Jenkinson, & Wilson, 1994). Furthermore, Blanchard et al. (1999) found that phallometric measures were accurate in this population concerning the correct identification of high risk sex offenders. They found that sexual interests for people with pedophilia who were lower functioning were less likely to show adult female erotic preference.

The DSM-5 description does not provide extensive diagnostic criteria for differentiating between *paraphilia* and what some authors have called "counterfeit deviance." This term was introduced by Hingsburger, Griffiths, and Quinsey in 1991. They provided case examples of sexual misbehavior of persons with intellectual disabilities who were often often the product of experiential, environmental, or medical factors, rather than a *paraphilia*. Diagnosis needs to carefully consider and evaluate the individual's environment, socio-sexual knowledge and attitudes, learning experiences, partner selection, courtship skills, and biomedical influences in order to differentiate *paraphilia* from *counterfeit deviance*. Such misbehavior can result from an environmental lack of privacy (structural), modeling, inappropriate partner selection or courtship, lack of sexual knowledge or moral training, a maladaptive learning history, medical disorders or medication effects (Hingsburger et al., 1991).

Counterfeit deviance is sometimes misunderstood to mean that paraphiliacs with intellectual disabilities are lacking in the above areas of knowledge or experience. The contrary is often noted; persons with intellectual disabilities who have paraphilic interests often demonstrate good sexual knowledge and are fully aware of the social norms and sanctions for their behavior. The differential diagnosis involving counterfeit deviance is based on identifying individuals whose apparently paraphilic behavior is not based on sexual interest but due to other factors.

Functional Consequences

In recent decades the field has seen several shifts in treatment models. Four different pathways have been identified as important to matching appropriate treatment to specific offender types (Ward & Hudson, 1998). According to this scheme of categorization, *avoidant/passive offenders* do not actively seek to reoffend but lack appropriate or functional skills or strategies; *avoidant/active offenders* similarly do not seem to actively intend to reoffend but engage in strategies that are ineffective to avoid reoffenses. In contrast *approach/automatic offenders* engage in illegal sex spontaneously and impulsively if the situation is presented. People categorized as *approach/explicit offenders* actively pursue opportunities to reoffend. Treatment would therefore be tailored to meet the individual needs of each type of offender based in part on their pathway to offence. Some require more focus on habilitative approaches whereas others focus on rehabilitative strategies as approaches to self-regulation (Ward & Ganon, 2006).

Andrews and Bonta (2007) described a three part model for consideration in the treatment of all offenders: risk, needs and responsivity. They suggested that the level of service provided should match the relative risk of reoffense, that treatment should be individualized to address the needs of the offender to overcome criminogenic vulnerabilities, and that treatment should be responsive to the needs and strengths of the specific individual, accounting for unique abilities and learning needs. For people with intellectual disabilities, the evaluation of each of these components of the model requires understanding of the nature of the offenses committed and the factors that may reduce recidivism while addressing the specific learning needs of the individual.

Comorbidity

The compounded effects of co-morbid conditions in regard to sexual behaviors have often been ignored especially concerning people with intellectual disabilities (e.g., epilepsy, autism spectrum disorder, etc.) (Fedoroff, Selhi, Smolewska, Ng, & Bradford, 2001).

Watson, Richards, Griffiths, Fedoroff and Miodrag (2012) discuss the relationship between genetics, behavioral phenotypes and inappropriate sexual behavior. For instance, impulsivity is a common characteristic of many genetic disorders. Cases of sexually inappropriate touching due to an impaired inability to refrain from such behavior due to impulsivity have been reported. People with Prader-Willi syndrome often have obsessions and compulsions and in some cases these can take on the form of sexual preoccupations leading to illegal behaviors such as stalking (Hartley, MacLean, Butler, Zarcone & Thompson, 2005). People with intellectual disabilities have an increased risk of having the full range of psychiatric disorders, in part due to their increased risk of genetic disorders (Allen & Davis, 2007). Therefore, all people with intellectual disability presenting with problematic sexual behaviors should be assessed not only for paraphilic disorders but also concurrent psychiatric and medical disorders, including genetic disorders.

Application of Diagnostic Criteria to People with Intellectual Disabilities

General Considerations

Griffiths et al. (2004) noted that much of what is known about the presentation of paraphilias or paraphilia-like syndromes in people with intellectual disabilities is based on clinical observations and extrapolation from clinical experience with nondisabled offenders. Haaven (2010) explains that accurate diagnoses are obtained through assessment that provides a complete picture of the nature and features of the offense and how it developed. The research for nondisabled offenders has generally been conducted with reasonable scientific rigor. However, generalization to people with intellectual disabilities requires caution.

Paraphilic disorders are diagnosed on the basis of clinical interviews together with review of collateral materials. Phallometric testing may be helpful but is not part of the DSM-5 diagnostic criteria. Tests of intelligence are not usually done on people undergoing assessment for paraphilias unless they have known or suspected intellectual disabilities. However assessment of problematic sexual behaviors in people with known or suspected intellectual disabilities requires additional consideration. Often individuals who have intellectual disabilities are given standardized intelligence tests While these measures may provide information regarding an individual's general cognitive functioning and specific strengths and weaknesses in learning, these tests are often misapplied in the prediction of the person's overall functioning and sexual development. Most standardized intelligence tests do not provide information regarding current functioning or what adaptations need to be made to support or improve the person's functioning. Moreover, the mental age, as identified in a test of intelligence, does not predict overall functioning or sexual interest or knowledge. Mental age only indicates age equivalence in ability to answer a comparable number of questions on the specific test. It is predictive of academic achievement and may globally describe the typical outcomes of individuals achieving the same score on the test. A forty year old man with a "mental age" of five but who also has forty years of life experience, including the physical and sexual development of a forty year old man, is not comparable to a five year old child on any real life dimensions.

There are several key areas of assessment regarding paraphilia in this population. They are social and sexual knowledge and attitudes, behaviors, cognitions, phallometry, risk assessment, and recommendations for recovery.

Sociosexual Knowledge and Attitudes[1]: Most adults with intellectual disabilities know less about sexuality and sexual abuse than teenagers and young adults without disabilities (Murphy, 2003; Griffiths & Lunsky, 2003); however, sex education has been shown to make a significant difference. Recent clinical examples have shown that a lack of education regarding sexually appropriate and responsible behaviors represents a critical vulnerability in the development of sexually inappropriate behavior (see Griffiths, 2002). Hingsburger, Griffiths, & Quinsey (1991) described case examples of people with intellectual disabilities with problematic sexual behaviors who were offered sex education alone. Since then, other cases representing even more clinically complex interventions in which sex education was found to be a critical vulnerability for the development of the problematic sexual behaviors. It remains one of Dr. Griffiths' main components for effective interventions in this population (Griffiths, 2002; Griffiths, et al., 1989).

Evaluation of the sociosexual knowledge and attitudes of sexual offenders with intellectual disabilities is a critical measure in establishing a comprehensive differential diagnosis of possible disorders contributing to problematic sexual behaviors. The Socio-Sexual Knowledge and Attitudes Tool – Revised (*SSKAAT-R*) (Griffiths & Lunsky, 2003) and the Sexual Knowledge, Experience, Feelings and Needs Scale (*Sex-Ken-ID*) (McCabe, 1994) are two of the assessment tools available to assess initial and subsequent changes in both knowledge and attitude. On both measures, the person being assessed answers questions that are not verbally demanding in response to a picture book.

The SSKAAT-R has been field-tested across North America and has excellent psychometric properties, including internal consistency, test-retest reliability, and content validity. This measure is especially useful as an aid to identify baseline knowledge and attitudes concerning a range of sociosexual behaviors and as an aid in establishing a comprehensive differential diagnosis that includes factors contributing to counterfeit deviance such as impaired awareness of social boundaries such as who and under what circumstances it is acceptable to hug and kiss.

The Sex Ken-ID reports high levels of internal consistency for all of its subscales with the exception of the needs and feeling subscales (McCabe, Cummins, & Deeks, 1999). Test-retest reliability data and validity data were less convincing. This assessment differs from the SSKAAT-R because it also includes information about past experiences. Whitehouse and McCabe (1997) stated that future programs need to consider the use of checklists and transcript analysis to cover both the more accurate but more limited assessment of sexual facts as well as the more complex analysis of feelings and attitudes. The SexKen-ID may be a more valuable tool for use in exploring experiences and feelings related to sexual dysfunction (physical problems having sex as opposed to problems in types of sexual interest). Although there are less complicated measures available (i.e. Timmers, Ducharme, & Jacob., 1981), the psychometric evaluation of these is often lacking (McCabe et al., 1999).

1 Disclaimer: *The SSKAAT-R was co-developed by one of the authors of this chapter; Dr. Griffiths in no way benefits from the sale of that product as her proceeds are directly donated to charity.*

Cognitions Assessment: Direct application of some testing procedures to this population may be misleading. Some measures have been adapted for persons with intellectual disabilities, for example the Abel and Becker Cognition Scale (ABCS, Abel, Becker & Cunningham-Rathner, 1984) was revised by Kolton, Boer & Boer (2001). The original instrument attempts to measure cognitive distortions that typically occur in individuals who sexually assault children. Although the scale was modified for people with intellectual disabilities in order to increase its readability and to enhance the assessment of cognitive distortions in offenders with an intellectual disability, it does not have demonstrated validity in people with intellectual disabilities and problematic sexual behaviors. The nature of the items on this measure may lead to individuals with intellectual disabilities giving responses that may be misleading because the individual is responding to please the examiner. Alternatively, Broxholme and Lindsay (2003) developed a questionnaire about the cognitions of persons with disabilities as they relate to sex offending. This assessment was updated and validated on groups of sex offenders, nonsexual offenders and nonoffenders (all with intellectual disability) and non intellectual disability males (Lindsay, Whitefield & Carson 2007) and has been used extensively in treatment trials for sex offenders with intellectual disability (Lindsay, Craig & Michie, unpublished assessment).

Phallometric Assessment: Murphy, Coleman and Abel (1983) suggested that, although phallometric assessment was useful with persons with intellectual disabilities who had committed a sexual offense, some individuals failed to show expected patterns or to respond to any stimuli. They hypothesized the following reasons for the findings they observed in people with intellectual disabilities: (i) they were less able to focus on the visual test stimuli, (ii) they had greater difficulty identifying deviant situations, (iii) they may require more concrete interview questions, (iv) they were on medications that interfered with the evaluation, (v) they may have had difficulty providing accurate self-report information, and (vi) they may present with physical, communication, and behavioral challenges that interfere with the evaluation (Murphy, Coleman & Abel, 1983). Use of phallometric assessment was demonstrated by Reyes et al (2006) when they presented 10 cases. The 10 cases were numbered from 1 to 47 suggesting that they had been picked specifically for illustration. They found that four cases showed specific deviant arousal, two cases were non-specific, and four cases showed arousal to adult stimuli. Another study employing phallometric assessment is the previously mentioned report by Rice, Harris, Langi, & Chalin (2008). There are however, very few studies that employ phallometric assessment in men with intellectual disability, and caution should be employed with any such use.

Typical interviewing and testing procedures require adaptation and caution when used with individuals from this group (i.e., phallometric testing, genetic testing, psychological testing) (Murphy, Coleman, & Haynes, 1983).

There are mixed results concerning deviant sexual interest, as measured in phallometric laboratory tests, for persons with intellectual disabilities. Some studies have found that people with intellectual disabilities do not present with deviant sexual interests, implying they are more likely to be opportunistic offenders (Day, 1994; Timms & Goreczny, 2002), while other studies have found that some do display deviant sexual interests. Harris and Rice (2002) studied 58 sexual offenders with intellectual disabilities matched with 45 normal IQ sexual offenders on various variables pertaining to sexual preference and risk assessment. They found that offenders who had an intellectual disability were more likely to show a sexual preference for male children and for prepubescent children than did the control group of sex offenders without intellectual disabilities. Green, Gray and Willner (2002) looked at differences between 16 criminally convicted and 30 non convicted men in the U.K., with learning disabilities (intellectual disabilities) who had sexually offended. Only having male children as victims was related to whether or not the men were prosecuted for their offenses. These results may explain why

Rice et al. (2008) found that offenders with intellectual disabilities were more likely to target male children. It is important to note that phallometric testing is not part of the DSM-5 diagnostic criteria for any of the paraphilias, including pedophilia. In addition, phallometric testing is a measure of sexual preference in the lab and not intended to establish innocence or guilt. Its use provides additional information to gain greater insight for a working diagnosis and to provide an objective measure of treatment success (Fedoroff & Richards, 2010).

Risk assessment: Mikkelsen & Stelk (1999) described a risk assessment protocol for relapse prevention in the community treatment of people with intellectual disabilities who criminally offend based on expert opinion and then current state of the field. However, researchers and clinicians are now moving towards empirically based actuarial risk assessments (e.g., the Sex Offender Risk Appraisal Guide (SORAG) (Quinsey, Harris, Rice & Cormier, 1998) or the Static-99-R (Hanson & Thornton, 2000)). Actuarial risk measures are more accurate in predicting sexual recidivism in large groups of sex offenders (Hanson & Bussiere, 1998); they have been used but to a lesser degree in sex offenders with intellectual disability. In a recent cumulative metaanalysis, Hanson, Sheahan, and VanZuylen (2013) reviewed the small number of studies using the STATIC-99 on offenders with intellectual disability. They also conducted their own study extracting information on 52 offenders with intellectual disability from a large database. The STATIC-99 has four iterations; AUC calculations for all four were essentially similar, with values of between .75 and .79. The authors concluded, "We are optimistic that these tools will continue to perform well with DD (developmentally delayed) sexual offenders given the consistency of the current results with the much larger research on non-DD sexual offenders" (p. 11).

Concerns about their predictive validity with this population have been examined but with mixed results (Fedoroff et al., 2001; Fedoroff, Curry, & Madrigrano, 2002). To counter these concerns, researchers have started to investigate the contribution of dynamic variables in risk assessment. Boer, Tough and Haaven (2004) developed the ARMIDILO-S consisting of dynamic items relating to the role of staff and the individual's environment in addition to those relating to the offender. Two studies have estimated the predictive accuracy of the ARMIDILO-S in comparison to general offender tools. Blacker et al (2011), found that the ARMIDILO-S was a good predictor of sexual reoffending amongst the intellectual disability sample (n=10) although the retrospective follow up design, small intellectual disability sample size, and failure to use the entire ARMIDILO-S limit the impact of this study. A further study by Lofthouse et al. (2013) found the ARMIDILO-S to be a very good predictor of sexual incidents (n=64, follow up average 6 years; AUC = 0.92). The ARMIDILO-S has an additional unique characteristic in that it has a protective scale as well as a risk scale.

The DSM-5 notes that identification of intensity and persistence may be difficult to apply, such as in the assessment of persons who are very old or medically ill and who may not have "intense" sexual interests of any kind. This could apply to some individuals with intellectual disabilities which therefore makes the issue of assessment an even more critical piece in the identification of paraphilia and especially in those cases where pedophilia has been identified forensically. Utilizing state-of-the-art validated tools that have been adapted to the population of individuals with intellectual disabilities is not only necessary but ethically responsible.

Methodology

An on-line search including MEDLINE and Academic Search Premier plus university library sources was conducted using key words of paraphilia, sexual offenses, intellectual disability, developmental disability, and counterfeit deviance. It produced approximately fifty peer reviewed papers.

Review of Research Applying to People with Intellectual Disabilities

In mainstream research on sex offenders, up to 6 different categories of sexually aggressive behavior have been suggested (Knight & Prentky 1990). However, in research on inappropriate sexual behavior (ISB) and sex offending in men with intellectual and developmental disabilities (IDD), two main categories have been suggested by several authors. Day (1994) reported on 47 sex offenders with intellectual disability. He noted that "serious offences are less common and there is a high percentage of minor or nuisance offences" (p 637). In a principal components analysis, two distinct groups emerged. The first was a group who committed sex offenses only and who are typically shy, immature individuals with little sexual experience. Their recidivism rate was high, but they tended to commit less serious crimes (less direct contact with victims). The second group committed sexual offences as part of a wider complex of offending and antisocial behavior. This second group had a higher prevalence of psychosocial deprivation and a history of poor parenting when they were growing up. They were found to be more likely to commit more serious sexual offenses. They also had high recidivism rates and the offenses they committed were on average more serious. Day (1994) reported that recidivists had low specificity for age of victims in that a number who had previously sexually abused children reoffended against adults and a number of patients who had previously abused against adults reoffended against children. While the sample was small (n=47), this was one of the first indications of a low specificity for sex offenders with intellectual disability. Gilby et al. (1989) also reported that sex offenders with intellectual disability generally commit less serious assault offenses but more non-contact problematic sexual behaviors such as public masturbation, exhibitionism, and voyeurism. In contrast to a non-disabled sample who targeted mostly females, men with intellectual disability offended equally against males and females. Both Day (1994) and Gilby et al. (1989) felt that these perpetrators may be more opportunistic in their offenses and less focused on particular types of victims. There was also evidence that sex offenders with intellectual disability were less likely to be violent during the offenses than sexual offenders without intellectual disabilities, and less likely to commit penetrative offenses (Murrey, et al., 1992).

These two categories were placed into sharper focus by Lunsky, Frijters, Watson, Willison, & Griffiths (2007) when they categorized a group of participants into those who had committed repeated or forced in-person sexual offenses and those who had committed less severely problematic sexual behaviors such as public masturbation or non-consensual touching. Comparing the two groups they found that the former had higher levels of sexual knowledge and more liberal attitudes than the less severe offenders. These findings support the need for further empirical studies into the validity of these two groups of sex offenders with IDD. In another study, Michie et al. (2006) found that while sexual knowledge was correlated with IQ in non-sexual offenders with intellectual disability, there was no significant relationship between sexual knowledge and IQ in a group of sex offenders with intellectual disability.

Blanchard et al. (1999) investigated patterns of sexual offending in 950 participants. They found that those sex offenders with lower intellectual functioning were significantly more likely to commit offenses against younger children and male children (see quote from Blanchard et al., 2009, below). Although the proportion of variance was not high, the study did suggest that inappropriate sexual preference might play a role in at least some of the sexual offending in this client group. They also reported that their results suggested that choices of male or female victims by offenders with intellectual disability were not primarily determined by accessibility or other circumstantial factors. Cantor et al. (2005) reported a detailed meta-analytic study of previous research that included reliable data on IQ in men charged with sexual and nonsexual offending. In a reanalysis of data on 25,146 sexual offenders and controls, they found a robust relationship between low IQ and sexual offending specifically, low IQ and pedophilia. They hypothesized that "A third variable – a perturbation of prenatal or childhood brain development-produces both pedophilia and low IQ" (p. 565). They went on to accept that psychosocial influences are likely to be important but incomplete in explaining pedophilia, emphasizing the value of investigating the range of hypotheses presented for the genesis of sexual offending. It is important, for this chapter, to note that the average IQs in the study were all in the normal range. The men who showed sexual attraction to children still had an average IQ of 93 which is two standard deviation above the range of intellectual disability.

Cantor et al. (2004) compared the IQs of different types of sexual offenders. They separated 298 sexual offenders into three groups comprising those who had offended against prepubescent children, pubescent teenagers, and adults. Those who had offended against prepubescent children had an average IQ of 90 while those who had offended against adults had an average IQ of 98. This was a highly significant difference but, as can be seen, the average IQ of those with a pedophilic interest was well above the cut-off for intellectual disability. In addition to average IQ, Cantor et al. (2004) also reported the standard deviations within each group. If there were more individuals in the range of intellectual disability (IQ<75) in the group who offended against prepubescent children, then in order to have an average IQ of 90, they would have needed more individuals with above average IQ's resulting in a larger standard deviation. In fact, the standard deviation for those who offended against prepubescent children was slightly less than those who offended against adults (sd 14.6 V sd 16.6) suggesting that there was not a higher percentage of individuals with IQ<75. In a further study in this series, Blanchard and Lippa (2007) employed a larger sample from different referral sources. They argued that the IQ differences could be a result of ascertainment bias because men with intellectual disability with a sexual interest in children may be more likely to be referred by care-providers who were concerned about their welfare. They found no evidence of ascertainment bias but once again found that while offenders against children had a lower IQ than offenders against adults, both groups fell in the normal range (IQ 90 v 100).

In a direct comparison, Rice et al. (2008) compared 69 sex offenders with intellectual disability and 69 control sex offender participants without intellectual disability. These researchers found that the offenders with intellectual disability had a higher rate of pedophilic interest than the control group but were no more likely than the comparison offenders to exhibit preferences for extremely coercive sex with children or to exhibit deviant adult activity preferences, nor were they more likely to reoffend. Therefore, while this study provided some evidence for an increase in pedophilic interest among sex offenders with intellectual disability, there was no evidence for an interest in coercive or deviant adult sexual interests. This latter finding was also reported by Day (1994) in his study of 47 men with intellectual disability (average IQ 60). They had committed 191 sexual offenses and acts of ISB but violence was used in only 3.6% of cases. In terms of offense type, 54% had committed offenses against both adults and children. Day (1994) concluded " that these findings "suggest that circumstances and opportunity, rather than sexual preference....., are the overriding factors in the choice of victim and type of offence committed in the vast majority of cases" (p. 637).

Langevan and Curnoe (2008) reported on 2286 male sex offenders referred to a university hospital and private clinic over a period of 39 years. Over half had a full intellectual assessment using a version of the WAIS and all participants had further assessments of learning disability. Across this population, there was no increase in the level of intellectual disability (2.4%) or borderline intelligence (7.2%) compared to the proportion expected in the general population. However, the rate of broadly defined learning disability including a heterogeneous group who had significant difficulties in speaking, reading, writing, reasoning, and mathematical abilities and organic disorders were recorded at a much higher rate (31%) than would be expected in the general population. Langevin and Curnoe (2008) also compared offense type in those with and without intellectual disability and found no differences. In particular, they found no increase in offenses against children. Summarizing their research, Blanchard and Lippa (2007) noted the small effect sizes and wrote "the statistical relations of IQ ... to paedophilia, although valuable as potential clues to the aetiology of this disorder, are far too small to permit these variables to be used as diagnostic indicators" (p 308).

As indicated above, phallometric measures have been used with this population by both the Blanchard research group and the Harris and Rice research group. Both of these research groups have found a small but consistent statistical effect size in that sex offenders with intellectual disability are more likely to have a sexual interest in prepubescent children and male children. Use of phallometric assessment has been useful as demonstrated by Reyes et al. (2006) when they presented 10 cases. The 10 cases were numbered from 1 to 47 suggesting that they had been picked specifically for illustration. They found that four cases showed specific deviant arousal, two cases were non-specific, and four cases showed arousal to adult stimuli. There are, however, very few studies that employ phallometric assessment in men with intellectual disability and caution should be employed due to limited experience with PTT in this population. Even strong proponents of phallometry (Harris & Rice, 2006) have recommended that phallometric testing should be used only in conjunction with a range of other assessments such as risk assessments.

Evaluating Level of Evidence

Much of what is known about the problematic sexual behaviors of people with intellectual disabilities is gained from clinical profiles (Griffiths et al., 2004). The diagnostic research in this area is based primarily on expert opinion, case file reviews and small clinical examples. Similarly, there is a growing body of clinical experience from specialized treatment providers who report that sex offenders with intellectual disabilities, particularly those individuals who were mildly and moderately intellectually disabled, have been surprisingly responsive to treatment (Lackey & Knopp, 1989). While there have been reports of minimal empirical demonstration of the treatment effectiveness with this population (Griffiths et al., 2004), some clinics have reported success rates at least as high as for sex offenders without intellectual disabilities (Fedoroff & Richards, 2010; Fedoroff & Richards, 2013)

Adults with Moderate Intellectual Disability

Day (1997) reviewed clinical records to find that persons with intellectual disabilities display a full range of deviant sexual behavior (i.e., fetishes to pedophilia) similar to that of the nondisabled population. Among 47 male sex offenders he found that the majority of offenses were committed by persons with mild or borderline intellectual ability, who showed a "high incidence of adjustment problems in school, delinquency, other behavior problems, psychiatric illness, organic brain damage, family psychology and psychosocial deprivation" (p. 279). However, he also found a higher incidence of nuisance and less serious crimes, less specificity for age and gender of victim, of offense type, with victims more often female under the age of 16, and offenses against adult women in the course of relationships to be rare.

Day (1997) noted that persons who commit a range of offenses, which may also include sexual offenses, are often higher functioning persons with intellectual disabilities (without associated psychopathology, brain damage, or generalized problem behaviors). This group commits less serious offences and is less specific in choice of offense behavior or victim then nondisabled offenders. Offenders in this group are typically shy, lacking sexual knowledge or experience, and often are from "sexually repressive" environments (Day, 1997).

Adults with Severe or Profound Intellectual Disability

There is no doubt that paraphilic-like behaviors can occur in individuals with severe and profound intellectual disabilities. Stripping (indecent exposure), sexual interference, sexual assault, and masturbation in public places may all be witnessed in establishments such as group homes for individuals with severe and profound intellectual disabilities. However, before diagnosing these as sexual or paraphilic disorders, it is important to consider three broad contexts for the sexualized or apparently sexualized behavior.

First, some sexual behaviors occur because the individuals involved simply do not understand the rules and laws governing those behaviors. For example, a man who has severe or profound intellectual disability might sexually assault a woman in the group home where they live simply because he wants to and has the opportunity, without having any understanding of the need for consent in sexual relationships. Even after issues of consent are explained to him, he may not understand what consent means or how it applies to him. Therefore, he might simply do it again the following week when he gets the opportunity. The same might happen in the case of a woman with severe or profound intellectual disability although it may be less likely. Even when it is explained to these individuals that non-consensual sex is wrong, they may not understand why it is wrong since issues of consent require considerable perspective taking abilities. The person who is perpetrating the sexual act must understand that consent requires the other person to have a similar desire to engage in sexual activity. Similar arguments are true for public masturbation. Some individuals might masturbate frequently in the dayroom of their home but when told that it is wrong simply do not understand why.

Secondly, there is no theoretical reason why a few men with severe or profound intellectual disability cannot have normal as well as aberrant sexual preferences, just like any other group of men. In the same way that some men of average ability have sexual preferences for children, so some men with severe or profound intellectual disabilities may have sexual interests in children. Quinsey (2003) gathered evidence to argue for the biological basis of certain aberrant sexual interests. His analysis implied there are universal biological principles that apply equally to people with and without intellectual disability that can result in problematic sexual interests and behaviors. There are no documented examples of men with severe/profound intellectual disability having a sexual preference for children, but there is no theoretical reason why this should not be the case. It may be more difficult for such individuals to organize their sexual feelings and direct them in a focused manner. Also, they are far less likely to have the opportunity to have unsupervised contact with children since they are more likely to live in group homes or with care-providers. They are therefore less likely to learn that their sexual feelings are towards children. Also, they are more likely to be monitored during the day so if they did make any advance towards a child, they would be redirected.

Finally, there are a number of behaviors that might appear to be paraphilic but, as already discussed in the sections on behavioral phenotypes and genetic disorders, may be non-sexually motivated self-stimulatory challenging behavior. Behaviors such as anal probing and vaginal or penile stimulation may fall into these categories. It is important to rule out medical diseases such as urinary tract infections that may contribute to self-stimulation, especially in people who are unable to verbalize their discomfort or who misattribute pain from disease in another area to their genitals. Even if the discomfort began due to a medical illness, genital stimulation may become a self-soothing mechanism that persists after the illness is treated. A common, and non-pathologic example, of this is using masturbation as an aid to sleep after a period of insomnia.

Children and Adolescents with Intellectual Disability

According to the DSM-5, the minimum age for a diagnosis of a paraphilia vary by type as summarized in Table A.

Table A

DSM-5 Paraphilia	Minimum age for diagnosis (years)
Voyeuristic Disorder (302.82)	18
Exhibitionistic Disorder (302.4)	No minimum age
Frotteuristic Disorder (302.89)	No minimum age
Sexual Masochism Disorder (302.83)	No minimum age
Sexual Sadism Disorder (302.84)	No minimum age

Table A (continued)

DSM-5 Paraphilia	Minimum age for diagnosis (years)
Pedophilic Disorder (302.2)	16 and at least 5 years older than the child unless the child is 12 or 13 (then the person can be in "late adolescence" and still NOT meet diagnostic criteria for pedophilia
Fetishistic disorder (302.81)	No minimum age
Transvestic Disorder (302.3)	No minimum age
Other specified disorder (302.89)	Age unspecified
Unspecified Paraphilic Disorder (302.9)	Age unspecified

While there are only two DSM-5 paraphilic disorders with specified minimum ages, diagnosis of paraphilia is not typically made in children. Care needs to be taken to apply the same standards of judging exploratory and reactive sexual behavior in children (see Johnson, 1993). It is important to be cautious about inadvertently stereotyping people with disabilites as "childlike" and thereby overlooking more typical factors: For example, a child with autism was placed on Depo medroxyprogesterone acetate (an injected antiandrogen) because he touched the genital area of young girls and teachers, despite repeated verbal correction to the contrary. The behavior could have many causes, not necessarily indicating a paraphilic disorder. For example, it could be a sign of bipolar disorder or a behaviorally motivated wish for attention or escape from an unwanted task. Or it could be a reaction to an abusive sexual experience or exposure to a sexually stimulating event that the child was not able to integrate due to age or disability. The type of the behavior would not necessarily provide sufficient evidence to establish the diagnosis of a paraphilia without further assessment. It is always more difficult to confidently and correctly diagnose a child, especially if the child is nonverbal and/or intellectually disabled. It is recommended that diagnoses of paraphilias in children always be provisional. Treatment of children with anti-androgens should be avoided due to significant side effects, including interference with growth and physical maturation.

Maltreatment of children with disabilities is 1.5 – 10 times more frequent than the rates for children without disabilities (Sobsey & Doe, 1991; Sobsey & Varnhagen, 1991). The sexual victimization experiences often manifest themselves in severe behavioral problems. These experiences may be exhibited as seductive, promiscuous, and, at times, sexually aggressive behaviors (Cox-Lindenbaum, 1994). Over the past few years research has linked the experience of prior sexual abuse with increased sexualized behavior (Browne & Finkelhor, 1986; Cosentino, Meyer-Bahlburg, Albert, Weinberg & Gaines; 1995; Cunningham & McFarlane, 1991). Gale and colleagues (1988) found that 41% of sexually abused children under age seven displayed sexually inappropriate behaviors. Ryan (1997) states it is the relationship and interaction that define sexual abuse rather than isolated behavior out of context.

Much of the literature lacks congruence regarding what to call sexualized behavior in children. Cunningham and McFarlane (1991, 1996) call children who engage in sexual behaviors as "abuse-reactive"; Frederick and Luecke (1988) refer to them as "sexually aggressive or reactive"; Gil and Johnson (1993) call them "sexualized children," and Cunningham and McFarlane (1991) refer to them as "children who molest." Children and young people who manifest problematic sexual behaviors are not a uniform group because sexually abusive behavior by children is a behavior and not a diagnosis. The world has difficulty understanding children in this group, and when applied to children with disabilities, may even deny their existence (Johnson, 1993).

It is important to separate developmentally appropriate behaviors from those that are pathologic (Gil, 1993 a, 1993b; Johnson 1993). Guidelines for distinguishing age-appropriate from problematic behaviors have been provided by a number of authors (Johnson 1993; Ryan, 1991, Sgroi, Bunk & Wabrek, 1998). A child with sexualized behaviors is described as one who initiates sexual behavior in a manipulative or coercive way.

Etiology of sexualized behaviors in children with intellectual disabilities is similar to that of children without disabilities, but risk factors for dysfunction may be more apparent. For example, biological factors have been postulated as being causative in the development of sexual interest patterns. Becker, Cunningham-Rathner and Kaplan (1987) propose that sexually abusive behavior by children and juveniles results from a combination of individual characteristics (poor impulse control, history of victimization, lack of social interactional skills) and family variables such as poor bonding and attachment, domestic violence, child maltreatment, lack of boundaries, and lack of knowledge about appropriate interpersonal boundaries. These factors coupled with additional factors such as vulnerabilities presented by the disability itself, reliance on caretakers, immobility, and inability to communicate effectively, all place the child with a disability at higher risk. For example, transmission of values, attitudes, and feelings that are sexually positive may not be or communicated with children with intellectual disabilities in a manner in which information can be integrated, shared, and practiced.

Research regarding appropriate assessment, diagnosis, and treatment is limited in the area of paraphilic behaviors in children and is almost nonexistent in children with intellectual disabilities. Adaptations for treatment are indicated such as accommodations for verbal deficits and hyperactivity. It is important to note that children with disabilities are often excluded from treatment opportunities because they are seen as "disruptive" to the process of treatment, especially group therapy. The essential concern should be provision of necessary treatment in a manner that adapts to the needs of the child. It is important to note that sexualized behavior in children and adolescents might be secondary to sexual abuse. The sexualized behavior may be a sign of posttraumatic stress disorder which "can occur at any time after the first year of life" (American Psychiatric Association, 2013, p. 276).

Adolescent sex offenders who have an intellectual disability were largely ignored in research or intervention until recent years (Ross & Loss, 1991; Timms & Goreczny, 2002). However, there are many similarities between adolescent sex offenders with intellectual disabilities and those without. Both populations have a lack of fully developed social and sexual skills and cognitive processing. They may also have diminished self-esteem, poor empathy, and problems with assertiveness and impulse control (Swartz & Masters, 1983 or Haaven, Little, & Petre-Miller, 1990). However, Lane (1991) suggests that adolescent sexual offenders with intellectual disabilities may appear to be more opportunistic because of their comparative lack of control over their environment, lack of power, and a pattern of being concrete and rigid in their thinking. They are also more likely to have been victims. They tend to be unsophisticated in their "grooming" of victims (Timms & Goreczny, 2002). They are more likely to assault victims who are known, thereby limiting the range and diversity of their victims (Lane, 1991).

Timms and Goreczny (2002) suggest that by treating the causes of sexual offending behavior in people with intellectual disabilities during adolescence, there is an increased potential to prevent the paraphilia from developing. Haaven et al. (1990) asserts, based on their experience, that while persons with intellectual disabilities may cling to their cognitive distortions longer, when change occurs it is authentic.

Summary of Limitations in Applying the DSM5 Criteria to People with Intellectual Disabilities

The DSM-5 has widened the criteria that define paraphilias, thereby making it easier to be labeled as having a paraphilia. This is due to the fact that a paraphilia can now be "ascertained" or diagnosed. The former refers to a situation in which the clinician believes the person meets the Category A criteria for a paraphilia but not the Category B criteria. This means the new DSM-5 criteria are more sensitive (will include more true positives) but less specific (will include more false positives). This is of particular concern in the case of people with intellectual disabilities because they are already prone to fall into the false positive group (Griffiths, Hingsburger, Hoath, & Ioannou, 2013). A major problem is that once a person with intellectual disability has been *ascertained* to have a paraphilia, they are likely to be treated by care providers as if they have been *diagnosed* with a paraphilic *disorder*.

The dangers of mislabeling and/or misdiagnosis of paraphilias in people with intellectual disability are also increased by the text of the DSM-5 which uses terms like "hypersexuality" which is defined in the DSM-5's glossary of technical terms as, "A stronger than usual urge to have sexual activity" (P. 823). Individuals with intellectual disability are often falsely regarded as child-like. It is therefore easy for any sexual interest described or expressed by a person with intellectual disability to be labeled as "inappropriate" or "greater than usual" because they are compared to children instead of their true peers. This may lead to false labeling of person with intellectual disability as "paraphilic."

A further criticism of the DSM-5 is its confusion of non-consensual sadism and masochism with consensual bondage, discipline, sadism, masochism (BDSM). For example, in the DSM-5's discussion of the development and course of sexual sadism disorder the text quotes figures from a survey of men and women in the BDSM community rather than surveys of people with DSM-5 sadism or masochism. Individuals who engage in bondage as part of a self-soothing ritual are in danger of being misdiagnosed and therefore harmfully labeled under the current DSM-5 diagnostic criteria.

Of all the paraphilias, pedophilia is perhaps the one with the most significant consequences in terms of the social consequences of the label. In part this is due to misconceptions, such as the one implied by the DSM-5, that pedophilia cannot go into remission or respond to treatment. The DSM-5 permits a diagnosis of pedophilic disorder on the basis of having "sexually approached multiple children on separate occasions," even if the person does not describe a persistent sexual interest in children (p. 698). This criterion is based on a single study conducted by Blanchard et al., 1999 that did not include participants with intellectual disability. This is important because, as the DSM-5 acknowledges, it is important to distinguish between a persistent pathologic sexual interest, and, "age-appropriate puberty-related sexual curiosity and activity" (p. 688). Individuals with intellectual disability may experience delays in social maturation that result in increased social interactions with children that may transform into sexual interactions for reasons that are not related to pedophilic interests. The DSM-5 recommendation that repeated incidents of apparent pedophilic sexual activity can be interpreted as indicative of true pedophilia has not been proven in the case of individuals with intellectual disability.

There is clinical evidence that the behaviors described in the DSM-5 may occur but not be accompanied by recurrent fantasies or urges (Hingsburger et al., 1991). For example, age inappropriate sexual behavior learned while being abused may seem natural to an individual who has an intellectual disability who has not been afforded appropriate sexual education, personal experience, or social opportunity to learn otherwise. Learned institutional sexual behavior, while appearing inappropriate within the context of the community, may have functionality (or learned functionality) within the culture of the institution and as such may render no distress or impairment. Thus the DSM-5 must be used with caution in light of life experiences and learning/experiential deprivation which might account for the behavior. This is especially important because of the wide-spread but unproven belief that paraphilic disorders are untreatable, especially in people with intellectual disabilities.

Etiology and Pathogenesis

Risk Factors

Biomedical and psychological vulnerabilities together with social and environmental features place people with intellectual disabilities at higher risk to engage in paraphilic behaviors when confronted by specific instigating features. These can include psychological (e.g., deficit of anger control skills, deficit of social skills, or a lack of empathy skills), biomedical (e.g., mental illness, neurological, physical problems, or behavioral phenotypes), or socio-environmental (e.g., restricted opportunity for sexual expression). These risk factors, while not instigating the behavior, may serve to create a vulnerability that influences how an individual will respond when instigating conditions are present. Knowledge of these vulnerabilities may not only assist in differential diagnosis but are also critical to designing intervention approaches that are targeted to reduce the vulnerabilities that have contributed to the behavior. It is important to note that the fact that people with intellectual disabilities have a higher risk of engaging in problematic sexual behaviors does not mean that disorders such as pedophilia are caused by intellectual disability. This is analogous to the mistake of attributing the cause of drunk driving to being an adolescent male instead of alcohol due to the fact that this group has a higher incidence of being involved in drunk-driving accidents.

Biological Factors

People with paraphilias have been reported to show a higher rate of neurological abnormalities, sex hormone abnormalities, substance abuse, problems in socialization, as well as a history of violence having been noted (Langevin, 1992). However, there is disagreement in the field with regard to the relative influence of various factors in the development of paraphilias. This becomes even more complicated in the case of sexual offending by people with intellectual disabilities. Paraphilias may reflect the interactive effects of biomedical influences (e.g., physical neurological, biochemical, sensory, or psychiatric), psychological characteristics (e.g. cognitions, motivational features, communication skills, emotional expressions, anger management skills, coping skills), and socio-environmental influences (e.g. physical environmental features and social interactions).

The brain pathology of persons who are sexually aggressive is complicated by the fact that they represent such a heterogeneous group relative to their preference of sex, age, sexual acts, and the context of the offense. Due to the heterogeneity of the population it is questionable whether brain pathology is present in all offenders (Langevin, Wortzman, Wright, & Hardy, 1988). It appears that the presence of brain damage and dysfunction in some sex offenders may serve as an underlying vulnerability that interferes with psychological and biological functioning. However, the exact nature of the influence is still speculative and under investigation.

There is a well-documented extensive history of sexual victimization of people with disabilities, resulting in a significant degree of imposed harm (Mansell & Sobsey, 2001; Mansell, Sobsey, Wilgosh, & Zawallich, 1997; Razza & Tomasulo, 2005; Sobsey, 1994). According to Razza and Tomasulo (2005) the sexual trauma experienced by an individual with intellectual disability places him or her in a particularly exaggerated state of vulnerability. A study conducted by Sequeira, Howlin, and Hollins (2003) reported a higher incidence of depression, anxiety, and sexual maladjustment in people with intellectual disability who had been sexually abused. Specifically, they found a higher incidence of symptoms consistent with post-traumatic stress disorder in people with intellectual disabilities. Sequeira et al. (2004) found a significantly higher incidence of problematic sexual behaviors in the group of people studied with intellectual disabilities. Lindsay, Steptoe, and Haut (2012) also found that sex offenders with intellectual disability had a higher rate of being sexually abused than nonsexual offenders with IDD.

Genetic Syndromes

Some genetic syndromes, that are associated with intellectual disability, are also associated with behaviors that may appear to be paraphilic. Griffiths, Richards, Fedoroff and Watson (2002) found that individuals with intellectual disabilities, including some with genetic disorders, are more likely to experience physical and medical challenges that interfere with their sexual experience. The expression of the problematic behaviors, however, may not be directly related to the disability but to an aspect of the behavioral pheonotype. For example, clinicians report that inappropriate sexual behaviors found in Autism spectrum disorder, which has a high familial loading, may be due primarily to social skills deficits. Fetal alcohol spectrum disorder (FASD) is a familial but non-genetic syndrome in which a variety of problems result from a combination of mild intellectual disability and impulse control problems. Importantly, people with FASD also have a greater likelihood of dysfunctional family problems that can contribute to problematic sexual behaviors in adulthood. Tourette's syndrome is associated with complex motor tics and compulsions to touch and swear that can become sexualized. People with William's syndrome can find themselves in trouble due to indiscriminant socialization. Smith Magenis syndrome is associated with polyembolokoilamania (stuffing of objects into bodily orifices including ears, mouth, as well as anus or vagina). These latter expressions of "orifice stuffing" are often interpreted to be a sexual act rather than a behavior associated with the syndrome, although the exact function this serves to the individual is obscure (Grifftiths, et al., 2002). It should be noted that polyembolokoilamania itself is a behavior and not a diagnosis. Determination of whether a behavior is or is not sexualized must be part of the assessment.

Psychological Factors

Risk factors associated with the development of paraphilias, such as lack of attachment, neurologic impairments, and impaired pro-social skills, are also highly associated with intellectual disabilities. People who demonstrate problematic sexual behaviors have been found to have poorer attachment bonds (Lindsay et al. (2001), family relationships and low self-esteem, greater emotional loneliness, social skills difficulty, fewer friendships and intimate relationships, and difficulties with issues of power, and inhibition (Marshall, Hudson, & Hodkinson, 1993). People with intellectual disabilities may also be more vulnerable than nondisabled people to these psychological factors all of which may be associated with counterfeit deviance.

Psychological factors that may contribute to counterfeit deviance include but are not limited to impaired social skills and sociosexual knowledge, institutional learning, and communication problems. The lack of typical sexual learning and the nature of sexual and relationship experiences generally afforded by society to persons with intellectual disabilities have also been found to correlate with expressions of sexuality that were problematic and sometimes labeled deviant. People with intellectual disabilities are more likely to experience repressive, abusive, and culturally-distorted sexual learning, which may contribute to problematic expressions of their sexuality.

Sexual abuse of persons with intellectual disabilities is extremely prevalent. It has been suggested that 88% of persons with intellectual disabilities have been sexually exploited (Hill, 1987). Doucette (1986) states that although exact prevalence is difficult to determine due to problems in reporting and differences in methodology and definitions used, Sobsey (1994) found that persons with intellectual disabilities are at least one and one half times more at risk for sexual abuse than other members of society.

Early sexual victimization may condition some individuals to respond sexually to certain individuals or situations reminiscent of early experiences of abuse. The relationship between childhood violence and trauma and the development of sexual offending behavior is called the *traumagentic model*. Finkelhor and his associates (1986) have suggested that some sexual offenders may be motivated to recapitulate their own sexual victimization and that the content of the sexual fantasies of repeat offenders may be the result of "protracted sexually deviant and pathological experience first sustained at a young age" (Prentky & Burgess, 1991, p.241). According to the *traumagenic model*, for some sex offenders there is a correlation between the age of onset of fantasy-driven sexual aggression and the age of their own abuse, the duration of their abuse, and the level of invasiveness of the abuse (Pithers, 1993). However, as noted, the correlation between age of victim and victimizer is not high and the theory has been challenged (Fedoroff & Pinkus, 1996).

Griffiths (as cited in G. Allan Roeher Institute, 1988), in a survey of a sample of individuals participating in a clinic for sexual offenders with intellectual disabilities, reported that all individuals receiving treatment had past childhood experiences of abuse. Although this 100% rate was not present in subsequent samples, the high rates of abuse experienced by persons with intellectual disabilities who were referred for sexual offending behavior did continue. Similarly, Hingsburger (1987) reported that persons with intellectual disabilities with histories of institutionalization had experienced molestation or coercive sexual activity while in the institution and that many of these individuals later committed similar acts against individuals who were younger and more vulnerable.

In two empirical studies on this topic, Lindsay et al. (2001) reviewed the patterns of physical and sexual abuse in both offenders with intellectual disabilities who offend sexually (46) and non-sexually (48). They conducted comprehensive assessments over a period of a year regarding their experiences of childhood sexual and physical abuse. They found that 37% of the sexual offenders and 12.7% of the nonsexual offenders had been sexually abused, whereas 13% of the sexual offenders and 33% of the nonsexual offenders had experienced physical abuse. They concluded that sexual abuse in childhood was a significant variable in the history of sexual offenders, while physical abuse was more prevalent in the history of nonsexual offenders, but that a history of abuse does not invariably lead to offending behavior nor is it sufficient as an explanation of the abuse-offense cycle. These findings were replicated by Lindsay et al. (2012) with a larger sample. Hayes (2010) looked at the developmental pathways for sex offenders who have intellectual disabilities from childhood experiences to adult sex crimes and concluded that these pathways can be conceptualized as a chain of events revealed over time and influenced by either single or multiple factors. In other words, childhood sexual abuse, neglect, and attachment problems frequently play a synergistic role in the development and perpetuation of problematic sexual behaviors in this population, as they may in the offenders without intellectual disabilities. However, the higher rates of abuse, the lack of identification of abuse, and the lack of therapeutic intervention for abuse (Sobsey, 1994) make this an area that should be routinely explored with persons with intellectual disability.

Most individuals who have experienced childhood sexual abuse do not develop pedophilia; conversely most people who sexually offend against children were not sexually abused. Nonetheless, data do indicate that for some individuals the *traumagenic* experience may have "conditioned" certain stimuli to be sexually arousing (i.e., children of a certain age or specific situations). People with intellectual disabilities may be more likely to relive the traumagenic experience because their abuse is often repeated, it is often not addressed nor treated the individual is less likely to be able to escape the conditions, environment or victimizer associated with the event. In addition, there are less likely to be pro-social sexual experiences to replace the initial experiences. Thus to the extent that the abuse is currently affecting the problematic sexual behaviors, it can be said that the abuse affects the current issues.

People with intellectual disabilities may lack appropriate sociosexual knowledge. This could be directly related to behavioral phenotypes (Griffiths et al., 2002), lack of sociosexual education or social skills training (Griffithset al., 1989) or the result of exposure to environments where the sociosexual culture has promoted behaviors that may be inappropriate (Hingsburger, 1992). For example, a young man who has always lived in an institutional environment where privacy was not respected nor taught is now living in the community. He drops his pants when he needs to go to the bathroom to signal his discomfort; however he does so whether in private or public. This behavior could be misinterpreted as exhibitionistic disorder rather than a lack of information about how to behave in public.

These psychological risks can be even more apparent in individuals with more severe intellectual disabilities who may lack traditional communication skills or language to explain various types of distress or needs. This lack of communication could also lead to a misdiagnosis of a paraphilic disorder. For example, a woman with severe intellectual disabilities is experiencing distress due to vaginitis or a yeast infection. Without a means to communicate this distress to someone else she attempts to insert an object to scratch the itch or rubs up against objects or people. This could easily be misinterpreted as exhibitionistic disorder or frotteuristic disorder.

Socioenvironmental Risk Factors

Edgerton (1973) suggested that people with intellectual disabilities do not tend to demonstrate any more sexually inappropriate behaviors than non-disabled persons if they are provided a normative learning experience. In a discursive summary of the research literature on sexual aggression and those with an intellectual disability, Griffiths (2002) presented research both from the disability and the sex offender fields to demonstrate the potential relationship between known vulnerabilities for the development of sexual offending behavior and the life experiences that are afforded most people with intellectual disabilities. It is not uncommon for adolescent boys with intellectual disabilities to grow up in a non-familial, congregated environment where interpersonal violence and aggression is present (Grifftths, 2002; Hayes, 2010; Lindsay, 2002). All in all, it should be highlighted that the environmental factors in childhood and adolescence are potential risk factors for sexually aggressive and offending behaviors by individuals with intellectual disabilities.

In many environments that support persons with intellectual disabilities, consensual sexual activity may never have been taught, made available to, or permitted. In the environments in which most individuals with intellectual disabilities live, sexual activity is generally severely restricted or punished. Day (1997) has suggested that the high rates of sexual offense behavior committed by persons with intellectual disabilities may be a reflection of the generally repressive and restrictive attitudes toward the sexuality of persons with disabilities.

The restrictive nature of the environment can directly influence the development of problematic sexual behaviors in the form of erotophobia or institutionalized sexual behavior.

E*rotophobia:* Hingsburger (1992) suggested that the sexual experiences of individuals with intellectual disabilities may have been so suppressed, controlled, or punished that individuals may be conditioned to have a negative reaction to anything sexual. Symptoms of this *erotophobic* behavior include fear of the person's own genitals or sexual response, a negative reaction to any discussion, pictures ,or act involving sexual things, including denial and anger over their own developing sexuality, self-punishment following sexual behavior, and a conspiracy of denial (Hingsburger, 1992). Thus individuals with intellectual disabilities may experience differential conditioning of their sexuality as a result of punishment of the normal intellectual processing of their sexuality. This may alter their responses to the instigating factors for normal sexual experiences. In some cases the person may shift to response patterns that may appear abnormal. In addition, the erotophobia may alter an individual's response to interviewing and phallometric testing, which may account for the differential patterns of some persons with intellectual disabilities observed by Murphy et al. (1983).

Institutionalized Sexual Behavior: Many agencies still hold written or unwritten policies that fail to recognize the sexuality of the persons they serve or that prohibit and even punish sexual expression, appropriate or inappropriate, consenting or not. Consequently, there is no differential response for individuals who engage in consenting appropriate sexual expression from those who engage in coercive non-consensual expression. The only difference pragmatically is that inappropriate or non-consenting sexual behavior may have less of a probability of being detected by staff.

Application of Criteria

Although it is not suggested that the criteria for paraphilia be modified, several cautionary notes have been included to ensure that clinicians can rule out the rival hypothesis of counterfeit deviance or behaviors that are syndromicly related rather than sexually related. It should be noted that the recommended annotations are based on acceptance of the DSM-5 diagnostic criteria which themselves are deserving of many more criticisms that are listed here.

For further discussion see Fedoroff (2011).

Voyeuristic Disorder

DSM-5 Diagnostic Criteria	Applying Criteria for Persons With Mild And Moderate Intellectual Disability	Applying Criteria for Persons With Severe And Profound Intellectual Disability
A. Over a period of at least 6 months, recurrent and intense sexual arousal from observing an unsuspecting person who is naked, in the process of disrobing, or engaging in sexual activity, as manifested by fantasies, urges, or behaviors. B. The individual has acted on these sexual urges with a nonconsenting person, or the sexual urges or fantasies cause clinically significant distress or impairment in social, occupational, or other important areas of functioning. C. The individual experiencing the arousal and/or acting on the urges is at least 18 years of age.	**Cautionary note:** Rule out that the behavior is not due to lack of knowledge regarding private/ public or social norms. It may represent learned institutional behavior or curiosity.	**Note:** Sexually inappropriate behavior in this population is better understood as examples of counterfeit deviance since clearly linking the interest/behavior to a sexual motivation can be a stretch.

Exhibitionistic Disorder

DSM-5 Diagnostic Criteria	Applying Criteria for Persons With Mild And Moderate Intellectual Disability	Applying Criteria for Persons With Severe And Profound Intellectual Disability
A. Over a period of at least 6 months, recurrent and intense sexual arousal from the exposure of one's genitals to an unsuspecting person, as manifested by fantasies, urges, or behaviors. B. The individual has acted on these sexual urges with a nonconsenting person, or the sexual urges or fantasies cause clinically significant distress or impairment in social, occupational, or other important areas of functioning.	**Cautionary note:** Exhibitionism to be distinguished from exposure due to a lack of socio-sexual knowledge regarding public-private, institutionally learned behavior, abuse learned behavior, or a response to a medical discomfort (i.e., vaginal itch), or syndrome (i.e., disrobing characteristic of syndromes such as Smith Magenis or Tourette's). Public exposure in a person with intellectual disability when in the presence of an arousing stimuli may also be due to lack of access to sexual stimuli (i.e., erotica) combined with cognitive challenges in maintaining sexual fantasy without the presence of arousing stimuli (i.e., in private masturbation).	**Note:** Sexually inappropriate behavior in this population is better understood as examples of counterfeit deviance since clearly linking the interest/ behavior to a sexual motivation can be a stretch.

Frotteuristic Disorder

DSM-5 criteria for frotteuristic disorder mirror those of exhibitionist disorder, except they relate to touching or rubbing against a nonconsenting person.

Sexual Masochism Disorder

DSM-5 criteria for sexual masochism disorder mirror those of exhibitionist disorder, except they relate to the act of being humiliated, beaten, bound, or otherwise made to suffer. It is important to distinguish this disorder from BDSM.

Sexual Sadism Disorder

DSM-5 criteria for sexual sadism disorder mirror those of exhibitionist disorder, except they relate to the physical or psychological suffering of another person. It is important to distinguish this disorder from BDSM.

Pedophilic Disorder

DSM-5 Diagnostic Criteria	Applying Criteria for Persons With Mild And Moderate Intellectual Disability	Applying Criteria for Persons With Severe And Profound Intellectual Disability
A. Over a period of at least 6 months, recurrent, intense sexually arousing fantasies, sexual urges, or behaviors involving sexual activity with a prepubescent child or children (generally age 13 years or younger). B. The individual has acted on these sexual urges, or the sexual urges or fantasies cause marked distress or interpersonal difficulty. C. The individual is at least age 16 years and at least 5 years older than the child or children in Criterion A. **Note:** Do not include an individual in late adolescence involved in an ongoing sexual relationship with a 12- or 13-year-old	**Cautionary note:** A person with an intellectual disability may engage in a behavior that appears paraphilic but may not represent sexual preference rather than a history of punishment , and subsequent lack of education and restriction to age inappropriate interactions. Although this may occur in persons without intellectual disabilities, the higher rates of abuse and the abnormal learning and living environments of some individuals (i.e., institutionalization) make this a special consideration for this population. **Cautionary note:** Assessment of the individual's ability to identify the ages of self, child, and an appropriate sexual partner is important to determine if the behavior is complicated by challenges in age discrimination.	**Note:** Sexually inappropriate behavior in this population is better understood as examples of counterfeit deviance since clearly linking the interest/behavior to a sexual motivation can be a stretch.

Fetishistic Disorder

DSM-5 Diagnostic Criteria	Applying Criteria for Persons With Mild And Moderate Intellectual Disability	Applying Criteria for Persons With Severe And Profound Intellectual Disability
A. Over a period of at least 6 months, recurrent and intense sexual arousal from either the use of nonliving objects or a highly specific focus on nongenital body part(s), as manifested by fantasies, urges, or behaviors. B. The fantasies, sexual urges, or behaviors cause clinically significant distress or impairment in social, occupational, or other important areas of functioning. C. The fetish objects are not limited to articles of clothing used in cross-dressing (as in transvestic disorder) or devices specifically designed for the purpose of tactile genital stimulation (e.g., vibrator).	Cautionary note: Behaviors to be distinguished from object insertion in orifice (including genitalia) could be symptomatic of Smith-Magenis syndrome or physical distress related to a medical disorder (i.e., vaginitis).	**Note:** Sexually inappropriate behavior among this population is better understood as examples of counterfeit deviance since clearly linking the interest/behavior to a sexual motivation is a stretch.

Transvestic Disorder

DSM-5 criteria for transvestic disorder mirror those of exhibitionist disorder, except they relate to cross-dressing, do not involve criminal acts, or non-consent.

Other Specified Paraphilic Disorder

Unspecified Paraphilic Disorder

DSM-5 also provides options for other specified paraphilic disorder and for unspecified paraphilic disorder.

References

Abel, G.G., Becker, J.V. & Cunningham-Rathner, J. (1984). Compliance, consent and cognition in sex between children and adults. *International Journal of Law and Psychiatry, 7,* 89-103.

Abel, G.G. & Rouleau, J. (1990). The nature and extent of sexual assault. In W.L. Marshall, D.R. Laws, & H.E. Barbaree (Eds.), *Handbook of sexual assault* (pp. 9-21). New York: Plenum Press.

Allen, D., & Davis, D. (2007). Challenging behavior and psychiatric disorders in intellectual Disabilities. *Current Opinion in Psychiatry, 20,* 450-455.

American Psychiatric Association. (2000). *Diagnostic and statistical manual of mental disorders,* (4th ed., text rev.). Washington, DC: Self.

American Psychiatric Association, (2013). *Diagnostic and statistical manual of mental disorders* (5th ed.). Washington, DC: American Psychiatric Publishing.

Andrews, D.A., & Bonta, J. (2007). *The psychology of criminal conduct* (4th ed.). Cincinnati, OH: Anderson.

Becker, J., Cunningham-Rathner, J., & Kaplan, M. (1987). Adolescent sex offenders: demographics, criminal and sexual histories, and recommendations for reducing future offenses. *Journal of Interpersonal Violence, 1,* 431-445.

Blacker, J., Beck, A.R., Wicox, D., & Boer, D.F. (2011). The assessment of dynamic risk and recidivism in a sample of special needs sex offenders. *Psychology, Criminology and Law, 17,* 75-92.

Blanchard R., & Lippa, R.A. (2007). Birth order, sibling sex ratio, handedness and sexual orientation of male and female participants in a BBC internet research project. *Archives of Sexual Behaviour, 36,* 163-176.

Blanchard, R., Watson, M.S., Choy, A., Dickey, R., Klassen, P., Kuban, M., & Ferren, D.J. (1999). Pedophiles: Mental retardation, maternal age, and sexual orientation. *Archives of Sexual Behavior, 28,* 111-127.

Brown, B.S., & Courtless, R.F. (1971). *Mentally retarded offender.* Washington, D.C.: National Institute of Mental Health, Center for Studies of Crime and Delinquency.

Brown, A. & Finkelhor, D. (1986). Impact of child sexual abuse. A review of the research. *Psychological Bulletin, 99,* 66-77.

Brown, H. & Stein, J. (1997). Sexual abuse perpetrated by men with intellectual disabilities: A comparative study. *Journal of Intellectual Disabilities Research, 41(Pt 3),* 215-224.

Browne, A., & Finkelhor, D. (1986). Impact of child sexual abuse. A review of the research. *Psychological Bulletin, 99,* 66-77.

Boer, D. P., Tough, S., & Haaven, J. (2004). Assessment of risk manageability of intellectually disabled sex offenders. *Journal of Applied Research in Intellectual Disabilities, 17*(4), 275-283. doi:10.1111/j.1468-3148.2004.00214.x

Broxholme, S.L. & Lindsay, W. (2003). Development of questionnaire on cognitions related to sex offending. *Journal of Intellectual Disability Research, 47,* 472-482.

Buhrich, N., Barr, R., & Lam-Po-Tang, P.R. (1978). Two transsexuals with 47-XYY karyotype. *British Journal of Psychiatry, 133,* 77-81.

Campo, J., Nijman, H., Merkelbach, H., Evers, C. (2003). Psychiatric co-morbidity of gender identity disorders: A survey among Dutch psychiatrists. *American Journal of Psychiatry,160,* 1332-1336.

Cantor, J.M., Blanchard, R., Chistensen, B.K., Dickey, R., Klassen, P.E., Beckstead, A.L., ... Kuban, M.E. (2004). Intelligencee, memory and handedness in pedophilia. *Neuropsychology, 18*(1), 2-14.

Corbett, K., Shurberg Klein, S., & Bregante, J. L. (1989). The role of sexuality and sex equity in the education of disabled women. *Peabody Journal of Education,* 64(4), 198-212.

Cosentino, C. E., Meyer-Bahlburg, H. F. L., Albert, J. L., Weinberg, S.L., & Gaines, R. (1995). Sexual behavior problems and psychopathology symptoms in sexually abused girls. *Journal of the American Academy of Child and Adolescent Psychiatry, 34(3),* 1033-1042.

Cox-Lindenbaum, D. (1998). Children who molest children: Youth in treatment. International NADD Conference. Montreal, QC, Canada.

Craig, L.A. (2010). Controversies in assessing risk and deviancy in sex offenders with intellectual disabilities. *Psychology, Crime & Law, 16*(1-2), 75-101.

Cunningham, C. & McFarlane, K. (1991). *When children molest children.* Orville, VT; Safer Society.

Cunningham, C. & McFarlane, K. (1996). *When children abuse.* Brandon, VT: Safer Society.

Day, K. (1994). Male mentally handicapped sex offenders. *British Journal of Psychiatry, 165*, 630-639.

Day, K. (1997). Clinical features and offence behavior of mentally retarded sex offenders: A review of research (pp. 95-99). In R.J. Fletcher & D. Griffiths (Eds.), *Congress Proceedings- International Congress II on the Dually Diagnosed.* New York: NADD.

Doucette, J. (1986). *Violent acts against disabled women.* Toronto: DAWN Canada.

Edgerton, R. (1973). Socio-cultural research considerations. In F.F. de la Cruz & G.G. La Veck (Eds.), *Human_sexuality and the mentally retarded* (pp. 240-249). New York: Brunner/Maze.

Fedoroff J.P. (2011 Jun) Forensic and diagnostic concerns arising from the proposed DSM-5 Criteria for sexual paraphilic disorder. *The Journal of the American Academy of Psychiatry and the Law, 39*, 238–41.

Fedoroff, J. P. (2010) Paraphilic worlds. In: S. B. Levine (Ed), *Handbook of clinical sexuality for mental health professionals* (Chapter 23, pp. 401-424). New York: Routledge.

Fedoroff, J.P. & Blanchard, R. (2000). Is sex re-assignment surgery ethical? In D. Goldbloom (Ed.), P*sychiatry rounds* (pp.1-6). Toronto: Snell Medical Communication Inc.

Fedoroff, J.P., Curry, S., & Madrigrano, G. (2002). Risk assessment for developmentally delayed child molesters. Unpublished raw data.

Fedoroff J.P. & Pinkus S. (1996). The genesis of pedophilia: testing the abuse to abuser hypothesis. *Journal of Offender Rehabilitation, 23*, 85-101.

Fedoroff, J. P. & Richards, D. A. (2010). Sexual disorders and intellectual disabilities. In S. S. B. Levine, C. B. Risen, & S. E.-A. Hohof (Eds.), *Handbook of clinical sexuality for mental health professionals* (2nd Ed) (pp. 451-468). New York: Brunner-Routledge.

Fedoroff,J.P., & Richards, D. (2013). An experiment concerning ethical issues in the care of people with intellectual disabilities and potentially problematic sexual behaviours, *Journal of Ethics in Mental Health, 7, 1-9.*

Fedoroff, J.P., Selhi, Z., Smolewska, K., Ng, E., Bradford, J.M.W. (2001) Assessment of violence and sexual ofense risk using the "VRAG" and "SORAG" in a sample of men with developmental delay and paraphilic disorders: A case-controlled study. *International Academy of Sex Research Twenty-Seventh Annual Meeting Abstracts*, 17.

Fedoroff, J. P., Selhi, Z., Smolewska, K., & Ng, E. (2001). Risk assessment for men with paraphilias and developmental delay. Poster session presented at the twenty-seventh annual meeting of International Academy of Sex Research, Montreal.

Finkelhor, D. & Associates (1986). *A sourcebook on child sexual abuse.* Beverly Hills, CA: Sage Publishing.

Frederick, W.N. & Luecke. W.J. (1988). Young school aggression. *Professional Psychological Research, 19*(2), 155-169.

G. Allan Roeher Institute (1988). *Vulnerable: Sexual abuse and people with an intellectual handicap.* Downsview, Ontario: G. Allan Roeher Institute.

Gale, J., Thompson, R.J., Moran, T., & Sack, W.H. (1988). Sexual abuse in young children: Its clinical presentation and characteristic patterns. *Child Abuse and Neglect, 12*, 163-170.

Gil, E. (1993a) Age-appropriate sex play versus problematic sexualized behaviors. In E. Gil and T. C. Johnson, *Sexualized children: Assessment and treatment of sexualized children who molest* (pp. 21-40). Rockville, MD: Launch Press.

Gil, E. (1993b). Etiological theories. In E. Gill and T. C. Johnson (Eds.), *Sexualized children: Assessment and treatment of sex-*

ualized children who molest (pp. 53-66). Rockville, MD: Launch Press.

Gil, E., & Johnson, T.C. (1993). *Sexualized children: Assessment and treatment of sexualized children who molest.* Rockville, MD: Launch Press.

Gilby,R., Wolf, L. & Goldberg, B. (1989). Mentally retarded adolescent sex offenders: A survey and pilot study. *Canadian Journal of Psychiatry, 34*, 542-548.

Green, R. (1985). Gender identity disorder in childhood and later sexual orientation: follow-up of 78 males. *American Journal of Psychiatry, 142*, 339-341.

Green, R. (1987). *"The sissy boy syndrome" and the development of homosexuality.* New Haven, CT: Yale University Press.

Green, G., Gray, S., & Willner, P. (2002). Factors association with criminal convictions of sexually inappropriate behavior in men with learning disabilities. *The Journal of Forensic Psychiatry, 13*(3), 578-607.

Griffiths, D., (1999). Sexuality and people with developmental disabilities: Mythconceptions and facts. In L. Brown, & M. Percy, (Eds.), *Developmental disabilities in Ontario.* Toronto, ON: Front Porch Publishing.

Griffiths, D. (2002). Sexual aggression. In W. I. Gardner (Ed.), *Aggression and other disruptive behavioral challenges: Biomedical and psychosocial assessment and treatment* (pp.525-398). New York: National Association for Dual Diagnosis.

Griffiths, D., & Fedoroff, P. (2008) Persons with intellectual disabilities who sexually offend. In F.M. Saleh, A.J. Grudzinskas, J.M., Bradford, & D.J. Brodsky (Eds.), *Sex offenders: Identification, risk, assessment, treatment, and legal issues (pp. 352-374).* New York: Oxford University Press.

Griffiths, D., Hingsburger, D., & Christian, R. (1985, December). Treating developmentally handicapped sexual offenders. *Psychiatric Aspects of Mental Retardation Review, 4*, 49-52.

Griffiths, D., Hingsburger, D., Hoath, J., Ioannou, S. (2013). 'Counterfeit deviance' revisited. *Journal of Applied Research in Intellectual Disabilities, 26*, 471-480.

Griffiths, D. & Lunsky, Y. (2003). *Socio-sexual knowledge and attitude assessment tool (SSKAAT-R).* Wood Dale, IL: Stoelting.

Griffiths, D., Richards, D., Fedoroff, P., & Watson, S. (2002). Sexuality and mental health issues. In D. Griffiths, C. Stavrakaki, & J. Summers (Eds). *Dual diagnosis: An introduction to the mental health needs of persons with developmental disabilities* (pp. 419-454). Sudbury, ON: Habilitative Mental Health Resource Network

Griffitths, D. M., Ware. J., Haslam, T., Richards, D., Vyrostko, B., & Stranges, S. (1996) *Healthy boundaries: Sexual abuse prevention.* Unpublished Manuscript.

Griffiths, D., Watson, S., Lewis, R., & Stoner, K. (2004). Research in sexuality and intellectual disability. In E. Emerson, C. Hatton, T. Parmenter, & T. Thompson (Eds.), *Handbook of methods of research and evaluation in intellectual disabilities (pp. 311-334).* London: Wiley.

Griffiths, D.M., Quinsey, V.L., & Hingsburger, D. (1989). *Changing inappropriate sexual behavior: A Community based approach for persons with intellectual disabilities.* Baltimore: Paul H. Brookes Publishing.

Haaven, J., & Lindsay, W. (2013). *A summary of how to score the ARMIDILO – S instrument.* Workshop presented to ATSA 32nd annual research and treatment conference, Chicago, USA.

Haaven, J. (2010). Foreword. In L.A. Craig, W.R. Lindsay, & K.D. Browne (Eds.), *Assessment and treatment of sexual offenders with intellectual disabilities: A handbook (pp. ix-xxi).* West Sussex.

Haaven, J., Little, R., & Petre-Miller, D. (1990). *Treating intellectually disabled sex offenders: A model residential program.* Orwell, VT: Safer Society Press.

Hanson, K., Sheahan, C., & VanZuylen, H. (2013). STATIC-99 and RRASOR predict recidivism among developmentally delayed sexual offenders: A cumulative meta-analysis. *Sexu-*

al Offender Treatment, 8. Sexual-Offender-treatment.org. ISSN 1862-2941

Hanson, R.K., & Bussiere, M.T. (1988). Predicting relapse: A meta-analysis of sexual offender recidivism studies. *Journal of Consulting and Clinical Psychology, 66*(7), 348-362.

Hanson, R.K., & Thornton, D. (2000). Improving risk assessments for sex offenders. A comparison of three actuarial scales. *Law and Human Behavior, 24*(1), 119-136.

Harris, G.R. & Rice, M.E. (2002). Sex offenders with developmental disabilities: Sexual preferences and risk assessment. Paper presented at the meeting of the Association for the Treatment of Sexual Abusers. Montreal.

Harris, G.T., & Rice, M.E. (2006). Treatment of psychopathy: A treatment of empirical findings. In C.J. Patrick (Ed.), *Handbook of psychopathy.* New York: Guilford Press.

Hartley, S.I., MacLean Jr., W.E., Butler, M.G., Zarcone, J., & Thompson, T. (2005).Maladaptive behaviors and risk factors among the genetic subtypes of Prader-Willi syndrome. *American Journal of Medical Genetics, 136A*, 140-145.

Hayes, S. (1991). Sex offenders. *Australian and New Zealand Journal of Developmental Disabilities, 17*(2), 221-227.

Hayes, S.C. (2010). Developmental pathways in intellectually disabled sexual offenders. In L.A. Craig, W.R. Lindsay, & K.D. Browne (Eds.), *Assessment and treatment of sexual offenders with intellectual disabilities: A handbook* (pp. 37-46). West Sussex, UK: Wiley.

Hill, D. (1987). Sexual abuse and the mentally retarded. *Child Sexual Abuse Newsletter, 6*, 4.

Hingsburger, D. (1987). Sex counselling with the developmentally handicapped: The assessment and management of seven critical problems. *Psychiatric Aspects of Mental Retardation Reviews, 6*, 41-46.

Hingsburger, D. (1992). Erotophobic behavior in people with intellectual disabilities. *The Habilitative Mental Healthcare Newsletter, 11*, 31-34.

Hingsburger, D., Griffiths, D., & Quinsey, V. (1991). Detecting counterfeit deviance: differentiating sexual deviance from sexual inappropriateness. *The Habilitative Mental Healthcare Newsletter, 10*, 51-54.

Johnson, T. C. (1993). Assessment of sexual behavior problems in preschool-aged and latency-aged children. In A. Yates (Ed.), *Sexual and gender identity disorders* (pp. 431-449), Philadelphia: W.B. Saunders Co.

Klimicki, M.R., Jenkinson, J., & Wilson, L. (1994). A study of recidivism among offenders with intellectual disabilities. *Autstralia and New Zealand Journal of Developmental Disabilities, 19*(3), 209-219.

Knight, R.A. & Prentky, R.A. (1990). Classifying sexual offenders: The development and corroboration of taxonomic models. In W.L. Marshall, D.R. Laws, & H.E. Barbaree (Eds.*), The handbook of sexual assault: Issues, theories, and treatment of the offender* (pp. 27-52). New York: Plenum Press.

Koller, R. (2000). Sexuality and adolescents with autism. *Sexuality and Disability, 18(2)*, 125-135.

Kolton, D.J.C., Boer, A., & Boer, D.P. (2001). A revision of the Abel and Becker Cognition Scale for intellectually disabled offenders. *Sexual Abuse, 13*, 217-220.

Konstantareus, M.M. & Lunsky, Y. (1997) Sociosexual knowledge, experience, attitudes and interests in individuals with autistic disorder and intellectual delay. *Journal of Autism and Intellectual Disorders, 27*, 397-413.

Lackey, L.B., & Knopp, F.H. (1989). A summary of selected notes from the working sessions of the First National Training Conference on the Assessment and Treatment of Intellectual Disabled Juvenile and Adult Sexual Offenders. In F. Knopp (Ed.), *Selected readings: Sexual offenders identified as intellectually Disabled.* Orwell, VT: Safer Society Press.

Lane, S. (1991). Special offender populations. In G. Ryan & S. Lane (Eds.), *Juvenile sexual offenders: Causes, consequences and corrections* (pp. 299-307). Lexington KY: Lexington Books.

Langevin, R. (1992). A comparison of neuroendocrine abnormalities and genetic factors in homosexuality and in pedophila. *Annals of Sex Research, 6*, 67-76.

Langevin, R., & Curnoe, S. (2008). Are the mentally retarded and learning disordered over represented among sex offenders and paraphilics? *International Journal of Offender Therapy and Comparative Criminology, 52*(4), 401-415.

Langevin, R., Wortzman, G., Wright, P., & Hardy, L. (1988). Studies of brain damage and dysfunction in sex offenders. *Annals of Sex Research, 2*, 163-179.

Leicester M. & Cooke, P. (2002). Rights not restrictions for learning disabled adults: A response to Spiecker and Steutel. *Journal of Moral Education*, 31(2); 181-187.

Lindsay, W.R. (2002). Research and literature on sex offenders with intellectual and developmental disabilities. *Journal of Intellectual Disabilities Research, 46* (Suppl. 1), 74-85.

Lindsay, W.R., Hastings, R.P., Griffiths, D. M., Hayes, S.C. (2007). Trends and challenges in forensic research on offenders with intellectual disability. *Journal of Intellectual & Developmental Disability, 32*(2): 55–6.

Lindsay, W.R., Law, J., Quinn, K., Smart, N. & Smith, A.H. (2001). A comparison of physical and sexual abuse: Histories of sexual and non-sexual offenders with intellectual disability. *Child Abuse and Neglect, 25*, 989-995.

Lindsay W.R., Steptoe L., & Haut F. (2012) The sexual and physical abuse histories of offenders with intellectual disability. *Journal of Intellectual Disability Research, 56*, 326 -31.

Lindsay, W.R., Whitefield, E., & Carson, D. (2007). An assessment of attitudes consistent with sex offending for use with offenders with intellectual disabilities. *Legal and Criminological Psychology, 12*, 55-68.

Lofthouse, R. E., Lindsay, W. R., Totsika, V., Hastings, R. P., Boer, D. P., & Haaven, J. L. (2013b). Prospective dynamic assessment of risk of sexual reoffending in individuals with an intellectual disability and a history of sexual offending behaviour. *Journal of Applied Research in Intellectual Disabilities, 26*(5), 394-403. doi:10.1111/jar.12029

Lunsky, Y., Frijters, J., Watson, S., Willison, S., & Griffiths, D. (2007). Sexual knowledge and attitudes of men with intellectual disabilities who sexually offend. Special issue on offenders with ID/DD. *Journal of Intellectual and Developmental Disabilities, 32*(2), 74-81.

MacEachron, A.E. (1979). Mentally retarded offenders: Prevalence and characteristics. *American Journal of Mental Deficiency, 84*, 165-176.

Mansell, S., & Sobsey, D. (2001). Understanding the challenges associated with the sexual abuse of people with developmental disabilities. In S. Mansell & D. Sobsey (Eds.), *Counselling people with developmental disabilities who have been sexually abused* (pp. 15-68), Kingston, NY: NADD Press.

Mansell, S., Sobsey, D., Wilgosh, L., & Zawallich, A. (1997). The sexual abuse of young people with disabilities: Treatment considerations. *International Journal for the Advancement of Counselling, 19*, 293-302.

Marshall, W.L., Hudson, S.M, & Hodkinson, S. (1993). The importance of attachment bonds in the development of juvenile sex offending. In H. E.Barbaree, W.L. Marshall, & S.M. Hudson (Eds.), *The juvenile sex offender* (pp. 164-181). New York: Guilford Press.

McGee, J., & Menolasino, F.J. (1992) The evaluation of defendants with mental retardation in the criminal justice system. In R.W. Conley, R. Luckasson, and G.N. Bouthilet (Eds.) *The criminal justice system and mental retardation: Defendants and victims* (pp. 55-78). Baltimore: Paul. H. Brookes.

Michel, A., Mormont, C., Legros, J. (2001). A psycho-endocrinological overview of transexualsim. *European Journal of Endocrinology,145*, 365-376.

Mikkelsen, E.J. & Stelk, W.J. (1999). *Criminal offenders with mental retardation.* Kingston, NY: NADD Press.

Mohr, J., Turner, R.E., & Jerry, M. (1964). *Pedophilia and exhibitionism.* Toronto: University of Toronto Press.

Money, J. (1999). *Principles of developmental sexology continuum.* Buffalo, NY, Prometheus Press.

Moschella, S. (1982). The mentally retarded offender: Law enforcement and court proceedings. In M.B. Santamour & P.S. Watson (Eds.), *The retarded offender.* New York: Praeger.

Murphy, G.H. (2003). Capacity to consent to sexual relationships in adults with learning disabilities. *Journal of Family Planning and Reproductive Health Care, 28(3)*, 148-149.

Murphy, W.D., Coleman, E.M., & Haynes, M. (1983) Treatment and evaluation issues with the mentally retarded sex offender. In J. Greer & I. Stuart (Eds.), *The sexual aggressor: Current perspectives on treatment* (pp. 22-41). New York: Van Nostrand Reinhold.

Murphy,W.D., Coleman, E.M., & Abel, G.G. (1983). Human sexuality in the mentally retarded. In J.L. Matson & F. Andrasik (Eds.), *Treatment issues and innovations in mental retardation* (pp. 581-643). New York: Plenum.

Murrey, G.J., Briggs, D., & Davis, C. Psychopathic disordered, mentally ill, and mentally handicapped offenders: A comparative study. *Medical Law Science, 32(4)*, 331-336.

Nezu, C.M., Nezu, A.M. & Dudek, J..A. (1998). A cognitive behavioral model of assessment and treatment for intellectually disabled sex offenders. *Cognitive and Behavioral Practice, 5*, 25-64.

McCabe, M.P. (1994). *Sexual knowledge, experience, feelings and needs scale for people with intellectual disability* (Sex Ken-ID) (4th ed.). Burwood, Australia: Deakin University.

McCabe, M. (1999). Sexual knowledge, experience and feelings among people with disabilities. *Sexuality and Disability, 17*, 157-170.

McCabe, M. & Cummins, R. (1996). The sexual knowledge, experience, feelings, and needs of people with mild intellectual disability. *Education and Training in Mental Retardation and Developmental Disabilities, 31(1)*, 13-21.

McCabe, M.P., Cummins, R.A., & Deeks, A.A. (1999). Construction and psychometric properties of sexuality scales: Sex knowledge, experience, and needs scales for peoplewith intellectual disabilities (SexKen-ID), people with physical disabilities (SexKen-PD), and the general population. *Research in Intellectual Disabilities, 20*, 241-254.

McCabe, M., & Schreck, A. (1992). Before sex education: An evaluation of the sexual knowledge, experience, feelings and needs of people with mild intellectual disabilities. *Australia and New Zealand Journal of Developmental Disabilities, 18*(2), 75-82.

McCarthy, M. & Thompson, D. (1998). *Sex and the 3Rs: A guide to sex education work with people with learning disabilities* (2nd ed.). Brighton: Pavillion.

Michie, A.M., Lindsay, W.R., Martin, V., & Grieve, A. (20006). A test of counterfeit deviance: A comparison of sexual knowledge in groups of sex offenders with intellectual disabilities and controls. *Sexual Abuse: A Journal of Research and Treatment, 18*(3), 271-278.

Neiderbuhl, J. M., & Morris, D. C. (1993). Sexual knowledge and the capability of persons with dual diagnoses to consent to sexual contact. *Sexuality and Disability*, 11(4), 295-307.

Pithers, W. (1993). Treatment of rapists: Reinterpretation of early outcome data and explanatory constructs to enhance therapeutic efficiency. In G. G. Nagayama Hall, R. Hirrschman, J.R., Graham & M.S. zaragoza (Eds.), *Sexual aggression: Issues in etiology, assessment and treatment* (pp. 176-196). Washington DS: Taylor & Francis.

Prentky, R.A. & Burgess, A.W. (1991). Hypothetical biological substrata of fantasy-based drive mechanisms for repetitive sexual aggression. In W. Burgess (Ed.), *Rape_and sexual assault* (pp. 235-256). New York: Gaylord.

Quinsey, V.L. (2003). The aetiology of anomalous sexual preferences in men. *Annals of the New York Academy of Sciences, 989*, 1-13.

Quinsey, V. L., Harris, G. T., Rice, M. E., & Cormier, C. A. (1998). *Violent offenders: Appraising and managing risk.* Washington DC: American Psychological Association.

Razza, N. J., & Tomasulo, D. J. (2005). *Healing trauma: The power of group treatment for people with intellectual disabilities.* Washington, DC: American Psychological Association.

Reyes, J.R., Vollmer, T.R., Sloman, K.N., Hall, A., Reed, R., Jansen, G., ... Stoutimore, M. (2006). Assessment of deviant arousal in adult male sex offenders with developmental disabilities. *Journal of Applied Behavior Analysis, 39*(2), 173-188.

Rice, M. E., Harris G., Lang, C & Chaplin T. (2008) Sexual preferences and recidivism of sex offenders with mental retardation. *Sexual Abuse: A Journal of Research and Treatment. 20*, 409-25

Ross, R. & Losss, P.A. (1991). Assessment of the juvenile sex offender. In G. Ryan & S. Lane (Eds.), *Juvenile sexual offending: Causes, consequences and corrections* (pp. 199-251). Lexington, KY: Lexington Books.

Rowe, W., & Savage, S., (1986). *Sexuality and the developmentally handicapped: A guidebook for health care professionals.* Lewiston, N.Y.: Edwin Mellen Press.

Ruiter, I. D. (2000). *Allow me. A guide to promoting communication skills in adults with developmental delays.* Toronto, Ontario: The Beacon Herald Fine Print Division.

Ryan, G. (1997). Perpetration Prevention. *Juvenile Sexual Offending* (pp. 433-454). San Francisco, CA, Jossey-Bass.

Ryan, G. (1991). Perpetration prevention. In G. D. Ryan (Ed.), *Juvenile sexualized offending* (pp. 393-408) Lexington, MA; Lexington Books.

Santamour, W., & West, B. (1978). *The mentally retarded offender and cor*rections. Washington, DC: U.S. Department of Justice.

Selling, L.S. (1939). Types of behavior manifested by feeble minded sex offenders. *Proceedings from the American Association on Mental Deficiency, 44*, 178-186.

Sequeira, H., Howlin, P., & Hollins, S. (2003). Psychological disturbance associated with sexual abuse in people with learning disabilities. *British Journal of Psychiatry, 183*, 451-456.

Sgroi, S. M., Bunk, B.S. & Wabrek, C. J. (1998). children's sexual behaviors and their relationship to abuse. In S. M. Sgroi (Ed.) *Vulnerable populations (Volume I)* (pp. 1-24). Lexington, MA: Lexington Books.

Shapiro, S. (1986). Delinquent and disturbed behavior within the field of mental deficiency. In A.V.S. deReuck & R. Porter (Eds.), *The mentally abnormal offender (pp. XX-XX).* New York: Grune & Stratton.

Snaith, R.P., Penhale, S., & Horsfield, P. (1991). Male-to-female transsexual with XYY karyotype. *Lancet, 337* (8740), 557-8.

Sobsey, D. (1994). Sexual abuse of individuals with intellectual disabilities. In A. Craft (Ed.), *Practice issues in sexuality and intellectual disability* (pp. 91-112). London, UK: Routledge.

Sobsey, D. & Varnhagen, C. (1991). Sexual abuse, assault, and exploitation of Canadians with disabilities. In C. Bagley & J. Thomlinson (Eds.), *Child sexual abuse: Critical perspectives on prevention, intervention, and treatment* (pp. 203-216). Toronto, ON: Wall & Emerson.

Sobsey, D. & Doe, T. (1991). Patterns of sexual abuse and assault. *Sexuality and Disability*, 9, 243-259.

Steiner, J. (1984) Group counselling with retarded offenders. *Social Work, 29*, 181-182.

Strong, B., DeVault, C., Sayad, B. W., Yarber, W. L. (2001). *Human sexuality: Diversity in contemporary America, 4th Edition.* USA: McGraw-Hill Publishing.

Swartz, M. & Masters, W. (1983). Conceptual factors in the treatment of paraphilias: A preliminary report. *Journal of Sexual Marital Therapy*, 9, 3-18.

Taneja, N., Ammini A.C., Mohapatra, I. and Saxena, S. (1992). A transsexual male with 47,

XYY karyotype. *British Journal of Psychiatry, 16*(1), 698-699

Timmers, R.L., Ducharme, P., & Jacob, G. (1981). Sexual knowledge, attitudes and behaviours of intellectually disabled adults living in a normalized apartment setting. *Sexuality and Disability, 4*, 27-39.

Timms, S., & Goreczny, A.J. (2002). Adolescent sex offenders with mental retardation:Literature review and assessment considerations. *Aggression and Violent Behavior, 7*, 1-19.

Tudiver, J. Broekstra, S., Josselyn, S., & Barbaree, H. (1997). *Addressing the needs of developmentally delayed sex offenders: A guide.* Ottawa, Canada: Health Canada.

Valenti-Hein & Dura, J. R. (1996). Sexuality and sexuality development. In J.W. Jacobson & J.A. Mulich (Eds.), *Manual of diagnostics and professional practice in mental retardation* (pp 301-310). Washington DC: American Psychological Association.

Ward T. & Hudson S.M. (1998). A model of the relapse process in sexual offenders. *Journal of Interpersonal Violence, 13*, 700-725.

Ward T. & Gannon T. (2006). Rehabilitation, etiology, and self-regulation: The good lives model of rehabilitation for sexual offenders. *Aggression and Violent Behavior,11*, 77–94.

Watson, S., Richards, D., Griffiths, D., Fedoroff, J.P., Miodrag, N. (2012). Genes, misunderstanding, and rights: A biopsychosocial approach to sexuality and disability. *NADD Bulletin, 15*(3), 14-16.

Watson, S. L., Griffiths, D. M., Richards, D., & Dykstra, L. (2002). Sex education. In D.M. Griffiths, Richards, D., Fedoroff, P., & Watson, S. L. (Eds.) *Ethical dilemmas: Sexuality and developmental disabilities.* Kingston, NY: NADD Press.

Wender, P.H. *ADHD: Attention-deficit hyperactivity disorder in children, adolescents, and adults.* New York: Oxford University Press.

Westheimer, R. & Lopater, S., (2002). *Sexual dysfunctions: Incompatibility, inadequacy, or just inappropriately learned responses. Human sexuality: A psychosocial perspective.* Baltimore, MD.: Lippencott Williams & Wilkens,

Whitehouse, M.A., & McCabe, M.P. (1997). Sex education programs for people with intellectual disabilities: How effective are they? *Education and Training in Mental Retardation and Intellectual Disabilities, 32*, 229-240.

Zhon, J., Hofman, M., Gooren, L., Swaab, D. (1995). A sex difference in the human brain and its relation to transsexuality. *Nature*, 378, 68-70.

Zucker, K.J. (2000). Gender identity disorder. In A.J. Sameroff, M. Lewis & S. Miller (Eds.), *Handbook of developmental psychopathology* (2nd ed.) (pp. 671-686). New York: Kluwer Academic/Plenum Publisher.

Zucker, K.J., Green, R., Coates, S. Zuger, B. Cohen-Kettenis, P.T., Zecca, G.M.,... Blanchard, R. (1997). Sibling sex ratio of boys with gender identity disorder. *Journal of Child Psychology and Psychiatry, 38*, 543-551.

APPENDIX

Alphabetical Listing of DSM-5 Diagnoses with ICD-10-CM Codes

Academic or educational problem (Z55.9)
Acculturation difficulty (Z60.3)
Acute stress disorder (F43.0)
Adjustment disorder
    With anxiety (F43.22)
    With depressed mood (F43.21)
    With disturbance of conduct (F43.24)
    With mixed anxiety and depressed mood (F43.23)
    With mixed disturbance of emotions and conduct (F43.25)
    Unspecified (F42.20)
Adult antisocial behavior (Z72.811)
Adult-onset fluency disorders (F98.5)
Adult physical abuse by nonspouse or nonpartner, confirmed
    Initial encounter (T74.11XA)
    Subsequent encounter (T74.11XD)
Adult physical abuse by nonspouse or nonpartner, suspected
    Initial encounter (T76.11XA)
    Subsequent encounter (T76.11XD)
Adult psychological abuse by nonspouse or non partner, confirmed
    Initial encounter (T74.31XA)
    Subsequent encounter (T74.31XD)
Adult psychological abuse by nonspouse or non partner, suspected
    Initial encounter (T76.31XA)
    Subsequent encounter (T76.31XD)
Adult sexual abuse by nonspouse or nonpartner, confirmed
    Initial encounter (T74.21XA)
    Subsequent encounter (T74.21XD)
Adult sexual abuse by nonspouse or nonpartner, suspected
    Initial encounter (T76.21XA)
    Subsequent encounter (T76.21XD)
Agoraphobia (F40.00)
Alcohol-induced anxiety disorder
    With mild use disorder (F10.180)
    With moderate or severe use disorder (F10.280)
    Without use disorder (F10.980)
Alcohol-induced bipolar and related disorder
    With mild use disorder (F10.14)
    With moderate or severe use disorder (F10.24)
    Without use disorder (F10.94)
Alcohol-induced depressive disorder
    With mild use disorder (F10.14)
    With moderate or severe use disorder (F10.24)
    Without use disorder (F10.94)
Alcohol-induced major neurocognitive disorder,
    Amnestic confabulatory type
    With moderate or severe use disorder (F10.26)
    Without use disorder (F10.96)
Alcohol-induced major neurocognitive disorder,
    Nonamnestic confabulatory type
    With moderate or severe use disorder (F10.27)
    Without use disorder (F10.97)

Alcohol-induced mild neurocognitive disorder
- With moderate or severe use disorder (F10.228)
- Without use disorder (F10.988)

Alcohol-induced psychotic disorder
- With mild use disorder (F10.159)
- With moderate or severe use disorder (F10.259)
- Without use disorder (F10.959)

Alcohol-induced sexual dysfunction
- With mild use disorder (F10.181)
- With moderate or severe use disorder (F10.281)
- Without use disorder (F10.981)

Alcohol-induced sleep disorder
- With mild use disorder (F10.182)
- With moderate or severe use disorder (F10.282)
- Without use disorder (F10.982)

Alcohol intoxication
- With mild use disorder (F10.129)
- With moderate or severe use disorder (F10.229)
- Without use disorder (F10.929)

Alcohol intoxication delirium
- With mild use disorder (F10.121)
- With moderate or severe use disorder (F10.221)
- Without use disorder (F10.921)

Alcohol sue disorder
- Mild (F10.10)
- Moderate (F10.20)
- Severe (F10.20)

Alcohol withdrawal
- With perceptual disturbances (F10.232)
- Without perceptual disturbances (F10.239)

Alcohol withdrawal delirium (F10.231)

Amphetamine (or other stimulant) - induced anxiety disorder
- With mild use disorder (F15.180)
- With moderate or severe use disorder (F15.280)
- Without use disorder (F15.980)

Amphetamine (or other stimulant) - induced bipolar and related disorder
- With mild use disorder (F15.14)
- With moderate or severe use disorder (F15.24)
- Without use disorder (F15.94)

Amphetamine (or other stimulant) – induced delirium (F15.921)

Amphetamine (or other stimulant) – induced depressive disorder
- With mild use disorder (F15.14)
- With moderate or severe use disorder (F15.24)
- Without use disorder (F15.94)

Amphetamine (or other stimulant) – obsessive-compulsive and related disorder
- With mild use disorder (F15.188)
- With moderate or severe use disorder (F15.288)
- Without use disorder (F15.988)

Amphetamine (or other stimulant) – psychotic disorder
- With mild use disorder (F15.159)
- With moderate or severe use disorder (F15.259)
- Without use disorder (F15.959)

Amphetamine (or other stimulant) – sexual dysfunction

With mild use disorder (F15.181)
- With moderate or severe use disorder (F15.281)
- Without use disorder (F15.981)

Amphetamine (or other stimulant) – induced sleep disorder
- With mild use disorder (F15.182)
- With moderate or severe use disorder (F15.282)
- Without use disorder (F15.982)

Amphetamine or other stimulant intoxication

Amphetamine or other stimulant intoxication with perceptual disturbances
- With mild use disorder (F15.122)
- With moderate or severe use disorder (F15.222)
- Without use disorder (F15.922)

Amphetamine or other stimulant intoxication without perceptual disturbances
- With mild use disorder (F15.129)
- With moderate or severe use disorder (F15.229)
- Without use disorder (F15.929)

Amphetamine (or other stimulant) intoxication delirium
- With mild use disorder (F15.121)
- With moderate or severe use disorder

- (F15.221)
  - Without use disorder (F15.921)
- Amphetamine or other stimulant withdrawal (F15.23)
- Amphetamine-type substance use disorder
  - Mild (F15.10)
  - Moderate (F15.20)
  - Severe (F15.20)
- Anorexia nervosa
  - Binge-eating/ purging type (F50.02)
  - Restricting type (F50.01)
- Antidepressant discontinuation syndrome
  - Initial encounter (T43.205A)
  - Sequelae (T43.205S)
  - Subsequent encounter (T43.205D)
- Antisocial personality disorder (F60.2)
- Anxiety disorder due to another medical condition (F06.4)
- Attention-deficit/hyperactivity disorder
  - Combined presentation (F90.2)
  - Predominantly hyperactive/impulsive presentation (F90.1)
  - Predominantly inattentive presentation (F90.0)
- Autism spectrum disorder (F84.0)
- Avoidant personality disorder (F60.6)
- Avoidant/ restrictive food intake disorder (F50.8)
- Binge-eating disorder (F50.8)
- Bipolar I disorder, current or most recent episode depressed
  - In full remission (F31.76)
  - In partial remission (F31.75)
  - Mild (F31.31)
  - Moderate (F31.32)
  - Severe (F31.4)
  - With psychotic features (F31.5)
  - Unspecified (F31.9)
- Bipolar I disorder, current or most recent episode hypomanic
  - In full remission (F31.0)
  - In partial remission (F31.74)
  - Unspecified (F31.9)
- Bipolar I disorder, current or most recent episode manic
  - In full remission (F31.74)
  - In partial remission (F31.73)
  - Mild (F31.11)
  - Moderate (F31.12)
  - Severe (F31.13)
  - With psychotic features (F31.2)
  - Unspecified (F31.9)
- Bipolar I disorder, current or most recent episode unspecified (F31.9)
- Bipolar II disorder (F31.81)
- Bipolar and related disorder due to another medical condition
  - With manic features (F06.33)
  - With manic- or hypomanic-like episodes (F06.33)
  - With mixed features (F06.34)
- Body dysmorphic disorder (F45.22)
- Borderline intellectual functioning (R41.83)
- Borderline personality disorder (F60.3)
- Brief psychotic disorder ((F23)
- Bulimia nervosa (F50.2)
- Caffeine-induced anxiety disorder
  - With mild use disorder (F15.180)
  - With moderate or severe use disorder (F15.280)
  - Without use disorder (F15.980)
  - Caffeine-induced sleep disorder
  - With mild use disorder (F15.182)
  - With moderate or severe use disorder (F15.282)
  - Without use disorder (F15.982)
- Caffeine intoxication (F15.929)
- Caffeine withdrawal (F15.93)
- Cannabis-induced anxiety disorder
  - With mild use disorder (F12.180)
  - With moderate or severe use disorder (F12.280)
  - Without use disorder (F12.980)
- Cannabis-induced psychotic disorder
  - With mild use disorder (F12.159)
  - With moderate or severe use disorder (F12.259)
  - Without use disorder (F12.959)
- Cannabis-induced sleep disorder
  - With mild use disorder (F12.188)
  - With moderate or severe use disorder (F12.288)
  - Without use disorder (F12.988)
- Cannabis intoxication
- Cannabis intoxication, with perceptual disturbances

With mild use disorder (F12.122)
With moderate or severe use disorder (F12.222)
Without use disorder (F12.922)

Cannabis intoxication, without perceptual disturbances
With mild use disorder (F12.129)
With moderate or severe use disorder (F12.229)
Without use disorder (F12.929)

Cannabis intoxication delirium
With mild use disorder (F12.121)
With moderate or severe use disorder (F12.221)
Without use disorder (F12.921)

Cannabis use disorder
Mild (F12.10)
Moderate (F12.20)
Severe (F12.20)

Cannabis withdrawal (F12.288)

Catatonic associated with another mental disorder (catatonia specifier) (F06.1)

Catatonic disorder due to another medical condition (F06.1)

Center Sleep Apnea
Central sleep apnea comorbid with opioid use (G47.37)
Cheyne-stokes breathing (R06.3)
Idiopathic central sleep apnea (G47.31)

Child affected by parental relationship distress (Z62.898)

Child neglect confirmed
Initial encounter (T74.02XA)
Subsequent encounter (T74.02XD)

Child neglect suspected
Initial encounter (T76.02XA)
Subsequent encounter (T76.02XD)

Child or adolescent antisocial behavior (Z72.810)

Child physical abuse, confirmed
Initial encounter (T74.12XA)
Subsequent encounter (T74.12XD)

Child physical abuse, suspected
Initial encounter (T76.12XA)
Subsequent encounter (T76.12XD)

Child psychological abuse, confirmed
Initial encounter (T74.32XA)
Subsequent encounter (T74.32XD)

Child psychological abuse, suspected
Initial encounter (T76.32XA)
Subsequent encounter (T76.32XD)

Child sexual abuse, confirmed
Initial encounter (T74.22XA)
Subsequent encounter (T74.22XD)

Child sexual abuse, suspected
Initial encounter (T76.22XA)
Subsequent encounter (T76.22XD)

Childhood-onset fluency disorder (stuttering) (F80.81)

Circadian rhythm sleep-wake disorders
Advanced sleep phase type (G47.22)
Delayed sleep phase type (G47.21)
Irregular sleep-wake type (G47.23)
Non-24-hour sleep-wake type (G47.24)
Shift work type (G47.26)
Unspecified type (G47.20)

Cocaine-induced anxiety disorder
With mild use disorder (F14.180)
With moderate or severe use disorder (F14.280)
Without use disorder (F14.980)

Cocaine-induced bipolar and related disorder
With mild use disorder (F14.14)
With moderate or severe use disorder (F14.24)
Without use disorder (F14.94)

Cocaine-induced depressive disorder
With mild use disorder (F14.14)
With moderate or severe use disorder (F14.24)
Without use disorder (F14.94)

Cocaine-induced obsessive-compulsive disorder
With mild use disorder (F14.188)
With moderate or severe use disorder (F14.288)
Without use disorder (F14.988)

Cocaine-induced psychotic disorder
With mild use disorder (F14.159)
With moderate or severe use disorder (F14.259)
Without use disorder (F14.959)

Cocaine-induced sexual dysfunction
With mild use disorder (F14.181)
With moderate or severe use disorder (F14.281)

Without use disorder (F14.981)
Cocaine-induced sleep disorder
With mild use disorder (F14.182)
With moderate or severe use disorder (F14.282)
Without use disorder (F14.982)
Cocaine intoxication
Cocaine intoxication with perceptual disturbances
With mild use disorder (F14.122)
With moderate or severe use disorder (F14.222)
Without use disorder (F14.922)
Cocaine intoxication without perceptual disturbances
With mild use disorder (F14.129)
With moderate or severe use disorder (F14.229)
Without use disorder (F14.929)
Cocaine intoxication delirium
With mild use disorder (F14.121)
With moderate or severe use disorder (F14.221)
Without use disorder (F14.921)
Cocaine use disorder
Mild (F14.10)
Moderate (F14.20)
Severe (F14.20)
Cocaine withdrawal (F14.23)
Conduct disorder
Adolescent-onset type (F91.2)
Childhood-onset type (F91.1)
Unspecified type (F91.9)
Conversion disorder (functional neurological symptom disorder)
With abnormal movement (F44.4)
With anesthesia or sensory loss (F44.6)
With attacks or seizures (F44.5)
With mixed symptoms (F44.7)
With special sensory symptoms (F44.6)
With speech symptoms (F44.4)
With swallowing symptoms (F44.4)
With weakness/paralysis (F44.4)
Conviction in civil or criminal proceedings without imprisonment (Z65.0)
Cyclothymic disorder (F34.0)
Delayed ejaculation (F52.32)
Delirium
Delirium due to another medical condition (F05)
Delirium due to multiple etiologies (F05)
Medical-induced delirium (*for ICD-10-CM codes, see specific substances)*
Substance intoxication delirium (*see specific substances for codes)*
Substance withdrawal delirium (*see specific substances for codes)*
Delusional disorder (F22)
Dependent personality disorder (F60.7)
Depersonalization/ derealization disorder (F48.1)
Depressive disorder due to another medical condition
With depressive features (F06.31)
With major depressive-like episode (F06.32)
With mixed features (F06.34)
Developmental coordination disorder (F82)
Discord with neighbor, lodger, or landlord (Z59.2)
Discord with social service provider, including probation officer, case manager, or social service worker. (Z64.4)
Disinhibited social engagement disorder (F94.2)
Disruption of family by separation or divorce (Z63.5)
Disruptive mood dysregulation disorder (F34.8)
Dissociative amnesia (F44.0)
Dissociative amnesia, with dissociative figure (F44.1)
Dissociative identity disorder (F44.81)
Encopresis (F98.1)
Enuresis (F98.0)
Erectile disorder (F52.21)
Excoriation (skin-picking) disorder (L98.1)
Exhibitionistic disorder (F65.2)
Exposure to disaster, war, or other hostilities (Z65.5)
Extreme poverty (Z59.5)
Factitious disorder (F68.10)
Female orgasm disorder (F52.31)
Female sexual interest/ arousal disorder (F52.22)
Fetishistic disorder (F65.0)

Frotteuristic disorder (F65.81)
Gambling disorder (F63.0)
Gender dysphoria is adolescents and adults (F64.1)
Gender dysphoria is children (F64.2)
Generalized anxiety disorder (F41.1)
Genito-pelvic pain/ penetration disorder (F52.6)
Global developmental delay (F88)
Hallucinogens persisting perception disorder (F16.983)
High expressed emotion level within family (Z63.8)
Histrionic personality disorder (F60.4)
Hoarding disorder (F42)
Homelessness (Z59.0)
Hypersomnolence disorder (G47.10)
Illness anxiety disorder (F45.21)
Imprisonment or other incarceration (Z65.1)
Inadequate housing (Z59.1)
Inhalant-induced anxiety disorder
- With mild use disorder (F18.180)
- With moderate or severe use disorder (F18.280)
- Without use disorder (F18.980)

Inhalant-induced major depressive disorder
- With mild use disorder (F18.14)
- With moderate or severe use disorder (F18.24)
- Without use disorder (F18.94)

Inhalant-induced major neurocognitive disorder
- With mild use disorder (F18.17)
- With moderate or severe use disorder (F18.27)
- Without use disorder (F18.97)

Inhalant-induced mild neurocognitive disorder
- With mild use disorder (F18.188)
- With moderate or severe use disorder (F18.288)
- Without use disorder (F18.988)

Inhalant-induced psychotic disorder
- With mild use disorder (F18.159)
- With moderate or severe use disorder (F18.259)
- Without use disorder (F18.959)

Inhalant intoxication
- With mild use disorder (F18.129)
- With moderate or severe use disorder (F18.229)
- Without use disorder (F18.929)

Inhalant intoxication delirium
- With mild use disorder (F18.121)
- With moderate or severe use disorder (F18.221)
- Without use disorder (F18.921)

Inhalant use disorder
- Mild (F18.10)
- Moderate (F18.20)
- Severe (F18.20)

Insomnia disorder (G47.00)
Insufficient social insurance or welfare support (Z59.7)
Intellectual disability (intellectual developmental disorder)
- Mild (F70)
- Moderate (F71)
- Profound (F73)
- Severe (F72)

Intermittent explosive disorder (F63.81)
Kleptomania (F63.3)
Lack of adequate food or safe drinking water (Z59.4)
Language disorder (F80.9)
Low income (Z59.6)
Major depressive disorder, Recurrent episode
- In full remission (F33.42)
- In partial remission (F33.41)
- Mild (F33.0)
- Moderate (F33.1)
- Severe (F33.2)
- With psychotic features (F33.3)
- Unspecified (F33.9)

Major depressive disorder, Single episode
- In full remission (F32.5)
- In partial remission (F32.4)
- Mild (F32.0)
- Moderate (F32.1)
- Severe (F32.2)
- With psychotic features (F32.3)
- Unspecified (F32.9)

Major frontotemporal neurocognitive disorder, Possible (G31.9)
Major frontotemporal neurocognitive disorder, Probable (G31.9)
- With behavioral disturbance (F02.81)

Without behavioral disturbance (F02.80)
Major neurocognitive disorder due to another medical condition
With behavioral disturbance (F02.81)
Without behavioral disturbance (F02.80)
Major neurocognitive disorder due to HIV infection (B20)
With behavioral disturbance (F02.81)
Without behavioral disturbance (F02.80)
Major neurocognitive disorder due to Huntington's disease (G10)
With behavioral disturbance (F02.81)
Without behavioral disturbance (F02.80)
Major neurocognitive disorder with Lewy bodies, Possible (G31.9)
Major neurocognitive disorder with Lewy bodies, Probable (G31.83)
With behavioral disturbance (F02.81)
Without behavioral disturbance (F02.80)
Major neurocognitive disorder due to multiple etiologies
With behavioral disturbance (F02.81)
Without behavioral disturbance (F02.80)
Major neurocognitive disorder due to Parkinson's disease, Possible (G31.9)
Major neurocognitive disorder due to Parkinson's disease, Probable (G20)
With behavioral disturbance (F02.81)
Without behavioral disturbance (F02.80)
Major neurocognitive disorder due to prion disease (A81.9)
With behavioral disturbance (F02.81)
Without behavioral disturbance (F02.80)
Major neurocognitive disorder due to traumatic brain injury (S06.2X9S)
With behavioral disturbance (F02.81)
Without behavioral disturbance (F02.80)
Major vascular neurocognitive disorder, Possible (G31.9)
Major vascular neurocognitive disorder, Probable
With behavioral disturbance (F01.51)
Without behavioral disturbance (F01.50)
Male hypoactive sexual desire disorder (F52.0)
Malingering (Z76.5)
Medication-induced acute akathisia (G25.71)
Medication-induced acute dystonia (G24.02)
Medication-induced postural tremor (G25.1)
Mild frontotemporal neurocognitive disorder (G31.84)
Mild neurocognitive disorder due to Alzheimer's disease (G31.84)
Mild neurocognitive disorder due to another medical condition (G31.84)
Mild neurocognitive disorder due to HIV infection (G31.84)
Mild neurocognitive disorder due to Huntington's disease (G31.84)
Mild neurocognitive disorder due to multiple etiologies (G31.84)
Mild neurocognitive disorder due to Parkinson's disease (G31.84)
Mild neurocognitive disorder due to prion disease (G31.84)
Mild neurocognitive disorder due to traumatic brain injury (G31.84)
Mild neurocognitive disorder with Lewy bodies (G31.84)
Mild vascular neurocognitive disorder (G31.84)
Narcissistic personality disorder (F60.81)
Narcolepsy
Autosomal dominant cerebellar ataxia, deafness, and narcolepsy (G47.419)
Autosomal dominant narcolepsy, obesity, and type 2 diabetes (G47.419)
Narcolepsy secondary to another medical condition (G47.429)
Narcolepsy with cataplexy but without hypocretin deficiency (G47.411)
Narcolepsy without cataplexy but with hypocretin deficiency (G47.419)
Neuroleptic-induced parkinsonism (G21.11)
Neuroleptic malignant syndrome (G21.0)
Nightmare disorder (F51.5)
Nonadherence to medical treatment (Z91.19)
Non-rapid eye movement sleep arousal disorders
Sleep terror type (F51.4)
Sleepwalking type (F51.3)
Obsessive-compulsive disorder (F42)
Obsessive-compulsive personality disorder (F60.5)
Obsessive-compulsive and related disorder due to another medical condition (F06.8)
Obstructive sleep apnea hypopnea (G47.33)
Opioid-induced anxiety disorder

- Encounter for mental health services for victim of child sexual abuse by parent (Z69.010)
- Encounter for mental health services for victim of nonparental child sexual abuse (Z69.020)
- Personal history (past history) of sexual abuse in childhood (Z62.810)
- Encounter for mental health services for perpetrator of spouse or partner psychological abuse (Z69.12)
- Encounter for mental health services for victim of spouse or partner psychological abuse (Z69.11)
- Personal history (past history) of spouse or partner psychological abuse (Z91.411)
- Encounter for mental health services for perpetrator of spouse or partner neglect (Z69.12)
- Encounter for mental health services for victim of spouse or partner neglect (Z69.11)
- Personal history (past history) of spouse or partner neglect (Z91.412)
- Encounter for mental health services for perpetrator of spouse or partner violence, Physical (Z69.12)
- Encounter for mental health services for victim of spouse or partner violence, Physical (Z69.11)
- Personal history (past history) of spouse or partner violence, Physical (Z91.410)
- Encounter for mental health services for perpetrator of spouse or partner violence, Sexual (Z69.12)
- Encounter for mental health services for victim of spouse or partner violence, Sexual (Z69.81)
- Personal history (past history) of spouse or partner violence, Sexual (Z91.410)
- Other counseling or consultation (Z71.9)
- Other hallucinogen-induced anxiety disorder
  - With mild use disorder (F16.180)
  - With moderate or severe use disorder (F16.280)
  - Without use disorder (F16.980)
- Other hallucinogen-induced bipolar and related disorder
  - With mild use disorder (F16.14)
  - With moderate or severe use disorder (F16.24)
  - Without use disorder (F16.94)
- Other hallucinogen-induced depressive disorder
  - With mild use disorder (F16.14)
  - With moderate or severe use disorder (F16.24)
  - Without use disorder (F16.94)
- Other hallucinogen-induced psychotic disorder
  - With mild use disorder (F16.159)
  - With moderate or severe use disorder (F16.259)
  - Without use disorder (F16.959)
- Other hallucinogen intoxication
  - With mild use disorder (F16.129)
  - With moderate or severe use disorder (F16.229)
  - Without use disorder (F16.929)
- Other hallucinogen intoxication delirium
  - With mild use disorder (F16.121)
  - With moderate or severe use disorder (F16.221)
  - Without use disorder (F16.921)
- Other hallucinogen use disorder
  - Mild (F16.10)
  - Moderate (F16.20)
  - Severe (F16.20)
- Other medication-induced movement disorder (G25.79)
- Other medication-induced parkinsonism (G21.19)
- Other personal history of psychological trauma (Z91.49)
- Other personal risk factors (Z91.89)
- Other problem related to employment (Z56.9)
- Other problem related to psychosocial circumstances (Z65.8)
- Other specified anxiety disorder (F41.8)
- Other specified attention-deficit/hyperactivity disorder (G21.19)
- Other specified bipolar and related disorder (F31.89)
- Other specified delirium (R41.0)
- Other specified depressive disorder (F32.8)
- Other specified disruptive, impulse-control, and conduct disorder (F91.8)
- Other specified dissociative disorder (F44.89)
- Other specified elimination disorder
  - With fecal symptoms (R15.9)

With urinary symptoms (N39.498)
Other specified feeding or eating disorder (F50.8)
Other specified gender dysphoria (F64.8)
Other specified hypersomnolence disorder (G47.19)
Other specified insomnia disorder (G47.09)
Other specified mental disorder (F99)
Other specified mental disorder due to other medical condition (F06.8)
Other specified neurodevelopmental disorder (F88)
Other specified obsessive-compulsive and related disorder (F42)
Other specified paraphilic disorder (F65.89)
Other specified personality disorder (F60.89)
Other specified schizophrenia spectrum and other psychotic disorder (F28)
Other specified sexual dysfunction (F52.8)
Other specified sleep-wake disorder (G47.8)
Other specified somatic symptom and related disorder (F45.8)
Other specified tic disorder (F95.8)
Other specified trauma- and stressor-related disorder (F43.8)
Other (or unknown) substance-induced anxiety disorder
With mild use disorder (F19.180)
With moderate or severe use disorder (F19.280)
Without use disorder (F19.980)
Other (or unknown) substance-induced bipolar and related disorder
With mild use disorder (F19.14)
With moderate or severe use disorder (F19.24)
Without use disorder (F19.94)
Other (or unknown) substance-induced delirium (F19.921)
Other (or unknown) substance-induced depressive disorder
With mild use disorder (F19.14)
With moderate or severe use disorder (F19.24)
Without use disorder (F19.94)
Other (or unknown) substance-induced major neurocognitive disorder
With mild use disorder (F19.17)
With moderate or severe use disorder (F19.27)
Without use disorder (F19.97)
Other (or unknown) substance-induced mild neurocognitive disorder
With mild use disorder (F19.188)
With moderate or severe use disorder (F19.288)
Without use disorder (F19.988)
Other (or unknown) substance-induced obsessive-compulsive and related disorder
With mild use disorder (F19.188)
With moderate or severe use disorder (F19.288)
Without use disorder (F19.988)
Other (or unknown) substance-induced psychotic disorder
With mild use disorder (F19.159)
With moderate or severe use disorder (F19.259)
Without use disorder (F19.959)
Other (or unknown) substance-induced sexual dysfunction
With mild use disorder (F19.181)
With moderate or severe use disorder (F19.281)
Without use disorder (F19.981)
Other (or unknown) substance-induced sleep disorder
With mild use disorder (F19.182)
With moderate or severe use disorder (F19.282)
Without use disorder (F19.982)
Other (or unknown) substance intoxication
With mild use disorder (F19.129)
With moderate or severe use disorder (F19.229)
Without use disorder (F19.929)
Other (or unknown) substance-induced intoxication delirium
With mild use disorder (F19.121)
With moderate or severe use disorder (F19.221)
Without use disorder (F19.921)
Other (or unknown) substance use disorder
Mild (F19.10)
Moderate (F19.20)
Severe (F19.20)

Other (or unknown) substance withdrawal (F19.239)
Other (or unknown) substance withdrawal delirium (F19.231)
Other or unspecified stimulant use disorder
    Mild (F15.10)
    Moderate (F15.20)
    Severe (F15.20)
Overweight or obesity (E66.9)
Panic attack specifier
Panic disorder (F41.0)
Paranoid personality disorder (F60.0)
Parent-child relational problem (Z62.820)
Pedophilic disorder (F65.4)
Persistent (chronic) motor or vocal tic disorder (F95.1)
Persistent depressive disorder (dysthymia) (F34.1)
Personal history of military deployment (Z91.82)
Personal history of self-harm (Z91.5)
Personality change due to another medical condition (F07.0)
Phase of life problem (Z60.0)
Phencyclidine-induced anxiety disorder
    With mild use disorder (F16.180)
    With moderate or severe use disorder (F16.280)
    Without use disorder (F16.980)
Phencyclidine-induced bipolar and related disorder
    With mild use disorder (F16.14)
    With moderate or severe use disorder (F16.24)
    Without use disorder (F16.94)
Phencyclidine-induced depressive disorder
    With mild use disorder (F16.14)
    With moderate or severe use disorder (F16.24)
    Without use disorder (F16.94)
Phencyclidine-induced psychotic disorder
    With mild use disorder (F16.159)
    With moderate or severe use disorder (F16.259)
    Without use disorder (F16.959)
Phencyclidine intoxication
    With mild use disorder (F16.129)
    With moderate or severe use disorder (F16.229)
    Without use disorder (F16.929)
Phencyclidine intoxication delirium
    With mild use disorder (F16.121)
    With moderate or severe use disorder (F16.221)
    Without use disorder (F16.921)
Phencyclidine use disorder
    Mild (F16.10)
    Moderate (F16.20)
    Severe (F16.20)
Pica
    In adults (F50.8)
    In children (F98.3)
Posttraumatic stress disorder (F43.10)
Premature (early) ejaculation (52.4)
Premenstrual dysphoric disorder (N94.3)
Problem related to current military deployment status (Z56.82)
Problem related to lifestyle (Z72.9)
Problem related to living alone (Z60.2)
Problem related to living in a residential institution (Z59.3)
Problems related to multiparity (Z64.1)
Problems related to other legal circumstances (Z65.3)
Problems related to release from prison (Z65.2)
Problems related to unwanted pregnancy (F64.0)
Provisional tic disorder (F95.0)
Psychological factors affecting other medical condition (F54)
Psychotic disorder due to another medical condition
    With delusions (F06.2)
    With hallucinations (F06.0)
Pyromania (F63.1)
Rapid eye movement sleep behavior disorder (G47.52)
Reactive attachment disorder (F94.1)
Relationship distress with spouse or intimate partner (Z63.0)
Religious or spiritual problem (Z65.8)
Restless legs syndrome (G25.81)
Rumination disorder (F98.21)
Schizoaffective disorder
    Bipolar type (F25.0)
    Depressive type (F25.1)

Schizoid personality disorder (F60.1)
Schizophrenia (F20.9)
Schizophreniform disorder (F20.81)
Schizotypal personality disorder (F21)
Sedative-, hypnotic-, or anxiolytic-induced anxiety disorder
- With mild use disorder (13.180)
- With moderate or severe use disorder (F13.280)
- Without use disorder (F13.980)

Sedative-, hypnotic-, or anxiolytic-induced bipolar and related disorder
- With mild use disorder (13.14)
- With moderate or severe use disorder (F13.24)
- Without use disorder (F13.94)

Sedative-, hypnotic-, or anxiolytic-induced delirium (F13.921)
Sedative-, hypnotic-, or anxiolytic-induced depressive disorder
- With mild use disorder (13.14)
- With moderate or severe use disorder (F13.24)
- Without use disorder (F13.94)

Sedative-, hypnotic-, or anxiolytic-induced major neurocognitive disorder
- With moderate or severe use disorder (F13.27)
- Without use disorder (F13.97)

Sedative-, hypnotic-, or anxiolytic-induced mild neurocognitive disorder
- With moderate or severe use disorder (F13.288)
- Without use disorder (F13.988)

Sedative-, hypnotic-, or anxiolytic-induced psychotic disorder
- With mild use disorder (13.159)
- With moderate or severe use disorder (F13.259)
- Without use disorder (F13.959)

Sedative-, hypnotic-, or anxiolytic-induced sexual dysfunction
- With mild use disorder (F13.181)
- With moderate or severe use disorder (F13.281)
- Without use disorder (F13.981)

Sedative-, hypnotic-, or anxiolytic-induced sleep disorder
- With mild use disorder (F13.182)
- With moderate or severe use disorder (F13.282)
- Without use disorder (F13.982)

Sedative, hypnotic, or anxiolytic intoxication
- With mild use disorder (13.129)
- With moderate or severe use disorder (F13.229)
- Without use disorder (F13.929)

Sedative, hypnotic, or anxiolytic intoxication delirium
- With mild use disorder (13.121)
- With moderate or severe use disorder (F13.221)
- Without use disorder (F13.921)

Sedative, hypnotic, or anxiolytic use disorder
- Mild (F13.10)
- Moderate (F13.20)
- Severe (F13.20)

Sedative, hypnotic, or anxiolytic withdrawal
- With perceptual disturbances (F13.232)
- Without perceptual disturbances (F13.239)

Sedative, hypnotic, or anxiolytic withdrawal delirium (F13.231)
Selective mutism (F94.0)
Separation anxiety disorder (F93.0)
Sex counseling (Z70.9)
Sexual masochism disorder (F65.51)
Sexual sadism disorder (F65.52)
Sibling relational problem (Z62.891)
Sleep-related hypoventilation
- Comorbid sleep-related hypoventilation (G47.36)
- Congenital central alveolar hypoventilation (G47.35)
- Idiopathic hypoventilation (G47.34)

Social anxiety disorder (social phobia) (F40.10)
Social exclusion or rejection (Z60.4)
Social (pragmatic) communication disorder (F80.89)
- Somatic symptom disorder (F45.1)

Specific learning disorder
- With impairment in mathematics (F81.2)
- With impairment in reading (F81.0)
- With impairment in written expression (F81.81)

Specific phobia
- Animal (F40.218)

Blood-injection injury
Fear of blood (F40.230)
Fear of injuries and transfusions (F40.231)
Fear of injury (F40.233)
Fear of other medical care (F40.232)
Natural environment (F40.228)
Other (F40.298)
Situational (F40.248)
Speech sound disorder (F80.0)
Spouse or partner abuse, Psychological, Confirmed
Initial encounter (T74.31XA)
Subsequent encounter (T74.31XD)
Spouse or partner abuse, Psychological, Suspected
Initial encounter (T74.31XA)
Subsequent encounter (T74.31XD)
Spouse or partner neglect, Confirmed
Initial encounter (T74.01XA)
Subsequent encounter (T74.01XD)
Spouse or partner neglect, Suspected
Initial encounter (T74.01XA)
Subsequent encounter (T74.01XD)
Spouse or partner violence, Physical, Confirmed
Initial encounter (T74.11XA)
Subsequent encounter (T74.11XD)
Spouse or partner violence, Physical, Suspected
Initial encounter (T74.11XA)
Subsequent encounter (T74.11XD)
Spouse or partner violence, Sexual, Confirmed
Initial encounter (T74.21XA)
Subsequent encounter (T74.21XD)
Spouse or partner violence, Sexual, Suspected
Initial encounter (T74.21XA)
Subsequent encounter (T74.21XD)
Stereotypic movement disorder (F98.4)
Tardive akathisia (G25.71)
Tardive dyskinesia (G24.01)
Tardive dystonia (G24.09)
Target of (perceived) discrimination or persecution (Z60.5)
Tobacco-induced sleep disorder
With moderate or severe use disorder (F17.208)
Tobacco use disorder
Mild (Z72.0)
Moderate (F17.200)
Severe (F17.200)
Tourette's disorder (F95.2)
Transvestic disorder (F65.1)
Trichotillomania (hair-pulling disorder) (F63.2)
Unavailability or inaccessibility of health care facilities (Z75.3)
Unavailability or inaccessibility of other helping agencies (Z75.4)
Uncomplicated bereavement (Z63.4)
Unspecified alcohol-related disorder (F10.99)
Unspecified anxiety disorder (F41.9)
Unspecified attention-deficit/hyperactivity disorder ((F90.9)
Unspecified bipolar and related disorder ((F31.9)
Unspecified caffeine-related disorder (F15.99)
Unspecified cannabis-related disorder (F12.99)
Unspecified catatonia (F-06.1)
Unspecified communication disorder (F80.9)
Unspecified delirium (R41.0)
Unspecified depressive disorder (F32.9)
Unspecified disruptive, impulse-control, and conduct disorder (F91.9)
Unspecified dissociative disorder (F44.9)
Unspecified elimination disorder
With fecal symptoms (R15.9)
With urinary symptoms (R32)
Unspecified feeding or eating disorder (F50.9)
Unspecified gender dysphoria (F64.9)
Unspecified hallucinogen-related disorder (F16.99)
Unspecified housing or economic problem (Z59.9)
Unspecified hypersomnolence disorder (G47.10)
Unspecified inhalant-related disorder (F18.99)
Unspecified insomnia disorder (G47.00)
Unspecified intellectual disability (intellectual developmental disorder) (F79)
Unspecified mental disorder (F99)
Unspecified mental disorder due to another medical condition (F09)
Unspecified neurocognitive disorder (R41.9)
Unspecified neurodevelopmental disorder (F89)
Unspecified obsessive-compulsive and related

Index

B

C

D

E

P

R

S

T

V

W